Corporate Financial Accounting and Reporting

We work with leading authors to develop the strongest
educational materials in business and finance, bringing
cutting-edge thinking and best learning practice to a
global market.

Under a range of well-known imprints, including
Financial Times Prentice Hall, we craft high quality print
and electronic publications which help readers to
understand and apply their content, whether studying
or at work.

To find out more about the complete range of our
publishing please visit us on the World Wide Web at:
www.pearsoned.co.uk

Corporate Financial Accounting and Reporting

Second Edition

Tim Sutton

Prentice Hall

FINANCIAL TIMES

An imprint of **Pearson Education**

Harlow, England • London • New York • Boston • San Francisco • Toronto • Sydney • Singapore • Hong Kong
Tokyo • Seoul • Taipei • New Delhi • Cape Town • Madrid • Mexico City • Amsterdam • Munich • Paris • Milan

Pearson Education Limited

Edinburgh Gate
Harlow
Essex CM20 2JE
England

and Associated Companies throughout the world

Visit us on the World Wide Web at:
www.pearsoned.co.uk

First published 2000
Second edition published 2004

© Financial Times Management 2000
© Pearson Education Limited 2004

ISBN: 978-0-273-67620-1

British Library Cataloguing-in-Publication Data
A catalogue record for this book is available from the British Library.

10 9 8 7 6
08 07

Typeset in 10/12pt Minion by 35
Printed and bound in Malaysia, (CTP-VVP)

The publisher's policy is to use paper manufactured from sustainable forests.

Contents

List of boxes

Preface

Purpose and structure of the book

This book is an introductory financial accounting textbook. It is designed for use in business administration courses at undergraduate and graduate levels which are offered by European universities and business schools.

The book is directed at future managers and finance professionals. The aim is to help them understand and interpret the accounts which companies issue each year. The structure of the book reflects this goal. It has three parts following the introductory chapter:

- Part 1 'Foundations' (Chapters 2–6) introduces the main financial statements and the terms in them. It also shows where the numbers in them come from. It explains briefly the process by which transactions are recorded and summarised in financial statements. Certain accounting fallacies are exposed.
- Part 2 'The House of Accounting' (Chapters 7–17) considers in more depth the components of the financial statements: the assets and liabilities that appear on the balance sheet; the revenues and expenses, gains and losses that constitute the income statement. It shows how the accounting policies a company follows affect the numbers in the statements – and thus the financial ratios derived from them.
- How investors analyse financial statements is the subject matter of Part 3 'Perspectives' (Chapters 18–20). Widely used measures of performance such as earnings and cash flow are explored at length.

Focus of the book

Those using this book are likely to be a diverse group of people. They come from many different countries – and not just within Europe. Although English may not be their first language, their English-language skills are high. What they share in common is an international outlook.

The book caters to their needs in various ways. Its approach to the subject matter is open. For example, the chapters in the second part describe and illustrate the most common accounting practices that managers will encounter in the financial statements of larger companies, both European and non-European.

In many cases, these practices are the result of national laws. For companies in European Union (EU) member states, such laws are heavily influenced by EU directives. Additionally, an increasing number of larger companies, within and outside Europe, follow international accounting standards (IAS) when preparing consolidated accounts. Thus most chapters in the second part contain a section summarising the relevant EU and IAS requirements. The book does not set down the accounting rules that apply in each European country, although unusual national practices are mentioned.

For obvious reasons, the book has an Anglo-Saxon flavour. Given an international readership, this is not a disadvantage. As we've noted, many larger European companies base their consolidated accounts on IAS. These standards have Anglo-Saxon roots. Some European multinationals have adopted US accounting standards. In many cases these are similar to IAS. Significant differences between US and international standards are pointed out in the text.

The accounting practices described and illustrated are general in nature. They apply to companies in all industries. The book does not discuss accounting practices that are industry-specific.

Distinctive features

The book has distinctive features. Among them are the following:

- *Comprehensive coverage.* Included in the book are some topics – such as accounting for pension costs and foreign operations – which do not usually appear in introductory texts. Other topics like consolidation accounting and financial statement analysis are dealt with at greater length than is customary. As a result, the book can be used in an elective course on, say, corporate financial reporting as well as in a core financial accounting course.

  Moreover, it can serve as a reference book. Many students retain their accounting textbooks after their studies have finished for this reason. Because of its coverage and other features – such as easy-to-follow examples in each chapter and an extensive glossary – the book is well suited for this role.
- *Modular design.* Instructors have different preferences as to the topics covered in an introductory course and the order in which they are discussed. The book's design allows for this. In Part 2, each chapter is largely self-contained and an instructor can discuss topics in a different order from that presented. Moreover, Chapters 18 (on cash flow analysis) and 19 (on financial statement analysis) from Part 3 of the book can be scheduled for inclusion at any stage after the introductory material (Chapters 1–6) has been covered.

  In Parts 2 and 3 of the book, the chapters themselves are, in most cases, modular in construction. In some, 'core issues' are distinguished from 'specialised topics'. In others, the chapter is broken up into separate, 'stand-alone' sections. This gives instructors additional flexibility when drawing up a syllabus.
- *Clarity.* The book has been designed with a non-Anglophone audience in mind. It has been extensively tested in a major European business school where the majority of students are not native English speakers.

How to use the book

An accounting textbook is not like a consumer appliance. There is no need for 'instructions for use'. But students and instructors may find helpful some suggestions as to how to use it.

For students who have never opened an accounting book before, the secrets to mastering the material are patience and perseverance. Do not be in a hurry. Spend time on the examples in the text. Work through the numbers in them. Make sure you understand how the accounting transaction or event illustrated is recorded. As befits its name, accounting requires only simple mathematical (counting) skills. The logic behind 'double entry' (the recording of all accounting events twice – both the source of the resource flow and its destination) may take time to grasp – but is satisfying (and unforgettable) when it is. More troubling, perhaps, is the terminology. Some terms in everyday use, such as 'depreciation', have a different meaning in an accounting context.

Instructors have different concerns. Chief of these is the fit of text to course. The modular design of the book and the range of topics covered both help here. For example, in an introductory course of approximately 30 hours of class time, the following topics can be covered: 'Foundations' (Chapters 2–6); conceptual issues (7); and the 'core' sections of Chapters 8 to 14. Revisiting the cash flow statement (Chapter 18) is a helpful way of concluding the course and reviewing the material covered.

A second course on corporate financial reporting (of similar length) is likely to focus on more specialised topics. Examples are: leasing (Chapter 11); business combinations (Chapter 14); foreign operations (Chapter 15); pension costs (Chapter 16); and deferred tax accounting (Chapter 17). It can also serve to illustrate how investors use numbers in published accounts, drawing on material in Chapters 18–20.

An Instructor's Manual is available to instructors who adopt the text. It contains solutions to the end-of-chapter problem assignments and additional practice problems (with solutions).

Suggestions do not flow one way. Users of a book can make them too. If you have ideas about how the book can be improved, please send them to me. All constructive suggestions are appreciated and will be acknowledged.

Second edition

Much has changed in the financial landscape since the first edition was published. The first three years of the millennium (2000–2002) saw sharp falls in share values after the bull market of the 1990s. In some cases investors' losses could be traced to misleading company accounting or fraud: examples are Enron and WorldCom in North America and Daewoo in Asia. These scandals, in turn, prompted regulatory changes – witness the US's Sarbanes-Oxley Act. At the same time, moves to broaden world capital markets and lower companies' capital costs continued apace. A new international accounting standards-setting body, the IASB, was established. The European Commission announced that by 2005 all listed EU companies must prepare their accounts according to international accounting standards.

I have tried to capture the accounting fall-out from these events in the second edition. Other changes are more mundane, though no less important. Besides updating the text, examples and problem assignments, I have taken the opportunity to revise some of the chapters to make the exposition clearer. Regulatory changes have also prompted a major rewriting of two of them (11 and 13) to incorporate new international accounting and disclosure rules on financial instruments. An innovation in this edition is the inclusion of boxed material in many chapters. Their purpose is to broaden and enliven the discussion in the chapter. In some cases, I summarise interesting empirical research in accounting and related disciplines. In others, I illustrate financial accounting's 'long arm' – its influence in other fields such as environmental reporting, government budgeting and corporate governance. Apart from this, the structure of the book is unchanged.

Acknowledgements

Every author has debts – and not just monetary ones. Some of mine are of long standing. Among the creditors are Gerry Mueller who introduced international accounting to me and many others at the University of Washington, and Larry Revsine of Northwestern University whose teaching skills are legendary. I am indebted to faculty at IESE Business School, the University of Maastricht, and the Cass Business School of City University for their comments and feedback on the first edition. Special thanks are also due to the librarians of IESE Business School and the ICAEW in London for their assistance. The most numerous of my creditors are former IESE students who patiently endured the ambiguities and errors of the text before (and after) the first edition saw the light of day. The book is dedicated to them.

Abbreviations

A	asset
ABS	asset-backed security
ABV	accrued benefit valuation (pension costing method)
AC	absorption costing
AFS	available-for-sale
AG	Austrian/German public limited (liability) company
AMEX	American Stock Exchange
A/R	account receivable
A/S	Danish public limited (liability) company
ASB	Accountings Standards Board (UK)
AT	assets turnover
BB	beginning balance
BI	beginning inventory
BV	book value
BVCAP	book value of capital
BVE	book value of equity
C$	Canadian dollar
C & A	capitalising and amortising (costs)
CA	contra-asset
CAD	Canadian dollar
capex	capital expenditure
CC	(1) completed contract (method of revenue recognition) (2) cost of capital
CEO	chief executive officer
CFO	chief financial officer
CFS	cash flow statement
CIP	contracts in progress
CL	contra-liability
COGAFS	cost of goods available for sale
COGS	cost of goods sold
COS	cost of sales
CPP	current purchasing power
CR	current ratio
Cr.	credit
CV	current value
D	debt
D&A	depreciation and amortisation
DB	(1) declining balance (method of depreciation) (2) defined benefit (type of pension plan)
DC	defined contribution (type of pension plan)
DIV	dividends
DKr	Danish krone
DM	Deutschemark
Dr.	debit
DTA	(1) deferred tax asset (2) deferred tax accounting
DTL	deferred tax liability
DVFA/SG	Institute of Financial Analysts (German)
E	equity
EB	ending balance
EBIT	earnings before interest and tax
Ebitda	earnings before interest, tax, depreciation and amortisation
EC	European Commission
EDI	electronic data interchange
EEIG	European economic interest grouping
EI	ending inventory
EMH	efficient market hypothesis
EMU	European monetary union
EP	exercise price
EPS	earnings per share
ESO	employee share option
EU	European Union
EUR	euro
EV	enterprise value
EVA	economic value added
FA	financial asset
FASB	Financial Accounting Standards Board (USA)
FCC	fixed charge coverage (ratio)
FCM	financial capital maintenance
FG	finished goods
FIFO	first in, first out

FL	financial liability	NRV	net realisable value
FTE	full-time equivalent	NV	Dutch public limited (liability) company
FV	fair value	NYSE	New York Stock Exchange
GAAP	generally accepted accounting principles	OA	operating asset
		OCF	operating cash flow
GBP	Great Britain pound	OE	owners' equity
GDP	gross domestic product	OL	operating liability
GNP	gross national product	OWC	operating working capital
HC	historical costs	P&E	property and equipment
HFT	held-for-trading	P/B	price/book
HTM	held-to-maturity	P/E	price/earnings
IAS	International Accounting Standards	PB	provisional balance
IASB	International Accounting Standards Board	PBV	projected benefit valuation (pension costing method)
IASC	International Accounting Standards Committee	PC	(1) parent company (2) personal computer
IC	Interpretations Committee	PCM	physical capital maintenance
IE	immediate expensing (costs)	PLC	public limited (liability) company (UK/Ireland)
IFRS	International Financial Reporting Standard		
		PM	profit margin
IOSCO	International Organisation of Securities Commissions	POC	percentage of completion (method of revenue recognition)
IPO	initial public offering	POS	potential ordinary shares
IRR	internal rate of return	PPE	property, plant and equipment
IT	Information technology	PSC	past service cost
IWO	immediate write-off	PV	present value
JPY	Japanese yen	PVA	present value of annuity
L	liability	R&D	research and development
LBO	leveraged buyout	RC	replacement cost
LIBOR	London interbank offered rate	RI	residual income
LIFO	last in, first out	RM	raw materials
LOCOM	lower of cost or market	ROA	return on assets
LTD	long-term debt	ROCE	return on capital employed
M&S	materials and supplies	ROE	return on equity
MD&A	Management's Discussion and Analysis (USA)	ROFA	return on financial assets
		RONOA	return on net operating assets
MI	minority interest	ROOA	return on operating assets
MP	market price	RT	receivables turnover
MV	market value	SA	(1) French/Spanish public limited (liability) company
MVE	market value of equity		(2) selling and administrative (expenses)
N/R	note receivable		
NA	net assets		
NBC	net borrowing cost	SAR	share appreciation rights
NBV	net book value	SE	(1) shareholders' equity
NETFLEV	net financial leverage		(2) societas europea
NFE	net financial expense	SEC	Securities and Exchange Commission (USA)
NFI	non-financial indicator		
NOA	net operating assets	SFAS	Statement of Financial Accounting Standards (USA)
NOK	Norwegian krone		
NOPAT	net operating profit after tax	SFr	Swiss francs

SGA	selling, general and administrative (expenses)	TMT	telecoms, media and technology (industries)
SI	specific identification	TPA	taxes payable accounting
SKr	Swedish krona	UHG/L	unrealised holding gains/losses
SL	straight line (method of depreciation)	UoP	units of production (method of depreciation)
SME	small and medium-sized enterprise		
SoYD	sum-of-years' digits (methods of depreciation)	USD	US dollar
		VAT	value added tax
SpA	Italian public limited (liability) company	VC	variable costing
		WAAE	weighted average accumulated expenditures
SPE	special purpose entity		
STD	short-term debt	WAC	weighted average cost
TD	temporary differences (tax)	WACC	weighted average cost of capital
TIE	times interest earned	WIP	work-in-progress

Publisher's acknowledgements

We are grateful to the following for permission to reproduce copyright material:

Exhibit 6.4 from Barco, *Annual Report and Accounts 2001*, Barco NV; Exhibit 6.21 from OMV Group, *Annual Report and Accounts 2000*, reproduced with permission from OMV Aktiengesellschaft, any further reproduction with prior permission of OMV Aktiengesellschaft only; Exhibit 8.9 from Henkel Group, *Annual Report 2001*, Henkel KGaA; Exhibit 9.17 from BP Amoco, *Annual Report and Accounts 2001*, BP plc; Exhibit 9.18 from General Motors Corporation, *Annual Report and Accounts 2001*, General Motors Corporation; Exhibits 10.9 from Benetton Group, *Annual Report 2001*, Benetton Group; Exhibit 11.5 from BG Group, *Annual Report and Accounts 2001*, BG Group plc; Exhibit 11.8 from LVMH Group, *Annual Accounts 2001*, LVMH; Exhibit 12.4 from BMW Group, *Annual Report and Accounts 2001*, BMW Group; Exhibit 12.7 from PSA Peugeot Citroën, *Annual Report and Accounts 2001*, PSA Peugeot Citroën; Exhibit 13.5 from Novartis Group, *Annual Report and Accounts 2001*, Novartis Group; Exhibit 13.6 from Microsoft Inc., *Annual Report and Accounts 2002*, copyright Microsoft Corporation, reproduced with permission of Microsoft Corporation; Exhibit 13.7 from Allianz Group, *Annual Accounts 2001* and *Interim Report for 6 months to June 2002*, Allianz Aktiengesellschaft; Exhibit 14.17 from BT, Circular to Shareholders, September 2001, BT Group plc; Exhibit 15.4 from SCA Group, *Annual Report 2001*, Svenska Cellulosa Aktiebolaget SCA; Exhibit 16.5 from Roche Group, *Annual Report and Accounts 2001*, Roche Holding Ltd; Exhibit 16.8 from Toray Industries, *Annual Report and Accounts for year to March 31, 2002*, Toray Industries, Inc.; Box 18.1 Figure from Causes and consequences of earnings manipulation: An analysis of firms subject to enforcement actions by the SEC in *Contemporary Accounting Research*, 13(1), Canadian Academic Accounting Association (Dechow, P.M., Sloan, R.G. and Sweeney, A.P. 1996); Exhibit 18.2 adapted from *Financial Reporting and Statement Analysis: A Strategic Perspective, 3rd Edition*, reprinted by permission of South-Western, a division of Thomson Learning (Stickney, C. 1996); Exhibit 19.1 adapted from *Competitive Strategy: Techniques for Analyzing Industries and Competitors*, adapted with permission of The Free Press, a Division of Simon & Schuster Adult Publishing Group (Porter, M.E. 1980); Exhibit 19.2 from Canadean Beverage Market Research, Canadean Ltd; Appendix 19.2 from Carlsberg Group's financial statements for 2001, Carlsberg A/S; Exhibit 19.3 from *Statistical Handbook*, Brewing Publications Ltd (British Beer and Pub Association 2002), and *Demographic Yearbook*, United Nations (UN, various); Exhibit 19.4 from Carlsberg Group, *Report and Accounts 2001*, Carlsberg Group A/S; Exhibit 19.5 from Carlsberg A/S, *Report and Accounts 2001*, Carlsberg Group A/S, and Heineken NV, *Annual Report and Accounts 2001*, Heineken NV; Exhibit 19.17 from Kao Corporation, *Annual Report 2002*, Kao Corporation; Exhibit 19.21 from Deutsche Telekom, *Annual Report and Accounts 2001*, Deutsche Telekom AG; Exhibit 20.1 from Xstrata Group, *Annual Report 2001*, Xstrata plc; Exhibit 20.4 from Benetton Group, *Annual Report and Accounts 2001*, Benetton Group; Exhibit 20.8 from MyTravel Group plc, *Annual Report and Accounts 2001*, MyTravel Group plc; Exhibit 20.11 from Smith & Nephew plc, *Annual Report and Accounts 2001*, Smith & Nephew plc; Exhibit 20.13 from Nestlé, *Management Report 2001*, Nestlé S.A.

In some instances we have been unable to trace the owners of copyright material, and we would appreciate any information that would enable us to do so.

1 Financial accounting: an overview

INTRODUCTION

Shining a light on company accounts

'Fair value' accounting for all financial assets and liabilities is on its way. Banks and companies hate the idea.

(*The Economist*, 18 August 2001)

Amazon is all grown up, except for its accounting

Jeff Bezos [Amazon CEO] will get more credit if he drops pro forma from his routine.

(*BusinessWeek*, 5–12 August 2002)

Headlines like these are common in today's financial press. They serve to remind us how important it is for business people to have a sound grasp of the fundamentals of financial accounting. The aim of this book is to supply that knowledge.

This chapter sets the scene for the rest of the book. We start by answering certain basic questions. What is financial accounting? What are the accounts which managers must know how to interpret? What is the entity being accounted for? And who are the users of the accounts or, to put it another way, whom do the accounts serve?

Published accounts are, by definition, in the public domain: investors, creditors, employees, government agencies and public interest groups all consult them. Each of these groups has different information needs. How can one set of accounts serve so many different users? We assume – as do preparers of company accounts – that investors are the main users and that they consult the accounts for help in their investment decisions. This raises additional issues – what, for investors, are the characteristics of 'useful financial information'? which characteristics are considered the most important? – which we address in this chapter.

Accounting's influence is felt beyond the investment community. As we illustrate in the penultimate section, it is present in many aspects of economic and social life – in the details of contracts between lenders and borrowers as well as in 'macro' issues such as economic development and pension policy. We'll come across other examples of accounting's long arm later in the book.

The chapter concludes with a guide to the book's chapters and a key to help the reader understand the numbers in them.

What is financial accounting?

Financial accounting *is the process of summarising financial data taken from an organisation's accounting records and publishing it in the form of annual (or more frequent) reports for the benefit of people outside the organisation.*

Two ideas are of key importance in this definition. First, *financial data are taken from the accounting records and summarised in the form of financial statements.* The maintenance of accounting records, for example the recording of financial transactions in the books of account, is known as **bookkeeping**. The setting-up of accounting records and the devising of new structures of records (now increasingly computerised) to provide timely, reliable information at low cost are referred to as **accounting systems design**. Both systems design and bookkeeping tasks are often carried out or supervised by accountants. Both are essential to, but are different from, financial accounting.

Second, *financial reports are published and issued to outsiders.* Accountants also produce financial reports for use by an organisation's managers – to help them plan and control its activities. This process is known as **management accounting**. The job of producing financial reports for external use falls to the financial accountant, for internal use to the management accountant.

The published annual accounts issued by larger companies in the European Union (EU) – and by publicly quoted companies in the USA – are **audited**. Managers are responsible for preparing the company's financial statements. However, the owners (and others) use them to evaluate managers' performance. To protect the public from a potential conflict of interest on the part of managers, larger EU companies must have their accounts checked by an independent expert, the **external auditor**. The process of examination and verification of an organisation's accounts, accounting records and record-keeping system is known generally as **auditing**.

Organisations, especially larger ones, employ their own experts to carry out **internal audits** of their accounting systems. Such audits help an organisation to safeguard its resources and assist the external auditor in his or her duties: they are not required by EU law.

Overview of the company and its activities

We focus in this book on the financial accounting of a particular class of organisation, namely profit-seeking companies. Before outlining the accounting documents produced by a company and the purposes they serve, it's helpful to keep in mind the activities of a typical firm and their interrelations.

Consider the case of an entrepreneur who has a new business idea. She sets up a company (a business with its own legal identity), invests her own money in it and persuades others to contribute capital to it too. The company invests some of the capital in long-term resources – for example, it acquires buildings and equipment and purchases licences and patents. It then begins operations. It recruits staff, purchases materials and services (again, with the capital it has raised) and, using the long-term assets acquired, produces goods and services for sale. If the business is successful, the operations generate profits which are used to reward the providers of capital – in the form of interest and dividend payments – and to expand the business. The interrelation of the financing, investing and operating activities of the firm is illustrated in Exhibit 1.1.

For successful firms, the resource flow cycle is continuous. As Exhibit 1.1 makes clear, some of the profits from the firm's operations are ploughed back into the business. If internal funds are insufficient to pay for new long-term assets, additional capital is raised from owners and lenders (e.g. banks).

Exhibit 1.1 The activities of the firm: financing, investment and operations

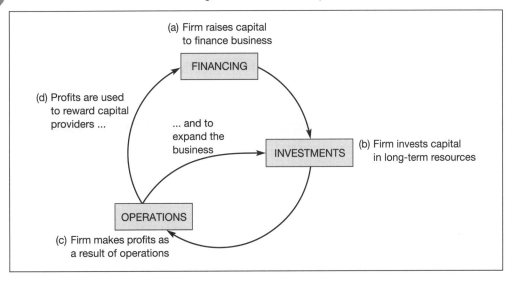

What are the accounts?

The term 'the accounts' has two meanings for managers. It can refer to *the summary financial statements which are produced for internal and external use on a periodic basis.* It's also used to describe *the collection of accounting records in which transactions are recorded and from which financial statements are prepared.* We use the term mostly in its first sense in this book. When referring to summary financial statements, we shall concentrate on the (published) annual accounts, since these are the most comprehensive set of periodic accounts companies produce for outsiders.

The **annual accounts** comprise, at a minimum, a balance sheet, an income statement (or profit and loss account) and accompanying notes to the accounts, together with the auditor's report on the accounts. The **balance sheet** lists in summary form a company's resources (assets) and claims to them (liabilities and shareholders' equity). It provides readers of the accounts with information about the company's financial condition on a particular day (usually the last day of the financial year).

Readers of accounts also want to know how the company has performed over the financial year. In particular, they want to know how and by how much its resources increased or decreased in this period as a result of its operations. For this information, they turn to the **income statement** which shows the company's revenues and expenses for the year. Revenues are the increases, expenses the decreases, in its net resources which arise largely from its operating activities. Profit (synonyms: income, earnings) is the excess of revenues over expenses. It is a widely used indicator of a company's performance in a period. Investors relate profit to some other figure in the accounts – to the previous period's profit, to the number of shares outstanding (earnings per share), or to the company's assets or capital (rate of return on investment) – to increase its utility as a performance measure.

Companies often include other statements in their annual accounts. One of the most useful is the **cash flow statement** which, as its name suggests, summarises the flows of cash into and out of the company during the financial year. In many European countries this is now a required part of the annual accounts of publicly quoted companies.

Relating these three financial statements to the resource flow cycle in Exhibit 1.1, only the cash flow statement records flows – specifically, cash flows – with respect to the three activities shown. The income statement is also a 'flow' statement but it focuses largely on flows arising from the operating activities of the firm. The balance sheet, by contrast, is a 'stock' statement. It shows the capital the firm has raised, the investments it has made and its trading position (e.g. its inventories and cash) – all in terms of the balances in these accounts on a given day. However, it does cover all three activities.

The **notes to the accounts** serve several purposes. They provide more detail on items in the balance sheet, income statement and cash flow statement. They also inform the reader about the accounting policies the managers of the company have followed when preparing its accounts.

Companies publish financial information in addition to the annual accounts. For example, publicly quoted companies are required by stock exchange rules to produce **interim accounts** either half-yearly or quarterly, depending on the stock exchange.

What is an accounting entity?

Published accounts must relate to some entity. What is it? For the purposes of this book, an **accounting entity** *is a company or group of companies under common control*. This is a narrow definition. The term 'accounting entity' can also embrace the business activities of an individual trader or of a partnership. Charitable organisations, government agencies and co-operatives are accounting entities, too. We limit our study to companies for two reasons. First, organisations like charities and government agencies have different accounting and reporting practices. Second, in many countries sole traders and partnerships are not required to publish accounts. However, the ideas in this book apply to not-for-profit organisations and unincorporated businesses which adopt corporate accounting practices.

An accounting entity is not necessarily the same as a legal entity. For example, in most countries a group of companies under common control is not a legal entity (although each individual company in the group is). It is, however, an accounting entity: it must prepare **consolidated accounts**. In contrast, the business activities of a sole trader or a partnership constitute an accounting entity even though, in law, the private and business activities of the trader or active partner cannot be separated. For example, the liability of such individuals for the debts of their business is unlimited, whereas in the case of most companies, the liability of the owners (the shareholders) is limited to the share capital for which they have subscribed.

Even with our narrow definition of accounting entity, there are practical problems applying it. How is control defined? Must the dominant company own a majority of the voting shares of the dominated company? Or can control be demonstrated in other ways, for example by means of contractual arrangements? There are other issues. For example, many companies in Europe and elsewhere have set up funded pension plans for their employees. Under the scheme, company cash is transferred to a pension fund which invests it on a long-term basis to meet future pension payments to retired employees. Should the pension fund be considered a separate accounting entity or is it really part of the company? We address these issues in the course of the book.

There are, in law, various types of company. The two most common in the European Union are the public and the private (limited liability) company. A **public company** differs from a **private company** in two important respects. First, it usually has a larger capital base because the law sets a higher minimum capital requirement for public companies. Second, there are usually no restrictions on the transfer of shares of a public company. Private companies can and do impose such restrictions. An EU company signals whether it is public or private by the abbreviation – or *extension* – attached to its name. This varies by country: for example, public companies in France and Spain carry the extension *SA*, in Austria and Germany *AG*, and in Ireland and the UK *PLC*.

A full listing of extensions – for non-European as well as European companies – can be found on the website www.corporateinformation.com.

Note that companies whose shares are listed on a stock exchange are public companies in the legal sense. A private company cannot be a quoted company. Stock exchanges impose high minimum capital requirements and usually outlaw restrictions on the transfer of shares.[1]

Who are the users of financial accounts?

The principal users of a company's published annual accounts are investors. 'Investors' is a broad term. When the president of a company writes an open letter to shareholders in the management report which accompanies the annual accounts, he or she is addressing not just existing owners of the company's shares but also the investment community at large.

There are other users of annual accounts, as Exhibit 1.2 shows.

Users are as varied as society itself. Banks and other creditors consult the accounts to check on the financial health of prospective borrowers. Unions use them in formulating wage claims. Tax authorities refer to them when calculating a company's income tax liability. When public interest groups campaign for corporate action on social and environmental issues, they often cite (high) profit figures – taken from the accounts – to justify their demands.

Since there are different user groups, why are there not different versions of the annual accounts to meet the specific information needs of each group? Multiple accounts are rejected on cost-benefit grounds. It's argued that by meeting the needs of investors, who are the primary users and the most demanding, the accounts will be comprehensive enough to serve the needs of other user groups. Moreover, the management report which accompanies the annual accounts often contains supplementary information – for example, on the health and safety of employees or on the company's environmental activities – which is of interest to other groups.

Governments acknowledge the public interest in annual accounts by regulating their format and content. For example, member states in the EU require all companies, public and private, to

Exhibit 1.2 Users of corporate financial accounts

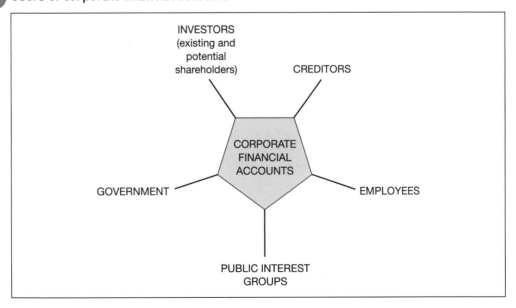

publish annual accounts, even if in abridged form. Additional disclosure burdens are placed on larger EU companies, private as well as public.

Government regulation of accounts is controversial. Supporters claim that investors as well as other user groups benefit from it. Standardising the form and content of accounts makes it easier for investors to compare the financial performance of different companies in the same industry in one country. This enables them to allocate investment resources more efficiently. The European Commission extended the argument to cross-border comparisons of companies. Making accounting and reporting practices similar across member states should improve the allocation of capital within the whole European Union, it asserts.

Those opposed to regulation take a different line. Companies compete for funds. They try to raise money at the lowest cost. Information reduces uncertainty and, as a result, the rate of return investors seek on the capital they supply. Thus it is in a company's interest, anti-interventionists maintain, to furnish investors with the information they demand. Opponents of accounting regulation have had limited success so far. But the debate illustrates an important point. Arguments on accounting matters are not always technical: they can enter the political arena as well.

The aim – and desirable qualities – of accounts

What is the aim of financial accounts? This appears to be a philosophical question – but, in fact, the answer has important implications for the way financial statements are prepared. The generally accepted view today is that *the main objective of published accounts is to provide financial information that users of accounts will find helpful in making economic decisions.*[2] This begs the question: what types of information do users find helpful in making such decisions?

Consider the process by which an investment decision is made. (We focus on investment decisions because, as argued earlier, investors use published accounts more than any other group.) An investor wants to allocate resources among various investment opportunities. A rational investor will choose those which offer the highest return for a given level of risk. **Return** is measured by the amount and timing of future cash flows expected from an investment, **risk** by the expected variability of those cash flows. Thus the investor needs information which will help him or her estimate the amount, timing and variability of future cash flows associated with an investment.

The (annual) accounts provide such information, it is claimed. The balance sheet helps the investor assess a company's financial strength and the income statement its financial performance. The cash flow statement offers additional clues about the company's ability to survive. (Even profitable companies can founder because of the cash flow strains of rapid expansion.) Armed with this picture of the company's financial past, an investor can better predict the cash flows it is likely to generate in the future.

This view of the objective of published accounts – the decision-usefulness view – has not gone unchallenged. Some people maintain that accounting is a control device and the main purpose of accounts is to monitor and influence behaviour. According to this 'monitoring' view, owners want to know whether the managers to whom they have entrusted their capital have invested it wisely. Creditors want to know whether owners have taken actions such as paying high dividends that have depleted the assets of the firm and threatened its ability to repay its debts. Existing accounts provide this information because they show owners and creditors what has happened to the firm in the past. Investors, however, want forward-looking information – information about a firm's new products and investment plans, for example – and they will not find it in conventional accounts, according to this view.[3] In later chapters, we see how this difference in viewpoint can have major practical consequences, especially in the valuation of assets and liabilities.

There is less disagreement about the desirable characteristics of financial information. For information to be useful, whether for investment decisions or for monitoring of managers, it should be:

1 *Understandable*. Financial reports are not designed for the benefit of experts alone. They should be accessible to the non-professional investor who is informed on business and economic matters and willing to spend time analysing them.

2 *Relevant*. Information is relevant if it has the potential to affect a user's beliefs: to confirm his beliefs about the past, or to shape his beliefs about the future. Relevant information is usually timely: delay reduces its utility.

3 *Reliable*. Information is considered reliable if it gives a faithful picture of what has occurred, if it's comprehensive (nothing material has been left out of the picture), and if it's verifiable (the contents of the picture can be checked against independent sources of information).

   Reliable information is neutral. Information loses its neutrality if it favours one user group at the expense of another. For example, the intentional understatement of assets results in biased information: creditors may benefit but investors suffer. Notice the inclusion of 'intentional'. Preparers of accounts are encouraged to be prudent in the way they account for assets (and liabilities). This may lead to a conservative valuation of assets – but not their deliberate understatement.

   It must be neutral in another way. It must 'tell it how it is'. Thus smoothing a firm's income (reducing its inherent variability by accounting devices) can also result in biased information.

4 *Comparable*. Assessing a company's performance requires investors and others to make comparisons – with the performance of the company's competitors and with its own performance in previous periods. To make valid comparisons, they need information which is consistent across firms and over time.

5 There is one general test which useful financial information must meet. Gathering and publishing it must be economically justifiable. Only if the benefits from the information exceed the costs of obtaining it should it be collected and disseminated.

The above is a (partial) list of the characteristics of useful information on which all can agree. It is when we come to operationalise these ideas that disagreement arises. For example, people disagree about the ranking of the various properties of useful information. Relevance and reliability are often cited as the most important, with neutrality, comparability and other characteristics being, in effect, related to these two (e.g. neutrality and reliability; comparability and relevance). But what if relevance and reliability are in conflict? Consider the case where, in order to obtain information quickly, a user may have to accept that it is tentative: there is a trade-off between timeliness (relevance) and completeness (reliability). Which should take precedence? Agreement on the answer to this question could have far-reaching consequences. Those who consider decision-usefulness the main aim of accounts rank relevance ahead of reliability. Those who emphasise the monitoring role of accounts put reliability before relevance.

Accounting fallacy no. 1: *'Published accounts, when accompanied by an unqualified auditor's report, give an accurate picture of the firm.'*

Novice investors arrive at this opinion usually on the strength of two observations. First, they see that the balance sheet of every company balances, no matter what its size. Second, they are struck by the fact that the values of items in the accounts – assets, liabilities, revenues, expenses – are stated, if not to the actual euro, dollar or yen, then to the nearest thousand, even in very large companies.

   Neither observation provides evidence that the accounts are accurate. The two sides of a company's balance sheet balance because of the way it records each accounting transaction or event. We illustrate this point at length in the following chapter.

The precision of the monetary amounts assigned to items in the accounts is not an inherent characteristic of accounts and is misleading. *Published accounts rest on estimates*, a fact which is rarely highlighted and of which readers of accounts are often ignorant. For example, management have to estimate the expected economic lives of buildings and equipment in order to determine the depreciation charge for the year. They must estimate what proportion of amounts owed by customers (receivables) will prove uncollectible and which inventory items will prove difficult to sell – and adjust the accounts accordingly.

Because a company's accounts are prepared on the assumption that the company will continue in business – known in the business world as the **going concern assumption**, judgements about the future have to be incorporated in the current period's financial statements. Thus management must make provision against current revenues for future (estimated) warranty costs associated with this period's sales. They must make provision for future (estimated) pension payments arising from employees' service in the current period.

One of the characteristics of useful financial information we identified was reliability. Note that we deliberately did not specify accuracy as a component of reliable information. In view of the pervasive use of estimates in the accounts, this is too much to expect.

The long arm of accounting

Accounting pervades business life. It is not surprising that it is described as the language of business. A good understanding of where the numbers in financial statements come from and what they tell us about the company is essential, therefore, for anyone pursuing a business career.

The way accounting is woven into the fabric of business life can be seen in its role in legal contracts. In many companies, the employment contract promises the employee a bonus in addition to his or her regular salary. The bonus is based on the company's reported profit in the year. The reason for linking pay to profit is to motivate employees and encourage them to think and act like company owners. Accounting numbers also appear in debt contracts – usually with the aim of constraining the borrowing company's behaviour. Thus the borrowing company may be required to maintain minimum levels of working capital or shareholders' equity or a ratio such as profit-to-interest payments. The terms 'profit', 'working capital', 'shareholders' equity' are usually not defined in the contract. (Fear not: we discuss these terms in later chapters.) Instead, the contracting parties rely on the numbers in the company's financial statements. The way these numbers are calculated – and any changes in their calculation for regulatory or other reasons – can have important economic consequences. For example, if the borrowing company's reported profit-to-interest ratio falls below the specified minimum, the company may be in breach of the debt contract. The lender may then impose tougher terms on the company (e.g. a higher interest rate) or, worse, demand immediate repayment of its loan.

The impact of accounting on the business world is not confined to contracts, however. Investors appraise a company's published accounts along with its products, management and business strategy. If it has 'transparent' accounts and makes full financial disclosure, it is easier for investors to evaluate the company, investment risks are reduced and investors demand a lower return. This has broader economic consequences. Rajan and Zingales, two University of Chicago economists, found that industries that are more dependent on external finance grow faster (than other industries) in countries with high-quality corporate accounting. The reason for this is that they can raise capital more cheaply. Rajan and Zingales illustrate their findings with two industries, tobacco and pharmaceuticals (pharma), in three countries, Malaysia, South Korea and Chile. Tobacco requires little external finance (companies generate more than enough cash internally to finance expenditures on plant and equipment), whereas pharma requires lots.

Malaysia, South Korea and Chile were at a similar stage of development in the 1980s: all were moderate-income, fast-growing countries. Malaysia's financial markets – as measured by its accounting disclosures and other aspects of corporate governance – were the most developed, followed by South Korea and then Chile. Rajan and Zingales found that Malaysia's pharma industry grew at a 4% higher annual rate than its tobacco industry in the 1980s, while in South Korea the margin of advantage was only 3%. By contrast, Chile's pharma industry grew at a 2.5% *lower* rate than tobacco in that decade.[4]

Accounting's reach extends beyond contracts and corporate governance. It can unsettle governments. A vivid example of this occurred in the UK in 2002. Early that year many UK companies announced they were closing their pension schemes to new employees and, in some cases, to existing employees as well. One reason management gave for their decision was the proposed introduction of a new UK accounting rule which would force a company to value its pension fund assets and liabilities at current value and show the resulting surplus or deficit on its own balance sheet. Most UK pension funds invest a large proportion of their assets in equities. As a result of the sharp fall in world stock markets in 2000 and 2001, many companies' pension funds moved from a surplus to a deficit in these years. Management argued that reflecting pension fund volatility on the balance sheet in the way the accounting rule proposed would increase the perceived riskiness of the company and raise its cost of capital. The companies' decision to modify their pension schemes, though understandable, alarmed trade unions and the government. Trade unions saw the changes as a disguised pay cut. The government was concerned that the changes would lead to less private pension provision and greater demand for state-funded benefits in the future. As a result, the finance ministry put discreet pressure on the (private) rule-making body to amend its pension accounting rules.[5]

War, declared Talleyrand, the nineteenth century French statesman, is too important to be left to the generals. Is accounting too important to be left to the accountants? The above examples suggest it is. If so, this is added incentive for business students who do not aspire to be accountants to study it.

The structure of the book

The book has three parts. In Part 1, which covers Chapters 2 to 6, we describe and illustrate the core of financial accounting. We learn how the two principal financial statements, the balance sheet and income statement, are constructed and what they tell us (Chapters 2 and 3). We describe the main accounting records and outline the way firms keep them: this helps explain key accounting terms managers use (Chapter 4). We discover what are the essential features of accrual-based accounting, the method of accounting used by most companies (Chapter 5). And we find out what financial information the typical European company discloses in its annual report and how it presents it (Chapter 6). This chapter also contains an overview of the cash flow statement, the third main financial statement.

In Part 2, we examine the way companies account for and report the various types of asset and liability identified in Part 1. We start by providing a framework for the discussion. Accountants are faced with two central questions: when should an asset (or liability) be recognised in the accounts? and how should it be valued? We describe the recognition criteria and valuation methods European companies currently follow in their accounts (Chapter 7) and we illustrate them in our later discussion of particular assets and liabilities (Chapters 8–17).

Making the most of all the financial data companies publish is our goal in Part 3. We try to show how an understanding of where the accounting numbers come from and how they are calculated can sharpen our skills – in interpreting the cash flow statement (Chapter 18) and analysing actual financial statements (Chapters 19 and 20).

Throughout the book we illustrate European accounting and reporting practice by means of examples. To avoid national bias, we do not usually specify a unit of currency in the examples. In those cases where clarity demands that a unit of currency be specified, we use the euro. When presenting financial data, we follow the conventions used in English-language accounts:

- summed amounts are shown at the foot of a column of numbers;
- commas are used to indicate thousands, periods to indicate decimals;
- a billion is a thousand million, thus 2,435.7 million reads: 2 billion, 435 million and 700 thousand units of currency.

We use certain terms frequently in the book. Defining them here may help you. Countries that have signed the Treaty of Rome (1957) (and subsequent amending treaties) are member states of the European Union (EU). An **EU company** is a company incorporated under the laws of an EU member state. A **European company** is one incorporated under the laws of any European country. The terms 'company' and 'firm' are used interchangeably.

Notes to Chapter 1

1 Beware: the terminology can be confusing here. In the financial press, companies whose shares are quoted on a stock exchange are often referred to as 'public companies'; however, a large, unquoted company can be, in legal terms, a public company.

2 International Accounting Standards Board, *Framework for the Preparation and Presentation of Financial Statements*.

3 For a summary of this view, *see* Watts, R. and Zimmerman, J. (1986), *Positive Accounting Theory*, Englewood Cliffs, NJ: Prentice Hall, chapter 8.

4 Rajan, R. and Zingales, L. (1998), Financial dependence and growth, *American Economic Review*, 88(3): 559–586.

5 Peel, M. and Shrimsley, R. (2002), Darling [UK finance minister] presses for rethink of controversial pensions rule, *Financial Times*, 3 March. Note that the pensions rule was not the only reason firms gave for changing their pension schemes. Other factors cited were minimum funding requirements, employees' longer life expectancy, and lower expected investment returns.

Foundations

2

The balance sheet: a financial picture of the firm

INTRODUCTION

In this chapter we introduce the balance sheet, one of the three principal financial statements issued by companies. The other two major financial statements – the income statement and the cash flow statement – are introduced in Chapters 3 and 6 respectively.

We begin our study of the balance sheet by asking what it is and what purpose it serves. We then look at the main components – assets, liabilities and owners' equity – of a balance sheet and provide accounting definitions for them. An example follows, in which we see how the balance sheet of a company changes over time as a result of transactions between the firm and others. Next, we present the actual balance sheet of a large company and illustrate the way assets and liabilities are classified. We end the chapter by discussing a popular misconception about what the numbers in the balance sheet really mean.

The purpose of a balance sheet

The balance sheet of a company – or of any organisation or individual – gives a listing of its resources and of its sources of capital, as of a particular day.

With this statement, financial statement users have a picture of the company – in two dimensions. They can see the composition of the resources under the firm's command. By examining the 'sources of capital' section, they can see how those resources have been financed.

The resources of a firm are described in the balance sheet as **assets**. Examples of typical corporate assets are buildings and equipment, goods held for sale (i.e. inventory) and cash. The sources of capital used to finance the assets are known as **equities**. They consist of the interests of creditors and owners. By supplying capital to the firm, creditors and owners have a stake in (or equity in) its assets.

The interests of creditors, such as banks and suppliers of goods or services, are of fixed duration. We shall refer to their interests as **liabilities**. Thus the liabilities of the firm are the amounts it owes to its creditors. The interests of owners are of indefinite duration. We describe them as **owners' equity**.

In a balance sheet, the assets of the firm are equal to the interests (equities) of creditors and owners in them.

There are two important features of the balance sheet which should be stressed at this stage. *First, it is a statement of the balances of the firm's assets and equities on a particular day.* Since the firm engages in business activities every working day, the balances of its individual assets and liabilities are likely to change as frequently. Hence it should specify the date on which its balance sheet is prepared.

Second, assets and equities are not equal by chance or good management: they are equal by definition. Recall that equities are the interests of creditors and owners in the firm's assets. Think of such interests as claims. A company's assets cannot go unclaimed. Creditors usually have a prior claim to the firm's assets. From a legal standpoint, their interests precede those of the firm's owners. Should a firm go out of business, then any proceeds from the disposal of its assets will be used first to satisfy the claims of its creditors. Any remaining assets belong to its owners. This is why owners are said to have a residual interest in (or residual claim to) their company's assets.

Company A
BALANCE SHEET
at 31 December year xx

ASSETS
– LIABILITIES   . . . (Prior) claims of creditors
OWNERS' EQUITY   . . . (Residual) claims of owners

The components of the balance sheet

Assets then are the resources of the company. Creditors and owners provide the capital necessary to acquire them. But what constitutes an asset? What characteristics must a resource have for it to be considered an asset of the firm? Similarly, what makes an obligation an accounting liability?

Assets

Consider assets first. An accounting asset usually has the following three characteristics:

1 *it is expected to provide future economic benefits to the firm;*
2 *it is owned or controlled by the firm; and*
3 *the firm acquired it as a result of a past transaction or event.*[1]

Let's explore this definition further. An asset yields *future economic benefits* if the company receives cash – or avoids paying cash – in future. (Cash itself is always considered an asset.) Thus an amount owed by a customer, described in the balance sheet as an 'account receivable', is an asset because the company expects to receive cash at a later date. Similarly, goods held for resale (known as 'inventory') are assets, assuming they can be sold and cash received. Buildings and plant generate cash indirectly. For example, equipment is used to produce the goods (or services) which themselves generate cash. A prepayment of, say, rent on a building is also an asset since the company occupying the building enjoys use of it during the rent term.

Assessing whether an investment today will yield benefits tomorrow is an essential task of management. It is not always an easy one and companies err on the side of caution. Thus if it is difficult to show that the benefits from an expenditure will extend beyond the current financial year or if the benefits themselves are highly uncertain, then no asset is recognised. This is why expenditures on basic research are rarely recorded as assets.

Ownership by the company is another feature of virtually all resources that are considered accounting assets. In this respect, the technical usage of the term 'asset' differs from its everyday one. Clearly, the employees of a company are one of its most important resources but, since it does not own them, they cannot be treated as an accounting asset. However, the right to use a resource, which may carry with it the same economic benefits as ownership, can be recorded as an accounting asset in some circumstances. For example, if a company leases a computer for a period equal to the computer's economic life, then in many countries the computer can be treated as its asset even though it doesn't own it.

Notice that in all the examples given so far, a *past transaction* has been assumed. This is the third common characteristic of accounting assets. A firm buys equipment in exchange for cash (or a promise to pay cash later). It records an asset, 'equipment', when the transaction has taken place.

This requirement prevents certain resources – for example, the goodwill a company has built up over the years from its own efforts – from being classified as accounting assets. Only if a firm buys a business or collection of assets from another and pays a premium over its market value can it record the premium as an asset, 'goodwill (on acquisition)'.

In the above examples, the transaction involves an exchange. Resources are swapped between two parties. However, sometimes a firm acquires a benefit without making a sacrifice. For example, charitable organisations receive gifts of land, buildings or shares of companies. Where such gifts meet the other conditions for asset recognition (future economic benefits, ownership), they should be recorded as accounting assets.

Liabilities

We turn now to accounting liabilities. Legally, a liability is an *obligation of one entity to deliver money, goods or services to another*. This definition embraces many accounting liabilities. An account payable, for example, represents an obligation to pay cash to a supplier. Note that the obligation may be expressed in goods or services rather than cash. British Airways reports an item 'Sales in advance of carriage' in the liability section of its balance sheet. This represents the airline's obligation at the balance sheet date to provide travel services to customers in the future.

However, the legal and accounting definitions of liability do not always coincide. Accountants usually insist that *for an accounting liability to exist, the firm must have a present obligation*. A commitment is not an accounting liability unless it is irrevocable. For example, a company places an order with a supplier for goods to be delivered in the future. At the time of the order, neither cash nor goods have changed hands. Only promises – to supply goods on the one hand, to pay for them on the other – have been exchanged. A legal liability may exist for both parties but in normal circumstances neither side recognises an accounting one. This occurs only when one party executes its part of the contract. Continuing our example, when the supplier delivers the goods contracted for, it has fulfilled its part of the agreement. The customer then has a present obligation. It recognises a liability 'Account payable (to company X)' on its balance sheet.

The exact amount of the accounting liability need not be known in advance. For example, a car manufacturer does not know at the time of sale of one of its products how much it will have to pay for repair costs while the vehicle is under warranty. It can estimate these repair costs, however. It records an estimated liability for them when the vehicle is sold.

We now have the essential features of an accounting liability:

1 *it is a present obligation of the firm to another party;*
2 *it arises from a past transaction or event;*
3 *to settle the obligation, the firm must give up assets of a known or estimated amount.*[2]

Owners' equity

You will remember we described the owners' interest as a residual one. It is the difference between accounting assets and accounting liabilities. It consists of two elements: contributed capital and earned capital. 'Contributed capital' represents the investments made by the owners when the firm is founded and when later it calls for new capital for expansion or to repay debts. 'Earned capital' represents the accumulated profits of the firm which have been reinvested in the business and not distributed as dividends to owners.

For most companies, assets exceed liabilities and the owners' residual interest is positive. The owners' equity can be negative, however. This is usually a temporary situation. When a company's liabilities exceed its assets, the company is technically insolvent. The balance sheet indicates it is unable to pay all its debts. If this is in fact the case, the company is bankrupt. One outcome is that the company will cease trading and its assets will be sold to meet creditors' claims. If, however, its assets generate sufficient cash flow to pay its debts when they fall due, its creditors will usually allow it to continue trading.

The balance sheet and transactions

The amounts shown against individual assets and equities are the result of a continuous record-keeping process, not of a calculation made once a year on the balance sheet date.

During a financial period many transactions occur which affect a firm's assets, liabilities and owners' equity, and thus its balance sheet. To ensure that these transactions are properly recorded, the firm sets up an account for each type of asset (A), liability (L) and owners' equity (OE). As a transaction takes place, it is recorded and the accounts updated. The balance in an account on any particular day captures the effect of all the transactions which have been recorded in it, from the date the account was first established up to that time.

Transactions, therefore, cause the balances in individual A, L and OE accounts to change – to increase or decrease. However, they do not upset the equation (strictly, the identity) underlying the balance sheet:

$$A = L + OE$$

How is this achieved? The explanation is simple. *Each transaction affects at least two accounts. The effect of a transaction on the left-hand side of the balance sheet equation is always the same as its effect on the right-hand side.*

The combinations of A, L and OE accounts affected are many. Here are some of those affecting two types of accounts only. A transaction can result in:

1 an increase in one asset, a decrease in another asset;
2 an increase in one liability, a decrease in another liability;
3 an increase in one owner's equity account, a decrease in another owner's equity account;
4 an increase in an asset, an increase in a liability;
5 an increase in an asset, an increase in an owner's equity account;
6 an increase in a liability, a decrease in an owner's equity account;

and so forth. More than two accounts can be affected. For example, a transaction can result in an increase in one asset, a decrease in another asset and an increase in a liability. *No matter how many accounts are affected, the transaction itself must balance.* The change to the asset side of the balance sheet must be equal to the change to the equity side. In this way, the balance sheet identity is preserved after each transaction.

We now illustrate the effect of transactions on the balance sheet. The example that follows concerns the establishment of a new company. In this chapter we illustrate the accounting effects of transactions the company enters into before it starts operations. (In the next chapter we focus on the transactions that occur during its first month of operations.) We first describe the transactions during the company's first week and, in Exhibits 2.1 and 2.2, show the effect of each on the individual balance sheet accounts. We then prepare a balance sheet at the end of the first week.

Illustration

Georgie Sand and Fred Chopin decide to move to Mallorca for health reasons. Shortly after their arrival in December, they open a shop selling stationery and other writing materials. The following events occur during the week prior to the shop's opening on 8 January year 1.

1 On 2 January, they complete the necessary legal steps to form a company, to be called 'Sun, C and Sand', and invest 20,000 of their own funds in the new business.

2 The next day, the company leases shop premises for three months. The rent for the period which amounts to 6,000 is paid in cash that day.

3 On 4 January, equipment is bought for 10,000 cash. It includes shop fixtures, a cash register and a new shop sign. The equipment is expected to have a life of several years.

4 That same day, the company borrows 12,000 from a bank for a three-month period.

5 On 5 January, the company buys merchandise for 35,000 of which 24,000 is acquired on credit and 11,000 for cash.

6 Defective merchandise costing 5,000 is returned to a supplier for full credit on 6 January. The company has not yet paid the supplier for the goods.

7 On 7 January, the company finds it has surplus shop fixtures costing 1,000 and exchanges them for merchandise of similar value with a neighbouring shop.

On 8 January, Sun, C and Sand Company opens its doors for business.

We consider first the balance sheet impact of transactions 1 to 4.

1 *Initial investment*

On 2 January, Sand and Chopin invest 20,000 of their own funds in a new company, Sun, C and Sand.

Financial statement impact (amounts in 000):

Assets	=	Liabilities + Owners' equity
+20	=	+20
Cash		*Contributed capital*

The company's cash increases by 20,000 (A+); the claims of its owners increase by the same amount (OE+). As a result of the investment, Sand's and Chopin's own assets go down by, and the company's increase by, 20,000. Note that the corporate entity, Sun, C and Sand, is legally distinct from its owners. What we record above is the effect of the transaction on the company's accounts.

2 *Lease of shop premises*

On 3 January, the company pays 6,000 in cash for the three-month lease of a shop.

Financial statement impact (amounts in 000):

Assets		=	Liabilities	+	Owners' equity
Prepaid rent	+6				
Cash	−6				
Net effect	0	=	0		0

The company acquires, for 6,000, the right to use shop space for three months. The prepayment of rent represents an accounting asset to the company because it will receive economic benefits beyond the current period. This transaction involves the exchange of one asset for another (Cash −; Prepaid rent +).

3 *Purchase of equipment*

On 4 January, the company pays 10,000 in cash for shop equipment.

Financial statement impact (amounts in 000):

Assets		=	Liabilities	+	Owners' equity
Equipment	+10				
Cash	−10				
Net effect	0	=	0		0

Again, the company acquires an accounting asset, since the equipment is expected to provide economic benefits for several years. As in 2, this transaction involves the exchange of one asset for another (Equipment +; Cash −).

4 *Bank loan*
Also on 4 January, the company borrows 12,000 from a bank for three months.

Financial statement impact (amounts in 000):

Assets	=	Liabilities	+	Owners' equity
+12	=	+12		
Cash		*Bank loan*		

By obtaining a loan from a bank, the company's cash balance increases (A+) and so, too, do the claims of creditors to the company's assets (L+). Note that, in this case, the bank's claim of 12,000 covers all the company's assets: it is not a claim to a particular asset.

Exhibit 2.1 shows the effect on Sun, C and Sand's accounts of transactions 1 to 4 individually and cumulatively.

Exhibit 2.1 Effect of transactions on the balance sheet

	Sun, C and Sand Company Transactions between 2 and 4 January				
	Transaction (amounts in 000)				
Account title	(1) *Initial investment*	(2) *Shop rental*	(3) *Equipment purchase*	(4) *Bank loan*	*Balance at 4/1*
Assets					
Cash	+20	−6	−10	+12	16
Prepaid rent		+6			6
Shop equipment			+10		10
Total assets	+20	0	0	+12	32
Liabilities					
Bank loan				+12	12
Owners' equity					
Contributed capital	+20				20
Total liabilities and owners' equity	+20	0	0	+12	32

We now consider the effect on the company's balance sheet of the three transactions that occur between 5 and 7 January.

5 *Purchase of inventory*

On 5 January, the company buys merchandise for 35,000, of which 24,000 is acquired on credit and the balance of 11,000 for cash.

Financial statement impact (amounts in 000):

Assets		=	Liabilities	+	Owners' equity
+24		=	+24		
Net effect of:			Account payable		
Inventory	+35				
Cash	−11				

The company acquires an asset, inventory, in part with cash and in part on account. ('On account' or 'on credit' is the phrase used to indicate that the buyer has bought goods or services under deferred payment terms offered by the seller.) By allowing the company to delay payment, the supplier has provided it with capital. Since this capital has to be repaid – within 30–45 days, depending on the credit terms – it is a liability of the company. Note that, in this case, more than two accounts are affected and yet the transaction balances:

$$\text{Inventory } +, \text{ Cash } - = +24{,}000 = \text{Account payable } +$$

6 *Return of goods*

On 6 January, the company returns defective goods costing 5,000 to a supplier and is reimbursed in full.

Financial statement impact (amounts in 000):

Assets	=	Liabilities	+	Owners' equity
−5	=	−5		
Inventory		Account payable		

By returning goods it has not yet paid for, the company reduces its inventory (Inventory –) and the amount it owes its supplier (Account payable –). Both asset and liability accounts decrease by the cost of the goods returned, 5,000.

7 *Exchange of equipment for inventory*

On 7 January, the company exchanges surplus equipment costing 1,000 for merchandise of the same value.

Financial statement impact (amounts in 000):

Assets		=	Liabilities	+	Owners' equity
Inventory	+1				
Equipment	−1				
Net effect	0	=	0		0

An exchange of one asset for another need not always involve cash. In this case, the inventory the company acquires (A+) is paid for with equipment (A–).

Exhibit 2.2 shows the effect on Sun, C and Sand's accounts of transactions 5 to 7. The balance in each of the accounts at the close of 7 January is also given.

Exhibit 2.2 Effect of transactions on the balance sheet

Sun, C and Sand Company
Transactions between 5 and 7 January

Transaction (amounts in 000)

Account title	Balance at 4/1	(5) Purchase of inventory	(6) Return of goods	(7) Inventory for equipment	Balance at 7/1
Assets					
Cash	16	−11			5
Merchandise inventory	0	+35	−5	+1	31
Prepaid rent	6				6
Shop equipment	10			−1	9
Total assets	32	+24	−5	0	51
Liabilities					
Bank loan	12				12
Account payable	0	+24	−5		19
Owners' equity					
Contributed capital	20				20
Total liabilities and owners' equity	32	+24	−5	0	51

Observe that the change in assets is equal to the change in equities for each transaction. Thus in transactions 2 and 7 the net change in assets and in equities is zero since one asset is exchanged for another. In transaction 5, the net increase in assets is 24,000 (the increase in inventory of 35,000 less the cash payment of 11,000 to the supplier of the merchandise) which is matched by a similar increase in liabilities (the balance of 24,000 still owing to the supplier).

Since each transaction balances, we can draw up a balance sheet after any one of the transactions. It will reflect all accounting events up to that time. You can see this in Exhibits 2.1 and 2.2 where the balances in the accounts at the end of 4 and 7 January are shown.

Exhibit 2.2 also illustrates the continuous nature of balance sheet accounts. Drawing up a balance sheet does not signal the close of asset and equity accounts. It simply indicates a reckoning of the state of those accounts at a particular time. The balance at the end of one period (e.g. that ending on 4 January) becomes the balance at the start of the next (that starting on 5 January). As new transactions are recorded (on 5 January), they alter the initial balance and create a new one.

The list of account balances at 7 January is presented as a formal balance sheet in Exhibit 2.3.

The format of the balance sheet in Exhibit 2.3 is similar to that used by US companies and by many non-US companies in the English-language version of their annual accounts. However, other balance sheet formats are permitted. We discuss the various ways companies present their financial statements, both balance sheets and income statements, in Chapter 6.

Exhibit 2.3

Sun, C and Sand Company
BALANCE SHEET
at 7 January year 1
(amounts in 000)

Current assets			Current liabilities		
Cash	5		Bank loan	12	
Merchandise inventory	31		Account payable	19	
Prepaid rent	6				31
		42			
Fixed assets			Owners' equity		
Shop equipment		9	Contributed capital		20
Total assets		51	Total equities		51

Balance sheet presentation

Now that we've defined what accountants mean by 'asset' and 'liability' and seen how transactions give rise to them, we look at an actual balance sheet to find out how a typical European company presents them. Exhibit 2.4 shows the consolidated balance sheet of a major European supermarket group, BestPrice Stores. Do not worry if you do not understand all the terms in it. We explain the main items in this section; the remaining ones will be discussed in later chapters. All that we're doing at this stage is setting out the basic structure of a balance sheet. What follows applies to all corporate balance sheets, European and non-European.

Note: We discuss BestPrice Stores as if it were a real company; it is not. BestPrice's accounts, extracts from its company report and discussions about its business activities (presented here, and later in chapters 3 and 6) together present an illustrative model of a large European retail group, and have been designed to depict many common aspects of such a business.

Meaning of 'consolidated'

The first noteworthy feature is the statement's title. The balance sheet illustrated is the **consolidated** balance sheet at the end of x2 and, for comparative purposes, that of end-x1. (Companies have to provide comparative figures for the previous year on the face of the balance sheet.) This means that the balance sheets of the parent company BestPrice Stores S.A. and its subsidiary companies (those over which it has management control, usually represented by a majority shareholding) have been combined. For example, the amount of €1,533mn. shown against 'inventories' is the sum of the inventories of the parent company and those of its subsidiary companies. BestPrice lists its principal subsidiaries in the notes to the x2 accounts.

Classification of assets and liabilities

Take a closer look at BestPrice's assets and liabilities. You'll notice that BestPrice distinguishes between those that are **current** and those that are **long-term** (or **fixed** in the case of assets). Classifying assets and liabilities in this way is common among retailing and industrial companies. One reason is to help investors gauge the liquidity of a firm's assets and the maturity of its debts.

Exhibit 2.4

BestPrice Stores
CONSOLIDATED BALANCE SHEETS
at end December x2 and x1
(amounts in € millions)

Assets	x2	x1
Current assets		
Cash	658	507
Marketable securities	708	528
Trade and other receivables	1,249	1,022
Inventories	1,533	1,358
Prepayments and accrued income	160	112
Total current assets	4,308	3,527
Fixed assets		
Property, plant and equipment	3,313	3,156
Long-term financial investments	1,084	946
Intangible assets	3,306	3,250
Total fixed assets	7,703	7,352
Total assets	12,011	10,879
Shareholders' equity and liabilities		
Current liabilities		
Short-term debt and current portion of long-term debt	874	1,545
Trade and other payables	2,694	2,608
Accrued expenses and deferred income	1,134	1,038
Total current liabilities	4,702	5,191
Long-term liabilities		
Long-term debt	3,315	2,379
Provisions for contingencies and charges	207	232
Other long-term liabilities	44	3
Total long-term liabilities	3,566	2,614
Minority interests	556	502
Shareholders' equity		
Share capital	135	126
Reserves and retained earnings	2,749	2,194
Net income for the year	303	252
Total shareholders' equity	3,187	2,572
Total shareholders' equity and liabilities	12,011	10,879

● Current assets

Current assets are of two types. The first is the asset which arises from operations and which the firm expects to consume or convert into cash within its operating cycle. Examples are **inventories** and **trade receivables** (amounts owed by customers). For a retailing company like BestPrice, inventories consist largely of **merchandise** (goods awaiting sale). For a manufacturing company, inventories include **raw materials**, **work in progress** (products in the course of manufacture) and **finished goods**. In many countries, **prepayments** (of operating costs such as rent) and **accrued income** (for example, interest earned on customers' debts but not received by the balance sheet date) are classified as current assets, too.

The second type is the asset held for trading purposes or for the short term. Examples are **cash** and **marketable securities**. The latter are usually securities the firm owns and which it plans to sell within one year of the balance sheet date.

Fixed assets

Fixed assets (or non-current assets) also fall into two types. One is the asset the firm plans to use on a continuing basis in its operations. Examples are **property**, **plant and equipment** (also known as 'tangible fixed assets'), and purchased patents, trademarks and goodwill (known as **intangible assets**). The other type is the financial asset which will not mature – or which the firm doesn't plan to sell – within the coming financial year. Examples are long-term loans to customers, investments in the shares of other companies (sometimes described as **long-term financial investments**) and the prepayment of future income taxes ('deferred tax asset'). BestPrice Stores has both types of fixed asset on its x2 consolidated balance sheet.

Note that an asset can be current in one context but fixed in another. The new and used cars on display in a motor dealer's forecourt are its inventory. Company-owned cars used by its sales representatives are its fixed assets. Remember: to an accountant, 'fixed' does not mean immobile!

Current and long-term liabilities

Liabilities are classified on the basis of their maturity. **Current liabilities** are obligations which the company will have to settle – through the payment of cash or the supply of goods or services – within one year of the balance sheet date (or the operating cycle, if longer). They include amounts payable to suppliers (**trade payables**), to banks and other lenders (**short-term debt**) and to governments (taxes payable). All non-current liabilities are grouped under **long-term liabilities**.

Sometimes an obligation exists even though there is no formal evidence of it in the form of an invoice or debt contract. For example, a firm consumes gas, water and electricity but has not received invoices from suppliers by the balance sheet date. Such liabilities, if current, may be described as **accrued expenses**. Similarly, estimated long-term liabilities – for example, for future pensions payable to retired employees – are reported separately as **provisions**. Again, there are examples of both types of liability in BestPrice's x2 consolidated balance sheet.

Minority interests

In preparing a consolidated balance sheet, the parent company – BestPrice Stores S.A., for example – combines all the assets and all the liabilities of its subsidiary companies with its own. The reason is that as a majority shareholder it controls the subsidiaries and their resources and access to capital. But what if it doesn't own 100% of the shares of every subsidiary?

In this event, the equities side of the consolidated balance sheet contains a separate item, **minority interests**. In European company balance sheets, it is usually shown next to 'shareholders' equity'. *It indicates the interests of minority shareholders in the net assets of those (consolidated) subsidiary companies which the parent company does not own outright.* The example in Exhibit 2.5 makes this clearer.

Parent company P has two subsidiaries S1 and S2. It owns 100% of S1's shares but only 80% of S2's shares. In its consolidated accounts, it combines 100% of S2's assets, as well as 100% of S1's, with its own. It does the same with S1 and S2's liabilities. It shows as 'Minority interest' (MI) the 20% of S2's owners' equity – and thus net assets $(OE = A - L)$ – it does not own.

Outside shareholders have a stake in the net assets of BestPrice's subsidiaries that amounts to €556 million at the end of x2. Note that these minority interests are not a liability of the BestPrice

Exhibit 2.5   Minority interest in subsidiary's net assets: illustration

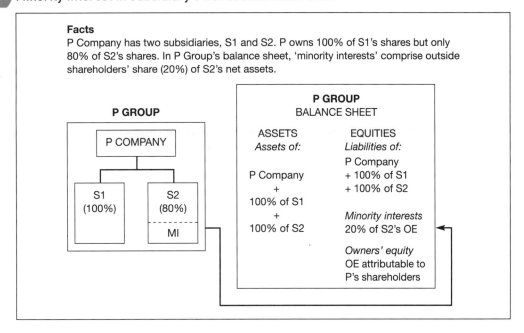

Facts
P Company has two subsidiaries, S1 and S2. P owns 100% of S1's shares but only 80% of S2's shares. In P Group's balance sheet, 'minority interests' comprise outside shareholders' share (20%) of S2's net assets.

group. They are part of the 'group equity' of BestPrice which includes the interests of both parent company (BestPrice Stores S.A.) and outside shareholders.

Shareholders' equity

The owners of public companies such as BestPrice are usually described as **shareholders** because their ownership interest is evidenced by shares. Thus the term **shareholders' equity** replaces 'owners' equity' in the balance sheet. Note that in a consolidated balance sheet, 'shareholders' equity' is the equity of the parent company's shareholders.

As we saw earlier, shareholders' equity has two components. Part represents capital *contributed* by individuals and organisations (e.g. other companies, pension funds, charitable foundations). The company seeks new capital from investors – to invest in new projects, for example – and issues shares to them in exchange for cash. If the company is a publicly quoted company, investors can sell their shares to others at a later date: such share trading has no effect on the company's contributed capital. More generally, changes in the market value of a company's shares have no effect on its reported contributed capital (although its ability to raise new capital will be affected).

Most of the owners' capital in a firm, however, has been *earned* by it through profitable operations. As we shall see in the next chapter, a firm increases its shareholders' equity (and its net assets) by operating profitably. Part of the profits are usually distributed in the form of dividends. The rest is retained and reinvested in the business. Accumulated **retained earnings** constitute the earned (and reinvested) capital of the firm.

Like most companies, BestPrice does not show contributed capital in one figure. The amount shown against **Share capital** is the *nominal* value of the shares it has issued (i.e. number of shares issued (and paid up) times the nominal value per share). However, at the issue date, the company received the *market value* of the shares, which was more than their nominal value. The difference – between market value (at the issue date) and nominal value – is known as **share premium** (or **additional paid-in capital**). BestPrice includes share premium in its reserves. Thus the caption 'Reserves and retained earnings' contains both contributed and earned capital.

In common with many other Continental European companies, BestPrice distinguishes, on the face of the balance sheet, profits earned in the current year (**Net income for the year**) from profits of previous years which it has retained in the business (included in 'Reserves and retained earnings'). Note that the 'net income for the year' figure is 'before appropriation', that is, before BestPrice's shareholders have decided in their annual general meeting (scheduled for x3) how much of the company's x2 profit should be distributed as dividend. The portion not distributed will be included in 'retained earnings' on its end-x3 balance sheet.

We summarise the main components of contributed and earned capital below:

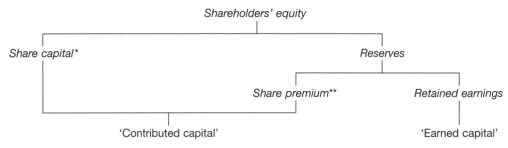

* Shares issued × Nominal value (per share)
** Shares issued × (Market price at issue – Nominal value)

The balance sheet and financial ratios

Financial ratios help us interpret financial statements better. By relating certain numbers to others within the financial statements and constructing ratios from them, we gain insight into a company's performance and financial condition which the numbers alone will not yield us. In this and succeeding chapters we describe the major ratios which are used in the analysis of financial statements. We defer discussion of the techniques of financial statement analysis until Chapter 19.

We start by considering two widely used balance sheet ratios, the current ratio and the debt-equity ratio. To illustrate their construction, we use BestPrice's end-x2 and end-x1 consolidated balance sheets. A condensed version is set out in Exhibit 2.6.

*The **current ratio** tells us the extent to which a company's short-term assets cover its short-term liabilities.* More precisely, it indicates how many euros (or dollars or yen) of current assets a firm has at the balance sheet date to pay each euro of current liabilities:

$$\text{Current ratio} = \frac{\text{Current assets}}{\text{Current liabilities}}$$

BestPrice's current ratio was less than one at the end of both x1 and x2. The ratio improved significantly between the two balance sheet dates, largely as a result of the decline in short-term debt:

			End x2	End x1
BestPrice group's current ratio	=	$\dfrac{(B)}{(D)}$ =	$\dfrac{4,308}{4,702}$	$\dfrac{3,527}{5,191}$
		=	0.92 : 1	0.68 : 1

Exhibit 2.6		

BestPrice Stores
CONDENSED BALANCE SHEETS
at end x2 and x1
(amounts in € millions)

Assets	x2	x1	Shareholders' equity and liabilities	x2	x1
Cash and marketable securities (A)	1,366	1,035	Short-term debt (C)	874	1,545
Other fixed assets	2,942	2,492	Other current liabilities	3,828	3,646
Total current assets (B)	4,308	3,527	Total current liabilities (D)	4,702	5,191
			Long-term debt (E)	3,315	2,379
			Other long-term liabilities	251	235
			Total long-term liabilities	3,566	2,614
			Shareholders' equity	3,187	2,572
			Minority interests	556	502
Fixed assets	7,703	7,352	Group equity (F)	3,743	3,074
Total assets	12,011	10,879	Total shareholders' equity and liabilities	12,011	10,879

The current ratio is a simple but informative measure of a firm's **liquidity**, that is to say its ability to pay its short-term debts when they fall due. Most firms report a current ratio greater than one. At the end of x1, BestPrice had only 68 cents of current assets to pay each euro of current liabilities. Supermarket chains like BestPrice can support a current ratio of less than one without suffering liquidity problems. Many of their sales are for cash but their purchases – which consist mostly of merchandise – are on account. Moreover, they carry relatively small inventories because of the short shelf-life of much of their merchandise.

An alternative guide to a firm's liquidity position is its **working capital**. This is calculated by subtracting current liabilities from current assets on the balance sheet date:

$$\text{Current assets} - \text{Current liabilities} = \text{Working capital}$$

Most firms have positive working capital: their current assets exceed their current liabilities. Supermarket chains like BestPrice often have negative working capital for the reasons given above.

Another balance sheet ratio you will encounter frequently is the **debt–equity ratio**. *It relates the capital provided by a company's financial creditors to that provided by its owners.*

$$\text{Debt–equity ratio} = \frac{\text{Net debt}}{\text{Shareholders' equity}}$$

'Net debt' is defined as short-term plus long-term interest-bearing liabilities, less cash and marketable securities. (Strictly, only cash in excess of operating needs should be deducted but this number isn't usually disclosed so analysts subtract all cash and cash equivalents.) 'Shareholders' equity' represents the company's share capital and reserves (including retained earnings). In a corporate group, it is the equity of both the parent company's shareholders and minority shareholders in its subsidiaries.

BestPrice's relative indebtedness declined between end-x1 and end-x2. Its net debt fell from 94% to 75% of group equity during x2.

		End x2	End x1
BestPrice group's debt–equity ratio $= \dfrac{(C) + (E) - (A)}{(F)} =$		$\dfrac{2{,}823}{3{,}743}$	$\dfrac{2{,}889}{3{,}074}$
In percentage terms		75.4%	94%

The improvement in BestPrice's debt–equity ratio is attributable to the increase in group equity which increased by €670 million between end-x1 and end-x2. Inspection of the accounts indicates that the company issued new shares in x2 to finance expansion of the business. The shares were issued at a price much in excess of their nominal value. BestPrice includes this share premium in 'Reserves'. It's likely that the share issue benefited the group's cash balances, too: 'cash and marketable securities' rose by €330 million in x2. The balance sheet also reveals that BestPrice changed the composition of its debt that year. As we've already noted, current debt fell – from €1,545 million to €874 million – but long-term debt rose almost €1 billion to €3,315 million between the start and end of x2.

Financial statement users calculate the debt–equity ratio to assess a company's financial risk. Remember that shareholders have a residual interest in the firm's assets: the claims of creditors must be satisfied first. If the firm encounters financial problems, creditors' claims may absorb all of its assets and shareholders are left with nothing. Thus the more a firm relies on debt to finance its activities, then, other things being equal, the greater is the risk of financial loss to shareholders.

The debt–equity ratio is often described as a measure of **financial leverage**. By supplementing equity with debt, a firm increases or 'levers up' the capital available to it without diluting the ownership interests of existing shareholders.

The current ratio is not the only way of assessing a firm's liquidity. Nor is the debt–equity ratio the only measure of financial leverage. Moreover, there are alternative versions of these ratios. For example, some analysts relate a firm's net debt to its financial capital (net debt + group equity) rather than the equity provided by the group's shareholders. *The important point is that, no matter how a liquidity or leverage ratio is formulated, it should be calculated consistently over time and across firms.*

Valuation fallacy

Accounting fallacy no. 2: *'The balance sheet indicates the current value of the firm's assets. From it we can derive the current value of the firm.'*

Many people who know little about how a balance sheet is constructed would agree with the above statement. At first sight, it seems reasonable. If a balance sheet is a statement of a company's resources, as we claimed at the beginning of this chapter, then surely all its resources should be shown. If monetary amounts are given against individual assets and liabilities, then is it not fair to assume that they represent current values? After all, an individual drawing up a personal balance sheet will automatically record assets (investments, property, car) and liabilities (mortgage, bank loan) at current market values.

The traditional corporate balance sheet in an annual report is not like an individual's balance sheet. It is not a statement of net worth – for two main reasons. First, most companies state their physical assets (i.e. buildings, equipment, inventory) at cost of acquisition or production. These historical costs will correspond to current values in limited circumstances only. They are most likely to do so when the asset is acquired. They will continue to be equivalent only if prices do not change. In the past, prices of most physical assets have risen because of inflation. Use of historical costs has resulted in the values of these assets being understated.

Second, even if current prices were used to value all assets and liabilities, the book value of the firm – derived from the values of its reported assets and liabilities – would not equal its market value. The main reason for this is that the accounting definition of an asset is narrow. The skills of a company's employees, the reputation of its products, the abilities of its management, these are some of the 'assets' of the firm which are not usually captured on its published balance sheet but which help to determine its market value.

If the balance sheet is not a statement of value (not even the value of accounting assets and liabilities), how do we interpret it? It is useful to think of the historical costs (HC) of assets as representing minimum values. A key assumption underlying HC-based financial statements is that a company is a going concern, that is to say its survival in the foreseeable future is not in doubt. As a result, it should be able, at a minimum, to recover through profitable operations the cost of the inputs used. *Historical costs represent those minimum recoverable costs.*

Of course, there may be circumstances when historical costs fail this test. For example, economic conditions may have caused the value of assets such as plant or inventory to fall permanently below acquisition cost. In this case, only these lower market values may be recoverable and the assets affected must be written down below cost to market value. Where the company's very survival is at risk, liquidation values may be a better guide to amounts recoverable from disposal of its assets. Thus the guiding principle behind the valuation convention in the traditional balance sheet is a conservative one: to state assets at no more than the minimum amount the company expects to receive from their sale or use.

What we have outlined in this chapter is the typical balance sheet of today. It is currently under attack. Some critics argue that by omitting important resources of the firm and by recording physical assets at historical cost, it does not provide relevant information to users of financial statements. We consider in later chapters the reforms to the balance sheet these critics have proposed. Others are more radical. They want additional statements – in balance sheet form – that will provide information about a company's social and environmental resources and obligations (*see* Box 2.1).

Summary

Here are the key ideas that we introduced in this chapter.

- The balance sheet of a company is a statement of its assets, and the claims of its creditors and owners to those assets, on a particular day.
- Most assets listed on a company's balance sheet share three characteristics:
  - they are expected to provide future economic benefits to the company;
  - they are owned or controlled by it; and
  - they were acquired as a result of a past transaction or event.
- The claims of creditors are known as liabilities. Most liabilities listed on a company's balance sheet also have three characteristics in common:
  - they are present obligations of the firm to outside parties;
  - they arise from a past transaction or event; and
  - to settle such obligations, the firm must give up assets of a known or estimated amount.
- The claims of owners are residual claims to the company's assets after those of creditors have been satisfied. The claims of a company's owners are known as owners' (or shareholders') equity. Owners' equity usually has two components: the capital contributed by the owners and the capital earned by the company on their behalf and reinvested in it.

BOX 2.1   The ecobalance

Organisations are devising new types of balance sheet. In addition to the traditional financial one described in the chapter, you'll encounter human resource, environmental and social balance sheets. Common to all of them are the following two features: first, a *listing* of those things that are the focus of the balance sheet (in the case of the traditional balance sheet, the organisation's accounting assets) and second, a *balancing* – of resources and claims on resources, of sources and uses of capital, or of inputs and outputs.

These two features – a listing and a balancing – can be seen in the ecobalance. Researchers at the IÖW (Institut für Ökologische Wirtschaftsforschung) in Berlin developed the ecobalance concept in the 1980s, building on the ecological accounting work of Müller-Wenk in the 1970s. The aim of the ecobalance is to show the inputs into – and outputs from – a production process over a period. The ecobalance lists the various inputs (materials, energy, water, air) and the outputs (products, solid waste, waste heat, waste water, air emissions) usually in physical units (kg, m^2, megawatt-hours). By definition, all inputs become outputs, either of saleable product or waste/emissions. Note that the balancing here is of *flows* rather than of stocks as in the traditional financial balance sheet.

Kunert AG, a German hosiery manufacturer, is a pioneer of environmental accounting in Europe. Set out below is its summary group ecobalance for 1996.

Kunert Group
SUMMARY ECOBALANCE
for 1996

Input	1996	Output	1996
Raw materials (kg)	2,992,878	Hosiery (kg)	4,432,403
Ancillary material (kg)	1,325,893	Outer wear (kg)	339,823
Semi and finished goods (kg)	1,954,433		
		Transport packaging (kg)	735,196
Dyes (kg)	60,310	Product packaging (kg)	1,808,171
Chemicals (kg)	1,071,012		
		Special waste (kg)	83,687
Product packaging (kg)	1,824,532	Waste for recycling (kg)	1,472,896
Product applications (kg)	85,553	Waste for disposal (kg)	171,040
Energy (MWh)	101,635	Waste heat (MWh)	not recorded
Water (m^2)	373,620	Waste water (m^2)	284,662
		Heavy metals (kg)	30
Air (m^2)	not recorded	NO_x (kg)	52,159
		SO_x (kg)	192,029
		CO_2 (kg)	30,837,598

Source: Kunert AG Umweltbericht 1995/96

Interestingly, Kunert's ecobalance is incomplete. Air inputs and waste heat output were not fully quantified in 1996. This is not surprising in view of the scale of the analysis (nine sites are involved) and the difficulty in measuring certain inputs and outputs accurately. Kunert's management adopted an incremental approach when they began the ecobalance exercise in the 1990s. They focused first on those areas such as materials and packaging where reductions in use would yield large environmental benefits and also offer cost savings.[3]

- A balance sheet must always balance. Claims to assets can never be more or less than the assets themselves. Every transaction balances, too. Any change in assets is matched by a change in equities.
- Transactions shape the balance sheet. They cause individual asset, liability and owners' equity accounts to increase or decrease. The balance in a balance sheet account represents the cumulative movement in that asset, liability or owners' equity account up to a particular time.
- The conventional balance sheet is not intended to be a statement of the firm's current value. Key resources are excluded from it. Moreover, the assets which are reported are usually stated at historical cost or at a valuation which, like historical cost, is intended to indicate the minimum amount expected to be recovered from the asset's sale or use.

Problem assignments

P2.1 Balance sheet equation illustrated

In the course of a commentary on property prices, wealth and perceptions of wealth, a columnist made the following statements in a newspaper article:

> In spite of their great tumble, the Reichmann brothers [the principal shareholders in the failed property company, Olympia and York] are perceived as being richer than me, so, therefore, they are richer. This means that they still have far more chance of squeezing $100m out of a friendly banker than I do, and, although by that act they would become $100m poorer (still more debts), the world would think of them as $100m richer.

Suppose you borrow $10,000. Are you $10,000 poorer as a result of this transaction? Discuss.

P2.2 Nature of the balance sheet

The recent annual accounts of a famous European football club reveal that at the end of its financial year the club had total debts of €66 million, of which €45 million were current. Its total assets at that date were €104 million but only €15 million of these were current.

An official of the club is quoted as follows:

> We need to set the record straight here. Although it's true the reported debt is €66 million, the *real* debt is only around €48 million, given that in the near future we expect cash inflows of €18 million. It's very easy to quote numbers but you have to know how to read the small print in order to interpret them.

Comment on the official's statement. Is the club's true debt at year-end 'only around €48 million'?

P2.3 Identifying transactions

Set out below are the balances in Holmes Company's asset and equity accounts at the end of each day in a nine-day period. You'll notice that two or more of the account balances change each day. *Identify for each day the transaction which occurred (there was only one), based on the movement in the balance sheet accounts from the previous day.* For example, by comparing the balances at the close of 1 June with those at the close of 31 May, we see that the company borrowed 6,000 in cash from its bank on 1 June. (No transactions occurred during the weekend of 3–4 June.)

		Balances at the close of . . .						
	31/5	1/6	2/6	5/6	6/6	7/6	8/6	9/6
Holmes Company								
(amounts in 000)								
Assets								
Cash	2	8	6	3	3	3	13	5
Accounts receivable	24	24	24	24	24	24	14	14
Inventories	15	15	22	22	22	20	20	20
Prepaid rent	3	3	3	6	6	6	6	6
Property and equipment	10	10	10	10	14	14	14	14
Total	54	60	65	65	69	67	67	59
Shareholders' equity and liabilities								
Accounts payable	20	20	25	25	25	23	23	15
Bank loans	7	13	13	13	13	13	13	13
Shareholders' equity	27	27	27	27	31	31	31	31
Total	54	60	65	65	69	67	67	59

P2.4 Recording transactions I

Dick Dewy decides to start a road haulage business. He forms a company, Greenwood Transport Company, on 1 June year 1. Set out below are the transactions the company enters into in its first week of operations.

1 Dewy and associates invest 40,000 of cash in the company on 1 June.
2 The company buys a truck for 20,000 in cash on 2 June.
3 The same day it purchases with cash one year's insurance on the vehicle for 1,200.
4 On 5 June, it rents an office for three months and pays in cash 1,500 to the landlord.
5 It purchases on credit office equipment costing 600 and supplies costing 200 on 6 June.
6 The following day it returns faulty office equipment costing 100 to a supplier for full credit.
7 On 8 June, it pays to suppliers 500 of the 700 balance outstanding.
8 That same day, it invests, in short-term interest-bearing securities, 5,000 of cash which is surplus to its immediate operating needs.

Required

(a) Record the above transactions on a worksheet similar to that in Exhibits 2.1 and 2.2.

(b) Draw up a balance sheet for Greenwood Transport Company at the close of 8 June year 1.

> Check figures:
> Total assets at 8/6   40,200
> Cash at 8/6   11,800

P2.5 Recording transactions II

Peerless Company is formed on 1 September x1. A distributor of TV and video equipment, it specialises in the sale of widescreen, high-definition televisions. It enters into the following transactions in September.

1 On 1 September, the firm issues 3,000 shares for 45,000 cash.
2 It leases shop premises for one year from 1 October. The rental payments are structured as follows:
   – a fixed monthly charge of 2,000; and
   – a variable charge of 1.5% of monthly sales.
   It pays three months of the fixed charge in advance on 5 September. (It will not make any variable rental payments until October when sales begin.)

3 It acquires shop fittings on 5 September. The bill for the fittings is 14,000 but the supplier gives a discount of 1,000 since the firm makes a full payment on 10 September.

4 It purchases merchandise (televisions for resale) on account at a cost of 38,000 on 15 September.

5 It receives a cheque of 800 from a customer on 20 September as a deposit on an order for a top-of-the-line television set. The contract price is 4,000.

6 The labour costs of installing the fittings in 3 are 6,000 and are paid in cash on 25 September.

7 The company hires two employees who will begin work in the shop on 1 October. It makes a cash advance of 300 to one of the employees on 27 September.

8 It purchases office equipment costing 7,400 on 30 September. It pays a deposit of 2,000 in cash on that date and agrees to pay the balance within 30 days.

9 Peerless's lawyer submits a bill amounting to 9,000 for legal services in connection with the formation of the firm. The company gives her 600 shares in payment.

Required

(a) Record the above transactions on a worksheet similar to that in Exhibits 2.1 and 2.2.

(b) Prepare a balance sheet for Peerless Company at the close of 30 September, prior to the opening of the company's first shop on 1 October.

Check figures:
Cash at 30/9   18,500
Total assets at 30/9   98,200

P2.6 Drawing up a balance sheet

Goliath Motors (name disguised) is a large manufacturer of cars in Europe. Listed below are account balances taken from the group's 20x2 balance sheet. All amounts are in € million.

Trade and other receivables	36,133
Short-term debt	24,035
Intangible assets	5,277
Share capital	?
Inventories	7,956
Minority interests in subsidiaries' net assets	42
Long-term debt	10,200
Prepayments and deferred charges	1,443
Trade payables	5,644
Property, plant and equipment	17,388
Cash and marketable securities	6,316
Reserves	18,326
Provisions and other long-term liabilities	19,265
Long-term financial investments	3,199
Other current liabilities	5,157
Leasing and rental assets	5,827

Required

Draw up a balance sheet for the Goliath Motors group at 31 December 20x2, showing current and fixed assets, current and long-term liabilities and shareholders' equity. ('Leasing and rental assets' comprise Goliath vehicles which the group leases or rents out to companies or individuals. Decide how these should be presented in Goliath's balance sheet.)

Check figure:
Total assets   83,539

P2.7 Comparison of balance sheet data

France Telecom, the dominant fixed line and wireless telecommunications company in France, expanded its international operations in 2000. In August it acquired UK-based Orange plc and combined its wireless business with that of Orange to form a pan-European group with 30 million subscribers. It also made investments in Internet-related businesses and data communications companies outside France in the same year. The condensed balance sheets in Exhibit 2.7 are taken from its 2001 English-language annual report.

Exhibit 2.7

France Telecom
CONSOLIDATED BALANCE SHEETS (CONDENSED)
at 31 December 1999, 2000 and 2001
(amounts in € million)

| | 31 December | | |
	2001	2000	1999
ASSETS			
Current assets			
Cash and marketable securities	4,081	2,256	2,635
Trade and other receivables	10,285	8,783	6,884
Inventories	900	1,216	621
Prepayments and other current assets	7,755	6,391	3,353
	23,021	18,646	13,493
Fixed assets			
Intangible assets	53,152	52,338	2,131
Property, plant and equipment	31,728	34,623	28,964
Long-term financial investments	12,152	20,724	6,739
Other long-term assets	7,305	3,254	2,728
	104,337	110,939	40,562
Total assets	127,358	129,585	54,055
LIABILITIES AND SHAREHOLDERS' EQUITY			
Current liabilities			
Short-term debt	12,961	32,707	5,030
Trade and other payables	15,890	15,347	9,538
Other current liabilities	6,113	10,571	2,800
	34,964	58,625	17,368
Long-term liabilities			
Long-term debt	54,543	30,547	12,233
Pension plan and other long-term liabilities	8,663	5,220	4,182
	63,206	35,767	16,415
Minority interest	8,101	2,036	1,369
Shareholders' equity			
Share capital	4,615	4,615	4,098
Additional paid-in capital	24,228	24,228	6,629
Retained earnings	5,526	2,807	5,408
Net income (loss) for the year	(8,280)	3,660	2,768
Own shares	(5,002)	(2,153)	–
	21,087	33,157	18,903
Total liabilities and shareholders' equity	127,358	129,585	54,055

(*Source*: France Telecom SA, *Annual Report and Accounts 2001*.)

Required

(a) Calculate France Telecom's current ratio and debt–equity ratio at 31 December 1999 and 2001. Is France Telecom better able to pay its current liabilities at the end of 2001 than at the end of 1999? Has its financial leverage increased between these two dates?

(b) Examine the three balance sheets in Exhibit 2.7 more closely. Why have the current and debt–equity ratios changed between end-1999 and end-2001?

Notes to Chapter 2

1 International Accounting Standards Board, *Framework for the Preparation of Financial Statements*, para. 49(a).
2 IASB, *Framework*, para. 49(b).
3 Rainer Rauberger and Bernd Wagner give a fuller description of the ecobalance and Kunert's experience using it – see their article 'Ecobalance analysis as a managerial tool at Kunert AG' in Bennett, M. and James, P. (eds) (1999), *Sustainable Measures*, Sheffield: Greenleaf Publishing. Since 1997, Kunert has published an abbreviated environmental report, with only extracts from the full ecobalance for the year.

3

The income statement

INTRODUCTION

In this chapter we turn our attention to the income statement. We first ask what purpose it serves. This leads us to consider its structure and to define key terms in it – revenue, expense and profit. Through these definitions we see the link between the income statement and the balance sheet. An example follows which reinforces this idea. It shows how transactions which yield profit to the firm also increase its net assets.

Revenues often get mistaken for receipts and expenses are muddled with expenditures. The confusing of income statement numbers with cash flows is another popular accounting fallacy which we expose. In the final section we look at a published income statement, explain some of the more common terms in it, and describe and illustrate key profitability ratios.

The purpose of the income statement

An income statement shows the performance of an enterprise over a period of time. In the case of a profit-seeking company, it reveals the profit or loss generated by the company and how that profit or loss arose. In the case of a non-profit-seeking organisation, for example a charitable institution, it shows the surplus or deficit arising from the organisation's activities.

Profit-seeking companies which are publicly owned measure their performance at regular intervals – usually yearly, but often half-yearly or quarterly as well – and publish the results. This is very important. Modern corporations have long, in many cases legally indefinite, lives. Investors want progress reports at predetermined intervals, in the form of an income statement, to determine whether the company is earning a profit on their investment. They are not prepared to wait until the company's dissolution to find out whether the capital they invested has grown or not. Notice that by demanding periodic reports investors can also monitor better the managers they have appointed to operate the business for them.

Periodic monitoring of corporate performance serves other purposes. It helps investors make resource allocation decisions. By comparing the profitability of company A with that of company B, investors discover which one has generated a higher return on the capital invested in it. This influences where they direct their investment funds. Although past profitability is not necessarily a good guide to future profitability, it nonetheless provides useful information for investment decisions.

The format of the income statement

An income statement has a very simple form. *It shows, for a particular period (a year, a month), the output of the company and the inputs used to achieve that output.* The difference between the output and the related inputs is the profit (or loss) which the company has earned (sustained) in the period.

How do we measure 'output'? There are two approaches in use in Europe. One way, and the most popular, is to define output in terms of sales. This is the approach used by all retailing companies and most manufacturing companies. The other way is to define output in terms of production. This is the approach employed by many German manufacturing companies. The difference in approach does not affect the calculation of income, however. To keep the discussion simple at this stage, we will concentrate on the first approach (output = sales) and discuss the second (output = production) in a later chapter.

A sales-based income statement measures the firm's accomplishments in a period in terms of the revenues it obtains from goods or services sold to customers. *Revenue from a sale is usually recognised in the accounts when goods have been delivered to a customer or a service has been performed.*

Sales are only part of the performance of the firm. There is little point in selling goods or services at a loss. To find out whether a sale is profitable, we need to know the costs of the good or service sold. These costs cover production, marketing, distribution and administrative activities. They represent the effort the company made to obtain the sale. *By deducting the costs incurred in generating a sale from the revenues from it, we can determine whether it yielded a profit or a loss.*

The costs that relate to a period's sales are known as expenses. They are recorded in the income statement either at the time the revenues are recognised or in the same financial period. Thus an income statement can be summarised as follows:

Company A
STATEMENT OF INCOME
for the financial year xx

ACCOMPLISHMENTS ——————→ REVENUES FROM SALES
less
EFFORTS ——————————→ – EXPENSES
equals
PERFORMANCE ——————→ PROFIT (or LOSS)

If revenues exceed expenses, the company reports a profit for the period. If expenses exceed revenues, it reports a loss.

For the profit or loss figure to be a useful indicator of the firm's performance, it is important that outputs and inputs are related. Deducting year 2 costs from year 1 revenues yields a meaningless measure of year 1 – and of year 2 – performance. By deducting only year 1 costs from year 1 revenues, the firm *matches* its expenses with its revenues. The resulting income number better reflects the value it has created (or destroyed) that year.

The link between income statement and balance sheet

When a company reports a profit (or loss), it is not only its income statement that is affected. The balance sheet changes, too. Recall the balance sheet equation in its net asset form: $A - L = OE$. The net profit reported by a company (net, that is, of interest and taxes) belongs to its owners. The amount of their capital in the company increases as a consequence. If OE increases, then, for a balance to be maintained, $(A - L)$ must also increase. Similarly, if a firm reports a loss, both owners' equity and net assets must decrease. The link between income statement and balance sheet is set out below.

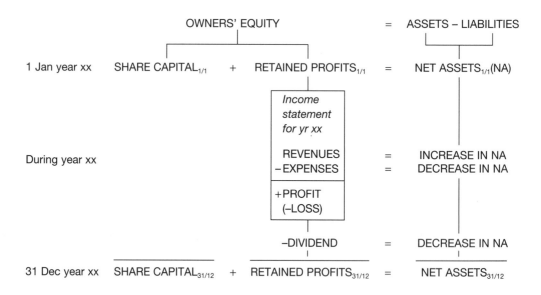

As can be seen from the table, revenues and expenses have balance sheet consequences. When revenues from a sale are recognised in the accounts, reported owners' equity and net assets increase. When an expense is recorded, owners' equity and net assets decrease.

How are revenues/expenses and retained profits linked? We assume, for simplicity, a temporary account, 'Profit/loss for the year'. During the year, a company records revenues and expenses in this account. At year-end, it determines the annual profit or loss and transfers the balance to a balance sheet account, 'Retained profits'. Profits are accumulated and distributed (as dividend) through this account.

Examples make clearer the link between income statement and balance sheet. Four transactions, taken from one firm's accounts, are set out below. We show the impact of each on the firm's income statement and balance sheet.

	OE	=	A	–	L
1 A firm sells goods on credit for 2,000	+2,000 *P/L for yr* *(Sales revenue)*	=	+2,000 *Accounts receivable*		
2 The goods sold cost the firm 1,200	−1,200 *P/L for yr* *(Cost of goods sold)*	=	−1,200 *Inventory*		
3 It incurs wage costs of 500 but its staff have not yet been paid	−500 *P/L for yr* *(Wage expense)*	=		–	(+500) *Wages payable*
4 It earns rental income of 800 from a tenant who paid in advance	+800 *P/L for yr* *(Rent revenue)*	=		–	(−800) *Unearned revenue*

In 1, the sale of goods on credit increases owners' equity (sales revenue) and assets (accounts receivable), since customers now owe the firm 2,000. (If the goods had been sold for cash, another asset account, Cash, would have increased.)

The goods sold in 1 are shipped out of the company's warehouse to the customer. Thus in 2, a reduction in inventory is recorded and the related production cost of the sale (cost of goods sold) is recognised as an expense.

An expense can give rise to an increase in a liability rather than be the result of a reduction in an asset. In 3, the cost of wages earned during the period the sales were generated is treated as an expense of that period. Since the wages are unpaid, the firm's liabilities increase and hence its net assets decrease.

The firm's liabilities are also affected in example 4. The rent received in advance is a liability of the firm, since it is under a contractual obligation to provide space for the tenant. The firm recognises rental revenue, as the rental period elapses and the obligation is satisfied. As a result, its liabilities fall and both net assets and owners' equity increase.

We can generalise from these examples. *A **revenue** increases net assets.* Net assets increase either because an asset increases (e.g. accounts receivable rise) or because a liability decreases (e.g. unearned rent revenue falls). *An **expense** decreases net assets.* Net assets decrease either because an asset decreases (e.g. a reduction in inventory) or because a liability increases (e.g. an increase in wages payable). It follows that ***profit***, *being an excess of revenues over expenses, results in an increase in net assets. When a **loss** is reported (expenses exceed revenues), net assets decrease.*

Usually a retail or manufacturing firm's annual profit or loss comes mostly from its operations. It is likely to report other sources of profit or loss, however. It may receive income from investments in the form of interest or dividends. If it has borrowed money from a bank, it incurs interest charges on the loan. Other activities may also affect its reported profit. For example, should it sell a fixed asset at a price greater (less) than the book value, it will record a gain (loss) on disposal. In each of these cases, the revenue, expense, gain or loss is accompanied by an inflow or outflow of net assets. Operations, investing and financing are a firm's *ordinary* activities. *We define ordinary profit or loss for a period as the increase or decrease in a firm's net assets arising from operations and other activities incidental to them.*

The effect of transactions

We return now to the company, Sun, C and Sand, whose initial activities we analysed in the last chapter. The transactions and events we consider here are those that occur between 8 January, the date it begins trading, and 31 January. They illustrate, among other things, the key features of revenues: the firm's accomplishments, mainly from operating activities, which lead to an

Exhibit 3.1 Effect of transactions on financial statements

	Sun, C and Sand Company				
	Transactions 9 and 10 in January year 1				
	Transaction (amounts in 000)				
Account title	*Balance 8/1/x1*	*(9(a)) Sale of goods*	*(9(b)) Cost of goods sold*	*(10) Payments to suppliers*	*Balance after event 10*
Assets					
Cash	5	+40		−14	31
Accounts receivable	0	+10			10
Inventory	31		−30		1
Prepaid rent	6				6
Equipment	9				9
Total assets	51	+50	−30	−14	57
Liabilities					
Bank loan	12				12
Accounts payable	19			−14	5
Owners' equity					
Contributed capital	20				20
Profit/loss in January	0	+50 *Sales revenue*	−30 *Cost of goods sold*		20
Total liabilities and owners' equity	51	+50	−30	−14	57

Note: The employment of the (part-time) employee (event 8) has no impact on Sun, C and Sand's accounts on the date of hiring.

inflow of net assets, and expenses; the costs incurred in generating the revenues, which result in an outflow of net assets.

We look at the effect of each transaction on the accounts, alone and cumulatively, using the same worksheet format we employed in the previous chapter. The transaction worksheet is displayed in Exhibits 3.1, 3.2 and 3.3. An income statement and balance sheet similar to those the company would prepare at the end of January are set out in Exhibit 3.4.

Illustration

Georgie and Fred's saga continues. Sun, C and Sand opens its doors to the public on 8 January. During the remainder of January, the following financial events occur.

8 The company hires a student on 9 January on a part-time basis. He starts work on 10 January. His salary is 1,600 a month.

> *Financial statement impact:* On 9 January, none.

At the time the student is hired, there is no effect on the accounts. On the contract date, only promises have been exchanged – his promise to perform services in exchange for the company's promise to make payment for them. An exchange of promises is not usually recognised in financial accounts.

9 Between 8 and 31 January, the company sells, for 50,000, goods that cost it 30,000; 40,000 of the goods are sold for cash, the balance of 10,000 on credit.

> *Financial statement impact* (amounts in 000):
>
> 9(a) *Sale of merchandise*

Assets		=	Liabilities	+	Owners' equity
+40	+10	=			+50
Cash	Accounts receivable				P/L in January (Sales revenue)

> 9(b) *Cost of merchandise sold*

Assets	=	Liabilities	+	Owners' equity
–30	=			–30
Inventory				P/L in January (Cost of goods sold)

When the sales are made, Sun, C and Sand records an increase in its owners' equity (to highlight its results in January, we call the temporary account 'Profit/Loss in January') and a corresponding increase in its assets ('Accounts receivable' and 'Cash'). Since it knows the cost of the merchandise sold at the time of sale, it records the expense then – as a decrease in owners' equity (again, using the 'P/L in January' account) and a decrease in assets ('Inventory'). In practice, individual income statement accounts (e.g. 'Sales revenue', 'Cost of goods sold') are established to permit the various types of revenue and expense to be identified.

Exhibit 3.2 Effect of transactions on financial statements

Sun, C and Sand Company
Transactions 11 to 13 in January year 1

Transaction (amounts in 000)

Account title	*Balances after event 10*	(11) *Cash from customers*	(12) *Wages earned by employee*	(13) *Cost of utilities*	*Balances after event 13*
Assets					
Cash	31	+6	−1	−0.35	35.65
Accounts receivable	10	−6			4
Inventory	1				1
Prepaid rent	6				6
Equipment	9				9
Total assets	57	0	−1	−0.35	55.65
Liabilities					
Bank loan	12				12
Accounts payable	5				5
Wages payable	0		+0.1		0.1
Owners' equity					
Contributed capital	20				20
Profit/loss in January	20		−1.1 *Wage expense*	−0.35 *Utilities expense*	18.55
Total liabilities and owners' equity	57	0	−1	−0.35	55.65

10 During this period Sun, C and Sand makes payments of 14,000 to suppliers for merchandise purchased on credit on 5 January.

Financial statement impact (amounts in 000):

Assets	=	Liabilities	+	Owners' equity
−14		−14		
Cash		Accounts payable		

This transaction does not affect the firm's income statement. No revenues have been earned nor expenses incurred. The payment of cash to suppliers reduces an asset and a liability.

11 Of the 10,000 owed by customers, the company collects 6,000 in cash.

Financial statement impact (amounts in 000):

Assets		=	Liabilities	+	Owners' equity
+6	−6	=	0		0
Cash	Accounts receivable				

As with transaction 10, the company's income statement is not affected. The credit sale has already been recorded (transaction 9(a)). With the receipt of cash from credit customers, the amount owed to the company diminishes. One asset (Accounts receivable) is exchanged for another (Cash).

12 The employee is paid 1,000 in cash in January. On 31 January, the firm owes him 100 for wages earned but not paid during the last few days of the month.

Financial statement impact (amounts in 000):

Assets	=	Liabilities	+	Owners' equity
−1	=	+0.1		−1.1
Cash		Wages payable		P/L in January (Wage expense)

The cost of the services the employee performs for the company in January is 1,100. The company records the cost as 'wage expense'. It does not pay the whole of this amount in January, however. The wages earned but not paid (100) represent an obligation of the company: hence the increase in a liability account, 'Wages payable'. As a result, wage payments in February will include unpaid January wages as well as wages earned in February.

13 The cost of utilities (e.g. electricity, gas, water) for January totals 350. This amount is paid in cash in the month.

Financial statement impact (amounts in 000):

Assets	=	Liabilities	+	Owners' equity
−0.35	=			−0.35
Cash				P/L in January (Utilities expense)

The cost of the utilities consumed in January is an expense ('Utilities expense') and thus a reduction in owners' equity that month. The services are all paid for in cash in January: hence the corresponding reduction in an asset, 'Cash'. What the company has done here is to compress two transactions into one. In reality, utility 'assets' (electricity, gas, water) have been purchased – in the same way that equipment is purchased. However, such assets (unlike equipment) cannot be stored. They are consumed immediately. Since acquisition and consumption of a utility 'asset' occur almost simultaneously, the company records only the expense and not the asset.

Exhibit 3.3   Effect of transactions on financial statements

Sun, C and Sand Company
Transactions 14 to 16 in January year 1

Transaction (amounts in 000)

Account title	Balances after event 13	(14) Interest on bank loan	(15) Use of shop space	(16) Use of equipment	Balance at 31/1
Assets					
Cash	35.65	–0.1			35.55
Accounts receivable	4				4
Inventory	1				1
Prepaid rent	6		–2		4
Equipment	9			–0.25	8.75
Total assets	55.65	–0.1	–2	–0.25	53.3
Liabilities					
Bank loan	12				12
Accounts payable	5				5
Wages payable	0.1				0.1
Owners' equity					
Contributed capital	20				20
Profit/loss in January	18.55	–0.1 *Interest expense*	–2 *Rent expense*	–0.25 *Depreciation expense*	16.2
Total liabilities and owners' equity	55.65	–0.1	–2	–0.25	53.3

14 The company pays the first month's interest on the 12,000 bank loan on 31 January. The annual interest rate is 10%.

Financial statement impact (amounts in 000):

Assets	=	Liabilities	+	Owners' equity
–0.1	=			–0.1
Cash				P/L in January
				(Interest expense)

Interest expense, the cost of using the capital provided by the bank, is time-based. Given a 10% annual interest rate and approximately one month's use of the 12,000 loan, the cost is 100 ((10% × 1/12) × 12,000). Since the interest is paid in January, the reduction in owners' equity is matched by a reduction in cash.

15 By the end of January, the company has had one month's use of the shop space which it rented on 3 January for three months at 6,000.

16 Also by that date, the company has enjoyed one month's services of the shop equipment. The equipment (the balance remaining after the exchange of surplus equipment for inventory) costs 9,000, has a three-year economic life and is expected to have no scrap value.

Financial statement impact (amounts in 000):

15 *Use of shop space*

Assets	=	Liabilities	+	Owners' equity
–2	=			–2
Prepaid rent				*P/L in January*
				(Rent expense)

16 *Use of equipment*

Assets	=	Liabilities	+	Owners' equity
–0.25	=			–0.25
Equipment				*P/L in January*
				(Depreciation expense)

In each case, the company acquires an asset in early January and consumes part of its services in the month. Assets ('Prepaid rent' and 'Equipment') and owners' equity are reduced. Both assets are valued at their historical cost. The company assumes it will use up the benefits from each asset at a constant rate each period. Thus each asset is amortised on a straight-line basis. Rent expense in January is 2,000, one-third of the amount paid for the right to use the shop space (1/3 × 6,000). The equipment has a three-year life. Depreciation expense in January is therefore 250, one thirty-sixth of the amount paid for the equipment (1/36 × 9,000).

Items 15 and 16 are updating entries. The company has consumed part of the services of two assets – prepaid rent and equipment – during January. It must adjust its accounts during or at the end of the month to reflect this. Such updating entries are examples of 'accrual adjustments' and are an essential feature of accrual-based accounts. We look more closely at such adjustments in Chapter 5.

We can now draw up an income statement and balance sheet for Sun, C and Sand Company covering its first month's operations. These are set out in Exhibit 3.4.

To construct Sun, C and Sand Company's January income statement in Exhibit 3.4, we consult the row titled 'Profit/loss in January' in Exhibits 3.1–3.3. This is the balance sheet account which contains details, by transaction, of the company's revenues and expenses in that month. We classify the revenues and expenses – in this case, by their nature – and list them in the income statement. The net amount of profit in January, the 'bottom line' of 16,200, appears as part of 'Owners' equity' on the company's end-January balance sheet.

With our example, we have illustrated the link between the income statement and balance sheet described earlier. In Sun, C and Sand's case, the company has net assets of 20,000 at the close of 7 January. As a result of its trading and financial activities, it recognises revenues of 50,000 and expenses of 33,800 between 8 January and 31 January, a net profit of 16,200 in the month. At the same time, it records changes in its assets and liabilities which lead to an increase of 16,200 in its net assets during this period. Thus its net assets at 31 January stand at 36,200. The increase in net assets is illustrated in Exhibit 3.5.

Note that profitable operations are not the only source of increases in net assets. If Georgie and Fred contributed more capital to the company, this would cause its net assets to rise.

Exhibit 3.4

Sun, C and Sand Company
FINANCIAL STATEMENTS
for January year 1
(amounts in 000)

Statement of income
for period 8 January to 31 January year 1

Revenue from sales		50
Less Expenses:		
Cost of goods sold	30	
Rent expense	2	
Wage expense	1.1	
Utilities expense	0.35	
Depreciation expense	0.25	
Interest expense	0.10	
Total expenses		−33.8
Profit for the period		16.2

Balance sheet at 31 January year 1

Current assets			*Current liabilities*	
Cash	35.55		Bank loan	12
Accounts receivable	4		Accounts payable	5
Inventory	1		Wages payable	0.1
Prepaid rent	4		Total	17.1
Total	44.55			
Fixed assets			*Owners' equity*	
Shop equipment, net of depreciation	8.75		Contributed capital	20
			Profit in January	16.2
			Total	36.2
			Total liabilities	
Total assets	53.3		and owners' equity	53.3

The fallacy of profit and cash flow equivalence

Accounting fallacy no. 3: *'Revenues show the cash received by the company and expenses show the cash paid out by the company in a financial period. It follows that the net profit or loss figure in the income statement indicates the company's net cash inflow or outflow during that period.'*

Many people view the income statement incorrectly as a statement of cash flows. A major reason for confusing income with cash flow lies in the terms 'revenue' and 'expense'. In popular speech, 'revenue' is often equated with 'receipt of cash' and 'expense' is considered a synonym for 'expenditure'. But the terms 'revenue' and 'expense' in technical use have no necessary connection with cash flows. As we have seen, revenues (expenses) result in an inflow (outflow) of net assets, of which cash is only a part.

To see the distinction between revenue and receipt more clearly, let's look again at our example. In January, Sun, C and Sand sells merchandise of 50,000 to customers. These sales are an indicator – and a widely used one – of the firm's operating accomplishment. The company therefore reports revenues of 50,000. It receives 46,000 of cash with respect to these sales in

Exhibit 3.5

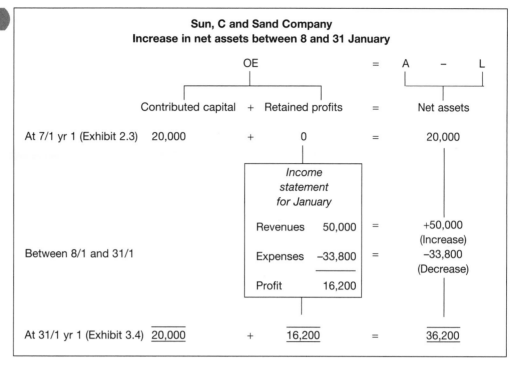

Sun, C and Sand Company
Increase in net assets between 8 and 31 January

	Contributed capital	+	Retained profits	=	Net assets
At 7/1 yr 1 (Exhibit 2.3)	20,000	+	0	=	20,000

Income statement for January

Revenues	50,000	=	+50,000 (Increase)
Expenses	−33,800	=	−33,800 (Decrease)
Profit	16,200		

At 31/1 yr 1 (Exhibit 3.4)	20,000	+	16,200	=	36,200

January. Thus receipts fall short of revenues by 4,000. Since January is the first month of trading, this is the balance in 'Accounts receivable' at the end of the month.

	Net assets (A − L)		=	Owners' equity
	Accounts receivable	Cash		Profit in January
Transaction				
9(a)	+10,000	+40,000	=	+50,000 (Sales revenue)
11	−6,000	+6,000	=	0
Net effect by 31/1/yr 1	+4,000	+46,000	=	+50,000

When the company recognises revenue from sales, net assets increase by 50,000. Ignoring the cost of the sales (and other expenses), net assets continue to be higher by that amount at the end of January, even though the composition of the 50,000 has changed – and will continue to change – as credit customers pay off their debts.

A similar picture emerges when we consider the expenses reported by Sun, C and Sand in January. In two cases – rent and depreciation – the outlays of cash for the lease of shop space and for the purchase of equipment exceed the charges for rent and depreciation in the income statement. Since the lease term and the life of the equipment both extend beyond January, it would be misleading to treat all of the expenditures on these items as part of the effort necessary to generate January revenues. Rent and depreciation expenses therefore reflect only one month's use of the underlying assets.

By the same token, the logical measure of matched effort with respect to the goods sold in January is the cost of the items sold. It is not the cost of the inventory purchased nor the payment made in January for merchandise.

Exhibit 3.6		

Sun, C and Sand Company
STATEMENT OF CASH FLOWS
from 8 January to 31 January year 1
(amounts in 000)

Receipts from:		
Cash sales		40
Collections of amounts owed by credit customers		6
Total inflows of cash		46
Less: Expenditures on:		
Merchandise inventory purchased on credit	14	
Wages	1	
Utilities	0.35	
Interest on bank loan	0.1	
Total outflows of cash		−15.45
Net cash inflow in period		30.55
Cash balance on 7 January		5
Cash balance on 31 January		35.55

Remuneration of the part-time employee provides a further example of how expense and expenditure can diverge. The wage expense of 1,100 represents the cost of the services the employee renders the company during January. This would be so even if none of this amount was paid to him in January. In fact, wage payments – the company's expenditure – amount to 1,000. The difference of 100 represents the company's liability to him at the month's end.

Sometimes expense and expenditure coincide (as can revenue and receipt). Sun, C and Sand Company consumes 350 of utilities in January: this is its utilities expense that month. Interest on its 12,000 bank loan accrues day by day: the cost in January amounts to 100. In each case, the amount recognised as expense in January is paid by the month's end.

To highlight the difference between profit and cash flow, we set out, in Exhibit 3.6, a cash flow statement for Sun, C and Sand for the period from 8 January, when operations began, to 31 January.

Notice how the cash flow statement ignores events which have no cash flow impact. The above statement ignores rent, for example, because Sun, C and Sand made no rent payments between 8 and 31 January. Similarly, it ignores 4,000 of January sales because cash for them was not received that month.

On the other hand, the cash flow statement highlights events such as the issuance of new shares or outlays on new plant which have a delayed and often multi-period effect on a firm's operations. Net cash flows can fluctuate markedly from period to period depending on the timing of such major cash events. It's for these reasons that cash flow is not considered a useful barometer of a company's operating performance.

Income statement presentation

Sun, C and Sand's January income statement is short and straightforward; the published income statements of large public companies are often long and complex. We illustrate the different ways in which income data are presented in practice – and the meanings of common income statement terms – using BestPrice's x2 consolidated income statement. This is set out in Exhibit 3.7. (You'll recall from Chapter 2 that BestPrice Stores is a European supermarket group.)

Exhibit 3.7

BestPrice Stores
CONSOLIDATED INCOME STATEMENTS
for x2 and x1
(amounts in € millions)

Year to 31 December	x2	x1
Net sales	17,587	15,258
Cost of sales	–13,707	–11,990
Gross profit	3,880	3,268
Selling expenses	–2,629	–2,258
General and administrative expenses	–583	–511
Exceptional charges	–26	–
Operating profit	642	499
Investment income	37	51
Interest expense, net	–121	–101
Income before tax	558	449
Income tax expense	–203	–157
Income after tax	355	292
Minority interests	–51	–40
Net income	304	252
Weighted average number of shares outstanding (x 1,000)	73,103.8	66,436.4
Earnings per share	€4.16	€3.79

Meaning of 'consolidated'

The title declares that this is a consolidated income statement. It brings together the revenues and expenses of the parent company, BestPrice Stores S.A., and those of all the subsidiaries over which it has management control. In accordance with EU law, BestPrice presents comparative figures for the previous financial year, x2, alongside the x1 figures.

Note that BestPrice combines all the revenues and expenses of the subsidiaries it controls, even where it owns less than 100% (but more than 50%) of the shares of these companies. To ensure that the 'Net income' number reflects only the profit attributable to parent company shareholders, BestPrice deducts from group profits ('Income after tax') the after-tax profits of subsidiary companies which are attributable to outside shareholders. These profits – €51 million in x2 – are described as 'Minority interests'.

Multiple-step and single-step analysis of profit

BestPrice shows not one but five profit numbers on the face of its x2 income statement. This is an example of a **multiple-step** income statement. Moving down the statement – with each succeeding step – the profit number becomes more inclusive. Thus only merchandise costs (i.e. cost of sales) are deducted in calculating 'gross profit' while merchandise and other operating costs (i.e. selling, general and administrative expenses) are deducted in calculating 'operating profit'. 'Exceptional charges' are shown with operating expenses because in this case they are operating in nature. (According to the notes to the accounts, BestPrice incurred exceptional restructuring charges of €26 million in x2 arising from the integration of a retailing business acquired during the year.) The income before tax figure is more inclusive yet. It is arrived at after combining the income effects of operating and financial activities. The latter include investment income (for example, dividends received), interest expense and interest income. The most inclusive group profit number is income after tax: tax expense reflects the tax impact of all the group's revenues and expenses recorded in earlier steps.

Under the alternative **single-step** income statement, net earnings is arrived at in one step. The company groups all expenses together. If it has more than one type of revenue, these too are combined. Total expenses are then deducted from total revenues to arrive at one income number.

The advantage of the multiple-step income statement is that it allows investors to see more clearly the burden of each type of cost. Moreover, as we will see in a later section, different income numbers are used in different profitability ratios.

Classification of expenses

BestPrice groups costs by functional activity. For example, all the costs of inputs (materials, labour, depreciation of equipment, etc.) used by the sales department are shown against 'Selling expenses' while those used by administrative departments are shown against 'General and administrative expenses'. In a retail company like BestPrice, 'Cost of sales' represents simply the cost of the merchandise sold. In a manufacturing company, however, 'Cost of sales' includes all the production costs relating to the goods sold in the period.

An alternative approach is to classify expenses by their nature. Where a natural format is used, separate figures are given for each major input, e.g. materials, labour (wage expense), equipment (depreciation) and so forth. Sun, C and Sand's January year 1 income statement shown in Exhibit 3.4 illustrates the natural format.

The natural format is widely used in Europe. US companies, however, must use the functional format. We look at both formats in greater detail in Chapter 6.

Income statement terminology

Some income statement terms in English-language accounts present special problems. Some words have a similar meaning – for example, income, earnings, profit – but cannot be used interchangeably in every context. For example, although we can apply the term 'profit' to one transaction or many, 'earnings' is usually only used to describe the (successful) results of all of a firm's activities over a period.

The terms 'gain' and 'loss' warrant additional explanation. They can be used in various contexts. Perhaps the most common usage is to describe *the net effect of a transaction which is not part of the normal operating activities of the firm*. For example, suppose BestPrice sells a building. The company is not in the business of selling buildings: this is not part of its normal operations. Thus it does not show the cash proceeds as part of sales revenue, nor the cost (more precisely, the book value) of the building as part of 'Cost of sales'. Instead, the transaction is reported net. Any difference between the sale amount and the asset's book value is described as 'Gain (or loss) on disposal of fixed asset' and, if material, is shown separately on a multiple-step income statement as part of operating profit (or loss).

Gain and loss are also used in connection with both changes in the values of assets and liabilities and the effects of 'windfalls'. Thus if some of BestPrice inventory is damaged or spoilt, the reduction in value is recorded as 'loss from inventory write-down'. If merchandise disappears from the shelves and cannot be traced (one possible reason is theft), BestPrice records a 'loss from inventory shrinkage'. If such losses are small, they are absorbed within 'Cost of sales' on the income statement.

Exhibit 3.8

BestPrice Stores
Condensed x2 consolidated accounts
(amounts in € millions)

Consolidated income statement for x2

Net sales	(A)	17,587
Gross profit	(B)	3,880
Operating profit	(C)	642
Net income	(D)	304

Consolidated balance sheet	*End x2*		*End x1*
Total assets	12,011		10,879
Average total assets		(E) 11,445	
Liabilities and minority interests	8,824		8,307
Shareholders' equity	3,187		2,572
Total equities	12,011		10,879
Average shareholders' equity		(F) 2,880	

A postscript on the term 'net' in the income statement: when applied to corporate earnings, it means 'after deduction of corporate income taxes'; when applied to sales, it means 'after deduction of value added (and similar) taxes, customs duties and sales discounts'. In broad terms, 'net sales' indicates the cash the company expects to receive and retain from sales transactions.

Key profitability ratios

At the outset of this chapter we noted that financial statement users turn to the income statement to learn about the performance of the company in past periods. Most income statement-related ratios are designed to help them in this task. We describe four such ratios in this chapter and introduce additional ones in later chapters. To illustrate the four ratios, we use BestPrice's x2 consolidated accounts, a condensed version of which is given in Exhibit 3.8.

Profit-to-sales ratio

*The **profit-to-sales ratio** shows how many cents of profit are earned on each euro of sales.* It is also known as the (**rate of**) **return on sales** or – the term we use often in this book – the **profit margin ratio**. It can be calculated using various measures of profit, e.g. gross profit, operating results, net earnings. We give below two examples, the gross profit- and net income-to-sales ratios, and illustrate both with numbers from BestPrice x2 consolidated income statement:

$$\frac{\text{Gross profit}}{\text{Net sales}} \, (\times 100) = \frac{\text{(B)}}{\text{(A)}} = \frac{3,880}{17,587} \, (\times 100) = 22.1\%$$

$$\frac{\text{Net income}}{\text{Net sales}} \, (\times 100) = \frac{\text{(D)}}{\text{(A)}} = \frac{304}{17,587} \, (\times 100) = 1.73\%$$

In x2 BestPrice made a profit of 22.1 cents on every euro of sales at the check-out. However, selling, administrative and financial costs – as well as the government's income tax take – ate up around 20 of those 22.1 cents.

BestPrice's x2 ratios provide striking illustration of both the strength and weakness of the profit margin ratio as a performance measure. First, the strength: *the ratio provides insight into a firm's cost structure.* The disparity between BestPrice's gross and net profit margins tells us how important non-merchandise costs are in BestPrice's cost structure. By comparing individual types of cost with sales – over time for the same firm and in one time period across firms in the same industry – we gain a better understanding of why margins change over time and why they differ across firms.

Rate of return on shareholders' equity

Now the weakness: *the profit margin ratio is inadequate as a complete measure of profitability because it takes no account of how much capital is used in the business.* Shareholders want to know what is the return on the investment they have made in an enterprise. (Profit represents a positive return; a loss a negative return.) We measure this return by relating the profit attributable to the firm's owners to the owners' capital, both contributed and earned, which the enterprise has had use of during a period. We call this the **rate of return on shareholders' equity** or, simply, the **return on equity (ROE)**.

$$\text{Return on equity (ROE)} = \frac{\text{Net profit (to shareholders)}}{\text{Average shareholders' equity}} \times 100$$

The **return on equity** shows the profit the company generates in a period on the capital invested in it by its owners.

From Exhibit 3.8 we see that the capital at BestPrice's command in x2 that belongs to shareholders is €2,880 million. (This is an average figure. We have approximated it by taking a simple average of the start- and end-year stockholders' equity figures.) Using the same net income figure we used in the net income-to-sales ratio calculation, we can now compute BestPrice's x2 ROE as follows:

$$\text{Return on equity of BestPrice's shareholders} = \frac{\text{(D)}}{\text{(F)}} = \frac{304}{2,880} (\times 100) = 10.6\%$$

BestPrice's shareholders did not earn a healthy return on their investment in x2. In fact, it's quite likely that the ROE of around 10% that year fell short of the minimum return they were seeking on such an investment. This minimum return is, in effect, the cost of equity capital to BestPrice. For most large supermarket chains, the cost of equity capital was in the 10–15% range in the early 2000s.[1]

Assets turnover

The profit margin ratio and ROE are not the only corporate performance indicators that investors (and managers) monitor. They also check the efficiency with which a company uses its assets. A widely used measure of asset efficiency is the **turnover rate** (or **total activity ratio**), the number of times in the year the company 'turns over' its assets. It's computed as follows:

$$\text{Assets turnover rate} = \frac{\text{Net sales}}{\text{Average total assets}}$$

The higher the turnover rate, the more sales each euro of assets generates. Assuming the margin on each sale is positive, it's easy to see how, by raising its turnover rate, a company can boost its overall profits.

We set out below the calculation of BestPrice's assets turnover in x2 using data from Exhibit 3.8. We assume the average assets controlled by the group in x2 are a simple average of start- end-x2 figures.

$$\text{Assets turnover in x2} = \frac{(A)}{(E)} = \frac{17{,}587}{11{,}445} = 1.54 \text{ times}$$

BestPrice turned over its assets at a modest rate in x2. It generated around 1.5 euros of annual sales from each euro of assets that year. Most European supermarket chains do better.

Rate of return on assets

The **rate of return on assets** (or **return on assets (ROA)**) is another measure of profitability. *It shows the profit the company generates in a period on the total assets employed by it.* By contrast, ROE focuses on the return on *net* assets, that is those assets financed by the firm's owners $(A - L = OE)$.

ROA links both the profit margin ratio and the assets turnover rate in one ratio:

$$\text{Return on assets (ROA)} = \frac{\text{Operating profit}}{\text{Average total assets}}$$

$$= \frac{\text{Operating profit}}{\text{margin ratio}} \times \frac{\text{Assets turnover}}{\text{rate}}$$

$$= \frac{\text{Operating profit}}{\text{Net sales}} \times \frac{\text{Net sales}}{\text{Average total assets}}$$

We compute below BestPrice's ROA for x2. The group's average total assets in x2 are €11,445 million (Exhibit 3.8). Dividing BestPrice's operating profit (€642 million) by its average total assets yields a ROA for x2 of 5.6%:

$$\text{BestPrice's return on assets in x2} = \frac{(C)}{(E)} = \frac{642}{11{,}445} (\times 100) = 5.6\%$$

BestPrice's substandard return on assets is the result of both low margins and slow assets turnover:

$$\text{Return on assets} \quad = \quad \frac{\text{Operating profit}}{\text{margin ratio}} \times \frac{\text{Assets turnover}}{\text{rate}}$$

$$\text{BestPrice's x2 ROA} \quad = \quad \frac{632}{17{,}587} (\times 100) \quad \times \quad \frac{17{,}587}{11{,}445}$$

$$= \quad 3.59\% \quad \times \quad 1.54 \text{ times}$$

$$= \quad \underline{5.5\%}$$

Each euro of assets yielded BestPrice operating profit of around five and a half cents on average in x2. Note that, at 10.6%, BestPrice's ROE is well above its x2 ROA. A major reason for this is the company's successful use of leverage. Much of its capital comes from its suppliers. Trade payables represent over 20% of its end-x2 equities. These are liabilities that carry no explicit interest charge. We explore this and related issues in a later chapter on financial statement analysis.[2]

The four profitability ratios we've looked at in this chapter are summarised in Exhibit 3.9.

Exhibit 3.9	Key profitability ratios: method of calculation and purpose

Ratio	Calculation	Purpose
Profit margin ratio	$\dfrac{\text{Profit*}}{\text{Net sales}}$	Shows the return on each euro of sales.
Assets turnover (rate)	$\dfrac{\text{Net sales}}{\text{Average total assets}}$	Measures efficiency with which firm uses its assets.
Return on equity	$\dfrac{\text{Net profit**}}{\text{Average shareholders' equity}}$	Shows the return on each euro of capital invested by owners.
Return on assets	$\dfrac{\text{Operating profit}}{\text{Average total assets}}$	Shows the return on each euro of assets employed by firm.

* *Profit* can be gross, operating or net.
** *Net profit* = after-tax profit attributable to (parent company) shareholders.

Profitability and wealth creation

The income numbers used in the above profitability ratios have a financial focus. Net income shows the returns flowing to shareholders; operating profit the returns flowing to shareholders and lenders. In effect, the income numbers reflect the wealth the firm has created for financial capital providers.

Economists favour a broader measure of wealth creation. They calculate a firm's **value added**. This is the difference between a company's output (i.e. its sales) and the inputs of materials and services it has purchased. Under this view, a company creates wealth by turning inputs into higher valued output. Some companies publish a supplementary 'value added statement' in their annual report. The statement shows both the source of value added by the company in a period and its distribution – to employees and government as well as shareholders and creditors (*see* Box 3.1).

BOX 3.1	The value added statement

The value added statement (VAS) and the income statement are alternative ways of portraying a firm's performance. In practice, the numbers in the former are derived from those in the latter. This can be easily demonstrated. Define retained profits (RP) as follows:

$$S - PGS - W - DEP - I - T - DIV = RP \qquad (1)$$

where: S   = sales
PGS = purchased goods and services
W   = wages and salaries
DEP = depreciation
I   = interest charges
T   = tax
DIV = dividends paid to shareholders

Box 3.1 *continued*

Equation (1) can be rearranged to yield value added – and its distribution:

$$S - PGS = W + [I + DIV] + T + [DEP + RP] \tag{2}$$

The left-hand side of equation (2) shows the source of value added, namely sales less purchased inputs. The right-hand side of equation (2) shows how value added has been distributed – to employees (wages and salaries), providers of financial capital (interest and dividends), government (tax) – with the undistributed portion reinvested in the business (depreciation and retained profits).[3]

A VAS usually has a structure similar to that in equation (2). The example below is taken from Singapore Airlines' annual report for 2000/01. It has been condensed.

STATEMENT OF VALUE ADDED AND ITS DISTRIBUTION

In Singapore $m	*Year to 31 March 2001*
Revenue	9,951
– Purchase of goods and services	–5,366
Value added by Group	4,585
Investment and other non-operating income	595
Total value added available for distribution	5,180
Applied as follows:	
To employees (salaries and other staff costs)	2,093
To government (corporate income taxes)	317
To suppliers of capital	
Dividends	321
Interest on borrowings	38
Minority interests	38
Retained for future capital requirements	
Depreciation	1,145
Retained profits	1,228
	5,180

There is no legal requirement on companies to publish a VAS. Why, then, do firms like Singapore Airlines do it? One reason is that showing corporate performance in this way is more understandable to employees. Some managers believe it even contributes to better labour relations. The statement views employees, capital providers and government as equal beneficiaries of the wealth created by a firm. It is not surprising that the VAS enjoyed a surge in popularity in Europe in the late 1970s when corporate profitability was damaged by oil-price-induced inflation and labour relations deteriorated as managements resisted union-backed demands for wage increases. Interest waned in the 1990s but the rise of the SEEAR (social, environmental and ethical accounting and reporting) movement in recent years may well bring about a revival in the popularity of the VAS.

Note that, in practice, the value added statement is easy for companies to prepare since, to a large extent, it involves simply recasting the income statement.

Summary

What are the main lessons we can draw from our examination of the income statement?

First, its purpose. Investors and other users study the income statement to assess the performance of an enterprise in a particular time period. With information from this and other sources, they can make better resource allocation decisions – whether to invest funds, how much credit to extend, where to pitch a wage claim. Thus the corporate income statement serves an important economic role in our society.

Second, its construction. Performance is measured by comparing a company's operating accomplishments with the efforts it makes to achieve them. Operating accomplishments are indicated by the firm's output in the form of its production or sales during a period. The inputs used to generate the production or sales are the related efforts. Revenue and expense are the terms used to give financial expression to the firm's operating accomplishments and its 'matched' efforts. If, over a period, revenues are greater than expenses, the company reports a profit; if less, it reports a loss.

Third, the inextricable link between the income statement and the balance sheet. When revenues are recognised, net assets increase. When expenses are recognised, net assets decrease. If, over a period, total revenues exceed total expenses and a profit is reported, the resulting increase in owners' capital is mirrored in an overall increase in net assets.

Finally, the distinction between income and cash flow. Revenues are not necessarily inflows of cash (receipts); nor are expenses necessarily outflows of cash (expenditures). They may be but they need not be. Revenues (expenses) lead to an inflow (outflow) of net assets. Thus they can alter non-cash assets and liabilities. Hence the income statement is not equivalent to a statement of cash flows.

Problem assignments

P3.1 Recording transactions I

After gaining experience of the cloth trade in France, Francesco Datini returns to his native Tuscany in x3 and opens his own wholesale cloth business in Prato, specialising in fine imported materials. From his business records, you learn the following facts about operations in January, the first month of operations.

1 Datini and associates set up a company, Datini SpA, and invest 25,000 in it.
2 The company rents a warehouse with offices at the start of January, paying 14,400 for six months rent in advance.
3 The company purchases equipment costing 15,000 for the warehouse and offices. It makes a 20% cash downpayment and agrees to pay the balance in 60 days.
4 The company buys 20,000 of merchandise on credit.
5 It sells cloth costing 15,000 for 25,000. All of the sales are on account, save for 2,000 which are for cash.
6 Company employees earn salaries of 2,500 in January; 200 is unpaid at month-end.

7 A (credit) customer returns and receives full credit for cloth with a sale price of 1,000 which was shipped in error. The gross margin on the merchandise is the same as the average on the month's sales (*see* 5).

8 Other operating expenses in the month amount to 600, which are all paid in cash.

9 Equipment depreciation of 100 is recognised. So, too, is rent for the month (*see* 2).

10 The company's profits are taxed at 30%. None of the liability has been paid by the end of January.

Required

(a) Record the above transactions on a worksheet similar to that used in Exhibits 3.1–3.3.

(b) Prepare an income statement for January and a balance sheet at 31 January for the company.

Check figure:
Total assets, 31/1/x3   61,200

P3.2 Identifying transactions

Set out below are the balances in Poirot SA's asset and equity accounts after each of eight accounting transactions or events in the week beginning 12 June. You'll notice that two or more of the account balances change with each transaction. Identify each transaction or event, based on the movement in the account balances. Transactions 1 and 2 are related.

Poirot SA (amounts in 000)	Balance at 12/6	Balances after transaction/event						
		1	2	3	4	5	6	7
Assets								
Cash	5	10	10	19	13	13	13	18
Accounts receivable	14	21	21	21	21	21	21	16
Inventories	20	20	12	12	12	12	12	12
Prepaid rent	6	6	6	6	6	6	5	5
Property and equipment	14	14	14	10	10	10	10	10
Total	59	71	63	68	62	62	61	61
Shareholders' equity and liabilities								
Accounts payable	15	15	15	15	9	9	9	9
Wages payable	0	0	0	0	0	2	2	2
Bank loan	13	13	13	13	13	13	13	13
Share capital	31	31	31	31	31	31	31	31
P/L for period	0	12	4	9	9	7	6	6
Total	59	71	63	68	62	62	61	61

P3.3 Recording transactions II

Dick Dewy forms a company, Greenwood Transport plc, on 1 June. During the first week of its existence, it invests in the assets necessary to begin operations as a haulage company. Its balance sheet on 8 June is set out below:

Greenwood Transport plc
Balance sheet at 8 June year 1

Assets			Equities	
Current assets			*Current liabilities*	
Cash		11,800	Accounts payable	200
Short-term securities		5,000		
Office supplies		200		
Prepaid insurance				
(for one year)		1,200		
Prepaid rent				
(for three months)		1,500		
		19,700		
Fixed assets			*Shareholders' equity*	
Truck	20,000			
Office equipment	500		Share capital	40,000
		20,500		
Total		40,200	Total	40,200

The company makes its first shipments on 9 June. The following is a summary of the transactions and events that occur between 9 June and the end of the month.

1 Revenues from haulage of goods in June amount to 3,500, of which 500 represents cash business and the balance is undertaken on the company's normal credit terms (in this case, unpaid amounts are due within 30 days of invoice date).
2 Fuel costs during June total 300, all paid in cash.
3 When Dewy bought the truck, the dealer agreed to provide free servicing, valued at 240, in the first six months. No service work was performed in June. (Dewy obtains fuel and servicing work from separate suppliers.)
4 The company buys a further 50 of supplies on credit. The cost of the supplies on hand at the end of the month is 150.
5 Wages earned by company staff in June total 1,800. By the end of June, the company has paid 2,000 of wages, including 200 of advance wages to staff who'll be on vacation in early July.
6 By month-end, customers have paid 1,000 of the 3,000 they owe to the company.
7 At the end of June, the company recognises depreciation of 300 on the truck. (Depreciation on the office equipment is very small and is considered immaterial to the monthly accounts.)
8 At the same time, it recognises one month's use of rented office space and one month's benefit from insurance coverage on the truck.
9 Short-term securities yield 50 of interest revenue, all of which is received in cash.
10 Income tax on company profits in June is expected to be 150. None of this estimated liability has been paid by the end of the month.

Required

(a) Record the relevant transactions and events in 1 to 10 on a worksheet similar to that used in Exhibits 3.1–3.3.

(b) Prepare accounts (income statement and balance sheet) for the month of June for Greenwood Transport plc.

Check figure:
Total assets, 30/6/yr 1   40,700

P3.4   Financial statement relationships

Key figures have been taken from the x8 accounts of three separate companies. They are given below under columns 1, 2 and 3. The accounts, however, are incomplete. Fill in the blanks which are letter-coded. (Amounts are in millions.)

	Company 1	Company 2	Company 3
Total liabilities, end x8	50	(E)	30
Expenses in x8	(A)	65	90
Total owners' equity, start x8	60	40	(I)
Total assets, end x8	(B)	70	(J)
Revenues in x8	95	(F)	100
Capital contributed by owners in x8	0	15	10
Total liabilities, start x8	(C)	10	(K)
Total owners' equity, end x8	(D)	50	85
Profit or loss in x8	20	(G)	(L)
Total assets, start x8	100	(H)	120

P3.5   Recording transactions III

Peerless Company is a distributor of wide-screen, high-definition television sets and related equipment. The company was formed in September x1 and its balance sheet just prior to the start of trading is as follows:

Peerless Company
Balance sheet at 30/9/x1

Current assets		Current liabilities	
Cash	18,500	Accounts payable	43,400
Advance to employee	300	Deposit from customer	800
Inventory	38,000		44,200
Prepaid rent			
(for three months)	6,000		
	62,800		
Fixed assets		Shareholders' equity	
Shop fittings	19,000	Share capital	54,000
Office equipment	7,400		
Organisation costs	9,000		
Total assets	98,200	Total equities	98,200

The company's first retail outlet opened its doors for business on 1 October. The company's transactions in October are summarised below.

1 TVs and videos are sold for 40,000 (euros), 22,000 on account, the balance for cash. Cash sales include delivery of the TV set to the customer who paid a deposit of 800 in September. The cost of items sold is 20,000.
2 The company collects 7,000 of amounts owed by customers.
3 It pays 34,000 to suppliers for inventory and office equipment it purchased on account in September.
4 The company has two employees. Each earns a salary of 1,000 in the month. Because of the 300 advance to one of them in September, salary payments in October are only 1,700.

5 Rent expense is recognised. Rent consists of a monthly fixed charge of 2,000 and a variable charge of 1.5% of sales revenue. The rent prepayment at end-September represents three months of the fixed charge which was paid in advance in late September. The variable charge is to be paid in cash.

6 The company recognises depreciation of 200 on the shop fittings and 100 on the office equipment. (The shop fittings are expected to have a 7½-year life and salvage value of 1,000; the office equipment a six-year life and salvage value of 200. The straight-line method of depreciation is used. The assets are depreciated from the start of October when operations begin.)

7 Organisation costs are amortised at the rate of 100 a month.

8 The income tax rate is 40%. No tax is paid in October.

Required

(a) Record the above transactions and events in 1 to 8 on a worksheet similar to that used in Exhibits 3.1–3.3.

(b) Prepare for the benefit of the company's management an income statement for October and a balance sheet at 31 October x1.

Check figure:
Total assets at 31/10/x1   78,400

P3.6 Deriving financial data and calculating ratios

(1) Profit and profit margin data

The following income figures have been taken from Mitica Company's accounts for year 7. (Amounts are in millions.)

Income tax expense	1.8	Administration expense	9.3
Distribution expense	6.9	Revenues from sales	162.5
Interest income	0.9	Interest expense	1.0
Cost of goods sold	140.7	Dividends paid	4.6

Required

A venture capital company, Croesus International, is thinking of investing in the company. It asks you to calculate, for year 7, Mitica Company's:

(a) operating profit;

(b) net profit or loss;

(c) gross profit-to-sales ratio (in percentage terms).

(2) Balance sheet figures and profitability ratios

You are then given the following balances, also taken from Mitica Company's year 7 accounts. (Amounts are in millions.)

Cash	11.4	Provisions for liabilities	4.0
Accounts payable	32.5	Share capital	10.8
Retained profits	36.9	Accounts receivable	41.6
Long-term investments	3.1	Long-term debt	6.8
Inventories	26.9	Property, plant and equipment	43.0
Short-term bank loan	3.2	Other current liabilities	17.6
Share premium	14.2		

Required

Croesus International now asks you to calculate Mitica Company's:

(a) end-year 7 current assets;

(b) end-year 7 fixed assets;

(c) end-year 7 shareholders' equity;

(d) return on assets for year 7 in percentage terms (use end-year 7 assets in the denominator).

Check figure:
End-year 7 total assets   126.0

P3.7 Constructing an income statement

Banting Corporation (name disguised) is a major international pharmaceutical company. Listed below are items and amounts taken from the company's consolidated accounts for the year to 31 December 20x2. All amounts are in millions of US dollars. (Note that not all items listed are drawn from the income statement.)

Financial income, net of financial expense	147
Share premium	1,026
Cost of goods sold	2,392
Licence fees and other operating income	347
Trade receivables	1,553
Research and development costs	1,588
Sales revenue	9,510
Investment income	20
Employee costs payable	430
Provision for deferred tax	543
Sales and distribution costs	2,886
Administration expenses	746
Corporate income tax	866
Work-in-progress	1,072

Required

(a) Prepare a multiple-step income statement for Banting Corporation for calendar year 20x2, showing separately gross profit, operating profit, profit before tax and net profit.

(b) Comment on Banting Corporation's cost structure in 20x2. What is unusual about it?

Check figure:
(a) Net profit   1,546

P3.8 Basic profitability ratios

Grupo Inditex is a fast-growing Spanish-owned clothing retailer. Its leading store brand is Zara but it owns several other well-known chains – Massimo Dutti, Pull & Bear, Bershka, Stradivarius. At the end of 2001, the group had almost 1,300 stores in 39 countries. Inditex launched an initial public offering of its shares in May 2001. By the end of the financial year (31 January 2002), the share price had risen 45% above the issue price and the company's market capitalisation was €13.8 billion.

Set out in Exhibit 3.10 are income statements and balance sheets condensed from those reported in the group's 2000 and 2001 accounts.

Exhibit 3.10

Grupo Inditex
CONDENSED INCOME STATEMENTS AND BALANCE SHEETS
from 2001 and 2000 consolidated accounts
(amounts in € million)

Consolidated income statement for year to 31 January:	2002	2001
Net sales	3,249.8	2,614.7
Cost of sales	−1,563.1	−1,277.0
Gross profit	1,686.7	1,337.7
Other operating expenses	−1,169.2	−957.8
Operating income	517.5	379.9
Net financial expense	−21.3	−13.7
Exceptional items	−1.1	+2.6
Profit before tax	495.1	368.8
Taxes	−149.9	−106.9
Profit after tax	345.2	261.9
Minority interests	−4.8	−2.7
Net profit	340.4	259.2

Consolidated balance sheet at 31 January	2002	2001	2000
Assets			
Current assets	853.7	600.3	481.9
Fixed assets	1,751.3	1,507.3	1,291.0
Total assets	2,605.0	2,107.6	1,772.9
Liabilities and shareholders' equity			
Current liabilities	834.2	670.3	551.7
Long-term liabilities	263.5	255.1	313.9
Minority interests	21.1	11.3	14.1
Shareholders' equity	1,486.2	1,170.9	893.2
Total liabilities and shareholders' equity	2,605.0	2,107.6	1,772.9

(*Source*: Grupo Inditex, *Annual Report and Accounts 2000 and 2001*.)

Required

(a) Calculate the following ratios for Grupo Inditex in 2001 (year to 31 January 2002):
   (i)   gross profit-to-sales ratio;
   (ii) net profit-to-sales ratio;
   (iii) assets turnover;
   (iv) return on assets;
   (v)   return on equity.

(b) Grupo Inditex reported improved performance in 2001 on the following measures of profitability:
profit margin ratio, ROA and ROE. However, the scale of improvement differed across the various
measures. For example, ROA was 19.6%, and ROE 25.1%, in 2000 (year to 31 January 2001).
From the information in Exhibit 3.10, identify one or more reasons why the increase in ROA rose
faster than the increase in ROE between 2000 and 2001.

Notes to Chapter 3

1 The cost of a firm's equity capital depends in part on investors' assessment of the risk of investing in the firm. Standard finance textbooks show how to estimate this risk and derive equity capital's cost.

2 The ROA calculation shown here is simplified. In practice, many analysts compute the numerator, operating profit, on an after-tax basis since tax is a cost that a company making operating profits will bear. In addition, to make the denominator consistent with the numerator, analysts define it as 'net operating assets' (i.e. operating assets less operating liabilities) since this is the capital that generates *operating* profits. We show in Chapter 19 (on financial statement analysis) how ROA is calculated under this more precise approach.

3 Equation (2) shows 'gross' value added. An alternative is to present value added 'net', that is after deducting depreciation, on the grounds that the fixed assets that are the source of depreciation are themselves a purchased input. For a fuller discussion of this and other issues relating to the VAS, *see* Morley, M. (1979), The value added statement in Britain, *The Accounting Review*, 54(3): 618–629.

4

Accounting records: structure and terminology

INTRODUCTION

Accounting record-keeping is the theme of this chapter. In the previous two chapters, we used a worksheet to illustrate the effect of transactions on, first, balance sheet accounts and, then, income statement accounts. In practice, companies do not use a worksheet. Instead, they have developed over many years a ledger-based record-keeping system which is less cumbersome and has built-in checks to guard against error.

In the next two chapters, we'll outline this system. In this chapter, we follow the record-keeping path from source documents through the journal and ledger to the trial balance; in Chapter 5, from trial balance to the actual financial statements. On the way we introduce accounting terms and expressions which are in everyday use in the business world and which we'll encounter often later in the book. We illustrate both the mechanics and the terminology of a ledger-based system by means of an example.

The manner of recording transactions, be it on a worksheet or in journals and ledgers, doesn't alter the basis of accounting. Both worksheet and ledger-based systems are double-entry accounting systems: all transactions are recorded twice. Many small businesses, however, use a single-entry accounting system, which we describe briefly in the last section of the chapter.

The general ledger and ledger accounts

The problem with the worksheet approach to recording transactions is that, for most companies, it cannot cope with either the variety or the number of transactions to be processed. Accounting records have been invented to overcome both difficulties. We look at each in turn.

The more varied the activities of the company, the larger are the number of accounts needed. *An account*, you'll recall, *is a record which brings together, in monetary terms, all the transactions and events which affect a particular asset, liability or category of owners' equity*. In our worksheet, each account is represented by a row. For a company where the number of accounts may well number in the hundreds, use of a worksheet with one row per account is not realistic, certainly in the absence of a computerised system. Accountants devised a system appropriate to the manual records then available. *They assigned a separate document to each account*.

What form did the document take? In essence, it was the page of a blank book. A company set up a **ledger**, a book specially designed to receive accounting information. One or more pages of the ledger were assigned to each account. The term ledger is still used. A company's **general ledger** is the collection of its account documents (or **ledger accounts**), be they in the form of pages of a book, cards or, most common today, computer files. Exhibit 4.1 contrasts the account form in the worksheet and the general ledger.

The general ledger is a special kind of book. First, *it's expandable*. As the company embarks on new activities, it may well have to establish new accounts – insert new pages in the book – to reflect a broader set of assets and liabilities. Moreover, new types of asset and liability arise as a result of changes in business practice. Fifty years ago, the leasing of equipment in Europe was rare. Twenty years ago, brand names were not considered accounting assets. Companies have created new ledger accounts in which to record transactions in leased assets, lease liabilities and brand names.

Second, *the ledger contains a detailed referencing system*. Every company has a **chart of accounts** in which each type of asset, liability and owners' equity is given a code number. When it initially records a transaction, it uses the code numbers to refer to the accounts affected. An

Exhibit 4.1 **The form of the account: worksheet and general ledger contrasted**

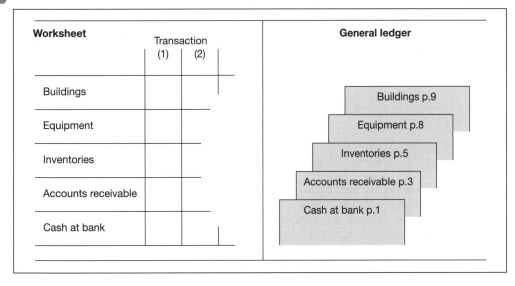

Exhibit 4.2 **Account codes: extract from Spanish National Chart of Accounts**

Group 1 *Basic financing*
  10. Capital
  11. Reserves
  ⋮

Group 2 *Fixed assets*
  ⋮

  22. Tangible fixed assets
      220. Land and natural resources
      221. Buildings
      ⋮

Group 5 *Financial accounts*
  ⋮

  57. Treasury
  ⋮

      572. Banks . . . . , sight accounts, domestic
      ⋮

extract from the Spanish national chart of accounts is set out in Exhibit 4.2. Thus, a Spanish firm that buys land for cash uses codes 220 and 572 to record the increase in land and decrease in cash respectively.

National charts of accounts are common in Continental Europe, especially in countries influenced by French accounting practice. The aim is to standardise the accounting for and presentation of financial transactions. This allows the government to compile statistics on the corporate sector that have a high degree of internal consistency. In some countries (e.g. Belgium, France), use of the chart and its coding system is mandatory. The chart and coding system are contained in a national accounting plan that also lays down how companies are to value assets and liabilities and present them in the financial statements. Other countries are more flexible. For example, Spanish companies must follow the valuation and presentation rules in the national accounting plan but need not follow the coding system laid out in it. Where there is no national accounting plan (e.g. north European countries, USA), individual companies devise their own charts of accounts.

Advocates of uniform account codes claim that since transactions are treated in the same way, firms' accounts are likely to be more comparable. Opponents argue that a national code is less flexible than a company-specific one which can be modified as the company's environment – and the types of transactions it enters into – change. However, all agree on the merits of account coding. It makes it easier for management to record transactions and to trace them through the accounting system. As a result, they can find and correct errors more quickly.

The format of a ledger account

All ledger accounts have a two-column format. Increases to the account are recorded in one column, decreases in the other. It is a convention that *increases in asset accounts are recorded in the left-hand column*. Similarly, by convention, *increases in equity accounts (owners' equity and liabilities) are recorded in the right-hand column*. Thus decreases in asset accounts are shown in the right-hand column and decreases in equity accounts are shown in the left-hand column. These points are made pictorially in Exhibit 4.3.

Exhibit 4.3 **Format of balance sheet accounts**

Balance sheet equation	Assets (A)	=	Equities (L + OE)	
Examples of balance sheet accounts	Cash		Bank loan	Share capital

Balance sheet accounts (T format):

Cash		Bank loan		Share capital	
+	−	−	+	−	+

Notice how ledger accounts have a T format. It's for this reason that they're often referred to as **T accounts**.

Why record movements in equity accounts in the opposite way from movements in asset accounts? Consider the balance sheet more closely. For it to balance, the balances on all 'left-side' accounts (assets) must agree in total with the balances on all 'right-side' accounts (equities). Assigning asset increases to the left side of the ledger account and equity increases to the right side ensures that assets carry a left-side balance and equities a right-side one. If the left-side/right-side equality is observed in each accounting transaction, then the sum of the asset balances should equal the sum of the equity balances. The link between account balances and balance sheet is illustrated in Exhibit 4.4.

Exhibit 4.4 **Link between account balances and balance sheet**

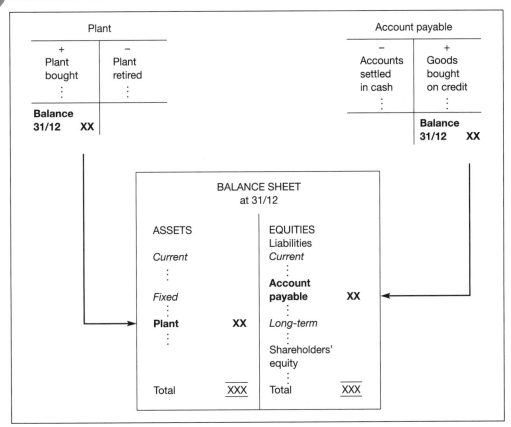

| Exhibit 4.5 | Format of income statement accounts |

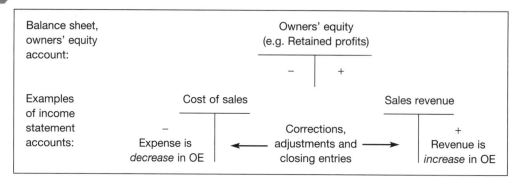

The same convention applies to income statement accounts. You'll recall from Chapter 3 that we showed Sun, C and Sand's revenues and expenses in January as part of its 'Profit or loss in January' account. The ledger system allows us to set up separate ledger accounts for each type of revenue and expense, rather than group them all in one account. *Revenues being increases in owners' equity are recorded in the right-hand column of the specific revenue account; expenses being decreases in owners' equity are recorded in the left-hand column of the specific expense account.* Exhibit 4.5 illustrates this. (The left-hand (right-hand) column of the revenue (expense) account is used only for corrections, adjustments and closing entries.)

Debit and credit: accounting shorthand

Accountants and managers use shorthand to indicate the left-hand side and right-hand side of T accounts. In English, *the term **debit** is used to indicate the left-hand side of a ledger account, **credit** to indicate the right-hand side.* The abbreviations used are **Dr.** and **Cr.**[1] The terms apply equally to asset and equity accounts:

```
        Inventory                    Wages payable
        (Asset)                      (Liability)
    ─────────────────            ─────────────────
    Dr.    │   Cr.               Dr.    │   Cr.
    (+)    │   (–)               (–)    │   (+)
```

Thus the purchase of merchandise, an increase in the firm's assets, is recorded as a debit to Inventory. When wages earned are finally paid, a liability is reduced: the Wages payable account is debited. (The terms 'debit' and 'credit' are very flexible: they can be used as noun, verb or adjective.)

Here's a useful tip regarding the commercial usage of debit and credit. Should you refer to your account when in correspondence with your bank, remember the account referred to is the one in *its* books. For example, the sum you ask your bank to 'credit to your account' is an addition to its liability, 'Customer deposits', even though in your books it's an addition to one of your assets, 'Cash at bank'.

The journal and the journal entry

We've seen how use of separate records for individual asset and equity accounts overcomes the problem of the variety of such accounts. We turn now to the problem of the number of transactions and see what measures accountants take to deal with it.

Most companies have to record thousands of transactions each year. In some companies, the transactions number in the millions. To keep track of individual transactions and reduce the risk of error, companies maintain a record of all transactions as they occur. The titles used for this record – **daybook**, **journal**, **'diario'** – underline the point that entries are made to it daily.

What does the journal look like? Exhibit 4.6 contains a specimen page from a journal used in a manual accounting system.

Exhibit 4.6 The role of the journal in accounting records

| Document | → | Journal | → | Ledger |

Journal			(page) 45	
Date	Accounts	Ledger ref.	Debit amount	Credit amount
8 May	Accounts receivable, customer A	430	5,000	
	Revenue from sale	700		5,000
	Cash	572	3,000	
	Accounts receivable, customer B	430		3,000

430: Accounts receivable

Date	Ref.	Dr.	Date	Ref.	Cr.
1/5	Balance	xx			
8/5	J45	5,000			
			8/5	J45	3,000

Note:
The ledger account 'Accounts receivable' is a master account. The sale to A and the cash received from B must also be recorded in the individual accounts the firm maintains for A and B. In this way, the firm knows the amount owed by each customer as well as the total receivables due.

Two transactions are illustrated: the sale, on account, of goods priced at 5,000 to customer A on 8 May; and the receipt, the same day, of 3,000 of cash from customer B with respect to a previous credit sale. Observe that each transaction is recorded chronologically. Each entry contains details of the date of the transaction, the accounts affected and their code numbers, and the effect of the transaction on those accounts, by amount and direction (increase or decrease, using the Dr./Cr. shorthand).

The key element within the journal is the individual **journal entry**. In fact, many managers when discussing the effect of a transaction on the accounts will usually do so in journal entry terms. A journal entry has the following format:

Date	*Account(s) debited*	*Amount(s) debited*
	Account(s) credited	*Amount(s) credited*
	Description of the transaction	

Although, in practice, entries to journals are more abbreviated (e.g. accounts may be referred to by code number only), they contain essentially the same information.

Note two fundamental features of every journal entry in a double-entry system. First, *at least two accounts are affected*. Second, *the amounts debited must equal the amounts credited*, whether on an individual entry basis or after grouping together many transactions of a similar type (e.g. the total of the day's sales). Both features are also present when we use a worksheet approach to analyse transactions. They're necessary for the balance sheet to balance.

Consider the journal entry for the following purchase transaction. Kaufmann Company purchases 20,000 of merchandise from Venedor Company on 12 February year 7. It makes an initial cash payment of 8,000 that day and agrees to pay the balance within 30 days. Kaufmann records the transaction in journal entry form as follows:

	Dr.	Cr.
12/2/year 7		
Dr. Merchandise inventory (300)	20,000	
Cr. Cash (572)		8,000
Cr. Accounts payable, Venedor (400)		12,000
To record the purchase of 20,000 of merchandise from		
Venedor, 8,000 in cash, 12,000 on credit		

The journal entry states the date of the transaction, the accounts affected (including their code numbers), and the amounts and direction (Dr./Cr.) by which they have changed. The explanation of the transaction is optional.

Use of a journal has several advantages. First, *it reduces the incidence of error*. Transactions are recorded with a minimum of delay. This means they are less likely to be overlooked or misrecorded. Another advantage is *the easier tracking of transactions*. Note how they are referenced both in the journal and in the ledger. Exhibit 4.6 illustrates this. As a result, it is easier to follow the trail of transactions, whether from ledger account back to source document or from source document forward to ledger account. Errors, if they do arise, can be spotted more quickly.

A company using a manual-based accounting system may keep more than one journal. It may establish a separate journal for a particular type of transaction (e.g. sales, purchases, cash receipts, cash payments).

The replacement of manual by computer-based accounting systems has changed the form of record-keeping but not its substance. A computer file in which accounting transactions are recorded as they occur is in effect a journal.

The journal and ledger accounts

In our example in Exhibit 4.6, we record the sale and cash receipt transactions in both the journal and the relevant ledger accounts at the same time. This is what effectively takes place in a computer-based system. A company codes each transaction so that, as details of the transaction are entered in the system, the ledger accounts are automatically updated. In a manual system, however, the ledger accounts are summary documents. The firm records individual transactions in a journal and transfers totals – for example, of sales and cash receipts – to the relevant ledger accounts at periodic (e.g. weekly) intervals.

The trial balance

We've shown how transactions are first recorded in the journal and then posted to ledger accounts. We now examine the final step that's taken, namely the drawing up of a trial balance, before financial statements are prepared.

The **trial balance** is a listing of the balances in all the general ledger accounts as of a particular day. To find the balance in a ledger account on a given day, the entries in the debit (left-hand side) column are added and compared with the summed entries in the credit (right-hand side) column. Where the difference is a net debit balance (as with asset and expense accounts), this amount is carried to the debit column of the trial balance. Similarly, net credit balances (from liability, revenue and other capital accounts) are taken to the credit column of the trial balance. The layout of a typical trial balance is given in Exhibit 4.7.

Why do companies construct a trial balance at the end of the financial period? Why don't they prepare the income statement and balance sheet directly from the ledger accounts? The main

Exhibit 4.7 The format of the trial balance

	Debit balances	Credit balances
Trial balance at 31 December year 1		
Ledger accounts:		
Cash	xxx	
Inventory	xxx	
Equipment	xxx	
Accounts payable		xxx
Share capital		xxx
Sales revenue		xxx
Cost of sales	xxx	
Utilities expense	xxx	
Totals	XXX	XXX

reason can be found in the name given to this listing of balances. It's a *trial* balance. It provides a test of the accuracy of the company's record-keeping. If one transaction alone – out of the thousands or possibly millions the company processes – does not balance, then the totals in the debit and credit columns will not agree and the trial balance will not balance. Of course . . .

> if the totals agree,
> this is no guarantee
> the books are error-free.

(Sorry. The rhyme was unintended.) A transaction may have been misclassified (for example, an expense account rather than an asset account is debited) or even totally omitted.

A company guards itself against record-keeping errors in several ways. First, it designs its accounting system so that there are built-in safeguards against certain kinds of error. For example, a retailer checks its till records against cash balances, cheques and credit card slips at least daily. A firm that sells goods or services on credit maintains a separate record of transactions – sales, returns and cash collected – for each customer. (This is known as the (subsidiary) sales ledger.) The sum of the individual account receivable balances in the sales ledger is checked periodically against the overall account receivable balance in the general ledger. Second, computerised systems eliminate arithmetic error – although they do not prevent error at the point of data entry. Third, the accounting records of independent organisations with which the company does business (for example, statements from its bank and suppliers) are also used to check the accuracy of its own records.[2]

Exhibit 4.8 summarises the major steps in the record-keeping process, from source document to the drawing up of the trial balance.

Exhibit 4.8 **The recording process**

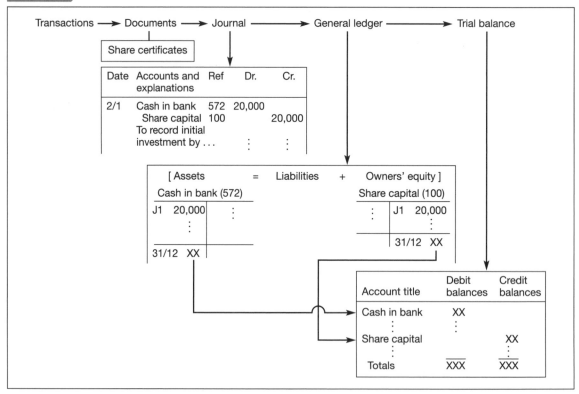

Exhibit 4.9	**Out of Babel Company**

Out of Babel Company
Balance sheet at 31 December year 1
(amounts in 000)

Assets			*Liabilities and shareholders' equity*		
Current assets			*Current liabilities*		
Cash		11			
Accounts receivable		6	Accounts payable		2
Supplies inventory		1			
Prepaid rent		8			
		26			
Fixed assets			*Shareholders' equity*		
Equipment at cost	10		Share capital	30	
– Year 1 depreciation	–2		Profit in year 1	2	
Equipment, net		8			32
			Total liabilities and		
Total assets		34	shareholders' equity		34

The recording process: from transaction to trial balance

We now illustrate the points raised so far in this chapter. We use journal entries to record typical transactions of a period in the ledger accounts of a fictitious company. At the end of the period, we transfer the balances in the ledger accounts to the company's trial balance.

Sam Beckett and Carrie Blixen open a language school for business executives in mainland Europe in year 1. They incorporate the school but have difficulty choosing a name for the company. Putting hope before experience, they call it 'Out of Babel'. The balance sheet which the company issues at the end of its first year of operations is set out in Exhibit 4.9.

The balances in the ledger accounts at the end of year 1, from which the balance sheet at 31 December has been prepared, are also the balances at the start of year 2. The company's ledger accounts with their opening year 2 balances are shown in T account form in Exhibit 4.10.

The transactions the company records in its accounts in year 2 are described in summary form below. We show the journal entry corresponding to each of the transactions and then post the amounts to the ledger accounts (Exhibits 4.10–4.12).

1 The company decides to expand its facilities. Before buying new equipment, it issues new shares to investors in mid-year 2 for 10,000 in cash and borrows 15,000 from a bank. The loan is for one year and interest at a 12% annual rate is payable when the loan matures.

Journal entry (1)
Dr. Cash (Asset +)   25,000
   Cr. Share capital (Owners' equity +)   10,000
   Cr. Bank loan (Liabilities +)   15,000

Discussion
The company raises cash (debit to 'Cash') by issuing shares (an increase in owners' equity, hence the credit to 'Share capital') and by borrowing money (an increase in a liability, hence the credit to a new account, 'Bank loan'). (The amounts are posted to the ledger accounts using the reference (1). All later entries are referenced in this way.)

2 The company invests the cash raised in (1) in new equipment costing 25,000.

Journal entry (2)
Dr. Equipment (A+)   25,000
   Cr. Cash (A–)   25,000

Discussion
The company buys equipment for cash. The increase in one asset – the debit to 'Equipment' – is matched by a decrease in another – the credit to 'Cash'.

3 The company earns 80,000 in fee revenues from short language courses during the year. Companies which sponsor students (35,000 of revenues) are granted a credit period of 30 days before payment is due. Non-sponsored students (45,000 of revenues) pay in cash when registering for the course.

Journal entry (3)
Dr. Accounts receivable (A+)   35,000
Dr. Cash (A+)   45,000
   Cr. Revenue from tuition fees (OE+)   80,000

Discussion
The company earns fee revenues which it recognises in its accounts. Revenues represent an increase in owners' equity: hence the credit to the income statement account, 'Revenue from tuition fees'. They also represent an inflow of net assets. In this case, the company receives cash and claims to cash: hence the debits to 'Cash' and 'Accounts receivable'.

Exhibit 4.10

Out of Babel Company
LEDGER ACCOUNTS
Recording of journal entries (1) to (3)
(all amounts in 000)

Assets	**Liabilities**	**Owners' equity**

Cash

Dr.		Cr.
1/1	11	
(1)	25	(2) 25
(3)	45	

Accounts payable

Dr.	Cr.
	1/1 2

Share capital

Dr.	Cr.
	1/1 30
	(1) 10

Bank loan

Dr.	Cr.
	(1) 15

Profit in year 1

Dr.	Cr.
	1/1 2

Income statement account
Revenue from fees
Dr.   Cr.
(3) 80

Accounts receivable

Dr.		Cr.
1/1	6	
(3)	35	

Supplies inventory

Dr.		Cr.
1/1	1	

Prepaid rent

Dr.		Cr.
1/1	8	

Equipment (net)

Dr.		Cr.
1/1	8	
(2)	25	

4 The company buys 6,000 of supplies on account during year 2.

> *Journal entry (4)*
> Dr. Supplies inventory (A+)   6,000
>   Cr. Accounts payable (L+)   6,000

Discussion
By purchasing supplies, the company acquires an asset: hence the debit to 'Supplies inventory'. Because the goods are bought on account, the company has a liability to the supplier: hence the credit to 'Accounts payable'.

5 The company receives 32,000 from other companies in payment of amounts owing for their employees' tuition fees. Of this amount 6,000 relates to year 1 fees and 26,000 to year 2 fees.

> *Journal entry (5)*
> Dr. Cash (A+)   32,000
>   Cr. Accounts receivable (A–)   32,000

Discussion
The company receives cash in settlement of customers' debts. An increase in one asset – the debit to 'Cash' – is matched by a decrease in another – the credit to 'Accounts receivable'.

6 The company pays 5,000 to suppliers in payment of amounts owing for supplies purchased. Of this amount 2,000 is in payment of year 1 credit purchases and 3,000 in payment of year 2 credit purchases.

> *Journal entry (6)*
> Dr. Accounts payable (L–)   5,000
>   Cr. Cash (A–)   5,000

Discussion
The company pays cash in settlement of its debts. The decrease in an asset – the credit to 'Cash' – is equal to the decrease in a liability – the debit to 'Accounts payable'.

7 Payments by the company for salaries in year 2 amount to 47,000. Salaries are paid monthly and the final payment date is 24 December.

> *Journal entry (7)*
> Dr. Salary expense (OE–)   47,000
>   Cr. Cash (A–)   47,000

Discussion
The company recognises an expense for the cost of employees' services in the period. Expenses represent a decrease in owners' equity: hence the debit to 'Salary expense'. They also represent an outflow of net assets. In this case, 'Cash' decreases and the account is credited.

Exhibit 4.11

Out of Babel Company
LEDGER ACCOUNTS
Recording of journal entries (4) to (7)
(all amounts in 000)

Assets	Liabilities	Owners' equity

Assets

Cash

	Dr.		Cr.
1/1	11		
(1)	25	(2)	25
(3)	45	(6)	5
(5)	32	(7)	47

Accounts receivable

	Dr.		Cr.
1/1	6		
(3)	35	(5)	32

Supplies inventory

	Dr.		Cr.
1/1	1		
(4)	6		

Prepaid rent

	Dr.		Cr.
1/1	8		

Equipment (net)

	Dr.		Cr.
1/1	8		
(2)	25		

Liabilities

Accounts payable

	Dr.		Cr.
		1/1	2
(6)	5	(4)	6

Bank loan

	Dr.		Cr.
		(1)	15

Owners' equity

Share capital

	Dr.		Cr.
		1/1	30
		(1)	10

Profit in year 1

	Dr.		Cr.
		1/1	2

Income statement account

Revenue from fees

	Dr.		Cr.
		(3)	80

Salary expense

	Dr.		Cr.
(7)	47		

8 The costs of telephone, electricity and water total 7,000 in year 2 and all bills are paid by the company by year-end.

> *Journal entry (8)*
> Dr. Utilities expense (OE–)   7,000
>   Cr. Cash (A–)   7,000

Discussion

This journal entry summarises utilities-related transactions in year 2. It is similar to (7). The same reasoning applies.

9 In September, the company launches a nine-month three-term language course, to run from October year 2 to the end of June year 3. Students have the option of paying for the whole course in advance at a discounted price. The new course and the special payment terms are popular. The company receives 18,000 by early October as advance payment for the course.

> *Journal entry (9)*
> Dr. Cash (A+)   18,000
>   Cr. Unearned fee revenue (L+)   18,000

Discussion

The company receives cash for services it promises to perform in the future. 'Cash' is debited. A liability, the obligation to provide tuition services, is incurred: hence the credit to 'Unearned fee revenue'.

10 At the beginning of November, the company invests 24,000 in short-term securities. This is cash which is surplus to its operating needs. The securities bear interest at an annual rate of 10%. Interest is receivable on maturity on 1 May year 3.

> *Journal entry (10)*
> Dr. Short-term investment (A+)   24,000
>   Cr. Cash (A–)   24,000

Discussion

The company acquires one asset with another. The increase in (debit to) 'Short-term investment' is offset by a decrease in (credit to) 'Cash'.

Exhibit 4.12

Out of Babel Company
LEDGER ACCOUNTS
Recording of journal entries (8) to (10)
and calculation of provisional balances
(all amounts in 000)

Assets

Cash

	Dr.		Cr.
1/1	11		
(1)	25	(2)	25
(3)	45	(6)	5
(5)	32	(7)	47
(9)	18	(8)	7
		(10)	24
31/12	23		

Short-term investment

	Dr.		Cr.
(10)	24		
31/12	24		

Accounts receivable

	Dr.		Cr.
1/1	6		
(3)	35	(5)	32
31/12	9		

Supplies inventory

	Dr.		Cr.
1/1	1		
(4)	6		
31/12	7		

Prepaid rent

	Dr.		Cr.
1/1	8		
31/12	8		

Equipment (net)

	Dr.		Cr.
1/1	8		
(2)	25		
31/12	33		

Liabilities

Accounts payable

	Dr.		Cr.
		1/1	2
(6)	5	(4)	6
		31/12	3

Bank loan

	Dr.		Cr.
		(1)	15
		31/12	15

Unearned fee revenue

	Dr.		Cr.
		(9)	18
		31/12	18

Owners' equity

Share capital

	Dr.		Cr.
		1/1	30
		(1)	10
		31/12	40

Profit in year 1

Dr.			Cr.
		1/1	2
		31/12	2

Income statement accounts

Revenue from fees

	Dr.		Cr.
		(3)	80
		31/12	80

Salary expense

	Dr.		Cr.
(7)	47		
31/12	47		

Utilities expense

	Dr.		Cr.
(8)	7		
31/12	7		

		Exhibit 4.13

Out of Babel Company
INITIAL TRIAL BALANCE
at 31 December year 2
(all amounts in 000)

	Debit balances	Credit balances
From balance sheet accounts:		
Cash	23	
Short-term investment	24	
Accounts receivable	9	
Supplies inventory	7	
Prepaid rent	8	
Equipment	33	
Bank loan		15
Accounts payable		3
Unearned fee revenue		18
Share capital		40
Profit in year 1		2
From income statement accounts:		
Revenue from fees		80
Salaries expense	47	
Utilities expense	7	
Totals	158	158

Exhibit 4.12 also shows the first step towards constructing the company's year 2 accounts. The debit and credit columns of each ledger account are totalled and a provisional balance in each account determined. The balances are then transferred to an initial trial balance, shown in Exhibit 4.13. Happily for us, the sum of the debit balances in the trial balance agrees with the sum of the credit balances, so one source of error – the omission of part of a journal entry – has been avoided.

This is only the first step. Before financial statements can be drawn up for year 2, we have to adjust the company's accounts for the effect of 'accounting events' on its income and net assets. Accounting events give rise to revenues and expenses – and changes in assets and liabilities – which do not involve exchanges with parties outside the firm. Such adjustments to the accounts are known as **accrual adjustments**. We discuss how and when they are recorded in a company's books in the next chapter.

Accounting record-keeping in European companies

The double-entry system described in this chapter has been the dominant method of accounting record-keeping in large companies in Europe and elsewhere for at least 100 years (*see* Box 4.1). However, it's not the only method currently in use. The types of records European companies keep are largely a function of the scale and complexity of their operations. Government regulations also play a part.

BOX 4.1	Luca Pacioli, double-entry bookkeeping and capitalism

The origins of the double-entry system of bookkeeping are a mystery. Surviving account books of merchants in Florence, Genoa and Venice show that double-entry records were in use in these cities by the early fourteenth century. However, the first full exposition of the double-entry system did not appear until 1494 with the publication in Venice of Luca Pacioli's *Summa de Arithmetica, Geometria, Proportioni et Proportionalita*. Pacioli was a mathematician, and as the title suggests, *Summa* is in large part a mathematical treatise. However, in keeping with the spirit of the place and age – this was Renaissance Italy – Pacioli included in the book a section on commercial bookkeeping that contains the essential features of the double-entry system as we know it today. It's for this reason that he is known as the 'father of modern accounting'.[3]

The double-entry system began to be used at the same time that capitalism, in its mercantile, pre-industrial form, took hold. During this phase of capitalism (1300–1750), merchants invested capital in goods, sold them for cash and then reinvested the proceeds in more goods. Since manufacturing was not factory-based, there was little investment in plant. Some economic historians – Werner Sombart is the best known – have argued that the double-entry system played a pivotal role in western Europe's capitalist development in this era. They claimed it provided accurate, timely information about an enterprise's profits and capital and thus made possible the more efficient allocation of resources.

The evidence does not support this theory, however. Although Pacioli's ideas were disseminated through texts on bookkeeping that appeared in Italy, Flanders, France, Germany and England in the first half of the sixteenth century, adoption of the double-entry system was patchy. From the accounting records of the sixteenth, seventeenth and eighteenth centuries that survive, it appears that many business ventures in Europe (and North America) continued to use a single-entry system. At that time, the capitalist was both owner and manager, his business was small in scale and he could judge its profitability from observation and changes in his cash balance. The double-entry system only became popular in the nineteenth century during the industrial phase of capitalism when the size and complexity of business operations increased and the advantages of double entry – above all, its ability to process large numbers of transactions in an orderly way – began to be appreciated.[4]

Small companies and single-entry accounting systems

Large and medium-sized companies use a double-entry system. They find that, despite its cost, such a system enables them to control their operations better. The alternative, a single-entry system, is only used by very small businesses, where transactions are few in number and most of them involve the receipt or payment of cash. The principal accounting record under a single-entry system is the cash book. The cash book is so designed that receipts and payments can be broken down by type. Exhibit 4.14 shows in outline the payments page of the cash book of a small service company.

A company can still prepare an income statement and balance sheet if it uses a single-entry system. At periodic intervals, say once a year, it takes an inventory (i.e. a count) of all its assets and liabilities. To calculate the year's sales revenue and cost of sales, it adjusts operating receipts and payments for the change in accounts receivable, accounts payable and inventory over the year. Other income and expenses are derived in the same way.

For example, suppose Elbegast Company wishes to prepare an income statement for year 9. It recorded cash receipts of 15,000 that year – from cash sales and from collections of its small

Exhibit 4.14 Single-entry accounting system: cash payment record illustrated

			CASH PAYMENTS				
		Control	Analysis of expenditure				
Date	Ref.	total	Salaries*	Supplies	Utilities	. . .	Other**
⋮							
21/5	813	750		50			700 . . .
23/5	814	115			115		
28/5	815	1,300	1,300				
⋮	⋮	⋮	⋮				

  * May be further analysed, e.g. income tax withheld, social security deductions, net pay.
** For irregular payments such as capital expenditures. Description is usually provided, e.g.
    700 Office equipment.

number of accounts receivable. At 31 December year 8, a listing of unpaid customer invoices revealed an accounts receivable balance of 300. A similar exercise on 31 December year 9 reveals a balance of 800. Revenues from year 9 sales are therefore 15,500, as calculated below:

Sales revenue	=	Cash sales and receipts from credit customers	+	Increase in accounts receivable (– Decrease in A/R)
	=	15,000	+	500

The increase in receivables between the start and end of year 9 indicates that the company's sales exceeded its cash receipts that year. If Elbegast's receivables balance had declined, the decrease would have been subtracted from cash receipts to arrive at sales revenues.

Using the same logic, expenses can be derived from operating expenditures. Calculating a retailing company's cost of sales requires a further step. First, purchases of merchandise on account are derived from the movement in accounts payable:

Purchases on account = Cash payments to suppliers + Increase in accounts payable
                               granting credit   (– Decrease in A/P)

Then the change in inventory over the year combined with purchase data yields the 'cost of sales' figure:

Cost of sales = Purchases on account –   Increase in inventory
                 (and for cash)   (+ Decrease in inventory)

We illustrate these accounting adjustments with data from our Elbegast Company. Assume that it's a retailer and buys all its merchandise on account. It recorded cash payments to suppliers (in its single-entry accounts) of 10,000 in year 9. At 31 December year 8, a listing of unpaid supplier invoices showed an accounts payable balance of 900. A year later, unpaid supplier invoices total 1,200. Elbegast carries out an inventory count at the end of each year. At end-year 9, the company has merchandise costing 1,000 in inventory, up from 800 a year earlier. With this information, management can derive Elbegast's cost of sales for year 9.

Purchases on account	=	Payments to suppliers	+	Increase in accounts payable		
	=	10,000	+	300	=	10,300
Cost of sales	=	Purchases on account (and for cash)	–	Increase in inventory		
	=	10,300	–	200	=	10,100

The company's cost of sales of 10,100 in year 9 is computed by adjusting cash payments to suppliers for the changes in accounts payable and merchandise inventory over the year. Note that an increase in inventory indicates the company purchased more than it sold and is therefore *subtracted* from the purchases figure to arrive at cost of sales.

Computerisation of accounting records

Computerisation of accounting records is now widespread. Software packages are available for even the smallest business. The record-keeping framework, in particular the use of general and subsidiary ledgers, is the same for both manual and computer-based systems.

Major advantages of computer-based records are the low marginal costs of storing information and the speed with which it can be accessed. Fast retrieval of data has led companies to produce reports more frequently and in shorter time. The case of Cisco Systems, the US networking equipment group, illustrates just how rapidly an efficient computerised system can yield information about a company's operations. Cisco produces daily sales and profit reports – by region, product line, salesperson – for top management. It can also draw up group financial statements within a day of the end of the financial quarter.[5]

Companies have used low information storage costs to expand data gathering beyond that required for accounting purposes. Consider the receivables ledger. A firm can store and retrieve quickly not just general data about a customer's account – recent credit sales and cash received – but also the content of each sales invoice. Details of which goods a customer has bought and when can then be used by other departments (e.g. the marketing department). What begins as an accounting information system becomes a general one.

The information exchanged *between* companies has also been computerised. Companies are abandoning paper documents and communicating with each other electronically. This process is known as 'electronic data interchange' – or EDI. Initially, EDI took place on proprietary networks owned by large IT companies. Increasingly, however, companies exchange data via the Internet. Among the early users of EDI were car manufacturers, pharmaceutical companies and large retailers. They order goods from suppliers – often on a 'just-in-time' basis – and receive shipping and invoice information from them, all electronically. EDI offers several advantages over paper documentation: faster information flows, fewer errors and – once the set-up costs have been recovered – lower bookkeeping costs. Storage and interest costs should also fall as inventories are reduced. Companies also employ EDI to convey non-financial information such as sales volume forecasts and future sales promotions.

Some companies that use EDI 'self-bill', that is, they pay suppliers on the basis of information in their own accounting system, rather than wait for receipt of an invoice. Commentators wonder whether EDI will lead eventually to the sharing of accounting systems. If a supplier can accept self-billing by a customer, why should they not set up a common ledger account?

Government regulation in Europe

European companies are required by national law to maintain certain business records. One reason is to enable the tax authorities to verify the information in a company's financial statements and tax declarations. This applies to payroll taxes and value added tax as well as corporate income taxes. In most EU member states, companies must keep key documents on file for at least six years and, in some (e.g. France, Germany), for up to ten years.

For the most part, the record-keeping burden imposed by governments is not onerous. Rarely are companies required to keep more records than they would keep voluntarily as part of an effective internal control system. The Dutch Civil Code, for example, requires companies to maintain 'proper books of account'. The Code does not specify which books must be maintained: the only stipulation is that they should be sufficient to produce the annual accounts required by law. French law is more specific. The required accounting records are a journal, general ledger and a book of balances (similar to a trial balance).

Summary

Accounting record-keeping systems differ markedly across firms. A company's size, the complexity of its business and the degree of computerisation of its records, these are some of the factors affecting the way it keeps track of its financial activities.

There are certain features which are common to double-entry record-keeping systems, however:

1 Companies operating such a system keep a chronological record of financial transactions as they occur. This record, especially in its manual form, is referred to as a journal.
2 Financial transactions and accounting events are also recorded in a ledger. Each ledger account contains a summary record of all the accounting transactions and events affecting a particular asset, liability or category of shareholders' equity. The aggregate of a company's ledger accounts is known as the general ledger.
3 Before a company prepares financial statements for a period, it constructs a trial balance. This is a listing of the balances in the ledger accounts. It acts as a check on the accuracy of the company's record-keeping process.

Managers and accountants employ certain terms when referring to the recording of transactions in the journal and the posting of amounts to the ledger accounts. Debit (Dr.) is the term used for the left-hand side of an account; credit (Cr.) is the term used for the right-hand side. An entry to the left-hand side of the account signifies an increase (decrease) in an asset (equity). The debit and credit amounts for each entry to the journal (journal entry) must balance if the accounts for the period are to balance.

Problem assignments

P4.1 Meaning of debit and credit

The Minister of Finance of Euroland announces the introduction of a 20% research and development (R&D) tax credit for all Euroland-based companies. Under the scheme, a company will receive a 20 cent reduction in its annual corporate income tax liability for every euro it spends on 'qualifying' R&D in the year.

Required

(a) Show in outline the journal entries a (profitable) company makes to record:
   (i)   its income tax liability for the year, without the R&D tax credit;
   (ii) the impact of the R&D tax credit on its income tax liability.

(b) A manager asks you: 'How can a tax credit reduce our company's tax liability? Credits represent increases in equities – therefore a tax credit should mean an increase in the tax we owe. Does the government use the terms "debit" and "credit" in the opposite sense to the way we use them?' Explain the reason for the term 'tax credit' in this context.

P4.2 Record-keeping in community bartering schemes

Community bartering schemes maintain books of account even though money is not used as a medium of exchange. People join such schemes out of conviction (they believe such schemes foster a sense of community) or out of necessity (they are unemployed and short of money). The *Financial Times* describes how one such scheme called 'Lets' (Local Exchange and Trading System) operates in the UK.

> To start up a Lets a group of people produce a directory of services offered. Each item is priced according to the local unit. In some schemes the unit is linked to an hourly standard. The beak (an example of a local unit) is worth 10 minutes of labour.
>
> Members of the schemes are given cheque books and a central record keeper debits or credits their accounts after each transaction.
>
> (Rich, M. (1994), 'How to barter a massage for didgeridoo expertise', Financial Times, 27 August 1994)

Members of a Lets are encouraged to run up debts ('go into debit' is the phrase used). A co-ordinator of a local scheme remarks to the *Financial Times*:

> It is the people with large credits and no debits who let the system down. If people do a lot of work for other people but cannot think of anything they want, it creates a lot of people with large negative balances who then become disinclined to trade.
>
> (Ibid.)

Required

(a) Assume that a community bartering scheme has two members, A and B. B performs services for A. Show in outline how the scheme's bookkeeper records this transaction – in the general ledger and in the subsidiary ledger (i.e. the individual members' accounts). Confirm that, by running up a debt, A has a debit balance.

(b) Comment on the coordinator's observation that the people who let the system down are those with large credits and no debits. How can a community bartering scheme overcome this problem?

P4.3 Recording transactions by journal entries I

Carmen opens a *tabaquería* in Seville in September. She records her initial investment of 10,000 in the business as follows:

Cash			Capital, Carmen		
Dr.		Cr.	Dr.		Cr.
(1) 10,000					(1) 10,000

She asks your help in setting up additional accounts and recording the following transactions in September:

2 The bank lends the company 7,500 at 8% annual interest.
3 The *tabaquería* pays 4,800 in advance to the owner of the property for a six-month lease of the shop space.
4 It buys 12,000 of merchandise, 4,000 for cash, the rest on account.
5 1,000 of the goods purchased on account are received spoilt and have to be discarded. The supplier issues the company a credit note for this amount. (Remember: from the supplier's point of view, Carmen's *tabaquería* is a debtor.)
6 The *tabaquería* sells merchandise costing 9,000 at an average mark-up on cost of two-thirds (66.67%), all for cash.

7 It pays 6,000 of the amount owing to suppliers.

8 Friends and well-wishers provide free advertising services (e.g. printing and distributing of leaflets) which Carmen reckons would have cost the company 500.

9 Her one assistant has earned one month's salary of 1,500. Only two-thirds of this is paid by the end of September.

10 One month's interest on the bank loan is paid.

Required

(a) Set up the accounts Carmen's *tabaquería* must establish, based on the transactions listed above.

(b) Prepare the journal entries to record the transactions in September.

(c) Post the entries to the accounts.

P4.4 Journal entries, ledger posting and trial balance

As we discovered in this chapter, Sam Beckett and Carrie Blixen have established a language school in mainland Europe. Listed below is a summary of the financial transactions and events that took place in year 1, the first year of the school's operation.

1 The Out of Babel Company was formed in early January year 1. Beckett, Blixen and associates invested 30,000 in it.

2 The company leased premises for five years. It paid two years' rent totalling 16,000 in advance in January.

3 In the same month the company spent 10,000 in cash to acquire equipment for a language laboratory.

4 During the year 300 students enrolled at the school. They attended, on average, ten sessions at a per-session charge of 20. Of the total fees of 60,000, 40% came from students sponsored by organisations which were billed for the tuition provided. The other 60% of students paid cash for each session attended.

5 The company hired two language teachers during the year. Total salary payments in the year amounted to 40,000. All year 1 teaching services were paid for by year-end.

6 The company bought supplies costing 4,000 on credit.

7 Utility and miscellaneous expenses amounted to 5,000 in year 1. All were paid in cash by 31 December.

8 Of the 24,000 owing to the company for sponsored students' tuition, all but 6,000 was collected by year-end.

9 The company paid suppliers 2,000 of the amount it owed them.

Required

(a) Prepare journal entries to record each of the above transactions.

(b) Post the entries to the ledger accounts.

(c) Draw up a trial balance at 31 December year 1.

(d) Compare your trial balance with the end-year 1 balance sheet in Exhibit 4.9. What can you deduce about the use of supplies in year 1 and the expected life of the equipment, from the comparison?

Check figure:
(c) Total debit balances   92,000

P4.5 Derivation of revenues and expenses I

Alain ('Al') Addin runs a shop in Brussels, specialising in the sale of handmade lamps from the Orient. He comes to you early in year 6 with the following balance sheets and extracts from his cash book. Addin wants to find out the annual income for year 5 from the shop's activities and to determine the income tax which will have to be paid (at the rate of 40%) on year 5 profits.

Balance sheets at start and end of year 5
(amounts in 000)

	1/1	31/12 (provisional)
Assets		
Cash	15	26
Accounts receivable	10	15
Merchandise inventory	55	57
Equipment, net of depreciation	25	27
Total assets	105	125
Equities		
Accounts payable for merchandise	14	19
Share capital	60	60
Retained profit	31	46
Total equities	105	125

(The 31 December balance sheet is provisional because the income tax liability for the year has not been established.)

Extracts from year 5 cash book (amounts in 000)

Cash sales	+81
Collections from credit customers	+65
Payments to suppliers of lamps	−70
Cash purchases of equipment	−7
Salaries and other operating outlays	−58

There were no disposals of equipment in year 5. No taxes have yet been paid.

Required

Compute each of the following for year 5:

(a) revenue from credit sales;

(b) cost of lamps purchased (all purchased on account);

(c) cost of lamps sold;

(d) depreciation expense;

(e) before-tax profit;

(f) tax expense and liability for the year.

Check figure:
Net profit   9

P4.6 Derivation of revenues and expenses II

'Rollers' is a shop selling bicycles, skateboards, and rollerblades. Its balance sheets at the beginning and end of the first quarter of x7 are shown in Exhibit 4.15.

The owner of Rollers wants you to prepare an income statement for quarter 1, x7 (i.e. the three months to 31/3/x7). You ask to see the cash records. Unfortunately, there was a flood in the shop in March and, as a result, the cash records are incomplete. You find the following cash information (amounts are in thousands):

Exhibit 4.15

Rollers Company
Balance sheet at start- and end-quarter 1, x7
(amounts in 000)

	Quarter 1, x7 Start	Quarter 1, x7 End		Quarter 1, x7 Start	Quarter 1, x7 End
Current assets			*Current liabilities*		
Cash	11	10	Accounts payable,		
Accounts receivable	63	56	merchandise suppliers	83	101
Merchandise inventory	168	181	Salaries payable	14	6
	242	247		97	107
Fixed assets			*Shareholders' equity*		
Shop and equipment,			Share capital	270	270
net of depreciation	240	253	Retained profits	115	123
				385	393
			Total liabilities and		
Total assets	482	500	shareholders' equity	482	500

Cash receipts		*Cash payments*	
Cash sales	94	Suppliers of merchandise	90
Cash collected from credit sales	80	Salaries paid	52
		Other expenses (including tax)	9
		Suppliers of equipment	?

The company made payments to suppliers of equipment but the total figure is lost. There are no other cash receipts or payments in the year.

Required

Compute each of the following for quarter 1, x7:

(a) sales revenue;

(b) cost of goods sold;

(c) salary expense;

(d) depreciation expense.

Check figures:
Gross profit   72
Net profit   8

P4.7   Recording transactions by journal entries II

Refer to P3.1. Set out in the problem are details of Datini SpA's transactions in January x3.

Required

(a) Set up ledger accounts for Datini's wholesale business.

(b) Prepare journal entries to record the transactions of the company in January x3.

(c) Post the amounts to the ledger accounts.

(*Note*: the balances in the accounts at the end of January should agree with the balances in the worksheet you prepared for P3.1.)

P4.8 Errors in recording transactions

Charlie Cheeryble of Cheeryble Brothers and Company called Tim Linkinwater, the company controller, into his office one day. 'This fellow, Nickleby, we've hired recently as an accountant – does he know his stuff? I've been looking through the journal and have come across some entries he's made that don't look quite right to me. Here, take a look.' The following are the entries Cheeryble has circled with his pen.

1 Dr. Cash   500
    Cr. Sales revenue   500
500 cash received from Customer B in settlement of her account.

2 Dr. Cost of sales   1,400
    Cr. Account payable, X   1,400
Purchase of merchandise on account at a cost of 1,400.

3 Dr. Bank loan   11,200
    Cr. Cash   11,200
Payment of 10,000 principal, together with total annual interest of 1,200, on maturity of a one-year loan.

4 Dr. Bad debt expense   300
    Cr. Cash   300
Write-off of 300 balance of unpaid account of bankrupt customer H.

5 Dr. Account payable, X   200
    Cr. Gain on return of goods   200
Return of defective goods costing 200 to supplier, who gives full credit for them. Cheeryble has not yet paid for them.

6 Dr. Wage expense   250
    Cr. Wages payable   250
250 promised by Cheeryble to family of sick worker.

Required

Help Tim Linkinwater. What is the entry that he must make in each case in order to correct any error of Nickleby's?

Notes to Chapter 4

1 Dr. is the abbreviation for 'debitor' (later shortened to 'debtor') and Cr. 'creditor'. For merchants and banking houses that were the first users of double-entry bookkeeping, receivables or 'debtors' (i.e. amounts owing by customers) were their principal asset. Showing debit balances on the left-hand side of a ledger account is a convention that's not observed everywhere. It's customary among family businesses in some parts of India to reverse the presentation and show debit balances (and by extension, asset balances on the balance sheet) on the right-hand side.

2 A company faces a trade-off when designing its accounting system. The more detailed the system, the lower the incidence of error (and the risk of fraud) but the more costly it is to run. These issues are discussed at length in textbooks dealing exclusively with accounting system design.

3 Hatfield, H.R. (1950), An historical defence of bookkeeping, in Baxter, W.T. (ed.), *Studies in Accounting*, London: Sweet & Maxwell, p. 1.

4 Edwards, J.R. (1989), *A History of Financial Accounting*, London: Routledge, chapters 5 and 6.

5 Taylor, R. (1999), Mind of the money tracker, *Financial Times*, 12 April. Cisco's much lauded information system did not give management advance warning of a build-up in inventories as sales slowed in the winter of 2001, however. The company was forced to write down its stocks by $2.2 billion in April that year to reflect their lower market value.

5

Accrual adjustments and financial statement preparation

INTRODUCTION

This is the second of two chapters dealing with the accounting cycle. In the last chapter we looked at the accounting records within a double-entry system. In this chapter we focus on the final stages of the record-keeping process: the adjustments to the initial trial balance, the closing of income statement accounts and the preparation of the income statement and balance sheet.

Adjustments are made to the initial trial balance to remove errors and to update the accounts for certain events which have an economic impact on the company in the period. We call the latter **accrual adjustments**. They are an essential part of accrual-based accounts. We start the chapter by reminding ourselves of the key elements of accrual accounting.

We discuss several other topics in this chapter. We introduce a new type of account, the contra (or offset) account, and show how and why it is used. We also take our first look at the accounting for dividends. A cash dividend is a distribution of profit – and corporate assets – to the owners of a company. Lastly, in the fourth of our 'accounting fallacy' series, we define the terms 'ordinary' and 'extraordinary' as they are used in an accounting context and show why investors value ordinary profits more highly than extraordinary ones.

The accrual basis of accounting

The method of accounting we have outlined in the last three chapters is known as the **accrual basis of accounting**. It's the method of accounting most widely used by large and medium-sized companies in Europe and elsewhere.

What is the aim of the accrual basis of accounting? It is simply this. *A company's financial statements should reflect all transactions and events which have an economic impact on the firm in the period.* A transaction or event can have an economic impact even when there has been no flow of cash to or from the firm. *Thus 'accrual basis' means the recognition of the accounting effect of a transaction or event when it occurs* – which may not be the same as when cash is received or paid.[1]

The accrual basis rests on two guidelines or 'principles': the revenue realisation principle and the matching principle. The first governs the recognition of revenues, the second the recognition of expenses.

According to the **revenue realisation principle**, *a company recognises revenue only when the earning process is complete.*[2] Since this principle is concerned with the timing of revenues, it is sometimes called the **timing principle**. The decision to recognise revenue is of crucial importance under the accrual basis because it also determines when the company recognises profit (or loss) on its operating activities. Under the **matching principle**, *at the time the company recognises revenue, it recognises in the income statement the costs of generating that revenue.* These matched costs are described as 'expenses'. Revenue and expense recognition together determine how much profit a company reports in a period.

Revenue recognition

Identifying when the earning process is complete can be difficult. Consider the operating cycle of a typical manufacturing company. It consists usually of five stages. The company:

1 buys raw materials;
2 transforms them into products by the addition of labour and capital;
3 stores the finished products;
4 delivers them to the customer; and
5 receives cash for them, part of which it then reinvests in more materials.

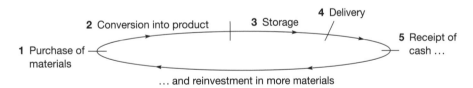

Most of the value of the product is added during production (stage 2). Why then do most manufacturing companies delay recognition of revenue until delivery (stage 4)?

Accountants insist that a company should recognise revenue – from the sale of goods or rendering of services – only when certain conditions are met. Under international accounting standards, these conditions are:

● *The company is expected to receive economic benefits from the transaction.*
● *It can measure reliably the revenues from the transaction and the related costs.*

And, in the case of the sale of goods:

● *It has transferred the significant risks and rewards of ownership to the buyer.*

When these conditions are met, the earning process is considered complete.

Manufacturing companies usually choose delivery (stage 4) as the revenue recognition point because this is the earliest time when all three conditions are met. For most firms, even for those that manufacture to order, the risks of ownership are not transferred at the production stage. Note that some risks may still remain even after the firm has delivered the goods – for example, the risk of costs it may incur under a warranty agreement with the buyer – but they are usually small and can be quantified.

In some industries where goods or services are supplied under a long-term contract (e.g. major projects in the construction industry), companies may recognise revenue during the course of the production (stage 2). When such a contract is signed, the company knows the customer and the contract price. Assuming future costs are estimable, it can determine, with reasonable accuracy, the profits earned at each stage of the contract. Thus it can recognise revenue and profit on a pro rata basis over the contract's life.

A company may delay revenue recognition until it receives cash from the customer (stage 5). Suppose a company that invests in and trades real estate sells land to a property developer and agrees to be paid for it out of the proceeds of the development. The risk of non-payment may be high and not quantifiable. As a result, at the time of delivery of the land significant risks remain with the real estate company and it should not recognise revenue then.

We illustrate the effect on the accounts of these alternative recognition points in a later chapter. In this chapter, however, we assume that firms recognise revenue at the point of delivery (or performance, in the case of services).

Expense recognition

When a company recognises revenue, it recognises as expenses the costs incurred in generating the revenue. How strictly is this matching principle applied? Do companies try to determine how much of, say, labour, depreciation or interest costs are attributable to individual sales? The answer is that matching is, in many instances, approximate.

Manufacturing companies do attempt to match *production* costs with units sold. We'll see in a later chapter how they do this. However, their *non-production* costs (e.g. selling, administration, financing) are rarely matched with revenue on a product basis. Instead, they're matched on a time basis.

Selling costs (e.g. the salaries, equipment depreciation and utilities costs of the sales department) are charged to the income statement *in the period they are incurred*. The justification is that the efforts of the sales department help generate all the sales in a financial period and the benefits of a more precise matching – on a product basis – are less than the costs of data collection and analysis associated with it.

Practice in other industries varies. Retail and wholesale companies follow manufacturers in matching the cost of merchandise with each unit sold while other costs are charged against revenues on a periodic basis. In some sectors (e.g. banking), key sources of both revenue (e.g. interest revenue) and expense (interest expense) accrue on a time basis so that matching occurs implicitly.

Expenses are not always matched. Sometimes they are anticipated. For example, companies provide for expected future costs such as environmental liabilities. They also make provision for possible overstatement of assets: examples are adjustments to receivables for 'doubtful' debts and to inventories for slow-moving items. The underlying principle in these cases is that of **prudence**. *Under this principle, an expense is recognised as soon as a liability is incurred or a potential loss is sustained.* Note that if prudence and the matching principle conflict, prudence usually takes precedence.

Advantages of accrual basis

Investors use accounting numbers in deciding whether to invest in (or disinvest from) a company. Such a decision involves valuing the company and valuation in turn requires investors to make predictions about the company's future cash flows. Empirical evidence indicates that an accrual-based number, current earnings, generally provides more accurate predictions of future cash flows than current cash flows.[3] Why is this? The two accrual accounting principles – the revenue realisation and matching principles – are largely responsible for the better predictive performance of earnings. Cash-based accounting lacks such a framework. Current inflows of cash are a poor predictor of future inflows because they may relate to economic events that have already taken place (e.g. credit sales of an earlier period) or that have yet to occur (e.g. goods or services to be supplied in a later period).

Accrual-based financial statements also encourage the improved allocation of resources. By identifying and recording an organisation's assets, management can better determine the cost of using them. This should lead to more efficient use of the assets themselves (*see* Box 5.1).

BOX 5.1

The accrual basis and government accounts

Traditional government accounts are cash-based. They show receipts and expenditures only. Moreover, no distinction is made between capital and revenue expenditures. Outlays on bridges and bureaucrats' salaries are accounted for in the same way. A consequence of this is that the government has no record of the resources it owns. This means that government departments that use fixed assets such as motor vehicles and buildings are not aware of their cost (except for their purchase price in the year of acquisition) and may use them inefficiently. In addition, certain government obligations are not recognised. One example is the liability for state pensions. These are accounted for on a pay-as-you-go basis. By not recording the liability today, the government risks underestimating payments it will have to make in the future to settle it.

Recently, governments have discovered the merits of accrual-based accounting. New Zealand led the way when its government adopted the 'resource basis of accounting' – the term used in government circles for the accrual basis – in the 1980s. New Zealand made several important innovations. First, government accountants there distinguished 'working assets' from Crown assets. Working assets are assets used by government departments or agencies in order to provide services to citizens (e.g. schools, hospitals, roads). Crown assets are state-owned assets that have cultural value such as works of art, national monuments and national parks. The second innovation was to attribute working assets to individual government departments and charge the departments for their use by means of depreciation and interest charges. Since government departments had to pay these charges out of their budgets, they began to use the assets more efficiently, selling some they didn't need and replacing others with less costly alternatives.

Other governments have followed New Zealand's example and published accrual-based balance sheets. Few have yet introduced resource-based budgeting, however. Moreover, there is continuing disagreement about what should be included as assets and liabilities in government accounts – and how to measure them. For example, are teachers' salaries an expense of the year – or does the outlay represent an investment because it yields benefits (a more productive workforce) in the future? How should land used by the army for training purposes be valued? At cost? Replacement value? Alternative use value? Governments face problems implementing the accrual basis similar to those that companies encounter.

Accrual-based numbers have limitations, however. It may not be possible to implement the revenue realisation and matching principles as formulated. As we've seen, some costs cannot be matched on a product basis for practical reasons. Furthermore, accrual-based numbers rely on estimates made by management – estimates of the lives of depreciable assets or the collectibility of receivables, for example – and management may make inaccurate or misleading estimates.

Accrual adjustments

It's not just transactions which give rise to revenues and expenses under accrual accounting. Events occur which have an economic impact on the firm but which do not involve an exchange with an individual or firm. Recall from Chapter 3 that the costs of generating Sun, C and Sand's January revenues include the use of shop space (rent expense) and equipment (depreciation expense) in the month. In both cases, there is no transaction during January that signals the use of the asset. Similarly, revenue can be earned on interest-bearing investments even though, during the period, no cash is received.

By recording the effect of events such as the using up of assets, we adjust the accounts. The associated journal entries are therefore known as **adjusting entries**. Adjustments can be made as frequently as the company wishes – weekly or even daily if the informational benefits from up-to-date accounts exceed the marginal bookkeeping costs. It's usual, however, to record accrual adjustments when the accounts are prepared at the end of a financial period, be it a month, quarter or year. We follow this practice in this chapter.

Adjusting entries are of two types. First, there are those *adjustments which reflect the **passage of time***. Then there are *adjustments which reflect the **expiry of an asset or liability***. We look at each type in turn.

Passage-of-time adjustments

Consider, for example, the cost of borrowed money. Interest on debt outstanding is usually paid at regular intervals – monthly, half-yearly or yearly. However, the cost of borrowing does not arise only when interest is paid. It is incurred (and the liability mounts up) day by day. Interest expense, therefore, should not be recorded by the borrower only when interest is paid. It should be recognised, along with the liability for unpaid interest, as time passes.

A similar process occurs in the books of the lender. Interest on a loan is received at regular intervals. But interest is earned on a daily basis. Thus the lender should recognise interest revenue and the accompanying asset, accrued interest receivable, with the passage of time.

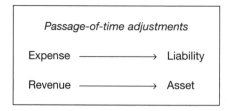

In both cases, the impetus for the adjustment comes from the need to recognise revenue or expense. Recognition of a revenue or expense leads to recognition of a related asset or liability.

The following example illustrates the accrual process. On 31 October year 5, Verleiher AG lends Emprunteuse SA 15,000 for one year at an interest rate of 12%. Interest will be received at the time of loan repayment. Verleiher's financial year ends on 31 December. It makes the following entries in year 5:

31 October year 5
Dr. Short-term investment (or loan receivable) (A+)   15,000
    Cr. Cash (A–)   15,000
To record a one-year loan to Emprunteuse SA at a 12% interest rate.

31 December year 5 (adjusting entry)
Dr. Accrued interest receivable (A+)   300
    Cr. Interest revenue (OE+)   300
To record interest earned in the two months to 31 December year 5 (2/12 × (12% × 15,000)).

The adjusting entry on 31 December reflects the event, the earning of interest, that has occurred between 1 November and 31 December. If monthly accounts are prepared, an adjusting entry will be made at the end of each month to recognise interest earned at the rate of 150/month. (We assume, for ease of calculation, a 30-day month, 360-day year.)

What happens in year 6? Assuming adjusting entries are not made monthly during year 6, Verleiher will record, on 31 October, the earning of interest in the first ten months and the collection of cash from Emprunteuse, as follows:

31 October year 6
Dr. Cash (A+)   1,800
    Cr. Interest revenue (OE+)   1,500
    Cr. Accrued interest receivable (A–)   300
To record interest earned in the ten months to 31 October year 6 and the receipt of one year's interest on the Emprunteuse loan.

Dr. Cash (A+)   15,000
    Cr. Short-term investment (A–)   15,000
To record the collection of the principal on the Emprunteuse loan.

Notice that, although Verleiher collects one year's interest of 1,800 on 31 October year 6, the company earns only ten months' interest in year 6. Under the accrual basis, the accounts reflect the economic impact of the loan each period: interest of 300 earned in year 5, interest of 1,500 earned in year 6. The year's interest collected on 31 October year 6 includes the three months' accrued interest at the end of year 5 – hence the credit to (reduction of) 'Accrued interest receivable'.

Let's summarise. If, for the borrower, the date of interest payment does not coincide with the end of the financial period, it must make an adjustment to reflect the interest expense and liability that have accrued from the last payment date to the current balance sheet date. Similar adjustments must also be made for other time-based expenses (e.g. salaries and wages). Lenders must also record an adjusting entry for interest earned between the last receipt date and their current balance sheet date.

Expiry-of-asset/liability adjustments

As we saw with the Sun, C and Sand Company, a firm can acquire resources which yield benefits over several financial periods. These resources can be tangible fixed assets like equipment or services paid for in advance like prepaid rent.

How do such assets 'expire'? Think of equipment or prepaid rent as a bundle of services. Over the course of the asset's useful life the company owning it will consume all these services in order to generate revenues. What a company records as expense in a period reflects management's assessment of the portion of the asset's total expected services which are consumed that period. Of course, the bundle of services has to be valued. Let's assume it's valued at the asset's historical cost. Thus, if management reckon the company uses up, in the first year, 40% of the services from a piece of equipment and the cost of that equipment is 10,000, the depreciation expense is 4,000 that year. The 4,000 is, in effect, the expired cost of the equipment in its first year.

Liabilities can expire, too. This occurs when a company fulfils an obligation it has incurred to provide goods or services to customers. As the liability is satisfied – through the delivery of goods or performance of services – revenue is earned and should be recognised in the company's accounts.

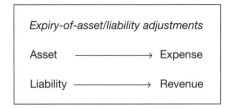

Expiry-of-asset/liability adjustments

Asset ⟶ Expense

Liability ⟶ Revenue

A change in a balance sheet account provides the spur for this type of adjustment. Expiry of an asset or liability results in the recognition of an expense or revenue.

Again, an example helps make these ideas more concrete. In April year 8, Dueño SA rents a building to Tenant plc for one year. Tenant pays Dueño 24,000 in advance. The lease commences on 1 May. Dueño's financial year ends on 31 December. Dueño records the cash received as follows:

30 April year 8
Dr. Cash (A+)   24,000
   Cr. Unearned rental revenue (L+)   24,000
To record the advance receipt from Tenant of one year's rent.

Note that no revenue is recognised by Dueño in April. By accepting the advance payment, Dueño has incurred a liability in that month – to supply Tenant with a service, the use of a building, for one year from 1 May. As it performs this service each month, it fulfils part of its obligation and can recognise rental revenue of 2,000. Unearned revenue becomes earned.

31 May year 8 (and monthly to 30/4/year 9) (adjusting entry)
Dr. Unearned rental revenue (L–)   2,000
   Cr. Rental revenue (OE+)   2,000
To record the earning of one month's revenue on Tenant's lease.

If Dueño prepares financial statements only once a year and has a calendar year-end, then it would make just one adjusting entry in year 8. This would reflect the earning of eight months' rental revenue to 31 December:

31 December year 8 (adjusting entry)
Dr. Unearned rental revenue (L–)   16,000
   Cr. Rental revenue (OE+)   16,000

Whether Dueño makes adjusting entries monthly or only at the end of its financial year, the effect on its income statement is the same – revenue of 16,000 is recognised in year 8 and 8,000 in year 9.

Companies can use an alternative method of recording expiry adjustments, especially for assets and liabilities with short lives. They record the initial cash outlay (or receipt) as an expense (revenue) and adjust the expense (revenue) account at the financial statement date for the unexpired portion of the asset (liability). In the case of Dueño – and assuming only one adjusting entry is made at 31 December – the entries in year 8 would be:

30 April year 8
Dr. Cash (A+)   24,000
    Cr. Rental revenue (OE+)   24,000

31 December year 8 (adjusting entry)
Dr. Rental revenue (OE–)   8,000
    Cr. Unearned rental revenue (L+)   8,000
To record as a liability the one-third of rent received but not yet earned.

Note that the effect on Dueño's year 8 and year 9 financial statements is still the same. The company recognises revenue of 16,000 in year 8 and 8,000 in year 9 with respect to this lease. It records a current liability in its year 8 balance sheet for 'deferred' revenue.

One small but revealing point: the transactions and events that Dueño records are also recorded by Tenant – but from the point of view of the user of the building space rather than its supplier. The journal entries in Tenant's books are the mirror image of those recorded by Dueño. Dueño's liability 'Unearned rental revenue' is Tenant's asset 'Prepaid rent'. As Dueño's liability expires, so too does Tenant's asset. Both make adjusting entries to recognise in one case rental revenue, in the other rental expense.

Dueño SA (amounts in 000)	[Dr.]	[Cr.]	*Tenant plc* (amounts in 000)	[Dr.]	[Cr.]
30 April year 8					
Cash	24		Prepaid rent	24	
Unearned revenue		24	Cash		24
Adjusting entry at 31 December year 8					
Unearned revenue	16		Rent expense	16	
Rental revenue		16	Prepaid rent		16
30 April year 9					
Unearned revenue	8		Rent expense	8	
Rental revenue		8	Prepaid rent		8

In sum, passage-of-time and expiry-of-asset/liability adjustments are essential if a company's accounts are to be accrual-based. They ensure that all revenues earned and all expenses incurred in a period are captured on the income statement. At the same time, the balance sheet is updated – and on a consistent basis. It shows assets and liabilities – accrued or unexpired – accounted for on the same basis as at previous balance sheet dates. The result is that, subject to the somewhat restrictive assumptions companies make when recognising and valuing certain assets and liabilities (a topic we'll explore in a later chapter), the financial statements reflect all events with an economic impact in the period.

Error adjustments

At the same time that accrual adjustments are being recorded, the trial balance is also being corrected for any **errors** in the accounts that have come to light.

Despite the best endeavours of accountants, errors can arise. Sometimes they are easy to see – for example, the trial balance does not balance – although it may be difficult to find the source of the error. There are occasions when they're not easy to spot (e.g. self-balancing errors). How companies identify accounting errors is not pursued here as it lies outside the scope of this book. Our concern is with the effect of errors on the accounts.

Errors in financial statements fall into two types. The first occurs within one financial statement, the **within-statement error**. It usually represents a misclassification of an asset or liability (for example, a short-term investment reported as a long-term one) or of a revenue or expense (for example, a production cost classified as distribution expense). Although neither the 'profit for the year' nor the total asset figure is misstated, components of both these figures will be. For example, misclassification of production cost as distribution expense results in the overstatement of gross profit. This may convey a misleading signal about product profitability.

The second – and more common – type of error is the **between-statement error**. It involves both the income statement and the balance sheet. Totals (e.g. profit for the year, total assets) as well as components of the financial statements are misstated. For example, the failure to record accrued interest on debt leads to the overstatement of net income (through the understatement of interest expense) and net assets (through the understatement of a liability, accrued interest payable).

Some between-statement errors are permanent: charging an expense against a contributed capital account may go unnoticed throughout the company's existence. Many such errors, however, are self-correcting. In the case of short-term accruals, the error is likely to correct itself in the following period.

Consider this example. A company with a 31 December year-end borrows 100,000 on 1 August year 1 for one year at an annual rate of 12%. It pays interest at the time of principal repayment on 31 July year 2. Exhibit 5.1 shows the effect on its year 1 and year 2 balance sheets of (1) accruing and (2) failing to accrue interest in year 1.

Failure to record interest expense in year 1 results in an overstatement of the company's year 1 profit and an understatement of its end-year 1 liabilities. When it pays interest in year 2 and recognises a full year's expense of 12,000, its income statement that year bears a double burden. By the same token, its net assets decrease in year 2 by more than they would have done if it had recorded the accrual correctly in year 1 (12,000 instead of the correct figure of 7,000). Over the two years together, however, the effect on its owners' equity and net assets is the same, whether it accrues interest in year 1 or not.

The self-correcting nature of many accounting errors should not make us complacent. Sometimes, as with misrecording of depreciation on long-lived assets, it may take many years for the error to be corrected. More importantly, such errors in periodic financial statements can distort trends in company earnings and assets. They may undermine intercompany comparisons of profitability and financial strength. As a result, they render financial statements less useful to investors.

| Exhibit 5.1 | Illustration of self-correcting error: failure to accrue interest on debt |

	(1) Accrual of interest (amounts in 000)				(2) No accrual of interest (amounts in 000)			
				OWNERS'				OWNERS'
	NET	ASSETS	=	EQUITY	NET	ASSETS	=	EQUITY
		Accrued interest		Interest		Accrued interest		Interest
	Cash	payable		expense	Cash	payable		expense
Year 1 31/12		− (+5)	=	−5		0	=	0
Year 2 31/7	−12	− (−5)	=	−7	−12	0	=	−12
Combined effect, years 1 and 2	−12	0	=	−12	−12	0	=	−12

Closing entries

With the trial balance updated by accrual adjustments and corrected for errors, we can now draw up the income statement and balance sheet for the period. At the end of its financial year, however, a company will take a further step: it will **close** its income statement accounts for the year. The overall profit or loss for the year is established and the end-of-year balance sheet can be prepared.

Why, at year-end, are income statement accounts closed but balance sheet accounts are not? The reason lies in the nature of the two types of account. From income statement accounts, we learn about a company's performance during a particular financial year. We do not want events of, say, year 4 to be confused with those of year 3 or year 5. To ensure separation, revenue and expense accounts are treated as **temporary** in nature. In effect, they are **dated**. Thus, at the end of its year 4 financial year, a company closes the year 4 revenue and expense accounts; at the start of year 5, it opens new accounts, that is year 5 revenue and expense accounts.

By contrast, balance sheet accounts tell us the state of the company on a particular day. The process of updating the balances in asset and equity accounts for new transactions and events continues each day for as long as the company is in existence. Since balances can be determined each and every day, the balance sheet accounts are **permanent** in nature.

The income statement accounts are closed to a balance sheet account. In Chapter 3, we called this owners' equity account, 'Profit or loss in the year'. The closing entries are straightforward. We take the totals in each of the revenue and gain accounts (e.g. sales revenue, interest revenue, gain on sale of buildings) to the owners' equity account by debiting the revenue and gain accounts and crediting 'Profit or loss in the year'.

Similarly, we transfer the totals in each of the expense and loss accounts (e.g. cost of sales, depreciation expense, loss on disposal of investment) to 'Profit or loss in the year' by crediting the income statement accounts and debiting the balance sheet account.

If total revenues and gains exceed total expenses and losses in the year, the balance sheet account, now shortened to 'Profit in the year', will have a credit balance. If revenues and gains are less than expenses and losses, it will have a debit balance, a reduction in owners' equity, and will be reported in the balance sheet as 'Loss in the year'. Exhibit 5.2 shows the procedure for closing income statement accounts in both journal entry and T account form.

Exhibit 5.2 Closing of income statement accounts: journal entries and effect on ledger accounts

Illustration

La Cenerentola, a company in the home cleaning business, has only two income statement accounts, revenues from services and salaries expense. Revenues are 6,000 a month; salaries are 5,000 a month. At the end of year 1, the company makes the following closing entries.

Journal entries

		Dr.	Cr.
31 Dec.	Service revenues	72,000	
	Profit or loss in year 1		72,000
	Profit or loss in year 1	60,000	
	Salaries expense		60,000

Ledger accounts

OWNERS' EQUITY

Salaries expense

	Dr.		Cr.
Jan.	5,000	To:	
:	:	P/L	
:	:	in	
:	:	yr 1	60,000
Dec.	5,000		

Service revenues

	Dr.		Cr.
		To:	
		P/L	
		in	
	yr 1	72,000	
		Jan.	6,000
		:	:
		:	:
		:	:
		Dec.	6,000

Profit or loss in year 1

		Dr.			Cr.
From:			From:		
Salaries			Service		
expense	60,000		revenues	72,000	
			Balance,		
			31/12/yr 1	12,000	

As a result of closing the 'Service revenues' and 'Salaries expense' accounts, the company finds that it has made a profit of 12,000 in year 1 – represented by a credit balance of that amount in the 'Profit or loss in year 1' account.

The recording process: from trial balance to financial statements

It's time to return to our mythical language school, Out of Babel Company. In Chapter 4, we took leave of the company after having drawn up the initial trial balance at 31 December year 2, which is set out again in Exhibit 5.3 below.

The company's ledger accounts – with their provisional balances at 31 December year 2, as shown in Exhibit 4.12 – are reproduced in Exhibit 5.4.

Inspection of the accounts in the trial balance reveals that adjustments must be made to reflect the passage of time and the partial expiry of certain assets and liabilities. Taking the accounts in the order listed in the trial balance, we'll

- explain the adjustments required;
- show by journal entry which accounts are affected and by how much; and
- post the adjustments to the ledger accounts, as set out in Exhibits 5.4 and 5.5.

The income statement accounts are then closed (Exhibit 5.6), the final trial balance for year 2 drawn up (Exhibit 5.7), and financial statements for year 2 prepared (Exhibit 5.8). Let battle commence!

Exhibit 5.3			

Out of Babel Company
Initial trial balance
at 31 December year 2
(all amounts in 000)

	Debit balances	*Credit balances*
From balance sheet accounts:		
Cash	23	
Short-term investment	24	
Accounts receivable	9	
Supplies inventory	7	
Prepaid rent	8	
Equipment	33	
Bank loan		15
Accounts payable		3
Unearned fee revenue		18
Share capital		40
Profit in year 1		2
From year 2 income statement accounts:		
Revenue from fees		80
Salaries expense	47	
Utilities expense	7	
Totals	158	158

● Adjustments to the accounts of Out of Babel Company

A1 Interest earned

Interest on the 24,000 of short-term securities the company acquires in early November year 2 accrues at an annual rate of 10% or 200 a month. Since the company will not receive any interest until the investment matures at the end of April year 3, it records the interest earned in November and December as a receivable.

> *Journal entry (A1)*
> Dr. Accrued interest receivable (A+)   400
>   Cr. Interest revenue (OE+)   400

A2 Supplies consumed

As a result of an inventory count on 31 December, the company discovers that only 3,000 of the 7,000 of supplies purchased remain in stock. Assuming no losses from theft or wastage, this means the company has consumed 4,000 of supplies. It records an expense of this amount in year 2:

> *Journal entry (A2)*
> Dr. Supplies expense (OE–)   4,000
>   Cr. Supplies inventory (A–)   4,000

A3 Rent expense

The company paid 16,000 for two years' rent of its premises at the start of year 1. Half of the asset, 'Prepaid rent', expired in year 1. The company makes an adjustment at the end of year 2 to record the expiry of the remaining half.

> *Journal entry (A3)*
> Dr. Rent expense (OE–)   8,000
>   Cr. Prepaid rent (A–)   8,000

A4 Depreciation of equipment

The company recognises a second year's depreciation of 2,000 on the equipment it purchased (for 10,000) in year 1. In addition, it recognises depreciation on the equipment it bought for 25,000 in year 2. We assume this equipment also has an expected life of 5 years and the services from it will be the same each year. Since it was purchased in mid-year, only half a year's depreciation is charged in year 2. Thus total depreciation expense recognised in year 2 amounts to 4,500 ($2,000 + (1/2 \times 5,000)$).

> *Journal entry (A4)*
> Dr. Depreciation expense (OE–)   4,500
>   Cr. Equipment (A–)   4,500

The total cost of the two assets is 35,000. Accumulated depreciation charged to the end of year 2 is 6,500. Thus at 31 December year 2, the equipment has a net book value of 28,500, the balance shown in the equipment account then.

Exhibit 5.4 shows the posting of adjustments A1–A4 to Out of Babel's ledger accounts.

Exhibit 5.4

Out of Babel Company
Recording of adjustments A1 to A4
at the end of year 2
(all amounts in 000)

Assets	**Liabilities**	**Owners' equity**
Cash	Bank loan	Share capital
PB 23	PB 15	PB 40
Accrued interest receivable	Accounts payable	Profit in year 1
(A1) 0.4	PB 3	PB 2
Short-term investment	Unearned fee revenue	
PB 24	PB 18	

Accounts receivable

PB   9

Supplies inventory

PB   7 | (A2)   4

Prepaid rent

PB   8 | (A3)   8

Equipment (net)

PB   33 | (A4) 4.5

Year 2 income statement accounts

Revenue from fees

PB   80

Salaries expense

PB   47

Interest revenue

(A1) 0.4

Utilities expense

PB   7

Supplies expense

(A2)   4

Depreciation expense

(A4) 4.5

Rent expense

(A3)   8

Note: PB = Provisional balance at 31 December year 2.

A5 Interest incurred

The company borrowed 15,000 from the bank for one year on 1 July year 2. By 31 December, it has had six months' use of the money. The loan bears interest at an annual rate of 12%, payable on maturity. The company has incurred an expense and a liability (for unpaid interest) of 900 by the end of year 2 (a monthly rate of 1% on 15,000 for six months).

Journal entry (A5)
Dr. Interest expense (OE–)	900	
Cr. Accrued interest payable (L+)		900

A6 Tuition fees earned

In early October year 2, the company received in advance 18,000 of tuition fees for its nine-month language course. By the end of December, the company had earned one-third of the fees – and 6,000 of the 18,000 liability recognised in October has expired.

Journal entry (A6)
Dr. Unearned fee revenue (L–)	6,000	
Cr. Revenues from fees (OE+)		6,000

A7 Salary costs incurred

The last salary payment date in year 2 was 24 December. The company's financial year does not end until 31 December. Given that employees earn salaries in the final week of the year, the company must accrue the cost of the services they perform in that period. Its normal monthly wage bill is approximately 4,000. Assuming a four-week month, the company has to recognise an expense and liability of 1,000 for salaries earned but not paid in the last week of year 2.

Journal entry (A7)
Dr. Salaries expense (OE–)	1,000	
Cr. Accrued salaries payable (L+)		1,000

Exhibit 5.5 shows the posting of adjustments A5–A7 to the company's ledger accounts.

Exhibit 5.5

Out of Babel Company
Recording of adjustments A5 to A7
at the end of year 2
(all amounts in 000)

Assets	Liabilities	Owners' equity
Cash	**Bank loan**	**Share capital**
PB 23	PB 15	PB 40
Accrued interest receivable	**Accounts payable**	**Profit in year 1**
(A1) 0.4	PB 3	PB 2
Short-term investment	**Unearned fee revenue**	
PB 24	(A6) 6 | PB 18	
Accounts receivable	**Accrued interest payable**	**Year 2 income statement accounts**
PB 9	(A5) 0.9	
Supplies inventory	**Accrued salaries payable**	**Revenue from fees**
PB 7 | (A2) 4	(A7) 1	PB 80 / (A6) 6
Prepaid rent	**Salaries expense**	**Interest revenue**
PB 8 | (A3) 8	PB 47 / (A7) 1	(A1) 0.4
Equipment (net)	**Utilities expense**	
PB 33 | (A4) 4.5	PB 7	
	Supplies expense	**Depreciation expense**
	(A2) 4	(A4) 4.5
	Rent expense	**Interest expense**
	(A3) 8	(A5) 0.9

Note: PB = Provisional balance at 31 December year 2.

Note that the adjustments the company makes at the end of year 2 include all four types of adjustment we identified earlier. The charges for depreciation, rent and supplies are examples of the consumption of an asset. The revenue earned on the tuition fees paid in advance is an example of the (partial) fulfilment of an obligation. The accrual of interest and salaries incurred as well as the accrual of interest earned illustrate the effect of the passage of time on both liabilities and assets.

Assuming the company's accounts are judged to be error-free, no further adjustments are necessary. Given that this is the end of its financial year, the next steps are, first, to *determine the adjusted ending balances* in the ledger accounts and, next, to *close the revenue and expense accounts*.

The first step is straightforward. Each account's adjusted ending balance is calculated by updating the provisional balance for the accrual adjustments of the period. The second step requires a new balance sheet account to be set up to which income statement accounts can be closed. The company titles it 'Profit or loss in year 2'. The company closes year 2 revenue and expense accounts to this account in order to arrive at the profit or loss for the year. The closing entries are set out below.

Closing of year 2 revenue accounts at 31 December (C1)

Dr. Revenue from tuition fees	86,000	
Dr. Interest revenue	400	
Cr. Profit or loss in year 2		86,400
(balance sheet account)		

Closing of year 2 expense accounts at 31 December (C2)

Dr. Profit or loss in year 2	72,400	
(balance sheet account)		
Cr. Salary expense		48,000
Cr. Utilities expense		7,000
Cr. Depreciation expense		4,500
Cr. Supplies expense		4,000
Cr. Rent expense		8,000
Cr. Interest expense		900

Exhibit 5.6 shows the calculation of the adjusted ending balances at the end of year 2 and the posting of the closing entries to the company's ledger accounts.

The journal entries presented above are summary entries. Entries can be made to close individual revenue and expense accounts separately. Whichever method is used, the *total* of each revenue or expense account for the year is computed and transferred to 'Profit or loss in the year'.

There are two important consequences of closure. First, the balance in each of the revenue and expense accounts is now zero. As a result, when Out of Babel Company records year 3 revenues and expenses, it will do so in new accounts. It will not mix year 3 results with those of year 2.

Second, the balance in the 'Profit or loss in the year' account indicates whether the company has made a profit or loss. In our example, the company's revenues in year 2 exceed its expenses that year. The credit balance of 14,000 in the 'Profit or loss in year 2' account indicates the profit which the company reports in its year 2 accounts.

Exhibit 5.6

Out of Babel Company
Closing income statement accounts and
computing ending balances at 31/12/year 2
(all amounts in 000)

Assets	Liabilities	Owners' equity

Cash

EB	23	

Short-term investment

EB	24	

Accrued interest receivable

(A1)	0.4	
EB	0.4	

Accounts receivable

EB	9	

Supplies inventory

PB	7	(A2)	4
EB	3		

Prepaid rent

PB	8	(A3)	8
EB	0		

Equipment (net)

PB	33	(A4)	4.5
EB	28.5		

Bank loan

		EB	15

Accounts payable

		EB	3

Unearned fee revenue

(A6)	6	PB	18
		EB	12

Accrued interest payable

		(A5)	0.9
		EB	0.9

Accrued salaries payable

		(A7)	1
		EB	1

Salaries expense

PB	47		
(A7)	1		
EB	48	(C2)	48

Utilities expense

EB	7	(C2)	7

Supplies expense

(A2)	4		
EB	4	(C2)	4

Rent expense

(A3)	8		
EB	8	(C2)	8

Share capital

		EB	40

Profit in year 1

		EB	2

Profit/loss in year 2

(C2)	72.4	(C1)	86.4
		EB	14

Year 2 income statement accounts

Revenue from fees

		PB	80
		(A6)	6
(C1)	86	EB	86

Interest revenue

		(A1)	0.4
(C1)	0.4	EB	0.4

Depreciation expense

(A4)	4.5		
EB	4.5	(C2)	4.5

Interest expense

(A5)	0.9		
EB	0.9	(C2)	0.9

Notes: PB = Provisional balance at 31 December year 2.
EB = (Adjusted) ending balance at 31 December year 2.

With the ending balances determined and income statement accounts closed, a final trial balance can be drawn up prior to preparing the company's year 2 financial statements. We show in Exhibit 5.7 the final (or post-closing) trial balance and the link via adjusting and closing

Exhibit 5.7

Out of Babel Company
Effect of adjusting and closing entries
on the trial balance at 31/12/year 2
(all amounts in 000)

Account	Initial trial balance Dr.	Initial trial balance Cr.	Adjusting entries Dr.	Adjusting entries Cr.	Closing entries Dr.	Closing entries Cr.	Final trial balance Dr.	Final trial balance Cr.
Cash	23						23	
Short-term investment	24						24	
Accrued interest receivable			(A1) 0.4				0.4	
Accounts receivable	9						9	
Supplies inventory	7			(A2) 4			3	
Prepaid rent	8			(A3) 8			0	
Equipment	33			(A4) 4.5			28.5	
Bank loan		15						15
Accrued interest payable				(A5) 0.9				0.9
Accounts payable		3						3
Unearned fee revenue		18	(A6) 6					12
Accrued salaries payable				(A7) 1				1
Share capital		40						40
Profit in year 1		2						2
Profit/loss in year 2					(C2) 72.4	(C1) 86.4		14
Fee revenue		80		(A6) 6	(C1) 86			0
Interest revenue				(A1) 0.4	(C1) 0.4			0
Salaries expense	47		(A7) 1			(C2) 48	0	
Utilities expense	7					(C2) 7	0	
Depreciation expense			(A4) 4.5			(C2) 4.5	0	
Supplies expense			(A2) 4			(C2) 4	0	
Rent expense			(A3) 8			(C2) 8	0	
Interest expense			(A5) 0.9			(C2) 0.9	0	
Totals	158	158	24.8	24.8	158.8	158.8	87.9	87.9

entries between it and the initial trial balance. An additional intermediate trial balance (e.g. after adjustments have been made but before closing entries have been posted) can be drawn up to ensure the adjusting entries have been correctly recorded.

Exhibit 5.8 contains the company's income statement for year 2 and its balance sheet at 31 December year 2. Certain accounts have been combined to simplify presentation. For example, 'Short-term investment' includes accrued interest receivable on the investment. 'Retained earnings' comprises the profits earned (and retained) by the company in both years 1 and 2.

Exhibit 5.8

Out of Babel Company
Annual accounts for year 2
(all amounts in 000)

Income statement for year 2
(1 January to 31 December)

Revenue from fees		86
Operating expenses:		
Salaries	48	
Rent of premises	8	
Utilities	7	
Depreciation of equipment	4.5	
Supplies	4	
Less: Operating expenses		−71.5
Operating profit		14.5
Interest expense	0.9	
Less: Interest revenue	−0.4	
Less: Interest expense, net		−0.5
Profit for the year (before tax)		14.0

Balance sheet
at 31 December year 2

Current assets		*Current liabilities*	
Cash	23	Bank loan (including	
Short-term investment		accrued interest)	15.9
(incl. accrued interest)	24.4	Accounts payable	3
Accounts receivable	9	Fees received in advance	12
Supplies inventory	3	Accrued salaries payable	1
Total current assets	59.4	Total current liabilities	31.9
Fixed assets		*Shareholders' equity*	
Equipment at cost	35	Share capital	40
Less: Accumulated		Retained earnings	16
depreciation	−6.5		
		Total shareholders' equity	56
Equipment, net	28.5		
		Total liabilities and	
Total assets	87.9	shareholders' equity	87.9

The role of the contra account

The presentation of 'equipment' in the balance sheet displayed in Exhibit 5.8 differs from its treatment in the ledger accounts in Exhibits 5.4 to 5.6. In the ledger, we show the consumption of the equipment (depreciation) as a direct reduction of the equipment account, in the same way that we record consumption of prepaid rent and supplies. In practice, however, a separate record is maintained for accumulated depreciation charges. It is known as a **contra account** (or **offset account**).

A company employs a contra account when, for information reasons, it wishes to record (downward) adjustments to the value of an asset or liability separately. Consider the case of depreciable fixed assets. Managers and investors want to be able to distinguish any changes in the holdings of such assets – through acquisitions and disposals – from the effects of wear and tear or obsolescence on them.

In the case of depreciable fixed assets, the method chosen is to accumulate in a separate balance sheet account the depreciation charges on a particular fixed asset. Thus, instead of periodic depreciation charges on equipment being credited to the equipment account itself, they are credited to an account 'Accumulated Depreciation – Equipment' which offsets (is 'contra' to) the equipment account. (In their published accounts, companies group fixed assets and related accumulated depreciation charges by category – e.g. buildings, equipment, vehicles – to simplify presentation.)

Using the facts in our example, we set out in Exhibit 5.9 first the journal entries and then the effect on the ledger accounts of both the 'net' approach (the method used up to now) and the more widely used 'contra' approach.

The contra account 'Accumulated depreciation' behaves like an equity account: increases in the account are recorded on the right-hand side (as credits), decreases on the left-hand side (as debits). This is true of all contra-asset accounts. (By the same token, entries to contra-liability accounts are recorded in the same manner as entries to asset accounts.)

The accumulated depreciation account is debited when the related asset is retired (i.e. sold or scrapped): then all accumulated depreciation on the asset disposed of must be removed from the account. For example, suppose that at the start of year 3 the equipment purchased in year 1 is sold for its (depreciated) book amount of 6,000. The disposal will be entered in the journal as follows (amounts in 000):

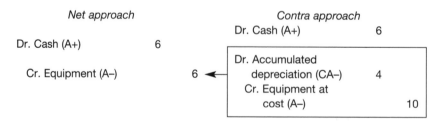

Under the contra approach, the balance in the equipment account represents the cost of the asset throughout the holding period (assuming the asset is not revalued or written down). Thus when the company retires the asset, the equipment account is credited for its cost. Since the accumulated depreciation account is debited for the total depreciation charged on this asset (4,000, or two years at 2,000 a year), the net effect is to reduce fixed assets by the net book value (6,000) of the asset disposed of. Thus the net and contra approaches have the same overall impact on the accounts.

Exhibit 5.9   **Accounting for depreciation: net and contra approaches contrasted**

Facts

Out of Babel acquires for cash equipment costing 10 in year 1 (event 1) and 25 in year 2 (event 3). Depreciation expense is 2 in year 1 (event 2) and 4.5 in year 2 (event 4). (All amounts are in 000.)

Journal entries

Event	Net approach	Dr.	Cr.	Contra approach	Dr.	Cr.
(1)	Equipment (A+)	10		Equipment (A+)	10	
	Cash (A–)		10	Cash (A–)		10
(2)	Depreciation expense (OE–)	2		Depreciation expense (OE–)	2	
	Equipment (A–)		2	Accumulated depreciation (CA+)		2
(3)	Equipment (A+)	25		Equipment (A+)	25	
	Cash (A–)		25	Cash (A–)		25
(4)	Depreciation expense (OE–)	4.5		Depreciation expense (OE–)	4.5	
	Equipment (A–)		4.5	Accumulated depreciation (CA+)		4.5

Note: CA = contra-asset.

T accounts – for equipment and related accounts

	Net approach			Contra approach				
	Equipment, net			Equipment, at cost			Accumulated depreciation	
	+		–	+		–	–	+
During year 1	(1)	10	(2) 2	(1)	10			(2) 2
Balance, end-year 1	8			10				2
During year 2	(3)	25	(4) 4.5	(3)	25			(4) 4.5
Balance, end-year 2	28.5			35				6.5

Equipment, net 28.5

Dividends: the distribution of profits

The income number not only indicates how well the company has performed in the financial period under view: it also provides essential information to the board of directors when they consider what dividend should be paid to shareholders.

A dividend is normally a distribution of profit. The firm's accumulated profits are its earned capital. Until profit has been determined, neither the directors who recommend the amount of the dividend nor the shareholders who, in general meeting, approve it can know whether the proposed dividend represents a distribution of earned capital or a return of contributed capital.

Consider the position of Out of Babel Company in year 2. Suppose that, as directors, Sam Beckett and Carrie Blixen propose that the company pay a dividend of 14,000 to shareholders in year 2. Until the financial statements have been prepared and the profit earned in year 2 has been determined, it is possible that a dividend of this magnitude would result in a return of part of the company's contributed capital of 40,000.

From a legal and accounting standpoint, a dividend is an appropriation (allocation) of profit and not an expense incurred in arriving at it. The company decides, at the annual general meeting of shareholders, how the profit for the year is to be allocated: how much must be set aside to reserves by law; how much will be retained in the business; and how much will be distributed to shareholders. From this perspective, the dividend is a discretionary payment to shareholders. Of course, in economic terms, a dividend represents, along with capital gains, the return a shareholder expects on his or her investment in the same way that interest is the return on the debtholder's investment. In this light, both dividends and interest are costs of doing business. But whereas the cost of debt capital is treated by accountants as an expense, the cost of equity capital is never treated this way. There is no such thing as 'dividend expense'.

The accounting for cash dividends reflects this. The dividend is charged against the profit for the year – or profits retained from previous years if the current year's profit is insufficient (or the firm makes a loss). For example, suppose Out of Babel Company decides to distribute, as cash dividend, all of its year 2 profit, it will make the following entry at the date of payment in, say, March year 3:

> *March year 3*
> Dr. Profit in year 2 (OE–)   14,000
>   Cr. Cash (A–)   14,000

(In practice, a firm may record the dividend in a temporary owners' equity account ('Dividend in year xx'), which it closes to the balance sheet account 'Profit/loss in year xx' at year-end.)

A company can also distribute profits earned (and retained) in prior years. For example, Out of Babel can declare a year 2 dividend of up to 16,000, the total of its year 1 and year 2 reported profits, assuming the company's statutes permit it.

> *March year 3*
> Dr. Profit in year 2 (OE–)   14,000
> Dr. Profit in year 1 (OE–)   2,000
>   Cr. Cash (A–)   16,000

Companies following Anglo-Saxon accounting practice do not distinguish between profits earned in the current year and profits brought forward from previous years. Both are combined in one account 'Retained earnings', as we saw in Exhibit 5.8. In this case, the above journal entry would read:

March year 3
Dr. Retained earnings (OE–)   16,000
    Cr. Cash (A–)   16,000

Dividends: the effect on corporate assets

Notice the credit side of the above journal entries. With the exception of a share dividend where shareholders receive additional shares of the company in place of cash, *a dividend represents a distribution of cash (or other corporate assets)*. That cash has alternative uses. It can be used to repay debt or to finance investments in plant and equipment. Thus a company may restrict the amount of its profits it pays out as dividends (its payout ratio) if management reckon – and shareholders agree – that there are other, more profitable ways of employing the cash.[4]

The restriction on profit – and cash – distribution may be externally imposed. In many European countries, the government requires all public companies to transfer a percentage (usually 5%) of their annual profit to a legal reserve until a specified minimum balance in the reserve has been reached. Covenants in loan agreements may also place restrictions on the annual dividend a company can declare. Both measures are designed to protect the interests of creditors. Once corporate assets have been distributed to shareholders, they are no longer available to meet creditors' claims.

We look more closely at the accounting for dividends – and alternative ways of distributing corporate cash to shareholders – in a later chapter.

The extraordinary items fallacy

Accounting fallacy no. 4: *'Extraordinary profits are more important than ordinary ones.'*

In everyday speech, 'extraordinary' suggests something special. When an individual is referred to as 'extraordinary', we think of the person as being *above* the ordinary, rather than simply *out of* the ordinary. However, in accounting the term has a narrower meaning.

In Chapter 3, we defined a firm's ordinary profit or loss as the profit or loss arising from its operations and other activities incidental to them. Thus the firm's operations and related activities (e.g. financing, investing) are its 'ordinary activities'. It follows that *extraordinary profits or losses result from events that are distinct from the firm's ordinary activities. Moreover, such events occur infrequently and irregularly*. For example, the loss which a company sustains when it sells a fixed asset at an amount less than its book value is ordinary; the loss arising from earthquake damage to its plant in southern France is extraordinary.

Investors prize recurring or 'permanent' profits. They estimate a company's value by reference to its current – and expected future – recurring profits. The most important source of recurring profit is the profit from its continuing operations which are part of its ordinary activities. Extraordinary profits, by definition, occur infrequently and irregularly. Investors view them as temporary and attach a lower value to them. Thus, for investors, extraordinary profits are *less* important than ordinary ones.

The layout of the income statement reflects the relative importance of the various types of profit and loss. Although companies use different income statement formats (we illustrate the ones found in EU and US company accounts in the next chapter), in most cases the income statement has the general structure shown in Exhibit 5.10.

The results of the firm's operating activities (operating profit/loss) head the statement. Shown next are income from investments (the result of investing activities) and interest income or expense (the net effect of financing activities). (The order here may be reversed: interest income/expense

| Exhibit 5.10 | General structure of income statement |

Type of activity		Income statement caption
Ordinary activities:		
Operations		Operating profit/loss
Investing	+	Investment income
Financing	+/–	Interest income/expense
Other ordinary activities	+/–	Other gains/losses (e.g. gain or loss on sale of fixed asset)
		Profit/loss before tax
Tax cost of profits	–	Tax expense
(Tax benefit of losses	+	Tax credit)
Total ordinary activities		Net profit/loss from ordinary activities*
Extraordinary events or transactions	+/–	Extraordinary gains/losses, net of tax
Ordinary and extraordinary activities		Net profit/loss after extraordinary gains/losses

* In a consolidated income statement, this figure is shown after deducting 'minority interests' (outside shareholders' share of the net profits/losses of subsidiaries).

may precede investment income.) 'Other gains and losses' are sometimes described as 'exceptional items' – to distinguish them from 'extraordinary items'. Exceptional items are unusual or occur irregularly – but not both. They are treated as part of the firm's ordinary activities.[5]

'Net profit/loss from ordinary activities' is a key number in the income statement. It's used in profitability ratios such as return on equity. It is sometimes referred to as 'the bottom line'. Extraordinary gains and losses are shown beneath this figure – or 'below the line', as financial journalists like to put it. Because the bottom line profit or loss is an after-tax figure, extraordinary gains and losses must be shown net of their associated tax cost or benefit.

The income statement is becoming more detailed. For example, under new international rules, companies must split the operating result between profits or losses from continuing operations and those from operations discontinued in the year. In some countries this is already required under national rules. More confusingly, another recent innovation is the supplementary income statement, in which a company records certain gains and losses which otherwise it would book directly to its reserves in the balance sheet. We illustrate this statement in the next chapter.

Summary

In this chapter we completed the journey we began in Chapter 4.

The accrual basis of accounting rests on timing and matching 'principles' or guidelines which determine when revenues and expenses – and thus profit – are recognised.

To prepare accrual-based accounts, a company makes accrual adjustments to the initial trial balance at the end of a financial period. These adjustments capture accounting events such as the effect on the accounts of the passage of time and the expiry of assets and liabilities during the period. In addition, the company adjusts the trial balance for any errors it uncovers in the accounts.

At the end of the financial year, once it has updated the accounts and corrected any errors, it closes the income statement accounts. This ensures that the profit or loss it reports is the result of revenues and expenses arising in that year alone.

The record-keeping cycle, from source document to end-of-year financial statements, can be summarised as follows:

$$\text{Source document} \rightarrow \text{Journal} \rightarrow \text{Ledger} \rightarrow \text{Trial balance} \rightarrow \text{Adjusting and closing entries} \rightarrow \text{Financial statements}$$

We introduced a new type of account, the contra account. A company sets up a contra account when, for information reasons, it wants to record separately adjustments to the value of an asset or liability. We use the example of depreciation to illustrate how a contra account works.

We also looked at the accounting treatment of cash dividends. Two interesting points emerge from the discussion. First, a dividend is, from a legal and accounting standpoint, a distribution of profit, not an expense incurred in arriving at it. Second, a cash dividend results in a reduction of corporate assets as well as owners' capital. Thus creditors as well as shareholders are affected by the company's dividend decision. And the company's own cash operating needs will influence its payout policy.

Finally, we exposed the extraordinary items fallacy. A firm's extraordinary activities are, from an accounting perspective, unusual and non-recurring. By contrast, its ordinary activities, in particular its continuing operations, are the main source of its recurring profits and the basis of its market value. Thus investors attach more importance to the profits arising from its ordinary than its extraordinary activities.

Problem assignments

P5.1 Accrual adjustments and accounting records

Governments at local and national level are examining new ways of charging motorists directly for road use. One proposal is based on an automatic vehicle identification (AVI) system. A device is fitted to a car's windscreen which enables a radio signal from a roadside beacon to identify the car as it's moving.

A problem for governments is how to collect the toll from the user of the vehicle in an efficient way. An individual may well drive cars other than the one(s) he or she owns. Two alternatives have been proposed. The first is a 'smart card'. An individual can get into any car, insert his smart card into a device connected to the AVI and have the bill for road use charged to his account. He then settles his account monthly or quarterly.

The second alternative is the prepaid card. The card entitles the buyer to a specified number of 'road use units'. It works in the same way as the smart card except that charges for road use are deducted directly while the card is in radio contact with the AVI. (As *The Economist* (7 August 1993) points out, one advantage of the prepaid card is that it is more private. There is no record of where a particular driver has been and when.)

Required

Consider the accounting implications of the two charging methods for the company collecting the road tolls. What are the balance sheet and income statement accounts it must set up in its books? Show the entries for road use and payment (not necessarily in that order) under the two methods.

P5.2 Accrual accounting and debt payments

In the 1990s, some of Poland's fastest growing companies were former foreign trade organisations (FTOs) which turned themselves into conglomerates. Keeping control of the finances of their subsidiaries proved a difficult task for top management. The chairman of one FTO/conglomerate, Universal, told *The Economist* (5 August 1995) that a subsidiary was able to show a profit in a period only because it skipped debt payments.

Required

Is the chairman's statement (as reported) correct? What is the effect on a firm's accounts if it fails to make scheduled debt payments?

P5.3 Accrual adjustments I

'Autovalet' is a successful chain of car cleaning centres. Some of the centres are owned by the company while others operate under a franchise arrangement – where Autovalet is the franchisor and the proprietor of the centre is the franchisee. During x5 Autovalet enters into the following transactions. The company's financial year ends on 31 December.

1 On 31 May, Autovalet loans 75,000 to a franchisee for two years at an annual interest rate of 8%. Under the agreement, the franchisee is to pay interest every six months and to repay the principal of 75,000 on 31 May x7.
2 Autovalet buys supplies costing 11,000 during the year. It has supplies costing 2,000 in inventory at the end of x5. The year before (end x4), it had supplies costing 3,000 in inventory.
3 Autovalet receives 360,000 of advance fees from franchisees on 1 September x5, covering services it will render them in the year to 31 August x6. The services consist mainly of advertising and promoting the Autovalet brand and will be provided evenly over the year. The equivalent sum it received on 1 September x4, was 336,000.
4 As a result of expansion, Autovalet has to rent additional office space for its staff in x5. On 1 March x5, it enters into a contract with the owner of the office building and pays 135,000 for three years' rent in advance.

Required

Compute the following amounts Autovalet reports in its annual accounts for x5:

(a) interest income;

(b) supplies expense;

(c) unearned franchise fee revenue at 31 December;

(d) rent expense.

P5.4 Accrual adjustments II

We learned about Sun, C and Sand in Chapters 2 and 3. The company's balance sheet on 31 January year 1 – the end of its first month of operations – is set out in Exhibit 5.11.

Fred Chopin and Georgie Sand opened a bottle of Cava to celebrate the success of their store in January. February, by contrast, was a disaster. Unseasonably cool, wet weather kept the winter visitors away. Here's what happened to the business that month:

1 The company made no sales of goods in February. Moreover, the customer who owed 4,000 at the end of January also experienced business problems. After lengthy negotiations the customer signed a six-month note agreeing to pay, at the end of July, the principal of the note plus accrued interest. Interest is to accrue from 1 February at the rate of 1.5% a month.
2 In desperation, Georgie started a monthly magazine for resident foreigners like herself. Remembering the Cava, she decided to call it 'Grapevine'. The annual subscription was 24, payable in advance. Five hundred subscriptions were sold in February. The first issue came out at the end of February.

Exhibit 5.11

Sun, C and Sand Company
Balance sheet at 31 January year 1

Current assets		Current liabilities	
Cash	35,550	Bank loan	12,000
Accounts receivable	4,000	Accounts payable	5,000
Inventory	1,000	Accrued wages payable	100
Prepaid rent	4,000	Total	17,100
Total	44,550		
Fixed assets		*Shareholders' equity*	
Shop equipment	9,000	Contributed capital	20,000
Less: Accumulated		Profit in January	16,200
depreciation	–250	Total	36,200
Net book value	8,750		
		Total liabilities	
Total assets	53,300	and shareholders' equity	53,300

Notes (*see also* Chapter 3):
Equipment: Purchased early January; has expected useful life of three years.
Prepaid rent: Three months' rent of 6,000 paid at start of January.

3 The magazine generated 750 of advertising revenue in February (although Sun, C and Sand received no cash from advertisers that month).

4 The costs of printing and distributing the magazine were 3/copy, all paid in cash during the month.

5 Utility costs paid in February were 350, the same as in January.

6 Payments in February to the part-time employee (whose duties now included writing a gossip column, *Sotto voce*, in the magazine) were 1,200, including 100 of unpaid January wages. In view of his additional duties, the wages earned by him in February were 1,350.

7 Despite the company's operating difficulties, the amount owing to suppliers at 31 January was paid in February. So too was February's interest on the 10% bank loan.

8 Adjustments were made in the accounts for the use of shop space and equipment in the month. There were no other transactions or accounting events in February.

Required

(a) Prepare journal entries to record the above.

(b) Post the entries to ledger accounts.

(c) What is the company's profit or loss in February?

Check figure:
Cumulative profit
at 28 February year 1   12,460

P5.5 Financial statement relationships

By coincidence, three separate companies report the same summary balance sheet at the end of year 4.

Assets		Liabilities	+	Shareholders' equity
105,000	=	50,000	+	55,000

Shareholders' equity comprises share capital and retained earnings. End-year retained earnings are equal to start-year retained earnings adjusted for the profit/loss and dividend in the year:

$$RE_{end} = RE_{start} +/- P/L - DIV$$

In other respects the accounts of the three companies diverge. Key figures have been taken from their year 5 accounts. They are given below under columns 1, 2 and 3. As you can see, the accounts are incomplete.

	Company		
	(1)	(2)	(3)
Share capital, end year 5	25	(F)	(K)
Revenues in year 5	125	(G)	114
Liabilities, end year 5	(A)	51	53
Expenses in year 5	115	115	112
Retained earnings, end year 4	(B)	(H)	(L)
Assets, end year 5	110	(I)	111
Dividend in year 5	(C)	2	3
Share capital, end year 4	(D)	11	(M)
Retained earnings, end year 5	36	39	42
New investment by owners in year 5	0	(J)	(N)
Shareholders' equity, end year 5	(E)	53	(P)

Required

Fill in the blanks which are letter-coded. (Amounts are in 000.)

P5.6 Effect of errors on the accounts

It's early in x3. You are examining the financial records of Les Gaulois Company with a view to making an (amicable) bid for the company. You discover that the company, formed in x1, has made the following errors in x1, perhaps because of its preoccupation with hostile manoeuvres by Les Romains Company.

In each case, determine the effect of the error on reported profit in x1 and x2 and on retained earnings at the end of x1 and x2, and indicate which other balance sheet accounts, if any, were in error at the end of x1 and x2. Use the following notation: U (understated); O (overstated); NE (no effect). The solution to item 1 is given as an example (the 'asterix' is optional).

1 The company failed to accrue interest revenue in x1 on a loan it made to another company. It receives the interest (and the principal) in x2.

Profit		Retained earnings		Other balance sheet accounts	
x1	x2	end-x1	end-x2	end-x1	end-x2
				*Interest	
U	O	U	NE	receivable U	NE

2 Employees earned salaries in x1 which the company did not record until x2 when the salaries were paid.

3 The company purchased and received goods at the end of x1 but failed to make accounting entries to record the (credit) purchase and receipt until January x2.

4 It neglected to record annual depreciation on equipment in x1. The annual depreciation charge in x2 was correctly recorded.

5 In x1 customers made payments of 2,000 in advance for Les Gaulois products. Of this, only 500 worth of goods were shipped in that year (and the balance in x2). The company reported all 2,000 as revenues of x1. (Cost of sales was correctly recorded in both years.)

6 The company purchased 1,200 of office supplies in x1 and recorded all of it as an expense of that year. A physical count of supplies revealed inventory of 700 and 100 at the end of x1 and x2 respectively. There were no purchases of supplies in x2.

P5.7   Derivation of balance sheet

Poseidon Company specialises in the leasing of holiday apartments with boating facilities in the Greek islands. It has asked for your help. It's January year 3, and there's been a serious fire in its administrative offices. Many records have been destroyed. The company wants you to reconstruct the balance sheet at 31 December year 2. The balance sheet at the start of year 2 is available, cash records for year 2 have escaped the fire and a copy of the year 2 income statement has been discovered in the briefcase belonging to the managing director's husband. Information from these three items is set out in Exhibit 5.12.

Exhibit 5.12

Poseidon Company
Extracts from year 2 accounts
(amounts in 000)

Balance sheet at 1 January year 2

Assets			Equities		
Cash and short-term			Rentals received in advance		24
investments		32	Utilities payable		3
Property	828		Income tax payable		4
Less: Accumulated			Current liabilities		31
depreciation	−192		Long-term loan		560
		636			
			Share capital	40	
			Retained earnings	37	
			Shareholders' equity		77
Total assets		668	Total equities		668

Extracts from year 2 cash account

Cash receipts			Cash payments	
			Dividend paid	4
Holiday rentals received		93	Salaries paid	12
Interest received		2	Utilities paid	10
Increase in long-term loan		50	Interest paid	48
			Purchase of property	75
Total receipts		145	Total payments	149

Income statement for year 2

Depreciation expense	14	Revenue from holiday rentals	96
Salaries expense	13	Interest income from short-term	
Utilities expense	9	investments	3
Interest expense	51		
Income tax expense	6		
	93		
Net profit	6		
	99		99

Required

Reconstruct Poseidon's balance sheet at 31 December year 2.

Check figure:
Total assets, 31/12/year 2   726

P5.8 Cash-based and accrual-based accounts compared

Daedalus runs a small airline. He keeps his records on a cash basis. Learning that you are a master of the basics of accrual accounting (MBAA), he asks you to show him how the following items should be accounted for on an accrual basis, assuming updating entries are made once a year at year-end. The company has a 31 December year-end.

1 The company rented an aircraft for two years on 31 March x8. Daedalus recorded the 1.68 million rental payment for the two years as follows:

> *31 March x8*
> Dr. Rent expense   1,680,000
>   Cr. Cash   1,680,000

He made no further entries with respect to the rental.

2 The company received 200,000 from ticket sales in December x8. Ten per cent of the receipts were advance payments by customers for flights to be taken in January x9. Daedalus made the following entry in December:

> *December x8*
> Dr. Cash   200,000
>   Cr. Sales revenue   200,000

3 Some of the airline's staff are paid weekly. Their last pay day in x8 was Friday, 27 December. Daedalus made the following entry for the weekly payroll on that date.

> *27 December x8*
> Dr. Wage expense   2,800
>   Cr. Cash   2,800

The next payroll payment date is Friday, 3 January x9. (Ignore holidays and assume a seven-day work week.)

4 The company invests 100,000 in short-term government securities on 1 September x8. When the securities mature on 1 March x9, the company will receive 104,500. Daedalus recorded the following entry on 1 September.

> *1 September x8*
> Dr. Short-term investment   100,000
>   Cr. Cash   100,000

He made no further entry in the company's books in x8, since no cash was received that year. (Assume each month has 30 days.)

Required

For each of the four items above, show the entries that need to be made to convert the company's x8 accounts to an accrual basis.

Notes to Chapter 5

1 In practice, not all events are accounted for when they occur. For example, firms face restrictions on when they can recognise increases in the values of certain assets.

2 When a company sells an asset for more (less) than it paid for it, it *realises* a gain (loss), that is it converts the gain or loss into cash (or its equivalent). 'Realisation' has a broader meaning in the context of revenue recognition: it implies the securing of measurable economic benefits.

3 Using data from 1960 to 1989, a US researcher found that over various reporting intervals (quarterly, annual, four-yearly), US companies' stock market returns were more closely associated with earnings than cash flows (Dechow, P. (1994), Accounting earnings and cash flows as measures of firm performance: the role of accounting accruals, *Journal of Accounting and Economics*, 18: 3–42).

4 Dividend policy is a complex area. In addition to considering financial and strategic implications, firms must also weigh up the tax effect of dividend income on shareholders. Finance textbooks contain a full treatment of this subject.

5 Look out for differences in terminology across countries. Items described as extraordinary may, in fact, be merely exceptional and should be included in ordinary profits.

6

The annual report and accounts

INTRODUCTION

In previous chapters we described the purpose and form of the two key financial statements, the balance sheet and the income statement, and showed how they are prepared from accounting records. The aim of this chapter is to put a company's published financial statements in their usual context, the context of the annual report and accounts.

We review the contents of the annual report and accounts of a typical large European company and emphasise the parts of greatest interest to investors. These include, in addition to the financial statements, management's report to shareholders, the notes to the accounts, the governance statement and the auditors' report. We point out a common misconception about the income statement, the fifth in our accounting fallacy series.

We illustrate the different formats of balance sheet and income statement to be found in company accounts. EU law specifies the formats EU member states may permit or require firms to use. We provide a brief guide to the EU's company law harmonisation initiative in an appendix.

We introduce the third major financial statement, the statement of cash flows, explaining its form and function. (The discussion is short. We devote a whole chapter to the topic later.)

Finally, since the annual accounts are an important source of information for those buying and selling the securities of quoted public companies, we describe certain earnings- and dividend-based financial ratios which are widely used by stock market investors.

Note that the annual report and accounts are a part – albeit a very important part – of a quoted company's continuous 'dialogue' with investors. Quoted firms communicate with investors in other ways during the financial year – for example, through publication of interim accounts and announcements of significant changes to the company.

Overview

As the name suggests, the annual report and accounts contains two parts. The annual accounts comprise the financial statements and explanatory notes, and the auditors' report on them. The annual report which normally precedes the accounts is more varied in format. It usually contains:

1 a review of the company's activities over the past year and of its prospects for current and future ones; and
2 a discussion and analysis of the accounts.

Both the accounts and the report are prepared by management and are addressed to shareholders. Together these represent management's 'scorecard' for the year. In addition, the annual report contains other information and reports (e.g. the directors' report or the report of the supervisory board) which the company is legally obliged to publish.

The law influences the content of the annual report and accounts. Consider the case of EU firms. They must present the balance sheet and income statement according to a prescribed format. The annual accounts of all but small companies must be audited. The content of the annual report is also regulated. For example, a company must disclose any important events – examples are the acquisition or disposal of a subsidiary – that occur between its financial year-end and the date the accounts are signed. The report need not be audited but the auditor should ensure that it is consistent with the accounts. These requirements are summarised in Exhibit 6.1.

The disclosure and audit requirements are laid down in the EU's 4th Directive.[1] They are minimum requirements. Member states are free to demand additional disclosures. The Directive imposes less onerous requirements on smaller companies. We summarise these later in the chapter.

Other industrialised countries lay down similar disclosure and audit requirements. For example, publicly quoted companies in the USA must submit to the Securities and Exchange Commission (SEC) audited annual accounts which include a review by management of the company's activities over the year.

EU law also requires companies to make copies of their annual report and accounts available to the public (at a price no greater than administrative cost). When written, the law assumed this

---

Exhibit 6.1 ▶ **Annual report and accounts: EU disclosure and audit requirements**

	Minimum disclosures	Audit requirement
Annual report	● Review of past year's operations and financial position ⎤	
	● Information on:	**None**
	– post-balance-sheet events	(but auditor should
	– likely future development	check consistency
	– R&D activities	with annual accounts)
	– purchase of own shares ⎦	
Annual accounts	● Balance sheet ⎤	**Yes**
	● Income statement	(for medium-sized
	● Notes to the accounts ⎦	and large firms only)

(*Source*: Fourth Company Law Directive 78/660/EEC.)

would be a paper document. However, in order to disseminate the information more widely, many quoted companies in the EU and elsewhere now file the annual report and accounts on their corporate website as well.[2]

Management's report to shareholders

Management's report to shareholders comprises the largest part of a company's annual report and accounts. It's also the most colourful part, since unlike the accounts section it carries glossy pictures or even specially commissioned artwork illustrating company products, happy customers, contented staff and, increasingly, broader themes of current interest such as the environment. The reader is left with the impression that the accounts themselves are of secondary importance. They are relegated to the end of the document, often with a different typeface and sometimes printed separately on poorer quality paper.

BestPrice's x2 report and accounts share many of these characteristics. The management report runs to 40 pages. It's liberally sprinkled with pictures of smiling customers and 'associates' (employees). By contrast, the 30 pages of financial statements and accompanying notes are consigned to the back of the document and are printed with a smaller typeface. The report and accounts are also available on the company's website. They are simply a reproduction of the printed version, but readers are able to download the document by section so they need not be aware of the ordering of the material in the report.

Besides its promotional role, the management report is also a source of information about the company. Investors gain valuable insights from a well-written one. BestPrice's x2 management report is a good example. Each of the various parts of the report sheds light on different aspects of the company.

- *The chairman's letter to shareholders.* In addition to summarising the financial results for the year, the chairman of BestPrice's board of directors sets out in an introduction to the report the major strategic decisions the company has taken during the year. Important ones in x2 were the decision to expand its operations in emerging markets – BestPrice opened new stores in Asia and Latin America during the year – and the development of new lines of business in Europe, in particular, in-store banking and other financial services.
- *Review of operations.* BestPrice's management review developments in each of the company's markets (Western and Central Europe, South East Asia, and Latin America) in the year. These include acquisitions and disposals, new joint ventures, and new retailing concepts (e.g. internet-based home delivery service, smaller store formats in city centres and at petrol stations). The company discloses sales and operating results by market. In the case of sales, it highlights 'organic' sales growth (i.e. excluding the effect of new businesses acquired in the year). For its retail operations it gives information about sales, sales area and sales per square foot – a key performance indicator in the retail sector – by company within each country for both x1 and x2.

  BestPrice has one main line of business, retailing. When a company has more than one, it usually structures its review of operations by product or industry rather than by market.
- *Financial review.* BestPrice's management provide more detail about the financial performance, especially the earnings, of operations in each of the company's markets. They also use this section to link the operating review with the annual accounts. They refer back to events described in the operating review – for example, new store openings, the raising of new equity capital via a share offering, the devaluation of the Argentine peso – to explain key numbers in the accounts.

  Investors may also learn about a company's financing policies from this section. Some companies – but not BestPrice – disclose a target debt–equity ratio.

● *Outlook for current year (x3)*. BestPrice's management outline the company's prospects for x3 and provide sales and operating profit margin forecasts for the year. They give little cash flow information, however: for example, they do not indicate how much the company expects to spend on fixed assets in x3. There is also a separate section in the report dealing with significant post-balance sheet events (i.e. events that occurred after 31 December x2 but before the publication of the x2 report). For example, BestPrice made an acquisition of another retail group in January x3. Investors find information about such events useful in developing their own earnings forecasts.

The management reports of other large companies have a similar structure. However, the quality of the analysis in them varies considerably. One reason is the conflict of interest that management face: the report they write is a commentary on their own performance as managers. It is not surprising, therefore, if they emphasise the company's achievements in the year and downplay its failings.

In recent years, management reports have improved, thanks to the efforts of regulatory agencies. For example, publicly quoted firms in the USA have to include, in annual information filed with the SEC, a section in which management discuss and analyse the company's financial condition and operating results for the past three years. This is known as the MD&A (Management's Discussion and Analysis). The SEC has issued guidelines as to the content of the MD&A. Many US firms reproduce the MD&A in their annual report to shareholders. The UK's Accounting Standards Board has also issued guidelines to help UK listed firms prepare the 'operating and financial review' section of the management report.

Alternative balance sheet and income statement formats

Under EU law, the annual accounts comprise a balance sheet, income statement, explanatory notes and, for larger companies, an auditors' report. Comparative figures from the previous year must be given for all items in the balance sheet and income statement. As mentioned earlier, these are minimum requirements. In some EU member states, firms must publish a cash flow statement (or equivalent) as part of the annual accounts.

Although balance sheets and income statements are in principle the same across all countries, their formats differ. We describe below the formats found in EU company accounts and contrast them with those used by US and other large international firms.

Format of balance sheet

Look back at BestPrice's end-x2 balance sheets in Chapter 2 (Exhibit 2.4). It is laid out in **account format**. Where the balance sheet is presented on one page, assets head the page. On a two-page layout, assets are shown on the left, equities on the right. *The focus of attention is the entity's financial position.* Thus, whether a one- or two-page layout is used, all equities are grouped together.

The assets are listed in *descending* order of liquidity, with the most liquid assets, current assets, at the top of the asset column and fixed assets at the bottom. In a similar but more approximate way, equities are listed in descending order of maturity: liabilities with the shortest maturity head the equities' column while shareholders' equity (equity with an indefinite life) is shown last. US companies present their balance sheets in this way. Many non-US multinationals like BestPrice Stores adopt the US format because US investors are the largest national group of users of their English-language accounts.

The EU's 4th Directive permits two balance sheet formats: the account format and the statement format. The EU's **account format** is similar to a US-style balance sheet (e.g. assets first/on

Exhibit 6.2 EU balance sheet: account format

Assets	Equities
Fixed assets	Shareholders' equity
	Long-term liabilities and provisions
Current assets	Current liabilities

the left) save that it's upside down. Assets are listed in *ascending* order of liquidity and equities in ascending order of maturity. The format is summarised in Exhibit 6.2.

The Directive also permits the use of the **statement format**. In this format, *the focus of interest is the position of the owners* (in equation terms, A − L = OE). Assets and equities are listed vertically, with assets shown first, followed by liabilities and then shareholders' interests. The asset section is so arranged that the company's working capital ('net current assets') is highlighted, as Exhibit 6.3 demonstrates.

Exhibit 6.3 EU balance sheet: statement format

(1)   Fixed assets
(2)   + Current assets
(3)   − Current liabilities
(4)   Net current assets [(2) − (3)]
(5)   Total assets − current liabilities [(1) + (4)]
(6)   − Long-term liabilities and provisions
(7)   Net assets [(5) − (6)]

(8)   Shareholders' equity [= (7)]

Note that both formats contain the same information. A balance sheet can easily be converted from one basis to another. The asset side of an account-format balance sheet consists of items (1) and (2) above, while the equities side consists of items (8), (6) and (3).

The account format is the one most companies in continental Europe employ in their original-language balance sheets. Custom and law are responsible. In Spain, for example, under the 1989 law implementing the EU's 4th (and 7th) Directive companies must use this format. The statement format is popular only in Ireland and the UK.

Exhibit 6.4 illustrates the EU version of an account-format balance sheet. It shows the 2001 consolidated balance sheet of the Barco group, a Belgian manufacturer of visual display, imaging and projection equipment. In common with other Belgian companies, it provides detailed information on the face of the balance sheet. By contrast, the balance sheet of BestPrice Stores (*see* Exhibit 2.4) contains summary information only. BestPrice publishes detailed information in the notes to the accounts. Thus Barco breaks down its 'stocks' (inventories) figure on the face of the balance sheet; BestPrice provides this detail in the notes. These are two contrasting (and acceptable) ways of meeting EU disclosure requirements. (Note that Barco has a full range of manufacturing inventories (VII.A.1–3 and B) but, since it is not a retailer, no merchandise inventories (VII.A.4 represents 'goods for resale').)

Exhibit 6.4 Barco consolidated balance sheet (after appropriation) at 31 December 2001: account format

In thousands of euros

	2001
FIXED ASSETS	**224,737**
II. Intangible fixed assets	**50,946**
III. Consolidation differences	**42,974**
IV. Tangible fixed assets	**116,457**
A. Land and buildings	62,427
B. Plant, machinery and equipment	34,764
C. Office furniture and vehicles	13,052
D. Leasing and other similar rights	177
E. Other tangible fixed assets	2,466
F. Assets under construction and advance payments	3,571
V. Financial fixed assets	**14,360**
B. Companies accounted for by the equity method	7,023
1. *Shares*	2,023
2. *Amounts receivable*	5,000
C. Other enterprises	7,337
1. *Shares*	4,043
2. *Amounts receivable and cash guarantees*	3,294
CURRENT ASSETS	**530,438**
VI. Amounts receivable after one year	**463**
A. Trade debtors	227
B. Other amounts receivable	236
VII. Stocks and contracts in progress	**157,078**
A. Stocks	149,134
1. *Raw materials*	73,925
2. *Work in process*	36,153
3. *Finished goods*	39,056
B. Contracts in progress	7,945
VIII. Amounts receivable within one year	**259,565**
A. Trade debtors	220,903
B. Other amounts receivable	38,662
IX. Investments	**54,789**
X. Cash at bank and in hand	**51,921**
XI. Deferred charges and accrued income	**6,667**
TOTAL ASSETS	**755,220**

	2001
SHAREHOLDERS' EQUITY	**352,339**
I. Capital	**53,065**
A. Issued capital	53,065
II. Share premium account	**120,471**
IV. Reserves	**168,241**
VI. Translation differences	**7,629**
VII. Investment grants	**2,933**
MINORITY INTERESTS (VIII)	**882**
PROVISIONS AND DEFERRED TAXES	**60,850**
IX. A. Provisions for liabilities and charges	**51,930**
1. *Pensions and similar obligations*	3,791
2. *Taxes*	260
3. *Major repairs and maintenance*	2,638
4. *Other liabilities and charges*	45,241
B. Deferred taxes and latent taxation	**8,921**
CREDITORS	**341,148**
X. Amounts payable after one year	**16,833**
A. Financial debts	15,548
2. *Bonds*	12,354
3. *Long-term leases and similar obligations*	202
4. *Credit institutions*	2,967
5. *Other loans*	25
D. Other amounts payable	1,285
XI. Amounts payable within one year	**290,707**
A. Current portion of amounts payable after one year	1,735
B. Financial debts (*1. Credit institutions*)	77,629
C. Trade debts	76,296
1. *Suppliers*	75,345
2. *Bills of exchange payable*	951
D. Advances received on contracts in progress	29,946
E. Taxes, remuneration and social security	72,258
1. *Taxes*	32,831
2. *Remuneration and social security*	39,427
F. Other amounts payable	32,842
X11. Accrued charges and deferred income	**33,609**
TOTAL LIABILITIES AND SHAREHOLDERS' EQUITY	**755,220**

(Source: Barco, Annual Report and Accounts 2001. Comparative figures for 2000 have been omitted. Reproduced by permission of Barco NV.)

Format of income statement

The 4th Directive offers EU countries four different formats for the corporate income statement. The key difference concerns the classification of expenses: expenses can be classified on either a functional or a natural basis within either a vertical or horizontal layout.

Expense classification

You'll recall that *under the **functional** basis, expenses are grouped by department or functional activity.* Thus the merchandise (or, for manufacturing companies, the production) costs of goods sold are shown under 'cost of sales', all the costs of the sales and marketing departments under 'distribution expense', and the costs of head office and other administrative departments under 'administration expense'.

The EU version of the functional income statement is summarised in Exhibit 6.5. BestPrice's x2 consolidated income statement, shown in Exhibit 3.7, is an example of this format.

Exhibit 6.5 Income statement: functional basis/vertical layout

```
 (1)  Revenue from sales
 (2)  Cost of sales
 (3)  Gross profit or loss [(1) – (2)]
 (4)  Selling and distribution expense
 (5)  Administration expense
 (6)  Other operating income
 (7)  Operating profit or loss [(3) – (4) – (5) + (6)]
 (8)  Investment income
 (9)  Financial expense, net
      (interest expense less interest income)
(10)  Income tax
      (expense or credit)
(11)  Net profit or loss on ordinary activities
      [ = (1) – (2) – (4) – (5) + (6) + (8) –/+ (9) –/+ (10)]
(12)  Extraordinary gain or loss, net of tax
(13)  Net profit or loss for the year [(11) +/– (12)]
```

Under the **natural** basis, expenses are reported by their type or nature. In practice, only the costs of key inputs – materials, labour and depreciation – are shown separately. Firms rarely break down these input costs by department. Thus the reader cannot find out from the financial statements the labour costs incurred in, say, the production department. Exhibit 6.6 shows the format of an income statement under the natural basis.

Note that this is the income statement of a retailing company. The natural-basis income statement of a manufacturing company is more complex and is illustrated in a later chapter.

The operating and net profit figures should be the same under both the functional and natural bases. Accrual-based operating costs are the same in total under the two bases: they are simply classified differently. Thus the cost of sales figure of a retail company (item 2, Exhibit 6.5) incorporates both the cost of purchased merchandise (but not services) and the variation in merchandise inventories (item 3 (part) and item 2 (part), Exhibit 6.6).

Exhibit 6.6   Income statement (retailing company): natural basis/vertical layout

(1) Revenue from sales
(2) Increase/decrease in inventories
(3) Costs of purchased merchandise and services
(4) Personnel costs
(5) Depreciation (and asset writedowns)
(6) Other operating costs
(7) Other operating income
(8) Operating profit or loss
      [= (1) +/– (2) – (3) – (4) – (5) – (6) + (7)]
(9) Investment income
(10) Financial expense, net (*see* Exhibit 6.5)
(11) Income tax (*see* Exhibit 6.5)
(12) Net profit or loss on ordinary activities
(13) Extraordinary gain or loss, net of tax
(14) Net profit or loss for the year

A simple example illustrates this. Assume Snug, a hardware store, holds merchandise costing 2,000 at the beginning of April. It purchases goods for 10,000 and sells goods costing 9,000 for 16,000 in the month. Inventories therefore increase by 1,000. Its only other costs are the salary of a sales person (1,500) and depreciation of shop fittings (500). Its April operating profit is 5,000 under either basis of expense classification, as Exhibit 6.7 makes clear.

Which basis of expense classification do investors prefer? Each method has its champions. Supporters of the natural basis claim that the cost information provided is more reliable and comparable across firms. Even firms in the same industry can define a function such as production or marketing differently. Supporters of the functional basis argue that it yields information that is more relevant to investors. For example, gross profit and marketing expenses are key figures which investors like to monitor.

In fact, in countries where companies can choose how to classify expenses, many select the natural basis in order to *avoid* disclosing sensitive information. It's impossible to determine the gross profit of a manufacturing firm under this basis, because materials, labour and overheads

Exhibit 6.7   Comparison of expense classification bases

Snug
Operating statement for April
(in 000)

Functional basis		Natural basis	
Revenue from sales	16	Revenue from sales	16
Cost of sales	–9	Increase in inventories	+1
		Cost of merchandise bought	–10
Gross profit	7	Personnel costs	–1.5
Distribution and		Depreciation	–0.5
administration expense	–2		
Operating profit	5	Operating profit	5

are not broken down into production and non-production categories. As a result, competitors have difficulty estimating the profitability of a company's manufacturing operations and calculating the amount it spends on marketing its products.

Layout of income statement

The outline income statements shown in Exhibits 6.5 and 6.6 have a vertical layout. The firm's revenues and expenses are presented in a single column, starting with those from its operating activities. In the alternative horizontal layout found in EU company accounts, revenues and expenses are shown in separate columns. Expenses being debits are in the left-hand column, revenues being credits in the right-hand one – just like a T account, in fact. As in the vertical layout, operating revenues and expenses head the statement. Exhibit 6.8 shows in outline an EU income statement in horizontal layout.

Note that net profit is shown in the left-hand column. In effect, it is the amount that balances the debit and credit entries to that point. For this reason, a loss-making firm reports a net loss and any related tax credit in the right-hand column.

Exhibit 6.8 Income statement (retailing company): horizontal layout/natural basis

Debit	Credit
Costs of purchased merchandise and services	Revenue from sales
Decrease in inventories	[or Increase in inventories]
Personnel costs	
Depreciation	
Other operating costs	Other operating income
	Investment income
Interest expense	Interest income
Income tax expense	
———————————	———————————
Net profit on ordinary activities	
Extraordinary charges/losses	Extraordinary income/gains
———————————	———————————
Net profit for the year	
———————————	

EU and international practice

Income statement presentation differs widely in the EU. Some countries such as Belgium, Italy, Portugal and Spain require firms to classify expenses by nature. In countries where both natural and functional bases are permitted (e.g. Germany, UK), there has been a shift towards use of the functional basis in recent years, especially in the English-language accounts of larger companies. One reason is the influence of international investors whose proportionate stake in EU-quoted firms has been growing. These investors are accustomed to US-style income statements: all US companies classify expenses by function.

As for the layout of the income statement, there's less diversity of practice. The vertical layout is the most widely used, certainly in the English-language income statements of large European companies, since this is the layout best understood by international investors. Spain, however, requires its firms to use the horizontal layout – but even here, larger quoted companies usually provide supplementary 'analytical' income statements (i.e. vertical layout, functional basis of expense classification) for the benefit of investors.

The income statement fallacy

Accounting fallacy no. 5: '*All items of income appear on the income statement.*'

In Chapter 3 we said that a firm's ordinary profit is the increase in its net assets arising from operations and activities incidental to them. In Chapter 5 we extended the definition of profit to include extraordinary items. We now summarise that definition. *Profit (or loss) is the overall change in net assets (NA) in the year, excluding the effects of dividends (DIV) and changes in share capital.* Thus, for year t:

$$\text{Profit}_t \text{ (or loss}_t) = (\text{NA}_t - \text{NA}_{t-1}) - \text{Capital increase}_t + \text{DIV}_t$$
$$(+ \text{ Capital decrease}_t)$$

Profit defined in this way is known as *comprehensive income* (or *clean surplus*).

Is the 'bottom line' net profit figure in Exhibits 6.5, 6.6 and 6.8 equal to comprehensive income? In practice, no. Companies do not report the whole of the comprehensive income on the income statement. The main reason is the legal requirement that revenues and gains should be *realised* before they can be reported on the income statement. It is argued that, on grounds of prudence, the profit number in the income statement should be limited to the amount that can be distributed to shareholders as a cash dividend. Unrealised revenues and gains are, in this view, not distributable.

As a result, gains from the revaluation of fixed assets – a practice permitted in some EU countries – are not reported on the income statement at the time of revaluation because they are not realised then. (The gains are only realised when the revalued asset is sold or consumed.) There are other types of gain and loss – certain foreign exchange gains and losses, for example – which for technical reasons are not recorded on the income statement when they arise. We encounter more examples of non-income statement gains and losses in later chapters.

Where do these non-income statement gains (or losses) go? The usual practice is for firms to take them directly to reserves in the balance sheet. For example, a surplus arising on the revaluation of a fixed asset such as property is credited to a revaluation reserve account. This is a non-distributable reserve and is therefore shown separately from retained earnings.

It is sometimes hard to calculate a company's comprehensive income for the year. Not all firms disclose the movement in the components of shareholders' equity over the year. Moreover, the amount of non-income statement gains and losses is increasing as new accounting rules are introduced which extend the use of current valuations in the accounts. For these reasons, accounting regulators have concluded that the existing financial statements should be extended. A firm following international accounting standards can extend the statements in one of two ways. It can include a formal 'statement of changes in shareholders' equity' in the annual accounts. With information about the changes in retained earnings and other reserves, anyone reading the accounts can derive the firm's comprehensive income. Alternatively, the firm can attach a 'statement of recognised gains and losses' to the income statement. This combines the 'bottom line' of the income statement (i.e. net profit) and non-income statement gains and losses to give the firm's total recognised gains (or losses) in the year. This is equivalent to comprehensive income. Exhibit 6.9 shows how this statement is linked to the income statement and balance sheet.

Exhibit 6.9 Statement of recognised gains and losses: form and links to other financial statements

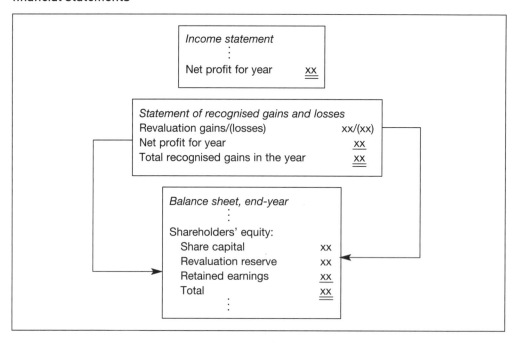

Notes to the accounts

The notes provide vital information to help the reader improve his or her understanding of a company's accounts. In fact, in an exposé of the creative accounting practices of UK companies in the 1990s, the author, a financial analyst, advises investors to read annual reports from the back – by starting with the notes.[3]

The notes help investors in several ways. First, they put flesh on skeletal information in the financial statements. They contain details which it is inconvenient or impossible to disclose on the face of the balance sheet or income statement. BestPrice, for example, gives in the notes to its x2 accounts a breakdown of the long-term debt of €3,315 million shown on its end-x2 balance sheet. Part of the note on long-term debt is shown in Exhibit 6.10.

With information in this footnote we can estimate the x3 interest charges on BestPrice's long-term debt, since we are given the interest rate and amount of each category of long-term debt. In addition, BestPrice discloses how much of the end-x2 total debt is repayable in each of the following five years. All this information is useful in estimating the company's future profits and cash flows.

Second, the notes give us information about the accounting methods the company has used and any estimates or assumptions it has made in deriving the numbers in the accounts. Financial statements are not uniform. In preparing accrual-based accounts, a company has to make estimates – for example, about the lives of its fixed assets and the amount of its trade debts which it reckons will be uncollectible. Estimates differ across companies. In addition, there are different methods of accounting for certain assets and liabilities, as we'll see in later chapters. In many cases, accounting methods are prescribed – by law or accounting standards. In some cases, a company is allowed to choose which method to adopt. The note to the accounts in which a company's **accounting policies** (its accounting methods and estimates) are disclosed is therefore of major interest to financial statement users.

Exhibit 6.10 BestPrice: extract from note on long-term debt in x2 accounts (amounts in €mn)

Loan details	Gross proceeds	Term	x2	x1
Fixed rate				
6% bonds, due December x2	500	4 years	–	500
4.5% bonds, due August x6	400	6 years	**400**	400
5.75% bonds, due May x5	450	5 years	**450**	450
5.5% bonds, due April x9	400	7 years	**400**	–
5.5% bonds, due April x9	200	7 years	**200**	–
5.5% bonds, due April x9	350	7 years	**350**	–
Floating rate				
EUR bonds, average 4.3%, due October x4	500	3 years	**500**	500
EUR bonds, average 4.1%, due June x3	200	2 years	**200**	200
Other loans, average 4.6%			**1,279**	1,041
			3,779	3,091
Current portion of long-term debt			**−464**	−712
Long-term debt			**3,315**	2,379

Exhibit 6.11 contains an extract from the 'accounting policies' note to the 2001 English-language accounts of Carrefour, a leading French retailer. It describes how the group values its fixed assets and the method it uses to depreciate them. The estimated lives of the main classes of fixed asset are also disclosed.[4]

Investors often review the accounting policies of firms in the same industry before comparing their financial results. Differences in profitability may be attributable to differences in accounting methods or estimates. For example, Carrefour depreciates its buildings more rapidly than BestPrice – over 20 years against BestPrice's 33 years. This may reflect differences in the market segments the two firms are in: Carrefour operates hypermarkets which have simpler structures and shorter expected lives. Tax rules may also be responsible: Carrefour's depreciation rates may be a legacy of the rates allowed under French tax law. Whichever is the explanation, investors must be aware of the likely impact on Carrefour – higher building depreciation charges, lower book value of property – when comparing the two firms' profitability and leverage.

Exhibit 6.11 Carrefour: note on accounting policies for (owned) fixed assets

Property and equipment

Land, constructions and equipment are valued at their original cost price. Depreciation is calculated according to the straight-line method based on average life, i.e.:

- Constructions:
  - buildings .... 20 years
  - land .... 10 years
  - parking lots .... $6^{2}/_{3}$ years

- Equipment, fittings and fixtures .... $6^{2}/_{3}$ years to 8 years

- Other property, plant and equipment .... 4 years to 10 years

(*Source*: Carrefour, *Annual Report and Accounts 2001*.)

Third, the notes contain additional information which helps investors interpret the numbers in the financial statements and make more reliable projections from them. Here are some examples:

- *Segmental data.* Larger diversified companies provide a breakdown of sales, profit and, increasingly, assets, by both industry and geographical area. These disclosures help explain past changes in a firm's aggregate sales (and earnings) and make possible more accurate forecasts of its future performance.
- *Post-balance sheet events.* A firm should give details of events such as the acquisition or disposal of a business, a disaster (e.g. fire, flood) or a discovery (e.g. oil strike) which are likely to have a major impact on the business and which occur *after* the balance sheet date but before the accounts are released. Such events affect investors' estimates of a company's future sales, earnings and cash flow. (EU firms may give this information in the management report rather than the notes to the accounts.)
- *Contingencies and commitments.* Investors want to know – again for forecasting purposes – if the company has any major potential liabilities at the balance sheet date (contingencies) or any contractual agreements which involve large future cash outlays (commitments). Under existing rules, these are unlikely to appear on the face of the published balance sheet or income statement.
- *Related party transactions.* These can include any type of transaction – from purchase of goods to loans – with individuals (e.g. directors) or companies (e.g. associated companies) with which the firm is linked. The extent and nature of such transactions interest investors. Are they undertaken at arm's length? What risks does the firm bear as a result?

All larger EU firms provide at least some information in each of these areas, thanks to the 4th Directive. But except in the case of firms quoted on the major international stock exchanges, which have more extensive disclosure rules, the information is often scanty.

Governance statement and auditors' report

With the exception of family-run firms, shareholders do not usually get involved in the day-to-day running of the companies in which they invest. Instead, they appoint managers for this task. This creates a dilemma. Managers want the freedom to manage – to run the company without having to get approval for every decision they take – but shareholders want to prevent managers from misusing or even stealing their capital.

Over the years, shareholders have found ways to protect their investments in management-run companies. The law helps them. Company law in all countries gives outside shareholders certain rights – for example, to appoint directors, receive periodic financial statements and vote on major business decisions in general meeting. We look at shareholder rights in more depth in later chapters. In this section we draw attention to two features of published financial statements that illustrate those rights in action. They are the corporate governance statement provided by directors and the auditors' report.

Corporate governance statement

An effective board of directors is a vital governance mechanism. It is the voice of shareholders (and, in companies with employee-elected directors, of staff, too). The board appoints the company's top managers and holds them to account for their actions. In recent years, many stock exchanges have introduced governance regulations for listed companies. In some cases, these take the form of a 'comply-or-explain' code of conduct (i.e. directors must state, in the annual report, the reasons for not complying with any of the code's provisions).

The directors provide in the annual report a statement of corporate governance. The statement gives background information about the board and how it functions and sets out its responsibilities, especially with regard to the company's internal financial controls. For example, more than half of BestPrice's board consist of independent directors (i.e. directors who have no executive role and no business or family ties to executive directors or other managers). These independent directors serve on special committees of the board that are responsible for appointing new directors (nominations committee), setting their pay (remuneration committee) and liaising with the firm's auditors (audit committee). BestPrice also gives information about individual directors' pay – in total and by type (salary, bonuses, pension benefits, share options) – in this section of the report.

● Auditors' report

Another key protection for investors is the right to receive audited financial statements annually. In an external audit, independent accountants examine the financial statements of a company (and the record-keeping system from which the numbers in them are drawn) and express an opinion on them. The 4th Directive requires that all but very small EU companies must have their annual accounts audited by an individual or organisation authorised under national law. Unlike in the USA, the EU's audit requirement covers unquoted as well as quoted companies (so long as they meet certain size tests).

The auditors' report accompanies the annual accounts. It is addressed to the company's shareholders. The report on BestPrice's x2 accounts is set out in Exhibit 6.12.

Exhibit 6.12 **BestPrice Stores: report of the auditors on the x2 accounts**

Auditors' report

Introduction
We have audited the financial statements of BestPrice Stores S.A. for the year ended December 31, x2. These financial statements are the responsibility of the company's management. Our responsibility is to express an opinion on these financial statements based on our audit.

Scope
We conducted our audit in accordance with auditing standards generally accepted in Euroland. Those standards require that we plan and perform the audit to obtain reasonable assurance about whether the financial statements are free of material misstatement. An audit includes examining, on a test basis, evidence supporting the amounts and disclosures in the financial statements. An audit also includes assessing the accounting principles used and significant estimates made by management, as well as evaluating the overall financial statements presentation. We believe that our audit provides a reasonable basis for our opinion.

Opinion
In our opinion, the consolidated financial statements of BestPrice Stores S.A. give a true and fair view of the consolidated financial position of the company as of December 31, x2 and of the consolidated results of operations for the year then ended, in accordance with International Accounting Standards, and comply with the financial reporting requirements of the Euroland Civil Code.

Tick, Foot & Sample, Certified Accountants
Eurocity, March 28, x3

The wording of BestPrice's auditors' report follows that set out in international auditing standards. (Auditors following national standards use different wording but the structure of the report is the same.) There are two sections of the report to which investors pay close attention. *The first indicates the scope of the audit, that is to say, which items have been audited and by whom.* BestPrice's auditors state explicitly that they have audited the x2 financial statements of the parent company (BestPrice Stores S.A.). Since they make no reference to other auditors' work, we can infer that they audited those of BestPrice's subsidiaries as well. 'Financial statements' here include the notes to the accounts. We should not assume, however, that supplementary financial information shown outside the accounts has been audited. The auditors may also state which auditing standards have been followed. Usually, as in BestPrice's case, they are national standards.

The second, the opinion paragraph, contains the auditors' judgement on the items audited. European countries, both within and outside the EU, usually require auditors to state whether the accounts comply with national legislation. The 'compliance audit' has been the traditional form of audit in most of continental Europe. (Scandinavian countries go further. In Finland and Sweden, the auditors must decide whether or not to recommend that the accounts be approved by shareholders and the directors be relieved of further responsibility for them for the financial period just ended.)

In the Netherlands and Anglo-Saxon countries, auditors have long been concerned with the integrity of the numbers in the published financial statements as well as their compliance with the law. The EU has adopted this point of view. The 4th Directive requires a company's auditors to state whether the accounts for the period 'give a true and fair view' of its profit for the year and its state of affairs at year-end.

What is meant by 'give a true and fair view'? The phrase has not been defined but a widely held view is that accounts which, according to auditors, meet this test 'reflect the underlying commercial reality' of the company and its business. Note that compliance with the law and accounting rules does not guarantee the accounts will give a true and fair view. Commercial practices change constantly; laws and rules are modified only periodically. Moreover, laws and rules are not omniscient: they cannot anticipate every unusual commercial event. For these reasons, the 4th Directive and international accounting standards contain a 'true and fair view override'. This states that, in exceptional cases, a company can override a provision of the 4th Directive (or an international accounting standard) and apply an accounting policy that is not generally accepted if, only by so doing, will its accounts give a true and fair view.[5]

The auditors may qualify their (good) opinion of the accounts, withhold it or issue an adverse opinion. They may take issue with management's accounting treatment of a particular asset or liability. If they consider it a minor point, they will simply draw attention to it in their report. If it has a material impact on the accounts, they may give an adverse opinion on them. They withhold their opinion when they are unable to obtain the information they need – perhaps because of a breakdown in the company's record-keeping system.

One final point: a company's managers, not its auditors, are responsible for the preparation of its financial statements. The introduction to BestPrice's auditors' report reminds shareholders of this fact. Statements by auditors – and managers – of their respective responsibilities are an increasingly common sight in the accounts of international companies. Such statements, though they do little more than express the long-standing legal duties of both parties, are a response to investor criticism of the way many companies are governed.

EU disclosure and audit requirements

Disclosure and audit requirements for small and medium-sized companies in EU member states are less onerous than those for large companies. Most of the companies enjoying this concession are private.

Under the 4th Directive, small companies are only required to publish an abridged balance sheet and abridged notes to it. An abridged balance sheet need only contain totals by type of asset and equity. Using Barco's balance sheet (Exhibit 6.4) as a guide, a small company must disclose the information shown against the roman numerals (I, II, III, . . .) only. It need not publish an income statement. An annual report is not required: nor, too, is an audit.

Under the same Directive, medium-sized companies are required to publish an abridged balance sheet, abridged income statement and abridged notes to them. A medium-sized company is allowed to begin the income statement with the gross profit (or loss) figure. Information about turnover, its total amount and its breakdown (by product line and geographical area) need not be disclosed. An annual report and audit are mandatory.

The Directive defines size on the basis of three criteria – net turnover (operating revenues, net of sales rebates and sales-related taxes), 'balance sheet total' (i.e. total assets) and average number of employees in the year. To qualify as small or medium-sized, a company must not exceed the upper limits of two of the three criteria for that size category in two successive years:[6]

Upper limits for size category of firm

Size category	Net turnover (€ m)	Balance sheet total (€ m)	Average number of employees
Small	7.3	3.65	50
Medium-sized	29.2	14.6	250

The upper limits for net turnover and balance sheet total are revised every five years to allow for the effects of inflation. Remember that these are minimum disclosure requirements. EU member states can and do impose more stringent ones.

The cash flow statement

Background

The third major corporate financial statement is the **statement of cash flows**. The purpose of the statement is to show where the cash flowing into a company has come from and how it has been used. In fact when first conceived it was known as the 'where from? where to?' statement.[7]

The term 'cash' has a broad meaning in this context. It usually covers both cash and cash equivalents, that is to say, cash invested in short-term highly liquid investments. Sometimes cash is a net figure: amounts borrowed under a bank overdraft facility may be deducted.

EU companies are not required under the 4th Directive to publish a cash flow statement. In some EU countries (e.g. Spain, UK) and elsewhere (e.g. Canada, USA), publication is mandatory, however. Companies in other countries that prepare their accounts according to international accounting standards are also required to publish the statement as part of their accounts. In these cases, the statement is audited. An alternative practice is to include the (unaudited) statement in the annual report. Some stock exchanges require its publication as a condition of listing a company's securities on the exchange.

Our task in this chapter is to show in outline how the statement is prepared and to try to interpret the numbers in it. (We look at the statement in more depth in a later chapter.) Preparing a cash flow statement involves three steps. First, overall cash flow, the 'bottom line' of the statement, must be calculated. Cash flow is the change in cash and cash equivalents over the period. Next, the reasons for the change in cash and cash equivalents are identified. Cash inflows and outflows are usually classified according to the activity to which they relate – operating, investing and financing. Finally, the operating cash flows are recast into the form in which the majority of companies currently present this information.

We illustrate these steps using Out of Babel Company, the language school whose year 2 financial statements we derived in Chapters 4 and 5. The company's income statement and start- and end-year balance sheets are reproduced in Exhibit 6.13.

Calculating 'cash flow'

The simplest approach to calculating cash flow is to use information in the cash ledger account – or cash and short-term investments accounts, where 'cash' is defined more broadly.

Exhibit 6.13

Out of Babel Company
Annual accounts for year 2
(amounts in 000)

Income statement for year 2

Revenue from fees		86
Less: Operating expenses		
Salaries	48	
Rent of premises	8	
Utilities	7	
Depreciation of equipment	4.5	
Supplies	4	
		−71.5
Operating profit		14.5
Less: Financial expense, net		
Interest expense	0.9	
Interest revenue	−0.4	
		−0.5
Profit for the year (before tax)		14.0

Balance sheets at 31 December year 2 and year 1

	Year 2	Year 1		Year 2	Year 1
Current assets			*Current liabilities*		
Cash	23	11	Bank loan	15	0
Short-term investment	24	0	Accrued interest payable	0.9	0
Accrued interest receivable	0.4	0	Accounts payable	3	2
Accounts receivable	9	6	Fees received in advance	12	0
Supplies inventory	3	1	Accrued salaries payable	1	0
Prepaid rent	0	8	Total current liabilities	31.9	2
Total current assets	59.4	26			
Fixed assets			*Shareholders' equity*		
Equipment at cost	35	10	Share capital	40	30
Accumulated depreciation	−6.5	−2	Retained earnings	16	2
Equipment, net	28.5	8	Total shareholders' equity	56	32
			Total liabilities and		
Total assets	87.9	34	shareholders' equity	87.9	34

(*Source*: Exhibits 4.9 and 5.8.)

Out of Babel begins year 2 with a cash balance of 11,000. At year-end, the company has cash of 23,000 and a short-term investment of 24,000. (We treat the short-term investment as part of cash since we know that the company invests, on a short-term basis, cash which is surplus to its operating needs.) The company therefore increases its cash and cash equivalents by 36,000 in year 2. This represents its cash flow for the year. The movement in the 'Cash' and 'Short-term investment' accounts in year 2 is shown in Exhibit 6.14.

Exhibit 6.14

Out of Babel Company
Cash and Short-term investment: Ledger accounts year 2
(amounts in 000)

Cash

	Dr.		Cr.
Balance, 1/1/year 2	11		
(1) Issue of shares	10	(2) Equipment purchase	25
Bank loan	15	(6) Payment for supplies	5
(3) Fees in cash	45	(7) Payment of salaries	47
(5) Collection of debts	32	(8) Payment for utilities	7
(9) Fees received in advance	18	(10) To Short-term investment	24
Balance, 31/12/year 2	23		

Short-term investment

	Dr.		Cr.
Balance, 1/1/year 2	0		
(10) From Cash	24		
Balance, 31/12/year 2	24		

(*Source*: Exhibit 4.12.)

Classifying cash flows by activity

Using the information in the ledger accounts in Exhibit 6.14 we can draw up a cash flow statement.[8] Although there are various ways of classifying a firm's cash flows – the simplest is to split them into 'sources' and 'uses' of cash – the standard approach is to classify them by activity. The cash flow statement highlights three types. The sale of goods and services – and related trading costs – are a firm's **operating activities**. The purchase and disposal of fixed assets are its **investing activities**. The issuance of debt or equity securities – and their retirement or repurchase – are its **financing activities**.

The year 2 cash flow statement of Out of Babel Company is shown in activity form in Exhibit 6.15.

What does the activity-based cash flow statement tell us about Out of Babel? The company generated a healthy cash flow from operations in year 2. The tuition fees received exceeded operating outlays (on salaries, supplies and utilities) by 36,000. This was more than sufficient to finance its investment in equipment in the year (25,000) (and, incidentally, to renew the 8,000 a year lease on its premises, for which payment is due at the start of year 3). The external capital raised – by bank loan (15,000) and share issue (10,000) – suggests the company is planning to make larger investments in year 3.

Exhibit 6.15	

Out of Babel Company
Cash flow statement for year 2: direct approach
(amounts in 000)

Operating activities		
Tuition fees received [(3) + (5) + (9)]*	95	
Less: Payments for supplies, salaries and utilities		
[(6) + (7) + (8)]	–59	
Cash inflow from operating activities		36
Investing activities		
Purchase of equipment (2)	–25	
Cash outflow on investing activities		–25
Financing activities		
Bank loan (1)	15	
Issuance of shares (1)	10	
Cash inflow from financing activities		+25
Net increase in cash		36
Cash and cash equivalents, 1/1/year 2		11
Cash and cash equivalents, 31/12/year 2		47
End-year balance comprises:		
Cash in hand and at bank		23
Short-term investment		24
Total		47

* References are to cash account entries (*see* Exhibit 6.14).

Cash flows from operations: the indirect approach

Presentation of operating cash flow in published financial statements is regrettably not as straightforward as the direct approach illustrated in Exhibit 6.15. In practice, companies show operating cash flow, not as the difference between operating receipts and payments but as the sum of reported profit and 'accruals'. Accruals here are operating revenues and expenses which in part or in whole have no cash flow impact in the period. Presenting operating cash flow in this way is known as the **indirect approach**.

The calculation of operating cash flow under the indirect approach proceeds as follows:

- Take the (post-tax) *profit* figure from the income statement.
- *Adjust it for revenues and expenses, gains and losses, which have no impact on the company's operating cash flow.* (The most common example is depreciation. The depreciation charge involves no cash outlay. That occurred when the building or equipment was bought.)
- Finally, make a further set of adjustments to convert revenues and expenses, the components of profit, into operating receipts and expenditures. How? *Adjust the profit figure for changes in operating working capital accounts,* such as inventories and accounts payable.

Strictly, further adjustments should be made. Income received from investments should be reclassified as an investing inflow, interest and dividend payments as a financing outflow. And, as a consequence, tax payments (or refunds) should be apportioned among operating, investing and financing cash flows. In practice, many companies classify interest and dividends received, interest paid and tax paid (or refunded) as operating flows to make clearer the link with net profit. Dividend payments, however, are usually shown as a financing outflow. This is the practice followed in this chapter.

We illustrate the indirect approach using Out of Babel Company's accounts for year 2. We first calculate the change in non-cash working capital accounts between end-year 1 and end-year 2. Exhibit 6.16 shows the movement in the balances of individual current assets and liabilities between the start and end of year 2.

Exhibit 6.16

Out of Babel Company
Year 2 change in non-cash working capital accounts
(amounts in 000)

	31 December			Effect of
	year 1	year 2	Change	change on cash
Current assets (excl. cash and short-term investment)				
Accounts receivable	6	9	+3	−3
Accrued interest receivable	0	0.4	+0.4	−0.4
Supplies inventory	1	3	+2	−2
Prepaid rent	8	0	−8	+8
Current liabilities (excl. bank loan)				
Accounts payable	2	3	+1	+1
Accrued interest payable	0	0.9	+0.9	+0.9
Fees received in advance	0	12	+12	+12
Accrued salaries payable	0	1	+1	+1
Total effect on cash				+17.5

Notice that *increases in current assets (and decreases in current liabilities) reduce cash.* Similarly, *increases in current liabilities (and decreases in current assets) increase cash.* Why is this? Think of current operating assets as investments and current operating liabilities as capital. An investment uses corporate cash; new capital provides cash for the company.

The company's cash flow statement for year 2 is shown in indirect form in Exhibit 6.17.

Compare Exhibits 6.15 and 6.17. The operating activity section differs in format between the direct and indirect approaches. *However, the 'cash inflow from operating activities' figure is the same* (in this case, 36,000), despite the convoluted way of calculating it under the indirect approach. Adjusting the accrual-based income number for non-cash revenues and expenses and for the movement in operating working capital is equivalent to deducting operating outlays from operating receipts. The investing and financing activity sections of the statement are identical under the two approaches.

A simple example will help to demonstrate the equivalence of the two layouts. Consider the tuition fees of 95,000 the company receives in cash in year 2. Exhibit 6.18 shows how that number can be obtained either from the cash account (the direct approach) or from the tuition fee revenue and related working capital accounts (the indirect approach).

The link between accrual-based expenses and operating expenditures can be demonstrated in a similar manner.

Exhibit 6.17

Out of Babel Company
Cash flow statement for year 2: indirect approach
(amounts in 000)

Operating activities		
Profit for year		14
Add back expenses/deduct revenues not involving cash:		
+ Depreciation		+4.5
Adjust for changes in non-cash working capital:		
– Increase in accounts receivable	–3	
– Increase in accrued interest receivable	–0.4	
– Increase in supplies inventory	–2	
+ Decrease in prepaid rent	+8	
+ Increase in accounts payable	+1	
+ Increase in accrued interest payable	+0.9	
+ Increase in fees received in advance	+12	
+ Increase in accrued salaries payable	+1	
		+17.5
Cash inflow from operating activities		36
Investing activities		
Purchase of equipment	–25	
Cash outflow on investing activities		–25
Financing activities		
Bank loan	+15	
Issuance of shares	+10	
Cash inflow from financing activities		+25
Net increase in cash		36
Cash and cash equivalents, 1/1/year 2		11
Cash and cash equivalents, 31/12/year 2		47

(*Sources*: Exhibit 5.8 for 'profit for year' and depreciation, and Exhibits 6.15 and 6.16.)

Exhibit 6.18

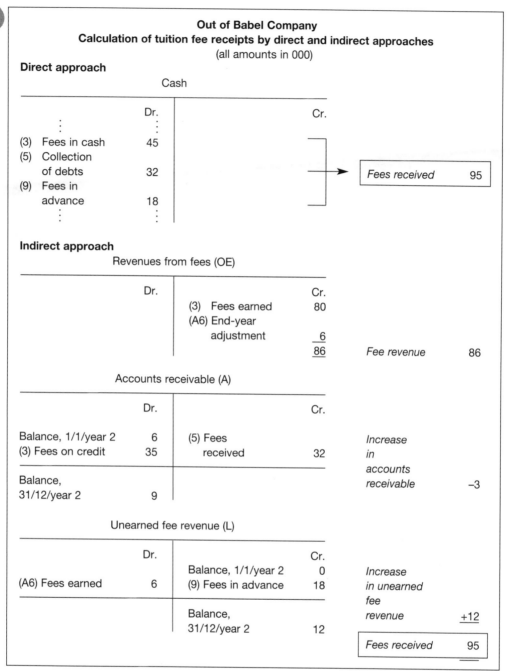

Out of Babel Company
Calculation of tuition fee receipts by direct and indirect approaches
(all amounts in 000)

Direct approach

Cash

	Dr.		Cr.	
(3) Fees in cash	45			
(5) Collection of debts	32		Fees received	95
(9) Fees in advance	18			

Indirect approach

Revenues from fees (OE)

	Dr.		Cr.	
		(3) Fees earned	80	
		(A6) End-year adjustment	6	
			86	Fee revenue 86

Accounts receivable (A)

	Dr.		Cr.	
Balance, 1/1/year 2	6	(5) Fees received	32	Increase in accounts receivable −3
(3) Fees on credit	35			
Balance, 31/12/year 2	9			

Unearned fee revenue (L)

	Dr.		Cr.	
		Balance, 1/1/year 2	0	Increase in unearned fee revenue +12
(A6) Fees earned	6	(9) Fees in advance	18	
		Balance, 31/12/year 2	12	Fees received 95

Analysing the cash flow statement: an illustration

In earlier chapters we looked at the income statement and balance sheet of the European super-market chain, BestPrice Stores. The cash flow statement in its x2 accounts is set out in Exhibit 6.19.

BestPrice follows majority practice. It presents cash flows by activity and uses the indirect approach to calculate operating cash flow.

Exhibit 6.19	BestPrice Stores		
	Consolidated cash flow statements for x2 and x1		
	(amounts in € millions)		
Year to 31 December		*x2*	*x1*
Cash flows from operating activities			
Income after tax		**355**	292
Adjustments for:			
Depreciation, amortisation and changes in provisions		**+376**	+317
Deferred taxes		**+30**	−3
Gains on disposal of fixed assets		**−16**	−27
Other adjustments		**−12**	−44
		733	535
Changes in operating working capital:			
Inventories		**−188**	−84
Receivables		**−466**	−240
Payables		**+379**	+328
Net cash inflow from operating activities		458	539
Cash flows from investing activities			
Purchases of tangible and intangible fixed assets		**−689**	−701
Disposals of tangible and intangible fixed assets		**+84**	+53
Purchases of long-term financial investments		**−184**	−78
Disposals of long-term financial investments		**+39**	+69
Acquisitions of businesses, net		**−53**	−502
Net cash outflow on investing activities		−803	−1,159
Cash flows from financing activities			
Dividends paid		**−136**	−115
Proceeds from issuance of shares for cash		**+622**	−
Additions to debt		**+1,980**	+1,426
Retirements of debt		**−1,806**	−610
Net cash inflow from financing activities		+660	+701
Impact of exchange rate fluctuations		**+2**	+35
Net change in cash and cash equivalents		**+317**	+116
Cash and cash equivalents at start of year		825	709
Cash and cash equivalents at end of year		1,142	825

BestPrice's statement is similar to those of other companies in another respect – the apparent jumble of items within each cash flow activity. Unlike the income statement, the cash flow statement does not have an easily understandable structure. There is no equivalent to 'operating revenues' which provides an anchor for the analysis of the income statement. How then do investors make sense of the cash flow statement? Here is an approach they use – and you may find helpful.

● Start with operating cash flow (OCF). This is a key number in the statement. Operations are the company's motor and usually the main source of its cash inflows. Is OCF positive? If yes, is it greater than profit for the year? The OCF of a mature company usually exceeds profit owing to depreciation and other non-cash expenses. For a fast-growing firm, however, OCF is likely to be low or even negative because of its large investment in operating working capital. Note that negative operating cash flow is not necessarily a sign of poor health. Fast-growing firms have a big appetite for cash – payments for inputs to be manufactured and sold next period exceed the receipts for goods sold in this and previous periods – even when their operations are highly profitable.

BestPrice's OCF exceeds the group's after-tax income in both x1 and x2. This is largely thanks to non-cash charges ('depreciation, amortisation and changes in provisions'). The changes in operating working capital had little overall impact on OCF in x1 (the increases in payables offset the increases in inventories and receivables) but *decreased* it by €275 million in x2 (because inventories and receivables grew at a faster rate than payables). As a result, OCF fell by 15% between x1 and x2 (from €539 million to €458 million) even though after-tax income rose by over 20% during this period.

- Compare OCF with dividends and net capital expenditures (purchases less disposals of tangible and intangible fixed assets) in the period. A profitable, mature firm is likely, over the business cycle, to finance regular cash dividends and capital expenditures out of OCF. It has positive 'free cash flow'. A fast-growing or loss-making firm cannot finance both outlays internally. It has negative free cash flow.[9]

  BestPrice's free cash flow was negative in x1 and x2. The company invested heavily in tangible and intangible fixed assets in both years. In fact, net capital expenditures (i.e. net of disposals) exceeded OCF even before taking account of dividend payments (which rose in line with profits).

- Determine the effect of the company's positive or negative free cash flow on its investments and finances. Suppose it has surplus funds. How does it use them? Is it expanding (by acquiring other firms)? Is it returning capital to creditors (repayment of long-term debt) and owners (special dividends, share repurchase)? Suppose it has negative free cash flow. How does it finance the shortfall? Is it selling financial investments? Is it raising new capital?

The analysis can be extended. Suppose the company makes a major acquisition which requires external financing. Which type of capital does it choose – debt or equity?

BestPrice's investing outlays in x1 and x2 were swollen by acquisitions of businesses (in x1) and purchases of shareholdings in other companies (in x2). To finance these outlays – and the negative free cash flows in both years, the company resorted to outside finance. It relied on borrowings in x1 but turned to its shareholders for funds in x2. New equity and borrowings in x2 covered the cash flow shortfall of €481 million and bolstered the company's cash balances as well. BestPrice's cash flows in x1 and x2 are summarised below:

(In € million)	x2	x1
Operating cash flow	458	539
Capital expenditures, net*	–605	–648
Dividends paid	–136	–115
'Free cash flow'	–283	–224
Acquisitions of business, net	–53	–502
Net purchases of long-term financial investments	–145	–9
	–481	–735
Issuance of shares for cash	+622	–
Borrowings (net of debt repayments)	+174	+816
Impact of exchange rate fluctuations	+2	+35
Net increase in cash and cash equivalents**	+317	+116

* Purchases less disposals of tangible and intangible fixed assets
** The company defines cash and cash equivalents as cash + marketable securities – short-term bank loans.

The simple framework shown above can be used to analyse the cash flows of all non-financial institutions. We return to the subject of cash flow analysis and examine it in greater depth in a later chapter.

Popular financial ratios among investors

European companies often disclose financial ratios in the annual report voluntarily, usually in management's report to shareholders or as part of the 'financial highlights' of the year. The ratios presented vary from company to company: measures of profitability, liquidity and leverage like those described in Chapters 2 and 3 are the most popular.

Earnings per share

One ratio which many large European quoted companies publish is **earnings per share** (**EPS**). It shows the company's profit for the period on a per-share basis. More precisely, it is:

$$\text{EPS} = \frac{\text{After-tax profit or loss in period, attributable to ordinary shareholders}}{\text{Weighted average ordinary shares outstanding during period}}$$

Note the calculation of the numerator. *In consolidated accounts, it is the profit or loss attributable to the parent company's ordinary shareholders.* Thus group income attributable to subsidiary companies' outside shareholders ('minority interests') is excluded; so too are dividends earned by preference shareholders.

Controversy surrounds the purpose of the ratio. Should EPS show profits attributable to existing shares only – or to existing and likely future shares as well? Consider the effect of **dilutive securities** on EPS. These are securities such as convertible bonds and share options which, when converted or exercised in the future, may increase the number of outstanding shares relative to reported earnings. This reduces (dilutes) EPS. Should the current EPS figure reflect the impact of such future dilution? Under new international rules, quoted companies are required to disclose actual EPS ('basic EPS') and, if potential dilution is material, a hypothetical EPS number ('diluted EPS'). We discuss the calculation of EPS in more detail in a later chapter.

For quoted companies, EPS is an important statistic. It's often cited in the annual report – along with sales, operating profits and dividends. Some firms set a minimum annual percentage growth in EPS as a financial target. Its influence is greater still because it's employed in other key ratios. One of these is the **price/earnings ratio** (P/E ratio or multiple):

$$\text{P/E ratio} = \frac{\text{Current market price per ordinary share}}{\text{Most recent 12 months' EPS}}$$

The ratio is unusual in that it combines market and accounting data. It tells potential investors how many years it will take them to recover, through corporate earnings, an investment made in a company at today's market price, assuming those earnings remain at current levels. Thus a P/E ratio of 12 indicates that the investment recovery period is 12 years at the firm's current level of earnings.

Of course, earnings are not expected to remain at current levels. Investors expect them to grow. The faster the expected rate of growth of earnings, the higher the price investors will pay for them. *Thus the P/E ratio is an indicator of a company's growth prospects, as perceived by the market.* (Not all shares with high P/E multiples are 'growth stocks'. A company recovering from a period of low profits can also enjoy a high P/E ratio.)

P/E ratios can change daily, as the market price of a company's shares fluctuates. The impact of earnings changes is felt less frequently. The EPS figure is updated each quarter or half-year, depending on how frequently the company publishes interim accounts. It's based on the earnings over the immediate previous 12 months (the four most recent quarters or two most recent half-years).

Analysts often estimate prospective P/E ratios. *A prospective P/E ratio relates a firm's current share price to (the analyst's) forecast of its earnings for the current financial year.* Since the share price is itself forward-looking (it's the discounted value of the firm's expected future earnings), analysts argue this version of the P/E ratio is a better guide to market sentiment about a company's future performance.

Dividend cover

As we've seen, a company's directors propose, and shareholders approve, the distribution of its profits. The dividend is expressed as an amount per share (hereafter DIV). Investors monitor a firm's **dividend cover**, which is calculated as follows:

$$\frac{\text{Dividend}}{\text{cover}} = \frac{\text{EPS}}{\text{DIV}} = \frac{\text{Per-share earnings in period attributable to ordinary shareholders}}{\text{Per-share cash dividend paid/proposed to ordinary shareholders in period}}$$

The ratio shows the number of times current earnings cover dividend payments.

Dividend cover can be less than one. An uncovered dividend indicates that the company draws on past years' retained profits to meet the dividend. Many companies try to ensure that the dividend (for a given investment in ordinary shares) grows steadily over time. Only in times of economic difficulty will a company cut its dividend. Dividend cover is therefore an indicator of investment risk.

The reciprocal of dividend cover is the **payout ratio** (DIV/EPS). You will find both terms employed in annual reports and the financial press.

Accounting and market rates of return

A postscript to our discussion of stock market-oriented financial ratios: the rates of return discussed in Chapter 3, ROE (return on equity) and ROA (return on assets), are accounting rates of return. Investors in publicly quoted companies use an additional performance measure. They calculate, for each company, the **market return** on the capital they have invested. *The market rate of return in a period is the sum of:*

- *the per-share dividend paid by the firm in the period; and*
- *the change (increase or decrease) in the share's market price between the start and end of the period;*

all deflated by the share's start-of-period market price. Thus for period *t*:

$$\text{Market rate of return} = \frac{\text{DIV}_t + (P_t - P_{t-1})}{P_{t-1}}$$

where the dividend (DIV) is received at the end of the period.

A firm's ROE and market rate of return will not be the same, except by coincidence. They measure different things. ROE (and ROA) measure past performance, using accounting numbers. The market rate of return incorporates, through the change in the share price, the change in the market's expectations about the company's future prospects.

Differences in UK/US accounting terms in financial reports

It's said of the UK and the USA that they are two nations divided by a common language. Investors are reminded of this saying when reading English-language accounts. To minimise confusion, we've used American terminology up to now. Exhibit 6.20 gives the British equivalent of key accounting terms in order to help you 'translate' accounts from British English.

Exhibit 6.20 Differences in accounting terminology: American and British English

American English (AE)	British English (BE)
Balance sheet	
Account receivable	Trade debtor
Inventory	Stock
Account payable	Trade creditor
Stockholders' (or shareholders') equity	Shareholders' funds (or Capital and reserves)
(shares of) Common stock	Ordinary shares
(shares of) Preferred stock	Preference shares
Additional paid-in capital	Share premium account
Retained earnings	Profit and loss account
Income statement (AE)/Profit and loss account (BE)	
Operating revenue (i.e. from sales of goods and services)	Turnover
Interest income	Interest receivable
Interest expense	Interest payable
Financial analysis	
Leverage	Gearing

We'll continue to use American terminology because you are more likely to find it in the English-language financial reports of European companies. However, in certain circumstances – for example, when discussing shareholders' equity in EU company accounts – we employ British English terms because of their legal significance.

Summary

We turn from core to context in this chapter. In previous chapters, we focused on how a company constructs its balance sheet and income statement. In this chapter, we look more broadly at the corporate annual report of which these financial statements form a part.

We first outlined the contents of the annual report and accounts of a typical (large) EU company. We then discussed key sections in them, in particular management's report to shareholders, the main financial statements and their format, the notes and the auditors' report, using BestPrice's x2 annual report and accounts as an example. Here are some key points from our discussion:

● The management report is of great help to investors. They can check whether management's explanation of the company's results is consistent with the numbers in the annual accounts. The report also contains information investors use in forecasting its future profits and cash flows.
● The balance sheets of EU companies do not share the same format, nor do their income statements. Yet the accounting is not affected. A company's total assets and net profit are still the same, whichever format is used. If it classifies expenses by nature, however, it may not be possible to calculate its gross profit.
● Not all items of income are in the income statement. Some like unrealised gains go direct to reserves in the balance sheet. Companies following international accounting standards now

include a new statement within the accounts which shows the company's comprehensive income in the period or allows investors to compute it more easily.

● Management prepare the accounts; auditors express an opinion on them. From an investor's standpoint, what matters is the auditors' judgement as to the picture those accounts convey – do they give a 'true and fair view' of the company's financial results and condition for that period.

Next, we introduced a third financial statement, the cash flow statement, which many EU companies include in their annual accounts. This is not yet a legal requirement in all EU countries. We showed how the statement is usually presented and illustrated an approach commonly used by investors when interpreting the numbers in it.

We described certain financial ratios which are widely cited in the financial press and often disclosed in the annual report. The most important is earnings per share. It's used alone as a performance measure and, in combination with the company's share price (via the P/E ratio), as an indicator of the company's expected growth prospects. We concluded the chapter with a list of accounting terms where the British version differs from the American one used in this book.

APPENDIX 6.1 The EU's company law harmonisation programme

The European Union is a federation of European countries, 15 in number as of 2003, that have signed the Treaty of Rome (1957) and amending treaties.[10] Its aim, in broad terms, is to foster economic and political union within Europe.

The main political institutions of the Union are the Commission, the Parliament, the Council of Ministers, and the Court of Justice. Each is involved in legislative programmes such as company law harmonisation. The European Commission proposes new laws (it has other responsibilities and powers). Parliament debates them, amending or, in some cases, rejecting them. The Council – which brings together national ministers in charge of each policy area – decides them. The Court of Justice plays a key role in the enforcement of EU law. The majority of its rulings concern the non-implementation or incorrect implementation of directives by member states.

What form does EU law take? The Treaty of Rome specifies three types of instrument the Council of Ministers can use to establish law in member states. They are:

1 *Directives.* A directive specifies the result to be achieved by legislation. National authorities can decide how it is implemented. It applies only to the member state(s) addressed. Company law directives implemented to date are addressed to all member states.
2 *Regulations.* A regulation applies directly in all member states. It does not require national legislation.
3 *Decisions.* A decision also applies directly – but only to the entity addressed. This may be a member state, a company or even an individual.

The Council can also make *recommendations* (and issue *opinions*). These have influence but no legal force.

The Council has issued various directives to promote the harmonisation of company law within the Community. It's argued that such harmonisation is essential if goods, services, labour and capital are to move freely among member states. For example, companies may be reluctant to supply goods and services to firms in other member states if they cannot obtain financial information about them. Company law directives cover the following matters:

- disclosure of constitutional information about the firm, e.g. its charter and by-laws (1st Directive, 1968);
- minimum requirements for the formation and continuing operation of public companies (2nd Directive, 1977);
- mergers and demergers of public companies within member states (3rd Directive, 1978, and 6th Directive, 1982);
- format and content of annual accounts (4th Directive, 1978). Separate directives have been issued dealing with the accounts of banks and other financial institutions (1986) and of insurance companies (1991);
- consolidated accounts (7th Directive, 1982);
- qualification of auditors (8th Directive, 1984);
- disclosure requirements for branches of companies (11th Directive, 1988);
- establishment of single shareholder companies (12th Directive, 1988).

Directives have been drafted (but not yet adopted) on the structure and management of public companies (5th), on cross-border mergers (10th) and on public offers (i.e. takeover bids) (13th).

The 4th and 7th Directives are known as the 'accounting directives'. They apply to all limited liability companies within the EU. Because companies in some member states sought to avoid the requirements of the accounting directives – for example, by forming a partnership of which one or more of the partners is a limited liability company – the Commission extended their reach in 1990. They now cover partnerships, limited partnerships and unlimited companies as well.

The Commission has long believed that the EU needs a single large securities market to allow firms to raise debt and equity capital at lower cost. One of the steps needed to create such a market, in its view, is greater comparability of financial statements, so that investors can compare companies' financial results and condition more easily and allocate their capital more efficiently. To this end it drafted a regulation requiring that by 2005 all listed EU firms prepare consolidated accounts according to international accounting standards (IAS). In 2001 it amended the 4th and 7th Directives (and those relating to banks' and insurance companies' accounts) to bring their valuation rules in line with IAS.

There are two other EU initiatives which may have a significant effect on the legal form of European business organisation in the future. Since 1989, small and medium-sized enterprises (SMEs) from different member states can set up a form of partnership called a 'European economic interest grouping' (EEIG). The aim is to make it easier for SMEs to pursue joint activities such as research and development projects across borders. An EEIG is a new entity. It's incorporated directly into EU law, although it's governed by the laws of the member states in which it is registered and operates. It has full legal capacity, i.e. it can enter into contracts in its own name but, as a form of partnership, profits are taxed in the hands of its corporate members.

In addition, the Council of Ministers approved in 2001 a regulation permitting the establishment of a European company (Societas Europea, or SE). The regulation allows firms from different member states to create a corporate vehicle – by merger, setting up a joint subsidiary or forming a holding company – to pursue cross-border ventures. The advantage of an SE, it's claimed, is that it overcomes the problems associated with national legal entities for such ventures. National law has limited territorial reach and this can make disputes among corporate shareholders from different member states difficult and costly to resolve.

Problem assignments

P6.1 Earnings, cash flow and dividends

(1) The following item appeared in the financial section of a European newspaper:

Cash flow behind rise at Kerry

KERRY GROUP, the west of Ireland-based meat, dairy and food ingredients company, achieved a 28 per cent increase in pre-tax profits to I£13.6 m (£12.8 m) for the six months to June 30. . . .

The profits increase was largely due to strong cash flow of I£29 m and lower interest rates in the US, UK and Ireland, where Kerry has a geographically even spread of business. . . .

Required

Comment on the above news item. Under what circumstances does an increase in cash flow lead to an increase in profits?

(2) In an article on Tele-Communications Inc. (TCI), a major US cable-TV company, a business newspaper drew attention to the company's high operating cash flow and the way it is employed:

Like many cable firms, TCI ploughs that cash back into the business instead of paying dividends: it has not made a profit [in the past four years].

Required

(a) What is the likely reason that TCI has a high operating cash flow but reports losses?

(b) The newspaper states that TCI could have paid a dividend but chose to 'plough that cash back into the business'. Under what circumstances can a loss-making company pay a dividend?

| Exhibit 6.21 | OMV Group: consolidated statement of income for 2000 |

In €000		2000
1.	Sales, including petroleum excise tax	9,218,454
2.	Petroleum excise tax	(1,763,986)
3.	**Subtotal of items 1 to 2 (Net sales)**	**7,454,468**
4.	Changes in inventories of finished products, work in progress and services not yet invoiced	6,907
5.	Other own work capitalised	19,078
6.	Other operating income	86,372
7.	Cost of material and services	(5,623,733)
8a.	Personnel expenses	(409,695)
8b.	Expenses for severance payments and pensions	(177,550)
9.	Depreciation and amortisation	(320,063)
10.	Other operating expenses	(545,291)
11.	**Subtotal of items 3 to 10 (Earnings before interest and tax)**	**490,493**
12.	Income from investments	16,737
13.	Income from other securities and loans shown under financial assets	15,870
14.	Other interest and similar income	37,524
15.	Income from the disposal and write-up of financial assets and securities held as current assets	1,989
16.	Expenses arising from financial investments and securities held as current assets	(8,864)
17.	Interest and similar expenses	(101,013)
18.	**Subtotal of items 12 to 17 (Financial items)**	**(37,757)**
19.	**Income from ordinary activities**	**452,736**
20.	Taxes on income	(130,174)
21.	**Net income for the year**	**322,562**
22.	Allocation to revenue reserve	(205,010)
23.	Minority interests	(1,448)
24.	Income brought forward	5
25.	**Unappropriated income**	**116,109**

(*Source*: OMV Group, *Annual Report and Accounts 2000*. Reproduced by permission of OMV Aktiengesellschaft.)

P6.2 Income statement format and terminology

OMV Group is one of Austria's largest listed companies and a leading European oil and gas group. The English-language version of its 2000 consolidated income statement is set out in Exhibit 6.21.

Required

Find or derive the following income numbers for the OMV Group in 2000. If the number cannot be derived, explain why.

(a) Gross profit.

(b) Operating profit.

(c) Net profit of the group.

(d) Net profit attributable to the parent company's shareholders.

(*Hint*: Items 4 and 5 on the income statement can be considered adjustments to operating expenses.)

P6.3 Balance sheet format and terminology

Set out below is the consolidated balance sheet at 23 February 2002 of Tesco plc, a large UK retailer:

	£m
Fixed assets	
Intangible assets	154
Tangible assets	11,032
Investments	317
	11,503
Current assets	
Stocks	929
Debtors (of which 81 due after more than one year)	454
Investments	225
Cash at bank and in hand	445
	2,053
Creditors falling due within one year	(4,809)
Net current liabilities	(2,756)
Total assets less current liabilities	8,747
Creditors falling due after more than one year	(2,741)
Provisions for liabilities and charges	(440)
Net assets	5,566
Capital and reserves	
Called up share capital	350
Share premium account	2,004
Other reserves	40
Profit and loss account	3,136
Equity shareholders' funds	5,530
Minority interests	36
Total capital employed	5,566

Required

You want to compare Tesco's balance sheet with that of a large non-UK retailer which uses a US-style format and US terminology in the English-language version of its annual accounts. To do so, you have to make certain adjustments to the format and wording of Tesco's balance sheet. As part of this exercise, determine the following balances at 23 February 2002:

(a) total assets;

(b) working capital;

(c) equity attributable to parent company's shareholders;

(d) retained earnings.

P6.4 Identifying operating, investing and financing cash flows

Van Baerle Company, a seed and bulb producer, is famous for its tulips, especially the almost black variety, *Tulipa 'A. Dumas'*.

The company wants to prepare a cash flow statement for x9 and asks you to calculate the key numbers in it. It gives you a summary of the company's cash account for the year. This is shown in Exhibit 6.22.

Exhibit 6.22

Van Baerle Company
Cash account: transactions in x9
(amounts in 000)

Cash

Balance, 1/1/x9	32		
		Salaries paid	124
Disposal of building	37	Dividends paid	4
Increase in long-term debt	181	Payments to suppliers of goods	
Receipts from customers	432	and services	204
Disposal of long-term investment	11	Short-term debt repaid	39
Issue of new shares	135	Corporate income taxes paid	16
		Purchase of equipment	406
		Payment of rent	18
Balance, 31/12/x9	17		

Required

Calculate the following totals for x9:

(a) after-tax operating cash flow;

(b) investing cash flow;

(c) financing cash flow.

P6.5 Construction of simple cash flow statement

Sonne AG is a magazine publisher and distributor. Set out in Exhibit 6.23 are the company's balance sheets at the start and end of year 7, together with its income statement for year 7.

A summary of the company's ledger account, Cash, is presented below. The amounts are also in thousands.

Cash

	Dr.		Cr.
Balance, 1/1/year 7	37	Purchase of buildings and equipment	49
Sale of land	14	Purchase of investments	3
Collection of debts from credit		Payments for paper and other inventories	185
customers	58	Payments for rent	12
Long-term loan	50	Payments of dividends	8
Receipts from new subscriptions	98	Tax payments	7
Cash sales of magazines	80	Other operating outlays	16
		Interest payments	6
Balance, 31/12/year 7	51		

Exhibit 6.23

Sonne AG
Summary accounts for year 7
(amounts in 000)

Balance sheet at 31 December

	year 6	year 7		year 6	year 7
Fixed assets			*Shareholders' equity*		
Land	26	20	Share capital	75	75
Building and equipment	53	102	Retained profits	38	45
Less: Accumulated				113	120
depreciation	−29	−41	Long-term liabilities	0	50
	24	61		113	170
Investments	25	28			
	75	109	*Current liabilities*		
			Accounts payable, paper		
Current assets			suppliers	53	59
Inventories	54	65	Taxes payable	4	7
Accounts receivable	9	11	Unearned subscription		
Prepaid rent	5	8	revenues	10	8
Cash	37	51		67	74
	105	135			
Total assets	180	244	Total equities	180	244

Income statement for year 7

Revenues from: cash sales		80
credit sales		60
subscription sales		100
Total revenues		240
Less: Cost of sales		−180
Gross profit		60
Less: Operating expenses		
Rent on leased asset	−9	
Depreciation on buildings and equipment	−12	
Other operating expense	−16	
Gain on sale of land	+8	
		−29
Operating profit		31
Interest expense		−6
Profit before tax		25
Income taxes		−10
Net profit		15

Required

(a) Explain the change in each of Sonne's balance sheet accounts between the start and end of year 7, using information from the year 7 income statement and the movement in the cash account during the year. For example:

	Land			Cash			Gain/loss on asset disposal	
BB	26			⋮	⋮			
		Sale 6 (at cost)	Sale of land 14				Gain on land sale 8	
				⋮	⋮			
EB	20							

(b) Prepare a cash flow statement for Sonne for year 7, showing separately cash flows from operating, investing and financing activities. Calculate its cash flow from operations by the direct approach. Classify interest payments and tax payments as operating outflows and dividend payments as financing outflows.

(c) Calculate Sonne's year 7 cash flow from operations using the indirect approach.

(d) What does the cash flow statement tell us about Sonne's activities in year 7?

Check figure:
(c) Cash flow from operations   10

P6.6   Understanding cash flow terminology

'MetroModa is getting to be as laid back as its clothes. Operating working capital soared by over €200 million in x1, absorbing cash needed for expansion and contributing to negative free cash flow that year. The company has a great product line. If only its financial management were in the same league . . .'

MetroModa, a specialist designer and manufacturer of 'smart casual' clothes, is enjoying rapid growth, thanks to the movement towards less formal attire in the office. However, the company has attracted criticism among professional investors for its poor working capital management and high financial leverage.

This criticism attracts the notice of the company's non-executive directors. One of them saw the above comment in the *Green Eye Shade* column of the *Business News*, a prominent weekly newspaper, shortly after the company released its x1 results. He contacts the chief financial officer of the company and asks some questions (see below). The CFO is busy negotiating several acquisitions at present and, knowing your financial analysis skills, she asks you to deal with them. Extracts from MetroModa's x1 accounts are given in Exhibit 6.24.

Required

Answer the following questions raised by the non-executive director, using information in MetroModa's x1 accounts.

(a) 'How can working capital have increased by over €200 million in x1? By my calculations, working capital was €150 million at the end of x0 and €322 million at the end of x1. That's an increase of only €172 million – a big increase, to be sure, but less than the figure quoted in *Business News*.'

(b) 'What is "free cash flow"? It's not stated anywhere on the cash flow statement. Is it the same as "net increase in cash"? If so, this is a positive, not a negative, figure.'

(c) 'Is the figure for depreciation in the cash flow statement correct? According to the balance sheet, depreciation was €786 million in x1. I assume that's the number that should be in the cash flow statement. It can't be the change in depreciation between end-x0 and end-x1. That's only €136 million.'

Exhibit 6.24

MetroModa SA
Extracts from x1 accounts
(amounts in € million)

Balance sheet at 31 December

	x1	x0		x1	x0
Current assets			*Current liabilities*		
Cash and marketable securities	122	110	Accounts payable	211	170
Accounts receivable	243	140	Accrued expenses	51	55
Inventories	348	200	Taxes payable	33	25
Prepaid expenses	57	50	Bank loans	153	100
	770	500		448	350
Fixed assets			*Long-term loans*	430	300
Property, plant and equipment	1,819	1,600			
Less: Accumulated depreciation	−786	−650	*Shareholders' equity*		
	1,033	950	Contributed capital	200	200
			Retained profits	725	600
				925	800
			Total liabilities		
Total assets	1,803	1,450	and shareholders' equity	1,803	1,450

Cash flow statement for x1

Operating activities	
Net profit	175
Depreciation	150
Changes in operating working capital:	
Accounts receivable	−103
Inventories	−148
Prepaid expenses	−7
Accounts payable	41
Accrued expenses	−4
Taxes payable	8
Net cash inflow from operations	112
Investing activities	
Purchase of plant and equipment	−240
Sale of property	7
Net cash outflow on investing activities	−233
Financing activities	
Increase in bank loans	53
Increase in long-term loans	130
Dividends paid	−50
Net cash inflow from financing activities	133
Net increase in cash	12
Cash and marketable securities, start-x1	110
Cash and marketable securities, end-x1	122

P6.7 Ratios in the financial press

Newspapers such as the *Financial Times* and the *Wall Street Journal* publish share price and dividend data for quoted companies every day. Set out below are data for three large international retailers. The companies have their headquarters in France, UK and USA respectively. Although the business strategy each pursues is slightly different, investors benchmark each company's performance against the others'. The share price and market capitalisation figures are taken from the 29 April 2002 edition of the *Financial Times*.

	Share price (closing)	Mkt cap. (in million)	Yield, gross	P/E ratio
Carrefour	€49.52	€35,216	1.1	29.1
Tesco	£2.63	£18,214	2.1	21.8
Wal-Mart	$55.80	$248,378	0.5	37.4

Notes:

(i) Mkt cap.: Shares outstanding × share price

(ii) Yield, gross: $\dfrac{\text{Per-share dividend (before withholding tax)}}{\text{Share price}} \times 100$

Required

(a) Estimate Carrefour's net income (in euros) in the latest 12 months (to end-March 2002).

(b) Calculate the dividend cover (or its reciprocal, the payout ratio) as of end-April 2002 for each of the three companies.

(c) Wal-Mart's P/E ratio in April 2002 is much higher than that of the other two companies. Suggest possible reasons for this.

Check figure:
(b) Wal-Mart: Dividend cover 5.3 times

Notes to Chapter 6

1 The full title is 'Fourth Company Law Directive'. The appendix to the chapter lists the directives already implemented under the EU's company law harmonisation programme.

2 Documents filed with the SEC are now available on the SEC's EDGAR website. These documents include quarterly and annual reports, prospectuses and reports recording occurrence of 'material' events. The filing requirements apply to all companies, non-US as well as US, whose securities are listed on a recognised US stock exchange.

3 Smith, T. (1996), *Accounting for Growth*, 2nd edition, London: Random House, chapter 19.

4 The 'land' that Carrefour depreciates represents the premium (over alternative use value) that the company has paid to acquire a site for retail development. Land itself is not usually depreciated.

5 Both the 4th Directive and international accounting standards require firms that invoke the 'true and fair view override' to explain the reasons for departing from 4th Directive (IAS) requirements and to state the effect of the departure on their accounts (4th Directive, Art. 2 (4) and (5); IAS 1, *Presentation of Financial Statements*, para. 13). For an interesting discussion of the 'true and fair view' concept in a European context, see *The European Accounting Review* (1997), 6(4): 673–730.

   Note that the phrase found in US-style audit reports, namely 'present fairly in accordance with generally accepted accounting principles (GAAP)', is similar in intent to the European wording. However, there is no 'present fairly override': US firms must follow US GAAP in all circumstances.

6 The upper limits for net turnover and balance sheet total apply from July 2003 (EU Council Directive 2003/38/EC).

7   In some European countries, companies include in their accounts a statement showing sources and uses of *funds* rather than cash. 'Funds' in this context means working capital and is a less liquid measure of resource flow than cash. We illustrate the funds flow statement when we revisit the cash flow statement in Chapter 18.

8   Note that most investors and analysts are unable to use this approach since they don't have access to the company's ledger accounts. In this case, they must derive an approximate cash flow statement using balance sheet and income statement data.

9   There is no agreed definition of 'free cash flow'. All versions contain at least two elements: operating cash flow or equivalent (i.e. profit plus depreciation and amortisation) less capital expenditures in the same period. We look again at this concept in Chapter 18.

10   As of 2003, the member states are: Belgium, France, Germany, Italy, Luxembourg, Netherlands (founder members); Denmark, Ireland, UK (joined in 1973); Greece (1981); Portugal and Spain (1986); Austria, Finland, and Sweden (1995). Countries due to join the EU in 2004 are: Cyprus, the Czech Republic, Estonia, Hungary, Latvia, Lithuania, Malta, Poland, Slovenia and the Slovak Republic.

PART 2

The house of accounting

7

Key conceptual issues in financial accounting

INTRODUCTION

Let's take stock of where we are. In the previous chapters, we learned about the foundations of the accounting 'building'. We identified the main financial statements: we discovered what purpose each statement serves and how it's constructed. We found out where the numbers in the statements come from by following the accounting cycle from transaction through to trial balance. These foundations are common to all companies.

Our task now is to explore the building, floor by floor. This involves examining each category of asset and equity to see what particular accounting and reporting problems each gives rise to. The notes to the accounts are of great help here. They tell us the accounting policies the firm follows, that is, how it has accounted for various types of transactions. Policies are, in some cases, the result of management decisions and are company-specific. In many cases, however, they are dictated by accounting standards and corporate law and apply to all firms. We aim to shed light on firms' accounting policies – what they mean, what effect they have on the financial statements – in Chapters 8 to 17.

Before exploration of the building begins, we need to know more about its structure. This is the aim of this chapter. We discover at the outset that the financial statements of all companies rest on certain general 'principles': the going concern assumption, consistency, prudence, the accruals concept. These affect, directly or indirectly, each firm's accounting policies. Today these principles are considered insufficient. They leave unanswered important questions such as:

- What should be the objectives of financial reporting?
- What are desirable characteristics of information in financial statements?
- How should key elements such as assets and liabilities be defined? When should they be recognised? How should they be valued? And what's the impact of valuation on profit?

Accounting standard-setters have completed a major project to tackle these questions. The project's goal was to provide a 'conceptual framework' for accounting – a plan of the accounting building, if you like – which would guide standard-setters and corporate management and thus influence the form and content of firms' accounting policies in the future. We raised some of the issues in this conceptual framework in earlier chapters. We explore others in this one. In particular, we investigate the various ways assets and liabilities can be valued and the effect of different valuation methods on the calculation of corporate income.

Accounting policies and their origins

Companies draw up their annual accounts according to a set of accounting policies. As we saw in the last chapter, each firm sets down its accounting policies in the notes to its accounts. Accounting policies comprise the methods a company uses to account for specific types of transactions or events – for example, the method of costing its inventory – and the estimates it must make, given that events this period are affected by uncertain events in future periods. For example, a company's annual depreciation charge is determined in part by managers' estimates of the useful lives of its fixed assets. Management are responsible for making accounting estimates. What about accounting methods? Who or what decides them?

Accounting methods are the result of:

- corporate and tax law;
- accounting standards issued by national and international standard-setting bodies;
- custom; and
- professional and management judgement.

We see examples of each of these factors in the accounting policies disclosed by Eni, Italy's leading oil and gas company. Exhibit 7.1 contains extracts from the notes on accounting policies in Eni's 2001 English-language consolidated financial statements.

- *Corporate law.* Eni consolidates the financial statements of all companies in which it directly or indirectly holds a majority of the voting rights or which it otherwise controls. (Insignificant subsidiaries and those about to be sold have not been consolidated.) This is consistent with the EU's 7th Company Law Directive which has been incorporated into Italian law. Similarly, fixed assets have been revalued as required by Italian monetary revaluation laws.
- *International accounting standards.* Eni follows IAS in the absence of applicable Italian accounting rules. Thus it prepares the cash flow statement in line with *IAS 7*. (Note that, from 2005, IAS will supersede national accounting rules for EU listed companies like Eni.)
- *Business custom.* Eni recognises revenue from the sale of products when ownership is transferred. This usually occurs when the customer takes delivery of them. As we saw in Chapter 5, recognising revenue at the time of delivery is a long-standing practice.
- *Management judgement.* Management must decide how the services provided by depreciable fixed assets are likely to be consumed. Eni considers they will be consumed evenly over the assets' lives, since it uses the straight-line method of depreciation.

Historical background

Eni is an Italian company. To the extent that company law and business custom affect its accounting policies, it is Italian law and Italian custom. Does this mean that, to understand a company's accounts, investors must be familiar with the legal system and business customs of the company's home country?

The answer is a qualified no. Many features of accrual accounting are universal. Moreover, in the EU, company law directives have removed or narrowed accounting differences between member states. In addition, certain accounting practices are common to countries with a similar legal and economic history. Only a few aspects of a firm's accounts are unique to its home country.

Consider the accounting and reporting practices of European and North American companies, for example. In the past, there were marked differences between the practices of 'Anglo-Saxon' and those of 'Continental European' firms. Within Europe, Ireland, the Netherlands

Exhibit 7.1   Eni: extracts from notes to consolidated 2001 financial statements

---

2) Summary of significant accounting and reporting policies

Basis of presentation
The consolidated financial statements of Eni have been prepared in accordance with Eni's group accounting policies which are in accordance with accounting principles prescribed by Italian law and supplemented by the accounting principles issued by the Consiglio Nazionale dei Dottori Commercialisti e dei Ragioneri or, in the absence thereof and if applicable, the International Accounting Standards Committee. . . .

Principles of consolidation
The consolidated financial statements include the statutory accounts of Eni SpA and all Italian and foreign companies controlled by Eni SpA, directly or indirectly, either by holding the majority of the voting rights or sufficient votes to enable it to exercise control at ordinary shareholders' meetings. . . .

:

Fixed assets
Fixed assets are stated at cost as adjusted by revaluations in accordance with various Italian laws: revaluations are included in the consolidated shareholders' equity. . . .

Depreciation of fixed assets, except on those related to exploration and production activities, is computed on the revalued cost, using the straight-line method by applying depreciation rates that are based on the estimated remaining lives of the fixed assets.

:

Recognition of revenues and costs
Revenues from sales of products are recognised upon transfer of title. Revenues from services are recognised when the services have been provided. . . .

:

Statements of cash flows
The cash flow statements are prepared in accordance with International Accounting Standards, using the indirect method.

:

(*Source*: Eni SpA, *Annual Report 2001*.)

and the UK form the Anglo-Saxon group and Belgium, France, Germany, Italy and Spain are the principal members of the Continental European group. (From an accounting perspective, most western European countries belong to the Continental European group. Danish accounting practice, however, shows strong Anglo-Saxon influence.) A brief overview of the two different accounting traditions follows.[1]

Continental European accounting tradition

In Continental European countries, government has been the main influence on corporate financial accounting. Firms' published accounts reflect more the interests and concerns of government agencies (e.g. the tax authorities, the ministry of economic planning) and creditors than those of equity investors.

Why is this? A major reason is the ownership of firms and its effect on the way they finance their activities. In the past, most firms in these countries were either family- or state-owned. They financed growth from reinvested profits or with debt. Because outside shareholders played a small role in company financing, there was little demand for investor-oriented information.

Another reason is the legal system in these countries. A code law tradition prevails. Laws are framed according to a code, a set of general principles, formulated by the legislature. This means that only government (through its legislative branch) can initiate law.

What were the consequences for corporate accounting?

- First, the government prescribed the format of accounts and the valuation rules to be used in their preparation. In some countries the government drew up a national chart of accounts which firms had to use for record-keeping purposes. The tax authorities reinforced this. They insisted on 'uniform reporting', that is a firm's taxable profit should be the same as the profit figure shown in its published accounts.
- Second, published accounts revealed a creditor bias. The balance sheet was considered the key financial statement. Assets were conservatively valued and provisions for future liabilities encouraged. Mandatory appropriations of profit to legal reserves restricted firms' ability to distribute profits to shareholders. Firms were not required to publish consolidated accounts or disclose per-share earnings, information that equity investors value.

Anglo-Saxon accounting tradition

In Anglo-Saxon countries, the form and content of published accounts owe more to the initiatives of management, the accounting profession and the stock exchange than to government.

The main reason is, as before, the ownership of firms and its effect on corporate financing. Legal innovations (e.g. the joint-stock company, limited liability) and active financial markets – originally in commodities and insurance, later in stocks – enabled firms to raise equity capital cheaply. In time, ownership became diffuse as founder-owners sold their holdings to outside shareholders. The latter demanded audited accounts and greater disclosure.

Another factor in England, Ireland and Wales (and, outside Europe, the USA and British Commonwealth countries) is the legal system. These countries have a common law tradition. Courts as well as the legislature shape the law. Judges consult precedent and custom when framing their decisions. Thus good accounting practice influenced judges' decisions and was incorporated later into company law. (The impact of the legal system on corporate ownership and financing is explored in Box 7.1.)

In what ways did these factors affect accounting practice in Anglo-Saxon countries?

- First, published accounts were varied in format and content. For example, initially there was no standard layout to the balance sheet or income statement. Historical cost accounting was not universal: for example, some Dutch firms valued fixed assets at replacement cost.
- Second, many accounting innovations introduced by firms – consolidated accounts, expenses classified by function, interim reports – were geared to the needs of equity investors.
- Third, the tax authorities had minor influence over the preparation of accounts. They permitted 'separate reporting': a firm did not have to follow the tax code in determining its published profits.
- Lastly, the accounting profession became large and influential. By requiring firms to have their accounts independently audited, the British government encouraged the growth of an accounting profession and British accountants later exported their skills to other English-speaking countries. To aid its members, the profession in each country drew up guidelines for the preparation and audit of accounts. These formed the basis of accounting and audit 'standards' which later acquired stock exchange and government backing.

BOX
7.1 ## Legal tradition, investor protection and company financing

Recent empirical work confirms that countries with a common law tradition have more developed equity markets and that companies in these countries have broader share ownership than those in code law countries. A major Harvard-based study of 49 countries found that common law countries on average had more firms and more initial public offerings of equity per head of population than code law countries in 1994. The value of shareholdings held by 'outside' shareholders as a proportion of gross national product (GNP) was also higher in common law countries that year.[2]

Why is this? The economists conducting these studies (La Porta, Lopez-de-Silanes, Shleifer, Vishny) argue that *outside investors*, that is, creditors and shareholders who neither have a controlling stake in the company nor are managers, have stronger legal rights in common law countries. Laws in these countries enable them to challenge 'insiders' (i.e. managers and controlling shareholders) who attempt to misappropriate the company's assets, for example by diverting them to other companies they control. As a result, outside investors are willing to invest in companies they don't control (and demand a lower return for doing so). In turn, existing controlling shareholders (e.g. entrepreneurs who have built up their own businesses) are willing to become outside investors – by reducing or disposing of their stakes in their own companies and investing in other firms – knowing that there's less risk of their assets being misappropriated.

La Porta *et al.* provide persuasive evidence that outside investors are better protected in common law countries. In the case of equity investors, they identify six measures of shareholder protection and they construct an 'antidirector rights index' based on them. The index is formed by adding one when each of the following holds:

1 Shareholders can mail their proxy vote to the firm rather than have to show up in person or send an authorised representative to the shareholders' meeting: this makes it easier for them to cast their votes.
2 Shareholders are not required to deposit their shares several days prior to a shareholders' meeting: this means they're not prevented from selling the shares during this period.
3 The law allows cumulative voting for directors or proportional representation of minority (i.e. outside) shareholders on the board.
4 There are legal mechanisms to protect minority shareholders from oppression by directors. Minority shareholders can challenge directors' decisions in the courts or force the company to repurchase their shares in certain circumstances (e.g. mergers or asset sales).
5 Shareholders have a pre-emptive right to buy new issues of shares. This means insiders can't dilute the interests of minority shareholders by issuing shares to selected investors at favourable prices.
6 The percentage of share capital needed to call an extraordinary shareholders' meeting is low (La Porta *et al.* set the cut-off at 10% in their studies), thereby making it easier for minority shareholders to challenge management.

La Porta *et al.* classify 49 countries by legal tradition. The 18 countries with a common law tradition have an average antidirector rights index score of 4 (out of 6), whereas the 31 countries with a code law tradition have an average score of 2.42.[3]

What role does accounting play here? La Porta *et al.* argue that strong legal rights are of little value if enforcement mechanisms are weak. To exercise their rights, outside investors rely not only on efficient and 'clean' courts but also on full and fair disclosure of financial information. La Porta *et al.* find that, based on their 1990 annual reports, companies in common law countries disclose more financial information than their code law counterparts.[4]

Exhibit 7.2	Continental European vs Anglo-Saxon accounting: main factors responsible for differences

Factor	Continental European countries	Anglo-Saxon countries
Corporate ownership	Concentrated: state-owned or family-owned	Diffuse – through public share offerings
Taxation	Uniformity of tax and book income	Separate tax/book income calculation
Legal tradition	Code law	Common law (most English-speaking countries)

Non-European countries can be incorporated in this simple framework. Other English-speaking countries (e.g. the USA) and countries which, in the past, have been in the US or UK sphere of influence (e.g. Israel, British Commonwealth countries), usually follow Anglo-Saxon accounting. Countries whose commercial and legal systems have been influenced by those of Continental European countries (e.g. Japan, Francophone countries in Africa) have, in the main, adopted their corporate accounting practices, too. Exhibit 7.2 summarises the main factors which are responsible for the differences between Continental European and Anglo-Saxon accounting.

In recent years, accounting practices in Continental European countries have moved closer to those found in Anglo-Saxon countries. Several forces are at work.

- *EU company law directives have narrowed differences within Europe.* Anglo-Saxon countries within the EU have adopted standard formats for the balance sheet and income statement. Continental European countries have accepted that a company's accounts must give a 'true and fair view' of its financial position and its profit or loss in the period.
- *The influence of international accounting standards is increasing.* As mentioned earlier, all listed companies in the EU must prepare their consolidated accounts according to IAS from 2005. (Member states have the option to impose a similar requirement on unlisted companies and individual company accounts.) Even before this EU regulation was announced, many of the larger companies in Continental European countries had switched to international or US standards – or were reconciling key numbers such as net profit and shareholders' equity to them – in order to gain access to international capital markets. IAS have Anglo-Saxon roots. However, they are less prescriptive (and, for Europeans, more acceptable politically) than US standards.
- *Accountants in public practice have grown in number and wield more influence in Continental European countries.* EU law is partly responsible: we've seen already that the accounting directives require larger EU companies, private and public, to have their annual accounts audited. The big international public accounting firms have taken a large share of this new market, especially in southern European countries, and brought Anglo-Saxon accounting and auditing practices with them.

In addition, accounting rules in Continental European countries – whether in the tax code or in the accounting plan – have not kept pace with best practice in financial reporting. For example, they were silent on how pension costs, deferred income taxes and environmental liabilities should be accounted for. Accountants have stepped into the breach. They have formed new private-sector associations (e.g. the Spanish Accounting and Business Administration Association, the Norwegian Accounting Standards Board) to draw up accounting standards and to lobby governments on accounting issues – in the same way that their counterparts in the UK and USA do.

In later chapters we emphasise the accounting practices that unite European firms rather than those that divide them. For this reason we focus on EU directives and international accounting standards. We describe and illustrate unusual national practices if they are likely to have a material impact on a firm's accounts.[5] In the remaining sections of this chapter, we review the accounting framework that underlies international standards and the EU's accounting directives.

Fundamental accounting principles

'Principle' is an overused term in accounting. It can refer to a norm or assumption that underlies the accrual basis of accounting. This is the sense we use it in this chapter. It's also found in the phrase 'generally accepted accounting principles' or GAAP. This is a US term. It refers to the set of accounting methods in general use in that country, including the accounting rules laid down by the US standard-setting body, the FASB.

The accounting policies a firm follows rest on certain fundamental principles. They are:

- *The going concern assumption.* The financial statements are prepared – and assets and liabilities are valued – on the assumption that the company is able to continue trading for the foreseeable future. This means that it is expected to recover its investment in fixed assets through normal operations and sell its inventory in the same way.
- *Consistency.* The company applies the accounting policies it has adopted on a consistent basis. Like transactions and events are accounted for in the same way from one period to the next. This increases users' confidence in a firm's accounts and allows them to make interperiod comparisons.
- *Prudence.* The financial statements are prepared on a prudent basis. More specifically, profits are only recognised in the income statement when they are 'realised' or 'realisable', that is when cash or claims to cash are received. In addition, prudence requires liabilities and potential losses to be provided for as soon as they arise.
- *The accruals concept.* A company recognises revenues and expenses in the period they occur. This may not coincide with the date of cash receipt or payment. The 'matching principle' is an illustration of the accruals concept at work: the expense of a sale (cost of goods sold) is recognised in the same period as the revenue from it. Note that if prudence and the accruals concept conflict, prudence usually takes precedence.

These are the most important of the general principles set down in the EU's 4th Directive (Art. 31.1).[6] A company can depart from them 'in exceptional circumstances' but it must state the reason for, and the effect of, the departure (Art. 31.2). Interestingly, principles similar to these were in force in all EU member states prior to the issuance of the 4th Directive. They form the bedrock of international accounting standards, too.[7]

How did these principles arise? Although they are set down in commercial and tax codes in many countries, their origins are found in long-accepted business practice. Consider the timing of revenue recognition under accrual accounting. The practice of recognising revenue at the time of delivery – the dominant practice in the case of goods – took hold for legal and practical reasons. Legal title is usually transferred when the buyer receives the goods. In addition, shipment prompts changes to the seller's books: a shipping note and invoice are issued and the inventory records are adjusted, too. To recognise sales revenue at that time minimises the number of entries the seller must make to its records.

Accountants derived a general principle from this specific practice. The general principle is that revenues are recognised in the income statement when they have been earned. We saw in Chapter 5 how this principle is given substance in practice, in particular what conditions must be met before the earning process is considered complete (i.e. measurable economic benefits to seller, risks and rewards of ownership transferred to buyer). The revenue recognition principle is an important one – in fact, it's a key component of the accruals concept.

Once a rationale for revenue recognition was established, it could then be applied to new situations. With the growth of the service sector in the past 30 to 40 years, there are many of these. Take the case of the initial fee a franchisor charges each new franchisee. To the extent that it relates to tangible assets (for example, special equipment the franchisee must use), the franchisor can recognise it as revenue when it delivers the assets. If it's a charge for future services, the franchisor should defer recognition until it performs them. The reasons for the initial fee affect when revenue is considered 'earned' and can be recognised. In each case, the franchisor is implicitly applying fundamental accounting principles when deciding how to account for the initial fee.

Problems with fundamental accounting principles

The fundamental principles listed above have had, and continue to have, a powerful influence on accounting practice. For example, legislators and rule-making bodies cite prudence as a justification for valuing physical assets at historical cost (in most countries, the dominant basis of valuation). Until an asset such as property or inventory has been sold, any gain from an increase in its value has not been realised. It is therefore imprudent to recognise the gain as profit, they argue.

Thirty years ago, people began to question whether these principles provided an adequate conceptual basis for accounting. Important questions had been ignored. For example, what should be the objectives of financial statements? What are the key elements in those statements, when should they be recognised, and how should they be valued? Meanwhile, the business world was changing fast. Economic growth brought new products and industries, new methods of financing and expanding stock markets. Unfortunately, it was accompanied by inflation. As a result, answers to basic questions such as: what is an asset? how should it be valued? became more pressing. The old structure of financial accounting was found wanting. A new one was called for.

The 'conceptual framework': a new agenda for accounting

When the FASB, the current US accounting standard-setting body, was established in 1973, one of its first tasks was to begin constructing a 'conceptual framework' for financial accounting and reporting. Since then, the IASB and rule-making bodies in other countries have undertaken similar ventures. In the FASB's case, the project lasted over ten years and provoked considerable controversy.

The idea behind the conceptual framework is simple and can be best understood by analogy. We've talked already of the 'accounting building'. A building is constructed according to a plan. Among other things, the plan sets out the shape and form of the building and ensures that, from a design standpoint, the structure is sound and internally consistent.

In principle, a conceptual framework is financial accounting's architectural plan. It sets the shape and form of the accounting building by giving answers to key questions such as: what are the objectives of financial statements? what are the qualities of 'useful' information? It provides guidance for accounting standard-setters. They try to ensure new standards are consistent with it. They cite it in support of their decisions – to outlaw 'inferior' accounting methods and to decree the use of 'superior' ones.

One difference between an architect's plan and accounting's conceptual framework is that the conceptual framework was drawn up after work on the accounting building had been proceeding for many years. As a result, it's not clear what the framework is intended to be: a redesign of the financial accounting building, or, as some critics claim, a plan which allows the existing building to be modified and extended but avoids fundamental alteration.

Conceptual framework: main components

We now take a closer look at a particular conceptual framework, that of the IASB. Exhibit 7.3 summarises the main issues as the IASB sees them and its position on each.[8] The IASB's framework is similar to that of other standard-setting bodies. (An overview of the IASB and its predecessor, the IASC is given in Appendix 7.1.)

Exhibit 7.3 A conceptual framework for financial accounting: issues and the position of the IASB

Issues	IASB's position summarised
What are the objectives of financial statements?	*To provide information about a firm that is useful to a wide range of people making economic decisions.* 'Useful information' is information on a company's financial position, performance and liquidity.
What are the characteristics of 'useful financial information'?	Four main characteristics are identified: – *understandability*; – *relevance*; – *reliability*; – *comparability*.
What are the main elements of financial statements?	The main elements are: *asset, liability, equity* (of owners), *income and expense.* 'Income' includes revenue and gain; 'Expense' includes loss.
How are they defined?	Asset – *resource controlled by a firm as a result of past events and from which economic benefits are expected to flow in future.* Liability – *present obligation of a firm arising from past events, settlement of which is expected to result in a future outflow of resources.* Other elements are defined in terms of these two.
What are the criteria for recognising them?	Criteria for recognising elements (i.e. incorporating them in financial statements) are: – *it's probable that future economic benefits associated with the item will flow to/from the firm*; and – *item has cost or value that can be measured reliably.*
How should assets and liabilities be valued?	IASB lists four valuation bases now in use but does not favour one over the others: – *historical cost*; – *current cost*; – *realisable (settlement) value*; – *present value.*
Which type of capital should a firm seek to maintain?	IASB identifies two capital maintenance objectives but expresses no preference. – *financial capital maintenance, in nominal monetary units or units of constant purchasing power*; – *physical capital maintenance.*

(*Source:* IASB, *Framework for the Preparation and Presentation of Financial Statements.*)

We discussed some of these issues at length in earlier chapters. The IASB's position on them provokes little comment today. 'Usefulness for economic decision-making' is widely accepted as the main objective of financial statements. (However, as we saw in Chapter 1, there's a minority view which holds that the objective should be more restrictive: to provide owners and creditors with financial information that lets them monitor managers' past actions.) There's general agreement that accounts should be understandable, relevant, reliable and comparable. These are considered to be desirable characteristics of financial information (*see* Chapter 1).[9]

More questionable are the definitions of the elements of financial statements. Recall that owners' equity and income statement items are all defined in terms of assets and liabilities (Chapters 2 and 3). Critics argue that the balance sheet focus of the definitions is at odds with the way investors use financial statements. For them, the income statement is the most important statement as it provides more useful information for earnings and cash flow prediction.

Moreover, the definitions of asset and liability are too narrow, it's claimed. They appear to exclude certain deferred costs from assets and certain accrued costs from liabilities. For example, it's doubtful whether the legal and related costs of setting up a firm – an asset according to the EU's 4th Directive – can be considered a 'resource . . . from which future economic benefits are expected to flow'. Again, not all the provisions shown as liabilities in European company balance sheets represent 'present obligations' that will cause a future outflow of resources.

The views of the IASB (and other rule-making bodies) on recognition and valuation also arouse controversy. As we haven't addressed these issues before and they'll colour our discussion of assets and liabilities in future chapters, we devote much of the rest of this chapter to exploring them.

A recognition test for assets and liabilities

Recognition, in an accounting context, means inclusion on the face of a primary financial statement (balance sheet, income statement, cash flow statement). Not all items that meet the definition of asset or liability appear on the balance sheet. A firm's accounting assets (liabilities) can be viewed as a subset of its resources (obligations). Exhibit 7.4 shows this pictorially.

To be included on the balance sheet, assets and liabilities must pass a recognition test. According to the IASB, the test has two parts:

- *It must be probable that the item gives rise to future economic benefits which flow to the firm (assets) or future economic costs which flow from the firm (liabilities).*
- *The cost or value of the item can be measured reliably.*

Exhibit 7.4 Accounting assets/liabilities: subset of a firm's resources/obligations

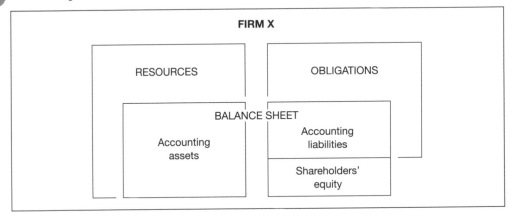

An asset or liability is not recognised on the balance sheet if it fails either part of this test. For example, company A guarantees certain borrowings of B, a travel firm specialising in tour holidays in the Middle East. In 2000, when the guarantee was given, B's financial position was sound. In the aftermath of the terrorist attacks in the USA in September 2001 and growing tensions in Israel and adjacent occupied territories, demand for the firm's products slumps. B's finances deteriorate and it declares bankruptcy in 2002. In its 2000 accounts, A reports no liability with respect to the guarantee since it is not probable then that it will have to pay B's debts. (It may disclose a contingent liability in the notes to its accounts, however.) It *may* report a liability in its end-2001 balance sheet – this depends on its judgement of B's financial position and future cash flows – but it will definitely report a liability at the end of 2002 since by then the recognition test is met.

Sometimes it is difficult to measure the cost (or value) of an asset or liability reliably. This is likely to be the case with internally developed intangibles such as brands or customer lists. The IASB has concluded that because it's difficult to distinguish outlays on these items from those incurred in developing the business as a whole, they fail the measurement part of the test and cannot be recognised as accounting assets.

The same recognition criteria apply to revenues and expenses – and thus profit. Recall that revenues are inflows – and expenses outflows – of net assets arising from a firm's operations or activities incidental to them.

The recognition criteria are a screening device. They prevent 'soft' assets and revenues (soft with respect to existence or amount) from appearing in the accounts. However, they are flexible. Management and auditors must judge the probability of future costs and benefits and the reliability of valuation.

The way in which the IASB defines assets and liabilities and the recognition criteria it lays down give standard-setters flexibility, too. For example, the definitions and the recognition test have been drafted so as to cover virtually all existing accounting assets. But they are loose enough that in future they may allow companies to recognise as assets resources which hitherto have been excluded from the balance sheet (e.g. assets leased under short-term contracts).

Measurement of assets and liabilities

Alternative valuation bases

Once a company decides to recognise an asset or liability, it is then faced with the problem of measuring it. There are two measurement issues. One issue is how the boundaries of the asset or liability are determined. For example, if a company constructs a building for its own use, what costs should it capitalise in the fixed asset account? The other – which we address in this section – is how the asset or liability is valued. (We deal with the first issue in later chapters when we study the accounting problems associated with individual assets and liabilities.)

Up to now, we have assumed that assets and liabilities can be valued in one of two ways – at **historical cost (HC)** or at **current value (CV)** (also known as **fair value**). At the time an asset is acquired or an obligation incurred, HC and CV should be identical. Thereafter, cost and value diverge as the prices of goods and services change and interest rates fluctuate.

Current value, however, is an ambiguous term. It can be estimated by calculating any of the following:

● *The cost today of acquiring a similar asset or the cash that would be obtained if the same obligation were incurred today.* (Note that as interest rates rise (fall), the same debt terms will command less (more) cash.) This version of current value is better known, for assets at least, as **replacement cost (RC)**. (The IASB prefers the term **current cost**.)

- *The proceeds from disposing of the asset or the amount required to settle the liability today.* This can be determined by finding the current **market value (MV)** – realisable value in the case of an asset and settlement value in the case of a liability. Disposal (or settlement) is assumed to occur in the normal course of business and without duress.
- *The discounted value today of the expected cash flows to or from the company which are attributable to the asset or liability.* This is also known as the **present value (PV)** of the asset or liability. (Appendix 7.2 contains an explanation of how the present value of a stream of expected cash flows is derived.)

Each of the above may yield a different estimate of current value. The reason lies largely in imperfections in the markets for assets and liabilities. Custom-built machinery, for example, is expected to generate healthy cash flows – it has a high 'value in use' – and is costly to replace but its realisable value may be low because of its specialised nature. Box 7.2 outlines the approach a company should use to determine the current value of an asset or liability when the value estimates under the three bases differ.

Effect of alternative valuation bases on profit

The impact of alternative valuation bases goes beyond the balance sheet. A different asset (or liability) value may result in a different profit figure.

An example demonstrates this. Charon is a Greek ferry operator. At the start of year 1, he invests 30,000 in a new venture, Charon Chauffeuring. With that sum the company buys a large car in order to drive dignitaries around Athens and, as Mr Charon puts it, 'to and from the Styx'. The car has an expected economic life of four years and its disposal value then is expected to be minimal. Charon expects annual revenues from chauffeuring to be 50,000 and annual outlays on fuel, wages, insurance and taxes to be 40,540, an annual net cash flow of 9,460.

On 2 January, the purchase date, the car's historical cost, replacement cost and market value are, by definition, 30,000. Using a 10% discount rate, the present value of the expected annual net cash flows from the chauffeuring service is approximately 30,000 (9,460 × 3.17, the end-year annuity factor for four years at 10%). Thus its balance sheet on 2 January is the same under all four valuation bases. It is shown in Exhibit 7.5.

Consider now the situation at the end of year 1. The company's year 1 revenues and expenditures are in line with its forecasts at the start of the year. There are no other receipts or payments during the year so its end-year cash balance is 9,460. The company's only other asset is the car. It has no liabilities.

The value of the car at 31 December differs, depending on which valuation method the company uses.

- Under HC accounting, the net book value of the car is 22,500. The car's services are expected to be consumed evenly over the four years of its expected life. Annual HC depreciation is therefore 7,500 (30,000/4).

Exhibit 7.5	
Charon Chauffeuring
Balance sheet at 2 January year 1
under HC, RC, MV and PV valuation bases

Fixed asset	30,000	Owner's equity	30,000

BOX 7.2   Deprival value

How should a company choose among the three bases – replacement cost (RC), market value (MV), or present value (PV) – when determining the current value of an asset or liability? A popular approach is to try to determine the 'value to the company' of each asset and liability. One economist has defined this for assets as follows:

> The value of a property to its owner is identical in amount with the adverse value of the entire loss, direct and indirect, that the owner might expect to suffer if he were deprived of the property.[10]

Using the same approach, the value of a liability to the debtor company is the gain it would enjoy if it were relieved of the liability.

The next step is to operationalise *deprival value*. Consider the case of an asset where RC, MV and PV differ. The most likely situation is PV > RC > MV: the value of an asset in use exceeds its replacement cost which in turn exceeds its sale value. In this case, the asset's deprival value is its replacement cost. Because PV > RC, it's worthwhile for the company to buy a new asset if it's deprived of the old – but the maximum loss it sustains is the cost of the replacement. In fact, whenever PV or MV (or both) exceeds RC, the deprival value is replacement cost. (If MV > RC, the company should buy and then immediately sell the asset!) In these cases, it pays to replace the asset and the loss the company sustains is the cost of the replacement.

What if replacement cost exceeds present value and market value? In these cases, replacement is not worthwhile. Then the value of the asset to the firm – what it would lose from being deprived of the asset – is the *higher* of the asset's present value and market value.[11]

These ideas are summarised below. Note that 'recoverable amount' is, by definition, the higher of PV and MV. As we'll discover in a later chapter, a company forced to write down a fixed asset below cost because it's impaired must value it at recoverable amount under IAS.

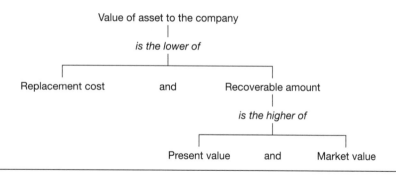

- We learn that the same model costs 32,000 new at the end of year 1. Given the vehicle's four-year life, this means the replacement cost of a similar one-year-old car is 24,000. RC depreciation is 8,000 (32,000/4) at end-year 1 values.
- We discover from an authoritative guide to second-hand car prices that the disposal value of an equivalent 1-year-old car is 21,500. The decline in the car's market value in year 1 is therefore 8,500.
- With expectations about business unchanged from 1 January forecasts, the present value of expected net cash flows in the remaining three years is 23,530 (9,460 × 2.487, the end-year annuity factor for 3 years at 10%). Thus the reduction in the present value of these cash flows is 6,470 (30,000 − 23,530).

Exhibit 7.6

Charon Chauffeuring
Annual accounts for year 1
under HC, RC, MV and PV valuation bases
(all amounts in 000)

	Historical cost	Replacement cost	Market value	Present value
Income statement for year 1				
Revenues from chauffeuring	50	50	50	50
Expenses of fuel, wages, etc.	−40.54	−40.54	−40.54	−40.54
Depreciation or value diminution*	−7.5	−8	−8.5	−6.47
Holding gain**	–	2	–	–
Profit in year 1	1.96	3.46	0.96	2.99
Balance sheet at 31/12/year 1				
Fixed asset				
– at valuation or				
depreciated cost	22.5	24	21.5	23.53
Cash	9.46	9.46	9.46	9.46
Total assets	31.96	33.46	30.96	32.99
Owner's equity:				
At 1 January	30	30	30	30
Profit in year 1	1.96	3.46	0.96	2.99
At 31 December	31.96	33.46	30.96	32.99

* Depreciation/value diminution is calculated as follows:

HC: 25% × historical cost of 30.

RC: 25% × 31/12/year 1 replacement cost of 32.

MV: Difference between market values at 2/1 and 31/12.

PV: Difference between present values at 2/1 and 31/12.

** By buying the car on 1 January, Charon saved 2 on what he would have spent by delaying purchase until 31 December, i.e. 30 against 32. This cost saving is known as a holding gain.

Exhibit 7.6 shows Charon Chauffeuring's annual accounts for year 1 under the four valuation bases.

Choice of valuation method affects the income statement as well as the balance sheet. Notice the different charges for depreciation under the four methods in Charon Chauffeuring's year 1 accounts. In addition, under replacement cost accounting, the company records the cost saving in year 1 – from buying the car a year earlier at a lower price – as a 'holding gain'. The differences in reported profit also appear as differences in end-year owner's equity.

Valuation methods: IASB's and EU's position

The IASB expresses no preference for any of the valuation methods (or 'measurement methods') illustrated in Exhibit 7.6. It merely notes that historical cost is the most widely-used method and that companies often use more than one valuation method in their accounts. The IASB's own standards are partly responsible for this diversity. The accounting standard on financial instruments *requires* firms to carry certain financial assets and liabilities at fair value (i.e. market value) in the balance sheet. Other standards *allow* firms to revalue tangible and purchased intangible fixed assets.

The EU's accounting directives are similarly permissive. Although the EU's 4th Directive requires assets to be valued at historical cost (specifically, 'purchase price or production cost' (Art. 32)), it gives member states the right to sanction other valuation methods. According to Article 33, member states can allow companies to:

(a) value tangible fixed assets and inventories at RC;
(b) revalue tangible and financial fixed assets; and
(c) use methods 'designed to take account of inflation'.

Use of market values and present values is permitted under method (b). Method (c) allows firms to make adjustments to all accounts, in both balance sheet and income statement, for changes in general prices. The accounting directives were amended in 2001 to allow EU companies to carry certain financial assets and liabilities at fair value. This brings the directives into line with IAS.

In practice, historical cost is still the dominant valuation method in Europe (and elsewhere). Many member states do not take advantage of the alternative methods the 4th Directive allows. As of 2003 fair value accounting for investments is widespread only in North America. We look more closely at how specific categories of asset and liability are valued in later chapters.

Recognition and measurement controversies

The IASB has come under fire over its conceptual framework project, especially the criteria it lays down for recognising assets and liabilities and its position on how they should be valued.

Despite the apparent flexibility of the recognition test, the effect in practice is to make it difficult for certain key resources to be recognised as accounting assets. Critics argue that most internally developed intangibles that are marketing-related (e.g. brand names, publishing titles) are likely to fail the second part of the test (absence of a reliable cost figure). In addition, some research and development spending, in particular outlays on basic research, fail the first part of the test (probability of future economic benefits) as well. Given that, for many companies, internally developed intangibles represent a growing proportion of corporate resources, failure to account for them undermines the utility of company balance sheets, according to this view.

As for measurement, the charge is that the IASB's seeming neutrality on this issue is a smokescreen. Because of the way the IASB defines assets and liabilities in its conceptual framework (i.e. as inflows and outflows of future economic benefits), use of current values is encouraged, critics claim. And they point to new accounting rules – such as the use of fair values to value certain financial assets and liabilities and the inclusion of a present value calculation in valuing impaired fixed assets – as evidence that the IASB favours current value methods of measurement. Since current values are not always based on actual market transactions, they may be less reliable than the historical cost figures they replace. Critics fear that investors will then lose confidence in the reported numbers in financial statements and the resulting uncertainty will drive up firms' capital costs.

Capital maintenance and the measurement unit in accounts

One further issue in the IASB's conceptual framework concerns the type of capital a firm should seek to maintain. This is important. *Profit represents the return on the capital invested in a business. A firm cannot be said to have made a profit during a period if it has not maintained the capital with which it started the period.* The IASB identifies three ways of defining invested capital:

- financial capital measured in nominal monetary units;
- financial capital measured in units of constant purchasing power; and
- physical capital.

We review here the differences between financial and physical capital and explain the concept of 'units of constant purchasing power'.

Capital can be defined as:

- the investment (initial contribution plus reinvested profits) made in the firm by its owners; or
- the productive capacity of the firm.

The first is known as **financial capital**, the second as **physical capital**. The two versions of capital can result in quite different profit figures.

Financial capital maintenance

Consider Charon Chauffeuring. Charon invested 30,000 in the business. This is the firm's financial capital at the start of year 1. Charon Chauffeuring generates a profit in year 1 if Charon's equity at the end of the year, after adjusting for any further capital contributions or distributions, is greater than 30,000. The excess over 30,000 is the amount the company can distribute as dividend without impairing Charon's investment. (Any distribution *above* that amount is a return *of* his capital.)

Where financial capital maintenance (FCM) is the firm's objective, the profit it reports depends in part on the way it values its assets and liabilities. Look again at Exhibit 7.6. Each one of the profit figures is consistent with FCM. So long as the company applies consistently the valuation method adopted and restricts any dividend to the profit reported, Charon's investment will be preserved. Thus, if it values assets at HC and restricts the year 1 dividend to 1,960, Charon's end-year equity in the business, *valued at HC*, will be 30,000, the amount he initially contributed. (Of course, different profit figures and dividend payments will result in different end-year cash balances.)

Physical capital maintenance

The company's physical capital at the start of year 1 is the car it purchased new on that date. To maintain its physical capital, the company must have, at year-end, either a similar car (i.e. one with the same productive capacity) or the resources equivalent to the cost of one. We know that the replacement cost of the same model is 32,000 at the end of year 1. Thus Charon's net assets must not fall below 32,000 at the end of year 1.

Where the firm's objective is to maintain its physical capital (PCM), it must value its assets and liabilities at replacement cost. It must also exclude from distributable profit any holding gains or losses that have arisen in the year. For example, when an asset's value increases relative to its historical cost, the firm gains from holding it. However, if it must replace the asset, it cannot distribute the holding gain as dividend without impairing its physical capital. Thus under PCM, holding gains and losses are not part of distributable profit of the period.

Charon Chauffeuring's circumstances in year 1 demonstrate this. Its year 1 financial statements under PCM are summarised in Exhibit 7.7.

At 31 December, the company's assets – the sum of its cash and the car at net replacement cost – are 33,460. They exceed the replacement cost of a similar car by 1,460 (33,460 – 32,000). This is also the amount by which the company's current revenues (50,000) exceed its current costs in the year (48,540). By excluding the holding gain of 2,000 from year 1 distributable profit and thus limiting any dividend to 1,460, Charon ensures that the company retains in the business the equivalent of the productive capacity (the car) it began the year with.

Exhibit 7.7

Charon Chauffeuring
Annual accounts for year 1
under PCM objective
(amounts in 000)

Income statement for year 1

Operating revenues	50
Operating expenses at current cost	
(fuel, wages, depreciation)	−48.54
Profit for year	1.46

Balance sheet at end-year 1

Fixed asset, at RC	32	Owner's equity:	
– Year 1 depreciation	−8	At 1 January	30
Fixed asset, net	24	Holding gain	2
Cash	9.46	Profit for year	1.46
Total assets	33.46	Total equities	33.46

Nominal currency or constant purchasing power units

In the last section we saw how a company, to maintain its capital, may – and, in the case of physical capital maintenance, must – take account of changes in the prices of specific assets and liabilities. Replacement cost, market value, and present value are alternative ways of measuring the changes in those prices. However, we said nothing about the effect of changes in *general* prices on a company's accounts. For example, in drawing up the year 1 balance sheet and income statement of Charon Chauffeuring, we use the nominal currency (e.g. the euro) as the **measurement unit**. By so doing, we assume that there is no change in general prices in Greece in year 1.

In practice, general prices do change: in most countries they rise year by year. As a result, a given nominal amount of currency buys fewer goods and services in the current year than it did in a prior one. Its purchasing power falls. This undermines its role as a measurement unit. It becomes impossible for a financial statement user to disentangle the effect of inflation on a company's accounts and to discover whether the firm has maintained its capital (financial or physical) in real terms.

To overcome this problem, a measurement unit is needed whose purchasing power is constant over time. Accountants have invented the **constant purchasing power unit**. The way it works is quite simple. First, a company (or the government on behalf of all companies) decides on a date on which it will measure its accounts in constant purchasing power (CPP) terms. It is known as the **measurement date**. The measurement date can be the end of the current financial year or some earlier date (e.g. 1 January 2000). Then the company adjusts its accounts for the change in purchasing power of the currency between the dates of the transactions and events underlying its nominal currency accounts and the measurement date. The adjusted financial statements are then stated in terms of the purchasing power of the currency on the measurement date.

Historical cost/CPP-based accounts

We illustrate **historical cost/CPP-based accounts** with a simple example. Elysian Fields, a property investment company, is founded on 1 January x6 with equity capital of 60. It borrows 40 on that date and invests its total cash of 100 in land. At the end of the year, it sells, for 120 in cash, part of the land costing 80. In nominal currency terms, it records a profit of 40 in that year. However, general prices rose 10% in x6. What is the company's profit in inflation-adjusted terms? How much can it distribute as dividend and preserve the owners' initial investment in real terms?

Exhibit 7.8 shows Elysian Fields' x6 accounts in nominal terms and restated on a CPP basis. The company chooses 31 December x6 as the measurement date for its CPP-based accounts. The accounts are simplified: interest on debt, administrative expenses and taxes are ignored.

Exhibit 7.8   Elysian Fields: x6 accounts on HC/CPP basis

Facts

Elysian Fields is founded on 1 January x6 with total capital of 100, of which 60 is equity and 40 debt. It invests 100 in land. At the end of x6, it sells, for 120 cash, land costing 80. Administrative expenses, interest and taxes are ignored. General prices rise 10% in x6. Constant purchasing power (CPP) accounts assume 31/12/x6 measurement date.

Financial statements for x6

	In nominal currency	Adjustment[1]	In CPP units
Income statement for x6			
Revenue	120	–	120
Cost of land sold	–80	110/100	–88
Profit	40		32
Purchasing power gain from holding debt[2]			+4
Profit including purchasing power gain			36
Balance sheet at 31/12/x6			
Land	20	110/100	22
Cash	120	–	120
Total assets	140		142
Owners' equity:			
Initial investment	60	110/100	66
Profit in x6	40	(see above)	36
	100		102
Debt	40	–	40
Total equities	140		142

Notes:

1. Assume general price level index stands at 100 on 1/1 and 110 on 31/12. No CPP adjustment is made to revenues since the land is sold at year-end. No CPP adjustment is made to cash or debt since the measurement date is 31/12/x6.
2. The company holds net debt throughout x6 while prices rise 10%. The cash required to pay off the debt has less purchasing power at year-end. In CPP terms, the company enjoys a gain of 4 (10% × 40).

The nature and timing of transactions and events determine the CPP adjustments a firm must make to its nominal accounts. Elysian Fields makes no adjustment to revenues in x6 since it sells land at the end of the year. The cost of the land sold must be adjusted, however. The general price index has increased by 10% since the date of purchase so the cash of 80 used to buy that parcel of land on 1 January x6 has purchasing power of 88 at 31 December x6.

The new item, 'Purchasing power gain', warrants explanation. If a company holds cash or other monetary assets during a period of general price increase, it suffers a loss in purchasing power because a given nominal amount of cash buys fewer goods at the end of the period than at the start. On the other hand, if it holds debt or other monetary liabilities during that period, it enjoys a gain in purchasing power: to repay the debt it gives up cash which has less buying power at the end of the period than at the beginning. In our example, Elysian Fields enjoys a purchasing power gain in x6 because it holds debt throughout the year when prices are rising. (It receives cash from the sale of land only at the end of x6.)

In drawing up a balance sheet in CPP units, firms distinguish between monetary and non-monetary items. *Monetary items consist of those assets and liabilities where the cash to be received or paid is contractually fixed.* (Cash is, of course, a monetary asset.) Where the measurement date is the balance sheet date, no CPP adjustments to monetary items are necessary. Elysian Fields' cash of 120 commands purchasing power of that amount at the end of x6. Similarly, the nominal amount of the company's debt (40) reflects the purchasing power it would give up to repay it at that date. Non-monetary items must be adjusted, however. The currency's purchasing power has declined by 10% since the company raised equity of 60 from its shareholders and bought the land (of 20) it still holds. In CPP terms, these balances should be 66 and 22 respectively.

We can look at the CPP-based accounts in another way. The currency of 60 invested in Elysian Fields by its owners at the start of x6 can purchase 66 of goods and services in end-x6 purchasing power terms. Any increase in the net assets of the firm (capital contributions and distributions excepted) above the 6 needed to preserve the purchasing power of the owners' investment is profit. The company's net assets at the end of x6 are, in fact, 102 in historical cost/CPP terms (142 less 40). Thus it reports CPP profits of 36 (102 – 66) that year. This is the maximum amount it can distribute without impairing the purchasing power of the owners' initial investment.

Current value/CPP-based accounts

In our example, we assume that Elysian Fields values its land at historical cost. However, it could use a current value basis and still seek to maintain the financial capital of its owners in real terms. The resulting accounts are then **current value/CPP-based** accounts.

For example, suppose that between the date the company buys the land (1/1/x6) and the date it sells it (31/12/x6) land prices increase 25%. Thus the replacement cost of the land sold is 100 (80 × 1.25) and that of the land still held at the end of the year is 25 (20 × 1.25). Exhibit 7.9 shows Elysian Fields' x6 accounts prepared on a RC/CPP basis.

Elysian Fields' RC/CPP profit of 39 in x6 is 3 greater than its HC/CPP profit (36: *see* Exhibit 7.8) because it takes into income the real holding gain on the land still held at year-end (25 – 22). The company could distribute that gain and the owners' financial investment – 66 in end-x6 purchasing power terms – would still be preserved.

Exhibit 7.9 illustrates a key point: the way a company values its assets is quite separate from its choice of measurement unit. The former captures *specific* price changes, the latter *general* price changes. Specific and general prices may move in different directions. It's quite possible for the replacement costs of a firm's inventories and plant to decline while prices in general are rising. (This has been the experience of the electronics industry in the last two decades.) Current value/CPP-based accounts capture both types of price movement.

| Exhibit 7.9 | Elysian Fields: x6 accounts on replacement cost/CPP basis |

Facts

As for Exhibit 7.8. In addition, land prices increase 25% during x6.

Financial statements for x6

Income statement for x6

Revenue from land sale		120
Current cost of land sold		−100
Current cost profit		20
Gain on holding land during x6:		
Nominal gain (100 × 25%)	25	
Less: Inflation element (100 × 10%)	−10	
Real holding gain		+15
Purchasing power gain from holding debt (Exhibit 7.8)		+4
Replacement cost/CPP profit		39

Balance sheet at 31/12/x6

		Owners' equity:	
Land (20 × 1.25)	25	Initial investment (restated at	
		CPP amount)	66
		Profit in x6	39
			105
Cash	120	Debt	40
Total assets	145	Total equities	145

Capital maintenance objective and measurement unit: accounting practice in Europe

EU company law directives make no explicit reference to financial or physical capital maintenance as a corporate objective. Implicitly, financial capital maintenance is the objective – in Europe and elsewhere – since historical cost (proceeds) is the principal basis of valuing assets (liabilities) in all countries.

An EU member state can permit firms to present CPP-based accounts since this is a method 'designed to take account of inflation' (4th Directive, Art. 33). In practice, EU firms (and those in other low-inflation countries) use the nominal currency as the measurement unit in their accounts. It's a different story in high-inflation economies. 'Indexation' of accounts – which usually involves making CPP adjustments to HC- or RC-based accounts – has been common in Latin American countries with a history of high inflation. International accounting standards require firms in a hyperinflationary economy to restate their accounts on a CPP basis.[12]

Subtle changes to this long-standing accounting model are occurring, however. New international accounting standards are altering the way firms implement the financial capital maintenance objective. Hitherto, where asset revaluations were permitted, any surplus on revaluation was taken directly to a reserve account in the balance sheet. Prudence, one of the fundamental accounting principles we discussed earlier, precludes the recognition of unrealised holding gains in income. Under fair value accounting which companies following IAS must use to value certain financial assets and liabilities (and may use to value properties held as investments), unrealised holding gains have to be reported in the income statement in certain circumstances. The EU's accounting directives have been modified to allow for this. However, the prudence principle still applies when other types of asset are revalued.

Summary

Management must make accounting decisions when they prepare their company's financial statements for publication. They must decide the firm's accounting policies – the methods to be used and estimates to be made when accounting for the many different types of transaction and event – and state them in the notes to the accounts. For some transactions, only one accounting method can be used; for others, management has a choice.

Accounting methods have many sources: company and tax law, accounting standards, custom, professional and management judgement. Underpinning the set of accounting methods in current use are four main 'principles' which have been distilled from accepted accounting practice. These are: *the going concern assumption, consistency, prudence* and *the accruals concept.* Management and auditors refer to these principles whenever they seek a solution to a new accounting problem.

In recent years, investors have campaigned for an improvement in the quality of corporate financial reports. In response, the IASB and other regulators launched a new programme: to issue tougher accounting standards which specify the method firms must use to account for a particular transaction and the disclosures it must make. (We explore these new standards in depth in later chapters.) To guide them in this task, regulators first set down a conceptual framework of accounting. This states that:

- *Providing useful information to investors is the main objective of financial reporting.*
- *Understandability, relevance, reliability and comparability are the principal qualities of useful information.*
- *Assets (resources controlled by the firm) and liabilities (obligations to transfer such resources) are the key elements of financial statements.* Other elements such as owners' equity and income statement items can be defined in terms of these key elements.
- *Assets and liabilities should be recognised in financial statements only if it is probable that a resource or obligation exists and it can be measured reliably.*

Unresolved are two key issues: *how should assets and liabilities be valued?* and – given that the firm aims to maintain its capital (income is, after all, the return on capital) – *what type of capital should it seek to maintain?* Although various valuation bases are in current use, most assets and liabilities are carried in the balance sheet at historical amounts. Maintenance of the owners' financial capital rather than the company's productive capacity is the objective – usually implicit – of management. However, in measuring financial capital, firms rarely adjust for changes in the purchasing power of the currency, except in high-inflation economies.

APPENDIX 7.1   An overview of the IASB and its predecessor, the IASC

The International Accounting Standards Board (IASB) was set up in 2001. It replaces the International Accounting Standards Committee which was established in 1973. The goals of the Board and the Committee are the same: to improve and, at the same time, harmonise accounting and reporting practices worldwide through the issuance of accounting standards.

Structure of IASB

The IASB is responsible for developing new international accounting standards. The standard-setting structure is designed to ensure the Board is both independent and expert. Board members are chosen largely for their technical expertise. Twelve of the fourteen work full-time at the Board. The Board is supported by technical staff and advised by an international council. It is also assisted by an Interpretations Committee (IC), a body of twelve experts chaired usually by a Board member or senior member of the technical staff, that provides guidance on how to apply or interpret existing accounting standards.

Board (and IC) members are appointed by an international foundation. The foundation is also responsible for fund-raising. Trustees of the foundation are chosen to ensure diversity of geographical and professional background. A trustee cannot be a Board or IC member.

The IASB and IC follow accepted due process procedures. Meetings are open to the public. Exposure drafts of standards (and interpretations) are published and comments are invited from interested parties. When a new standard is issued, the Board publishes an explanation of its decisions.

The IASC's achievements and the challenge for the IASB

The decision in 1973 to set up an agency, the IASC, to produce global accounting rules was a private initiative. (It still is – hence the need for fund-raising.) At that time, international investors and financial institutions were concerned about the variation in the quality of financial accounting and reporting across countries. It made capital allocation more difficult and costly – and this raised the cost of capital for firms.

In its first 15–20 years, the IASC made little impact. Few companies used IAS either in their primary accounts or in supplementary statements. As standards became more numerous and rigorous, however, support for them in the investment and political communities grew. In 1995, IOSCO, the organisation representing international securities' regulators, agreed to accept IAS-based financial statements submitted by companies seeking cross-border listings of their securities – on condition that the IASC developed a tougher set of standards. International standards received a further fillip in 2000 when the European Commission decided to require all listed EU companies (estimated at 6,700 that year) to file consolidated accounts according to IAS from 2005. This was a major coup for the IASC: only 275 EU companies were using IAS in 2000. The final hurdle, not yet achieved, is SEC acceptance of the equivalence of IAS-based and US GAAP-based financial statements: then non-US companies with securities listed on a US stock exchange need prepare only one set of consolidated accounts.

The IASC issued 41 standards (and 24 interpretations) in its 28-year existence. The 34 standards – or IAS – in force in mid-2002 are listed in Exhibit 7.10. It also published a conceptual framework of financial accounting, *Framework for the Preparation and Presentation of Financial Statements*, to assist it in developing new standards.

Despite its achievements, the IASC faced considerable criticism, especially from the North American investment community. It was accused of having poor governance, many of its standards were allegedly lax, and its efforts to enforce its standards were ineffective. The structure of the IASB, the IASC's successor, is designed to overcome the first criticism. Note especially the separation of fund-raising from standard-setting activities. The new agency plans to address the second criticism by revising existing standards and introducing new ones. (These will be known as International Financial Reporting Standards, or IFRS.) Topics on the initial agenda include: business combinations, consolidation, leases, reporting business performance and share-based compensation.

Exhibit 7.10 International Accounting Standards issued as of June 2002

IAS no.*	Title
1	Presentation of Financial Statements
2	Inventories
7	Cash Flow Statements
8	Net Profit or Loss for the Period, Fundamental Errors and Changes in Accounting Policies
10	Events After the Balance Sheet Date
11	Construction Contracts
12	Income Taxes
14	Segment Reporting
15	Information Reflecting the Effects of Changing Prices
16	Property, Plant and Equipment
17	Leases
18	Revenue
19	Employee Benefits
20	Accounting for Government Grants and Disclosure of Government Assistance
21	The Effects of Changes in Foreign Exchange Rates
22	Business Combinations
23	Borrowing Costs
24	Related Party Disclosures
26	Accounting and Reporting by Retirement Benefit Plans
27	Consolidated Financial Statements and Accounting for Investments in Subsidiaries
28	Accounting for Investments in Associates
29	Financial Reporting in Hyperinflationary Economies
30	Disclosures in the Financial Statements of Banks and Similar Financial Institutions
31	Financial Reporting of Interests in Joint Ventures
32	Financial Instruments: Disclosure and Presentation
33	Earnings Per Share
34	Interim Financial Reporting
35	Discontinuing Operations
36	Impairment of Assets
37	Provisions, Contingent Liabilities and Contingent Assets
38	Intangible Assets
39	Financial Instruments: Recognition and Measurement
40	Investment Property
41	Agriculture

* Seven standards (3, 4, 5, 6, 9, 13 and 25) have been superseded.

The third criticism is more difficult for the IASB to deal with. Accounting standard-setting agencies do not usually have policing powers. These rest with separate bodies (e.g. the SEC in the USA, the Financial Services Authority in the UK). There is recent evidence that some companies have applied international standards incorrectly and have not observed all IAS disclosure requirements.[13] This may be due in part to company financial officers and auditors not being familiar with international standards. A more likely explanation is the absence of an agency enforcing international standards: national financial regulators or stock exchanges may have to assume this role.

Present value concepts – an introduction

The aim of this appendix is to explain briefly the concept of present value and to illustrate its application in financial accounting. A more detailed presentation can be found in a finance textbook.

You are familiar with the old saying: 'A euro (or dollar, yen, peso, etc.) today is worth more than a euro tomorrow'. The reason is simple. A euro can be invested today and by tomorrow it will be worth today's euro plus the interest earned in the intervening period. Given an interest rate of r in a period and an investment of C, the future value, F, of that investment at the end of the period will be:

$$F = C\,(1 + r)$$

With positive interest rates, F is clearly greater than C. The future value of a euro invested today is expected to be greater than its present value.

There is another side to this coin. An investor will pay *less* than one euro today for an investment that is expected to yield one euro tomorrow. Using our notation:

$$C = F \times \frac{1}{(1 + r)}$$

If F is the amount expected in the future, the investor will only pay C, the fraction $1/(1 + r)$ of F, today in order to secure that return.

An example will help here. Suppose Marianne, a Dijon mustard supplier, has a customer, John Bull, an English producer of roast beef dinners, who is experiencing financial difficulties. Bull offers to pay 20,000, the current balance on his account, in one year's time. If Marianne receives that money now, she can invest it, say at 10%, for that period. How much is Bull's offer worth to Marianne? The answer is:

$$C = 20{,}000 \times \frac{1}{(1 + 0.1)}$$

$$= 20{,}000 \times 0.9091$$

$$= \underline{18{,}182}$$

The 20,000 in one year's time is clearly worth less than 20,000 received today. In fact, the present value of that future sum is only 18,182, given the current annual interest rate of 10%.

The logic can be extended. A euro tomorrow is worth more than a euro received the day after tomorrow. Suppose Bull's financial condition deteriorates. He asks Marianne for a *two*-year extension to pay the debt of 20,000. This means Marianne will forgo two years' interest on this sum. We can express the present value of this future sum as:

$$C = F \times \frac{1}{(1 + r)^2}$$

If the interest rate on a two-year investment (of 20,000) is still 10% a year, the present value of John Bull's proposed payment terms is:

$$20{,}000 \times \frac{1}{(1 + 0.1)^2}$$

$$= 20{,}000 \times 0.8264$$

$$= \underline{16{,}528}$$

The manager of Marianne's credit department reckons that a two-year extension is too generous and suggests Bull repay half the 20,000 in one year's time and the balance at the end of the second year. Would Marianne be better off under her manager's proposal or under Bull's? The present value of the credit manager's proposed payment terms is:

$$\left(10{,}000 \times \frac{1}{(1 + 0.1)}\right) + \left(10{,}000 \times \frac{1}{(1 + 0.1)^2}\right)$$

$$= (10{,}000 \times 0.9091) \quad + (10{,}000 \times 0.8264)$$

$$= \underline{17{,}355}$$

(We assume a 10% interest rate can be earned each year.)

Not surprisingly, the manager's suggestion is more advantageous to Marianne. This is because the 10,000 received at the end of year 1 can be reinvested then, yielding an expected 1,000 (10,000 × 10%) at the end of year 2. When discounted to today, this is equivalent to 826 (1,000 × 0.8264), the difference (after rounding) between the present values of the two proposals (17,355 − 16,528).

We introduced a new term, 'discounted', in the last paragraph. The procedure of finding the present value of future cash inflows or outflows is referred to as **discounting**. The interest rate on investment opportunities forgone, which is used in present value calculations, is often known as the **discount rate**. And the multiples applied to future cash sums – in our example, 0.9091 and 0.8264 (or, more generally, $(1 + r)^{-1}$, $(1 + r)^{-2}$, ... $(1 + r)^{-n}$) – are described as **discount factors**.

Discounting is the obverse of compounding. Where compound interest rather than simple interest is in force, interest is earned or incurred on prior interest as well as the principal of the investment or debt. Similarly, discount factors reflect interest forgone not just on the principal but also on the prior interest.

Over long time periods, the effect of 'lost interest on interest' can be substantial. Suppose a company issues ten-year bonds which pay no interest. (Such bonds are known as 'zero coupon bonds'.) The purchaser of a bond receives on the maturity of the bond (at the end of ten years) 1,000, the par value of the bond. How much would an investor pay for one such bond, assuming that, at the time of issuance, the market rate of interest for bonds of equivalent risk is 12% a year?

To answer this question, we need to find the present value of a future sum, 1,000, where the discount factor, $1/(1 + r)^n$, is based on an interest rate r of 12% and a period n of ten years. The investor should pay no more than 322 for the bond:

$$1{,}000 \times \frac{1}{(1 + 0.12)^{10}} = 1{,}000 \times 0.322$$

$$= \underline{\underline{322}}$$

The 1,000 the investor receives on the bond's maturity will exactly compensate her for the loss of interest (compounded annually) on her 322 in the intervening ten years.

Use of present value tables

How do we obtain discount factors in practice? After all, computing $1/(1 + 0.12)^{10}$ by hand is a time-consuming and error-prone exercise, though many hand calculators and computer spreadsheet packages contain present value computational routines. Present value tables are presented in Exhibit 7.11 for the benefit of those who don't have access to other sources. They're also of help to the calculator- and computer-blessed, because they provide a way of checking calculations.

A short explanation of the tables follows. Table 1 presents discount factors. It shows the present value of one unit of currency (euro, dollar, yen, etc.) received or paid in the future, for a range

Exhibit 7.11 Present value tables

Table 1 Present value (PV) of 1 euro (or other currency unit)

Periods	1%	1.5%	2%	2.5%	3%	4%	5%	6%	7%	8%	9%	10%	12%	15%	20%
1	0.990	0.985	0.980	0.976	0.971	0.962	0.952	0.943	0.935	0.926	0.917	0.909	0.893	0.870	0.833
2	0.980	0.971	0.961	0.952	0.943	0.925	0.907	0.890	0.873	0.857	0.842	0.826	0.797	0.756	0.694
3	0.971	0.956	0.942	0.929	0.915	0.889	0.864	0.840	0.816	0.794	0.772	0.751	0.712	0.658	0.579
4	0.961	0.942	0.924	0.906	0.888	0.855	0.823	0.792	0.763	0.735	0.708	0.683	0.636	0.572	0.482
5	0.951	0.928	0.906	0.884	0.863	0.822	0.784	0.747	0.713	0.681	0.650	0.621	0.567	0.497	0.402
6	0.942	0.915	0.888	0.862	0.837	0.790	0.746	0.705	0.666	0.630	0.596	0.564	0.507	0.432	0.335
7	0.933	0.901	0.871	0.841	0.813	0.760	0.711	0.665	0.623	0.583	0.547	0.513	0.452	0.376	0.279
8	0.923	0.888	0.853	0.821	0.789	0.731	0.677	0.627	0.582	0.540	0.502	0.467	0.404	0.327	0.233
9	0.914	0.875	0.837	0.801	0.766	0.703	0.645	0.592	0.544	0.500	0.460	0.424	0.361	0.284	0.194
10	0.905	0.862	0.820	0.781	0.744	0.676	0.614	0.558	0.508	0.463	0.422	0.386	0.322	0.247	0.162
11	0.896	0.849	0.804	0.762	0.722	0.650	0.585	0.527	0.475	0.429	0.388	0.350	0.287	0.215	0.135
12	0.887	0.836	0.788	0.744	0.701	0.625	0.557	0.497	0.444	0.397	0.356	0.319	0.257	0.187	0.112
13	0.879	0.824	0.773	0.725	0.681	0.601	0.530	0.469	0.415	0.368	0.326	0.290	0.229	0.163	0.093
14	0.870	0.812	0.758	0.708	0.661	0.577	0.505	0.442	0.388	0.340	0.299	0.263	0.205	0.141	0.078
15	0.861	0.800	0.743	0.690	0.642	0.555	0.481	0.417	0.362	0.315	0.275	0.239	0.183	0.123	0.065
16	0.853	0.788	0.728	0.674	0.623	0.534	0.458	0.394	0.339	0.292	0.252	0.218	0.163	0.107	0.054
17	0.844	0.776	0.714	0.657	0.605	0.513	0.436	0.371	0.317	0.270	0.231	0.198	0.146	0.093	0.045
18	0.836	0.765	0.700	0.641	0.587	0.494	0.416	0.350	0.296	0.250	0.212	0.180	0.130	0.081	0.038
19	0.828	0.754	0.686	0.626	0.570	0.475	0.396	0.331	0.277	0.232	0.194	0.164	0.116	0.070	0.031
20	0.820	0.742	0.673	0.610	0.554	0.456	0.377	0.312	0.258	0.215	0.178	0.149	0.104	0.061	0.026
25	0.780	0.689	0.610	0.539	0.478	0.375	0.295	0.233	0.184	0.146	0.116	0.092	0.059	0.030	0.011
30	0.742	0.640	0.552	0.477	0.412	0.308	0.231	0.174	0.131	0.099	0.075	0.057	0.033	0.015	0.004
40	0.672	0.551	0.453	0.372	0.307	0.208	0.142	0.097	0.067	0.046	0.032	0.022	0.011	0.004	0.001
50	0.608	0.475	0.372	0.291	0.228	0.141	0.087	0.054	0.034	0.021	0.013	0.009	0.003	<.001	<.001

Discount rate across the top.

Table 2 Present value of an annuity (PVA) of 1 euro (or other currency unit) in arrears*

Payments	1%	1.5%	2%	2.5%	3%	4%	5%	6%	7%	8%	9%	10%	12%	15%	20%
1	0.990	0.985	0.980	0.976	0.971	0.962	0.952	0.943	0.935	0.926	0.917	0.909	0.893	0.870	0.833
2	1.970	1.956	1.942	1.927	1.913	1.886	1.859	1.833	1.808	1.783	1.759	1.736	1.690	1.626	1.528
3	2.941	2.912	2.884	2.856	2.829	2.775	2.723	2.673	2.624	2.577	2.531	2.487	2.402	2.283	2.106
4	3.902	3.854	3.808	3.762	3.717	3.630	3.546	3.465	3.387	3.312	3.240	3.170	3.037	2.855	2.589
5	4.853	4.783	4.713	4.646	4.580	4.452	4.329	4.212	4.100	3.993	3.890	3.791	3.605	3.352	2.991
6	5.795	5.697	5.601	5.508	5.417	5.242	5.076	4.917	4.767	4.623	4.486	4.355	4.111	3.785	3.326
7	6.728	6.598	6.472	6.350	6.230	6.002	5.786	5.582	5.389	5.206	5.033	4.868	4.564	4.160	3.605
8	7.652	7.486	7.325	7.170	7.020	6.733	6.463	6.210	5.971	5.747	5.535	5.335	4.968	4.487	3.837
9	8.566	8.361	8.162	7.971	7.786	7.435	7.108	6.802	6.515	6.247	5.995	5.759	5.328	4.772	4.031
10	9.471	9.222	8.983	8.752	8.530	8.111	7.722	7.360	7.024	6.710	6.418	6.145	5.650	5.019	4.192
11	10.368	10.071	9.787	9.514	9.253	8.760	8.306	7.887	7.499	7.139	6.805	6.495	5.938	5.234	4.327
12	11.255	10.908	10.575	10.258	9.954	9.385	8.863	8.384	7.943	7.536	7.161	6.814	6.194	5.421	4.439
13	12.134	11.732	11.348	10.983	10.635	9.986	9.394	8.853	8.358	7.904	7.487	7.103	6.424	5.583	4.533
14	13.004	12.543	12.106	11.691	11.296	10.563	9.899	9.295	8.745	8.244	7.786	7.367	6.628	5.724	4.611
15	13.865	13.343	12.849	12.381	11.938	11.118	10.380	9.712	9.108	8.559	8.061	7.606	6.811	5.847	4.675
16	14.718	14.131	13.578	13.055	12.561	11.652	10.838	10.106	9.447	8.851	8.313	7.824	6.974	5.954	4.730
17	15.562	14.908	14.292	13.712	13.166	12.166	11.274	10.477	9.763	9.122	8.543	8.022	7.120	6.047	4.775
18	16.398	15.673	14.992	14.353	13.754	12.659	11.690	10.828	10.059	9.372	8.756	8.201	7.250	6.128	4.812
19	17.226	16.426	15.678	14.979	14.324	13.134	12.085	11.158	10.336	9.604	8.950	8.365	7.366	6.198	4.844
20	18.046	17.169	16.351	15.589	14.877	13.590	12.462	11.470	10.594	9.818	9.129	8.514	7.469	6.259	4.870
25	22.020	20.720	19.525	18.424	17.413	15.623	14.094	12.783	11.654	10.675	9.822	9.077	7.843	6.464	4.948
30	25.808	24.016	22.396	20.932	19.600	17.292	15.372	13.765	12.409	11.258	10.274	9.427	8.055	6.566	4.979
40	32.835	29.916	27.355	25.104	23.115	19.793	17.159	15.046	13.332	11.925	10.757	9.779	8.244	6.642	4.997
50	39.196	35.000	31.424	28.364	25.730	21.482	18.256	15.762	13.801	12.233	10.962	9.915	8.305	6.661	4.999

Discount rate across the top.

* To calculate the present value of an annuity in advance, find the annuity in arrears for one less payment and add 1.

of periods n and interest rates r. To determine the discount factor where $n =$ ten years and $r = 12\%$, find the intersection of row $n = 10$ and column $r = 12\%$. The discount factor rounded to three decimal places is 0.322.

Table 2 presents annuity factors. This table can be used when a constant sum is expected to be received (or paid) each period for n periods. The formula for the annuity factor:

$$\frac{1}{r} - \frac{1}{r(1+r)^n}$$

is simply the difference between the factor for an annuity received in perpetuity from today $(1/r)$ and that for an annuity to be received n periods hence and discounted back to today:

$$\frac{1}{r} \times \frac{1}{(1+r)^n}$$

Table 2 has a direct relationship to Table 1. You'll notice that the annuity factors are equivalent to the discount factors for a particular r accumulated up to period n. We can see this from the example of John Bull, the slow-paying debtor. Remember the proposal of Marianne's manager – that Bull pay 10,000 at the end of each of the next two years? Originally we used discount factors to find the present values of these cash flows:

$$(10,000 \times 0.9091) + (10,000 \times 0.8264) = 17,355$$

Using the annuity factor table, we find the annuity factor for $n = 2$ and $r = 10\%$ which is 1.736. Thus the present value of this two-year stream of constant cash flows is:

$$10,000 \times 1.736 = 17,360$$

In effect, the annuity factor in this case is the sum of the two discount factors for $n = 1$ and $n = 2$. (The difference is due to rounding to three instead of four decimal places.) The annuity factor table is particularly useful where we need to determine the present value of constant amounts which are to be received or paid over long periods (e.g. interest on long-term fixed-rate debt).

Timing of cash flows

The factors shown in Tables 1 and 2 are derived under the assumption that the cash flows to be discounted occur at the end of the period. This raises two issues. First, what is meant by a 'period'? Second, what discounting procedure should be used if cash flows occur other than at the end of the period?

A period can be a year or a fraction of it. If the latter, the discount rate r must be adjusted so that it's based on the same interval of time. For example, if interest on long-term debt is paid semi-annually at a 12% nominal annual rate, this is equivalent to compounding at a 6% rate every six months or 12.36% $[\{(1.06)^2 - 1\} \times 100]$ compounded annually. Generalising from this, a nominal interest rate of $r\%$ a year compounded m times a year is equivalent to an annually compounded rate of $[\{(1 + [r/m])^m - 1\} \times 100]$. It follows that, where the interest rate is compounded m times a year, the discount factor for period n is:

$$\frac{1}{(1 + [r/m])^{mn}}$$

We can use the tables to handle different compounding multiples m. For example, if we wish to find the present value of a ten-year stream of semi-annual interest payments on a ten-year 12% bond issued at par value of 100, we go to the intersection of the 20 period row and the 6% (12%/2) column of Table 2 to obtain the annuity factor (in this case 11.470) to apply to the constant semi-annual interest payment.

End-of-period discount factors are widely used, even when strictly they are not appropriate. The error from employing end-of-period factors when the cash flows occur during the period is likely to be small, especially in relation to the potential error from mis-estimating future cash flows. There are two circumstances when companies abandon end-of-period discount factors: first, when it is known that cash will be received or paid at the start of the period; second, where cash flows are expected to occur continuously (and evenly) over the period.

The first case is easy to accommodate. The start of period n is equivalent to the end of period $n - 1$. Where $n = 1$, the cash flows occur at time zero, i.e. today, and the discount factor is 1.0. Tables 1 and 2 can be adapted easily, too. For Table 1, simply add 1 to the numbering of the rows. Thus the factors shown against the '$n = 5$' row in Table 1 are equivalent to '$n = 6$' when cash flows occur at the start of the period. As we've seen, where $n = 1$, the discount factor for all r is 1.0. As for Table 2, to determine the annuity factor for n payments when cash flows occur at the start of the period, find the annuity factor for $n - 1$ payments in Table 2 and add 1.0 to it.

Where cash flows are expected to be continuous and even, discount and annuity factors based on a continuous compounding assumption should be used. Consult a finance text for more details. We shall assume cash flows occur only at the start or end of periods in this book.

Problem assignments

P7.1 Unusual events: accounting treatment

Consider the following events. How do you think each should be accounted for in the light of the IASB's conceptual framework described in the chapter?

(a) A company buys 1,000 national lottery tickets at 1 euro each. (To win, a punter must choose six correct numbers between 0 and 90.) There is no secondary market for lottery tickets.

(b) An oil company is unsure how and when it should account for future field abandonment costs. It has just installed a production platform to develop a large oil field it has discovered in the Baltic Sea. Under environmental regulations governing oil production in these waters, it must remove and dismantle the platform at the end of the field's economic life in 20 years' time. The company reckons it can estimate the dismantlement and other abandonment costs reasonably accurately.

(c) A quoted company pays an annual bonus to senior managers, based on its profit performance in the year. To save cash, it decides to pay the bonus in the form of new shares – which in the current year involves the distribution of 100,000 shares. At the date of the award, it recognises compensation expense at the nominal value of the shares issued. Each share's nominal value is five euros. Its market value at this time is 20 euros.

P7.2 Accounting for pre-contract costs

Amey is a UK-based support services group. It provides a range of services – from IT support to property maintenance – for public sector and private sector organisations that have decided to outsource these activities. According to the chief executive, 2001 was a good year. Group revenues increased 19% to £786 million. The company had an 80% bid success rate, winning contracts with a total value of £1,890 million that year. However, 2002 saw it competing for major London Underground modernisation contracts and there were doubts whether it could maintain this bid success rate.

The company changed the way it accounted for pre-contract costs in its 2001 accounts. Until then, it had capitalised as an asset (under 'deferred charges') the costs incurred in bidding for new contracts where it was reasonably certain it would recover the costs. (Evidence of 'reasonable certainty' was a cost indemnity or the company's appointment as preferred bidder.) Capitalised costs were amortised against income arising on the related contracts. The new policy is to expense immediately all pre-contract costs unless reimbursement is assured.

The effect of the change in policy on the group's 2001 accounts was significant. Profit before tax was reduced by £28.5 million. Together with other accounting changes introduced at the same time, this turned a £15 million profit into a loss (before tax) of £18.2 million.

Amey's management justified the change in policy on the grounds that it was consistent with proposed UK accounting guidelines on the topic. However, the draft rules only required companies to expense immediately pre-contract costs that did not meet specified cost recovery tests. Moreover, Amey's competitors did not change their accounting policies in 2001 and continued to capitalise certain pre-contract costs. An analyst commented at the time:

> 'Amey has interpreted [the draft rules] very prudently indeed, more so than any other company has contemplated before.'

Required

(a) Under what circumstances should pre-contract costs be recorded as an asset in your view?

(b) Why do you think Amey changed its accounting policy on pre-contract costs in 2001?

P7.3 Effect of alternative valuation bases on accounts

On 1 January x1, Exprés Company, a distributor of ultra-fast ('Josep') coffee-making machines, has 30 in stock with a unit historical cost (and current value) of 2,500 (units of local currency). The company's balance sheet on that date is as follows:

Inventory	75,000	Shareholders' equity	75,000

The company sells, for cash, 20 machines at 4,000 each at the end of December x1. It has no other revenues or expenses that year.

Because of the strong demand for the Josep coffee-making machines, the manufacturer increases the price to distributors by 20% to 3,000 at end-x1.

Required

Draw up Exprés Company's x1 income statement and end-x1 balance sheet, assuming it values the coffee-making machines at:

(a) historical cost;

(b) replacement cost.

Assume any holding gains arising under (b) are included in profit for the year.

Check figure:
(b) Total assets 110,000

P7.4 Effect of alternative capital maintenance objectives on accounts

Assume the same facts as in P7.3. In addition, general prices increase by 10% between the start and end of x1.

Required

(1) Draw up Exprés Company's x1 accounts assuming it uses, as the measurement unit, the purchasing power of the currency at the end of x1 and it values its coffee-making machines at:
(a) historical cost;
(b) replacement cost.

(2) What is the maximum amount of x1 profit that the company can distribute as dividend on 1 January x2, and still maintain:

(a) its financial capital in nominal currency?

(b) its financial capital in end-x1 purchasing power terms, assuming:

(i) it values inventory at HC?

(ii) it values inventory at RC?

(c) its physical capital in nominal currency?

Check figure:
(2)(b)(ii) 27,500

P7.5 CPP accounting: purchasing power gains and losses

Exprés Company decides to finance part of its assets with debt. Assume its start-x1 balance sheet is as follows:

Inventory	75,000	Shareholders' equity	50,000
		Debt	25,000
Total assets	75,000	Total equities	75,000

The annual interest rate on the debt is 15%. Interest is paid in cash at year-end. All other facts are the same as in P7.3 and P7.4, i.e. start-x1 inventory comprises 30 machines at 2,500 each, 20 are sold at end-x1 – each for 4,000 cash – when the replacement cost is 3,000, and general prices increase 10% in x1.

Required

Draw up Exprés Company's x1 accounts, assuming it uses the end-x1 purchasing power of the currency and it values the coffee-making machines at:

(a) historical cost;

(b) replacement cost.

Check figure:
Profit for year: (a) 23,750; (b) 26,250

P7.6 Long-term debt: impact of alternative valuation bases

On 1 January x1, Sylvie Company borrows €750,000 for five years at a fixed interest rate of 6% from Old Goriot Bank. Under the terms of the agreement, it pays interest of €45,000 on 31 December each year between x1 and x5 and repays the principal of €750,000 on 31 December x5.

During x1, market interest rates fall. By end-x1, when Sylvie Company prepares its accounts for the year, the interest rate on debt of equivalent maturity and risk is 5%. As a result, the current value of the loan at 31 December x1 (after payment of interest for the year) is €776,595. (This is the present value, as of 31/12/x1, of future loan payments discounted at 5%.)

Required

(a) Show the impact of the €750,000 loan on Sylvie Company's x1 income statement and end-x1 balance sheet, assuming the debt is valued at:

(i) historical cost;

(ii) current value.

(b) Suppose the current market interest rate remains at 5% in x2. What is the impact of the €750,000 loan on Sylvie Company's x2 income statement and end-x2 balance sheet, assuming the debt is valued at current value? The current value of the loan at 31 December x2 is €770,424.

P7.7 Effect of falling prices on corporate financial statements

General prices can decrease as well as increase. The most notable example of a country that has experienced falling prices in recent years is Japan. After rising slightly between 1990 and 1994, general prices – as measured by the GDP deflator – declined by 2.3% between 1994 and 1999. They fell by 1.5% in 1999 alone.

A decline in the general price level undermines reported numbers in company accounts. The effect is the opposite of that of rising prices. Set out below are summary 1999 financial statements for Japan Inc. – the combined income statements and balance sheets of some 2.5 million non-financial companies in Japan, before adjustment for changing prices. (Amounts are in billions of yen.)

Japan Inc.
Summary 1999 accounts

Income statement for year

Sales	1,383,464
Cost of sales (including depreciation of 41,690)	−1,076,441
Sales and general management costs	−277,753
Operating profits	29,270
Financial and other non-operating income	+19,432
Financial and other non-operating expenses	−21,778
Recurring profits	26,924
Special profits and losses	−14,281
Profit before tax	12,643
Corporate income tax and inhabitant tax	−10,475
Net profit	2,168

Balance sheet, end-year

Assets	1999	1998	Liabilities and capital	1999	1998
Cash and deposits	134,657	133,415	Bills and accounts payable	182,315	204,494
Bills and accounts receivable	224,076	225,886	Short-term borrowings	180,978	189,511
Inventories	115,793	134,470	Other current liabilities	171,655	182,466
Other current assets	113,599	138,097	Current liabilities	534,948	576,471
Current assets	588,125	631,868			
			Long-term borrowings	322,518	369,046
Tangible fixed assets, net	495,943	498,514	Other long-term liabilities	140,212	114,711
[of which: Land	170,314	162,374]	Long-term liabilities	462,730	483,757
Intangibles	15,158	17,923			
Investments and other	183,039	161,954	Share capital	81,482	78,131
Fixed assets	694,140	678,391	Share premium	47,594	42,581
			Revenue reserves	157,903	131,606
Deferred charges	2,650	2,540	Special legal reserve	257	253
			Capital and reserves	287,236	252,571
Total assets	1,284,915	1,312,799	Total liabilities and capital	1,284,914	1,312,799

Source: Statistics Bureau, Government of Japan, *Statistical Yearbook 2002*, Table 5-11.

Required

Assess the impact of the decline in general prices on Japan Inc's reported 1999 income. What is the likely effect of the decline – in directional terms (i.e. + or −) – on (a) operating profits and (b) recurring profits that year, assuming HC/CPP accounting? Give reasons for your answers.

P7.8 Valuation using present value methods*

(1) Valuation of bonds at issuance

Company X raises €20 million in cash by issuing five-year 5% bonds to investors on 2 January x1. (Bonds are interest-bearing securities with, in most cases, a stated maturity date.) The company will pay interest annually in the amount of 1 million euros at the end of each of the five years x1 to x5. The principal of the bonds (€20 million) will be paid in full on 31 December x5.

Required

What is the present value of the bonds, at time of issuance, if the market rate of interest for bonds of equivalent risk at that date is:

(a) 5%?

(b) 6%?

(2) Valuation of leased equipment and effect on accounts

Company Y is considering leasing computer equipment. The annual lease payment is €100,000 which the company must pay at the start of each year of the lease contract. The term of the lease is four years, which is also the expected economic life of the equipment. If the company buys the equipment with debt, the annual cost of borrowing will be 8%.

Required

(a) What is the present value of the lease payments under this contract?

(b) Assume the present value of the lease payments represents the market value of the computer equipment at the date the lease contract is signed (and the first payment is made). If Company Y is viewed as the economic owner of the computer equipment (because it will enjoy the economic benefits the equipment is expected to provide), how do you think Company Y should report the lease in its financial statements at the contract date?

(3) Calculation of pension contribution

Company Z wants to set up a pension scheme for its current president that will give her (and her surviving spouse) an annual income of €250,000 for 20 years, starting when she retires in five years' time. She will receive her pension at the end of each year. To ensure there are sufficient assets available to meet these payments, the company plans to make annual contributions to its pension fund over the next five years. Assume the annual discount rate used by the pension fund to discount its liabilities and the expected annual rate of return on fund investments are both 6%.

Required

(a) How much should the company contribute each year to the fund during the president's remaining working life? Assume the annual contribution is made at the end of the year.

(b) How do you think the company and the pension fund should record the annual contribution to the fund?

* Problem draws on material in Appendix 7.2.

Notes to Chapter 7

1 The discussion in this section owes much to work by Nobes (*see* Nobes, C. (1992), *International Classification of Financial Reporting*, London: Routledge). The best known early attempt to classify accounting regimes was made by Mueller (*see* Mueller, G. (1967), *International Accounting*, New York: Macmillan).

2 La Porta, R., Lopez-de-Silanes, F., Shleifer, A. and Vishny, R. (1998), Law and finance, *Journal of Political Economy*, 106: 1113–1155. In a separate study, the authors found that debt markets were also larger and broader in common law countries (*see* La Porta, R., Lopez-de-Silanes, F., Shleifer, A. and Vishny, R. (1997), Legal determinants of external finance, *Journal of Finance*, 52: 1131–1150).

3 La Porta *et al.* derive an antidirector rights index separately for French code law, German code law and Scandinavian code law countries (ibid. (1998), table 2, pp. 1130–1131). I have combined the index scores for all code law countries here.

4 To construct the disclosure index, the authors examined annual reports for inclusion or omission of 90 items covering general information, income statement, balance sheet, cash/funds flow statement, accounting standards, stock data and special items. The average score for common law countries is 69.6, that for code law countries 56.9 (ibid. (1998), pp. 1142–1143).

5 There are now many English-language sources of information on national accounting practice within Europe. Among the most up-to-date are: Roberts, C., Weetman, P. and Gordon, P. (2001), *International Financial Accounting*, 2nd edition, London: FT/Prentice Hall; Alexander, D. and Archer, S. (eds) (2001), *European Accounting Guide*, 4th edition, New York: Aspen Law & Business; Ordelheide, D. and KPMG (eds) (2001), *Transnational Accounting*, 2nd edition, Basingstoke: Palgrave; and the tax and business guides of the major international public accounting firms.

6 The directive mentions two other general 'principles'. The components of individual assets and liabilities must be valued separately. And the beginning balance sheet of a period should agree with the ending balance sheet of the previous period.

7 In addition to the going concern assumption, the accruals concept and consistency, the IASB includes materiality ('Each material item should be presented separately in the financial statements') and offsetting ('Assets and liabilities should not be offset [unless permitted or required by an IAS]') among the 'overall considerations' that should underlie financial statements (*IAS 1: Presentation of Financial Statements*).

8 The IASB's position is set out in full in its *Framework for the Preparation and Presentation of Financial Statements*. (In fact, the *Framework* was drawn up by the IASB's predecessor, the IASC.) One issue not addressed in the *Framework* is the meaning of 'entity', in accounting. We know from our discussion of sole proprietorships and corporate groups in Chapter 1 that an accounting entity is not necessarily the same as a legal entity. We investigate this issue further in a later chapter on consolidation accounting.

9 Relevance and reliability are considered the two most important characteristics of useful information and the IASB explores the accounting dimensions of each. For example, materiality and relevance are linked. 'Information is material if its omission or misstatement could influence the economic decisions' of financial statement users (IASB, *Framework*, para. 30). Thus information must be material to be relevant. Similarly, reliability is linked to another hallowed concept in accounting, 'substance over form'. The IASB argues that only when accounts reflect the economic substance of transactions do they 'faithfully represent' events. Faithful representation, along with neutrality and completeness, are key aspects of reliable information.

10 Bonbright, J.C. (1937), *Valuation of Property*, Charlottesville, VA: Michie, p. 71.

11 Report of the Inflation Accounting Committee (Chairman: F.E.P. Sandilands) (1975), *Inflation Accounting*, London: HMSO, pp. 57–60.

12 IASB, *IAS 29: Financial Reporting in Hyperinflationary Economies*. One indicator of a hyperinflationary economy, according to the IASB, is a cumulative three-year inflation rate that approaches, or exceeds, 100%.

13 Cairns, D. (2000), *The International Accounting Standards Survey 2000*. The Survey is updated annually: *see* www.cairns.co.uk.

8

Fixed assets, tangible and intangible

INTRODUCTION

Accounting for, and reporting of, tangible and intangible fixed assets is the subject of this chapter. (The accounting for financial fixed assets is covered in later chapters.) *Tangible and intangible fixed assets are resources of the firm which are expected to generate future benefits indirectly: they are used to produce the goods or services which themselves generate cash.*

Fixed assets with physical substance – land, buildings, equipment – are referred to as 'tangible assets'. Non-monetary assets without physical substance – purchased patents, trademarks, licences – are described as 'intangible assets'. To keep the terminology simple, we shall often refer to tangible and intangible fixed assets collectively as fixed assets.

In section 1 of the chapter we consider the accounting for tangible assets at the three stages of their existence: formation, working life and retirement. A company must make accounting decisions when a fixed asset is 'born' and during its life. These decisions concern the costs to include as part of the asset (the capitalisation decision), the method and period of amortisation (the depreciation decision), and the basis of valuing the asset during its economic life (the valuation decision). We illustrate the effect of each of these decisions on a firm's accounts. We also describe the way it accounts for fixed asset disposals.

The above decisions concern the measurement of fixed assets. A company must first decide whether an 'investment' has created a fixed asset. This raises definition and recognition issues. They lie at the heart of the controversy over the accounting for intangibles such as goodwill, brands and research and development costs. We look at the accounting problems created by outlays on intangibles in section 2 of the chapter.

Firms following international accounting standards must make extensive disclosures about their fixed assets. In section 3 of the chapter, we learn what information IAS require firms to make and discover how investors use it when analysing a company's accounts.

Tangible assets

The capitalisation decision

A company recognises an item of property, plant or equipment as an accounting asset using the same criteria we set out in Chapter 7. It expects to obtain economic benefits from the asset in future periods and the asset's cost or value can be measured reliably. For items of low value, like tools or dies, management must decide whether to treat them singly or to group them when applying the criteria.

Property, plant and equipment are valued initially at cost. But what is 'cost'? Companies follow the general principle that *cost should include the purchase price and 'any directly attributable costs of bringing the asset to working condition for its intended use'.*[1]

An example shows how this general principle is applied. Quixote, an electricity-generating company, decides to construct a windmill of advanced design to generate electricity in a remote area of Spain. It incurs the following costs in acquiring land and installing the windmill:

Purchase price of land	10,000
Cost of razing old buildings on land, net of salvage value	15,000
Cost of windmill, including transport to and assembly at site	1,000,000
Cost of initial tests, including salaries of technicians involved	48,000
One year's insurance premium, of which one tenth relates to test period	20,000

The cost of the land is recorded at 25,000. Site clearance costs of 15,000 should be capitalised, since the land cannot be put to its intended use without incurring such costs.

Under international accounting rules, the cost of the windmill is recorded at 1,050,000. The costs of testing the equipment (48,000), including the relevant share of the insurance premium (2,000), should be capitalised, since, again, these outlays are necessary before the windmill can be brought into service.

Companies follow the same general principle when constructing their own plant and buildings. Included in the cost of a self-constructed asset are direct costs, such as materials and labour, and indirect costs which are allocated to it. Examples of such indirect costs are depreciation on equipment used in making the asset and the cost of management time spent supervising its construction.

There are grey areas, however. Take financing costs as an example. How should a company treat the cost of debt incurred to finance the asset's construction? Is it part of the cost of financing the business as a whole and thus expensed in the period incurred? Or is the cost of borrowing no different from other indirect costs which have to be incurred for the asset to be usable? And if the latter, should not a company that relies on equity capital to finance the asset's construction be allowed to charge an imputed cost of equity to the asset?

Opinion, at present, is divided – and practice reflects this.

- Under the 4th Directive, EU member states can permit firms to capitalise borrowing costs incurred to finance production of fixed assets. Interest capitalisation is not a common practice in Europe except in certain industries (e.g. construction).
- Under IAS, companies can either expense all borrowing costs immediately ('benchmark' treatment) or capitalise those borrowing costs incurred to finance the acquisition, construction or production of a 'qualifying' asset (allowed alternative treatment). (A qualifying asset

is one that 'necessarily takes a substantial period of time to get ready for its intended use or sale'. It can be a building, manufacturing plant or long-production-cycle inventory.[2]) Whichever policy is adopted must be applied consistently.

● US GAAP requires interest capitalisation in those cases where IAS permit it.

No country permits the capitalisation of imputed equity costs. Thus the complaint remains that own-constructed assets which are equity-financed and those which are debt-financed may be treated inconsistently.

In the event a company elects to capitalise borrowing costs, how does it determine capitalised interest in a period? IAS apply an 'opportunity cost' approach. A company should capitalise

---

Exhibit 8.1   Capitalisation of borrowing costs: illustration

Facts

Quixote makes the following payments on the windmill during year 1: 210,000 on 1 March; 390,000 on 1 June; 320,000 on 1 October; and 130,000 on 31 December. The total cost of the windmill is 1,050,000. It enters service on 1 January year 2. Quixote's total debt outstanding during year 1 is 2,000,000. The average annual interest rate on the debt is 6%.

Calculation of windmill's capitalised interest cost

To calculate the interest costs to be capitalised, first calculate the *weighted average accumulated expenditures* (WAAE) on the asset during the construction period. The windmill's WAAE is 482,500.

Date	Expenditures	Expenditure weight*	Weighted average accumulated expenditures
1 March year 1	210,000	10/12	175,000
1 June	390,000	7/12	227,500
1 October	320,000	3/12	80,000
31 December	130,000	–	–
	1,050,000		482,500

* Months between date of expenditure and date interest capitalisation ceases (31 December), divided by 12.

Next, determine the cost of financing the WAAE. WAAE are financed first by specific borrowings and the balance by general borrowings. The total cost of these borrowings is *avoidable interest*. Interest capitalised is the lower of (a) avoidable interest and (b) actual interest costs incurred in the capitalisation period. Quixote has not raised debt to finance the windmill specifically. All its borrowings are general. Thus interest capitalised is 28,950, the avoidable interest.

Capitalisation period	Avoidable interest	Actual interest incurred
1 March–31 December year 1	28,950 (482,500 × 6%)	100,000 (2,000,000 × 6% × $^{10}/_{12}$)

(The expenditure figure of 482,500 is computed after weighting expenditures during the 10-month capitalisation period so the interest rate itself is not adjusted.)

Balance sheet presentation

The cost of the windmill is recorded as 1,078,950 (1,050,000 + 28,950) in Quixote's balance sheet at 31 December year 1.

those borrowing costs that would have been avoided if expenditures on the qualifying asset had not been made. Exhibit 8.1 illustrates how this approach works in practice, using Quixote's windmill acquisition as an example.

Based on the numbers in the example, the interest Quixote would have avoided if the windmill had not been acquired is 28,950. This is the product of the average interest rate on the company's debt (6%) and the average accumulated expenditures on the windmill during the capitalisation period (482,500). The revised cost of the windmill is thus 1,078,950 which is the sum of the acquisition cost (1,050,000) and the capitalised interest (28,950).

Note that interest is only capitalised while the asset is being made ready for use (or sale). When it is ready, capitalisation ceases and all interest costs after this date are expensed as incurred.

The depreciation decision

Once a company begins to use a fixed asset (strictly, when the asset becomes available for use), it must decide how to depreciate the asset. Assets such as buildings, machinery and equipment have limited useful lives, at the end of which the economic benefits they provide the firm are all consumed. Regardless of how such an asset is valued, its **carrying amount** (or **net book value**) is reduced as the firm uses the asset and consumes the benefits. The firm records the reduction as 'depreciation expense' in its income statement. In this way, reported profit reflects the cost of fixed asset inputs used to generate revenues in the period.[3]

'Amortisation' is a synonym for depreciation. It is usually applied only to intangible fixed assets. The term 'depletion' refers to the using up of exhaustible natural resources such as oilfields and copper mines.

Asset life

When calculating depreciation, management's first task is to estimate an asset's useful life. To do this, they have to consider the effects of future changes in economic conditions and technology and, in the case of tangible fixed assets, the effects of physical wear and tear. Note that the useful life of a fixed asset to a company may well be less than its economic or physical life. For example, a commercial aircraft may have utility to a charter airline even after its useful life to a scheduled carrier has ended.

Not all fixed assets are depreciated. For example, a firm will not depreciate land if it considers its useful life to be indefinite.

Depreciation method

Managers must decide on a systematic method of allocating an asset's cost or value over its useful life. They determine the method of depreciation at the outset of the asset's life and then apply it consistently. Strictly, the method should reflect *when* the firm expects to consume the asset's benefits. Thus, if proportionately more of the asset's benefits will be enjoyed in the earlier years of its life, it makes sense to charge more depreciation in the early years and less in the later years.

In practice, other factors, such as ease of calculation, likely impact on profits and, in uniform reporting countries, tax considerations, influence management's choice of depreciation method. Nonetheless, *systematic* methods are always used. This is important. They make it more difficult for management to adjust depreciation expense in the light of operating conditions. Manipulating profit by altering the periodic depreciation charge was a favourite ploy in the early days of corporate accounting.

Several systematic methods of depreciation are in use in Europe. Two popular ones are the **straight-line method** and the **declining-balance method**. We explain and illustrate both below.

Two other methods, namely the sum-of-years'-digits and units-of-production methods, are described in Appendix 8.1.

Straight-line method (SL method)

Under the SL method, the depreciation charge is a constant amount each period. It is an appropriate method when an asset's economic benefits are expected to be consumed evenly over its life.

The SL depreciation charge is computed by applying a predetermined, fixed percentage to the asset's depreciable amount. The depreciation percentage (or rate) is based on the asset's expected useful life:

$$\text{SL depreciation rate} = \frac{1}{\text{Asset's expected useful life}} \times 100$$

The **depreciable amount** is the asset's cost less the expected end-of-life salvage value. **Salvage value** (or **residual value**) is not depreciated because the company expects to recover this portion of the asset's cost. Thus the SL depreciation charge on equipment costing 12,000 with an expected four-year life and estimated salvage value of 2,000 is 2,500:

$$\text{SL depreciation charge} = [12,000 - 2,000] \times 25\%$$
$$\qquad\qquad\text{Cost}\quad\text{Salvage}\quad\text{Depreciation}$$
$$\qquad\qquad\qquad\quad\text{value}\qquad\text{rate}$$
$$= 2,500$$

Declining-balance method (DB method)

Under the DB method, the depreciation charge is a decreasing amount each period. The DB method is an example of a **reducing charge method**. In North America it's described as an **accelerated method**. A reducing charge method is appropriate when the economic benefits from an asset are expected to be concentrated in the early years of its life.

The DB depreciation charge is computed by applying a predetermined, fixed percentage to the start-of-year carrying amount of the asset. (In the first year, the percentage is usually applied to the asset's cost.) The percentage should be that rate which ensures that the asset is written down to its expected salvage value at the end of its useful life. In practice, the declining-balance depreciation rate is calculated as a multiple of the straight-line rate. Thus the 'double declining-balance' rate for an asset with a ten-year life is 20%. In short:

$$\text{DB depreciation charge} = \text{Start-of-period carrying amount} \times \text{DB depreciation rate}$$

Since over the asset's life depreciation accumulates while the cost remains unchanged, an asset's carrying amount diminishes over time. As a result, the depreciation charge also diminishes each period in absolute terms.

Exhibit 8.2 charts the effect of the SL and DB methods on both the annual depreciation charge and the carrying amount of a typical asset. The asset is valued at cost and is expected to have no salvage value at the end of its useful life.

Note that under the DB method an asset's NBV – and thus the depreciation charge – declines by a decreasing amount each period.

Depreciation methods illustrated

We now illustrate these two methods. Quixote buys a Rocinante van for use by its windmill-based personnel. The van cost the company 10,000 and is expected to have a useful life of five years. The straight-line depreciation rate is therefore 20%. The depreciation rate used in the

Exhibit 8.2 Straight-line vs declining-balance methods: effect on depreciation charge and net book value of typical fixed asset

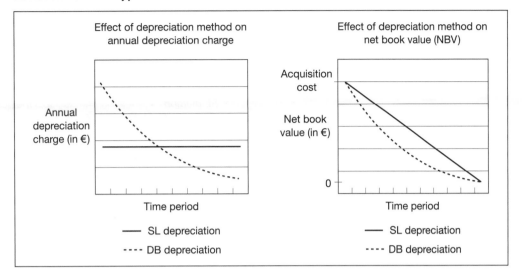

declining-balance calculation is set at double the straight-line rate or 40%. The van's salvage value at the end of five years is expected to be minimal and can be ignored in the depreciation calculation.

Exhibit 8.3 shows the yearly depreciation charges and end-year net book value figures for the Rocinante van, which Quixote would report under the two depreciation methods. The company measures the asset at (depreciated) cost.

Under the SL method, the annual depreciation charged on the van each year is 2,000 (10,000 (the depreciable amount) × 20%).

Under the DB method, the depreciation charge is a function of the van's net book value which declines over its life. For example, at the start of year 2, the van's net book value (NBV) is 6,000, the asset's cost of 10,000 less year 1 depreciation of 4,000. The DB rate of 40% is then applied to this NBV to give a year 2 depreciation charge of 2,400 (40% × 6,000). By the start of year 3, the van's NBV is 3,600 (the asset's cost less depreciation in years 1 and 2) which in turn yields a year 3 depreciation charge of 1,440 (40% × 3,600).

Notice that in year 4, the company switches from the declining-balance to the straight-line method. This is a common practice in some continental European countries when the SL depreciation charge, *calculated from the date of change*, is higher than the DB charge for the year. In year 4, the DB charge is 864 (40% × 2,160); the SL charge that year (calculated from the start of year 4) is 1,080 (50% × 2,160). Switching to SL depreciation avoids a large depreciation charge in the year of disposal, which would occur under the DB method when the remaining book value is written off.

The choice of depreciation method does not affect the type of accounting records kept nor the entries to them. For example, the entry to record depreciation in year 3 under the two methods is as follows (amounts in 000):

	Depreciation method	
	SL	*DB*
Dr. Depreciation expense (OE–)	2.0	1.44
Cr. Accumulated depreciation (CA+)	2.0	1.44

Exhibit 8.3 Straight-line (SL) and declining-balance (DB) depreciation methods: illustration (amounts in 000)

Facts

Quixote buys a Rocinante van for 10. It has an expected useful life of five years and expected residual value of zero.

Annual depreciation charge and net book value (NBV)

	SL method		DB method	
	Depreciation expense	Net book value	Depreciation expense	Net book value
Acquisition		10		10
Year 1 depreciation	2	−2	4	−4
End-year 1 NBV		8		6
Year 2 depreciation	2	−2	2.4	−2.4
End-year 2 NBV		6		3.6
Year 3 depreciation	2	−2	1.44	−1.44
End-year 3 NBV		4		2.16
Year 4 depreciation	2	−2	1.08*	−1.08
End-year 4 NBV		2		1.08
Year 5 depreciation	2	−2	1.08*	−1.08
End-year 5 NBV		0		0

Calculations

Straight-line (SL) method:
- Five-year life implies depreciation rate of 20% a year.
- Annual depreciation is 2 (20% × 10).

Declining-balance (DB) method:
- Depreciation rate is assumed to be *double* the SL rate.
- Apply rate to start-of-year NBV.
- Thus, year 2 depreciation is: 40% × 6 = 2.4

* It is common practice in Continental European countries to switch from the DB method to the SL method when the SL depreciation charge – calculated from that date – exceeds that under the DB method. Year 4 is the first year in which the SL charge is *greater* than the DB charge (because the SL *rate* is greater than the DB rate) – hence the switch to the SL method that year:

		DB method	SL method
Depreciation:	year 2	2.4	1.5 (6.0 × 25%)
	year 3	1.44	1.2 (3.6 × 33%)
	year 4	0.86 (2.16 × 40%)	1.08 (2.16 × 50%)

Practical aspects of depreciation calculation

Depreciation calculations are not as exact or as time-consuming as they appear at first sight. Rather than estimating expected life on an individual asset basis, a company often determines the average expected life for each class of fixed asset – for example, industrial buildings, motor vehicles, office equipment – using industry data and its own past experience.

Companies can and do use different depreciation methods for different types of asset. This is logical since assets differ in the pattern of benefits they yield. However, depreciation methods must be consistently applied over time. Management should justify any change in depreciation: for example, they should explain why the new policy is preferable to the old.

Companies usually bring assets into service during the financial year rather than at the start. How is depreciation expense calculated in these cases? The most logical approach is to charge depreciation for the part of the financial year an asset is in service. Assume Quixote prepares annual accounts on a calendar year basis. If the company acquires the Rocinante van on 15 September year 1, the van is in service for only 3.5 months in that year. Given that it depreciates such assets on a double declining-balance basis (in this case, 40%), it charges depreciation of only 1,167 in year 1 ((10,000 × 40%) × 3.5/12). The asset's net book value at the end of year 1 is 8,833 (10,000 − 1,167) and the depreciation charge in year 2 is 3,533 (8,833 × 40%). Quixote charges the balance of the depreciable amount at the end of year 5 as depreciation in year 6. Note that other, simpler methods (such as charging half a year's depreciation in the financial year the asset enters service, irrespective of when in the year it does so) are also used.

Depreciation and residual values

If a company expects to sell a fixed asset at the end of its useful life for more than a nominal sum, then, under international rules, the expected residual value should be deducted from the asset's cost in calculating the amount to be depreciated. The expected residual value is the net proceeds from disposal (that is, net of any estimated disposal costs), as estimated at the date of the asset's acquisition.[4]

In practice, companies base depreciable amount on the asset's cost if residual value is expected to be immaterial. Tax authorities in Europe rarely take account of it in determining tax depreciation.[5]

Depreciation and cash flow

Depreciation is a non-cash expense. It has no direct effect on a company's cash flow. Consider Quixote. Suppose it forecasts profit before tax of 2 million in year 9. This forecast is based on expected (cash) revenues of 10 million and expected expenses of 8 million of which the only non-cash expense is depreciation of 500,000. As a result of a change in depreciation method, actual depreciation in year 9 is 750,000. Other things being equal, Quixote's year 9 pre-tax profit will fall to 1.75 million but its operating cash flow (ignoring working capital changes) will be unchanged at 2.5 million.

Quixote: Year 9 profit and cash flow before tax (in m)

	Forecast		Actual	
Revenues		10		10
Expenses: Cash-based	7.5		7.5	
Depreciation	0.5		0.75	
		−8		−8.25
Profit before tax		2		1.75
+ Depreciation		+0.5		+0.75
Operating cash flow before tax		2.5		2.5

Depreciation has an *indirect* effect on corporate cash flow – through its impact on taxes. If a company can increase its depreciation charge for tax purposes in a period, it lowers its taxable income and thus the income taxes it pays that period. Continuing with our Quixote example, assume the company's taxable income in year 9 is equal to its profit before tax that year and the tax rate is 40%.

Quixote: Year 9 profit and cash flow after tax (in m)

	Forecast	Actual
Profit		
Profit before tax	2	1.75
Less: Income tax at 40%	−0.8	−0.7
Profit after tax	1.2	1.05
Operating cash flow		
OCF before tax	2.5	2.5
Less: income tax paid	−0.8	−0.7
OCF after tax	1.7	1.8

Higher depreciation of 250,000 reduces Quixote's after-tax profits by 150,000 (250,000 × (1 − tax rate)). But it lowers the tax the company pays in year 9 by 100,000 and thus *raises* its after-tax operating cash flow from 1.7 million to 1.8 million that year.

Quixote's tax bill is not permanently lowered. Under HC accounting, higher depreciation in the current period means lower depreciation in future periods. Thus the company postpones rather than avoids tax of 100,000. Of course, in present value terms, the company benefits from the tax deferral.

Up to now we have assumed that the depreciation a company reports on its tax return (**tax depreciation**) is the same as the depreciation it charges in its published accounts (**book depreciation**). This is rarely the case in separate reporting countries. Governments and companies have different goals when determining depreciation policy. A government may allow firms to depreciate certain types of asset at a rapid rate for tax purposes so that they can lower their after-tax cost of investment. Management, however, estimate asset lives with the aim that the accounts portray fairly ('give a true and fair view of') the results and position of the firm. In separate reporting countries, a change by a firm in its book depreciation is unlikely to affect its tax depreciation and thus will have no impact on its after-tax cash flow.

In sum, a change in book depreciation always affects reported profits. It only affects cash flow if tax and book depreciation are linked. In this case, the effect on cash flow is the opposite of the effect on profits. We return to this topic in a later chapter when we discuss the accounting for income taxes.

Depreciation of fixed assets: EU practice

Empirical evidence indicates that the SL method is the most popular depreciation method in Europe and elsewhere. In a survey of listed and unlisted EU companies in the 1990s, over 90% of those that reported property in their accounts – and almost 90% of those reporting plant and machinery – used the SL method. (This does not mean that only 10% of firms use other methods. In some countries, firms use both SL and DB methods for different types of equipment.)[6]

One obvious reason for the SL method's popularity is its simplicity and ease of calculation. Moreover, when a company's fixed asset base is growing and asset prices are rising, the SL method results in a lower aggregate depreciation charge and the company reports higher profits. In the past, this is more likely to have influenced managers in separate reporting countries. Higher profits mean higher pay – whether directly via profit-related bonuses or indirectly via the premium they command as 'successful' managers. However, higher profits from this source have no effect on a firm's tax liability (since tax depreciation and thus taxable income are computed differently from the book numbers).

By contrast, we should expect to find reducing charge methods more popular in those uniform reporting countries which permit their use for tax purposes. Empirical evidence bears this out. For example, France and Germany come from a uniform reporting tradition, the Netherlands and the UK from a separate reporting one. French and German companies can opt to use the declining balance method to depreciate plant and machinery for tax purposes. In the survey mentioned above, over two-thirds of German companies and almost half of French firms disclosing plant and machinery in their balance sheets reported using the DB method for some types of equipment whereas none of the equivalent Dutch and UK companies reported using it.[7]

Repairs and improvements

Sums are often spent on a building or machine during its life. How should such outlays be accounted for? Under IAS, expenditures which raise the performance of an asset beyond its initial level are treated as **improvements**. *Improvements are capitalised and depreciated over the asset's remaining useful life.* Examples of improvements are expenditures that extend an asset's useful life, increase its capacity, raise substantially the quality of its output or reduce substantially its operating costs. If the expenditure maintains rather than adds to the benefits expected from the asset initially then the costs are treated as **repairs**. *Repairs are expensed in the period they're incurred.*

Consider the case of Quixote's windmill. It costs 1,078,950 and enters service at the start of year 2. Suppose Quixote spends a further 228,700 on it in late year 2 in order to extend its useful life from three to five years. The expenditure improves the asset's performance and is therefore capitalised. Quixote must also revise the annual depreciation charge, starting in year 3. In year 2, it charged SL depreciation of 359,650 against revenues. Depreciation in year 3 (and subsequent years) is now reduced to 237,000. The calculation is shown below (all amounts in thousands):

	Windmill at cost	Accumulated depreciation	Net book value
Cost, at 1/1/year 2	1,078.95		1,078.95
Year 2 depreciation (1,078.95/3 years)		359.65	−359.65
End-year 2 improvement	228.7		+228.7
Balance, end-year 2	1,307.65	359.65	948
Year 3 depreciation (948/4 remaining years)		237	−237
Balance, end-year 3	1,307.65	596.65	711

The revised depreciation charge is calculated by allocating the windmill's net book value (948,000) at the end of year 2 over the remaining four years of its life.

Retirement

A company retires a fixed asset when it is economically advantageous for it to do so. This date may not coincide with the disposal date forecast at the time of acquisition. Changes in economic conditions or the level of usage may result in a company selling a fixed asset earlier (or later) than planned. If the company foresees this, it should write off the asset at a faster (slower) rate. Past financial statements are not restated: only future depreciation charges are modified.

There are occasions when an asset may continue to be used after it's fully depreciated. In this event, the company no longer charges depreciation since the asset's cost has been fully recovered. It does not adjust prior years' financial statements if it can show that the calculation of depreciation in those years was made in good faith. Managers can only be expected to use information currently available when estimating assets' useful lives.

The accounting for a fixed asset's retirement is straightforward. We learned earlier that, at the time of disposal, the balances in the asset and accumulated depreciation accounts relating to the asset sold must be removed. In addition, the company records a gain (loss) in its income statement if the asset's disposal value is greater (less) than its net book value at that date. Consider Quixote's Rocinante van. The company decides to retire it at the end of the fourth year of its life for economic reasons. It sells the van for 1,500. The van's net book value then is 2,000 under the SL method. A 'loss on disposal' of 500 is recorded, since the cash received from the sale is less than the net book value of the asset by that amount:

Dr. Accumulated depreciation, van (CA–)	8,000	
Dr. Cash (A+)	1,500	
Dr. Loss on disposal of fixed asset (OE–)	500	
Cr. Van, at cost (A–)		10,000

The result of this entry is that the balances in the ledger accounts, with respect to both the van and the accumulated depreciation on it, are eliminated. Exhibit 8.4 illustrates this.

Exhibit 8.4 Retirement of Rocinante van at end-year 4 – extracts from Quixote's ledger accounts (amounts in 000)

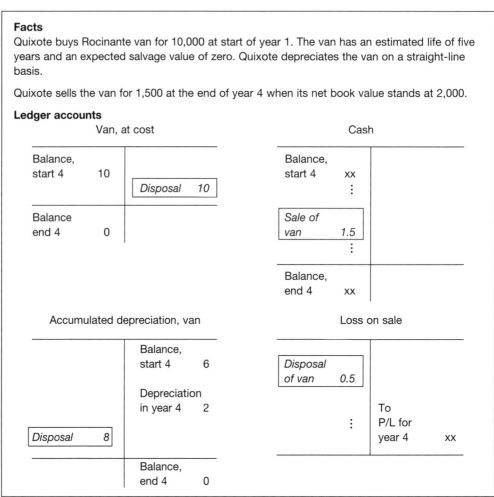

Facts

Quixote buys Rocinante van for 10,000 at start of year 1. The van has an estimated life of five years and an expected salvage value of zero. Quixote depreciates the van on a straight-line basis.

Quixote sells the van for 1,500 at the end of year 4 when its net book value stands at 2,000.

Ledger accounts

Van, at cost

Balance, start 4	10	Disposal	10
Balance end 4	0		

Cash

Balance, start 4	xx		
Sale of van	1.5		
Balance, end 4	xx		

Accumulated depreciation, van

Disposal	8	Balance, start 4	6
		Depreciation in year 4	2
		Balance, end 4	0

Loss on sale

| Disposal of van | 0.5 | To P/L for year 4 | xx |

If Quixote had sold the van for 2,500 at the end of year 4, it would have recorded a 'gain on disposal' of 500 (the excess of cash proceeds over net book value).

Think about the nature of this entry for a moment. Quixote is not worse off as a result of reporting the loss on disposal. Nor would it have been better off if it had reported a gain. A gain or loss arises because of errors in the calculation of depreciation charges in previous periods. Rather than reopen previous periods' accounts, a company corrects the error when it retires the asset and records the correction as a gain or loss then.

The valuation decision

The main accounting adjustment to a fixed asset during its life is depreciation. But it's not the only one. A company may make other adjustments to an asset's carrying amount. In some countries, firms can write up their tangible fixed assets when the market values of those assets increase. In all countries, firms must write down fixed assets whose values are impaired. We consider each case in turn.

Increase in value during holding period

Consider first the case where a fixed asset's current value is greater than its depreciated cost. *Under historical cost accounting, the increase in value is not recognised in the accounts, except in rare circumstances.* (One such circumstance is when a company's assets are purchased by another in a takeover and the 'purchase' method is used to account for the acquisition. We describe the purchase method in a later chapter on intercorporate investments.)

Under current value accounting, however, the increase in value of fixed assets is recognised in the accounts. The company restates the asset to its current value and takes the surplus on revaluation to a non-distributable reserve. It calculates depreciation on the basis of the asset's current value from the date of revaluation.

Quixote's Rocinante van can provide us with the vehicle (forgive the pun) to illustrate these points. Assume that at the start of year 3 the price of a new Rocinante van increases to 12,000. By then, 40% of the van's estimated five-year service life has expired. (We assume SL consumption of the van's benefits.) The replacement cost (RC) of an equivalent van with three years' life remaining is therefore 7,200 (12,000 − (40% × 12,000)). Quixote adjusts both asset and accumulated depreciation accounts on a proportionate basis: the asset account by 20% to reflect the RC of a new van (12,000); the accumulated depreciation account by 20% (from 4,000 to 4,800) to reflect two years of use, where the services consumed are valued at RC.[8] It credits the net increase of 1,200 in the carrying value of the van – from 6,000 to 7,200 – to a revaluation reserve account.

Start year 3
Dr. Van, at replacement cost (A+)   2,000
   Cr. Accumulated depreciation (CA+)   800
   Cr. Revaluation reserve (OE+)   1,200

The annual depreciation charge in year 3 is 2,400, one-fifth of the van's start-year 3 RC of 12,000. If there is no further change in the van's RC, this will be the depreciation charge in years 4 and 5 as well.[9]

Exhibit 8.5 shows the movement in Quixote's asset and equity accounts in year 3 as a result of the revaluation and depreciation of its van.

The (net) surplus on revaluation of 1,200 is an unrealised holding gain. Under 4th Directive rules and IAS, *holding gains on revaluation of fixed assets cannot enter the calculation of profit and*

Exhibit 8.5 Revaluation and subsequent depreciation of the Rocinante van in year 3 – extracts from Quixote's ledger accounts (amounts in 000)

Van, at (replacement) cost				Revaluation reserve		
Balance, start 3	10			Balance, start 3		0
Revaluation	2			Revaluation		1.2
Balance, end 3	12			Balance, end 3		1.2

Accumulated depreciation, van			Year 3 depreciation expense		
	Balance, start 3	4			
	Revaluation 0.8			To 'P/L for	
	Year 3 depreciation 2.4		Year 3 depreciation 2.4	year 3'	2.4
	Balance, end 3	7.2			

be distributed as dividend until they are realised. The revaluation reserve is therefore a non-distributable reserve.

A surplus on revaluation is realised when the underlying asset is sold. It's also considered realised when the benefits from the asset are consumed. Thus as a fixed asset is depreciated, the excess of RC over HC depreciation in the year (400 in the case of the Rocinante van) is a realised holding gain. Quixote has the option, therefore, of transferring the realised gain with respect to annual depreciation to distributable profits at the end of year 3 (and of years 4 and 5 also).

End-year 3		
Dr. Revaluation reserve (OE–)	400	
Cr. Retained profits (OE+)		400

Note that the realised holding gain is credited directly to a balance sheet account. International rules prohibit firms from passing it through the income statement.

Decrease in value during holding period

We turn now to the situation where a fixed asset declines in value. Traditionally, under HC accounting, a company would write down a fixed asset only if fair value fell below carrying amount and management judged the decline to be permanent. In this case the asset is said to be *impaired.*

The accounting for *asset impairments* has long been considered unsatisfactory. The old accounting rules were vague and open to abuse. Investors often had the uneasy feeling that asset write-downs were recorded when it was advantageous for the company (or, more particularly, the management) to do so rather than when the impairment of the asset had taken place. There was evidence that in some countries a company was more likely to write down fixed assets when its profits were already low or losses had been incurred. In such years, earnings are said to 'take a bath'. Since investors expected results to be poor, management, often newly installed, took the opportunity to lower the book value of the firm's fixed assets and described the charge against profits as the cost of 'corporate restructuring'. In subsequent years, profits benefited from a lower depreciation charge and the new management took credit for the profit 'improvement'.

A recent international accounting standard restricts management's discretion over the timing and size of asset write-downs.[10] The key features of the standard are as follows:

● *Annual impairment review of fixed assets.* Companies must check all their fixed assets each year to find out if any have been impaired. *An asset is impaired if its recoverable amount is below its carrying amount.*
● *Definition of recoverable amount.* The standard defines an asset's **recoverable amount** as *the higher of its net selling price and its value in use.* 'Net selling price' is simply market value in an arm's length transaction, net of disposal costs. 'Value in use' is the present value of estimated future cash flows from the asset's continued use by the company (and its ultimate disposal). The standard gives guidance as to the calculation of net selling price and value in use. Note that both must be below carrying amount for an asset to be impaired.[11]
● *Immediate recognition of impairment losses.* Impairment loss is the excess of an asset's carrying amount over its recoverable amount. It must be recognised as an expense on the income statement immediately. Impairment losses are accumulated either in the 'Accumulated depreciation' account or in a separate contra-asset account in the balance sheet.

We illustrate the accounting for asset impairments using our Quixote example. Assume a change in local economic conditions late in year 2 leads to a reduction in the demand for electricity from Quixote's windmill. You'll recall that the windmill entered service at the start of year 2, cost 1,078,950 and has an expected life of three years. The windmill's net book value at the end of year 2 is 719,300.

Management estimate that the windmill's value in use (based on estimated future discounted cash flows) is 400,000 at the end of year 2. This is also its recoverable amount since management estimate the net selling price is only 250,000. As the windmill's recoverable amount (400,000) is less than its carrying amount (719,300), Quixote has sustained an impairment loss of 319,300. The loss is recognised in the year 2 income statement as follows:

End-year 2		
Dr. Loss from windmill write-down (OE–)	319,300	
Cr. Accumulated impairment losses (CA+)		319,300

The asset's revised carrying amount is now 400,000, the difference between its cost (1,078,950) and the sum of its accumulated depreciation (359,650) and impairment losses (319,300). Quixote must reduce the depreciation charge in year 3 – from 359,650 to 200,000 (400,000/2) – to take account of the windmill's lower depreciable amount.

What if an asset's recoverable amount increases in a later period owing to, say, higher expected cash flows or a higher net selling price? Under the new international standard, a company records the reversal of the impairment loss as a 'write-back' and recognises it as income. There is a cap on such write-backs, however. The new carrying amount of the asset cannot be increased above what it would have been in the absence of earlier impairment losses.

Accounting for asset impairments under *current value accounting* is similar to that under HC accounting. Annual revaluations include an impairment review. Recoverable amount is defined in the same way. Decreases in current value are recognised immediately. The main difference concerns the accounting treatment of the value decrease. *Where the decrease represents a reversal of a previous increase, the write-down is charged against the already established revaluation reserve.* Once the revaluation reserve is exhausted, any further write-downs must be charged against profit, as occurs under HC accounting.

Valuation of fixed assets: EU and international practice

Although the 4th Directive lays down that fixed assets must be valued at purchase price or production cost, it gives member states the power to permit or require companies to value such assets on another basis. As we saw in Chapter 7, the Directive mentions three alternative bases:

1 replacement cost;
2 a valuation; or
3 cost adjusted for changes in the general price level.

IAS designate (depreciated) historical cost as the 'benchmark' method of valuing tangible fixed assets. However, an allowed alternative method is to carry them at a revalued amount. This is carefully defined. It's the fair value at the revaluation date less subsequent accumulated depreciation (and impairment). Revaluations must be carried out regularly so that the asset's carrying amount does not differ materially from its fair value at the balance sheet date.[12]

Companies refer to suppliers' current price lists or industry-specific price indices to estimate replacement cost. They use professionally qualified experts to provide valuations of assets. In some countries, valuation by the company's directors is permitted. In most cases, experts (or directors) estimate an asset's value on the basis of its market value in its existing use.

EU countries differ in their response to the 4th Directive's concession. They fall into one of three groups.

1 *Prohibitionist.* Commitment to HC accounting is strong. Upward valuations of fixed assets are not permitted except in rare circumstances. Germany is the principal 'prohibitionist'.
2 *Liberal.* Companies are free to state some or all tangible fixed assets at RC or at a valuation. Denmark, Ireland, the Netherlands and the UK belong to this group. There are no tax consequences from revaluation, since in these countries the calculation of taxable income is separate from that of book income.
3 *Dirigist.* The government requires – or, through the tax system, encourages – companies to update the values of their fixed assets in the balance sheet. The adjustment is usually based on government-specified index numbers. It occurs infrequently: for example, 13 years elapsed before the Spanish government introduced the latest voluntary revaluation (*actualización de balances*) in 1996. Where revaluations are compulsory, any surplus arising is usually tax exempt. Under Italy's 1991 compulsory revaluation, the surplus was taxed (at 16%) but, offsetting this, the increased depreciation charges were tax deductible immediately.

   Belgium, France, Greece and Portugal – in addition to Spain and Italy – have mandated nationwide revaluations in the past. Belgian and French companies are free to revalue each year: they do not do so because, unless the revaluation is an official one, any surplus on revaluation is taxable as income.

Most non-EU countries can be classified in the same three groups. For example, Canada, Japan and the USA support the prohibitionist line. Many Commonwealth countries (e.g. Australia, India, Singapore) permit revaluations of fixed assets. China and Russia display dirigist tendencies: asset revaluations, when permitted, must be in accordance with government decrees. Countries that in the past had (Mexico), or currently have (Turkey), a high rate of inflation require companies to use constant purchasing power adjustments to update the carrying amounts of their fixed assets.

Evidence from surveys of EU company accounts indicates that revaluation of fixed assets is common among firms in countries with a history of legal restatement (e.g. France, Italy, Spain). As for 'liberal' EU countries, UK firms appear keen to revalue property but not plant. More surprisingly, revaluation is a minority practice among Dutch firms, despite long acceptance of current value accounting in the Netherlands.

Fixed assets at RC or valuation: rationale

Why do companies voluntarily revalue their fixed assets? One reason is that management consider that *the accounts provide more up-to-date and therefore more relevant information when assets are stated at current values*. The impact of inflation on asset values is especially marked for assets with long or indefinite lives, such as buildings and land, in high-inflation countries. This explains, in part, the popularity of property revaluations in the UK where inflation in the past has been higher than in, say, the Netherlands, another 'liberal' country.

It's not just the balance sheet which is made more relevant. Supporters of current value methods argue that the income statement is more useful, too. Under current value accounting, the current costs of inputs – and that includes depreciation – are matched against current revenues. As a result, the operating profit figure provides a more accurate measure of the company's performance, so supporters maintain. Under HC accounting, the historical costs of inputs are matched against current revenues. As we saw in Chapter 7, the HC profit figure fails to distinguish gains from *holding* assets from the profit from *operating* them.

A second reason is that *revaluation can improve the way a company looks*. Consider the effect of an upward valuation of fixed assets on the accounts. Total assets as well as shareholders' equity are greater by the surplus on revaluation. As a result, the company appears stronger: its reported financial leverage falls.

If the assets revalued are depreciable, there is an income statement price to be paid. (There is no cash benefit because, as already mentioned, in countries where revaluation is voluntary, the additional depreciation is usually not tax deductible.) Higher asset values spell higher depreciation charges and thus lower reported profits. One attraction of revaluing property – but not plant and equipment – is that the income statement 'cost' is slight: land is rarely depreciated and the depreciation charge on a building is usually small in relation to its cost or value, owing to its long life. (Companies that hold property as an investment and follow IAS do not depreciate it if they opt to carry it at current market value in the balance sheet. Appendix 8.2 summarises the international accounting standard on investment property.)

Can a company use revaluations selectively to give itself a balance sheet 'facelift'? International accounting rules try to prevent this. If it chooses this alternative, a firm must revalue an entire class of assets and carry out revaluations regularly so that asset values are up to date. Since asset values can decrease as well as increase – witness the fall in property values in London, Paris and Tokyo in the early 1990s – it is difficult, if not impossible, for a firm to earmark only value-increasing assets for revaluation.

SECTION 2 · Intangible assets

Intangible assets are long-term assets used in a company's business which have no physical substance and are not financial in nature. In many cases the benefits which they yield have a common source. They flow from *rights which a company owns or controls*, for example, rights over:

- an invention or discovery (**patent**);
- the expression of ideas (**copyright**); or
- a commercial name or symbol (**trademark**).

These rights usually have a contractual basis and are therefore verifiable. Not all intangibles share this characteristic, however. An important exception is purchased goodwill. We identify others in this section.

In many respects, the accounting for intangibles is similar to that for their tangible cousins.

- A company records an intangible asset, on acquisition, at cost.
- It amortises the asset over its estimated useful life (which, for contractually based intangibles, may be shorter than its legal life).
- It writes down the asset's carrying amount (net book value) to its recoverable amount when the asset is impaired and the recoverable amount is below carrying amount.
- On disposing of the asset, it compares the asset's carrying and disposal amounts and records a gain or loss.

The accounting rules for intangibles are tougher, however. Recognition criteria are more demanding and measurement rules more restrictive. To understand why, we look at certain expenditures made by firms and outline the arguments for and against capitalising them as intangible assets.

Intangibles: the recognition debate

Consider the following three situations. A consumer products company incurs heavy advertising and promotional costs to launch a new product. A photocopier manufacturer spends large sums training its customer service personnel in copier maintenance. A pharmaceutical firm undertakes an expensive research effort to discover new drug compounds. How should the outlays on advertising, training and research in these three cases be accounted for?

One school of thought argues that such outlays meet the definition of an asset. They are expected to yield future economic benefits. Why else would a firm make them? They should therefore be capitalised as intangible fixed assets and then amortised over their expected useful lives.

For example, suppose Quixote spends 200,000 in year 1 on development of a new design of windmill. Outlays cover the costs of researchers' salaries as well as materials and equipment specific to the project. If Quixote capitalises the expenditure and amortises it over four years, the entries are:

Year 1
Dr. Development costs (A+)   200,000
   Cr. Accrued payroll (L+), Cash (A–), etc.   200,000
To record outlays of 200,000 on windmill development as an intangible asset.

Years 2–5
Dr. Development expense (OE–)   50,000
   Cr. Development costs (A–)   50,000
To record one year's amortisation of the 'Development costs' asset.

Another school of thought maintains that advertising, training and non-contractual research and development (R&D) should not be considered accounting assets. First, it is often hard to isolate the benefits from outlays on these activities. For example, other factors besides advertising outlays – for example, the firm's overall marketing efforts and its reputation – contribute to the success of an advertising campaign. Second, the firm may not be able to appropriate the benefits from these expenditures. Employees gain skills from in-company training which they take with them to other jobs. Finally, the benefits may be highly uncertain. As a result, cost is an unreliable guide to value. For a purchased patent, the market price in an arm's length transaction provides an objective measure of the patent's value. For a patent developed internally as a result of a company's own R&D efforts, no such external check is available.

How would the accounting look, assuming immediate write-off of costs? Consider Quixote's outlays on new windmill development. If it expenses development costs as it incurs them, the entries it makes in year 1 are, in sum:

> *Year 1*
> Dr. Development expense (OE–)   200,000
>   Cr. Accrued payroll (L+), Cash (A–), etc.   200,000
> To record outlays of 200,000 on windmill development as an expense of the year.

It will make no entries in years 2 to 5 with respect to its year 1 development outlays.

Accounting for intangibles: international rules

In recent years, accounting regulators have tried to resolve the debate over recognition of intangibles by issuing a new accounting standard on the topic. We summarise its key features below.[13]

- *Intangibles must be identifiable.* Intangible assets are 'non-monetary assets without physical substance' which a company holds in order to produce goods and services. In addition to the usual characteristics of an asset (i.e. controlled by the firm; expected to yield future benefits), an intangible must also be 'identifiable'. Clearly, intangibles containing transferable legal rights (patents, trademarks, licences) are identifiable. But so, too, are intangibles where a verifiable value can be assigned to them at the date of acquisition (e.g. purchased goodwill).
- *Probable future benefits must be demonstrable.* The recognition criteria for intangibles are similar in form to those for other assets. The expected future benefits to the company from controlling the asset must be probable. Intangibles are measured at cost initially and the cost measure must be reliable. However, the criteria for internally generated intangibles are more demanding. These intangibles must pass a 'demonstration test'. A firm must demonstrate how an internally generated intangible will increase the flow of probable future benefits. It must also demonstrate the ability and means to exploit those benefits.

As with recognition criteria, the measurement rules for intangibles have much in common with those for tangibles. For example, the initial cost of an intangible includes the costs necessary to create, produce or prepare it for its intended use. Subsequent to acquisition, intangibles are carried in the balance sheet at amortised cost. But, once again, the rules are tougher:

- *A ceiling on estimated useful life.* The maximum useful life of an intangible is assumed to be 20 years – unless the firm can provide evidence the asset's life is longer.
- *Valuations must be market-based.* Fair value accounting is permitted as an alternative to amortised cost – but only if there is an active market in that type of intangible.

These are the major differences between tangible and intangible asset accounting. (There are additional, minor differences in measurement rules.) Why are recognition criteria and measurement rules more stringent for intangibles? The reason lies in their nature. It's hard for a firm, let alone an auditor, to verify the existence and amount of an intangible if there's no legal contract or other external evidence to support it.

For firms following international accounting standards, the new rules are likely to reduce the amount of costs capitalised under 'Intangible assets' on their balance sheets. Consider the effect of the standard on the following types of expenditure.

Training costs

The costs incurred by the firm to train its staff must be expensed as incurred. The firm does not control the benefits from this expenditure. Staff are free to leave the firm and take their new skills with them. (Note that this accounting treatment follows from the definition of an asset given in the conceptual framework (*see* Chapter 7). The new standard simply reinforces this point.)

Research and development costs

The IASB distinguishes 'research' from 'development' activity. It defines work undertaken to gain new scientific or technical knowledge as 'research'. The application of such knowledge to the plan or design of new products or processes is considered 'development'.

The new standard requires research costs to be expensed as incurred. They fail a recognition criterion: in the IASB's view, a firm can never demonstrate that expected future benefits from such outlays are probable.

Development costs, by contrast, can be capitalised in some circumstances. Consider a project – for, say, a new computer software product – which is in the development phase. In this case, an intangible is identifiable. Assume the project has reached a critical juncture: management judge the new product to be both technically feasible and commercially viable and the firm can finance development through to the product's launch. Thus the demonstration test is met. *From this point, development costs can be capitalised (up to the launch date).* Development costs prior to this point should have been expensed and IAS do not allow costs already expensed to be reinstated and capitalised.

Goodwill

Goodwill is the excess of the total value of a business entity over the fair values of the individual, identifiable assets (less liabilities) on its balance sheet. Firms generate goodwill internally – in the form of resources such as employee skills, product reputation, customer loyalty – as a result of successful business operations. They can acquire goodwill, too. If a company buys part or all of the (net) assets of another and the purchase price exceeds the fair value of those net assets, the premium is described as 'purchased goodwill'. In both cases, we can think of goodwill as representing the present value of future above-normal returns (or economic rents) which the assets in combination are expected to generate.

Internally-generated goodwill cannot be recognised as an asset in the accounts. This has long been accounting practice and the new international standard reaffirms it. The main reasons are that the asset is not identifiable and its cost cannot be measured reliably.

By contrast, the accounting for purchased goodwill is less clear-cut. Capitalisation (and amortisation) is the benchmark practice under the EU's 7th Directive. US accounting rules require it. However, in some countries it is customary for firms to write off purchased goodwill immediately against reserves. This practice, permitted under the EU's 7th Directive, is on the decline. Countries where the practice was once common (e.g. Netherlands, UK) now ban it.

The accounting effect of the two approaches – capitalisation versus immediate write-off – at the time of asset purchase is contrasted below:

Capitalisation			*Immediate write-off*		
Dr. Assets*	xx		Dr. Assets*	xx	
Dr. Goodwill (A+)	xx		*Dr. Reserves (OE–)*	xx	
Cr. Cash		xx	Cr. Cash		xx

* 'Assets' include identifiable assets (e.g. property, plant, inventory, receivables). If the acquirer firm takes over identifiable liabilities (loans, payables, provisions), it credits the accounts affected at the purchase date.

Immediate write-off has a balance sheet cost: assets and shareholders' equity are smaller and thus financial leverage is greater. (These balance sheet effects are still evident in the accounts of firms that have recently abandoned the practice.) However, there is an income statement benefit as goodwill amortisation charges are avoided.

International accounting standards ban the immediate write-off of goodwill. Purchased goodwill must be recognised initially as an intangible asset. A transaction has occurred which, in the IASB's view, allows a company to identify an asset and measure its cost reliably. Note that it is not possible for the firm to verify the value of purchased goodwill. There's no market for this type of asset. If the firm pays more than the assets are worth, the overpayment is captured in the carrying amount of goodwill. However, international measurement rules for intangibles (mandatory amortisation, annual impairment reviews) should limit the risk of goodwill overstatement.[14]

Brands and related costs

In its simplest form, a brand is the registered trademark of a particular product. Examples are Perrier bottled water and the EVA financial performance measure. For accounting purposes, the term refers not just to the name of a product but also other resources dedicated to supporting it (e.g. logo, product-specific advertising, product-specific distribution channels). The term is used loosely in other contexts. For example, companies whose name enjoys worldwide recognition – for example, Coca-Cola, Mercedes-Benz, Microsoft – are said to be brands.

Controversy over the accounting for brands first arose in the 1980s. In that decade, some consumer goods firms were acquired by other companies at a large premium to the fair value of their net assets. Examples are Guinness's purchase of Distillers (Scotch whisky producer) and LVMH's acquisition of Parfums Christian Dior. Instead of accounting for the whole premium as goodwill, the acquirer companies estimated the values of the acquiree's major brands – using discounted cash flow or earnings multiple techniques – and created a new intangible asset 'Acquired brands'. These brand values were then included with the fair values of other identifiable assets acquired. As a result, the amount of the purchase price assigned to goodwill was reduced:

$$\text{Goodwill} = \text{Purchase price} - \text{Fair value of net assets acquired } \textit{including brands}$$

Acquirer firms justify this accounting treatment on the grounds that brands are an important – if not the most important – resource of most consumer goods companies. For example, in 1996 when LVMH (Louis Vuitton Moët Hennessy) acquired majority control of Loewe, the leading Spanish leather and textile goods producer, it assigned 73% of the €168 million investment to the Loewe brand. To deny accounting recognition of this resource would be to mislead investors, it's claimed.

Another reason, rarely acknowledged publicly by acquirer firms, is the reporting benefit from this accounting treatment. There is no income statement cost from brand recognition because brand assets are not usually amortised. Management claim that the large marketing outlays they make each year to promote individual brands maintain or even enhance their value and thus the brands have an indefinite life. Moreover, for those firms that write off goodwill immediately, brand recognition reduces the amount of the goodwill write-off and thus the damage this inflicts to their balance sheets.

The international accounting standard on intangible assets makes recognition of brand assets harder. The standard states explicitly that the cost of developing brands internally – for example, the advertising and promotion costs incurred on them – must be expensed as incurred. The IASB argues that such expenditures benefit the business as a whole and thus the cost of internally developed brands cannot be measured reliably. In addition, these expenditures may not pass the demonstration test. A company will have difficulty showing how advertising increases the inflow of future benefits. Lever (of Unilever) famously remarked that one half of all advertising is wasted: the problem is to know which half.

Under international rules, brands acquired in a separate transaction – for example, Bacardi-Martini's purchase of certain Scotch whisky and gin brands from Diageo in 1998 – can be recognised as an intangible asset. In this case, all the conditions for asset recognition are met. Where brands are acquired with other assets – for example, in a business combination, they should only be recognised as a separate intangible asset if their cost can be measured reliably. This is a difficult test to pass. There is no active market for brands and it is often hard to attribute corporate cash flows *specifically* to them. If a brand's cost cannot be measured reliably, then the brand is viewed as part of purchased goodwill and accounted for as such.

Intangibles: the accounting controversy continues

The international accounting standard on intangibles is relatively recent – it came into force in 1999 – and it's still too soon to judge its impact on company accounts. Supporters hope it will lead to greater harmonisation of accounting practice in this area and make it easier for investors to compare the financial statements of companies in different countries.

Critics are less sanguine. In their view, the standard takes too cautious an approach to the recognition of certain internally generated intangibles such as R&D. As a result, important resources do not appear on company balance sheets. This leads to misstatement of profits – and profitability – and undermines comparisons of returns on capital across firms. These arguments are developed more fully below.

A notable feature of recent decades is the growth in spending on knowledge-based activities. These are defined as R&D, software and higher education. Investment in knowledge-based activities by OECD countries – comprising 30 of the world's richest countries – increased on average by 3.4% a year in the 1990s. By contrast, investment in tangible fixed assets grew by only 2.2% a year on average over the same period.[15] Much of the expenditure on knowledge-related activities is expensed as incurred under current accounting rules. As a result, investments by companies in these activities – though growing as a proportion of their total investments – are often not recorded as assets on their balance sheets.

Companies would not undertake investments in knowledge-based activities if they did not expect them to yield future economic benefits. The stock market shares management's expectations. A recent US study estimates that the benefits from R&D investment accrue over five to nine years and the internal rate of return on investment in R&D ranges from 15% in the machinery and computer hardware sector to 28% in the chemicals and pharmaceuticals sector.[16] This indicates that the stock market implicitly capitalises R&D expenditures and applies different amortisation rates depending on the industry source of the R&D.

Accountants' conservatism in recognising R&D investment as an asset biases accounting measures of profitability. In fast-growing companies, ROA and ROE are likely to be *understated*. Companies may even report losses because of the immediate expensing of the costs of intangibles (e.g. start-up companies in high-technology industries). By contrast, when companies are mature and sales are growing slowly, reported ROA and ROE may be *overstated*. In this case, intangible costs expensed immediately approximate the amortisation of capitalised intangibles: thus profit is little different under the two alternatives. However, assets and shareholders' equity are *lower* under immediate expensing (because of the earlier write-off of intangibles), leading to ROA and ROE overstatement.

An example illustrates this. Consider Quixote's efforts to develop a new windmill. Suppose it projects development costs of 200,000 a year for at least the next five years. Exhibit 8.6 contrasts the effect on Quixote's forecast accounts of the alternative treatments of (a) immediately

Exhibit 8.6 Development costs: alternative accounting treatments and effect on income statement, balance sheet and profitability (amounts in 000)

Facts

Quixote spends 200 a year on the development of a new windmill design. Because of the nature of the expenditure, it can either capitalise or expense it immediately. Under the first alternative, the asset is amortised over four years.

Assume that Quixote has net assets of 3,000 at the start of year 1. Forecast pre-R&D annual profit – 500 in year 1 – is expected to grow by 50 each year for the next five years. Taxes are ignored. Dividends are assumed to be zero.

Profitability is defined as: Profit/End-year net assets.

Alternative accounting treatments

	Year				
	1	2	3	4	5
(a) Immediate expensing					
Profit excluding R&D	500	550	600	650	700
R&D expense	−200	−200	−200	−200	−200
Profit	300	350	400	450	500
Net assets	3,300	3,650	4,050	4,500	5,000
Profitability	9.1%	9.6%	9.9%	10%	10%
(b) Capitalisation and amortisation					
Profit excluding R&D	500	550	600	650	700
R&D expense	−50	−100	−150	−200	−200
Profit	450	450	450	450	500
R&D costs, net	150	250	300	300	300
Other net assets	3,300	3,650	4,050	4,500	5,000
Net assets	3,450	3,900	4,350	4,800	5,300
Profitability	13%	11.5%	10.3%	9.4%	9.4%

expensing (IE) and (b) capitalising and amortising (C&A) these costs. (A four-year amortisation period is assumed.)

Quixote's income statement and balance sheet suffer when it expenses R&D costs immediately. Year 1 profit and net assets are 150,000 less than the figures reported under the C&A method. In subsequent years the difference in profit shrinks as annual amortisation under C&A increases. By year 4, profit is the same under the two accounting methods. However, reported net assets under IE continue to be less – by the amount of the R&D asset (unamortised R&D costs) on the C&A balance sheet. In our example, this amount is 300,000 at the end of year 4 and, given our assumptions, remains at this level in year 5.

The impact of the two accounting methods on Quixote's reported profitability is revealing. Profitability under IE is lower initially (years 1–3) because of higher R&D expense. Once the expense (and profit) figures are the same under the two methods (years 4 and 5), profitability is higher under IE because of the smaller asset base.

The Quixote example also shows how current accounting rules on intangibles can undermine comparisons of profitability. If two R&D intensive companies, one mature, the other young, earn similar *economic* returns on investment, the mature company will report higher *accounting* returns – and may find it easier to attract capital as a result.

The critics of the IASB's approach to intangibles accounting have a powerful case. We would expect, therefore, that companies would capitalise expenditures on intangibles in those situations where they were allowed to. This rarely occurs, however. One reason is that investors are suspicious of firms that capitalise intangibles. They believe capitalisation gives management greater scope to manipulate earnings – through altering capitalisation and amortisation policies – and they may well demand a higher return to compensate them for the additional risk from investing in a 'capitaliser'. As a result, even where firms can capitalise expenditures on a specific category of intangible, they rarely do so. For example, few pharmaceutical companies that have adopted international standards capitalise product development costs, although this is permitted under IAS. Like other large US computer software companies, Microsoft expenses *all* software development costs as incurred, even though US accounting rules allow it to capitalise development costs incurred after it has established technological feasibility of a new software product.

How do investors overcome the problems associated with the existing accounting for intangibles? Some construct pro forma financial statements and account for intangibles such as R&D costs as if they had been capitalised and amortised *ab initio*. (For these investors, it's not capitalisation in itself they object to but who oversees it.) Another approach is to devise non-financial indicators (NFIs) of performance covering, for example, innovation, product quality and customer satisfaction and use them to supplement traditional financial measures of performance. NFIs may better explain changes in the market values of intangible-rich companies than financial indicators of performance (*see* Box 8.1).

BOX 8.1 **Non-financial indicators: making intangibles tangible**

Non-financial indicators (NFIs) are measures of corporate performance that, as the name suggests, rely wholly or partly on non-financial data. NFIs come in many forms. Some shed light on how efficiently a company uses fixed assets or labour (e.g. hotel occupancy rate, annual steel production per employee): these are productivity measures. Others focus on innovation and product quality. For example, investors may monitor a pharmaceutical company's patent filings or check surveys of customer satisfaction on a range of products from banking services to cars. NFIs are usually industry-specific, as the above examples demonstrate.

Empirical evidence suggests investors are likely to find NFIs particularly helpful when appraising companies that are rich in intangibles. In these cases, traditional financial statements may be misleading: expenditures on intangibles are expensed as incurred and profits and net assets of growing companies are understated. A study by Amir and Lev of 14 US mobile phone companies in the early 1990s illustrates this point well. They found that although these companies were, on average, loss-making, their market capitalisation to reported net assets (or 'market-to-book' ratio) was much higher than that of other New York Stock Exchange (NYSE) firms. They also found that selling, general and administrative (SGA) expenses and depreciation and amortisation (D&A) expenses of these companies were much higher than those of NYSE firms during this period. Table 1 below contrasts earnings yields, market-to-book ratios and SGA and D&A expense ratios of the 14 mobile phone companies and NYSE firms during the four years 1990–1993.[17]

Box 8.1 *continued*

Table 1   Selected median financial ratios for 14 mobile phone companies and NYSE firms, 1990–1993

		1993	1992	1991	1990
EPS/Price (%)	Mobile phone companies	−1.6	−4.0	−3.5	−0.4
	NYSE firms	4.6	5.1	5.0	7.2
Mkt-to-book	Mobile phone companies	12.3	6.6	9.3	11.2
	NYSE firms	2.1	1.8	1.7	1.4
SGA/Sales (%)	Mobile phone companies	42.1	46.1	52.7	46.4
	NYSE firms	20.1	20.2	20.2	19.5
D&A/PPE (%)	Mobile phone companies	15.4	15.2	15.7	12.8
	NYSE firms	6.8	6.8	6.9	6.9

The mobile phone companies in Amir and Lev's sample had SGA expense ratios of 42–53% between 1990 and 1993, over twice the level of NYSE firms. D&A as a proportion of property, plant and equipment (PPE) was over 15% in 1993, again more than twice the level of NYSE firms. Amir and Lev argue that part of these expenses represent investments and are viewed as such by investors. SGA expenses include customer acquisition costs. D&A comprise mostly amortisation of intangibles such as licences and goodwill. Mobile phone companies reporting high expenses in these areas were expanding, acquiring new licences, buying businesses and taking on new customers. In a regression of their sample companies' market value (more precisely, the market-to-book ratio) on earnings (pre-SGA and D&A), SGA expenses and D&A expenses, Amir and Lev found that the SGA and D&A variables had significant *positive* coefficients, consistent with these costs being viewed as value-creating investments by the stock market. By contrast, the coefficient for the earnings variable was not significant.

To overcome the deficiencies of traditional financial statements, investors often turn to NFIs. Those used to evaluate the performance of mobile phone companies include average revenue per user, churn rate, and costs of acquiring and retaining subscribers. Where mobile phone operators are awarded licences for defined geographic areas, as was the case in the USA in the 1980s, the population in the licence areas (POPS) and the penetration rate (ratio of subscribers to POPS) are additional NFIs investors monitor. POPS is a measure of a mobile phone company's growth potential while the penetration rate is an indicator of its operating performance. Only these two NFIs were available to Amir and Lev on a quarterly basis for their sample of mobile phone companies in the 1984–93 period. They found that in quarterly regressions of share price on financial and non-financial indicators, POPS and penetration rate both had statistically significant positive coefficients. The financial variables they used (net assets per share and EPS) were only statistically significant in combination with the non-financial indicators.

An extension of Amir and Lev's work is to use NFIs to value specific intangibles such as brands. Investors face problems doing this, however. Companies often don't publish NFI information. When they do, the NFI data can't be compared across firms because of measurement differences. There have been calls in the investment community for companies to standardise the calculation of widely used NFIs and disclose them in their published financial reports.[18]

SECTION 3

Fixed assets and financial statement analysis

Disclosure

Companies following international accounting standards provide extensive information about their fixed assets in the annual accounts. They disclose, under 'Accounting Policies', the basis (or bases) of valuing fixed assets, the estimated lives of the different classes of tangible fixed asset and the depreciation methods used. In addition, they are required to disclose the movement in the carrying amounts of tangible and intangible fixed assets over the year. Investors find this useful. They cannot tell from knowledge of beginning and ending balances alone whether, for example, a small net increase represents a small addition to fixed assets or the offsetting of large additions and large disposals.

Mining and petroleum companies usually disclose supplementary information about their natural resource properties. Under conventional accounting, such firms do not recognise in their accounts new ore bodies or petroleum reserves they discover. They only show as assets the costs incurred in developing them (and, in some cases, in exploring for them). They also capitalise the cost of properties purchased. Since accountants have not yet found an acceptable way of incorporating discovery values into corporate accounts, some stock exchanges now insist that listed firms in the oil and gas industry provide information about the size and location of their reserves and the reasons for changes in them during the year.

Fixed asset utilisation

Fixed asset information is used in analyses of asset efficiency. Recall from Chapter 3 that a profitability measure such as return on assets is the product of two elements, profit margin and assets turnover. A company's profitability is thus affected by the rate at which it turns over its assets in the year. We can explore the changes in a company's assets turnover over time (or the differences in asset turnover across firms) by breaking it down by type of asset, in particular by fixed assets, inventories and receivables.

Fixed assets turnover is usually computed as:

$$\text{Fixed assets turnover} = \frac{\text{(Net) sales revenues in year}}{\text{Average tangible and intangible fixed assets, at net book value}}$$

The higher the ratio, the more sales each unit of fixed assets generates and thus, other things being equal, the more intensively the company is using its buildings, plant and capitalised intangibles. (Intangible fixed assets are not always included in the calculation of fixed assets turnover.)

Note that the ratio is sensitive to the business cycle. In a recession, fixed assets turnover is likely to fall as sales remain static or decline and management are reluctant to cut production capacity in case the company's post-recession recovery is hindered. In periods of rapid economic growth, the ratio will rise as capacity utilisation increases and companies squeeze more sales out of existing plant and equipment.

Average age and life of tangible fixed assets

Depreciation data shed light on the age of a company's fixed assets and its policy on asset replacement. The plant and equipment of a newly formed company are young: accumulated depreciation is a small proportion of asset cost. Similarly, an established firm that invests heavily in new equipment reports a lower ratio of accumulated depreciation to asset cost than a competitor that replaces assets more slowly.

We can estimate the average age and life of a company's fixed assets directly. Assume for the moment that it uses straight-line depreciation and that price changes are small so that cost approximates current value. Then the average age of its depreciable fixed assets (at year-end) is:

$$\text{Average age (in years)} = \frac{\text{Accumulated depreciation, end-year balance}}{\text{Depreciation expense for the year}}$$

The average life of such assets is:

$$\text{Average life (in years)} = \frac{\text{Gross cost of depreciable assets at end-year}}{\text{Depreciation expense for the year}}$$

We can compute average age and life by class of fixed assets (buildings, plant, vehicles, office equipment) if the company breaks down the cost, depreciation and accumulated depreciation figures in this way.

The above calculations of average age and life are only approximate. They are sensitive to large increases or decreases during the year in the firm's fixed asset base. They are also sensitive to the rate of inflation and the depreciation method used. For example, when prices are rising but the firm values its fixed assets at HC, the average age of its assets is understated: older, lower-valued assets carry greater weight in the numerator (accumulated depreciation) than in the denominator (depreciation expense).

Fixed asset ratios and accounting policy differences

When comparing companies' fixed assets turnover, age and life, it is advisable to check their accounting policies beforehand. We saw earlier that differences can arise in the three main areas of fixed asset accounting.

- *Capitalisation*. Firms differ with respect to the costs they capitalise as part of tangible fixed assets. Examples are plant set-up costs (e.g. French companies may show them separately as a 'deferred charge') and interest on asset construction.
- *Depreciation/amortisation*. Differences in depreciation policy are a major reason for lack of international comparability of financial statements. Companies in countries with a uniform reporting tradition tend to depreciate tangible fixed assets faster. Tax rules allow them to use accelerated methods and/or to be conservative in their estimates of asset lives. The result is that, relative to sales, depreciation charges are higher and book values of fixed assets are lower. The effect of the latter is to raise fixed assets turnover.
- *Valuation*. Valuation differences can also undermine interfirm comparability. Recall that company accounts in France, Italy and Spain contain fixed assets at indexed amounts. Some Dutch companies record fixed assets at RC. Many UK companies state property assets at a valuation. In each case, the firms affected report lower fixed assets turnover than their HC-based rivals.

Differences in capitalisation, depreciation and valuation create problems for investors when they make cross-border comparisons of profitability. One solution is to use a 'cash earnings' number in profitability calculations. (Cash earnings is simply profit before deducting non-cash charges such as depreciation and amortisation.) Such adjustments are not usually necessary when making *within-country* comparisons of firms' profitability or when observing trends in a company's profitability over time.

Warning signals

A company has scope, through its accounting policies on fixed assets, to flatter its 'bottom line'. Investors are mindful of this, especially when reviewing the accounts of companies from separate reporting countries. Among the techniques in this area that firms use to raise short-term profits are:

- *Extending the boundaries of capitalisation.* A firm may alter slightly its measurement rules and capitalise more costs. For example, the notes in last year's accounts may state that interest is capitalised on own-constructed assets 'up to the date an asset is completed' whereas in this year's they state that interest is capitalised 'up to the date it is put into service'. The company should flag such changes if they have a material impact on the accounts. Nonetheless, it is wise to compare the phrasing of the fixed asset note in successive years' accounts, as the change may have a delayed impact on profits.
- *Changing the method of depreciation.* A firm with a fast-growing asset base may switch from an accelerated to a straight-line method to lower the annual depreciation charge. Once again, it should flag such a change and show the impact on the current year's accounts, if material.[19]
- *Lengthening assets' expected useful lives.* Amortising an asset over a longer period lowers the periodic charge. Firms do not always highlight the change in the accounts. Instead, they may disguise it by making the change within a broad asset category (e.g. plant and equipment with estimated lives of 10–20 years). As a check, investors calculate the average life of a firm's fixed assets (i.e. gross cost divided by the annual depreciation charge) over several years: if the figure is rising, especially in comparison with that of rival firms, they view it as a warning signal.

Note that a change in the accounting for fixed assets that increases short-term profits is not evidence, in itself, of profit manipulation. A firm may have a *bona fide* reason for making the change. For example, a slower than expected rate of technological change justifies extending the useful life of a class of assets. Thus more than one alarm bell must sound before investors conclude that management are manipulating profits.

Summary

As with other assets, tangible and intangible fixed assets are expected to provide future benefits to the firm. The benefits are mostly indirect. They arise from the use of the asset in the production of the goods a firm sells and the services it performs.

All costs incurred to bring a fixed asset to 'working condition for its intended use' are capitalised. So too are costs incurred to enhance its productive capacity. In some countries, the cost of borrowing to finance the asset's construction in-house can be capitalised as well.

Depreciation is the systematic allocation of the asset's cost or value over its useful life. Depreciation has no direct effect on corporate cash flow. There are various permitted methods of depreciation. Relative to the widely used straight-line method, accelerated methods such as the declining balance and sum-of-years'-digits methods lower profits and assets when introduced – but only continue to do so, if the asset base is expanding. Accelerated methods, if permitted for tax purposes, can postpone taxes and thus indirectly improve cash flow.

Some EU countries permit the revaluation of tangible fixed assets. Any surplus on revaluation is usually taken direct to reserves and is not distributable until the asset is depreciated or sold. Upward revaluation strengthens reported balance sheet ratios by increasing assets but depresses profitability for the same reason – and, in the case of depreciable assets, by lowering income through higher depreciation charges.

In the majority of European countries, tangible and intangible fixed assets are stated at (depreciated) cost. Under international accounting rules management must assess each period the amount recoverable from a fixed asset's use or sale. When the asset is impaired, it must be written down to the lower recoverable amount. Management now have less scope for manipulating income through altering the timing and magnitude of asset write-downs.

Internally generated intangibles such as employee skills, product design and brand names form a growing proportion of a firm's total resources. Accountants are reluctant to recognise them as assets because the future benefits they provide are uncertain or not appropriable by the firm. Some investors prepare their own pro forma financial statements for intangible-rich companies in which expenditures on key intangibles are capitalised rather than expensed as incurred.

Given the importance of tangible fixed assets to many firms, investors monitor carefully key statistics about them, such as their expected useful lives, age and productivity.

APPENDIX 8.1   Sum-of-years'-digits and units-of-production depreciation

We described two popular methods of depreciation in section 1 of the chapter: the straight-line and declining-balance methods. Two other systematic methods which you may encounter in published accounts are the **sum-of-years'-digits method** and the **units-of-production method**.

Sum-of-years'-digits (SoYD) method

The SoYD depreciation rate is calculated by relating the remaining life of an asset to its initial expected life. The asset's initial expected life is expressed in digits and the digits are then summed:

$$\text{SoYD depreciation rate} = \frac{\text{Number of remaining years of asset's life}}{\text{Asset's initial expected life, expressed in digits and summed}}$$

The SoYD depreciation charge is the SoYD rate times the asset's depreciable amount:

$$\begin{array}{c}\text{SoYD depreciation}\\\text{charge in year } t\end{array} = [\text{Cost} - \text{Salvage value}] \times \begin{array}{c}\text{SoYD depreciation}\\\text{rate in year } t\end{array}$$

Thus for an asset with a four-year expected life, the denominator of the SoYD depreciation rate is 10 (the sum of the digits of the asset's life: $4 + 3 + 2 + 1$). The fraction applied to the depreciable amount in the first year, with four years remaining, is 4/10; in the second year, with three years remaining, 3/10; and so forth.

The SoYD method is a reducing charge (or 'accelerated') method of depreciation. One advantage it offers over the rival declining-balance method is ease of calculation. However, this is now a minor consideration in today's computer age.

Units-of-production (UoP) method

Under the UoP method, the depreciation charge is a function of the asset's output or usage in the period. The depreciation rate is the ratio of the asset's output (or usage) in a period to its total expected output (or usage):

$$\text{UoP depreciation rate for year } t = \frac{\text{Output (usage) in year } t}{\text{Total expected output (usage)}}$$

The rate is applied to the asset's depreciable amount to give the depreciation charge for the period:

$$\begin{array}{c} \text{UoP depreciation} \\ \text{charge in year } t \end{array} = [\text{Cost} - \text{Salvage value}] \times \begin{array}{c} \text{UoP depreciation} \\ \text{rate in year } t \end{array}$$

This method results in a depreciation charge which fluctuates with output or asset use. It is favoured where an asset's useful life is conditioned more by physical usage than by economic or technological change. It's widely used by companies in natural resource industries to depreciate exploration and on-site production equipment.

● Illustration

Exhibit 8.7 illustrates the SoYD and UoP depreciation methods. It shows the calculation of annual depreciation and end-year net book value for Quixote's Rocinante van which we introduced in Section 1 of the chapter. The Rocinante van, you'll recall, cost 10,000 and has a five-year expected life and zero residual value. To calculate UoP depreciation, we need to know its expected and actual usage as well. Quixote reckons it will cover 150,000 km during its five-year life. Actual kilometres driven in each of the five years are: 45,000 in year 1; 30,000 in year 2; 22,500 in year 3; 37,500 in year 4; and 10,000 in year 5; a total of 145,000 km.

Given Rocinante's initial expected life of five years, the denominator of the SoYD depreciation rate in all years is 15. The depreciation rate in the first year, with five years' life remaining, is 33% (5/15). The numerator – and the depreciation rate – declines as the remaining years of life diminish. Thus in year 4, with two years' life remaining, the SoYD depreciation rate is 13.3% (2/15).

Under the UoP method, the depreciation rate varies with production each period. In this case, production is measured by kilometres driven. For example, in year 2, the van covered 30,000 kilometres. The van is expected to cover 150,000 kilometres over its useful life. Thus one-fifth of the van's total expected services were consumed that year and the depreciation charge is 2,000. In practice, an asset's actual total output rarely corresponds with expectations and an adjustment must be made in the final period, as in the Rocinante van's case.

APPENDIX 8.2   Investment property

A company may hold property as an investment rather than for its own use. It expects the land and/or building to yield a return in the form of rental income and capital appreciation. In the past, differences in accounting practice made it difficult for investors to compare the performance and condition of companies with significant investment property assets. Their task is now easier as a result of a new IAS on the topic.

The standard includes familiar recognition and measurement rules. As with other types of property, an investment property is recognised as a (fixed) asset when it is probable it will yield future economic benefits to the company owning or controlling it and its cost can be measured reliably. It should be measured initially at cost but thereafter it can be measured at either depreciated cost or fair value. A property's fair value is usually its market value as of the balance sheet date. A company must choose one of these two valuation bases and apply it consistently across all its investment properties. If it chooses depreciated cost as the valuation basis, it must disclose the fair value of investment properties in the notes to the accounts.[20]

The innovation in the accounting standard lies in how fair value accounting is applied. *A company must recognise in the income statement any gain or loss arising from a change in the fair value of investment property.*[21] This contrasts with the accounting treatment of unrealised holding gains

Exhibit 8.7 **Sum-of-years'-digits and units-of-production depreciation methods: illustration** (currency amounts in 000)

Facts

Quixote buys a Rocinante van for 10. It has an expected useful life of five years and expected residual value of zero.

Annual depreciation charge and net book value (NBV)

	SoYD method		UoP method	
	Depreciation expense	Net book value	Depreciation expense	Net book value
Acquisition		10		10
Year 1 depreciation	3.33	−3.33	3	−3
End-year 1 NBV		6.67		7
Year 2 depreciation	2.67	−2.67	2	−2
End-year 2 NBV		4		5
Year 3 depreciation	2	−2	1.5	−1.5
End-year 3 NBV		2		3.5
Year 4 depreciation	1.33	−1.33	2.5	−2.5
End-year 4 NBV		0.67		1.0
Year 5 depreciation	0.67	−0.67	1.0*	−1.0
End-year 5 NBV		0		0

Calculations

SoYD method:

- With five-year life, denominator of SoYD rate is 15 (5 + 4 + 3 + 2 + 1).
- Depreciation rates by year are:

Year 1	33%	(5/15)
2	26.7%	(4/15)
3	20%	(3/15)
4	13.3%	(2/15)
5	6.7%	(1/15)

UoP method:

- 'Production' is assumed to be 'number of kilometres driven'.
- Van will cover 150,000 km over its expected life.
- Depreciation rates by year are:

Year 1	30%	(45,000 km/150,000 km)
2	20%	(30,000 /150,000)
3	15%	(22,500 /150,000)
4	25%	(37,500 /150,000)
5		* Remaining balance charged as depreciation. Total actual usage rarely corresponds with expected usage.

and losses (UHG/L) on revalued fixed assets that are used in a company's business. As we saw in the chapter, these gains and losses are taken to a revaluation reserve in the balance sheet and unrealised holding losses (and their reversal) are recognised in the income statement only when the revaluation reserve is exhausted.

As a result of this and other international standards, there are different measurement rules depending on whether property is held as inventory, as an investment or for the company's own use. These differences are summarised in diagrammatic form below:

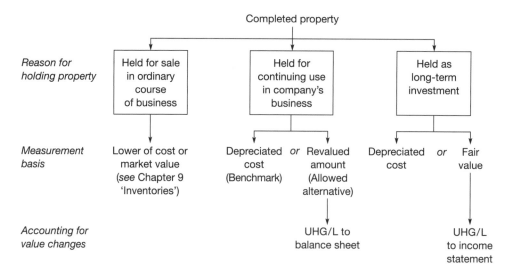

Note that the reason for holding property can change – and this too can give rise to an unrealised holding gain or loss. For example, if a company decides to hold a property as an investment that was previously held for sale – and the investment is to be carried at fair value, the transfer from inventory to investment is treated as equivalent to a sale. Any UHG/L at the date of transfer is recognised in income.

Real estate companies have been most affected by this accounting standard. For example, those in the UK and many Commonwealth countries have traditionally carried properties at market value – but the revaluations have not always been annual and unrealised holding gains and losses have usually been taken directly to a shareholders' equity account ('revaluation reserve') in the balance sheet.

Problem assignments

P8.1 Fixed asset measurement: which costs to capitalise?

Diafoirus, Purgon and Argan (two established doctors, one newly qualified) run a health clinic, Les Médecins Imaginaires (MI). Their practice is expanding and they decide to move the clinic's operations to larger premises.

The building they acquire is 15 years old and in need of modernisation. It cost 200,000 to build and the seller carries it in its books at depreciated cost of 80,000. MI pay 250,000 for it. Legal costs associated with the purchase are 6,000. MI obtain a ten-year 7% loan of 150,000 from their bank to finance the purchase.

The building requires extensive alterations. Before moving in, MI spend 50,000 on these alterations. They create new office space by altering internal walls and fitting partitions. They lower the ceilings of many of the rooms in order to house cable for medical and computer equipment. The alteration work takes two months. At the same time, they replace the air-conditioning system at a cost of 20,000. Toinette, MI's office manager, who spends half her time supervising the alteration work, receives an annual salary of 42,000.

Within a month of moving in, MI receive an annual property tax assessment of 3,000 and vandals smash some windows on the ground floor of the building. The cost of replacing the glass, 2,500, is covered by insurance but MI decide to fit external roller blinds to all the windows at a cost of 12,000 in order to reduce the risk of further damage and to improve the security of the building.

Required

MI record fixed assets at (historical) cost. In your opinion, which of the above costs should be capitalised and why?

P8.2 Introduction to depreciation methods

The Tivoli Company has just opened a pizza restaurant in Copenhagen. The restaurant contains a new pizza oven which cost 110,000 to buy and install. The oven has an expected life of ten years. The expected residual value is minimal and can be ignored.

You have been asked to illustrate the effect of different methods of depreciating the pizza oven on the company's income statement and balance sheet.

Required

Calculate the depreciation charge on the oven and its end-year carrying amount for years 1, 2 and 5 under the following methods of depreciation:

(a) the straight-line (SL) method;

(b) the declining-balance (DB) method. (The DB rate is assumed to be 150% of the SL rate);

(c)* the sum-of-years' digits (SoYD) method. (A formula for finding the denominator of the SoYD rate quickly is: $[n(n + 1)/2]$, where n is the initial expected life (in years) of the asset);

(d)* the units-of-production (UoP) method. (Total expected output of the oven over ten years is 600,000 standard-size pizzas. Forecast output in each of years 1 to 5 is: 30,000; 48,000; 66,000; 78,000; and 84,000 pizzas respectively.)

* **(c)** and **(d)** are based on material in Appendix 8.1.

P8.3 Depreciation: alternative methods and change in estimated useful life

Early in January x1, Ionian Airlines purchases a new wide-bodied aircraft for its short- and medium-haul routes in Europe. The aircraft cost 30 million. It has an expected useful life of 15 years and an estimated residual value of 3 million (in x1 values).

Ionian is pleased with its purchase. The aircraft proves to be more reliable and have lower operating costs than expected. At the start of x5, Ionian extends the estimated life by three years. However, it does not change its estimate of the aircraft's residual value.

Ionian encounters financial difficulties in x6 as a result of increased competition following the entry of low-cost airlines into its markets. It sells the aircraft for 18 million in late December x6. Ionian's financial year ends on 31 December.

Required

(a) Assume Ionian uses the SL method of depreciation. Calculate the depreciation that Ionian charges each year on this aircraft between x1 and x6. What is the gain or loss on disposal it recognises in its x6 accounts?

(b) Assume Ionian uses the DB method of depreciation. It sets the DB rate at 150% of the SL rate but ignores estimated residual values in determining the annual DB charge. Recalculate the annual depreciation Ionian charges on this aircraft between x1 and x6 and the gain or loss on disposal at the end of x6.

Some companies switch to SL depreciation when the SL charge, calculated on the basis of the remaining depreciable amount, exceeds the DB charge. If Ionian follows this practice, will it switch over to SL depreciation before it sells the aircraft in x6 and, if so, when?

(c) While reviewing the published accounts of Alpair, another European regional airline, you notice that it owns aircraft of a similar type but depreciates them over 12 years. Suggest reasons why the two airlines assume a different useful life for the same class of aircraft.

Check figure:
(a) Annual depreciation x5 – x6 1.414 million

P8.4　Depreciation, profits and cash flow

Sensing that the business world would profit from closer acquaintance with his fables, Aesop decides to launch a management consulting firm. It begins trading on 1 January year 1 with cash and capital of 100 and immediately acquires, for cash, office equipment costing 75. Trading is all cash-based: year 1 revenues are expected to be 200 and year 1 expenses (other than depreciation) 150. No dividend will be paid to shareholders that year.

The equipment has an expected useful life of five years. The company can depreciate the equipment using either straight-line or accelerated depreciation. Under the SL method, annual depreciation is 15. Under the accelerated method, depreciation is 30 in the first year (and 18, 11, 8 and 8 in the remaining four years).

The company's choice has tax consequences, however. Under the country's tax code, it must use the same depreciation method to calculate its income tax liability as it uses in its published accounts. Its tax position in year 1 is uncertain. It may be able to avoid tax altogether. At the other extreme, it may have to pay it at the full rate of 40%.

Required

(a) Aesop asks Leopard, a new employee, to investigate the effects of different depreciation and tax assumptions on the company and to draw up projected year 1 accounts using the framework in Exhibit 8.8.

The two depreciation alternatives are the SL method and the accelerated method. The two tax assumptions are tax rates of zero and 40% respectively. Help Leopard complete the exhibit.

(b) After preparing the projected accounts, Leopard reckons the numbers all tell the same story. The company should select the SL depreciation method because reported profit is higher under this method at tax rates of zero and 40% and, as far as he can see, at all tax rates in between. Do you agree with his conclusion?

P8.5　Economist's view of depreciation

Milton Keynes is puzzled by the accountant's calculation of depreciation. As an economist, he views depreciation as the decline in an asset's market value over a period. If an active market for an asset does not exist, market value can be approximated by the present value of the expected cash flows the asset will generate. In this case, depreciation is the fall in the present value of those cash flows.

'For example,' says Milton, 'suppose an asset has a three year life and is expected to generate cash flows of 100 at the end of each year. Assuming a 10% discount rate and no salvage value, the asset has a value now of 248.7. Annual depreciation is then the decline in the discounted amount of those cash flows over the year. I estimate annual depreciation for this asset for years 1 to 3 as follows:

	Expected cash flows	Present value (at 10%)	Depreciation in year
Now		248.7	
End-year 1	100	173.6	75.1 (year 1)
End-year 2	100	90.9	82.7 (year 2)
End-year 3	100	0	90.9 (year 3)

'Simple, isn't it? And, unlike many economic ideas, so easy for the business man or woman to understand!'

Required

Comment on Milton's method of calculating depreciation. It is known as the 'annuity method'. What are the key differences between this method and the methods (e.g. straight-line, declining-balance) which companies normally use? Why do you think Milton's method is rarely used by companies in their published accounts – or by tax authorities in determining a company's taxable income?

| Exhibit 8.8 | Effect of depreciation method on the accounts under different tax regimes |

	Aesop Year 1 accounts			
			Depreciation method	
	Straight-line		*Accelerated*	
	(1)	(2)	(1)	(2)
Tax rate	0%	40%	0%	40%
Income statement for year 1				
Revenues	200	200	200	200
Expenses:				
Depreciation	. . .	. . .	. . .	. . .
Other	−150	−150	−150	−150
Profit before tax	. . .	. . .	. . .	. . .
Income tax	. . .	. . .	. . .	. . .
Net profit	. . .	. . .	. . .	. . .
Balance sheet, end-year 1				
Assets				
Fixed assets	75	75	75	75
Less: Accumulated depreciation	. . .	. . .	. . .	. . .
Fixed assets, at NBV	. . .	. . .	. . .	. . .
Cash	. . .	. . .	. . .	. . .
Total assets	. . .	. . .	. . .	. . .
Shareholders' equity				
Share capital	100	100	100	100
Retained profit	. . .	. . .	. . .	. . .
Total equities	. . .	. . .	. . .	. . .

P8.6 Extracting fixed asset information from the accounts

Henkel is a German-owned manufacturer of personal care and household products. Among its best-known international brands are Loctite adhesives, Fa cosmetics and Persil and Dixan laundry detergents. In 2001, Henkel sold its Cognis chemical business and its stake in the Henkel–Ecolab industrial and institutional hygiene joint venture in order to focus production and marketing efforts on its branded products.

Henkel draws up its financial statements according to IAS. It provides in the notes to the consolidated accounts a schedule showing the movement in fixed assets (including financial fixed assets) during the year. The schedule for 2001 is set out in Exhibit 8.9. All amounts are in € million.

Required

(a) What is the carrying amount of Henkel Group's tangible fixed assets at 31 December 2001?

(b) (i) Henkel reports in a separate note that it made a gain of 98 from the disposal of fixed assets in 2001. (This figure excludes the gains from disposal of its Cognis business and its stake in the Henkel–Ecolab joint venture.) Calculate the sale value of the fixed assets disposed of in 2001.

(ii) Henkel reports as an investing inflow in the 2001 consolidated cash flow statement 'proceeds from disposal of fixed assets' of 182. (Again, this amount does not include the proceeds from the sale of the Cognis and Henkel–Ecolab investments.) Why is this figure not the same as your answer to (b)(i)?

Exhibit 8.9 Henkel Group: changes in fixed assets schedule for 2001 (extract)

	Intangible assets	Property, plant and equipment	Financial assets	Total
Cost				
At January 1, 2001	3,687	7,386	925	11,998
Changes in the group*	−145	−2,944	−12	−3,101
Additions	40	534	731	1,305
Disposals	382	275	49	706
Reclassifications	3	−2	−1	−
Translation differences	66	49	34	149
At December 31, 2001	3,269	4,748	1,628	9,645
Accumulated depreciation				
At January 1, 2001	1,085	4,615	3	5,703
Changes in the group*	−44	−1,961	1	−2,004
Write-ups	−	2	−	2
Depreciation and amortization	512	481	2	995
Disposals	371	226	−	597
Reclassifications	−	−	−	−
Translation differences	42	18	−	60
At December 31, 2001	1,224	2,925	6	4,155
Fixed assets (net) at December 31, 2001	2,045	1,823	1,622	5,490

* Disposal of Cognis chemical business and stake in Henkel–Ecolab joint venture.

(*Source*: Henkel Group, *Annual Report 2001*. Reproduced by permission of Henkel KGaA.)

(c) In preparing the consolidated accounts, Henkel's management must translate into euros the financial statements of subsidiaries located outside the eurozone, before combining them with those of the company's eurozone subsidiaries. In most cases, it translates all assets and liabilities – including fixed assets – at the exchange rate prevailing on the balance sheet date. If, as is likely, exchange rates between the subsidiary's currency and the euro change between the start of the year (or the date of asset acquisition/disposal during the year) and the end of the year, exchange gains and losses arise. These are reported as a 'translation difference' in the 'Changes in fixed assets' schedule.

From inspection of the translation differences reported in Exhibit 8.9, did the euro strengthen or weaken overall against the currencies of Henkel's foreign subsidiaries? Give reasons for your answer.

P8.7 Revaluation and impairment of fixed assets

Garter Inns is a hotel chain with small but fast-growing international operations. Early in x2 it buys a hotel in Thailand for cash. The fair value of the hotel building then is 50. (All amounts are in millions of euros.) Garter Inns depreciates hotel buildings on a straight-line basis over 25 years and assumes a zero residual value. The following events occur over the five years to end-x6:

1 Professional valuers carry out a valuation of all Garter Inns hotels at the end of x2. These external valuations usually occur every three years. The valuers estimate the current market value of the Thai hotel building at 54.
2 There is an economic crisis in Asia in x4. Hotel occupancy rates fall sharply. Garter's management carry out an impairment review at the end of x4 (after recording depreciation for the year). They estimate the value of the Thai building in its existing use to be 30. But developers express interest in the property for conversion to mixed office and residential use and their net offer price is 33.

3 Economic conditions are still difficult at the end of x5 when the triennial valuation of Garter's properties occurs. No revaluation of the Thai hotel occurs then.

4 The Asian economy rebounds in x6. Management carry out an impairment review at the end of x6
(after recording depreciation for the year) and estimate the Thai building's recoverable amount at
42 then.

Garter Inns prepares its accounts according to international accounting standards.

Required

(a) Assume Garter Inns measures its land and buildings at depreciated cost. Show the effect on the
company's accounts of:
  (i) the purchase of the Thai hotel building in x2;
  (ii) the changes in its carrying amount each year over the five years to end-x6.

Use journal entries or the balance sheet equation.

(b) Assume Garter Inns measures its land and buildings at revalued amounts. It carries buildings in
its accounts at their net amount (i.e. it does not show accumulated depreciation separately). Show
the effect on the company's accounts of the changes in the carrying amount of the Thai hotel
building each year over the five years to end-x6.

> *Check figures:*
> Loss (in x4) from asset write-down
> (recognised in income statement): (a) 11; (b) 10.5

P8.8 Intangible assets: the recognition controversy

SnapHappy is a Canadian mail-order film developer. Although the photo developing business in
Canada is growing slowly, SnapHappy has reported large increases in sales and earnings in recent
years. Sales jumped from C$46m in x0 to C$118m in x6. Net profit rose even faster – from C$2.9m
to C$11m over the same period. The stock market thinks the company has a great future. In early x7
the company was valued at C$350m – three times x6 sales and 26 times estimated x7 earnings.

What is the secret of SnapHappy's success? Many investors (and management) attribute it to
the company's marketing flair. Rather than compete on price, the company focuses on service. The
following are some of the company's innovations:

- Customers are offered a set of slides and a set of prints from the same roll of film.
- They also receive a 'picture index', showing miniphotos of every picture on the roll.
- A replacement roll of film is included with every development order.

As a result, customers accept prices 60% above those of discount film developers and the company
reports a 40% gross margin.

Some investors have doubts. They take issue with the company's accounting practices.
SnapHappy capitalises the costs of its direct mailings to prospective customers and amortises them
over three years. This is a questionable practice since SnapHappy's marketing innovations are easy
to copy and retaining customers is difficult. The company's end-x6 balance sheet has C$15m of mar-
keting costs under 'fixed assets'. If it expensed all marketing costs as incurred, x6 earnings would
have been C$7.5m instead of the C$11m reported.

SnapHappy counters that the company's accounting is prudent. Marketing costs are amortised at
an accelerated rate – 55% in the first year, 29% in the second, 16% in the third. These figures are based
on 15 years' experience of customer purchasing behaviour. And the company is still innovating. Its
latest service is to provide a photo finishing service for customers with digital cameras. They can send
images over the Internet using a personal computer and the resulting prints are then returned to them
by post.

Required

Consider SnapHappy's policy of accounting for direct mailing costs to prospective customers. How
do you think these costs should be accounted for? Give reasons for your decision.

P8.9 Intangible assets: from capitalisation to write-off

Helius Software is a fast-growing company specialising in environmental management software. Helius capitalises certain software development costs – in particular the costs of improving or extending existing software products – and amortises them over a 3–5 year period. Management are firm supporters of capitalisation. They maintain that the development costs they capitalise meet the definition of an asset and fulfil asset recognition criteria. They also claim that, if they had expensed such costs, the firm would not have grown as fast as it has. Raising capital, especially debt capital, would have been more difficult since the firm's asset base would have been smaller.

Helius was founded in x1. Summary accounts for the six years from x2 to x7 are set out in Exhibit 8.10.

Required

(a) You discover that Helius's competitors write off all software development costs as incurred. What would Helius's operating profit and capital employed (fixed assets plus working capital) have been in the five years x3 to x7 if the firm had followed a similar policy of immediate write-off of development costs? Assume the change in accounting method has no effect on the income taxes the company pays.

(b) In the light of your answer to (a), suggest another reason why Helius's management favour capitalisation.

Check figure:
(a) Operating profit, x5   78

Helius Software
Summarised income statements and balance sheets
for the six years, x2–x7
(amounts in 000)

	x2	x3	x4	x5	x6	x7
Income statement						
Operating revenues	308	425	649	1,070	1,767	2,340
– Amortisation of development costs	–20	–32	–31	–47	–72	–174
– Other operating expenses	–246	–324	–507	–857	–1,425	–1,973
Operating profit	42	69	111	166	270	193
Net profit	29	31	52	90	221	164
Balance sheet, end-year						
Capitalised software	145	200	290	425	780	1,530
Less: Accumulated amortisation	–38	–70	–101	–148	–220	–394
Capitalised software at net book value	107	130	189	277	560	1,136
Property and equipment	95	131	120	175	341	1,946
Working capital	2	6	95	233	935	950
Capital employed	204	267	404	685	1,836	4,032
Shareholders' equity	119	170	227	650	1,672	1,842
Long-term debt	85	97	177	35	164	2,190
Long-term capital	204	267	404	685	1,836	4,032

Notes to Chapter 8

1   International Accounting Standards Board, *IAS 16: Property, Plant and Equipment*, para. 16. The requirements of the 4th Directive are similar (Art. 35(2) and (3)).

2   International Accounting Standards Board, *IAS 23: Borrowing Costs. See also* the 4th Directive, Art. 35(4).

3   Depreciation may form part of the cost of another asset rather than being expensed in the period incurred. We illustrate this in the following chapter on inventories.

4   This means that the firm should estimate the residual value using prices ruling at the time of the asset's purchase.

5   Many firms ignore salvage value when computing the depreciable amount under the DB method. This is because the actual depreciation rate they use is inaccurate. The DB rate should be the rate which ensures that the asset's NBV declines to expected salvage value by the end of its life. This rate can be determined exactly as

$$(1 - \sqrt[n]{s/c})$$

where n is the asset's estimated useful life, s is its salvage value and c is its acquisition cost. Since this formula can result in a different depreciation rate for each asset, it's rarely used in practice.

6   Fédération des Experts Comptables Européens (1993), *1992 FEE Analysis of European Accounting and Disclosure Practices*, London: Routledge, tables 6.9 and 6.15.

7   Ibid., table 6.9.

8   IAS also allow firms to eliminate the existing accumulated depreciation balance against the cost of the asset and revalue the *net* amount.

9   Notice that Quixote's income statement bears the higher depreciation expense of 2,400 from year 3 only. The adjustment to RC depreciation for years 1 and 2 (800 total) is taken to the balance sheet: the credit to revaluation reserves is the net increase in replacement cost of 1,200, not the gross increase of 2,000. An alternative, more conservative approach is to charge the additional depreciation for prior years – known as **backlog depreciation** – to the income statement which, of course, depresses profits.

10   International Accounting Standards Board, *IAS 36: Impairment of Assets*. The standard covers certain investments (e.g. investments in associated companies and joint ventures) as well as tangible and intangible fixed assets.

11   It may not be possible to estimate the recoverable amount of an asset in isolation (e.g. because of its interdependence with other assets). In this event, the firm applies the impairment test to the asset's 'cash-generating unit' (i.e. the group of assets of which it is a part).

12   *IAS 16*, op. cit. *See also* 4th Directive, Art. 33(1).

13   International Accounting Standards Board, *IAS 38: Intangible Assets*.

14   In 2002, the IASB issued a draft standard on business combinations that, if implemented, would eliminate mandatory amortisation of goodwill but would require companies to test the goodwill asset for impairment each year.

15   Organisation for Economic Cooperation and Development (2001), *Science Technology and Industry Scoreboard of Indicators 2001: Towards a Knowledge-based Economy*, Paris: OECD.

16   Lev, B. and Sougiannis, T. (1996), The capitalization, amortization, and value-relevance of R&D, *Journal of Accounting and Economics*, 21: 107–138.

17   Amir, E. and Lev. B. (1996), Value-relevance of non-financial information: the wireless communications industry, *Journal of Accounting and Economics*, 22: 3–30.

18   Some managers are in favour of standardising the calculation of NFIs. A widely used indicator in the retail sector is 'like-for-like' (or 'organic') sales, a figure that removes the contribution of new store openings to reported total sales. Carlos Criado-Perez, then chief executive of Safeway, a large UK supermarket chain, criticised London analysts for misrepresenting the company's trading performance in the first half of 2002. He argued that rivals Sainsbury and Tesco had inflated their like-for-like sales numbers in the same period by including extra selling space they'd installed in existing stores (Voyle, S. (2002), Safeway chief launches attack on City analysts, *Financial Times*, 1 November).

19　Some firms pursue a more subtle strategy. They switch to the units-of-production (UoP) method for certain types of asset. Investors are suspicious of this method (except in the natural resources industry where it's an accepted practice). The reason is that the company may overestimate total production or usage during the asset's useful life – thereby inflating the denominator of the depreciation factor and reducing the annual charge. Moreover, the UoP depreciation charge is conveniently low in periods of low activity – which are usually periods of low profits, too.

20　International Accounting Standards Board, *IAS 40: Investment Property*.

21　*IAS 40*, para. 28. Under the fair value approach, the property is accounted for in the same way as certain financial investments. We discuss the accounting for financial investments in Chapter 13.

9

Inventories

INTRODUCTION

In this chapter, we examine the accounting for and reporting of inventories. For retailing companies, inventories consist largely of goods held for resale. For manufacturing companies, inventories include materials to be used directly and indirectly in production ('raw materials and consumables'), completed products ready for sale ('finished goods') and products which are still in the course of manufacture ('work in progress'). They are an important asset of retailing and manufacturing companies: for example, inventories make up 10–20% of the total assets of most manufacturing companies.

The central issue companies face when reporting inventories is how to measure them. Specifically, companies must decide:

- which costs to include in inventories; and
- how to value them.

Manufacturing firms usually capitalise all production costs – including production overheads – when determining the cost of work in progress and finished goods. We explain and illustrate this method of costing which is known as **absorption costing**. (An alternative method, **variable costing**, is used by a minority of companies. We describe it in the appendix to this chapter.)

Most European (and all US) companies value their inventories at historical cost (HC), that is the cost of purchase or production. Some, however, value them at replacement cost. We illustrate both valuation methods. HC valuation is not straightforward. Purchase and production costs change over time. Most firms make an assumption about the way these changing costs flow through inventory to sales: on a first-in, first-out (FIFO) basis, on a last-in, first-out (LIFO) basis, or a weighted-average basis. We explain these various cost-flow assumptions and show the impact of each on corporate income and cash. We also describe an end-of-period valuation adjustment – writing down inventories to their lower market value – which most firms using HC apply.

Investors monitor inventories closely. We explain a key ratio, **inventory turnover**, which they employ to do this. They also calculate firms' cost-to-sales ratios. Because European firms classify costs differently, some by function, others by nature, intercompany comparison may not be possible. We look once again at the two ways of classifying costs, this time in a manufacturing context.

We begin the chapter, however, on a bookkeeping note. We outline the two principal ways companies maintain their inventory records. These are known as the **periodic** and the **perpetual** systems of record-keeping. How a company keeps its inventory records can affect the types of cost included in inventories and thus the way they are measured.

Inventory records: perpetual and periodic systems

A company can maintain its inventory records in one of two ways. *Under the 'perpetual system', it enters all movements of inventory, both inflows and outflows.* It updates its records on a continuous basis. Thus it can determine, at any time, the amounts consumed or sold by consulting its records. *Under the 'periodic system', it records only additions to inventory.* To find the amounts consumed or sold in a period, it must count (and value) the inventory at the start and end of the period. Thus it updates its records only periodically.

A simple example shows how the two systems operate in practice. Gretel and Hansel both make a device known as a 'witchit', an important component in certain food processing equipment. Witchits are made from steel and other materials. Consider the way each of them accounts for movements in steel inventory.

Gretel updates her steel inventory records on a continuous basis (*perpetual system*). Her accounts show steel costing 25,000 in stock at 31 December year 4. During year 5, she records the purchase of steel costing 35,000 and the use of 40,000 worth in witchit manufacture. Thus her records show end-year 5 steel inventory with a book value of 20,000.

By contrast, Hansel updates his inventory records only at the end of each year (*periodic system*). He begins year 5 with steel holdings of 10,000, this being the cost of the steel in stock which was counted on 31 December year 4. He acquires steel for 55,000 during year 5. A count by Hansel at 31 December year 5 shows his steel holdings to be 20,000 in cost terms. These details are summarised in T account form in Exhibit 9.1.

From Exhibit 9.1 we see that under the periodic system there is an unknown quantity which has to be derived. It is the cost of inventory used (or, in the case of a retailing company, sold) in the period. This can only be derived accurately by counting the inventory on hand at the end of the period, costing it and deducting the amount from the cost of inventory available for use (or sale). In Hansel's case:

	Inventory counted and costed at end-year 4	10,000
+	Inventory purchased	+55,000
	Cost of inventory available for use	65,000
−	Inventory counted and costed at end-year 5	−20,000
	Cost of inventory used in year 5	45,000

By contrast, Gretel can consult her (perpetual) inventory records at any time to discover the amount and cost of steel used in previous periods and currently on hand.

The perpetual system of record-keeping offers managers several advantages. *First, it provides them with up-to-date information about inventory movements and inventory levels.* By contrast, under the periodic system, management must resort to frequent stock counts to obtain similar information (although, if there is a stable relationship between material inputs and output of final product, it can estimate material usage from sales data).

Second, when supplemented by stock counts, it yields information – about inventory 'shrinkage' – which a periodic system does not normally supply. Companies using a perpetual system also count their inventories at regular intervals. A stock count provides a check on the accuracy of a

Exhibit 9.1 Perpetual and periodic systems: inventory accounts contrasted

Gretel and Hansel
Summarised inventory accounts
(all are currency amounts and in 000)

	Gretel *(Perpetual system)*			*Hansel* *(Periodic system)*	
	Inventory (steel)			Inventory (steel)	

Balance, 1/1/yr 5	25	Used in witchit manufacture	40	Balance, 1/1/yr 5	10	Used in witchit manufacture	x
Purchases	35			Purchases	55		
Balance, 31/12/yr 5	20			Balance, 31/12/yr 5	20		

x = cost of inventory used in year.
= beginning balance
  + purchases of inventory
  − ending balance
= 45

company's records and can indicate to management the incidence and scale of unexpected decreases in inventory. Shrinkage can be the result of deterioration, damage or theft. Once its existence is known, management can investigate the reasons for it.

For example, suppose an end-year 5 stock count at both companies indicates the closing balance has a cost of 18,000. Under his periodic system, Hansel records the cost of steel used at 47,000 (10 + 55 − 18) instead of 45,000. However, Gretel's perpetual system reveals a discrepancy between the records and physical inventory levels. Assuming the records themselves are not in error, the unexpected decrease of 2,000 cannot be attributed to normal usage. This will prompt Gretel to investigate the reason for the unexplained variation. Under a periodic system, the inventory records cannot provide such a signal. As a result, stock controls are weaker.

There are other accounting implications, in particular for the costing of finished goods. Consider what happens to the 2,000 of shrinkage. Under a periodic system, it is treated as part of the cost of material used in the manufacture of witchits. As such, it enters into the cost of finished units and is charged to the income statement – as part of 'cost of sales' – only when those units are sold. Under a perpetual system, the amount is not capitalised since it provides no future benefit: instead, it is written off as a loss in the period when it's identified.

A perpetual record-keeping system does have one disadvantage. It's more costly to operate than a periodic system. Where inventories are of low value or change little over the period, the costs of running a perpetual system may outweigh the benefits from the additional information it provides. Note that a firm can employ both systems – for different types of inventory – within the same plant.

The capitalisation decision

Companies with material holdings of inventory face the question: which costs should be treated as part of inventory and capitalised? We had a foretaste of this in the previous section when considering the 'cost' of shrinkage. Firms in Europe and elsewhere follow a long-standing principle accepted worldwide. *All costs are capitalised which are incurred in order to bring the inventories to 'their present location and condition'.*[1]

For retailing and wholesaling companies, this means that, in addition to the purchase price, any specific, non-reclaimable duties (such as import tariffs) are capitalised. So, too, is the cost of shipping the goods *into* the store or warehouse. (Freight-*out* costs, however, are treated as distribution costs and are expensed in the period incurred.)

For manufacturing companies, the principle is more ambiguous. Clearly, the raw materials – and the production labour incurred to convert them into saleable product – are inputs necessary to bring inventories of finished goods to their completed state. But how should a company account for costs which are not directly associated with the manufacture of each unit of product? Such costs are often described as 'overhead costs' or simply 'overheads'.

Overheads cover a wide range of costs. They include production-related costs such as plant depreciation, plant maintenance and the costs of utilities and insurance associated with the factory. They also extend to selling, distribution and administrative costs. Firms distinguish between production and non-production overheads. The salary of a foreman is considered a production overhead. That of a senior manager with production and administrative responsibilities is in part a production overhead and in part an administrative overhead. Strictly, the cost of her salary should be apportioned between the two, based (this is one obvious allocation basis) on the time she spends on each of the two types of duties.

The distinction between production and non-production overheads is an important one in practice. The method of costing products used by most manufacturing companies is **absorption**

Exhibit 9.2 Absorption costing: impact of product and period costs on accounts

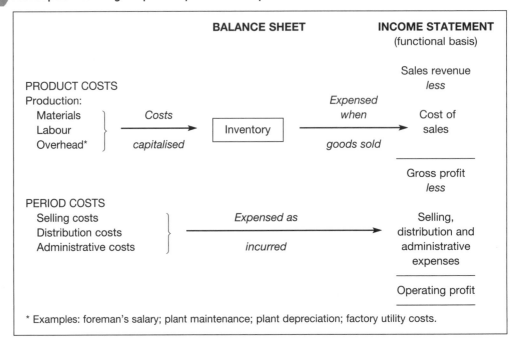

* Examples: foreman's salary; plant maintenance; plant depreciation; factory utility costs.

costing. *Under this method, a firm capitalises all production costs – material, labour and overheads – when determining the cost of manufactured inventory in its published accounts.* All other costs are charged to the income statement in the period when they're incurred. (We show how it's applied in a later section.) Costs capitalised in inventory are known as **product costs**. Non-capitalised costs – those charged to the income statement immediately – are known as **period costs**. Exhibit 9.2 summarises the various types of product and period cost under absorption costing and the impact of both on the accounts.

The practice of capitalising production costs and expensing immediately all non-production costs is of long standing. The justification is that only production costs add value directly to the product. There are also practical reasons for limiting capitalisation to production costs. The link between selling or administrative costs and individual products is often hard to show. In addition, there is less risk of valuing inventories above their fair value in the balance sheet since clearly their book values are lower than they would be if non-production costs were capitalised.

Firms following international accounting standards must use absorption costing.[2] An alternative method of costing which is used by some firms in their internal accounts is **variable costing**. *Under this method, only production costs directly attributable to the product's manufacture (mainly production materials and labour) are capitalised and shown as the cost of inventory.* Other production costs (and all non-production costs) are expensed in the period incurred. It yields lower inventory values than absorption costing but it allows readers of accounts to see more clearly the link between sales and profits. We illustrate this method in the appendix.

Flow of product costs: retailer and manufacturer

How do manufacturing companies record production costs? It's helpful to contrast the ways product costs flow through the manufacturer's and the retailer's inventory accounts. We look first at the retailer and then the manufacturer.

Flow of retailer's costs

Recall for a moment the essential features of a retailer's operations. He buys goods, stores them and later sells them. The goods themselves are not (intentionally) physically altered during the period between purchase and sale. The accounting mirrors the physical movement of the goods.

1 During the period of storage, the costs of the goods are held in a balance sheet account, 'merchandise inventory'.
2 At the time of sale (perpetual system) or at the end of the financial period when the inventory is counted (periodic system), the costs of the goods sold are removed from inventory and transferred to the income statement. They are recorded as an expense ('Cost of goods sold') and matched against the revenues generated by the sale.

The flow of product costs for the retailer (or wholesaler) is charted in Exhibit 9.3.

Flow of manufacturer's costs

Now consider the operations of a manufacturer. She buys raw materials and employs people and equipment to convert those materials into a product which is then sold. Under absorption costing, she records *in inventory* the costs of converting the materials to finished product. Thus inventoried costs consist of:

Exhibit 9.3   Flow of product costs in a retailing company

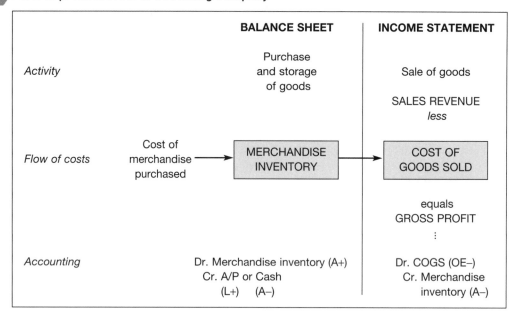

- raw materials (sometimes known as direct materials);
- direct production labour; and
- production overhead (i.e. plant depreciation, factory utility costs, plant maintenance, foreman's salary and other indirect labour costs of production).

There are various ways in which the manufacturer can record the production costs in her books. Exhibit 9.4 illustrates one approach which is common where production is by job or batch. The accounting assumes continuous updating of inventory records (perpetual system).

For this manufacturing company, product costs flow as follows:

1 Materials when purchased are stored in an inventory account 'Raw materials inventory' (RM).

2 When production begins, the costs of the materials *used* are transferred from RM to another inventory account, 'Work-in-progress inventory' (WIP).

3 The production costs of converting the materials into saleable product, namely the costs of direct labour and production overhead, are recorded in WIP as they're incurred. In effect, these conversion costs are *capitalised* (made into an asset).

4 When a unit of product is completed, the production costs attached to it are transferred from WIP to a third inventory account, 'Finished goods inventory' (FG), and stored there until the item is sold.

5 When the product is sold, its costs are transferred from the balance sheet ('Finished goods inventory') to the income statement ('Cost of goods sold'). The manufacturer, like the retailer, recognises revenue from the sale and matches against it the (production) cost of the item sold.

Thus while a good is being made or, once made, is in store awaiting sale, its production costs are viewed as an asset of the firm (Inventory). When it is sold, the firm gives up the asset (in exchange for cash or a claim to cash). As revenue from the sale is recognised, the cost of the relinquished asset is recorded as an expense (Cost of goods sold).

| Exhibit 9.4 | Flow of product costs in a manufacturing company |

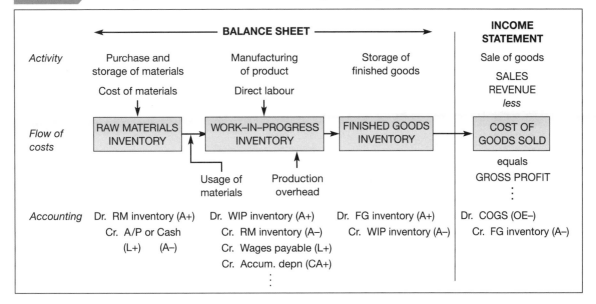

Absorption costing illustrated

We can follow the flow of costs – from purchase of raw materials to sale of finished goods – in Gretel's accounts for year 5. Assume Gretel begins the year with net assets of €125,000, of which €25,000 represent the cost of raw materials inventory. The key year 5 production facts are that Gretel:

- starts manufacture of 8,000 witchits,
- completes 7,000, and
- sells 6,000 (for €16 each).

Each witchit requires €5 of materials, €2 of labour, and €4 of overhead. The 1,000 witchits in end-year 5 WIP inventory need no further materials but are half-complete with respect to labour and overhead.

The events in Gretel's production-to-sale cycle in year 5 are described below and referenced by number to the worksheet in Exhibit 9.5.

[1] Gretel buys €35,000 worth of raw materials in year 5 . . .
[2] and issues materials costing €40,000 for the 8,000 units on which production starts in year 5 (8,000 units × €5).
[3] Gretel incurs production labour costs of €15,000 [(7,000 units × €2) + (1,000 units × 0.5 × €2)] . . .
[4] and production overhead of €30,000 [(7,000 units × €4) + (1,000 units × 0.5 × €4)].
[5] Gretel completes the 7,000 witchits at a unit cost of €11 (5 of materials, 2 of labour and 4 of overhead) and transfers the costs (€77,000) to finished goods inventory.
[6] The company records the €66,000 cost of the units sold (6,000 at €11) . . .
[7] when it recognises the revenue of €96,000 (6,000 units at €16) from those sales.

At year-end, 1,000 witchits are 'in progress', half-complete with respect to labour and overhead. Their unit cost is €8 (5 of materials, 1 of labour and 2 of overhead). In addition, 1,000 finished witchits with a unit cost of €11 await sale.

Exhibit 9.5   Production cost flows under absorption costing: transaction analysis format

Gretel Company

| | Inventory | | | Other net | Shareholders' |
Amounts in €000	RM	WIP	FG	assets	equity
Balance,1/1/year 5	25	0	0	100	125
[1] RM purchased	+35			−35	
[2] RM used	−40	+40			
[3] Production labour					
costs incurred		+15		−15	
[4] Production overhead					
costs incurred		+30		−30	
[5] Units completed		−77	+77		
[6] Cost of sales			−66		−66
[7] Sales revenue				+96	+96
Balance, 31/12/year 5	20	8	11	116	155

We show in Exhibit 9.6 how these events affect Gretel Company's ledger accounts. The journal entries recording, for example, direct labour and plant depreciation costs have the following form:

Dr. WIP inventory (A+)	xx	
Cr. Wages payable (L+)		xx
Dr. WIP inventory (A+)	xx	
Cr. Accumulated depreciation (CA+)		xx

Notice how the production costs incurred in year 5 are accounted for. They are capitalised (i.e. made into an asset) in a balance sheet account 'WIP inventory'. Gretel Company does not record production wage and depreciation costs in income statement accounts, 'wage expense' and 'depreciation expense'.[3] Only when the witchits are sold are the capitalised labour and other production costs expensed – through the 'Cost of goods sold' account. This may well occur in the financial period *after* the costs were incurred. For example, the 8,000 euros of materials, labour and overhead in WIP inventory at the end of year 5 were *incurred* that year but will not be *expensed* until the 1,000 witchits to which they relate are sold – in year 6 or possibly later.

Inventory record-keeping of manufacturing firms

Inventory systems differ across industries. Industries where production flow is rapid and work-in-progress is minimal dispense with a perpetual system to track the costs of a product during production. All production labour and overhead are charged to a 'production expense' account. End-of-period inventory is determined by a count and an adjustment is then made to both the production expense and inventory accounts.

Inventory systems also change over time. For example, many companies now require 'just-in-time' delivery of materials to their production centres. In this case, a separate raw material inventory serves no purpose. Instead, material costs are charged directly to work-in-progress (or production expense). Again, an end-of-period count is made to adjust expense and inventory accounts.

Exhibit 9.6 Production costs flows under absorption costing: ledger account entries

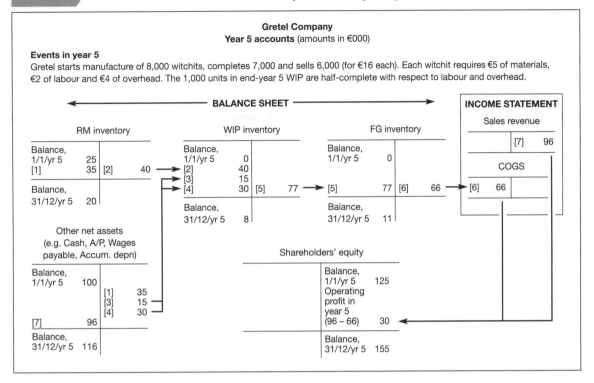

Gretel Company
Year 5 accounts (amounts in €000)

Events in year 5
Gretel starts manufacture of 8,000 witchits, completes 7,000 and sells 6,000 (for €16 each). Each witchit requires €5 of materials, €2 of labour and €4 of overhead. The 1,000 units in end-year 5 WIP are half-complete with respect to labour and overhead.

Inventories at historical cost

Up to now we've assumed that the unit costs of inventories, be they goods for resale or goods under production, are constant. In Gretel's case, for example, the manufacturing cost of a witchit is €11 a unit throughout year 5. In reality, even when overall inflation is negligible, the costs of purchased merchandise and production inputs change over time. How does the manufacturer determine the cost of units produced and the retailer the cost of units sold in these circumstances?

Companies that follow the HC convention use one of two approaches to determining cost. The first, and less common, is known as the **specific identification** (SI) approach. Where inventories are not interchangeable (e.g. the 'one-of-a-kind' piece of furniture, the unique piece of jewellery) or where they're project-specific, merchandise or production costs are identified with a particular good or project.

In other cases, however, specific identification of costs with goods is impractical and, as we show later, can lead to profit manipulation. As a result, most companies follow the second approach. *They make an assumption about the way costs flow through inventories.* Three cost-flow assumptions are in general use. Companies can assume that:

1 the *first* costs to flow in are the *first* costs to flow out (the FIFO cost-flow assumption);
2 the *last* costs to flow in are the *first* costs to flow out (the LIFO cost-flow assumption); or
3 the costs which flow out are a *weighted average* of the costs that flow in (the weighted average cost-flow assumption).

Each of these cost-flow formulas offers a systematic way of assigning costs to products, one that's easy to implement and less prone to manipulation than the SI approach. Note that in principle the cost flow assumed does not have to correspond to the *physical* flow of goods. A food retailer, for example, may use weighted-average cost when valuing goods in inventory, even though, to minimise losses from spoilage, the company follows a 'first-in, first-out' policy of inventory management.

Cost-flow assumptions: FIFO, weighted average and LIFO

An example will help illustrate the way the three cost-flow assumptions work and the effect of each on a company's accounts. We'll inject some realism in the example by assuming prices of goods are rising, a phenomenon which has occurred continuously in most countries over the past 20 years.

Jack Falstaff is a London wine merchant. He imports and sells sherris-sack through his wholesale business. Sherris-sack is a Spanish fortified wine which is finding growing favour among the 'taverna' crowd in the city.

He has two casks of sherris-sack in inventory at the start of x1. Each cost him 30. During the first half of the year, he buys three casks: one in February for 35, the second in April for 40 and the third in June for 45. He sells two casks of wine (for 75 each) during the second half of x1.

Falstaff wants to know what the costs are of the two casks sold in x1 and of the three casks remaining in inventory at 31 December. Exhibit 9.7 shows that these costs differ, depending on the cost-flow assumption – FIFO, weighted average or LIFO – the company makes when valuing inventory.

Each cost-flow assumption assigns production or merchandise costs to the income statement (cost of goods sold) or balance sheet (inventory), using a simple, unchanging formula. *Under FIFO, the earliest costs (the first costs in) are assigned to the units sold (the first goods out), while the most recent costs are assigned to the units remaining in inventory.* In Falstaff's case, the earliest costs assignable to the two casks sold are those of beginning inventory (2 casks at 30). The casks in ending inventory are valued at 120, the costs associated with the February, April and June purchases (35, 40 and 45 respectively).

Under the weighted average cost assumption, an average cost is computed, based on the costs of the goods or merchandise available for sale (or use). Merchandise available for sale comprises items in beginning inventory and items purchased for resale. The weighted average cost (WAC) per unit is calculated as:

$$\text{WAC/unit} = \frac{\text{Total costs of units available (for sale)}}{\text{Number of units available (for sale)}}$$

We use total costs and total units available in the calculation of unit WAC. The *number* of units in the beginning inventory and in each purchase act as weights in determining weighted average cost. The resulting WAC is applied to both units sold and units in ending inventory. In Falstaff's case, the total costs of casks available are 180 ((2 casks @ 30) + (1 @ 35) + (1 @ 40) + (1 @ 45)) and the WAC per cask is 36. Thus the unit cost of the casks in beginning inventory carries double the weight of each of the Falstaff's purchases during x1.

LIFO reverses the FIFO cost-flow assumption. *Under LIFO, the most recent costs are assigned to the units sold; the earliest costs are assigned to the units remaining in inventory.* For Falstaff, the costs assignable to the two casks sold are – going from most recent to next most recent – that of the June purchase (1 cask at 45) and then that of the April purchase (1 at 40). The costs assigned to the three casks in ending inventory are those of the February purchase (1 at 35) and beginning inventory (2 at 30) – 95 in total.

Exhibit 9.7 Falstaff's sherris-sack: costs of sales and ending inventory in x1, under FIFO, WAC and LIFO cost-flow assumptions

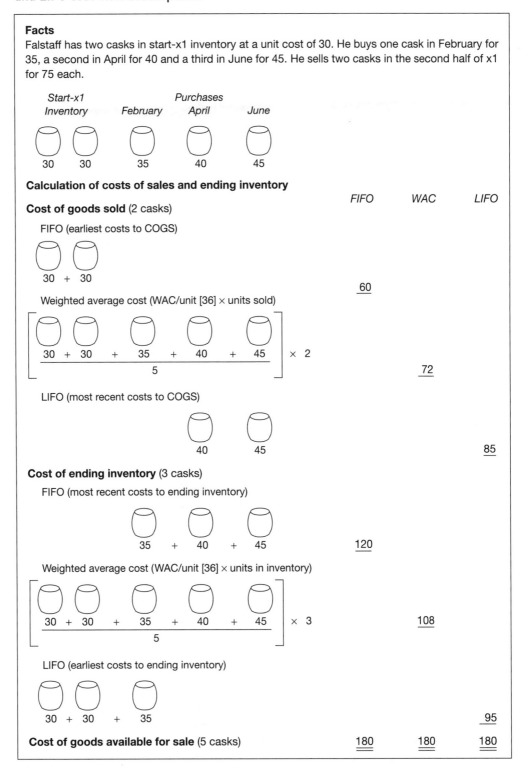

Facts

Falstaff has two casks in start-x1 inventory at a unit cost of 30. He buys one cask in February for 35, a second in April for 40 and a third in June for 45. He sells two casks in the second half of x1 for 75 each.

		Purchases	
Start-x1 Inventory	*February*	*April*	*June*

Calculation of costs of sales and ending inventory

	FIFO	WAC	LIFO
Cost of goods sold (2 casks)			
FIFO (earliest costs to COGS) — 30 + 30	60		
Weighted average cost (WAC/unit [36] × units sold) — $\left[\dfrac{30 + 30 + 35 + 40 + 45}{5}\right] \times 2$		72	
LIFO (most recent costs to COGS) — 40 + 45			85
Cost of ending inventory (3 casks)			
FIFO (most recent costs to ending inventory) — 35 + 40 + 45	120		
Weighted average cost (WAC/unit [36] × units in inventory) — $\left[\dfrac{30 + 30 + 35 + 40 + 45}{5}\right] \times 3$		108	
LIFO (earliest costs to ending inventory) — 30 + 30 + 35			95
Cost of goods available for sale (5 casks)	180	180	180

The flow of Falstaff's sherris-sack costs – to sales and ending inventory – under the three assumptions is also shown in T account form below:

Sherris-sack inventory, assuming:

FIFO		WAC		LIFO	
BI　　60 (2@30) Buy　120 (1@35; 1@40; 1@45)		BI　　60 Buy　120		BI　　60 Buy　120	
	COGS　60 (2@30)		COGS　72 (2@36)		COGS　85 (1@45; 1@40)
EI　　120 (1@35; 1@40; 1@45)		EI　　108 (3@36)		EI　　95 (2@30; 1@35)	

Notice that, in our example, the cost of goods sold (COGS) and the cost of ending inventory (EI) sum to 180 in all three cases. This is not a coincidence. The cost of purchases is by definition the same (120) under all three cost-flow assumptions. Since the book value of beginning inventory (BI) is assumed to be the same across the alternatives in our example, it follows the cost of goods available for sale must be identical and hence the sum of the costs of sales and ending inventory will be equal, too:

$$\begin{array}{ccc} \text{Beginning inventory} & & \text{Cost of goods sold} \\ + & = \text{Cost of goods available for sale} = & + \\ \text{Purchases} & & \text{Ending inventory} \end{array}$$

Even though, in practice, the book value of beginning inventory and thus the cost of goods available for sale (COGAFS) will differ across the three cost-flow assumptions, the relationships shown above still hold. *For any given COGAFS, a cost-flow assumption which assigns more of such costs to cost of goods sold will assign less of them to ending inventory.*

Effect of cost-flow assumption on income

When the costs of merchandise or production inputs are changing, the cost flow assumed by management affects corporate income and, the tax code permitting, corporate cash flow. We can deduce from Exhibit 9.7 the direction of the link between price changes and income. *When costs are rising (and, an important proviso, inventory levels are constant or increasing), use of FIFO will lead to higher reported profits and higher book values for inventory than those reported under the WAC or LIFO assumptions.* The difference will be greatest between FIFO and LIFO, with reported profits and inventory values under WAC at levels between the two.

The way the three cost-flow assumptions work provides the clue to these results. Under FIFO, 'old' costs are assigned to units sold – hence the lower cost of goods sold figure – while 'new' costs are captured in ending inventory. The lower cost of sales leads to higher reported profits. The reverse occurs under LIFO. Under WAC, the unit cost assigned to both inventory and cost of goods sold is a (weighted) average of the 'old' and 'new' costs. Of course, when prices are

Exhibit 9.8 Falstaff's sherris-sack: x1 gross profit, before- and after-tax, under FIFO, WAC and LIFO cost-flow assumptions

	FIFO	WAC	LIFO
Sales revenue (2 casks at 75)	150	150	150
Less: Cost of goods sold (Exhibit 9.7)	60	72	85
Gross profit (before tax)	90	78	65
Less: Income tax at 30%	27	23.4	19.5
Gross profit (after tax)	63	54.6	45.5

falling, we should observe the opposite result: reported profits and inventory values will be *lower* under FIFO.

Falstaff's figures for x1 confirm these findings. Exhibit 9.8 shows the gross profit, before and after tax, on his sherris-sack line, under the three cost-flow assumptions. Falstaff sold two casks of wine in x1 at a per-cask price of 75. A tax rate of 30% is assumed.

Falstaff's gross profit under FIFO is higher than that under WAC or LIFO in x1. We can generalise from Exhibit 9.8. In periods of rising prices (and constant/rising inventory levels), FIFO yields higher reported profit and, as a result, higher reported tax expense than the WAC and LIFO alternatives.

● Effect of cost-flow assumption on cash flow

Choice of cost-flow assumption has no effect on before-tax corporate cash flow: it will affect after-tax cash flow, if the tax code permits the use of alternative cost-flow assumptions. A switch from, say, FIFO to LIFO does not change the retailer's purchase costs or the manufacturer's outlays on production inputs. It does change the calculation of reported profit, as we have seen. In this case, the lower profit translates into a lower tax charge, assuming the new cost-flow assumption, LIFO, is accepted by the tax authorities. Given an unchanged before-tax cash flow and lower tax payments, the switch from FIFO to LIFO results in higher after-tax cash flows.

This is evident from Falstaff's x1 cash flow statement for its sherris-sack line summarised in Exhibit 9.9. We assume for simplicity that all transactions are cash-based.

Falstaff's tax payments under FIFO are greater in x1 – and its after-tax cash flows lower that year – than those under LIFO. Thus *use of LIFO in inflationary periods can result in lower reported profits but, tax authorities willing, higher cash flows than prevail under FIFO or WAC.* By the same

Exhibit 9.9 Falstaff's sherris-sack: x1 cash flow, under FIFO WAC and LIFO cost-flow assumptions

	FIFO	WAC	LIFO
Receipts from sales	150	150	150
Less: Payments for casks purchased in February, April and June*	120	120	120
Before-tax cash flow	30	30	30
Less: Income tax (Exhibit 9.8)	27	23.4	19.5
After-tax cash flow	3	6.6	10.5

* The beginning inventory was paid for in an earlier period.

token, when prices are falling, corporate income will be higher and after-tax cash flows lower under LIFO than under the alternative cost-flow assumptions.

These results only hold when inventory levels are constant or rising. When inventory levels fall, 'old' costs which, under LIFO, are 'preserved' in inventory are released into the income statement. As a consequence, the cost of goods sold is lower and income higher: higher than if inventory levels had been maintained – and higher, possibly, than income reported under FIFO or WAC. At this point, taxes hitherto postponed become payable. Note that *any tax benefits from the adoption of LIFO stem from the (present value) effect of tax deferral*. The company's tax bill is not permanently reduced.

Flaws in HC-based inventory costing methods

Each of the HC cost-flow assumptions can be criticised for misstating reported income and the value of inventories. FIFO, it is argued, overstates income in inflationary periods since the cost of sales figure is based on 'old' costs. LIFO, on the other hand, understates the value of inventories: 'new' costs are channelled to the income statement and thus the balance sheet becomes the repository of 'old' costs. WAC accounts suffer from both faults, but to a lesser degree.

LIFO and WAC are susceptible to profit manipulation. In both cases, profit can be affected by the timing of inventory purchases. For example, suppose Falstaff decides to buy another cask of wine (at, say, 45). By bringing forward the purchase date from early x2 to late x1, he can raise cost of goods sold and lower profits in x1, *assuming the company determines the costs of sales and ending inventory on a periodic (end-of-year) basis*.

How does this happen? The cost of the December x1 purchase is included in periodic-based cost of sales, even though the cost is incurred *after* the last sale. As a result, the x1 LIFO cost of sales increases to 90 (2 casks at 45) and the x1 WAC cost of sales to 75 (2 casks × (225/6)). Falstaff's x1 FIFO profit is unaffected by the above purchasing strategy. FIFO cost of sales is based on the earliest costs which don't alter as a result of an additional purchase at year-end.

Specific identification (SI) of costs with goods is not a satisfactory alternative to a cost-flow assumption. Where products are interchangeable and large in number, identifying costs with individual items makes record-keeping unnecessarily expensive. Where products are interchangeable and few in number, the method is still unsatisfactory because of the potential for profit manipulation.

Suppose Falstaff uses the SI method to determine the cost of sales and the book value of inventory. Assuming the casks of sherris-sack are interchangeable, he can choose to draw the two casks he sells in x1 from the five available in such a way as to report any one of several (before-tax) gross profit figures between 65 and 90. Moreover, even if the casks he draws from stores in x1 exhibit a recognised physical flow, e.g. FIFO, he is not bound, under the SI method, to follow that pattern of usage in later periods. By contrast, *a cost-flow assumption such as FIFO, once adopted, must be adhered to in subsequent periods*. The company's auditors draw attention in their report to any change in cost-flow assumption – on the grounds that the company has not applied accounting policies consistently. They require it to disclose the effects of the change on its accounts, if material.

In a later section, we describe an alternative method of valuing inventories, the replacement cost method, which avoids the flaws of HC-based methods.

Lower of cost or market rule

Inventories may decline in value. Supply may exceed demand, perhaps because of a change in competitive conditions in the industry. An advance in technology may render a product or process obsolete. In consumer goods industries, changes in fashion or taste can lead to a fall in demand for a product. Goods may be damaged. In each case, the manufacturer or retailer is forced to mark down the price of the goods in order to sell them. Note that materials and work-in-progress may be affected as much as finished goods.

What are the accounting implications? A company that values its inventories at historical cost usually applies an impairment test to them on the balance sheet date. The test is known as the 'lower of cost or market' – or LOCOM – rule. IAS define 'market' as **net realisable value (NRV)**, that is, *the amount the inventories are expected to realise in the normal course of business, net of future costs necessary to complete and sell them.* Assume the carrying amount of a company's inventories is their cost of purchase (or production), as determined using specific identification or a cost-flow assumption like FIFO. If, at the end of a financial period (i.e. year, quarter), the NRV of its inventories falls below cost, it's doubtful whether the company can recover its investment under current market conditions and so it should write the inventories down to NRV and recognise the unrealised loss in its income statement immediately. The inventories' NRV becomes the new carrying amount when applying the LOCOM rule at the end of the next period (assuming the goods remain unsold).

We illustrate the operation of the LOCOM rule using Jack Falstaff's sherris-sack line. Suppose as a result of a change in consumer tastes the demand for sherris-sack falls away in late x1 and Falstaff estimates that the NRV of each cask is only 35 at year-end. Assume, too, that FIFO is the cost-flow assumption Falstaff uses in his HC-based accounts. Inspection of Exhibit 9.7 shows that, of the three casks in ending inventory, two must be written down to market value. The cask purchased in June must be written down by 10 (45 − 35) and the one purchased in April by 5 (40 − 35). The total write-down at the end of x1 can be recorded as follows:

December x1
Dr. Loss from inventory write-down (OE–)	15	
Cr. Valuation allowance, inventories (CA+)		15

In a functional-based income statement the loss is usually absorbed in 'Cost of goods sold'. If, however, it is material, it is reported separately as an exceptional loss.

As for the credit entry, the asset itself can be written down (i.e. Cr. Inventories) or, as in the journal entry above, a contra-asset account can be established. When the goods are sold, both the inventory and valuation allowance accounts are adjusted. For example, suppose Falstaff sells the three remaining casks for 42 each in x2. He will make the following entries:

x2
Dr. Accounts receivable/Cash (A+)	126	
Cr. Sales revenue (OE+)		126
(3 casks at 42)		
Dr. Cost of goods sold (OE–)	105	
Dr. Valuation allowance, inventories (CA–)	15	
Cr. Inventories (A–)		120

Falstaff charges COGS for the carrying amount of the units sold (3 at 35) but reduces inventories by the original cost of those units (1 each at 35, 40, and 45).

One advantage of recording the valuation adjustment in a separate account is that the company retains a record of the costs of its inventories. This is useful if the market value of written-down inventory recovers. In this event, the write-down is reversed to the extent of the recovery – but not above 'cost'. The company increases the carrying amount of inventory (directly or by reducing the valuation allowance) and recognises the benefit in income (e.g. via lower COGS). If it takes the write-down to the inventory account directly, it may have difficulty determining whether a subsequent write-up breaches 'cost'.

The LOCOM rule is in keeping with a long-standing practice in accounting: that current assets should not be carried in the balance sheet above their fair value. Defenders of LOCOM claim it is a control device since it puts bounds on management. By having to reveal unrealised losses, managers have less incentive to take risky actions to overturn the losses but which may make them larger. Note that the rule is not applied restrictively. For example, if the market value of materials falls below cost but that of the final product is not expected to do so (i.e. the manufacturer expects to recover the cost of materials), it is not required to write them down, so long as the quantities it holds are not abnormally high.

Nonetheless, the rule has its critics. They argue it is one-sided. Investors, they maintain, want to know the fair value of inventory when it's *above* cost as well as when it's below. They want information about unrealised holding *gains* as well as losses. A valuation method which provides this information is the replacement cost method, the subject of the next section.

Inventories at replacement cost

We've already identified some of the weaknesses of historical cost methods of valuing inventory: they may misstate the cost of sales or of inventories (or both) and they open the door to manipulation of both numbers.

Valuing inventories at current value avoids the distortions of HC valuation. By charging against revenues (which are by definition current) the *current* cost of the goods sold, like is matched with like. The income number is then a more trustworthy indicator of corporate performance. By valuing inventories at their current worth, the balance sheet provides a more realistic picture of the company's assets. Stating inventories at current value is more costly than using an HC cost-flow assumption, however. At low rates of inflation, the higher costs of collecting and verifying current value data may outweigh the informational benefits to investors and managers.

Although there are various methods of determining the current value of inventories, we discuss only the replacement cost (RC) method in this chapter. It's the only current value method of valuing inventory which the EU permits. We show how HC accounts are adjusted to an RC basis and how investors interpret RC data.

Determining replacement cost of inventory

Under the RC method, a company charges against revenues the replacement cost of the goods sold and values inventories in the balance sheet at their replacement cost. Replacement cost can be determined in various ways. Suppliers' price lists provide one source of information. Companies also employ external or internally developed index numbers to restate the historical costs of work-in-progress or finished goods inventories to current reproduction cost.

Falstaff uses information from his sherris-sack suppliers to determine the replacement cost of casks sold and in inventory. Let's assume that, in the second half of x1, the RC per cask is 47. When the two casks are sold, the cost of the sales is recorded as 94. As a result, Falstaff reports a before-tax gross profit of 56 on this product line in x1.

Sales revenue (2 casks × 75)	150
Cost of goods sold, at RC (2 × 47)	94
Gross profit, at RC	56

Assuming no change in RC, the three casks in ending inventory are also valued at 47 each or 141 in total.

Mechanics of RC accounting for inventories

How does a company like Falstaff incorporate RC valuations in its accounts? One way is to revalue inventory to RC at periodic intervals, for example monthly or at the time of each sale. For example, at the start of the second half of x1, Falstaff has five casks available for sale, at a total historical cost of 180 (Exhibit 9.7). At the time the two casks are sold, he can revalue the five casks in inventory to their RC of 47 a cask. The carrying amount of inventory is now 235, resulting in a surplus on revaluation of 55 (235 – 180). This amount is credited to a non-distributable reserve:

(1)	Dr. Inventory, sherris-sack (A+)	55
	Cr. Revaluation reserve (OE+)	55

When the two casks are sold, Falstaff records the expense and the reduction in inventory at the casks' replacement cost (i.e. 2 units at 47).

(2)	Dr. Cost of goods sold (OE–)	94
	Cr. Inventory, sherris-sack (A–)	94

This yields a post-sale balance in inventory of 141 (3 casks at 47), as can be seen in the inventory ledger account below.

Inventory, sherris-sack

Balance, 1/1/×1	60		
(2 casks at 30 each)			
February purchase	35		
April purchase	40		
June purchase	45		
		(2) Cost of goods sold	94
(1) Revaluation	55	(2 casks at 47 each)	
(235(RC) – 180(HC))			
Balance, 31/12/x1	141		
(3 casks at 47 each)			

The excess of the RC cost of goods sold over the HC cost of goods sold represents the realised **holding gains** on inventory. (An alternative term is (realised) **inventory profits**.) If the RC cost of goods sold is less than HC cost of goods sold, the company realises a holding loss. Holding gains or losses on items that remain in inventory are *unrealised*. According to 4th Directive rules, only inventory holding gains that have been realised are distributable.

Suppose Falstaff wants to distribute holding gains realised on the sale of the two casks in x1. Assuming the HC of the casks sold is 36 a cask (WAC assumption: *see* Exhibit 9.7), the realised holding gains in x1 total 22 (2 casks × (47 – 36)). Falstaff can transfer this amount from non-distributable to distributable reserves:

(3)	Dr. Revaluation reserve (OE–)	22
	Cr. Retained profits (OE+)	22

Note this transfer is unlikely to have any tax effect in practice. Countries that permit RC valuation of inventories calculate taxable income independently of book income.

Exhibit 9.10 Falstaff's sherris-sack: effect on x1 accounts of accounting for inventory at RC

| | Net assets | | = | Shareholders' equity | |
	Inventory	*Other*		*Revaluation reserve*	*Retained profits*
Balance, 7/x1 (partial)	180	. . .		0	. . .
(1) Revaluation	+55		=	+55	
Sales revenue		+150			+56
(2) COGS	−94		=		(Gross profit)
(3) Realised holding gain	0		=	−22	+22
Balance, end-x1 (partial)	141	. . .		33	. . .

After (optional) entry (3), there is a balance in Falstaff's revaluation reserve of 33. It represents the unrealised holding gains on the three casks in ending inventory (3 casks × (47 − 36)). The movement in 'Revaluation reserve' is shown below. (We assume that the RC and HC of the casks in beginning inventory are the same: hence the zero balance in revaluation reserve at 1/1/x1.)

Revaluation reserve, inventory			
		Balance, 1/1/x1	0
		(1) Revaluation	55
(3) Realised holding gains	22		
		Balance, 31/12/x1	33

We show the effect of entries (1) to (3) on Falstaff's x1 accounts in balance sheet equation form in Exhibit 9.10.

Under HC accounting, realised holding gains and losses are automatically included in profit. In fact, they are incorporated in HC cost of goods sold. One advantage of gathering RC information on inventories is that, by separating 'old' from 'new' (i.e. current) costs, the magnitude of realised inventory holding gains or losses in total HC profits is revealed. In Exhibit 9.11, the HC (WAC) gross profit of Falstaff's sherris-sack line in x1 is broken down into its current profit and holding gain components.

Exhibit 9.11 Falstaff's sherris-sack: HC (WAC) income statement for x1 with disclosure of realised holding gains

Sales revenue	150
Less: Cost of sales at RC	−94
Gross profit, at RC	56
Plus: Realised holding gains	+22
HC (WAC) gross profit before tax (Exhibit 9.8)	78

In this case, over a quarter of Falstaff's x1 HC gross profits are attributable to savings in purchase costs from buying sherris-sack when prices were low. This information can be useful to investors (and Falstaff himself) when evaluating the performance of the company's managers.

Valuation of inventories: rules and custom

EU and IAS requirements

Companies following IAS must measure inventories at the lower of cost or market. The 4th Directive imposes a similar requirement on EU companies. Under IAS, a cost-flow assumption must be used where items are not ordinarily interchangeable or set aside for specific projects. FIFO and WAC are the benchmark cost-flow assumptions; LIFO is an allowed alternative. The 4th Directive allows the use of FIFO, WAC or LIFO wherever items to be valued are 'fungible': this includes certain financial investments as well as inventories. The Directive also gives member states the power to permit or require firms to value inventories at RC instead of HC. IAS are silent on this issue: the applicable standard deals with inventories in an HC system only. As for the 'market' term in LOCOM, we've already seen that IAS define this as net realisable value. Normally the LOCOM rule is applied on an item-by-item basis but the standard permits inventory items with similar purposes or end uses to be grouped when the test is carried out.

Country and industry practice

Most companies value inventories at LOCOM. Japan is the exception: according to a 1990s survey, only one-quarter of Japanese firms test inventories for impairment. FIFO and WAC are the most commonly used cost-flow assumptions, certainly in Europe.[4] LIFO is popular in the USA thanks mainly to tax rules (*see* Box 9.1).

The IAS definition of 'market' in the LOCOM test, namely NRV, is widely observed. However, there are interesting national nuances. In the USA and some Asian countries, 'market' is defined as replacement or reproduction cost, subject to upper and lower limits based on NRV.

Although 'liberal' EU countries such as the Netherlands and the UK allow inventories to be valued at RC, few companies in these countries use this valuation basis now as EU inflation is so low. In countries with a history of high inflation, valuing inventories at RC is permitted under IAS rules – and may be required under national rules (e.g. in Mexico).

In addition to national differences in inventory valuation, there are specialised industry practices. Those in agriculture, mining and retailing are of long standing and are accepted by accounting regulators.

- *Agriculture and mining.* Agricultural produce and mineral ores are usually valued at net realisable value at the point of harvest or extraction. This applies not only when the produce has been sold under a forward contract but more generally when there is an active commodity market and minimal risk of the produce or ore being unsaleable.
- *Retailing.* Retailers often value their inventories at expected sales value less normal gross margin. (The gross margin deduction is adjusted if the sale price is marked down.) The 'retail method' is usually applied on a departmental basis because stock within a department tends to have a similar shelf life and carry similar gross margin ratios.

Note that in all three industries, the valuation basis used is, in effect, market value adjusted for either selling costs or gross margin. A recent international standard on agriculture extends the NRV basis of inventory valuation to 'biological assets', defined as living animals (e.g. cattle) or plants (e.g. orchards).[5]

BOX 9.1 The US LIFO puzzle

Valuing inventories on a LIFO basis is a minority practice worldwide. One reason is that the LIFO cost-flow assumption is not acceptable for tax purposes in many countries. An exception is the USA. What makes US accounting unusual is that a company can only use LIFO for tax purposes if it uses the method in its published accounts. Inventory valuation is one of the few areas in US accounting where tax and book treatment are not separated.

LIFO has been permitted for US tax purposes since the 1940s. In the low inflation 1950s and 1960s few companies costed their inventories on the LIFO assumption. A sample of large firms in 1970 revealed that only 25% used LIFO for any of their inventories and even fewer (10%) used it for more than 50% of them. LIFO's popularity rose sharply in the 1970s as inflation surged in the aftermath of the oil price shocks of 1973 and 1979. The chart below compares on an annual basis between 1969 and 2000 the percentage change in the US producer price index with the percentage of companies – from a sample of 600 large US firms – that use LIFO for more than 50% of their inventories.[6]

Note that the rate of LIFO usage remained high even after inflation fell in the 1980s and 1990s. Once a firm has adopted LIFO, it usually has an incentive to continue using it. LIFO *postpones* US firms' tax liabilities: it doesn't reduce them permanently. Switching back to FIFO (or WAC) carries a tax penalty since the postponed liabilities then become payable.

As we saw in the chapter, when prices rise (and inventories are growing), LIFO lowers income tax payments, resulting in higher after-tax cash flows and more wealth for shareholders. Why, then, didn't *more* US firms switch to LIFO when inflation rose steeply in the 1970s? Various explanations have been advanced. First, tax benefits from switching may have been small or non-existent because the firm's input prices were declining, it had unused tax losses, or its inventory levels fluctuated markedly thereby increasing the risk of liquidating old LIFO inventory layers. Second, LIFO bookkeeping costs are high and fixed: this places a proportionately greater burden on small companies and may have discouraged them from switching. Third, LIFO weakens key balance sheet ratios (lower reported inventories and retained earnings reduce the current ratio and lift the debt–equity ratio) so firms that were financially strained avoided LIFO to reduce the risk of breaching debt covenants. Although US researchers find evidence to support all three hypotheses, they are unable to explain fully the reluctance of many US firms to embrace LIFO.[7] Other factors – inertia, management's fixation on reported earnings rather than cash flows – may also have played a part. The US LIFO puzzle remains unsolved.

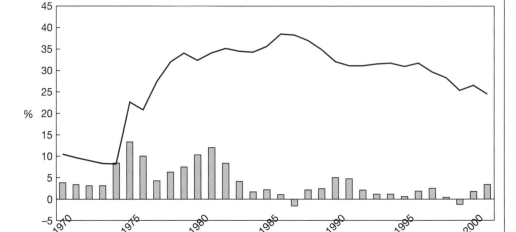

LIFO usage in sample of large US firms, 1969–2000

▭ Producer price index, annual change   —— Heavy LIFO users

Financial statement presentation and analysis

General disclosures in annual accounts

Companies following IAS must break down their inventories by type – for example, raw materials, supplies, work-in-progress, finished goods and merchandise. (The 4th Directive requires similar disclosures by larger EU companies.) This breakdown can be revealing. For example, firms with a long production cycle are likely to report high work-in-progress relative to sales.

IAS require firms to state how they measure inventories, including which cost-flow assumption they use. If a company values inventories at LIFO, it must disclose the difference between this value and the LOCOM amount under FIFO or WAC. If a firm has preserved old costs in inventory and costs are rising, the LIFO value of its inventory may well be materially less than the LIFO or WAC value.

Classification of costs by manufacturing companies

As we saw in Chapter 6, companies usually classify costs either by function or by nature. What does this mean for manufacturing companies? In a functional income statement, manufacturing costs are captured in the 'Cost of goods sold' figure. Non-manufacturing costs are broken down further – into, for example, sales, administration, research and development. Where costs are classified by nature, they are shown by type of input, e.g. materials, labour, depreciation. These costs are not assigned to functional areas. Thus 'personnel costs' in a natural income statement include both manufacturing and non-manufacturing labour costs incurred. Because of adjustments made for costs capitalised in inventories (and fixed assets), operating profit (and all subsequent profit figures) should be the same under the two bases of cost classification.

This last point is best demonstrated by an example. Flute, a musical instrument maker, reports the following inventory balances at the start and end of x4 (all amounts are in €000).

	Start-x4	End-x4
Materials and supplies (M&S)	4	8
Work-in-progress (WIP)	7	5
Finished goods (FG)	6	14
Total	17	27

The company buys 33 of materials and supplies in the year and uses 24 in production and 5 in sales and administration. It incurs 31 of payroll costs, 12 on production and 19 on sales and administration. Depreciation and other overheads amount to 25, of which 14 relate to production and 11 to sales and administration. The company sells instruments for 100 in x4. Exhibit 9.12 shows the flow of costs through Flute's ledger accounts and the presentation of the company's operating results for x4 under both expense classification approaches.

Under the natural basis, a company reports all operating costs it incurs in a period on the face of its income statement. This is in contrast to the functional basis, where production costs (COGS) are matched against revenues on a product rather than on a time basis. But the basis of expense classification does not change the method of costing. A firm classifying costs by nature still capitalises the production costs of incomplete and unsold goods in WIP and FG inventories. To avoid miscounting these production costs, it includes in its income statement an adjustment for the change in the book values of WIP and FG inventories over the period. *If the book values of such inventories increase, the increase is subtracted from operating costs incurred; if they decrease, the decrease is added to operating costs.* In Flute's case, WIP and FG inventories amount to 13 at the start of x4 (7 + 6) and 19 at the end (5 + 14), a net increase of 6. Therefore, production of

Exhibit 9.12   Classifying a manufacturing company's costs by nature or by function: illustration

Facts

Flute, a musical instrument maker, has the following inventory balances at the start and of x4 (all amounts in €000):

	End-x4	End-x4
Materials and supplies (M&S)	4	8
Work-in-progress (WIP)	7	5
Finished goods (FG)	6	14

The company buys 33 of materials and supplies in the year and uses 24 in production and 5 in sales and administration. It incurs 31 of payroll costs, 12 on production and 19 on sales and administration. It incurs 25 of depreciation and other overheads, 14 on production and 11 on sales and administration. It sells goods for 100 in the year.

Flow of costs and calculation of operating profit

Materials and supplies inventory

Balance, 1/1	4	Used: in WIP	24
Purchases	33	in SA	5
Balance, 31/12	8		

Payroll costs

Total labour costs incurred	31	To WIP	12
		To SA	19

Overhead costs

Total overhead costs incurred (e.g. depreciation, utilities, insurance)	25	To WIP	14
		To SA	11

WIP inventory

Balance, 1/1	7	Cost of goods completed	52
M&S used	24		
Labour	12		
Overheads	14		
Balance, 31/12	5		

FG inventory

Balance, 1/1	6	Cost of goods sold	44
Cost of goods completed	52		
Balance, 31/12	14		

FLUTE: Statement of operating income for x4

Expenses classified by function

Sales revenue	100
less:	
Cost of goods sold	−44
Gross profit	56
less:	
Selling and administrative (SA) expenses [5 (M&S) + 19 (Payroll) + 11 (O'head)]	−35
Operating profit	21

Expenses classified by nature

Sales revenue		100
Materials and supplies used	29	
Staff costs	31	
Other operating costs	25	
less:		
Increase in WIP & FG inventories	−6	−79
Operating profit		21

instruments exceeds sales by 6 in x4. To match costs with revenues, Flute deducts the net increase in WIP and FG inventories from total operating costs of 85 and the resulting figure, 79, is the amount of total operating *expenses* in x4.

Firms sometimes link the change in inventories to revenues rather than costs. They describe the adjusted figure as 'output' or 'operating performance'. Exhibit 9.13 shows the 2001 consolidated income statement of the Bosch Group, a large (and privately owned) German auto components supplier. Bosch reports total operating performance of €34,200 million in 2001. Operating performance is equal to sales plus the increase (less the decrease) in WIP and FG inventories plus other capitalised costs. This number is hard to interpret since sales are recorded at market prices while inventories, and changes in them, are recorded at cost.

Note that Bosch's operating performance figure includes not only the change in inventories but also 'other capitalized costs'. A note to the consolidated accounts, summarised below, gives more details of both items:

(million euro)	2001	2000
Change in finished goods and work-in-progress inventories	−164	161
Other capitalized costs	335	208
	171	369

What are 'Other capitalized costs'? Bosch constructs new plant and equipment each year for its own use. It incurs costs – of materials, labour (including management time) and overheads – which total €335 million in 2001. These costs do not belong on the income statement – they do not relate to goods sold in the period – and hence they are transferred to fixed asset accounts.

Exhibit 9.13

Bosch Group
CONSOLIDATED STATEMENT OF INCOME FOR 2001

(million euro)	2001	2000
Sales	34,029	31,556
Changes in finished goods and work-in-progress inventories and other capitalized costs	171	369
Total operating performance	34,200	31,925
Other operating income	2,195	2,046
Cost of materials	−16,284	−15,428
Personnel costs	−9,959	−8,950
Depreciation and amortization of intangible and tangible fixed assets	−2,502	−2,250
Other operating expenses	−6,419	−6,078
Net income from investments	155	83
Amortization of financial investments and securities included with current assets	−101	−72
Interest income, net of expenses	126	138
Income from ordinary business activities	1,411	1,414
Taxes on income	−761	−34
Net income for the year	650	1,380

(*Source*: Bosch Group, *Annual Report and Accounts 2001*. Robert Bosch GmbH.)

The alternative way of presenting the natural income statement makes clearer the transfer by Bosch of costs to fixed asset accounts (and from inventory) in 2001:

		€ million
Sales		34,029
Less:		
Operating costs*	35,164	
– Changes in FG/WIP inventories and other capitalized costs	−171	
		−34,993
Other operating income		2,195
Operating profit		1,231
Net income from investments		155
⋮		
Income from ordinary business activities (before tax)		1,411
⋮		

* Comprising costs of materials and personnel, depreciation and other operating expenses.

Expense classification: EU and US companies

Classifying expenses by nature is a common practice among EU companies. However, the functional basis is increasingly popular among larger international firms. US companies, on the other hand, classify expenses only by function. Historical differences in the use of, and audience for, corporate accounts are largely responsible. In many EU member states, the tax authorities, government statisticians and other official agencies – historically, the dominant external users of accounts in these countries – have long insisted that companies classify expenses by nature. And some still do (e.g. Italy, Spain). By contrast, the US Securities and Exchange Commission requires listed companies to provide a breakdown of expenses by function, on the grounds that investors – the key external users of accounts in the USA – find income statements prepared on this basis easier to understand.

IAS permit either method of expense classification. However, if a firm classifies expenses by function, it must disclose the amounts of staff costs and depreciation and amortisation expense in the period. The IASB claims investors find this information useful when predicting a firm's future cash flows.

Financial statement analysis

Investors monitor inventories to gauge both general economic trends – traditionally an economic downturn is accompanied by a rise in inventory levels relative to output – and the efficiency with which individual companies use this asset.

The principal inventory-specific ratio they employ is the **inventory turnover rate** or **stock turn**. This ratio is similar in form to other asset turnover ratios. It is normally computed by dividing annual sales revenue (or cost of goods sold) by the average level of inventories held during the year.[8] In the absence of more detailed information, the average holding is usually estimated by taking the simple average of start- and end-year inventories:[9]

$$\text{Inventory turnover rate} = \frac{\text{Sales revenue (or Cost of goods sold) in year}}{\text{Average inventories in year}}$$

As the name implies, *the ratio shows how many times in a year the company turns over its inventories*. The rate of turnover of inventory differs across industries – it's clearly much faster for a food retailer than a manufacturer of process plant – but changes in the ratio are often more revealing than its level. A drop in the turnover rate often accompanies a fall in sales (or even a decline in their rate of growth), as production fails to adjust quickly to lower demand. A rise in the ratio may signal a revival of demand. It's for this reason that economists monitor sectoral inventory-to-sales ratios when preparing economic forecasts.

Note that at the individual company level a change in the ratio can arise for one of several other reasons. Deliberate overstatement of ending inventories by management in order to boost reported profits causes the turnover rate to fall. But so too does a build-up in inventories in advance of expected sales growth. Recent changes in inventory management have disturbed historical relationships between inventories and sales. For example, introduction of just-in-time methods in purchasing and production have raised turnover rates to a higher level. Thus investors need to look behind the ratio, at the changes in underlying inventories and sales, to understand the reasons for changes in it.

How inventories are measured can affect all ratios and comparisons made from them. Consider the case of manufacturing firms in the same industry when prices of inputs are rising (and inventory levels are constant or rising). Those firms using the FIFO cost-flow assumption or valuing inventories at RC will report stronger balance sheet ratios (higher current ratio, lower debt ratios) than their rivals using LIFO. Firms using FIFO (but not firms using RC) will also enjoy higher reported margins. Thus it's wise to check firms' accounting policies on inventories before comparing their financial performance and strength. We've noted already that those using LIFO must disclose the FIFO cost (strictly, the current cost) of their ending inventories. Likewise, firms valuing inventories at RC are expected to provide HC-based numbers as well.

Summary

Two questions dominate our discussion of inventories. The first is: which costs do companies treat as part of the cost of inventory? The second is: how do firms value their inventory?

Firms are required to capitalise all costs they incur to bring the inventory to its 'present location and condition'. For manufacturing companies, this means that production costs – the costs of materials, labour and usually all overheads related to a product's manufacture – are capitalised as part of the cost of inventory. This method of costing is known as absorption costing. Under the alternative method, variable costing, only variable manufacturing costs are capitalised. In both cases, certain production costs are not charged to the income statement as they're incurred. They are stored in inventory accounts (first, work-in-progress, then finished goods) and expensed only when the products to which they attach are sold.

Most firms value their inventories at the actual (historical) cost of purchase or production. Since actual costs change over time, firms usually assume costs flow through inventory in a particular pattern: on a first-in, first-out (FIFO); last-in, first-out (LIFO); or weighted average (WAC) basis. In periods of rising prices (and constant or rising inventory levels), reported profits are higher under FIFO than under WAC or LIFO because a higher proportion of older, lower costs are captured in the cost of sales. After-tax cash flows are lower under FIFO, if the same cost-flow assumption is used for tax and book purposes. Whichever flow of costs is assumed, firms sailing under the HC flag usually observe the LOCOM rule: they write down inventories to their net realisable value when the latter falls below cost.

Some firms value inventories at replacement cost. Others disclose the replacement cost of goods sold. Disclosing the current cost of goods sold and in inventory allows investors to separate the gains or losses a firm makes from holding goods, both realised and unrealised, from the income earned from producing and trading them. Under LOCOM, only unrealised holding losses are reported.

Investors calculate the inventory turnover rate to monitor the efficiency with which a firm manages its inventories. This and other financial ratios are sensitive to the method(s) the firm uses to value them. Interfirm comparisons are also made more difficult by the alternative approaches – natural and functional – to expense classification.

<table>
<tr><td>APPENDIX
9.1</td><td>**Variable costing**</td></tr>
</table>

As mentioned in the chapter, manufacturing companies in some European countries establish the costs of work-in-progress and finished goods using **variable costing** rather than absorption costing. *Under variable costing (VC), only production costs which vary in proportion to output are capitalised and included in the cost of inventory. Fixed production costs are expensed in the period they're incurred rather than allocated to products as occurs under absorption costing (AC).*[10]

We can use our Gretel example to show how VC works and to contrast its impact on the accounts with that of AC. Recall that in year 5 Gretel produces more witchits than she sells. She starts manufacture of 8,000, completes 7,000, and sells 6,000 units. Per-unit material and labour costs are €5 and €2 respectively. We assume the production overheads of €30,000 are fixed but under AC these are allocated to witchits at the rate of €4 per finished unit. Exhibit 9.14 shows the calculation of Gretel's year 5 profit (at the production stage) under VC and AC.

Exhibit 9.14	Variable and absorption costing contrasted: production exceeds sales

Facts

During year 5 Gretel starts manufacture of 8,000 witchits, completes 7,000 and sells 6,000. There are no WIP or FG inventories at the start of year 5. The witchit sale price is €16 and the production costs are:

- materials (M)   €5/unit
- labour (L)   €2/unit
- (fixed) overhead (O)   €30,000 in total

Gretel Company
(Partial) income statement for year 5 (in €000)

Variable costing			*Absorption costing*		
Sales (6,000 × €16)		96	Sales		96
Start WIP and FG inventory	0		Start WIP and FG inventory	0	
Variable production			Total production		
costs incurred:			costs incurred:		
M + L (Exhibit 9.5)	+55		M + L + O (Exhibit 9.5)	+85	
− End WIP/FG inventory	−13		− End WIP/FG inventory	−19	
Variable COGS		−42	COGS		−66
Fixed production costs		−30			
Profit (at production stage)		24	Gross profit		30

Cost of ending inventory

Variable costing			*Absorption costing*		
M L			M L O		
WIP: 1,000 × (5 + 1*)		6	WIP: 1,000 × (5 + 1* + 2*)		8
FG: 1,000 × (5 + 2)		7	FG: 1,000 × (5 + 2 + 4)		11
Total		13	Total		19

* WIP is half complete with respect to labour and overhead.

Gretel reports profit of €30,000 under AC but only €24,000 under VC. Why the €6,000 difference? The reason is simple. Under VC, all fixed production costs of year 5 (€30,000) are expensed in the year. Under AC, €6,000 of these costs are capitalised in inventories. They are the overheads assigned to the 1,000 units still in progress (note that WIP_{AC} is €2,000 greater than WIP_{VC}) and to the 1,000 units completed but not sold (FG_{AC} is €4,000 greater than FG_{VC}). *Because Gretel produces more witchits than she sells in year 5, overhead costs of €6,000 get captured in ending WIP and FG inventories and escape the income statement that year.* As a result, its year 5 profits – and its ending WIP and FG inventories – are €6,000 greater under AC.

Suppose in year 6 Gretel sells more witchits than she produces. She completes the 1,000 units in WIP, starts and completes 6,000, and sells these 7,000 and the 1,000 in FG inventory. The witchit's sale price and production costs are assumed to be the same as in year 5. Exhibit 9.15 shows the calculation of Gretel's year 6 profit (at the production stage) under VC and AC.

In year 6, when sales exceed production, Gretel reports profits of €42,000 under VC, €6,000 higher than under AC. The reason is that, under AC, fixed production costs of that amount which were inventoried in year 5 are expensed in year 6 when Gretel sells the witchits to which they are attached.

Exhibit 9.15 Variable and absorption costing contrasted: sales exceed production

Facts
Gretel produces and sells witchits in year 6 as follows:

	WIP	FG	Total
Beginning inventory (units)	1,000	1,000	2,000
Production			6,000
Sales			8,000
Ending inventory	0	0	0

The witchit sale price and production costs are the same as in year 5 (*see* Exhibit 9.14).

Gretel Company
(Partial) income statement for year 6 (in €000)

Variable costing			*Absorption costing*		
Sales (8,000 × €16)		128	Sales		128
Start WIP/FG inventory			Start WIP/FG inventory		
(Exhibit 9.14)	13		(Exhibit 9.14)	19	
Variable production			Total production		
costs incurred	43[1]		costs incurred	73[2]	
– End WIP/FG inventory	0		– End WIP/FG inventory	0	
Variable COGS		–56	COGS		–92
Fixed production costs		–30			
Profit (at production stage)		42	Gross profit		36

Notes:	*Production costs incurred in year 6*		
	Materials	6,000 units × €5	30
	Labour	1,000 units in WIP × €1 ⎫	
		6,000 units × €2 ⎬	13
	1. Variable production costs incurred		43
	Overheads (fixed production costs)		30
	2. Total production costs incurred		73

We can generalise from this example. *Profits reported under VC are a function of the level of sales; they are not influenced by the level of production.* Thus the increase in profits of €18,000 between years 5 and 6 under VC – from €24,000 to €42,000 – is the result of Gretel selling 2,000 more witchits at a **contribution** of €9 a unit. (Contribution is defined as sale price (in this case, €16) less unit variable cost (material and labour, totalling €7).)

Profits reported under AC are a function of both the production rate and sales. A company with stable sales can increase its profits under AC by raising its production rate. By so doing, it diverts part of the year's fixed production costs from the income statement (COGS) to the balance sheet (WIP and FG inventory). (Of course, this is not a viable long-term strategy. The company must finance the extra production and will incur higher inventory carrying costs.)

The main advantage of VC over AC is the clearer signal it sends the reader of financial statements about the source of change in a company's profits. Without the detailed information we had access to in Gretel's case, it is hard to disentangle the effects of production and sales on corporate profits. However, VC suffers as a costing method. It yields unit values for inventory items which, in most cases, are severely understated because they include only variable production costs. It is largely for this reason that many regulatory agencies forbid its use in published accounts.

Variable costing and financial statement analysis

Although absorption costing is the method of costing used by most manufacturing firms worldwide (and is required under international accounting standards), its use is not universal. Some EU companies continue to favour VC (it is permitted under the 4th Directive) and, until recently, it was popular with Scandinavian firms. Many firms use VC in their internal accounts.

Some investors try to adjust the financial statements of firms using VC to an AC basis. This is not an easy task. To do it, they must estimate the proportion of fixed costs in the company's production cost structure. Note that in most cases the adjustment will have a greater impact on the balance sheet than the income statement. For a company experiencing little change in its inventory levels (i.e. sales and production are roughly in balance), VC profits approximate AC profits. However, even in this case, inventories (and retained profits) under VC are understated, relative to those under AC, because the company has expensed fixed production costs earlier.

Problem assignments

P9.1 Manufacturer's income statement: alternative expense classification

Narcissus makes mirrors. N asks for your help in preparing an income statement for the third quarter of x2, using the information below. The company is short-staffed and N is preoccupied with quality inspection.

In €000	Quarter 3, x2 Start	End
Raw materials	13	9
Work-in-progress	22	15
Finished mirrors	21	34

	During quarter 3, x2	
	Production department	Sales and admin. departments
Materials purchased	50	–
Supplies purchased and used	–	2
Salaries and employee benefits	46	28
Depreciation	23	11
Utilities and other overheads	8	4

The company sells 25,000 mirrors at a unit price of €8. The corporate income tax rate is 30%.

Required

(a) Calculate Narcissus Company's gross profit for quarter 3, x2.

(b) Draw up an income statement for Narcissus Company for the third quarter of x2. Assume the company classifies expenses:
(i) by function; and
(ii) by nature.

> *Check figure:*
> Cost of goods sold   €125,000

P9.2 Costs of sales and inventory under absorption costing

'I don't know whether this product line is profitable or not. We're selling the Bauhaus line of bus passenger shelters for €900 each but our accounting records don't tell us what the unit cost is. Can you work this out for us?'

UrbanFurniture Company is a small firm that specialises in the fabrication and assembly of 'street furniture' (shelters, kiosks, pavilions, seats) and playground equipment. Amparo, the manager in charge of the street furniture division, asks you to determine the unit cost of the Bauhaus line of shelter (*see below*) and the costs of shelters installed in x5 and being made at year-end.

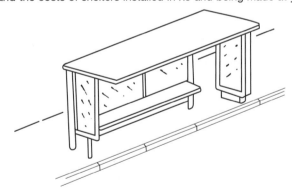

She gives you the following information about the Bauhaus bus passenger shelter. The product line was introduced during x5. Sales have been brisk, due in part to the growth in bus usage as a result of the deregulation of scheduled bus services in the country. Forty units were fabricated and installed in the year and work had been started on a further six units. Amparo estimates that the units in progress at year-end are, on average, two-thirds complete with respect to materials and one-half complete with respect to fabrication labour and overhead. There are no shelters finished and awaiting installation at year-end.

According to UrbanFurniture's records, the company purchased materials (sheet and tubular steel, acrylic panels, plastic seating, lighting) for this new product line at a cost of €12,800 in x5. The records also show that the cost of materials is €275 per shelter. To fabricate each shelter requires 20 hours of labour and the average hourly labour cost is €12. Fabrication overheads (such as depreciation and utilities) on this product line totalled €3,870 in x5. As for the costs of installing the 40 units (i.e. transport, site preparation, and assembly of shelters), these amounted to €2,880 for labour and €2,520 for overhead.

Required

Calculate the costs of the Bauhaus shelters installed in x5 and of the inventory – both materials and work-in-progress – with respect to these shelters at end-x5. What is the gross profit margin ratio on the Bauhaus line in x5?

P9.3   Production costs and income statement presentation

Pirelli SpA is a large Italian tyre and cable manufacturer. Exhibit 9.16 shows part of the company's 2001 consolidated income statement (in the English-language version).

Exhibit 9.16

Pirelli SpA
Consolidated 2001 income statement (extract)
(amounts in € million)

	2001
(A) Production value	
Revenues from sales and services	7,509,220
Changes in inventories of work-in-process, semi-finished and	
finished products	(99,559)
Changes in contract work-in-progress	(37,988)
Increase in property, plant and equipment	16,313
Other revenues and income:	
(a) Miscellaneous	193,770
(b) Government grants	7,516
Total production value	**7,589,272**
(B) Production costs	
Raw materials, supplies and goods for resale	(3,822,787)
Service expenses	(1,181,035)
Lease and rent expenses	(80,077)
Personnel	(1,501,738)
Amortization, depreciation and write-downs:	
(a) Amortization of intangible assets	(46,571)
(b) Depreciation of property, plant and equipment	(324,062)
(d) Write-downs of receivables included in current assets and	
cash and banks	(77,174)
Changes in inventories of raw materials, supplies and goods for resale	(6,511)
Other accruals	(30,521)
Other operating expenses	(223,881)
Total production costs	**(7,294,357)**
Difference between production value and production costs	**294,915**

⋮   ⋮

(*Source*: Pirelli SpA, *Annual Report and Accounts 2001*.)

Required

(a) Did the group's inventories of work in process, semifinished and finished products increase or decrease in 2001? By how much?

(b) What is the meaning of 'Raw materials, supplies and goods for resale' under 'Production costs'? Is it the cost of purchases? Or is it the cost of items consumed and sold? Give evidence for your answer.

(c) Under 'Production value', Pirelli shows the item 'Increase in property, plant and equipment'. What is this? What would happen to profit (before tax) in 2001 if this item were not in the income statement?

(d) Pirelli describes a line item as 'Difference between production value and production costs'. What is the more usual name for this?

P9.4 Sensitivity of income to production levels under absorption costing*

Hansel has devised a more advanced (wicked?) witchit, to be known as a 'widget'. His company plans production of this product for the coming year (year 1). Sales are expected to be 20,000 units at a price of 20/unit. Material and labour costs are production-related and variable: combined, they're forecast to be 10/unit. Production overhead costs are all fixed and are estimated at 100,000 in total. There are no widget-related inventories at the start of year 1. All units started will be completed in the year. The company continues to use absorption costing when costing products.

Required

(a) Hansel asks you to calculate expected gross profit on the new widget line if:
- (i) production is set *equal* to sales of 20,000 units; and
- (ii) production is set at 25,000 units, 5,000 *higher* than sales.

(b) Why is expected gross profit under (a) (ii) greater than expected gross profit under (a)(i)? Is the company better off by producing more units than it expects to sell?

(c) Hansel looks ahead to year 2. Suppose production strategy (a) (ii) is followed in year 1 (i.e. production of 25,000 widgets exceeds sales by 5,000 units) but in year 2, sales show no growth (they remain at 20,000 units) so production is cut to 15,000 units to clear stocks. There's no change in sale price, unit costs or total production overhead.

Calculate the widget line's expected gross profit in year 2. Why is it different from the expected gross profit figures you calculated under (a) (i) and (a) (ii)?

Check figures:
(a) (ii) Expected gross profit   120,000
(c) Expected gross profit in year 2   80,000

* Problem assignment draws on material in the appendix to this chapter.

P9.5 Costs of sales and inventory under alternative cost-flow assumptions

Naiad distributes equipment for yachts and small boats. It decides to stock the EauK, a new type of desalinator that uses the boat's own motion through the sea to operate the device. The following table shows the company's purchases of EauK units in the second quarter of x4.

April	5	at €2,340 each
May	5	at €2,100
June	6	at €2,050

Naiad sells 12 EauK units in this quarter. It calculates the cost of sales on a periodic basis at the end of the quarter.

Required

(a) Compute the costs of second quarter sales and of units in inventory at end-June x4, under FIFO, WAC and LIFO cost-flow assumptions.

(b) Assume the company uses the WAC cost-flow assumption. A consultant urges Naiad to purchase additional units of the desalinator before the end of the second quarter. He argues that the extra purchases will reduce the risk of stock-outs in the busy third quarter and, in addition, will increase second quarter profits.

Recalculate WAC cost of sales in the second quarter, assuming the company buys an extra four units of EauK in late June at a unit price of €2,050 (making purchases of 10 units in the month). Why is cost of sales lower than under the WAC case in (a)? Is the company better off purchasing the additional four units at end-quarter 2?

Check figure:
(b) Unit average cost   €2,135

P9.6   Effect of cost-flow assumptions on income and tax

The Švejk Company is a wholesaler of beer tankards. The table below shows the company's purchases and sales of its (1 litre) Pilsener Special tankard.

	Purchases		Sales		Balance in inventory	
31/12/x5					500	at 4/tankard
During x6:						
February	300	at 5				
April			600	at 7		
July	700	at 5.5				
August			800	at 7.5		
October	500	at 6				
Total	1,500		1,400			
31/12/x6					600	at ?

Required

(a) Calculate the x6 gross profit and end-x6 inventory for this product line under FIFO, LIFO and WAC cost-flow assumptions. Assume the company uses a perpetual system to keep track of inventory quantities and values. Compare the results. Which method yields the highest gross profit and why?

(b) Assume all three methods are permitted for tax purposes. Would Švejk's income tax liability for x6 be greater or less if it used LIFO rather than FIFO – and by how much? Assume a 40% tax rate.

(c) On investigating Švejk's accounting systems, you discover that it uses a *perpetual* inventory system to keep track of inventory quantities but uses a *periodic* system to establish the costs of tankards sold during the year. (Under the periodic system, COGS is calculated at year-end: thus purchases made (and other costs incurred) after the last sale date are included in the COGS calculation.)

Recalculate the x6 gross profit for the Pilsener Special product line under FIFO, LIFO and WAC cost-flow assumptions. Compare the resulting gross profit figures with those you calculated in (a). Why does gross profit differ between (a) and (c) under LIFO and WAC? Under what circumstances would you expect a company to choose the system outlined in (c)?

Check figures:
(a) WAC gross profit   3,375
(c) LIFO gross profit   2,350

P9.7 Effect of LOCOM rule on income

Refer to P9.6. As a result of European Commission health warnings, demand for large beer tankards falls sharply. Švejk estimates their net realisable value (that is, sale price, net of selling costs) is 5/unit in December x6.

Required

(a) What is the effect of the above events on Švejk's x6 gross profit if the company values inventory (i) at FIFO cost; (ii) at the lower of FIFO cost or market?

(b) Švejk sells the remaining tankards in x7 for 6/unit. It makes no further purchases in x7. What is the gross profit it reports on this product line in x7 under (i) FIFO cost; (ii) LOCOM? Looking at Švejk's x6 and x7 results under the two valuation assumptions, what conclusions can we draw about the impact of the LOCOM rule on company accounts?

P9.8 Valuing inventory at replacement cost

Refer to P9.6. Švejk is considering whether to change the basis of valuation of its inventory from historical cost to replacement cost (RC). Assume that, at the time of the April x6 sale, the tankard's RC is 5; at the time of the August sale, it's 5.5; and at year-end, it has risen again to 6.5.

Required

(a) Calculate the x6 gross profit for the Pilsener Special tankard on an RC basis. What is the effect on Švejk Company's end-x6 balance sheet of valuing its tankard inventory at RC rather than at FIFO HC?

(b) Determine the holding gains which Švejk realised in x6 as a result of purchasing tankards when the price was low. Assume that in determining the historical cost of inventory sold, Švejk assumes a FIFO flow of costs.

Check figure:
(a) RC cost of sales 7,400

P9.9 RC information in HC accounts

BP Amoco, a large Anglo-American oil company, is the result of a merger between BP and Amoco that took effect at the end of 1998. Financial statements for 1997 and prior years were restated as if the two companies had been united then. In 2000, the group acquired ARCO, a US oil company. This was accounted for as an acquisition and prior years' accounts were not restated.

BP Amoco provides replacement cost information in its historical cost accounts. Exhibit 9.17 contains summary income statement and operating data that have been taken from the notes to the company's 2001 consolidated accounts.

Required

(a) What can we learn about BP Amoco's operations between 1997 and 2001 from the stock holding gains and losses it reports in those years?

(b) BP Amoco is not the only major oil company to publish RC data in its accounts. Oil companies are not required to do so by law or accounting standards. Why do you think they voluntarily provide this information?

Exhibit 9.17

BP Amoco plc
Group income statement and operating data for calendar years 1997–2001

	1997	1998	1999	2000	2001
Income statement (condensed) (in $m)					
Group turnover	91,760	68,304	83,566	148,062	**174,218**
Replacement cost operating profit	10,683	6,521	8,894	17,756	**16,135**
Exceptional items	128	850	(2,280)	220	**535**
RC profit before interest and tax	10,811	7,371	6,614	17,976	**16,670**
Stockholding gains (losses)	(939)	(1,391)	1,728	728	**(1,900)**
HC profit before interest and tax	9,872	5,980	8,342	18,704	**14,770**
Interest expense	1,035	1,177	1,316	1,770	**1,670**
Profit before taxation	8,837	4,803	7,026	16,934	**13,100**
Taxation	3,013	1,520	1,880	4,972	**5,017**
Profit after taxation	5,824	3,283	5,146	11,962	**8,083**
Minority shareholders' interest	151	63	138	92	**73**
Profit for the year	5,673	3,220	5,008	11,870	**8,010**
Operating data					
Crude oil and liquids production (000 bbl/day)	1,930	2,049	2,061	1,928	1,931
Natural gas production (m ft³/day)	5,858	5,808	6,067	7,609	8,632
Total production (000 boe*/day)	2,940	3,050	3,107	3,240	3,419
* boe = barrel (bbl) of oil equivalent					

Average realisations	*1996*					
BP crude oil and liquids price ($/bbl)	19.5	18.3	12.1	16.7	26.6	22.5
Henry Hub gas price ($/000 ft³)	2.6	2.6	2.2	2.3	3.9	4.3

(*Source*: BP Amoco, *Annual Report and Accounts 2001*. Reproduced by permission of BP plc.)

P9.10 Converting LIFO-based accounts to a FIFO basis

General Motors (GM) is the largest vehicle producer in North America. It is also a leading provider of financial services. Set out below are key numbers from its 2001 accounts relating to its industrial activities ('Automotive, communications services, and other operations'). Amounts are in US$ million.

	2001	2000
Net sales	151,491	160,627
Gross profit	15,871	22,324

	End-2001	End-2000
Current assets	37,063	41,147
(of which: Inventories	10,034	10,945)
Total assets	323,969	303,100
Current liabilities	56,346	55,740
Total liabilities	126,171	116,704

Exhibit 9.18

General Motors Corporation Extract from 2001 accounts		

Note 6   Inventories

Inventories included the following for Automotive, Communications Services, and Other Operations (dollars in millions):

December 31	2001	2000
Productive material, work in process, and supplies	$ 5,069	$ 5,544
Finished product, service parts, etc	6,779	7,257
Total inventories at FIFO	11,848	12,801
Less: LIFO allowance	1,814	1,856
Total inventories (less allowances)	$10,034	$10,945

Inventories are stated generally at cost, which is not in excess of market. The cost of approximately 90% of U.S. inventories is determined by the last-in, first-out (LIFO) method. Generally, the cost of all other inventories is determined by either the first-in, first-out (FIFO) or average cost methods.

(*Source*: General Motors Corporation, *Annual Report and Accounts 2001*. Reproduced by permission of General Motors Corporation.)

You wish to compare GM's financial performance with that of other major car producers. You discover that although car companies value inventories in different ways, most provide FIFO information in the notes to the accounts. You decide therefore to convert key GM numbers to a FIFO basis. Exhibit 9.18 contains the note on inventories taken from GM's 2001 accounts.

Required

(a) Calculate GM's inventory turnover rate (cost of sales/average inventories), current ratio and gross profit margin ratio in 2001, using the unadjusted numbers in GM's accounts.

(b) Adjust GM's inventory and gross profit figures to a FIFO basis, using the information in Exhibit 9.18. Recalculate the ratios in (a). Contrast the unadjusted and adjusted ratios. Why is inventory turnover lower but the gross profit margin ratio barely changed under the FIFO basis?

Notes to Chapter 9

1   International Accounting Standards Board, *IAS 2: Inventories*, para. 7.
2   *IAS 2*, op. cit. Under international rules, borrowing costs can be treated as a production overhead and capitalised, subject to two conditions. First, production of the good or service requires a substantial period of time (examples are the ageing of whisky and the construction of property for sale). Second, the company's borrowing costs are lower if production doesn't take place (*IAS 23: Borrowing Costs*).
3   In practice, companies collect costs such as depreciation and wages in a temporary account (e.g. Depreciation, Payroll) and then distribute them to production (WIP inventory) and non-production departments (Selling expense, Administrative expense).
4   Fédération des Experts Comptables Européens (1993), *1992 FEE Analysis of European Accounting and Disclosure Practices*, London: Routledge, chapter 6.
5   International Accounting Standards Board, *IAS 41: Agriculture*. The standard uses the phrase 'fair value less estimated point-of-sale costs' instead of 'net realisable value'.

6 American Institute of Certified Public Accountants (1970–2001), *Accounting Trends and Techniques*, 24th–55th editions, New York: AICPA. The sample of 600 large quoted US firms – and the industry composition of the sample – changes over time as firms drop out owing to mergers, takeovers and bankruptcy, and are replaced by others of comparable size but, in many cases, from a different sector.

7 Cushing, B.E. and LeClere, M.J. (1992), Evidence on the determinants of inventory accounting policy choice, *The Accounting Review*, 67: 355–366.

8 Using cost of goods sold in the numerator is preferred since both numerator and denominator (average inventories) are then stated on the same basis: cost. If a company classifies expenses by nature, however, the COGS figure may not be available and sales revenue must be used.

9 Using start- and end-year figures may overstate inventory turnover if a company chooses its financial year-end at a time when its inventories are low (e.g. at the end of its major selling season).

10 Variable costing is also known as 'direct costing'. *Direct costs are those which can be traced directly to products*. Each of Gretel's witchits, for example, requires a specific quantity of steel and a specific amount of labour time in its manufacture: the costs of the steel and the production labour are direct costs of the witchit. (Costs which cannot be traced in this way and which must be assigned to products by means of an allocation mechanism – examples are depreciation, repairs, insurance, supervisory labour – are 'indirect' costs.) At one time, direct production costs were all variable. Nowadays, the production labour costs of many firms do not vary in direct proportion to output. Nonetheless, the synonym lives on.

10

Recognition of revenue and valuation of receivables

INTRODUCTION

Sales and receivables are linked. When a company sells goods or services on account and recognises revenue, its receivables increase. In this chapter, we return to the issue of revenue recognition we first discussed in Chapter 5 and, in addition, we look at how receivables are valued in the balance sheet.

Revenues are gross inflows of economic benefits. Most companies reckon they can be sure of these benefits and can measure them reliably only when they deliver goods to customers or perform services for them. As a result, this is the point in the operating cycle when most companies recognise revenue. But some manufacturing and construction companies recognise revenue before delivery – and some, more rarely, after. And service companies often have problems in practice determining when services have been performed. We begin section 1 of the chapter by exploring these issues and showing the impact of alternative recognition dates on a company's accounts.

Trade receivables arise because companies extend credit to customers. A company faces problems measuring its receivable asset. Receivables are valued initially at cost. But what is a receivable's cost when the invoice amount includes taxes and the company offers discounts? Subsequently, the amount at which the company carries a receivable on its books should be reduced if it exceeds realisable value, that is the amount the company expects to collect in cash from the customer. How do companies estimate realisable value in this case? We consider in the remainder of section 1 the effects of value added tax, cash discounts, bad debts and sales returns on the valuation of receivables.

We turn to more specialised topics in section 2. We discuss the accounting for long-term contracts and contrast the financial statement effects of two widely used methods of recognising revenue from them, the percentage-of-completion and completed contract methods. The remaining two topics concern receivables. Cash-constrained firms sell receivables to a third party before the debts mature. Cash-rich firms, on the other hand, offer long-term credit to customers at below-market interest rates. Each situation gives rise to accounting problems. We explain current international standards in these areas.

In section 3 of the chapter we consider what investors look for when reviewing a company's revenue and receivables figures. We describe a key ratio, receivables turnover, which links credit sales and receivables and which, in adjusted form, shows how many days a firm's customers take to pay their bills.

SECTION 1

Core issues

Revenue recognition revisited

General

A company generates revenue from selling goods or performing services. It also earns revenue – in the form of interest, royalties and dividends – when others pay for the use of its assets. In each case, what occurs – and this is the definition of revenue – is a 'gross inflow of economic benefits' to the company arising from its ordinary activities. Note that the company only records as revenue inflows received (or receivable) *on its own account*. Amounts collected on behalf of others are not revenues. Thus value added taxes are excluded from revenue. Similarly, a company acting as an agent shows as revenue only the commissions it earns – not the gross amount collected on behalf of the principal.

At what point does a company recognise revenue? Accounting regulators have laid down certain conditions that must be met before it can do so. The key ones for the sale of goods are:

- it's probable that economic benefits associated with the transaction will flow to the company;
- the amount of revenue – and related costs – can be measured reliably; and
- the company has transferred to the buyer the significant risks and rewards of ownership.[1]

These revenue recognition conditions are general. They apply in all industries. In some cases, however, there is uncertainty about whether one or more of the conditions is met.

Consider, for example, the transfer of ownership risks and rewards. Often it is clear when the risks have *not* been transferred. For example, where goods are sold on consignment, the seller/consignor should not recognise revenue until the consignee has sold the goods to a third party, since, until then, the seller is still the owner of the goods.

Sometimes we need to look more closely at the sale contract. Suppose the buyer has the right to return the goods. In this case, the seller still retains some ownership risk. What matters then is how large is the risk retained. For example, the risk to a retailer that accepts returned merchandise and offers to refund dissatisfied customers is usually small: in this case it recognises revenue at the point of sale and establishes a provision for estimated returns. But if a company sells goods on approval, then, under international accounting standards, it should recognise revenue only when the buyer has accepted the goods and the time period for rejection has passed.[2]

In most cases, a company transfers the main risks and rewards of ownership when legal title passes to the buyer. This usually occurs when the goods are delivered to the buyer. It's for this reason that delivery is the point in the operating cycle when most companies that sell goods recognise revenue. But note that there are circumstances when recognition of revenue can occur before the delivery date or be delayed until after it. An agricultural producer must measure its produce (e.g. milk, corn, grapes) at fair value net of estimated point-of-sale costs *at the time of harvest*.[3] This is equivalent to recognising revenue on completion of production. Accounting regulators claim there are active markets for most types of agricultural produce and thus fair value, a more relevant measure of value than historical cost in this case, can be easily established at the harvest date. By contrast, a landowner selling land to a property developer under extended payment terms faces a different environment. Suppose that payments are structured so that, in essence, the developer pays for the land out of the proceeds of development. In this case, it would be prudent of the landowner to recognise revenue from the land sale only as it receives each instalment of cash.

Exhibit 10.1 Revenue: financial statement impact of alternative recognition points

Facts

Beatrix makes the McGregor line of earthenware pots at a (cash) cost of €12/unit and sells them for €20/unit. All sales are on account. Key operating data for year 1 are as follows:

Production	600 units
Delivery	550 units
Cash collected from credit customers	€9,000

There are no inventories at start-year 1 and only finished goods inventories at end-year 1.

Recognising revenue on production, delivery and cash collection: impact on accounts

Revenue recognised on:	Completion of production	Delivery	Cash collection
Units	600	550	450
Effect on Beatrix's year 1 profit			
Revenues	€12,000	€11,000	€9,000
Matched costs	7,200	6,600	5,400
Gross profit	€4,800	€4,400	€3,600
Effect on Beatrix's net assets (and owners' equity), at end-year 1			
Finished goods inventory (50 units)	€1,000*	€600	€600
Accounts receivable (100 units)	2,000	2,000	1,200**
Cash***	1,800	1,800	1,800
Total	€4,800	€4,400	€3,600

  * Inventory at fair value (50 units at €20)
 ** A/R at cost (100 units at €12). Profit is excluded because cash has not yet been collected.
*** Cash collected (€9,000) less production costs (€7,200 [600 units × €12]).

The following example contrasts the financial statement effects of recognising revenue at three different dates: completion of production, delivery, and cash receipt. Beatrix makes pots. The McGregor, one of her favourite lines, costs €12 each to produce and sells for €20. In year 1, she produces 600 units, delivers 550 to customers, and collects €9,000 cash from them. Exhibit 10.1 shows the effect on Beatrix's year 1 income and net assets under each of the three revenue recognition points. (To keep the example simple, we assume no beginning inventories – and only finished goods in ending inventory. All production costs are paid in cash and there are no selling costs.)

Earlier recognition of revenue results in higher profits and net assets so long as products are profitable and output is expanding. Bringing forward recognition of revenue – from delivery to production – increases Beatrix's year 1 profit and end-year 1 net assets by €400, the product of units in inventory (50) and the excess of sales price over cost (€8). By contrast, postponement of revenue recognition – from delivery to cash collection – lowers the profits and net assets of profitable firms. In Beatrix's case, profit deferred on uncollected credit sales in year 1 is €800 (100 units × €8). The key word here is 'deferred'. Delaying (advancing) the revenue recognition date doesn't permanently lower (raise) profits. It simply alters their timing.

● Revenues from services

A company that supplies a service recognises revenue when it performs it. The conditions for revenue recognition are similar to those for goods. The company must show there's a strong likelihood it will receive economic benefits from the transaction and it can measure the revenue and related costs reliably. The third test – the transfer of ownership risks and rewards – does not apply to service transactions. Instead, accounting regulators impose a different test. Where a company performs services under a contract over more than one financial period, it should recognise revenue based on the stage of completion of the contract at the balance sheet date.[4] This assumes the company can make reliable estimates of both the outcome of the contract and its progress. If it can't, the company should recognise revenue only to the extent that contract costs are recoverable.

An example illustrates how the **percentage-of-completion method**, as it's known, is applied in practice. Delphi Consulting is awarded a contract to carry out a strategic study for the European Commission. The contract has a value of €600,000 which the EC will pay on completion. Expected contract costs are €500,000: these will be paid as they are incurred. Delphi expects to complete 30% of the contract in year 1, 50% in year 2 and the balance in year 3. These percentages are based on the costs Delphi expects to incur each year. The contract turns out as expected. Exhibit 10.2 shows the effect of the contract on the company's income and balance sheet in each of the three years.

The contract revenue and profit Delphi recognises in its income statement reflects the work done in the year. Thus in year 1 Delphi recognises as revenue 30% of the contract's value – or

Exhibit 10.2 Recognising revenues from services: the percentage-of-completion method

Facts

The European Commission awards Delphi Consulting a three-year contract at a value of €600,000 (to be received in cash on completion). Expected contract costs are €500,000: all costs are paid in cash as they're incurred. Delphi expects to complete 30% of the contract by end-year 1 and 80% by end-year 2. The stage of completion is based on costs incurred (relative to total expected costs).

Percentage-of-completion method: expected effect on Delphi's accounts
(currency amounts in €000)

	Year 1	Year 2	Year 3	
Expected % completed	30	80	100	
Expected effect on profit				
Contract revenues	180	300	120	
Contract expenses	−150	−250	−100	
Contract profit	30	50	20	
[Cumulative contract profit	30	80	100]	

Expected effect on end-year net assets			On contract completion	Receipt of cash
Contract in progress (at fair value)	+180	+480	+600	0
Cash	−150	−400	−500	+100
Total	+30	+80	+100	+100

€180,000 – since this is the proportion of the contract completed that year. As the cost of this work is €150,000, Delphi recognises profit on the contract of €30,000. Delphi's balance sheet shows the uncompleted contract at fair value (i.e. cost plus recognised profits). This is recorded as 'Contract in progress', an inventory account. Note how by the end of year 2, Delphi's net assets have increased by €80,000, the excess of the contract's inventory value (€480,000) over cumulative cash outlays on it (€400,000). This is also the cumulative profit on the contract at that date.

Our Delphi example is simple. Long-term contracts are more complicated in practice. Contracts rarely go according to plan. Actual contract costs – and work done each period – differ from expectations. In addition, customers make progress payments rather than pay only when the contract is completed. We illustrate the accounting for these features of long-term contracts in section 2.

Problem areas

Revenues can give rise to recognition and measurement problems for a wide range of companies. Sometimes the problems are industry-specific. For example, when should an insurance company recognise revenue from an insurance premium? How should a film production company account for revenues and expenses from film production and distribution? We focus here on general issues. Nonetheless, the principles derived can help answer revenue questions in specific industries like insurance and film production.

A company may provide both goods and services in one transaction. For example, a retailer sells audio equipment which carries an extended warranty. How does it account for a composite transaction like this? The recommended approach in these circumstances is to split the transaction into its component parts and account for each separately. Thus the retailer should estimate the fair value of the goods without the extended warranty and recognise revenue from this part of the transaction at the time of sale. The fair value of the extended warranty is estimated separately and recognised, usually on a time basis, over the term of the warranty. The difficulty in practice is in determining the fair values of the components of the transaction. Published prices may mislead because the retailer may cut the price of the equipment in the hope of recouping the lower profit margin by signing up the customer to a higher margin warranty contract.

The revenue figure needs to be adjusted whenever a vendor supplies a range of products or services and cross-subsidisation occurs. Consider the case of the franchisor. It usually charges a new franchisee an initial fee to cover the costs of staff training, advertising and other start-up services. It may also supply goods or services – for example, pizza dough to franchised pizza restaurants – in the early years of the franchise contract at a price below market. In this event, it should defer part of the initial franchise fee (equal to the value of the subsidy) and recognise it as revenue when it supplies the subsidised goods or services to the franchisee.

Revenue recognition problems can also arise when a company swaps goods and services with another. Where the goods or services swapped are similar in nature, neither party should recognise revenue since there's no additional inflow of economic benefits. For example, a European oil company arranges an oil swap with an American competitor: it supplies crude oil to its competitor's refinery in Europe and, in return, receives crude oil for its US West Coast refinery from the American company. Both parties avoid shipment costs. The transaction is an exchange of inventory. Any difference in the value of the oil exchanged is settled in cash.

If the goods or services exchanged are dissimilar in nature, however, revenue *is* recognised. Thus a mining company that barters, say, bauxite for equipment recognises revenue from the sale of bauxite.

Dr. Equipment (A+)	xx	
Cr. Revenue from sale of bauxite (OE+)		xx
Dr. Cost of bauxite sold (OE–)	xx	
Cr. Inventory (A–)		xx

Barter is common where the costs of using money as the medium of exchange are high (e.g. the mining company's operations are in a country with multiple foreign exchange rates). The mining company measures the revenue at the fair value of the consideration *received* (in this case, the equipment). If, however, the fair value of the equipment can't be measured reliably, it should use the fair value of the goods *given up* (i.e. the bauxite) as the basis for measuring both the revenue and the equipment received in exchange.

Revenue recognition: international practice

Companies that sell goods usually recognise revenue at the point of delivery. Earlier recognition of revenue is rare. In agriculture and in some natural resource industries, revenue is recognised on completion of production where the fair value of the agricultural produce or commodity can be measured reliably. Delaying recognition until after delivery is also unusual, except in tax accounts. The tax authorities in many countries allow firms to defer recognition of revenue (and profit) on instalment sales until cash is received. For the taxpaying company, the advantage is clear. Tax is postponed until the company has collected the cash from customers to pay it.

As for companies providing services, the nature of the service determines the timing of revenue recognition. Where the service consists of one transaction (e.g. a loan placement, a theatre performance), the usual practice is for the provider to recognise revenue when the transaction takes place. Where the service consists of a series of transactions or is time-related (e.g. course tuition, a loan commitment facility), practice varies. IAS favour a percentage-of-completion or time-apportioned basis of revenue recognition – and the popularity of this method is growing, even in countries with a uniform reporting tradition that hitherto have delayed recognition of revenue until contract completion. (We contrast the percentage-of-completion and completed-contract methods in section 2.) However, the percentage-of-completion method should come with a health warning: there is a risk that the service provider may 'front-load' revenue and profits by claiming that it performs services earlier than is in fact the case.

Credit sales: terms and methods of payment

For most manufacturing companies and increasingly for many retailing companies too, it is common to grant customers a period of credit before they have to pay their debts. A firm sets **credit terms** (a credit limit and a credit period), which may vary with the perceived riskiness of the customer. However, there is a growing tendency to standardise the credit period within an industry. In some industries, the period is stated cryptically as 'net monthly': this is usually interpreted as one month after the end of the month in which the invoice is received.

There are country differences, too. The European Commission surveyed firms in EU member states in 1996 and found that, among the larger states, French and Italian companies offer a longer credit period than those in Germany and the UK:

	Contractual credit period (average)	Days accounts are overdue (average)
Germany	23	11
UK	31	18
France	48	10
Italy	65	22

Notice that in all the above countries customers on average exceed the permitted credit period. In fact, the Commission found that the overdue period in the EU (plus Norway) was on average 15 days in 1996.[5]

Some companies offer **cash discounts** for early payment. An example is '1/10, net 30' (1% cash discount for payment within 10 days; otherwise, the invoiced amount within 30 days). We review the accounting for cash discounts in the next section. Companies may charge **interest** on overdue accounts. In August 2000, the European Commission issued a directive which gives all firms in the EU a legal right to interest on overdue debts.[6]

The terms of sale discussed above refer to sales **on open account**. Such a sale involves an unwritten contract in which the purchaser agrees to pay the seller the net amount stated on the invoice within the credit period granted. Sales can also be made by **draft**, using a **promissory note** or a **bill of exchange**. In this case, purchaser and seller are parties to a written agreement in which the sum owing, the date of payment and other conditions (for example, the date from which interest is charged and the rate of interest) are explicitly stated. Drafts and the accounting for them are discussed in section 2 of this chapter.

Some companies *sell* their receivables before the due date. A company may discount a bill (or note) it holds before the maturity date. It presents the bill to its bank and receives funds at a discount to the bill's maturity value. A firm may sell its trade accounts receivable *en bloc* to a **factor** or, in special cases (e.g. credit card receivables), it may be able to securitise them.

A factor offers several services to client companies. It will take over part or all of a client's credit management tasks – assessing credit risk, setting credit limits for individual customers, managing the sales ledger – for a fee (which may range between 0.75% and 3% of sales). It can collect customers' debts directly. And it will make a cash advance equivalent to a high percentage (80–85%) of a client company's outstanding debts at an interest rate little higher than the company's usual bank borrowing rate. A client can select one or more of these services. Factoring is popular among smaller firms in industries where there are many suppliers and many customers (e.g. shoe, textile, carpet and toy manufacturing). Credit card companies offer, in effect, a factoring service to retailers. In both cases, the factor enjoys economies of scale in credit risk assessment and debt collection.[7]

Trade debts may be sold **with recourse**. This means that in the event that the debtor does not pay the amount owing when due, the factor can demand payment from (has recourse to) the seller of the receivables. Likewise, bills and notes may be discounted with recourse. We discuss the accounting implications of this in section 2 of this chapter.

Offering credit to customers brings risks as well as rewards. Sales and profits are likely to increase but some customers will default on their debts. The loss the company sustains is, at the limit, the sale price of the good or service. Not surprisingly, firms take various measures to reduce the incidence and thus the cost of bad debts:

- assessing potential customers' credit risk and setting credit terms accordingly;
- monitoring carefully credit actually taken and chasing overdue accounts;
- using specialist services for risks that are hard to assess (e.g. obtaining letters of credit from small export customers); and
- buying insurance to protect against non-payment of certain types of debt.

Despite these precautions some debts are never collected. Later in this section we describe and illustrate the various ways firms account for bad debts.

Receivables valuation

When accounting for receivables, companies face measurement as well as recognition problems. We've already seen that when a company recognises a trade receivable depends on when it recognises revenue. Once the receivable is recognised, it must then be valued. *First, the company must decide at what amount it should record the receivable initially.* For example, how should it account for any cash discount it offers a customer who pays early? *Second, it must decide what adjustments it should make to the receivable if it is impaired.* For example, what should it do if collection of the receivable becomes doubtful?

The 4th Directive offers no specific guidance on these issues. International accounting standards do. The main IAS valuation rules for receivables are summarised below. They reflect current best practice.

- State receivables at cost. 'Cost' is the fair value of the consideration given. In the case of trade receivables, this is the invoiced amount of the goods or services supplied (i.e. net of trade and quantity discounts given at the time of invoicing).
- Measure long-term receivables at the present value of the future cash receipts specified in the contract. The discount rate should be the market rate of interest for a similar loan at the date of the contract.
- Write down a receivable to its recoverable amount when it's probable the contractual amounts can't be collected when due. Recognise the loss (or bad debt expense) in income immediately. 'Recoverable amount' is the total of revised future cash flows. In the case of long-term receivables, the cash flows are discounted.[8]

We now show how firms put these principles into effect.

Value added tax

The cost of a receivable includes any taxes borne on the sale of goods and services and which the seller collects on behalf of the government. It therefore includes value added tax (VAT) and excise duties. VAT is an indirect tax, similar to a sales tax, which is levied by all EU member states. Any business that carries out an economic activity (production, trading, supply of services) must charge VAT on the (taxable) goods and services it supplies (known as 'output tax'). However, it can recover VAT charged on the goods and services it purchases ('input tax'). The amount it pays to the government each tax period is the net of its output and input taxes. *VAT is thus a tax on the value a firm adds in its operations.*

How does VAT affect the reporting of credit (and cash) sales? The company recognises as revenue the sale of goods or supply of services net of VAT. The invoice the customer receives – and thus the amount he or she must pay – *includes* VAT. The difference is recorded by the firm as a VAT liability. Customs and excise duties are treated the same way. For example, suppose retailer Y sells a computer to customer Z on account at a price excluding VAT of 1,000. The VAT rate is 15%. Y records the sale as follows:

Dr. Account receivable, Z (A+)	1,150	
Cr. Revenue from sale (OE+)		1,000
Cr. VAT payable (L+)		150

Y's *net* VAT liability is less than 150. It can recover any VAT included in the price it pays for the computer. Assume the ex-factory price of the computer, net of VAT, is 600 and the VAT rate is 15%. Y records the purchase from manufacturer X as follows:

Dr. Inventory (A+)	600	
(later: Cost of sales (OE–))		
Dr. VAT receivable (A+)	90	
Cr. Account payable, X (L+)		690

Thus Y's net VAT liability with respect to the purchase and sale of the computer is 60 (150 – 90).

As with any tax, the devil lies in the detail – of which there is much, given the differences in the way VAT is administered across the European Union. For example, in most member states there are different rates of VAT for different types of goods and services. Certain goods such as food, books and pharmaceutical supplies attract a reduced rate of VAT in many states. Exports are zero-rated (i.e. carry a VAT rate of 0%). It is possible, therefore, for a firm to report a net VAT *receivable*: the VAT reclaimable on its inputs exceeds the VAT charged on its output.[9]

Cash discounts

Where a supplier offers a customer a cash discount for early payment, it is common practice for the supplier not to recognise the discount unless the customer pays within the discount period. Initially, the supplier reports revenue and receivable gross. If the customer takes the discount and pays early, the cost to the supplier is recorded as an expense (or as a deduction from sales revenue). Similarly, the customer is also likely to record the purchase and the payable at the gross amount and recognise as income the benefit from any cash discount when it's taken. This is known as the **gross method** of accounting for cash discounts. Note that in most EU countries, discounts for early payment are excluded from the VAT calculation.

To illustrate, suppose Buddenbrook sells goods costing 80,000 to Hagenstroem for 100,000 and offers a 1.5% discount if payment is made within ten days of the invoice date. Hagenstroem takes advantage of the discount, in view of the high opportunity cost of forgoing it.[10] Under the **gross method**, Buddenbrook records the sale of goods and the recognition of the discount as follows. (To keep the numbers simple, VAT is ignored. Currency amounts are in thousands.)

Buddenbrook (Supplier)			**Hagenstroem (Customer)**		
Sale of goods			*Purchase of goods*		
	Dr.	Cr.		Dr.	Cr.
Account receivable (A+)	100		Inventory (A+)	100	
Sales revenue (OE+)		100	Account payable (L+)		100
Cost of sales (OE–)	80				
Inventory (A–)		80			
Receipt of cash within ten days			*Payment of cash within ten days*		
Cash (A+)	98.5		Account payable (L–)	100	
Sales discount[1] (OE–)	1.5		Cash (A–)		98.5
Account receivable (A–)		100	Purchase discount[2] (OE+)		1.5

[1] Shown as expense or deduction from revenue.
[2] Shown as income or deduction from related expense.

Both Buddenbrook and Hagenstroem record the transaction initially at the gross amount of 100,000. Neither recognises the discount – an expense to the former, income to the latter – if Hagenstroem does not settle his debt within ten days.

An alternative, less widely used method – but one which results in an initial receivable value closer to the realisable amount – is known as the **net method**. The supplier records the sale and receivable at the amount net of discount (e.g. 98,500 in the above example) and treats any cash discount forfeited by the customer as *income*. Similarly, the customer can also (independently) use this method: in this case, the purchase is recorded at the net amount and, should payment not be made within the discount period, the lost discount (1,500 in our example) is shown as an *expense*. One advantage of the net method is that it highlights the benefit (to the supplier) and the cost (to the customer) of forfeited discounts.

If a supplier grants a customer a **volume rebate** (for example, a percentage reduction in the normal unit price when the number of items a customer orders in a specified period exceeds a stated level), it adjusts the customer's account only when the volume level is exceeded. It acknowledges the rebate either by adjusting the current invoice or by issuing a credit note. VAT must also be adjusted.

Bad and doubtful debts

Not all receivables are converted into cash. A customer may go bankrupt. From the standpoint of an unsecured creditor (which is the unfortunate fate of most suppliers of goods and services), amounts owed by a bankrupt customer are likely to be partially or wholly unrecoverable. Debts may prove uncollectible for other reasons. For example, a customer may dispute an invoice and the legal and administrative costs to the seller of pursuing its claim exceed the debt outstanding. When debts are considered uncollectible, they are described as 'bad'.

Direct write-off and allowance methods

There are two general ways in which a company can account for its bad debts. It can write them off when management decide they are not collectible. We call this the **direct write-off** method. Alternatively, it can estimate each period the percentage of debts which it reckons will prove uncollectible and make a provision in the accounts for them. We call this the **allowance** method.

Let's illustrate these two methods. Ragueneau is a poet and a pâtissier. Although a master of his trade – he has been called the 'Apollo of the kitchen' – his business skills do not match his culinary ones. In particular, credit management is weak. Some customers are slow to pay; some do not pay at all (at least, not in cash – a few try to pay for their pastries with poems).

Ragueneau records credit sales of 3.2 million in year 1, his first year of operations. At the end of the year, he estimates that 5% of the receivables balance of 400,000 is likely to prove uncollectible. In year 2 his company collects 380,000 of the end-year 1 receivables balance and writes off the remaining debts of 20,000 as bad. The accounting entries Ragueneau makes in years 1 and 2 under the two methods are as follows (amounts in 000):

(a) *Direct write-off method*

(b) *Allowance method*

End-year 1

	Dr.	Cr.
Bad debt expense (OE–)	20	
Allowance for bad debts (CA+)		20
To record the cost of estimated bad debts and make allowance for them		

No entry

During year 2

	Dr.	Cr.		Dr.	Cr.
Bad debt expense (OE–)	20		Allowance for bad debts (CA–)	20	
Accounts receivable (A–)		20	Accounts receivable (A–)		20
To record the cost of bad debts at the time of write-off			To record the write-off of bad debts previously allowed for		

Under the direct write-off method, the cost to the firm of uncollectible accounts ('Bad debt expense') is recognised only when management have judged particular debts 'bad' and authorised their write-off. In Ragueneau's case, this decision is taken in year 2. The write-offs are made direct to the specific customer accounts in 'Accounts receivable'.

Under the allowance method, uncollectible accounts are estimated – during or at the end of the financial period. (At this stage they are 'doubtful' accounts.) The cost to the firm of such accounts is recognised in the period when the estimate is made – year 1 in our example. Because the firm cannot identify which accounts will prove uncollectible at that date, it cannot credit 'Accounts receivable' directly since this would involve adjusting individual customer accounts. Thus the adjustment is recorded in a contra-asset account, 'Allowance for bad debts' (or 'Allowance for doubtful accounts').

When the firm identifies actual bad debts, it adjusts individual customer accounts – by crediting 'Accounts receivable' – and utilises the allowance. In Ragueneau's case, this occurs in year 2. Note that under the allowance method, the entry to write off bad debts has no income statement impact.

The allowance method is the preferred method of accounting for bad debts. It ensures that the carrying amount of receivables is reduced by the amount of estimated uncollectible accounts and is thus closer to their realisable value. For example, at the end of year 1, Ragueneau reports net receivables of 400,000 under the direct write-off method and 380,000 under the allowance method. The latter figure better reflects the cash which will be collected from this asset.

In our example, the allowance for bad debts at the close of year 1 (20,000) is the same as the debts actually written off in year 2. In reality, estimated and actual bad debts rarely correspond exactly. Where a difference occurs, management usually adjust the bad debt expense figure in the period the difference is discovered. If, for example, only 18,000, not 20,000, of Ragueneau's year 1 receivables prove uncollectible, the expense in year 2 is reduced by the 2,000 overestimate. The company does not restate its year 1 accounts since they reflect the information available to it at the time. In practice, the adjustments are usually small, especially for an established company, since it can draw on its past experience to refine its bad debt estimates.

Estimating the bad debt allowance

The percentage-of-receivables method

How do companies determine the allowance for bad debts? Most companies use a balance sheet approach. A simple method is to apply a percentage to the end-year receivables balance, as we showed in our example. The percentage itself will vary depending on trading conditions, being higher, for example, during an economic recession and its aftermath.

Ageing analysis

A more complicated, but potentially more accurate, method is to analyse the end-period receivables balance by the length of time accounts are outstanding. A different percentage is then applied to each 'age' category of receivable. The older the debt, the higher is the percentage applied. The percentages are derived from the company's past experience. Assume Ragueneau performs an ageing analysis of his company's receivables balance of 400,000 at the end of year 1. Its normal credit period is 30 days from the invoice date. The breakdown of its end-year 1 receivables, together with the percentage it applies to each age category of receivable, is set out in Exhibit 10.3.

By applying a predetermined percentage to each age category of end-year 1 receivables, Ragueneau estimates his firm needs an allowance for bad debts of 19,000 (after rounding). As a result, net receivables reported in its end-year 1 balance sheet are 381,000.

Exhibit 10.3 Ragueneau Company: ageing analysis of end-year 1 receivables
(currency amounts in 000)

	Due (within 30 days of invoice date)	Number of days past due			
		1–30	*31–60*	*over 60*	*Total*
Receivables, 31/12/year 1 (A)	170	160	50	20	400
Percentage (B) expected to be uncollectible	0.6%	1.8%	10%	50%	
Allowance required, end-year 1 (A) × (B)	1.02	2.88	5	10	18.9

An ageing analysis offers management informational benefits. They can identify which customers are slow payers. They can even distinguish habitual slow-payers from the more risky group of customers whose payment record has deteriorated sharply. They can then use the information to take action – for example, to chase slow payers, lower credit limits for high-risk customers or, more generally, alter the company's credit terms.

Calculating bad debt expense under the allowance method

Under balance sheet methods of determining the allowance for bad debts, the cost of bad debts recorded in the income statement is a derived number. *Bad debt expense under these methods is equivalent to the net write-offs in the period (write-offs less recoveries of bad debts previously written off), adjusted for the change in the estimated required allowance between the start and end of the period.*

We use our Ragueneau example to illustrate the calculation. Assume that in year 2 the company writes off bad debts of 20,000 but recovers a previously written-off debt of 2,000 from Cyrano, a loyal but impoverished customer.

Write-offs of bad debts		
Dr. Allowance for bad debts (CA–)	20,000	
Cr. Accounts receivable (A–)		20,000
Recovery of bad debt		
Dr. Account receivable, Cyrano (A+)	2,000	
Cr. Allowance for bad debts (CA+)		2,000
Dr. Cash (A+)	2,000	
Cr. Account receivable, Cyrano (A–)		2,000

(Cyrano's debt is first reinstated before the cash collected is recorded. In this way, Ragueneau's management can distinguish, at the individual customer level, bad debts recovered from those unrecovered. This information will prove valuable when they review the company's credit policy towards individual customers at a later date.[11])

We discover from Ragueneau's books that its end-year 2 gross receivables are 450,000, up from 400,000 at the end of year 1. An ageing analysis indicates that the company needs a bad debt allowance of 24,000 at end-year 2, an increase of 5,000 over the allowance established at the end of year 1. As a result, the company recognises bad debt expense of 23,000. The calculation and journal entry are shown below:

Net write-offs in the year (20,000 – 2,000)	18,000
Increase in required allowance (24,000 – 19,000)	+5,000
Year 2 bad debt expense	23,000

Dr. Bad debt expense (OE–)	23,000	
Cr. Allowance for bad debts (CA+)		23,000

The bad debt expense figure can also be derived from the 'Allowance for bad debts' contra-asset account, shown in ledger account format below.

Allowance for bad debts (CA)

	Dr.(–)		Cr.(+)
		(Required) Balance,	
		1/1/year 2	19,000
Bad debts written off in year 2	20,000	Recovery of Cyrano's debt	2,000
		Year 2 expense	
		(derived)	*23,000*
		(Required) Balance,	
		31/12/year 2	24,000

Ragueneau shows the accounts receivable balance at its net amount (i.e. net of the allowance for bad debts) in its end-year balance sheet:

	At 31 December	
	Year 2	Year 1
Accounts receivable, gross	450,000	400,000
Less: Allowance for bad debts	–24,000	–19,000
Accounts receivable, net	426,000	381,000

Some companies determine bad debt expense using *income statement* data. On the basis of past experience, a firm estimates what proportion of its credit sales will prove uncollectible and, at the time of sale, records an expense and an allowance based on that percentage. Bad debt expense calculated in this way is provisional, however. At the end of the financial period, the firm should correct the provisional expense figure using the findings of its ageing analysis – and other data such as actual write-offs and recoveries in the period.

Accounting for bad debts: international practice

How firms account for bad debts is not well documented. We do know that in uniform reporting countries the national tax code influences corporate accounting in this area. Companies may be required to distinguish, for tax purposes, specific from general bad debts. A tax deduction is usually available for losses arising from debts written off in the period. However, some countries restrict the tax deduction a company can claim for *general* bad debts. For example, the general bad debt deduction that Italian companies can claim in their annual tax return is limited to 0.5% of gross end-year receivables. In many countries (e.g. France, Mexico, Singapore, UK, USA), a general provision for bad debts is not tax deductible.

Note that tax authorities in Europe usually take no account of a firm's provision for bad debts in assessing VAT. The taxable amount for VAT purposes is the cost or purchase price of the good or service. Only when the supplier writes off a customer's debt on the grounds that the amount is uncollectible, is it entitled to a VAT refund.

Sales returns and allowances

Companies adjust revenues (and, in the case of credit sales, receivables too) for sales returns and sales allowances. In the case of a **sale return**, the supplier permits a customer to return merchandise if it is defective, unsuitable or, in the case of a customer who is a retailer, unsaleable. It then cancels the amount owing on the goods (or grants the customer a refund). In the case of a **sale allowance**, it grants the customer an allowance, for example a voucher to be used against future purchases, in place of returning the goods.

Where returns or allowances are sizeable in relation to sales, a prudent company provides for them at the time of sale. The accounting is similar to that for bad debts. Take the case of a toy manufacturer which may have to accept unsold stock from retailers in the post-Christmas season. At the time of sale, the company records the amount of the estimated returns as a deduction from revenues. At the same time, it provides for future returns by means of a contra-asset account, 'Allowance for sales returns'. This is usually shown as an adjustment to its receivables.

Dr. (Estimated) sales returns (OE–)	xx	
Cr. Allowance for sales returns (CA+)		xx

When the company accepts returned toys from a retailer, the provision is used and the retailer's debt to the company is reduced. (In the case of cash sales – or credit sales fully paid for – a refund is given.)

Dr. Allowance for sales returns (CA–)	xx	
Cr. Account receivable, retailer X (A–)		xx
(or Cash)		

If the returned goods are resaleable, the toy manufacturer will also adjust its 'inventory' and 'cost of sales' accounts.

Many companies, however, do not provide for estimated sales returns and allowances – for practical reasons. In contrast to bad debts, it's hard to estimate the amount of returns and allowances – or their nature (i.e. can the goods be resold? is rework necessary?). Moreover, except in certain industries, the amounts involved are not material. Thus firms account for such items as they occur, even though this can result in mismatching of cost (e.g. sales return) and revenue.

Whichever method of accounting a company uses – the direct or the allowance method – it reports sales revenues net of returns and allowances.

Specialised topics

Long-term contracts

In certain industries (e.g. construction, aerospace), a company produces an asset or assets (e.g. a bridge, an oil refinery, military aircraft) under contract to a customer. Contracts come in two forms. Under a **fixed-price contract**, the contractor accepts a fixed contract price (in total or per unit of output). In some cases, cost escalation clauses permit an increase in the price if specified costs increase. Under a **cost-plus contract**, the client reimburses the contractor for costs incurred and pays a mark-up (which may be a percentage of contract costs or a fixed fee). The costs to be reimbursed are carefully defined in the contract.

If the term of the contract covers more than one accounting period, the issue arises: when should the contractor recognise revenue? Firms in the service sector that win long-term contracts (e.g. architects, management consultants) face a similar question. Note this accounting issue applies to both fixed price and cost-plus contracts.

Methods of recognising revenue on long-term contracts

There are two main ways that a contractor can account for revenue from a long-term contract: the **percentage-of-completion method** and the **completed contract method**. We use an example from section 1 to illustrate both methods. Delphi Consulting, you'll recall, is awarded a fixed-price contract to carry out a strategic study for the European Commission (EC). The impact of each method on Delphi's accounts is outlined below.

1 *Percentage-of-completion (POC) method.* Delphi recognises as revenue each period a portion of the contract's value, based on the work done on it during the period. Delphi calculates this on an incremental basis. Thus if it reckons it has completed 30% of the work on the contract by the end of the first year and 80% by the end of the second, it recognises revenue equal to 30% of the contract's value in the first year and 50% (80% – 30%) in the second year. 'Work done' can be estimated using a physical measure (e.g. Delphi consultants' time on the job) or a monetary one (e.g. contract costs incurred for work performed). Delphi matches against contract revenue the costs incurred to generate that revenue.

2 *Completed-contract (CC) method.* Delphi waits until the contract is completed before recognising revenue. In the first two years, it stores costs incurred on the EC contract in an inventory account, 'Contract in progress'. When it completes the contract in year 3, it recognises the total contract revenue and matches against it all the stored costs relating to the contract. Thus it records no revenue or expense with respect to this contract in years 1 and 2 when the contract is in progress.

Income statement impact

We now put flesh on Delphi's EC contract to see what effect each method has on its accounts. (To illustrate better the operation of the POC method, the example here is more complex than that in Exhibit 10.2.) Assume the value of the contract is 600,000 – based on 6,000 expected manhours at a billing rate of 100/hour. The billing rate includes profit as well as labour and contract-related overheads. Initially, Delphi estimates contract costs at 500,000. It revises them upwards to 520,000 early in year 2: this proves to be the contract's actual cost. Exhibit 10.4 sets out the costs

Exhibit 10.4 Long-term contracts: illustration of income statement impact under (a) percentage-of-completion method and (b) completed contract method (amounts in 000)

Facts

The European Commission awards Delphi Consulting, a management consulting company, a three-year contract. The value of the contract is 600. At the outset, Delphi estimates total contract costs will be 500. It revises these upward at the end of year 2 to 520 and this is the contract's actual cost. Costs incurred by year, originally estimated and revised, are:

	Year 1	Year 2	Year 3	Total
Estimated, at start of year 1	150	250	100	500
Revised (start-year 2) and actual	150	240	130	520

Costs incurred reflect work done in the year.

Calculation of contract revenue and profit by year

(a) *Percentage-of-completion method*

(i) Cumulative costs incurred	150	390	520	
(ii) Total expected costs	500	520	520	
(iii) % completed by end-year ((i)/(ii))	30%	75%	100%	
(iv) % completed during year	30%	45%	25%	

Contract revenue ((iv) × 600)	180	270	150	600
Contract expense	150	240	130	520
Profit on contract	30	30	20	80

(b) *Completed contract method*

Contract revenue	0	0	600	600
Contract expense	0	0	520	520
Profit on contract	0	0	80	80

---

incurred in each of years 1–3 and shows the calculation of revenue and profit by year under the two revenue recognition methods.

In the case of profitable contracts, the POC method results in the earlier recognition of revenue and profit. This can be seen in Exhibit 10.4. Under the POC method Delphi recognises profit of 30,000 in each of years 1 and 2 and 20,000 in year 3. Under the CC method it recognises no profit in the first two years. Instead, the whole profit of 80,000 is recognised in year 3 when the contract is completed. (For loss-making contracts, the accounting under the two methods is similar: in each case the loss must be recognised in full as soon as it arises.)

Safeguards are built into the calculation of periodic revenue and profit under the POC method to prevent a firm from overstating profit in a contract's early years. For example, contract delays and future increases in cost are incorporated immediately into the calculation of current profit. Consider our example. Under its original estimate, Delphi expected to have completed 80% ((150,000 + 250,000)/500,000) of the contract by the end of year 2. Because of higher spending and a shift in work to year 3, only 75% of the contract is completed by the end of that year. As a result, Delphi must revise down its year 2 profit – from the original estimate of 50,000 ((80% × 100,000) – (30% × 100,000)) to the reported figure of 30,000 ((75% × 80,000) – (30% × 100,000)).

Moreover, a firm cannot boost profits by simply bringing forward contract spending. In calculating the percentage of a contract completed, the emphasis is on the *work done*, specifically:

$$\frac{\text{Work done on the contract to date}}{\text{Total past work done and future work required on the contract}}$$

rather than on the outlays made. For example, buying materials does not raise the percentage of the contract completed. This occurs only when the materials are *used*. In our example, we assume for simplicity that the costs Delphi incurs on the EC contract represent work done on it.

The CC method is clearly more conservative than the POC method. A contractor using the CC method recognises revenue and earnings on a profitable contract at a later date. However, if its business is growing slowly and the profitability of its contract portfolio is stable, there may be little difference in the total annual profit it reports under the two methods. In these circumstances, revenues and profit recognised on completed contracts are similar in total to revenues and profit recognised on contracts in progress.

Balance sheet impact

So far we have looked at the income statement effects of the two methods. What is the impact of each on the balance sheet? *Simply stated, a company that uses the POC method and whose contracts are profitable reports higher assets and retained profits than if it had used the CC method. This is because it recognises revenue at an earlier date.*

We demonstrate this using our Delphi example. Consider the accounting entries it makes with respect to the EC contract. Note that the cash outflows and inflows it records are common to both revenue recognition methods (all amounts are in thousands):

● Delphi records the costs incurred on the contract (materials, labour, overhead) in an inventory account, 'Contracts in progress (CIP), at cost', during the year. These amount to 150, 240 and 130 in years 1, 2 and 3 respectively. We assume all are paid in cash.

	Year 1		Year 2		Year 3	
	Dr.	Cr.	Dr.	Cr.	Dr.	Cr.
POC and CC methods						
CIP, at cost (A+)	150		240		130	
Cash (A–)		150		240		130

● It bills the Commission for – and the Commission makes payments of – 100, 200 and 300 in each of the three years. Note that the billing terms are set down in the contract. The amount and timing of the bills do not necessarily correspond to costs incurred (or revenue recognised).

	Year 1		Year 2		Year 3	
	Dr.	Cr.	Dr.	Cr.	Dr.	Cr.
POC and CC methods						
Billing						
Accounts receivable (A+)	100		200		300	
Progress billings (CA+)		100		200		300
Cash receipt						
Cash (A+)	100		200		300	
Accounts receivable (A–)		100		200		300

'Progress billings' are accumulated in a contra-asset account. Usually they are offset against the (cumulative) 'Contract in progress' account and the net amount is shown as an asset (or liability, if billings exceed the CIP balance). Note that, in practice, a contract is likely to have a positive receivable balance since there is a delay between billing and cash receipt.

Delphi's balance sheet differs between the POC and CC methods solely because of the timing of revenue recognition.

● Under the POC method, Delphi recognises revenue during the course of the contract. It records the revenue recognised in an asset account – we call it 'CIP, at fair value' – and, at the same time, removes the related costs from the 'CIP, at cost' account.[12] The revenue and expense figures are taken from Exhibit 10.4. When the contract is completed, the balances in 'Progress billings' and 'CIP, at fair value' with respect to this contract are eliminated.

	Year 1		Year 2		Year 3	
	Dr.	Cr.	Dr.	Cr.	Dr.	Cr.
POC method						
CIP, at fair value (A+)	180		270		150	
Contract revenue (OE+)		180		270		150
Contract expense (OE–)	150		240		130	
CIP, at cost (A–)		150		240		130

	End-year	
	Dr.	Cr.
Progress billings (CA–)	600	
CIP, at fair value (A–)		600

● Under the CC method, Delphi recognises revenue only when the contract is completed at the end of year 3. At that point, the costs stored in 'CIP, at cost' expire and, assuming all work has been billed, the balance in the 'Progress billings' account (which should equal the contract's value) is eliminated.

	End-year 3	
	Dr.	Cr.
CC method		
Progress billings (CA–)	600	
Contract revenue (OE+)		600
Contract expense (OE–)	520	
CIP, at cost (A–)		520

Exhibit 10.5 shows the effect of the EC contract on Delphi's end-year balance sheets for years 1, 2 and 3 under both the POC and CC methods. Remember that the balance sheet shows the *cumulative* effect of the contract. For example, the balance in the 'CIP, at fair value' account at the end of year 2 (namely, 450) represents the cumulative costs incurred (390) plus the profits recognised in years 1 and 2 (60).

Our example assumes a contractor has one contract. What if it has a large contract portfolio giving it stable revenues and profits? In this case, choice of revenue recognition method still affects its balance sheet. If it opts for the CC method in place of the POC method, it reports lower assets and retained earnings since no profits are recognised on the contracts currently in progress.

Note that both methods have the same impact on a firm's (pre-tax) cash flows. Delphi's EC contract illustrates this. We assume all contract costs are paid in cash as incurred and the Commission makes progress payments of 100, 200 and 300 at the end of each of the three years. As a result, Delphi experiences a net outflow of 50 and 40 in years 1 and 2 and a net inflow of 170 in year 3, *irrespective of the revenue recognition method it uses.* The yearly net outflow or inflow is the difference between the cash payments on the contract and the cash received from the Commission.

Exhibit 10.5 Long-term contracts: illustration of balance sheet impact under (a) percentage-of-completion method and (b) completed contract method (amounts in 000)

Facts

The value of Delphi's three-year contract with the European Commission is 600. At the outset, Delphi estimates total contract costs will be 500. It revises these upward at the start of year 2 to 520. Actual costs incurred each year are: year 1 – 150; year 2 – 240; year 3 – 130. All are paid in cash. Delphi bills the Commission – and the Commission makes payments of – 100, 200 and 300 in years 1, 2 and 3 respectively. Profits on contract recognised under POC method are: year 1 – 180; year 2 – 270; year 3 – 150.

Balance sheet impact under revenue recognition methods:

	1	End-year 2	3
(a) *Percentage-of-completion method*			
Cash	−50	−90	80
Contract in progress, at fair value	180	450	
Less: Progress billings	−100	−300	
	80	150	0*
Cumulative effect on net assets (and retained profits)	30	60	80
(b) *Completed contract method*			
Cash	−50	−90	80
Contract in progress, at cost	150	390	
Less: Progress billings	−100	−300	
	50	90	0**
Cumulative effect on net assets (and retained profits)	0	0	80

* Net effect. 'CIP, at fair value' and 'Progress billings' are both 600 at date contract is completed.
** Balances in 'CIP, at cost' (520) and 'Progress billings' (600) are both eliminated when contract is completed and revenue is recognised at end of year 3.

Accounting for long-term contracts: international practice

There has long been a marked difference in the way companies account for long-term contracts. In countries where Anglo-Saxon accounting is the norm, 'percentage-of-completion' is the dominant method. Profit on individual contracts is recognised earlier but there is no tax cost – in the form of earlier tax payments – as the tax authorities determine a firm's taxable income according to their own rules. By contrast, companies in most continental European countries, where a uniform reporting tradition prevails, have traditionally used the CC method in order to postpone tax payments (or because the law requires it). Accounting practice in these countries is changing, however, in response to new national and international accounting rules.

Companies following international standards must account for long-term construction and service contracts by the POC method *so long as the outcome of the contract can be estimated reliably.* As with the sale of goods, this occurs when:

- it is likely the rewards from the contract will flow to the company; and
- contract revenues and costs can be measured reliably.[13]

When a contract's outcome cannot be estimated reliably, the contractor should apply a modified version of the POC method. It should:

● distinguish costs that are likely to be *recoverable* from those that are not;
● recognise revenues in the amount of recoverable costs incurred; and
● recognise *all* contract costs as expenses in the period they are incurred.

At the point in the contract's life when the contractor can estimate the outcome reliably, it should apply the POC method in unmodified form.

We illustrate this 'recoverable cost' modification using our Delphi example. Assume that, because of cost uncertainties, Delphi feels unable to estimate the total profit on the EC contract at the end of year 1. Moreover, it has doubts about whether 10 of the 150 costs incurred that year are recoverable (amounts are in thousands). Assume, too, that by the end of year 2 when cumulative costs incurred are 390, Delphi feels confident that the 10 of costs will be recoverable, the contract is 75% complete and contract profits will be 80. Contract revenues and expenses recognised in years 1–3 are as follows (amounts are in thousands):

	Year			
	1	2	3	Total
Contract revenues	140	310*	150	600
Contract expenses				
(costs incurred)	150	240	130	520
Profit/(loss) on contract	(10)	70	20	80

* [(75% × 600) − 140]

Thus while cost uncertainties exist, Delphi recognises no profit on the contract – in fact, it recognises a loss in year 1 because costs incurred exceed its estimate then of recoverable costs. When, in year 2, the uncertainties are removed, it recognises profit on a percentage-completed basis. Cumulative profits recognised at the end of year 2 (60) are the same as if it had applied the standard POC method from the outset.

The CC method is no longer an acceptable method under international accounting standards. Use of the POC method (in its standard and modified forms) is set to grow in Europe and elsewhere but in countries where national accounting rules override international ones, the CC method will endure.

Transfer of receivables

A company that supplies goods or services on account can raise cash from the resulting receivables before its customers pay their debts. There are various ways it can do so. It can **pledge** or **assign** receivables, that is, use them as collateral for a loan. (Assignment is a more formalised procedure than pledging: the lender investigates the receivables portfolio and selects the best credit risks as collateral.) Alternatively, it can sell them – either on an individual basis or *en bloc*. The **discounting** of a bill of exchange is an example of the sale of an individual receivable. One of the services offered by a **factor** (usually an arm of a bank or a specialist finance company) is the provision of short-term finance through the purchase of a block of receivables.

The distinction between pledging/assigning and factoring carries over into accounting. Where a company pledges or assigns its receivables as security for a loan, they remain on its balance sheet – it is still the owner – but it discloses in the notes to the accounts their use as collateral. Where a company discounts a bill or factors receivables, the accounting is less clear cut. If the company gives up all the significant risks and rewards of ownership, the transfer is clearly an asset sale. In many cases, however, the company retains certain risks. Suppose, for example, it has the right to reacquire the receivables at a predetermined price that is more than their fair value at the reacquisition date. How should it account for the initial transfer? Is it a sale – or a disguised loan, with the receivables acting as security?

(a) *Transfer of receivables as sale*	Dr.	Cr.	(b) *Transfer of receivables as loan*	Dr.	Cr.
Cash (A+)	xx		Cash (A+)	xx	
Financial asset (A–)		xx	Loan (L+)		xx

Note that a company has an incentive to structure a transfer of assets as a sale in order to reduce reported debt. A transfer that is in substance a loan but is accounted for as an asset sale is a form of off-balance-sheet financing.

Under new international accounting rules, a company must 'derecognise' a financial asset (i.e. record it as a sale) only when it surrenders control of the contractual rights contained in the asset.[14] Usually this is evident from the terms of the contract. For example, if, at the time of transfer, a company agrees to repurchase the asset in the future on terms that give the transferee a lender's return on the cash exchanged for the asset, it clearly has *not* surrendered control. Sometimes, however, there's room for debate. For example, what if the company transfers receivables **with recourse**, that is, it agrees to reimburse the factor for some or all of the uncollectible accounts? Accounting regulators argue that, in this case (and assuming other conditions are met), the company has handed over control of the asset but has assumed a financial liability in respect of the recourse obligation. It reports as a gain or loss in the income statement the difference between the cash received and the carrying amount of the receivables *plus the value of the recourse obligation.*

We illustrate below the accounting for factoring of receivables and discounting of bills and highlight the treatment of recourse obligations.

Factoring of receivables

We return to our Ragueneau example. Ragueneau has gross accounts receivable of 450,000 at end-year 2. Given the strained finances of his business, he decides to raise cash by selling them. A factor, Lise Asset Finance, agrees to pay 370,000 for a large group of them with a face value of 390,000, on condition that Ragueneau reimburses it for bad debts up to a limit of 20,000. (Ragueneau's end-year 2 accounts show an allowance for bad debts of 24,000.) Lise will charge a fee of 2.5% plus interest at 10% on the average time to maturity of the receivables (estimated at 30 days). Ragueneau records the factoring of the receivables as an asset sale:

Dr. Cash (A+)	370,000	
Dr. Factoring fee (OE–) (390,000 × 2.5%)	9,750	
Dr. Interest expense (OE–) (390,000 × 0.10 × 30/360)	3,250	
Dr. Loss on sale of receivables (OE–)	7,000	
Cr. Accounts receivable (A–)		390,000

and at the same time recognises an estimated liability with respect to the recourse obligation:

Dr. Allowance for bad debts (CA–)	20,000	
Cr. Recourse obligation (L+)		20,000

BOX 10.1   Securitising receivables

A company may be able to remove receivables from its balance sheet by securitising them. Securitisation is simply the issue of claims on the cash flows of a financial asset. The claims are represented by securities such as shares and bonds. (These securities are often known as asset-backed securities, or ABS.) Traditionally, trade receivables, mortgages, loans and leases were the principal assets securitised. Recent offerings have been more innovative: they include rental income from student accommodation and season ticket sales of major football clubs. The feature all these assets share is a relatively stable and predictable stream of cash flows.

How does a company securitise a financial asset like trade receivables? The first step is for it to set up a special purpose entity (SPE) or trust. The SPE (or trust) issues securities to third parties and uses the cash to purchase a pool of receivables from the company. It then services the securities – for example, paying interest and principal on debt securities – with the cash it collects from the company's credit customers.

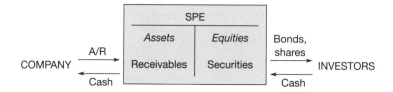

Why do companies securitise their financial assets? The main advantage is lower financing costs. Note that the alternatives are either selling the assets to one investor or borrowing using the assets as collateral. Securitisation gives many investors the opportunity to participate in the financing and, at the same time, allows them to diversify their investments. As a result, they demand a lower return. Another advantage is that it lightens the balance sheet. Low-yielding assets are sold off and the cash from them is deployed more productively. This benefits banks in particular since, under existing capital adequacy rules, they're required to support their principal asset (loans) with expensive risk capital. SPEs are usually highly leveraged – the stability and predictability of their cash inflows allows this – so securitisation can take debt as well as assets off the company's balance sheet.

International accounting rules require companies to account for securitised assets in the same way as other financial asset transfers. The securitisation is recorded as a sale only if the transferor loses control of the contractual rights that comprise the asset. Sometimes part of the asset is retained – for example, a bank may retain the right to service the loans securitised – and in this case, the carrying amount of the asset (loans) is allocated between the part sold and the part retained, based on their relative fair values at the date of sale. Note that the transferor must not control the SPE. If it does, the accounting benefits of securitisation – removing assets (and debt) from the balance sheet – no longer apply since the SPE's accounts would then be consolidated with those of the company.

Enron, the US energy company that collapsed in 2001, made extensive use of SPEs to securitise its assets. Under US accounting rules then in force, it was able to remove the assets (and the related debt) from its balance sheet even though in effect it controlled the SPEs.

When a factored debt is deemed uncollectible, Ragueneau reimburses the factor and the liability is reduced (Dr. Recourse obligation, Cr. Cash). If the liability proves to be an overestimate (i.e. bad debts on the factored receivables are less than 20,000), Ragueneau recognises a gain in the amount of the residual liability.

Our example is simplified. A company factoring its receivables may well bear other costs besides the factor's fee and interest charges. Examples of such costs are sales returns and sales discounts. To cover them, the factor may hold back 5% or so of the invoice amount of the receivables, charge the costs against the monies retained, and pay the balance to the company when all the factored receivables have been collected.

Note that if Ragueneau transfers the receivables **without recourse**, the credit in the above journal entry is to 'Bad debt expense' rather than 'Recourse obligation'. In this case, the factor bears the cost of bad debts. Ragueneau writes back that part of the previously established provision for bad debts (Dr. Allowance, Cr. Bad debt expense) that relates to the receivables sold to Lise Asset Finance.

An alternative to factoring that's available to larger companies is to securitise receivables. Box 10.1 outlines how and why firms securitise financial assets.

Discounting of bills

A **bill of exchange** (or **draft**) represents an order to pay, drawn up by a supplier of goods or services instructing the customer to pay specified amounts on specified dates to either the seller or a third party (e.g. the seller's bank).[15] A bill signed (accepted) by the customer is known as an 'acceptance'. A sale evidenced by a bill of exchange offers the seller two advantages over a sale on open account: greater legal security and, since the bill is negotiable, greater liquidity. Bills are widely used in international trade.

A bill can be discounted (sold) before maturity. The holder – either the original supplier or someone to whom he has transferred the bill, usually for consideration, by endorsing it – presents the bill to his bank and receives funds at a discount to the bill's maturity value. Exhibit 10.6 summarises the key events that occur during the life of a typical bill.

Companies account for bills in the same way as trade debts on open account. When a bill is issued in exchange for goods, it is stated initially at cost. Interest accrues from the issue date, usually on a simple rather than a compound basis. If the bill is impaired (i.e. part of the amounts owing is uncollectable), the holder of the bill writes it down to the recoverable amount.

Discounting of bills may give rise to accounting problems. If a supplier discounts a bill, he records the transfer as a sale on the grounds that he has relinquished control of the asset. If the bill is discounted with recourse, the supplier accounts for it in the same way but, in addition, recognises a liability with respect to the recourse obligation. For example, suppose that on 1 May, Louis accepts a three-month bill for 20,000 presented by Ragueneau for food and wine he has supplied at a recent banquet. The bill carries an interest rate of 0.5% a month. On 1 July, Ragueneau discounts the bill at Crédit Hollandais: the discount rate is 0.625% a month. The discount rate on similar 'no recourse' bills is 0.75% a month. (Assume for simplicity a 30-day month, 360-day year.) The cash proceeds from the sale and the carrying amount of the bill in Ragueneau's books at 1 July are calculated as follows:

Cash proceeds from discounting of bill

Maturity value:	20,000 + [3 × (20,000 × 0.5%)]	20,300
	(face value) (3 months' interest)	
Less: Discount [1 month × (20,000 × 0.625%)]		−125
		20,175

Exhibit 10.6   Key events during the life of a bill of exchange

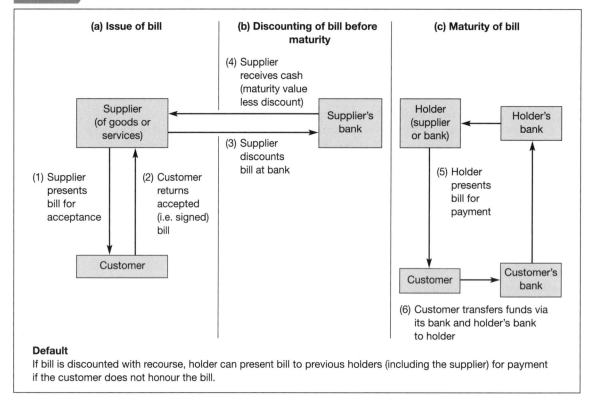

Default

If bill is discounted with recourse, holder can present bill to previous holders (including the supplier) for payment if the customer does not honour the bill.

Carrying amount of bill	
Face value	20,000
Plus: Accrued interest [2 months × (20,000 × 0.5%)]	+200
	20,200

The fair value of the recourse obligation is 25, the difference between the actual discount at 1 July (125) and that on a similar 'no recourse' bill (150, or 1 month × (20,000 × 0.75%)). Thus Ragueneau recognises a loss of 50 on the discounting of Louis's bill: this is the excess of the sum of the carrying amount of the bill (20,200) and the recourse obligation (25) on 1 July over the cash proceeds from discounting (20,175) on that date.

Dr. Cash (A+)	20,175	
Dr. Loss on discounting of bill (OE−)	50	
Cr. Bill of exchange (A−)		20,200
Cr. Recourse obligation (L+)		25

It is common practice in some countries (e.g. Italy, Brazil, Japan) to formalise receivables through promissory notes or bills of exchange and to discount them at financial institutions as a means of financing. Under national accounting rules, the discounted receivables are treated as an asset sale and, if they're transferred with recourse, the recourse obligation is not recorded as a liability on the balance sheet. For companies in these countries, discounting of receivables will carry a balance sheet cost when they implement new international accounting rules in this area.

Long-term receivables

A supplier of goods or services may grant a customer an extended period of credit. If the payment period stretches over more than one year, it's customary for the supplier to state the receivable at the present value of future scheduled receipts. (The customer records the payable in the same way.) The discount rate that the supplier uses to find the present value of future receipts is the market rate of interest prevailing at the date the sale transaction takes place. Since receivables are accounted for at (historical) cost, this rate should be used throughout the credit period. The 'market rate' is the rate of interest applicable to financial instruments of similar risk and maturity.

If, under the terms of sale, an interest rate is specified and the rate is equivalent to the market rate, the accounting for the receivable is straightforward. The face and present values of the receivable are the same and the interest income the supplier recognises each period is equal to the interest it receives in cash. For example, suppose that Jacques Perron sells equipment to Liège Mines for 550,000. It agrees to defer collection for two years and, in exchange, Liège Mines will pay interest each year at 8%, the market rate of interest at the date of sale. Perron records the sale and the receivable at 550,000 and in each of the following two years he receives – and recognises as income – interest of 44,000.

At date of sale		
Dr. Note receivable, Liège Mines (A+)	550,000	
Cr. Revenue from equipment sale (OE+)		550,000
(Dr. Cost of equipment sold (OE–)	xxx	
Cr. Inventory (A–)		xxx)
Each year, during the two-year credit period		
Dr. Accrued interest receivable (later, Cash) (A+)	44,000	
Cr. Interest income (OE+)		44,000
On collection date		
Dr. Cash (A+)	550,000	
Cr. Note receivable, Liège Mines (A–)		550,000

Perron computes interest income at 8%, the rate specified in the contract, even though the current market rate of interest during the two years is a rate other than 8%. (The term 'Note receivable' is used in place of 'Account receivable' where the sale contract is supported by a formal agreement specifying the amount and timing of future payments.)

● Measuring receivables carrying below-market interest rate

Consider now the case where the supplier offers a customer highly attractive financing terms on the long-term receivable. Suppose it specifies in the sale contract a below-market interest rate – or no interest at all. For example, car manufacturers sometimes offer customers 0% financing as a sale promotion device. When this occurs, the face value of the receivable is no longer equal to the present value of future scheduled receipts discounted at the historical market rate of interest. How does the supplier measure the receivable (and the sale revenue) in these circumstances?

The new international accounting standard on financial instruments (*IAS 39*) supports long-standing practice in this area. Recall the basic measurement rule: a receivable (or other financial asset) should be measured initially at cost and cost is equal to the fair value of the consideration given for it. If fair value isn't readily determinable – because, for example, product specifications (and credit terms) differ from one customer to another, the supplier measures the receivable by discounting future cash receipts at an *imputed* market interest rate.

We return to our Jacques Perron example. Suppose that, in response to its customer's request, Perron changes slightly the equipment's specifications and financing terms. Under the new deal, Liège Mines will pay 600,000 two years after the sale date plus interest at only 3% a year. The company accepts the revised offer. Perron estimates the market rate of interest on such financing is 8%. The fair value of the deal based on the new financing terms is 546,500. This amount is derived by discounting at 8% interest received at end-year 1 and interest and principal received at end-year 2. This is the only way of readily determining fair value in this case.

$$[18,000 \times PV \ (8\%, 1 \ \text{period})] + [618,000 \times PV \ (8\%, 2 \ \text{periods})] = 546,500$$

Perron measures the revenue from the sale and the initial receivable at this amount. (The cost of equipment sold and reduction in inventory are recognised at the same time.)

Dr. Note receivable, Liège Mines (A+)	546,500	
Cr. Revenue from equipment sale (OE+)		546,500

Alternatively, the note can be stated at its face amount (600,000) and the difference between the face and present values (53,500) recorded in a contra-asset account, 'Discount on note receivable':

Dr. Note receivable, Liège Mines (A+)	600,000	
Cr. Discount on note receivable (CA+)		53,500
Cr. Revenue from equipment sale (OE+)		546,500

In this case, Perron still shows the note receivable on the balance sheet at the net amount of 546,500. (We ignore VAT here.)

To calculate annual interest income, Perron applies the historical market rate of interest of 8% to the start-of-year carrying amount of the receivable. Exhibit 10.7 shows the calculation of interest income in years 1 and 2.

In year 1, Perron recognises interest income of 43,720 (8% of the start-of-year carrying amount of the receivable) but receives in cash only 18,000 (3% of the receivable's face value).

Exhibit 10.7 Imputed interest on note receivable: illustration

Facts
Perron sells equipment to Liège Mines at start-year 1. Liège Mines is to pay Perron 600,000 two years after sale date plus annual interest (on 600,000) at 3%. Market interest rate on such financing is 8% a year. Present value of note receivable (N/R) at start-year 1 is 546,500.

Perron: calculation of interest income and end-year receivable

	(A) N/R, start-year	(B) Interest income (A) × 8%	(C) Interest received 600,000 × 3%	(D) Increase in N/R (B) − (C)	(E) N/R, end-year (A) + (D)
Year 1	546,500	43,720	18,000	25,720	572,220
Year 2	572,220	45,780 (rounding)	18,000	27,780	600,000

The difference between the interest income recognised and the interest received in cash is recorded as an increase in the receivable (or, under the alternative presentation, as a reduction in the 'discount' contra-asset). By the end of year 2, the carrying amount of the receivable in Perron's books is 600,000, the face value of the bill.

These are the mechanics. What is the conceptual basis for this accounting? Think of the 'discount' contra-asset as unearned interest income. With the passage of time, the unearned interest becomes earned and is recognised within interest income: 25,720 in year 1 and 27,780 in year 2. Perron could bring the unearned interest into income in a different way – on a straight-line basis, for example. The advantage of the 'interest method' is that the interest income Perron reports each period reflects the market rate of interest for this form of financing (i.e. 8%) at the time the receivable arose.

Using the information in Exhibit 10.7, we reconstruct the journal entries Perron makes to record interest earned and received in years 1 and 2 and the receipt of principal at the end of year 2:

End-year 1

Dr. Cash (A+)	18,000	
Dr. Note receivable, Liège Mines (A+)	25,720	
(or: Discount on N/R (CA–))		
Cr. Interest income (OE+)		43,720

End-year 2

Dr. Cash	18,000	
Dr. Note receivable, Liège Mines	27,780	
(or: Discount on N/R)		
Cr. Interest income		45,780

Dr. Cash (A+)	600,000	
Cr. Note receivable, Liège Mines (A–)		600,000

Impairment of long-term receivables

What if a long-term receivable is impaired? For example, suppose a customer experiences financial difficulties and the supplier/creditor no longer feels reasonably assured of collecting the amounts owing when due. In this event, the accounting is clear. The supplier/creditor normally reduces the carrying amount of the receivable to its recoverable amount and recognises the reduction in that period's income. It determines the recoverable amount in the same way as before – by calculating the present value of revised scheduled receipts (which are likely to be smaller and/or later than under the original contract).

What makes the accounting for impaired receivables unusual is the way they are measured. IAS require that, in calculating present value, the discount rate used should be the rate applied initially when the receivable was first recognised, i.e. the historical market rate. This is likely to be less than the market rate at the time of impairment. Usually, a debtor forced to restructure its debt because of financial difficulties pays a *higher* interest rate to compensate lenders for the greater credit risk they bear. Thus the *accounting* loss a supplier recognises on writing down a note receivable is likely to be less than the *economic* loss it sustains. Accounting regulators argue that use of a current market rate implies fair value accounting and this is not consistent with the way receivables (and other financial assets carried at cost) are measured. It is also worth noting that the most receivables-intensive companies and the ones most likely to suffer receivables impairment are banks (loans are a bank's receivables) and they lobbied hard against use of a current market rate to value their troubled loans.

Revenues, receivables and financial statement analysis

Disclosures

Companies usually give a breakdown of their revenues by category – e.g. sale of goods and rendering of services, interest, royalties and dividends – in their accounts. They also state in the notes the revenue recognition policies they follow for each type of revenue.

Disclosures for long-term contracts are more extensive. Under international rules, companies must show the amount of contract revenue recognised in the period and the method(s) used to determine it (e.g. percentage-of-completion method). In addition, they must disclose for contracts in progress at the balance sheet date:

- contract costs incurred and profits (less losses) recognised to date;
- advances (i.e. amounts received from customers in advance of work done); and
- retentions (i.e. amounts retained by customers until contract conditions have been satisfied).

A contractor must disclose a contract asset or liability at the balance sheet date. It may be that it must disclose both. An asset is recorded in the case of contracts where costs incurred (plus recognised profits) exceed progress billings – and a liability in the case of contracts where the reverse applies. (Progress billings are amounts billed for work done on a contract, irrespective of whether or not they've been paid.) The asset and liability can't be netted.

Disclosure requirements for receivables are not as explicit. Under international rules, firms must break down receivables by category. As a result, investors can distinguish trade from other receivables (e.g. receivables from related parties such as affiliated companies, loans receivable, tax refunds receivable). IAS also require firms to reveal impairment losses on receivables. In some countries, national rules require firms to disclose the end-year balance in the allowance for bad debts. Exhibit 10.8 provides an example of these disclosures. It shows the breakdown, at end-2001, of the accounts receivables balance of Telefónica, the large Spanish telecommunications group.

Telefónica highlights those customer receivables at year-end that are 'doubtful'. Given the balance in the allowance for bad debts, it appears the company has made specific provision for these debts – but only a small general provision for others. Bad debts were a growing problem for Telefónica in 2001. Note the 47% increase in bad debt expense in the year (from €701 million to €1,032 million) and the 17% increase in the doubtful receivables balance between end-2000 and end-2001. The economic crisis in Argentina, where the company has extensive operations, contributed to customers' worsening payment record.

Non-financial firms rarely explain the movement in the allowance account (unless national rules demand it). In many countries, however, banking regulations require banks to explain the movement in the equivalent account for bad loans, known as the 'allowance for credit losses'.

Revenue recognition and the front-loading of profit

When a company recognises revenue can affect the amount of profit it reports in a period. For a growing, profitable business, the earlier in the operating cycle it recognises revenue, the larger is its reported profit then. Investors always check a company's policy on revenue recognition in the notes to its accounts. Companies in Anglo-Saxon countries – and others where book income is uncoupled from taxable income – are more likely to recognise revenue earlier in the operating cycle. The resulting higher profit carries no tax penalty and may benefit managers and other staff receiving profit-related bonuses.

Exhibit 10.8   Telefónica Group: extract from notes to accounts, 2001

Note 10.   Customer receivables

The detail of the balances of this caption as of December 31, 2001 and 2000, is as follows:

Millions of euros	Balance at 12/31/01	Balance at 12/31/00
Services billed		
Customer receivables billed	3,005.49	3,688.67
Doubtful customer receivables	1,606.11	1,340.97
Other receivables	47.16	46.09
	4,658.76	**5,075.73**
Unbilled services	2,124.48	1,903.33
	6,783.24	**6,979.06**
Allowance for bad debts	(1,692.89)	(1,449.76)
Total	**5,090.35**	**5,529.30**

The 'Unbilled services' account includes the connection, monthly and metered service charges not yet billed by the Group operators. This amount arises because these companies' subscriber billing schedules do not coincide with December 31.

The balance of the public-sector customer receivables in the countries in which the Group operates amounted to €410.16 million as of December 31, 2001 (€486.29 million as of December 31, 2000).

In 2001 provisions amounting to €1,032.62 million (€701.09 million in 2000) were recorded in this connection.

(*Source*: Telefónica Group, *Annual Accounts 2001.*)

Because of the link between revenue and profit, firms in separate reporting countries are tempted to exploit it. Investors watch out for the practice of 'front-loading' – *stealing revenues from a future period in order to boost revenues (and profits) in the current one.* Box 10.2 describes other ways in which firms inflate their current revenues.

How can investors tell when managers are playing this game? Receivables provide a clue. If a firm's receivables grow at a faster rate than its credit sales in a period – and there are no convincing business explanations for the divergence (e.g. new product lines with different credit terms or loosening of credit terms on existing lines), this suggests that the firm has changed the way it recognises or measures revenues.

Receivables turnover

As we've already seen, investors and managers assess the efficiency with which a company uses its resources by monitoring the rate at which it turns over its assets in a period. In the case of receivables, the turnover rate is usually expressed in a more readily interpretable form as the average credit period taken by customers. We set out both versions of the ratio in this section.

To compute the **receivables turnover**, credit sales in the year are divided by the average level of accounts receivable outstanding during the year:

$$\text{Receivables turnover (in year)} = \frac{\text{Annual credit sales, net}}{\text{Average net accounts receivable}}$$

BOX 10.2　Revenue games

According to the FASB, the US accounting regulator, revenue recognition is the most common issue in cases of fraudulent accounting and accounting restatements in the USA. Anecdotal evidence based on news stories in the international business press suggests that revenues are a major source of creative accounting in other countries, too.

Revenue misstatement usually takes one of two forms – recording revenues early or over-stating them. (We consider only non-fraudulent accounting here: in fraudulent cases, revenues are fabricated.) Premature recognition is a problem in both the manufacturing and the service sectors. In the case of goods, it usually arises because companies bring forward the delivery date artificially – or recognise revenue before delivery. A US maker of household appliances, provides an example of this. It achieved notoriety in the 1990s for its policy of 'bill and hold'. Under the policy, a retailer agreed to buy the appliances subject to later delivery and payment. The company recognised revenue on the contract date and stored the goods in a warehouse until the retailer called for them. This accounting policy came to light in 1998 and the company was forced to restate its 1996 and 1997 results. (It later filed for bankruptcy protection in 2001.)

In the case of services, long-term contracts are often the reason for early recognition of revenue. The supplier books revenue in full when a service contract is signed or the customer makes non-refundable payments, even though it has continuing obligations under the contract. Instances of premature revenue recognition have increased in recent years because of the growth of outsourcing. Companies (and governments) now contract out many activities previously performed in-house and these contracts often extend over several accounting periods.

Revenue misstatement can also be traced to aggressive measurement practices. The dotcom bubble of 1999–2000 produced some interesting examples. Priceline, an Internet company that offered discounted airline tickets and hotel rooms, reported as revenues the gross amount of the booking (e.g. the price of the hotel room or airline ticket) even though most of the cash went to the hotel or airline. By contrast, travel agencies report as revenue only their commission on the booking. Priceline claimed that, unlike a travel agent, it assumed the risks of owning the ticket/hotel booking, even if for a short period, and its commission was not fixed. (The SEC accepted this argument.) Promotional discounts offer another means of revenue inflation. For example, an online flower service offers all customers an electronic coupon that cuts 20% off the €25 posted price of a floral bouquet. What is the revenue from a sale, €25 (and marketing expenses of €5) or €20? Note that, in both examples, operating profit (or, more likely, loss) is not affected.

Why do companies misstate revenues in these ways? 'Channel stuffing' (i.e. pushing goods onto distributors) and 'bill and hold' practices can often be traced to sales-based compensation schemes. Divisional managers are awarded bonuses based on meeting sales targets. Top management stretches the targets to encourage 'outperformance'. Top managers themselves have an economic interest in raising sales. Higher revenues usually result in higher profits and their wealth is linked either directly (via profit-related bonuses) or indirectly (e.g. value of share options, market earnings power) to the level and rate of increase of their company's profits. For start-up companies that make losses and have negative cash flows, the link between revenues and management wealth is more direct. These companies cannot be valued on the basis of current earnings or cash flows. A practice common in the dotcom bubble years was to use a price/revenue multiple to value them. To the extent that top management believe their firms are valued in this way, they have an incentive to boost reported revenues, even if there is no impact on the bottom line.

By dividing the resulting turnover figure into the number of days in the year, the average time (in days) a firm's customers take to pay their accounts can be computed:

$$\text{Average credit period taken by customers (in days)} = \frac{365}{\text{Receivables turnover}}$$

This version of the receivables turnover ratio is sometimes known as (the number of) **days' sales in receivables**.

The above ratios are used to assess how long it takes a firm to collect cash from customers to whom it has granted credit. Obviously, for cash sales collection occurs at the time of sale. Thus the numerator of the receivables turnover ratio should be based on *credit* sales only. Moreover, the gross amount of credit sales is usually greater than the cash actually received and retained: thus in the ratio, credit sales (and receivables) should be shown net of VAT, duties, discounts and returns. For similar reasons, numerator and denominator should be adjusted for estimated bad debts.

As with all ratios, care should be taken when interpreting a company's receivables turnover rate. 'Average receivables' is usually a simple average of start- and end-year figures. If a company chooses its year-end at that point in the year when cash is normally high and non-cash working capital low, its receivables turnover will appear high.

There can be many reasons for changes in the turnover rate over time. For example, a reduction in the credit period (and thus a faster turnover rate) may indicate tighter credit management. It can also be the consequence of the firm factoring part of its receivables.

Summary

A company recognises revenue – from selling a good or performing a service – when it expects the transaction will bring it economic benefits and it can measure them reliably. In the case of goods, this usually occurs at the point of delivery, since the risks (and rewards) of ownership are transferred to the buyer then. An exception is when goods are produced under long-term contract and the profit on the contract can be estimated with a reasonable degree of accuracy. In this event, the preferred approach is for the firm to recognise revenue during production on the basis of work completed (percentage-of-completion method). Revenues from services should be recognised in the same way, that is, by reference to the stage of completion of the service transaction.

A company records a trade receivable when it recognises revenue from a credit sale. Receivables are stated in the balance sheet at realisable value. For short-term receivables, realisable value is the invoice amount of the receivable. For long-term receivables, it is the present value of future scheduled payments by the customer, discounted at the market rate of interest on equivalent loans when the receivable arose.

Realisable value falls if receivables are uncollectible. A company must write down its receivables to their recoverable amount when they're impaired in this way. The usual procedure is to make a provision for bad debts on an estimated basis and write off actual bad debts against the provision (allowance method). Where a long-term receivable is impaired, the company writes down the carrying amount to the present value of the revised scheduled payments – using the original discount rate – and recognises a loss.

Receivables transferred before maturity, whether factored or discounted, are recognised as a sale only if the transferor has relinquished control over the asset. Otherwise, the transfer is accounted for as a borrowing, with the receivables acting as security for the loan.

Investors monitor revenues and receivables closely. Aggressive revenue recognition practices can lead to the 'front-loading' of profit. Careful monitoring of receivables can help unmask 'hollow' revenues. Where this occurs, a firm's receivables grow faster than its revenues and its receivables turnover falls.

Problem assignments

P10.1 Recognising revenue: innovative practices

New revenue recognition practices emerge as companies seek to adapt traditional methods to new circumstances. The following are examples of new practice.

(a) A van hire company acquires a large number of vans for use in its business. The supplier gives it a discount in view of the number of vehicles purchased. The van hire company reports the bulk vehicle discount as revenue. In the year to 30 April 2001, revenue from bulk purchase discounts represents 48.8 million of the company's total revenues of 310.6 million.

(b) A biotechnology company undertakes substantial research to discover new drug compounds. To help finance its research efforts, it enters into drug delivery agreements with major pharmaceutical companies. In addition, it licenses to other drugs companies products and technology that it has developed in-house.

The drug delivery and licensing agreements result in substantial licensing income. Where the amounts received are non-refundable or the potential risk of repayment is remote, the company recognises income from licensing on the date the contract takes effect. Where the licensing income is receivable in stages, the company defers part of the licensing income until conditions specified in the contract have been met.

(c) Newtel is a recently established telecoms company that markets itself as an alternative carrier to existing national telecoms companies such as AT&T, Deutsche Telekom and NTT. It has invested heavily to build a 'backbone' network to carry Internet traffic which is growing rapidly. In order to give customers global communications cover, it leases capacity on other companies' networks where there are gaps in its own. (These leases are known as IRUs or indefeasible rights of use.) It pays for the long-term leases through reciprocal arrangements in which other carriers lease capacity on its network to fill gaps in their networks. Although the exchanges are referred to as 'swaps' in the business press, Newtel insists that they are separate transactions since each sale or purchase is priced individually and evaluated separately.

Newtel records capacity leased out as a sale and books the whole revenue from the long-term lease at the date of the contract. Other carriers account for Newtel's lease of capacity on their networks in the same way.

Required

Is the method of revenue recognition used in each of the above situations acceptable in your opinion? Explain why (or why not). If the method is unacceptable, how should the company account for the transaction?

P10.2 Revenue and profit recognition: the film industry

In addition to its theme parks in the USA, Europe and Japan, the Walt Disney Company is a major producer of feature films and television programmes. It follows industry practice when recognising revenue and profit from film production and distribution. Its accounting policies concerning film production and distribution are set out below; they're taken from the notes to its 2001 accounts.

Revenue recognition Revenues from the theatrical distribution of motion pictures are recognized when motion pictures are exhibited. . . . Revenues from the licensing of feature films and television programming are recorded when the material is available for telecasting by the licensee and when certain other conditions are met. [. . .]

Film and television costs   Film and television production and participation costs are expensed based on the ratio of the current period's gross revenues to estimated total gross revenues from all sources on an individual production basis. . . . Estimates of total gross revenues can change significantly due to a variety of factors, including the level of market acceptance of film and television products, advertising rates and subscriber fees. Accordingly, revenue estimates are reviewed periodically and amortization is adjusted, if necessary.

Required

Comment on the way Disney (and other film companies) calculate periodic expense when determining the profit from the distribution and licensing of films. What are the risks to investors from the accounting methods used?

P10.3 Alternative revenue recognition points

The Tell Company manufactures a novel apple-shaped archery target. Each archery target costs €6 to produce and €1 to sell. The selling costs are period costs and are incurred (and recognised) when targets are delivered to retailers. Tell sells them at a price of €10 each. All sales are on account. Data on production, delivery and cash collection in the first and second years of the company's existence are summarised below:

	Year 1	Year 2
Units produced	10,000	8,500
Units delivered	8,000	9,500
Cash collected	€75,000	€87,000

Required

Calculate revenues, expenses (production and selling expenses) and operating profit in years 1 and 2, assuming Tell recognises revenue:

(a) when units are produced;

(b) when units are delivered;

(c) when cash is collected.

P10.4 Revenue recognition issues in a dotcom company

ESoccer is an Internet-based media company serving soccer enthusiasts worldwide since its founding four years earlier in x1. It provides up-to-the-minute information on the soccer world (teams, players, games etc.) in audio and video form and sells soccer-related merchandise and memorabilia.

The company generates revenue from four main sources: advertising, e-commerce, content licensing and membership services. ESoccer charges advertisers for displaying advertisements on its websites. It sells soccer-related products and services (e-commerce). It licenses its content (e.g. soccer news, feature articles) to third parties. Finally, for members of its ESoccerClub schemes, it offers bonus points for viewing pages and making purchases and, for additional fees, the opportunity to participate in contests with cash prizes.

The company reported total revenues of €30 million in x5, a 100% increase on the x4 figure. Operating losses were €28 million that year, up from €19 million in x4.

Part A   Advertising revenues

According to the company's statement of accounting policies, 'advertising revenue is recognised in the period the advertisement is displayed, provided that no significant company obligations remain and collection of the resulting receivable is probable'. Company obligations typically include guarantees of a minimum number of 'impressions', or times that an advertisement is viewed by users of the company's websites.

Required

Suppose that ESoccer bills an advertiser €100,000 at the start of the fourth quarter of x5, based on a certain number of impressions being delivered by end-x5. Only 85% of the impressions are delivered by year-end, however. Assuming the number of impressions delivered is above the guaranteed minimum and the advertiser has not yet paid the bill, show the effect on ESoccer's accounts of:

(a) the initial billing; and

(b) the end-year adjustment ESoccer makes to its x5 accounts.

How would your answers to (a) and (b) differ if the guaranteed minimum number of impressions was equivalent, in billing terms, to €90,000?

Part B   Membership scheme and bonus points

The company launched a points scheme in x5 for members of its ESoccerClub. Members of the club can earn points – from registering as members, spending time on the company's websites and making purchases. For example, members can earn 10 points for every €1 spent at the company's online store. They can then spend the points on further purchases or on special soccer-related events promoted by the company. For every 100 points earned, a member can save €1 on his or her next purchase at the company's online store. When making purchases, a member has the choice of using points or allowing them to accumulate. Points expire two years after they are earned. The company recognises the cost of points earned when members use them. It makes a year-end adjustment in its accounts for the estimated cost of the change in unused points over the year.

Required

Prepare the accounting entries ESoccer makes to record the following events in December x5.

(a) Members purchase merchandise for cash from ESoccer's online store. The goods have a market value – before discounts – of €500,000 and cost the company €400,000. Members use 2 million previously earned points when paying for the goods.

(b) According to the company's records, there are 20 million unused points at end-December x5. The company estimates that 16 million of these points will be used before the expiry date. Since the points scheme only began in x5, the company has not yet recognised any cost of unused points in its accounts.

Part C   Barter transactions

ESoccer exchanges advertising space – and content – on its web pages for advertisements on other websites as well as on TV and radio. According to the notes to the company's x5 accounts, barter transactions accounted for 17% of total revenues in x5 and slightly higher proportions in x4 and x3. The revenues are stated at the fair value of the services (e.g. advertising space) that ESoccer receives in exchange.

Required

(a) What would be the effect on the company's x5 income statement if it were not permitted to recognise barter transactions in its published x5 accounts? State any assumptions you've made in answering this question.

(b) Barter transactions are common among media companies. For traditional media firms, barter deals are usually no more than 5% of sales. Among some start-ups, however, barter may represent half of revenues and even for established Internet companies like ESoccer, the proportion can reach 15–20%. Some investors claim that counting barter deals as revenue is fraudulent accounting. Why are investors suspicious of web-based barter transactions?

P10.5 Recognising revenue on long-term contracts I

The Stevin Company has just won a major land reclamation contract from the Dutch government. The value of the contract is €800 million and the work is expected to take four years. The expected contract cost is €550 million. Stevin recognises revenue on long-term contracts on a percentage-of-completion basis.

Required

(a) Stevin estimates that the percentage of the total work that will be completed each year is as follows:

Year 1	Year 2	Year 3	Year 4
18%	28%	32%	22%

Estimate the profit or loss the company will recognise on the contract in each of years 1–4.

(b) Year 1 outcomes are as forecast. However, during year 2, Stevin encounters major difficulties with the contract. The estimated cost rises to €700 million. Only 40% of the contract work will be done by end-year 2 and 75% by end-year 3. Stevin still reckons it can complete the whole of the contract by the end of year 4.
   The time is mid-year 2. Revise the estimates of contract revenue and profit for years 2–4.

Check figure:
(b) Cumulative profit, end-year 3   €75m

P10.6 Recognising revenue on long-term contracts II*

Early in x4 Hephaestus Construction Company was awarded a three-year contract by the French and Spanish governments to build a road tunnel through the Pyrenees. The value of the contract was 5,100. (All amounts are in millions of euros.) The tunnel was completed on schedule by late x6. Information about costs incurred, billings made and payments received is set out below:

(In millions)	x4	x5	x6
Cumulative costs incurred	1,000	2,520	4,100
Costs to be incurred (estimated at year-end)	3,000	1,680	–
Progress billings in year	1,000	1,500	2,600
Progress payments received in year	900	1,400	2,000

Required

(a) Compute the profit or loss Hephaestus recognises on the contract each year in x4, x5 and x6 under:
   (i) the percentage-of-completion (POC) method (assume 'costs incurred' approximate work completed);
   (ii) the completed contract method.

(b) Show the effect of this contract on the company's x4–x6 balance sheets under each revenue recognition method. Assume all costs incurred are paid in cash in the year.

Check figure:
(b) Cumulative profit on contract,
     end-x5, POC method   540

* Problem assignment draws on material in section 2 of this chapter.

P10.7 Calculation of bad debt expense

Harpagon is known to be a miser. One of his great worries is the customers to whom he extends credit. He's concerned that they will take advantage of his credit terms of 'net 30 days' (which he describes as 'generous') and delay payment to the very end of the period or even beyond it.

The balance sheet of Harpagon's company shows the following balances at the end of x7 (all amounts are in euros):

	End x7
Accounts receivable, gross	410,000
Less: Allowance for bad debts	(22,000)
Accounts receivable, net	388,000

During x8, the company makes cash sales of 1.8 million and credit sales of 3 million. It collects 2.85 million from credit customers. It writes off 30,000 of bad debts (these relate to both x7 and x8 sales). At the end of x8, Harpagon carries out an ageing analysis of receivables. The results are as follows:

			Numbers of days past due		
	Total	Current	1–30	31–60	>60
Percentage of x8 receivables	100	45	35	12	8
Percentage expected to be uncollectible		0.5	1.5	10	40

Required

(a) Calculate the following for the company:
  (i)   gross accounts receivable at end-x8;
  (ii) allowance for bad debts at end-x8 (round to nearest 000);
  (iii) bad debt expense recognised in x8.

(b) How would your calculations in (a) differ if the company recovered, at the end of x8, 3,000 of the bad debts written off earlier in the year?

Check figure:
(a) (iii) 35,000

P10.8 Accounts receivable data in published accounts

Benetton is a large Italian clothing manufacturer and retailer. Accounts receivable are a significant asset, amounting to a third of the group's total reported assets of €2.82 billion at the end of 2001. The end-year receivables figures for 2000 and 2001 are analysed below. They are taken from the group's 2001 balance sheet and are shown net of the allowance for bad debts.

	At 31 December	
(In €000)	2001	2000
Accounts receivable		
Trade receivables	849,504	815,319
Due from subsidiaries, associated companies and the parent company	2,782	5,850
Other receivables	94,677	116,368
Total accounts receivable	946,963	937,537

Benetton provides additional information on its receivables in a note to its accounts (Note 5) reproduced in Exhibit 10.9.

Required

(a) Benetton gives information about the allowance for bad debts ('doubtful accounts') in Note 5 to its 2001 accounts. What is the charge the company made for bad debts in its 2001 income statement?

(b) Benetton reports the following sales in 2000 and 2001.

(In €000)	2001	2000
Revenues from sales and services	2,097,613	2,018,112

Benetton's year-end trade receivables appear high in relation to sales in both 2000 and 2001. Why?

(c) Suggest a reason for the large VAT receivable at year-end.

Exhibit 10.9   Benetton Group: extract from notes to 2001 accounts (amounts in €000)

Note 5   Accounts receivable

Trade receivables.   As of December 31, 2001, trade receivables, net of the allowance for doubtful accounts, amount to 849,504 (815,319 as of December 31, 2000), of which 209,012 are in foreign currency. Of currency hedging transactions, valued at year-end exchange rates, 125,803 refer to accounts receivable and 74,138 to orders from customers.

   Trade receivables also include 46,287 (90,321 as of December 31, 2000) of bank receipts and notes deposited with financial institutions.

   The allowance for doubtful accounts as of December 31, 2001 amounts to 67,326 (62,836 as of December 31, 2000). 17,149 of this reserve was used during the year. A prudent assessment of the specific and generic risks associated with receivables outstanding at year-end has resulted in an additional provision of 23,051 to take account of the aging of certain balances and the difficult economic conditions in a number of markets.

Due from subsidiaries, associated companies and the parent company.   Accounts receivable from subsidiary companies, amounting to 2,739, are financial receivables, while those from associated companies (41) and the parent company (2) are trade receivables.

Other receivables.   These mainly include:

- VAT recoverable from the tax authorities of 17,851 (18,943 as of December 31, 2000), of which 987 is due beyond 12 months;
- Tax credits of 7,837 (9,191 as of December 31, 2000), of which 313 is due beyond 12 months;
- Other amounts due from tax authorities of 36,382 (33,201 as of December 31, 2000), of which 409 is due beyond 12 months. The item includes 32,240 of net deferred tax assets;
- Accounts receivable from disposals of fixed assets of 3,878 (3,567 as of December 31, 2000), of which 174 is due beyond 12 months.

The remaining amount relates to advances to agents and receivables from funded projects.

(*Source*: Benetton Group, *Annual Report 2001*. Reproduced by permission of Benetton Group.)

P10.9   Accounting for long-term receivables*

Mobile phone operators in Europe were financially stretched in the early 2000s as a result of large payments on third-generation (3G) licences and the cost of establishing 3G networks. Many asked for – and received – favourable financing terms from telecom equipment makers such as Nokia and Motorola.

   In one such deal with a face value of €500 million, Mapletel provides vendor financing on the sale of equipment to Eco, a Spanish mobile phone operator. Under the terms of the contract, Eco receives the equipment in the final quarter of 2003. It pays for the equipment in two equal instalments of €250 million at the end of 2004 and 2005. Interest accrues from 1 January 2004 at the rate of 2% a year and is payable on 31 December 2004 and 2005 on the balance outstanding in the previous 12 months. The market rate of interest on loans of equivalent risk and maturity is 6% a year.

Required

(a) How should Mapletel account for the Eco equipment sale and financing? Show, via journal entries or the balance sheet equation, the effect of the contract on Mapletel's accounts at the time of sale in late 2003 and at the end of 2004 and 2005?

(b) Eco experiences liquidity problems in 2004. At the end of the year, Mapletel agrees to defer collection of the annual instalments by one year – to end 2005 and 2006, respectively. Interest continues to accrue at the rate of 2% a year and is payable at the end of each year of the revised agreement (2004–06) on the balance outstanding in the previous 12 months. To secure equivalent financing, Eco would have to pay 12% a year. What is the effect of the receivable restructuring on Mapletel's 2004 accounts? Assume Eco has paid 2004 interest (of 10) to Mapletel by the end of 2004.

* Problem assignment draws on material in section 2 of this chapter.

Notes to Chapter 10

1 International Accounting Standards Board, *IAS 18: Revenue.*
2 It is standard practice in many countries for a company to specify in the contract of sale that it retains title to the goods until the buyer has paid for them. This makes it easier for it to recover the goods in the event the buyer defaults on its debts. A 'retention of title' clause does not mean that the seller retains significant ownership risks and should not affect when it recognises revenue.
3 International Accounting Standards Board, *IAS 41: Agriculture.*
4 *IAS 18: Revenue,* op. cit.
5 European Commission (1997), Communication from the Commission: Report on late payments in commercial transactions, *Official Journal* C216, 17 July, pp. 10–24.
6 European Commission (2000), Directive 2000/35/EC on combating late payment in commercial transactions, *Official Journal* L200, 8 August, pp. 35–38. Under the Directive, interest is to accrue from 30 days after the invoice date (or goods receipt date, if later), unless the contract specifies an alternative date. The interest rate is a penalty rate of seven percentage points above the European Central Bank refinancing rate (or the equivalent national rate in countries outside the eurozone).
7 Mian, S. and Smith, C.W. (1994), Extending trade credit and financial receivables, *Journal of Applied Corporate Finance,* Summer: 75–84.
8 International Accounting Standards Board, *IAS 39: Financial Instruments: Recognition and Measurement.*
9 Foreign trade gives rise to special problems. For imports from non-EU countries, the importer bears the cost of VAT (and customs duties). The customs office will not release goods until VAT and duties have been paid. The EU abolished customs controls within the EU when the single market was introduced in 1993, so 'imports' from EU states can no longer be taxed in this way. Nonetheless, the destination principle still applies to intra-Union trade. Exports to other EU states continue to be zero-rated. As for imports from member states, the *purchaser* now declares and pays VAT on them, at the local rate. This self-assessed VAT can then be recovered as input tax. The intention is that, whether goods and services are acquired locally or from other EU states, they bear the same VAT rate.
10 The opportunity cost in this case is almost 32% on an annual basis. Hagenstroem saves 1.5 on every purchase costing 100 by paying 20 days early (10 days rather than 30 days after the invoice date). This is a return of 1.523% (1.5/98.5) in a 20-day period. The annual return is 31.76% ($1.01523^{18.25}$), given that there are 18.25 periods of 20 days in a year (365/20) and the periodic return is compounded.
11 Recoveries can be credited to a separate income statement account (e.g. 'Gain from recovery of bad debts written off'). In this case, recorded bad debt expense is 25,000. Note, however, that the net impact is still a reduction of 23,000 in before-tax profit.
12 The asset account 'CIP, at fair value' carries other titles – for example, 'Contract costs incurred and recognised profits to date'.
13 International Accounting Standards Board, *IAS 11: Construction Contracts.* Contract revenues cover not only amounts initially agreed in the contract but also variations in contract work (e.g. changes in specification or design), claims made by the contractor and incentive payments (when the contractor meets or exceeds specified performance standards), so long as these additional amounts are likely to result in revenues and can be estimated reliably. Contract costs include direct costs (e.g. labour, materials), indirect costs that are related to contracts in general (e.g. overheads such as insurance and

payroll processing costs) and any other costs specifically chargeable to the customer under the terms of the contract.

14   *IAS 39*, op. cit. As each instalment is received, the supplier determines the sale and interest components and recognises the revenue from each separately. We ignore interest here, to keep our example simple.

15   The terminology can be confusing. In essence, a bill or draft involves three parties: the first (the 'drawer') instructs a second (the 'drawee') to pay a third (the 'payee'). The drawer is the initiator of the bill: he or she can be either seller or customer. For example, a cheque is a form of bill, initiated by the customer: he or she, as drawer, instructs his or her bank (the drawee) to pay the seller of the goods or services (the payee) the sum stated on the cheque.

Sometimes the instrument contains a promise rather than an order. In a promissory note, the customer promises to make specified payments on specified dates to the supplier. Like bills of exchange, promissory notes can be discounted.

11

Liabilities, on and off balance sheet

INTRODUCTION

In this chapter we study the accounting for and reporting of liabilities. Liabilities are a source of capital for companies. They differ from equity capital in that they are of fixed term. A common feature of all liabilities is that the debtor must, at some future date, transfer resources – cash or goods or services – to the creditor to settle the debt. Because of the breadth of the subject, we adopt a selective approach here. We review the general features of all liabilities and examine in more depth the accounting for long-term debt and lease commitments.

Section 1 of the chapter deals with general issues. We return to the conceptual framework described in Chapter 7 and recall how a liability is defined, when it's recognised and how it's measured. This framework applies to estimated as well as firm liabilities. Not everyone accepts it, however. We discuss briefly four areas of continuing controversy: provisions, off-balance-sheet debt, financial commitments and measurement of non-monetary liabilities.

In section 2 of the chapter we explore in greater depth the accounting for long-term debt. The key question we address here is a measurement one: what is the cost of debt? The question is particularly important when a company issues debt at a discount (or premium) to its face value.

Leasing – and, in particular, the accounting for lease commitments by the lessee – is the subject matter of section 3 of the chapter. (We consider the topic from the lessor's angle in an appendix to the chapter.) We distinguish two types of lease – the operating and the finance lease – and illustrate the accounting for each.

Presentation and disclosure also matter. In section 4 of the chapter we look at the way a company presents liabilities on the face of its balance sheet and indicate what additional information about long-term debt and leases an investor can expect to obtain from the notes. We also describe certain balance sheet and income statement ratios investors employ to assess a firm's financial leverage.

General issues

Definition, recognition and measurement

● Definition of liability

There are many types of accounting liability. Some are contractual (e.g. amounts owed to suppliers); others are non-contractual (e.g. amounts owed to government agencies for taxes). Some are for known amounts (e.g. a bank loan); others are estimated (e.g. a provision for pension benefits). However, all share the following elements: in all cases, the company:

- has a present obligation . . .
- arising from a past transaction or event . . .
- that is expected to result in an outflow of economic resources to settle it.[1]

An accounting liability is an obligation, that is 'a duty or responsibility to act in a certain way'.[2] As we saw in an earlier chapter, an obligation need not be legally enforceable: it can arise from custom. A company that has a policy – but no contractual commitment – to give awards to long-serving employees has a constructive liability and should provide for the future cost of awards as employees earn them.

A future commitment is not a present obligation. When a customer places an order with a supplier, each party makes a commitment: the supplier to furnish the goods and the customer to pay for them. As one side carries out its promise, the other records an accounting liability. On delivery of the goods, the customer records the amount owing to the supplier as an account payable. Should the goods be paid for in advance, the supplier records the payment as deferred revenue. The delivery of goods or the advance payment is the *past* event which gives rise to the *present* obligation.

Normally, a company settles a liability by paying cash or providing goods or services to another party. These are the 'economic resources' it gives up. But settlement can take other forms. A company can swap debt for equity or new debt. And a debtor in financial difficulties may find its liability extinguished by a kindly creditor that waives its rights. In this case, although the debtor *expected* to transfer resources, the creditor's action means it avoids doing so.

● Recognition and measurement

An obligation may meet the definition of an accounting liability but not be *recognised* by the debtor. Recall that, under IAS, a company should record an obligation as a liability on its balance sheet if two conditions are met. These are:

1 it's probable that resources will flow out of the company; and
2 the resource outflow can be estimated reliably.

'Probable' is defined as 'more likely than not'. If one or both conditions are not met, recognition is not required.

The way a liability is measured differs according to its nature. A monetary liability – one which is settled in money, such as a loan or account payable – is measured by the *amount of cash the debtor is contracted to pay to settle it*. A non-monetary liability – examples are a prepaid airline ticket or rent received in advance – is usually recorded at the *amount of cash received for the goods or services the debtor is contracted to supply in future.* If the liability is long-term and involves scheduled payments of fixed amount, then it is usually stated at the *present value of the scheduled payments.* Under HC accounting, the rate used to discount future payments is *the yield on the debt when it was incurred,* that is the interest rate that equates the present value of future payments to the cash the debtor receives initially.

Contingent liability

A contingent liability is a *possible* obligation. Its existence depends on the occurrence (or non-occurrence) of future events that aren't fully under the control of the company.[3] Examples of contingent liabilities are a legal action against the company and a debt guarantee it gives to an affiliated company. In both cases there is a past event – the initiating of legal proceedings by the plaintiff, the giving of the guarantee – but whether the company has an obligation depends on a future event – an adverse legal opinion or court decision, the bankruptcy of the affiliate – that it can't control.

So long as a liability is contingent, it's not recognised in the financial statements. Instead, information about it, in particular its nature and amount, is usually disclosed in the notes to the accounts. If and when the obligation becomes probable – and assuming it's measurable, then the company recognises a liability. Thus a company that receives an adverse legal opinion on a lawsuit it's defending makes the following entry:

Dr. Loss arising from legal claim (OE–)	xx	
Cr. Provision for legal claims (L+)		xx

The provision represents management's best estimate of the payments the company will have to make to settle the legal action (Dr. Provision (L–), Cr. Cash (A–)).

In practice, legal claims against a company present management with an accounting dilemma. Information about them is of value to potential investors. However, management do not wish to publish any details which could prejudice the company's financial position. Thus although they are willing to disclose the amount of a claim in the notes (assuming it is material), they may be reluctant to show separately the amount of any provision made in the accounts since other parties to the lawsuit may use this information against the company. There is a risk, therefore, that management may delay recognising a liability for a legal claim in the company's accounts by claiming that one or both of the recognition criteria are not met by the balance sheet date.

Problem areas

The accounting framework for liabilities given above – which is based on IAS – is not universally accepted. Controversy persists. Accountants and managers disagree about what liabilities are, when they should be recognised and how they should be measured. We illustrate these disagreements below.

Provisions

What is a provision? There are two competing definitions – we'll call them the balance sheet view and the income statement view.[4]

Balance sheet view

Under the balance sheet view, a provision is an estimated liability.[5] It shares the same characteristics as a firm liability with the exception that the amount or timing of the obligation is uncertain. In some cases the identity of the creditor is not known when the provision is established.

An example of an estimated liability is the provision a company makes for future costs arising under a warranty agreement. Consider the case of Dukas Company, a household appliance manufacturer which offers a one-year warranty against certain types of fault in its 'Sorcerer' electric brooms. Past experience (with apprentices) indicates that it's probable that claims will arise. Moreover, the amount of the claims can be estimated with reasonable accuracy, based on the average claims-to-sales ratio in the past. Thus, even though the exact amount and timing of the obligation are not known, the two conditions for liability recognition are met.

Suppose Dukas estimates in year 1 that the costs of warranty claims amount to approximately 1.25% of sales. During year 1, it accrues this expected cost, probably on a monthly basis. Assuming its year 1 sales are 8 million, it records a total charge for warranty costs of 100,000 in year 1:

Dr. Warranty expense (OE–)	100,000	
Cr. Provision for warranty costs (L+)		100,000

Repairs made to brooms under warranty in year 1 amount to 55,000 and are charged against the provision as incurred.

Dr. Provision for warranty costs (L–)	55,000	
Cr. Cash (A–)		55,000

At the end of year 1, the company reviews the balance (of 45,000) in the provision account to determine if it is sufficient to meet expected warranty claims in year 2 on year 1 sales. The provision is adjusted if the balance is considered under- or overstated.

Income statement view

Many managers and accountants reckon that the balance sheet view of provisions is too restrictive. They argue that, in addition to providing for estimated liabilities, a company should also provide for other business costs that it has incurred in generating revenues of the period. They claim this is a long-standing business practice that can be defended on matching grounds. *Under this income statement view, a provision represents accrued costs.* Consider, for example, plant maintenance. It is customary for a firm to accrue the expected costs of such work (by debiting repair expense and crediting a provision for repair work), even if actual repairs are not carried out until a later period for scheduling reasons.

Many EU companies apply this version of provision in their accounts. Under the 4th Directive, EU member states can allow firms to create provisions for costs 'which have their origin in the (current) financial year' but which are uncertain as to amount and timing (Art. 20). Moreover, the legal and tax regimes in some EU countries encourage firms to establish generous provisions for uncertain costs. For example, German companies have traditionally prepared their financial statements with creditors' interests foremost. They are required by law to provide for 'all probable risks'. The resulting charges against income reduce their taxable profits (and thus their income tax liability) and the profits available for distribution to their shareholders.

IASB position

The IASB supports the balance sheet view of provisions. In its view, a provision is an estimated liability. In order to be recorded in the accounts, it must pass the definition and recognition tests of a liability. In measuring the provision, a company should use the 'best estimate' – at the balance sheet date – of the outlay necessary to settle the obligation. In the case of long-term provisions (e.g. for dismantling nuclear power stations or clean-up of contaminated sites), estimates of future outlays can incorporate expected technological advances and the liability should be measured at present value.

The voluntary adoption of IAS by many Continental European companies in recent years has revealed the extent to which reported provisions in their national GAAP accounts comprise accrued costs. For example, BMW, the car and motorcycle producer, reported a near-doubling of start-2001 shareholders' equity – from €4,896 million to €9,432 million – as a result of switching from German to international accounting standards in 2001. Almost 15% (€673 million) of this increase is attributable to the 'derecognition and different measurement of other provisions'.[6]

Restructuring provisions

In principle, a restructuring provision is an estimated liability. When a firm restructures its operations because it is making low profits or even losses, it takes certain steps – for example, the dismissal of employees and the closing down of factories – which are likely to result in future liabilities (redundancy payments, plant closure costs). For reasons of prudence, management set up a provision for such costs when the restructuring decision is taken.

In recent years, firms have been accused of using restructuring provisions to manipulate their income. A favourite ploy of a firm embarking on a restructuring is to bring forward future operating costs and include them in the restructuring provision. The provision is often combined with other actions such as large asset write-downs. As a result, the firm reports a smaller profit (or even losses) in the year of restructuring but larger ones in following years. The tactic is often employed by new management just after they've been appointed. It's also used by an acquirer firm as a way of depressing an acquiree firm's net assets at the time of takeover and thereby boosting its post-acquisition profits.

Accounting regulators are keen to prevent misuse of restructuring provisions. According to IAS, for a restructuring provision to qualify as a (constructive) liability, a firm must have a detailed, formal restructuring plan, indicating the businesses and employees affected, likely costs and timescale. In addition, the firm must have either announced the plan publicly or started implementing it. Only direct expenditures arising from the restructuring can be provided for.[7]

Hidden and disguised debt

Companies like debt as a source of external capital. It has several advantages. First, it is flexible: a company can structure the debt's duration and repayment terms to suit its needs. Second, interest is tax-deductible. Third, existing owners' voting power is not diluted. However, debt carries a penalty. It increases a company's financial risk and thus the return owners demand. As a result, firms with high financial leverage have an incentive to conceal the extent of their indebtedness by raising debt but not reporting it as such on the balance sheet.

Hidden or disguised financing involves the raising of cash. A heavily-indebted firm may seek to *disguise* borrowing by presenting it as an issue of equity (a), a sale of existing assets (b), or a forward sale of assets (c). Or it may raise the debt through a non-consolidated affiliated company, in which case the debt is *hidden*: neither the cash nor the debt appears on its balance sheet (d).

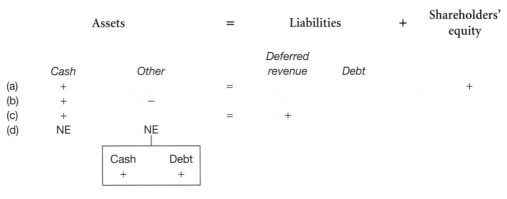

(NE = No effect)

- *Issue of quasi-equity.* The 1980s saw the launch of many new financial products which, the inventors claim, need not be classified as long-term debt but can be shown in or near shareholders' equity. Some are debt with equity characteristics (e.g. the perpetual bond). Others are equity with debt characteristics (e.g. preference shares redeemable at the option of the holder).
- *Sale of existing assets with recourse.* A company sells marketable assets such as receivables, inventories of finished goods or investments in shares and bonds in order to raise cash. However, it retains an economic interest in the assets. Under the 'sale' agreement, it must – or may be required to – repurchase the assets and recompense the buyer for holding and financing costs. In this case, the transaction is, in substance, a loan by the asset 'buyer' to the 'seller'.
- *Forward sale of assets.* These are known as 'prepay' transactions. A bank pays cash up front in exchange for the delivery of a commodity such as natural gas or oil at a future date. The supplier records the advance payment as 'deferred revenue'. This is an *operating* liability and is not considered 'debt' in financial leverage calculations. A Senate investigative committee discovered in 2002 that leading US banks had offered prepay transactions to energy companies such as Enron, Occidental Petroleum and Ocean Energy in the late 1990s.
- *Unconsolidated debt.* A company with non-consolidated subsidiaries or associates has additional scope for raising debt off balance sheet. An investor company records such investments in its balance sheet at its share of the net assets of the investee (or at cost). It does not combine the investee's liabilities (or assets) with its own. If the investee company raises cash by means of debt, its cash and debt increase but *its net assets do not change*. For the investor company, the carrying amount of its investment is unchanged but the cash it can control (and its real financial leverage) have increased.

Accounting regulators are trying to stop companies using the above techniques to hide or disguise debt. First, they have tightened the definition of a liability. According to IAS, a company has a financial liability if it has 'a contractual obligation to deliver cash or another financial asset' to another party.[8] Second, they have limited the ability of companies to record asset transfers as sales. A company can recognise a transfer of inventory as a sale only if certain revenue recognition criteria are met. One of those criteria is that 'the significant risks and rewards of ownership' have been transferred to the buyer.[9] Similarly, a transfer of a financial asset like receivables can only be considered a sale if the transferor surrenders control of the contractual rights contained in the asset. A company has not given up control of – and cannot derecognise – a financial asset if, for example, it retains the right to repurchase the asset on favourable terms or it's obligated to repurchase the asset on terms that ensure the 'buyer' a fair return on its investment.[10] Third, they have restricted the circumstances in which an investor company can avoid consolidating an investee. For example, consolidation is now required whenever one company *controls* another. Control can exist even in the absence of majority ownership.[11]

Commitments, including lease commitments

According to the definition of a liability we gave earlier, a commitment is not an accounting liability. Accountants argue that, at the time two parties enter into a commitment (e.g. by signing a contract for the supply of goods), no economic benefits have flowed from one to the other. There is no *present* obligation.

Some lease commitments *are* recognised as liabilities, however. What is a lease? It is a contract for the use of a fixed asset. One party (the lessee) rents property or equipment from another (the lessor) for a stipulated period. The lessee agrees to make specified payments to the lessor in return for unhindered use of the asset during that time.

In many countries, companies account for a 'finance lease' in the same way as an asset purchased with debt. *A finance lease is one where substantially all of the risks and rewards associated with ownership have been transferred from lessor to lessee.* It is usually a long-term, non-cancellable lease that runs for most, if not all, of an asset's economic life. At the time such a lease contract is signed, the lessee *capitalises* the lease: it records a fixed asset and a long-term liability on its books. The lessor, although still the legal owner of the asset, recognises the sale of an asset and a long-term receivable at this date. We show the balance sheet effect of the transaction in simplified terms below:

Lessee	
Assets	
⋮	
Fixed asset under lease	+xx
⋮	
Equities	
⋮	
Lease liability	+xx
⋮	

Lessor	
Assets	
Buildings and equipment	−xx
⋮	
Lease receivable	+xx
⋮	
Equities	
⋮	
Profit in year (gain/loss on sale)	+/−xx
⋮	

During the lease term, the lessee makes payments according to the contract. As a result, its lease liability is reduced; so, too, is the lessor's receivable. At the same time, both recognise the cost of the asset's financing: part of each lease payment is shown as interest expense in the lessee's income statement and interest income in the lessor's. (Hence the name 'finance lease'.) In addition, the lessee, as economic owner, depreciates the asset. The balance sheet impact of these events is summarised below:

Lessee	
Assets	
Fixed asset under lease	−xx
Cash	−xx
Equities	
Profit in year (depreciation and interest expense)	−xx
Lease liability	−xx

Lessor	
Assets	
Lease receivable	−xx
Cash	+xx
Equities	
Profit in year (interest income)	+xx

All other lease commitments are viewed, for accounting purposes, as 'operating leases'. In this case, the asset under lease remains on the lessor's books: the lessor is considered both economic and legal owner. It recognises rental income as rent is earned – and depreciation as the asset is consumed. The lessee reports neither asset nor liability on its books. It recognises rental expense as it uses the asset.

Accounting for commitments is controversial. Some investors and analysts think lessees should capitalise more of their leases. They argue that it is too easy for a lessee to circumvent accounting rules and account for *de facto* finance leases as operating leases. Such leases do not appear on the lessee's balance sheet. They are a form of *off-balance-sheet financing*.

Others go further and advocate the capitalisation of other types of commitment. At present, a company that enters into a long-term lease (involving the use of an asset) recognises a liability (and an asset) while one that enters into a long-term commitment to purchase goods or services does not. In the latter case, the most the purchaser must do is disclose the nature and amount of the commitment in the notes to its accounts. The danger is that the long-term purchase commitment, like the operating lease, may become a vehicle for off-balance-sheet financing.

We discuss the accounting for leases in greater depth in section 3 of this chapter and in the appendix.

Measurement problems

Liabilities, like assets, cause measurement problems. Consider the case of the liability to provide goods or services. How should this non-monetary liability be measured? One school of thought – we'll call it the 'cost' view – argues that the liability should be measured at the *cost of providing the good or service*. Thus a magazine publisher who accepts a new annual subscription to one of its monthly magazines – for, say, €120 – should measure the initial liability at the cost of providing the magazines during the subscription period (say, €90) Any difference between this amount and the cash received in advance for the annual subscription can be recognised as revenue immediately because it's already earned.

Dr. Cash (A+)	120	
Cr. Unearned revenue from magazine subscription (L+)		90
Cr. Revenue from magazine subscription (OE+)		30

The magazine publisher will then reduce the liability – and recognise revenue – at the rate of €7.50/month as it delivers the magazine to the subscriber.

The alternative school of thought – the 'fair value' view – maintains that non-monetary liabilities should be valued at the *fair value of the goods or services provided*. In the case of our example, the magazine publisher should measure the initial liability at €120, the price of the annual subscription. This is also the cash it receives in advance.

```
Dr. Cash (A+)                                                      120
    Cr. Unearned revenue from magazine subscription (L+)                    120
```

As it delivers the magazine to the subscriber, it recognises revenue – and reduces its liability – at the rate of €10/month, the fair value of each month's issue.

Accounting regulators favour the fair value view on theoretical and practical grounds. Fair value represents the least amount that the company would have to pay to settle a non-monetary obligation – or transfer it to a third party. Thus if the publisher couldn't meet its obligation to supply the magazine, it would have to either reimburse the subscriber or find another company to perform the service. The minimum price it would pay would be the fair value of the unfulfilled contract. There are also practical grounds for measuring non-monetary liabilities at fair value. The alternative, cost, is hard to determine. Which cost figure should be used – incremental cost? full production cost? full production and selling cost? Companies would end up using different cost measures and this would undermine the comparability of financial statements, it's claimed.[12]

SECTION 2   Long-term debt

Economic and legal background

For many companies, short-term and long-term borrowings are a major source of finance. A company issues debt in order to reduce its cost of capital and to safeguard existing shareholders' interests, among other reasons.

Debt is usually less costly than equity and more flexible. Interest is the cost of debt; dividends a cost of equity. In most countries in Europe and elsewhere, interest is tax-deductible; by contrast, dividends are not. In these countries debt is a lower-cost source of finance on an after-tax basis. Moreover, companies may need external capital for a short period only. A company with a seasonal pattern of sales, for example, will find it cheaper to borrow than to issue new shares to cover a cash shortfall *within* the year.

Corporate debt also has advantages for the *owners* of a firm. Debtholders have no voting rights. Thus, by borrowing funds, a company can raise additional capital without the ownership stake of existing shareholders being diluted. Moreover, debt has a disciplining function, especially in mature firms that generate large, stable cash flows. By requiring that the firm's investments be financed with debt rather than equity, owners ensure that managers evaluate new projects carefully since the cash flows from them must be sufficient to meet scheduled debt payments.

Debt carries risks, however. Debt payments such as interest are contractually fixed. They are not postponable. Owners – and managers – pay a heavy price if the company is unable to make debt payments when due. Owners may lose most, if not all, of their investment and managers their jobs. This may influence managers' investment decisions, especially in highly leveraged firms. Managers in these firms may forgo profitable but risky investments to reduce the likelihood of the company defaulting on its debts.[13]

Debt takes many forms. Companies borrow direct from banks by means of loans and overdrafts. Companies also issue debt securities to investors. There are different forms of debt security: we refer to them collectively as **bonds**.

Bonds are partitioned debt. Each bond represents a fraction of the total sum borrowed. Debt packaged in this way is more attractive to investors: they can spread their risk by allocating their capital across different bonds and can trade them in the secondary market. As a result, a company can secure better terms (e.g. a lower interest rate) when it raises debt capital.

In economic terms, a bond is like a share: it's a claim on the future cash flows of the firm. It differs from a share in the nature of the claim. A bond is a debt claim. It usually has a fixed term: the bondholder must be repaid in full by the maturity date. A company is in default – and at risk of legal action by bondholders – if it fails to pay interest or principal when due. By contrast, a share is an ownership claim. It usually has an indefinite life. Shareholders cannot seek legal redress if the company does not pay a dividend (but they may sell their shares or seek to change the management).

A bond also differs from a share in its ranking. On liquidation of a company, amounts owing to bondholders (and other creditors) must be paid first; shareholders receive the residue of the company's liquidated assets. Bonds themselves have a pecking order: senior debt ranks before subordinated debt in the queue for the borrower's assets and is judged less risky (carries a lower interest rate) as a result.

Whatever the form of the debt, lender and borrower must agree its terms. The contract will specify the following:

- the amount borrowed (the **principal**): for bonds, this is simply the product of the number of bonds issued and their **face value** (the amount stated on the face of the bond certificate). The principal is usually the amount the borrower must *repay* on the debt's maturity; it is not necessarily equal to the cash the borrower *receives* from the lender initially;
- the life (the **term**) of the debt: the contract states the date or dates the debt must be repaid (**maturity** dates);
- the interest (if any) to be paid each period: interest may be fixed or variable (in the case of floating-rate debt). For fixed-rate debt, the **coupon rate** is the annual interest payment divided by the principal;
- the dates on which interest payments are due;
- the **security** the borrower must offer the lender (e.g. corporate assets or personal guarantees of the owners);
- the restrictions on future borrowing (e.g. maximum debt ratios not to be exceeded and minimum working capital ratios to be maintained).

Bond and loan agreements may contain other provisions: examples are a **call provision** (the terms under which the company issuing the bonds can 'call' them, that is require the holders to sell their bonds back to the company), and a **sinking fund requirement** (the transfer of cash to a segregated account to finance the repayment of principal). There may also be a **conversion** option: in this case, bondholders have the right to convert their bonds into shares at a specified conversion rate within a specified period.

Initial recognition and measurement

The accounting issues surrounding long-term debt (or debt, for short) are similar to those for depreciable fixed assets. Management must decide how to account for debt at 'birth' (when the company incurs the liability), during its life and on 'death' (when the liability is extinguished). In the following sections we set out current accounting practice at each of these stages of debt's existence. We assume companies measure debt at cost, that is, they do not account for changes in its market value during its life.

Debt is a form of financial liability. A financial liability contains a contractual obligation on one party to deliver cash (or another financial asset) to another. Note that this obligation is a *contractual* one. Thus a company recognises debt as a liability when the contract with the lender takes effect and the company has the legal right to receive the cash. It measures the debt initially at the amount of cash received. This is the debt's cost (and fair value) at that date.[14]

Issue of bonds at par

We illustrate these recognition and measurement principles with an example. (The example is framed in terms of bonds but the concepts apply to all forms of long-term debt.) In early January x1, Lopakhin Company buys some land (including a cherry orchard) from Ranevskaya Company. It issues 4,000 bonds to finance the development of a tourist project (summer cottages with river frontage) on the land. The bonds have a face value of €1,000 each. They carry a fixed coupon rate of 6%, payable annually, and mature at the end of x5. They are issued at par. Thus Lopakhin receives €1,000 for each bond – or €4,000,000 in total. (We ignore issuance costs for the moment.) It recognises a liability for €4 million on the date the bonds are issued:

Issuance in January x1		
Dr. Cash (A+)	€4,000,000	
Cr. Bonds payable (L+)		€4,000,000

The company gives summary details of the bonds either on the face of the balance sheet or, more usually, in the notes to the accounts. The description it uses – '€4 million 6% bonds due December x5' – captures the essential features of the bonds: their face value, coupon rate and term (five years).

Issue of bonds at a discount

Companies do not always issue fixed-rate bonds at par. Recall that the coupon – stated in the bond contract – determines the interest bondholders receive in cash each year. If the market rate of interest on similar debt is *greater* than the coupon rate at the date of issue, an investor will offer a price *less* than the bond's face value because the interest stream is less than that on other companies' bonds. In this case, the bonds are **issued at a discount**. The amount by which the cash paid by investors falls short of the bonds' face value is known as the **bond discount** on issue.

Suppose that, when Lopakhin issues five-year 6% bonds, investors can earn a 10% return on bonds of similar risk and maturity. They will not pay face value (of €1,000) for a Lopakhin bond. A rational investor will pay no more than €848.5 for it. To find this price, the investor determines the cash flows offered by each Lopakhin bond and discounts them at the prevailing market interest rate of 10%:

	Cash flow per bond	Discount factor	Present value
Annual interest payment for five years	€60	3.791	€227.46
Principal repaid at end of fifth year	€1,000	0.621	€621.00
			€848.46

The present value of €848.5 (rounded) is the maximum price an investor is prepared to pay Lopakhin for one of its bonds at the date of issue. Since this price is less than face value, the bonds are issued at a discount. The initial discount is €151.5 on each €1,000 bond.

Note that investors express bond prices in percentage terms. Lopakhin's bonds are issued at 84.85% of their face value – so their price is 84.85%, or 84.85 for short.

How does Lopakhin record these bonds issued at a discount? Recall the general rule: financial liabilities are measured initially at the cash amount received. Lopakhin receives €3,394,000 at the date of issue (4,000 bonds × €848.5/bond), so the entry it makes then is *in substance* as follows:

Issuance in January x1 ('Bonds payable' shown net)

Dr. Cash (A+)	€3,394,000	
Cr. Bonds payable (L+)		€3,394,000

In practice, Lopakhin would account separately for the bond discount. It would record the face value of the bonds (€4 million) in a 'Bonds payable' account – this is its legal liability – and the difference between the face value and issuance price (€606,000) in a 'Bond discount' account. The bond discount is a contra-liability account (CL).

Issuance in January x1 ('Bonds payable' shown gross)

Dr. Cash (A+)	€3,394,000	
Dr. Bond discount (CL+)	606,000	
Cr. Bonds payable (L+)		€4,000,000

Note that, under this alternative version, the bonds are shown *on the balance sheet* net of the discount. Were Lopakhin to prepare a balance sheet immediately after the bond issue, it would report a liability of €3,394,000. Recording 'bonds payable' at the net amount simplifies the accounting so we'll use this approach in our examples.

Issue of bonds at a premium

If the market rate of interest is *less* than the coupon rate at the date of the bonds' issue, an investor is willing to pay *more* than the bond's face value because the interest stream is greater than that on other bonds. In this case, the bonds are **issued at a premium**. The amount by which the cash paid by investors exceeds the bonds' face value is known as the **bond premium** on issue. For example, suppose that, when Lopakhin issues five-year 6% bonds, investors can earn only 5% on bonds of similar risk and maturity. In this case, they are willing to pay €1,043.70 for each €1,000 bond. (This is the rounded sum of the present values, discounted at 5%, of interest payments over five years (€60 × 4.329) and of the principal in the fifth year (€1,000 × 0.784).) Lopakhin records the issue of the 4,000 bonds at the issue price of €1,043.70 as follows:

Issuance in January x1

Dr. Cash (A+)	€4,174,800	
Cr. Bonds payable (L+)		€4,174,800

The premium on issue is €174,800. As with bond discount, this can be accounted for separately, in which case 'Bonds payable' will be recorded at their face value of €4 million.

Why would a company issue bonds at a price other than face value? There may be technical reasons: market rates may move after the date the coupon is set. Sometimes the issuing company deliberately sets the coupon low. Suppose it finances an investment project with debt and the project is expected to generate low cash flows initially and high cash flows in later years. It may be advantageous for the issuer to structure debt payments so that they too are low in the early years and higher later.

Determining the periodic cost of debt

Companies that raise capital by means of long-term loans or bond issues face an accounting problem: how to determine the periodic cost of the debt – interest expense – over its term. We assume in the following discussion that interest, once computed, is expensed immediately. However, the accounting described below applies equally to interest that is capitalised.

When debt carries a fixed interest rate and its face value and fair value at date of issue (i.e. cash received) are the same, determining periodic cost is straightforward. The interest charge each year is simply the product of the stated interest rate on the debt and its face value. The interest is accrued over the year on a time basis. Thus if Lopakhin Company issues €4 million of five-year 6% bonds at par in early January x1, it will accrue interest of €240,000 (6% × €4 million) during each of the years x1 through x5 and pay it at year-end. The first year's entries are:

Interest accrual during x1		
Dr. Interest expense (OE–)	€240,000	
Cr. Accrued interest payable (L+)		€240,000
Interest payment at end-December x1		
Dr. Accrued interest payable (L–)	€240,000	
Cr. Cash (A–)		€240,000

The accounting for floating-rate debt is similar. In this case, the interest rate is linked to a reference rate such as the local interbank offered rate. At regular intervals (say, every three months), the interest rate is adjusted for changes in the reference rate. The borrowing company calculates interest expense (and payment) for the following three months by applying the new rate to the face value of the debt.

Lifetime cost of debt

Determining the periodic cost of debt is more complicated when bonds are issued at a discount or premium. The discount (premium) represents a cost (benefit) to the borrower. It's part of the total cost of the debt and should be reflected in interest expense. The question is: how? Under accrual accounting, the discount or premium is spread – or 'amortised' – over the life of the debt rather than recognised in the period the debt is redeemed – in the same way that tangible fixed assets are depreciated over their useful lives.

The first step in calculating amortisation is to work out the **lifetime cost** of the debt. This is simply the difference between the cash the company receives as a result of the borrowing and the scheduled payments it must make over the term of the loan or bonds. In the case of Lopakhin's five-year 6% bonds issued at a price of 84.85, the lifetime cost is €1,806,000.

In January x1, Lopakhin receives in cash	+3,394,000
Between x1 and x5, it makes cash payments totalling	–5,200,000
[4,000,000 + (5 × 240,000)]	
Principal Interest	
Lifetime cost of 6% five-year bonds	–1,806,000

The payments comprise interest of €240,000 a year – or €1,200,000 in total – and the principal of €4 million which is paid when the bonds mature in December x5.

Straight-line method of amortisation

The next step is to allocate the lifetime cost over the term of the debt to arrive at the interest charge each period. Failure to amortise gives a misleading picture of the debt's annual cost. For example, consider how Lopakhin would record the cost of its 6% five-year bonds if it accounted for them on a cash basis.

(Amounts in €000)			Year			
	x1	x2	x3	x4	x5	Total
Interest expense	240	240	240	240	846	1,806

Under the cash basis, the bond discount of €606,000 is only expensed in x5 when the bonds mature. As a result, the cost of debt is understated – and profits overstated – in years x1–x4 whereas the reverse is true in x5. The carrying amount of the bonds is also understated until the date of redemption.

Profit and liability misstatement are avoided if the accrual basis is used and the lifetime cost is amortised over the debt's term. The simplest method of amortisation is the straight-line (SL) method: each period bears an equal share of the debt's lifetime cost. Applying this to Lopakhin's five-year 6% bonds yields an annual interest charge of €361,200.

(Amounts in €000)			Year			
	x1	x2	x3	x4	x5	Total
Interest payments	240	240	240	240	240	1,200
Amortisation of bond discount	121.2	121.2	121.2	121.2	121.2	606
Interest expense (A)	361.2	361.2	361.2	361.2	361.2	1,806
Carrying amount of bonds, start-yr (B)	3,394	3,515.2	3,636.4	3,757.6	3,878.8	
Cost of debt (A)/(B), as %	10.6	10.3	9.9	9.6	9.3	

Since interest payments on the bonds are the same each year, the initial discount is also amortised on a SL basis. The carrying amount of the bonds increases each year by €121,200, the annual amortisation of the discount. (By the end of x5, the carrying amount will be €4 million, the maturity value of the bonds.)

The SL method, although simple to apply, has a major flaw according to accounting regulators. Reported interest expense doesn't reflect the historical cost of the debt, that is, the interest rate on debt of similar risk and maturity at the time of issue. For example, Lopakhin's five-year 6% bonds were priced to give investors a return of 10% over the debt's lifetime. But reported interest expense of €361,200 is not equal to 10% of the start-of-year carrying amount of the bonds in x1 – nor is it in any other year.

Interest method of amortisation

The method of amortisation favoured by accounting regulators is the **interest method**.[15] This method ensures, by design, that the interest expense the borrower reports each period reflects the market rate of interest on equivalent debt at the time it signed the debt contract. Here's how it works – in three easy steps:

1 Find the internal rate of return (IRR) that equates the present value (at contract date) of scheduled debt payments to the cash received by the borrower. This rate is also known as the 'level yield to maturity' or 'effective interest rate'.

2 Apply the IRR to the start-of-period carrying amount of the debt (initial carrying amount in the first period) to give the interest expense for the period. The difference between interest expense and interest paid is the discount or premium amortised in the period.

3 Adjust the carrying amount of the bonds for the discount or premium amortised. Amortised discount (premium) is added to (subtracted from) the start-of-period carrying amount. The adjusted figure is the carrying amount at the start of the following period.

Steps 2 and 3 are then repeated until the bonds mature or are retired.

Are your eyes glazing over? Once again, we call Lopakhin's bonds to our aid. Exhibit 11.1 shows the calculation of interest expense and discount amortisation under the interest method for each of the five years of the bonds' life.

We already know that the bonds' IRR is 10%. Each year Lopakhin applies this rate to the bonds' start-of-year carrying amount ('net liability') to determine the annual interest charge. The difference between interest expense and interest paid (€240,000) is the discount amortised in the year – and this is the amount by which the bonds' carrying amount *increases* between the start and end of the year. Note that the carrying amount is always the present value of future payments discounted at the initial IRR. For example, at the start of x3, the present value of the remaining scheduled payments is €3,602,700:

Exhibit 11.1   Cost of debt: interest method illustrated

Facts

Early in x1, Lopakhin Company issues €4 million five-year 6% bonds and receives €3,394,000 in cash. The bonds pay interest annually and yield 10% to maturity. The company uses the interest method to determine the annual cost and the carrying amount of the bonds. Amounts are in €000.

Calculation of annual interest expense and end-year carrying amount of bonds

	x1	x2	x3	x4	x5
(1) Net liability, start-year	3,394	3,493.4	3,602.7	3,723	3,855.3
(2) Interest expense: 10% × (1)	339.4	349.3	360.3	372.3	384.7*
(3) Interest paid: 6% × 4,000	240	240	240	240	240
(4) Discount amortised: (2) − (3)	99.4	109.3	120.3	132.3	144.7
(5) Net liability, end-year: (1) + (4)	3,493.4	3,602.7	3,723	3,855.3	4,000

* Rounded.

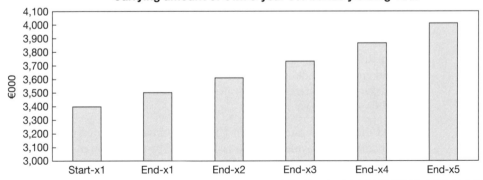

Carrying amount of €4m 5-year 6% bonds yielding 10%

[€240,000 × PVA(10%, 3 payments)] + [€4,000,000 × PV(10%, 3 periods)] = €3,602,700

This is also the start-x3 carrying amount of the bonds according to the amortisation table in Exhibit 11.1. By end-x5, the initial discount (of €606,000) is fully amortised and the bonds' carrying amount is €4 million. Lopakhin is obligated to repay this sum to bondholders when the bonds mature in December x5.

The interest method, like the SL method, ensures that the lifetime cost of debt is fully amortised. Where bonds are issued at a discount, interest expense increases in absolute terms each period since a constant interest rate is applied to a growing liability. Lopakhin's 6% bonds illustrate this.

(Amounts in €000)			Year			
	x1	x2	x3	x4	x5	Total
Interest payments	240	240	240	240	240	1,200
Amortisation of bond discount	99.4	109.3	120.2	132.3	144.7	606
Interest expense	339.4	349.3	360.2	372.3	384.7	1,806

By contrast, where bonds are issued at a premium, the liability *declines* as the premium is amortised, resulting in a *decreasing* interest charge each period.

Financial statement impact of interest method

We've seen already how bonds issued at a discount affect a company's accounts at the time of issue. We turn now to the accounting impact of such bonds over their life. Exhibit 11.2 shows the pre-tax effect of the 6% bond issue on Lopakhin's accounts for x1 through x5 using a worksheet approach.

Exhibit 11.2 Interest method: financial statement impact illustrated

Facts

Early in x1, Lopakhin Company issues €4 million five-year 6% bonds and receives €3,394,000 in cash. The bonds pay interest annually and have a yield to maturity of 10%. The company uses the interest method to determine the annual cost and carrying amount of the bonds. Amounts are in €000.

Financial statement impact of bonds

	Issuance Jan x1	x1	x2	x3	x4	x5	Redemption Dec x5	Net effect over 5 years
Assets								
Cash	+3,394	−240	−240	−240	−240	−240	−4,000	−1,806
Total	+3,394	−240	−240	−240	−240	−240	−4,000	
Equities								
Liabilities								
Bonds payable, net	+3,394	+99.4	+109.3	+120.2	+132.3	+144.7	−4,000	0
Shareholders' equity								
Profit for the year [Interest expense]		−339.4	−349.3	−360.2	−372.3	−384.7		−1,806
	+3,394	−240	−240	−240	−240	−240	−4,000	

Lopakhin's cash balance declines by €240,000 each year as interest is paid. However, the impact on profit – via interest expense – is greater by the amount of the discount amortised in the year. This is evident from the journal entries Lopakhin makes to record interest expense and payment each year. Here are specimen entries for x2.

Interest accrual during x2
Dr. Interest expense (OE–)   €349,300
    Cr. Accrued interest payable (L+)   €240,000
    Cr. Bonds payable (L+)   109,300

Interest payment at end-December x2
Dr. Accrued interest payable (L–)   €240,000
    Cr. Cash (A–)   €240,000

In our example, we've assumed that Lopakhin accounts for the bonds on a net basis. In practice, the company would record 'Bonds payable' at their face value (i.e. €4 million) and (unamortised) 'Bond discount' in a separate contra-liability account. In this case, the credit for €109,300 in the above entry would be to 'Bond discount', thereby *reducing* the contra-liability. Amortisation results in a zero balance in this account by the date the bonds mature. Full balance sheet presentation of the bonds illustrates this:

(In €000)	Issuance Jan x1	x1	x2	End year x3	x4	x5
Bonds payable, at face value	4,000	4,000	4,000	4,000	4,000	4,000
Less:						
Unamortised discount	–606	–506.6	–397.3	–277	–144.7	0
Bonds payable, net of discount	3,394	3,493.4	3,602.7	3,723	3,855.3	4,000

One final point. *Over debt's lifetime, the impact, pre-tax, on cash and income should be the same.* Lopakhin's 6% bonds demonstrate this. We can see from Exhibit 11.2 that Lopakhin's cash balance is lower by €1,806,000 after the bonds' redemption in x5. The company's cumulative profits are also lower by this amount. Of course, these calculations ignore the *benefits* – in cash and profit terms – which Lopakhin enjoys from the property investment financed by the bonds.

Other applications of interest method

The interest method can be used to amortise other types of financing cost. **Debt issuance costs** is one. For example, suppose that Lopakhin incurs costs of €100,000 when issuing the 6% bonds and thus the cash it receives in January x1 is €3.294 million, not €3.394 million. This increases the effective interest rate on the bonds to 10.74%, as can be seen by solving for x in the following equation:

$$(€240{,}000 \times \text{PVA } (x\%, 5 \text{ payments})) + (€4{,}000{,}000 \times \text{PV } (x\%, 5 \text{ periods})) = €3{,}294{,}000$$
    Annual   Principal
    interest

Lopakhin records the issuance of the bonds in January x1 as follows:

Issuance of bonds in x1
Dr. Cash (A+)   €3,294,000
    Cr. Bonds payable (L+)   €3,294,000

In effect, Lopakhin accounts for the issuance costs by increasing the initial discount from €606,000 to €706,000. By applying the effective interest rate of 10.74% to the start-of-year carrying amount, Lopakhin amortises the €100,000 issuance costs over the five-year term of the debt through the annual interest charge. The following journal entry summarises interest expense, interest paid and discount amortised in x1. The figures are rounded:

> *Interest expense and payment in x1*
> Dr. Interest expense (OE–)   €353,800
>   (10.74% × 3,294,000)
>   Cr. Bonds payable (L+)   €113,800
>   Cr. Cash (A–)   240,000

Approximately €14,400 of the x1 interest charge represents amortisation of issuance costs.

There are other kinds of bonds where the interest method can be used to calculate periodic cost. **Zero coupon bonds** are bonds which pay no interest. They are an unusual example of a debt security issued at a discount: annual interest expense is *equal* to discount amortised in the year. **Stepped interest bonds** (i.e. where scheduled interest payments increase over the debt term) and **bonds with a stated redemption premium** are two further examples. In both cases, the effective interest rate at time of issuance is greater than the (initial) coupon rate.

The interest method has found other applications. Companies that *invest* in debt securities and plan to hold them to maturity usually account for them at amortised cost. In this case, the difference between the purchase price and face value of the securities is usually amortised by the interest method. The accounting is the mirror image of that used by the *issuer* of the debt securities. The interest method is also used to determine the financing charge contained in the periodic payments of a **finance lease**, as we'll discover in section 3 of the chapter.

Derecognition

A company removes a financial liability from its balance sheet when the obligation is discharged, cancelled or expires.[16] For most financial liabilities, there is no uncertainty about when a financial liability is settled. The company that has purchased goods on account removes the payable from its accounts when it pays the supplier; the borrower clears a debt off its books when it repays the lender. So it is with Lopakhin and its 6% bonds. When the bonds mature in December x5, it records the repayment of the €4 million principal as follows:

> *Redemption of bonds in December x5*
> Dr. Bonds payable (L–)   €4,000,000
>   Cr. Cash (A–)   €4,000,000

Note that the entry is the same whether or not Lopakhin's bonds are issued at par. If bonds are issued at a discount, the discount is fully amortised by the end of their life and the carrying amount of the bonds is equal to their face value then.

Early retirement of debt

Accounting for retirement of debt is not always straightforward, however. Consider the case of the borrower that decides to retire debt early – by, say, replacing the debt with equity or by using surplus cash. Where the debt is in the form of bonds, the borrower can do this by buying them back (through negotiation with bondholders or purchases in the secondary market) or by calling them if the bond contract allows. The fair value of fixed-rate debt will not be the same as its carrying amount if the market rate of interest at this early retirement date is different from the effective interest rate on the debt. If market rates have risen (fallen) since the issue date, fair value will be less (greater) than carrying amount. The borrower will recognise a 'gain (or loss) on early retirement of debt' for the difference.[17] *Note that the impact on the income statement of settling a liability early is the opposite to that of disposing of an asset: where the liability's fair value is greater than its carrying amount, the company records a loss.*

An example best illustrates this point. Recall that at the start of x1 Lopakhin issues five-year 6% bonds at an effective interest rate of 10%. Suppose market interest rates fall in x1 and x2 and by the end of x2 the interest rate on bonds similar to Lopakhin's is only 8%. Early in x3, Lopakhin decides to buy back all 4,000 bonds.

The cost to Lopakhin of redeeming the bonds (i.e. their fair value) in January x3 exceeds their value on the company's books then. The bonds' fair value is €3,794,500, the present value (in January x3) of scheduled debt payments over the remaining three years, discounted at 8%:

$$[\text{€240,000} \times \text{PVA(8\%, 3 payments)}] + [\text{€4,000,000} \times \text{PV(8\%, 3 periods)}] = \text{€3,794,500}$$

    Annual   Principal
    interest

Assuming the company uses the interest method of amortisation, the carrying amount of the bonds at that date is €3,602,700 (*see* Exhibit 11.1). Thus Lopakhin recognises an accounting loss of €191,800. (We ignore transaction costs incurred in repurchasing the bonds.) The rise in the bonds' market value results in a *holding loss* that, under historical cost accounting, is realised – and thus recognised in the income statement – only when they're retired.

January x3	
Fair value of 6% bonds	€3,794,500
Carrying amount	−3,602,700
Loss on early retirement	€191,800

Lopakhin records the repurchase of the bonds as follows:

Repurchase in January x3 ('Bonds payable' shown net)		
Dr. Bonds payable (L–)	€3,602,700	
Dr. Loss on early retirement of bonds (OE–)	191,800	
Cr. Cash (A–)		€3,794,500

If, on repurchase, market rates of interest are *higher* than those prevailing when the debt was issued, the borrower records a *gain* on early retirement.

Think carefully about the nature of this gain or loss. Does Lopakhin suffer an economic loss by retiring its high-cost bonds when interest rates fall? Surely it would be better off replacing 10% debt with 8% debt? In fact, if taxes and transaction costs are ignored, the company is neither better nor worse off by replacing the debt. Over the five-year term of the original debt contract, the cost will be 10% regardless of the refinancing terms: in this case the effective interest rate on the new debt is lower but annual interest payments are higher.[18]

Accounting for debt: international practice

Most companies measure long-term debt at amortised cost. Thus bonds payable are shown on the balance sheet net of unamortised discount (or including unamortised premium). However, EU rules permit – and national rules in some countries (Belgium, Spain) require – firms to report on the balance sheet the amounts for which they're legally liable. In this case, bonds payable are shown at their maturity value and any initial discount (premium) is shown as a deferred charge (deferred income). We contrast the two presentations below, using our Lopakhin example.

Lopakhin Company: Extracts from January x1 balance sheet (in €000)

(a) Debt at legal liability

Assets		Liabilities and shareholders' equity	
⋮		⋮	
Deferred charge (Bond discount)	606	Long-term liabilities	4,000
⋮		⋮	

(b) Debt at amortised cost

Assets		Liabilities and shareholders' equity	
⋮		⋮	
		Long-term liabilities	3,394
		⋮	

The practice of reporting debt at its maturity value will decline in Europe after 2005 when IAS become mandatory for listed EU companies.

Debt discount or premium is always amortised, regardless of the way it's presented on the balance sheet. For example, the 4th Directive requires EU companies to amortise the discount by a 'reasonable amount' each year and write it off completely by the date the debt is repaid (Art. 41). The Directive does not specify the method of amortisation, however. The interest method appears to be the dominant practice among listed companies, in Europe and elsewhere. It's required under US and international rules. The straight-line method is acceptable only when the amount of the initial discount or premium is small and the interest charge is not materially different from that reported under the interest method.

The gain or loss arising from the early retirement of debt is usually shown as a component of financial income or expense. However, companies following US GAAP must report any material gain or loss as an extraordinary item.

SECTION 3

Leasing

Types of lease

*A lease is a contract under which the owner of a fixed asset (the **lessor**) grants another (the **lessee**) the right to use the asset for a specified period at a specified rental.* Assets leased are usually tangible and can range from office equipment to buildings.

From the user's standpoint, leasing has advantages over the alternative, asset purchase.

1 It offers flexibility: the lease period can vary from days to years. Some airlines make heavy use of short-term aircraft leases: they can adjust their capacity quickly to changes in demand for air travel.

2 It lowers risk: for assets subject to rapid technological change, leasing on a short-term basis allows the user to avoid being locked into outdated technology.

3 The lessee's initial cash outlays are reduced. The lessee needs cash to cover only the first lease payment, not the whole cost of the asset. Moreover, it receives 100% financing of the asset. The lessor provides a loan as well as an asset. Each lease payment includes both a capital charge for the asset and a financing charge.

4 Lastly, a lease can yield tax benefits. A lessor with large taxable income shares with the lessee the benefits of the tax depreciation and investment incentives it receives as owner. These benefits are passed on in the form of lower lease payments. The lessee's own taxable income may be too low for it to utilise tax benefits if it buys the asset.

Leases can be divided into two main types, operating leases and finance leases. An **operating lease** is a rental agreement. It has a short duration and cancellation penalties are small. A **finance lease** (capital lease) is akin to a purchase contract with debt financing. The lessor expects to recover the cost of the asset – and be recompensed for financing it – over the lease term. Thus the lease runs for years, often for the economic life of the asset. It may contain a purchase option. Cancellation results in heavy penalties.

In practice, the dividing line between the two types of lease is not always clear-cut. The key test – and the one accountants apply – is whether the lessee faces the same risks and rewards as an owner. If the answer is yes, the lease is judged to be a finance lease.

Lessee accounting

From an accounting perspective, the distinction between operating and finance leases is important because, under international rules, the two types of lease are accounted for differently.

An operating lease is viewed as a commitment: the lessee recognises neither liability nor asset when it signs the lease contract. The asset under lease remains on the lessor's books (and is depreciated there). Lease payments are accounted for as rent: they're recorded by the lessor as income when earned and by the lessee as an expense when the cost is incurred.

A finance lease is considered to be the equivalent of a purchase of a fixed asset by instalment. In this case, the lessee records a fixed asset and long-term liability on its books when the lease contract is signed. It charges the costs of the asset (depreciation) and of the liability (interest expense) to its income statement each period. Meanwhile, the lessor, though still the legal owner, records the sale of the asset under lease and its replacement by a (long-term) receivable, on which interest is earned.

In this section we illustrate the two treatments from the *lessee's* perspective. (Accounting by the lessor is illustrated in the appendix.) Consider the case of Jupiter Bus Company. On 1 January year 1, it decides to lease a bus from the manufacturer, Offenbach, for its Mount Olympus to Hades run. Here are details about the bus and the lease agreement:

- The fair value of the bus on 1 January is 309,250. It has a three-year economic life. Its expected residual value is zero. It is depreciated on a straight-line basis.
- Annual lease payments of 120,000 are payable at the end of each year. (Normally, payments are made at the start of the lease period. Our assumption simplifies Jupiter's bookkeeping.) The payments do not include maintenance and insurance costs which are covered by a separate contract.
- The interest rate implicit in the annual lease payments is 8%. (Solving $[120,000 \times PVA_3^{x\%} = 309,250]$ yields $x = 8$.)

Accounting for operating leases

How would Jupiter account for the lease if it were an operating lease? We assume the benefits from the lease are spread evenly over the three years: thus the cost of the lease each year (rent expense) is equal to the annual payment. The summary journal entry each year is as follows:

31 December year 1 (and years 2 and 3)
Dr. Rent expense (OE–)   120,000
   Cr. Cash (A–)   120,000

It makes no other entries. It records no liability at 1 January year 1, even though it is contractually bound to make payments to Offenbach for the following three years.

Accounting for finance leases

Consider now the case where the lease is accounted for as a finance lease. On 1 January year 1, the date of signing the lease, Jupiter records a fixed asset and a liability of 309,250, which is both the fair value of the leased asset and the present value of its lease payment obligations:

	Assets	=	Liabilities	+	Shareholders' equity
	Leased asset		Lease liability		
1 January year 1	+309,250	=	+309,250		

Jupiter reports the leased vehicle as a fixed asset on its balance sheet. The lease liability is equivalent, in economic terms, to a loan from Offenbach to Jupiter. If Jupiter were to draw up a balance sheet on 1 January, it would show the principal portion, 95,260, of the first payment of 120,000 as a current liability and the balance, 213,990, as a long-term liability. (This can be seen from the 'Lease liability' column in Exhibit 11.3.)

During each of the three years 1 to 3, Jupiter recognises in its income statement the amortisation of the asset and the cost of Offenbach's loan (interest expense).[19] The asset's life is, in this case, equal to the lease term (three years). Amortisation is on a straight-line basis. Thus the annual amortisation Jupiter records is 103,083 (309,250/3).

The cost of the implicit loan is calculated using the interest method. To determine annual interest expense, Jupiter applies the discount rate implicit in the lease (in this case 8%) to the start-of-year carrying amount of the liability. In year 1, the interest charge is 24,740 (309,250 × 8%). This may be accrued during the year or recognised at the time of the first annual lease payment of 120,000. The balance of that payment (95,260) represents part repayment of the lease liability. The entries Jupiter makes in year 1 in connection with the Offenbach lease are summarised below:

Amortisation of asset in year 1
Dr. Amortisation expense (OE–)   103,083
   Cr. Accumulated amortisation,
      leased asset (CA+)   103,083

Annual lease payment at end-year 1
Dr. Interest expense (OE–)   24,740
Dr. Lease liability (L–)   95,260
   Cr. Cash (A–)   120,000

Exhibit 11.3 Jupiter Company (lessee): financial statement impact of finance lease

	Assets		=	Liabilities +	Shareholders' equity
	Leased asset	Cash		Lease liability	Profit for year
Balance, start year 1	309,250	⋮		309,250	⋮
During year 1					
Amortisation of asset	−103,083		=		−103,083 (Amortisation expense)
Lease payment (and recognition of interest)		−120,000	=	−95,260	−24,740 (Interest expense)
End 1 balance	206,167	⋮		213,990	⋮
During year 2					
Amortisation	−103,083		=		−103,083
Lease payment		−120,000	=	−102,881	−17,119
End 2 balance	103,084	⋮		111,109	⋮
During year 3					
Amortisation	−103,084		=		−103,084
Lease payment		−120,000	=	−111,109	−8,891
End 3 balance	0			0	
Effect of lease on cash and SE, years 1–3		−360,000			−360,000

Calculation of interest expense and end-year liability

Year	(1) Lease liability at 1/1	(2) Lease payment at 31/12	(3) Interest expense 8% × (1)	(4) Reduction in liability (2) − (3)	(5) End-year liability (1) − (4)
1	309,250	120,000	24,740	95,260	213,990
2	213,990	120,000	17,119	102,881	111,109
3	111,109	120,000	8,891*	111,109	0

* Rounded.

Calculation of annual amortisation expense

$$\frac{\text{Amortisable cost of leased vehicle}}{\text{Economic life (in years)}} = \frac{309{,}250}{3} = 103{,}083$$

The carrying amount of the lease liability at the end of year 1 is 213,990, the initial liability (309,250) less the repayment of principal in year 1 (95,260). This is the basis for calculating interest expense in year 2.[20]

Exhibit 11.3 sets out the effect of the finance lease on Jupiter's accounts in each of years 1 to 3, using the balance sheet equation. A table at the bottom of the exhibit shows the calculation of annual interest expense and the end-year balance in the lease liability account.

The total cost of the lease – in terms of amortisation and interest charges – is 360,000, the same as the total lease payments. Of course, the exhibit ignores the *benefits* which the leased bus yields Jupiter. (Rumour has it that the Mount Olympus to Hades route is a lucrative one.)

Financial statement impact

The difference in impact of the two methods on a lessee's income is, in most cases, small. Initially, and also when the use of leasing is increasing, **lease capitalisation** (as the finance lease method is known) leads to *lower* income, because amortisation and interest charges combined exceed the rental charge. However, over time the interest charge diminishes and in later periods the total annual expense is likely to be less under lease capitalisation.

Exhibit 11.4 contrasts the impact of the two leasing methods on Jupiter's pre-tax income, by year and in total. Notice that the expenses recognised over the three years total 360,000 in each case. This is because we assume both Offenbach and Jupiter use the same discount rate, Offenbach to determine the annual lease payment and Jupiter to determine the cost of the loan. What is also evident from Exhibit 11.4 is that the choice of method affects the *timing* of expense recognition. As a general rule, a lessee's expenses in the early years of a lease are likely to be higher under a finance than an operating lease – assuming operating lease charges are constant each period and the leased asset under a finance lease is amortised on an SL basis.

It's the balance sheet impact of lease capitalisation which causes lessee companies most concern. Under the finance lease method, an additional asset and liability are created. Since the liability is interest-bearing, *the result is an increase in reported financial leverage.* Consider Jupiter Company's position. Assume that, on 1 January year 1, *before* signing the lease contract with Offenbach, its shareholders' equity and debt are 2 million and 1 million respectively, giving a debt–equity ratio of 0.5:1. By the end of the day (and ignoring other events and transactions), the ratio rises to 0.57:1 (1.309/2.309) if Jupiter capitalises the lease.

Notice that the lessee's (pre-tax) cash flows are the same under both the operating and the finance lease methods.

Exhibit 11.4 Jupiter Company (lessee): income statement impact of leased asset under operating and finance lease methods

Year	Operating lease		Finance lease	
1	Rent expense	120,000	Amortisation expense	103,083
			Interest expense	24,740
				127,823
2	Rent expense	120,000	Amortisation expense	103,083
			Interest expense	17,119
				120,202
3	Rent expense	120,000	Amortisation expense	103,084
			Interest expense	8,891
				111,975
	Total	360,000	Total	360,000

● Lease capitalisation under IAS

Companies cannot choose between the operating and finance lease methods. National and international rules state explicitly when a lessee should capitalise a lease. For example, IAS state: 'A lease is classified as a finance lease if it transfers substantially all the risks and rewards incident to ownership.'[21]

Under what circumstances are 'substantially all the risks and rewards' considered transferred? The international accounting standard offers the following examples (US rules in this area which many international companies follow are more specific and are given in parentheses):

1 *Ownership of the asset is transferred to the lessee by the end of the lease term.*
2 *The lease contains a 'bargain-purchase' option,* i.e. the lessee has the right to buy the asset at the end of the lease and the price is so advantageous that the lessee is expected to exercise the option.
3 *The lease term covers the major part (USA: 75% or more) of the asset's economic life.*
4 *The present value of the lease payments at the start of the lease is greater than or equal to substantially all (USA: 90%) of the fair value of the asset.*
5 *The leased asset is of a specialised nature and can only be used (in its existing form) by the lessee.*[22]

Under condition 1, the lease is, in form, the purchase of an asset by instalments. Under conditions 2 to 4, it is, in substance, an instalment purchase, since the lessor expects to recoup most, if not all, of its investment during the lease term. *If any one of these conditions is met, the lessee must recognise a leased asset and lease liability in its accounts.*

National and international regulators define carefully the terms used in the accounting rules for leases. Here are the international standard's definitions of the more important ones:

● *Lease term.* This includes not just the initial lease period but also *any renewal term if the lessee has the option to renew and is likely to exercise that option* (e.g. because the lease payments in the renewal term are low).
● *Lease payments.* These include the minimum annual payments (excluding service costs and taxes) and *any residual value which is guaranteed by the lessee or a related party.* If the lease contains a bargain-purchase option, lease payments include the amount of the option in place of the guaranteed residual value.
● *Initial valuation of leased asset and lease liability under finance lease.* At the start of the lease, the lessee should measure the leased asset and lease liability at the fair value of the asset or, if lower, at the present value of the lease payments.
● *Amortisation period of asset under finance lease.* If it's likely ownership will transfer to the lessee at the end of the lease term, the lessee should amortise the asset over its useful life. If the lessor is likely to retain ownership, the amortisation period should be the shorter of useful life or the lease term. Note that, because land has an indefinite life, a lease of land always fails condition 3 and is treated as an operating lease.
● *Discount rate* (in PV and interest expense calculations). This should be the interest rate implicit in the lease (from the standpoint of the lessor). If the lessee does not know this rate – and it may well not, given that it is unaware of both the *unguaranteed* residual value the lessor expects and the lessor's tax position – it should use its incremental borrowing rate (for debt of similar risk and maturity).

Regulators introduced capitalisation tests – and the accompanying definitions – because lessee companies were reluctant to capitalise finance leases on a voluntary basis. Even now, many lessee companies structure their leases in order to avoid capitalisation and its impact on reported leverage. The IASB is so concerned about the extent of avoidance that it plans to draft new rules that will extend capitalisation to a broader set of leases.

Sale-and-leaseback agreements

Accounting rules have been introduced to cover new types of leasing products. One of the most popular is the **sale-and-leaseback agreement**. This enables a company (the seller-lessee) to raise cash by selling a major asset such as land or commercial property while retaining use of it.

Sale-and-leaseback arrangement

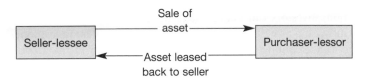

As with ordinary leases, the key issue is: is the lessee (still) the economic owner of the asset? If the 'leaseback' is judged to be a finance lease, the answer is yes: the seller-lessee has, in effect, borrowed funds against the asset. As a result, under international rules any gain on disposal of the asset is considered unrealised at the time of sale. Instead, the seller-lessee defers and spreads the gain over the lease term.

Lessee accounting: international practice

Capitalisation of finance leases has long been mandatory in countries with an Anglo-Saxon accounting tradition (e.g. UK, USA, Commonwealth countries). In countries with a Continental European accounting tradition, the distinction between operating and finance leases is relatively new: until recently all leases in these countries were accounted for as rentals. This is still the way French and Italian companies account for leases in their *individual* (i.e. non-consolidated) accounts.

Despite growing acceptance that finance leases should be capitalised, accounting practice is still not harmonised in this area. For example, national rules lay down different capitalisation criteria. Many follow international and US rules and lay down ownership transfer and investment recovery tests (i.e. present value of lease payments approximates fair value of leased asset). A Japanese company, however, must capitalise only those leases where it gains – or is likely to gain – ownership of the asset (i.e. those containing a transfer-of-title clause or a bargain purchase option). It *may* – but is not required to – capitalise other types of finance lease.

SECTION 4
Liabilities and financial statement analysis

Financial statement presentation

Virtually all companies, in Europe and elsewhere, distinguish **current** from **non-current liabilities**, either on the face of the balance sheet or in the notes to the accounts. *Current liabilities are those that are expected to be paid or settled within one year of the balance sheet date.* Included within them is the current portion of long-term liabilities. If, however, the company intends to refinance the debt on a long-term basis and there is evidence (e.g. a refinancing agreement) that it is able to do so, it can classify the current portion as long-term.[23] Given information about current assets as well as current liabilities, investors can better assess the ability of the firm to meet its short-term debts.

Companies also distinguish **creditors** from **provisions** on their balance sheets. In principle, this is a useful distinction: payments to creditors are more certain in terms of both amount and timing. However, as we've seen, certain provisions shown on the equity side of the balance sheet may not represent an estimated liability but simply expenses accrued in the period. Moreover, a firm may use provisions for income-smoothing purposes. Investors are better able to identify the estimated liabilities among provisions if the firm gives a breakdown of provisions by type (e.g. restructuring, environmental costs, employee benefits). IAS require firms to provide this breakdown – and to show the *movement* in each type of provision over the year. With this information, investors can better gauge whether a firm is using provisions to smooth income (i.e. increasing provisions in fat years and reducing them in lean ones).

Since contingent liabilities are not recognised in the accounts, investors must consult the notes for information about them. IAS require firms to give summary information about each class of contingent liability. For example, a firm will disclose for each major lawsuit the plaintiff's name, the nature and amount of the claim, and a brief history of the legal proceedings to date. Disclosure of a contingent liability isn't required if management reckon the likelihood of the firm making future payments to settle it is remote.[24]

Disclosures and long-term debt

Investors want to know not just the amount of financial liabilities but also when they're due and how much it costs to service them. The information EU companies are required to disclose on debt payment is limited. Under the 4th Directive, larger firms must state in the notes the *amounts due and payable more than five years after the balance sheet date* (Art. 43(6)). Using this and other information in the accounts (e.g. current/non-current liabilities), an investor can determine the following:

- debt payable within one year of . . .
- debt payable between two and five years of . . .
- debt payable more than five years after . . .

the balance sheet date. Larger firms must also state the amount of debt which is secured and the nature and form of the security.

IAS are more demanding. Companies following international standards must disclose, by class of financial liability, information about the 'significant terms and conditions that may affect the amount, timing, and certainty of future cash flows'. As a result, such firms now provide key details of major debt issues such as face value, coupon rate, currency, maturity date and – where applicable – sinking fund payments or call dates. To help investors assess interest rate risk, IAS require firms to disclose the effective interest rate (for fixed-rate debt) and repricing dates (for floating-rate debt). And they must also disclose the fair values of their financial liabilities (and assets) by class, so long as it is practicable to do so.[25]

There is also a growing trend among quoted companies – in response to stock exchange regulations as well as accounting standards – to explain in the annual accounts the financial risks they are bearing and the steps they have taken to reduce or contain them. An example of such disclosure can be found in the published accounts of BG Group, a medium-sized integrated gas company with headquarters in London but most of its assets outside the UK. BG's net borrowings rose almost 50% in 2001 – from £360m to £538m – to finance a heavy capital expenditure programme but the group's debt-to-capital ratio was still a modest 13% at end-2001. In the notes to its 2001 accounts, BG discloses the types of its borrowings, their maturity profile and currency and interest rate composition, and summary information on all its financial instruments (e.g. the fair values of financial liabilities and assets, notional principal amounts of derivatives). Extracts from the relevant notes are set out in Exhibit 11.5.

Note 16 Borrowings

Amounts falling due	2001		2000	
	Within one year £m	After more than one year £m	Within one year £m	After more than one year £m
Other loans – commercial paper	12	–	118	–
– bonds	113	379	57	178
Bank loans and overdrafts	216	84	146	55
Bills of exchange payable	152	–	–	–
Gross borrowings	493	463	321	233

Note 17 Currency and interest rate composition of the Group's borrowings

The following tables analyse the currency and interest rate composition of the Group's gross borrowings of £956m (2000 £554m) and net borrowings of £538m (2000 £360m) before and after taking swaps into account. Net borrowings comprise gross borrowings less current asset investments and cash at bank and in hand.

Currency composition

	Gross borrowings				Net borrowings			
	% after taking swaps into account		% before taking swaps into account		% after taking swaps into account		% before taking swaps into account	
	2001	2000	**2001**	2000	**2001**	2000	**2001**	2000
Currency:								
Sterling	–	4	**37**	4	**(12)**	(30)	**(53)**	(30)
US dollars	**86**	88	**47**	79	**96**	126	**28**	111
Euros	–	–	**7**	11	–	(5)	**13**	13
Other	**14**	8	**9**	6	**16**	9	**6**	6

Interest rate composition

	Gross borrowings				Net borrowings			
	% after taking swaps into account		% before taking swaps into account		% after taking swaps into account		% before taking swaps into account	
	2001	2000	**2001**	2000	**2001**	2000	**2001**	2000
Basis:								
Fixed rate	**65**	84	**83**	86	**41**	77	**74**	79
Floating rate	**35**	16	**17**	14	**59**	23	**26**	21

The effective interest rates as at 31 December 2001 were between 2% and 19% (2000 5% and 17%). The interest rates on those Group borrowings which are at floating rates are determined mainly by the prevailing LIBOR (London Interbank Offered Rate) for the relevant currency and maturity at the time of determination plus or minus an agreed margin.

Currency and interest rate composition (after the effect of swaps)

	Fixed rate weighted average period years	Fixed rate weighted average interest rate %	Fixed borrowings £m	Floating borrowings £m	**2001 Total £m**	2000 Total £m
Currency:						
Sterling	–	–	–	–	**–**	21
US dollars	1.1	6.1	609	209	**818**	490
Brazilian reals	–	–	–	126	**126**	30
Indian rupees	1.2	12.3	12	–	**12**	13
Gross borrowings			621	335	**956**	554

For the purposes of the above tables, debt with a maturity within one year, such as commercial paper, bills of exchange and other money market borrowings, has been treated as fixed rate. Borrowings falling due after more than one year of £463m (2000 £233m) (after currency and interest rate swaps) can be analysed as fixed rate 47% (2000 69%) and floating interest rate 53% (2000 31%).

(*Source*: BG Group, *Annual Report and Accounts 2001*. Reproduced by permission of BG Group plc.)

BG uses derivative instruments such as swap agreements and forward exchange contracts to hedge its exposure to interest rate and exchange rate movements. From the disclosures in Exhibit 11.5, it is evident that BG swapped fixed-rate for floating-rate debt and sterling for US dollar debt in 2001. Management state in the operating and financial review that the group has large dollar-denominated assets and conducts much of its business in that currency. Dollar debt – and the associated payments – act as a natural hedge for these dollar inflows. As a UK company, BG can secure better terms raising debt in its home currency and then swapping the sterling debt into dollars. The swap into floating-rate debt suggests management expected interest rates to fall.

BG makes other helpful debt-related disclosures in the 2001 report not shown in Exhibit 11.5. Three stand out. First, BG reveals the credit ratings given by the main credit rating agencies – Moody's, Standard & Poor's and Fitch – to its borrowing entities. These ratings influence the interest rate a company pays on its debt. Investors find a change in rating especially informative: it signals an improvement or deterioration in the company's debt-servicing ability and has implications for profit and cash flow forecasts. Second, BG reports its share of the net borrowings of joint ventures with other companies. This is a large figure (around £600m) and, given that BG accounts for investments in these ventures on a *net* basis, is not included in its consolidated debt. Investors are concerned about the level of joint-venture debt: the larger such debt, the greater is a company's effective leverage. (In BG's case, the risk is less since the debt is non-recourse.) Third, BG discloses the amounts of its unutilised borrowing facilities. They are extensive (around US$3 billion). Investors view untapped lines of credit as an indicator of the company's debt capacity – and of its ability to move quickly if new investment opportunities arise.

Disclosure of lease commitments

Under international rules, companies are required to indicate the fixed assets under lease and the related lease liabilities. In addition, they have to show the minimum payments they're committed to make under both long-term finance and non-cancellable operating leases (a) within one year; (b) between one and five years; and (c) more than five years of the balance sheet date.[26] Companies following US GAAP provide payment data *by year* for the five years following the balance sheet date for all non-cancellable leases.

Information about future lease payments is of double benefit to investors. It helps them improve their forecasts of a company's cash flows. Moreover, they can estimate, on an approximate basis, the present value of a firm's (non-cancellable) *operating* lease commitments and incorporate the capitalised amount in their leverage calculations.

Financial leverage

A firm must give up assets, usually cash, to settle its liabilities. As a result, the more liabilities a company has relative to its assets (i.e. the greater its **financial leverage** or **gearing**), the more risky it's perceived to be. There's then a greater chance that the company will be *insolvent,* that is, unable to pay its debts when they are due. If the company is liquidated, shareholders may fail to recover their investment.

Analysts employ various measures to assess a firm's financial risk. We look first at *asset-based* ratios and then at ratios based on *earnings*. Companies may account for the same type of liability in different ways. Thus financial statement users must be able to make adjustments to the numbers in the accounts to render the liability figures more comparable.

Asset-based debt ratios

The most widely used balance sheet measure of leverage is the **debt–equity ratio**. We defined it in Chapter 2 as the ratio of net debt to group equity:

$$\text{Debt–equity ratio} = \frac{\text{Net debt}}{\text{Group equity}}$$

'Net debt' is short- and long-term interest-bearing liabilities less liquid assets (e.g. cash and marketable securities) surplus to operating requirements. (In practice, analysts deduct all liquid assets since it's difficult to separate out the non-operating portion.) It's quite common for companies to borrow and carry large liquid assets at the same time. For example, a firm may borrow in a foreign currency to hedge its foreign assets but maintain large cash balances – say, to finance corporate acquisitions – in its domestic currency. 'Group equity' is the sum of shareholders' equity (i.e. the equity of *parent company* shareholders) and minority interests (the equity of *outside shareholders* in subsidiary companies).

Investors calculate balance sheet leverage in other ways. A popular ratio is the **debt-to-capital ratio**:

$$\text{Debt-to-capital ratio} = \frac{\text{Net debt}}{\text{Net debt} + \text{Group equity}}$$

'Capital' as defined here is equal to net operating assets (operating assets less operating liabilities).[27] So the ratio tells us what proportion of the firm's net operating assets is financed with debt.

A broader gauge of balance sheet leverage is the **liabilities–assets ratio**. In this case, total operating and financial liabilities are divided by total assets. This is a useful measure of leverage where a company treats operating liabilities as a source of finance (e.g. suppliers' credits in the case of retailers and customer deposits in the case of banks).

Balance sheet leverage ratios may be inverted. In this form, they indicate the degree of protection a firm's assets afford its creditors. Consider the inverse of the liabilities–assets ratio: total assets/total liabilities. The creditor can see from this by how much assets can decline from their present level before liabilities are 'uncovered' by assets. The greater the cover, the greater is the 'margin of safety' for creditors.

Industry conditions affect the margin of safety creditors seek. Companies in industries with relatively stable cash flows – because of a low income elasticity of demand for their products (food retailing) or because of regulation (electric utilities) – can carry relatively high debt ratios without alarming creditors.

Traditionally, investors have calculated balance sheet leverage using book values of debt and equity. Many financial analysts argue that this understates a firm's debt capacity – especially if the firm is in a knowledge-based industry – since key resources are not recognised as (intangible) assets on its balance sheet. They prefer using market values when calculating debt ratios. One version is the **debt-to-capitalisation ratio**:

$$\text{Debt-to-capitalisation ratio} = \frac{\text{Net debt (at market value)}}{\text{Shareholders' equity (at MV)} + \text{Minority interests (at MV)}}$$

The market value of a firm's equity is the product of the current price of its ordinary (common) shares and the number of shares outstanding. If the market (or fair) value of debt or minority interests is not known, analysts use book value instead.

The debt-to-capitalisation ratio has yet to find favour with creditors. Leverage calculations in loan covenants still tend to be expressed in book value terms. One reason may be that when a firm gets into financial difficulties, its market value – and thus the value of its intangibles – shrinks rapidly. If the firm is liquidated, it is its tangible and tradeable assets which provide most of the cash to settle creditors' claims.

A note of warning before you compare debt ratios across firms and over time. Check the way assets and liabilities are calculated in company accounts. Companies may define liabilities (or assets) differently. We have already seen how provisions may inflate the reported liabilities of some European companies. Companies may also have different recognition and measurement policies, too. Adjusting company financial statements for national accounting differences reveals surprising variation in cross-border financial leverage, as Box 11.1 shows. The reasons for the variation in leverage are not well understood yet.

Earnings-based debt ratios

Healthy companies service their debt from earnings rather than asset disposals. Investors therefore check to see whether and by how much a company's operating earnings cover its financial fixed charges. The ratio they commonly use is the **interest cover**. It's also known as the **times interest earned ratio**. In its basic form it shows earnings (pre-interest and pre-tax) expressed as a multiple of interest expense.

$$\text{Interest cover} = \frac{\text{Net profit} + \text{Income tax expense} + \text{Interest expense}}{\text{Interest expense}}$$

'Interest expense' can be a net figure, i.e. net of interest income. It's customary to calculate interest expense in this way where a company carries large balances of cash and other interest-bearing financial assets.

A firm operating at break-even (i.e. making zero pre-tax profit) has an interest cover of 1: it makes profits just sufficient to meet interest charges. Loan agreements often set a minimum cover (as well as a maximum debt–equity ratio). Healthy companies usually have an interest cover of at least 2.

To make valid comparisons of interest cover across firms and over time, earnings and interest expense must be calculated consistently. In addition to general adjustments to earnings to eliminate differences in accounting policies (on depreciation, inventory costing, etc.), investors often make two specific adjustments. These are designed to broaden the ratio to cover all (financial) fixed charges. First, they estimate the interest element in lease and other rental payments and add it to both numerator and denominator. In addition, they include in the denominator interest charges that have been capitalised in the year. (As a capitalised cost, it is not charged against earnings and thus the numerator, which represents adjusted earnings, is not affected.)

The resulting **fixed charge coverage ratio** is calculated as follows:

$$\text{Fixed charge coverage ratio} = \frac{\substack{\text{Net} \\ \text{profit}} + \substack{\text{Income} \\ \text{tax expense}} + \substack{\text{Interest} \\ \text{expense}} + \substack{\text{Interest portion} \\ \text{of rental costs}}}{\substack{\text{Interest expense} + \text{Capitalised interest} \\ + \text{Interest portion of rental costs}}}$$

Notice that we've moved away from a pure earnings-based ratio. The denominator of the fixed charge coverage ratio is, in essence, the interest *paid* in the year. Some investors go further and define the coverage ratio solely in cash-flow terms. We look at the use of cash-flow-based ratios to assess financial risk in a later chapter.

Concealed debt: warning signals

Companies with high reported leverage may try to conceal the extent of their indebtedness. We saw earlier in the chapter how firms do this. They issue quasi-equity (debt masquerading as equity). They 'sell' assets with recourse. They borrow through unconsolidated subsidiaries. And they lease fixed assets long-term using operating leases.

How can debt disguised in these ways be unmasked? The simple answer is: check a firm's accounts, especially the notes, carefully. We give some examples below.

● *Issue of quasi-equity.* Check the balance sheet. Are there any preference shares – or other shares with debt characteristics – outstanding? If so, find out from the notes what the repayment terms are. Redeemable preference shares, where redemption is not under the control of the issuing firm, are effectively debt securities.

BOX 11.1

Financial leverage: international differences

Are there international differences in corporate financial leverage, and if so, why? Economists have long believed that leverage is higher in countries with a large banking sector (e.g. France, Germany, Japan) and lower in countries with large stock markets (e.g. Canada, UK, USA). The evidence doesn't support this, however. Instead, the data suggest that other factors are at play.

Rajan and Zingales calculated various balance sheet and income statement leverage ratios for firms in seven large countries in 1991.[28] In their study, they compute the ratios twice – first, using reported numbers (unadjusted ratios) and then after making adjustments for certain key accounting differences across countries (adjusted ratios). The adjustments to shareholders' equity are:

1 Add deferred income taxes. In 1991 these were mostly long-term undiscounted liabilities, which analysts judged to be small in present value terms.
2 Deduct intangibles (including goodwill). Capitalisation criteria for R&D differed across countries. Moreover, treatment of goodwill differed: UK companies wrote it off against reserves while North American and Japanese companies capitalised it.
3 Add other provisions. In countries with a Continental European accounting tradition, these consisted largely of accrued costs in 1991.

Rajan and Zingales also use net rather than gross debt in the adjusted ratio calculations. The chart below shows the unadjusted and adjusted versions of one of Rajan and Zingales' ratios – average debt to capital (at book values) – for all non-financial firms in G7 countries that published consolidated accounts in 1991.

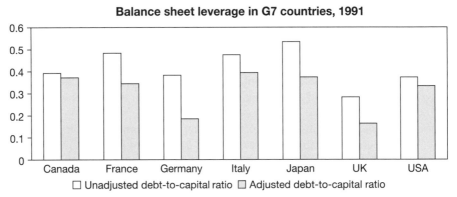

Balance sheet leverage in G7 countries, 1991

□ Unadjusted debt-to-capital ratio □ Adjusted debt-to-capital ratio

The adjustments reduce leverage in all seven countries, in four cases significantly (France Germany, Japan, UK). However, after adjustment, the ratio is similar in five of the seven countries (0.33–0.39). Only in Germany (a bank-oriented country) and the UK (a stock market-oriented country) is it much lower (0.18 and 0.16 respectively). Why? Rajan and Zingales suggest institutional differences – such as the tax code, bankruptcy law and restrictions on hostile takeovers – are responsible for cross-country differences in leverage. Differences in creditor rights are especially significant. Bankruptcy law is more creditor-friendly in Germany and the UK than in the other five countries. For example, only Germany and the UK allow secured creditors to try to collect their debts (by, for example, seizing their collateral) *after* the company files for bankruptcy. Moreover, in the UK, managers of the debtor company are automatically replaced at the time of liquidation. These important creditor rights effectively raise the cost of debt for the company's insiders (i.e. managers and controlling shareholders) and help explain why financial leverage is lower in Germany and the UK.[29]

- *Unconsolidated debt.* Check the financial fixed assets (or 'investments') note, together with the listing of the firm's subsidiaries and associates. Does the firm have any large investments in associated companies or joint ventures? More unusually, does it have any significant unconsolidated subsidiaries? It should provide in the notes to the accounts a summary balance sheet and income statement for each major affiliate or joint venture.
- *Leased assets.* Consult the 'commitments' note. If the firm has entered into lease contracts, whether of a finance or of an operating nature, it is committed to making lease payments in future years and these should be disclosed, if material.

This is not a complete list. Debt can be disguised in other ways. For example, a firm may enter into a long-term purchase agreement with a supplier in which the agreement contains a 'take-or-pay' clause. It may guarantee the debt of a third party (e.g. a key supplier). Long-term purchase agreements are commitments; guarantees are contingent liabilities. Thus the commitments and contingencies notes should be studied carefully. The financial effects of these and other hidden liabilities can then be estimated and incorporated into leverage ratios.

Summary

We surveyed general issues concerning liabilities in section 1 of the chapter. Liabilities come in many forms but the accounting for them has a common framework. In all cases, the debtor has an obligation to another, as a result of a past transaction, and expects to sacrifice resources (cash, goods or services) in the future to settle it. The debtor recognises the obligation, whether known or estimated, on the face of the balance sheet so long as the sacrifice is both probable and measurable. Liabilities like assets are usually valued at historical cost, that is the cost – in cash, goods or services – of settling the liability at the time it was incurred.

The above framework is not always honoured. Firms include items in the liabilities section of the balance sheet that aren't present obligations (e.g. certain accrued costs) and exclude items which are (e.g. liabilities disguised as equity or asset sales). Moreover, many people question the framework. At present, financial commitments (other than certain lease commitments) are not considered accounting liabilities. Changes in the market value of a liability are not usually recognised.

We explored in section 2 of the chapter the accounting problems that arise when firms raise long-term debt capital. The cash a firm issuing debt securities receives at the time of issuance may be less than the amount it must repay on maturity. This initial discount increases the lifetime cost of the debt. Rather than recognising it in one period, the firm amortises it – by the SL or interest method – over the debt term through a higher interest charge. We showed how these ideas can be applied to other types of debt and debt-related costs.

Firms often choose to lease rather than buy fixed assets. We discussed lessee accounting in section 3 of the chapter (and lessor accounting in the appendix). Where the lessee is considered the economic owner of the asset under lease, the transaction is accounted for as an instalment purchase. The lessee recognises a fixed asset and a long-term liability when the lease contract is signed. It amortises the asset over the lease term and recognises as interest expense the cost of the implicit loan.

Accounting for long-term debt and leases in Europe is in a state of flux. National rules differ and international standards are not yet widely observed. Under pressure from investors, quoted firms are disclosing more information, in particular, the market values of their financial liabilities and the interest rate, currency and other risks associated with them. We summarised IAS disclosure requirements in section 4 of the chapter. To assess a firm's ability to service its debts, investors supplement asset-based leverage ratios with income-based ones. We described both types of ratio in section 4 of the chapter and pointed out their strengths and weaknesses.

APPENDIX 11.1   Leasing–lessor accounting

Leasing is a profitable activity for the *owner* as well as the user of an asset. For the manufacturer, it can help promote sales. For example, a long-term lease can be marketed as a cheaper alternative to outright purchase. Financial institutions act as lessors, too. They buy assets from the manufacturer and then lease them on to users. (If the lessor-bank borrows funds to finance the purchase of the asset, the lease is known as a **leveraged lease**.) Leasing is often preferable to the alternative, a loan to the user to finance the asset's purchase. First, the lessor-bank has greater security for its loan: it, not the user, owns title to the asset. Second, it can take advantage of the tax benefits (tax depreciation and credits) available to owners and reduce its tax bill.

The distinction between operating and finance leases we identified in the chapter has accounting implications for lessors, too. In the case of an operating lease, the asset remains on the lessor's books. It records each period the rental income earned and the depreciation of the asset. With a finance (or capital) lease, however, the lessor disposes of the asset and records a lease receivable, the counterpart to the lease liability recognised by the lessee.

If the lessor is a manufacturer or distributor, the finance lease is known as a **sales-type lease**. The transfer is viewed as a sale and the lessor recognises, at the time of the contract, a profit (or loss) based on the difference between the 'sale' price (fair value) of the asset and its cost.

If the lessor is a financial institution, the finance lease is known as a **direct financing lease**. No profit or loss arises on the transfer of the asset to the lessee, because its fair value is equivalent to its cost to the lessor-bank. It is the loan element in the lease transaction which provides the lessor-bank with a return (in the form of interest) on its investment.

Accounting for sales-type leases

We look first at the accounting for sales-type leases. You'll recall from our discussion of lessee accounting that Jupiter, a bus company, leases a bus from Offenbach, the manufacturer. Here are the main details of the bus and the lease:

- The fair value of the bus at the start of the lease is 309,250. The cost of manufacture is 225,000. The bus has a three-year life and its expected residual value is zero. Offenbach depreciates fixed assets on a straight-line basis.
- The lease has a three-year term. Jupiter must make a payment of 120,000 to Offenbach at the end of each year. The implicit interest rate in the lease is 8%.

Offenbach accounts for the lease in the same way as an instalment sale. At the start of the lease, it recognises revenue from the 'sale' of the bus and records an increase in its receivables. At the same time, it recognises the cost of the sale and records a reduction in its inventory. The journal entries are summarised below:

'Sale' of bus on 1/1/year 1		
Dr. Lease payments receivable (A+)	309,250	
Cr. Sales revenue (OE+)		309,250
Dr. Cost of sales (OE–)	225,000	
Cr. Finished goods inventory (A–)		225,000

For balance sheet classification purposes, the lease payments receivable should be split into its current (95,260) and long-term (213,990) components.[30]

Offenbach recognises profit on the sale of 84,250 on 1 January year 1. It also earns interest on the outstanding lease receivable over the term of the lease contract. *A lessor uses the interest method to calculate interest income. It applies the interest rate implicit in the lease to the start-of-period receivable.* Using this method, Offenbach recognises interest income of 24,740 in year 1 (309,250 × 8%). The entries Offenbach makes to record the receipt of the year 1 lease payment and to recognise interest earned that year are summarised below:[31]

Cash receipt & interest earned in year 1		
Dr. Cash (A+)	120,000	
Cr. Lease payments receivable (A–)		95,260
Cr. Interest income (OE+)		24,740

With each lease payment received, the receivable outstanding falls and so, too, does the interest Offenbach earns in the following period. Exhibit 11.6 shows the effect of the Jupiter sales-type lease on Offenbach's accounts in years 1 to 3.

At the end of year 3, all instalments have been paid and the balance in 'Lease payments receivable' is zero. As a result of the lease transaction, Offenbach's assets and retained profits are 135,000 higher at the end of the three years.

Exhibit 11.6 **Offenbach Company (lessor): financial statement impact of sales-type lease**

		Assets			Equities
		Lease payments			*Profit*
	Inventory	*receivable*	*Cash*		*for year*
'Sale' of bus on 1/1/year 1		+309,250		=	+309,250 *(Sales revenue)*
	–225,000			=	–225,000 *(Cost of sales)*
Lease payment received, yr 1		–95,260	+120,000	=	+24,740 *(Interest income)*
Balance, end 1	⋮	213,990	⋮		⋮
Lease payment received, yr 2		–102,881	+120,000	=	+17,119
Balance, end 2	⋮	111,109	⋮		⋮
Lease payment received, yr 3		–111,109	+120,000	=	+8,891
Balance, end 3		0			
Effect of lease on accounts, years 1–3	–225,000		+360,000	=	+135,000

Calculation of interest income and end-year receivable

Year	(1) Lease payments receivable at 1/1	(2) Lease payment at 31/12	(3) Interest income 8% × (1)	(4) Reduction in receivable (2) – (3)	(5) End-year receivable (1) – (4)
1	309,250	120,000	24,740	95,260	213,990
2	213,990	120,000	17,119	102,881	111,109
3	111,109	120,000	8,891*	111,109	0

* Rounded.

Financial statement impact

Classifying a lease as a sales-type (finance) lease rather than an operating lease usually increases the lessor's reported income in the first year of the lease term. The reason is that the lessor reports a profit on the sale of the asset at the start of the lease. Such *front-loading* of income makes finance lease treatment popular among lessors. (This assumes there are no adverse tax consequences. In some countries, tax rules are kind to lessors. Income tax is levied only when lease payments are received, irrespective of whether the lease is accounted for as an operating or a finance lease.)

Our Offenbach example illustrates the potential size of the income benefit of a sales-type lease in the first year. Exhibit 11.7 contrasts the impact of the Jupiter lease on Offenbach's income statement in years 1 to 3, assuming the lease is treated as an operating lease (column A) and as a sales-type lease (column B).

If the lease is an operating one (column A), Offenbach reports income (before tax) of 45,000 a year. This comprises rental revenue from the bus (120,000 a year) less depreciation which, assuming a manufacturing cost of 225,000, a three-year life and SL depreciation, amounts to 75,000 a year. If the lease is a sales-type lease (column B), Offenbach reports income (before tax) of almost 109,000 in year 1 and only 17,000 and 9,000 in years 2 and 3 respectively. Year 1 income is 80% of the three-year total of 135,000. Note that the difference in accounting treatment affects the *timing* of income from the lease but not its total amount.

The balance sheet impact of a sales-type lease is less dramatic. The lessor simply reports the exchange of one asset (inventory or property) for another (receivable). In addition, its shareholders' equity changes by the amount of profit or loss recognised on the sale. This in turn will affect its debt–equity ratio but the effect on reported leverage is likely to be minor compared

Exhibit 11.7 Offenbach Company (lessor): income statement impact of leased asset, assuming lease is: (A) operating lease; (B) sales-type lease

(A) *Operating lease*		(B) *Sales-type lease*	
Year 1		*Year 1*	
Rental revenue	120,000*	Profit on sale	84,250
– Depreciation	–75,000**	Interest income	24,740
Income (net)	45,000	Income	108,990
Year 2		*Year 2*	
Rental revenue }		Interest income	17,119
– Depreciation }	45,000		
Year 3		*Year 3*	
Rental revenue }		Interest income	8,891
– Depreciation }	45,000		
Total income (net)	135,000	Total income	135,000

* Journal entry:
  Dr. Cash (A+)   120,000
    Cr. Rental revenue (OE+)   120,000

** Calculation assumes:
  Cost of manufacture to Offenbach: 225,000
  Depreciation: SL method; 3 year life; zero residual value.

to the effect on profitability. Note that the lessor's pre-tax cash flow is identical under both accounting treatments.

Accounting for direct financing leases

If a bank acquires the bus from Offenbach (at fair value) and then leases it to Jupiter, the lease, if capitalised, is a direct financing lease. In effect, the bank provides a loan to Jupiter for the asset's purchase. The bank's accounting reflects this. It records a loan (lease receivable) on which it earns interest. (Offenbach recognises profit on the sale of the bus to the bank.)

Lease capitalisation is likely to lead to earlier recognition of income by the bank but the effect is less marked than with a sales-type lease. Consider the Jupiter lease. Assuming the bank calculates interest income as a constant percentage of the start-of-period receivable (as illustrated in Exhibit 11.7), it reports interest income of 24,740 in year 1 under a direct financing lease against rental revenue, net of depreciation, of 16,917 in the same year under an operating lease. (Rent revenue is still 120,000 but depreciation (of 103,083) is based on the bus's fair value of 309,250.) Note that banks in some countries must structure leases of assets to third parties as finance leases because they are prohibited from carrying tangible fixed assets – other than those for their own use – on the balance sheet.

Lessor accounting under IAS

International accounting standards require lessors and lessees to apply the same tests. A lease is classified as a finance lease by the lessor only if 'substantially all the risks and rewards incident to ownership' are transferred to the lessee. In practice, this means that not only must the lease meet at least one of the capitalisation conditions given in section 3 of the chapter but also, in the case of sales-type leases, the lessor should apply the usual revenue recognition criteria. Thus the lessor should not recognise revenue and, by extension, profit on the sale if, for example, doubts exist about whether the lessee can make the lease payments when they are due. In this case, it should classify the lease as an operating one and recognise revenue when cash is received.

Lessors and lessees define key terms such as lease payment and lease term in the same way, too. However, the lessor's receivable may be different from the lessee's payable. First, lessor and lessee may use different discount rates. Recall that the lessee must use its incremental borrowing rate if it does not know the rate used by the lessor to set lease payments (the implicit interest rate). Second, the lessor includes in its receivable (and sales revenue) calculation any **unguaranteed residual value**, that is, cash it expects to receive on disposing of the asset at the end of its life but which has not been underwritten by the lessee.

A manufacturer or distributor wishing to front-load its reported income is tempted to structure its leases so that they are *in form* sales-type leases. In the past, some lessors, in the USA and more recently in the UK, have abused the rules in this way. One tell-tale sign of lease misclassification is a rapid growth of a lessor's sales and profits without a concomitant increase in its cash flow. The increase in sales is matched by an increase in the lessor's receivables. By contrast, lessors in countries with a uniform reporting tradition will choose, if they can, to structure their leases as operating leases. In this way, they defer tax payments as well as income.

One final point. Although lessor and lessee usually classify a lease symmetrically for accounting purposes, there is no requirement for them to do so. Indeed, some investment banks, in promotional material, offer to structure a lease in such a way that it is a finance lease for the manufacturer-lessor and an (off-balance-sheet) operating lease for the customer-lessee. The consequence is that the asset under lease disappears from both the lessor's and the lessee's balance sheet!

Problem assignments

P11.1 The nature of accounting liabilities

In some cases, it is not clear whether a company has an accounting liability and, if it has, how it should be measured. Consider the following (independent) situations.

(1) Self-insurance

A retail chain has traditionally purchased insurance cover from an insurance company to meet claims, by customers and staff, for personal injury in company stores. In view of the size of the annual premiums paid and the absence of claims in recent years, the company is considering insuring itself. The chief executive officer (CEO) has suggested the company set up a provision for injury claims along the following lines:

Dr. Insurance expense (OE–)	xx	
Cr. Provision for injury claims (L+)		xx

When claims are submitted and accepted, the company would then charge the amount against the provision (Dr. Provision; Cr. Cash).

Required

The controller has doubts about whether the above accounting treatment is acceptable. Advise her.

(2) Post-employment compensation

The date is end-March x5. As a result of a boardroom clash, the board of directors of a pharmaceutical company dismissed the CEO earlier in the month. Under the terms of his contract, the ex-CEO is entitled to receive his annual salary of 900,000 until June x8. However, the contract also states that the payments may cease – at the company's option – if he accepts employment from another pharmaceutical company during this period. The ex-CEO is well-regarded in the industry. Under his leadership, the company's share price has doubled in the last three years.

The company's financial year runs to 30 June. Therefore, the total salary payments the ex-CEO might receive, subsequent to his dismissal, could be 3 million:

Financial year x4/x5	300,000	(1/3 × 900,000)
x5/x6	900,000	
x6/x7	900,000	
x7/x8	900,000	

The controller believes the company has a liability and expense of 3 million in March x5. The board, however, would prefer not to record a liability of that amount then. They feel the company should recognise an expense (of 75,000) each month only when a salary payment is made.

Required

How should the company account for the ex-CEO's post-employment compensation?

(3) Lawsuit

In x2 a law firm launches legal action against Sonia, a manufacturer of mobile phones, seeking substantial damages on behalf of customers who, it's claimed, have developed brain tumours as a result of radiation emitted by the company's phones. Sonia contests the claim. Lawyers acting for the company advise management that, because scientists have not yet established a link between mobile phone use and incidence of brain tumours, the company will probably win the case.

Required

(a) How should Sonia report the lawsuit in its x2 accounts? (Assume the size of the plaintiffs' claim is material to its accounts.)

(b) Consider the following scenario. The year is x3 and the case is still in progress. Damaging new scientific evidence has emerged. Sonia's lawyers put the probability of the company winning the case at only 40%. They recommend the company seek an out-of-court settlement. However, management are fearful that a settlement could encourage a rash of lawsuits from other customers and this would have severe financial consequences for the firm and its shareholders. They decide to continue contesting the suit. How should Sonia report the lawsuit in its x3 accounts?

P11.2   The nature of accounting liabilities II

Altran Technologies is a fast-growing French R&D consulting firm. In x1 its revenues soared to €1.3 billion, a 40% increase on the x0 figure, and it maintained its operating profit margin ratio at a healthy 18%. However, its share price fell 65% during the second quarter of x2 as doubts emerged about its accounting policies. Some analysts accuse the company of understating its liabilities, a charge which management vigorously deny.

The main area of controversy surrounds Altran's treatment of acquisitions. The company has grown rapidly by acquiring smaller consultancies in other countries – it bought 28 businesses in x1 alone – in order to increase market share. In most cases it pays for the acquired business with cash: part is paid when the contract is signed and part is deferred and linked to the increase in the acquisition's annual earnings over the following five years. The total price paid is usually twice the initial payment. Altran does not recognise the 'earn-out payments' as a liability until the acquired company has generated the increase in profits. 'It's impossible to quantify these earn-out payments in advance, so they shouldn't be held as debts,' argues Michel Friedlander, the company's chief executive.

Altran paid €78 million in earn-out payments in x1. Analysts claim the company's end-x1 indebtedness including estimated earn-out payments was €956 million rather than the €337 million reported in the x1 balance sheet. This gives a debt–equity ratio of over 240% which puts the company's bonds in the 'junk' category, according to analysts.

Required

How should Altran account for future estimated earn-out payments at the balance sheet date, in your view? Give the reason(s) for your decision.

P11.3   Frequent-flier miles: accounting issues

Three Englishmen, George, Harris and J., are flying to Canada on a Kingston Airlines flight to enjoy a boating holiday in Northern Ontario. They're travelling for free, using the frequent-flier miles they've accumulated (at the rate of one mile earned for each mile flown) with the airline. Somewhere over the Atlantic Ocean, the conversation turns to frequent-flier programmes and J., being a curious fellow, wonders how Kingston accounts for the miles he and other programme members have earned.

George: It's simple: they record a liability. The liability is the product of (1) the free miles earned and (2) their cost. I expect they measure the cost on an 'opportunity cost' basis. For example, in our case the opportunity cost is the revenue Kingston forgoes from a fare-paying customer wishing to fly from London to Toronto.

J.: Surely not the *full* fare. After all, look around you. The plane is half-empty. The airline isn't turning away full-fare customers to allow us to fly. It would make more sense to measure the liability on an incremental cost basis – the additional costs the airline incurs when a frequent flier occupies one of those empty seats.

Harris: You're both forgetting something. Not all miles earned are redeemed. I read the other day that at the end of 2001 frequent fliers had accumulated almost 8 trillion unused miles. So Kingston needs to apply a probability factor – the probability of the frequent flier redeeming the miles earned – to J.'s cost figure. This makes the actual liability so small the airline can forget about it for all practical purposes.

George: But miles don't expire – unless they're not used within three years of being earned. Airlines can't ignore those unredeemed miles you mention. It was easy to get free seats on this flight but you can't get them on the popular routes.

J.: That's Harris's point, isn't it? The reason there are so many unredeemed miles is that frequent fliers can't get the flights they want. In fact, once capacity starts filling up on a particular route, the airline usually restricts the number of free seats available. But I don't agree the liability can be ignored. The 8 trillion figure is an industry total. Some airlines may have a high redemption rate.

Harris: Perhaps – but that doesn't mean they have a legal liability. Look at the small print of Kingston's frequent-flier programme. 'The accumulation of mileage credits does not entitle members to any vested rights. . . . In accumulating mileage, members may not rely on the continued availability of any award.' That's pretty clear, I reckon. Kingston can cancel its programme tomorrow and the miles we've earned but not used are worthless. Where is Kingston's 'obligation to transfer resources to a third party' then? I wouldn't be surprised if the airline accounts for the cost of air miles as and when they're used rather than accrue a liability.

Required

How do you think an airline like Kingston should account for frequent-flier miles and other travel awards? Does the company have a liability as the awards are earned and, if so, how should it measure it?

P11.4   Bonds: terminology and basic accounting

On 1 January x3, Ajax Steel Company issues, at a price of 101, €150 million of 6% bonds due 31 December x7. Interest is payable annually. Ajax Steel values the bonds in the balance sheet at amortised cost and uses the straight-line method to amortise any initial discount or premium. The company's financial year ends on 31 December.

Required

(a) What is: (i)   the term of the bonds?
  (ii) the coupon rate?
  (iii) the amount Ajax Steel must pay bondholders when the bonds mature?

(b) Show the effect on Ajax Steel's accounts of:
  (i)   the issuance of the bonds (ignore issuance costs);
  (ii) the recognition of interest expense in x3 and the payment of interest on 31 December x3.
  Use journal entries or the balance sheet equation.

(c) When Ajax Steel issued the 6% bonds, was the market interest rate on debt of similar risk and maturity higher or lower than the coupon rate on Ajax's bonds? Explain.

P11.5   Early retirement of bonds

Refer to P11.4. Ajax Steel issued €150 million of 6% bonds on 1 January x3 at a price of 101. Two years later, on 1 January x5, Ajax decides to retire the bonds. The company has a large cash balance and management decide to use part of it to reduce the company's debt. At this time, the market interest rate is 7.15% and Ajax's 6% bonds trade at a price of 97.

Required

(a) What is the market value of Ajax's 6% bonds on 1 January x5?

(b) Assume Ajax Steel is able to buy back all the bonds at their market value on that day. Show the effect of the repurchase on the company's accounts. Use journal entries or the balance sheet equation. Ignore transaction costs.

Check figure:
(b) Carrying amount   €150.9 million

P11.6   Interest method of amortisation

On 1 January x2, Dorrit Company issues €5 million of 2.5% bonds, due 31 December x5. They are priced at 91.14 to yield 5% to maturity. Dorrit amortises any initial discount (or premium) by the interest method and reports the bonds on the balance sheet at amortised cost. The company's financial year ends on 31 December. Interest is payable annually.

Required

(a) How much cash does Dorrit receive from the sale of the bonds?

(b) What is the total lifetime cost of the bonds to Dorrit over the four years to 31 December x5?

(c) What is the interest expense Dorrit reports in its income statement for x2 and for x3 with respect to the bonds?

(d) What is the carrying amount of the bonds in Dorrit's balance sheet at the end of x2 and at the end of x3?

Check figure:
(c) Discount amortised in x2   €102,850

P11.7   Debt instruments: deriving information from published accounts

At end-2001, Roche, the Swiss pharmaceutical company, had total bonds payable of SFr14 billion out of total borrowings of SFr18 billion. Unusually, each of the bond issues bore a name – e.g. 'Sumo' yen exchangeable bonds, 'Bullet' Swiss franc bonds – and was packaged so as to appeal to a particular investor group, marketing innovations introduced by Roche's finance director, Henri Meier, in the 1990s.

The company discloses information about each of the outstanding bond issues in the notes to its 2001 accounts. Details of three, including their Swiss franc carrying values at end-2000 and end-2001, are given below. Roche uses the interest method to amortise the cost of the bonds.

	Effective interest rate	2001	2000
Swiss franc bonds			
'Rodeo' 1.75% due 2008, principal 1 billion Swiss francs	2.83%	933	923
US dollar bonds			
'Bull Spread' 3.5% due 2001, principal 1 billion US dollars	5.13%	–	1,610
Zero coupon US dollar exchangeable notes			
'LYONS V' due 2021, principal 2.051 billion US dollars	4.18%	1,544	–

Roche provides the following additional information about the 'Bull Spread' and 'LYONS V' bonds:

Repayment of 'Bull Spread' US dollar bonds
On the due date of 18 May 2001 the Group repaid the principal amount of 1 billion US dollars of the 3.5% US dollar bonds originally issued in 1991. The resulting cash outflow was 1,734 million Swiss francs.

Issue of 'LYONS V' US dollar notes exchangeable into non-voting equity securities
On 25 July 2001 the Group issued zero coupon US dollar exchangeable notes due 25 July 2021 with a principal amount of 2,051 million US dollars. The notes are exchangeable into non-voting equity securities, at any time prior to maturity.

Net proceeds from the issue were 980 million US dollars (1,689 million Swiss francs). These have been initially allocated as 3,535 million Swiss francs of debt, 1,978 million Swiss francs of unamortised discount, 86 million Swiss francs of equity (in respect of the conversion option embedded in the bonds) and 46 million Swiss francs of deferred tax liability.
(*Source*: Roche Group, *Annual Report and Accounts 2001*.)

According to the accounts, the exchange rate between the US dollar and Swiss franc was US$1 : SFr1.68 at end-2001 and US$1 : SFr1.64 at end-2000. The average exchange rate in 2001 was US$1 : SFr1.69.

Required

(a) What is the interest expense Roche incurs on the 'Rodeo' bonds in 2001? What is the interest payable on them that year? (Assume interest is payable annually.)

(b) What is the gain or loss, if any, that Roche recognises on the repayment of the 'Bull Spread' bonds? Note that gains and losses from exchange rate changes are recorded separately from gains and losses on (early) retirement of bonds.

(c) Estimate the interest expense – in Swiss francs or US dollars – that Roche incurs on the 'LYONS V' notes in 2001. Show how Roche derives the end-2001 carrying amount of SFr1,544 million.

(d) Roche has made several large issues of zero coupon exchangeable notes in recent years. Why do you think it has chosen to issue debt in this form?

P11.8 Accounting for lease by lessee

Dogberry Security Services wins a five-year contract in late x1 to provide routine police services to Messina's municipal government. Rather than buy all the equipment it needs, it decides to lease some of it. Polease, a vehicle dealer, offers to lease to Dogberry an armoured van for the transport of prisoners. The van has a fair value of 39,925 and is expected to yield economic benefits evenly over its five-year life. Under the terms of the proposed lease, Dogberry will pay Polease 10,000 at the end of each of the five years which indicates an implicit interest rate in the lease of 8% (39,925/10,000 = 3.9925 = PVA (8%, 5 payments)). At the end of the lease term, Dogberry will return the vehicle to Polease. There is no transfer-of-title clause or bargain purchase option in the lease contract.

Dogberry's management are concerned about the financial implications of Polease's offer. They ask you to determine the financial statement impact of the lease under two assumptions – that it's classified as (i) an operating lease and (ii) a finance lease. Dogberry plans to sign the lease contract on 1/1/x2. The company has a 31 December financial year-end.

Required

(a) What is the effect of the lease on Dogberry's accounts at the start of x2 when the contract is signed if the lease is:
  (i) an operating lease?
  (ii) a finance lease?

(b) How should Dogberry account for the lease in its x2 and x3 accounts (income statement and end-year balance sheet) if the lease is:
  (i) an operating lease?
  (ii) a finance lease?

(c) Is the lease an operating lease or a finance lease under IAS? Give reasons for your answer.

Check figure:
(b) (ii) Interest expense, x3 2,650

P11.9   Accounting for lease by lessor

Refer to P11.8. Consider the proposed lease of the van from the point of view of Polease, the lessor. The van cost Polease 32,000. Its estimated residual value at the end of the five years is zero. The company has a 31 December financial year-end.

Required

(a) What is the effect of the lease on Polease's accounts at the start of x2 when the contract is signed if the lease is:
(i)   an operating lease?
(ii) a sales-type lease?

(b) How should Polease account for the lease in its x2 and x3 accounts (income statement and end-year balance sheet) if the lease is:
(i)   an operating lease?
(ii) a sales-type lease?

(c) Assume now that Polease estimates the van – which Dogberry is to hand back at the end of the five-year lease term – will have a residual value of 4,000 then. The residual value is not guaranteed by either Dogberry or a third party. (The annual lease payment remains at 10,000. The van's initial fair value is still 39,925.)

Explain in general terms how this additional information alters your answers to (a) and (b) above? (You need not make any fresh calculations.)

P11.10   Debt, lease commitments, and financial statement analysis

The French group, LVMH, produces and distributes a range of branded luxury goods such as Louis Vuitton leather and luggage goods, Christian Dior perfumes, Moët & Chandon champagne and Hennessy cognac. It also owns a chain of airport duty-free shops through which it sells some of its own merchandise (as well as that of other companies). Its 2001 sales and pre-tax income were €12.2 and €0.7 billion respectively. Exhibit 11.8 contains a condensed end-2001 balance sheet for the group as well as details of its lease commitments taken from note 28 of its 2001 accounts.

Required

(a) In the financial review accompanying the 2001 accounts, management state that net debt increased from €7.4 billion at end-2000 to €8.3 billion a year later.
(i)   Using information from the condensed balance sheet in Exhibit 11.8, show how these numbers are derived.
(ii) What is the group's debt–equity ratio at the end of 2001?

(b) What is the lease liability LVMH reports on its 2001 balance sheet? (The liability is included in 'Long-term debt'.) In the note on tangible fixed assets, LVMH discloses that assets acquired or financed under capital leases amount to €249 million (at net book value) at end-2001. Why does this number differ from the lease liability LVMH reports on that date?

(c) Many analysts argue that minimum payments under non-cancellable operating leases and similar contracts are no different in substance than required payments under debt agreements.
(i)   If this reasoning were applied to LVMH's accounts, estimate by how much the group's end-2001 net debt would increase. (*Hint*: Assume that the group will make annual operating lease payments of €195 million for four years after 2006 and annual concession fees of €58 million in 2007 and 2008, all the payments are made at year-end and the rate used to discount them is 6%.)
(ii) Would capitalisation of operating lease and concession fee payments have a significant impact on the group's end-2001 debt–equity ratio?

Exhibit 11.8 LVMH Group: extracts from 2001 accounts

Condensed balance sheet at 31 December 2001

(in € billions)

	2001	2000		2001	2000
Fixed assets			**Shareholders' equity**		
Tangible	4.2	3.4	Capital and reserves	6.9	7.0
Intangible: Goodwill	3.5	3.8			
Brands and other	4.3	3.4	Minority interests	1.8	1.5
Financial	2.3	2.4			
Total	14.3	13.0	**Long-term liabilities**		
			Long-term debt (LTD)	5.7	3.8
Current assets			Provisions and other	1.4	1.3
Inventories	3.7	3.4	Total	7.1	5.1
Trade accounts receivable	1.5	1.6			
Prepaid expenses and other	1.9	1.9	**Current liabilities**		
Treasury shares*	1.0	1.3	Short-term debt and current		
Cash and short-term			portion of LTD	4.0	5.6
investments	1.4	2.0	Accounts payable and accrued		
Total	9.5	10.2	expenses	4.0	4.0
			Total	8.0	9.6
			Total liabilities and		
Total assets	23.8	23.2	**shareholders' equity**	23.8	23.2

* LVMH shares purchased and held by the company

Note 28   Lease commitments

At December 31, 2001, a total number of 1,501 stores were used by the group worldwide, particularly for Fashion and Leather Goods and Selective Retailing business groups.

In a large number of countries, rentals for these stores are contingent on payment of minimum amounts, especially when the leases include revenue-indexed rent clauses; this is particularly valid in cases where airport concession fees are paid. In addition, the leases may also include non-adjustable minimum terms. [. . .]

At December 31, 2001, the breakdown of future non-cancellable commitments arising from these arrangements is as follows:

In € millions	Operating leases	Concession fees	Capital leases
2002	287	278	99
2003	243	257	31
2004	226	185	11
2005	213	152	9
2006	187	53	9
2007 and subsequent years	781	116	33
Total minimum lease commitments	1,937	1,041	192
Less amounts representing interest	–	–	(14)
Present value of minimum lease commitments	1,937	1,041	178

(*Source*: LVMH Group, *Annual Accounts 2001*. Reproduced by permission of LVMH.)

Notes to Chapter 11

1 International Accounting Standards Board, *Framework for the Preparation and Presentation of Financial Statements*, para. 49. Note that this definition excludes balance sheet accounts which have credit balances but which are not part of shareholders' equity.

2 *Framework*, para. 60.

3 International Accounting Standards Board, *IAS 37: Provisions, Contingent Liabilities and Contingent Assets*. Contingent assets share the same features as contingent liabilities. In this case, it's the *resource* that is 'possible'. The resource is not recognised as an asset unless and until the firm can demonstrate that the future inflow of economic benefits is 'virtually certain' as well as measurable.

4 English terminology is confusing. Adjustments to asset values are also referred to as provisions (e.g. provision for bad debts, provision for inventory obsolescence).

5 An obligation for goods or services received but not yet invoiced by the supplier is also an estimated liability. This is usually described as an 'accrual' rather than a provision.

6 BMW Group, *Annual Report and Accounts 2001*, note 7. The other major reasons for the €4.5 billion increase in BMW's shareholders' equity under IAS are: capitalisation of development costs, absorption costing of inventory (in place of variable costing), and use of SL method of depreciation of plant and equipment (in place of accelerated methods).

7 *IAS 37*, paras 72, 80. By announcing the plan or starting to implement it, the company raises expectations among customers, employees, and suppliers that it will carry out the restructuring – hence the *constructive* nature of the liability.

8 International Accounting Standards Board, *IAS 32: Financial Instruments: Disclosure and Presentation*, para. 5.

9 International Accounting Standards Board, *IAS 18: Revenue*, para. 14.

10 International Accounting Standards Board, *IAS 39: Financial Instruments: Recognition and Measurement*, paras 35, 38.

11 International Accounting Standards Board, *IAS 27: Consolidated Financial Statements and Accounting for Investments in Subsidiaries*, paras 7, 12.

12 *IAS 37*, paras 36, 37. The arguments for the 'fair value' view are set out more fully in Foster, J.M. and Upton, W. (2001), The case for initially measuring liabilities at fair value, in *Understanding the Issues*, Vol. 2, Series 1, Stamford, CT: FASB.

13 For a fuller but non-technical discussion of the reasons for corporate borrowing, *see* Barclay, M.J. and Smith, C.W. (1999), The capital structure puzzle: another look at the evidence, *Journal of Applied Corporate Finance*, 12(1): 8–20.

14 Note that bonds may be issued between interest payment dates. In this case, the price the company pays includes accrued interest. A company issuing bonds at par records the issue as follows:

Dr. Cash (A+)	xx	
Cr. Bonds payable (L+)		xx
Cr. Accrued interest payable (L+)		xx

On the first interest payment date, bondholders receive a full period's interest *payment* but the company recognises interest *expense* only for the period from the issuance date to the interest payment date.

15 The interest method is also known as the 'actuarial method'.

16 A debtor *discharges* a liability by paying it. Under IAS, it isn't released from its obligation by paying a third party in place of the creditor, unless there's a *legal* release. ('In-substance defeasance' is not permitted under IAS.) A creditor may *cancel* a debt if the debtor is in financial difficulties and is unable to pay. Where one party guarantees the debt of another for a limited period, its liability *expires* when the guarantee does.

17 A gain or loss can arise on floating-rate debt if it is retired early. With such debt, the interest rate is reset at the start of each new interest period. If the market rate of interest changes between that date and the date the debt is retired, the market value and carrying amount will differ.

18 The revised pattern of cash flows over five years, if Lopakhin replaces the 6% bonds with 8% (three-year) bonds at the start of x3 is as follows (amounts in €000):

	Start	End				
	x1	x1	x2	x3	x4	x5
Interest payments	–	−240	−240	−303.56	−303.56	−303.56
Principal payments 6% bonds	+3,394		−3,794.5			
8% bonds			+3,794.5			−3,794.50
Total payments	+3,394	−240	−240	−303.56	−303.56	−4,098.06

The rate of return which equates the present value of the inflow at start x1 with the present value of the outflows of interest and principal at the end of each of the five years x1–x5 is 10%, the effective interest rate on the original 6% bonds.

19 A leased asset is 'amortised' rather than 'depreciated' since what is being used up is an intangible, the lessee's right to use a fixed asset. (In fact, Spanish companies must show assets under lease as *intangible assets*.)

20 Note that the carrying amount is equal to the present value of future lease payments, discounted at the implicit interest rate of 8%. Thus lease liabilities are measured in the same way as long-term debt carried at amortised cost.

21 International Accounting Standards Board, *IAS 17: Accounting for Leases*, para. 3.

22 *IAS 17*, para. 8. This is not a comprehensive list. The standard describes other situations where a lease should be classified as a finance lease. A common feature is that the risks and rewards associated with ownership are passed to the lessee.

23 International Accounting Standards Board, *IAS 1: Presentation of Financial Statements*, para. 63.

24 *IAS 37*, para. 86. The standard permits a company to avoid disclosure in the 'extremely rare' case that publishing the information could 'seriously prejudice' it in a dispute with other parties (para. 92).

25 *IAS 32*, paras 47, 56, 77. Where the company has a number of debt instruments, the standard recommends that it tabulates their maturities, grouping them into current (within one year of the balance sheet date), medium-term (between two and five years) and long-term (more than five years). Companies are also encouraged to indicate the sensitivity of their annual interest charges to a 1% change in market interest rates.

26 *IAS 17*, para. 23. IAS-based disclosure rules for long-term debt apply equally to finance leases since a lease liability is a financial liability.

27 The balance sheet equation can be presented as follows:

Operating assets + Financial assets = Operating liabilities + Financial liabilities + Shareholders' equity

Operating assets consist of plant and equipment, inventories, and trade receivables and financial assets cash and short-term investments. Similarly, operating liabilities comprise trade payables and accrued expenses and financial liabilities debt. Rearranging the above equation gives:

Operating assets − Operating liabilities = (Financial liabilities − Financial assets) + Shareholders' equity

Thus a firm's capital (net debt plus equity – and, in the case of a group, minority interests) is, by definition, equal to its net operating assets.

28 Rajan, R.G. and Zingales, L. (1995), What do we know about capital structure? Some evidence from international data, *Journal of Finance*, 50: 1421–1460.

29 *See also* La Porta, R., Lopez-de-Silanes, F., Shleifer, A. and Vishny, R.W. (1998), Law and finance, *Journal of Political Economy*, 106(6): 1113–1155. La Porta *et al.* constructed a creditors' rights index for each of the 49 countries in their sample. Of the G7 countries, Germany and the UK had the highest scores.

30 In practice, the accounting for the receivable is more complicated. Offenbach records the total undiscounted payments (360,000) as a receivable and the unearned interest income (50,750, on 1 January year 1) in a separate contra-asset account:

Dr. Lease payments receivable (A+)	360,000	
Cr. Sales revenue (OE+)		309,250
Cr. Unearned interest income (CA+)		50,750

In the balance sheet, it reports a *net* receivable of 309,250. The IASB favours this accounting treatment.

31 Under the more complicated accounting noted above, the contra-asset account, 'Unearned interest income', is reduced as interest is earned. The end-year 1 entries to record interest earned and the lease payment received are as follows:

Dr. Unearned interest income (CA−)	24,750	
Cr. Interest income (OE+)		24,750
Dr. Cash (A−)	120,000	
Cr. Lease payments receivable (A−)		120,000

The end-year 1 net receivable is still 213,990 (240,000 less unearned interest income of 26,010 (50,750 − 24,750)).

12 Shareholders' equity

INTRODUCTION

The shareholders' equity section of the balance sheet shows the capital of the company provided by its owners. Part they contribute directly, part they provide indirectly when they approve the reinvestment of the company's earnings. The total amount represents their equity – or interest – in the net assets of the company.

In this chapter we look at the way a company accounts for its shareholders' equity. We start by trying to answer basic questions about business organisations. What are the major forms of business organisation? Why do entrepreneurs – and investors – prefer the corporate form? Investors receive shares as evidence of their ownership interest in a company. This prompts additional questions. What are the various classes of share a company can issue? What are their respective rights?

We have already seen how the way a firm accounts for its assets and liabilities – when it recognises them and how it measures them – affects owners' interests through their impact on profits and reserves. In this chapter, we concentrate on accounting and reporting issues which are unique to shareholders' equity. These issues include:

- the issuance of shares;
- the distribution of profits;
- the appropriation of profits to reserves; and
- the write-down of capital.

In these areas accounting practice is heavily influenced by national legal requirements. EU company law directives have reduced but not eliminated the differences among member states. Our discussion in section 1 of the chapter reflects the continuing legal diversity within Europe.

In section 2 of the chapter we turn to specialised topics. In particular, we describe the accounting for:

- the purchase by a company of its own shares;
- convertible securities and warrants; and
- government grants.

In our discussion we try to answer broader questions. Why, for example, do companies buy back their own shares? Why do firms issue convertible securities? The answers shed light on the way companies now account for these transactions.

An 'equity' number appears in measures of profitability (return on equity) and leverage (debt–equity ratio) and in valuation calculations (price-to-book ratio). In section 3 we consider how investors define 'equity' in these ratios. We also review the form and content of a new financial statement, the statement of changes in equity, that an increasing number of companies publish as part of their annual accounts.

Core issues

Different forms of business organisation

Batavus Droogstoppel has been a coffee broker on the Amsterdam Exchange for the past 17 years. For long an aficionado of coffee in all its forms, he's keen to expand the market for the humble bean. He's considering starting a business to produce and market coffee-flavoured yoghurt and ice cream, with decaffeinated variants for consumers concerned about their caffeine intake.

Sole proprietorship

He has yet to decide on the form his business should take. One possibility is to register the name of his venture 'Coffee Cornucopia' and begin producing his coffee-flavoured desserts on his own. As the **sole proprietor** of his business, he enjoys the following advantages.

- He retains total control of the management of the business.
- He saves the legal and economic costs of forming and running a company. One such cost is the required disclosure of information about the business which may help competitors.

Partnership

Friends of his are willing to invest in his business. A second possibility, therefore, is to form a **partnership** with them. If his fellow partners are **general partners**, they will participate in the day-to-day running of the business and he will no longer have total control of it. However, if he can persuade them to be **limited partners**, they will be investors only and their liability for partnership debts will be limited to their capital contributions to the partnership. In this case, he will:

- enjoy all the advantages of sole proprietorship;
- have access to additional capital to expand the business.

The partnership agreement sets out the rights of each partner. In particular, it states how each partner is to share in the profits and losses of the business.

Incorporation

A third possibility is for Droogstoppel to **incorporate** his business.[1] In this case, a **company** is formed, Coffee Cornucopia Company. CCC is a separate legal entity – with a name, residence and set of powers which specify the activities it can engage in – all contained in its (legally approved) charter of incorporation. As a separate entity, it can enter into contracts with individuals and other companies. In addition, a company has a constitution which governs the way it functions. For example, the constitution lays down rules governing meetings of shareholders (frequency of meetings, tabling of resolutions, voting procedures).

Droogstoppel and his friends can benefit from investing in a company rather than a partnership. Two important benefits are:

1 a limit to their liability to the company; and
2 easier transfer of their ownership rights.

Limited liability

A shareholder is, in most cases, only liable for the nominal (or par) value of the shares he has subscribed for. Once this capital has been paid in, the company's creditors must look to the company, not the shareholders, for satisfaction of their claims. By contrast, the sole proprietor and the partners (other than limited partners) have unlimited liability for the obligations of their respective businesses.

Ease of transfer of ownership

If the company is a public company (EU) or corporation (USA), *a shareholder can transfer his ownership interest usually without hindrance* – by selling his shares to outside investors without the prior consent of other shareholders.[2] By contrast, to withdraw capital from a partnership, a partner must first get the agreement of other partners. This can disrupt the running of the business. For example, in some cases, the retirement of one partner may force the dissolution of the old partnership and the creation of a new one.

A consequence of incorporation is that investors are more willing to put their capital into the business. Their liability is limited and they can withdraw their capital easily. As a result, an enterprise like CCC can raise equity capital at a lower cost if it's incorporated.

The advantages of incorporation should not be overstated. Banks and other creditors often require the owners of small companies to guarantee the company's debts personally. As a result, shareholders' liability is no longer limited. *Private* companies place restrictions on the transfer of shares. For example, a holder of a private company's shares may be required to gain the consent of a majority of other shareholders before selling his shares to a third party. Moreover, the EU requires that, except in the case of very small firms, companies must publish their annual accounts and certain other information (e.g. the names of directors). In the words of one UK official, 'disclosure of the accounts is the price companies pay for limited liability'.

In the EU, most companies are either public or private companies. We've already identified the major feature distinguishing the two. The shares of a public company are freely transferable (in principle). This enables it to raise capital through the stock market if it wishes to. To protect investors, the EU's 2nd Company Law Directive lays down a minimum share capital (of €25,000) for a public company. (Member states are free to set the minimum at a higher amount.) For example, the minimum share capital for a UK public company is £50,000 (€75,000 approximately). The minimum share capital required of private companies varies across EU member states.

Share capital

Terminology

A share is a proportionate interest in the net assets of a company. Assume CCC, the company founded by Droogstoppel, issues 100,000 shares. An investor holding 1,000 shares has a 1% stake in the company.[3]

A company usually assigns a **par value** (nominal value) to its shares when it is incorporated.[4] Suppose CCC assigns a par value of 5 euros to its shares. Then the share capital of CCC for legal purposes is €500,000. A share's par value has little relation to its market price, which is a function of the firm's expected earnings and market interest rates.

The term 'share capital' is often prefixed, particularly in European company accounts, by an adjective such as 'subscribed', 'called-up' or 'paid-up'. It's helpful to know what these terms mean. Let's start at the company's creation. Its statutes specify the number (and type) of shares it can **issue**. The directors of the company must obtain the consent of shareholders in general meeting before this limit can be increased. The reason for this is clear. Shareholders incur a cost as a result of a capital increase – either directly if they buy the additional shares or indirectly through dilution of their ownership stake if they don't. They need to be persuaded of the need for the capital increase before agreeing to it.[5]

A quoted company may raise new capital through a public offering of its shares. Investors **subscribe** for shares. Shares are **allotted** – on a proportionate or scaled basis if the offer is over-subscribed. To encourage interest among small investors, the company may decide that payment for the shares issued is to be made by instalment. The first payment accompanies subscription, second and later instalments (after allotment has taken place) are **called** by the company. Between the first and last instalment, the shares are **partly-paid**. Once all the cash is received, the share capital is subscribed for, allotted, called-up and fully paid!

Par value and its significance

Share capital (total issued shares at par value) is the permanent capital of a company. It can be returned to shareholders only under restrictive conditions – for example, a court's permission may be necessary before a company's capital can be reduced. Similar restrictions may apply to a firm's non-distributable reserves. It is argued that this affords protection to creditors since the company must maintain net assets equal to its share capital and non-distributable reserves. However, in some countries firms set par value low. If a firm's non-distributable reserves are also small, then its creditors enjoy little effective protection.

Par value can be of significance to individual shareholders in some circumstances. Recall that a shareholder is not liable to the company except to the extent that par value on his shares is unpaid. When is par value unpaid? One circumstance is when shares are issued 'partly paid'. Under the EU's 2nd Directive, only one-quarter of a public company's minimum share capital must be paid in on incorporation. Another circumstance is when a company issues shares at a discount to par value. This practice is banned under the EU's 2nd Directive which states that shares must be issued at a price equal to or above par value. However, it is permitted in certain US states.

Ordinary share capital: ownership rights

A share is an ownership claim. As a part-owner of a company, a shareholder has certain rights. *An ordinary shareholder (US: common stockholder) generally has the right to share proportionately in:*

1 *the earnings of the company;*
2 *the management of the company;*
3 *new issues of shares of the company;* and
4 *its assets, should the company be liquidated.*

These rights have the following practical force.

1 Shareholders share in the earnings of the firm through corporate dividend payments. An ordinary dividend is not a fixed amount per share. Each year the directors propose, and the shareholders approve, the amount of corporate earnings to be distributed as dividend. This amount can vary from year to year, depending on the company's economic circumstances.[6]

2 Directors are ultimately responsible for the management of the company. Through votes cast at general meetings, shareholders appoint and may dismiss the directors. They also amend the constitution of the company in the same way.[7]

3 Existing shareholders have the right of first refusal when new shares are issued. This ensures their ownership stake in percentage terms is not diluted without their consent. A company's shareholders can vote in general meeting to waive their 'preemptive right'. Note that company law in some countries does not grant shareholders this right.[8]

4 Should the company be wound up and the assets sold, any cash remaining after the creditors' claims have been met is distributed among shareholders in proportion to their equity stake.

Other classes of share

Companies can usually issue other classes of share besides voting ordinary shares. Each class has a different set of rights. In some cases, the aim is to offer investors securities carrying less risk: in return, investors accept lower potential rewards. In other cases, the intention is to raise equity capital from new shareholders while allowing existing shareholders to retain control of the company.

Preference shares

One popular alternative class of share is the **preference share** (USA: **preferred stock**). *A company's preference shareholders have priority over its ordinary shareholders when it distributes profits.* The preference dividend must be paid first before ordinary dividends can be paid. Hence preference shares carry less risk than ordinary shares.

The preference dividend is usually a stated amount per share which is fixed at the time of issuance. As a result, preference shareholders forgo the higher returns which ordinary shareholders may earn. If the preference shares are **participating** shares, then the holder participates with ordinary shareholders in the residual profits of the company once the prescribed dividend has been paid.

In most cases, the preference dividend is **cumulative**: any unpaid preference dividends accumulate from one year to the next and must be paid off in full (along with the current preference dividend) before the company can resume payment of the ordinary dividend. Note that any preference **dividend in arrears** is not a legal obligation of the company. The amount is not reported as a liability on the balance sheet but is disclosed in the notes to the accounts.

Preference shareholders have different rights from ordinary shareholders in other ways. They take precedence when the company's assets are distributed on liquidation. In Anglo-Saxon countries, preference share capital usually carries limited voting rights: holders do not have the right to vote in general meeting, except in certain circumstances (e.g. when their dividends are in arrears).

Shares with differential voting rights

As a general rule, one ordinary share carries one vote. However, a company may be allowed under its statutes to issue ordinary shares that carry more – or less – than one vote per share. Shareholders' rights in other respects – for example, to share in the profits of the company and in its assets on liquidation – are unaffected.

Issuing shares with differential voting rights is one means by which a group of shareholders, usually the founding family and its descendants, can bring in new risk capital to the business

BOX 12.1   Corporate ownership and control: international perspectives

Imagine you run a large and successful family company. Most of your wealth and that of other family members is tied up in the business. Some of the younger generation who are not involved in the management of the company are growing restless. They want to sell their stakes and invest the capital elsewhere. You are in a quandary. You can't afford to buy them out, either with your own capital or with borrowed money. However, if you allow them to sell their shares to outsiders, you risk losing control of the company.

Many companies that are family controlled or have a dominant shareholder need to raise outside equity capital at some point in their history. It may be to finance growth or, as in our example, to replace the equity provided by certain shareholders. There are, in principle, various ways they can do so and still allow the family (or dominant shareholder) to retain control. We describe three below. They can be used individually or in combination. Legal and tax considerations may limit the choice in practice.

1 *Differential voting rights.* The company issues different classes of ordinary share – for example, A shares and B shares. A shares may have multiple votes (say, 10 votes per share) whereas B shares carry just one. Alternatively, only holders of A shares are enfranchised (one vote per share): B shares are non-voting.
2 *Cross-shareholdings.* One or more firms with close business ties to the company acquire a stake in it. The company reciprocates. The stakes held by friendly investors may be small individually but together they protect the company from takeover and allow it to raise additional capital.
3 *Pyramid structure.* The family establishes a holding company – or chain of holding companies – which it controls usually by means of a significant minority holding (e.g. more than 20%). Each holding company attracts outside shareholders. The result is that the family can obtain outside capital and still control the business through the holding company or companies.

In a recent study of corporate ownership in 27 countries using 1995 data, La Porta, Lopez-de-Silanes and Shleifer found that many large as well as medium-sized companies have a dominant shareholder.[9] (The study employs two measures of dominance: direct and indirect control of more than (a) 20% and (b) 10% of voting rights.) Moreover, the shareholder usually exercises control by means of one or more of the above techniques and, in the case of families, through involvement in the company's management as well. They found evidence of a dominant shareholder in some of the world's biggest companies. Examples are:

- Samsung Electronics (South Korea). Lee Kun-Hee, the son of Samsung's founder, controls more than 10% of the votes through a pyramid structure.
- ABB (Sweden) and Fiat (Italy). In each case, a family (Wallenberg for ABB, Agnelli for Fiat) controls more than 20% of the votes through a combination of pyramid structure and differential voting rights.
- Toyota Motor Corporation (Japan). Companies within the Mitsui Group control more than 10% of the votes directly. Toyota itself holds shares in Mitsui Group companies.

Two of La Porta *et al.*'s findings are especially interesting. First, concentrated ownership appears to be the rule rather than the exception. Only in 36% of their large firm sample and 24% of their medium-sized firm sample are shares widely held. The traditional model, popularised by Berle and Means in the 1930s, that ownership of large companies is diffuse, applies in only a few countries (UK, USA). Second, ownership is significantly more concentrated in countries with weak shareholder rights. In these countries, families control over half of the sampled medium-sized firms and they do so mainly through pyramid structures (and involvement in management). Families' reluctance to relinquish control is understandable given the poor legal protection they would enjoy as minority shareholders.[10]

without diluting their voting power. There are other ways they can achieve the same result – for example, through cross-shareholdings and using a pyramid of companies. A recent study of corporate ownership around the world found that family control of companies, even of large ones, is widespread, especially in countries with weak shareholder protection. However, the device most commonly used by families to maintain control is a pyramid structure rather than shares with differential voting rights (*see* Box 12.1).

Shareholder rights and European companies

Departure from the one share, one vote principle is common in Europe. In addition to issuing shares with differential voting rights, companies may place a voting cap on individual shareholders or grant additional voting rights to long-term shareholders. For example, no shareholder can hold, directly or indirectly, more than 3% of the share capital of Nestlé, the Swiss food and beverage giant. PSA Peugeot Citroën shares that are registered in the name of the same holder for at least four years carry double voting rights.

These discriminatory practices are under attack. The European Commission argues that they are inconsistent with the free movement of capital, a key aim of the EU. Minority (i.e. non-controlling) shareholders oppose them because they depress the value of their investment. There are small signs of progress. Some companies like GUS, a major UK retailer and owner of Burberry's, the clothing store, have voluntarily enfranchised their non-voting shares. A determined bidder can surmount a voting cap, as Vodafone's purchase of Mannesmann in 2000 demonstrates. But getting all EU member states to accept the principle of one share, one vote is proving harder. The difficulty the Commission experienced in the early 2000s securing passage of its takeover directive illustrates this. Some governments and boardrooms opposed the 2002 draft directive because they feared its insistence that a target firm's shareholders should have equal voting rights during a takeover bid would make it easier for foreign companies to acquire key national firms.

Accounting for share issues and profit appropriation

Droogstoppel decides to incorporate his business as a public company, Coffee Cornucopia Company. Many of his friends and relatives subscribe for shares in the company. In this section we trace the first year of the life of CCC, focusing on those events which affect the shareholders' equity section of the balance sheet. The events we examine are:

- the issuance of shares for cash;
- the payment of dividends;
- the transfer of profits to reserves;[11]
- share dividends and share splits; and
- the write-down of capital.

Much of the accounting for shareholders' equity is determined by company law. This varies from country to country (or from state to state in countries with a federal structure like the USA or Canada). Our example emphasises practices found in EU countries.

Issuance of shares for cash

At the start of year 1, CCC issues for cash 100,000 ordinary shares with a par value of 5. (All currency amounts are in euros.) The price paid by subscribers is 8 a share. All shares are fully paid at the time of issue. The company makes the following journal entry.

Issuance of shares on fully-paid basis

Dr. Cash (A+)	800,000	
Cr. Share capital (at par) (OE+)		500,000
Cr. Share premium (OE+)		300,000

CCC credits the total par value of the shares issued (100,000 shares × 5) to 'Share capital'. It credits the excess of the proceeds from issue (800,000) over par value (500,000) to 'Share premium'.[12]

Jurisdictions differ in the restrictions they place on **share premium** (USA: additional paid-in capital). In most countries it is considered a non-distributable reserve. However, it can be *capitalised*, that is, new share capital can be created from it. We illustrate the capitalisation of reserves later.

All issues of shares for cash are accounted for in the manner shown above. The accounting is the same whether the shares are ordinary or preference, or whether they are issued at the time of incorporation (the initial offering) or at a later date. Where the company receives assets other than cash (e.g. property or investments in other companies) as consideration for the shares, the shares issued are usually valued at the market value of the assets received.

Public offerings of shares can be costly. Banks or securities firms often underwrite issues of shares by quoted companies. For smaller issues, underwriting fees can amount to 5–10% of the gross proceeds from the sale of shares – to which must be added legal and accounting costs incurred preparing the prospectus. The usual practice is for the issuing company to write off the transaction costs associated with a share issue against share premium.

As we have mentioned, EU companies can issue partly-paid shares. There are restrictions on this practice, however. At least 25% of the par value (and 100% of the share premium) must be paid in at the time of share allotment. In its share offer document, the company states on which date or dates it will call the remaining balance from shareholders. EU companies usually show the total capital subscribed, whether called or uncalled, as 'Share capital' on the equity side of the balance sheet. The uncalled portion (plus any called portion that has not yet been received) is shown as an asset.[13]

Remember that the transfer or trading of shares after issuance has no impact on the issuing company's accounts. In the case of registered shares, the company – or the registrar of its shares – simply notes the change in share ownership in its records. (No record of change of ownership is – or can be – made for bearer shares.)

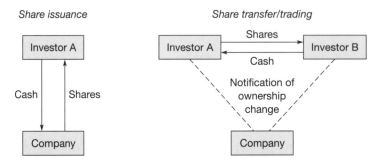

● Payment of dividends

CCC has a good beginning. It reports profits of 80,000 in year 1 and 200,000 in year 2. When the year 2 results are published in March year 3, the directors propose the payment of a cash dividend of 100,000 (i.e. 1 a share). This is the company's first profit distribution. The shareholders duly approve the dividend at the annual general meeting in May year 3. CCC makes the following entry when the dividend is paid in June:

Payment of dividend in June year 3
Dr. Profit for year 2 (OE–)   100,000
   (or: Retained profits (OE–))
   Cr. Cash (A–)   100,000

(A company may set up a temporary owners' equity account, 'Dividends', record profit distributions in it, and then close it to a permanent owners' equity account at year-end.)

The presentation of the profit earned and distributed by CCC in its year 2 balance sheet will differ depending on which country CCC is based in. In Exhibit 12.1 we show three different formats. Many EU companies (i.e. those in Belgium, France, Italy and Spain) follow the first format. The remaining two correspond to the formats used by UK/Irish and North American companies.

Under the 'dominant EU' format, companies distinguish, on the face of the balance sheet, between 'Profit for the year' and profit retained from previous years (format 1). In most EU

Exhibit 12.1 **Presentation of shareholders' equity following announcement of profit and dividend: illustration of EU and US formats** (amounts in euros)

Facts

CCC reports net income in year 1 of 80,000 and net assets at the end of the year of 880,000. No dividend is paid out of year 1 income. In year 2 it reports net income of 200,000. The directors propose a dividend of 1 a share (or 100,000) in March year 3 when the year 2 results are published. The year 2 accounts and proposed dividend are approved by shareholders at the annual general meeting in May year 3.

The following are alternative ways of presenting the shareholders' equity section of CCC's year 2 balance sheet.

Shareholders' equity

In 000		End-year 2	End-year 1
Format 1	Share capital	500	500
(Dominant	Share premium	300	300
in EU)	Profit retained	80	0
	Profit for the year	200	80
		1,080	880
Format 2	Share capital	500	500
(UK and	Share premium	300	300
Ireland)	Profit and loss account	180*	80
		980	880
Format 3	Common stock	500	500
(USA)	Additional paid-in capital	300	300
	Retained earnings	280**	80
		1,080	880

* Retained profits of years 1 and 2, after deducting proposed year 2 dividend of 100. Dividend payable of 100 shown as current liability in year 2 balance sheet.

** Dividend not declared at balance sheet date.

countries, the 'Profit for the year' number on the balance sheet is the same as that reported in the income statement since shareholders have not yet approved the appropriation of the year's profit. When this occurs, the dividend is recognised. Since, at the end of year 2, CCC's shareholders have not yet approved the year 2 dividend, it is not deducted from shareholders' equity in the end-year 2 balance sheet.

By contrast, UK and US companies combine the retained profits of the current and previous years and show them as one line on the balance sheet. Increasingly, this is the presentation favoured by all large international companies. UK/Irish and US companies differ in their accounting for dividends, however. *A UK/Irish company recognises a dividend in the accounts of the period to which it relates (format 2).* As a UK/Irish firm, CCC records the dividend proposed in March year 3 in its year 2 accounts – before the latter are closed in year 3 – on the grounds that the dividend is a distribution of its year 2 profit.

```
Proposed dividend (UK/Ireland):
adjustment to year 2 accounts
Dr. Profit and loss account (OE–)          100,000
    Cr. Dividend payable (L+)                           100,000
```

As a result, CCC reports lower shareholders' equity and higher current liabilities in its end-year 2 balance sheet than if it had followed the dominant EU practice (format 1).

A US company recognises a dividend (and the related liability) on the date when its board of directors declares it (format 3). CCC announces the dividend in year 3 and so, under US practice, there is no effect on its year 2 accounts.

Interim dividends

Companies often pay an interim dividend in addition to the final one. (Most US quoted companies declare dividends on a quarterly basis.) In some countries, the dividend that can be paid during the year is restricted. For example, French public companies can pay an interim dividend only if audited accounts show profits at least equal to the interim dividend.

The accounting for interim dividends varies across Europe. A common practice in continental European countries is to show the interim dividend as a deduction, 'Dividend on account', in the shareholders' equity section of the balance sheet. Once shareholders have approved the appropriation of the year's profit, the 'dividend on account' is eliminated and retained profits reduced. UK and US companies follow national practice, as shown in Exhibit 12.1, when accounting for interim dividends.

Transfer of profits to reserves

EU public companies are required by law to transfer profits to reserves in certain circumstances. First, most Continental European countries, and many Latin American, African and Asian countries with a Continental European accounting tradition, require public companies to establish a **legal reserve**. *A legal reserve is intended to protect the company's creditors by reducing the profits available for distribution.* This should reduce the profits actually distributed, thereby conserving the company's assets. A company must transfer a percentage (usually 5%, in some cases 10%) of its annual after-tax profits to a legal reserve until the reserve reaches a specified minimum level, usually expressed as a percentage of share capital. (The percentage varies – from 10% in France to 100% in Taiwan.) Beyond that level, transfers are voluntary.[14]

Suppose CCC is a French company. It makes a transfer of 5% of year 2 profits to reserves when shareholders approve the annual dividend in May year 3. Year 2 profits amount to 200,000 so the transfer to legal reserve is 10,000.

> *Transfer of profit to legal reserve*
> Dr. Profit for year 2 (OE–)   10,000
>   Cr. Legal reserve (OE+)   10,000

Second, the EU's 2nd Company Law Directive requires public companies to establish a reserve *when they buy back their own shares*. This 'Reserve for own shares' is created by transferring an amount from retained profits equivalent to the cost of the shares repurchased. We examine why and how companies acquire their own shares in section 2 of this chapter.

Companies transfer profits to reserves for other reasons. Company statutes may require it. Or the directors may propose it on a voluntary basis – for example, when a heavy capital investment programme is in progress. *Transferring profits to reserves, whether by law or by choice, does not involve the setting aside of cash. It merely signals to investors that not all the profits earned in current and past periods are available for distribution.*

Revaluation of assets, where permitted, can also result in the creation of a reserve. As we saw in our discussion of fixed assets and inventories, any unrealised holding gain from the increase in the market value of such assets above cost is credited to a revaluation reserve. Under the EU's 4th Directive, such gains are not distributable until the related assets are used up or sold and the gains realised. (Unrealised losses are charged first to this reserve and, when it is exhausted, to current year's profits.)

Non-cash dividends

Dividends need not be in cash. If its statutes permit it, a company can distribute to shareholders a **dividend in kind** (for example, shares it holds in other companies) or a **share dividend** (that is, additional shares in itself). A share dividend goes by several names: stock dividend, bonus issue, capitalisation issue. Although dividends in kind are unusual, share dividends are common.

Dividend in kind

There is no agreed accounting treatment. Many companies follow US practice and record a dividend in kind *at the fair value* of the non-cash assets distributed. If the assets are not already carried at fair value in the company's accounts, a gain or loss must be recognised at the time of distribution. For example, suppose a company plans to distribute an investment in debt securities to shareholders and it carries this asset at an amount less than fair value. It makes the following entries:

> *Revaluation of investment to fair value*
> Dr. Investment in debt securities (A+)   xxx
>   Cr. Gain on revaluation of investment (OE+)   xxx
>
> *Dividend in kind*
> Dr. Retained profits (OE–)   xxx
>   Cr. Investment in debt securities (A–)   xxx

The company recognises the gain in the income statement since the asset is 'derecognised' and the gain is realised. (To simplify presentation, we assume no time lag between dividend declaration and payment.)

Share dividend

Most EU firms record a share dividend *at the par value* of the shares issued. For example, suppose CCC's shareholders approve in May year 3 a 20% share dividend – that is a distribution of one new share for every five held. CCC's share dividend is in place of its cash dividend. The issuance of the 20,000 shares (remember, CCC has 100,000 shares outstanding) is recorded as follows:

Share dividend: EU practice		
Dr. Retained profits (OE–)	100,000	
Cr. Share capital (OE+)		100,000
(20,000 × 5 par value)		

Thus retained profits (or, in some countries, share premium) are reduced by the par value of the 20,000 shares issued.

US companies, by contrast, must record share dividends *at the fair value* of the shares distributed. For example, if CCC observes US GAAP and the market price of its shares is 9 at the date the 1:5 share dividend is declared in year 3, it makes the following entry in its US-style accounts:

Share dividend: US practice		
Dr. Retained earnings (OE–)	180,000	
Cr. Common stock (OE+)		100,000
(20,000 shares × 5 par value)		
Cr. Additional paid-in capital (OE+)		80,000
(20,000 shares × (9 – 5))		

The excess of the market value over the par value of the shares issued is credited to the US equivalent of share premium. As the example shows, a US company finds it more 'costly', in terms of *distributable* profits, to pay a share dividend than its European counterpart.[15]

Notice a common feature of both the European and US treatment of share dividends. *Companies convert reserves (usually retained profits) into shares.* In effect, they capitalise (make capital out of) reserves – hence the term 'capitalisation issue'.

Why do companies declare dividends in the form of shares? We have seen already (in Chapter 6) that companies can be profitable and yet short of cash. A fast-growing company, for example, may face a cash constraint as it seeks to finance investment in new plant and working capital. To avoid the outflow of funds which a cash dividend will cause, it 'rewards' its shareholders with additional shares. As a result, shareholders have tangible evidence of their share of the firm's accumulated profits.

But are shareholders rewarded? In theory, they should be no better off. The company has not distributed assets to them. In fact, its own net assets are unchanged. (Look at the journal entry CCC makes in May year 3: shareholders' equity has not changed in total.)

An individual shareholder's net assets should also be unchanged. For example, Mevrouw Last, an investor, holds 1,000 shares of CCC. At a market price of 9 a share, her investment is valued at 9,000. After receiving a 20% share dividend, she now holds 1,200 shares. However, the market value of her investment should still be 9,000: the price per share should fall to 7.5. In practice, this does not occur. Announcement of a share dividend is viewed by investors as information ('news') about the company. They may interpret it as good news (faster growth and a higher cash dividend in future) or bad news (inability to pay cash dividend because of difficult trading conditions), depending on the company's circumstances. They will buy or sell the shares accordingly. As a result, the market price will not adjust to its theoretical value of 7.5 a share and the value of Mevrouw Last's investment will not remain at 9,000.

Scrip dividend

Some companies allow shareholders to take a cash dividend in shares. The shareholder may enjoy a tax advantage from taking the dividend in 'scrip' (i.e. shares) and, if she wants to increase her shareholding in the company, she also avoids the transaction costs associated with share purchase.

There is no agreed accounting treatment for scrip dividends (also known as 'optional stock dividends'). Many companies account for them at fair value. They debit 'Retained profits' for the *fair value* of the shares taken in lieu of cash (measured at the date the cash dividend is declared). The par value of the shares distributed is credited to 'Share capital' and the difference between fair and par value to 'Share premium'.

Share splits

Companies often split their shares when the market price per share rises above a certain level. They do so to make their shares more liquid and marketable. By increasing the number of shares outstanding, a share split usually results in more share transactions, a larger shareholder base – and hence greater liquidity. Moreover, a high share price may deter the small investor. He or she cannot afford to buy a large number of shares and the transaction costs (e.g. brokers' charges) are proportionately higher for small purchases. A share split lowers the price and makes the shares attractive to a wider range of investors.

A company which splits its shares issues new shares in exchange for old ones. The new shares carry a lower par value. Thus if CCC declares a 2:1 share split, it will issue 200,000 new shares with a par value of 2.50 a share, in place of the 100,000 old shares (with a par value of 5 a share).[16]

A share split has no accounting implications. No accounts are adjusted. The book amount of the firm's shareholders' equity does not change. Share capital is simply recalibrated. Thus CCC's share capital account now consists of double the number of shares (200,000) at half the par value (2.5).

Note the difference between a share split and a share dividend. If CCC declares a 100% share dividend, it issues 100,000 *additional* shares *at the existing par value of 5*. To do so, it capitalises 500,000 of reserves. Its accounts *are* adjusted. Although the balance in 'Shareholders' equity' does not change in total, its share capital increases at the expense of its reserves.

In theory, the market value of a company should be unaffected by a share split. In our CCC example, 100,000 shares valued at, say, 9 a share should become 200,000 shares at 4.5 a share: CCC's total market value should still be 900,000. In practice, the share price may not adjust fully (i.e. halve to 4.5). It should benefit from the shares' greater liquidity and from the positive signal – about the company's future earnings and dividends – conveyed by the split.

If the market price of a company's shares falls to very low levels, the company faces a different problem. Regular investors spurn the shares and price volatility increases as day-traders speculate on them. Some stock exchanges may delist shares when the price falls below a specified minimum ($1 in the case of Nasdaq and the New York Stock Exchange). To drive up the price, management may decide to **consolidate** the shares, issuing fewer new shares in exchange for old ones. A 'reverse share split', as it's known, is accounting-neutral. There is no change to shareholders' equity. Share capital consists of fewer shares at a higher par value. However, the share price may not respond as expected. Fewer shares in circulation mean the market for them is likely to be less liquid. Moreover, management appear to be telling investors that the share price is unlikely to increase unaided.

Shareholder accounting for dividend received

How does a shareholder account for a dividend received? If the dividend is in cash, the shareholder recognises investment income and records an increase in his or her cash balance:

Receipt of cash dividend
Dr. Cash (A+)   xxx
    Cr. Investment income (OE+)   xxx

If the dividend is a share dividend, the shareholder adjusts the cost base of his or her investment in the company. The shareholder does not record any income from the share dividend. Consider the case of Mevrouw Last. She acquired 1,000 shares of CCC at a price of 8 a share (the initial issue price). After CCC's declaration of a 20% share dividend, she now has 1,200 shares, still with a carrying amount of 8,000. She recognises no income. Should she sell any CCC shares at a later date, the cost per share in the calculation of the gain or loss on disposal will be 6.67 (8,000/1,200 shares).

Share dividend: adjustment to cost base

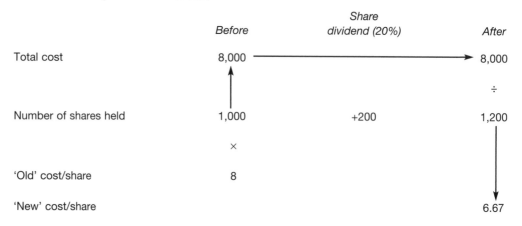

	Before	Share dividend (20%)	After
Total cost	8,000		8,000
Number of shares held	1,000	+200	1,200
'Old' cost/share	8		
'New' cost/share			6.67

Capital write-down

As mentioned earlier, a share dividend is sometimes known as a 'capitalisation issue'. Retained profits (or other reserves such as share premium) are converted into share capital. The reverse can occur. A company in financial difficulties may, as part of a capital restructuring, convert contributed capital into earned capital. Why would it do this? After all, the conversion has no effect on its shareholders' equity in total. *The main reason a company writes down its capital is to eliminate its accumulated book losses.*

Consider the case of a firm whose operations are profitable – or have been made so as a result of an operational restructuring – but which has accumulated losses. It wishes to attract new capital, preferably on favourable terms. This requires the early resumption of dividend payments. Without a capital restructuring, the company would have to dedicate future profits to 'paying off' past losses. Cash dividends would be delayed.

How is the write-down carried out? After obtaining shareholders' approval and, in some circumstances, the court's permission, the company cuts the par value of its shares and cancels part or all of the share premium. The aim is to reduce contributed capital to the extent necessary to eliminate the accumulated losses:

Dr. Share capital (OE–)   xxx
Dr. Share premium (OE–)   xxx
    Cr. Accumulated losses (OE+)   xxx

The court may lay down additional conditions, for example, the appropriation of part of the future profits of the firm to a special (non-distributable) reserve. The court's intention is to protect the interests of the firm's creditors. As we have noted, a capital write-down makes possible the early resumption of dividend payments. The special reserve is designed to restrict the outflow of corporate assets to shareholders when this occurs.

Shareholders' equity and IAS

IAS address the accounting for shareholders' equity in two main areas only: the definition of an equity instrument and the disclosure of share capital and reserve balances (and their movement) in the accounts. We look at definitional issues here and at disclosure issues in section 3.

Accounting regulators view shareholders' equity as a residual. As we saw in earlier chapters, IAS carefully define what is an asset and a liability and set out recognition and measurement rules for them. Shareholders' equity is then simply the difference between total assets and total liabilities. IAS apply the same approach to financial instruments. They define what is a financial liability. A financial instrument that is not debt is considered to be equity.

According to the IASB, a financial liability is 'any liability that is a contractual obligation to deliver cash or another financial asset to another enterprise'.[17] Ordinary share capital is clearly not a financial liability since the company is not obligated to make payments to shareholders. However, certain types of preference share are equity instruments in name only. Examples are redeemable preference shares where redemption is either mandatory or at the option of the shareholder. In these cases, the issuing company has a contractual obligation to repay the share capital at some future date. Under IAS, it must classify such redeemable preference share capital as debt on its balance sheet and report dividend payments as a financing expense on its income statement. Other equity securities with debt-like features (e.g. fixed-term securities paying tax-deductible 'dividends') must also be accounted for as a financial liability if the contract requires the issuer to make payments to security holders. Where a financial instrument contains both a liability and an equity element – as in the case of convertible securities, IAS require the issuing company to present the two elements separately in its financial statements.

IAS also impinge on the accounting for share issues and profit distributions. International rule-makers support the current practice of writing off share issuance costs against reserves: only the costs of failed share issues should be expensed.[18] More significantly, a company following IAS may not recognise as a liability at the balance sheet date dividends that it proposes or declares *after* that date. This is likely to have a major impact on UK and US companies. As we noted earlier, it's common practice for directors of UK and US firms to propose or declare the final dividend rate (on ordinary or common shares) at some date between the balance sheet date and the date the accounts are published. Under IAS, firms must *disclose* the amount of this proposed or declared dividend but not book a liability for it at the balance sheet date.[19]

SECTION 2 Specialised topics

Purchase of own shares

Reasons for share repurchase

Share buybacks can take one of two forms. A company that repurchases its own shares either cancels them after purchase or holds them in treasury for later resale.

Why would a company want to buy back and cancel its shares? The main reason is to shrink its business. Management may reckon they can't find sufficient profitable investment opportunities for shareholders' funds. Just as companies raise equity from investors to pursue wealth-creating investments, so they return it when such opportunities disappear.

Management usually have different motives for buying the company's shares for treasury. They may believe its shares are undervalued. The acquisition is then a temporary investment of corporate cash: management hope to sell the shares at a higher price in the future (assuming the market comes to accept management's view of the share's worth). Another reason is to make shares available to employees under company-sponsored share purchase and share option plans. The alternative, a special issue of new shares, involves higher transaction costs for the company. Note that, if the law allows, the company may use the treasury route even if its aim is to shrink the business. Buying shares for treasury is more flexible than share repurchase and immediate cancellation: the company has the option to cancel the shares at a later date.

From the company's perspective, a share repurchase is equivalent to a cash dividend. In both cases, equity and cash are reduced. However, shareholders may view them differently. All shareholders receive a dividend; only those that proffer their shares receive cash from a buyback. Moreover, the tax impact of each is likely to differ. A share repurchase is more advantageous for shareholders than a dividend if the tax rate on the capital gain from the share sale is less than the income tax rate on dividend income.

EU and US practice

Share repurchase is a common practice among US firms; it is less so in the EU. EU law places restrictions on its use. In general, an EU public company must:

1 obtain shareholder authorisation before a repurchase can take place;[20]
2 limit the amount of shares repurchased to 10% of its subscribed capital;
3 ensure that non-distributable capital (share capital plus non-distributable reserves) is preserved.

Some EU member states impose tougher rules on share repurchase.

Why are there restrictions on EU firms buying back their own shares? One reason is that in many European countries the law takes a narrow view of what are the legitimate actions a company can take. It's argued that shareholders never intended that managers should invest their capital in the company's own shares. Such a practice has been described as 'autophagy' (eating oneself). Hence, shareholder approval is required before a repurchase can occur (condition 1).

In addition, there is a fear that if given the right to buy and sell their own shares freely, companies will abuse it. For example, shareholders are not privy to the same information about the company as managers: the latter may use their inside information to buy back and then reissue the company's shares to their advantage. Because of tough US laws against insider trading, investors in US listed companies enjoy better protection against such risks than investors in European firms.

Nonetheless, an increasing number of European firms are buying back their own shares and those EU states that place additional restrictions on share repurchase are coming under pressure to lift them. (Some, for example Germany and the UK, have already done so.) International investors form a growing proportion of shareholders of large European listed firms. They consider a company's primary goal is to increase its shareholders' wealth. Among the measures a company can take to achieve this is to identify surplus equity in the business and return it, in a tax-efficient manner, to shareholders.

Accounting for share repurchase

Shares held in treasury

Under IAS, shares repurchased and held in treasury should be accounted for as a deduction from equity. The usual practice is to show the cost of the shares as a one-line adjustment within shareholders' equity. For example, suppose CCC buys back 5,000 of its own shares at a price of 12 and does not cancel them. It records the transaction as follows:

> *Repurchase of shares for treasury*
> Dr. Shares held in treasury (Contra-OE+)   60,000
>   Cr. Cash (A–)   60,000

CCC shows the 60,000 cost of the treasury shares as a debit balance, either below contributed capital or at the bottom of the shareholders' equity section of the balance sheet.

IAS also require that any gain or loss from later resale of the treasury shares should not be recognised in income, on the grounds that the gain or loss represents a transfer between shareholders.[21] IAS do not specify how gains or losses should be recorded in the balance sheet, largely because of differences in national law regarding the creation and utilisation of individual reserve accounts. Some companies take all gains and losses to retained profits. An alternative approach is to credit all gains to share premium (USA: additional paid-in capital) and charge losses first to share premium up to the amount of previous treasury gains and then the balance to retained profits.

Note that some companies do not account for treasury shares as a deduction from equity. Instead, they record the investment in 'Own shares' as an asset and recognise any gain or loss from later resale on the income statement. This treatment is no longer acceptable under IAS.

Shares held in treasury are considered to be 'issued but not outstanding'. They are excluded from the calculation of earnings per share (only *outstanding* shares are included in the EPS denominator). They do not qualify for dividends although they are adjusted for share splits.

Cancelled shares

Shares repurchased and cancelled result in a reduction in share capital and, usually, share premium. Any share premium recorded on the issuance of the shares is reversed on their cancellation. If the shares are repurchased at a price greater than the issue price, the difference is usually charged against retained profits.

In certain circumstances, EU law requires firms to establish a special (non-distributable) reserve when buying back their own shares. This must be done when the shares are repurchased for cancellation and there's no fresh issue of shares to offset those cancelled. We illustrate this with our CCC example. Recall that the company originally issued the 5 par shares at 8 a share. If it buys back 5,000 shares at 12 each and cancels them, it makes the following entries:

> *Repurchase and cancellation of shares*
> Dr. Share capital (OE–)   25,000
>   (5,000 shares × 5 par)
> Dr. Share premium (OE–)   15,000
>   (5,000 shares × (8 – 5))
> Dr. Retained profits (OE–)   20,000
>   Cr. Cash (A–)   60,000
>   (5,000 shares × 12)
>
> Dr. Retained profits (OE–)   40,000
>   Cr. Reserve for own shares (OE+)   40,000
>   (5,000 shares × 8)

The purpose of the above entries is to preserve the capital of the firm. CCC's non-distributable capital is maintained at 800,000 after the share repurchase, as can be seen below:

	Before repurchase (100,000 shares)	After repurchase (95,000 shares)
Non-distributable capital:		
Share capital (5 par)	500,000	475,000
Share premium	300,000	285,000
Reserve for own shares	0	40,000
	800,000	800,000

Under EU law, a company can only reduce its capital if it has the approval of its shareholders and creditors' interests have been safeguarded. It cannot use a share repurchase and cancellation to circumvent these legal requirements.

Convertible securities and warrants

Companies issue securities which contain both debt and equity components. They are known as 'compound' financial instruments. Examples include:

1 *Convertible securities.* These comprise convertible bonds and convertible preference shares. A holder has the right to convert each bond (or preference share) into a predetermined number of ordinary shares during a specified future period. The conversion price (implicit in the conversion rate of convertible stock for ordinary shares) is usually set higher than the market price of ordinary shares at the date of the convertible's issue. A holder will convert the stock only if the market price per share rises above the conversion price. If it does not, the bonds or preference shares remain outstanding until they mature or are redeemed.

2 *Warrants.* A company issues straight bonds or preference shares with warrants attached. A warrant is a long-term call option: it entitles the holder to buy a specified number of ordinary shares at a predetermined price (the exercise price) during a future period (the exercise term). A holder will exercise the warrant only if the market price of the ordinary share is above the exercise price. If this does not occur, the warrant will expire unused at the end of the exercise term. Warrants are sometimes 'detachable': in this case, they can be separated from their host bonds or shares and traded independently.

What is the attraction of convertible securities or warrants to the issuing company and investors? Consider the companies that make frequent use of such instruments. They are often small and fast-growing. Internal cash flow is insufficient to finance growth so they must seek outside capital. Issuing straight equity is costly. The market fears the issue signals an overvalued share price (management have an information advantage which the market believes they're trying to exploit) and forces the company to issue new shares at a discount, thereby depressing the value of existing shareholders' stakes. As for straight debt, the high coupon the company must pay increases the risk of financial distress. Compound instruments like convertible bonds alleviate these problems. They enable small firms to invest and, if the investments are successful, build up their equity base.[22]

As for investors, convertibles and warrant-carrying securities offer a relatively secure income stream – in the form of bond interest or preference dividends – and the opportunity to share in profits as ordinary shareholders, if the company does well.

Accounting for convertibles and warrants

Many companies still account for convertibles and warrants according to their form. Thus convertible bonds are treated as straight debt and non-detachable warrants are not recognised separately. Under new international rules, however, firms must account for compound instruments according to their substance. The liability and equity components of such instruments must be recognised and valued separately. This new approach will replace traditional accounting over time. We illustrate both approaches below.

Traditional approach: no separation of liability and equity components

Consider, first, the case of convertible securities. Suppose that early in year 3 CCC issues at par 500 of five-year 4% convertible bonds with a nominal value of 1,000. (All currency amounts are in euros.) Under the terms of the bond issue, from the start of year 5 holders can convert each 1,000 bond into shares at the rate of 65 shares to each bond. Thus bondholders have no incentive to convert the bonds until the share price reaches the conversion price of 15.4 (1,000/65 shares = 15.3846). (Assume CCC's shares are trading at a price below this when the bonds are issued.)

Under traditional practice, CCC accounts for the bonds as debt. It assigns all the issue proceeds to a liability account. (Issuance costs are ignored.)

> *Issue of convertible bonds, start year 3*
> Dr. Cash (A+)   500,000
>   Cr. Convertible bonds payable (L+)   500,000

CCC applies the coupon rate to the face amount of the bonds to determine their periodic cost. Annual interest expense is 20,000 (4% × 500,000).

> *Annual cost of convertible bonds*
> Dr. Interest expense (OE−)   20,000
>   Cr. Cash (A−)   20,000

If conversion takes place, the issuing company usually records the shares issued at the carrying amount of the convertible securities exchanged. Assume bondholders convert the 500 bonds into CCC ordinary shares at the start of year 5. CCC records the 32,500 shares issued at 500,000, the carrying amount of the bonds. (In effect, each share is valued at the conversion price of 15.4.)

> *Conversion of bonds at start year 5*
> Dr. Convertible bonds payable (L−)   500,000
>   Cr. Share capital (OE+)   162,500
>   (32,500 shares × 5 par)
>   Cr. Share premium (OE+)   337,500
>   (32,500 shares × (15.3846 − 5))

If the bonds are not converted, they remain, as debt, on CCC's balance sheet until they mature or are redeemed.

The accounting for securities issued with non-detachable warrants is similar to that for convertible securities. At the time of issue, the equity component (in this case, the warrant) is not recognised. If the warrants are exercised, the company records the issue of shares at the exercise price:

> Dr. Cash (at exercise price)   xxx
>   Cr. Share capital (at par)   xxx
>   Cr. Share premium (exercise price − par)   xxx

Where the warrants are *detachable*, they are recognised, as equity, at the time of issue. The method that issuing companies use to value securities with detachable warrants, namely the residual value method, is also used in the new approach to measuring compound financial instruments which we describe and illustrate below.

New approach: separation of liability and equity components

A company following international accounting standards must show separately on the balance sheet the liability and equity components of any compound financial instrument it issues. This involves recognising, at the time of issue, the value of the conversion option implicit in a convertible bond or preference share and the value of the call option implicit in a warrant. The issuing company measures the compound instrument using a 'residual value' approach. It values the liability component of the instrument as if it were a 'straight' security (i.e. one without a conversion option or warrant attached). The difference between the value of the compound instrument at the issue date and the value of the liability component is the residual value assigned to the equity component (i.e. the option or warrant).

We illustrate the residual value approach using our CCC example. An investment bank advises CCC that it would have to offer investors an 8% return if the five-year bond contained no conversion option: this is the prevailing interest rate for straight bonds of this risk class and maturity. Exhibit 12.2 shows how the value of the conversion option of CCC's 4% five-year convertible bonds is established.

CCC records the issue of the convertible bonds as follows:

Issue of convertible bonds, start year 3		
Dr. Cash (A+)	500,000	
Dr. Bond discount (CL+)	79,640	
Cr. Convertible bonds payable (L+)		500,000
Cr. Equity component of convertible bonds (OE+)		79,640

The bonds are stated in CCC's start year 3 balance sheet at 420,360, the fair value of equivalent straight debt then. The conversion option is valued at 79,640, the difference between the fair value of the whole convertible (500,000) and the fair value of the liability component.

Exhibit 12.2 Valuation of equity and liability components of convertible bonds: residual value approach (amounts in euros)

Facts
CCC issues 500,000 of five-year 4% convertible bonds at the start of year 3. If it issues straight debt then, it must offer investors an 8% yield to maturity. (Each 1,000 bond is convertible into 65 CCC ordinary shares from year 5.)

Valuation of equity and liability components of convertible

	Amount	PV factor (at 8%)	Present value	
Value of five-year 4% convertible bonds at issue				500,000
Less: Value of liability component:				
Annual interest	20,000	3.993	79,860	
Principal	500,000	0.681	340,500	
				−420,360
Value of equity component (conversion option)				79,640

How will CCC measure the liability and equity components during the life of the convertible bonds? The liability component is accounted for in the same way as debt issued at a discount. Thus the debt discount of 79,640 is amortised over the five-year life of the bonds, using the interest method of amortisation as illustrated in Chapter 11. The interest charge each period is based on the cost of straight debt at the time of issue, namely 8%. Under HC accounting, the bonds are reported in CCC's balance sheet at amortised cost (principal amount less unamortised discount). Meanwhile, the equity component does not alter. It is included with reserves in CCC's shareholders' equity.

On conversion of the bonds, the liability component is eliminated while the equity component is absorbed into share premium. No gain or loss arises on conversion: the shares issued are valued at the combined carrying amounts of the liability and equity components. Thus if CCC's bondholders convert all the bonds at the start of year 5 and the carrying amount of the liability component then is 448,540 (or 500,000 less unamortised discount of 51,460), CCC records the conversion as follows:

Conversion of bonds at start year 5		
Dr. Convertible bonds payable (L–)	500,000	
Dr. Equity component of convertible bonds (OE–)	79,640	
Cr. Bond discount (CL–)		51,460
Cr. Share capital (OE+)		
(32,500 shares × 5 par)		162,500
Cr. Share premium (OE+)		365,680

The 32,500 shares issued in exchange for the 500 bonds are valued at 528,180, the sum of the unamortised cost of the debt (448,540) and the value assigned initially to the conversion option (79,640).

The merit of the new approach is that it recognises explicitly the equity component of a compound financial instrument and attempts to measure both liability and equity components accurately at the date of issue. Note, however, that the liability component is measured at amortised cost and thus changes in fair value during its life are not recognised in the issuing company's financial statements.

State aid to companies

In virtually all countries, governments offer financial assistance to companies. They do so for several reasons. They seek to stimulate investment and reduce unemployment, especially in poorer regions. They want to encourage research and development in industries which are held to be of 'national importance' (e.g. defence, aerospace, information technology, energy). And they try to forestall bankruptcy, especially of large companies. Government financial assistance takes many forms, ranging from grants and subsidies to tax holidays and low-interest loans. We focus in this section on the accounting for equity-related aid.

Where there is evidence that the government has ownership rights (e.g. the company issues shares to it in exchange for financial aid), the company accounts for the aid in the same way as any other issue of share capital.

When the assistance is in the form of a cash grant or subsidy, the company should not record the amount received as permanent capital. *Under international accounting rules, it should recognise the assistance as income on an accrual basis, that is, in the period or periods it expects to benefit from it.*[23] In the case of a grant towards the cost of new equipment, it can establish a liability account, 'Deferred income', on the balance sheet and amortise it to income over the asset's expected life (the deferred income approach). Alternatively, it can deduct the grant from the cost of the asset acquired (the net-of-grant approach). The accounting benefits from the grant are captured in the income statement in the form of lower depreciation charges.

An example contrasts the two accounting methods. Tasman Company offers survey services to mining and oil companies. At the start of x1, it has capital of 3 million. Early in the year, it purchases remote sensing equipment, at a cost of 2 million, for use in aerial surveys and receives a government grant of 10% towards the cost. The equipment is expected to have a four-year life. Exhibit 12.3 shows the effect of the grant on Tasman's x1 accounts under the deferred income and net-of-grant approaches.

Exhibit 12.3 Accounting for government grants: deferred income and net-of-grant approaches

Facts

Tasman Company offers survey services to mining and oil companies. Early in x1, it purchases remote sensing equipment for use in aerial surveys. The equipment costs 2 million. It receives a government grant of 10% towards the cost. The equipment is expected to have a four-year life.

Tasman's capital at the start-x1 is 3 million. x1 profits before depreciation are 700,000. (Income taxes are ignored.)

Accounting for receipt of grant and amortisation of benefit (amounts in 000)

Deferred income approach	Dr.	Cr.	Net-of-grant approach	Dr.	Cr.
Start x1					
Equipment	2,000		Equipment	2,000	
Cash		2,000	Cash		2,000
Cash	200		Cash	200	
Deferred income (L+)		200	Equipment		200
End years x1–x4					
Depreciation expense	500		Depreciation expense	450	
Accumulated depreciation		500	Accumulated depreciation		450
Deferred income (L–)	50				
Other income (OE+)		50			

Tasman's end-x1 balance sheet (amounts in 000)

Deferred income approach		Net-of-grant approach	
Assets		*Assets*	
Plant	2,000	Plant	1,800
– Accumulated depreciation	– 500	– Accumulated depreciation	– 450
	1,500		1,350
Other assets	1,900	Other assets	1,900
Total assets	3,400	Total assets	3,250
Equities		*Equities*	
Capital, start-x1	3,000	Capital, start-x1	3,000
Profit in x1	250	Profit in x1	250
Shareholders' equity	3,250	Shareholders' equity	3,250
Deferred income	150		
Liabilities and shareholders' equity	3,400		

The 'bottom line' impact of the two methods is the same. Consider Tasman's profit in x1. Assuming profit before depreciation is 700,000 and the remote sensing equipment is the only depreciable asset, Tasman's x1 before-tax profit is 250,000 in both cases:

	Deferred income approach	Net-of-grant approach
Profit before depreciation	700,000	700,000
– Depreciation	–500,000	–450,000
+ Other income	+50,000	–
Profit before tax	250,000	250,000

During the amortisation period, Tasman's balance sheet differs between the two approaches. The carrying amount of fixed assets and total equities are lower under the net-of-grant approach. At the end of the amortisation period (end-x4 in Tasman's case), the balance sheets should be the same.

Ignoring indirect effects, government financial assistance clearly benefits a company's shareholders. The accounting reflects this. Shareholders' equity is higher each year by the amount of the amortised grant or subsidy. Moreover, because the aid flows into shareholders' equity by way of reported earnings, it can be distributed. Other things being equal, Tasman's retained profits – and thus its distributable capital – are 200,000 greater at the end of x4 than if no grant had been received.

SECTION 3   Shareholders' equity and financial statement analysis

Disclosure

The published annual accounts are a rich source of information about a firm's capital structure. National law usually requires firms to disclose the following:

- The number and par value of shares issued at the balance sheet date. This information is given for each class of share (e.g. ordinary, preference).
- The composition of reserves. For example, EU companies break down this figure into: share premium; revaluation reserve; retained profits (identifying separately the profit or loss for the year); and other reserves required by national law (e.g. legal reserve).
- The dividends declared – or proposed to be paid – with respect to the current year's profits.

IAS go further. Companies following IAS must disclose *changes* in their capital structure, in particular the change in shares outstanding and the changes in share capital (including treasury shares) and reserves. They can show these changes in equity either in a separate statement or in the notes to the accounts. They must also provide information about 'off-income-statement' gains and losses – either in the statement of changes in equity or separately – so that readers of the financial statements can determine the firm's **comprehensive income or loss** for the period.[24]

Most companies following IAS now include a statement of changes in equity as a fourth statement after the balance sheet, income statement and cash flow statement. Exhibit 12.4 shows an extract from the statement in the BMW Group's 2001 accounts.

What were the main events affecting BMW's equity in 2001?

Exhibit 12.4 BMW Group: extracts from 2001 consolidated accounts

Balance sheet (part) at 31 December
(in euro million)

	Notes	**2001**	2000
Subscribed capital		**673**	672
Capital reserves		**1,937**	1,914
Revenue reserves		**9,405**	7,849
Accumulated other equity		**−1,245**	−1,003
Equity	[26]	**10,770**	9,432

Statement of changes in equity (part)
(in euro million)

	Subscribed capital	Capital reserves	Revenue reserves	Accumulated other equity			Total
				Translation differences	Fair value measurement of marketable securities	Derivative financial instruments	
Balance at 31 December 2000	672	1,914	7,849	−261	−23	−719	9,432
Subscribed capital increase	1	–	–	–	–	–	1
Additional paid-in capital on preferred stock	–	23	–	–	–	–	23
Dividends paid	–	–	−310	–	–	–	−310
Translation differences	–	–	–	−165	–	−23	−188
Financial instruments	–	–	–	–	−92	38	−54
Net profit 2001	–	–	1,866	–	–	–	1,866
Balance at 31 December 2001	673	1,937	9,405	−426	−115	−704	10,770

Note 26   Equity (part)

Number of shares issued
At 31 December 2001, issued BMW AG common stock was divided, as in the previous year, into 622,227,918 shares with a par value of one euro. Issued BMW AG preferred stock was divided into 50,638,232 (2000: 49,597,812) non-voting shares, with a par value of one euro. All of the company's stock is issued in the form of bearer shares. Preferred stock bears an advance profit (additional dividend) of €0.02 per share.

At the Annual General Meeting held on 18 May 1999, authorised capital was created with a total nominal amount of €5 million for the issuance of 5 million preferred stock shares. During the fiscal year 2001, this was used for the subscription of 1,040,420 (2000: 1,138,000) employee shares. . . .

Capital reserves
Capital reserves comprise additional paid-in capital on the issue of shares. The addition to capital reserves of €23 million (2000: €21 million) arose in the year from the subscription of employee shares.

Revenue reserves
Revenue reserves are disclosed in accordance with the disclosure requirements contained in German commercial law. They comprise the post-acquisition and non-distributed earnings of consolidated group companies. In addition, revenue reserves include both positive and negative goodwill arising on the consolidation of group companies prior to 31 December 1994 and the effect, recognised as an adjustment to the opening balance of revenue reserves, of the first-time application of IAS.

(*Source*: BMW Group, *Annual Report and Accounts 2001*. Reproduced by permission of BMW Group.)

- First, the company raised only a small amount (€24 million) of additional capital. Note 26 to the accounts tells us employees subscribed for around 1 million shares of preferred stock in 2001. (BMW's preferred stock does not have a fixed dividend rate. Holders share in the earnings of the company in the same way as common stockholders but they receive an additional dividend of €0.02/share to compensate them for the loss of voting rights.)
- Second, BMW's revenue reserves (i.e. retained profits) rose over €1.5 billion, the net effect of net profits in the year of €1.8 billion and dividends paid (out of 2000 profits) of €0.3 billion.
- Third, cumulative off-income-statement losses – described as 'Accumulated other equity' on BMW's balance sheet – increased by €242 million to €1,245 million at end-2001. They consist of unrealised losses (net of gains) arising from investments held in other currencies ('Translation differences') and from certain financial instruments measured at fair value. Changes in exchange rates give rise to 'differences' (i.e. gains or losses) when BMW translates its foreign subsidiaries' financial statements into euros before consolidating them. (We illustrate the accounting in Chapter 15.) And IAS require firms to value certain financial instruments at fair value and take unrealised holding gains and losses on them directly to equity, as we'll see in Chapter 13.

BMW's comprehensive income is the sum of its reported net profit and off-income-statement gains and losses in the year. Given the company reported €242 million of such losses in 2001, comprehensive income was only €1,624 million that year. Moreover, off-income-statement losses increased sharply between 2000 and 2001, offsetting in part the rise in net profit:

(In € million)	2001	2000	% change
Net profit	1,866	1,209	+54
Off-income-statement losses, net	−242	−18	
Comprehensive income	1,624	1,191	+36

(The comparative figures for 2000 are taken from BMW's 2001 consolidated accounts.)

An alternative way of presenting off-income-statement gains and losses is to provide a statement of comprehensive income as an adjunct to the regular income statement. UK companies, for example, include a 'Statement of recognised gains and losses' beneath the income statement. The statement, known locally as the 'struggle' after its initials (st_rgl), combines the net profit or loss recognised in the income statement with other gains and losses recognised directly in shareholders' equity on the balance sheet.

Definition of 'equity' in key financial ratios

'Equity' in profitability ratios

When investors speak of 'equity' in a profitability context – as in 'return on equity' (ROE) – they're usually referring to the capital provided by a company's ordinary (common) shareholders. These are the owners of the firm and ROE is designed to measure the return they've earned on their investment. That investment consists of their contributions (paid-up share capital and share premium) and the cumulative profits attributable to them that have been reinvested in the firm on their behalf. From a profitability perspective, it is irrelevant whether the reinvested capital has a restricted use (e.g. legal reserve, reserve for own shares) or is available for immediate distribution (e.g. retained profits).

$$\text{Return on equity} = \frac{\text{Net income attributable to ordinary shareholders in period}}{\text{Share capital and reserves attributable to ordinary shareholders (period average)}}$$

Preference share capital is not included in the denominator of ROE and income attributable to these shareholders is excluded from the numerator. Similarly, in the case of a group, 'equity' is usually defined as the capital provided by the *parent* company's ordinary shareholders. The interests of minority shareholders in subsidiaries' net assets and income are excluded from denominator and numerator, respectively. Note that since treasury stock is deducted from equity, the denominator represents the capital attributable to *outstanding* shares.

Book value per share and price-to-book ratio

Investors also refer to ordinary shareholders' equity as stated in the accounts as 'book value'. By contrast, 'market value' represents the interests of the same ordinary shareholders measured at current market value. Book value is often expressed on a per-share basis:

$$\text{Book value per share} = \frac{\text{Share capital and reserves attributable to ordinary shareholders (end-period)}}{\text{End-period ordinary shares outstanding}}$$

Investors compare a company's per-share book value (taken from the most recent accounts) with the current market price of its shares, by means of the **price-to-book ratio**:

$$\text{Price-to-book ratio} = \frac{\text{Current market price per share}}{\text{Book value per share (end of most recent quarter or year)}}$$

Profitable and growing companies have a price-to-book ratio of greater than one. This is evident when we analyse the price-to-book (P/B) ratio: the ratio is the product of return on equity and the price–earnings ratio.

$$\text{Price-to-book ratio} = \frac{\text{Earnings per share}}{\text{Book value per share (end period)}} \times \frac{\text{Current market price per share}}{\text{Earnings per share}}$$

We learned in Chapter 6 that investors use the P/E ratio as an indicator of a company's growth prospects. The P/B ratio serves the same role – but it's a richer measure because it includes the firm's current profitability as well. And it's a more reliable measure in the case of companies whose earnings are cyclical or that suffer short-term earnings declines. PSA Peugeot Citroën's recent history illustrates this well. The French vehicle manufacturer made losses in 1997. It returned to profit in 1998 and improved its profitability in each of the following three years. The company's P/B ratio for the five years to 2001 is analysed below:

	1997	1998	1999	2000	2001
PSA Peugeot Citroën					
P/B ratio	0.72	0.78	1.23	1.20	1.20
Return on equity (end-year)	(0.05)	0.057	0.084	0.15	0.162
P/E ratio	–	13.6	14.7	8.0	7.4

The company's P/B ratio was less than unity in 1997 and 1998: the company's return on equity was less than its cost in both years. The P/B ratio rose above unity in 1999 as the company increased its ROE. Despite the company's rising profitability in subsequent years, the market judged its growth prospects to be limited: the P/B ratio remained around 1.2 in 2000 and 2001. (Note that French share prices were declining in these years and PSA's share price was affected by the change in market sentiment.) By contrast, the P/E ratio tells a less clear story. It was relatively high in 1998 and 1999 – because earnings were low but recovering – but fell back in 2000 and 2001 as earnings stabilised. (It can't be computed for 1997 because PSA made losses that year.)

Investors combine information about current book value with forecasts of future earnings in their valuations of companies. Box 12.2 describes one such valuation model they use – it's known as the **residual income model** – and the insights it provides.

BOX
12.2

Valuing companies using book value and residual income

How do investors value a company? The traditional approach is to forecast the dividends it will pay during its lifetime and discount them to the present time. The dividend discount model has the following form:

$$MVE_0 = \sum_{t=1}^{\infty} \frac{DIV_t}{(1 + r_e)^t} \tag{1}$$

where:

MVE$_0$ is the market value of a firm's equity at time 0;

DIV$_t$ is the dividends it pays in period t; and

r_e is the cost of the firm's equity capital (i.e. the minimum return investors demand for investing in the firm).

Dividends are the cash return investors expect to get from their investment. Should they sell the investment in the future, the price they will receive will be based on the dividends the market expects the company to pay thereafter. All firms can be valued on this basis. Even those that don't pay dividends currently because they can profitably reinvest all their earnings will pay them at some point in the future as investment opportunities diminish.

Economists have shown that the above model can be expressed in terms of accounting numbers.[25] If we assume 'clean surplus accounting', that is, income in the period is 'comprehensive income' and includes off-income-statement gains and losses, then the dividends a company pays in a period are equal to net income (NI) adjusted for the change in the book value of equity (BVE) over the period. (Capital transactions can be ignored because of their offsetting effects on the book value of equity each period.)

$$BVE_t = BVE_{t-1} + NI_t - DIV_t$$

Thus:

$$DIV_t = NI_t + BVE_{t-1} - BVE_t \tag{2}$$

Substituting (2) into (1) and rearranging terms gives the following 'residual income' model:

$$MVE_0 = BVE_0 + \sum_{t=1}^{\infty} \frac{NI_t - r_e BVE_{t-1}}{(1 + r_e)^t} \tag{3}$$

Residual income – or **abnormal earnings** as the term is also known – is equal to reported net income (NI) less a capital charge (r_eBVE). The capital charge is, in effect, the minimum income shareholders demand given the investment they've made in the firm. Thus the second term on the right-hand side of equation (3) is the discounted value of future abnormal earnings. The market value of equity today is the sum of these discounted future abnormal earnings and the book value of equity today.

The residual income valuation model yields important insights. First, if a company can earn a return on equity no greater than its cost, the second term on the right-hand side of equation (3) is zero and the market value of equity is equal to its book value. It is current and expected abnormal earnings that cause market value to exceed book value. Second, the larger the abnormal earnings the firm can generate, the faster they grow and the longer they're expected to last, the greater is the market premium over book value (MVE$_0$ – BVE$_0$). Note, however, that abnormal earnings usually have a limited life. Other firms become aware of them, enter the market and compete them away. Third, the present value of expected abnormal earnings is sensitive to the firm's cost of capital. A fall in the risk premium that investors demand for investing in equities leads to a fall in the cost of capital for all firms. Some economists attribute the bull market of the 1990s and its reversal in the early 2000s to the way changes in expectations about corporate earnings growth and changes in the equity risk premium were mutually reinforcing.

'Equity' in leverage ratios

When calculating financial leverage, investors opt for a broader definition of equity. In addition to ordinary shareholder's equity, they include other sources of non-repayable capital such as (non-redeemable) preference shares. In the case of a group, 'equity' embraces minority interests as well as those of parent company shareholders. Thus the consolidated debt–equity ratio is usually calculated as follows:

$$\text{Debt–equity ratio} = \frac{\text{Net debt at end-period}}{\begin{array}{c}\text{Shareholders' equity} \\ \text{(of ordinary and non-redeemable} \\ \text{preference shareholders), end-period}\end{array} + \begin{array}{c}\text{Minority interests,} \\ \text{end-period}\end{array}}$$

There is disagreement about how to classify equity with debt characteristics. For example, is preferred stock redeemable at the option of the holder debt or equity? Companies following IAS account for it as debt. Companies following US GAAP, however, must show such redeemable preferred stock and other types of 'quasi-equity' (also known as 'temporary equity') in a separate section – between long-term debt and shareholders' equity – on the balance sheet. How might an investor deal with debt-like equity securities in leverage calculations? A useful approach is to check the terms of the contract between issuing company and security holder (the company usually provides summary details in the notes to the accounts) and decide on the classification of each type of security on a case-by-case basis.

Summary

Investors favour the corporate over other forms of business organisation because their liability for an enterprise's debts is limited and they can transfer their ownership interest more easily. Firms exploit these advantages to raise equity capital more cheaply.

Shares are evidence of ownership of a company. There are various classes of share. Investors who hold ordinary shares enjoy the greatest potential returns but bear the greatest risk of loss. Ordinary shares carry certain rights, in most cases the rights to participate in the firm's earnings and to vote. Shares that carry a different set of rights, such as preference shares, offer investors a different risk–return prospect.

The shareholders' equity of a company comprises contributed capital and earned capital. Equity and net assets increase when the firm issues new shares for consideration (increase in contributed capital) or generates profits (increase in earned capital). Both decrease when it buys back and cancels its shares (decrease in contributed capital) or generates losses (decrease in earned capital).

Dividends in cash or in kind are distributions of earned capital and decrease shareholders' equity and net assets. Share dividends, transfers of profit to reserves and capital write-downs alter the composition of shareholders' equity but not its overall amount.

Companies purchase shares for treasury as a financial investment, to fund employee share schemes, and as an alternative to paying a cash dividend. Whatever the reason, the accounting is the same. Shares held in treasury are a deduction from equity and any gains or losses on trading should not be recognised on the income statement.

Government grants are not viewed as contributed capital. They are recorded as deferred income or as a reduction in the cost of the grant-financed asset. Either way, they serve over time to increase income and thus distributable capital.

Until recently, form rather than substance governed the accounting for compound instruments such as convertible securities. This is now changing. Under new international rules, companies must account for the liability and equity components of such instruments separately.

Investors use 'equity' – or 'book value' – in profitability, leverage and valuation calculations. They also monitor the change in shareholders' equity over the year, using the 'statement of changes in equity' now provided by many companies. Information in this statement allows them to calculate a company's comprehensive income, a broader measure of performance that incorporates off-income-statement gains and losses arising in the year.

Problem assignments

P12.1 Accounting for share issue and profit appropriation

In year 5, a group of business school graduates decide to launch a courier service in an unnamed EU country. They call their company Iris and its logo shows a pair of winged (and nimble) feet.

Listed below are key events in years 6 and 7 which affect Iris's shareholders' equity. (All currency amounts are in euros.)

1 The company issues 400,000 shares for 15 a share on 2 January year 6. The shares are fully paid in year 6. The par value of a share is 5.
2 The company has a 31 December year-end. At the end of year 6, it reports a net profit of 1 million. This is recorded in a 'Profit for the year' account in the year 6 balance sheet.
3 Iris's shareholders approve the following appropriation of profits in June year 7:
   – a cash dividend of 1 a share;
   – a transfer of 10% of profits to a legal reserve, as required by law;
   – the balance of the year 6 profit to be retained.
4 Iris's shareholders also approve the declaration of a 10% share dividend in June. The company accounts for the dividend by capitalising retained profits at the par value of the shares issued.

Required

(a) Show the effect of the events listed above on the company's accounts, using journal entries or the balance sheet equation. Specify the shareholders' equity account(s) affected. If assets or liabilities are affected, assume the entry is to 'Net assets'.

(b) An investor buys 8,000 Iris shares on 2 January year 6, and is still holding them in June year 7. What journal entries does he make in his own accounts at the time of the above events? Assume he has a 31 December year-end and accounts for investments at cost. What is the cost per share of his investment in Iris at the end of June year 7?

Check figure:
(a) Share capital, June year 7   2.2 million

P12.2 Reporting changes in share capital

FlySavvy is a low-cost airline based in Europe. Revenues and profits have grown rapidly since it started operations in x1. The company has invested heavily in new aircraft as it has expanded its route network. To finance these investments, it has had to raise additional capital from its shareholders and borrow funds from financial institutions. The company launched an initial public offering of its shares in x3 and made a secondary issue of shares in x4. The shareholders' equity section of its end-x4 balance sheet is set out below (all amounts, save per-share amounts, are in €000).

Shareholders' equity	At end-x4
Share capital (€0.05 par value ordinary shares, 147.1 million issued and outstanding)	7,355
Share premium	297,479
Retained earnings	231,084
	535,918

Net profit for x4 of 83,586 is included in the retained earnings figure. The company pays no dividends on its shares.

The following events affect FlySavvy's shareholders' equity in x5 (again, all amounts are in €000, save per-share amounts):

- The company issues 5.5 million ordinary shares in March x5 at a price of €22.8 a share. Issue costs of 4,213 are charged against the share premium account.
- The company carries out a 2:1 split of its shares in July x5.
- It reports net profit for the year of 120,328.

Required

(a) Prepare the shareholders' equity section of FlySavvy's x5 balance sheet. What is the number of issued and outstanding shares at the end of x5?

(b)* Consider the effect of the following additional event in x5. FlySavvy buys back 3 million shares in November x5 and holds them in treasury. (The company has a share option scheme for executives and wants to ensure there are sufficient shares available should executives exercise the options in x6 when they're allowed to.) The repurchased shares were issued at an average price of €7.63 and FlySavvy buys them back at a price of €12.08. Revise the shareholders' equity section of the company's x5 balance sheet prepared in (a). What is the book value per FlySavvy share at end-x5?

* Part (b) of the assignment draws on material in section 2 of this chapter.

P12.3 Dividends and other appropriations of profit: impact on the accounts

Repsol YPF is a large Spanish integrated oil and gas company that has extensive oil and gas holdings in Argentina. Exhibit 12.5 contains an extract from the note on 'Stockholders' equity' in the English-language version of its 2001 accounts.

Under Spanish corporation law, a company must transfer 10% of its net income each year to a legal reserve until the balance in the reserve reaches at least 20% of capital stock (i.e. share capital). 'Paid-in surplus' is another term for the share premium account. The column 'Translation differences' shows the exchange gains or losses that arise from translating the net assets of Repsol YPF's foreign businesses, including its investments in Argentina, into euros.

Repsol YPF paid interim dividends of €232 million (€0.19 per share) in 2000 and €257 million (€0.21 per share) in 2001. Shareholders at the company's annual general meeting in 2001 approved a supplementary dividend of €378 million (€0.31 per share) for 2000 but the following year accepted management's recommendation that none be paid for 2001.

Required

(a) Why didn't Repsol YPF transfer 10% of 2000 net income to legal reserve in 2001?

(b) Why does the company show an 'interim dividend' as a deduction in the shareholders' equity section of the balance sheet each year?

(c) What was the dividend paid by Repsol YPF to its shareholders in 2001?

(d) What is the company's dividend pay-out ratio in 2000? in 2001?

(e) With the information Repsol YPF discloses in its 2001 accounts, it is possible to determine the distribution of its 2001 income in 2002.

Exhibit 12.5   Repsol YPF: Movement in stockholders' equity in 2001 (in € millions)

| | Capital stock | Paid-in surplus | Legal reserve | Other reserves of the parent company | | Reserves of consolidated companies | Translation differences | Income for the period | Interim dividend | Total |
				Voluntary and other reserves						
Balance as of										
December 31, 2000	**1,221**	**6,428**	**224**	**1,114**		**3,397**	**562**	**2,429**	**(232)**	**15,143**
Distribution of 2000 income:										
Legal reserve	–	–	20	–		–	–	(20)	–	–
Interim dividend	–	–	–	–		–	–	(232)	232	–
Supplementary dividend	–	–	–	–		–	–	(378)	–	(378)
Voluntary reserves	–	–	–	39		1,760	–	(1,799)	–	–
Translation differences & other	–	–	–	–		21	(1,016)	–	–	(995)
Net income for the year	–	–	–	–		–	–	1,025	–	1,025
Interim dividend	–	–	–	–		–	–	–	(257)	(257)
Balance as of										
December 31, 2001	**1,221**	**6,428**	**244**	**1,153**		**5,178**	**(454)**	**1,025**	**(257)**	**14,538**

(*Source:* Repsol YPF, *Annual Report and Accounts 2001.*)

> (i) What is the amount the company must transfer to legal reserve in 2002?
> (ii) What is the expected transfer to voluntary reserves in 2002?

(f) Why do you think management recommended no supplementary dividend be paid out of the company's 2001 income?

P12.4 Share splits, share repurchases, and conversion of debentures*

PSA Peugeot Citroen is one of Europe's largest and most successful vehicle manufacturers. Net sales of its manufacturing and sales companies exceeded €50 billion in 2001, earnings per share increased almost 28% and the share price bucked the downward trend in world stock markets by rising 18% over the year.

There were a number of transactions and events causing changes to shareholders' equity in 2001. Unusually, the company's issued and outstanding shares declined over the year. Extracts from the 2001 consolidated accounts relating to shareholders' equity are set out in Exhibit 12.6.

Required

(a) PSA split its stock in July 2001. A shareholder asks: "Why is there no entry in the accounts to record the share split? Surely this is a capitalisation of reserves and there should be a transfer from 'Capital in excess of par value of stock' or other reserve to 'Common stock'." Explain to the shareholder why 'Common stock' has not increased as a result of the share split.

(b) When PSA buys shares for capital reduction purposes, it records the purchase as a deduction from equity. (Shares purchased for employee stock option schemes – the other main reason the company buys back its shares – are recorded as an asset.)
> (i) Reconstruct the journal entries the company made in 2001 to record the purchase and cancellation of shares as part of its capital reduction programme.
> (ii) Under EU law, the company should transfer distributable reserves to 'reserve for own shares' when it buys back shares for cancellation. What is the amount of the transfer to 'reserves for own shares' the company should make in 2001 to ensure it preserves its capital? (Although there is no evidence of a transfer in 2001, PSA may have done so. 'Retained earnings' includes legal and statutory reserves.)

Exhibit 12.6 PSA Peugeot Citroën: extracts from accounts on stockholders' equity, 2001

CONSOLIDATED STATEMENT OF STOCKHOLDERS' EQUITY

(in € millions)	Stockholders' equity	Common stock	Capital in excess of par value of stock	Retained earnings	Treasury stock	Cumulative translation adjustment
Balance, as of December 31, 2000	9,361	278	276	9,515	(507)	(201)
2001 net income	1,691	–	–	1,691	–	–
Dividend (€5 per €6 par value share)	(217)	–	–	(217)	–	–
Issuance of shares	109	4	105	–	–	–
Purchases of treasury stock	(458)	–	–	–	(458)	–
Cancellations of treasury stock	–	(23)	(381)	(510)	914	–
Translation adjustment	(204)	–	–	–	–	(204)
Balance, as of December 31, 2001	10,282	259	–	10,479	(51)	(405)

Note 29 – Stockholders' equity (extracts). Common stock, capital in excess of par value of stock.

a – Common stock
As of December 31, 2001, the Company's capital stock amounted to €259,109,146, represented by common shares with a par value of €1 (note 29-c), all fully paid. The shares may be held in bearer or registered form, at the choice of stockholders. Shares registered in the name of the same holder for at least four years carry double voting rights (article 38 of the bylaws).

b – Changes in the number of shares issued and outstanding

(in euros)	2001
As of January 1	278,223,630
Cancelled shares	(23,450,000)
Shares issued on conversion of debentures	4,335,516
As of December 31	259,109,146

c – 2001 stock split
On July 2, 2001, existing €6 par value shares were exchanged for new €1 par value shares, on a six-for-one basis. This stock split was authorized by stockholders at the Extraordinary Meeting of May 16, 2001.

e – Capital reduction
On November 23, 2001, the Company cancelled 23,450,000 new €1 par value shares under a stockholder-approved program. . . . The difference between the cost of the shares and their par value was charged against 'Capital in excess of par value of stock' in the amount of €381 million . . . and against 'Retained earnings' for €510 million.

j – Treasury stock
Effective from December 31, 1999, treasury stock corresponds to the cost of all the Peugeot S.A. shares purchased on the open market, net of cancelled shares and shares held for allocation on exercise of management and employee stock options which are reported under 'Short-term investments' (in the balance sheet).

Share and shareholder data: supplementary information

Buyback and cancellation of shares
The share buyback program launched in 1999 was actively pursued in 2001 when a net total of 10,424,509 Peugeot SA shares were bought back at an average price of €46.40. Under the authorization granted at the Annual Stockholders' meeting on May 16, 2001, 23,450,000 shares representing 8.3% of shares outstanding, were cancelled as of November 23, 2001. . . At December 31, 2001, the Company held 2,994,287 of its shares in treasury, of which 1,940,100 were allocated to stock option plans.

(*Source*: PSA Peugeot Citroën, *Annual Report and Accounts 2001*. Reproduced by permission of PSA Peugeot Citroën).

(c) Holders of PSA convertible debentures converted most of the debentures to shares in 2001. The company gives details of its convertible debentures in note 34 of the accounts:

> "In March 1994, Peugeot S.A. issued convertible debentures for a total of €604 million. The four million debentures were issued at a price of €150.92 and were convertible at any time on the basis of one share per debenture.
>
> The debentures matured on January 1, 2001. Of the 747,329 debentures outstanding as of December 31, 2000, 722,586 were converted into shares and 24,743 were redeemed for cash."

According to the 2000 consolidated balance sheet, the carrying amount of the convertible debentures outstanding at end-2000 was €113 million. The company classifies the convertibles as straight debt in its accounts.

(i) How many shares were issued in 2001 on conversion of the debentures?

(ii) Reconstruct the journal entries the company made in 2001 to record the conversion and redemption of debentures.

* Assignment draws on material in section 2 of this chapter.

P12.5 Accounting for share repurchase and cancellation*

Iris Company started a courier service in year 5 (*see* P12.1). Following a reappraisal of the company's investment opportunities in year 9, management decide to return some of its capital to the owners. After obtaining shareholder approval, they buy back 50,000 shares at a price of €19 a share and cancel them.

Assume the cost of the shares bought back is €13.6 a share. Iris's shareholders' equity just before the share repurchase stands at €7.7 million. It consists of 440,000 issued ordinary shares (with a par value of €5/share), share premium of €4 million and retained profits of €1.5 million.

Required

Show the effect of the share repurchase and cancellation on Iris's year 9 accounts, using journal entries or the balance sheet equation. Assume the company establishes a non-distributable reserve, 'Reserve for own shares', in order to maintain its permanent capital.

* Assignment draws on material in section 2 of this chapter.

P12.6 Accounting for convertible securities*

Suizo-Hispania, a designer and builder of luxury automobiles, issues at par 15 million of 3% ten-year convertible bonds at the start of year 7. (All currency amounts are in euros.) Holders can convert each 1,000 bond into 250 Suizo-Hispania ordinary shares (of 1 par value) from year 9. The company would have had to offer investors an 8% yield if it had issued debt without the conversion option.

Required

(a) How does Suizo-Hispania (S-H) record the issue of bonds in year 7, assuming:

(i) it accounts for them as debt only?

(ii) it recognises the equity component of the securities separately?

Use journal entries or the balance sheet equation. Ignore issuance costs. Assume the residual value approach is used to measure the equity component of the securities.

(b) What is the interest expense Suizo-Hispania records in year 7 under assumption (a) (i)? under assumption (a) (ii)? The company has a calendar financial year and a full year's interest is charged in year 7. The company uses the interest method to determine interest expense under (a) (ii).

(c) Bondholders convert all the bonds to ordinary shares at the start of year 9. The market price of an ordinary S-H share then is 5. How does S-H record the issue of ordinary shares in exchange for bonds, assuming that on issue of the bonds in year 7:

(i) it accounts for them as debt?

(ii) it recognises the equity component of the securities separately?

Check figure:

(a) (ii) Equity component   5.03 million

* Assignment draws on material in section 2 of this chapter.

P12.7 Capital provided by risk- and revenue-sharing partnerships: accounting issues

Rolls Royce, the UK aero-engine maker, was criticised for some of its accounting policies in 2002. One area of controversy was its treatment of risk- and revenue-sharing partnerships (RRSPs). These are designed to help the company fund development of new jet engines, which are often costly and risky investments. Management explain in the notes to the 2001 accounts how the group accounts for them.

> *Risk- and revenue-sharing partnerships.* From time to time the Group enters into arrangements with partners who, in return for a share in future programme turnover or profit, make cash or other payments in kind which are not expected to be refundable. Sums received are credited to other operating income and payments to partners are charged to cost of sales.

Many analysts challenge this accounting treatment. They argue that an RRSP is a source of financing and should be accounted for as such on the balance sheet. Some think it is equity capital; others claim it is a loan.

Rolls Royce's management disagree. They maintain it has none of the features of a loan. 'Is it repayable? No. Does it accrue interest? No. It has no attributes of a loan, which is why it is not treated as a loan,' says Paul Heiden, the company's then finance director.

RRSPs had a significant impact on Rolls Royce's 2001 results. The group reported sales of £6,328 million (€10,206 million) and pre-tax profit (excluding exceptional items) of £422 million that year. The pre-tax profit figure was struck after crediting £126 million for RRSPs:

	£m
RRSPs – receipts (credited to 'other operating income')	239
– payments (charged to 'cost of sales')	(113)
Net impact of RRSPs on pre-tax profit	126

Required

Comment on the way Rolls Royce accounts for its RRSPs. Explain why its accounting treatment is – or is not – correct, in your view. If you disagree with the company's treatment, outline the way you think it should account for the RRSPs.

P12.8 Unusual types of security: debt or equity?

Some companies issue unusual types of security that are difficult to classify as either debt or equity. Details of three such issues are given below. They are taken from the notes to the 2001 accounts of certain large international companies.

(1) Redeemable preference shares of a subsidiary company

On 30 March 2001, a wholly owned subsidiary of Company A issued perpetual, cumulative, non-voting preference shares for a total amount of €205 million.

The preference shares have no voting rights. They are not redeemable, except at the exclusive option of the issuer, in whole but not in part, on or after the fifth anniversary of the issue date or at any time in case of certain limited specific pre-identified events including changes in taxation laws. Should redemption occur, the redemption price would be equal to the par value together with dividends accrued, but not yet paid.

From the issue date to the fifth anniversary of the issue date the preference shares will carry a dividend based on a variable 6-month Euribor rate. Beyond the fifth anniversary, the dividend rate will increase by an additional 2% per annum, in line with market conditions for such instruments.

The dividends are payable semi-annually from the issue date. The preference shareholders will benefit from a limited Company A guarantee covering the subsidiary's obligations under its shares.

(2) Undated subordinated notes

Company B issued, on 29 Septem illion Auction Rate Coupon Undated Subordinated Notes. These notes may be redeemed at the option of the issuer except in certain exceptional circumstances, including any failure to pay interest when due, when they may be redeemed at the option of their holders. They rank *pari passu* (i.e. equally) with holders of other subordinated indebtedness. Interest is payable semi-annually, at variable rates based on Euribor. The payment of accrued interest may be suspended if both of the following conditions are satisfied:

(i)   the annual non-consolidated accounts of Company B show an absence of income available for distribution;

(ii) the annual consolidated accounts of Company B show that the consolidated net income available for distribution to common shareholders is less than or equal to zero.

(3) Non-voting participating securities

Company C issued 100,000 non-voting participating securities in ecus in 1984. The non-voting participating securities are not redeemable. Their remuneration is included in financial charges. These securities were converted into euros in 1999.

Each security carried a coupon that gave the holder the right to subscribe to a new non-voting participating security until February 1987. There were 94,633 securities resulting from the exercise of the coupons.

The remuneration of the 194,633 non-voting participating securities comprises a fixed interest element of 60% of the nominal value of the security and equal to 7.5% per annum and a variable amount on the remaining 40% based on the consolidated net income of the previous year within the limits fixed in the prospectus.

Required

Consider each of the above issues of securities. How should the issuing company present the securities in its accounts under IAS? Give reasons for your decision.

Notes to Chapter 12

1   Other forms of business organisation may be available. For example, in some countries investors can structure the business as a hybrid of partnership and company. Examples are the German GmbH & Co. and the US limited liability company (LLC). These are partnerships for tax purposes but some (GmbH & Co.) or all (LLC) of the members enjoy limited liability.

2   The term 'public' is used in its legal sense here. It signifies a company of a certain size which meets EU legal requirements for that designation. However, investors also use the term to describe companies whose shares are listed on a stock exchange. We refer to these as *quoted companies*.

3   Evidence of ownership can take different forms. In the case of **registered shares**, the company knows who the owners are, since it (or its representative) maintains a register of shareholders and shareholdings. In the case of **bearer shares**, the share certificate itself is the only evidence of ownership. Only public companies – and, even then, in some but not all EU member states – can issue bearer shares.

4   In some jurisdictions in Europe and the USA, companies are allowed to issue shares without a par value.

5   In some countries, there's a two-stage approval process. A company's statutes specify the shares it is **authorised** to issue. Its **issued** share capital is usually less than its authorised capital. Shareholders approve, by simple majority, a proposal of the directors to increase the number of shares issued – up to the authorised level. Any increase beyond the authorised level requires further shareholder

approval, this time by super-majority vote, to amend the firm's statutes and set a new limit on authorised share capital.

6   Note that firms are not required to distribute earnings. Shareholders may decide in general meeting that, because of the high returns available from investments within the firm, all profits should be reinvested.

7   Many companies in northern Europe have a management board and a supervisory board. In this case, shareholders (and employees) elect members to the supervisory board which in turn appoints and may dismiss members of the management board.

8   This is not the only example of a shareholder right that is available in some countries but not in others. For other examples, *see* Box 7.1 'Legal tradition, investor protection and company financing' in Chapter 7.

9   La Porta, R., Lopez-de-Silanes, F. and Shleifer, A. (1999), Corporate ownership around the world, *Journal of Finance*, 54: 471–517. Another method of maintaining control available in some countries is to use a special legal vehicle, the 'partnership limited by shares' (KGaA in Germany; SCA in France). This is a quoted company with a separate legal personality. The majority of its shareholders have limited liability (they are, in effect, limited partners) but there is at least one that has unlimited liability and management control (the general partner). Family-controlled firms such as Henkel and Merck in Germany and Michelin in France use this legal structure.

10   La Porta *et al.*, op. cit., tables II, III and IV.

11   The payment of dividends and the transfer of profits to reserves are examples of 'profit appropriation', the setting aside of profits for a particular purpose.

12   Should a company issue 'no par value' shares, it will credit the whole proceeds of the issue to 'Share capital'. In some jurisdictions, however, the company may assign an 'accounting value' to the no par value shares, in which case the entry is as shown.

13   Practice is different in some countries. UK and Irish firms show 'called-up capital' on the balance sheet. They disclose subscribed capital not yet called in the notes to the accounts. US firms show 'subscriptions receivable' as a deduction within shareholders' equity rather than as an asset.

14   Companies face other legal hurdles preventing them from depleting assets through 'excessive' profit distributions. For example, the EU's 2nd Directive requires firms to transfer from retained profits to a non-distributable reserve the effect of accrual adjustments which increase profits but not cash (e.g. capitalisation of R&D costs). The non-distributable reserve is reduced as these adjustments reverse (e.g. through amortisation).

15   Under US GAAP, the term 'share dividend' can strictly only be used where the shares issued as a result of the dividend amount to 25% or less of the shares previously outstanding. A distribution larger than this is considered to be, in effect, a share split since management's intent is to reduce the market price per share – the same rationale as for a share split. (In fact, US companies refer to a large share dividend as a 'stock split effected in the form of a stock dividend'.) US companies account for large share dividends by capitalising retained profits or share premium at par, not fair value.

16   Be careful of the phrase '*x* for *y*' when applied to share issues. We have used it here in the sense of 'in exchange for'. However, it can also be used in the sense of 'in addition to'. In a 1:1 share split, one new share is issued in exchange for one old. In a 1:1 (or 100%) share dividend, an additional share is distributed for every one share held.

17   International Accounting Standards Board, *IAS 32: Disclosure and Presentation*, para. 5. An equity instrument is defined in the same paragraph as 'any contract that evidences a residual interest in the assets of an enterprise after deducting all of its liabilities'.

18   Standing Interpretations Committee [of the IASC], *SIC 17: Equity – Costs of an Equity Transaction*, para. 6.

19   International Accounting Standards Board, *IAS 10: Events After the Balance Sheet Date*, paras 11 and 12.

20   This condition need not apply if shares are purchased for an employee share ownership scheme or to 'prevent serious and imminent harm to the company' (2nd Directive, Art. 19).

21   Standing Interpretations Committee [of the IASC], *SIC 16: Share Capital – Reacquired Own Equity Instruments (Treasury Shares)*, paras 4 and 5.

22   For a fuller discussion of these ideas, *see* Jen, F.C., Choi, D. and Lee, S.-H. (1997), Some new evidence on why companies use convertible bonds, *Journal of Applied Corporate Finance*, Spring, pp. 44–53.

23 International Accounting Standards Board, *IAS 20: Accounting for Government Grants and Disclosure of Government Assistance.*

24 International Accounting Standards Board, *IAS 1: Presentation of Financial Statements.*

25 For an extensive discussion of the model and a comparison with other methods of valuing companies, *see* Palepu, K.G., Healy, P.M. and Bernard, V.L. (2000), *Business Analysis and Valuation*, 2nd edition, South-Western College Publishing, chapter 11.

13

Financial investments

INTRODUCTION

Companies as well as individuals can be investors. They buy and sell debt and equity securities issued by other companies and governments. These are primary financial instruments. They also invest in secondary (or derivative) instruments such as options or futures. They may acquire non-financial assets – commodities, real estate, works of art – for investment purposes. In this chapter and the next we focus on the accounting for and reporting of financial investments.

The way a company accounts for a financial investment depends in part on management's reasons for acquiring it. Thus investments in debt securities purchased for trading purposes are valued differently from those that management plan to hold to maturity. In addition, the method of accounting for long-term *equity* investments depends on the power the investor company can exert over the investee's operating and financing decisions. Investments in debt securities, (passive) investments in equity securities and derivatives are the subject matter of this chapter. We discuss the accounting for long-term equity investments where the investor has influence or control in Chapter 14.

The accounting for financial investments is changing. New international rules require companies to value them at fair value. Traditionally, companies measured them at cost or LOCOM. We focus on the new approach in this chapter, illustrating how fair value accounting is applied and explaining why it has found favour with investors and regulators alike. We also look at the way derivatives are accounted for. Derivatives are widely used as a means of hedging against adverse price or cash flow movements and we show how companies account for both hedging instruments (e.g. derivatives) and items being hedged (e.g. existing financial assets and liabilities or expected future transactions) under new IAS.

In the final section we discover what information investors can glean about a firm's financial investments from the annual accounts and how they use it to analyse the returns from the investments and their risk.

Types of financial investment

Companies' financial investments take many forms. Companies buy other firms' bonds, shares and short-term securities such as commercial paper. They purchase derivative instruments such as futures and options. They also invest in government securities – from treasury bills to long-term government debt. They make loans to other firms: companies within a group do this, as well as banks.

Reasons for investing in financial assets

Why does a company make such investments? One obvious reason is that the expected return is high relative to the risk assumed. But there may be other considerations and these affect the type of investment made.

1 *Cash management.* A company usually invests cash that is surplus to its operating requirements in the short-term debt of governments (treasury bills) or companies (commercial paper) or in funds which invest in such securities (money market funds). It may invest such cash in a portfolio of actively traded equity securities, too. It chooses these investments because they are highly liquid and involve small price risk.[1]

 The amount of these investments can be large. For example, a company may raise long-term capital through a debt or equity issue just before the balance sheet date but not spend the cash on the purchase of long-term assets until after it. Sometimes a company purposely carries large cash balances. Acquisition-hungry companies maintain high levels of liquid assets – to buy target firms on advantageous terms – if they find it costly to raise external capital quickly.

2 *Business strategy.* Often a company acquires a shareholding in another for strategic reasons. For example, it may want to gain access to new technology. The shareholding may be defensive – to prevent the investee's takeover by another. Or the investment could be in the nature of an option – giving the firm the opportunity to enlarge its stake at a later date if the initial investment proves worthwhile. The investments by some pharmaceutical giants in small biotechnology start-ups can be viewed in this way.

 In all the above cases, the shareholding in percentage terms is likely to be small. The investor has a voice in the investee's affairs but no power. Power, from an investment perspective, is usually correlated with the size of a shareholding. A company acquires a large stake in another as a means of exercising influence or control over it.

3 *Risk protection.* A company may acquire a financial asset as a hedge. It wishes to protect itself against adverse movements in asset prices or cash flows. For example, it buys a put option (the right to sell at a specified price) on a shareholding to hedge against a decline in the share's market price. An exporter enters into a forward exchange contract to limit losses arising from the appreciation of its home currency. A firm that borrows funds at a floating rate signs a swap agreement to cap its interest charges: under the swap it receives interest at a floating rate but pays interest at a fixed rate. Note that in this case it acquires a financial asset (a stream of variable receipts) and incurs a financial liability (a stream of fixed payments).

4 *Funding of liabilities.* Companies set aside cash – and invest it – to meet future liabilities. For example, a firm may establish a sinking fund in order to repay the principal of a loan when it matures. A company that offers a defined benefit pension scheme to its employees invests cash – internally or via a separate pension fund – to meet future pension payments to retirees.

Balance sheet presentation

Financial statement users can often deduce the reason for a financial investment by the way it is presented on the balance sheet. Investments which are held for trading purposes or which management expect to realise within the year are shown as current assets. Those which management plan to hold to maturity (debt securities) or for more than one year are shown as financial fixed assets. Thus investments which are strategic in nature are usually classified as long-term; those which serve a cash management role are classified as current.

Users can also learn more about the nature of the company's *equity* investments from their description on the balance sheet. Various types of equity investment are illustrated in a partial balance sheet in Exhibit 13.1. Note that this is company X's *individual* balance sheet, not the consolidated balance sheet of the X group.

It's helpful to know the terms used to describe the various types of equity investment. Where company X has a large minority stake in another, C, and *participates* in its management, it has a 'participating interest' in C. C is an **associate** (or **associated company**) of X. Where X has a majority stake in another, B, and *controls* its operations, X is B's **parent company** and B is X's **subsidiary** (or **affiliate**).

Exhibit 13.1 Equity investments: description and balance sheet presentation

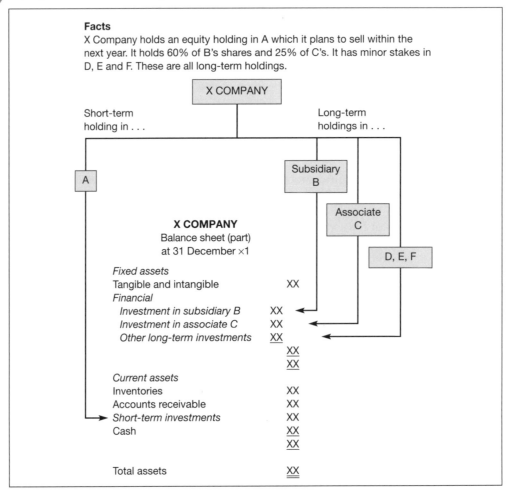

Facts

X Company holds an equity holding in A which it plans to sell within the next year. It holds 60% of B's shares and 25% of C's. It has minor stakes in D, E and F. These are all long-term holdings.

X COMPANY

Short-term holding in . . .

Long-term holdings in . . .

A

Subsidiary B

Associate C

D, E, F

X COMPANY
Balance sheet (part)
at 31 December ×1

Fixed assets		
Tangible and intangible		XX
Financial		
Investment in subsidiary B	XX	
Investment in associate C	XX	
Other long-term investments	XX	
		XX
		XX
Current assets		
Inventories		XX
Accounts receivable		XX
Short-term investments		XX
Cash		XX
		XX
Total assets		XX

Exhibit 13.1 can be adapted to cover non-equity investments. 'Other long-term investments' include investments in debt securities which the company plans to hold to maturity and other assets (e.g. real estate, works of art) held for investment purposes. All investments which are held for trading purposes and/or have a short life are 'short-term investments'.

Recognition and measurement

The accounting for financial investments is in transition. The major change concerns their measurement. Companies following IAS must now value many of their investments in debt and equity securities and derivative instruments at fair value. Traditional methods of valuation – namely, the cost method and the lower of cost or market (LOCOM) method – are outlawed (LOCOM) or can be used in limited circumstances only (cost). US GAAP impose similar requirements on US companies. The European Commission introduced a fair value directive in 2001 amending the main accounting directives (4th and 7th) to permit EU companies to record certain investments at fair value. However, outside North America, cost and LOCOM continue to be widely used. (Listed EU companies are not required to adopt IAS until 2005.) In our discussion of financial investments, we outline all the main valuation methods now in use – cost, LOCOM, fair value – but place special emphasis on the fair value method.

Recognition and initial measurement

Recognition of financial investments poses few problems. A company usually records an investment on its balance sheet on acquisition, that is, when it acquires legal title to the asset.[2] The standard criteria for recognising assets are met at this point: the risks and rewards of ownership have passed to the company and the cost or fair value of the asset can be measured reliably.

Where an investor company acquires a compound financial instrument (i.e. an investment containing an *embedded derivative*), IAS require the derivative and the host contract to be recognised and measured separately. Thus a company that buys another firm's convertible securities as an investment should account for the two components – the straight debt element and the conversion option – as separate investments. However, it can account for the compound instrument as one investment if (a) the two components share similar economic characteristics and (b) each would be accounted for in the same way (i.e. at fair value and changes in fair value taken to income) if separated.

Companies record investments initially *at cost*.[3] This holds under both traditional and new approaches to investment accounting. 'Cost' includes transaction costs, such as purchase commissions. In addition, certain adjustments may have to be made. For example, a company acquiring debt securities must show separately any unpaid interest that has accrued up to the date of purchase. Assume Grandet Company buys, at par, 40 million of 7% French government bonds on 1 October x1. Assume the government pays interest on these bonds annually on 30 June. Thus the price Grandet pays for the bonds is 40.7 million. It records the accrued interest of 700,000 (40 million × 7% × 3/12) separately as a receivable (amounts shown are in millions):

Investment in bonds with accrued interest		
Dr. Investment in 7% bonds (A+)	40	
Dr. Accrued interest receivable (A+)	0.7	
Cr. Cash (A–)		40.7

Similarly, a company making an equity investment should record separately, as dividend receivable, any distributions by the investee from its pre-acquisition profits. In each case, the accrued interest or dividend is an adjustment to the investment's cost and should not be reported as income by the investor. Thus, assuming Grandet has a 30 June year-end, it records the interest of 2.8 million received on 30 June x2 as follows:

Payment of first-period's interest

Dr. Cash (A+)	2.8	
Cr. Accrued interest receivable (A–)		0.7
Cr. Interest income (OE+)		2.1
(40 million × 7% × 9/12)		

Grandet recognises interest income for only the nine months to end-June x2 that it holds the bonds.

Measurement subsequent to acquisition

How are financial investments measured *after* acquisition? Here the accounting becomes more complicated. There are several ways of valuing an investment. From Exhibit 13.2 we see that the valuation method depends partly on management's intentions when the investment was acquired (e.g. to hold it for trading or for other purposes) and partly on the nature of the investment (e.g. size of shareholding, in case of equity investments).

We consider below the accounting for small equity shareholdings and investments in debt securities. (We discuss methods of accounting for large equity stakes in other companies in Chapter 14.) We outline the traditional cost-based approach to valuing these investments and then explain and illustrate the new fair value-based approach.

Exhibit 13.2 Financial investments: principal valuation/accounting methods*

	NATURE OF INVESTMENT				
	Debt securities	←	**Equity securities**	→	
		Passive minority < 20%	*Active minority 20–50%*	*Joint venture*	*Active majority > 50%*
Traditional accounting (dominant practice)	← LOCOM / Cost → *(short-term investments) (long-term investments)*			Equity method *or* Proportionate consolidation	
New accounting	← IAS 39 →		Equity method		Global consolidation
Classification of investments	*Held-to-maturity Held-for-trading Available-for-sale*				
Valuation method	Amortised ← Fair value → cost				

* In consolidated accounts.

Traditional cost-based approach

Until recently, most companies in Europe and elsewhere accounted for short-term investments at LOCOM and long-term investments at cost. The main features of the two valuation methods are summarised below.

- *Cost*. Under the cost method, the investor company carries the asset at cost throughout the holding period. It recognises interest income as it accrues and dividend income on receipt. Changes in the asset's market value are generally not recognised until disposal. Only if the asset is impaired does the investor company write it down to its lower recoverable amount. When the company sells the asset, it recognises the difference between the net proceeds from sale and the asset's carrying amount (cost or lower recoverable amount) as a realised gain or loss.
- *LOCOM* (lower of cost of market). Under the LOCOM method, the investor company carries the asset at cost – or market value if lower. Where market value is below cost, the company writes down the asset and recognises a loss for the amount of the write-down.

Dr. Loss from decline in market value of investment (OE–)	xxx
Cr. Investment in ABC Company (A–)	xxx

Should the asset's market value recover in a later period, the company recognises as a gain the recovery of the asset's value – but only up to its cost.

Dr. Investment in ABC Company (A+)	xxx
Cr. Gain from recovery in market value of investment (OE+)	xxx

The LOCOM rule may be applied on an individual investment or a portfolio basis. In the latter case, a loss is recognised only when the *portfolio*'s market value is less than its cost. The carrying amount of the portfolio is adjusted through a valuation allowance (similar to that used for inventory write-downs): the individual investments themselves are still carried at cost.

In other respects, the accounting is similar to that under the cost method. The investor company accrues interest income but recognises dividend income on receipt. On the sale of the asset, it records as a gain or loss the difference between the net proceeds from sale and the asset's carrying amount.

What is the rationale for these two valuation methods? Consider the cost method first. Supporters argue that an investor company – and by extension, its owners – want to know the return generated by an asset or set of assets. In the case of an equity investment held for the long-term, the return will be mainly in the form of dividends. Where a debt investment is held to maturity, the return will consist of interest. Given the expected holding period, changes in the market value of the investment from one period to the next are of little economic interest to the investor company or its shareholders, it's claimed.

Advocates of LOCOM point to weaknesses in the cost method. Investments are overstated when market value is below cost. LOCOM provides a prudent basis for valuation: declines in market value are recognised, but increases (above cost) aren't. Moreover, it deters management from gambling with company assets. Managers who are not required to reveal unrealised losses may be tempted to make risky investments in the hope of generating offsetting gains. Such investments may result in yet larger losses. This was the experience of some Japanese companies in the early 1990s. LOCOM forces management to disclose – and account for – all unrealised losses.

New fair value-based approach

Under the fair value method, the investor company carries the investment on the balance sheet at end-of-period market value. It recognises in income any change in the asset's market value that arises in the period. Interest and dividend income – and realised gains and losses – are accounted for in the same way as they are under the cost and LOCOM methods.

Fair value accounting is often described in the financial press as 'mark-to-market' accounting. The fair value of an investment traded in an active market is clearly its quoted market price.

Where an active market does not exist – as in the case of unquoted securities, fair value is estimated using accepted valuation techniques (e.g. discounting of future cash flows).

Accounting for financial investments at fair value is not new. It has long been popular in parts of the financial sector (e.g. mutual funds). What is new is the growing demand from the investment community that *all* companies should account for financial investments in this way. Why is this? What are the merits of fair value accounting for this class of asset? Supporters point to its informational benefits. Most of the expected return on *short-term* investments takes the form of capital gain. For this reason, investors want to know the changes in the market value of such investments from period to period. The market values of *long-term* investments are also of interest: investors can determine the opportunity cost to the company of retaining the investments (i.e. the benefit forgone by not selling them.)

Companies can provide these informational benefits by *disclosing* the fair values of investments in the notes to the accounts. Why require companies to *recognise* fair values in their accounts? Supporters make the following argument in defence of recognition. By having to include unrealised gains and losses in income, management have less scope to manipulate corporate profits. Under the cost and LOCOM methods, a gain is shown in the income statement only when an investment is sold. (Under the cost method, most losses are recognised only then too.) As a result, management can alter reported profit by delaying or bringing forward the sale of an investment whose market value is greater than its cost. Under fair value accounting, management cannot do this: all changes in value are recognised as they occur.

This argument has added force owing to stock market developments in recent years. The world's stock markets have grown in size and depth. Market capitalisation soared from US$9.4 trillion in 1990 to US$36 trillion in 1999, a 280% increase. (World GDP grew 34% in the same period.) The markets are also broader and more liquid. There are now many more quoted securities and they are traded in more active markets. For example, the number of listed companies on the world's stock markets almost doubled in the 1990s – from 25,400 in 1990 to 49,600 in 1999. Value traded increased, too – from US$5.5 trillion in 1990 to US$31 trillion in 1999.[4] As a result, information about the current values of many financial investments is easier to obtain and more reliable.

Fair value accounting under IAS

General framework

Current IAS do not insist on full fair value accounting for all financial investments.[5] Companies following IAS must classify investments into one of three categories and account for them as follows:

1 *Held-to-maturity (HTM) investments.* These are investments in debt securities that the investor company has the 'positive intent and ability' to hold to maturity. *HTM investments must be accounted for at amortised cost.*
2 *Held-for-trading (HFT) investments.* These are investments that the investor company designates as such on acquisition. They can be debt or equity securities and are usually held for the short-term. *HFT investments must be accounted for at fair value; all changes in fair value should be recognised in income.*
3 *Available-for-sale (AFS) investments.* All other financial investments are described as AFS investments. They can be investments in debt or equity securities and presented as either current or non-current assets, depending on the expected holding period. *AFS investments are accounted for at fair value; changes in fair value are recognised directly in shareholders' equity in the balance sheet.* Unrealised gains and losses are transferred to the income statement when an investment is sold (or if it's impaired).

Thus IAS require the investor company to measure all financial investments at fair value with the exception of HTM investments. If fair value cannot be reliably determined (i.e. there is no active market from which to obtain a quoted price and it is not feasible to estimate fair value in other ways), then IAS require that the investment be measured at cost (at amortised cost if it has a fixed maturity).

Illustration

How a company classifies an investment – as HTM, HFT or AFS – can have a significant impact on its accounts. We use a simple example to illustrate this. Rosaura's company designs and makes family games: her most successful product is the board game *Battle of the Sexes*. With the growing integration of national markets in Europe, she decides to invest in other EU countries. At start-x3, her company buys small equity stakes in Castiglia and Runebif, quoted Spanish and UK companies respectively, and invests in the debt securities of Lebleu and Bosco Nero, a French and an Italian company. Acquisition prices and end-x3 fair values of the four investments are set out below. All currency amounts are in euros. Note that the effective interest rate on the Lebleu and Bosco Nero securities is 6% at the date of acquisition in x3. (Transaction costs are ignored.)

Category and investment	Face or nominal value	Acquisition price (in x3)	Amortised cost at end-x3
Held-to-maturity investment			
Bosco Nero 5% bonds, due end-x7	400,000	383,157	386,146
			Fair value at end-x3
Held-for-trading investment			
Castiglia ordinary shares, €5 par	75,000	126,000	140,000
Available-for-sale investments			
Lebleu 8% bonds, due end-x15	200,000	235,400	215,880
Runebif ordinary shares, €2.50 par	125,000	300,000	311,000

Rosaura accounts for the investment in Bosco Nero bonds as a held-to-maturity investment. She views the small equity stake in Castiglia as a speculative investment – the shares were undervalued at start-x3 in her view – and accounts for it as a held-for-trading investment. The other two investments are classified as available-for-sale investments: Rosaura considers both to be long-term investments but does not plan to hold the Lebleu bonds to maturity.

The accounting entries Rosaura makes in x3 with regard to these four investments are explained below.

Bosco Nero bonds: held-to-maturity investment

Rosaura acquires the 400 Bosco Nero bonds for cash.

Start-x3:	Dr. Investment in Bosco Nero 5% bonds (A+)	383,157	
	Cr. Cash (A–)		383,157

Bosco Nero pays interest on the bonds annually at the end of December so there is no accrued interest in the purchase price. The bonds purchased have a face value of €400,000. Rosaura must amortise the discount of €16,843 at the purchase date over the remaining five years of the bonds' life, using the interest method. Rosaura records interest income of €22,989 in x3: this is based on an effective interest rate of 6% at the start of x3 when the bonds were purchased and includes €2,989 of amortised discount. (Note that the creditor's accounting for investments in fixed-rate bonds mirrors that used by the debtor to account for fixed-rate liabilities – and which we described in Chapter 11.)

During x3:	Dr. Accrued interest receivable [5% × €400,000] (A+)	20,000	
	Dr. Investment in Bosco Nero 5% bonds (A+)	2,989	
	Cr. Interest income [6% × €383,157] (OE+)		22,989
End-x3:	Dr. Cash (A+)	20,000	
	Cr. Accrued interest receivable (A–)		20,000

The carrying amount of the bonds in Rosaura's balance sheet at the end of x3 is €386,146. The market value of the bonds is only €372,900 because the market interest rate on these bonds was 7% at year-end. However, the bonds are not written down to this lower value because the increase in interest rates does not indicate an impairment of the investment.

Castiglia ordinary shares: held-for-trading investment

Rosaura's Castiglia investment (15,000 ordinary shares) is also acquired for cash.

Start-x3:	Dr. Investment in Castiglia ordinary shares (A+)	126,000	
	Cr. Cash (A–)		126,000

Castiglia does not pay a dividend in x3. The shares increase in value during the year. At year-end, Rosaura revalues the investment and recognises the unrealised holding gain in income. (We assume Rosaura's company prepares annual financial statements only. If it prepares accounts every six or even every three months, it will record the change in value of AFS (and HFT) investments half-yearly or quarterly.)

End-x3:	Dr. Investment in Castiglia ordinary shares (A+)	14,000	
	Cr. Unrealised holding gain in income (OE+)		14,000

Rosaura carries the investment in the end-x3 balance sheet at €140,000. The €14,000 unrealised gain is shown on the income statement under 'Financial income'.

Lebleu bonds and Runebif ordinary shares: available-for-sale investments

As with her other investments, Rosaura pays for the 200 Lebleu bonds and 50,000 Runebif ordinary shares with cash.

Start-x3:	Dr. Investment in Lebleu 8% bonds (A+)	235,400	
	Dr. Investment in Runebif ordinary shares (A+)	300,000	
	Cr. Cash (A–)		535,400

Runebif declares and pays a dividend of 18 cents a share in June x3. Interest on Lebleu's 8% bonds is paid at the end of the year. Rosaura records dividend income when received but accrues interest income as it's earned over the year.

June x3:	Dr. Cash (A+)	9,000	
	Cr. Dividend income [18¢ × 50,000 shares] (OE+)		9,000
During x3:	Dr. Accrued interest receivable (A+)	16,000	
	Cr. Interest income [8% × €200,000] (OE+)		16,000
End-x3:	Dr. Cash (A+)	16,000	
	Cr. Accrued interest receivable (A–)		16,000

At the end of x3, Rosaura adjusts the carrying amounts of the two investments to fair value (Runebif +€11,000; Lebleu –€19,520). The decline in the fair value of the Lebleu bonds is due to the rise in market interest rates during x3. Rosaura recognises the unrealised holding gain (Runebif) and loss (Lebleu) directly in shareholders' equity in the balance sheet.

End-x3:		
Dr. Unrealised holding loss in equity (OE–)	19,520	
Dr. Investment in Runebif ordinary shares (A+)	11,000	
Cr. Investment in Lebleu 8% bonds (A–)		19,520
Cr. Unrealised holding gain in equity (OE+)		11,000

The *net* unrealised holding loss of €8,520 is recorded in a separate reserve account – under the caption 'Accumulated fair value adjustments' or 'Unrealised holding gains/losses (UHG/L) in equity'. (The loss should be stated net of tax.) The impact of the revaluation on Rosaura's end-x3 balance sheet is illustrated below:

BALANCE SHEET
Assets

⋮

	Cost	Revaluation	End-x3 fair value
Investments			
– in Runebif shares	300,000	11,000	311,000
– in Lebleu bonds	235,400	(19,520)	215,880
		(8,520)	

Shareholders' equity

⋮

	Start-x3	Revaluation	End-x3
Unrealised net holding loss in equity	0	(8,520)	(8,520)

⋮

Impairment, disposal and transfer of financial investments

In the previous section we presented the basic framework of fair value accounting under IAS. We now extend it by showing how companies account for impairments of investments, disposals, and transfers between categories of investment. We use our Rosaura example to illustrate the accounting for each of these events. The key facts on which we'll base our discussion are summarised below (amounts are in euros):

Category and investment	Acquisition price (in x3)	Amortised cost at end-x3	Impaired value at end-x4	Disposal value in x4	Fair value on transfer to AFS
Held-to-maturity investment					
Bosco Nero 5% bonds, due end-x7	383,157	386,146			372,900
		Fair value at end-x3			
Held-for-trading investment					
Castiglia ordinary shares, €5 par	126,000	140,000		136,000	
Available-for-sale investments					
Lebleu 8% bonds, due end-x15	235,400	215,880	96,000		
Runebif ordinary shares, €2.50 par	300,000	311,000		318,000	

Impairment

An investor company must carry out an impairment test on its financial investments at each balance sheet date. *An investment is considered impaired if its carrying amount is greater than the (discounted) cash flows the company can expect to recover from sale (HFT and AFS investments) or holding the asset (HTM investments).* For evidence of impairment, the company must first assess the health of the investee (i.e. the issuer of the debt or equity securities). Warning signals include sustained periods of losses, continuing restructuring of the business and renegotiation of loan agreements. *If evidence of impairment exists, the company must write down the investment to recoverable amount and recognise the impairment loss in income.*

Impairment of AFS investments can have a significant income statement impact. If the company has any unrealised holding gains on such investments, impairment results in the transfer of these gains from the balance sheet to the income statement. Suppose, for example, that Lebleu encounters financial difficulties in late x4 and Rosaura estimates the recoverable amount of its Lebleu 8% bonds at only €96,000 at the end of the year. Rosaura records the impairment loss as follows:

End-x4:	Dr. Loss from impairment (OE–)	139,400	
	Cr. Unrealised holding loss in equity (OE+)		19,520
	Cr. Investment in Lebleu 8% bonds (A–)		119,880

The loss from impairment is the difference between the acquisition cost (€235,400) and the estimated recoverable amount from selling the AFS investment (€96,000) at end-x4. The unrealised loss of €19,520 recorded in x3 is removed from equity and the investment itself is written down by €119,880 – from its end-x3 carrying amount (€215,880) to the recoverable amount. This is shown below:

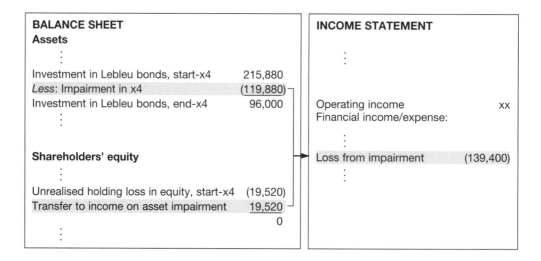

Disposal

Under IAS, a company 'derecognises' a financial investment (or other financial asset) when:

1 *it gives up its rights to the asset's cash flows;*
2 *it transfers those rights to another party and has no continuing involvement in them; or*
3 *the rights expire.*

Event 1 occurs when a company sells an investment; event 3 occurs when an option expires. (The reason for including event 2 is to prevent a company disguising a loan – with financial assets transferred to the lender as collateral – as a sale of assets.) On disposal of an investment (the most common form of derecognition), the company realises a gain or loss and books it in the income statement. The gain or loss is the difference between the net proceeds from sale and the carrying amount of the investment. A further adjustment may be needed if the investment sold is an AFS investment. Any unrealised holding gains or losses that have accumulated in equity are realised then and must be recognised in income.

Rosaura disposes of two investments in x4. She grew disenchanted with her equity stakes in Castiglia and Runebif during the year and decides to sell them both. Castiglia is an HFT investment, Runebif an AFS one. The market value of Rosaura's stake in Castiglia falls back – from €140,000 at end-x3 to €136,000 at the date of sale in March x4. By contrast, Runebif's share price continues to rise but at a slow rate. By November x4, when Rosaura decides to get rid of it, her stake in Runebif is worth €318,000. Rosaura makes the following entries in x4 to record the sale of both investments. (Transaction costs are ignored.)

March x4:	Dr. Cash (A+)	136,000	
	Dr. Loss on sale of HFT investment (OE–)	4,000	
	Cr. Investment in Castiglia ordinary shares (A–)		140,000
Nov. x4:	Dr. Cash (A+)	318,000	
	Dr. Unrealised holding gain in equity (OE–)	11,000	
	Cr. Investment in Runebif ordinary shares (A–)		311,000
	Cr. Gain on sale of AFS investment (OE+)		18,000

In the case of the HFT investment (Castiglia), a loss arises because the net proceeds from the sale (€136,000) are less than the carrying amount of the investment (€140,000, the fair value at end-x3). As for the AFS investment (Runebif), disposal results in a reported gain of €18,000: this is the difference between the net proceeds (€318,000) and the acquisition cost (€300,000). The gain includes the unrealised holding gain accumulated in equity (€11,000) and the change in the investment's fair value between the last balance sheet date and the date of sale (€318,000 – €311,000). Note, though, that the net impact on shareholders' equity *in x4* is only €7,000. The above calculations of gain and loss ignore tax effects. The financial statement impact of the disposal of the Runebif shares is shown below:

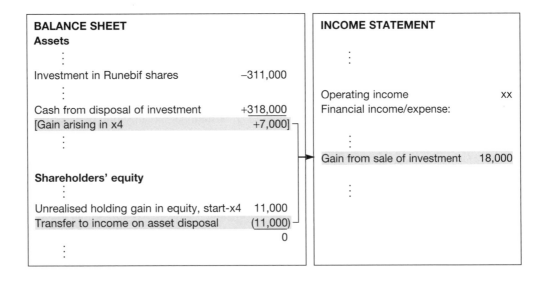

Transfer

Current international accounting rules create a new problem for investor companies: how to account for transfers of investments between categories. Such transfers occur for *bona fide* reasons (e.g. a change in management's intentions with regard to the holding period) and for suspect ones, too. For example, if a company is nursing unrealised holding losses on an HFT investment, management might seek to reclassify it as an AFS investment – or an HTM investment, in the case of a debt instrument – before the balance sheet date, in order to avoid recognising the losses in income. Regulators have devised rules for transfers that limit the opportunities for earnings management in this way.

Two features of international rules on investment transfers stand out. *First, an HFT investment should never be reclassified.* By electing to classify an investment in this category at the time of acquisition, the company commits itself to recognising in income all unrealised gains and losses on the investment until disposal. *Second, all permitted reclassifications must be carried out at fair value. The new classification determines the treatment of the unrealised holding gains or losses.* For example, where a company transfers an HTM investment to the AFS category (because of a change in intent or ability), it recognises unrealised gains and losses in equity. Where it transfers an AFS (debt) investment to the HTM category it designates the fair value at date of transfer as the new amortised cost and amortises past gains and losses, along with the discount or premium at date of transfer, over the remaining life of the investment.

Rosaura's portfolio of investments allows us to illustrate the accounting for transfers. At the start of x4, she reclassifies the investment in Bosco Nero's 5% bonds to the AFS category since she no longer intends to hold them to maturity. The market value of the bonds at that time is €372,900 (since the market interest rate has risen to 7%) and the amortised cost of the bonds is €386,146 then. She makes the following entry to record the transfer:

Start-x4:	Dr. Investment in Bosco Nero 5% bonds [AFS] (A+)	372,900	
	Dr. Unrealised holding loss in equity (OE–)	13,246	
	Cr. Investment in Bosco Nero 5% bonds [HTM] (A–)		386,146

The above entry ensures that the transfer of the bonds occurs at fair value and the unrealised loss (€386,146 – €372,900) is taken to equity, in the same way as other unrealised gains and losses on AFS investments.

Exhibit 13.3 summarises the effect of the above-mentioned events in both x3 and x4 on the company's key ledger accounts.

New international standards on financial investments: a review

The new international accounting rules on financial instruments are a compromise. The then IASC had originally planned to introduce fair value accounting for *all* financial assets and liabilities but its draft proposals encountered considerable opposition when they were published in 1997. To meet the deadline of IOSCO (International Organisation of Securities Commissions) for a core set of international accounting standards to be issued by 1998, the IASC scaled back its ambitions. The resulting standard on the recognition and measurement of financial instruments, IAS 39, is similar in essentials to US GAAP on the topic. The three-way split of investments – held-for-trading (HFT), held-to-maturity (HTM), and available-for-sale (AFS) investments – is taken directly from the US standard. Many companies were concerned that fair value accounting would lead to greater income volatility, investors would perceive companies to be more risky, and corporate capital costs would rise. As a result, US GAAP (and IAS) restrict pure fair value accounting – where changes in fair value pass through the income statement – to HFT investments only.

Key events in x3 and x4

1 Rosaura accounts for 400,000 5% Bosco Nero bonds at amortised cost in x3. Bonds yield 6% to maturity. x3 amortisation is 2,989 [(6% × 383,157) – (5% × 400,000)].
2 Castiglia shares are a held-for-trading investment. End-x3 fair value is 140,000. Unrealised gain of 14,000 is recognised in income.
3 Runebif shares and Lebleu bonds are available-for-sale investments. End-x3 fair values are 311,000 and 215,880 respectively. Unrealised gain (11,000) and loss (19,520) are recognised in equity.
4 Lebleu bonds are impaired in x4. End-x4 fair value is 96,000. Impairment loss (of 139,400) is recognised in income. It includes previous unrealised losses recorded in equity (19,520).
5 Rosaura sells Castiglia (5a) and Runebif (5b) shares in x4. Realised loss (4,000) and gain (18,000) are recognised in income. Gain on Runebif sale includes previous unrealised gain recorded in equity (11,000).
6 Rosaura transfers Bosco Nero bonds to 'available-for-sale' category at start-x4. Bonds are adjusted down to fair value (372,900) and unrealised loss (of 13,246) is recognised in equity.

Fair value and other adjustments to financial investments: ledger entries

ASSETS

Investment in Bosco Nero 5% bonds

Purchase, x3	383,157		
[1] Discount amortised, x3	2,989		
Balance, end-x3	386,146	[6] Revaluation on transfer	13,246
Fair value, start-x4	372,900		

Investment in Castiglia ordinary shares

Purchase, x3	126,000		
[2] Revaluation	14,000		
Balance, end-x3	140,000	[5a] Disposal	140,000
Balance, end-x4	0		

Investment in Lebleu 8% bonds

Purchase, x3	235,400		
		[3] Revaluation	19,520
Balance, end-x3	215,880		
		[4] Impairment	119,880
Balance, end-x4	96,000		

Investment in Runebif ordinary shares

Purchase, x3	300,000		
[3] Revaluation	11,000		
Balance, end-x3	311,000		
		[5b] Disposal	311,000
Balance, end-x4	0		

OWNERS' EQUITY ('Profit for the year')

Unrealised gain/loss in income

		[2] Revaluation of C shares, end-x3	14,000

Impairment loss

[4] Impairment of L bonds, x4	139,400	

Realised gain/loss on disposal

[5a] Loss on sale of C shares, x4	4,000	[5b] Gain on sale of R shares, x4 18,000

OWNERS' EQUITY ('Reserves')

Unrealised gain/loss in equity ('Accumulated fair value adjustments')

[3] Revaluation of L bonds, end-x3	19,520	[3] Revaluation of R shares, end-x3	11,000
Balance, end-x3	8,520		
[5b] Sale of R shares, x4	11,000	[4] Impairment of L bonds, x4	19,520
[6] Transfer of BN bonds, start-x4	13,246		

Fair value accounting in its IAS 39 form is not problem-free, however. First, companies still face the risk of increased volatility – but to their balance sheets rather than their income statements. The rise and fall in world stock markets at the turn of the millennium had a corresponding impact on companies' assets and shareholders' equity – and the impact was most marked in companies that accounted for investments at fair value. Banks are required, under national and international regulations, to maintain minimum capital adequacy ratios: these ratios, in effect, relate shareholders' equity to assets. Many companies that borrow funds agree (or 'covenant') not to let the debt–equity ratio exceed a specified limit. For these companies, fair value accounting increases the risk that these limits will be breached. The French Banking Federation appealed to the European Commission in October 2002 not to adopt IAS 39 in its current form because it would increase banks' balance sheet volatility.[6]

Second, the new standard increases the risk of income manipulation. As mentioned earlier, prior to IAS 39 companies usually accounted for short-term investments at LOCOM and long-term (passive) investments at cost. A criticism of the cost method is that companies are encouraged to time disposals of investments so that the resulting realised gains or losses smooth their bottom-line income. LOCOM reduces the scope for doing this, however, since companies must recognise in income *all* declines in investments' fair value. By classifying all its investments as AFS (and thereby deferring unrealised gains and losses in equity), a company can ensure that the income statement impact will be identical to that under the cost method. Moreover, the new rules put added strain on the impairment test. Recall that if an investment is impaired, the decline in value is considered permanent and the investor company must recognise it in income immediately. How will managers decide – and auditors verify – that a large decline in market value is temporary (and therefore deferrable) rather than permanent? Although IAS 39 offers guidance, managers will try to interpret the rules to their company's advantage.

Finally, many analysts and investors question the reliability of 'synthetic' fair values. International rules allow firms to estimate an investment's fair value – using the market value of a comparable asset, discounted cash flow analysis or an option pricing model – if a quoted market price (from an active market) is not available. Following Enron's collapse in 2001, evidence came to light that US energy trading companies had misused such estimation techniques.[7]

Derivatives and hedge accounting

Companies invest in **derivative financial instruments** – or derivatives, for short – as well as primary ones such as debt and equity securities. Derivatives include share options, forward contracts for foreign exchange ('currency forwards'), commodity futures contracts and interest rate swaps. Companies invest in these instruments mainly for hedging purposes. We focus in this section on the accounting problems that derivatives as hedges give rise to.

Derivatives: definition and terminology

According to IAS, a derivative is a financial instrument:

1 whose value changes in response to the change in a specified price, rate or index;
2 that requires little or no initial net investment; and
3 that is settled at a future date.

The price, rate or index to which a derivative's value is linked is known as the *underlying*. Thus the market price of the ABC share is the underlying of the ABC share option; the euro-yen exchange rate is the underlying of the euro-yen currency forward. A derivative contract usually specifies a *notional amount*: it could be the number of shares in the case of a share option or the number of currency units in the case of a currency forward. The amount to be exchanged on the settlement date – the *settlement amount* – is a function of the notional amount of the derivative and the underlying's price or value. Thus the settlement amount of a euro-yen currency forward is: (Forward euro-yen exchange rate – Spot euro-yen exchange rate on the settlement date) × Number of currency units.

Hedging

Exposure to risk is an unavoidable aspect of commercial life. A company that buys or sells goods in a foreign currency bears the risk of adverse exchange rate movement while the transaction is outstanding. A firm that borrows money at a floating rate of interest runs the risk that the interest rate will rise during the life of the loan. Companies can try to offset these risks – in part or in whole – through hedging activities. Alternatively, they can accept the risk exposure. Hedging can be costly. Moreover, if a company's shareholders hedge their own investment risks, corporate hedging may simply duplicate their efforts.

Hedging can take many forms. Generally, there are two types of economic hedge: natural hedges and derivative-based ones. A company with US dollar revenues decides to borrow money in that currency: the cash inflows in dollars provide a natural hedge for the debt payments it must make in them. Derivatives provide another means of hedging. Consider the case of a metal refining company with large quantities of copper in inventory. It has agreed to deliver the metal to a customer six months hence at the spot price then. It decides to sell the copper forward, using a futures contract that matures on the delivery date. The futures contract is thus a hedge against a decline in the copper price over the six months.

This second example illustrates the two essential elements of an economic hedge. First, there must be a **hedged item** – the copper inventory in our example. This is an asset or liability, commitment or expected future transaction that exposes the company to the risk of changes in the future cash flows or in the fair values of an asset or liability. Second, there must be an **effective hedging instrument** – the futures contract in our example. This is usually a designated derivative whose fair value or cash flows are expected to offset, to a high degree, changes in the fair value or cash flows of the hedged item.

Hedge accounting

There are essentially two ways to account for a hedging instrument. Under hedge accounting, the hedging instrument is measured in the same way as the hedged item. Under fair value accounting, it is 'marked to market' each period, irrespective of the way the hedged item is measured. Consider our copper inventory example. Under hedge accounting, the copper and the futures contract are both measured in the same way – at fair value, under IAS – and changes in the values of each are recognised in the same period. Under fair value accounting, the futures contract is measured at fair value and changes in value are recognised in income each period while the inventory is measured at cost and holding gains and losses are deferred until it is sold.

An example illustrates how hedge accounting works in practice. On 1 January x1, Bottom borrows €10 million from General Weavers Capital (G.W. Capital) to finance expansion of his business. The loan is for three years at a floating rate of interest equivalent to Euribor (European Interbank Offered Rate) and interest is reset (and paid) annually.[8] Being a cautious weaver, Bottom wants to guard against interest rate increases during the term of the loan. He enters into a swap contract with Wild Thyme Bank on the same day, under which he pays interest at a fixed rate of 7% a year and receives interest at a floating rate equivalent to Euribor. The notional principal of the swap is €10 million, the term is three years and the (variable) interest rate is reset annually, so the swap is an effective hedging instrument. Interest under the loan and swap contracts flows as follows:

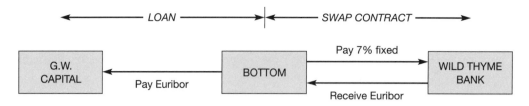

The swap in this case converts a variable-rate loan into a fixed-rate one.

Now to the accounting for the swap. First, we must establish its fair value each period. At 1 January x1, Euribor is 7% so the swap contract has a fair value of zero. The Euribor rate at each interest payment (and resetting) date and the fair value of the swap contract then are given below:

Date	Euribor	Net swap receipt (payment)	Fair value of swap asset (liability)
31 December x1	6.5%	€(50,000)	€(90,400)
31 December x2	7.15%	15,000	14,025
31 December x3	6.75%	(25,000)	0

In calculating the fair value of the swap contract at subsequent balance sheet dates, we assume, for simplicity, that Euribor remains at the then current rate for the remainder of the contract and the resulting stream of net swap receipts or payments is discounted at the fixed rate under the contract. Thus at end x1, the swap contract liability of €90,400 is based on assumed net payments of €50,000 (€650,000 floating rate receipt less €700,000 fixed rate payment) in x2 and x3 discounted at 7%.

Under hedge accounting, changes in the fair value of the interest rate swap are not recognised in income as they arise. Instead, they're deferred in a hedging reserve account and released to the income statement when 'settling up' occurs. Thus, as the hedging company recognises interest expense each period, it records as a gain or loss the net amount it receives or pays under the swap contract and adjusts the carrying amount of the swap at that time. Exhibit 13.4 shows, in simplified form, the entries Bottom makes each year between x1 and x3 in connection with the G.W. Capital loan and related swap contract.

Note that the swap has an offsetting effect on Bottom's income. For example, when Euribor is greater than 7% – as in x2, the gain on the hedging instrument (i.e. the net amount of €15,000 Bottom receives under the swap contract) offsets the 'loss' on the hedged item (the additional €15,000 interest payment under the loan agreement). As a result, the cost of the loan is fixed at 7%.

Hedge accounting is controversial. Supporters argue that it reflects management's intent in acquiring the hedge. Moreover, the income number is more meaningful. Gains from the hedging instrument are matched with losses arising on the hedged position; they are not recognised in different periods. Opponents criticise hedge accounting on practical grounds. They claim it gives too much discretion to management. By choosing the manner and timing of hedging, management can manipulate profits. New international accounting rules permit hedge accounting but, as we show below, seek to address the concerns of critics by imposing restrictions on its use.

Derivatives and hedge accounting: international rules

Like other financial investments, derivatives are measured initially at cost. For derivatives such as forward and futures contracts and interest rate swaps, there's usually no net investment initially so cost at that time is zero. For call options, however, the initial asset is the premium paid to the writer of the option for accepting the risk.

After the initial recognition date, derivatives must be 'marked to market' each balance sheet date.[9] If they're held for trading or speculative purposes, changes in fair value are recognised in income, as with other held-for-trading investments. If they're held for hedging purposes,

Exhibit 13.4 Interest rate swap contract and hedge accounting: illustration

Facts

At start-x1, Bottom borrows €10 million from G.W. Capital for three years at Euribor. Interest is paid and reset annually. Bottom enters into a swap contract with Wild Thyme Bank on the same date. The terms of the swap (notional principal of €10 million, three-year term, variable interest rate, Euribor-linked, reset annually) match those of the loan. Under the swap Bottom pays interest at a fixed rate of 7% and receives interest at a rate equivalent to Euribor.

Annual swap receipts and payments – and end-year fair values of the swap contract – in the three years x1–x3 are set out below (currency amounts are in euros).

Date	Euribor	Floating rate receipt	Fixed rate payment	Net receipt (payment)	Fair value of swap A/(L)
1 Jan x1	7%				Nil
31 Dec x1	6.5%	650,000	700,000	(50,000)	(90,400)
31 Dec x2	7.15%	715,000	700,000	15,000	14,025
31 Dec x3	6.75%	675,000	700,000	(25,000)	0

Loan- and swap-related accounting entries (in €000)

		x1 Dr	x1 Cr	x2 Dr	x2 Cr	x3 Dr	x3 Cr
Date							
1/1	Cash (A+)	10,000					
	Loan (L+)		10,000				
	To record loan from GW Capital						
31/12	Interest expense (OE–)	650		715		675	
	Cash (A–)		650		715		725
	To record interest paid on loan						
	Loss on hedge (OE–)	50				25	
	Cash (A–)		50				25
	Cash (A+)			15			
	Gain on hedge (OE+)				15		
	To record net payment or receipt under swap contract						
	Hedging reserve (OE–)	90.4				14.025**	
	Swap contract asset/liability		90.4				14.025
	Swap contract asset/liability			104.425*			
	Hedging reserve (OE+)				104.425		
	To record *change* in fair value of swap contract						
	Loan (L–)					10,000	
	Cash (A–)						10,000
	To record repayment of loan						

* Entry to adjust swap contract liability of 90.4 at end-x1 to swap contract asset of 14.025 at end-x2.
** Entry to adjust swap contract asset of 14.025 at end-x2 to nil value at end-x3.

unrealised gains and losses are either recognised in income or deferred in equity, depending on the nature of the hedge and its effectiveness.

IAS identify three categories of hedge and specify the way companies must account for each.

1 A company uses a **fair value hedge** when it seeks to protect itself against changes in the fair value of an asset or liability that are attributable to a particular risk. The change in fair value must affect net income. The hedge of copper inventory using a commodity futures contract that we discussed earlier is an example of a fair value hedge.

   In the case of a fair value hedge, IAS require the company to recognise the gain or loss on the hedging instrument in income. The company must also adjust the asset or liability being hedged for the change in fair value attributable to the hedged risk. Thus, in the case of the hedge of copper inventory, not only must the metal refiner mark the futures contract to market and take unrealised gains and losses to income but it must also adjust the carrying amount of the copper inventory to fair value and record these gains and losses in income as well.

2 A company uses a **cash flow hedge** when it seeks to protect itself against changes in future cash flows due to risks connected with (a) an existing asset or liability or (b) a forecast transaction. Variable rate debt is an example of (a): this is an existing liability where the company is exposed to the risk of variation in interest rates in future. An interest rate swap – in the form of a 'pay fixed, receive variable' contract like the one Bottom entered into with Wild Thyme Bank – is a cash flow hedge. A planned future purchase of a fixed asset in a foreign currency is an example of (b): this is a probable future transaction where the company is exposed to the risk of variation in exchange rates in the future. Purchasing foreign currency forward represents a cash flow hedge against this risk.

   With a cash flow hedge, IAS require a company to defer the gain or loss on the hedging instrument in equity (assuming the hedge is effective). The company brings the gain or loss into income in a future period when the hedged cash flow affects the income statement. Thus, as we saw in our Bottom example, changes in the fair value of its interest rate swap are deferred in 'Hedging reserve'. They are released into the income statement when the hedged interest payments are reflected – as interest expense – in Bottom's income statement.

3 A company may also designate a financial asset or liability as a **hedge of a net investment in a foreign entity**. Thus, under IAS, a eurozone-based parent with a US subsidiary can earmark a US dollar loan – raised by the parent company – as a hedge of the US subsidiary's net assets. As with cash flow hedges, the company must defer gains or losses on the hedging instrument (in this case, the exchange gains and losses on the dollar loan) in equity. The gains or losses are 'recycled' in income when the company disposes of the investment.

We mentioned earlier that hedge accounting is open to abuse. Management may try to set up a hedge retrospectively – by designating a derivative as a hedging instrument *after* sustaining unrealised holding losses on a financial asset or liability. In addition, the derivative designated as a hedge could be ineffective because, for example, the hedging instrument and the hedged item are in different currencies. Accounting regulators have sought to reduce the scope for abuse by laying down strict conditions when hedge accounting can be used. Under IAS, a company can use hedge accounting only if:

- it prepares formal documentation, at the outset, identifying the hedging instrument, the hedged item or transaction, and the nature of the risk being hedged; and
- the hedge is expected to be highly effective – that is, the company *expects* changes in fair value or cash flows of the hedging instrument to 'almost fully' offset those of the hedged item and *actual* results are within a range of 80–125% of expected results.

A hedge can have both an effective and an ineffective portion. Hedge accounting can be applied only to the effective portion. The gain or loss on the ineffective portion of the hedging instrument must be reported in income immediately (if the hedging instrument is a derivative). In practice, this limits a company's ability to defer gains and losses on cash flow hedge and hedges of net investments in foreign entities.

Disclosure and analysis of financial investments

Disclosures

Firms in the EU and elsewhere usually distinguish current from long-term investments ('financial fixed assets') on the balance sheet. They also disclose the income from these investments in the income statement. Larger EU firms must provide additional information. They give a breakdown of long-term investments, showing separately investments in subsidiaries (unconsolidated subsidiaries in the case of group accounts), associated companies and other firms (i.e. investments in debt securities and passive minority shareholdings in other companies). They must also report loans to companies in these three categories. Moreover, they are required to disclose interest income, dividends received, realised gains and losses and value adjustments (e.g. losses from impairment of long-term investments). They must show separately the interest and other income they receive from subsidiary and associated companies.

Companies following IAS must provide similar information about their financial investments. New standards impose additional disclosure requirements, however.[10] As we've already seen, IAS now require most investments to be carried at fair value in the balance sheet. Companies must state the methods and assumptions used in estimating fair value. In the case of available-for-sale investments, they must state the unrealised gains and losses arising in the period and the amounts transferred to the income statement. For those financial assets and liabilities accounted for at amortised cost, companies must *disclose* their fair values in the notes (unless these can't be measured).

The new international standards also deal with disclosures relating to hedging activities. For example, companies must describe their risk management objectives and policies. Where they use hedging, they should give the following information for each of the three types of hedge (fair value, cash flow, and investment in foreign entity):

- the nature of the risks being hedged, including when hedged forecasted transactions are expected to occur;
- the hedging instruments used – and their fair values at the balance sheet date; and
- where gains and losses on hedging instruments are deferred in equity, the amounts transferred in and out of hedging reserve in the period.

Illustration

Novartis, a large Swiss pharmaceutical company, prepares its accounts in accordance with IAS. It reports on its 2001 balance sheet SFr 11 billion of marketable securities – shown as a current asset – and over SFr 2 billion of long-term investments. Together they represent 20% of total assets.

The marketable securities comprise equity and debt securities – classified as available-for-sale investments – and time deposits longer than 90 days. Long-term investments are likewise available-for-sale investments. At the start of 2001, when Novartis adopted *IAS 39*, net unrealised gains, pre-tax, on all AFS investments were SFr 1.9 billion.

Novartis makes extensive disclosures about its investments in derivatives. According to management, the company is exposed to risks from changes in exchange rates, interest rates and the market values of short-term investments. It uses derivatives to manage the resulting volatility. Specifically, it uses forward contracts and foreign currency option contracts to hedge expected foreign currency revenues and its net investment in foreign subsidiaries. It uses interest rate swap agreements to hedge interest rate risk and options to hedge price risk on investments. It does not use derivatives for purposes other than hedging. Panel A of Exhibit 13.5 contains an extract from

Exhibit 13.5 Novartis: extracts from 2001 accounts concerning financial instruments

---

Panel A Derivative financial instruments

In SFr millions	Contract or underlying principal amount		Positive fair values		Negative fair values	
	2001	2000	2001	2000	2001	2000
Currency-related instruments						
Forward foreign exchange rate contracts	7,114	8,191	94	355	(214)	(5)
Over-the-counter currency options	13,259	13,815	90	119	(157)	(155)
Cross-currency swaps	1,332	–	–	–	(33)	–
Total of currency-related instruments	21,705	22,006	184	474	(404)	(160)
Interest-related instruments						
Interest rate swaps	3,700	2,854	29	21	(5)	(30)
Forward rate agreements	6,450	2,950	–	1	(17)	(6)
Interest rate options	150	300	–	–	(4)	(2)
Total of interest-related instruments	10,300	6,104	29	22	(26)	(38)
Options on equity securities	12,018	10,386	79	503	(539)	(528)
Total derivative financial instruments	44,023	38,496	292	999	(969)	(726)

Panel B Fair value adjustments in 'Statement of changes in equity'

In SFr millions	Retained earnings	Fair value of deferred cash flow hedges	Total
January 1, 2001 fair value adjustments			
Available-for-sale marketable securities	1,891		1,891
Derivative financial instruments	265	138	403
Deferred tax on above	(213)	(35)	(248)
Effect of introducing IAS 39 on January 1, 2001	**1,943**	**103**	**2,046**
Changes in fair value:			
– Available-for-sale marketable securities	(150)		(150)
– Cash flow hedges		18	18
Realised gains or losses transferred to the income statement:			
– Marketable securities sold	(648)		(648)
– Derivative financial instruments	(265)	(152)	(417)
Impaired securities and investments	101		101
Deferred tax on above	73	11	84
Fair value adjustments at December 31, 2001	**1,054**	**(20)**	**1,034**

(*Source*: Novartis Group, *Annual Report and Accounts 2001*. Reproduced by permission of Novartis Group.)

Novartis's 2001 accounts showing derivatives' underlyings and their fair values – positive and negative – at the end of 2000 and 2001. The 'contract or underlying principal amount' shows the end-year notional amount of each derivative instrument that Novartis uses: it doesn't represent the amount at risk. The fair values are based on market prices or values derived from standard pricing models. The company states that the use of derivatives did not have a material impact on the 2000 and 2001 accounts.

Exhibit 13.5 also contains a note to the statement of changes in equity, showing the movement in fair value adjustments during 2001 (panel B). Fair value adjustments relate to both AFS investments and derivative financial instruments. Unrealised gains, net of tax, are SFr 2 billion at the start of 2001. Half of these gains are realised in the year and released to the income statement, either because marketable securities have been sold or because transactions that were hedged in advance occur that year. (Impairment losses of SFr 101 million represent unrealised losses on AFS investments that are recognised in income in 2001 because they are judged to be no longer temporary.) Note that the derivative-related fair value adjustments shown in panel B are a subset of the gains and losses on derivatives that Novartis recognises in 2001. Because they relate to (effective) cash flow hedges, they are deferred in equity until realised; gains and losses on fair value hedges (and ineffective cash flow hedges), however, are recognised in income as they arise.

Analysis of financial investments

In valuing a firm, investors focus on its operating activities and estimate the returns its operating assets will generate in the future. The investment income (of a non-financial firm) is of secondary importance. The returns on its financial assets are rarely as large as those on its operating assets. Moreover, they are harder to forecast. The income from financial assets comprises dividends received, interest income and recognised gains less losses. This last figure is the hardest for outside investors to estimate because it's influenced by management decisions. For example, it can be boosted or depressed simply as a result of the timing of decisions to sell investments (and realise gains or losses) or recognise asset impairment.

Despite these earnings forecasting problems, the stock market does not ignore a company's financial assets when valuing its shares. Moreover, investors appear to consider fair value information reliable and use it in their valuation decisions, according to studies of market reaction to publication of this information by Danish and US banks (*see* Box 13.1).

In the past, differences in the way companies accounted for financial investments made it difficult to compare returns on these assets across companies. Publication of fair value information should make this task easier now. However, it does require a further adjustment to the calculation of financial income. In addition to the elements mentioned above – dividends received, interest income, realised gains less losses and impairment losses – investors must include a **fair value adjustment**. This is, in effect, the unrealised holding gains less losses on the investments that arise in the period. Thus, to be comparable across firms, total financial income should be computed as follows:

> Dividends received
> + Interest income earned
> +/– Realised gains less losses on investments sold
> – Losses on impairment of investments (less recoveries)
> +/– <u>Fair value adjustment (i.e. unrealised holding gains less losses in the period)</u>
> <u>Total financial income (on fair value basis)</u>

Note that, even if a company classifies an investment as 'available-for-sale' (thereby deferring unrealised gains and losses in equity) or simply discloses fair value information in the notes (as in the case of held-to-maturity investments), the investor can still determine the 'fair value adjustment' and, by extension, financial income on a fair value basis.

Fair value accounting and banks: stock market lessons

Among the sectors most affected by the switch to fair value accounting of financial instruments is the financial sector. Financial assets represent a large proportion of the assets of banks and other financial institutions. Financial liabilities dominate the equities side of their balance sheets, too. Set out below are aggregated (and condensed) balance sheets of US and German commercial banks at end-1999, scaled by total assets.

	US	German		US	German
Cash and balance with Central bank	3.4	1.6	Capital and reserves	8.3	4.6
Interbank deposits	3.0	19.9	Interbank deposits	0.9	27.7
Loans	63.8	50.3	Customer deposits	66.2	42.8
Securities	20.2	21.8	Bonds	1.3	16.1
Other assets (incl. premises)	9.6	6.4	Other liabilities	23.3	8.8
	100.0	100.0		100.0	100.0

Source: OECD (2001), *Bank Profitability: Financial Statements of Banks 2000.*

International (and US) standards on financial instruments require companies to disclose the fair values of *all* financial assets and liabilities (unless reliable estimates of fair value can't be obtained). Thus even though banks can continue to *account* for major financial assets and liabilities such as loans to customers, deposits and borrowings at (amortised) cost, they must show the fair value of these assets and liabilities in the notes to the accounts.

Do investors find such fair value disclosures useful? One way of addressing this question is by looking at the impact of such disclosures on share prices. In a study of US banks in the early 1990s, Barth, Beaver and Landsman found that some of the fair value information that banks were disclosing for the first time was definitely 'value-relevant'. In regressions of the *difference* between the market and book values of equity on the *difference* between the fair and book values of banks' assets and liabilities, the fair value information in loans – and to a lesser extent, in securities and long-term debt – helped explain banks' share prices in those years.[11]

If investors value this information, why not require its inclusion in the financial statements themselves? Critics of fair value-based accounts for banks argue that:

1 the numbers are more easily manipulable and therefore less reliable than cost-based ones; and
2 they increase the volatility of reported earnings (because changes in fair value are recognised in the income statement). As a result, banks' capital adequacy ratios are violated more often, regulators are forced to intervene more frequently and the value of banks' assets – especially their intangibles – declines.

Bernard, Merton and Palepu carried out a comparative study of Danish and US banks in the late 1980s to test the validity of these arguments. Danish banks have long used mark-to-market accounting to measure investment securities, loans and derivatives, whereas US banks at that time accounted for these assets at cost or LOCOM (and did not disclose fair value data). The researchers found no evidence that Danish banks manipulated fair values (but like their US counterparts they did tend to smooth the recognition of loan losses). As for income volatility, Danish banks' earnings were clearly more variable when fair value adjustments were included but this did not change large banks' behaviour. (Small Danish banks, however, maintained a larger equity 'cushion'.) Based on the history of failed Danish banks in the late 1980s, there was no evidence that regulatory interventions had reduced banks' asset values. In sum, the Danish experience does not support the arguments of the fair value critics, according to Bernard *et al.*[12]

Summary

Financial investments comprise investments in debt and equity securities and in derivative instruments. Companies invest in such assets: to increase returns on surplus cash, to develop or protect long-term business relationships, to gain influence over or control of other firms, to fund future liabilities and to hedge risks. The nature of the investment and management's reasons for acquiring and holding it affect the way it is accounted for.

We focus in this chapter on debt investments, passive equity investments and derivatives. The accounting recognition and initial measurement of such investments are straightforward. A company recognises an investment as an asset when it becomes a party to the contract for it. The investment is measured initially at cost. What is unusual is how such assets are measured subsequently. Under new international rules, most financial investments must be measured at fair value. The only exceptions are investments in debt securities to be held to maturity and investments where fair value can't be reliably determined. The former must be measured at amortised cost, the latter at cost.

The new valuation rules represent a major change in accounting for investments. Traditionally, short-term investments were measured at LOCOM and long-term investments at cost. But the change in measurement affects companies' balance sheets more than their income statements. Unrealised holding gains and losses must be recognised in income only in the case of investments held for trading purposes. Most financial investments, however, are classified as 'available-for-sale' investments and companies defer unrealised gains and losses on them in equity. Only when such investments are sold or impaired, are the resulting gains or losses recognised in income.

Companies invest in derivatives largely to hedge risk. New international rules permit firms to use hedge accounting but only in clearly defined circumstances. Under hedge accounting, a company accounts for the hedging instrument (e.g. a derivative such as an interest rate swap or currency forward) in the same way as the hedged item (interest payments under existing debt, a future foreign currency payable). When a company hedges its exposure to changes in asset or liability values (fair value hedge), it measures both the hedging instrument and the asset or liability at fair value and recognises all gains and losses in income. When it hedges its exposure to fluctuations in future cash flows (cash flow hedge) or to exchange rate changes affecting a foreign investment (investment-in-foreign-entity hedge), it defers the gains and losses on the hedging instrument in equity until the hedged cash flows affect the income statement or the foreign investment is sold. To minimise abuse of hedge accounting, international rules require firms to designate all hedging instruments in advance and apply hedge accounting only to effective hedges.

The accounts of larger firms contain a wealth of information on financial investments. Investments are broken down by type, investment income by source. Reporting of fair value information allows investors to recast investment income and asset numbers on a fair value basis. Disclosures about derivatives shed light on the scale and focus of a firm's hedging activities.

Problem assignments

P13.1 Equity investments: LOCOM and fair value accounting

At the start of x1, Deriganov, a diversified industrial group, buys 80,000 shares of Pishchik, a china clay producer, at a price of 50 a share. Although the holding is only 5% of Pishchik's issued share capital, Deriganov views the investment as a strategic move since it has a majority stake in another company that makes porcelain.

Pishchik reports earnings of 5/share and pays a dividend of 2.5/share in x1. At the end of x1, the market value per share has risen to 60.

There is an economic downturn in x2. Pishchik's EPS falls to 4.2/share but the company maintains its dividend. The end-x2 market price is 47/share.

Pishchik's earnings recover in x3 as the economy rebounds. In response to shareholder dissatisfaction with the low returns they've received, Deriganov decides to focus on its core activities and dispose of its porcelain and related operations. It sells all its shares in Pishchik at a price of 55/share in x3 – prior to earnings and dividend announcements for the year.

Required

(a) Deriganov accounts for its investment in Pishchik at LOCOM. Show the effect of the investment on Deriganov's accounts in each of the three years x1 to x3. Use journal entries or the balance sheet equation.

(b) Deriganov accounts for its investment in Pishchik at fair value. It classifies Pishchik as an available-for-sale investment and records unrealised holding gains and losses in equity. The decline in the market value of Pishchik's shares in x2 is not an impairment of the investment. Show the effect of the investment on Deriganov's accounts in each of the three years x1 to x3. Use journal entries or the balance sheet equation.

Check figures:
Gain on disposal, x3 (a) 640,000
(b) 400,000

P13.2 Accounting for financial investments under new IAS: basic framework

Chisme Company makes certain investments in debt and equity securities at the start of year 4. The acquisition cost of the investments and their end-year 4 market values are set out below. (Amounts are in €000.)

	Acquisition cost	End-year 4 market value
Dingsda AG, 30,000 ordinary shares	750	570
Thingummy plc, 20,000 ordinary shares	680	700
Truc SA, 1,500 8% preference shares	120	not available
Coso SpA, 6% bonds, due end-year 7	356.1	360

The Thingummy shares Chisme holds are a held-for-trading investment; the Dingsda shares are an available-for-sale investment. As for the Truc investment, the (non-redeemable) preference shares are accounted for at cost as they are unquoted and their end-year 4 market value cannot be determined reliably. Chisme plans to hold the Coso bonds to maturity and therefore accounts for them at amortised cost. The bonds have a face value of €350,000 and pay interest annually. The effective interest rate at the date of purchase was 5.5%.

None of the companies in which Chisme holds shares pays a dividend in year 4.

Required

Show the effect of the following events on Chisme's year 4 accounts:

(a) purchase of the four investments at the start of the year;

(b) accrual and receipt of interest during the year;

(c) fair value adjustments at year-end.

Use journal entries or the balance sheet equation.

Check figure:
Total carrying amount of investments,
end-year 4 (in €000)   €1,744.7

P.13.3 Accounting for financial investments under new IAS: extensions

Chisme Company (*see* P13.2) makes certain changes to its investment portfolio in year 5. These changes – and the end-year 5 fair values of its investments – are set out below.

1 Chisme sells half of its Thingummy shares for €355,000 in May year 5. The market value of the remaining shares is €33/share at the end of year 5.

2 Dingsda experiences financial problems in year 5. At year-end, the market value of the shares is only €10/share. Chisme's management consider the investment impaired and decide to recognise the loss in income that year.

3 After a review of the company's investments at end-year 5, Chisme's management decide to reclassify the Coso bonds as an available-for-sale investment as they no longer plan to hold them to maturity. The fair value of the bonds then is €363,200.

4 As a result of an overhaul of its business by new management, Truc makes profits in year 5 and resumes paying a dividend (of €8/share) on its preference shares. (The preference dividend is not cumulative.) Although the company is unquoted, Chisme's management use cash-flow-based valuation techniques to value the investment. They estimate its end-year 5 value at €160,000 and classify Truc as an available-for-sale investment.

Required

Show the effect on Chisme's year 5 accounts of the following events:

(a) Accrual and receipt of interest (on Coso bonds) and receipt of dividend (on Truc's preference shares) during the year. Neither Dingsda nor Thingummy pays a dividend in year 5.

(b) Sale of Thingummy shares in May.

(c) Recognition of impairment of Dingsda investment at year-end.

(d) Transfer of Coso bonds to AFS category at year-end.

(e) Fair value accounting of Truc shares and fair value adjustment of other investments at year-end.

Use journal entries or the balance sheet equation.

P13.4 Hedge accounting: fair value hedge using an interest rate swap

In the example of hedge accounting in the chapter, the borrower, Bottom, swaps floating payments for fixed ones to hedge fluctuations in interest rates and therefore in its cash flows. But what if Bottom swaps fixed payments for floating ones? In this case, it's the fair value of the debt that is being hedged since the value of fixed-rate debt is sensitive to interest rate changes. The key facts of Bottom's new interest rate swap are summarised below.

At start-x1, Bottom borrows €10 million from G.W. Capital for three years at a fixed rate of 7%. Interest is paid annually. Bottom enters into a swap contract with Wild Thyme Bank on the same date. Under the swap Bottom pays interest at a floating rate equivalent to Euribor and receives interest at a fixed rate of 7%. The swap has a notional principal of €10 million and a three-year term and the variable interest rate is reset annually.

Annual swap receipts and payments – and end-year fair values of the swap contract – in the three years x1–x3 are set out below. (Currency amounts are in euros.)

Date	Euribor	Fixed rate receipt	Floating rate payment	Net receipt (payment)	Fair value of swap A/(L)
1 Jan x1	7%				Nil
31 Dec x1	6.5%	700,000	650,000	50,000	90,400
31 Dec x2	7.15%	700,000	715,000	(15,000)	(14,025)
31 Dec x3	6.75%	700,000	675,000	25,000	0

Bottom designates changes in the fair value of the swap as a hedge of changes in the fair value of the debt due to changes in Euribor. Under *IAS 39*, the swap contract must be separately recognised and measured at its fair value. (Initially, this is zero as the Euribor rate is 7% at the start of x1.) The carrying amount of the loan is also adjusted for changes in its fair value due to changes in Euribor. All gains and losses are recognised in the income statement.

Required

Show the entries Bottom must make in its accounts to record the loan payments and the changes in fair values of both swap and loan over the three years x1–x3. What is the net cost of the loan to Bottom in each of the three years?

P13.5   Investments: converting accounts from LOCOM to fair value basis

Orkla a.s., one of Norway's largest listed companies, has three main areas of activity: branded consumer goods, chemicals and financial investments. Its portfolio of investments, with a book value of NOK 11,400 million, represents over 20% of the group's end-2001 assets. The company classifies the portfolio investments as a current asset and accounts for them at the lower of portfolio cost or market. However, it provides market value information in the notes to the accounts. Set out below are key data from its 2001 accounts. Amounts are in NOK million.

	2001	2000	1999
Income statement			
Operating revenues	44,799	34,083	31,492
Operating profit	3,260	2,607	2,177
Dividends	545	555	325
Portfolio gains/(losses)*	(760)	2,727	595
Other financial items, net	208	(718)	(778)
Profit before tax	3,253	5,171	2,319

* These comprise gains and losses on disposal of investments and asset write-downs.

	2001	2000	1999	1998
Notes to the accounts				
Securities portfolio				
Market value	14,140	18,053	20,875	12,624
Book value	11,394	12,622	11,340	8,495
Unrealised gains before tax	2,746	5,431	9,535	4,129

Required

What is the profit before tax Orkla would have reported in the three years 1999–2001 if it had accounted for its securities portfolio at fair value? What do the fair value-based profit numbers reveal about the performance of its financial investments division in these years?

P13.6   Computing returns on financial assets under fair value accounting

Microsoft is the world's largest computer software company and, according to a *Financial Times* survey in May 2002, the world's second most valuable company by market capitalisation. Extracts from its 2002 accounts (year ended 30 June) are set out in Exhibit 13.6.

As a US company, Microsoft prepares its accounts according to US GAAP. The accounting for financial investments under US GAAP is similar to that under IAS. Microsoft classifies all short-term financial investments and most long-term financial investments as 'available-for-sale securities' and defers unrealised gains and losses in equity. Equity securities that are not publicly traded are recorded at cost.

Exhibit 13.6   Microsoft: extracts from 2002 accounts

In US$ millions		2001		2002
INCOME STATEMENTS (for year ended 30 June) (part)				
Revenue		25,296		28,365
Operating income		11,720		11,910
Investment income (loss):				
Dividends	377		357	
Interest	1,808		1,762	
Net recognised gains/(losses) on investments	(2,221)		(2,424)	
		(36)		(305)
Income (loss) on equity method investments		(159)		(92)
Income before taxes		11,525		11,513
⋮				
BALANCE SHEETS (at 30 June) (part)				
Cash and equivalents		3,922		3,016
Short-term investments		27,678		35,636
Other current assets (including A/R, deferred taxes)		7,610		9,924
Total current assets		39,210		48,576
Equity and other investments		14,361		14,191
Other long-term assets (including Property and equipment)		5,259		4,879
Total assets		58,830		67,646
STOCKHOLDERS' EQUITY STATEMENTS (part)				
⋮				
Retained earnings				
Balance, beginning of year (1 July)		18,173		18,899
Net income	7,346		7,829	
Other comprehensive income:				
Cumulative effect of accounting change	(75)		–	
Net gains on derivative instruments	634		(91)	
Net unrealised investment gains (losses)	(1,460)		5	
Translation adjustments and other	(39)		82	
Comprehensive income		6,406		7,825
Common stock repurchased		(5,680)		(6,191)
Balance, end of year (30 June)		18,899		20,533
NOTES TO THE ACCOUNTS (extract)				
Other comprehensive income (part)				
⋮				
Net gain on derivative instruments:				
Unrealised gains/(losses), net of tax effect of 246 in 2001 and 30 in 2002		499		55
Reclassification adjustment for (gains)/losses included in net income, net of tax effect of 67 in 2001 and (79) in 2002		135		(146)
		634		(91)
Net unrealised investment gains/(losses)				
Unrealised holding gains/(losses), net of tax effect of (351) in 2001 and (955) in 2002		(1,200)		(1,774)
Reclassification adjustment for (gains)/losses included in net income, net of tax effect of (128) in 2001 and 958 in 2002		(260)		1,779
		(1,460)		5

(*Source*: Microsoft Inc., *Annual Report and Accounts 2002*. Copyright Microsoft Corporation. Reproduced by permission.)

The line item 'Net recognised gains/(losses) on investments' in the income statement includes impairment losses, realised gains and losses on disposal of investments, and unrealised losses on derivatives (mainly with respect to those not designated as hedging instruments). Using information in the notes to the accounts, the net recognised gains/(losses) on investments can be broken down as follows (amounts in US$ billions):

Year ended 30 June	2001	2002
Impairment losses	(4.80)	(4.32)
Realised gains/(losses), equity and other investments	3.00	2.12
Realised gains/(losses), short-term investments	0.17	0.26
Unrealised losses, derivatives	(0.59)	(0.48)
Net recognised gains/(losses) on investments	(2.22)	(2.42)

Required

(a) Calculate Microsoft's pre-tax financial income *on a fair value basis* for 2001 and 2002 (i.e. include investment-related unrealised gains and losses arising in the year).

(b) After reviewing the accounts for 2001 and 2002, an analyst remarks: 'Microsoft's financial performance is being adversely affected by the poor returns it's earning on its investments.' Calculate the company's return on total assets, return on operating assets (ROOA) and return on financial assets (ROFA) for both years. ROOA and ROFA are defined as follows:

$$ROOA = \frac{\text{Operating income}}{\text{Operating assets}} \qquad ROFA = \frac{\text{Financial income}}{\text{Financial assets}}$$

Use pre-tax income numbers in the numerator and end-year asset figures in the denominator of the ratios. Assume financial income (and therefore total income) is computed on a fair value basis. Assume also that financial assets consist of short-term investments and equity and other investments and all other assets are operating assets. Comment on the ratios you've calculated. Is the analyst correct? What do you think Microsoft's response might be – to the analyst's comments and to your calculations?

P13.7   Investments and insurance companies: impact of stock market decline

Allianz is Germany's – and Europe's – largest insurance group. Premiums earned exceeded €50 billion in 2001 and total assets were almost €1,000 billion at the end of that year. Yet the group experienced difficulties throughout 2001 and 2002. Its banking unit, Dresdner Bank, which it acquired in 2001, made losses in both years. Its main property and casualty insurance business was hit hard – by asbestos claims in the USA and flood damage claims in central Europe. And the decline in the stock market wiped off billions of euros from its investment portfolio.

The group's problems are reflected in its annual 2001 and interim 2002 financial statements. Return on equity fell from 10.6% in 2000 to 4.8% in 2001, below the cost of equity capital. Performance continued to be weak in the first half of 2002. Operating cash flow was negative in that period and the parent company made a loss in the second quarter. The company's equity base was further eroded by the decline in share prices. Shareholders' equity (of the parent company) fell €3 billion (to €28.7 billion) in the first half of 2002: unrealised investment losses more than offset the small retained income in the period. Exhibit 13.7 gives a breakdown of the group's investments at end-December 2001 and end-June 2002 and shows the change in unrealised gains on equity investments between December 2000 and June 2002. (Allianz prepares its accounts according to IAS.)

In September 2002 Allianz was forced to deny reports that it needed to raise new equity capital to support its business. At the time its share price was €100, down from €400 at the end of 2000.

Required

(a) Analyst A reckons that Allianz has no need to raise new equity. The group can simply sell some of its investments. By doing this, it would raise cash and increase shareholders' equity – since the realised gains would boost profits. Is the analyst's reasoning correct? If not, explain why.

Exhibit 13.7   Allianz Group: extracts from annual 2001 and interim 2002 report

Condensed balance sheet (in €bn)

ASSETS	30/6/02	31/12/01	EQUITY AND LIABILITIES	30/6/02	31/12/01
Intangible assets	18.5	16.9	Group equity	38.3	49.0
Investments	361.3	380.2	Subordinated debt	12.1	12.2
Loans to customers/banks	310.7	301.0	Insurance reserves	325.1	324.2
Trading assets	117.6	128.4	Customer and bank deposits	303.9	312.7
Cash and cash equivalents	17.0	21.2	Certificated liabilities	124.9	134.7
Other assets	95.4	95.2	Other liabilities	116.2	110.1
Total assets	920.5	942.9	Total equity and liabilities	920.5	942.9

Investments	30/6/02	31/12/01
Investments in affiliates, associates and joint ventures	10.3	10.2
Investments held on account and at risk of life insurance policyholders	25.4	24.7
Other investments:		
Securities held to maturity	7.2	7.7
Securities available for sale		
Equity securities	65.8	81.5
Government bonds	113.5	112.3
Corporate bonds	84.3	86.3
Other	40.9	42.1
	304.5	322.2
Real estate used by third parties	11.6	12.0
Funds held by others under reinsurance contracts assumed	2.3	3.4
Total	361.3	380.2

Equity securities	30/6/02	31/12/01	31/12/00
Market value	65.8	81.5	91.7
Cost	62.4	69.9	62.4
Unrealised gains	3.4	11.6	29.3
Unrealised (loss) in period		(8.2)	(17.7)

(*Source*: Allianz Group, *Annual Accounts 2001* and *Interim Report for 6 months to 30 June 2002*. Reproduced by permission of Allianz Aktiengesellschaft.)

(b) Analyst B notes that the company's market capitalisation in September 2002 is below the fair value of its principal listed equity investments (as set out in the notes to the annual accounts).

In € bn	Sept 2002	End-Dec 2001
Market capitalisation	26	64
Listed equity investments (MV ≥ €100m or % stake ≥ 5%)	36 (estimate)	55

The analyst considers the company is vulnerable to a takeover bid since it is trading on a price-to-book ratio of less than one. A bidder could buy the company, sell the listed investments and earn a profit on its investment. Comment on this argument. What are the assumptions the analyst is making?

Notes to Chapter 13

1   A company is also likely to hold surplus cash on deposit with a financial institution. For the purposes of this chapter, we treat bank deposits as 'cash' rather than as an investment.

2   Recognition should occur only when a company becomes a party to the contract for the financial instrument (*IAS 39: Financial Instruments: Recognition and Measurement*). This can be either the date the company commits to purchase the asset (the *trade date*) or the date it takes delivery of it (the *settlement date*). Under settlement date accounting, the company must account for the change in value between the trade and settlement dates for investments carried at fair value.

3   More precisely, at the fair value of the consideration given. This is important to remember when a financial investment is acquired for other than cash.

4   Standard & Poor's (2001), *Emerging Stock Markets Factbook 2000*; United Nations (2002), *Statistical Yearbook 55th issue*.

5   The relevant international standards are: *IAS 32: Financial Instruments: Disclosure and Presentation*, and *IAS 39: Financial Instruments: Recognition and Measurement*. The procedures described in this section incorporate the main amendments to these two standards proposed by the IASB in an exposure draft issued in June 2002. One goal of the amendments is to align international standards on financial instruments with the US standard on this topic (FAS 133).

6   Parker, A. and Pretzlik, C. (2002), French banks go to EU over rule changes, *Financial Times*, 8 October.

7   In testimony to the (US) Senate governmental affairs committee in January 2002, Frank Partnoy, a university professor and former derivatives trader, alleged that some Enron employees 'used dummy accounts and rigged valuation methodologies to create false profit and loss entries for the derivatives Enron traded' (reported by McNulty, S. and Hill, A. (2002), Mark-to-market accounting: energy groups under renewed pressure, *Financial Times*, 31 January). A former controller of Dynegy, another US energy trading company, claimed the company sacked him when he refused to manipulate forward gas prices in 2000 to reduce 'mark-to-market' losses (McNulty, S. (2002), Former executive accuses Dynegy of civil conspiracy, *Financial Times*, 5 August).

8   In practice, the Euribor-based interest rate would be reset semi-annually rather than annually. In addition, we assume that, in calculating the fair value of the swap contract each period, future swap receipts or payments are based on the current Euribor rate. But, in practice, the expected interest rate in future periods may be higher or lower than the current rate and these future rates will be reflected in the current value of the swap contract.

9   The rules governing derivatives and hedge accounting are set out in *IAS 39: Financial Instruments: Recognition and Measurement*.

10   Although *IAS 32* is nominally the disclosure standard for financial instruments, *IAS 39* also contains disclosure provisions, especially in relation to hedge accounting. This can lead to confusion. It is expected that the IASB will combine the two standards into one comprehensive standard on financial instruments at a future date.

11   Barth, M., Beaver, W.H. and Landsman, W.R. (1996), Value-relevance of banks' fair value disclosures under SFAS No. 107, *The Accounting Review*, 71(4): 513–537.

12   Bernard, V.L., Merton, R.C. and Palepu, K.G. (1995), Mark-to-market accounting for banks and thrifts: lessons from the Danish experience, *Journal of Accounting Research*, 33(1): 1–32.

14

Equity accounting and consolidations

INTRODUCTION

A company may acquire a stake in another in order to play an active role in its operations. This involves buying a sizeable shareholding: shares usually carry votes and votes spell power. In these circumstances, the methods of accounting for investments we described in Chapter 13 are considered deficient. They provide the investor company's shareholders with insufficient information about the profitability and risk of the investee. As a result, alternative methods of accounting for 'active' investments have been devised.

Under these methods, an investor company must distinguish investees whose operating and financial policies it *influences* from those whose policies it *controls*. The former are its associates, the latter its subsidiaries. It accounts for associates by the equity method of accounting. In the case of subsidiaries, it prepares an additional set of accounts – known as consolidated accounts – for the group of companies it controls.

We describe and illustrate, in broad terms, both the equity method and global consolidation accounting in section 1 of the chapter. Goodwill can arise on the acquisition of associates and subsidiaries, and we explain the two main ways of accounting for it.

Section 2 of the chapter deals with more specialised topics. First, we extend the discussion of consolidation accounting and show how shares in a subsidiary company not owned by the parent – 'minority interests' – are accounted for. Next, we look at investments in incorporated joint ventures and describe proportionate consolidation, the preferred method of accounting for them under IAS. Finally, we examine the way companies account for divestments.

Consolidated accounts bring informational gains and losses. Shareholders benefit from seeing the total picture – the performance and health of a group of companies under common control. However, they are deprived of information about the components of the group. In section 3 of the chapter we look at the difficulties shareholders face when analysing consolidated accounts and the ways in which they try to overcome them.

Exhibit 14.1 summarises the circumstances in which each of the various methods of accounting for investments – from fair value to consolidation – is used. Note that the equity method and consolidation accounting apply only to *long-term* investments in which the investor company has an active minority or majority stake respectively.

Exhibit 14.1 Financial investments: principal valuation/accounting methods*

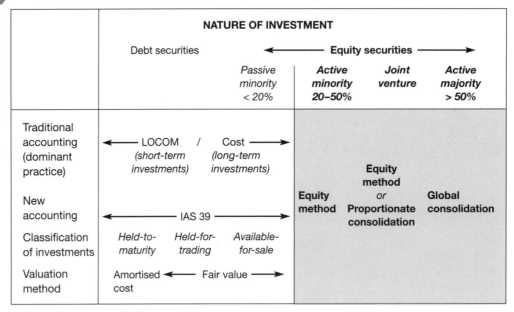

* In consolidated accounts.

Core issues

Equity method of accounting

A company acquires a shareholding in another which is large enough for it to exercise influence over, but not sufficient for it to control, the investee's operations. The investee is then an **associate** of the investor company. How should the investor account for its (long-term) investment? Accountants argue that, since it is able to shape the associate's operating and financial policies, it should use the **equity method** (or **equity accounting**).

Equity method: basic structure

*Under the equity method, an investment in another company's shares is considered equivalent to an interest in (**equity in**) the net assets of that company.* As the net assets of the investee change, so the carrying amount of the investment changes too. Thus when the investee operates profitably and increases its net assets, the investor company's books should reflect this: the carrying amount of the investment increases. When the investee pays a dividend (or reports a loss), its net assets decrease: so in proportionate terms does the investor company's assets. This is illustrated in diagrammatic form in Exhibit 14.2.

Assume X acquires 40% of Y's shares at a price of 40. Y has net assets of 100 at the date of acquisition so X buys the shares at their book value. Y earns a profit of 10 in the year following X's investment. As a result, its net assets increase by that amount – from 100 to 110. Under the

Exhibit 14.2 The equity method: link between investee's net assets and carrying amount of investor's asset

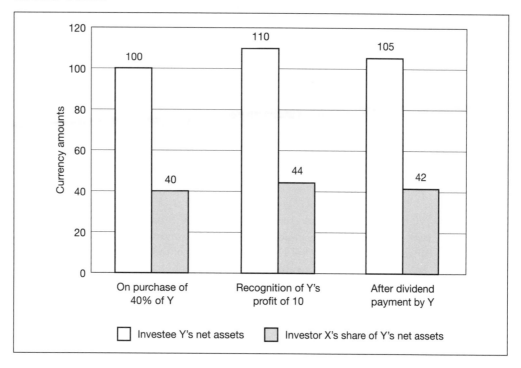

equity method, the carrying amount of X's investment in Y increases proportionately – from 40 to 44. When Y pays a cash dividend of 5 and its net assets decline from 110 to 105, the carrying amount of X's investment decreases by 40% of the dividend – from 44 to 42.

The investor company applies the same logic in determining the annual profit or loss from its investment. *Under the equity method, it reports in its income statement its share of the investee's reported profit or loss in the period. Any dividend received from the investee has no effect on its income.* The dividend is a distribution of the investee's profit. The investor company would count the same income twice if it recognised as income both its share of the investee's profit and the dividend it received.

Mechanics of equity method: illustration

Consider the case of Pangloss Company, a newspaper publisher whose journals all carry upbeat editorials. It decides to diversify its operations. On 1 January x1, it acquires 50,000 shares of Candide Company, manufacturer of garden products, for 5/share. Candide's total issued share capital is 200,000 shares and its reported net assets on that date are 1 million. Pangloss's 25% stake gives it influence over Candide's operating policies. Candide reports after-tax profit of 180,000 (or 0.9/share) in x1. It pays a dividend of 60,000 (0.3/share) in December x1.

Pangloss makes the following entries in x1 with respect to its investment in Candide:

(a) *Acquisition of 25% stake in Candide*
1/x1
Dr. Investment in Candide (A+)   250,000
    Cr. Cash (A–)   250,000

Pangloss reports its 'Investment in Candide' as a financial fixed asset in its balance sheet.

(b) *Recognition of 25% share of Candide's x1 profit*
End x1

Dr. Investment in Candide (A+)	45,000	
Cr. Investment income (OE+)		45,000

Pangloss recognises as income its share of Candide's x1 profit, namely 45,000 (25% × 180,000). Its asset, 'Investment in Candide', increases by this amount, reflecting the increase in Candide's net assets of which it owns a 25% share.

(c) *Receipt of dividend from Candide*
12/x1

Dr. Cash (A+)	15,000	
Cr. Investment in Candide (A–)		15,000

Candide's net assets decrease by 60,000 when it pays a dividend of this amount. Pangloss's asset, 'Investment in Candide', declines in proportionate terms (25% × 60,000). Overall, Pangloss's net assets do not change: the receipt of the cash dividend offsets the decrease in the carrying amount of its investment.

At the end of x1, Candide reports net assets of 1.12 million. (We assume there are no changes to its capital during the year.) On that date, the carrying amount of Pangloss's asset, 'Investment in Candide', stands at 280,000, 25% of Candide's reported net assets:

CANDIDE		PANGLOSS	
	Net assets		*Investment in Candide*
Balance, 1/1/x1	1,000,000	Cost of acquiring 25% stake	250,000
Profit in x1	+180,000	Share of Candide's x1 profit	+45,000
Dividend in x1	−60,000	Share of Candide's x1 dividend	−15,000
Balance, 31/12/x1	1,120,000	Carrying amount of investment, 31/12/x1	280,000

The 45,000 increase in Pangloss's financial fixed asset is its share of Candide's *after-tax* profit. If it so chooses, it can report its share of Candide's profit or loss on a *before-tax* basis in its income statement. Either way, it should disclose separately the tax expense (or benefit) attributable to this profit (or loss). Note that Pangloss is unlikely to have a current tax liability of this amount. The tax authorities usually tax an investor company on the dividend it receives rather than on its share of the investee's profit.

Suppose Candide reports a *loss* of 180,000 in x1. Pangloss recognises its share of the loss (45,000) and reduces the carrying amount of its investment by this amount:

Dr. Investment loss (OE–)	45,000	
Cr. Investment in Candide (A–)		45,000

Pangloss continues applying the equity method to account for Candide's losses in later periods until the carrying amount of the investment is reduced to zero.[1] However, before this occurs, there may be evidence that the investment is impaired. As with other fixed assets, Pangloss should carry out an annual impairment test of each of its equity-method investments. If the estimated recoverable amount (based on discounted expected cash flows) is below the carrying amount of the investment, it should write down the asset and recognise an impairment loss.

As with other financial investments, the investor company records a realised gain or loss on disposal of part or all of its stake in an associate. The gain or loss recognised is the difference between the consideration received and the carrying amount of the investment. Thus if Pangloss sells its stake in Candide for 300,000 cash at the end of x1 when the carrying amount of its investment is 280,000, it recognises a gain of 20,000.

Equity and cost methods contrasted

What impact does the equity method have on the investor company's accounts? One way to answer this is to compare it with the cost method – a common method used by investor companies to account for associates in their individual (unconsolidated) accounts. Thus, where the investee is profitable and does not distribute all its earnings, the investor company reports higher income and assets under the equity method than under the cost method. This is evident from Pangloss's x1 accounts (amounts are in thousands).

	Assets		=	Equities
	Investment in Candide	Cash		Profit in year (Investment income)
Equity method				
Purchase of investment	+250	−250		–
Share of C's profit	+45			+45
Share of C's dividend	−15	+15		–
Balance, end-x1	280	−235		45
Cost method				
Purchase of investment	+250	−250		–
Share of C's profit	–	–		–
Share of C's dividend	–	+15		+15
Balance, end-x1	250	−235		15

Under the cost method, Pangloss recognises as income only its share of Candide's *dividend*. Under the equity method, Pangloss recognises as income its share of Candide's *profit* in the year. As for the balance sheet, the carrying amount of Pangloss's investment under the equity method exceeds that reported under the cost method by its share of Candide's *retained* profits accumulated since acquisition.

Application of equity method: international rules

A company following IAS must use the equity method to account for its investments in associates when it prepares consolidated accounts. (The 7th Directive lays down a similar requirement on EU companies.) In its own accounts, it carries the investment at either cost or fair value.[2]

An associate is a firm over which the investor exercises 'significant influence'. *Significant influence* is defined as the *power to participate in the investee's financial and operating policy decisions.* An investor company is usually considered to have significant influence if it owns 20–50% of the investee's (voting) shares. However, the investee company may be able to prevent an investor with a shareholding of this size from exercising influence. Under international rules, the investor company must demonstrate (to its auditor's satisfaction) that its power is real. Here are situations where significant influence is evident:

- representation on the investee's board of directors;
- participation in its 'policy-making processes';
- 'material transactions' between investor and investee;
- interchange of managers; and
- supply by the investee of 'essential technical information'.[3]

Without such evidence, holdings larger than 20% should be accounted for in accordance with IAS 39 (i.e. at fair value – or cost, if fair value is not determinable). *With* such evidence, holdings smaller than 20% can be accounted for by the equity method. The 20% figure is a guide, not a cut-off.[4]

The equity method is the most widely used method of accounting for investments in associates in consolidated accounts. Even in Australia where national rules require that such investments be accounted for at cost, companies still must provide supplementary information showing the effect on the financial statements of accounting for them by the equity method. However, countries differ in their implementation of the method. An investor company may be deemed to exercise significant influence over a *quoted* investee company with a much smaller shareholding than 20%. For example, the lower limit is 3% in Spain and 10% in Italy. A common feature in all countries is that companies tend to decide on the accounting for associates based on a quantitative measure (e.g. the standard 20–50% shareholding guideline) rather than on a qualitative assessment of influence.

Rationale for equity method

Why is a company allowed to report as income its share of the profits of other companies over which it has influence? This question appears to trouble the general public if press comment is any guide. Commentators consider the equity method 'loose' accounting since 'all that is really arriving is dividends' (*The Economist*, 13 January 1990).

There are two major arguments in support of the equity method. The first is conceptual. Measurement of a company's performance is better served by an accrual- rather than a cash-based measure of income. What applies to an investor company's own performance applies equally to the performance of other firms which its management are able to shape.

There's a practical argument, too. In the past, equity investments were usually accounted for at cost or LOCOM. Under these methods, readers of financial statements are at a disadvantage. They lack information about the results of the investor company's associates (and subsidiaries). In addition, the investor company's management have greater scope to manipulate profits. They can bring its 'significant influence' to bear on the dividend policy of the investee. When the investor company's profits are high, the investee will be persuaded to hold, or moderate the increase in, its dividend rate. When the investor company's profits are low, the investee will be encouraged to raise its dividend. In this way, the underlying variability in the investor company's own profits is concealed.

Of course, the equity method can also give rise to abuse. A company may claim to wield influence over an investee when it does not, in order to inflate its reported profits. We have already noted that, to guard against this, management must show evidence of significant influence. Less obvious is abuse in the opposite direction, namely denying significant influence when it exists. This may arise when the investee is unprofitable and the investor company wants to avoid including in income its share of the investee's losses. For this reason, some firms restrict their holdings in new ventures (to, say, 10–15%) where large losses are expected initially (e.g. biotechnology ventures) and claim they are passive investors.

Consolidation accounting: the basic structure

Form and purpose of consolidated accounts

Consider now the case of a company that acquires a majority (51% or more) of the voting shares of another. Such a shareholding gives it *control* of the investee. (It can gain control in other ways – as we'll see later.) It may be a short step – in terms of share ownership – for an investor company to move from 'significant influence' to 'control' but the difference in accounting is profound.

Accountants argue that when one firm acquires control of another, a new economic entity (a **group**) is created. A group consists of the investor company (the **parent**) and the investee company or companies (its **subsidiaries**). *The parent company prepares accounts for the group: these are known as **consolidated accounts**. In addition, the parent and each of the subsidiary companies, being legal entities, continue to prepare separate accounts.*

Thus, if P Company controls S Company, three sets of accounts are produced: for P alone (showing, as an asset, its investment in S), for S and for the P group (P and S combined). We illustrate the links between the accounts of parent, subsidiary and group in Exhibit 14.3.

In the annual accounts of a group (e.g. P Group), the income statements and balance sheets of the individual subsidiary companies are not presented. However, EU companies usually disclose, with their consolidated accounts, the balance sheet and, UK and Irish companies excepted, the income statement of the parent company.

A group of companies under common control has, in most countries, no legal personality – for example, contracts cannot be signed in its name. However, it clearly has economic significance. *Consolidated accounts provide financial statement readers with information about all the resources under one company's command: what form they take, how they're financed and how successfully they've been employed in the year.* This is the *raison d'être* of consolidated accounts.

Global consolidation

Global consolidation involves the combining of the accounts of parent and subsidiaries. Conceptually, it is simple. *The assets and liabilities of the various companies are added together to form a consolidated balance sheet. Similarly, their revenues and expenses are summed to give a consolidated income statement.* In practice, the exercise is more complicated. In preparing consolidated accounts, management must make adjustments to the accounts of the parent and subsidiary companies. The adjustments are of three types:

1 *Alignment of accounting policies.* Consolidated accounts assume group companies follow a common set of accounting policies. The first adjustment is to apply group accounting policies to the accounts of all subsidiary companies.
2 *Elimination of intercompany balances.* Intercompany balances must be eliminated when combining the accounts of group companies in order to avoid double-counting. Examples are intercompany sales and loans.
3 *Accounting for consolidation-only balances.* Certain items arise only on consolidation and must be accounted for in group accounts. Examples are goodwill on consolidation and minority interests.

In this chapter we illustrate the latter two adjustments. We start with the first consolidation adjustment a company makes – to remove the share capital and reserves (at acquisition) of its subsidiary companies.

Exhibit 14.3 Parent, subsidiary and group: illustration of accounting links

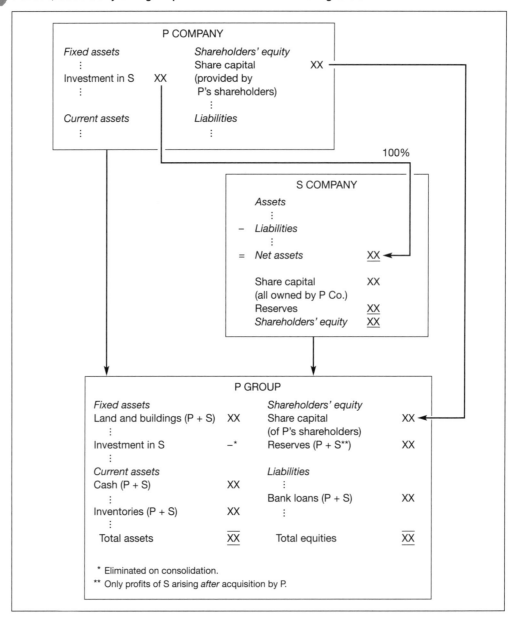

* Eliminated on consolidation.
** Only profits of S arising *after* acquisition by P.

Illustration 1: Initial consolidation

Glawari Industries, currently run by Hanna Glawari, the widow of the founder, is rumoured to be the subject of a takeover by an unnamed French company. The Pontevedrian government betrays the spirit of the EU's single market and seeks a national solution. It persuades Danilo Corporation (CEO: Graf Danilo) to make an offer for Glawari. At first, Danilo hesitates. He's not sure there's much synergy between his company's leisure business (principally, the restaurant/nightclub, Maxim's) and Glawari's Vilja timber interests. Hanna has her doubts,

Exhibit 14.4 Danilo Company and Glawari Company: summary balance sheets at start of year 1
(amounts in 000)

	Danilo		Glawari
	Before buying G	After buying G	
Assets			
Investment in Glawari	–	1,000	–
Other assets	5,000	4,000	1,800
Total	5,000	5,000	1,800
Equities			
Shareholders' equity	3,600	3,600	1,000
Liabilities	1,400	1,400	800
Total	5,000	5,000	1,800

too. They become convinced of the merits of union, however, when each discovers the quality of the other's assets.

Danilo acquires for cash all of Glawari Industries' share capital of 200,000 shares at 1 January year 1. It pays 5 for each share, the book amount of Glawari's net assets at that date. (To begin with, we'll assume the book values of Glawari's assets and liabilities are the same as their current values.) Exhibit 14.4 shows Danilo's own balance sheet, immediately before and after the acquisition of Glawari, as well as Glawari's balance sheet at that time.

We now construct a consolidated balance sheet at 1 January. To do this, we must eliminate the balances at that date in Glawari's shareholders' equity accounts and in Danilo's 'Investment in Glawari' account. Consider why. Glawari's share capital is now owned by Danilo's shareholders. *Their* interests, however, are already accounted for in Danilo's shareholders' equity. By the same token, Glawari's assets of 1.8 million and liabilities of 0.8 million are included in the consolidated assets and liabilities of the Danilo group. To include Danilo's asset 'Investment in Glawari' in consolidated assets as well would be to count Glawari's net assets twice. Exhibit 14.5 shows the construction of the consolidated accounts of the Danilo group at the start of year 1.

Exhibit 14.5 Danilo Group and group companies: summary balance sheets at 1 January year 1
(amounts in 000)

	Danilo (after buying G)	Glawari	Eliminations and other adjustments*	Danilo Group
Assets				
Investment in G	1,000	–	–1,000	–
Other assets	4,000	1,800	0	5,800
Total	5,000	1,800	–1,000	5,800
Equities				
Shareholders' equity	3,600	1,000	–1,000	3,600
Liabilities	1,400	800	0	2,200
Total	5,000	1,800	–1,000	5,800

* Elimination entry on consolidation:

Dr. Shareholders' equity (of Glawari)	1,000	
Cr. Investment in Glawari (Danilo's asset)		1,000

Note that the elimination entry does not appear in either Danilo's or Glawari's books. The group's accounts comprise a worksheet (usually computer-based), listing balances from parent and subsidiary company books together with the elimination (and other) entries needed to create the consolidated financial statements.

Two further points on Exhibits 14.4 and 14.5. First, Danilo offers Hanna cash for her shares in Glawari Industries. He could have offered her securities – shares or bonds of Danilo Company, for example. The market value of those securities would then determine the cost of the acquisition. Second, Danilo accounts for the purchase of Glawari as an acquisition in its group accounts, since it gains voting control of the company. Should neither party to a business combination dominate, the transaction is viewed as a merger. We describe merger accounting, the approach once widely used to account for such business combinations, at the end of this section.

Illustration 2: Consolidated year 1 income statement

Danilo and Glawari trade separately for most of the year. However, in the final quarter, Glawari sells goods to Danilo on account for 320,000 which had cost Glawari 240,000 to produce. By year-end, Danilo has sold the goods for 375,000 to outside entities and has paid Glawari all but 50,000 of the amount it owes its subsidiary. Exhibit 14.6 shows the derivation of the group's year 1 income statement from the (assumed) revenues and expenses of Danilo and Glawari. Income taxes are ignored. The income statements are extended to include the effect of dividend payments by Glawari (60,000) and Danilo (220,000). In Danilo's own accounts, the dividend received from Glawari is shown as investment income.

The Danilo group's year 1 consolidated income is 700,000, the difference between consolidated revenues and consolidated expenses. After taking account of the 220,000 dividend to Danilo's shareholders, the group's retained income for the year is 480,000.

Two adjustments are made in calculating consolidated income. The purpose of elimination entry (a) is to avoid the double-counting of intercompany sales. Goods sold by Glawari to Danilo are also included in Danilo's accounts (as sales of 375,000 to outside entities). Since Glawari recognises the 240,000 cost of its sales to Danilo in its own accounts, an adjustment must be made in the consolidated accounts to avoid the counting of those costs twice.

Exhibit 14.6 Danilo Group and group companies: summary year 1 income statements
(amounts in 000)

	Danilo	Glawari	Eliminations and other adjustments*		Danilo Group
Operating revenues	6,600	3,000	(a)	–320	9,280
Operating expenses	–6,100	–2,800	(a)	+320	–8,580
Operating income	500	200		0	700
Investment income	60	–	(b)	–60	0
Total income	560	200		–60	700
Dividend paid	–220	–60	(b)	+60	–220
Retained income	340	140		0	480

* Elimination entries on consolidation:

(a) Dr. Sales revenue (Glawari)	320	
Cr. Cost of sales (Danilo)		320

(b) Dr. Investment income (Danilo)	60	
Cr. Retained income (Glawari)		60

	Glawari	Danilo	Elimination	Group
Sales revenue	320 ⎯	375	–320	375
Cost of sales	–240 ⎯⎯▶	–320	–(–320)	–240
Operating income	80	55	0	135

Elimination entry (b) serves a similar purpose. Distribution of part of Glawari's year 1 profit to its owner, Danilo, is an internal transaction from the group's perspective.

In our example, we assume Danilo sells in year 1 all the goods it purchased from Glawari that year. If, however, part of Glawari's sales to Danilo are still in Danilo's inventory at the end of the period, Glawari's profit on those sales must be excluded from consolidated income – and consolidated inventory. For example, suppose Danilo sells to outside entities only 256,000 (i.e. 80%) of the goods it purchased from Glawari for 320,000. Then the elimination entry at end-year 1 is:

Dr. Sales revenue	320,000	
Cr. Cost of sales		304,000
Cr. Inventory		16,000

Consolidated income and inventory are both reduced by 16,000, one-fifth of the gross profit of 80,000 (320,000 – 240,000) which Glawari recognises on its intercompany sale. Only profits *realised* from sales to outsiders should be recognised on consolidation.

Illustration 3: Consolidated balance sheet at end-year 1

Of course, Danilo's and Glawari's operations in year 1 also affect their end-year balance sheets – and that of the group. Exhibit 14.7 sets out all three, together with the consolidation adjustments. To simplify calculations, we assume that for both companies the balance in 'Liabilities' is the same at the start and end of year 1.

On consolidation, Danilo's asset 'Investment in Glawari' and Glawari's *pre-acquisition* shareholders' equity are eliminated (entry (c)) to avoid double-counting. Amounts owing between group companies are also eliminated (entry (d)). As a result, consolidated receivables and payables reflect only those amounts owed by and to outside entities. Note the consistency between the consolidated year 1 income statement and balance sheet. The consolidated net assets increase during year 1 by 480,000, the amount by which profits retained by the group increase.

Consolidation adjustments are made to other intercompany transactions, for example intercompany loans (and related interest) and sales of fixed assets between group companies. In each case, the purpose is the same: to avoid double-counting assets and liabilities (and revenues and expenses) and to ensure that the consolidated accounts reflect only profits realised from transactions with outside entities.

Fair value adjustments and goodwill

A parent company rarely acquires a subsidiary at a price equal to the book value of the latter's net assets. The price it pays reflects its assessment of the cash flows those net assets are expected to generate. The amount may be more or less than book value. As a result, a positive or negative 'consolidation difference' arises. How is this difference accounted for?[5]

In most countries the difference is accounted for in two steps. First, the investor company *revalues the individual assets and liabilities of the acquired company to fair value* at the date of acquisition. (In countries which observe historical cost accounting strictly, this is a consolidation exercise only: the subsidiary's books are not altered.[6]) 'Fair value' means market value or a current

Exhibit 14.7 Danilo Group and group companies: summary balance sheets at 31/12/year 1 (amounts in 000)

	Danilo		Glawari	Eliminations and other adjustments*		Danilo Group
Assets						
Investment in G		1,000	–	(c)	–1,000	–
Other assets						
Start year 1	4,000		1,800			
Year 1 increase	340		140			
		4,340	1,940	(d)	–50	6,230
Total		5,340	1,940		–1,050	6,230
Equities						
Shareholders' equity:						
at 1 January		3,600	1,000	(c)	–1,000	3,600
Year 1 income retained		340	140		0	480
		3,940	1,140		–1,000	4,080
Liabilities		1,400	800	(d)	–50	2,150
Total		5,340	1,940		–1,050	6,230

* *Elimination entries on consolidation:*

(c) Dr. Shareholders' equity (of Glawari)	1,000	
Cr. Investment in Glawari (Danilo's asset)		1,000
(d) Dr. Accounts payable (Danilo's liability)	50	
Cr. Accounts receivable (Glawari's asset)		50

valuation. The reason for this adjustment is clear. If the investor company purchased assets from the investee on an individual basis, it would record them at their fair value at the date of exchange.

Any remaining difference between purchase price and the fair value of net assets at acquisition is described as 'goodwill' ('negative goodwill' if the purchase price is *less* than fair value). Goodwill represents the capitalised value of the 'above-normal' earnings attributable to an acquired company or collection of assets. In the second of the two steps, the goodwill is usually recognised as an intangible asset in the consolidated balance sheet. A minority practice is to write it off against consolidated reserves at the date of acquisition. There are also different ways companies account for negative goodwill. It may be deducted from the positive goodwill balance, shown as 'deferred income' on the equities side of the consolidated balance sheet or, in the case of a bargain purchase, recognised as a gain in the consolidated income statement.

An upward valuation of assets will lead, via higher cost of sales and depreciation charges, to lower consolidated income in later periods. Where goodwill is capitalised and amortised, consolidated income will be further reduced by the amortisation charge. (It will be *increased* if there is negative goodwill and it is amortised into income over time.)

Illustration 4: Goodwill on consolidation

We now illustrate both treatments of goodwill. Let us suppose that Danilo pays 8 per share, or 1.6 million, for the net assets of Glawari which on 1 January have a book value of 1 million. (Danilo's 'other assets' fall to 3.4 million as a result.) We also assume that, of the positive consolidation difference of 600,000:

Exhibit 14.8 Danilo Group and group companies: summary balance sheets at 1 January year 1 assuming (a) capitalisation and (b) immediate write-off of goodwill (amounts in 000)

	Danilo (after buying G)	Glawari	Eliminations and other adjustments*	Danilo Group
(a) *Goodwill capitalisation*				
Assets				
Goodwill	–	–	+400	400
Investment in G	1,600	–	−1,600	–
Other assets	3,400	1,800	+200	5,400
Total	5,000	1,800	−1,000	5,800
Equities				
Shareholders' equity	3,600	1,000	−1,000	3,600
Liabilities	1,400	800	0	2,200
Total	5,000	1,800	−1,000	5,800
(b) *Write-off of goodwill*				
Assets				
Investment in G	1,600	–	−1,600	–
Other assets	3,400	1,800	+200	5,400
Total	5,000	1,800	−1,400	5,400
Equities				
Shareholders' equity	3,600	1,000	−1,400	3,200
Liabilities	1,400	800	0	2,200
Total	5,000	1,800	−1,400	5,400

* *Eliminations and other adjustments:*

	Panel (a)	Panel (b)
Dr. Goodwill on consolidation	400	–
Dr. Fixed assets ('Other assets')	200	200
Dr. Shareholders' equity (of Glawari)	1,000	1,400
Cr. Investment in Glawari (Danilo's asset)	1,600	1,600

- 200,000 is attributable to a revaluation of Glawari's fixed assets to fair value; and
- the balance of 400,000 represents goodwill.

Exhibit 14.8 shows how the start-year 1 consolidated balance sheet of the Danilo group is derived under each of the two treatments of goodwill: capitalisation (panel (a)) and immediate write-off (panel (b)).

Notice how, under capitalisation, an intangible asset is recognised. 'Goodwill' appears *only* in the consolidated balance sheet. Under the alternative treatment, immediate write-off (IWO), group reserves are reduced by the amount of the (positive) goodwill. Thus in panel B, the consolidation adjustment to shareholders' equity of 1.4 million includes the goodwill of 400,000 arising from the purchase of Glawari.[7]

What is the effect on the group accounts of later periods if goodwill is capitalised? Exhibit 14.9 shows the consolidated accounts of the Danilo Group for year 1, prepared under the assumption that Danilo capitalises and amortises the goodwill arising on the acquisition of Glawari Industries. We also assume Danilo's and Glawari's operating results are the same as those illustrated in Exhibits 14.6 and 14.7 but, for simplicity's sake, we exclude intercompany transactions (other than the dividend payment from Glawari to Danilo).

Exhibit 14.9 Danilo Group and group companies: summary year 1 accounts assuming goodwill capitalisation and amortisation (amounts in 000)

Summary year 1 income statements

	Danilo	Glawari	Eliminations and other adjustments*		Danilo Group
Operating income	500	200		–	700
Investment income	60	–		–60	–
Total income	560	200		–60	700
Additional depreciation			(a)	–25	–25
Goodwill amortisation			(b)	–80	–80
Consolidated income					595
Dividend	–220	–60		+60	–220
Retained income	340	140		–105	375

Summary balance sheets at end-year 1

	Danilo	Glawari	Eliminations and other adjustments*		Danilo Group
Goodwill	–	–		+400 ⎫	320
			(b)	–80 ⎭	
Investment in G	1,600	–		–1,600	–
				+200 ⎫	
Other assets	3,740**	1,940**	(a)	–25 ⎭	5,855
Total assets	5,340	1,940		–1,105	6,175
Shareholders' equity					
Start year 1	3,600	1,000			
Year 1 income retained	340	140			
	3,940	1,140		–1,000 ⎫	3,975
			(a)&(b)	–105 ⎭	
Liabilities	1,400	800		0	2,200
Total equities	5,340	1,940		–1,105	6,175

* *Additional depreciation and goodwill amortisation adjustments:*

(a) Dr. Depreciation expense (200/8 years)	25	
Cr. Accumulated depreciation, fixed assets		25
(b) Dr. Goodwill amortisation expense (400/5 years)	80	
Cr. Accumulated amortisation, goodwill		80

** *Derivation of end-year 1 'Other assets':*

	Start year 1	+	Year 1 income retained	
Danilo	3,400	+	340	= 3,740
Glawari	1,800	+	140	= 1,940

Danilo makes two additional consolidation adjustments during year 1. First, depreciation is charged on the revalued assets. The assets are assumed to have a remaining life of eight years and are depreciated on a straight-line (SL) basis. This results in additional depreciation expense of 25,000 (200,000/8 years). (To keep things simple, we assume the revaluation and additional depreciation are consolidation entries.) Second, goodwill is assumed to have a five-year life. This yields an annual charge, assuming SL amortisation, of 80,000 (400,000/5 years). This, too, is a consolidation entry. As a result of these adjustments, year 1 group income and end-year share-holders' equity are 595,000 and 3,975,000 respectively – or 105,000 less than the amounts reported in Exhibits 14.6 and 14.7. As before, we assume that the liabilities' balance is unchanged and therefore the increase in shareholders' equity from the companies' profitable operations flows through to 'other assets'.

Consolidation and acquisition accounting under IAS

Consolidation requirements

International standards lay down simple rules to ensure consolidated accounts are consistent and timely. As already mentioned, parent and subsidiaries should apply similar accounting policies; if policies are different, the accounts should be adjusted before they are consolidated. In addition, consolidated and parent company accounts should be drawn up to the same date. If this is not feasible, then the reporting date of a subsidiary's accounts should be no more than three months before that of the consolidated accounts. The accounting effect of any significant events that occur between these reporting dates should be incorporated in the consolidated accounts.

A company prepares consolidated accounts if it controls another. What is meant by 'control'? According to IAS, evidence of control exists when:

● *the investor company owns a majority of the investee's voting shares*; or
● *it controls a majority of the voting rights of the investee's shares as a result of an agreement with other shareholders*; or
● *it can exercise a dominant influence on the investee's policy-making under a statute or an agreement*; or
● *it can appoint or remove a majority of the investee's directors*; or
● *it can cast a majority of the votes at meetings of the board of directors.*[8]

Thus in some circumstances a company can exercise control over another without owning a majority of its voting shares.

Certain companies may be *exempted* from the consolidation requirement. One example is the *intermediate parent company*, that is, a company with subsidiaries that is itself owned by another – so long as the ultimate parent company prepares consolidated accounts and minority shareholders of the intermediate parent consent.[9] The EU's 7th Directive also exempts the '*small*' (EU-based) group, i.e. one where two of the following three criteria are not exceeded in two consecutive financial years: total assets of €14.6 million; total sales of €29.2 million; and average employees in the year of 250 (art. 6). The exemption does not apply to quoted companies.

Consolidation of some subsidiaries is forbidden. IAS require *exclusion* of a subsidiary where:

● control is intended to be short-term; or
● the parent's ability to receive funds from the subsidiary is constrained because of severe restrictions on its operations.[10]

Under IAS, the parent company accounts for such unconsolidated subsidiaries at fair value – or at cost, if fair value can't be determined reliably.

Subsidiaries that have activities very different from those of other group companies present a special accounting problem. Consider, for example, the car manufacturer that has a finance subsidiary that lends money not just to car buyers but also to purchasers of other products and services. The balance sheet and income statement characteristics of the finance subsidiary are closer to those of a bank than those of a manufacturer. It was long felt that consolidation of all subsidiaries in these circumstances would distort the group accounts. Thus under earlier international standards, companies had to account for subsidiaries pursuing dissimilar activities by the equity method rather than fully consolidate them.

Non-consolidation can lead to distortion of another kind, however. As we've seen, the equity method provides limited information about the investee's performance and financial condition. All that appears in the consolidated accounts is one line on the income statement ('Share of profit or loss of unconsolidated subsidiary') and one line on the balance sheet ('Investment in unconsolidated subsidiary'). As a result, investors can't determine the profit margin or financial leverage of the equity-accounted subsidiary. For this reason, IAS now require full consolidation of subsidiaries pursuing dissimilar activities.[11] Companies with such subsidiaries must provide disaggregated balance sheet and income statement information – either on the face of the consolidated financial statements or in the notes – to allow investors to understand better how the components of the group have performed. We describe these disclosures in section 3 of the chapter.

Acquisitions

Under IAS, the acquirer accounts for the purchase of another company or business *at cost*. 'Cost' is the cash paid, or the fair value of the consideration given, for the net assets acquired. The assets and liabilities acquired or assumed comprise only those *existing at the date of acquisition*: thus the acquirer can't include within assumed liabilities a provision for restructuring the acquired business, unless it puts forward a restructuring plan at or before the acquisition date.[12]

Assets and liabilities acquired or assumed must be measured *at fair value*. The excess of cost of acquisition over the fair value of net assets acquired is 'goodwill'. The acquirer must capitalise goodwill in the consolidated accounts and amortise it on a straight-line basis over its useful life. 'Useful life' is the period over which the acquirer expects to receive economic benefits from the goodwill asset. IAS lay down a 20-year upper limit for useful life but this can be extended if the acquirer can justify it. Like other fixed assets, goodwill must be assessed annually for impairment and written down when the recoverable amount is less than the carrying amount.

When the cost of acquisition is *less* than the fair value of net assets acquired, the acquirer records 'negative goodwill' – as a deduction under intangible assets – in the consolidated accounts. If negative goodwill relates to future losses or expenses the acquirer expects to incur as a result of the acquisition, it's recognised as income when the losses or expenses are recognised (i.e. it has an offsetting effect). Any remaining negative goodwill should be amortised (usually on a straight-line basis) over the remaining average useful life of the acquired depreciable assets.[13]

The EU's 7th Directive on consolidated accounts is more permissive than IAS in some respects. EU member states can allow companies to write off goodwill against reserves, instead of capitalising it. The 4th Directive (on annual accounts) lays down a maximum amortisation period of five years, but member states can permit companies to write off capitalised goodwill over a longer period provided the amount doesn't exceed the asset's estimated useful life.[14]

Goodwill: international practice

Most companies today capitalise goodwill arising on consolidation. Until recently, some EU member states (Denmark, Ireland, the Netherlands, UK) and certain countries with a UK legal and accounting tradition (Hong Kong, Malaysia, Singapore) permitted immediate write-off (IWO) as an alternative to capitalisation and it was widely used. As a result of new national standards introduced in the late 1990s, however, the IWO alternative was banned in most of these countries. The arguments of those favouring capitalisation – that goodwill represents part of the investment made by the acquirer and the asset can be identified and measured reliably at the date of acquisition – have prevailed. Although the use of IWO is now rare, its impact can still be seen in company accounts: reported goodwill and reserves are lower, and balance sheet leverage higher, than in companies that have always capitalised goodwill.

Goodwill remains a controversial issue. Currently the debate centres on whether goodwill should be amortised on a systematic basis. Those who oppose the practice argue that the amortisation calculation is arbitrary. It's not possible to determine the estimated life of the asset or how its benefits will be consumed in this period. The consolidated balance sheet will contain a more accurate measure of goodwill if the carrying amount is based on an annual impairment review. Those in favour argue that it is no more difficult to estimate the useful life of goodwill than it is to estimate that of other (amortisable) intangibles. Moreover, systematic amortisation provides less scope for managers to manipulate company earnings. Impairment reviews rely heavily on estimates by managers of future corporate cash flows which, by their nature, are hard to verify and therefore to audit.

The IASB has already indicated that it accepts the anti-amortisers' arguments. It published in the summer of 2002 a summary of Board discussions on business combinations. The Board plans to issue new standards on this topic in 2003 and 2004. The following are among the key proposed changes to the existing standard:

● Merger accounting is to be banned (*see* Box 14.1). All business combinations are to be accounted for by the purchase method.
● Goodwill (and other intangible assets with indefinite useful lives) should not be amortised. Instead, they should be tested for impairment at each financial year-end.
● Intangibles with finite useful lives that are acquired in a business combination should be recognised separately so long as the asset is separable and arises from contractual or legal rights. In-process research and development costs are one such intangible.
● Negative goodwill should not be carried forward. The acquirer should reassess the net assets acquired and recognise all liabilities – including contingent liabilities – arising as a result of the business combination. Valuations should be checked for measurement error. Any remaining negative goodwill represents a bargain purchase and should be recognised immediately as a gain.[15]

SECTION 2

Specialised topics

Minority interests

An investor company may acquire less than 100% of the investee's shares. In principle, it can gain control of the investee by purchasing a majority (more than 50%) of its voting shares. Moreover, outright purchase may be neither desirable nor feasible. For example, it may want certain shareholders (e.g. former owner-managers) to continue to be involved in its new subsidiary – or it may be forced to accept them. National law in many developing countries requires local participation in a domestic company controlled by a foreign investor.

The interests of outside shareholders in a group's subsidiary companies are known as **minority** (or **third-party**) **interests**. *Under global consolidation, the parent company consolidates 100% of the subsidiary's net assets and income, even when it does not own 100% of the shares.* A company with a controlling stake has control over *all* the investee's assets and liabilities. Thus all the assets

BOX
14.1

Merger accounting

The pooling-of-interests method – or merger accounting – was a popular method of accounting for business combinations in the USA until it was banned in 2001. Why was it popular – and why was it banned?

Accountants devised the pooling method because it was felt that the alternative, the purchase method, was an inappropriate method of accounting for mergers. In a merger, two companies join together – or 'pool their interests'. To effect the merger, one company – the offeror, A – offers its shares in exchange for those of B, the offeree. The ratio of shares exchanged is based on the market values of the two companies' shares at that date (and whether or not there is any cash or other consideration as well). Unlike in an acquisition, there's no major outflow of cash or other resources. All that occurs in substance is a change in the ownership of B's shares: B's shareholders become part of A's. Since the now-united entities continue trading as before, there's no need to distinguish pre-combination from post-combination activities, so it's argued.

The pooling method reflects this 'uniting of interests'. Here are its essential features.

1 *Revenues and expenses of the two companies are combined from the start of the period in which the merger takes place.* The consolidated income statement for calendar year x1 includes the full x1 revenues and expenses of both companies even if the merger takes place in December.
2 *Assets and liabilities are combined at their carrying amounts.* There are no fair value adjustments. No goodwill arises on consolidation.
3 *Consolidated retained profits include the retained profits of the combining companies from their inception.* Both companies' accumulated profits are available for distribution.

Not surprisingly, the pooling method found favour with acquisition-hungry companies, especially during the merger wave of the 1960s. They liked its financial effects. The offeror's earnings per share is boosted by a full year's earnings of the offeree firm in the year of merger. Reported profitability is raised: assets are lower (no goodwill) and income is higher (no goodwill amortisation charges). And the offeree's pre-combination retained profits can be distributed as dividend.

As a result, a growing number of US companies accounted for *acquisitions* as well as mergers by the pooling method. To halt the abuse, US regulators introduced rules in the early 1970s designed to limit its use. The key requirement was that the combination had to be largely share-based: A must offer shares (with identical voting rights to its existing ones) in exchange for substantially all of B's. 'Substantially all' was defined as 90% or more. B's shareholders could be offered cash but pooling could only be applied if the actual cash element of the deal was 10% or less. The rules included anti-avoidance measures – preventing, for example, creeping purchases of shares followed by an all-share offer or major cash distributions to the offeree's shareholders either before or after the merger.

US companies responded to the new rules by structuring many acquisitions as mergers. All-share offers became popular, especially in periods of high share prices: in the late 1990s, the pooling method was used in 30% of all merger and acquisition transactions. Some companies went to great lengths to secure its use. According to Lys and Vincent, AT&T reportedly offered to pay NCR's shareholders an extra US$450 million (increasing the purchase price to US$7.5 billion) if it could account for the acquisition of their company by the pooling method. AT&T's managers estimated that accounting for NCR as a purchase would have cut consolidated 1990 earnings by around 20% (because of goodwill amortisation charges) and they were concerned about the impact of the earnings decline on AT&T's share price.[16]

The continued abuse of the pooling method troubled investors and companies. There was little support for the method outside the USA, even though it was permitted under IAS (and the EU's 7th Directive). After much study, US and international regulators concluded that all business combinations should be accounted for by the purchase method. True mergers – where no party dominates the combined entity – are rare. Any criteria used to distinguish such transactions would be arbitrary and companies would find ways of circumventing them.

Exhibit 14.10 Parent company and outside shareholders: interests in group entity

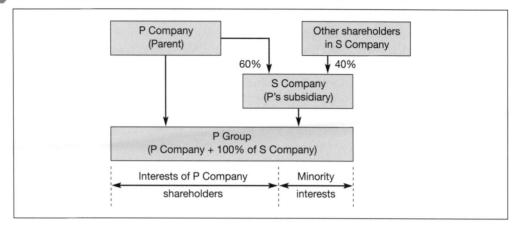

and liabilities (and revenues and expenses) of the subsidiary should be combined with those of the parent, it's argued. *The interests of the subsidiary's minority shareholders are then recognised separately in the consolidated accounts – as a deduction from group income in the income statement and as a separate equity account on the balance sheet.* Exhibit 14.10 shows diagrammatically how minority interests arise under global consolidation.

Illustration

To illustrate the accounting for minority interests, we return to our original example outlined in Exhibit 14.4 in which Danilo acquires shares in Glawari at book value. Assume now that Danilo acquires only 75% of Glawari's 200,000 shares at a price of 5/share at the start of year 1. Danilo's consolidated balance sheet at that date is derived in Exhibit 14.11.

Exhibit 14.11 Danilo Group and group companies: summary balance sheets at 1 January year 1 assuming Danilo has 75% interest in Glawari (amounts in 000)

	Danilo	Glawari	Eliminations and other adjustments*	Danilo Group
Assets				
Investment in G	750	–	–750	–
Other assets	4,250	1,800	0	6,050
Total	5,000	1,800	–750	6,050
Equities				
Shareholders' equity	3,600	1,000	–1,000	3,600
Minority interest in G's net assets	–	–	+250	250
Liabilities	1,400	800	0	2,200
Total	5,000	1,800	–750	6,050

* *Eliminations and other adjustments:*

Dr. Shareholders' equity (of Glawari)	1,000	
Cr. Investment in Glawari (Danilo's asset)		750
Cr. Minority interest in G's net assets (25% × 1,000)		250

Danilo's cash outlay is 750,000 (150,000 × 5/share), not 1 million, and its 'other assets' fall from 5 to 4.25 million. We assume Hanna Glawari retains a 25% stake in Glawari Industries. On consolidation, the subsidiary's capital and reserves at the date of acquisition and the parent's investment in the subsidiary are both eliminated as before.

What's new in this case is that Hanna's minority stake is recognised in the group accounts as 'Minority interest in G's net assets' at that date. It is valued at 250,000, 25% of Glawari's net asset value, and forms part of the Danilo group's equity. (We assume that the book values of Glawari's assets and liabilities at the start of year 1 reflect their fair values then and thus no adjustments need be made to them in the consolidated accounts.)

We now move forward a year and examine Danilo's consolidated accounts for year 1. We make the same trading assumptions as we made in our goodwill example (Exhibit 14.9):

- Danilo and Glawari have operating incomes of 500,000 and 200,000 respectively;
- Danilo distributes 220,000 and Glawari 60,000 of their respective profits;
- there are no intercompany transactions.

The group's income statement for year 1 and its end-year 1 balance sheet are derived in Exhibit 14.12.

How does Hanna's minority stake affect the group accounts? First, the group income statement distinguishes between the *total* consolidated income and the consolidated income *attributable to the parent company's shareholders*. In year 1, one-quarter of Glawari's 200,000 income or 50,000 accrues to Hanna, the minority shareholder. Thus while total income is still 700,000, consolidated income attributable to *Danilo's* shareholders is only 650,000.

Second, Glawari's 60,000 dividend is shared 75:25 between Danilo's shareholders and Hanna. As a result, Danilo reports investment income of 45,000 in its own accounts: this is eliminated on consolidation. At the same time, the equity account 'Minority interest' on the group balance sheet is adjusted. 'Minority interest' represents, in approximate terms, *the minority shareholders' interest in the net assets of subsidiaries*. In our example, the book amount of this equity account increases in year 1 by Hanna's share of Glawari's *retained* income that year, namely 35,000 (50,000 income *less the 15,000 dividend* Hanna receives). The end-year 1 balance in the account is 285,000, the initial 250,000 plus the 35,000 share of retained income. Note that this balance is also 25% of Glawari's net assets of 1,140,000 on that date.

Focus of consolidated accounts: parent company or entity?

There is a wider issue here: what should be the focus of consolidated accounts? Should they highlight the interests of the parent company's shareholders? After all, it's they who control the destiny of the group. Or should the interests of parent company and minority shareholders be treated equally, given that the entity depends on the capital of both?

This issue affects the way consolidated accounts are prepared. If consolidated accounts are to focus on the interests of the parent company's shareholders, then only the *parent company's* share of fair value adjustments and goodwill is recorded when a subsidiary is acquired. The minority shareholders' stake is recorded at book value. (The argument is that the purchase transaction values directly only the parent company's stake.) If, however, the focus of consolidated accounts is the entity, then the minority shareholders' share of fair value adjustments and goodwill must also be recognised.

There are differences in presentation, too. 'Minority interests' on the balance sheet may be shown separately from the equity of parent company shareholders (parent company approach) or as part of group capital and reserves (entity approach).

Current international standards favour the parent company approach. It's not mandatory, however. Some companies prepare consolidated accounts on an entity basis, on the grounds that this is more in keeping with the aim of consolidation.[17]

Exhibit 14.12 Danilo Group and group companies: summary year 1 accounts assuming Danilo has 75% interest in Glawari (amounts in 000)

Summary year 1 income statements

	Danilo	Glawari	Eliminations and other adjustments*		Danilo Group
Operating income	500	200		–	700
Investment income					
(75% of G's dividend)	45	–	(a)	–45	–
Total income	545	200		–45	700
Minority interest in G's income			(b)	–50	–50
Income attributable to D's shareholders					650
			(a)	+45 ⎫	
Dividend	–220	–60	(c)	+15 ⎬	–220
Retained income	325	140		–35	430

Summary balance sheets at end-year 1

	Danilo		Glawari	Eliminations and other adjustments*		Danilo Group
Investment in G		750	–		–750	–
Other assets:						
Start year 1	4,250		1,800			
Year 1 increase	325		140			
	4,575		1,940		0	6,515
Total assets	5,325		1,940		–750	6,515
Shareholders' equity						
Start year 1	3,600		1,000		–1,000	3,600
Year 1 income retained	325		140	(b)&(c)	–35	430
	3,925		1,140			4,030
Minority interest in G's net assets	–		–		+250 ⎫	285
				(b)&(c)	+35 ⎬	
Liabilities	1,400		800		0	2,200
Total equities	5,325		1,940		–750	6,515

* *Post-acquisition eliminations and other adjustments*:

(a) Dr. Investment income (of Danilo)   45
      Cr. Retained income (of Glawari)   45
     To eliminate intercompany dividend.

(b) Dr. Minority interest in G's income (25% x 200)   50
      Cr. Minority interest in G's net assets   50
     To recognise minority interest in G's income.

(c) Dr. Minority interest in G's net assets (25% x 60)   15
      Cr. Retained income (of Glawari)   15
     To record effect of G's dividend on minority interest.

Joint ventures

In recent years, it has become common for companies to enter into **joint ventures** with other firms. *A joint venture is a contractual arrangement in which two or more companies agree to work together on, and accept joint control over, some economic activity, for example producing or marketing a product.* Such an alliance can take one of several forms. Sometimes, assets are jointly owned (for example, an oil pipeline and pumping equipment) or operations are carried out jointly (for example, the marketing and distribution of a drug in a foreign market). In other cases, a separate company is formed with the 'joint venturers' as shareholders. A joint venture allows participants to share risks when embarking on a new line of business or expanding an existing one. It also means, of course, that returns are shared too.

Incorporated joint ventures pose an interesting accounting problem. Since the company is jointly owned, no one shareholder exercises dominant influence over it: thus no shareholder should use global consolidation to account for its investment.

Investor companies use either the equity method or **proportionate consolidation** (**pro-rata consolidation**) to account for their investment in an incorporated joint venture. The mechanics of equity accounting – and its rationale – are discussed in section 1 of the chapter. *Under proportionate consolidation, each investor includes in its consolidated accounts its share of the assets, liabilities, revenues and expenses of the jointly controlled company.*[18] It does not include its share of profits on transactions between it and the joint venture, since such gains are not realised.

Incorporated joint venture: accounting by venturer

We contrast the two ways of accounting for a joint venture, proportionate consolidation and the equity method, in the venturer's books. Candide, our garden products manufacturer, and Martin, a potter, decide that garden ornaments – and red sheep in particular – have good sales prospects. They set up a new entity, Eldorado Company, to market them. Each invests 500,000 cash in the company. Eldorado borrows 800,000 and acquires plant, inventory and other assets with the 1.8 million capital.

We illustrate the accounting for the joint venture in Candide's books. (The same issues apply to Martin, the other venturer.) Prior to the investment, the company has assets of 3 million and liabilities of 1.4 million. Exhibit 14.13 shows the effect of the investment on its accounts on 1 January before Eldorado begins operations.

Under proportionate consolidation, Candide combines 50% of Eldorado's assets (900,000) with its own (2.5 million, after the investment of 500,000 cash in Eldorado). Candide's consolidated liabilities figure is calculated in the same way ((50% × 800,000) + 1.4 million). Under the equity method, Candide records as an asset its investment in Eldorado (500,000 at 1 January).

As for the income statement, under proportionate consolidation, Candide includes its share (50%) of Eldorado's revenues and expenses in its consolidated income statement. Under the equity method, it shows, as investment income, its share of Eldorado's profit or loss.

Thus Candide's reported assets and liabilities and revenues and expenses are higher under proportionate consolidation. However, its total profit or loss – and, by extension, its end-year shareholders' equity – are the same under the two accounting methods.

Advocates of proportionate consolidation argue it better reflects the investor's financial performance and position. Use of the equity method results in a loss of information: Candide's share of Eldorado's liabilities, for example, are concealed in the asset 'Investment in Eldorado'. Critics, however, maintain it is misleading for a company to consolidate assets and liabilities (and revenues and expenses) where it has *full* control with those where it has *joint* control. To have a 50% stake in a building valued at 1 million is not the same as owning outright a building

Exhibit 14.13 Candide's accounting for Eldorado joint venture: summary balance sheets at 1 January under proportionate consolidation and equity method (amounts in 000)

Facts

Candide and Martin each owns 50% of Eldorado's shares. Each invests 500 in Eldorado. Eldorado borrows 800. Thus Eldorado's initial total assets are 1,800.

Summary balance sheets at 1 January

	Eldorado	Candide (pre-Eldorado)	Candide: proportionate consolidation of Eldorado	Candide: equity accounting of Eldorado
Assets				
Investment in Eldorado	–	–	–	500
Other assets	1,800	3,000	3,400*	2,500
Total	1,800	3,000	3,400	3,000
Equities				
Shareholders' equity	1,000	1,600	1,600	1,600
Liabilities	800	1,400	1,800	1,400
	1,800	3,000	3,400	3,000

```
*   3,000      –     500     +     900  ⎫
  Assets pre-   Investment   50% of  ⎬
   Eldorado    in Eldorado  E's assets ⎭
```

valued at 500,000. Under this view, joint control implies the ability to exercise significant influence and no more. Investments in joint ventures should therefore be accounted for by the equity method.

International rules and practice

Under IAS, proportionate consolidation is the preferred method of accounting by venturers for incorporated joint ventures; the equity method is an 'allowed alternative'.[19] (The EU's 7th Directive also permits both methods.) Where proportionate consolidation is used, the venturer's share of the joint venture's assets, liabilities, revenues and expenses can be shown separately in the consolidated accounts or combined with like items. Separate presentation overcomes the objection to proportionate consolidation mentioned above.

The choice of accounting treatments under IAS reflects differences in national accounting practice. For example, Dutch and French companies have long used proportionate consolidation to account for incorporated joint ventures; US companies normally account for such ventures by the equity method. The consequence is that two venturers – Candide and Martin, for example – may account for their investments in a jointly controlled company (Eldorado) using different accounting methods.

Divesting a business

Companies dispose of businesses as well as acquire them – and for similar reasons. Management hope to create wealth for shareholders by selling off subsidiaries that are performing poorly or are not part of the company's core operations. (The stock market, we're told, values more highly the earnings of 'focused' companies.) In addition, companies in financial difficulties sell businesses to raise cash. Divesting businesses became popular in the USA in the 1980s and spread to other countries in the 1990s. Recent examples include DuPont's carve-out of its Conoco oil business in 1998 and Telmex's spin-off of its mobile phone business in 2001. Research shows that the average demerger benefits shareholders. A study of 38 European spin-offs in the 1990s found that the share price of companies announcing a demerger outperformed the market by 5.5% on average at the time of the announcement.[20]

Divestment can take several forms. The divesting company (i.e. the parent) can sell an unwanted business to another company (or a private equity fund) via a **trade sale**. Alternatively, it can offer shares in the business to stock market investors in an **initial public offering** (**IPO**). However, when stock markets are depressed, it may decide that demerging the business creates more value for shareholders. There are two main types of demerger.[21] In a **spin-off**, the parent company distributes new shares representing 100% of the unwanted business directly to its shareholders on a pro-rata basis (e.g. one share in the spun-off entity for every share held in the parent). The spun-off entity lists its shares on the stock market and shareholders can then trade them. In an **equity carve-out**, the parent offers shares in part of the demerged entity via an IPO. It can spin off or sell the rest of the now quoted company at a later date. The diagram below contrasts the two types of demerger.

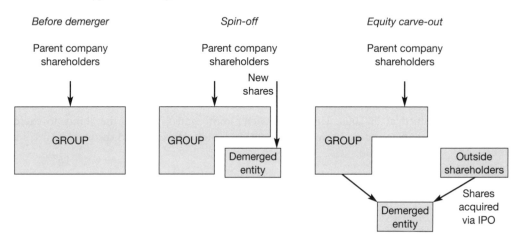

Note that both pure spin-offs and equity carve-outs are structured so that shareholders can postpone or avoid tax on the distribution of shares in the demerged entity.

How do companies account for divestments? This depends on the divestment route taken. In the case of a trade sale or IPO, the parent company receives cash, removes the assets and liabilities of the divested business from the consolidated balance sheet and records a gain or loss on disposal. If, in an IPO, the parent loses control of the divested business but doesn't sell all its shares to public investors, it deconsolidates the business and records the net assets retained as an investment. An example may help here. Suppose SpiceFolk, a spice-trading company based in South East Asia, decides to sell 70% of its shares in TeaTotal, a fully owned tea-trading subsidiary. It raises 350 in cash from an IPO. TeaTotal has net assets of 400 then. SpiceFolk records the IPO transaction in its consolidated accounts as follows. (All amounts are in millions. Taxes and transaction costs are ignored.)

Dr. Investment in TeaTotal	120	
Dr. Cash	350	
Cr. Net assets of TeaTotal		400
Cr. Gain on disposal of TeaTotal shares		70

The credit to 'Net assets of TeaTotal' is a summary entry. In practice, SpiceFolk removes from the consolidated accounts the carrying amounts of TeaTotal's individual assets and liabilities. As for its remaining investment in TeaTotal, SpiceFolk accounts for this by the equity method – assuming it exercises significant influence over the company.

In the case of an equity carve-out, the parent company retains control of the subsidiary after the IPO. Outside shareholders have a minority interest in the subsidiary's net assets and this is reflected in the parent's consolidated accounts. Thus if SpiceFolk sells 30% of TeaTotal in an IPO and receives cash of 130, it makes the following entry in the consolidated accounts to record the transaction.

Dr. Cash	130	
Cr. Minority interest (in TeaTotal's net assets)		120
Cr. Share premium		10

'Minority interest' reflects outside shareholders' 30% stake in TeaTotal's net assets of 400. The price SpiceFolk receives for each TeaTotal share is assumed to be less in an equity carve-out than in a sale of a majority stake because there's no control premium (and less liquidity). SpiceFolk credits the gain on disposal of TeaTotal shares to the share premium account. TeaTotal is still part of the SpiceFolk group. Gains and losses from trading own shares – whether the parent company's or a subsidiary's – should not be recognised in income since this undermines the earnings number as a measure of corporate performance.

A spin-off is treated in the consolidated accounts as a 'dividend in kind'. The parent company distributes part of its assets – by way of shares – to its shareholders and the distribution is recorded as a reduction in retained earnings. SpiceFolk records a dividend in kind of 400 on distribution of its shares in TeaTotal to its shareholders:

Dr. Retained earnings	400	
Cr. Net assets of TeaTotal		400

No gain or loss is recorded since, under current accounting practice, the shares distributed to the parent company's shareholders are valued at the carrying amount of the underlying net assets of the demerged entity.

To help investors gauge the effect of a divestment on future consolidated earnings and cash flows, IAS require firms to show separately the assets and liabilities, revenues and expenses of operations that are to be 'discontinued' – either on the face of the financial statements or in the notes. We illustrate IAS-required disclosures for discontinued operations in Chapter 20.

SECTION 3   Consolidated accounts and financial analysis

Disclosures related to equity/consolidation accounting

Most companies include a statement of consolidation policy in the notes to their consolidated accounts. The statement sets out, at a minimum:

- the criteria used to determine which investee companies are consolidated – and when;
- the consolidation procedures followed; and
- the accounting treatment of associated companies.

Exhibit 14.14 BestPrice Stores: statement of consolidation policy in ×2 accounts

---

Consolidation principles

The consolidated accounts include those of the parent company, BestPrice Stores S.A., and all companies in which it held directly or indirectly more than 50% of the voting power at the end of the year. Changes in the consolidation scope take effect from the date of acquisition or divestment. The global consolidation method has been applied. The minority interests of third parties in equity and income are shown separately in the balance sheet and income statement.

Investments in associated companies have been accounted for in the consolidated financial statements under the equity method. An associated company is a company in which the group holds between 20% and 50% of the voting power and exercises significant influence over its operating and financial decisions. Under the equity method, the group's share of the profit or loss of an associated company is shown in the consolidated income statement under 'investment income' and the group's share in the associated company's equity is shown in the consolidated balance sheet under 'long-term financial investments'.

All material intercompany balances and transactions have been eliminated in the consolidated financial statements.

Intercompany shareholdings have been eliminated by deducting the amount of each subsidiary's equity at the time of acquisition from the acquisition cost of its shares. The difference between a subsidiary's acquisition cost and the fair value of its net assets at the time of acquisition has been entered as goodwill in the consolidated balance sheet.

(*Source*: Nokia Corporation, *Annual Report and Accounts 2002*.)

BestPrice Stores, the fictitious Euroland retailer we encountered in earlier chapters, provides such a statement in its x2 accounts; *see* Exhibit 14.14.

BestPrice lists in its annual report its principal subsidiaries and associates, giving the name, country of incorporation and its percentage stake in each. This is common practice. The information helps financial statement users in several ways. They learn more about the geographical spread – and the related operating and financial risks – of the company's business. In addition, by comparing the listing of subsidiaries and associates in successive annual reports, they discover how the composition of the group is changing – for example, which subsidiaries and associates have been acquired and sold and in which companies the group's stake has increased or decreased during the year.

With this information, users can better explain changes in the consolidated numbers. For example, a reduction in a majority holding in a subsidiary is reflected in an increase in 'Minority interests' in the balance sheet.

Another important disclosure concerns **related-party transactions**. *Two parties are 'related' if one is able to control or exercise significant influence over the other in making financial and operating decisions.* Note that, in this context, an individual such as a large shareholder or a director of a company – or a close family member – can be a related party of a company. 'Transactions' include purchases and sales of goods and services, licence agreements, loans, guarantees and management contracts. Under international rules, a company must disclose the nature and extent of related-party transactions.[22]

Analysing consolidated accounts: problem areas

Investors value consolidated accounts. Empirical evidence suggests that they prefer them to unconsolidated ones.[23] However, they encounter problems using them. We identify three and discuss how they try to overcome them.

Performance of components of group

Consolidated accounts are, by definition, aggregated accounts. They show the *combined* financial results and condition of the companies in the group. It is difficult to find out from them how the various affiliates have performed. The problem is particularly serious when the group is diversified by product line or market. In this case, there is a greater likelihood that the aggregated results mask differences in performance within the group.

How do investors get accounting data on a group's components? Companies sometimes help. Under EU and international rules, certain companies must disclose, in the notes to the accounts, key financial numbers like sales broken down by line of business and geographical area. (We discuss segmental reporting in detail in Chapter 20.)

A second line of attack is to look at the accounts of the parent and subsidiary companies. As we mentioned earlier, a European company that produces consolidated accounts often includes part or all of the parent company's accounts in the annual report. To get financial information about subsidiary companies is more difficult. In most European countries, however, public companies, whether quoted or unquoted, must file their accounts with a government agency and the public can inspect them. Investors have two options: they can consult this source directly or they can purchase the products of information providers – such as credit rating agencies and financial database producers – who make use of it.

Change in composition of group and effect on accounts

When a company sells part of its business or takes over another firm, the composition of the group changes. The consolidated sales and profit figures reported after the change may not be comparable to those reported before. Without additional information, investors will have difficulty judging how well the group has performed in the current period relative to the past. Trends in sales, margins and asset efficiency are likely to be distorted. Future profits are harder to forecast.

Once again, investors can turn to the accounts of the individual companies in the group – including those bought or sold – and try to unravel the effects of changes in the group's make-up. But they often find valuable information in the consolidated accounts themselves. Under IAS, a company must show the effects of major business disposals – on sales and profits, for example – on the face of the consolidated income statement. (We illustrate the disclosures companies make concerning their 'discontinuing' operations in Chapter 20.) In the case of acquisitions, it may provide pro forma financial statements (showing, for example, what sales and profits would have been in the absence of the acquisition) in the notes.

Off-balance-sheet debt

Highly indebted firms are risky investments for creditors and shareholders alike. They are at greater risk of bankruptcy and bear higher capital costs as a result. Management of these firms have an incentive to conceal corporate debt. One approach, as we saw in Chapter 11, is to ensure that debt is carried by affiliates that are equity-accounted and not fully consolidated.

Accounting for investments by the equity method is often described as **one-line consolidation**. The company's shares of the investee's revenues and expenses are netted and shown as one line ('Investment income' or 'Equity in earnings of investee') on its income statement. Similarly, its shares of the investee's assets and liabilities are netted and shown as one line ('Financial fixed asset') on its balance sheet.

Under one-line consolidation, the company reports profitability and leverage ratios different from – and usually more favourable than – those it reports under global or proportionate consolidation. For example, total revenues and assets are lower under one-line consolidation. Net profit, however, is not affected. The result is that reported net margins are higher but total asset turnover is lower. *More importantly, the liabilities of the equity-accounted affiliates are not included in consolidated liabilities because they are set off against assets in the 'Investment' account.* The effect? Reported leverage ratios are lower.

Contrast the effect on Danilo's accounts of accounting for its (100%) stake in Glawari under the equity method and global consolidation. Exhibit 14.15 presents, in summary form,

Exhibit 14.15 Danilo's investment in Glawari: equity accounting and global consolidation contrasted (amounts in 000)

Danilo Company		Equity method		Global consolidation
Year 1 income statement				
Operating revenues		6,600		9,280
Operating expenses		−6,100		−8,580
Operating profit		500		700
Share of Glawari's profit		+200		−
Net profit		700		700
Dividend		−220		−220
Retained profit in year		480		480
End-year 1 balance sheet				
Investment in Glawari:				
Cost of acquisition	1,000			
Share of retained profit	140			
		1,140		−
Other assets:				
Start-year 1	4,000		5,800	
Year 1 increase	340		480	
		4,340		6,280
Total assets		5,480		6,280
Shareholders' equity:				
Start-year 1	3,600		3,600	
Year 1 retained profit	480		480	
		4,080		4,080
Liabilities		1,400		2,200
Total equities		5,480		6,280
Ratios				
Net profit margin ratio (in %)		10.6%		7.5%
(Net profit/Operating revenues)				
Total asset turnover		1.2×		1.5×
(Operating revenues/Assets at end-year)				
Liabilities-to-equity ratio (in %)		34.3%		53.9%
(Total liabilities/Total shareholders' equity)				

Danilo's year 1 accounts under both accounting methods. (The underlying figures are taken from Exhibits 14.6 and 14.7. We assume no intercompany transactions have taken place.) Key financial ratios are also given. If Danilo were to account for its investment in Glawari by the equity method, its year 1 profit margin ratio would be higher (10.6% against 7.5% under full consolidation) and its end-year 1 liabilities-to-equity ratio would be lower (34.3% against 53.9%).

Companies also have an incentive to ensure that newly acquired affiliates that are highly leveraged qualify for equity method treatment. Thus Renault acquired only a 37% stake in Nissan in 1999 when the Japanese vehicle manufacturer was in financial difficulties. Renault's stake was judged to be a participating rather than a controlling one: it was forced to report its share of Nissan's losses but avoided consolidating Nissan's debts.[24]

How does an investor discover the extent of debt raised off balance sheet via associated companies? Where the associate is publicly quoted, as in Nissan's case, the information is readily available. Failing this, the investor must unearth the accounts of the associated companies to discover the extent of their financial leverage. Sometimes the parent company comes to the investor's rescue and provides, in the notes, condensed accounts of each of its principal equity-accounted investments.[25]

In some countries, companies can use special purposes entities (SPEs) to hide debt. An SPE is a trust, partnership or other legal vehicle set up to hold and manage financial assets such as receivables. For example, a company that securitises its receivables can transfer them to an SPE and the latter then raises debt to finance them (see Box 10.1 in Chapter 10). Companies also use SPEs to avoid capitalising lease obligations. An SPE acquires assets – with debt or under a finance lease – and the company sponsoring the SPE then 'rents' them under an operating lease arrangement.

Under US accounting rules, the sponsor of the SPE does not consolidate the SPE's accounts with its own so long as the SPE meets certain conditions. Among these conditions is the requirement that providers of outside capital to the SPE – that is, parties unconnected with the sponsoring company – must have made a substantial investment in it. This is defined as at least 3% of the SPE's total assets.[26] Given that the percentage of required outside capital is so low, it is quite possible for the sponsoring company to control an SPE and yet avoid consolidating it. Enron, the failed energy trading company, made extensive use of SPEs. It's estimated that by the end of 1999 it had removed US$27 billion – the equivalent of 45% of its total assets – from its balance sheet in this way. There was little information in Enron's accounts about the assets of the SPEs or the debt used to finance them but, in some cases, the SPEs' own financial statements were publicly available.

Summary

When a company owns a large proportion of another's shares, the financial investment is of a special kind. The accounting reflects this.

A company that has an active minority stake in another – normally in the range of 20% to 50% – can usually exercise significant influence over its affairs. The investee is then its associate. It accounts for the associate by the equity method (in its consolidated accounts). It recognises as income its share of the profit or loss of the associate. The carrying amount of the investment is approximately its share of the associate's net assets. One advantage of equity accounting for investors is that a company is unable to manipulate its reported profits through its associate's distribution policy.

A company that controls another prepares, in addition to its own accounts, consolidated accounts for the two companies. The most common way for a company to acquire control is by buying a majority of another's voting shares. Under consolidation accounting, parent company and subsidiaries combine their accounts, eliminating intercompany balances and unrealised profits or losses on intercompany transactions in the process. Under global consolidation, 100% of a subsidiary's assets and liabilities, revenues and expenses are included in the consolidated accounts. If the parent owns less than 100% of the subsidiary's shares, the interests of outside shareholders in the subsidiary's income and net assets are recorded as 'minority interests' in the consolidated accounts.

A thorny problem is the accounting treatment of 'goodwill'. In consolidation accounting, this is the difference that arises when the price an investor company pays for its shareholding is greater than the fair value of the net assets it acquires. IAS require firms to capitalise and amortise goodwill. In some countries, however, firms can substitute an annual impairment review for systematic amortisation of the goodwill asset. Analysts overcome accounting differences by adjusting firms' accounts for goodwill amortisation.

Business combinations may take other forms and the accounting must adapt to them. In the case of joint ventures, firms share control. Such ventures are proportionately consolidated or accounted for by the equity method. Mergers, however, are accounted for in the same way as a purchase: it's argued that even in mergers of equals one firm effectively controls another. But where a firm demerges an entity by spinning it off to shareholders, the spin-off is viewed as a dividend in kind and its assets and liabilities are removed from the consolidated accounts at their carrying amounts.

Investors benefit from consolidation accounting. Consolidated accounts show the financial performance and condition – the total liabilities as well as the total assets – of an economic entity under common control. They pay a price, however. Consolidated accounts are aggregated accounts. In the absence of additional disaggregated data, it is hard for investors to discover how the components of the group are performing.

Problem assignments

P14.1 Equity method and consolidation accounting: general issues

Equity method and consolidation accounting are not always straightforward as the following (independent) situations demonstrate.

(1) Oceana, an investment company, increases its stake in Etam, a retailer, from 24% to 34.4% and announces that it will begin using the equity method to account for the investment in its consolidated accounts. Etam, a quoted (and profitable) company, files a complaint with the regulatory arm of its national stock exchange, arguing that Oceana's proposed accounting treatment is misleading since it doesn't exercise significant influence over Etam. Oceana has no representatives on Etam's board of directors and doesn't have any cooperation agreements with the company. In reply, Oceana's management maintain they can exert significant influence. First, Oceana is Etam's largest shareholder. In addition, its shareholding gives it the power to block special resolutions (which require a 75% majority in general meetings of shareholders).

(2) The Photowell Group manufactures, sells and operates coin-operated automatic photobooths. The group has operations throughout the world, with photobooths in metro stations, airports and shopping malls in every major country. Photowell's reported turnover in x7 was 170 million (in local currency). 'Turnover' comprises revenues from manufacturing and selling photobooths as well as revenues from operating and servicing them. The company presented its consolidated turnover in its x7 accounts as follows:

Turnover	Millions
Manufacture and distribution of photobooths:	
Sales to other divisions and companies within the Group	10.3
Sales to third parties	35.8
	46.1
Operation and servicing of photobooths	123.9
	170.0

The company explains its treatment of turnover in the notes to its x7 accounts:

Turnover

Turnover includes sales, by the Group's manufacturing divisions to Group undertakings [i.e. other divisions and companies within the Group], of equipment which is then capitalised with the accounts of the Group's undertakings. . . . Inter-company profit arising on such sales is excluded from the Group's profit.

(3) Koopman, a Dutch trading house, is preparing consolidated accounts for calendar year x1. Just before year-end, a Latin American subsidiary, Lamsa, collapses with large debts. Koopman's management want to exclude the subsidiary from the consolidated accounts for x1 and account for the investment at cost. They argue that, given the bankruptcy of Lamsa, Koopman's investment will be sold off or liquidated in x2 and thus its control of Lamsa is 'temporary'.

Required

Consider the accounting issue in each of the above cases. How should Oceana account for its investment in Etam in its consolidated accounts? How should Photowell report consolidated turnover in x7? How should Koopman account for its investment in Lamsa in its consolidated x1 accounts? Give reasons for your answers.

P14.2   The nature of goodwill

During the so-called bubble years in the late 1990s, many companies in the telecoms, media and technology (TMT) sectors used their highly valued shares to acquire other companies. They accounted for the acquisitions by the purchase method in most cases. Since the acquired companies often had few tangible assets, much of the purchase price was attributed to goodwill. When share prices in the TMT sectors collapsed in 2001/02, the acquirers were forced to write down the goodwill on their acquisitions, following interim and year-end impairment reviews. The sums involved were huge in some cases. Examples are given below.

Acquirer	Target(s)	Goodwill on acquisition	Goodwill write-downs in 2001/02
America Online	Time Warner	US$128bn	US$54bn
JDS Uniphase	SDL ⎱ E-Tek ⎰	US$56.5bn	US$54.3bn
Vivendi	Canal Plus	€14.1bn	€11.2bn
France Telecom	Mobilcom	€2.7bn	€2.5bn

Many managers argue that goodwill write-downs are bookkeeping adjustments and have little or no economic significance. According to Tony Muller, then chief financial officer of JDS Uniphase, big accounting charges like goodwill write-downs have no impact on 'real-world issues like cash flow or the company's bank covenants' (*Financial Times*, 18 June 2001).

Required

(a) What is the economic significance, if any, of a goodwill write-down? If a write-down has no economic significance, what is the economic significance of the goodwill asset itself?

(b) Some analysts argue that a distinction should be made between acquisitions for cash and acquisitions for 'paper' (i.e. using the acquirer's own shares). Goodwill write-downs represent value destruction in the former case but not in the latter. Comment on this argument. Why is it correct – or incorrect?

P14.3 Long-term equity investments: cost method and equity method

Olivia, a fashion house, acquires 1.2 million of the 4 million voting shares of Malvolio, a small textile company (best known product: yellow stockings) for €15 million at the start of year 6. The carrying amount of Malvolio's net assets is €50 million at that date. Malvolio reports net income in year 6 of €5 million and pays a cash dividend of €0.5 per share that year.

Required

(a) Assume Olivia does not exercise significant influence over Malvolio and uses the cost method to account for her investment. Show the effect on Olivia's year 6 accounts of:
   (i)   the acquisition of her stake in Malvolio;
   (ii) the reporting by Malvolio of net income in year 6; and
   (iii) the payment by Malvolio of cash dividends to his company's shareholders in year 6.

   Use journal entries or the balance sheet equation.

(b) Assume Olivia does exercise significant influence over Malvolio and uses the equity method to account for her investment. Show the effects on Olivia's year 6 accounts of the three events listed in (a) above.

(c) Suppose that Malvolio distributes a share dividend – of one share for every five shares held – to all shareholders in year 6. The share dividend is declared after the payment of the cash dividend. How does this affect your answers to (a) and (b) above?

Check figure:
(b) 'Investment in Malvolio'
    at end-year 6   } €15.9m

P14.4 Equity method, goodwill and losses

At the start of x1, Pasquale Company pays €10 million to acquire a 25% stake in Norina SpA. Norina's net assets at that date are €24 million. Pasquale exercises significant influence over Norina and accounts for its investment by the equity method. The company attributes the difference between the purchase price and its share of Norina's net assets to goodwill and proposes to amortise the asset on a straight-line basis over ten years. (It does not show the goodwill separately.)

The Norina investment is a disastrous one for Pasquale. Norina pays no dividends. It incurs losses of €4 million in calendar year x1 and further losses of €1.2 million in x2. Pasquale carries out an impairment review at the end of x2, as a result of which it writes off the remaining goodwill. In x3 Norina generates a small profit of €1.6 million. Pasquale takes advantage of the recovery in the value of its investment by selling its stake in Norina for €4.4 million at the end of x3.

Required

(a) Show the effect of its investment in Norina on Pasquale's accounts for each of the years x1–x3. Use journal entries or the balance sheet equation.

(b) Suppose that Pasquale carried out an impairment review at the end of x1 and wrote off *the whole of its investment in Norina* then. How would your answer to (a) differ?

Check figure:
(a) Investment in Norina,
    carrying amount at end-x2   €4.7m

Consolidation: basic structure

Impressed by the research and production skills of Fleurant Corporation, Argan SA decides at the end of x1 to buy a controlling interest in the pharmaceutical company for cash. The book value of Fleurant's net assets is 50 then. Argan's net assets prior to the acquisition are 350. (All amounts are in millions.)

In x2, Argan reports operating profit of 30 (i.e. before including income from Fleurant) and pays dividends of 14. That same year, Fleurant's profit is 6 and the dividend it pays is 4. (In its own accounts, Argan uses the cost method to account for its investment in Fleurant.) Any goodwill arising on consolidation is amortised on a SL basis over 10 years.

Required

Prepare (i) a summary consolidated balance sheet at end-x1 and (ii) summary x2 accounts (income statement and end-year balance sheet) for the Argan Group (Argan + Fleurant) under each of the following assumptions:

(a) Argan purchases 100% of Fleurant's shares for 50;

(b) Argan purchases 100% of Fleurant's shares for 80;

(c)* Argan purchases 80% of Fleurant's shares for 40.

> Check figure:
> (a) Argan Group:
>   Shareholders' equity, end-x2   372

* Assignment draws on material in section 2 of this chapter.

P14.6 Consolidation and intercompany sales

(1) At the start of year 8, Fireball Company pays 10/share in cash for all 3 million of Slowcoach Company's shares. Slowcoach has assets of 40 million and liabilities of 10 million at that date. Fireball's assets before the acquisition are 150 million and its liabilities 50 million.

Required

Draw up a summarised consolidated balance sheet for the Fireball Group at the start of year 8. Assume Slowcoach follows the same accounting policies as Fireball and its assets and liabilities are stated at fair value.

(2) In year 8, Fireball reports revenues of 80 and expenses of 60. (All amounts are in million.) Slowcoach's reported revenues and expenses are 37 and 34 respectively. During year 8, Fireball sells goods to Slowcoach on account for 10 which cost it 7 to make and for which Slowcoach has paid Fireball only 5 by year-end. Slowcoach sells all the goods to outside customers for 12 in year 8.

Fireball pays a dividend of 8 to its shareholders in year 8; Slowcoach pays a dividend of only 2 that year. The two companies' total liabilities at end-year 8 are unchanged from the start of the year.

Required

(a) Draw up summarised consolidated accounts for year 8 for the Fireball Group.

(b) How would your answer to (a) differ if Slowcoach had sold to outside customers only *half* of the goods purchased from Fireball and recognised revenues of 6 on them? ([Assume] Slowcoach's total reported revenues and expenses are still 37 and 34 respectively.)

> Check figures:
> (2)(a) Year 8 group profit   23.0m
>   (b) End-year 8 shareholders' equity   113.5m

P14.7 Consolidation: fair value adjustments and restructuring provision

At start year 5, Hardcastle pays 80 in cash to acquire 100% of Marlow's shares. The balance sheets of the two companies at end year 4 are set out below. (Amounts are in € million.)

	Hardcastle		Marlow	
Fixed assets				
Property, plant and equipment		184		142
Investments		76		83
		260		225
Current assets				
Inventories	72		29	
Receivables	135		75	
Cash and marketable securities	158		41	
		365		145
Total assets		625		370
Shareholders' equity		327		70
Debt		139		163
Provisions and other long-term liabilities		68		75
Accounts payable and accrued expenses		91		62
		298		300
Total equities		625		370

Hardcastle prepares consolidated accounts at start-year 5. It uses the purchase method to account for the acquisition and makes the following fair value adjustments to Marlow's accounts. (Amounts are in € million.)

Equipment: downward revaluation	−20
Investments: upward revaluation	+30
Inventories: reduction due to larger provision for slow-moving items	−3
Receivables: reduction due to increase in allowance for doubtful accounts	−5

Hardcastle plans to restructure the Marlow business and wants to include a restructuring provision of 12 with the fair value adjustments at the time of the initial consolidation.

Required

(a) Prepare an initial consolidated balance sheet for the Hardcastle Group at start-year 5. Include the restructuring provision in the fair value adjustments.

(b) Hardcastle and Marlow report year 5 income of 39 and 14, respectively. The fair value adjustment to equipment is depreciated over the assets' remaining life of 5 years. No further value adjustments are made to Marlow's investments in year 5. The adjustments to inventories and receivables are 'amortised' through COGS and bad debt expense in year 5. Goodwill is subject to an annual impairment test: no impairment is recorded in year 5. Compute the year 5 consolidated income of the Hardcastle Group. Ignore income taxes.

(c) The auditors disagree with Hardcastle's treatment of the restructuring provision. They note that there was no detailed formal plan for restructuring Marlow at the time of acquisition. They require Hardcastle to record the provision as an additional cost in Marlow's year 5 accounts and not include it with the fair value adjustments in the initial consolidation. How does this change in treatment affect (i) the initial consolidated balance sheet at start-year 5; and (ii) the calculation of consolidated income for year 5?

Check figure:
(a) Goodwill   20

P14.8 Joint ventures: alternative methods of accounting*

At the start of year 1, Zeus reports the following balance sheet:

Zeus Company

Assets		Equities	
Cash	20	Liabilities	100
Other assets	180	Shareholders' equity	100
	200		200

On that date Zeus enters into a joint venture with Maia. They establish a new firm, Hermes, and each invests cash of 10 in it. Hermes raises debt (on the strength of Zeus's and Maia's guarantees) to finance the purchase of fixed assets. When this investment is made, Hermes's balance sheet looks as follows:

Hermes Company

Assets		Equities		
		Liabilities		80
		Shareholders' equity:		
Cash and		Zeus	10	
other assets	100	Maia	10	20
	100			100

Required

(a) Zeus wants to know how to account for its investment in Hermes. Prepare a balance sheet for Zeus Company at the start of year 1, assuming the investment:

(1) is accounted for by the equity method;
(2) is consolidated on a proportionate basis;
(3) is consolidated on a global basis.

When should Zeus use each of the above methods?

(b) At the end of its first year, Hermes reports revenues of 70 and profit of 10. It pays a dividend of 8. Liabilities of 80 are unchanged. In the same period, Zeus reports revenues of 150 and profit (from its own activities) of 20. It pays a dividend of 12. Its end-year liabilities are still 100. There are no intercompany transactions between Zeus and Hermes except for the dividend. Ignore taxes.

For each of the methods listed in (a) above:

(i) calculate Zeus's total profit for year 1; and
(ii) prepare Zeus's balance sheet at the end of year 1. (Combine cash and other assets.)

Check figures:
(b) (ii) End-year 1 total assets
(1) 213 (2) 253 (3) 304

* Assignment draws on material in section 2 of this chapter.

P14.9 Acquisitions and disclosures: financial disclosures

Unilever, the giant Anglo-Dutch food and consumer products company, made major acquisitions and disposals of businesses in 2000 and 2001. Key cash flow statement information for both years is given below (amounts in € million).

	2001	2000
Cash flow from operating activities	**7,497**	**6,738**
Interest payments (net of financial income)	(1,805)	(760)
Taxation	(2,205)	(1,734)
Capital expenditures and financial investment	(1,358)	(1,061)
Acquisitions and disposals	3,477	(27,373)
Dividends paid on ordinary share capital	(1,420)	(1,365)
Cash flow before financing and treasury operations	**4,186**	**(25,555)**
Financing and treasury operations	(3,992)	25,366
Increase (decrease) in cash in year	**194**	**(189)**

Unilever's biggest acquisition was in October 2000. It paid €23.6 billion in cash for Bestfoods, a US food products company. In 2001 it raised almost €2 billion from the sale of Bestfoods' bakery businesses (and other businesses acquired in 2000 and held for resale) and €1.65 billion from the disposal of group companies. Details of the Bestfoods acquisition in 2000 and the disposal of group companies in 2001 are set out in Exhibit 14.16. They are taken from the notes to Unilever's 2000 and 2001 accounts.

Unilever uses the purchase method to account for acquisitions. Prior to 1998, it wrote off against reserves goodwill arising on acquisitions. Since 1998, the company capitalises goodwill and amortises it over 20 years.

Required

(a) What was the carrying amount – in the books of Bestfoods – of the net assets Unilever acquired in 2000?

(b) What was the main reason for the negative accounting policy adjustment of €1.1 billion to Bestfoods' intangible assets?

(c) Unilever paid €23.6 billion in cash for Bestfoods but the price of the business was €26.1 billion. How did it finance the difference?

(d) Unilever revalued 'acquired businesses held for resale' at the time of Bestfoods' acquisition. What would have been the effect on its accounts – in 2000 and in 2001 when it sold them – if it had not done so?

(e) Show in summary form the effect on Unilever's 2001 accounts of the businesses it sold that year. Account for 'net assets sold' as one item. Use a journal entry or the balance sheet equation.

P14.10 Divestment of a business: interpreting financial disclosures*

British Telecom (BT), the UK telecoms group, assembled all its wireless operations in a new subsidiary, mmO$_2$ plc. Because BT's fixed line and wireless operations had 'different market focus and expected growth characteristics', its board of directors decided in 2001 to split off mmO$_2$. Under the scheme, two new holding companies, BT Group and mmO$_2$, were established, one for fixed line and the other for wireless operations. A BT shareholder received one share in BT Group plc and one share in mmO$_2$ plc for every share they held in the old BT. Trading in the shares of the two companies began on the London Stock Exchange on 19 November 2001.

Exhibit 14.17 shows the pro forma balance sheet of BT Group plc – after adjustment for mmO$_2$ plc – at 30 June 2001.

BT's management decided that, in view of mmO$_2$'s current losses and its expected heavy capital outlays, it should carry less debt as an independent entity than it had as part of BT. As a result, debt was transferred from mmO$_2$ to BT Group (see third column of Exhibit 14.17).

Exhibit 14.16 Unilever's acquisitions and disposals in 2000/01: selective disclosures

Acquisition of Bestfoods in 2000

In € million	Balance sheets of acquired businesses	Provisional adjustments to align accounting policies	Provisional revaluations	Provisional fair values at date of acquisition
Intangible assets	1,504	(1,126)	(378)	–
Fixed assets	2,184	(361)	–	1,823
Acquired businesses held for resale	946	–	811	1,757
Other current assets	1,816	(71)	–	1,745
Creditors	(1,782)	(183)	–	(1,965)
Provisions for liabilities and charges:				
Pensions and similar obligations	(674)	237	–	(437)
Deferred taxation	450	(326)	–	124
Other provisions	(938)	–	–	(938)
Minority interest	55	(34)	–	21
Net assets acquired	3,561	(1,864)	433	2,130
Goodwill arising in subsidiaries				23,321
Goodwill arising in joint ventures				632
Consideration				26,083
Of which:				
Cash paid				23,623
Cash and current investments of Bestfoods				3,028
Translation adjustment between accounting rate and actual exchange rate at settlement date				(568)

The book values of the net assets acquired have been restated to provisional fair values as at the date of acquisition. The principal adjustments recognise acquired businesses held for resale at the present value of net expected proceeds and write off certain intangible assets. . . . The accounting policy alignment reflects the write-off of capitalised software, interest and certain intangible assets and the valuation of working capital, pension provisions and deferred tax in accordance with Unilever's accounting policy.

Disposals in 2001

. . . In 2001, disposed businesses principally comprised Unipath and Batchelors/Oxo in the United Kingdom, Royco in the Netherlands and Elizabeth Arden and Gortons in the USA.

	€ million
Fixed assets	279
Current assets	351
Creditors	(112)
Provisions for liabilities and charges	(11)
Minority interest	(2)
Net assets sold	505
Attributable goodwill	223
Profit on sale attributable to Unilever	927
Consideration	1,655
Of which:	
Cash	1,650
Cash, current investments and borrowings of businesses sold	(6)
Non-cash and deferred consideration	11

(*Source*: Unilever, *Annual Accounts 2000* and *2001*.)

Exhibit 14.17 BT: pro forma income and balance sheets on divestment of mmO₂

In € million	Historical BT	Adjustments for mmO₂	Adjustments for mmO₂ net debt	Pro forma BT Group
Profit (loss) for year to 30 March 2001	(2,378)	4,107 [loss]	–	1,729
BALANCE SHEET at 30 June 2001				
Fixed assets				
Intangible assets	18,297	(15,998)	–	2,299
Tangible assets	21,610	(3,877)	–	17,733
Investments	3,675	(30)	–	3,645
Total fixed assets	43,582	(19,905)	–	23,677
Current assets				
Stocks	289	(145)	–	144
Debtors	7,380	(1,602)	–	5,778
Investments	10,754	(495)	133	10,392
Cash at bank and in hand	388	(343)	343	388
Total current assets	18,811	(2,585)	476	16,702
Creditors: amounts falling due within 1 year				
Loans and other borrowings	(10,990)	5,777	(5,277)	(10,490)
Other creditors	(8,961)	2,107	–	(6,854)
Total creditors: amounts falling due within 1 year	(19,951)	7,884	(5,277)	(17,344)
Net current assets (liabilities)	(1,140)	5,299	(4,801)	(642)
Total assets less current liabilities	42,442	(14,606)	(4,801)	23,035
Creditors: amounts falling due after more than 1 year				
Loans and other borrowings	(17,633)	11,481	(11,119)	(17,271)
Provisions for liabilities and charges	(2,769)	191	–	(2,578)
Total net assets	22,040	(2,934)	(15,920)	3,186
Minority interests	82	–	–	82
Capital and reserves	21,958	(2,934)	(15,920)	3,104
	22,040	(2,934)	(15,920)	3,186

(*Source*: BT, Circular to shareholders, September 2001. Reproduced by permission of BT Group plc.)

Required

(a) What type of divestment is BT's splitting-off of its wireless operations – a trade sale, IPO, spin-off or equity carve-out? Give reasons for your answer.

(b) Show in summary form the entries BT made in its consolidated accounts to record the divestment of mmO₂ and adjustment of mmO₂'s net debt on 30 June 2001. Combine operating assets and operating liabilities in one line entry and debt and liquid assets in another. Why doesn't BT report a gain or loss from its divestment of mmO₂?

(c) What was mmO₂'s net debt at 30 June 2001 after adjustments?

* Assignment draws on material in section 2 of this chapter.

Notes to Chapter 14

1   If Candide starts making profits again, Pangloss can resume reporting its share of them – but only after making good its share of unrecognised losses.

2   International Accounting Standards Board, *IAS 28: Accounting for Investments in Associates*; European Commission, 7th (Company Law) Directive, Art. 33. If the investment is intended to be temporary, the investor should account for it at cost or fair value in accordance with *IAS 39*.

3   *IAS 28*, para. 5.

4   A change in shareholding may force an investor company to change the way it accounts for an investment. By increasing its shareholding, it may acquire significant influence over the investee's policies: the equity method is applied from the date this occurs. By reducing its shareholding, it may lose significant influence: the carrying amount of the investment is then its cost from that date.

5   The discussion that follows applies equally to an equity-accounted investment in an associated company. The investor company makes similar adjustments – first to the fair values of assets (and liabilities) acquired and then to goodwill – whenever the purchase price is greater (or less) than the investor's share of the book value of the associate's net assets.

6   Incorporating fair value adjustments into the *acquired company's accounts* is known as **push-down accounting**. Although it is not an accepted practice, certain listed US companies involved in business combinations have implemented it on the instruction of the Securities and Exchange Commission.

7   If the investor company sells part or all of the investee subsequently, it should include, in the carrying amount of the assets sold, the related goodwill written off. This is known as *goodwill write-back*. The effect of the write-back is to reduce the reported gain (or increase the reported loss) on disposal.

8   International Accounting Standards Board, *IAS 27: Consolidated Financial Statements and Accounting for Investments in Subsidiaries*, para. 12. Article 1 of the EU's 7th Directive contains similar phrasing.

9   Under IAS, an intermediate parent company must be at least 90% owned by another.

10 The EU's 7th Directive *permits* exclusion in these circumstances – and also in the case that consolidation of the subsidiary has no material effect on the financial statements (Art. 13).

11 *IAS 27*, para. 14. By contrast, the EU's 7th Directive requires exclusion of subsidiaries with activities dissimilar to those of other group companies (Art. 14). This will have to be amended before 2005 when EU listed companies must adopt IAS.

12 International Accounting Standards Board, *IAS 22: Business Combinations*.

13 This assumes negative goodwill is less than the fair value of acquired depreciable assets. Any amount greater than this should be recognised in income immediately.

14 IWO of goodwill is permitted under Art. 30(2) of the 7th Directive. Article 37(2) of the 4th Directive specifies the amortisation period for capitalised goodwill.

15 International Accounting Standards Board, *Project Summary – Business Combinations Phase 1*, July 2002. Note that the two key proposals – to ban merger accounting and to replace goodwill amortisation with an annual impairment test – are in line with new UK and US accounting standards on this topic.

16 Lys, T. and Vincent, L. (1995), An analysis of the value destruction in AT&T's acquisition of NCR, *Journal of Financial Economics*, 39: 353–379.

17 As part of its project on business combinations (*see* note 15), the IASB plans to eliminate the parent company approach. According to the Board's current thinking, the entity approach provides users with more useful information for assessing management's stewardship of the group's resources and should be the only basis for preparing consolidated accounts.

18 The assets, liabilities, revenues and expenses of *unincorporated* joint ventures are usually accounted for on a proportionate basis.

19 International Accounting Standards Board, *IAS 31: Financial Reporting of Interests in Joint Ventures*. Note that, as with subsidiaries and associates, a *temporary* interest in a joint venture should be accounted for according to IAS 39 (i.e. at fair value or at cost if fair value is not determinable).

20 Kirchmaier, T. (2001), Demergers – the way forward after M&A, *European Business Forum*, 2(1).

21 A third type of demerger, the issue of 'tracking stock', is similar in form to a spin-off. The parent issues shares to existing shareholders on a pro-rata basis. These shares represent claims to the profits of a particular segment of the business. The 'tracked' segment remains part of the parent's legal and

organisational structure, however. Many analysts believe the lack of managerial independence depresses the price of tracking shares. For further discussion of the various ways a company can divest a business and their financial implications, *see* Gilson, S.C. (2001), *Creating Value through Corporate Restructuring*, Chichester: Wiley Finance.

22 International Accounting Standards Board, *IAS 24: Related Party Disclosures*.

23 A study of German companies over the period 1981 to 1990 found, *inter alia*, that the association between stock market returns and consolidated earnings was higher than that between stock market returns and unconsolidated earnings (Harris, T., Lang, M. and Möller, H. (1994), The value relevance of German accounting measures: an empirical analysis, *Journal of Accounting Research*, Autumn: 187–209).

24 Renault increased its stake in Nissan to 44% in 2002 and the latter acquired a 15% stake in the French vehicle producer at the same time. Renault continued to account for its Nissan investment by the equity method. Although Nissan returned to profitability in 2001, its net debt remained high (Burt, T. and Ibison, D. (2001), Renault rules out full Nissan merger, *Financial Times*, 31 October).

25 The investor company may also disclose proportionate data on the face of its financial statements. For example, UK companies show the proportionate share of associated companies' turnover on the face of the consolidated income statement (but the amount is excluded from the group's *net* turnover).

26 The FASB announced in 2002 that the rules regarding consolidation of SPEs would be tightened. The percentage of required outside capital in an SPE is to rise from 3% to 10% of total assets. The FASB also introduced an 'independent economic substance' test: consolidation is not required if it can be shown that the SPE can function as a separate economic entity. By contrast, international rules are simpler: the sponsor must consolidate any SPE that it controls.

15

Transactions and operations in foreign currencies

INTRODUCTION

Up to now, we have assumed that the financial transactions a company enters into are all in one currency, its domestic currency. This is not usually the case. For countries in the eurozone, external trade (the average of exports and imports in euros) represented 15% of gross domestic product in 2001. For countries not part of a large currency bloc, the ratio was much higher – over 30% in the case of Canada, Denmark and South Korea. This means that for many companies, especially those engaged in manufacturing, purchases and sales in foreign currencies make up a significant portion of total transactions. In addition, the same companies have operations in foreign countries and thus have assets such as property and equipment denominated in foreign currencies.

In this chapter we study the impact of a firm's foreign currency transactions and operations on its accounts. Recognition and measurement problems arise because the rate of exchange between domestic and foreign currencies is not stable. For example, it may change while a transaction is open – a foreign credit sale is not yet collected or a foreign credit purchase is not yet paid – and this creates an exchange gain or loss on the foreign currency receivable or payable. How and when should this gain or loss be recognised? Similarly, a firm with a foreign operation may experience exchange rate changes. How does it measure in its domestic currency the foreign business's assets and liabilities? And how should any resulting translation gains or losses be accounted for?

We conclude the chapter by considering the implications, for investors, of a firm's foreign trade and investment. When a firm pursues such activities, shareholders enjoy the prospect of higher returns but they also bear additional risks. Even firms that focus exclusively on their home market are affected by exchange rate changes. Thus investors want information about a firm's exposure to foreign currency risks and the actions it is taking to reduce them.

Accounting for transactions in foreign currencies

Many firms import or export goods and services. These transactions often involve the purchase or sale of a foreign currency. A manufacturing firm buying raw materials from a foreign supplier purchases foreign currency in order to acquire them. A financial institution marketing financial services to foreign investors bills them in their local currency which it sells on receipt to obtain cash in its own.

At present, most exchange rates are not fixed. They can and do vary unpredictably from day to day. This poses difficulties for a company engaged in foreign currency transactions. It can hedge against exchange rate movements by, for example, buying (selling) in advance the foreign currency it needs (expects to receive). Or it can buy or sell foreign currency on the spot market when the transaction demands it. We describe the accounting for, first, unhedged and then hedged transactions.

Unhedged transactions

Consider the following example. Falkner, an Austrian ski-lift manufacturer, conducts most of its business in the eurozone and keeps its accounts in euros (*see* Box 15.1). The euro is its **functional currency**. On 1 December year 1 it imports machinery costing US$2.5 million when the exchange rate is €1.023 : US$1. Payment (in dollars) does not have to be made until 31 January year 2. Let's assume the euro weakens to €1.03 against the dollar by 31 December (Falkner's year-end)

BOX 15.1

Adoption of the euro: accounting implications

The euro is the official currency of countries within the EMU (economic and monetary union) of the European Union. All EU member states save Denmark, Sweden and the UK were in the EMU – or eurozone – in 2003. The two key features of the eurozone are: (a) one central bank, the European Central Bank, determines monetary and exchange rate policies for the zone and (b) national governments, though retaining control of fiscal policy, commit themselves to avoiding excessive government deficits (defined as no more than 3% of gross domestic product). The eurozone is likely to grow in future years: in addition to the above three EU member states, the ten applicant countries that are due to join the EU in 2004 are potential new members of the zone. Government ministers stress the economic advantages of membership: being part of a single currency zone reduces exchange rate risk for companies trading within it and fosters competition through greater price transparency.

Adoption of the euro has accounting as well as economic implications for companies in these countries. First, exchange gains and losses on open monetary transactions crystallise on the date a country enters the eurozone. This means that, in effect, exchange gains and losses are realised the day before and companies should recognise them in their accounts of that year. If, for example, the UK enters the eurozone on 1 January 2006 (unlikely, but miracles do happen), a UK company with a calendar year-end recognises exchange gains and losses on its outstanding euro receivables and payables in its *2005 accounts* (so long as the receivables/payables are not a designated hedge of an investment in a eurozone entity). The translation gains and losses on eurozone investments are not considered realised on 31 December 2005, however. UK companies will continue to defer them in equity until they sell the investments.

Box 15.1 continued

Second, par values of shares and bonds have to be converted and the resulting euro values may be awkward numbers. Companies may choose to renominalise shares (and bonds) to ensure the per-unit nominal value is a round number. For example, suppose a Hungarian company's ordinary shares have a par value of 1,000 forints and the exchange rate is fixed at 175 forints to the euro. This results in a euro par value of €5.7143 (after rounding). It decides to renominalise the shares to 875 forints – or €5. This has an administrative cost, however. Renominalisation results in an increase or decrease in share capital which, under EU law, requires prior approval of shareholders in general meeting. Note that the change in share capital following renominalisation also involves adjusting reserves. Suppose our Hungarian company has 2.5 million ordinary shares in issue. It must set up a non-distributable reserve of €1,785,750 [2.5 million × (€5.7143 − €5)] to offset the reduction in share capital of this amount.

Finally, companies must account for the costs of switching to the euro. These include the costs of altering equipment and computer software. Unless the expenditures meet the usual asset definition and recognition tests (i.e. they yield probable future benefits which can be measured reliably), they should be expensed as incurred. In practice, few euro conversion costs qualify for capitalisation. The reason is that, in most cases, companies incur such costs to *maintain* the capabilities of existing equipment and systems rather than to enhance them.

---

but then strengthens slightly to €1.027 by 31 January. How does the Austrian firm account for the effect on this transaction of the changes in the euro–dollar exchange rate between 1 December and 31 January?

International accounting rules require firms to account for *unhedged transactions* in a foreign currency as follows:

- *the transaction should be recorded in the company's functional currency using the exchange rate prevailing when the transaction takes place;*
- *at the balance sheet date, monetary items (e.g. receivables, payables) in a foreign currency should be translated at the **closing rate** (the spot exchange rate at the balance sheet date);*
- *at the balance sheet date, non-monetary items (e.g. tangible fixed assets, inventory) that are measured at cost in a foreign currency should be translated using the exchange rate at the date of the transaction. Those measured at fair value should be translated using the exchange rate at the date of valuation;*
- *exchange differences on monetary items should be recognised as income or expense when they arise. This applies to unrealised as well as realised gains and losses.[1]*

Thus Falkner records the machinery and the liability to the US supplier at €2,557,500, based on the 1 December exchange rate of €1.023 : US$1. At the balance sheet date, it increases the outstanding trade payable to €2,575,000, reflecting the weakening of the euro to €1.03 : US$1 by 31 December, and recognises an unrealised exchange loss of €17,500 in its year 1 accounts. When it pays the supplier the invoiced amount of US$2.5 million on 31 January year 2, only 1.027 euros are needed to buy a dollar and thus the cost of the payment is €2,567,500 ($2.5 million × 1.027). The strengthening of the euro in January results in a realised exchange gain of €7,500 that month. The entries the company makes in its accounts are (in €000):

1 December year 1:	Dr. Equipment (A+)	2,557.5	
	Cr. Account payable (L+)		2,557.5
31 December year 1:	Dr. Exchange loss (OE−)	17.5	
	Cr. Account payable (L+)		17.5

31 January year 2:	Dr. Account payable (L–)	2,575	
	Cr. Exchange gain (OE+)		7.5
	Cr. Cash (A–)		2,567.5

The book value of the equipment is not adjusted for the change in exchange rates. Assuming the company follows the historical cost convention, the fixed asset is stated at its (depreciated) historical cost. The difference between the value of the asset acquired (€2,557,500) and the cash paid for it (€2,567,500) represents a loss to the company of €10,000. This is the net amount of the year 1 exchange loss and the year 2 exchange gain.

Other types of monetary transaction are treated similarly. For example, exchange differences on foreign currency borrowings are recognised in income in the period when they arise.[2]

Hedged transactions

It is common practice now for firms to hedge foreign currency transactions. They use foreign currency loans or deposits, forward exchange contracts, currency swaps and currency options for this purpose. However, these instruments don't automatically qualify as accounting hedges. *A financial instrument (e.g. a forward exchange contract) can be considered a hedge for accounting purposes only if:*

- *it is formally designated a hedge from the outset;*
- *the item to be hedged – an asset, liability or cash flow – is identified at the same time;*
- *the hedge is expected to be effective: changes in the hedge's fair value or related cash flows are likely to largely offsets changes in the fair value or cash flows of the hedged item.*

As we saw in Chapter 13, IAS distinguish three types of qualifying hedge – the fair value hedge, the cash flow hedge, and the hedge of an investment in a foreign entity – and lay down how each should be accounted for.[3] Clearly, the last involves a foreign currency transaction by definition. But changes in exchange rates can expose a company to changes in future cash flows or changes in the fair value of an asset or liability which it can hedge using an effective hedging instrument. We illustrate foreign investment and fair value hedges in the two examples below.

Hedge of net investment in a foreign entity

Koivu, a Finnish forestry products company, has a profitable Canadian subsidiary which needs funds for expansion. Instead of the subsidiary raising the (Canadian) $50 million needed, Koivu uses its superior credit rating, borrows the funds in Canadian dollars, and invests them – through an increase in the subsidiary's share capital or an intercompany loan – in its Canadian operation. The Finnish firm designates the foreign currency borrowing as a hedge of (part of) its Canadian investment: a change in the dollar/euro exchange rate will have an effect on the debt payments opposite to that on the investment's cash inflows.

Suppose the euro weakens against the Canadian dollar, from C$ 1.7 : €1, when the investment was made, to C$ 1.65 : €1 at the balance sheet date. If Koivu translates its Canadian investment at the closing rate of C$ 1.65 : €1 when preparing its accounts, it will record a positive exchange difference, since its Canadian investment is worth more in euros. As we'll see in the next section, this exchange difference is taken direct to shareholders' equity on the balance sheet. As regards the dollar debt, Koivu sustains a loss from the euro depreciation as the euro cost of the debt is increased. Since the dollar borrowing is designated as a hedge of the Canadian investment, Koivu can defer the exchange loss of €0.89 million (C$ 50 million/C$ 1.7 – C$ 50 million/C$ 1.65) on the debt and set it off against the exchange gain (of a similar amount) on the asset. If it had not designated the borrowing as a hedge, it would have had to recognise the loss immediately.

Koivu oyj						
(Partial) balance sheet (in € million)						
	Exchange rate				Exchange rate	
	1.7 : 1	1.65 : 1			1.7 : 1	1.65 : 1
Assets				*Shareholders' equity*		
Additional investment				Deferred loss (borrowing)	0	(0.89)
in Canadian subsidiary	29.41	30.3		Deferred gain (investment)	0	0.89
(C$50m)				Net gain/loss		0
				Liabilities		
				Long-term debt (C$50m)	29.41	30.3

Hedging foreign currency transactions

In addition to hedging foreign investments, companies also hedge day-to-day transactions in foreign currencies. A common method of doing this is through the forward exchange market. A firm 'locks in' an exchange rate by buying (or selling) foreign currency in advance. Falkner, our Austrian ski-lift manufacturer, can do this for its purchase of US equipment. Suppose on 1 November year 1, the date it *orders* the equipment, it enters into a forward exchange contract with a bank under which the bank will provide it with US$2.5 million (the cost of the equipment) on the settlement date (31 January year 2). As a result of the contract, the firm protects itself during those three months against exchange losses caused by a depreciating euro.

How does Falkner account for the forward exchange contract? In the past, it might have recorded the equipment and the account payable at the contracted forward rate. Alternatively, it could have recorded the equipment at the spot rate (at the start of the forward contract) and the liability to the supplier at the forward rate. The difference, the premium paid on the forward contract, would be either booked as an expense immediately or amortised over the period of the forward contract on a straight-line basis. Both methods were popular. A common weakness is their failure to recognise the forward contract itself and the change in its value over time.

The new hedge accounting rules (in *IAS 39*) are designed to overcome the flaws in traditional accounting methods. Exhibit 15.1 sets out the entries Falkner makes to account for both the purchase of the equipment and the forward exchange contract. The euro–dollar spot and forward exchange rates are assumed.

Our example illustrates how the new rules work. The company recognises the hedging instrument – in this case, the forward contract receivable – at the contract date. The net fair value of the contract is zero initially since the forward contract receivable and dollar payable have the same value at this date. Thereafter, changes in the euro–dollar forward rate result in gains or losses on the forward contract. For example, the strengthening of the dollar against the euro makes the contract more valuable – hence the gains (and growing receivable) in November and December of year 1.[4]

At the same time, the strengthening dollar increases the cost of the liability Falkner has assumed. Because the company entered into the forward contract on the order date, it is hedging a *commitment* in the period from order to delivery of the asset and a *payable* in the period from delivery to settlement. *Falkner's hedge of its commitment to the US supplier is considered a fair value hedge.* The company recognises a temporary liability ('firm commitment') and recognises the cost of this liability ('loss on firm commitment') in income.

On delivery of the equipment on 1 December, Falkner records the asset and related liability (account payable) at the spot exchange rate. It eliminates the commitment and adjusts the equipment's value for the change in the fair value of the liability between the order and delivery dates. This means that the firm fixes the cost of the equipment at a value that approximates the 1 November forward rate.

Exhibit 15.1 Hedging of foreign currency payable via forward exchange contract

Facts

On 1 November year 1, Falkner, an Austrian ski-lift manufacturer, orders equipment costing US$2.5 million from a US supplier for delivery on 1 December. On the same day, it enters into a forward exchange contract with a bank to buy US$2.5 million on 31 January year 2, the date it has agreed to pay the supplier. Relevant euro–dollar spot and forward exchange rates are given below.

Date	Event	Spot rate	Forward rate (31 Jan year 2)
1 November, year 1 (US$1 = . . .)	Order	€1.015	€1.018
1 December	Delivery	1.023	1.025
31 December	Year-end	1.03	1.031
31 January, year 2	Settlement	1.027	(not applicable)

Accounting entries and explanations* (journal entry amounts in €000)

Date	Entry	Dr.	Cr.	Explanation
1 Nov, yr 1	–			Forward contract has zero fair value.
1 Dec	Dr. Forward contract receivable	17.5		Change in fair value of forward contract
	Cr. Hedging gain		17.5	[US$2.5m × (1.025 − 1.018)]. *Fair value hedge* so gain recognised in income.
	Dr. Loss on firm commitment	17.5		Weakening euro leads to exchange loss
	Cr. Firm commitment		17.5	on purchase order. 'Firm commitment' is temporary liability account.
1 Dec	Dr. Equipment	2,557.5		Asset and payable recorded at spot rate.
	Cr. Account payable		2,557.5	
	Dr. Firm commitment	17.5		Temporary liability (firm commitment)
	Cr. Equipment		17.5	eliminated and asset's fair value adjusted.
31 Dec	Dr. Forward contract receivable	15		Change in fair value of forward contract
	Cr. Hedging gain		15	[US$2.5m × (1.031 − 1.025)].
	Dr. Exchange loss	17.5		Adjust payable for change in spot rate
	Cr. Account payable		17.5	between 1 Dec and 31 Dec.
31 Jan, yr 2	Dr. Hedging loss	10		Change in fair value of forward contract
	Cr. Forward contract receivable		10	[US$2.5m × (1.027 − 1.031)].
	Dr. Account payable	7.5		Adjust payable for change in spot rate
	Cr. Exchange gain		7.5	between 31 Dec and 31 Jan.
31 Jan	Dr. Cash	22.5		Net settlement. Company pays €2.545m
	Cr. Forward contract receivable		22.5	to bank (based on €1.018 forward rate) and receives €2.5675m (based on €1.027 spot rate) to convert into dollars.
31 Jan	Dr. Account payable	2,567.5		Payable settled at spot rate.
	Cr. Cash		2,567.5	

* Entries for depreciation of equipment not shown. Depreciation begins as from date equipment is ready for use.

Once the equipment and payable have been recognised, the forward contract becomes a straightforward hedge of a foreign currency payable. Gains and losses on the forward contract are matched by exchange losses and gains on the foreign currency payable. The gains/losses do not offset exactly because spot and forward rates do not move in tandem.

On 31 January year 2, the settlement date, Falkner pays its US supplier US$2.5 million. This has a euro cost of €2,567,500 (based on the spot exchange rate at that date). But under the forward contract, the cost to the firm of the dollar liability is only €2,545,000. In effect, the bank gives the firm €2,567,500 to buy the dollars but, given the forward contract, receives only €2,545,000 in return. Thus the firm receives a net €22,500 in cash on the settlement of the forward contract.

In sum, by hedging its exposure to changes in the euro–dollar exchange rate, Falkner fixes the euro cost of the equipment. (The sum paid, €2,545,000, differs slightly from the initial carrying amount of €2,540,000, because the spot rate diverges from the forward rate in November.) The strengthening of the dollar against the euro after 1 December results in gains on the forward contract that are offset by exchange losses on the payable to the US supplier. Note that the entries the firm makes to record the amount payable initially and to adjust it subsequently for changes in the spot rate are identical to those it would make if the transaction were unhedged.

Accounting for foreign operations

Many European companies do more than import and export goods and services. They often make direct investments in other countries, within and outside Europe. For example, a company may establish a branch abroad – a sales office, for example – or it may incorporate its foreign business. Unlike a branch, a foreign subsidiary is a separate legal entity. Whichever legal form is chosen, the parent company incurs costs, earns revenues and holds assets and liabilities in a foreign currency. These must then be *translated* into the currency in which its accounts are prepared (the 'reporting currency') before being combined with its domestic revenues, earnings, assets and liabilities.[5]

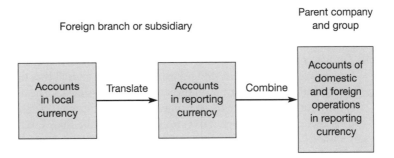

Accounting for foreign operations is a two-stage process of, first, translation and, then, consolidation. Our concern here is with the first part of the process: *how does the parent company translate the assets and liabilities, revenues and expenses of the foreign operation into its reporting currency?*

Nature of foreign operations

Under current international (and US) accounting rules, the way a company accounts for its investment in a foreign country depends on the nature of its operations there. *International and US standards distinguish two types of foreign operation: those which function as independent units and those which form an integral part of the parent company's operations.*[6] Classification of a foreign operation – as either autonomous unit or satellite of the parent's operations – affects both the exchange rate(s) used to translate foreign currency items and the presentation of any exchange gains or losses in the parent company's accounts.

The parent company's managers must weigh various factors when deciding how to classify a foreign operation. Here are the main ones they should consider, according to IAS:

- degree of local content in the good or service produced;
- proportion of purchases and sales that are intercompany (especially between foreign unit and parent company);
- proportion of sales made in the local market;
- reliance on local sources of finance.

For example, consider a foreign subsidiary that buys inputs, converts them into finished product and sells the output, all in its domestic market. It reinvests its profits to expand operations. Any debt finance it needs it raises locally. The parent company vets its annual budgets and major capital projects but devolves responsibility for most decisions to the subsidiary's managers. This subsidiary would be viewed as an autonomous unit of the parent company. Its functional currency is the local currency.

Contrast this with a manufacturing operation that a company sets up in a foreign country to supply it with components for its domestic plants. The foreign unit buys key inputs from – and sells most of its output to – the parent company. It relies on the parent for new capital. In this case the foreign unit would be viewed as the parent company's satellite, an integral part of the parent's operations. Its functional currency is the parent company's currency.

In practice, it is not always easy to classify a foreign operation. It may be neither wholly autonomous nor an integral part of its parent company but, instead, display features of both. However, once a classification decision is made, the accounting treatment must be followed consistently until the foreign unit's circumstances change.

Autonomous unit and closing rate method of translation

International standards require that the parent company should account for an autonomous unit by the **closing rate method**. Under this method, the parent company:

- *Translates all assets and liabilities in the foreign entity's balance sheet at the end-year exchange rate between the functional and reporting currencies.* (Recall that the functional currency is one in which the foreign entity conducts most of its business.) The end-year rate is known as the closing (or current) rate of exchange. Contributed capital (share capital, share premium) is translated at the exchange rate(s) prevailing when the shares were issued.
- *Translates all revenues and expenses in the foreign entity's income statement at the exchange rates prevailing when the revenues and expenses were recognised.* In practice, the average exchange rate for the period is often used.
- *Reports any net translation gain or loss as a direct adjustment to shareholders' equity in the consolidated balance sheet.* Succeeding years' translation gains and losses are accumulated in this balance sheet account.

Illustration

Let's see how the closing rate method is applied. Assume a UK company, Leicester plc, sets up a US subsidiary, Arkansas Inc, on 1 January x3, with share capital of $3 million.[7] Arkansas trades profitably during its first year. At the end of x3, Leicester prepares consolidated accounts. To do this, it must first translate Arkansas's dollar-based accounts into sterling. Leicester's management review the nature of Arkansas's operations and decide that it is an autonomous unit within the Leicester group. Exhibit 15.2 shows Arkansas's x3 accounts in US dollars (all the numbers are assumed) and translated into sterling. The translated accounts are then consolidated with those of Leicester and its other subsidiaries.

Calculation of the translated amounts in Exhibit 15.2 is straightforward. Since Arkansas's sales and production occur evenly over the year, Leicester translates Arkansas's dollar revenues and expenses at the average exchange rate for x3 (£0.7 : $1). The US firm's dividend is translated at the end-year exchange rate (£0.74 : $1), the rate when the dividend is paid. (The dividend is eliminated on consolidation but it is recorded as investment income in Leicester's own accounts.) All end-x3

Exhibit 15.2 Arkansas Inc: translation of x3 accounts to sterling under closing rate method

Key exchange rate information

At 1 January x3	£0.67	:	$1
Average for x3	0.7	:	1
At 31 December x3 (closing rate)	0.74	:	1

Arkansas's common stock is issued at the start of x3. Sales and production are even over the year. The dividend is paid at the end of x3.

	$000	Exchange rate	£000
Statement of income and retained earnings for x3			
Operating revenues	6,000	0.7	4,200
Less: Cost of sales	–4,200	0.7	–2,940
Depreciation	–500	0.7	–350
Other expenses	–700	0.7	–490
Net income	600		420
Dividend	–200	0.74	–148
Retained earnings, end-x3	400		272
Balance sheet at 31 December x3			
Assets			
Cash and receivables	1,700	0.74	1,258
Inventory	1,500	0.74	1,110
Property and plant, net	1,800	0.74	1,332
Total	5,000		3,700
Liabilities and stockholders' equity			
Payables (current)	1,000	0.74	740
Long-term debt	600	0.74	444
Common stock	3,000	0.67	2,010
Retained earnings	400	(see i/s)	272
Translation adjustment	–	*	234
Total	5,000		3,700

* *Derivation of translation adjustment:*

	$000	Exchange rate change**	£000
Net assets, 1 January x3	3,000	+0.07	210
Addition to net assets			
Net income in x3	+600	+0.04	+24
Reduction in net assets			
Dividend, end-x3	–200	0	0
Net assets, 31 December x3	3,400		
Translation adjustment			234

** 'Exchange rate change' is the change in exchange rate between the date of the event (e.g. net assets acquired on 1/1/x3, net income earned in x3) and the year-end.

assets and liabilities are translated at the closing rate. 'Common stock' is translated at £0.67 : $1, the rate prevailing on 1/1/x3 when Arkansas issues shares to Leicester in exchange for cash.

The translated amount of retained earnings and the translation adjustment are sometimes harder to understand. In Arkansas's case, it's easy to see how the sterling amount of x3 retained earnings is derived. Since x3 is its first year of operations, the balance sheet figure can be traced back directly to the income statement. In practice, the translated amount of retained earnings is a composite figure: it represents the sum of each year's retained profit as translated into the reporting currency that year. Thus at the end of x4, Leicester will translate Arkansas's x4 revenues, expenses and dividend payments in the same manner as in Exhibit 15.2 and add the sterling amount of Arkansas's x4 retained profit to the end-x3 figure of £272,000.

The cumulative 'translation adjustment' shows the cumulative gain or loss to the parent company from holding investments in foreign currencies when exchange rates change.[8] Consider Leicester's US investment in x3. Arkansas had a successful first year. It made a profit of $600,000, a 20% return on its initial equity of $3 million. The strengthening of the dollar during x3 meant that, in sterling terms, it did even better. Its profits (before dividend) are £18,000 higher than they would have been if the exchange rate had remained at £0.67 : $1. And, as can be seen from the translation adjustment, its net assets are £234,000 greater. Exhibit 15.2 shows how the translation adjustment is derived. Leicester has benefited because by end-x3 the dollar has gained 7 pence (£0.67 to £0.74) since it made its initial investment in Arkansas on 1 January and 4 pence (£0.7 to £0.74) over its average rate, the rate used to translate the increase in net assets in the year.

Rationale for closing rate method

A parent company views an autonomous foreign operation as a single investment, not as a collection of assets and liabilities held in a foreign currency. Although the various categories of asset and liability are translated separately (they have to be for consolidation purposes), *one* rate is applied to all end-year assets and liabilities because what matters to the parent company is the overall effect of an exchange rate change on its investment.

Translation at the closing rate is consistent with a firm's internal reporting system, proponents claim. Head office judges the financial performance of the foreign entity (and its management) on the basis of its financial statements. *Under the closing rate method, key financial ratios – for example, the profit margin and the current ratio – which are used in performance evaluation are the same after translation as they are in the original currency.*

Why are translation gains or losses not recorded in the income statement? Accounting regulators argue that, where a foreign operation is considered a long-term investment, an exchange rate change has no direct effect on the cash flows of the parent company. Thus translation gains and losses are taken to reserves. When the foreign entity is sold, the parent company's cash flow *is* affected. At that time the cumulative translation gains or losses with respect to that entity are realised. They should be included in the gain or loss on disposal and recognised in the consolidated and parent company income statements.

Integrated operation and temporal method of translation

Where a foreign operation is deemed to be integral to the parent's activities, the **temporal method** *of foreign currency translation is used.*[9] Under the temporal method, assets and liabilities are translated at the exchange rate appropriate to the valuation basis used in the foreign entity's accounts. Thus:

● *Monetary assets (e.g. cash, receivables) and monetary liabilities (e.g. payables, most kinds of debt) are translated at the closing rate of exchange.* Monetary assets and liabilities are items whose value is fixed in money terms: the balance sheet amount reflects their current value.

- *Non-monetary assets (e.g. inventory, plant) which are stated at historical cost are translated at the historical exchange rate, i.e. the exchange rate prevailing when the asset was acquired.* Those that are stated at current value are translated at the rate prevailing at the date of the most recent valuation. The same procedure is followed with non-monetary liabilities (e.g. deferred subscription revenues).
- *Revenues and expenses are translated at the exchange rates prevailing when the underlying events took place.* In practice, the average rate is used unless there are major within-year differences in revenues and expenses. HC-based cost of sales and depreciation are translated at historical rates, in keeping with the treatment of non-monetary assets in the balance sheet.
- *Translation gains and losses are recognised in the consolidated income statement as they arise.*

Illustration

We return to our example. Suppose Leicester's management decide that Arkansas's operations are well integrated with its own. Exhibit 15.3 shows Arkansas's x3 accounts, in US dollars and in sterling under this assumption.

How are the sterling amounts in Exhibit 15.3 arrived at? Consider first the balance sheet items. Monetary items (e.g. cash, long-term debt) are translated at the closing exchange rate (£0.74 : $1), since the balance sheet amounts indicate the current purchasing power which they command (monetary assets) or which must be sacrificed to settle them (monetary liabilities). Inventory and fixed assets are translated at historical rates – £0.72 for end-x3 inventory, £0.67 for fixed assets – as Arkansas values these assets at historical cost. Common stock is a non-monetary item and is translated at £0.67, the rate on 1/1/x3 when the shares were issued. As this is Arkansas's first year of operation, the translated 'retained earnings' figure can be traced directly to the income statement. (In later years, it will consist of the sum of each year's retained profit after translation.)

The cost of consuming or selling a non-monetary asset is treated in the same way as the asset itself. Thus depreciation is also translated at the historical rate (£0.67). Cost of sales is based on a FIFO flow of costs in this case. As a result, the costs assigned to ending inventory ($1,500) are the most recent costs and are translated at the rate prevailing when the inventory was acquired (£0.72). Arkansas uses the average rate to translate other income statement items since revenues are earned – and production inputs and other expenses are incurred – evenly over x3.

In HC-based accounts, the 'translation gain/(loss)' under the temporal method shows the effect of holding monetary items in a foreign currency when exchange rates are changing. The gain or loss is derived by applying to inflows and outflows of monetary items the change in the exchange rate between the date the inflow or outflow occurs and the year-end. A company gains when it holds cash and other monetary assets in an appreciating currency; it loses when it carries monetary liabilities in that currency. Arkansas's monetary assets exceed its monetary liabilities throughout x3 but as it invests its initial $3 million of cash in fixed assets and inventory, its net monetary asset position falls to only $100,000 at year-end. This explains why the translation gain in this case (£33,000) is so much smaller than the translation adjustment under the closing rate method (£234,000).

Rationale for temporal method

Where a foreign operation is bound closely to the parent company, then, in economic terms, its assets and liabilities are really the parent's assets and liabilities, even though the foreign unit has a separate legal identity. Accounting regulators argue that, in these circumstances, currency translation should change only the unit of measure (i.e. from dollar to sterling) and not the attribute of the item being measured. Thus if it is company policy to state property – domestic and foreign – at historical cost, the historical exchange rate should be used for translation purposes. In this way, the attribute (historical cost) of the asset is preserved.

Exhibit 15.3 Arkansas Inc: translation of x3 accounts to sterling under temporal method

Key exchange rate information

At 1/1/x3 (shares issued and property/plant acquired)	£0.67 : $1	
Average for x3	0.7 : 1	
At date when end-x3 inventory was acquired	0.72 : 1	
At 31/12/x3 (closing rate)	0.74 : 1	

	$000	Exchange rate	£000
Statement of income and retained earnings for x3			
Operating revenues	6,000	0.7	4,200
Less: Cost of sales	−4,200	*	−2,910
Depreciation	−500	0.67	−335
Other expenses	−700	0.7	−490
Translation gain/(loss)	–	**	+33
Net income	600		498
Dividend, end-x3	−200	0.74	−148
Retained earnings, end-x3	400		350
Balance sheet at 31 December x3			
Assets			
Cash and receivables	1,700	0.74	1,258
Inventory	1,500	0.72	1,080
Property and plant, net	1,800	0.67	1,206
Total	5,000		3,544
Liabilities and stockholders' equity			
Payables (current)	1,000	0.74	740
Long-term debt	600	0.74	444
Common stock	3,000	0.67	2,010
Retained earnings	400	(see i/s)	350
Total	5,000		3,544

* Calculation of cost of sales:

	$000		£000
Beginning inventory	0		0
Production costs (derived)	5,700	0.7	3,990
− Ending inventory	−1,500	0.72	−1,080
Cost of sales	4,200		2,910

** Derivation of translation gain:

	$000	Exchange rate change to end-x3	£000
Net monetary assets, 1/1/x3	3,000	+0.07	+210
Sources of net monetary assets			
Operating revenues	+6,000	+0.04	+240
Uses of net monetary assets			
Purchases of property and plant	−2,300	+0.07	−161
Purchases of production inputs	−5,700	+0.04	−228
Other operating expenses	−700	+0.04	−28
Dividend	−200	0	0
Net monetary assets, 31/12/x3	100		
Translation gain			+33

Why, under the temporal method, are translation gains and losses recognised in the income statement when they arise? Consider once again the relationship between the parent and the foreign operation. The foreign entity has no separate economic existence. Its assets and liabilities are those of its parent but in a foreign currency. Its net monetary position can be viewed as its parent's net foreign currency receivable or payable. (Remember: in HC-based accounts, monetary items are the source of all translation gains and losses under the temporal method.) Thus Leicester starts x3 with $3 million in cash (held via Arkansas). It ends the year with a (net, unhedged) receivable of $100,000 (Arkansas' end-x3 net monetary assets of that amount). In these circumstances, an exchange difference is similar to a *transaction* gain or loss. Because transaction gains and losses have a direct effect on the cash a company receives, they are recognised immediately in the income statement.

Special situations

The translation procedures described above are modified in certain circumstances. Here are two important ones.

Foreign operation in a high-inflation economy

If the foreign operation is an autonomous unit and is based in an economy experiencing a very high rate of inflation, the closing rate method may distort the operation's financial results and position. In particular, it understates the amount – and, via depreciation, the cost – of the foreign unit's long-lived property and plant in the reporting currency. For example, suppose a French company invests €1 million in plant and equipment in a new operation in Ruritania when the exchange rate is 100 Ruritanian bezants (RBz) to the euro. A year later, when accounts are drawn up, prices have doubled in Ruritania but have remained stable in the EU: the exchange rate has fallen to RBz200 : €1. If the Ruritanian operation's accounts are not adjusted, the value of its fixed assets in the parent company's accounts will have halved to €500,000 (RBz100 m/200) in one year, even though the productivity of those assets may be unchanged.

There are two ways of dealing with this problem. One is to adjust the local currency financial statements for the effects of inflation before they are translated:

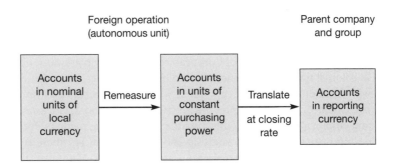

We explained how accounts are remeasured into units of constant purchasing power in Chapter 7.

The other approach is to assume that the foreign unit is an integral part of the parent company's operation and translate its accounts using the temporal method:

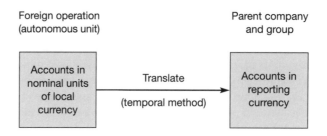

When changes in exchange rates reflect changes in relative prices alone, the two approaches yield the same result. Consider our Ruritanian example. Under the first approach, the fixed assets are restated to RBz 200 million in CPP terms and then translated at the closing exchange rate (RBz 200 : €1): the book value of the assets (before depreciation) is still €1 million. Under the second approach, the fixed assets are translated at the *historical* exchange rate (RBz100 : €1), so that the initial book value of €1 million is preserved.

Both approaches are in use. Under international rules, a company must use the first approach when it has an autonomous unit in a country experiencing hyperinflation.[10]

Intercompany balances

Intercompany receivables and payables are usually treated like other foreign currency transactions in the parent company's accounts. The exchange gain or loss (on an unhedged transaction) is recognised in the income statement when it arises. Note that this applies in the *consolidated* accounts as well: consolidation eliminates the intercompany balances but not the underlying currency exposure.

Not all intercompany balances are settled, however. For example, a parent may advance funds to a foreign operation for legal or tax reasons rather than invest equity capital in it. From an economic perspective, the loan represents part of the parent's permanent investment in the foreign unit. As a result, it should take any related exchange gain or loss direct to its reserves (as part of the translation adjustment) until it sells the foreign unit.

● Evolution of foreign currency translation practice

Current accounting rules on foreign currency translation represent a compromise between US and European accounting practices. These, in turn, reflect different experiences in foreign investment and different management styles.

The foreign operations of European companies often grew out of trading relationships forged in colonial times. Key decisions had to be taken by local management because communications with head office were difficult. Later, when communications improved, the political situation had changed. Former colonies became independent states. Governments objected to investment and employment decisions affecting the country being made by foreign companies and insisted on local participation in ownership and management. For these reasons, European companies came to view their foreign operations as autonomous. Moreover, there were pragmatic reasons for favouring the closing rate method. Many Continental European companies did not prepare consolidated accounts until recently. A parent company accounted for its foreign operations, in its own accounts, as a long-term investment. It was convenient to translate investments in foreign currencies, whether temporary or long-term, at the closing rate. When consolidation became mandatory in the 1980s, companies found the task of consolidating foreign subsidiaries' accounts easier under the closing rate method. Surveys of Dutch, French, German and UK firms carried out in the 1990s show that a large majority of companies in these countries used this method to translate the assets and liabilities of their foreign operations.

By contrast, the foreign operations of most US firms are of more recent origin. Many US firms first established an overseas unit to serve the parent company – as a sales outlet or a source of raw materials. Later, when the operation became more independent – with its own manufacturing base and markets – the parent company continued to maintain tight control. Local shareholdings were rare. US nationals occupied key management positions. The financial statements of foreign subsidiaries were consolidated with those of the parent from the outset and its performance was evaluated in dollars, not local currency. The temporal method – or a variant of it – was the logical method of translation in these circumstances.

What turned US business against the temporal method as the sole translation method was not the bases used to translate foreign assets but the treatment of exchange differences. Exchange rates became more volatile in the 1970s. For US firms with large foreign operations, this meant greater variability of reported earnings as exchange gains and losses were recognised immediately in the consolidated income statement. US firms protested to the FASB, the US accounting regulator, arguing that the increased variability was misleading. The closing rate method found favour because it provided a rationale for effectively deferring exchange gains and losses – if not indefinitely, then at least until the foreign operation was sold.

Problems with the closing rate and temporal methods

Since the introduction of the dual translation system, managers have softened their criticism. Investors are still uneasy, however. They have difficulty interpreting the translated numbers. What sense is there in translating at current rates items that are stated at historical cost? What does a 'positive translation adjustment' indicate? Is it just a bookkeeping entry or does it indicate an increase in the value of the firm's foreign operations?

To understand the problem faced by investors, it's helpful to ask what are the *properties of 'ideal' translated numbers*. Beaver and Wolfson reckon there are two.[11] *First, the translated numbers should have 'economic significance'*. For example, the book values of assets and liabilities after translation should be equal to the present value of expected cash flows attributable to them in the reporting currency. The return on foreign investment expressed in that currency should approximate the foreign assets' economic rate of return. *Second, the translated numbers should be unbiased*. The accounting numbers should not be affected by the location of the investment. Thus two identical investments in two different countries (using different currencies) yielding the same return should produce the same accounting numbers when expressed in a common currency.

Which translation method results in translated numbers having both properties? Beaver and Wolfson demonstrate that *the closing rate method meets the two tests, but it does so under very restrictive conditions*. First, all assets and liabilities must be valued at current market values. Second, changes in the exchange rates between any two currencies should be caused solely by changes in the currencies' relative purchasing power. When both conditions hold, any translation gain (loss) is a real economic gain (loss): it reflects the higher (lower) productivity of net assets held in the foreign currency.

Neither condition holds at present – or is ever likely to. Many assets and liabilities are measured at cost or amortised cost. Even if market values were to supplant historical costs, exchange rates would continue to be affected by interest rate differentials, political and economic uncertainties and other factors besides relative price inflation. In sum, only in rare circumstances will the translation adjustment in a period capture the change in value of a firm's foreign operations.

Financial statement disclosures and analysis

Disclosures

Most firms disclose the methods they use to account for foreign currency transactions and to translate the financial statements of foreign operations. Those that follow international accounting standards go further. They disclose:

- the exchange gains and losses included in profit for the period;
- the cumulative translation adjustment in reserves. The cumulative amount should be shown as a separate component of shareholders' equity and the movement in the account over the year explained; and
- the impact on the accounts of a change in the classification of a significant foreign operation (e.g. from satellite to autonomous unit) and the reason for the change.[12]

These disclosure requirements are similar to those in force in North America.

Investors check a firm's accounting policy on foreign currency translation carefully. It can be difficult comparing two companies in the same industry during periods of exchange rate turbulence if each has significant foreign operations but one classifies them as autonomous while the other considers them integral to the parent's operations.

Additional information sought by investors

Disclosures required under IAS are of limited help. Investors are forward-looking. They seek information about the expected risk and return from a company's foreign operations. A question that concerns them is: how will a company's transactions and operations in foreign currencies affect its *future* profits and cash flows? To answer this, they must assess its foreign currency exposure in the short and long term.[13]

Transaction exposure

A company's reported profits are sensitive to exchange rate changes in several ways. First, the company may have open transactions in a foreign currency. Examples are foreign currency receivables and borrowings. Companies in Indonesia, Malaysia, South Korea and Thailand suffered large foreign exchange losses during the currency turmoil of 1997. For example, Siam Cement, Thailand's largest industrial conglomerate, saw its 1997 baht profits wiped out as a result of foreign exchange losses on its $4 billion of (unhedged) foreign currency loans. This type of risk is known as 'transaction exposure'.

Transaction exposure can be managed. As we saw earlier, open transactions can be hedged. So, too, can future transactions. A company that plans to export goods to a country with a weak currency in the coming year can protect itself against devaluation by forward sale of the expected receipts in the weak currency. The first thing investors look for, then, is information in the annual report and accounts about the firm's hedging policies. SCA, a large Swedish paper and packaging producer, sets out its policies for managing currency risks in its annual report. Exhibit 15.4 contains an extract from the relevant section in its 2001 report.

SCA had consolidated sales of SEK 82 billion (€8.9 billion) in 2001. The group has production facilities in each of its major markets (Sweden, Germany, UK, USA) but the pulp and other raw materials for its European plants come mainly from Sweden. Thus it's exposed to exchange rate changes between the Swedish krona (SEK) and the euro (EUR) and between the krona and the pound (GBP). According to management, the company applies a decentralised system to

Exhibit 15.4   SCA Group: extracts from 'Financial risk management' in 2001 report

CURRENCY RISKS

Transaction exposure

Transaction exposure, defined as the commercial currency flow after net calculations of counterflows in the same currencies, amounts to SEK 8,451 million annually. The most important individual currency relations are SEK against EUR and GBP (see table below.).

SCA applies a decentralised system to manage the Group's transaction exposure, whereby each business area selects the most appropriate strategy for its subsidiaries within a centrally stipulated framework. A minimum requirement calls for the hedging of booked accounts receivable and accounts payable. Centrally, there is a mandate to deviate from the subsidiaries' positions within established risk limits.

During 2001, flows representing a maximum of 8.5 months and a minimum of 5.2 months were hedged against SEK. At year-end, flows representing 5.7 months were hedged, corresponding to a volume of SEK 4,026 million.

Foreign assets

Capital employed in foreign currencies at 31 December 2001 amounted to SEK 58,240 million. The distribution between different currencies is shown in the table below.

In accordance with SCA's policy for financing of foreign assets, capital employed is matched by borrowings and forward contracts so that the booked debt/equity ratio is unaffected by foreign exchange rate fluctuations. In combination with this policy, SCA strives to optimise capital structure based on the Group's tax situation in each country, which means that a higher debt/equity ratio is selected in certain countries. Overall, this means that, based on present currency distribution and debt/equity ratio, about 47% of the foreign capital employed must be matched.

On 31 December 2001, foreign assets were matched by loans in foreign currencies corresponding to SEK 28,620 million, equivalent to a matching ratio of 50%. . . .

Long-term currency sensitivity

The distribution of SCA's net sales and operating costs among different currencies shows the Group's long-term currency sensitivity. With the exception of SEK, SCA maintains a balance between revenues and expenses in all major currencies (see table below).

SCA Group earnings are also affected indirectly by changes in foreign exchange rates for USD, CAD (Canadian dollar) and EUR, since forest industry companies in North America and Finland are major exporters.

Currency	Transaction flows, SEK mn.	Capital employed, SEK mn.	Net debt, SEK mn.	Net sales, %	Operating expenses, %
Euro (EUR)	3,682	24,595	5,134	48	45
British pound (GBP)	2,035	12,567	5,909	16	13
Danish krone (DKK)	731	2,482	2,107	4	3
US dollar (USD)	112	14,210	14,179	15	16
Other	1,891	4,386	1,290	9	6
Swedish krona (SEK)	−8,451	12,341	−4,758	8	17
Total	**0**	**70,581**	**23,861**	**100**	**100**

(*Source*: SCA Group, *Annual Report 2001*. Reproduced by permission of Svenska Cellulosa Aktiebolaget SCA.)

manage transaction exposure but requires, at a minimum, that each business area hedges booked receivables and payables.

In the absence of a statement like SCA's (and not all firms provide one), investors must search in the accounts for indirect information about corporate hedging policy. Many companies try to use 'natural' hedges, where possible, since they are less costly than financial instruments such as forward exchange contracts which must be purchased.

A natural hedge is one where, as a result of regular operating and financing decisions, a firm's expected cash receipts in a foreign currency are equivalent to its expected payments in that currency. Thus oil companies often finance development of new fields with dollar loans because the US dollar is the currency in which most oil trading takes place. A strengthening of the dollar against other currencies results in exchange losses on the dollar debt but exchange gains on oil sales. By combining information in the accounts – for example, the currencies and payment profiles of borrowings – with an understanding of the company's business, investors can assess to what extent the firm is using natural hedges to protect itself against exchange rate changes.

Translation exposure

A second risk is that of 'translation exposure'. For a firm with operations in more than one country, exchange rate movements affect consolidated figures when the foreign units' accounts are translated into the group's reporting currency. Sometimes the reported translation gain or loss can be very large, especially after a major devaluation. Repsol YPF, a Spanish oil and gas company with large Argentinian operations, booked a translation loss of €1.45 billion in 2001 as a result of the devaluation of the Argentinian peso at the end of the year. This is equivalent to 10% of its end-2001 shareholders' equity and exceeds its reported 2001 net income of €1 billion.[14]

Investors often have difficulty interpreting the translation gain or loss – or 'translation adjustment', as it's also known. For example, there's general agreement that companies' Argentinian assets were impaired as a result of the 2001 economic crisis and accompanying peso devaluation. However, the translation adjustments that companies like Repsol reported that year were probably an unreliable indicator of the change in value of their Argentinian net assets since the latter were, in most cases, measured at (depreciated) cost. The translation adjustment usually captures the sign but rarely the magnitude of the gain or loss in net asset value from an exchange rate change.

Easier to understand is the effect of exchange rate changes on the income statement. Many multinational companies now provide this information voluntarily and investors find it helpful when preparing earnings forecasts. For example, Unilever, the Anglo-Dutch food and household products group, discloses in its 2001 accounts two calculations of turnover and trading result for the year: at average exchange rates prevailing in 2001 ('current rates') and at average rates prevailing in 2000 ('constant rates'). (Unilever defines trading result as operating profit before exceptional items and amortisation of goodwill and other intangibles.)

In €m	2001 current rates	2001 constant rates	2000	% change at current rates	% change at constant rates
Turnover	51,514	52,683	47,582	8.3	10.7
Trading result	6,579	6,688	3,753	75.3	78.2

Turnover and results were boosted in 2001 by the acquisition of Bestfoods, a US food products company. Restructuring also contributed to the sharp profit increase that year. The results were even better when measured using constant exchange rates. The strengthening of the euro in 2001 depressed the growth in group turnover and results: the sales and profit contributions of Unilever's US and UK operations had a lower translated value. (The opposite effect is evident in 2000 when the euro weakened against the dollar and sterling.)

Some firms hedge their translation as well as their transaction exposure. The most common practice is for the foreign unit to borrow funds in the local currency to finance its assets. As we saw earlier, under hedge accounting rules, a parent company can even designate its own borrowings in a foreign currency as a hedge of its investment in a foreign subsidiary. SCA goes further. According to its statement on currency risk management (set out in Exhibit 15.4), it uses forward contracts as well as foreign borrowings to achieve a target matching ratio of foreign debt to foreign capital employed. SCA may be required under loan covenants negotiated with its bankers to keep its debt–equity ratio below a specified upper limit and the company uses derivatives as well as natural hedges to ensure this.[15]

Economic exposure

As we saw with Unilever, firms with foreign operations often indicate the impact on past earnings of exchange rate changes during the year. However, investors are more interested in gauging the impact of those exchange rate changes on a firm's *future* earnings and cash flows. We can think of this impact as the firm's 'economic exposure' to currency shifts.

All firms – even those without foreign operations or even foreign transactions – are affected by exchange rate changes. Sometimes the effect is direct. For example, the appreciation of sterling against Continental European currencies in the late 1990s resulted in a fall in profits for UK-based companies with large export sales in these currencies. In other cases, the effect is indirect. SCA notes that its earnings are affected by the relative strength of the Swedish krona against the US dollar, Canadian dollar and the euro since these are the currencies of its main competitors (*see* Exhibit 15.4).

How can investors assess a firm's economic exposure to exchange rate changes? The first step is to check the annual report, in particular management's review of operations, to see whether the firm itself is aware of the risk and has a strategy to deal with it. For example, SCA – in common with other Swedish multinationals – shows the percentage of sales and operating expenses in each of the major currencies of its operations (*see* Exhibit 15.4). By maintaining a balance of revenues and costs in each currency, the company reduces the sensitivity of its earnings to exchange rate changes. It is for this reason that UK companies responded to the appreciation of sterling in the late 1990s by increasing the proportion of imported inputs. Car manufacturers such as Toyota and Nissan that had UK plants and large EU sales, shifted sourcing of components to eurozone countries. Note that the balancing of revenues and costs by currency reduces a firm's economic exposure to exchange rate changes but cannot overcome the effects of an overvalued exchange rate on its profitability.

In the absence of a formal statement by management, investors look for evidence of hedging of economic exposure in the firm's accounts. Where are its main operating assets? Where are its liabilities? In which currencies are most outlays made and in which are proceeds from sales received? To answer these questions, investors search for information about the following.

- *The geographical breakdown of the firm's sales and, if available, operating assets and liabilities.* This is part of the 'segmental reporting' disclosures that large quoted companies with foreign operations are required to make. The information is found either in the annual report or in the notes to the annual accounts. We discuss this topic further in Chapter 20.
- *The location of its major operating subsidiaries and associated companies.* National law usually requires firms to publish this information.
- *The currencies of its borrowings and the swap commitments it has entered into.* Firms following IAS or US GAAP are required to disclose borrowings by currency.

Investors then relate the information they've gathered from the accounts to the review by senior management of the firm's operations in the annual report. They also consult the annual reports of other firms in the industry to learn about the currency mix of their operations. In this way, they form a judgement about the risks to the target firm from exchange rate changes – and of the potential rewards, too.

Convenience translations

Some companies present their financial statements in more than one currency. Large Japanese companies, for example, present US dollar as well as yen numbers on the face of their financial statements. The figures in the foreign currency – usually, the US dollar – are for the benefit of international investors who may be unfamiliar with the company's reporting currency and use the US dollar numbers to gauge the magnitude of key numbers in the accounts such as sales and net profit. Such translations are known as **convenience translations**. The company translates all the numbers in the consolidated financial statements at one exchange rate (usually the spot exchange rate at its financial year-end). The translated numbers have no economic significance: they're simply a recalibration of those in the reporting currency.

Summary

In this chapter we have looked at the accounting for both transactions and operations in foreign currencies. The former is of broader interest. More companies trade – and borrow and lend – in foreign currencies than set up businesses abroad. However, foreign operations raise more tricky accounting problems.

Accountants distinguish hedged from unhedged foreign currency transactions. In the latter case, the company does not actively protect itself against loss from exchange rate changes. Under international rules, it must recognise unrealised foreign exchange gains and losses from such transactions immediately. If the company hedges the transaction – and the hedge is an effective one – it may be able to defer the unrealised exchange gain or loss. In the case of a cash flow hedge, the gain or loss is deferred until the asset or liability arising from the hedged cash flow is recognised. In the case of a foreign investment hedge, the gain or loss is deferred until the investment is sold.

A company with a foreign operation holds assets and liabilities in a foreign currency and must translate them into its reporting currency in order to prepare consolidated accounts. How it does this depends on the nature of the foreign operation. If it's an autonomous entity, the closing rate method is used: the entity's assets and liabilities are translated at the end-year exchange rate and any net translation gain or loss is deferred until it is sold. If the foreign operation is considered an integral part of the parent company's business, the parent uses the temporal method: assets and liabilities are translated at the exchange rate appropriate to the valuation basis used and the net translation gain or loss is recognised in income immediately. Both methods are flawed. The translation gain or loss under either method is unlikely to show the real change in value of the firm's foreign operations.

Firms engage in foreign trade and set up foreign operations in the search for higher returns. Such activities bring increased risk, in part because of exchange rate changes. Investors check the annual report for evidence that the firm is protecting itself against foreign currency risks. The hedges it employs may be artificial (e.g. forward exchange contracts) or natural (e.g. matching of cash inflows and outflows by currency). At a broader level, the currency mix of a firm's inputs and outputs and the geographical spread of its operations – and those of its rivals – give investors clues about the competitive impact on its business of exchange rate changes.

Problem assignments

P15.1   Unhedged transaction in a foreign currency

On 15 October x5, a Swiss retail co-op places a bulk order for 'Rosa' ragu sauce with Priore, an Italian food producer. The value of the contract is SFr 2 million. Priore delivers the goods on 1 December and the retail co-op pays the contract amount on 15 February x6, the due date. Priore's financial year-end is 31 December.

The rate of exchange between the euro (Priore's reporting currency) and the Swiss franc varies over this period. The spot rates on key dates are given below:

15 October x5	SFr 1.462 : €1
1 December	1.485
31 December	1.620
15 February x6	1.515

Priore does not hedge this foreign currency transaction. Its policy is to recognise unrealised exchange gains and losses on foreign currency transactions as they arise.

Required

Show the accounting entry Priore makes on 1 December x5 to record the sale. (Ignore the entry recording the cost of sales.) What is the exchange gain or loss on this contract that Priore recognises in x5? In x6?

> Check figure:
> Net exchange loss, x5 and x6   €26,669

P15.2   Hedged transaction in a foreign currency

Refer to the facts in P15.1. Suppose that on receipt of the order from the Swiss retail co-op on 15 October x5, Priore decides to hedge the SFr 2 million receivable to protect itself against appreciation of the euro. On that date, it enters into a four-month forward contract with its bank. The forward rates (for 15 February x6) on the order, delivery, and year-end dates are given below:

15 October x5	SFr 1.450 : €1
1 December	1.476
31 December	1.614

On 15 February x6, Priore receives SFr 2 million from the retail co-op. The bank pays Priore €59,178 [(SFr 2 million / SFr 1.45) – (SFr 2 million / SFr 1.515)] in settlement of the forward contract.

Required

Show the accounting entries that Priore makes on the order, delivery, year-end and settlement dates with respect to the sale and forward contracts. What is the hedging income or expense on the forward contract it recognises in x5? In x6? What is the exchange gain or loss on the sale contract it recognises in x5? In x6?

P15.3   Accounting for autonomous foreign operation

To better compete with low-cost imports, Sachs, a German footwear manufacturer, sets up a shoe-making company in an emerging economy, Pacifica, in January year 1, and invests 300 million pesos (€20 million) in it. Sachs Pacifica breaks even in its first year of trading. Its balance sheet at the end of year 1 is shown below (amounts are in millions of pesos).

Exhibit 15.5 Sachs Pacifica: annual accounts and key exchange rate data for year 2
(currency amounts in millions of pesos)

Sachs Pacifica
Income statement, year 2

Sales revenue		500
Less:		
Cost of goods sold:		
Beginning inventory	70	
Production costs	310	
– Ending inventory	−80	
		−300
Depreciation		−40
Other expenses		−120
Net profit		40

Balance sheet, end-year 2

Property and equipment	270*	Share capital	300
Inventories	80**	Profit for year	40
Accounts receivable	60		
Cash	40	Debt and other monetary liabilities	110
Total assets	450	Total equities	450

* Start year 2, at net book value	250
Purchases at 1/1	60
– Depreciation	−40
End year 2, NBV	270

** Purchased/produced in 4th quarter, year 2.

Exchange rate information:

	Year 1		Year 2		
	1/1	1/1	Average	4th qtr	31/12
Pesos to the euro	15	15	16.1	16	15.8

(There was no change in the exchange rate during year 1.)

Balance sheet, end-year 1

Property and equipment	250	Share capital	300
Inventories	70		
Accounts receivable	50		
Cash	30	Debt and other monetary liabilities	100
Total assets	400	Total equities	400

Sachs Pacifica trades profitably in year 2. Its financial statements for the year are set out in Exhibit 15.5. Information about the movement in the peso/euro exchange rate during years 1 and 2 is also given in the exhibit. Sachs follows international standards in accounting for foreign operations.

Required

Assume Sachs Pacifica is an autonomous unit for foreign currency translation purposes. Translate its year 2 accounts from pesos into euros.

Explain the reason for the change in the carrying amount of the investment. Why has it increased from €20 million at the start of year 2 to €21.52 million by the end?

P15.4 **Accounting for non-autonomous foreign operation**

Refer to the facts in P15.3 and Exhibit 15.5.

Required

Assume Sachs Pacifica's operations are an integral part of those of its German parent company – for foreign currency translation purposes. Translate its year 2 accounts from pesos into euros.

Why do Sachs Pacifica's operations give rise to a translation gain of €0.36 million in year 2 when the peso has weakened against the euro in that year?

P15.5 **Non-autonomous foreign operation: translation issues**

Ace, a South Korean electronics company, has a subsidiary, Diamond, in Puerto Grande, a Caribbean island. Diamond assembles computer hardware for sale in the region. Although Diamond keeps its accounts in doblón, the local currency, its functional currency is the South Korean won as it purchases parts and receives financing from its South Korean parent.

As a result of depressed economic conditions in the industry in x2, Diamond is forced to mark down its inventory to market value at 31 December. In addition, a year-end impairment review reveals that the recoverable amount of its plant and equipment is below the carrying amount.

(In millions of doblón)	*At 31 Dec x2*
Inventory, at cost	30
Valuation adjustment	−2
Inventory, at LOCOM	28
Plant and equipment, at cost	120
Accumulated depreciation	−24
Accumulated impairment losses	−15
Plant and equipment, net	81

Puerto Grande is an oil and gas producer and the doblón has strengthened against the won and other currencies in recent years as new reserves have been discovered. Key exchange rate data are given below:

Start x1 (purchase of plant and equipment)	162 won : 1 doblón
Average in Qtr 3, x2 (purchase of end-x2 inventory)	189
Average for x2	186
31 December x2	196

Required

Mae-Young, Ace's controller, is preparing the company's consolidated accounts for x2. She wants to know how to translate Diamond's fixed assets and inventory into won for consolidation purposes. Advise her.

P15.6 **Foreign operations in a hyperinflationary economy**

Portasports, an EU firm, assembles and markets portable sports facilities – or 'kits'. A kit allows sports matches – in, say, soccer, tennis or rugby – to be held in a village or town which lacks permanent facilities for that sport.

At the start of x3, Portasports establishes a subsidiary in the South Sea Islands (SSI). Portasports (SSI) imports 'portatennis' kits from Europe. Each kit contains the key elements of a competition tennis court – 'roll-away' court with net, scoreboard and spectator stands.

Portasports (SSI)'s initial balance sheet is as follows (amounts are in millions of pistoles):

Balance sheet at 1/1/x3

Inventory	9	Share capital	11
Cash	2	Liabilities	0
Total assets	11	Total equities	11

The inventory consists of three kits costing 3 million pistoles (or €500,000) each.

Portasports (SSI) trades profitably in its first year. It sells two of the three kits. Its x3 accounts are shown in Exhibit 15.6, together with relevant exchange rate and inflation data.

The South Sea Islands have experienced a rapid increase in prices in recent years. The cumulative rate of increase in the three years to the end of x3 is 125%.

Required

(a) Convert Portasports (SSI)'s x3 accounts from pistoles into euros. Either restate the accounts into end-x3 constant purchasing power units and translate the restated accounts at the closing rate or translate the unadjusted accounts using the temporal method.

(b) Portasports records a translation loss of €0.16 million in its consolidated x3 accounts with respect to its SSI subsidiary. Suggest ways in which it can reduce or eliminate future translation losses using a natural hedge.

Exhibit 15.6 **Portasports (SSI): summary x3 accounts and related data**
(currency amounts in millions of pistoles)

Portasports (SSI)
Income statement for x3

Sales revenue	15
(2 kits @ 7.5)	
Less:	
Cost of kits sold	−6
Other expenses	−6
Profit	3

Balance sheet at 31/12/x3

Inventory	10	Share capital	11
(1 kit @ 3, 2 kits @ 3.5)		Profit for x3	3
Cash	4	Liabilities	0
Total assets	14	Total equities	14

Inflation data:

		Index during x3		
	Start-year	End Qtr 2	End Qtr 3	End-year
Index of consumer prices	180	198	210	225
(start-x1 = 100)				

Exchange rate data in x3:

	Start-year	End Qtr 2	End Qtr 3	End-year
Pistoles per euro	6	6.6	7	7.5

Assumptions:
The 'portatennis' kits are imported at the start of x3. Sales are made and other expenses incurred at the end of quarter 2. Inventory is replenished (2 kits @ 3.5) at the end of quarter 3.

Exchange differences and published accounts

(1) Universal Electric (UE), a diversified US company with interests ranging from aero engine production to financial services, has extensive operations outside the USA. In the statement of changes in shareholders' equity in its x9 consolidated accounts, it reports the following balances at year-end (amounts are in US$ million):

	x9	x8	x7
Cumulative translation adjustment	279	(180)	(127)

Required

Did the US dollar, UE's reporting currency, strengthen or weaken overall relative to the currencies of countries where UE has operations: (a) in x8, (b) in x9? What assumptions underlie your answer?

(2) Geosonic, a large Japanese consumer electronics group, sold 80% of its stake in ACM, a US entertainment company, to Bourbon, a Canadian drinks group, in May x5 for US$5.7 billion. It had acquired its stake in ACM for US$6.1 billion five years earlier. However, because the yen had appreciated by more than 35% against the dollar since that date, it recorded a loss of ¥165 billion (then equivalent to US$1.9 billion) on the sale. ACM was an autonomous unit of Geosonic for foreign currency translation purposes.

Required

(a) Why did Geosonic recognise a foreign exchange loss of ¥165 billion in its income statement (for the year to 31 March x6), given that ACM was an autonomous unit of Geosonic?

(b) Geosonic's net assets declined by less than ¥165 billion as a result of the sale. Why?

Notes to Chapter 15

1 International Accounting Standards Board, *IAS 21: The Effects of Changes in Foreign Exchange Rates.* Where a non-monetary item is revalued, the exchange component of the revaluation is accounted for in the same way as the unrealised holding gain or loss – to reserves if the unrealised gain or loss is deferred in equity or to the income statement if it's recognised in profit or loss.

2 Not all unrealised exchange gains and losses on foreign currency monetary transactions must be recognised in income immediately. As we show later, a company can designate a foreign currency borrowing as a hedge of a net investment in a foreign entity under *IAS 21*. If the hedge is effective, the unrealised exchange gain or loss on the borrowing can be deferred in equity – along with the unrealised exchange loss or gain on the investment – until the investment is sold.

3 International Accounting Standards Board, *IAS 39: Financial Instruments: Recognition and Measurement.* Hedge accounting is discussed in greater depth in Chapter 13 (and the accounting for cash flow hedges is illustrated there).

4 In practice, the fair value of the forward contract is not necessarily equal to the notional amount of the forward contract times the change in forward exchange rates. The contract's fair value is influenced by other factors besides the change in forward rates (for example, the creditworthiness of the counter-party to the contract).

5 The currency in which the parent company prepares its accounts need not be the currency of its home country. For example, although BP is a UK-registered company, it prepares its consolidated accounts in US dollars. Most of its business is conducted in – or is referenced to – the US currency.

6 'Parent company' refers to the entity making the foreign investment. The US subsidiary of a Swedish firm that opens a factory in Mexico is the parent company of the Mexican operation – and the Swedish firm is the parent of the US one – for purposes of IAS 21.

7 Pronounced 'Lesster' and 'Arkansaw' respectively. Foreigners, as Mark Twain observed, 'always spell better than they pronounce' (Twain, M. (1869), *The Innocents Abroad*, Hartford, CT: American Publishing Company).

8   The accounting terminology here can be confusing. 'Exchange difference' is a general term which covers transaction and translation gains and losses, whether recorded in income or taken direct to reserves. A translation gain or loss which is taken direct to reserves is usually described as a (positive or negative) 'translation adjustment'.

9   *IAS 21* does not use the term 'temporal method' to describe these translation procedures. According to the standard, the accounting for non-autonomous foreign operations is considered to be equivalent to the accounting for (unhedged) foreign currency *transactions*.

10 One indicator of a hyperinflationary economy, according to IAS, is a cumulative inflation rate over three years approaching or exceeding 100% (*IAS 29: Financial Reporting in Hyperinflationary Economies*).

11 Beaver, W. and Wolfson, M. (1982), Foreign currency translation and changing prices in perfect and competitive markets, *Journal of Accounting Research*, 20: 528–550.

12 IAS 21 also encourages firms to disclose their foreign currency risk management policies.

13 Foreign operations entail other risks which investors must also assess. One example is political risk, a broad term which covers the risks of economic loss arising from government action (e.g. expropriation of corporate assets) or breakdown (e.g. civil unrest leading to suspension of business operations).

14 In addition to the translation adjustment, Repsol booked provisions of €1.3 billion in its 2001 income statement to cover the effects of the peso devaluation on its Argentinian operations (e.g. higher bad debts, impairment of assets, additional financial expenses). Repsol also discloses in the notes that the translation adjustment would have been €2.6 billion if it had applied the exchange rate prevailing at the date of issue of the financial statements rather than the rate prevailing at the balance sheet date.

15 Some companies try to minimise currency-induced swings in translated earnings through hedging. If a company expects its reporting currency to strengthen, thereby reducing its foreign unit's earnings on translation, it sells foreign currency forward. The exchange gain on the forward contract offsets the lower translated earnings. If the reporting currency does not appreciate as expected, the company forgoes the exchange gain on the forward contract but its foreign unit's earnings are higher in reporting currency terms. The popularity of such hedging has declined in recent years. It's costly and does not qualify for hedge accounting treatment. Under *IAS 39*, hedging foreign currency earnings is not a cash flow hedge so gains and losses must be recognised in income as they arise.

16

Employment costs

INTRODUCTION

Pay matters – and not just for employees. For many companies, especially those in labour-intensive service industries, wages and other employee benefits are the largest operating cost. On a national level, they represent 50–60% of the gross domestic product of developed countries.

Pay takes many forms. In section 1 of the chapter we survey the various types of compensation an employee may receive – from salary to share options, benefits to bonuses – and describe, in general terms, the accounting for each of them.

As a general principle, a company should recognise the cost of pay and other types of compensation as employees earn them and should measure that cost at fair value. In some cases, it is difficult to measure fair value when the compensation is deferred and is contingent on uncertain future events. We examine two examples of such compensation – post-employment benefits and employee share options – in depth in section 2.

In the final section we describe the information European companies disclose about employee numbers and costs in their annual accounts and show how it's used, by investors and others, in financial analysis.

SECTION 1

General issues

Types of employee benefit

Companies use pay and other forms of compensation to attract (and retain) staff, to motivate them and to reward them for good performance. The way staff are paid varies. Compensation can be fixed (salary) or variable (piece rate, sales commission). It is usually in cash but may be in goods and services (fringe benefits such as subsidised housing, transport and medical care) or the company's shares. Sometimes it is deferred – for example, merit increases that raise base salary in future periods, pensions and bonuses.

If the goals of pay policy are simple, why are there so many types of pay? One reason is that the goals require different pay mechanisms. For example, to motivate staff (and, indeed, to attract them to the company in the first place), the company must reduce their income uncertainties: this may require payment of a regular, fixed salary. To reward good performance, however, it needs to link part of an employee's pay to his or her accomplishments – hence the use of bonuses.

Another reason is the influence of a country's tax and welfare systems. For example, some countries provide tax incentives for company-sponsored pension plans: company contributions are tax-deductible but returns on plan assets are tax-exempt. Similarly, fringe benefits can offer tax advantages: they may be more lightly taxed than cash income in the hands of employees but the company is able to deduct their full value in its tax return.[1]

A third reason lies in the indirect, non-pecuniary effects of an organisation's pay policy. Pay involves issues of equity and status. For example, a company may increase the level of non-monetary rewards (e.g. certain fringe benefits, office size and location) relative to monetary ones if employees set great store by status.[2]

Accounting for employee benefits: an overview

Employee benefits comprise not only wages but also other forms of compensation such as bonuses, paid leave and pension benefits which an employee receives for services rendered to the company. The accounting for the cost of these benefits is straightforward. The company recognises the cost when the employee earns the benefit. The benefit is measured at fair value. In the following sections, we show how these recognition and measurement principles are applied with respect to the major types of employee benefit.

Wage and related costs

The principal employment cost for most firms is that of wages. (We use the term in its broad sense. The term 'salaries' is used more narrowly to refer to periodical (usually monthly) payments to employees.) A company recognises the cost of wages and the related liability as employees render services in exchange for them:

Dr. Wages expense (OE–)	xxx	
Cr. Accrued wages payable (L+)		xxx

Wages include overtime and other contractually agreed payments. For most companies, this is an *accrued* liability. The expense and liability accumulate (accrue) over time and payroll records are updated weekly or monthly. Periodically, the company settles the debt by paying its employees:

Dr. Accrued wages payable (L–)	xxx	
Cr. Cash (A–)		xxx

In practice, the structure of wage costs is more complicated and the accounting reflects this. *First, companies in all countries bear employment costs other than wages. The main additional cost is the* **employer's** *share of social security taxes.* Think of social security as a government-run multi-coverage insurance policy. Social security taxes are then a form of insurance premium. The range and scale of benefits offered by this insurance policy vary widely across countries: coverage can include medical care and sickness, disability, industrial injury and occupational diseases, maternity and paternity, family allowances, unemployment, retirement and death. As a result, national social security tax rates also differ markedly. *The other important non-wage cost is that of supplementary benefits the employer offers existing and former employees.* Examples are health care and pension benefits available under company-sponsored plans.

Second, the cash an employee receives is less than the wage he or she earns owing to taxes and other deductions withheld at source. The company may be required by law to withhold from pay both income taxes and its *employees'* share of social security taxes and forward them to the appropriate government agency. In addition, company pension and health care plans may be 'contributory' (the employee must make regular payments to the plan) and the employee's contributions are deducted at source from his or her pay.

How do employer costs and withholdings affect the accounting for wages? We can illustrate this with an example. Despina's clinic treats certain medical disorders using magnetic techniques. The January payroll records for two employees, Fiordiligi and Dorabella, are based on the following data:

Salary per employee	1,000
Withholding rate of income tax	20%
Social security tax:	
Employer contribution as % of salary	15%
Employee contribution as % of salary	8%
Pension plan: employer contribution/employee	100
Health care plan: employer contribution/employee	45
(Employees make no contributions to these plans:	
the plans are 'non-contributory'.)	

The journal entries the clinic makes to record the costs of the two employees' wages and benefits in January are as follows:

Wage costs

Dr. Salaries expense (OE–)	2,000	
Cr. Employee income taxes payable (L+)		400
Cr. Employee social security taxes payable (L+)		160
Cr. Salaries payable (L+)		1,440

Employee benefits cost

Dr. Employee benefits expense (OE–)	590	
Cr. Employer social security taxes payable (L+)		300
Cr. Employer pension contribution payable (L+)		200
Cr. Employer health care contribution payable (L+)		90

Despina pays Fiordiligi's and Dorabella's salaries at the end of January and settles the tax and contribution liabilities when they fall due, at monthly or quarterly intervals. Note that the total monthly cost to the clinic of the two employees is 2,590, of which 23% (590/2,590) represents the costs of employee benefits borne by Despina.

Compensated absences

Employment contracts usually stipulate that the employee continues to receive compensation when absent from work for certain specified reasons such as sickness, vacations, maternity or paternity leave, and jury or military service. In many cases, an employee's right to compensation 'accumulates', that is, the absences earned can be carried forward and used in future periods. (If the right to compensation 'vests', the employee receives a cash payment for absences earned and unused at the date he or she leaves the firm.)

Under IAS, a company should accrue the expected cost of compensated absences that are, by nature, accumulating, as employees earn them. Where the compensated absence does not accumulate (i.e. can't be carried forward), it should recognise the cost only when the absence occurs. Thus a company with ten employees that have each earned – and can carry forward – 15 days' vacation by its financial year-end should recognise an expense and a liability for the expected cost of these unused holidays:

Dr. Salaries expense (OE–)	xxx	
Cr. Accrued vacation pay (L+)		xxx

When the employees take the accumulated vacation, the company debits the liability and credits cash.

Accumulating compensated absences are measured at their *expected cost*. In the above example, the company should base the cost of the 15 days' earned vacation on the salaries the employees are expected to receive in the period when they take the vacation rather than when they earned it. In the case of accumulated sick-pay, a company measures its liability as the product of the days of carried-forward sick leave an employee is expected to claim times his or her expected salary rate at the time of claim.

Pension and other post-employment benefits

Post-employment benefits are benefits an employee receives after leaving the company's service or on retirement. They are a form of deferred compensation. The employee accepts a lower wage today in return for a lump sum or flow of payments in the future. *Post-employment benefits include pension, healthcare and insurance benefits.* The discussion in this section is framed in terms of pension benefits – for most companies, they are the largest post-employment cost – but the concepts apply to other post-employment benefits as well.

When setting up a company pension plan, management must make certain decisions. *One key one is whether or not the plan should be funded.* (In some countries, firms have no option: they have to fund.)

Where the plan is funded, the company, alone or with its employees, sets aside cash to meet future pension obligations. It does this by either contributing cash to a pension fund or purchasing dedicated insurance policies. The pension fund may be an independent entity (e.g. the fund management arm of a bank) or a unit legally separate from but controlled by the company. The fund (or insurance company) invests the cash (premiums) in income-yielding assets; later, it pays pensions to retired employees, drawing on those assets. Panel A of Exhibit 16.1 shows the pension-related cash flows between employer, pension fund insurance company and employee under a funded plan. (The plan is assumed to be non-contributory.)

Exhibit 16.1 Pension-related cash flows: funded and unfunded plans

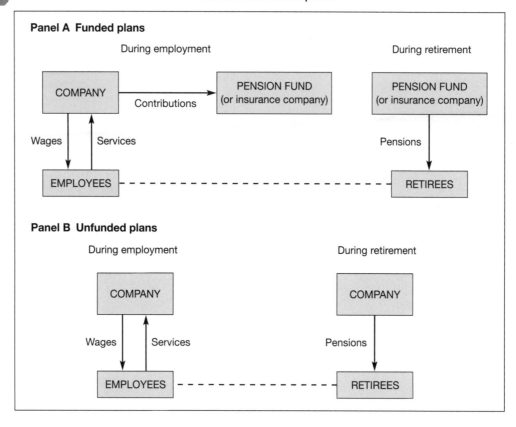

Where the plan is unfunded, the company pays pensions from its own resources. It may earmark its own assets (e.g. financial investments) for this purpose but it does not transfer funds to an independent entity. Panel B of Exhibit 16.1 shows the pension-related cash flows between employer and employee under an unfunded plan.

Another major decision for management is whether the pension plan should specify the pension benefits a retiree will receive. Company-sponsored plans fall into one of two groups:

1 **Defined contribution plans**. A defined contribution (DC) plan specifies the contributions which the employer (and, in some cases, the employee) must make to a separate pension fund each period. It does not specify the pension to be paid. Thus the sums an employee receives on retirement will depend on the amounts invested in the fund and the cumulative returns on those investments. In effect, the employee assumes the investment risk. **Money purchase plan** is another name for this type of plan.

2 **Defined benefit plans**. A defined benefit (DB) plan specifies the terms of an employee's pension – how it is to be computed, the starting date and duration. The pension is usually a function of length of employment and salary level, usually weighted towards the later years of employment. In fact, this type of plan is also referred to as a **final salary plan**.

A DB plan can be funded or unfunded. (A DC plan is, by definition, funded.) Note that, with a DB plan, the employer retains the investment risk. This is so even if the plan is funded. Although the contributions to the fund together with the returns on its investments are intended

Exhibit 16.2   Recognising the cost of pension benefits: accounting framework

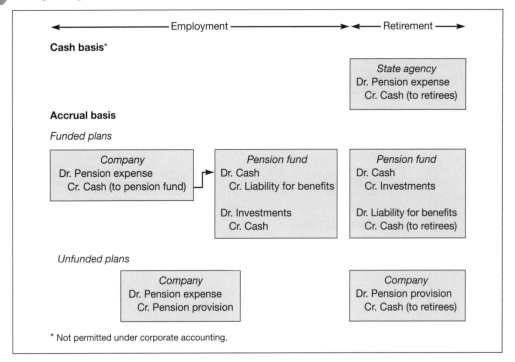

to be sufficient to meet retirees' pension benefits, the company bears the cost if they are not because the plan specifies the pensions to be paid.

A pension plan's form influences the way the company accounts for the cost of pension benefits. One principle, however, is universal. *Under international rules, a company must follow the accrual basis when accounting for pension (and other post-employment) costs.* It recognises the expense (and related liability) as employees earn the rights to these benefits. Most state pension schemes, however, are accounted for on a cash (or 'pay as you go') basis: pension expense is recognised when pensions are paid. Exhibit 16.2 shows in outline the accounting for pension costs under the accrual and cash bases and, within the accrual basis, contrasts the entries made under funded and unfunded plans.

Companies face problems measuring pension cost under DB plans. (In the case of DC plans, pension expense is usually equal to the periodic contribution the company is required to make to the plan.) There are two major sources of uncertainty. First, what are the future payments the company (or pension fund) will actually have to make to retirees? Remember: the pension liability of the company (or fund) is the present value of its expected pension payments to retirees. Those future payments must be estimated and the estimates themselves are sensitive to assumptions about future salary levels, employee turnover, life expectancy, interest rates and asset yields.

Second, how should the annual cost of the pension liability be determined? Even if there is agreement on what the pension liability is likely to be at the date of an employee's retirement, there are many ways in which that liability can be accrued over the employee's working life. Section 2 of the chapter explores these issues and explains how the international accounting standard on employee benefits has resolved them.

Termination benefits

Termination benefits are payments made by the company to staff on ending their employment before retirement. Usually the company has a legal obligation to make such payments – legislation or the employment contract itself requires them – but in some cases its obligation is a constructive one, based on business practice in the industry. A termination benefit usually comprises a lump-sum payment based on the employee's salary level and years of service but it can take other forms. For example, the company may improve the pension benefits of staff laid off.

From an accounting perspective, a company recognises a liability only when it ends an employee's service contract. Termination benefits are conditional on this event. It would be misleading, therefore, to accrue their cost over some arbitrary period of employee service. The problem is: what is the termination date? Mindful of the practice among some companies of smoothing income through selective timing of provisions (including provisions for redundancies), accounting regulators now require a firm to be 'demonstrably committed' to terminating employment before it can recognise a liability. Evidence of 'demonstrable commitment', according to IAS, is a detailed formal plan for termination and no 'realistic possibility of withdrawal'. A formal plan can include one in which employees agree to leave under voluntary redundancy terms.

The accounting entry to recognise the expense and liability of termination benefits is, in outline:

Dr. Termination benefits expense (OE–)	xxx	
Cr. Provision for termination benefits (L+)		xxx

Note that if the company makes an offer to encourage voluntary redundancy, it will have to estimate the number of employees likely to take up the offer in order to calculate the above expense and provision.

In some countries, companies grant termination *indemnities* to employees. These indemnities are payable regardless of how employment is terminated. In Italy, for example, the indemnity is payable on the employee's dismissal, resignation, retirement, disability or death. Such an indemnity is not a termination benefit. It is similar to a pension or other post-employment benefit and should be accounted for in the same way (i.e. the cost should be accrued each period as the employee earns his or her entitlement to the indemnity).

Other employee benefits

Employees receive compensation in ways other than those mentioned above. The accounting recognition and measurement principles are still the same. The cost of the benefit should be recognised as the employee earns it and measured at its fair value. Application of these principles can cause problems, however. We point out some of them below.

Non-monetary benefits

There are many types of non-monetary benefit. Examples are free or subsidised travel, accommodation and other services (e.g. club membership). The key issue here is the valuation of the benefit. For example, suppose a company rents a company-owned flat to an employee at a monthly charge of 500 when the market rate is 800. Assuming rent is received in arrears, the rental should be recorded as follows:

Dr. Cash (A+)	500	
Dr. Employee benefits expense (OE–)	300	
Cr. Rental income (OE+)		800

One benefit of using fair rather than cash values is that it highlights the cost to the firm of the subsidised goods or services.

Profit-sharing and bonus plans

Under these plans, employees receive a lump-sum payment at the end of a financial period. In some cases, they may only be entitled to the payment if they've worked for the firm for a specified period.

The terms of the plan indicate when the liability for the payment arises and its amount. For example, the plan may contain a formula linking the payment to reported profit or some other financial number. Only when the terms of the plan are met do employees earn the right to the payment. Note that the payment is treated as an expense, not a distribution, even when it's linked to *after-tax* profit, since it's awarded for employee services. The calculation in this case requires care. For example, suppose a bonus is set at a fixed percentage of after-tax profit (the 'bonus rate') and it is a tax-deductible expense. To find the amount of the bonus, the following simultaneous equations must be solved:

$$\text{Bonus} = \text{Bonus rate} \times (\text{Profit} - \text{Bonus} - \text{Tax})$$

$$\text{Tax (expense)} = \text{Corporate tax rate} \times (\text{Profit} - \text{Bonus})$$

The 'profit' figure in the above equations is profit *before* bonus and tax but after deducting all other expenses.

Share-based compensation

Employees may receive compensation in the form of shares or other equity instruments (e.g. share options) of the company. In Europe such compensation is often restricted to senior executives; in the USA, however, many start-up companies offer it to all employees. According to proponents, the main advantage of a share-based compensation scheme lies in its incentive effect. By linking their income to the market value of the company's equity, employees are encouraged to act in ways that will increase that value.

In principle, the accounting for share-based compensation should be governed by its substance. The company should recognise as compensation cost the fair value of the shares or other equity instruments granted to employees. In economic terms, it acquires (and consumes) an asset (employee services) for which it pays in shares rather than cash. In practice, however, either companies do not recognise compensation cost or, if they do, they measure it at an amount less than fair value. We look more closely at the accounting for employee share options in section 2 of the chapter.

Share-based compensation schemes should not be confused with employee share ownership plans. The main aim of the latter is to encourage share ownership among employees. The compensatory element is small – employees buy the company's shares at a small discount to the current market price – and is usually ignored.

SECTION 2

Specialised topics

Pension benefits

Company-sponsored pension plans, though widespread in the Netherlands, UK and North America, are still unusual in many countries. Citizens rely on state pension schemes and their personal savings for income provision in their old age. State pension schemes are usually unfunded: pensions are paid from current taxation.

Demographic changes are causing governments to rethink existing pension policies, however. People are living longer. Fertility rates have fallen, especially in Europe. The result is that Europe's dependency ratio, that is, the ratio of pensioners to those of working age, is expected to rise to 30% by 2040 from around 20% today. To pay pensions to this much larger group will require an increase in taxes, the burden of which will fall on the working population. It is partly for this reason that European governments are now promoting company-sponsored pension plans. As a result, the accounting methods illustrated in this section are likely to become more widespread in European company accounts in future.

Types of company-sponsored pension plan

The way a company accounts for pension benefits is heavily influenced by the type of pension plan it offers employees. As we saw in section 1 of the chapter, there are two types of plan. A *defined benefit (DB) plan* specifies the pension (or other benefits) the employee will receive on retirement: the benefit is usually a function of years of service and salary level. A *defined contribution (DC) plan* specifies the contributions the company (and, under a 'contributory' plan, the employee) will make to the plan during the employment period. A DC plan provides guidance as to the pension the employee is likely to receive given the amount of contributions and the investment performance of the fund but, in contrast to a DB plan, makes no commitment as to the amount.

In some countries, management face a further decision with respect to DB plans – whether to fund the plan or not. (DC plans are, by definition, funded.) Under a *funded DB plan*, the company transfers cash to an independent entity which is responsible for running the pension scheme (i.e. investing the cash, managing the investments and paying pensions to retirees). Under an *unfunded DB plan*, the company draws on its own assets to pay pensions. However, it provides for the cost as employees earn their pension rights.

Measuring the cost of pension benefits

We saw in section 1 that there's general agreement that the cost of pension benefits – like other employee benefits – should be accrued. Employees earn pension benefits under a company-sponsored plan while they're working for the company, and the company should recognise the expense and related liability during this period. Recognition should not be delayed until the pensions are paid. How the cost is measured is still a source of controversy, however. Before exploring the issues in this debate, we need to understand how a company with a pension plan calculates its pension expense and liability in a simple setting. The discussion below focuses on funded DB plans. Note that we're concerned solely with the accounts of the sponsoring company, not those of the pension fund itself.

Determining pension expense

The accounting for pension cost under DC plans is straightforward. *Annual pension expense is equal to the contributions the company must make to the plan with respect to the services performed by participating employees that year.* The journal entry at the date of payment to the fund is:

```
Dr. Pension expense (OE–)                                    xxx
     (or: Personnel cost, pensions)
   Cr. Cash (A–)                                                    xxx
```

Between payment dates, the cost is accrued. If additional contributions are made, these are recognised as expense in the periods when the employees perform the services to which they relate.[3]

By contrast, the accounting under DB plans can be complicated. The company's accountant must estimate the cost today of pension benefits which employees will receive some, maybe many, years later.

Under a DB plan, the entry the company makes to recognise pension expense is separate from the one it makes to record payments to the pension fund:

(a) *Expense recognition*
    Dr. Pension expense (OE–)   xxx
        Cr. Provision for pension costs (L+)   xxx
            (or: Accrued pension costs)
(b) *Funding*
    Dr. Provision for pension costs (L–)   xxx
        Cr. Cash (A–)   xxx

All companies with defined benefit plans, whether funded or unfunded, make entry (a). Only companies with funded plans make entry (b).[4] Note that the expense can be greater or less than the cash payment in any one period. If the cumulative charges in the income statement are greater than the cumulative payments to the fund, the company reports a liability ('Accrued pension costs') in its balance sheet. If the cumulative payments are greater than the cumulative charges, the company reports an asset ('Prepaid pension costs') in its balance sheet.

Companies usually get a tax deduction for contributions paid. In countries where unfunded schemes are the norm, special tax rules apply.

How is pension expense under (a) determined? Practice varies but the expense figure of a funded DB plan typically has the following components:

Current service cost	+ xx
Interest on plan liabilities	+ xx
Expected return on fund investments	– xx
Effects of plan amendments	+ xx
Net actuarial gains or losses	+/– xx
Total pension expense	xxx

We briefly discuss each component in turn.

1 *Current service cost.* This is the cost of pension benefits earned by employees as a result of services performed in the current period. It is usually the biggest component of pension expense.

   Actuaries have devised various methods of determining this cost, largely for funding purposes. Accountants have adapted these methods for their own use. A key difference among the methods is the assumption made about employees' future services.

   – Under accrued benefit valuation (ABV) methods, only services already rendered by employees are taken into account in determining the cost of current service.
   – Under projected benefit valuation (PBV) methods, future services are accounted for in determining current service cost. In effect, the cost of an employee's expected total service to the company is calculated and then spread over his or her working life.

   ABV methods result in an increasing current service cost per employee as the benefits he or she earns increase with each year of service; PBV methods, on the other hand, moderate the upward slope in the service cost calculation through their allocation mechanisms. Note that for companies with stable or slowly growing workforces, the difference in *aggregate* current service cost under the two valuation methods is not very marked.[5]

2 *Interest on plan liabilities.* To calculate the fund's liability (funded DB plans) or the company's provision (unfunded plans), the amounts and timing of pension payments to retirees in the future must be estimated and their present value determined. As retirement – and payment – approaches, the present value of those liabilities ('actuarial present value of future pension benefits') grows. The effect of the passage of time on the pension liability is usually captured in a separate 'interest' component of pension expense.

What discount rate is used to determine the present value? In some countries, the rate is specified by law. In others, management decide the rate, using as a guide the interest rate on long-term bonds of similar maturity.

3 *Return on investments.* In the case of funded DB plans, the investments of the fund earn returns – in the form of dividends, interest and capital gains – each period. These returns *reduce* the annual cost of the pension plan to the company: hence the credit to pension expense. To avoid sharp fluctuations in this number from year to year (pension investments may sustain capital losses in some years), companies estimate the expected long-run return on plan investments and use this figure in the pension expense calculation rather than the actual returns in the year.

4 *Effects of plan amendments.* A company may amend its DB plan. It may offer benefits for services rendered *before* the plan was introduced. In addition, it may give *additional* benefits to employees and retirees for each year of service. The cost to date of such amendments is known as **past service cost**. (Amendments may reduce benefits. In this case, past service cost is negative.)

5 *Net actuarial gains or losses.* These comprise experience gains and losses and the effects of changes in actuarial assumptions. Experience gains and losses arise because outcomes differ from expectations. Actual returns on investments are higher than expected (an 'experience gain'). Or the actuary's past assumptions about wage inflation or labour turnover prove to be too optimistic: the upward adjustment to the fund's liabilities is an 'experience loss'.

The actuary may alter his or her assumptions about *future* values of key variables (e.g. incidence of early retirement, life expectancy of plan participants). These can lead to increases or decreases in plan liabilities – and thus losses or gains.

Notwithstanding the netting of actuarial gains and losses, this component of pension expense can vary markedly from year to year. To minimise swings in reported pension expense, companies may not recognise the net gains or losses immediately but, instead, amortise them – as expense or income within pension expense – over a period of years.[6]

The above are the main components of pension expense. There are others. For example, if a company curtails a plan (when it lays off staff) or settles existing pension obligations (by granting plan participants a lump-sum payment in place of an annual pension), it recognises any gain or loss immediately – and usually within pension expense.

Illustration

We use a simple example to illustrate the calculation of pension expense. Lusitanian Shipping, a Portuguese company which specialises in the cargo trade between Europe and the Orient, starts a defined benefit pension scheme for its employees in x3. At the end of x7, the plan has assets and liabilities of 100 million. (This is unusual. Pension funds are normally in surplus (A > L) or in deficit (A < L).)

Lusitanian Shipping: Pension Fund Balance sheet, at end-x7			
Assets		*Liabilities*	
		Actuarial present value of future	
Investments	100	pension benefits	100

The company wants to calculate its pension expense for x8. It gives us the following information (all amounts are in millions):

- Current service cost in x8, calculated using an accrued benefit valuation method, is 10.
- At the start of x8, the company amends the plan. It grants additional pension benefits to employees for services rendered before the plan was started in x3. The cost of past service in present value terms is estimated at 8 at 1/1/x8. The company plans to recognise the cost immediately and raise its annual contribution over subsequent years in order to fund the higher pension liability.
- The interest rate used to discount future pension benefits is 6%.
- The expected long-term return on the fund's investments is 7%.
- There is a net actuarial gain of 1.5. Actual returns on fund investments are 5 higher than expected. However, changes in actuarial assumptions result in an increase of 3.5 in the plan's end-x8 liabilities.

What is the company's pension expense in x8?

The calculation is:

Current service cost	10
Past service cost	8
Interest on start-x8 plan liabilities	
$\quad$ (6% × (100 + 8))	6.5
Expected return on investments	
$\quad$ (7% × 100 (start-x8 plan assets))	−7
Net actuarial gain	−1.5
Total pension expense in x8	16.0

Note that the interest component increases – from 6 to 6.5 million – because of the additional liability caused by the plan amendment.

Lusitanian Shipping increases its contribution to the pension fund to 13 million in x8. (Contributions are assumed to be made at the end of the year.) The x8 entries to recognise pension expense and record the company's payment to the pension fund can be combined as follows:

Pension expense and contribution in x8		
Dr. Pension expense (OE–)	16	
$\quad$ Cr. Cash (A–)		13
$\quad$ Cr. Accrued pension cost (L+)		3

Determining the company's pension liability

In the simple framework we used in calculating pension expense, the pension liability ('Accrued pension cost') a company reports represents the excess of pension charges in current and previous periods over cumulative payments to the pension fund. If cumulative payments to the fund are greater than cumulative pension charges, the company reports a pension asset ('Prepaid pension cost') on its balance sheet.

The company's pension liability or asset is mirrored in the funding position of the pension plan. A reported liability indicates – given the assumptions in our example – that the pension plan is underfunded by that amount (i.e. pension fund liabilities exceed pension fund assets). If a company reports a pension asset, this means its pension plan is overfunded. The link between the pension fund's and the sponsoring company's balance sheets is illustrated in the diagram below. The numbers are taken from our Lusitanian Shipping example.

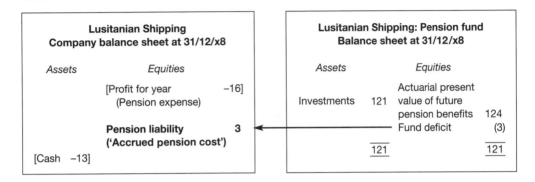

As we saw above, Lusitanian Shipping reports an increase in pension liability of 3 in x8. Since there is no pension asset or liability on the company's books at the end of x7, this is the balance of the liability at end-x8. The end-year pension liability of 3 is also the deficit in the company's pension fund at that date. Following a valuation at the end of x8, Lusitanian Shipping discovers the fund's investments have a fair value of 121 and its liabilities ('Actuarial present value of future pension benefits') are estimated at 124.

The fund has assets and liabilities of 100 at the start of x8. What are the reasons for the 21 increase in fund assets and the 24 increase in fund liabilities? Exhibit 16.3 shows the change in the fund's balance sheet during the year. From column 5 of the exhibit, we see that the fund's liabilities increase in x8 owing to a plan amendment (8), pension benefits earned by employees for service in the year (10), and the effects of time (interest) and changes in actuarial assumptions concerning wage inflation, labour turnover, and other factors (6.5 and 3.5, respectively). As for the fund's assets (column 4), these increase as a result of contributions to the fund (13) and returns generated on fund assets. Actual returns are 12, of which 7 are expected and 5 unexpected (described as 'actuarial gains on fund assets' in the exhibit). Pension payments to retirees (4) reduce both assets and liabilities. The net effect of these movements is that the fund's liabilities grow faster than its assets, resulting in a fund deficit of 3. (The movement in 'Fund equity' – the difference between fund assets and fund liabilities – is not shown for reasons of space.)

Exhibit 16.3 also shows how the changes in the fund's assets and liabilities (columns 4 and 5) directly affect the calculation of Lusitanian Shipping's pension expense (column 1) in the year. For example, the addition to the fund's liabilities as a result of the costs of current service and interest *increases* pension expense; the addition to the fund's assets arising from expected investment returns *reduces* it. The journal entry the company makes to record pension expense and contribution in x8 – set out above and shown also in the exhibit – summarises all the changes to the pension fund in the year (with the exception of pension payments to retirees, which is a transaction between the fund and retirees).

As mentioned above, the pension accrual or prepayment a company reports in its balance sheet indicates the funded status of its pension plan. Thus Lusitanian Shipping's accrued pension

Exhibit 16.3 Lusitanian Shipping: pension accounting by company and fund in x8
Base case: actuarial gains/losses recognised as they occur (amounts in millions)

	COMPANY			PENSION FUND	
	[1]	[2]	[3]	[4]	[5]
				Assets	**Liabilities**
			Prepaid/		*Actuarial PV*
	Pension		*(Accrued)*	*Cash and*	*of future*
	expense	*Cash*	*pension cost*	*investments*	*benefits*
	Dr./(Cr.)	*(Cr.)*	*Dr./(Cr.)*	*Dr./(Cr.)*	*Dr./(Cr.)*
Balance, start-x8			0	100	(100)
Pension expense:				Plan	
Past service cost	8			amendment 0	(8)
				Adjusted	
				balance 100	(108)
Current service cost	10				(10)
Interest on liabilities					
(6% × 108)	6.5				(6.5)
Expected return on					
assets (7% × 100)	(7)			7	
Actuarial losses on					
fund's liabilities	3.5				(3.5)
Actuarial gains on					
fund's assets	(5)			5	
Contribution to fund	–	(13)		13	
Journal entry	16	(13)	(3)		
Pension payments			–	(4)	4
Balance, end-x8			(3)	121	(124)
			'Accrued		
			pension		
			cost'	Fund deficit = 3	

Assumptions
- The fund has assets and liabilities of 100 at the start of x8.
- The plan is amended at the start of x8 to award employees pension benefits for past services. The cost of the amendment is 8.
- Pension benefits earned by employees for services in x8 ('Current service cost') are 10.
- The rate used to discount future pension benefits to their present value is 6%.
- Expected return on fund investments is 7%.
- The fund receives contributions of 13 from the company at end-x8 and invests them.
- It pays pensions of 4 to retirees at end-x8.
- Changes in actuarial assumptions (concerning wage inflation, labour turnover, mortality etc.) results in fund's estimated liabilities being 124 at end-x8 – hence 'Actuarial losses on fund's liabilities' of 3.5.
- The fair value of the fund's investments is 121 at end-x8. This implies actual returns exceed expected returns by 5 in the year – hence 'Actuarial gains on fund's assets' of 5.

cost of 3 at end-x8 reflects its pension plan's underfunding then. The company has contracted to provide pension benefits in the future and 3 million is the amount by which the expected cost of pension benefits earned by employees (and retirees) at end-x8 exceeds the resources earmarked to meet them. If a fund's assets exceed its liabilities, the pension plan is overfunded and the company reports a pension asset ('Prepaid pension cost'). The asset reflects the benefits to the company of making lower contributions to the fund in the future. In some countries, a company can realise the asset by terminating the existing plan and transferring accrued pension benefits – and fund investments *equal* to those accrued benefits – to a new plan.

Spreading the recognition of actuarial gains and losses

In the above example, we assume that Lusitanian Shipping recognises all actuarial gains and losses as they arise. This policy can lead to large variations in pension expense – and income – from year to year. For example, a company whose pension fund investments are weighted towards equities would have reported large actuarial gains and low or even negative pension expense (i.e. a pension credit) during the bull years of the 1990s and large actuarial losses and high pension expense in the stock market slump of the early 2000s. Many commentators claim the income statement effects are misleading. The income variability does not relate to a company's operations but is the result of its pension fund's investment decisions. Commentators also express doubts about recognising immediately actuarial gains and losses on pension fund liabilities. They argue there is so much uncertainty about the assumptions – concerning future labour turnover, inflation, life expectancy – underlying the present value calculations that it is unwise to recognise such gains and losses as they arise.

To overcome these problems, accounting regulators have introduced methods of spreading the recognition of actuarial gains and losses. One method favoured by international and US regulators is the **corridor treatment**. It works as follows:

- First, the firm determines the excludable portion of actuarial gains and losses. This is a band – or corridor – equal to the greater of 10% of the pension fund's assets or 10% of the fund's liabilities at the start of the year. Actuarial gains and losses are accumulated and netted at this date. If cumulative net actuarial gains or losses are within the corridor, they're not recognised in pension expense. If they exceed the limits of the corridor, only the *excess* is recognised, via an amortisation procedure, in pension expense. The corridor calculation is illustrated below:

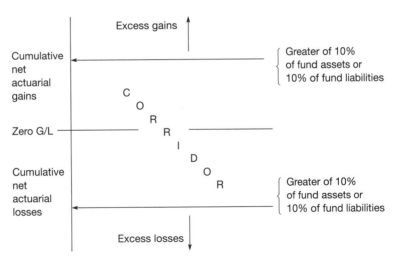

- Second, the firm amortises – or spreads – the excess net actuarial gains or losses. One accepted method of amortisation is to write them off on a straight-line basis over the expected average remaining working lives of plan participants. The amortised net gain or loss is then recognised as a component of pension expense.

We adapt our Lusitanian Shipping example to illustrate the corridor treatment of actuarial gains and losses. Suppose at the start of x8 the company has cumulative unrecognised actuarial gains of 20 (million). These are the result of higher than expected returns on plan assets in the past. The corridor limit is 12, i.e. the greater of 10% of fund assets (120) or 10% of fund liabilities (100). The excess gains of 8 are amortised on a straight-line (SL) basis over the average remaining working life of the company's employees. As Lusitanian Shipping's employees are, on average, ten years from retirement, this gives an amortisation charge of 0.8. The calculation is summarised below (amounts are in millions):

Cumulative actuarial gains at 1/1/x8	20
Corridor limit (10% of fund assets of 120)	–12
Excess gains	8
Average remaining working life of employees	10 years
Amortisation of actuarial gains (SL basis)	0.8

Given the net actuarial gains of 1.5 that arise in x8, the cumulative unrecognised gains increase to 20.7 million by year-end:

Cumulative actuarial gains at 1/1/x8	20
Actuarial gain in x8 (plan assets)	+5
Actuarial loss in x8 (plan liabilities)	–3.5
	21.5
Actuarial gain recognised in x8	–0.8
Cumulative actuarial gains at 31/12/x8	20.7

One consequence of the above treatment of actuarial gains and losses is that the pension asset or liability on a company's books no longer reflects exactly the funding position of its pension plan. This is evident in Lusitanian Shipping's case. Exhibit 16.4 builds on the example in Exhibit 16.3. Using revised data for x8, it shows how actuarial gains (and losses) are recorded off-balance-sheet and are recognised in the company's accounts over time.

The company's start-x8 pension liability is still zero. The actuarial gains of 20, though reflected in the pension fund's assets, are not recognised in the company's balance sheet. Instead, they're held off-balance-sheet in a memorandum account. Actuarial gains and losses arising in the year are accounted for in the same way. In this case, gains increase the fund's assets and losses increase its liabilities. However, the net gains of 1.5 in x8 are not recognised in the company's accounts that year but are transferred to the memorandum account. Only the amortised portion of the start-year gain is recognised in pension expense in x8. By recording changes in the fair values of pension fund assets and liabilities off-balance-sheet – and spreading them over time, Lusitanian Shipping reduces variability in both its income number (less variable pension expense) and its balance sheet (less variable pension liability – and shareholders' equity).

The company discloses in the notes to its x8 accounts the following analysis of the net pension liability at year-end (amounts in millions):

	End-x8	Start-x8
Funded plan		
Actuarial present value of future benefits	(124)	(100)
Fund's assets at fair value	142.4	120
Fund's assets in excess of fund's liabilities	18.4	20
Unrecognised actuarial net (gains)/losses	(20.7)	(20)
Net recognised liability	(2.3)	0

Thus the company's reported pension liability of 2.3 (million) at end-x8 is the net effect of a pension fund surplus of 18.4 and unrecognised net actuarial gains of 20.7 at that date.

Exhibit 16.4 Lusitanian Shipping: pension accounting by company and fund in x8
Revised case: amortisation of excess net actuarial gains/losses (amounts in millions)

	COMPANY			PENSION FUND		Memorandum account
	[1]	[2]	[3]	[4]	[5]	[6]
				Assets	**Liabilities**	
			Prepaid/		Actuarial PV	Unrecognised
	Pension		(Accrued)	Cash and	of future	net actuarial
	expense	Cash	pension cost	investments	benefits	gains
	Dr./(Cr.)	(Cr.)	Dr./(Cr.)	Dr./(Cr.)	Dr./(Cr.)	Dr./(Cr.)
Balance, start-x8			0	120	(100)	(20)
Pension expense:				Plan		
Past service cost	8			amendment 0	(8)	
				Adjusted		
				balance 120	(108)	
Current service cost	10				(10)	
Interest on liabilities						
(6% × 108)	6.5				(6.5)	
Expected return on						
assets (7% × 120)	(8.4)			8.4		
Amortisation of net						
actuarial gains	(0.8)					0.8
Contribution to fund	–	(13)		13		
Journal entry	15.3	(13)	(2.3)			
Pension payments			–	(4)	4	
Actuarial gains in year				5		(5)
Actuarial losses in year					(3.5)	3.5
Balance, end-x8			(2.3)	142.4	(124)	(20.7)
			'Accrued			
			pension			
			cost'			

Fund surplus = 18.4

Assumptions
- The fund has assets of 120 and liabilities of 100 at the start of x8. The company recognises no pension asset at this date.
- Actuarial gains and losses are recorded off-balance-sheet and are amortised, using corridor treatment, over the average remaining working life of employees (estimated at 10 years). Excess net actuarial gains at start-x8 are 8 (20 − (10% × 120)).
- The fair value of the fund's investments is 142.4 at end-x8. This implies actual returns exceed expected returns by 5 in the year.

Other assumptions are as in Exhibit 16.3.

International rules and practice

An international standard on the accounting for employee benefits was issued in the 1990s. The bulk of it deals with pension and other post-employment benefits under DC and DB plans.[7] In general, the standard follows the framework set out above. However, it contains detailed provisions that affect the way companies implement fair value accounting for DB plans. We list the more important ones below:

- *Benefit valuation method.* All companies must use a specific accrued benefit valuation method (known as the 'projected unit credit method') to measure pension liability and expense. The method incorporates expected wage inflation in the valuation of pension fund liabilities.[8]
- *Frequency of valuation.* A company should base the pension liability it recognises in the balance sheet on the current value of its pension fund assets and the present value of its pension fund obligations at the balance sheet date.
- *Discount rate.* In determining the present value of its pension fund obligations, a company should base the discount rate on the market yields at the balance sheet date of high quality corporate bonds (of similar currency and term).
- *Expected return on fund's assets.* This should be based on what the market expects an equivalent portfolio would earn over the entire period the pension obligations are being funded.
- *Past service cost.* Past service cost should be recognised in pension expense immediately if the additional benefits have already vested (i.e. they're not conditional on the employee's continued employment with the firm). If they haven't, the cost should be spread on a straight-line basis over the period to the vesting date.
- *Actuarial gains and losses.* A company can either recognise such gains and losses as they occur (our base case – *see* Exhibit 16.3) or amortise them using the corridor treatment (our revised case – *see* Exhibit 16.4).[9] It must apply the policy consistenty, however.

International rules on accounting for pension costs are of recent origin. As a result, national rules – where they exist – still have great influence. Summarised below are the main areas of difference between national and international rules in four countries where DB pension plans are common.[10]

Germany

Many plans are unfunded (they're known as 'book reserve' plans) but employees are protected since their benefits are insured. The calculation of pension cost is influenced by tax and legal rules. Companies determine current service cost using a projected benefit valuation method. Expected increases in salaries are not taken into account. The discount rate is fixed by law. Actuarial gains and losses are recognised immediately.

The Netherlands

Plans are funded. There are few rules governing the recognition and measurement of pension cost. A company can use either an accrued or a projected benefit valuation method – and can ignore expected wage inflation – in determining current service cost. It can recognise actuarial gains and losses immediately or defer them. Note that a Dutch plan is legally separate from the company. Employees are involved in its management – and in any decision to terminate it.

UK

Plans are funded. Under existing rules, companies have considerable discretion over how they measure pension liability and expense. The only requirement is that current service cost should be a substantially level percentage of payroll. New accounting rules – similar to IAS but requiring immediate recognition of actuarial gains and losses – have been proposed but their implementation has been deferred. However, companies must now disclose in the notes to the accounts the fair value of pension fund assets and the funded status of their DB plans.

USA

Again, all plans are funded. Accounting and reporting requirements correspond closely to international rules – in fact, US rules pre-date them and were the main influence on them. There are some unique features, however. For example, a company with an underfunded plan has to recognise a minimum pension liability in its balance sheet. This may involve recognising an intangible asset as an offset. However, the intangible cannot exceed unamortised past service cost. Any excess must be written off against shareholders' equity. The rationale for the pension intangible is that the firm enjoys a benefit – in the form of greater employee goodwill – equivalent to the cost of employees' enhanced pension rights.

As more countries align their national accounting rules with the international standard, cross-border differences in pension accounting should diminish and investors should find it easier to compare companies' pension costs and liabilities. Investors may face a moving target, however, as the international standard itself may be revised in the future. Its treatment of actuarial gains and losses is controversial. Critics argue that amortising such gains and losses using an off-balance-sheet mechanism means that the company's reported pension liability or asset does not reflect the actual funding position of the pension plan. Moreover, the average investor can't understand the accounting and loses confidence in the company's accounts, it's claimed. Supporters point out that the international standard reduces variability in income and balance sheet numbers – an important consideration when stock markets are volatile. As a result, companies are less likely to curtail or terminate their DB plans when the latter fall into deficit. In addition, investors can discover the actual funding position of a company's DB plans because it must disclose the assets and liabilities of its pension funds in the notes to the accounts. (We illustrate these disclosures in section 3.)

Employee share options

The practice of paying employees in the company's shares dates back to the nineteenth century and the early days of the joint-stock company. Using share options as a means of compensation is a more recent development, however. US companies began granting them to top executives in the 1950s. Their popularity grew in the 1980s and 1990s. Senior executives in non-US companies started receiving them in those decades and US start-up firms, especially in the information and biotechnology sectors, extended eligibility to all employees.

Employee share options (ESOs) are a controversial form of compensation. Although most compensation consultants support share-based pay on the grounds that it encourages employees to think and act like shareholders, many argue that companies should offer employees shares rather than share options. Share options may encourage employees to take excessive risks with company assets since the more volatile the price of the underlying share, the higher is the value of the option. Employee share options are a costly form of compensation for other reasons. Much of employees' wealth – pay, pensions and, more generally, the value of their human capital – is linked to the company they work for. Because employee share options are not tradable – so employees can't sell them to diversify their asset portfolios, their *value* to employees is less than their *cost* to the company. As a result, the company must offer more of them to yield the same benefit to employees as a tradable asset such as cash or company shares.[11] This has not deterred companies, especially in the USA, from awarding share options to employees, however. It's estimated that one-third of households in Silicon Valley in California hold them.

Mechanics of ESOs

All ESO plans share common features though they differ in detail. Employees who qualify for ESOs are each granted a certain number of options. These give them the right to buy shares of the company at a predetermined price ('exercise price') during a specified future period ('exercise term'). The number of options granted to an employee each year is restricted – in some cases to a multiple of salary. The exercise price (EP) is usually set close to – or equal to – the market price of the company's shares at the date of grant. National tax rules influence how the EP is set.

Under a 'fixed' ESO plan, employees must work for a period ('service period') before they earn the right to exercise the options. In the case of a performance-based plan, employees have to meet specified performance goals in addition before vesting can occur. The options may vest on one date ('cliff vesting') or in stages over time ('gradual vesting'). If an employee leaves the company before full vesting, he or she forfeits some or all of the options. Employees can exercise the options at any time between the vesting date and the date when they expire. Again, tax and investment rules influence the length of the exercise term. The key dates in a simple cliff-vesting share option plan are shown in the time line below:

Clearly, employees hope the share's market price will be above the exercise price at some point during the exercise term. Then they can realise a gain by exercising the options, acquiring shares and immediately selling them. (Of course, they can retain the shares in the hope of greater returns in the future.) If the market price remains below the exercise price throughout the exercise term, the options will expire unexercised.

ESOs are one form of share-based compensation. There are others. Here are three examples:

- *Share appreciation rights* (SARs). The employee is entitled to the increase in value on a specified number of share units over a specified period. The advantage of SARs is that employees do not have to buy any shares to capture the increase in share value. Thus they avoid the financing and transaction costs that would arise under an equivalent share option scheme.
- *Restricted shares.* The employee is granted shares directly or can buy them at a deep discount. Usually, ownership does not vest until certain performance goals have been met or a specified holding period has elapsed. (The term 'restricted' is also applied to schemes where legislation or the contract itself restricts the sale of the shares for a specified period.)
- *Phantom shares.* The employee receives notional shares as a reward for his or her performance. The shares entitle the holder to dividends and capital gains (in accordance with a predetermined formula) but carry no voting rights. Phantom shares are used by unquoted companies and in the divisions of large quoted firms.

In this section, we look at the accounting for employee share options (ESOs) only. However, companies apply similar recognition and measurement principles when accounting for other forms of share-based compensation.

Accounting issues

Accounting for ESOs – and other forms of share-based compensation – is contentious. People disagree on fundamental issues concerning their recognition and measurement. Preparers and users of financial statements are usually on opposing sides of the debate. We outline the two main areas of disagreement below.

Are ESOs a cost to the firm?

Most people accept that ESOs are a form of compensation to employees. Employees certainly view them that way. They hope to be able to exercise the options at a future date and enjoy a capital gain. The better the company performs (thanks, in part, to their efforts), the greater will be their gain. But on whom does the cost of the compensation fall? Many managers (and accountants) argue that the company doesn't incur an expense as there's no current or future outflow of corporate cash to employees. Instead, the cost falls on existing shareholders. They give up part of their share of the company's earnings when the options are exercised. They accept this earnings dilution because they expect corporate earnings to grow more rapidly in the future as a result of the option grant.

Investors and other users of financial statements challenge this reasoning. They note that the share option contract is between the company and its employees, not between shareholders and employees. The company agrees to grant employees rights to shares (ESOs) in return for labour services. The absence of any outlay of corporate cash is irrelevant. Companies engage in, and recognise in their accounts, many non-cash transactions. For example, start-up firms often pay for initial legal and banking services in shares rather than cash because of liquidity constraints.

How should the cost of ESOs be measured?

Some managers concede that ESOs are a cost to the firm but favour a method of valuation that effectively ensures that no cost is recognised in the company's accounts. There are two main ways in which the cost of ESOs can be measured – at their intrinsic value or at their fair value. The **intrinsic value** of a share option is the excess of the market price of the underlying share (MP) over the exercise price (EP) stated in the ESO contract. When MP ≤ EP, the intrinsic value is zero. Most companies organise their ESO plans so that, at the date of grant of the options, the exercise price is greater than or equal to the market price of the company's shares. Using intrinsic value as the measure of cost means that, when the options are granted, intrinsic value is zero and the company reports no compensation expense in its accounts.

An alternative measure of cost, favoured by users of financial statements, is the option's fair value. The **fair value** of an option comprises two elements: intrinsic value and time value. According to the widely used Black–Scholes option pricing model, **time value** captures the effect on an option's value of four main factors: the term of the option, the expected volatility of the share price, the expected dividends and the market rate of interest.[12] Other things being equal, the longer the term of the option, the more volatile the price of the underlying share, the lower the dividends or the higher the interest rate, the larger is an option's time value. Since time value is always positive – except at the end of the exercise term when it falls to zero, fair value can never be less than intrinsic value. Thus use of fair value in place of intrinsic value results in a positive compensation cost – and a cost figure that is always greater than that based on intrinsic value.

Some financial statement users favour basing the cost of compensation on the fair value of the services the company receives from its employees. They argue this provides a more reliable measure of fair value. The alternative approach, namely, basing the cost on the fair value of the ESOs granted, relies on option pricing models. The standard models assume that options are tradable and lapse only on expiry. ESOs, however, are non-transferable and lapse when an employee leaves (before vesting occurs) or fails to fulfil the performance criteria specified. But economists have modified the standard models to allow for the unique features of ESOs.

Fair value measurement illustrated

An example makes clearer the accounting for ESOs at fair value. (We assume fair value is determined by reference to the options rather than the services provided by employees.) Leeuwenhoek forms a company to develop a new type of microscope that he has devised. The company grants 20,000 share options to employees in January year 1. Each option gives the holder the right to buy one of the company's ordinary shares (par value €1). The exercise price is set at €7, the market price at the date of grant (so the options' intrinsic value is zero). The options vest in January year 4 at the end of the service period and, if unexercised, expire at the end of year 7.

The option's fair value is estimated at €3 in January year 1, using an option pricing model. The total cost of the options is therefore €60,000. The company doesn't recognise all this cost in year 1, however. Because the option award is for future employee services – and those services are assumed to be rendered evenly over the three years to the vesting date, the company allocates the cost on a straight-line basis over the period. (The cost can be spread on a different basis. For example, in the case of production staff, the costs of their compensation are usually matched with revenues on an output rather than a time basis.)

Recognition of annual expense, years 1 to 3
Dr. ESO-based compensation expense (OE–)	20,000	
Cr. Reserve – share options (OE+)		20,000

('Reserve – share options' is a temporary balance sheet account.) Suppose that in year 4, after vesting has occurred, the market price of Leeuwenhoek's shares is above the options' exercise price and employees exercise all their options. The company receives €7 a share in cash for each of the 20,000 shares it issues. The balance in 'Reserve – share options' is transferred into permanent shareholders' equity accounts when the shares are exercised or, if unexercised, when the options expire.

Exercise of options in year 4
Dr. Cash (A+)	140,000	
Dr. Reserve – share options (OE–)	60,000	
Cr. Share capital, €1 par (OE+)		20,000
Cr. Share premium (OE+)		180,000

If an employee leaves the firm during the service period and forfeits his or her options, the company reverses the expense recognition entry with respect to those forfeited options.

Reviewing the above entries, it appears that employee share options have no overall impact on reported shareholders' equity until they're exercised. (We ignore the tax effects of the options.) But closer inspection shows that by recognising the cost of ESOs in the accounts, a company reports lower profits – and lower distributable reserves.

International rules and practice

There are no international rules on accounting for ESOs at the time of writing (2002). The IASB plans to issue a standard on share-based payment in 2003/04. The standard will cover payment of *all* goods and services with equity instruments. The main features of the proposed standard are:

- The cost of share-based payment transactions should be recognised in the accounts. In the case of ESOs, the cost should be determined on the basis of their fair value, not their intrinsic value.
- Where the payment is for employee services, the cost should be measured by the fair value of the equity instruments (shares, share options) granted. In the case of ESOs, their fair value should be estimated using the Black–Scholes option-pricing model. For all other transactions, the cost should be measured by the fair value of the goods or services received. The IASB argues the latter is a more reliable measure of value where the transaction is with an outside party.
- Fair value should be estimated on the date the equity instruments are granted or, in the case of goods and non-employee services, on the date those goods or services are received.[13]

The new international standard is likely to have a major impact on corporate financial statements worldwide. Rewarding employees with shares or share options is common in the USA, especially among TMT (telecoms, media and technology) companies. The practice is growing in other countries, as tax rules are changed and employees are taxed when they exercise the options (or later when they sell the shares) rather than when the options are granted.

Currently, most companies follow US GAAP when measuring the cost of ESOs. Existing US rules permit either intrinsic value or fair value measurement of ESOs granted to employees. However, they require firms valuing such instruments at intrinsic value to disclose, in the notes to the accounts, the impact of fair value measurement on earnings and EPS. Until 2002, almost all companies recognised as compensation cost only the intrinsic value of ESOs. (Few non-US companies provided fair value disclosures.) In the wake of Enron's collapse and other corporate governance scandals that came to light in 2002, a number of leading US companies, including Citigroup and GE, announced their decision to account for such instruments on a fair value basis from 2003. But many US TMT companies remained resolutely opposed to fair value accounting and vowed to lobby against any change to US accounting rules, citing the dire economic consequences of fair value measurement (*see* Box 16.1).

BOX 16.1 'Economic consequences' of accounting standards

As with other regulations, accounting standards impose costs as well as confer benefits. In most cases, users of financial statements enjoy the benefits – fuller disclosure, clearer presentation, more relevant numbers – while preparers bear the costs. The costs of new standards include the direct costs of compliance – for example, the costs of altering the company's accounting system to produce the required information. They also include indirect costs which can be much more burdensome than direct ones. The most important indirect cost is the impact of a new standard on a company's contracts. It may alter key income statement or balance sheet numbers resulting in covenants in loan contracts being breached or higher bonuses being paid to employees under profit-sharing agreements. Managers are also concerned about the potential impact of a new standard on the company's cost of capital and on government decisions affecting the corporate sector (e.g. taxation). In addition, they have a personal interest in new standards since their wealth is linked – via profit-related bonuses – to the company's reported earnings and – via shares and share options – to its share price.[14]

Where managers perceive the expected costs of a proposed standard to be high, they will lobby to have it changed or withdrawn. Accounting standard-setting is a political as well as a technical activity: new rules can be implemented only if they enjoy majority support in society at large. So management use conventional lobbying techniques – letter-writing, representations through industry associations, and pressure exerted through elected representatives and government departments – to try to convince standard-setters that majority support for the proposed standard is lacking.

Among the most potent weapons that companies employ in their lobbying is the 'economic consequences' argument. The proposed accounting standard, it's claimed, will cause economic harm to an industry – or to the economy as a whole. US companies used the argument successfully in the early 1990s to thwart the FASB's attempts to require them to recognise as compensation expense the fair value of options granted to employees. They enlisted the support of Congress. The Senate even passed a resolution calling on the FASB to desist from pursuing its share option accounting standard because of the standard's 'grave economic

Box 16.1 *continued*

consequences particularly for business in new-growth sectors which rely heavily on employee entrepreneurship'. Senators were concerned that firms that made extensive use of share options to compensate employees would report sharply reduced profits (or increased losses) and this would impair their ability to raise capital for innovation and expansion.[15]

The 'economic consequences' argument has been employed in other countries. UK companies, through the Confederation of British Industry (CBI), lobbied the government in early 2002 to put pressure on the ASB, the UK standard-setting agency, to modify its standard on pensions. The standard requires companies to account for pension fund assets and liabilities at fair value and recognise the resulting fund deficit or surplus directly in equity. The CBI argued that the standard would make the shareholders' equity number more volatile, increasing the risk that a company would breach its loan covenants and, if assets fell below liabilities, making it technically insolvent. The UK government had its own concerns. A number of companies had announced they were closing their DB plans to new employees and introducing DC plans for them instead. (In addition to the new accounting standard, management cited the rising cost of supporting DB plans – retirees living longer, lower expected investment returns – as grounds for their decision.) DC schemes tend to be less generous than DB ones and the government feared that, as a result, retirees would rely more on state benefits in the future, increasing the burden on the government's purse. The ASB was prevailed upon in July 2002 to postpone the introduction of its accounting standard while the IASB reconsidered its own standard on the topic.[16]

The 'economic consequences' argument poses a challenge for accounting standard-setters. It involves them in a debate which lies outside their area of expertise. They have responded by commissioning academic research on the economic impact of proposed (and existing) standards. They're heeding the old maxim: forewarned is forearmed.

SECTION 3

Employment costs and financial analysis

Disclosures

Personnel, pay and pensions

Publicly quoted companies and larger private ones often state the size of their workforce in the annual report. In some countries, they're legally required to do so. Under EU accounting directives, all medium-sized and large firms must disclose:

- the average number of people employed during the financial year, broken down by category of activity; and
- staff costs for the financial year. This figure should be split between wages and social security costs. Pension costs within the latter should be separately identified (4th Directive, Art. 43(9)).

These are minimum required disclosures. Some EU member states go further. For example, Italian companies must disclose separately the annual cost of termination indemnities (and show the provision for them in the balance sheet). Large French companies give additional financial information about their employees in the *bilan social* (social report) which they must prepare each year and send to employees and shareholders alike. For example, the report reveals the payments made to temporary staff, the profit-related bonuses earned by employees and the costs incurred on staff training. (It also contains non-financial statistics on health and safety conditions and industrial relations.)

Companies following IAS must provide more detailed information about employees' pension and other post-employment benefits under DB plans. The international standard focuses on three areas: the company's pension liability, its pension expense and the key assumptions underlying the calculation of both. First, a company must reconcile its pension liability (or asset) to the net liability (or net asset) position of the pension fund. In particular, it must show, at the balance sheet date:

- present value of DB obligations (separating funded from unfunded liabilities);
- plan assets at fair value;
- unrecognised net actuarial gains or losses;
- unrecognised past service cost (non-vested benefits).

In addition, it must analyse the pension expense figure. We identified the main components in section 2 of the chapter (e.g. current service cost, past service cost, interest cost, expected return on plan assets, recognised net actuarial gains or losses). Finally, it should disclose the principal actuarial assumptions used in calculating the pension liability (or asset) and expense. These include the discount rate, expected rate of return on plan assets and expected rates of salary increase. Two other IAS-required disclosures are of interest to investors – and employees. The company must state how it recognises actuarial gains and losses (i.e. immediate recognition or spreading via the corridor treatment), and it must reveal how much of the pension fund's assets are invested in the company's own shares and bonds.

Exhibit 16.5 shows extracts from the note on employee benefits in the 2001 accounts of Roche, a large Swiss pharmaceutical company that follows IAS. The company incurred labour costs of SFr 7.4 billion in 2001. Most of this consists of wages and salaries (SFr 6 billion) and social security costs (SFr 0.7 billion). Pensions and other post-employment benefits under DB plans cost the company only SFr 264 million that year.

This last figure is the cost Roche *recognises* in its accounts. The notes reveal why it's so low. First, the company includes in the pension expense calculation an expected return on pension fund assets of SFr 761 million in 2001, which is around 7% of start-of-year plan assets of SFr 10,448 million. This more than offsets the interest cost in the year. The actual return on plan assets, however, was a negative SFr 1,334 million. Second, the actuarial losses the company sustains in 2001 – the decline in plan assets, the increase in plan liabilities – are not recognised immediately. According to the statement of accounting policies (not given in Exhibit 16.5), the company amortises only excess actuarial gains and losses outside the 10% corridor. The income statement benefit from avoiding recognising actuarial losses in 2001 is significant. The exhibit shows that Roche's funded plans moved from a net surplus (1,414) to a net deficit (–174) position between end-2000 and end-2001. The SFr 1.6 billion movement is reflected in 'Unrecognised actuarial (gains) losses' which also change by this amount – from gains of SFr 862 to losses of SFr 731 million at the end of 2001. The actuarial losses arising in 2001 (SFr 1.6 billion) represent 50% of Roche's group operating profits that year.

Thanks to its off-balance-sheet treatment of actuarial losses, Roche reports, on its balance sheet, a net *asset* of SFr 603 million with respect to its funded DB plans. Once *unfunded* plans are included, however, the overall balance is a net liability of SFr 1,837. (The SFr 2,440 liability on unfunded DB plans relates largely to health care benefits for its US employees.)

Share-based compensation

With no rigorous accounting standards (as yet) to guide them, investors must rely on footnote disclosures to assess the impact of share-based pay schemes on a company's accounts. Cost

[Note 8] Post-employment benefits (in millions of Swiss francs)

Most employees are covered by retirement benefit plans sponsored by Group companies. The nature of such plans varies according to legal regulations, fiscal requirements and economic conditions of the countries in which the employees are employed. Other post-employment benefits consist mostly of post-retirement healthcare and life insurance schemes, principally in the United States. Plans are usually funded by payments from the Group and by employees to trusts independent of the Group's finances. Where a plan is unfunded, a liability for the whole obligation is recorded in the Group's balance sheet.

The amounts recognised in arriving at operating profit for post-employment DB plans are as follows:

	2001	2000
Current service cost	362	333
Interest cost	685	675
Expected return on plan assets	(761)	(714)
Net actuarial (gains) losses recognised	(12)	2
Past service cost	5	3
(Gains) losses on curtailment	(15)	(1)
Total (included in 'Employees' remuneration')	264	298

The actual return on plan assets was a negative return of 1,334 million Swiss francs (2000: positive return of 1,175 million Swiss francs).

The movements in the net asset (liability) recognised in the balance sheet for post-employment DB plans are as follows:

	2001	2000
At beginning of year	(1,849)	(2,078)
Changes in Group organisation and Givaudan spin-off	–	84
Total expenses included in employees' remuneration (as above)	(264)	(298)
Contributions paid	177	174
Benefits paid (unfunded plans)	116	135
Currency translation effects and other	(17)	134
At end of year (as below)	(1,837)	(1,849)

Amounts recognised in the balance sheet for post-employment DB plans are as follows:

	2001	2000
Unfunded plans		
Recognised (liability) for actuarial PV of unfunded obligations	(2,440)	(2,423)
Funded plans		
Actuarial PV of funded obligations due to past and present employees	(9,575)	(9,034)
Plan assets held in trusts at fair value	9,401	10,448
Plan assets in excess of actuarial PV of funded obligations	(174)	1,414
Unrecognised actuarial (gains) losses	731	(862)
Unrecognised past service costs	46	22
Net recognised asset for funded plans	603	574
Asset (liability) recognised		
Deficit recognised as part of liabilities for post-employment benefits	(2,610)	(2,502)
Surplus recognised as part of other long-term assets	773	653
Total net asset (liability) recognised	(1,837)	(1,849)

The Group operates DB schemes in many countries and the actuarial assumptions vary based upon local economic and social conditions. The range of assumptions used in the 2001 actuarial valuations of the most significant DB plans . . . is as follows:

Discount rates	3–8%	Expected rates of return on plan assets	3–10%
Projected rates of remuneration growth	2–9%	Healthcare cost trend rate	5–10%

information is sparse. Outside the USA, few companies disclose the fair value of share options granted to employees. Companies following IAS give little value information about their equity compensation plans. They reveal the shares and share options in the plans at year-end and the movement in them over the year. In the case of share options, they also publish the average exercise prices for options granted and exercised during the year and for those outstanding at year-end. With this information, the investor can estimate the cash received – and receivable – from exercised (and exercisable) options.

Companies following US GAAP provide additional information about the cost of their ESOs under fair value accounting. In some cases, the effect on income is devastating. Yahoo! the US Internet business and consumer services company, is one such case. The company has separate share option schemes for employees and directors as well as an employee share purchase plan. Exhibit 16.6 contains key extracts from the note on share options and share compensation in its 2001 accounts.[17] Valuing options granted to employees at fair value (and recognising the cost over a four-year service period) results in additional compensation cost (net of tax) of almost US$900 million in 2001 (2000: over US$1.3 billion) and turns a small loss of US$92 million into a huge one of US$983 million.

Why does fair value accounting have such an impact in this case? First, the company grants a large number of options each year (e.g. 38 million in 1999, 27 million in 2000, 60 million in 2001). Second, the fair value of these options is high. Although the company does not disclose the options' fair value, it's possible to estimate it using the option pricing assumptions given. In the three years to 2001, the fair value of a Yahoo! ESO was at least 50% of the market price of its shares at the date of grant, thanks largely to the high expected volatility of the share price. Other US TMT companies with a history of generous ESO plans and volatile (and inflated) share prices report similar huge increases in compensation cost under fair value accounting. It's not surprising, therefore, that they have been so vociferous in their opposition to fair value measurement of ESOs.

Directors' compensation

Directors' remuneration is another issue that has become mired in controversy over the past decade. (The term 'directors' includes senior executives in this context.) In many countries, directors' remuneration has increased at a more rapid rate than average earnings during this time. This is due in part to the growing share of bonuses and other kinds of performance-related pay in directors' pay packages.

Companies vary in the information they disclose about directors' compensation in the annual report. Quoted firms in Anglo-Saxon countries provide fuller disclosure than those in other countries, thanks to stock exchange or government regulations. For example, the SEC requires domestic companies listed on a US stock exchange to provide a breakdown of the compensation of the CEO and the four highest paid senior executives (other than the CEO). The information disclosed covers annual compensation (salary, bonuses and perquisites), long-term compensation (e.g. share options granted, restricted shares awarded) and other compensation (e.g. pension contributions). The UK stock exchange demands that UK firms listed on the exchange disclose similar information for each of their directors.

Quoted firms in Continental Europe are less forthcoming about individual directors' pay but they're under pressure to reveal more. Under EU accounting directives, medium- and large-sized firms only have to disclose the *aggregate* pay and pension benefits of directors (and others with equivalent responsibilities) in the financial year.[18] However, a European Commission taskforce recommended in 2002 that such firms disclose the amount and composition of individual directors' pay, as part of its proposals to strengthen the governance of EU firms.[19]

Exhibit 16.6 Yahoo!: extracts from ESO disclosures in 2001 accounts

Note 8 STOCKHOLDERS' EQUITY
:

Stock option plans
:

Activity under the Company's stock option plans is summarized as follows (in thousands, except per-share amounts):

	2001		2000		1999	
	Options outstanding	Weighted average price per share	Options outstanding	Weighted average price per share	Options outstanding	Weighted average price per share
Balance, 1 Jan.	118,325	$49.83	124,790	$32.40	129,274	$10.60
Options granted	60,261	18.60	27,176	102.42	38,040	80.76
Options exercised	(15,317)	3.82	(23,795)	14.36	(33,732)	6.91
Options cancelled	(26,312)	60.45	(9,846)	63.93	(8,792)	11.09
Balance, 31 Dec.	136,957	39.22	118,325	49.83	124,790	32.40

:

Stock compensation

The company measures compensation expense for its stock-based employee compensation plans using the intrinsic value method. If the fair value-based method had been applied in measuring stock compensation expense, the *pro forma* effect on net income (loss) . . . would have been as follows (in thousands):

	Year ended December 31,		
	2001	2000	1999
Net income (loss)			
As reported	$ (92,788)	$ 70,776	$ 47,811
Pro forma	$(983,195)	$(1,264,987)	$(269,563)

:

Because additional stock options are expected to be granted each year, the *pro forma* disclosures are not representative of *pro forma* effects on reported financial results for future years. The fair value of option grants is determined using the Black–Scholes option pricing model with the following weighted average assumptions:

	Year ended December 31,		
	2001	2000	1999
Expected dividend	0.0%	0.0%	0.0%
Risk-free interest rate ranges	3.1%–4.8%	5.6%–6.7%	4.6%–6.1%
Expected volatility	79%	76%	71%
Expected life (in years)	3	3	3

(*Source*: Yahoo!, *Annual Report 2001*.)

Analysis of employment costs

This is a broad area. We look briefly at two issues – measuring labour productivity and assessing the impact of pension liabilities on financial leverage – which can cause problems for investors analysing company accounts.

Employee data and productivity analysis

Investors and others use employee data in financial reports to construct productivity ratios. The simplest is **sales per employee**. However, in its unadjusted form it is unsuitable for use in inter-company comparisons since it makes no allowance for differences in the following:

- *Employment patterns.* Some firms make heavy use of part-time labour while others rely exclusively on full-time staff. To make valid intercompany comparisons, the denominator (employees) should be expressed in terms of full-time equivalent (FTE) staff.
- *Outsourcing of activities.* Companies differ in the extent to which they contract out activities such as credit management or, more fundamentally, parts of the production process. Some car producers, for example, buy most of a vehicle's components from outside suppliers; others manufacture them in-house. An assembler – of any product – adds less value in its operations than an integrated manufacturer. Where there are likely to be large intercompany differences in 'value added' (output less the cost of purchased inputs) within an industry, a more appropriate measure of productivity is **value added per (FTE) employee**.

Productivity ratios like 'sales per employee' are not necessarily a good guide to cost competitiveness. High pay and benefits can more than offset high labour productivity, as some German manufacturers discovered to their cost in the 1990s. Thus investors and others monitor **labour cost ratios** as well as productivity ratios. Labour costs are expressed as a percentage of sales revenue or per unit of output. The latter is common in industries where output can be standardised (e.g. steel production in tonnes).

Pension liabilities and financial leverage

As we saw in Chapter 11, balance sheet measures of financial leverage usually relate interest-bearing debt to capital provided by shareholders (shareholders' equity plus minority interest). A company's obligations for pension and other post-employment benefits are operating liabilities – and thus not included in traditional measures of financial leverage. However, if a company has an underfunded DB plan and the deficit is large, investors may incorporate the unfunded pension liability in their calculation of its net debt. A key concern of investors – and of credit-rating agencies – is the additional cash contributions the company must make to reduce or eliminate the funding deficit. Such cash calls usually occur when the company's liquidity position is already weakened by difficult trading conditions. This was the experience of US auto, tyre and steel companies in 2002/03.

Summary

Companies reward employees in various ways. Compensation can be fixed or variable; in cash, in shares or in kind; current or deferred. The compensation package offered to an employee – the types of compensation and their relative weights – is the result of a balancing act. The firm wants to link pay to performance yet allay the employee's income anxieties, to reward individual achievement but also encourage team effort, to use the most efficient pay mechanisms yet take advantage of the prevailing tax and welfare systems in the country.

As a general rule, compensation should be recognised as a cost in the company's accounts as it is earned. In addition, it should be measured at fair value. These principles are sometimes difficult to apply, especially when the compensation is deferred and its amount is contingent upon uncertain future events. Two examples of such compensation are pension benefits under defined benefit plans and employee share options.

It is now accepted practice for companies (though not governments) to recognise the cost of pension benefits on an accrual basis. In the case of DB plans, accountants draw on the work of actuaries to estimate pension expense. However, they employ smoothing devices – by means of off-balance-sheet accounts – to spread the cost of large changes in the firm's pension liability from year to year.

Employee share options also pose measurement difficulties. As with DB pensions, assumptions must be made in order to value today a benefit that employees hope to receive in the future. Companies resist fair valuation of ESOs. Instead, they measure them at a lower intrinsic value. The unusual features of ESOs – the restrictive conditions (especially non-transferability) and, in the case of performance-based options, their contingent nature – render suspect the values produced by conventional option pricing models, it's claimed. The real reason for corporate opposition, however, is the effect of fair value accounting of ESOs on reported profits.

Disclosure of employee data – in terms of numbers and cost – permits investors to calculate labour productivity and cost ratios. Where a company's pension liability is significant, they adapt financial leverage ratios to incorporate it.

Problem assignments

P16.1 Cost of employee pay and benefits

D'Artagnan launches a personal bodyguard service at the start of x1. The company's name is 'Les Mousquetaires'. Its financial year ends on 31 December. The following three parts deal with payroll issues the company faces during the year. Assume each part is independent. All amounts are in euros.

Part A

'Les Mousquetaires' hires three employees: Athos, Porthos and Aramis. Set out below are the monthly pay, tax and benefits data for each of the three men in x1.

Salary	3,000
Income tax withheld	18%
Social security tax:	
Employer: % of salary	25%
Employee: % of salary	15%
Company-sponsored pension plan	
(a defined contribution plan):	
Employer contribution	75
Employee contribution	50
Supplementary medical care:	
Employer contribution	60

Required

Calculate the monthly salary expense and employee benefits expense of 'Les Mousquetaires' in x1. What is the net pay Athos, Porthos and Aramis receive in a typical month?

Part B

The salary Athos, Porthos and Aramis receive each month is based on the number of days worked. Assuming a month of 20 working days, this amounts to €150/day. 'Les Mousquetaires' grants them two paid days of holiday for each month (20 working days) of service. Unused days can be carried forward indefinitely and are paid off when employment ends.

In x1, the three each earn 24 days' paid holiday over the year. By the end of the year, each has used 20 days (Porthos to visit relatives in Brittany, Aramis a 'cousin' in Tours, and Athos – well, that's a mystery).

Required

Calculate the cost to 'Les Mousquetaires' of holiday pay earned during x1. What is the 'accrued holiday pay' liability at 31/12/x1? Ignore income tax and benefits.

Part C

'Les Mousquetaires' has a busy and successful first year. D'Artagnan decides the company will distribute a bonus to the three employees which will amount in total to 10% of its x1 after-tax profits. The corporate income tax rate is 35%. The bonus is tax-deductible.

Required

Complete the summary income statement for x1 set out below. What is the gross amount of bonus Athos, Porthos and Aramis will each receive?

'Les Mousquetaires'
Income statement for x1

Operating revenues	600,000
Operating expenses	–420,000
Profit before bonus	180,000
Profit-related bonus	———
Profit before tax	
Income tax (at 35%)	———
Profit after tax	———

Check figure:
Part C Income tax   59,155

P16.2 Company-sponsored pension plans: accounting and management issues

Despite their technical nature, the international rules on accounting for pension costs arouse strong feelings. Here's a sample of some of the criticisms.

(A) Reviewing the financial statements of companies with DB pension plans that have adopted IAS, an analyst remarks: 'The balance sheet figure for pension liabilities these companies report is meaningless. The smoothing techniques allowed under international rules mean that most of the actuarial gains and losses are off-balance-sheet. And there's no accounting or economic justification for this. After all, if a company has bank debt and the debt is increasing each year, it can't remove the increase from the balance sheet. Why should it be able to do this with pension liabilities?'

(B) A UK actuary queries the decision to value pension fund assets and liabilities at fair value at each balance sheet date. 'This doesn't give a true picture of the state of the pension fund since it only represents a snapshot of a fund's assets and liabilities on one day. People look at a pension fund deficit and assume that the company must inject cash of this amount into the fund to eliminate the deficit. But this isn't necessarily the case. The liabilities are long-term and the assets already invested in the fund may well be sufficient to cover them. For example, the aggregate deficit on UK corporate pension funds during the 2001 bear market was around £70 billion. However, if you assume fund assets earn a conservative stock market return – dividends and capital gains combined – of 6% a year, this deficit will be wiped out in a decade. It would be more sensible to value fund assets on a long-term actuarial basis, based on the present value of expected returns.'

(C) A director of a German company that has an unfunded pension plan complains that international standards are forcing German companies to introduce funded plans. 'Analysts say German unfunded plans aren't transparent. But where's the lack of transparency? We disclose a breakdown of our pension expense in the accounts. We also show the movement in the pension fund's liabilities over the year. Funding would be costly for us. We would have to hand over company cash to the fund each year. This would deprive us of flexibility – at the moment, we can choose to invest the cash destined for future pension payments either in financial investments or in our operations. As a result, we can finance our business more cheaply. And our employees are protected since, under German law, we have to insure against the risk of default on our pension liabilities.'

Required

Consider the above criticisms separately. According to accounting regulators, there are errors or misunderstandings in each of them. Identify them.

P16.3 Accounting for pension costs under a DB plan

Mirandolina Inns, a European chain of mid-price hotels, operates a DB pension plan for its employees. The company follows international standards when accounting for the costs of the plan. It has elected to use the corridor treatment to recognise net actuarial gains or losses in its accounts.

The company's pension fund has a deficit of 55 at the end of year 3. (All amounts are in € million.) The deficit has arisen because of the effect of the stock market decline on the value of plan assets. In addition, the fall in long-term interest rates has increased the present value of the pension obligations. Since unrecognised net actuarial losses amount to 50 at end-year 3, the company reports a pension liability of only 5 on its balance sheet then.

	In €m
Actuarial present value of pension obligations	(400)
Plan assets at fair value	345
Funded obligations in excess of plan assets	(55)
Unrecognised net actuarial losses	50
Net liability for funded obligations recognised	(5)

The following pension-related events occur in year 4. The cost of pension benefits earned by employees in the year ('Current service cost') is 15. The company contributes 10 in cash to the pension fund. It pays benefits of 8 to retirees. At the end of the year, the pension fund's assets have a fair value of 365 and the DB obligations of the fund have a present value of 433.

In calculating pension liability and expense, the company's actuaries assume a discount rate of 6.5% (the market yield on high-quality corporate bonds) and an expected rate of return on plan assets of 8%. The company estimates the average remaining working life of employees is 10 years.

Required

(a) Calculate Mirandolina Inns' year 4 pension expense and end-year 4 pension liability (or asset).

(b) Mirandolina Inns' management are concerned about the size of the pension fund deficit at the end of year 4. Fabrizio, the chief financial officer, is reviewing the pension scheme with a view to making changes to it in year 5. As input to this review, he asks you to determine the effects *on the company's year 4 accounts* if the following decisions had been made in year 4. Calculate the effect of each separately.

(i) The company contributes 15 in cash to the pension fund (instead of 10). The pension fund's assets at the end of the year are 5 higher (i.e. 370).

(ii) The company amends the plan at end-year 4 and *reduces* future benefits. The result is a negative past service cost of 5. This is recognised in income immediately.

Check figure:
(a) Pension expense, year 4 14.4

P16.4 Share-based compensation: a cost to the company?

Accounting regulators' attempts to require companies to recognise as an expense the shares and share options granted to employees have met with fierce resistance from the companies themselves. Management employ a variety of arguments. Here are two common ones.

(A) The finance director of a UK software company claims that requiring a company to recognise the cost of employee share options hits its earnings per share twice. 'EPS suffers a double whammy. The earnings figure is lower by the amount of the compensation charge and the number of shares outstanding, the denominator of the ratio, increases when the options are exercised. In reality, it's only the latter event that dilutes the interests of existing shareholders in the company's earnings.'

(B) The controller of a Belgian company questions whether recognising an expense from issuing shares as compensation to employees is consistent with the IASB's conceptual framework. 'In this framework, an expense is defined as an outflow of net assets. As I understand it, net assets flow out of a business when cash is paid out, an asset is consumed (depreciable fixed assets) or sold (inventory), or a liability is incurred. None of these events occurs when a company issues shares – or options on shares – to its employees as compensation. Since there's no outflow of net assets, the cost of share-based compensation can't be an accounting expense.'

Required

Consider each of the above arguments separately. Is it wrong – and, if so, why?

P16.5 Accounting for employee share options

Shareholders in Sif, a cosmetics company specialising in hair care products, agree to the establishment of a share option plan for employees at a general meeting in early x2. Up to 1.6 million €5 par shares may be issued under the plan.

The first tranche of 234,000 options (on an equivalent number of shares) is granted in early x2. The term of the options is ten years: it begins on the date of grant. Options may not be exercised before the end of a two-year period which begins on the day following the date of grant. This period is followed by an eight-year exercise period. The exercise price of the options granted in x2 is €25, equivalent to the average market price of Sif's shares on the 20 trading days prior to the issuance of the options. The fair value of the options at that date, based on the Black–Scholes option pricing model, is €10.5.

In early x4, 200,000 options are exercised when the market price of the shares is €31. The remaining 34,000 options lapsed in x3 because the employees left the company that year.

Required

(a) Assume Sif measures the cost of its employee share options at intrinsic value.
  (i) What is the compensation expense the company recognises in x2 with respect to the options granted that year?
  (ii) Show the entry the company makes to record the exercise in x4 of the options granted in x2.

(b) Repeat (a), assuming Sif measures the cost of its ESOs at fair value.

(c) A Sif manager wonders whether it's possible for the company to avoid recording compensation expense by hedging the exercise of the options. 'Suppose the company had bought back 234,000 of its shares at the time the options were granted in x2 and paid the market price then (€25) for them. The entry would have been:

Dr. Treasury shares (OE–)   €5,850,000
   Cr. Cash (A–)   €5,850,000

When the options are exercised, we reverse the above entry. Lots of companies do this. By buying back the shares at what is the exercise price, the company avoids having to buy them at a higher price later and incurring a loss as a result.'

Comment on the manager's idea. Can the company avoid recording compensation expense by buying back shares equivalent to the options granted? If not, why not?

P16.6 Analysis of pension plan disclosures I

Alice is puzzled by certain pension disclosures in Purdon Corporation's x3 accounts. Purdon is a (fictitious) US media company. 'Purdon's numbers are a complete wonderland to me', she says. 'Can you explain the information it provides about its defined benefit plans? I've highlighted the relevant note in its x3 accounts (*see* Exhibit 16.7).

'My first question concerns the company's income statement. If I understand it right, Purdon claims its DB plans generated net pension *income* in x3 – to the tune of US$290 million. (This is net of the cost of health-care and other post-employment benefit plans.) Pension income is a significant figure – around 10% of the company's before-tax profits. It appears to be due, in large part, to the income of some US$850 million the company earned on its pension fund investments that year. Yet, as the exhibit shows, Purdon's pension fund assets *declined* by US$930 million in x3. *How can Purdon earn a return of US$850 million on pension fund investments and report a decline in them of US$930 million in the same year?*

'The relationship between the pension fund and the company's balance sheet is the source of my next question. The numbers get curiouser and curiouser, the more I look at them. According to the numbers in the exhibit, Purdon's DB plans were in surplus by US$2.86 billion at the end of x3 – US$1.3 billion lower than a year earlier. Yet the company reports a net pension asset of US$2.4 billion at end-x3, a number that has grown by over US$400 million since end-x2. *How can Purdon's pension fund surplus decline year-on-year and yet the pension asset it reports on its balance sheet increase over the same period?*'

Required

Help Alice. Answer her two questions, using the information in Exhibit 16.7.

P16.7 Analysis of pension plan disclosures II

Toray Industries is a Japanese manufacturer of fibres, textiles, plastics and chemicals. The group reported worldwide sales of ¥1,016 billion (US$7.6 billion) and net profits of ¥3.8 billion in the year to 31 March 2002. It reported a pension liability of ¥115,671 million (and a pension asset of ¥67 million) on its end-March 2002 balance sheet.

Exhibit 16.8 contains extracts from the notes to the company's 2001/02 consolidated accounts. The company adopted a new national accounting standard on retirement benefits as of 1 April 2000. The standard brings Japanese accounting practice into line with IAS. According to the company, the net recognised liability represents 'the estimated present value of projected benefit obligations [i.e. including the effect of expected salary increases] in excess of the fair value of plan assets except that, as permitted under the new standard, unrecognised actuarial differences and unrecognised prior service cost are amortized on a straight-line basis over a period of 15 years' (*Annual Report 2001/02*, p.40).

The company also discloses that it contributed marketable equity securities to the retirement benefit plan in the year to 31 March 2002. The securities had a fair value of ¥22,005 million at the date of transfer.

Required

(a) Are Toray's retirement benefit plans over- or underfunded at 31 March 2002? What is the amount of the over- or underfunding?

Exhibit 16.7   Purdon Corporation: disclosures on DB pension plans in x3 accounts

Note 9   Pension benefits under defined benefit plans (extracts)

Effect on operations

In US$ mn	x3	x2
Service cost	173	153
Interest cost on benefit obligation	405	385
Expected return on plan assets	(848)	(736)
Amortization of transition asset*	–	(30)
Amortization of prior service cost	48	46
Net actuarial gain recognized	(188)	(160)
Pension income	(410)	(342)
Cost of other post-employment benefit plans	120	94
Pension income, net of cost of OPEB plans	(290)	(248)

Projected benefit obligation (PBO)

In US$ mn	x3	x2
Benefit obligation at 1 January	5,593	5,002
Service cost	173	153
Interest cost on benefit obligation	405	385
Plan amendments	–	227
Actuarial losses	174	190
Benefits paid	(382)	(364)
Benefit obligation at 31 December	5,963	5,593

Fair value of plan assets

In US$ mn	x3	x2
Fair value of plan assets at 1 January	9,752	9,848
Actual return on plan assets	(564)	252
Employer contribution	15	16
Benefits paid from pension fund	(382)	(364)
Fair value of plan assets at 31 December	8,821	9,752

Prepaid pension asset at 31 December

In US$ mn	x3	x2
Fair value of plan assets less PBO	2,858	4,159
Unrecognized prior service costs	269	317
Unrecognized net actuarial gain	(694)	(2,468)
Net pension asset recognized	2,433	2,008

Actuarial assumptions

At 31 December	x3	x2	x1
Discount rate	7.25%	7.5%	7.75%
Compensation increases	5.0	5.0	5.0
Return on plan assets	8.5	9.5	9.5

* 'Transition asset' is excess of plan assets over benefit obligation at date new US rules on pension accounting were introduced. Purdon's transition asset was fully amortised by end-x2.

Exhibit 16.8 Toray Industries: disclosures on retirement benefits in 2001/02 accounts

Note 8   Retirement Benefit Plan

The reserve for employees' retirement benefits as of March 31, 2002 and 2001 was analysed as follows:

	Millions of yen		Thousands of U.S. dollars
	2002	2001	2002
Projected benefit obligations	¥342,321	¥320,918	$2,573,842
Plan assets	172,687	154,322	1,298,398
	169,634	166,596	1,275,444)
Unrecognized actuarial differences	60,727	24,899	456,594
Unrecognized prior service cost	(6,697)	–	(50,353)
	115,604	141,697	869,203
Prepaid pension cost	67	37	504
	¥115,671	¥141,734	$ 869,707

The above table includes the amounts related to the portion subject to the Japanese Welfare Pension Insurance Law.

Net pension expense related to the employees' retirement benefits for the year ended March 31, 2002 and 2001 was as follows:

	Millions of yen		Thousands of U.S. dollars
	2002	2001	2002
Service cost	¥12,102	¥13,074	$ 90,992
Interest cost	10,493	10,342	78,895
Expected return on plan assets	(5,212)	(5,813)	(39,188)
Amortization of actuarial differences	1,667	–	12,534
Amortization of prior service cost	(420)	–	(3,158)
Amortization of transition amount	–	48	–
Net pension expense	¥18,630	¥17,651	$140,075

Assumptions used in calculation of the above information were as follows:

	2002	2001
Method of attributing projected benefits to periods of service	straight-line basis	straight-line basis
Discount rate	primarily 3%	3.5%
Expected rate of return on plan assets	primarily 3.5%	3.5%
Amortization period of prior service cost	primarily 15 years	–
Amortization period of actuarial differences	primarily 15 years	primarily 15 years
Amortization period of transition amount	–	1 year

(*Source*: Toray Industries, *Annual Report and Accounts for year to March 31, 2002*. Reproduced by permission of Toray Industries, Inc.)

(b) Toray reports 'Unrecognised actuarial differences' of ¥60,727 million at end-March 2002. Are these differences gains or losses? Suggest possible reasons why the differences more than doubled between end-March 2001 and end-March 2002.

(c) Compare Toray's retirement benefit disclosures with those of Roche (*see* Exhibit 16.5). What are the disclosures Roche makes but Toray doesn't that investors in Toray would find helpful, in your opinion?

Notes to Chapter 16

1　This can lead to major differences in the amount and composition of employment costs, even among countries with a similar per capita income. For example, according to a study of labour costs in the manufacturing sector, Denmark had the highest *wage* costs per hour worked (on average €19.57) in 2001 but Germany had the highest *labour* costs per hour worked (€27.33) that year. The reason? German firms sustained high non-wage costs (i.e. holiday pay, bonuses, social security contributions): at €12.58/hour, these costs were much heavier than those in other high-wage countries such as Denmark (€5.97/hour), Switzerland and the USA. (*See* Andersson, K.B. (ed.) (2002), *Industrial Outlook: Wages, Salaries, Labour Costs*, Confederation of Swedish Enterprise.)

2　For a fuller discussion of the link between compensation and motivation, *see* Milgrom, P. and Roberts, J. (1992), *Economics, Organization and Management*, Englewood Cliffs, NJ: Prentice Hall, Chapter 12.

3　In this chapter, we assume the firm expenses the cost of pensions (and other employee benefits) as incurred. In practice, the cost may be part of production costs and the firm capitalises it in inventory (or in fixed assets constructed for the firm's own use). How pension cost is calculated each period is not affected by its allocation, however.

4　Not all companies with funded plans make contributions to them each period. During the 1990s, many US and UK firms took contribution 'holidays'. The stock market boom in that decade resulted in pension funds that were heavily invested in equities reporting large surpluses.

5　The two types of actuarial valuation method are also applied to the calculation of other components of pension expense (e.g. past service cost).

6　Amortisation of actuarial gains – together with returns on fund investments – may outweigh the debit components of pension expense (current service cost and interest on plan liabilities), with the result that the company reports a pension *credit* instead of a pension expense in its income statement.

7　International Accounting Standards Board, *IAS 19: Employee Benefits*. The standard also deals with long-term *employment* benefits, such as long-service benefits, long-term paid leave and deferred compensation. These benefits are accounted for in the same way as pension benefits, except that past service costs and actuarial gains and losses are recognised immediately.

8　Under the Projected Unit Credit Method, each year of service gives rise to an additional unit of pension entitlement. Each unit is valued separately. The total pension benefit obligation is the sum of these units.

9　If a company has unrecognised net actuarial *losses* (or unrecognised past service costs), then in theory it could show a prepaid pension asset in its balance sheet. *IAS 19* limits the pension asset a company can report in these circumstances, however.

10　In countries with no tradition of company-sponsored pension plans for employees (e.g. France, Belgium, Italy), there are no accounting standards covering recognition and measurement of pension costs. Companies in these countries that offer DB pension plans to their employees apply US or international rules to account for the resulting costs.

11　For a full exposition of this argument, *see* Hall, B.J. and Murphy, K.J. (2002), Stock options for undiversified executives, *Journal of Accounting and Economics*, 33: 3–42.

12　For an explanation of the Black–Scholes and other option pricing models and their application, *see* Hull, J.C. (2002), *Options, Futures, and Other Derivative Securities*, 5th edition, Upper Saddle River, NJ: Prentice Hall.

13　*ED2: Share-based Payment*. The IASB published the exposure draft in November 2002.

14　For a fuller exposition of the costs (and benefits) of accounting standards, *see* Watts, R.L. and Zimmerman, J.L. (1986), *Positive Accounting Theory*, Englewood Cliffs, NJ: Prentice Hall.

15 For details of this and other examples of corporate lobbying of accounting standard-setting bodies in Australia, the UK, and the USA in the 1990s, *see* Zeff, S.A. (2002), 'Political' lobbying on proposed standards: a challenge to the IASB, *Accounting Horizons*, 16(1): 43–54.

16 The details in this paragraph are based on the following *Financial Times* reports in 2002: Peel, M. and Mackintosh, J., CBI to lobby government over [pensions standard] FRS17, *FT* 14 February; Peel, M. and Shrimsley, R., Darling [UK work and pensions minister] presses for rethink of controversial pensions rule, *FT* 4 March; Parker, A., Pensions accounting rule is set for delay, *FT* 2 July.

17 Yahoo! also discloses options outstanding and options exercisable at year-end at different exercise prices. The company's option 'overhang' is large: options outstanding at end-2001 represent 25% of the company's outstanding shares at that date.

18 4th Directive, Art. 43(12). *All* EU companies (including small ones) must report the amount and terms of any loans or guarantees to directors (Art. 43(13)). IAS also require disclosures about directors' pay and benefits. A director or key manager is a 'related party' to the company: he or she has 'the ability to control [the company] or exercise significant influence over [it] in making financial and operating decisions (*IAS 24: Related Party Disclosures*). Under the standard, all transactions between related parties, including payments for services, must be disclosed.

19 Winter Committee (2002), *A Modern Regulatory Framework for Company Law in Europe: Final Report of the High Level Group of Company Law Experts*, Brussels: European Commission. The committee also recommended that firms disclose their remuneration policy for directors in the annual report.

17

Accounting for corporate income taxes

INTRODUCTION

This chapter looks at the way companies account for their income taxes. It's said that taxes are, with death, the only things in life we can be certain of. Accountants add to corporate misery by making the accounting for them complicated.

We first discuss, in general terms, the framework of taxation of corporate income in industrialised countries. At present, countries differ in the way taxable profit is calculated, in the tax incentives available to companies, and in the treatment of losses and dividend payments. We outline these differences in section 1 of the chapter.

We then turn to the accounting for income taxes. As with other assets and liabilities, there are two major issues. First, when should a firm *recognise* the cost of income taxes in its financial statements? Second, how should it *measure* that cost?

It is now widely accepted that the cost of income taxes to the company is the tax impact, now and in the future, of the profit it reports in its annual accounts. This may not be the same as the income tax it pays in the year. When the tax authorities and the company calculate profit in different ways, the two numbers – tax payable and tax expense – diverge. Usually, this is because the tax authorities and the company value assets and liabilities differently. Such differences, though, are temporary. If the result is a delay in tax payment, the company reports a deferred tax liability. If taxes are paid early, it reports a deferred (or prepaid) tax asset. We devote much of part 1 and the whole of section 2 of the chapter to explaining how companies calculate income tax expense and determine their tax assets and liabilities under deferred tax accounting.

Investors monitor a company's tax figures closely. A company can increase its profits and cash flow by managing its tax affairs skilfully. We discuss in section 3 of the chapter the tax-related information investors look for in the accounts and a statistic they use, the effective tax rate, to assess a company's tax burden.

Core issues

Taxes on companies

Corporate income taxes are an important source of government revenue in industrialised countries. They are not the major source, however. Among developed countries, for example, only 5–10% of tax receipts comes from corporate income taxes while 20–30% comes from personal income taxes.[1]

Income taxes are one of several taxes a company must bear. The range and extent of taxes and levies on business vary from country to country. Some countries levy a tax on the transfer of assets in certain types of transaction (**transfer tax** or **stamp duty**): one example is the initial and subsequent issues of shares by the company. In many EU countries a firm must pay an annual tax on the assessed value of its property (**real estate** or **property tax**). Countries with a federal structure impose taxes at the local as well as national level: for example, German companies pay a municipal trade income tax to help finance municipal and regional (*Länder*) governments. More significant in national government revenue terms is the **value added tax** on domestic supplies of goods and services and imports. Among developed countries, around 30% of government revenues comes from this source.

Taxation of corporate income: general framework

In principle, the taxation of a company's income for a period is simple. The tax authorities first decide what is the taxable entity. In many cases, the taxable entity is the same as the legal entity.[2] (For simplicity, we assume the entity is resident and taxable in only one country.)

The tax authorities next calculate the entity's **taxable profit** in the year. In essence, taxable profit is calculated as follows:

$$\begin{array}{l} \text{Taxable revenues} \\ - \underline{\text{Tax-deductible expenses}} \\ \underline{\text{Taxable profit}} \end{array}$$

They then determine its tax liability by applying the corporate income tax rate (or rates) to taxable profit:

$$\text{Taxable profit} \times \text{Income tax rate} = \text{Income tax payable}$$

The company settles its income tax liability at the end of the year.[3]

Complications now set in. We list them below and discuss each briefly.

1 How do tax authorities determine taxable revenues and tax-deductible expenses?
2 How does a company's dividend policy affect its tax bill and that of its shareholders?
3 What happens if a company reports operating losses?
4 In what ways do tax-based incentives reduce a company's tax liability?

Our examples focus on EU member states and are based on tax rules in force in 2002.

Calculation of taxable profit

As a result of the 4th Directive, companies in the EU should now calculate **accounting profit** (the before-tax income number reported in the external accounts) independently of taxable profit. This is known as 'separate reporting'. Note, however, that in countries with a uniform reporting tradition (i.e. equivalence of accounting and taxable profits), the provisions of the national tax code still influence strongly the way accounting profit is calculated.

How does separate accounting work? The Directive requires that a company's accounts give a 'true and fair view' of the performance and position of the firm. Thus a company determines accounting profit according to 'fair presentation' principles as laid down in national (and international) accounting standards. It can then calculate taxable profit by adjusting accounting profit to meet the requirements of the tax code. In sum:

Taxable profit = Accounting profit +/− Tax code adjustments

Nature of tax code adjustments

The adjustments tax authorities make to accounting profit fall into two categories:

1 those which cause accounting and taxable profits to differ *permanently*; and
2 those which cause accounting and taxable profits to differ *temporarily*.

Permanent differences arise, in the main, because the government exempts certain revenues from tax and disallows a tax deduction for certain expenses. The latter is a more common occurrence. For an expense to be tax-deductible, a company must usually show that it is incurred 'wholly or exclusively' for the purposes of its business. This is the condition laid down by the UK tax authorities; similar phrasing is to be found in other countries' tax codes. But how is it applied? Most tax authorities agree that no tax relief should be provided for expenditures incurred because the firm breaks domestic law (e.g. fines, bribes). However, they disagree about the treatment of expenditures that break *foreign* law. And they question whether business entertainment expenses and contributions to charities should be tax deductible: are these incurred 'wholly and exclusively' for the purposes of the company's business?

Temporary differences arise because government and firms disagree about when (rather than whether) certain revenues and expenses should enter into the calculation of income. Bad debts and depreciation are two examples of important business costs where the tax authorities often substitute their own figures in place of the company's. The reasons are different. In the case of bad debts, governments suspect companies of trying to defer income (and thus tax) by overproviding for estimated bad debts. Thus, in many countries, a general provision is disallowed; only a specific provision (based on, say, an ageing analysis of receivables) or write-offs of known bad debts are tax-deductible.

By contrast, the tax deduction for depreciation is often more generous than that suggested by the economics of the business. Tax authorities allow companies to depreciate an asset at a faster rate than the rate at which the asset's services are consumed. This is the case in countries where the option of depreciating certain classes of asset at an accelerated rate for tax purposes applies to *all* assets within that class. Exhibit 17.1 provides an illustration.

Thus a French company purchasing plant which, for tax purposes, has a five-year life can apply an 'acceleration factor' of 1.75 and depreciate it (and all similar equipment) at a declining balance rate of 35%. Government intentions here are plain: to lower the after-tax cost of new fixed assets and thereby stimulate investment.

In many European countries (especially those with a uniform reporting tradition), the depreciation rates a firm uses in its tax accounts are often the result of negotiation with the tax authorities. Hence, in Exhibit 17.1, the straight-line (SL) rate for each asset class and the acceleration factor are usually shown as a range – save in the UK where negotiation of depreciation rates is rare.

We look at the accounting implications of permanent and temporary differences later in the chapter.

| Exhibit 17.1 | Typical tax depreciation rates by asset type, in selected EU member states |

(a) SL rate (%)

Asset class	France	Germany	Italy	Netherlands	Spain	UK*
Commercial buildings	2–5	3	3–5	2–4	2–3	4
Machinery	10–20	6–10		10–20	8–12	
Office equipment	5–20	12.5–33.3	10–40	10–33.3	10–25	25
Motor vehicles**	20–25	11–16		20	16	[DB]

* 4% SL for industrial buildings, 25% DB for general plant and equipment and 6% DB for long-life plant (>25 years).
** Special rules for cars in certain countries.

(b) Accelerated depreciation on plant and machinery*

	France	Germany	Italy	Netherlands	Spain	UK
Method	DB	DB	SL	DB	DB	***
Factor**	1.25 to 2.25	3.0 (max. 30%)	2.0 (first 3 years)	varies by asset class	1.5 to 2.5	

* Optional. DB = declining balance; SL = straight-line. Both the Netherlands and Spain permit firms to use sum-of-years'-digits (SoYD) method to calculate accelerated depreciation.
** To find the DB depreciation rate (Italy: the accelerated SL rate), apply the factor to the SL rate in (a). The factor varies depending on asset life and/or class of asset.
*** Certain types of company can deduct first-year allowance (of up to 100% of asset's cost) for certain types of asset. DB rate of 25% per year is applied to any remaining balance.

(*Source*: International Bureau of Fiscal Documentation (2002), *The Taxation of Companies in Europe*, Amsterdam: IBFD.)

Taxable profit and transfer pricing

A company with operations in more than one country faces a further problem – the allocation of its taxable profit among various tax jurisdictions. Tax authorities are suspicious of the prices companies charge for *internal*, cross-border transfers of goods and services. Countries with high tax rates fear that outward charges are set low and inward charges set high in order to divert taxable profits to low tax jurisdictions. Most tax authorities require internal transfers to be priced on an 'arm's length' basis (i.e. as if the good or service were sold to an independent party). In addition, they provide guidance as to how an arm's length price should be calculated. This is of help to firms producing specialised goods and services and other products for which there is no active market.

Tax treatment of dividends

Countries differ in their tax treatment of dividends. Dividends, you'll recall, are for legal and accounting purposes a distribution of profits rather than an expense. There are two important consequences. First, companies have an incentive to issue debt rather than equity because interest is a tax-deductible expense but dividends are not.[4] Second, in the absence of tax relief on dividend income, distributed profits are more heavily taxed than retained profits because they are taxed twice – once in the hands of the company and again in the hands of the shareholder. Most EU countries now provide at least partial protection against the double taxation of dividends.

The protection can take different forms. Under an **imputation system**, shareholders offset part or all of the corporate income tax paid on distributed profits against their individual income tax liability. In effect, income tax is *imputed* to the dividend the shareholder receives. Belgium, Denmark and France use this system. Countries differ in how they implement it. In some jurisdictions, shareholders may receive a tax credit for tax withheld when a dividend is paid: this credit is refundable if, for example, the shareholder is tax-exempt (e.g. a charity or pension fund). Under a **split-rate system**, there are two statutory corporate income tax rates: a higher rate that applies to retained profits and a lower rate that applies to distributed profits. Germany's pre-2001 tax regime was a combination of split-rate and imputation systems.

By contrast, under the **classical system**, distributed profits are in effect taxed twice, once at the corporate level (when the company declares taxable profits) and again when its shareholders receive a dividend. However, the effect of double taxation is mitigated if shareholders can exclude from taxable income part or all of the dividend they receive. This relief is usually applied differentially: it's greater for *corporate* than for individual shareholders. In fact, in many countries, dividends paid by a (domestic) subsidiary to its parent are tax-exempt. In recent years, changes in national tax regimes have seen a shift from imputation to classical systems. Germany switched in 2001, Italy did so in 2003, whereas the Netherlands and the USA have long had such a system.

An example illustrating the imputation and classical systems of taxation is given in Exhibit 17.2.

Exhibit 17.2 **Tax treatment of dividends: imputation and classical systems contrasted**

Assumptions
- Country A has imputation system. Shareholders receive tax credit of 36% of gross dividend (i.e. dividend + associated tax credit).
- Country B has classical system. There is no dividend relief in personal tax calculation.
- Corporate tax rate is 36% in both A and B.
- Two shareholders, one in A, the other in B, each receive dividend of €100 from a domestic company. Each has marginal personal tax rate of 40%.

Total tax on dividend of €100

	Country A (imputation)	Country B (classical)
Corporate income tax*	€56.25	€56.25
Personal income tax:		
Gross dividend**	€156.25	
Net dividend		€100
Income tax at 40%	62.5	40
– Tax credit	−56.25	–
Personal income tax due	6.25	40
Total tax on dividend	€62.5	€96.25
Tax as % of underlying income	$\dfrac{62.5}{156.25} \times 100$	$\dfrac{96.25}{156.25} \times 100$
	= 40%	= 61.6%

Notes:
 * Since dividends are a distribution of after-tax profits, in order to pay dividend of 100, company needs before-tax profit of 156.25 (100/(1 − 0.36)), assuming tax rate of 36%. Thus corporate income tax borne by dividend is 56.25.
 ** Under imputation system, shareholder reports gross dividend (i.e. dividend + associated tax credit) in tax return.

In our example, country A has a full imputation system: shareholders can claim a credit for all the corporate income tax a dividend has borne. Country B has a classical system with no tax relief on dividends. To keep our example simple, the corporate tax rate is the same (36%) in both countries. So too is the marginal personal tax rate (40%).

A dividend bears both corporate and personal income tax. We assume each company pays a dividend of 100. Given the corporate tax rate of 36%, the income necessary to support it is 156.25 (100/(1 − 0.36)). Under the imputation system in country A, the corporate and personal tax on that income is 62.5 or 40% of the underlying income. This is the sum of 56.25 of corporate income tax (36% × 156.25) and 6.25 of additional personal income tax ((40% − 36%) × 156.25). Under the classical system in country B, the total tax is 96.25 or 61.6% of the underlying income. This is made up of 56.25 of corporate income tax and 40 of additional personal income tax (40% × dividend of 100).

In our example, the tax burden on dividends is considerably higher under the classical system. In practice, the tax penalty is likely to be smaller. One reason is that governments in countries with classical systems set lower corporate and personal tax rates to offset the effect of double taxation.[5]

Tax treatment of losses

Governments usually give tax relief to companies which report operating losses. Countries differ, however, in the form and extent of the relief. Most EU member states permit companies to *carry forward* operating losses to set off against future years' profits. Some countries set a time limit – for example, five years in France and Italy; fifteen years in Spain. In many countries (the Netherlands, Sweden, the UK), there is no time limit.

Of greater potential benefit in present value terms is the right to *carry back* operating losses to set off against past years' profits. Fewer EU countries offer this concession and the period of carryback is restricted – usually to a maximum of three years (France, the Netherlands).

In many EU countries, group relief is available. A company and its domestic subsidiaries can elect to file a single tax return. This means that the operating losses of one subsidiary can be set off against the taxable income of another. As a result, the group can utilise losses earlier than if each subsidiary is assessed to tax separately.

Tax-based incentives

One of the major obstacles to tax harmonisation in the EU is governments' reluctance to accept restrictions on their right to use fiscal policy to influence companies' economic behaviour. At present, EU member states use tax measures to promote certain activities (e.g. investment in research and development) or certain regions (e.g. creation of new jobs in areas of high unemployment). These tax measures can take many forms – accelerated depreciation, tax credits, even tax holidays.

Spain, for example, offers a variety of tax-based incentives. A company undertaking research receives a 30% tax credit for such expenditures, i.e. it can deduct from its annual income tax liability ('credit against' the government's tax receivable) 30% of research outlays in the year. (This is for unchanged spending year-on-year: *increases* attract a 50% tax credit.) Investments in certain export activities, 'green' investments (anti-pollution devices, alternative energy sources), and expenditures on financing employees' continuing education also attract tax credits. Any unused tax credits can be carried forward and set off against future tax liabilities (for 15 years, in the case of research tax credits). The government also gives an incentive – in the form of a reduction in the corporate income tax rate – to firms that invest in designated Spanish regions or territories.

Recent changes in corporate taxation in the EU

The 1980s and 1990s saw major changes in the taxation of EU companies. Tax rates were lowered. The basic rate of corporate income tax (at national or federal level) is now less than 40% in all member states.[6] At the same time, subsidies and tax incentives favouring certain industries and regions were reduced. The overall corporate tax burden didn't fall but its distribution changed. It became, in the economists' phrase, more neutral.

Differences in corporate tax regimes within the EU are still significant. The European Commission believes they influence companies' investment decisions and distort competition. Its attempts to narrow those differences have met with only modest success to date. Some progress has been made. A parent–subsidiary directive in 1990 abolished double taxation of profit distributions between group companies in different member states. In a 1997 Code of Conduct, member states agreed not to engage in harmful tax competition – for example, by offering very low tax rates to foreign companies investing in 'greenfield' projects in the country. But the Commission has not yet persuaded member states to harmonise the main components of corporate income tax: tax rates, the calculation of taxable profit and the scheduling and collection of tax payments, as was recommended by a committee of experts in 1992.[7]

Putting corporate taxes in the EU on a common footing is likely to be a slow process. Any decision on taxation requires the unanimous approval of member states. Governments do not want to cede – or appear to cede – sovereignty over fiscal policy. However, the courts may achieve what politicians and bureaucrats cannot. In a number of recent cases covering transfer pricing, thin capitalisation, cross-border loss relief and controlled foreign companies, the European Court of Justice has struck down aspects of individual member states' tax regimes on the grounds that they do not comply with EU treaties.[8]

Exhibit 17.3 summarises the main features of corporate income taxation – from tax systems to tax rates – in the larger EU states at the end of 2002 and contrasts them with those in the Canada, USA and Japan. The exhibit illustrates the diversity of current corporate tax regimes *within* the EU as well as between EU and non-EU states.

The cost of income taxes: recognition issues

Accounting profit and taxable profit

Most business people view the corporate income tax as a regular cost – a cost they would rather avoid but one which, in most countries, is an inevitable consequence of profitable operations.[9] In this section we ask: how do companies account for this cost in their published accounts? We do not discuss, other than in general terms, how the company computes its tax liability. This requires detailed knowledge of national tax laws and is beyond the scope of this book.

The accounting for income taxes is not straightforward because, as we saw earlier, the (before-tax) profit a company reports to shareholders (its accounting profit) is not necessarily the same as the profit figure the tax authorities use to determine its tax liability (taxable profit). In separate reporting countries, a company calculates accounting profit according to national (or international) accounting rules and conventions; the tax authorities calculate its taxable profit according to the national tax code. Thus the tax return and the published accounts have the following form:

Tax return		*Published accounts*	
Taxable revenues	xx	(Accounting) revenues	xx
Tax-deductible expenses	xx	(Accounting) expenses	xx
Taxable profit	xx	*Profit before tax (accounting profit)*	xx

Exhibit 17.3 Corporate income tax in G7 countries: key features as of 2002

	Tax system[1]	Corporate tax rate standard[2] %	Corporate tax rate average[3] %	Net operating losses Carry-back (years)	Net operating losses Carry-forward (years)
France	I	33.33	35.43	3	5
Germany	C	25	38.38	1	Unlimited[4]
Italy	I[5]	36	40.25	0	5
UK	PI	30	30	1	Unlimited
Japan	PI	30	42.6[6]	1	5
Canada	PI	25[7]	39.7	3	7
USA	C[8]	35	39.3	2	20

Notes:
1 C = classical; I = imputation; PI = partial imputation (partial tax credit on dividends to individual shareholders; dividends to corporate shareholders usually tax-exempt).
2 Basic national or federal tax rate.
3 Includes temporary surcharge and (typical) state, provincial or local income tax.
4 Reduced to 7 years from 2003.
5 Replaced by classical system from 2003. Standard tax rate reduced to 33%.
6 Based on tax burden on Tokyo-based company. Includes inhabitants and enterprise taxes.
7 Net of provincial abatement. Reducing to 23% in 2003 and 21% in 2004.
8 US government proposed in 2003 to reduce personal income tax rate on dividend income.

(*Sources*: International Bureau of Fiscal Documentation (2002), *The Taxation of Companies in Europe*, Amsterdam: IBFD; PricewaterhouseCoopers (2002), *Corporate Taxes Worldwide Summaries*, London: PwC.)

Accounting and taxable profit differ if:

1 a revenue or expense is recognised in the tax return and published accounts in different periods;
2 the tax authorities disallow an expense or exempt a particular source of revenue from tax; or
3 items are treated as revenues/gains or expenses/losses in the tax return which are not recognised as such in the published accounts.

Type 1 differences are timing (or temporary) differences; types 2 and 3 are permanent differences.

An example will help here. Lazarillo is always hungry so he decides to open a restaurant. At the start of year 1, he forms a company, raises capital of 50 and invests it in a building, equipment and materials. We assume that all these assets, with the exception of kitchen equipment, are accounted for in the same way for tax and book purposes. The company depreciates kitchen equipment – which costs 20 and has a four-year expected life – on a straight-line basis in its published accounts (5/year) but on an accelerated basis in its tax return (8 in the first year and 6, 4 and 2 in the remaining three years). The company generates revenues of 100 and incurs expenses, other than depreciation on the equipment, of 85 in year 1. Exhibit 17.4 shows the calculation of Lazarillo's accounting and taxable profits for year 1.

In its first year of operations, Lazarillo Company reports book and tax profit *before* depreciation of 15. Because of the difference in calculation of depreciation, profit *after* depreciation is not the same. Accounting profit is 10 (15 − 5); taxable profit is 7 (15 − 8). Note that the reason for the difference between accounting and taxable profit is a timing difference: depreciation of 3 (8 − 5) is deducted from tax revenues in year 1 but will not be deducted from book revenues until a later year.

Exhibit 17.4 Taxable and accounting profit contrasted: Lazarillo Company's year 1 accounts

Assumptions
- Initial net assets 50, of which kitchen equipment 20.
- Kitchen equipment (KE) has four-year life and zero salvage value.
- Book depreciation: SL basis (5/year).
- Tax depreciation: accelerated basis (8, 6, 4, 2).
- Revenues 100; expenses, other than KE depreciation, 85.

Year 1 accounts

Statement of (pre-tax) income for year 1

Tax return		Published accounts	
Taxable revenues	100	(Accounting) revenues	100
Tax-deductible expenses,		(Accounting) expenses, save	
save KE depreciation	−85	KE depreciation	−85
Pre-depreciation profit	15	Pre-depreciation profit	15
Tax depreciation		Accounting depreciation	
on kitchen equipment	−8	on kitchen equipment	−5
Taxable profit	7	Accounting profit	10
		(Profit before tax)	

(Pre-tax) balance sheet at end of year 1

	Tax return	Published accounts
Net assets, except kitchen equipment	45	45
Kitchen equipment:		
Cost	20	20
Less: Accumulated depreciation	−8	−5
Kitchen equipment, net	12	15
Total net assets	57	60

Income tax expense under taxes payable accounting

The key accounting issue is: how should a company determine the cost of income taxes in the year? Two ways of calculating it have been proposed. Under **taxes payable accounting**, *the company records as expense (or credit) the income tax currently payable (or refundable) as a result of its activities in the year.* To find this amount, it applies the current tax rate to its taxable profit (or tax loss) for the year. For example, Lazarillo Company reports taxable profit of 7 in year 1. If the corporate income tax rate is 30%, it recognises a tax expense and liability of 2.1 that year. Exhibit 17.5 shows the link between its tax and published accounts.

Taxes payable accounting (TPA) is flawed. As can be seen from Exhibit 17.5, income tax expense is based on taxable, not accounting profit. It is thus a function not only of the profit of the period but also of the tax concessions the company receives (or tax penalties it bears). If these concessions or penalties are temporary, then income tax expense under TPA does not accurately reflect the total tax cost of the company's current profits. Lazarillo's low tax rate (tax expense/profit before tax) of 21% in year 1 is unsustainable. It arises because of the tax benefit from accelerated depreciation. But this is a temporary benefit. The total amount that the company can deduct from revenues over the equipment's four-year life is the same in both the published accounts and the tax return: it is the asset's cost of 20. If the tax deduction for depreciation

Exhibit 17.5 Lazarillo Company: year 1 income tax expense under taxes payable accounting

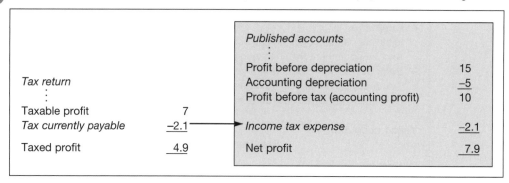

is larger in year 1, it will be smaller in, say, year 3 or 4. This will increase Lazarillo's tax bill in those years. This is the future tax cost of Lazarillo's year 1 profits which TPA ignores.

Income tax expense under deferred tax accounting

In view of the weaknesses of TPA, accountants devised an alternative approach. *Under* **deferred tax accounting**, *the company records as expense (or benefit) the tax impact, now and in the future, of its activities in the period.* In this case, income tax expense (or benefit) has two components:

1 the income tax currently payable or refundable (as in taxes payable accounting) – known, in this case, as **current tax expense** (or **benefit**); and
2 the future tax impact of the current year's accounting profit or loss – or **deferred tax expense** (or **benefit**).

Exhibit 17.6 shows the calculation of Lazarillo's income tax expense in year 1 under deferred tax accounting (DTA).

Lazarillo's total tax expense in year 1 under DTA is 3 – in this case, the tax rate (30%) applied to the company's accounting profit (10). Of the total expense, 2.1 is tax that is currently payable (current tax expense) and 0.9 is tax that is payable later (deferred tax expense). Lazarillo records the tax deferral of 0.9 as a 'deferred tax liability' on its balance sheet.

Exhibit 17.6 Lazarillo Company: year 1 income tax expense under deferred tax accounting

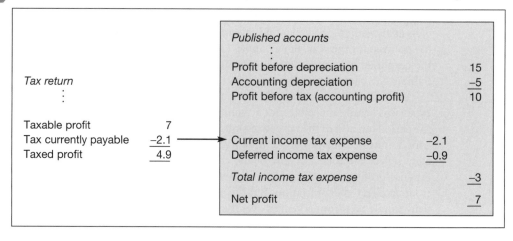

If Lazarillo depreciates the kitchen equipment at a faster rate in its books than in its tax return, accounting depreciation is greater than tax depreciation in year 1. In this case, taxable profit is higher than accounting profit and Lazarillo *prepays* part of its tax rather than deferring it. The prepayment is a deferred tax *asset* and the future tax impact of the current year's accounting profit (a *reduction* in the company's future tax liability) is recorded as a deferred tax *benefit* in the income statement.

Deferred tax accounting: balance sheet approach

How does a company calculate deferred tax expense (or benefit) and the related deferred tax liability (asset)? The main method used today is the balance sheet approach.[10] Under this approach, the company calculates the deferred tax liability and/or asset at the end of each financial year. This is the key step. To compute these balances, the company first determines the tax values of its assets and liabilities – taken from the balance sheet in its tax return – and compares them with their carrying amounts in the published accounts. The difference between an asset's (or liability's) tax value and its carrying amount is known as a **temporary difference**.

The company then applies the current tax rate to the end-year temporary differences. If it has 'taxable' temporary differences (i.e. the temporary differences increase future taxes), it recognises a deferred tax liability. If it has 'deductible' temporary differences (i.e. they reduce future taxes), it recognises a deferred tax asset – but only to the extent the tax asset is judged to be recoverable.[11] Deferred tax expense or benefit is the net change in the deferred tax balances over the year.

Exhibit 17.7 illustrates the balance sheet approach, using our Lazarillo example. The kitchen equipment is the only source of temporary difference between Lazarillo's tax and published balance sheets at the end of year 1. The asset's tax value then is 12; its carrying amount is 15. (Recall that tax depreciation is 8, book depreciation 5, in year 1.) As this is a taxable temporary difference, Lazarillo recognises a deferred tax liability of 0.9 ($3 \times 30\%$) in its end-year 1 balance sheet. The tax and book values of the equipment are the same (20) at the start of year 1 so the change in the deferred tax liability over the year is also 0.9. Thus Lazarillo reports deferred tax expense of 0.9 in its year 1 income statement.

Deferred tax numbers for later years are computed in the same way. Exhibit 17.8 shows the calculation of Lazarillo's deferred tax liability at the end of years 1–4 and the deferred tax expense it reports in those years. We assume the kitchen equipment remains the only source of temporary difference during that time.

Note the movement in Lazarillo's deferred tax liability over the four years. Taxes are postponed when taxable temporary differences increase in years 1 and 2. When those differences shrink in years 3 and 4, the deferred taxes become payable. This can be seen in the income statement. In years 3 and 4, the current tax charge (the amount currently payable) exceeds the total charge – hence the deferred tax expense reverses in those years. By the close of year 4 (the end of the equipment's life), the tax value and carrying amount are the same (0): the deferred taxes with respect to this asset have been paid.

Financial statement impact of deferred tax accounting

Exhibit 17.9 summarises the impact of deferred tax accounting on Lazarillo's income statement in years 1 to 4.

Lazarillo's total tax charge reflects the tax impact of annual profits now (current tax expense) and in the future (deferred tax expense). Since those profits are expected to remain constant (10/year) over the four years, the total tax charge is also constant (3/year). However, the composition of total tax expense changes over the period. Thanks to the effect of accelerated

Exhibit 17.7   Lazarillo Company: year 1 deferred tax liability/expense under balance sheet approach

	Tax return		Published accounts		
	(1)		(2)	(3)	(4)
				Deductible (Taxable)	**Deferred**
	Tax		Carrying	temporary	**tax asset**
	value		amount	difference	**(liability)**
				(1) – (2)	(3) × 30%
Deferred tax A/L calculation					
End-year 1					
Kitchen equipment:					
Cost	20		20		
Less: Accumulated depreciation	–8		–5		
Kitchen equipment, net	12		15	(3)	(0.9)
Start-year 1					
Kitchen equipment, net (= cost)	20		20	0	0
⋮					
(Increase) in deferred tax liability					(0.9)

Partial year 1 income statement

⋮	
Profit before tax	10
Current income tax expense	–2.1
Deferred income tax expense	–0.9
Total income tax expense	–3
Net profit	7

depreciation on taxable profits in the early years of an asset's life, Lazarillo's current tax liability (and current tax expense) is low initially but as the tax deduction for depreciation declines, so its tax bill and current tax expense increase.

Each component of tax expense has its counterpart in the balance sheet. We can see the link between income statement and balance sheet from the journal entries Lazarillo makes to record tax expense in years 1 to 4:

	Year							
	1		2		3		4	
	Dr.	*Cr.*	*Dr.*	*Cr.*	*Dr.*	*Cr.*	*Dr.*	*Cr.*
Current tax . . .								
Expense (OE–)	2.1		2.7		3.3		3.9	
Liability (L+)		2.1		2.7		3.3		3.9
(later, Cash (A–))								

Exhibit 17.8 Lazarillo Company: years 1–4 deferred tax liability/expense under balance sheet approach

Assumptions
- Kitchen equipment: cost 20; 4-year life; accounting depreciation 5/year.
- Tax depreciation (per year): 8, 6, 4, 2.
- Corporate income tax rate 30%

Deferred tax liability and expense in years 1–4

	[Start-year 1]	1	2	3	4
		Year			
Balance sheet, end-year					
Fixed asset (kitchen equipment):					
Tax value	20	12	6	2	0
Carrying amount	20	15	10	5	0
Deductible/(Taxable) temporary difference	0	(3)	(4)	(3)	0
Deferred tax asset/(liability)	0	(0.9)	(1.2)	(0.9)	0

Income statement for year
⋮

		1	2	3	4
Deferred tax expense (–)		−0.9	−0.3	+0.3	+0.9
[Deferred tax expense reversal (+)]					

Exhibit 17.9 Lazarillo Company: impact of deferred tax accounting on profit in years 1–4

Assumptions
- Profit before equipment depreciation is 15 each year.
- Accounting depreciation 5/year (for four years).
- Tax depreciation (per year): 8, 6, 4, 2.
- Income tax rate 30%.

Published accounts: summary income statements

	1	2	3	4
	Year			
Profit before equipment depreciation	15	15	15	15
Accounting depreciation on equipment	−5	−5	−5	−5
Profit before tax	10	10	10	10
Current tax expense*	−2.1	−2.7	−3.3	−3.9
Deferred tax expense (Exhibit 17.8)	−0.9	−0.3	+0.3	+0.9
Total tax expense	−3.0	−3.0	−3.0	−3.0
Net profit	7	7	7	7
* According to company's tax return:				
Profit before equipment depreciation	15	15	15	15
Tax depreciation on equipment	−8	−6	−4	−2
Taxable profit	7	9	11	13
Tax currently payable (at 30%)	2.1	2.7	3.3	3.9
(= current tax expense)				

	1		2		3		4	
	Dr.	Cr.	Dr.	Cr.	Dr.	Cr.	Dr.	Cr.
Deferred tax ...								
Expense (OE–)	0.9		0.3					
Liability (L+)		0.9		0.3				
Liability (L–)					0.3		0.9	
Expense (OE+)						0.3		0.9
[reversal]								

Advantages of deferred tax accounting

For the investor, deferred tax accounting has undoubted advantages over taxes payable accounting. It shows on the balance sheet the future tax obligations and benefits of a company. In addition, it sends a clearer signal about the profitability of the company's business. *The accrual accounting principles that are used to determine profit are also used to determine the tax cost of that profit.* As a result, after-tax profits are not distorted by the impact of tax concessions or penalties which affect the *timing* of tax payments but not their amount. Lazarillo's experience demonstrates this.

Sources of temporary difference

Tangible fixed assets are not the only source of temporary difference – although for many companies they are the most important one. Exhibit 17.10 sets out the various ways deferred tax assets and liabilities can arise under the balance sheet approach.

A deductible temporary difference arises under the following circumstances.

- *The tax value of an asset is greater than its carrying amount.* For example, a company makes a general provision for bad debts, thereby reducing the carrying amount of its receivables. The tax authorities only allow a tax deduction for actual bad debts. These are less than the provision in the year.

Exhibit 17.10 Deferred tax assets and liabilities: sources of temporary difference by type

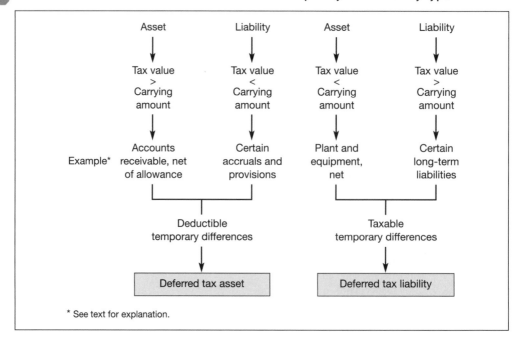

- *The tax value of a liability is less than its carrying amount.* A company with a funded defined benefit plan reports an accrued pension cost in its published accounts because cumulative payments to the fund are less than cumulative pension expenses. In the tax accounts, however, there is no pension liability. Cumulative expenses equal cumulative payments because the tax authorities only grant a tax deduction for contributions made to the fund.

A taxable temporary difference arises under the following circumstances.

- *The tax value of an asset is less than its carrying amount.* We've seen an example of this already. When a company (like Lazarillo) depreciates equipment in its tax accounts at a faster rate than in its books, the asset's tax value is less than its carrying amount.
- *The tax value of a liability is greater than its carrying amount.* A company issues debt securities at a discount. It accounts for the debt at amortised cost. Tax rules, however, require it to measure the debt in the tax accounts at the (higher) face value.

Temporary differences can also arise because of valuation changes. Suppose a company revalues its tangible fixed assets. This increases their carrying amount but not their tax value, resulting in a temporary difference in the year of revaluation. We discuss the tax effects of revaluations in section 2 of the chapter.

Permanent differences between accounting and taxable profit

Temporary differences are not the only reason for the difference between accounting and taxable profit. As we mentioned earlier, the difference may be of a continuing nature. For example, certain sources of income may escape tax: government grants may be treated as income for reporting purposes but are usually not subject to tax. Certain expenses may be disallowed for tax purposes: fines are usually non-deductible and so too, in many countries, are the costs of certain types of business entertainment.

What is the impact of permanent differences on a company's published accounts? Non-deductible expenses increase a firm's current tax expense and liability; tax-exempt revenues reduce them. For example, suppose Lazarillo incurs a fine (for sharp culinary practice?) of 1.5 in year 1. (The expense is already included in pre-depreciation profit of 15.) The fine is not tax deductible – though Lazarillo books it as an expense. As Exhibit 17.11 shows, this increases its current tax expense and liability by 0.45 (1.5 × 30%) that year.

Permanent differences, even when small in amount, upset the relationship between tax expense and profit. Without the fine, Lazarillo's effective tax rate is 30%, the same as the statutory tax

Exhibit 17.11 Lazarillo Company: effect of permanent difference on year 1 tax expense and liability

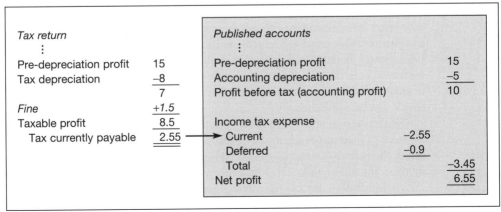

Tax return		Published accounts	
⋮		⋮	
Pre-depreciation profit	15	Pre-depreciation profit	15
Tax depreciation	−8	Accounting depreciation	−5
	7	Profit before tax (accounting profit)	10
Fine	+1.5		
Taxable profit	8.5	Income tax expense	
Tax currently payable	2.55 → Current		−2.55
		Deferred	−0.9
		Total	−3.45
		Net profit	6.55

rate. As a result of the fine, its effective tax rate increases to 34.5% (3.45/10). We look more closely at the relationship between statutory and effective tax rates in section 3 of the chapter.

International accounting rules and practice

Regulators have banned taxes payable accounting. National rules in most countries require companies to recognise the future tax effect of the current year's profit or loss. International rules go further. Companies following IAS must account for all temporary differences using the **balance sheet approach** outlined in the previous section. The standard also states that if the tax rate changes, deferred tax balances must be updated. Under this so-called **liability method**, companies must apply the *current* (or enacted) tax rate to their taxable and deductible temporary differences and adjust tax expense for the period.[12]

Although deferred tax accounting is now generally accepted, not all companies follow the international standard when applying it. Practice differs from international rules in two main areas.[13] First, companies in some countries (e.g. Germany, Spain) use the **income statement approach** to calculate deferred tax expense (or benefit) and the related liability (asset). Under this approach, deferred tax expense (benefit) arises when a company recognises a revenue or an expense in different periods for book and tax purposes. These book-tax differences are known as *timing differences*. Thus, using our earlier example, Lazarillo recognises a depreciation timing difference of 3 in year 1 – the difference between tax depreciation of 8 and book depreciation of 5 that year. This timing difference gives rise to a deferred tax expense of 0.9 (3 × 30%) in year 1. The deferred tax liability (or asset) that Lazarillo reports is the tax effect of *cumulative* timing differences at the balance sheet date.

The income statement and balance sheet approaches yield the same deferred tax figures in many situations. However, the balance sheet approach is more timely: there are differences between book and tax balance sheets that have no immediate income statement impact. For example, a revaluation of fixed assets that alters their carrying amounts but not their tax values gives rise to a temporary difference but will not be reflected in a timing difference until the revalued assets are depreciated. Likewise, changes in value of available-for-sale investments may lead to book-tax differences that are recognised earlier under the balance sheet approach.

The second area where practice may differ from international rules concerns the *scope* of deferred tax accounting. IAS require firms to account for *all* temporary differences (subject to certain exceptions). This is known as **comprehensive DTA**. However, in some countries (e.g. Italy), companies practise **partial DTA**. They do not recognise deferred tax liabilities when the likelihood of payment is remote. Supporters of partial DTA argue that growing companies can postpone for many years the deferred tax liability attributable to capital expenditures. Depreciation timing differences arising on new fixed assets more than offset reversing timing differences on old ones: as a result, the deferred tax liability increases year by year. Only when a company ceases growing and reduces its fixed assets base – which could be many years in the future – will its deferred tax liability decline. Opponents note that partial DTA confuses two separate events: the reversal of timing differences on existing assets which is bound to occur; and originating timing differences on *future* purchases of fixed assets which, for reasons of prudence, should not be anticipated.

The IAS version of deferred tax accounting is gaining ground. Norway and the USA adopted the balance sheet approach in the 1990s. The UK, Ireland, Hong Kong and Singapore followed suit in the early 2000s. All listed companies in the EU will be using the IAS version from 2005. By then, the minor differences that now exist between national and international versions of DTA – concerning, for example, recognition of deferred tax assets and measurement of long-term deferred tax balances – should have been resolved.

Deferred tax accounting: extensions

In this section we discuss certain accounting problems that can arise under the balance sheet approach to deferred tax accounting and describe how IAS deal with them.

Deferred tax assets

Recognition criteria

According to the international standard on income taxes, a company must recognise a deferred tax liability with respect to its taxable temporary differences. *However, deductible temporary differences give rise to a deferred tax asset only if the company expects to have taxable profits in the future when the differences reverse.* If the company reports losses and under existing tax legislation it is able to carry forward those losses to set against profits of future periods, it may also report a deferred tax asset if it is 'probable that future taxable profit will be available' against which to set the loss.[14]

The asset recognition tests for deductible temporary differences and tax losses carried forward appear to be similar. *In practice, a company is unlikely to recognise a deferred tax asset with respect to tax losses unless it can convince its auditors it is able to recoup the losses.* The auditors will be persuaded if the company:

- has sufficient taxable temporary differences in the same tax jurisdiction which, on reversal, will absorb the losses; or
- can show that the losses are attributable to specific factors (e.g. divestment of a loss-making activity) and are therefore unlikely to recur; or
- can create, through tax planning, taxable profits to offset the losses (e.g. via the sale of fixed assets and the realisation of taxable holding gains).

The company and its auditors must reassess the position each balance sheet date. If the probability of recouping the losses decreases, the deferred tax asset is written down and a deferred tax expense recorded. If, later, the company's trading position improves and the probability of recovery increases, the deferred tax asset is reinstated and a deferred tax benefit is recorded in the income statement.

Accounting for tax losses: illustration

We turn again to our Lazarillo example to illustrate the accounting treatment of tax losses. We move forward several years. The profits from the restaurant business have not grown as Lazarillo had hoped and when economic conditions worsen in year 9, the company records a loss. As for its tax position, it has deductible and taxable temporary differences. Deductible differences (the result of an underfunded pension plan) increase over the three years but taxable differences (attributable mainly to depreciation) fluctuate. Key figures for years 7 to 9 are set out below:

	Year 7	Year 8	Year 9
Before-tax accounting profit (loss)	11	13	(4)
Temporary differences at year-end:			
Deductible	10	12	17
Taxable	6	5	8

Lazarillo wants to know what are the tax figures the company must report in its year 9 accounts. Exhibit 17.12 shows the calculation of deferred tax balances and total tax expense for that year, under the assumption that the amount and timing of future profits are uncertain.

Our first task (*Step 1*) is to calculate the company's tax loss in year 9. The accounting loss of 4 is adjusted for increases in both deductible and taxable temporary differences. The result is a tax loss of 2. We assume the loss can only be carried forward and so no refund of past taxes paid is available. (Comparative figures are given for year 8. The company has taxable income of 16 that year and thus a current tax liability of 4.8.)

The next step (*Step 2*) is to determine the deferred tax balances at the end of year 9 and the change in these balances over the year. Normally we would apply the current tax rate to the taxable and the deductible temporary differences to find the end-year deferred tax liability and asset respectively. But since doubts exist about Lazarillo's future profitability, *the prudent course of action is for the company to recognise a deferred tax asset only up to the amount of the deferred tax liability it reports in year 9.* When the taxable temporary differences underlying the deferred tax liability reverse in a future period, they create taxable income against which reversing deductible differences can be set. Without them, the deductible differences (including the tax losses carried forward) cannot be used.

The company has taxable temporary differences of 8 at the end of year 9. Given its uncertain future prospects, it should restrict the deductible temporary differences accounted for to a similar number. As a result, it recognises a deferred tax asset of only 2.4 in its year 9 balance sheet – equivalent to its deferred tax liability then ($30\% \times 8 = 2.4$).

The deferred tax expense or benefit which a company records in the annual income statement is the net change in its deferred tax balances over the year. Between the start and end of year 9, Lazarillo's deferred tax liability increases by 0.9 while its deferred tax asset decreases by 1.2 (owing to the restriction on usable deductible temporary differences). The net effect is a deferred tax expense of 2.1 in year 9. Since the company has no current tax expense, this is also the total tax expense it reports that year (*step 3*).

Since the company incurs a tax *cost* in year 9, its reported loss is higher on an after-tax basis:

	Year 8	Year 9
Partial income statement		
⋮		
Profit/(loss) before tax	13	(4)
Tax expense	(3.9)	(2.1)
Net profit/(loss)	9.1	(6.1)

Lazarillo's deferred tax asset and liability have identical balances (of 2.4) at the end of year 9. Does this mean it can report a net deferred tax balance of zero that year? The answer is yes *if, and only if*, the tax asset and liability relate to taxes levied by the same tax authority.

Note that Lazarillo's unrecognised deductible temporary differences of 9 (17–8) and its tax loss carryforward of 2 are still available for future use. Their amounts should be disclosed in the notes to the accounts. If the company's trading position improves in a subsequent period, the deferred tax asset can be adjusted to include them.

Up to now we've assumed that future profits are uncertain. What if Lazarillo's year 9 losses are exceptional and the restaurant is expected to make money again in year 10 and later years? In this event, the restriction on the use of deductible temporary differences would be lifted. The company would account for the tax effect of *all* its deductible temporary differences (17) and its tax loss carryforward (of 2) at the end of year 9. As a result, it would recognise a deferred tax asset of 5.7 then ($19 \times 30\%$), an *increase* of 2.1 over the end-year 8 asset of 3.6.

Its year 9 income statement would show a tax *benefit* of 1.2, thereby reducing the accounting loss to 2.8 on an after-tax basis:

Exhibit 17.12   Lazarillo Company: impact of tax loss carryforward on year 9 accounts

Facts

Lazarillo reports the following earnings and end-year temporary differences (TD) in its years 7–9 accounts. The tax rate is 30%. *Future profits are uncertain.*

	Year		
	7	8	9
Before-tax accounting profit (loss)	11	13	(4)
Temporary differences (end-year):			
Taxable	6	5	8
Deductible	10	12	17
Restricted deductible	10	12	8

Calculation of tax payable and expense in years 8 and 9

Step 1: Calculate taxable income/(loss c/f)

	Year 8	Year 9
Before-tax accounting profit (loss)	13	(4)
Increase/(decrease) in deductible TD	2	5
(Increase)/decrease in taxable TD	1	(3)
Taxable income/(loss carried forward)	**16**	**(2)**
Current tax payable (at 30%)	4.8	–

Step 2: Calculate end-year DTL/DTA and change during year

	Year		
	7	8	9
End-year deferred tax liability (DTL):			
Taxable TD × 30%	**1.8**	**1.5**	**2.4**
(Increase)/decrease in DTL during year		0.3	(0.9)
End-year deferred tax asset (DTA):			
Restricted deductible TD × 30%	**3.0**	**3.6**	**2.4**
Increase/(decrease) in DTA during year		0.6	(1.2)

Step 3: Calculate tax expense for year

	Year 8	Year 9
Effect on deferred tax expense/benefit of:		
Change in deferred tax liability	0.3	–0.9
Change in deferred tax asset	0.6	–1.2
Deferred tax expense (–) / benefit (+)	0.9	–2.1
Current tax expense	–4.8	–
Total tax expense	**–3.9**	**–2.1**

	Year 9
Partial income statement	
⋮	
Loss before tax	(4)
Deferred tax benefit:	
(Increase) in deferred tax liability (Exhibit 17.12)	(0.9)
Increase in deferred tax asset	<u>2.1</u>
	1.2
Current tax expense (Exhibit 17.12)	<u>–</u>
Total tax benefit	<u>1.2</u>
Net loss	<u>(2.8)</u>

Notice that the income statement impact of taxes (under our assumption of assured future profits) is simply the tax rate (30%) times the accounting loss (of 4). This is because the company accounts for all temporary differences (and there are no other differences between its accounting and taxable profits).

Accounting for a tax loss carryback

There's a further twist to our tale of the accounting effects of tax losses. In some countries, as we learned in section 1 of the chapter, a company can carry back a tax loss, set it off against taxable profits of earlier years and claim a refund of taxes already paid. If this option were available to Lazarillo, how would it affect the company's year 9 accounts? The most noticeable impact would be in the calculation of the current portion of tax expense. *The company reports a current tax benefit in the amount of the tax refundable.* In addition, tax losses carried forward (and their deferred tax impact, if recognised) would be less by the amount of tax losses utilised through the carryback.

Assuming uncertain future profits (as in Exhibit 17.12), Lazarillo reports total tax expense of 1.5 in year 9, comprising deferred tax expense of 2.1 as before and a current tax benefit of 0.6 (30% × tax loss carryback of 2). At the same time, it recognises a current tax receivable for the 0.6 refundable in its year 9 balance sheet:

Dr. Tax refund receivable (A+)	0.6	
Cr. Current income tax benefit (OE+)		0.6

The total tax expense of 1.5 increases Lazarillo's year 9 loss to 5.5 on an after-tax basis:

	Year 9
Partial income statement	
⋮	
Loss before tax	(4)
Deferred tax expense (Exhibit 17.12):	
(Increase) in deferred tax liability	(0.9)
(Decrease) in deferred tax asset	<u>(1.2)</u>
	(2.1)
Current tax benefit from loss carryback	<u>0.6</u>
Total tax expense	<u>(1.5)</u>
Net loss	<u>(5.5)</u>

Carryback of the year 9 tax loss reduces the company's potential deferred tax asset. It discloses unrecognised deductible temporary differences of 9 in the notes to its accounts – but, of course, no tax loss carryforwards. Only if past profits in the permitted carryback period are insufficient to absorb this year's tax losses will the company have tax losses to carry forward.

Tax effects of revaluation and consolidation

Assets (and liabilities) carried at fair value

As we saw in earlier chapters, companies in certain European countries are allowed to measure assets at other than historical cost. For example, some Dutch companies value their inventories and fixed assets at replacement cost. Many Irish and UK firms revalue their land and buildings periodically. In addition, firms following IAS must carry certain financial investments at fair value.

What effect does an asset (or liability) revaluation have on deferred taxes? The answer is: none – if the tax base of the asset or liability is adjusted at the same time. *However, if when the asset or liability is revalued, the tax value remains the same, a temporary difference arises.* For example, an upward revaluation of a fixed asset – in the books but not in the tax return – results in a *taxable* temporary difference and thus an increase in the firm's deferred tax liability. The increase in value is recognised in the books at the time of the revaluation but is not subject to tax until the asset is sold or consumed.

The tax expense figure in the income statement is usually not affected, however. If the revaluation is booked direct to reserves, then the related tax effect is charged (or credited) to reserves too.[15] For example, suppose Lazarillo Company revalues land it owns and takes the revaluation surplus of 100 directly to reserves. If the tax value is unchanged and the tax rate is 30%, Lazarillo accounts for the increase of 30 in its deferred tax liability as follows:

Dr. Land (A+)	100	
Cr. Revaluation reserve (OE+)		70
Cr. Deferred tax liability (L+)		30

The revaluation reserve increases by the surplus of 100 net of the tax effect of 30.

The deferred tax liability is extinguished when the land is sold. For revalued depreciable fixed assets, the deferred tax liability diminishes each period in which book depreciation – higher as a result of the revaluation – exceeds tax depreciation.

Investments in subsidiaries

Under IAS, a company must usually prepare consolidated accounts (in addition to its own accounts) when it controls another firm. The consolidated accounts combine the accounts of parent and subsidiaries. However, the tax authorities may not accept the published consolidated accounts as the basis for taxing the companies within the group. One reason is that the tax code and accounting standards define a group – and thus its assets, liabilities and profits – differently. Another reason is that, under the tax code, only legal entities can be assessed to tax and the group is not a legal entity. As a result, each company within the group is taxed separately.[16]

In these circumstances, it is easy to see how book/tax differences can arise. Consider the following situations.

Fair value adjustments

On acquiring a firm, the parent company restates the assets and liabilities of the new subsidiary to fair value in the consolidated accounts. The tax values of the subsidiary's assets and liabilities (and their carrying amounts in its own accounts) are unchanged. The result? Taxable and deductible temporary differences arise. The parent recognises a deferred tax liability and asset in the consolidated accounts.

Goodwill on consolidation

The parent company pays more than fair value for the net assets it acquires. It reports goodwill in the consolidated accounts. If it capitalises goodwill as an intangible asset and there is no corresponding asset in the tax accounts, a taxable temporary difference arises. (It is temporary because it disappears when the goodwill is fully amortised or the investment is sold.)

In this case, however, no deferred tax liability is recognised. Accounting regulators argue that goodwill is a residual: if a deferred tax liability were recognised, the net assets of the acquired subsidiary would decrease and goodwill would increase. For example, suppose a company pays 100 for a subsidiary whose net assets have a fair value of 60. It recognises goodwill of 40 in the consolidated accounts. If it recognises a deferred tax liability with respect to the goodwill of, say, 12 (tax rate of 30% × 40), the subsidiary's net assets in the consolidated accounts fall to 48 and goodwill increases to 52. No deferred tax asset is recognised with respect to negative goodwill for the same reason.[17]

Intragroup transactions

Transactions between parent and subsidiaries are accounted for differently in the consolidated accounts and in the tax accounts of the separate companies. For example, profits on intercompany transactions are eliminated in the former but not in the latter. Probably the most important difference lies in the treatment of a subsidiary's profits. The parent company's share of these profits is included in consolidated profit. In the tax accounts of the parent company, however, only the profits *distributed* by the subsidiary are captured in the taxable profit of the parent. *Thus the parent company's share of the undistributed profits of its subsidiaries represents a taxable temporary difference in the consolidated accounts.*

In groups where most of the profits of subsidiaries are reinvested, the potential deferred tax liability may be huge. It is, however, *potential*: the liability only becomes payable if the subsidiary starts to distribute its retained earnings. So long as the parent company can control when a subsidiary distributes its profits and it's probable such profits will not be distributed in the foreseeable future (and thus the taxable temporary difference won't reverse), it should not recognise a deferred tax liability for them in the consolidated accounts. (It must disclose in the notes the amount of any unrecognised liability, however.)

Measurement issues

Effect of a change in the tax rate

When temporary book-tax differences arise, a company measures the deferred tax effect by applying the prevailing tax rate to those differences. But what happens when the tax rate changes? Does the company continue to value the temporary differences at the historical tax rate (the **deferred method**) or does it revalue them using the current tax rate (the **liability method**)?

Virtually all companies now use the liability method and IAS require it. Under the international standard, a company must measure its deferred tax asset and liability at the tax rate that is expected to apply when the asset is realised and the liability settled. (The rate must have been enacted or substantially enacted by the balance sheet date.) Thus, if the tax rate changes, the company adjusts its deferred tax balances by applying the new tax rate to its deductible and taxable temporary differences. The net adjustment to deferred tax balances is shown as an increase or decrease in its tax expense for the year.

We illustrate the effect of a tax rate change using our Lazarillo example. Suppose that at the start of year 8 the government enacts legislation under which the tax rate increases from 30% to 35%. Exhibit 17.13 shows the calculation of Lazarillo Company's tax expense and end-year deferred tax balances for year 8.

Exhibit 17.13   **Lazarillo Company: impact of increase in tax rate on year 8 accounts**

Facts

Lazarillo reports before-tax accounting profit of 13 in year 8. Temporary differences (TD) at the end of years 7 and 8 are as follows:

	Year 7	Year 8
Taxable temporary differences	6	5
Deductible temporary differences	10	12

The tax rate in year 7 is 30%. At the start of year 8, it increases to 35%.

Calculation of tax payable and expense in year 8

● *Current tax liability in year 8*

Before-tax accounting profit	13
Decrease in taxable temporary differences	+1
Increase in deductible differences	+2
Taxable profit	16
Current tax payable at 35%	5.6

● *End-year DTL/DTA and change during year*

	End-year 7		Start-year 8		End-year 8
Taxable TD	6		6		5
Tax rate	30%		35%		35%
Deferred tax liability (DTL)	1.8		2.1		1.75

	+0.3	−0.35
Change in DTL attributable to:	Change in tax rate	Decrease in taxable TD

	End-year 7		Start-year 8		End-year 8
Deductible TD	10		10		12
Tax rate	30%		35%		35%
Deferred tax asset (DTA)	3.0		3.5		4.2

	+0.5	+0.7
Change in DTA attributable to:	Change in tax rate	Increase in deductible TD

● *Tax expense in year 8*

	Year 8
Effect on deferred tax expense (−) or benefit (+) of:	
Decrease in taxable TD	0.35
Increase in deductible TD	0.7
Change in tax rate [increase in DTA, less increase in DTL]	0.2
Deferred tax benefit	1.25
Current tax expense	−5.60
Total tax expense	−4.35

Lazarillo must first adjust the deferred tax asset and liability at the start of year 8. Applying a higher tax rate to temporary differences, whether deductible or taxable, increases the deferred tax balances. In this case, the increase in deferred tax asset (0.5) outweighs the increase in deferred tax liability (0.3), so a deferred tax benefit of 0.2 flows into the year 8 income statement.

The remaining calculations are similar to those shown in Exhibit 17.12. The new tax rate is applied to the end-year 8 temporary differences to give the deferred tax asset (4.2) and liability (1.75) then. Comparing these figures with the amended start-year 8 balances, we find that the deferred tax asset has increased by 0.7 and the deferred tax liability has decreased by 0.35. The total deferred tax benefit (including the effect of the tax rate change) is 1.25.

The new rate is also applied to year 8 taxable profits in order to compute the current tax expense and liability. Total tax expense is the sum of current tax expense and deferred tax benefit. Not surprisingly, the higher tax rate increases Lazarillo's total tax expense (from 3.9 to 4.35). In this case, however, the increase in deferred tax benefit offsets in part the higher current tax expense.

In sum, a change in the tax rate alters not just the company's current liability but also the value of any deferred tax asset or liability. The company recognises the change in value of this future tax benefit or obligation immediately in the tax charge and discloses the amount, if material, in the notes.

Discounting

In some countries (e.g. the Netherlands, UK), companies are allowed under national accounting rules to discount their deferred tax balances. It's claimed that *when* a temporary difference reverses affects its current value: the greater the time to reversal, the lower is the value today of the future tax effect. The impact of discounting is especially significant for companies with large amounts of long-lived depreciable fixed assets.

International accounting standards forbid the discounting of deferred tax assets and liabilities (so, too, do US standards). *IAS 12* justifies the decision on practical grounds. Discounting requires 'detailed scheduling of the reversal of each temporary difference', a task that is considered too burdensome for a company to perform each financial period. Discounting has also been questioned on conceptual grounds. It's argued that the fair value of a deferred tax asset or liability is independent of when the underlying temporary difference will reverse (*see* Box 17.1).

SECTION 3
Corporate income taxes and financial analysis

Income taxes are a cost all profitable companies bear. As with any cost, managers try to minimise it. Investors check the accounts to see how successful they have been. Here are some tax-related numbers they pay special attention to.

Taxes paid

Knowing how much a company has paid in income taxes in the year is useful in building up a picture of its annual cash flow. A company that publishes a cash flow statement usually discloses payments (or refunds) of taxes in the year, either in the statement itself or in the notes.

BOX 17.1   Fair valuation of deferred tax assets and liabilities

Firms measure their deferred tax assets and liabilities by applying the current tax rate to deductible and taxable temporary differences. But what do the resulting deferred tax figures mean? Do they represent the fair values of those tax assets and liabilities? And if not, how are they to be adjusted to fair value?

Guenther and Sansing investigate the impact of deferred tax balances on a firm's value. A firm's value is, according to the standard finance model, the present value of its expected future cash flows. The latter must be expressed in after-tax terms. Using an analytical model, Guenther and Sansing show that, where there are book-tax differences, an adjustment to cash flows must be made, based on the *fair* value of the resulting deferred tax assets and liabilities.

The *reported* amounts of deferred tax assets (DTA) and liabilities (DTL) rarely equal their fair values. One situation where they do is when the underlying asset or liability is stated at fair value in the company's books but its tax value is zero. For example, suppose an oil company makes a provision for the abandonment of an oil field and measures it in its books at the present value of future outlays – say, 100. Assume, too, that the tax authorities only allow a tax deduction for payments made when the field is abandoned (i.e. at the end of its life): thus the tax value at the time the provision is made is 0. The deductible temporary difference then is 100 and, at, say, a 30% tax rate, the deferred tax asset is 30. In this case, the reported amount of the DTA is equal to its fair value.

Usually, however, the underlying asset or liability is not stated in the books at fair value (e.g. undiscounted provisions such as a provision for warranties) or its tax value is not zero (e.g. depreciable fixed assets). Where the asset has a positive tax value or the liability's book value is greater than its fair value, the fair value of the related DTL or DTA is *less* than the recorded amount (i.e. its book value). Guenther and Sansing show that, in the case of depreciable fixed assets valued at replacement cost, the adjustment coefficient is $[d / (d + r)]$ where d is the tax depreciation rate and r is the cost of capital. Thus $DTL_{FV} = DTL_{BV} [d / (d + r)]$.

Guenther and Sansing's second finding (which follows from their first) has significant policy implications. They show that the value of the firm is not affected by when temporary differences are expected to reverse. They use depreciable fixed assets to illustrate their finding. To delay reversal of depreciation temporary differences, a company must purchase new depreciable assets. If all new assets are zero net present value investments (a standard assumption where markets are competitive), buying a new one cannot increase the firm's value. Since the firm's value is insensitive to the reinvestment decision – it either reinvests and pays less in dividends or doesn't reinvest and pays more in dividends – it follows that the associated deferred tax liability has no valuation impact. Thus although reinvestment delays the reversal of temporary differences and postpones the payment of tax, the shareholders are not better off as the present value of those tax savings is captured in the price of the new asset. Guenther and Sansing conclude that requiring firms to discount DTA and DTL based on the expected time to reversal of temporary differences is not justified.[18]

Some companies do not disclose tax payments in the year. In these cases, investors must estimate the figure. This involves adjusting income tax expense for changes in tax liabilities and assets:

$$\text{Taxes paid} = \text{Tax expense} - \frac{\text{Increase (+ decrease)}}{\text{in current tax liability}} - \frac{\text{Increase (+ decrease)}}{\text{in deferred tax liability}}$$

(The signs are reversed for changes in current and deferred tax assets.)

● Effective tax rate

The **effective tax rate** is a corporate statistic which investors monitor.[19] It shows the company's income tax expense as a proportion of its accounting profit:

$$\text{Effective tax rate} = \frac{\text{Income tax expense}}{\text{Profit before tax}} (\times 100)$$

Tax expense is a better guide to the tax cost – in current and future years – of a firm's profits than the taxes it pays in the year. To discover how successful managers have been in lowering this cost, investors often compare a firm's effective tax rate with the **statutory tax rate** in its home country – or, in the case of a multinational, with the weighted average of the statutory tax rates in the countries in which it operates.

Why do effective and statutory rates diverge? Here are some of the main reasons:

- *Permanent differences.* As we saw earlier, some differences between taxable and accounting profits are permanent in nature. Certain expenses recognised in the books may not be tax-deductible. Certain revenues may be exempt from tax. Where permanent differences arise, the effective tax rate can never be the same as the statutory rate.

- *Income taxed at other than the statutory income tax rate.* In some countries, companies pay local (state, city) as well as national income tax. In addition, a capital gain (the excess of the sale price of a fixed asset over its original cost) may be taxed at a lower rate than operating profit. A company's effective tax rate will be lower than the statutory *income* tax rate when it realises capital gains in the year.

- *Investment and other tax credits.* A tax credit results in a direct reduction of a company's tax liability. For example, the government may allow a firm to claim a 5% tax credit when it invests in certain types of plant and equipment. This means a firm can reduce its tax liability by 5% of the cost of qualifying plant and equipment it buys that year. The purpose of such a scheme is to encourage investment by reducing its after-tax cost. Governments offer tax credits for regional investment, spending on research and development, and other economic activities they wish to promote. Note that a tax credit is more valuable to a company than a tax deduction: the latter only reduces the tax liability by the tax rate times the amount of the deduction.

  In *accounting* for a tax credit, a company can reduce tax expense for the year by the whole amount of the credit (the **flow-through method**). Alternatively, it can amortise the credit – to tax expense – over the life of the related asset (the **deferral method**). In both cases, the effective tax rate is lower in the year the credit is taken but is lowest under the flow-through method. *Regardless of the method of accounting used, the tax the company pays in the year the credit is received is reduced by the full amount of the credit.* A company may be able to carry forward (or back) an unused credit (e.g. where the credit available exceeds the tax liability for the year).

- *Unrecognised deferred tax asset.* As we saw in section 2 of the chapter, a company is not allowed to recognise a deferred tax asset for deductible temporary differences or tax losses carried forward if there is doubt about whether it will recover the asset. As a result, the effective tax rate will be higher in the period when such differences or losses arise (and are not recognised) and lower in the period when they are used. Similarly, a write-off of an existing deferred tax asset increases the effective tax rate.

For companies that account for deferred taxes on a *partial* basis (i.e. that recognise only those timing differences which will crystallise as a tax liability or asset in the near future), *unrecognised timing differences* are a further reason for a difference between statutory and effective tax rates. Since depreciation is usually the main source of unrecognised timing difference, the effective

Exhibit 17.14 BMW Group: effective tax rate and deferred tax disclosures in 2001 accounts

[A] Effective tax rate calculation

In euro million		2001	2000
Profit from ordinary activities (before tax)	[A]	**3,242**	2,032
Average German statutory tax rate		**38.9%**	52%
Expected tax expense		**1,261**	1,057
Variations due to different tax rates		**−94**	−348
Tax effects of non-deductible expenses		**82**	104
Tax payments (+) / refunds (−) relating to prior periods		**24**	−22
Other variances			
(mainly write-downs on deferred tax assets)		**103**	32
Actual tax expense*	[B]	**1,376**	823
Effective tax rate	[B]/[A]	**42.4%**	40.5%
* Of which: Current tax		**678**	425
Deferred tax		**698**	398

[B] Deferred tax disclosures

⋮

Deferred tax assets and liabilities at 31 December were attributable to the following positions:

In euro million	Deferred tax assets		Deferred tax liabilities	
	2001	2000	2001	2000
Intangible assets and property, plant and equipment	**1,464**	1,082	**3,859**	3,651
Financial assets	**27**	109	**52**	95
Current assets	**1,555**	719	**2,755**	1,388
Tax loss carry forwards	**2,263**	2,502	**–**	–
Provisions	**1,213**	1,121	**536**	177
Liabilities	**2,395**	2,011	**433**	364
Consolidations	**942**	1,018	**98**	149
	9,859	8,562	**7,733**	5,824
Write-downs	**−1,641**	−1,474	**–**	–
Netting	**−7,393**	−5,625	**−7,393**	−5,625
Total	**825**	1,463	**340**	199

The carrying value of deferred tax assets is reduced when recoverability is uncertain. In determining the level of the write-down, all positive and negative factors concerning the likely existence of sufficient taxable profit in the future are taken into account. These estimates can change depending on the actual course of events. Write-downs include €425 million (2000: €383 million) relating to tax loss carry forwards and €523 million (2000: €539 million) on losses on disposals . . . in Great Britain, which can only be set off against capital gains, but not against trading profits. In addition, there is a write-down of €653 million (2000: €552 million) on capital allowances [tax depreciation] in Great Britain, which are shown above in intangible assets and property, plant and equipment, and a write-down of €40 million (2000: 0) on consolidations.

(*Source*: BMW Group, *Annual Report and Accounts 2001*.)

tax rate of a firm using partial deferred tax accounting is likely to be lower than the rate it would report under full deferred tax accounting.

We illustrate some of these points using BMW Group's 2001 accounts. Section A of Exhibit 17.14 shows the calculation of the German vehicle manufacturer's effective tax rate in 2000 and 2001. Firms like BMW that follow IAS have to provide a reconciliation of their actual and expected tax expense (or a reconciliation of their effective and (weighted average) statutory tax rates) in their accounts.

BMW's effective tax rate rose slightly between 2000 and 2001, despite a decline in its average German corporate tax rate which, on a combined federal and local basis, fell from 52% to 38.9%. The main reason for the 1.9% increase in the effective rate is the write-down of deferred tax assets in 2001: management judged that certain tax losses could no longer be used. Note that the fall in tax rates in Germany narrowed the differential between BMW's German and foreign tax rates, reducing the benefit to tax expense from 348 to 94 (million euros).

Composition of tax expense and deferred tax balances

Investors find a breakdown of total tax expense helpful. Most firms distinguish current from deferred tax expense. Using the 'current tax expense' figure, investors can estimate the company's taxable profit for the year and thus the taxes it has paid or will shortly have to pay on that profit. If the deferred component of tax expense is large, total tax expense is a poor guide to a firm's current tax bill.

Multinational firms often show separately tax expense relating to domestic and foreign operations. By dividing domestic tax expense by the domestic tax rate, investors can estimate the profit earned from domestic operations and, by extension, from foreign operations. This is especially helpful if a firm provides a geographical breakdown of *sales* but not of profits as domestic and foreign profit margins can then be computed.

Some companies provide, in addition, an analysis of deferred tax expense and deferred tax balances. Again, this can yield useful information. Some temporary differences, like depreciation, reduce a firm's current tax liability for many years. As the firm expands and its fixed asset base grows, so the deferred tax liability with respect to depreciation grows too: new depreciation differences more than offset old reversing ones. Other temporary differences – such as those relating to provisions for restructuring costs – may be short term in nature. The higher tax liability in the year the provision is made is followed by a lower liability the next year as the company makes payments against the provision and obtains a tax deduction for them. Thus information about the *source* of temporary differences (e.g. depreciation, restructuring costs) helps investors predict a firm's future tax payments.

A company following IAS must disclose the components of tax expense and provide an analysis of its deferred tax assets and liabilities. It must also state the temporary differences for which *no* deferred tax asset or liability is recognised. These include *deductible* temporary differences (and unused tax losses and credits) where it's uncertain whether future profits will be available to utilise them and *taxable* temporary differences attributable to undistributed (and reinvested) profits of foreign subsidiaries.

BMW Group's 2001 accounts illustrate the tax disclosures required under IAS. The company breaks down tax expense into its current and deferred components and analyses its deferred tax balances at year-end (*see* section B of Exhibit 17.14). Where deferred tax assets and liabilities arise in the same tax jurisdiction, they're netted. BMW's accounts reveal a sharp increase in netting between 2000 and 2001, with the result that it reports a net asset of only €825 million and a net liability of only €340 million on its end-2001 consolidated balance sheet. 'Write-downs' (also known as **valuation allowance**) also increased in 2001. These represent the tax effect of deductible temporary differences or tax loss carry forwards that the company reckons it won't be able to utilise in the future. In BMW's case, over €1 billion of these write-downs relate to losses sustained on the disposal of its Rover car business in 2000 and its inability to set them off against profits and gains from its other UK operations.

BMW's tax disclosures are incomplete. Investors want to know more about the sources of its deferred tax assets and liabilities. For example, the tax assets and liabilities relating to 'current assets' amounted to €1.55 billion and €2.75 billion at end-2001. Which current assets are responsible for these deferred tax balances? Inventories? Receivables? And BMW doesn't reconcile the decline of €779 million in the *net* deferred tax asset in 2001 – from €1,264 million (1,463 – 199) to €485 million (825 – 340) – to the deferred tax expense of €698 million it reports on its 2001 income statement: what's the missing €81 million (779 – 698) attributable to? In addition, it provides no reconciliation of current tax expense, tax paid and current tax balances, as some companies do.

A word of warning. One consequence of new international rules is that companies have more discretion over the tax expense figure they report. A deferred tax asset can be recognised with respect to deductible temporary differences and tax losses carried forward only if management consider it probable that profits will be available in the future (in the same tax jurisdiction). Without future profits, the company cannot recover the tax asset. *A company whose managers are optimistic about its future prospects is more likely to recognise deductible differences and tax losses as a deferred tax asset. As a result, its tax expense will be lower and its after-tax profit higher than those reported by its more conservative rivals.*

Summary

The income tax a company pays is determined by the income it earns and the tax treatment of that income. Each country has its own tax code which spells out how the income of companies resident there is taxed. The tax code lays down, among other things, tax rates, definitions of taxable revenues and tax-deductible expenses, the treatment of losses and dividends, and the type and amount of tax concessions (such as tax credits) available to firms. Attempts to harmonise the codes of EU member states have not been successful so far.

Companies recognise, as an expense, the tax cost, now and in the future, of profits earned in the period. Where there are no differences between accounting and taxable profits, the tax cost is equal to the tax currently payable on the period's profits. Such equality is rare. In practice, book-tax differences arise. In some cases the differences are permanent: certain book revenues are not taxable; certain book expenses are not deductible. Of greater significance are temporary differences, that is, differences in the tax and book values of assets and liabilities. Temporary differences are the source of deferred tax balances. When temporary differences result in a postponement of taxes, the company reports a deferred tax liability. When they cause taxes to be paid early, it reports a deferred tax asset. The company recognises in tax expense the change in its deferred tax assets and liabilities.

Deferred tax accounting is complicated by the fact that companies determine deferred tax balances in different ways. Most account for all temporary differences between tax and book profit (comprehensive DTA) and value them at the current tax rate (liability method). However, some firms calculate deferred taxes by reference to revenue and expense *timing* differences. And there is variation in the way companies recognise the deferred tax benefits of tax loss carryforwards. As a result, the calculation of tax expense – and by extension post-tax profitability – may not be comparable across firms.

Quoted firms are disclosing more information in their consolidated accounts about their tax situation. Increasingly, investors are told how much tax the company paid in the period, why its effective tax rate differs from the statutory rate and what the reasons are for its deferred tax balances.

Problem assignments

P17.1   Calculation of taxable profit

Fremskridt Company reports before-tax profit of 750 in its x9 published accounts. (All amounts are in thousands.) This amount is arrived at after charging depreciation of 1,500, bad debt expense of 60 and entertainment costs of 25. Under the tax code of Norseland, Fremskridt's home country, these amounts must be adjusted in calculating taxable profit. Tax depreciation in x9 is 1,200, the deduction for bad debts is restricted to the actual debts written off in the year of 27 and only 8 of the entertainment costs is deductible. Norseland's corporate income tax rate is 30%.

Required

(a) Calculate Fremskridt Company's taxable profit and income tax liability in x9.

(b) Fremskridt's management want to know the impact on the company of each of the following situations. Recalculate the company's taxable profit and tax liability for x9 in each case. Each case is independent. (Amounts are in 000.)

  (i) Fremskridt receives a cash dividend of 56 from a (domestic) subsidiary. The dividend carries a tax credit of 24 (i.e. 3/7 of the dividend distributed). The dividend and related tax credit are not included in the company's before-tax profit of 750. Norseland has an imputation tax system.

  (ii) Fremskridt's before-tax profit of 750 is after deducting 240 that the company spent on research in x9. Under Norseland's tax code, Fremskridt can claim a tax credit of 20% against its income tax liability for research costs incurred in the year.

  (iii) Fremskridt can claim an investment deduction of 9% on investments in qualifying fixed assets in the year. (Certain investments, e.g. those in land, securities, goodwill, licences, concessions, do not qualify for the deduction.) Qualifying investments amount to 1,000 in x9. The investment deduction does not affect the depreciable base of the assets.

P17.2   Deferred tax accounting: taxable temporary differences I

Columbara is a textile producer with a reputation for very fast production and delivery of goods. The problem is that labelling of finished items is poor, which leads to customer frustration. The existing labels become detached from garments and customers can't remember the company's name. To remedy this, Columbara buys special labelling equipment at the start of x5. The equipment costs 120, has a four-year life and the expected salvage value is zero. For accounting purposes, the equipment is depreciated on a straight-line basis (with a full year's depreciation in the first year). It qualifies for accelerated depreciation under the tax code: the annual depreciation deduction over the four years is 48, 36, 24, 12.

Columbara expects profit before depreciation and tax to be 90 each year over the next four years. The current tax rate is 35%. The company takes a balance sheet approach when accounting for deferred taxes. It accounts for all temporary differences between book and taxable income. It expects no other book/tax differences in those years.

Required

(a) What is Columbara's expected income tax liability each year in the four years x5–x8, given the above facts?

(b) What is the annual income tax expense and net profit it expects to report in its published accounts between x5 and x8? What is the deferred tax liability or asset it expects to report in its balance sheet at the end of each of those years?

Check figure:
(b) Deferred tax expense, x6   2.1

P17.3 Deferred tax accounting: taxable temporary differences II

Refer to P17.2. Columbara is so pleased with the special labelling equipment it purchased in x5 that it decides to buy an additional machine each year until it has a stock of four. Each machine is expected to cost 120 and will be depreciated – for book and tax purposes – in the same way as the x5 purchase. Profit (before depreciation and tax) was 100 in x5. It is expected to grow by 30 a year until x8 and then remain at 190 in x9. The tax rate is 35% in x5 and is expected to stay at this level through x9.

Required

(a) Calculate Columbara's income tax payable, income tax expense and deferred tax liability or asset for each of the five years, x5–x9.

(b) An investor looks at your calculations and remarks:

'What the Columbara figures for x8 and x9 show is that when a company has stable earnings, most if not all of its total tax expense is current. Originating temporary differences on new assets and liabilities offset reversing temporary differences on old ones so that the company's deferred tax asset or liability shows little change and its deferred tax expense is zero or close to zero.'

Comment on these observations. Under what conditions is the deferred component of tax expense 'zero or close to zero'? Do these conditions only apply when earnings are stable?

Check figure:
(a) Taxable profit, x7   52

P17.4 Deferred tax accounting: comprehensive example

Tyr Company designs and manufactures military hardware. It has asked you to calculate its income tax expense for x3 and its current and deferred taxes at the end of that year.

Its provisional x3 accounts (with the exception of the tax and tax-related figures) are set out in Exhibit 17.15. Comparative end-x2 balance sheet numbers are also given.

On enquiry, you learn the following (all amounts are in millions):

- *Plant and equipment.* The depreciation rate is 20% SL in the books and 25% SL for tax purposes. The accumulated tax depreciation at the end of x2 is 50. The company purchases plant of 150 in x3. It records a full year's depreciation in the year of purchase.
- *Bribes.* The tax authorities have disallowed expenditures of 5 which the company describes in its accounts as 'Foreign sales commissions'.
- *Pension cost.* Under a new scheme, the company records pension expense of 14 and makes contributions to the plan of 11.5. Only pension contributions are tax deductible.
- *Bad debts.* The company makes a general provision for bad debts of 3 at the end of x3. Only bad debt write-offs are tax deductible. There are no bad debt write-offs in x3.

The tax rate is 40%. The company makes tax payments of 15 in x3. The company takes a balance sheet approach when accounting for deferred taxes and accounts for all temporary differences. Assume that deductible and taxable temporary differences arise in different tax jurisdictions.

Required

Complete Tyr's x3 accounts in Exhibit 17.15. Calculate income tax expense and deferred tax balances using the balance sheet approach.

Check figure:
Total assets, end-x3   279.2

Exhibit 17.15

Tyr Company
Provisional x3 accounts
(amounts in millions)

Income statement for x3

Sales revenue	300
Less: Cost of goods sold	
(including depreciation of 50)	−160
Gross profit	140
Less: Selling and administrative expenses	−80
Profit before tax	60
Less: Income tax expense	
Current	?
Deferred	?
Total	?
Profit after tax	?
Less: Dividend	−10
Retained profit for year	?

Balance sheets at end of x2 and x3

Assets	x2	x3	Equities	x2	x3
Plant and equipment	100	250	Share capital	90	90
−Accumulated depreciation	−40	−90	Retained profit	30	?
Plant and equipment, at			Shareholders' equity	120	?
net book value	60	160	Deferred tax liability	4	?
Accounts receivable	40	37	Pension provision	0	2.5
Deferred tax asset	0	?	Income tax payable	16	?
Other assets	70	80	Other liabilities	30	99.5
Total	170	?	Total	170	?

P17.5 Income taxes: analysis of disclosures I

Sandvik is a large engineering company with headquarters in Sweden. Its high-speed steel tools and mining equipment have a high reputation. Only 5% of its 2001 sales of SEK 48.9 billion (€5.3 billion) and one-third of its production that year were in its home market. Group profit before tax was SEK 5.6 billion in 2001 (2000: SEK 5.8 billion). Reported tax expense of SEK 1.7 billion in 2001 was broken down in the accounts as follows (negative sign indicates expense or debit):

In SEK million	2001	2000
Current taxes	−1,555	−1,662
Adjustment of taxes attributable to prior years	103	−71
Total current tax expense	−1,452	−1,733
Deferred tax expense	−241	−137
Taxes on participation in associated companies	−19	−11
Total reported tax expense	−1,712	−1,881

In common with other Swedish multinationals, Sandvik provides detailed information about its current and deferred taxes in its consolidated accounts. (The company follows Swedish GAAP which is similar to IAS in this area.) Exhibit 17.16 contains extracts from the tax note in the consolidated accounts.

Reconciliation of tax expense

The Group's weighted average tax rate, based on the tax rate in each country, is 30.7%. The tax rate in Sweden is 28%. The weighted average tax rate in the foreign subsidiaries is 33.2%.

The Group's weighted average tax rate is reconciled to its reported tax rate as follows:

	SEK m	%
Expected tax expense based on the Group's weighted average tax rate	−1,721	−30.7
Tax effects of:		
Goodwill amortization	−114	−2.0
Non-deductible expenses	−104	−1.8
Tax-exempt income	153	2.7
Overprovided in prior years	103	1.8
Effects of loss carryforwards, net	−34	−0.6
Other	5	0.1
Total reported tax expense	**−1,712**	**−30.5**

Out of the tax effect of tax-exempt income of SEK 153 m (2.7%), SEK 114 m (2.0%) pertains to non-recurring items.

Deferred tax assets and liabilities

The deferred tax assets and liabilities reported in the balance sheet are attributable to the following assets and liabilities, with liabilities shown with a minus sign.

Group 2001	Deferred tax assets	Deferred tax liabilities	Net
Intangible fixed assets	11	−3	8
Tangible fixed assets	57	−1,612	−1,555
Financial fixed assets	36	−2	34
Inventories	519	−13	506
Receivables	82	−28	54
Provisions	621	0	621
Interest-bearing liabilities	4	0	4
Non-interest-bearing liabilities	139	−22	117
Other	12	−679	−667
Loss carryforwards	26	0	26
Total	1,507	−2,359	−852
Offsetting within companies	−489	489	0
Total deferred tax assets and liabilities	**1,018**	**−1,870**	**−852**

Provisions within the 'Other' item pertain primarily to Swedish tax allocation reserves and similar untaxed reserves unrelated to specific assets or liabilities. . . . A reconciliation of the opening and closing balances of deferred taxes is presented below.

Deferred tax liabilities, net, 1 January 2001	−789
Acquisition of companies	−18
Reported in the income statement	−241
Translation differences and other items reported in Shareholders' equity	196
Deferred tax liabilities, net, 31 December 2001	−852

(*Source*: Sandvik Group, *Annual Report and Accounts 2001.*)

Required

(a) Investors use information in the analysis of a company's effective tax rate to forecast tax expense – and therefore profits – in future years. With the information Sandvik provides, it's possible to identify the recurring elements in the group's effective tax rate. Assuming Sandvik's weighted average (statutory) tax rate remains at 30.7%, estimate its effective tax rate for 2002. State any assumptions you have made.

(b) Sandvik reports a net deferred tax liability of SEK 852 million in its end-2001 consolidated balance sheet. There are four main sources of temporary difference. In addition to 'Other' (for which Sandvik provides an explanation), they are:
(i)   tangible fixed assets;
(ii) inventories;
(iii) provisions.

Suggest an explanation for each of these three major sources of temporary difference (taxable in the case of tangible fixed assets, deductible in the case of inventories and provisions). Note that the company values its inventories in its published accounts at the lower of FIFO cost or market, an acceptable method of valuation for tax purposes. 'Provisions' are long-term in nature and relate mainly to pension benefits and warranties.

(c) Not all the change in the Sandvik's net deferred tax liabilities in 2001 is reported in the income statement. Part relates to 'Translation differences and other items reported in Shareholders' equity'. Give examples of items reported directly in shareholders' equity that may have a deferred tax effect (besides translation differences).

P17.6 Income taxes: analysis of disclosures II*

Siam City Cement Company (SCCC) is Thailand's principal cement producer with consolidated 2001 revenues of Baht 16 billion (€360 million). The group was hit by the Asian financial crisis in 1997/98 and resulting devaluation of the baht. It incurred large operating losses in 1998/99 and did not return to profitability until 2000. The operating losses generated tax loss carry forwards which SCCC recognised as a deferred tax asset in its consolidated balance sheet. Key information concerning the tax effect of SCCC's past losses and current profits is given in Exhibit 17.17: it's taken from the company's consolidated accounts for calendar year 2001.

Required

(a) Calculate the group's effective tax rate for 2001.

(b) Why does the company report deferred but not current tax expense in 2001?

(c) How much tax did the group pay in 2001?

(d) Estimate the group's current and total tax expense for 2002. Assume the group makes consolidated before-tax profits of Baht 3,320 million (the same as in 2001) and the statutory corporate income tax rate in Thailand remains at 30%. State any other assumptions you have made.

* Assignment draws on material in section 2 of the chapter.

P17.7 Accounting for tax losses*

Few construction companies have as much experience of land reclamation and conservation as the Stevin Company which made its name on the Zuider Zee project. The company had been consistently profitable until x7 when, as a result of a fall in revenues and a large restructuring charge, it reported a before-tax loss of 200 in its published accounts (amounts are in millions).

Key details from the company's records are set out below. The taxable temporary differences are attributable largely to differences in the book and tax treatments of depreciation and profits on long-term contracts. Most of the deductible difference in x7 is attributable to the restructuring charge. There are no permanent differences.

Exhibit 17.17 Siam City Cement Company: tax-related disclosures in 2001 accounts

In baht million	Notes	**2001**	2000
Statement of income (condensed)			
Net sales		**15,927.8**	14,255.8
Income before tax*		**3,320.3**	1,597.2
Income tax	26	**−998.2**	−562.0
Group net income		**2,322.1**	1,035.2
Minority interest in income of subsidiary companies		**−72.7**	−83.1
Net income attributable to parent company shareholders		**2,349.4**	952.1

* Of which SCCC's share of income of associated companies is 235.9 (2000: 41.9 loss).

	Notes	**2001**	2000
Balance sheet, end year (condensed)			
Current assets		**6,705.7**	4,608.1
Property, plant and equipment, net		**12,817.0**	13,617.3
Investments in associated companies		**711.9**	544.2
Other assets		**4,129.3**	4,946.6
[of which: Deferred tax assets	26	832.7	1,830.9]
Total assets		**24,363.9**	23,716.2
Current liabilities		**1,884.1**	2,076.9
[of which: Income tax payable		–	71.1]
Long-term debt		**6,219.0**	6,892.4
Provident fund and employee resignation benefit plan		**358.2**	333.4
Group equity		**15,902.6**	14,413.5
Total liabilities and shareholders' equity		**24,363.9**	23,716.2

Note 26   Income tax (in baht million)

The provision for income tax is as follows:

	2001	2000
Current tax	–	82.4
Deferred tax	998.2	479.6
	998.2	562.0

The components of the deferred tax asset are as follows:

	December 31, 2000	Changes during year	December 31, 2001
Tax loss carry forwards	1,432.7	(861.0)	571.7
Allowance for doubtful accounts	71.1	1.1	72.2
Allowance for obsolete stocks	13.0	–	13.0
Equity in loss of associated companies	249.9	(142.3)	107.6
Provident fund and employee resignation benefit plan	64.2	4.0	68.2
Deferred income tax asset (net)	1,830.9	(998.2)	832.7

Note: 'Employee resignation benefit plan' and 'provident fund' represent estimated liabilities for employees' pension and termination benefits, respectively.

(*Source*: Siam City Cement Company, *Annual Report and Accounts 2001*.)

	x5	x6	x7
Accounting profit (loss)	600	700	(200)
End-year temporary differences:			
Taxable	270	380	540
Deductible	20	50	300

The corporate income tax rate is 40%. The company is uncertain about future profits and therefore recognises a deferred tax asset only up to the amount of its deferred tax liability at the balance sheet date.

Required

What is the income tax expense or benefit the Stevin Company will recognise in x6 and x7, assuming:

(a) it can carry tax losses forward but not back?

(b) it can carry tax losses back (one year only) as well as carry them forward?

In each case, determine the deferred tax balances Stevin will report in its end-x6 and end-x7 balance sheets.

Check figures:
(a) Deferred tax benefit, x7   80
(b) Deferred tax benefit, x7   36

* Assignment draws on material in section 2 of this chapter.

P17.8 Net-of-tax method: a simpler approach to deferred tax accounting?

'Why do we bother with deferred taxes?' asks the financial controller of a publicly quoted company. 'None of our investors – or the analysts covering our company – appears to take any notice of the deferred tax component of income tax expense or of the deferred tax asset and liability on the balance sheet. They just focus on the company's current tax expense and payable.

'Maybe accounting rule-makers should abandon the liability method and require companies to use the net-of-tax method instead. Under this method, a company reports the tax effects of temporary differences as adjustments to the carrying amounts of particular assets and liabilities and the related revenues and expenses. So, for example, equipment would be shown on the balance sheet net of the tax effect of any temporary differences between its tax and book values. And the depreciation expense for that equipment would be adjusted for the deferred tax expense or benefit relating to that asset (i.e. the tax effect of the *change* in temporary difference). The tax expense figure in the income statement would comprise current tax payable only but net profit would not be affected. This can be seen in my example below. (I assume a fixed asset costing 100 with book depreciation of 20 and tax depreciation of 33 in the first year, profit before depreciation of 120 and a tax rate of 30%.)

		Liability method	Net-of-tax method
Profit before depreciation and tax		120	120
Depreciation		–20	–24
Profit before tax		100	96
Current tax expense	–26		
Deferred tax expense	–4		
Total tax expense		–30	–26
Net profit in year 1		70	70
Fixed asset, at NBV, end-year 1		80	76

So the net-of-tax depreciation charge consists of two elements – book depreciation of 20 plus the tax effect of the excess of tax over book depreciation of 4.

'The main advantage of the net-of-tax method, in my view, is that the reported amount of an asset or liability incorporates the related tax benefit or cost directly. This gives a truer indication of its economic value. For example, the market value of the equipment described above is a function of both its service potential and the tax benefits available to the owner. In addition, the method simplifies the presentation of the income statement and balance sheet, removing the clutter of deferred tax items and making the accounts easier for a layperson to understand.'

Required

Comment on the financial controller's proposal. What are the potential weaknesses or disadvantages of the net-of-tax method, in your view?

Notes to Chapter 17

1   *OECD in figures 2002*, Paris: OECD.

2   It need not be, however. In some countries, a company owned and controlled by a few shareholders is treated as a partnership: the company's income is attributed directly to the owners and each is taxed on his or her share as if it were personal income. The individual owners are 'taxable entities'; the company is not.

3   In many countries, corporate income taxes are paid by instalment during the financial year. This means the company must estimate taxable profits for the year. It adjusts its profit estimate (and tax liability) when the accounts are closed after the year-end and actual taxable profits are known.

4   This can lead to an artificial capital structure. To counter this, tax codes in many countries seek to prevent firms from disguising equity capital as debt. Thus, in the case of a 'thinly capitalised' company, the tax authorities may deem part of its interest charge to be a distribution of profit and deny the company a tax deduction on it.

5   In our discussion, we've focused implicitly on the tax situation of *resident* shareholders. The differences among the various tax systems have less force for *non-resident* shareholders. Dividends (and other income payments such as interest and royalties) paid to non-residents bear a withholding tax, regardless of the tax system. The nominal rate is usually 25–30% but the actual rate is much lower (10% or less) thanks to tax treaties between countries. Moreover, in most countries taxpayers can claim a foreign tax credit for the withholding tax – or a tax exemption for the foreign-source dividend income – in their home-country tax return. They can't claim a tax credit for imputed (foreign) corporate income tax, however.

6   Many EU member states set a reduced rate for low corporate earnings. This is intended to help smaller companies.

7   Ruding Committee (1992), *Report of the Committee of Independent Experts on Company Taxation*, Brussels: European Commission.

8   Cussons, P. and Sylvester, C. (2002), ECJ round-up, *Tax Planning International: European Union Focus*, 4(2): 11–12.

9   Corporate income taxes have not always been considered a cost. In some European countries, it was common practice until recently to show income taxes in the same way as dividends – as a *distribution* of profits, rather than as a cost incurred in generating them.

10 The balance sheet approach is not the only way that a company can account for the future tax effects of current profits. In some countries, firms calculate deferred tax by reference to timing differences between the book and tax amounts of revenues and expenses (the income statement approach). Under yet another approach, the net-of-tax method, no separate deferred tax asset or liability is recognised. Instead, the carrying amounts of individual assets and liabilities are adjusted for the tax effect of any book/tax differences relating to them. Only the balance sheet approach is permitted under IAS.

11 Recoverability depends on future profits. If there are doubts about whether the company will generate profits in future periods, the deferred tax asset will be restricted – or not recognised at all.

12 International Accounting Standards Board, *IAS 12: Income Taxes*.

13 There is a third area where practice can differ. Instead of applying the *current* tax rate to temporary (or timing) differences (the liability method), a company values those differences at the tax rate(s)

prevailing when they arose (the deferred method). Thus, a change in tax rate does not result in the revaluation of deferred tax balances. Few companies use the deferred method today. It is not acceptable under IAS.

14   *IAS 12*. The previous international rules were tougher: there had to be 'assurance beyond any reasonable doubt' that future taxable profits would be available against which to set the loss before a deferred tax asset could be recognised.

15   More generally, the tax effect of any item that is charged or credited directly to shareholders' equity is also charged or credited there too. Thus the tax effect of a foreign currency translation adjustment is booked directly to reserves.

16   The tax code may grant concessions to corporate groups, however. As we saw in section 1 of the chapter, a parent company may obtain tax relief when it receives dividends from (domestic) affiliated companies. In addition, it may be possible to set off the operating losses of one company within the group against the operating profits of another.

17   This treatment is consistent with previous practice, where goodwill amortisation that was not deductible for tax purposes was considered a permanent rather than a timing difference.

18   Guenther, D.A. and Sansing, R.C. (2000), Valuation of the firm in the presence of temporary book-tax differences: the role of deferred tax assets and liabilities, *The Accounting Review*, 75(1): 1–12.

19   The accountant's effective tax rate is, in reality, an average tax rate. To an economist, the effective tax rate is the percentage of each additional currency unit (euro, dollar, etc.) of corporate income that is claimed by the tax authorities, i.e. its *marginal* tax rate.

PART 3

Perspectives

18

The cash flow statement revisited

INTRODUCTION

We have now finished our exploration of the accounting building. We have a better understanding of how a firm's balance sheet and income statement are put together and of the accounting policies that underlie their construction. Our attention now turns outward. In the next three chapters (Chapters 18–20), we consider how investors use financial statements to analyse a company's past and forecast its future.

We start by revisiting the cash flow statement which we first encountered in Chapter 6. Investors look at a company's cash flow statement to discover whether cash inflows are greater or less than cash outflows in the year. However, they learn more from it than just this. They gain insights into the nature of a company's business, its debt-paying ability and the impact of accrual adjustments on its accounts. We illustrate each of these points in the first part of the chapter.

We then turn to technical matters. We show how an approximate cash flow statement can be constructed, using balance sheet and income statement data only. This is a valuable skill to have, given that many smaller companies do not publish a cash flow statement.

The way companies present cash flow data is sometimes puzzling. We illustrate alternative ways of presenting operating cash flows. We close the chapter by explaining how foreign currency transactions and investments in associated companies, joint ventures and subsidiaries are dealt with in the cash flow statement.

Cash flow analysis: benefits to investors

Overview

Investors turn to the cash flow statement to find out how a company raised and spent cash during its past financial year. This information is not available directly from either the income statement or the balance sheet.

Format of cash flow statement

The cash flow statement comes in several guises. Increasingly, larger European firms present cash flows by activity. This is the format required by IAS. Exhibit 18.1 shows in outline an activity-based cash flow statement for a non-financial institution. (Financial institutions have separate reporting requirements.) As we saw in Chapter 6 (Exhibit 6.19), the 2001 cash flow statement of BestPrice Stores has a similar format.

The statement identifies three types of activity – operating, investing and financing. Exhibit 18.1 illustrates the main elements commonly found under each.

1 *Operating activities.* These comprise the sale of goods and services and their associated costs.[1] Cash receipts and payments from such activities are rarely shown directly. Instead, as

---

Exhibit 18.1   **Format of activity-based cash flow statement** (indirect approach)

*Operating activities**		
Net profit for the year	xx	A
Non-cash expenses	xx	B
(Increase) in operating working capital	(xx)	C
Cash inflow from/(outflow on) operations	xx/(xx)	D
Investing activities		
Purchase of tangible and intangible fixed assets	(xx)	
Disposal of tangible and intangible fixed assets	xx	
Purchase of financial investments	(xx)	
Disposal of financial investments	xx	
Cash (outflow on)/inflow from investments	(xx)/xx	E
Financing activities		
Issuance of shares and bonds	xx	
Repayment of debt/repurchase of own shares	(xx)	
Dividends to shareholders	(xx)	
Cash inflow from/(outflow on) financing	xx/(xx)	F
Net cash inflow (outflow) in year (D + E + F)	xx/(xx)	
Cash and equivalents, start-year	xx	
Cash and equivalents, end-year	xx	

* Net loss, non-cash revenues and decrease in operating working capital have the opposite signs.

Exhibit 18.1 shows, operating cash flow is derived indirectly, by adjusting profit for non-cash expenses (such as depreciation) and changes in operating working capital (mainly inventories, receivables and payables) during the year.

2 *Investing activities.* These embrace the purchase and disposal of tangible and intangible fixed assets such as property and equipment, trademarks and goodwill. In addition, the acquisition and disposal of financial investments such as government bonds or shares in other companies are also considered investing activities.

3 *Financing activities.* A firm raises outside capital by issuing shares or through borrowing. It reduces outside capital by repurchasing its shares and repaying debt. These along with the payment of dividends to shareholders are its principal financing activities.

The sum of the cash flows within an activity can be positive or negative. Note that the way cash flows are classified follows conventional accounting practice. Thus expenditures on research and development are shown as operating outlays even though, in economic terms, they are investing outlays like those on plant and equipment.

Initial analysis

The starting point for an initial analysis of a firm's cash flow is its operating cash flow (OCF). Is OCF positive or negative? OCF may be negative if the firm is making losses or if it is profitable but growing very rapidly. Fast-growing firms often invest heavily in operating working capital as well as in fixed assets. Negative OCF (or a trend of positive but declining OCFs) is a warning to investors that the firm may encounter financial difficulties in the future. Even profitable firms can experience liquidity problems.

For a firm with positive OCF, investors ask: is it self-financing? Can it pay for net capital expenditures (purchases less disposals of tangible and intangible fixed assets – known as *net capex*) and dividends to shareholders out of operating cash flow alone? If the answer is no, then the next question is: how is the firm financing the shortfall? Sources of cash besides operations include new debt, an issue of shares, a disposal of investments or a run-down of its cash balance. Of course, the firm may draw on more than one of these sources to meet the cash shortfall.

If the firm *is* self-financing, investors ask: how is it deploying the cash surplus? Ways of using the surplus include: early repayment of debt; returning cash to shareholders (via special dividends or share repurchases); making acquisitions (by buying the shares of other companies); and replenishing the firm's own cash balance. We summarise these alternatives below:

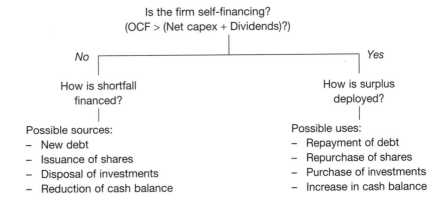

The cash flow statement yields other insights. By looking at the *composition* of a firm's operating, investing and financing flows, investors can see the effect of management decisions in those areas – more clearly than from inspection of the balance sheet and income statement alone. Here are some examples of questions about management policies which the statement can help answer:

- *Working capital management.* To what extent is a change in OCF attributable to a change in working capital levels? Is the change in working capital sales-related or the result of management action, e.g. tighter inventory control or (a negative OCF effect) the faster settlement of suppliers' accounts? Note that a reconciliation of profit to OCF – as provided by the indirect approach – is helpful here.
- *Investment strategy.* Is the company expanding internally – in which case expenditures on tangible fixed assets will be the major investing outlay – or through acquisition of stakes in other companies?
- *Financial structure.* Has the company altered the mix of debt and equity capital? Has it refinanced its debt? If so, has it changed the debt's term structure (e.g. by substituting long-term for short-term debt)?

Investors also turn to the cash flow statement for help with more specialised enquiries. In particular, they use cash flow data to:

1 assess a company's financial risk;
2 compare its performance with that of other firms which follow different accounting policies;
3 improve their forecasts of its future operating and investing cash flows; and
4 detect any manipulation of its earnings by management.

We illustrate each of these points in turn.

Assessing risk

Investors consult a firm's cash flow statement when assessing its credit risk – that is the risk it will be unable to pay its debts when they fall due.[2] The operating cash flow number is crucial here. A firm may be profitable and yet report a cash outflow from operations. Take the case of a company enjoying rapid growth in demand for its products. It makes profits but at the same time invests heavily in inventories and receivables (as well as fixed assets). In terms of Exhibit 18.1, negative C outweighs positive A and B.

Cash-based liquidity and leverage ratios

Investors have devised cash-based liquidity and leverage ratios to shed light on a firm's ability to pay its creditors. The **defensive interval**, a liquidity measure, relates a firm's defensive assets (i.e. cash and other liquid assets) to its non-avoidable outlays in the short run.[3]

$$\text{Defensive interval (in days)} = \frac{\text{Defensive assets}}{\text{Projected expenditures}} \times 365$$

where:
Defensive assets = Cash + Marketable securities + Accounts receivable (net), end-year t
Projected expenditures = Budgeted outlays (including capital expenditures) in year $t+1$.

Where information about budgeted outlays is not available, investors use the firm's reported outlays of the most recent year.

The ratio assumes a worst case scenario, namely, the company generates no cash from sales or other sources. It shows how long a firm can continue normal operations – in the absence of sales – without resorting to outside financing. The main advantage of the defensive interval over traditional liquidity ratios such as the current ratio is that it is forward-looking and focuses on future payments to creditors rather than on current liabilities. Moreover, it is less susceptible to manipulation: deferring until January the receipt of inventory purchased on credit raises the end-December current ratio (assuming it's greater than unity already) but has no effect on the defensive interval.

A variant of the defensive interval was widely used by analysts in the 'dotcom bubble' years of the late 1990s. Most start-up companies 'burn' cash initially: operating cash flow is negative as payments exceed receipts in the early years. Analysts estimate the rate of a start-up's **cash burn** (i.e. projected operating cash outflow (including capital expenditures) per quarter). By relating cash burn to the firm's liquid assets at the start of the quarter, analysts can work out how long it can survive until the next cash call – or liquidation.

$$\text{Cash call interval (in days)} = \frac{\text{Cash and marketable securities, end-quarter } t}{\text{Projected cash burn (in quarter } t + 1)} \times 90$$

Of course, those investing in the firm expect cash burn to diminish and eventually disappear. They assume that as revenues increase the firm will generate positive operating cash flow and further cash calls (or bankruptcy) will be avoided. As we now know, for many dotcom start-ups, this was wishful thinking.

Cash-flow leverage ratios have also become popular in recent years. One that's widely used is the **net debt-to-OCF ratio** which, as the title suggests, relates a company's net debt to its operating cash flow:

$$\text{Net debt-to-OCF ratio} = \frac{\text{Interest-bearing debt, less cash and cash equivalents, end-year } t}{\text{Operating cash flow in year } t}$$

The ratio shows how many years it will take for the company to pay off its debts given the current rate at which it generates cash from operations. Other versions of the ratio are in use. Analysts sometimes use projected OCF rather than the actual OCF of the most recent year. In the case of capital-intensive companies, they may deduct projected capital expenditures from OCF to give a more realistic measure of cash flow available to service the debt. Another variant, popular with credit-rating agencies, is to use cash earnings or Ebitda (earnings before interest, tax, depreciation and amortisation) in place of OCF on the grounds that OCF can be distorted by non-recurring changes in operating working capital in the year. (We discuss cash earnings and Ebitda in the next section.)

The net debt-to-OCF ratio – or variants of it – is steadily replacing the traditional debt/equity ratio as a measure of financial leverage. It has two main advantages. First, it reflects better the risks associated with debt. A company services – and repays – debt with cash. Operations are the main source of recurring cash flow. Thus a company with low OCF relative to net debt will find it harder to meet debt payments when they fall due. Second, new accounting standards have undermined balance sheet leverage ratios. Fair value adjustments to investments and impairment tests applied to goodwill and other fixed assets have made the book equity figure in the debt–equity ratio more volatile. Moreover, standards-driven charges against book equity do not necessarily indicate that a company's debt-servicing ability has worsened.

Available cash flows and committed outlays

Investors use cash flow data in other ways to assess a company's viability. Rather than calculating ratios, they construct a detailed forecast of its future cash flows. A bank, for example, may wish to estimate a potential borrower's cash flows before approving a loan. In these circumstances, it makes sense to distinguish the outlays the borrower *must* make from those it can avoid.

- *Committed outlays comprise existing scheduled debt payments and the minimum capital expenditures necessary to maintain operations.*
- *Discretionary outlays* (i.e. outlays the borrower can avoid) *include expansionary capital expenditures and investments in other firms.* (Strictly, ordinary dividends are, in terms of this analysis, a discretionary payment, but companies themselves may well view the existing level of dividends as a committed outlay.)

The cash flows available for servicing new debt (*net available cash flows*) are the borrowing firm's expected inflows from operations and other sources less its committed outlays:

Forecast available cash flows

Expected inflows from:	
Operations	xx
Asset disposals	xx
Return on investments	
(e.g. interest and dividends received)	xx
Available cash flow	xx
Committed outlays	
Scheduled debt payments:	
Debt servicing costs (e.g. interest payments)	−xx
Payments of principal	−xx
Non-cancellable contractual payments	
(e.g. lease payments)	−xx
Maintenance capital expenditures	−xx
Net available cash flow	xx

A healthy firm has positive net available cash flow even in the trough of the business cycle.

Investors in leveraged buyouts (LBOs) also make use of the above framework. In an LBO, the purchaser uses the target firm's own cash flow to service the debt used to finance the acquisition. The key number here is the target firm's expected **free cash flow**. *Free cash flow is (before-tax) 'available cash flow' less maintenance capital expenditures.* The larger this number, the greater is the cash available to meet payments of interest and principal and thus the more debt the purchaser can employ to fund the buyout.

Measuring performance

We argued in earlier chapters that profit is usually a better measure of financial performance than cash flow. Thanks to the timing and matching conventions of accrual accounting, profit (loss) more closely reflects the value added (or subtracted) by the firm's operations during a period than does cash flow.[4]

Nevertheless, investors use cash flow numbers in practice as a financial performance measure. In addition, they often base valuation multiples on cash flow rather than earnings. Some of the arguments they use for doing this are dubious, however.

Cash earnings and Ebitda margin ratios

Which cash flow ratios do investors use in interfirm comparisons of performance? One popular indicator is the cash earnings-to-sales ratio. Investors define **cash earnings** as 'profit plus depreciation (and other non-cash expenses)'. If they focus on the performance of the firm – rather than returns to shareholders, they add back interest expense – and tax – as well. This version of cash earnings is known as **Ebitda** (earnings before interest, tax, depreciation and amortisation).

Note that these measures of cash flow are not equivalent to operating cash flow. Recall that:

$$\text{Operating cash flow} = \text{Net profit (or loss)} +/- \text{Effect of accruals}$$

'Accruals' are of two types: long term (e.g. depreciation, changes in long-term provisions) and short term (e.g. changes in inventories, trade receivables and trade payables). Cash flow-based performance measures like Ebitda adjust profit for the effect of *long-term accruals* only:

$$\text{Ebitda} = \frac{\text{Profit (or loss) before}}{\text{interest and tax}} +/- \frac{\text{Depreciation, amortisation, and}}{\text{other long-term accruals}}$$

Why do investors use Ebitda (or cash earnings) rather than reported net profit as a performance measure? The main reason is its claimed versatility: it can be used to forecast future cash flows as well as measure past performance. Many investors believe that depreciation and amortisation don't have predictive value: using this information won't help them make more accurate forecasts of a firm's future cash flows, they argue. In addition, they cite international differences in the accounting for fixed assets. By excluding depreciation and amortisation from profit calculations, they allege they can better compare the performance of companies in different countries.

Both arguments are weak. Long-term accruals *do* have predictive value. Research shows that investors can improve their predictions of a company's future cash flows by breaking down its current earnings into cash flow and individual accruals components – long-term as well as short-term – and by building forecasts of future cash flows on these disaggregated amounts.[5] As for international accounting differences, these diminished considerably in the late 1990s, especially in the area of fixed assets, as a result of growing convergence in the accounting for intangibles and asset impairments.

Cash flow/share

Cash flow per share is another performance measure used in interfirm comparisons. As with the cash flow margin, financial commentators – and companies themselves – may define it as 'profit plus depreciation' or Ebitda rather than OCF.

From a conceptual point of view, the ratio is flawed no matter how it is calculated. In contrast to earnings, a firm's cash flow does not 'belong' to its shareholders. It is generated by *all* the company's assets, not that part which is financed by the owners. Nevertheless, cash flow per share is a popular performance measure, especially in the telecoms sector where many recent entrants currently report low or negative earnings owing to large non-cash charges (e.g. depreciation of cable and other long-lived assets, amortisation of licences and other intangibles).

Valuations and cash flow multiples

It's a short step from per-share cash flow to corporate valuations using cash flow multiples. A traditional method of valuing an unquoted company's shares is to apply a P/E ratio (based on that of quoted companies in its industry) to its prospective earnings per share. Recently, investors have begun to relate cash flow to 'enterprise value'. Enterprise value is the sum of the market values of a firm's debt as well as its equity. Cash flow is usually defined as Ebitda. This results in an EV/Ebitda ratio:

$$\text{EV/Ebitda ratio} = \frac{\text{Debt + Shareholders' equity + Minority interests (all at MV)}}{\text{Earnings before interest, tax, depreciation and amortisation}}$$

Investors use the EV/Ebitda ratio for the same purposes as the P/E ratio: to value an unquoted firm's equity and, more questionably, to look for mispricing of quoted companies' shares.[6] The advantage of a cash flow multiple is that it is less sensitive to accounting policy differences than an earnings multiple. However, be warned: in either form it is a crude valuation device. A more rigorous approach is to estimate a firm's future earnings or cash flows on a year-by-year basis and discount them using the appropriate risk-adjusted discount rate based on the firm's cost of capital.

Forecasting

Companies display different cash flow *profiles*. The way in which operating, investing and financing cash flows vary across firms is attributable in part to industry differences. Companies in fast-growing industries must usually rely on external capital (financing inflows) because internally generated funds are insufficient to meet investment needs. Companies in mature industries, however, 'self-finance' their capital expenditures and use surplus cash to acquire other companies, retire debt and/or buy back their own shares.

Investors use cash flow profiling to help them forecast a firm's future operating and investing cash flows. How do they do this? They start by relating a company's cash flow profile to the various stages in the lifecycle of its products. A product usually passes through (at least) four stages in its lifecycle: introduction, growth, maturity and decline.[7] A product's impact on the firm's income and cash flows during its lifecycle is shown in Exhibit 18.2.

At the time of the product's introduction, operating cash flows are negative because of heavy product development and launch costs. If the product is successful and becomes profitable, OCF may remain negative as the company invests in working capital to meet sales demand. During this period, the company relies on 'outside' capital, e.g. bank borrowings, new equity or even cash flows from the firm's other mature or declining products.

Exhibit 18.2 **Lifecycle of a product: income and cash flow impact**

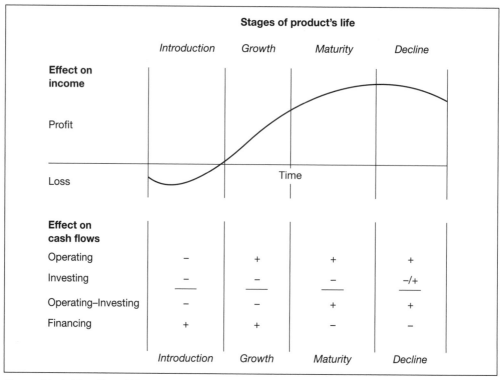

(*Source*: Adapted from *Financial Reporting and Statement Analysis: A Strategic Perspective, 3rd Edition* by Stickney. © 1996. Reprinted with permission of South-Western, a division of Thomson Learning: *www.thomsonrights.com*. Fax 800 730-2215.)

In the growth stage, the product generates positive OCF. However, these are not large enough to cover the growing outlays on fixed assets and outside capital is still needed.

When the product reaches maturity, it becomes self-financing. It generates sufficient cash from operations to meet investment needs (largely replacement in nature). Financing flows may well turn negative as the company repays debt using surplus cash flow.

It's harder to sketch the cash flow profile of products in decline since they are usually revamped, sold or abandoned before decline takes hold. Operating flows are likely to remain positive even if the product becomes unprofitable since key expenses like depreciation involve no cash outlay. They are lower than in the maturity phase, however. Investing outflows are modest: in fact, there may well be net inflows in some periods should the company dispose of productive capacity. Similarly, financing outflows – on debt repayment or equity transfers to new products – are small, reflecting declining operations and modest investment needs.

Estimating from actual cash flows the stage in the lifecycle that a *company* has reached is more difficult. A firm can be viewed as a portfolio of products. Not all products will be at the same stage of the lifecycle. Take the case of a pharmaceutical company. New drugs are in the 'introduction' or 'growth' stages while drugs that are off-patent are in the 'decline' stage. Even for a firm with products that are at a similar stage in their lifecycles, actual corporate cash flows may not correspond to expected flows in any one year. For example, in a recession a 'mature' company may well report falling profits and operating inflows. If operating cash flows fall below investment commitments, it will probably have to raise external capital in the period.

Nevertheless, cash flow profiling is a useful exercise. By first considering the growth trends in the industry and examining the cash flow statements of competitors, investors can construct an expected cash flow profile for the target company. This allows them to forecast its future operating and investing cash flows with more confidence.

Detecting earnings manipulation

Earlier we questioned the argument for using operating cash flow – or a variant such as Ebitda – as a performance measure. There is one circumstance, however, when OCF may be a more reliable indicator of a company's financial performance than reported earnings, and that is when investors suspect management of manipulating its profits.

To detect possible earnings manipulation, analysts investigate the amount and composition of a company's accruals. Rearranging the OCF equation given earlier yields:

Net profit (loss) = Operating cash flow –/+ Effect of accruals

Faced with slower growth – or even a fall – in a company's OCF, management may resort to accounting ploys to boost reported profits or stem their decline. The most popular ploy is to overstate operating revenues by recognising them early. Other widely used ones are to capitalise expenses or defer recognition of asset write-downs and provisions. These profit-boosting techniques have an effect on accruals. For example, bringing forward the recognition of revenues results in higher accounts receivable. Capitalising expenses manifests itself in an increase in reported inventory or deferred charges. (If the expenses are capitalised in a tangible or intangible fixed asset, the increase in accruals is reflected in higher depreciation in later periods.) Underproviding for bad debts and warranty costs also has a balance sheet effect (higher accounts receivable, lower provisions). Because management may use a variety of profit-boosting techniques involving more than one type of accrual, analysts monitor the movement in total accruals. There is empirical evidence that accruals are higher, in proportionate terms, among firms that are earnings manipulators. Moreover, the accruals of such firms tend to increase over time until the manipulation is discovered (*see* Box 18.1).

BOX
18.1

Using cash flow data to detect earnings manipulation

Despite being confusing to the novice investor, the indirect approach to deriving operating cash flow, namely, adjusting reported profit for non-cash charges and changes in operating working capital, does have one key advantage. It helps accounting sleuths. They can identify more easily a company's accruals in the period – by both type and amount – and use them to unmask manipulation of its earnings by managers.

Dechow, Sloan and Sweeney carried out interesting research in this area. They studied the characteristics of US firms that were subject to accounting enforcement actions by the SEC for alleged violation of US GAAP in the period 1982–92. In most cases, the alleged violation took the form of overstating revenues, understating expenses (or losses) or a combination of the two. The effect on accruals was significant. Dechow, *et al.* compared 66 alleged GAAP violators with 69 firms matched by industry, size and time period. For the former group, total accruals as a percentage of assets rose in the three years prior to the year the SEC alleged manipulation took place and then fell sharply in the following two years, as the previous accrual overstatements were reversed. By contrast, the accruals-to-assets ratio of the control group exhibited no systematic change over the same five-year period.

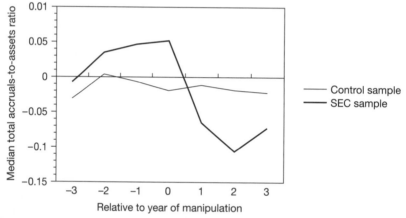

(*Source*: Dechow, P., Sloan, R. and Sweeney, A. (1996), Causes and consequences of earnings manipulation: an analysis of firms subject to enforcement actions by the SEC, *Contemporary Accounting Research*, 13(1), figure 1.)

What type of company manipulates its earnings? Dechow *et al.* reason that the activity is more likely to occur when management have both the incentive and the opportunity to do so. The *incentive* to manipulate is greater when a company needs to raise outside capital. A company that can demonstrate a history of strong and growing earnings should be able to obtain new capital at lower cost. Although many industries were represented in the SEC sample of alleged violators, one-third of the companies came from the capital-hungry high-tech sector (computer equipment, business services (including computer software) and instrumentation). Managers also manipulate earnings to prevent debt covenants being breached. Dechow *et al.* found that, relative to the control group, a significantly higher proportion of the SEC sample reported a technical violation of a debt covenant in the year of alleged manipulation and the two subsequent years.

As for the *opportunity* to manipulate earnings, this is greater in companies where the governance structure is weak. Dechow *et al.* investigated various indicators of corporate governance. They found that boards of directors in the SEC sample exercised less oversight over management than did boards in the control sample. Firms in the SEC sample were less likely to have an audit committee and had proportionately fewer non-executive directors. In addition, less of the board's shareholding was in the hands of non-executive directors and the CEO was more likely to be the founder of the company.[8]

(Reproduced by permission of Canadian Academic Accounting Association.)

SECTION 2	Specialised topics

Constructing a cash flow statement from balance sheet data

We've indicated some of the benefits to investors from the cash flow statement. What can investors do if a company doesn't provide one? Fortunately, it's possible to construct a cash flow statement using balance sheet and income statement data. The resulting statement is only approximate, however. If the company has large foreign operations or has made major acquisitions or disposals of businesses in the year, the derived cash flow statement may contain significant errors. It's not possible to isolate foreign currency cash flows from changes in balance sheet numbers that are all expressed in the reporting currency. And changes in working capital derived from balance sheet numbers include the working capital effects of businesses acquired (or disposed of) in the year. These are strictly investing cash flows and should not enter into the calculation of OCF. Nonetheless, in all other cases the statement should be sufficiently accurate to let the investor perform the kinds of analysis outlined in section 1 of the chapter.

As is evident from its title, the cash flow statement shows the *movement* in cash *over a period*. Thus the 'do-it-yourself' (DIY) preparer needs *two* balance sheets, at the start and end of the period, to identify why the company's cash balance has changed over the period. The income statement provides information – for example, about non-cash expenses – to supplement that in the two balance sheets.

● DIY construction of cash flow statement

To construct a cash flow statement (CFS) for a financial year, the DIY preparer must complete the following steps:

1 *Determine the change in the company's cash balance over the year.* This is the CFS's 'bottom line'.
2 *Calculate the changes in all other balance sheet accounts over the year.* The changes in these accounts must be equal, in sum, to the change in cash, if the balance sheet identity: A ≡ L + OE, is to be preserved.
3 *Identify the reasons for the changes in the non-cash accounts calculated in step 2.* Cash flows are then grouped by activity, specifically operating, investing and financing activities, as in Exhibit 18.1.

We show with an example how a CFS is prepared, using only balance sheet and income statement data. Figaro & Company is a conglomerate whose main interests – franchised hair salons, personal valet recruitment – are in the service sector. Figaro's x2 accounts, summarised in Exhibit 18.3, contain an income statement for x2 and comparative balance sheets for x1 and x2.

A cash flow statement for x2 is lacking: our task is to construct one. We do so by applying the three steps to Figaro's x2 accounts.

Step 1   Determine the change in cash and cash equivalents

'Cash' includes cash held by the company ('Cash in hand') and demand deposits held at banks and other financial institutions. 'Cash equivalents' are short-term, highly liquid investments – defined as those that mature within three months.[9] In Figaro's case, cash and cash equivalents – 'broad cash' for short – fall by 2 million in x2.

Exhibit 18.3

Figaro & Company
Annual Accounts for x2
(amounts in millions)

INCOME STATEMENT
for the year to 31 December x2

Operating revenues		154
Operating expenses (including depreciation of 8)		−129
Operating profit		25
Investment income	5	
Interest expense	−1	
Loss on sale of long-term investment	−2	
		+2
Profit before tax		27
Income tax expense		−10
Net profit		17
Dividend		−6
Retained profit for the year		11

BALANCE SHEETS
at 31 December x1 and x2

	x1	x2
Fixed assets		
Land, buildings and equipment	52	116
Less: Accumulated depreciation	−18	−26
Land, buildings and equipment, net	34	90
Long-term investments	41	38
Total fixed assets	75	128
Current assets		
Inventories	7	16
Accounts receivable	20	27
Short-term investments	8	5
Cash	2	3
Total current assets	37	51
Total assets	112	179
Shareholders' equity		
Share capital	9	12
Share premium	10	20
Retained profits	40	51
Total shareholders' equity	59	83
Liabilities		
Long-term debt	25	63
Provisions	12	14
Accounts payable, current	6	12
Taxes payable, current	10	7
Total liabilities	53	96
Total equities	112	179

(In millions)	x1	x2	Change
Cash	2	3	
Short-term investments	8	5	
Broad cash	10	8	−2

Step 2   Calculate changes in non-cash accounts

Recall the form of the balance sheet identity. It can be written in expanded form as:

$$\text{Cash} + \text{Non-cash assets} = \text{Liabilities} + \text{Shareholders' equity} \qquad (18.1)$$

'Cash' here is broad cash. Rearranging, equation 18.1 becomes:

$$\text{Cash} = \text{Liabilities} + \text{Shareholders' equity} - \text{Non-cash assets} \qquad (18.2)$$

Since equation 18.2 holds at any date, it must also be true of changes in the balance sheet between two dates:

$$\Delta\text{Cash} = \Delta\text{L} + \Delta\text{SE} - \Delta\text{Non-cash A} \qquad (18.3)$$

Thus in Figaro's case, the changes in balance sheet accounts other than cash during x2 must sum to a negative 2 million. This is shown in Exhibit 18.4.

Exhibit 18.4   **Figaro & Company: Change in cash and non-cash balances in x2**
(amounts in millions)

	x1	x2	Change	
Assets				
Land, buildings and equipment, net	34	90	+56	
Long-term investments	41	38	−3	+69
Inventories	7	16	+9	
Accounts receivable	20	27	+7	
Cash and short-term investments	10	8	−2	
Total assets	112	179		
Equities				
Share capital	9	12	+3	
Share premium	10	20	+10	+24
Retained profits	40	51	+11	
Long-term debt	25	63	+38	
Provisions	12	14	+2	+43
Accounts payable, current	6	12	+6	
Taxes payable, current	10	7	−3	
Total equities	112	179		

		Change in:			
		Shareholders'		Non-cash		Change in
Liabilities	+	equity	−	assets	=	(broad) cash
+43	+	24	−	(+69)	=	−2

Step 3 Explain why non-cash accounts have changed

We analyse next the movement in Figaro's individual liability, shareholders' equity and non-cash asset accounts to discover *why* (broad) cash declined by 2 million.

A helpful way to carry out this analysis is to set up a worksheet in columnar form. In the first two columns we list each non-cash balance sheet account and set down the net change in the account over the year. We then analyse the movement in each account in turn, showing in separate columns the cash flows attributable to operating, investing and financing activities. An example of such a worksheet is given in Exhibit 18.5 for Figaro & Company.

We start the worksheet with shareholders' equity – in particular, the retained profits account – since, for most companies, operating activities are the principal source of cash inflows. Thus the increase in retained profit of 11 in x2 (all amounts are in millions) is attributable to net profit of 17 (an operating inflow) and dividend payments of 6 (here shown as a financing outflow). We assume that the remaining increase of 13 in shareholders' equity is the result of an issuance of shares (a financing inflow). In practice, we would check this by consulting the notes to Figaro's accounts.

The movement in each liability and non-cash asset account is analysed in a similar way. Sometimes the explanation for the change in a balance sheet account can be found in the income statement. For example, the change in 'accumulated depreciation' (+8) is attributable to the annual depreciation charge on the company's fixed assets (*see* Exhibit 18.3). In many cases, however, we have to make assumptions, as we did with the increase in share capital and premium. Thus we assume that Figaro does not dispose of any property or equipment in x2: the gross increase of 64 is due solely to purchases of this amount. Other assumptions we make are:

● Figaro acquires no long-term investments in x2;
● interest expense and interest paid are the same; and
● the increase in provisions is the result of expenses accrued in the year (i.e. these have no cash impact).

Of course, if we have access to the notes to the accounts (not available in this case), we can prepare a more detailed cash flow statement.

Note that, in contrast to shareholders' equity and liability accounts, any movement in a non-cash asset account has the opposite effect on cash. This can be seen from equation 18.3. Thus the increase in Figaro's land, buildings and equipment (+64) indicates an investing cash *outflow*, the decrease in long-term investments (–3) an investing cash *inflow*.

Many of the changes in balance sheet accounts are the result of accruals and affect the calculation of operating cash flow. This is evident from the worksheet in Exhibit 18.5. The increases in accumulated depreciation and provisions reflect non-cash expenses. The movements in current liabilities (accounts payable, taxes payable) and current assets (inventories, accounts receivable) also represent the adjustment from expenses to expenditures, revenues to receipts.[10]

When the worksheet is complete and we can confirm that the sum of the cash flows by activity equals the change in broad cash, we are in a position to draw up a cash flow statement. Figaro and Company's x2 statement is set out in Exhibit 18.6.

The statement has three sections – for operating, investing and financing activities – corresponding to the three columns in the worksheet. The items in the 'operating activities' column are grouped in order to highlight non-cash items and changes in operating working capital. We look at alternative ways of presenting cash flows from operations in the next section.

What does the cash flow statement tell us about Figaro's activities in x2? The company appears to be growing strongly in x2. Although it is profitable and generates positive OCF that year, its internal cash flow is not sufficient to finance its heavy capital expenditure programme. Its free cash flow (defined here as OCF less net capex) is negative. It turns to outside sources – mainly long-term borrowing but also new equity capital – to meet the shortfall. As a result, its debt–equity ratio rises from around 40% to over 70% between the start and end of x2.

Exhibit 18.5 Figaro & Company: cash flow worksheet for x2 (amounts in millions)

Balance sheet account	Net change in x2	Cash inflow (+) from, outflow (–) on:		
		Operating activities	Investing activities	Financing activities
Shareholders' equity				
Retained profits	+11	+17 *Net profit*		–6 *Dividend*
Share capital	+3 ⎱			+13 *Issuance of shares*
Share premium	+10 ⎰			
Liabilities				
Long-term debt	+38			+38 *Additional loan*
Provisions	+2	+2 *Non-cash expense*		
Accounts payable	+6	+6 *Increase in A/P*		
Taxes payable	–3	–3 *Decrease in T/P*		
– Non-cash assets				
Land, buildings, and equipment (at cost)	+64		–64 *Purchase*	
– Accumulated depreciation	–(+8)	+8 *Non-cash expense*		
Long-term investments	–3		+3 *Disposal**	
Inventories	+9	–9 *Increase in inventories*		
Accounts receivable	+7	–7 *Increase in A/R*		
Totals, by activity		+14	–61	+45
Change in (broad) cash			–2	

* This is the *book value* of investments sold. *Cash* received is only 1, since investments are sold at a loss of 2 (*see* Exhibit 18.3). The disposal may also be shown as follows:

	Operating activities	Investing activities
Long-term investments	+2 'Loss on disposal' (Net profit adjustment)	+1 'Disposal, cash proceeds'

Presentation of cash flows

Exhibit 18.6 shows a simple cash flow statement. The one investors find in an annual report may well be more complicated. In this section we look more closely at the way cash flow data are presented. We focus on issues where the presentation appears strange or is difficult to

Exhibit 18.6

Figaro & Company
Cash Flow Statement for x2
(amounts in millions)

Operating activities

Net profit		17
Adjustments for items not involving cash:		
Depreciation		+8
Increase in provisions		+2
		27

Changes in operating working capital:

Increase in inventories	−9	
Increase in accounts receivable	−7	
Increase in accounts payable	+6	
Decrease in taxes payable	−3	
		−13
Cash flow from operations		14*

Investing activities

Purchase of land, buildings and equipment	−64	
Disposal of investments (at book value)	+3	
Cash outflow on investing activities		−61*

Financing activities

Issuance of shares	+13	
Increase in debt	+38	
Dividend paid	−6	
Cash outflow on financing activities		+45
Net cash flow in x2		−2
Cash and short-term investments, at start-x2		10
Cash and short-term investments, at end-x2		8

* If the disposal of investments is shown at the cash amount, the operating and investing activities'
sections are modified accordingly:

Operating activities

Net profit		17
Adjustments: Depreciation		+8
Increase in provisions		+2
Loss on disposal of investments		+2
		29
Changes in operating working capital (net)		−13
Cash flow from operations		16

Investing activities

Purchase of land, buildings and equipment	−64	
Disposal of investments, cash proceeds	+1	
Cash outflow on investing activities		−63
		⋮

The financing activities' section is unchanged and thus the 'net cash flow' is still −2.

understand. In each case, we describe the preferred treatment under international accounting rules.[11]

Presentation of operating cash flows: the direct approach

In calculating Figaro's x2 operating cash flow we used the indirect approach. Net profit is adjusted for the effects of accruals in the year. This is the approach used by most companies that publish cash flow statements.

Under the alternative direct approach, operating cash flows are stated gross. The first line of the 'operating activities' section shows operating receipts, which for most companies comprise cash collected from customers during the year. Operating payments – that is, payments for materials and services, including labour services, made during the year – are deducted from this figure. Exhibit 18.7 provides an example of this approach. It is taken from the 2001 consolidated accounts of Kone, a large Finnish company that makes, installs and maintains elevators and escalators.

Note that Kone, in line with IAS requirements, provides a reconciliation of profit to cash flow from operating activities. Investors can see at a glance the reasons why the two diverge. Thus they get the benefits of both approaches in one statement.

Investors prefer the direct approach. They find it easier to understand. Accounting regulators encourage firms to present operating cash flows in this way. Why then do companies persist in using the indirect approach? The main reason is cost. Many companies would have to alter their accounting systems to produce aggregate operating receipts and payments data. Since there is no internal demand for this information, they do not gather it.

Classification of interest and dividends received and paid

Figaro's net profit of 17 includes investment income and interest charges. As can be seen from Exhibit 18.6, we make no adjustment for them in the operating activities section of Figaro's x2 cash flow statement. As a result, they are, in effect, treated as operating cash flows. This is illogical. Interest and dividends received are part of the returns on investment: it would be more appropriate to show them as investing, not operating, cash inflows. Interest paid is the cost of debt: if dividends paid, a cost of equity capital, are shown as a financing outflow, then, logically, interest paid should be too.

IAS permit either the illogical treatment (i.e. that shown in Exhibit 18.6) or the logical one, so long as the company is consistent. Firms following US practice take the illogical route, since US rules require them to. One advantage is that income taxes do not have to be apportioned among operating, investing and financing activities. Taxes paid or refunded are shown as part of operating cash flows.

International rules do insist that, whichever treatment is adopted, the company should disclose the interest and dividends received and paid in the year. Interest cover, a key measure of financial risk, will be overstated if an investor fails to include in the denominator interest which has been paid but which has been capitalised in fixed assets or inventory rather than expensed as incurred.

Irish and UK firms follow a third route. Operating cash flow is stated before interest and tax. Interest and dividends received (returns on investment) and interest and preference dividends paid (servicing of finance) form a separate section. Income taxes are shown separately; so, too, are ordinary dividends paid. Exhibit 18.8 illustrates the Anglo-Irish version of the cash flow statement. It is taken from the 2001 consolidated accounts of Waterford Wedgwood, an Irish-owned producer of china and glassware.

Exhibit 18.7 OCF presentation under the direct approach
Kone: extracts from consolidated statement of cash flows, 2001

Million euros	2001	2000
Cash receipt from customers	2,892.2	2,604.0
Cash paid to suppliers and employees	(2,548.6)	(2,366.8)
Cash flow from financial items	1.3	(5.6)
Cash flow from taxes and other items	(90.4)	(60.3)
Cash flow from operating activities	254.5	171.3
Reconciliation of net income to cash flow from operating activities		
Net income	141.1	105.6
Depreciation	82.4	80.6
Minority interest	1.1	0.1
Income before change in working capital	224.6	186.3
Change in receivables	(30.7)	(74.0)
Change in payables	15.7	68.2
Change in inventories	44.9	(9.2)
Cash flow from operating activities	254.5	171.3

(*Source*: Kone Corporation, *Annual Report 2001*.)

Waterford Wedgwood's 2001 operating cash flow – before interest and tax – is €68.4 million. The company provides, in the notes to the cash flow statement, a reconciliation of this figure to operating profit.

Cash flows from equity method investments

Under the equity method of accounting, the investor company recognises as income its share of the investee company's profit or loss in the period. However, the cash return on the investment is the dividend it receives from the investee. Consider the case of an investor company which, like Figaro, uses the indirect approach to determine operating cash flow. If the starting point of its OCF calculation is profit including investment income, it must first *deduct* equity-method profit (or add back equity-method losses). It then *includes* dividends received from the investee as part of operating (or investing) cash flow. *Alternatively, it deducts, from net profit, its share of the investee's undistributed profit for the period.*

An example makes this clearer. A company recognises investment income of 9 (million): this is its share of the investee's profit. It receives a dividend of 3 from the investee. Thus the income it reports overstates the cash return on its investment by 6. It can adjust profit as follows:

Operating activities
Net profit   xx
Adjustments to profit:
　⋮
Less:
Share of undistributed profit of associated company   −6
　⋮
Cash flow from operations   xx

Exhibit 18.8 Presentation of cash flow statement under UK/Irish GAAP
Waterford Wedgwood: consolidated cash flow statement, 2001

In € million	Year ended 31 December 2001	2000
Net cash inflow from operating activities	**68.4**	90.2
Returns on investments and servicing of finance		
Interest received	**2.0**	2.1
Interest paid	**(28.0)**	(26.9)
	(26.0)	(24.8)
Taxation paid	**(9.3)**	(13.4)
Capital expenditure and financial investment		
Payments to acquire tangible fixed assets	**(38.0)**	(62.5)
Receipts from sales of tangible fixed assets	**13.7**	7.8
Net payments for financial assets	**(0.9)**	(0.9)
	(25.2)	(55.6)
Acquisitions and disposals		
Costs arising on acquisition of Ashling Corporation	**(0.7)**	–
Debt assumed on acquisition of Ashling Corporation	**(4.6)**	–
Acquisition of a further 5.2% of Rosenthal AG	**(5.3)**	–
Purchase of Hutschenreuther brand and related assets	**(2.3)**	(8.4)
	(12.9)	(8.4)
Equity dividends paid	**(20.2)**	(16.8)
Net cash flow before financing	**(25.2)**	(28.8)
Financing		
Issue of ordinary share capital	**1.8**	1.7
Sale of treasury shares	**–**	8.6
New long-term loans	**170.4**	230.4
Repayment of long-term loans	**(106.2)**	(250.8)
Repayment of capital element of finance lease rentals	**(0.2)**	(0.4)
	65.8	(10.5)
Increase/(decrease) in cash	**40.6**	(39.3)

(*Source*: Waterford Wedgwood plc, *Annual Report and Accounts 2001*.)

A simpler and clearer way of achieving the same result is for the company to start the operating activities section with 'Profit before investment income'. In this case, the investor company makes just one entry in the cash flow statement to record the dividend (of 3) it receives from the investee. (Exhibit 18.10 in the Problem Assignments contains an example of this approach. 'Income from associates' of SFr 133 million, shown under 'Investing activities', represents the dividends Nestlé received in 2001 from its associated companies (principally L'Oréal, the French cosmetics producer, in which Nestlé has a 26% stake). Nestlé excludes its share of these companies' profits from the 'Net profit of consolidated companies' figure which heads the 'Operating activities' section of the cash flow statement.)

Minority interests and joint ventures

A consolidated cash flow statement explains the movement in the group's cash balance over the year. This is more than just the parent company's cash balance. Under global consolidation, it includes 100% of the cash balances of subsidiary companies as well. As a result, the consolidated cash flow statement shows the operating, investing and financing cash flows of the parent company and all the companies under its control.

Should the parent own less than 100% of a subsidiary's shares, it must make adjustments in the statement for cash flows to and from minority shareholders. For example, where a subsidiary pays a cash dividend, the statement must show, as a group cash outflow, dividends paid to both parent company shareholders and the subsidiary's minority shareholders.

In addition, the consolidated cash flow statement may include a 'minority interests' adjustment under operating activities. If OCF is derived by the indirect approach and the starting figure is 'net profit attributable to parent company shareholders', the minority shareholders' interest in the subsidiary's profits (losses) must be added back (subtracted) to arrive at group OCF. We illustrate these points below:

	Operating activities	
	Net profit to parent company shareholders	xx
+	Minority interests (in subsidiary's profits)	+xx
+/–	Non-cash expenses (of group)	+/–xx
+/–	Change in operating working capital (of group)	+/–xx
	Cash flow from (group) operations	xx
	Investing activities	
–	Capital expenditures (of group)	–xx
	⋮	⋮
	Financing activities	
	⋮	
–	Dividends paid to parent company shareholders and minority shareholders in subsidiary companies	–xx
	⋮	⋮
	Change in cash (and equivalents) of group	xx

The accounting treatment of joint ventures dictates the cash flow presentation. Where a joint venture is consolidated on a proportionate basis, the cash flow statement includes the venturer's share of the venture's operating, investing and financing cash flows. Where the joint venture is accounted for under the equity method, only the venturer's investments in, and dividends from, the venture are shown in the cash flow statement.

Acquisitions and disposals of subsidiaries

Consolidated cash flow figures can be distorted if a company does not report separately the purchase or sale of a subsidiary (or other business unit, e.g. the net assets of a division). For example, the OCF figure is misstated if, in adjusting net profit for changes in operating working capital, the company includes the working capital contributed by subsidiaries acquired in the year. Such working capital should be viewed as part of the net assets acquired and classified as an *investing* cash outflow. International standards require firms to show, under investing activities, the net cash flows associated with the acquisition and disposal of subsidiaries. In the notes to the cash flow statement, the firm must disclose the total purchase or sale consideration and provide a breakdown of the assets acquired or sold and any liabilities assumed or transferred.

Interbrew's 2000 accounts illustrate international disclosure requirements well. Belgium-based Interbrew is one of the world's largest beer producers and has grown rapidly in recent years largely through acquisitions. Exhibit 18.9 contains details of the investing activities section of its 2000 consolidated cash flow statement and the note giving details of the net assets acquired

Exhibit 18.9   Investing cash flows and analysis of acquisitions
Interbrew Group: extracts from 2000 accounts

In € million	2000
Cash flow from operating activities	**871**
Investing activities	
Proceeds from sale of property, plant and equipment	59
Proceeds from sale of intangible assets	3
Proceeds from sale of investments	205
Acquisition of subsidiaries, net of cash acquired	(4,445)
Acquisition of property, plant and equipment	(465)
Acquisition of intangible assets	(22)
Acquisition of other investments	(65)
Payments of loans granted	(402)
Cash flows from investing activities	**(5,132)**
Cash flows from financing activities	**4,594**
Net increase in cash and cash equivalents	**333**
Cash and cash equivalents at beginning of year	321
Effect of exchange rate fluctuations on cash held	9
Cash and cash equivalents at end of year	**663**

Note 3 (condensed)   **Acquisitions of subsidiaries**

Net assets acquired:	
Property, plant and equipment	1,292
Intangible assets other than goodwill	10
Financial assets, non-current	368
Prepaid employee benefit costs	237
Provisions	(134)
Minority interests	(4)
Financial creditors, long-term	(25)
Net working capital	82
Cash and cash equivalents	95
	1,921
Goodwill on acquisition	2,619
Consideration paid	4,540
Less: Cash and cash equivalents acquired	(95)
Net cash outflow	**4,445**

(*Source*: Interbrew SA, *Annual Report and Accounts 2000.*)

during the year. The investing activities section shows that Interbrew spent around €400 million net on property, plant and equipment in 2000, but over ten times that amount – €4,445 million – acquiring other brewers that year. The firms involved were Whitbread and Bass in the UK and Rogan in the Ukraine. The notes to the accounts give a breakdown by asset (and liability) of the purchase cost of these businesses. (These details have been condensed for the purposes of this exhibit.) Interestingly, Interbrew assigns almost 60% (2,619/4,540) of the purchase cost to goodwill.

Cash flows in foreign currencies

A company with foreign operations – or one that simply conducts business with foreign companies – has cash flows denominated in foreign currencies. How does it record these flows in its cash flow statement? *The general principle under international rules is that a cash flow in a foreign currency should be translated into the reporting currency at the exchange rate prevailing when the cash flow occurs.* (If transactions take place evenly during the year, an average rate can be used.) Thus, unrealised foreign currency gains and losses do not appear in the cash flow statement.

We illustrate this with a simple example. Suppose an Italian company has a South African subsidiary whose principal asset at the start of x1 is land amounting to R100 million. The subsidiary neither buys nor sells land during x1 but the rand weakens from R8.6 : €1 to R9.1 : €1 between the start and end of the year. Translating foreign assets at end-year exchange rates (the South African subsidiary is an autonomous unit), the Italian group reports a decrease in its South African asset of €0.6 million (11.6 – 11.0) in its x1 consolidated accounts. However, the €0.6 million does not appear in its x1 cash flow statement since no cash transaction has occurred.

Companies with foreign operations usually show an item labelled 'Exchange rate effect on cash' (or similar wording – *see* Exhibit 18.9) next to the start-year cash balance in the cash flow statement. The purpose of this adjustment is to take account of the effect of exchange rate changes over the year on start-year foreign currency cash balances. In the case of Interbrew, the foreign currencies in which it held cash at the beginning of 2000 appreciated against the euro during the year – hence the €9 million positive adjustment to start-year cash in the 2000 cash flow statement.

Non-cash transactions

Some accounting transactions bypass the cash account completely. A company may swap capital (e.g. debt for equity) or assets (property for investments). It may acquire another company by issuing and distributing its own shares to the owners. Such transactions involve neither the receipt nor the payment of cash. As a result, they are not recorded on the cash flow statement. IAS, however, requires companies to disclose separately the impact of material non-cash transactions in order to give the financial statement user a fuller picture of a firm's investing and financing activities in the period.

New developments in the presentation of cash flow data

The cash flow statement is still evolving. As we have already seen, accounting rule-makers in certain countries require domestic firms to present cash flow data in a different form and in greater detail than international rules demand. Some firms are voluntarily providing additional cash flow information in response to investor requests. We look at two recent innovations which may well be adopted by international regulators in the future.

The first concerns the firm's capital expenditures on tangible and intangible fixed assets – or 'capex' for short. Some firms estimate the maintenance and expansion components of capex.

This allows investors to calculate the firm's free cash flow directly. (In an earlier section, we defined free cash flow as available cash flows less maintenance capital expenditures. OCF is often used as a proxy for available cash flows.) Orkla, a large Norwegian group with industrial and financial interests, breaks down capital expenditures in its industrial division in this way. In fact, it reports the division's free cash flow on the face of the group's cash flow statement.

In the second innovation, firms link the change in their cash balance to the change in their net indebtedness. 'Net indebtedness' is simply debt (i.e. interest-bearing liabilities including finance leases) less liquid assets (broad cash and short-term marketable securities). Why is this figure of interest to investors? We noted in Chapter 11 that many investors measure leverage in terms of net debt since debt-laden companies may carry large amounts of cash for hedging or investment reasons. Moreover, companies themselves often combine the management of cash and debt. This is one of the key tasks of a firm's treasury department. For these reasons the separation of flows of short-term financial investments, debt and cash on the face of the IAS-style cash flow statement may be artificial and potentially misleading. Irish and UK companies are required under national accounting rules to analyse the change in net debt over the year in a supplementary note to the cash flow statement. Swedish companies define the bottom line of the cash flow statement in broad terms: where the firm has net debt, the bottom line is the change in financing (or net debt) rather than the change in cash.

Summary

Here's a nice irony: cash is a well-understood asset that has been around for millennia; the cash flow statement is a new financial statement which perplexes many readers of annual accounts.

Investors are alive to the benefits from analysing a company's cash flows. As we discuss in the chapter, they use cash flow data to:

- *assess a company's debt-paying ability* – they monitor its cash-based liquidity and leverage ratios and estimate the future cash flows that are available for servicing its debts;
- *construct alternative performance measures* – cash-based ratios can provide more comparable measures of corporate performance than accrual-based ones, because they overcome differences in accrual accounting practices among firms;
- *gain strategic insights* – investors look at a company's cash flow profile to better predict its growth prospects. The composition of its cash flows sheds light on management's investment and financing decisions;
- *gauge incidence and extent of earnings manipulation* – by monitoring the size and direction of accruals, investors get early warning of any attempts by management to increase or smooth the company's earnings.

So useful are cash flow data that investors will construct an approximate cash flow statement if a company does not provide one. We showed how this can be done, using start- and end-period balance sheets and income statement data.

Why then do many investors find published cash flow statements puzzling? The main reason is the way cash flow data are presented.

- Most firms use the indirect approach to calculate operating cash flow: gross operating receipts and payments are not disclosed.
- Some investing and financing flows (e.g. interest received and paid) may be shown as operating flows.
- The emphasis on the cash flow impact of transactions (e.g. corporate acquisitions and operations in foreign currencies) may make it difficult for investors to reconcile cash flow numbers with those in the balance sheet and income statement. We illustrated these points in the chapter.

But there is another reason for investor confusion. The activity-based cash flow statement lacks the hierarchical structure of the income statement or balance sheet. The statement's 'bottom line' – the change in cash in the period – is not easy to interpret, unlike net profit or loss, its income statement counterpart. Investors must rearrange the data (and on occasion make estimates) to calculate key numbers such as free cash flow.

Problem assignments

P18.1 Cash flow statements: initial analysis

Swiss-based Nestlé is the world's largest consumer foods company with 2001 sales of €56 billion. It's best known for its beverage (Nescafé), bottled water (Perrier, Vittel) and confectionery (Kit Kat) brands. In recent years, it has expanded its petfood business through acquisitions of companies (Spillers (1998), Ralston Purina (2001)). Its consolidated cash flow statement for calendar 2001 is set out in Exhibit 18.10.

Nestlé prepares its cash flow statement according to IAS. The statement has certain unusual features, however. 'Net profit of consolidated companies' (the first item under 'Operating activities') is group net profit, i.e. before taking account of minority interests in subsidiaries' profits and Nestlé's share of associated companies' profits. (The dividend Nestlé received from associated companies is shown against 'Income from associates' under 'Investing activities'.) Nestlé shows changes in marketable securities and short-term investments under 'Financing activities': management view liquid assets as part of net debt and thus changes in these assets are presented alongside changes in debt.

Required

(a) Prepare an initial analysis of Nestlé's cash flows in 2000 and 2001. Condense the company's cash flow statement and calculate the following key numbers for both years:
  (i)   Free cash flow (defined as OCF less net capex and dividends paid);
  (ii) Net cash flow before financing;
  (iii) Net increase or decrease in debt;
  (iv) Net increase or decrease in liquid assets.

(b) As part of your analysis, answer the following questions:
  (i)   Was the company self-financing in 2000 and 2001? If it was, how did it deploy the cash surplus? If it was not, how did it finance the shortfall?
  (ii) Were there any major events affecting the company's investment strategy or financial structure in either year? If so, how did they affect the company's cash flows?

P18.2 Assessing financial risk using cash flow data

Franz, an analyst at a large insurance company, receives the following e-mail from Sylvie, his boss.

'Can you take a look at Unilever's financial leverage for me? I'm concerned about the impact of the Bestfoods acquisition in 2000. It played havoc with their balance sheet. Their profitability seems to have recovered in 2001 but their debt levels still look very high.

'I'm particularly interested in the group's net debt-to-Ebitda ratio. I read that Procter & Gamble, Unilever's big rival in the household products market, had a net debt-to-Ebitda ratio of only 1.37 in 2001/02 and it's been pretty steady in recent years (2000/01: 1.39; 1999/2000: 1.33). How does Unilever compare with P&G on this ratio?

Exhibit 18.10 Nestlé Group: consolidated cash flow statement, 2001

In millions of Swiss francs	*2001*	*2000*
Operating activities		
Net profit of consolidated companies	**6,338**	5,580
Depreciation of property, plant and equipment	**2,581**	2,737
Impairment of property, plant and equipment	**222**	223
Amortisation of goodwill	**494**	414
Depreciation of intangible assets	**150**	179
Impairment of goodwill	**184**	230
Increase/(decrease) in provisions and deferred taxes	**(92)**	(4)
Decrease/(increase) in working capital	**(870)**	(368)
Other movements	**(393)**	(140)
Operating cash flow	**8,614**	8,851
Investing activities		
Capital expenditure	**(3,611)**	(3,305)
Expenditure on intangible assets	**(288)**	(188)
Sale of property, plant and equipment	**263**	355
Acquisitions	**(18,766)**	(2,846)
Disposals	**484**	780
Income from associates	**133**	107
Other movements	**143**	39
Cash flow from investing activities	**(21,642)**	(5,058)
Financing activities		
Dividend for the previous year	**(2,127)**	(1,657)
Purchase of treasury shares	**(1,133)**	(765)
Sale of treasury shares and options	**880**	1,837
Premium on warrants issued	**209**	81
Movements with minority interests	**(172)**	(221)
Bonds issued	**3,338**	1,016
Bonds repaid	**(380)**	(1,143)
Increase/(decrease) in other long-term financial liabilities	**(71)**	(155)
Increase/(decrease) in short-term financial liabilities	**16,754**	921
Decrease/(increase) in marketable securities and other liquid assets	**(2,330)**	(2,788)
Decrease/(increase) in short-term investments	**216**	1,452
Cash flow from financing activities	**15,184**	(1,422)
Translation differences on flows	**60**	(175)
Increase/(decrease) in cash and cash equivalents	**2,216**	2,196
Cash and cash equivalents at beginning of year	**5,451**	3,322
Effects of exchange rate changes on opening balance	**(29)**	(67)
Cash and cash equivalents retranslated at beginning of year	**5,422**	3,255
Fair-value adjustment on cash and cash equivalents	**(21)**	–
Cash and cash equivalents at end of year	**7,617**	5,451

(*Source*: Nestlé Group, *Annual Accounts 2001*.)

'There's another cash flow measure of financial leverage I'd like you to calculate. It's called the cash flow adequacy ratio – or CFAR. The folks at Fitch, the credit rating agency, devised it.[12] It's calculated as follows:

$$CFAR = \frac{\text{Annual net free cash flow}}{\text{Average annual debt maturities over next 5 years}}$$

where:

Net free cash flow = Ebitda – Taxes paid – Interest paid – Preference dividends – Capex, net
Average annual debt maturities . . . = (Debt principal payments due in next five years)/5

'Fitch claims CFAR is a reliable indicator of changes in corporate credit quality. P&G had a CFAR of 2.9 in 2001/02. According to Fitch, that shows financial strength: in effect, the company's free cash flow covered average debt payments 2.9 times that year.'

Franz collects income and balance sheet data from the 1999–2001 accounts of the Anglo-Dutch food and household products group (*see* Exhibit 18.11). In addition, he extracts the following cash flow information from the group's cash flow statements for these years.

	2001	2000	1999
Income taxes paid	1,887	1,734	1,443
Interest paid (net of interest received)	1,651	620	58
Capital expenditures (net of disposals)	957	890	1,249

He's about to start work on the assignment when he gets called away on another project. He asks you to complete the assignment for him.

Required

(a) Calculate Unilever's net debt-to-Ebitda and CFAR ratios for each of the three years 1999–2001. Identify the main reasons for the changes in the two ratios over this time. Do the two ratios send the same signals about the group's credit quality and changes in it? If not, why not?

(b) Compare the two ratios, net debt-to-Ebitda and CFAR. Which of these ratios, in your opinion, provides a more accurate and reliable measure of a firm's debt-paying ability – and why?

P18.3 Detecting earnings manipulation with cash flow data

Managers sometimes try to inflate reported corporate earnings using dubious accounting techniques. Careful inspection of the cash flow statement may help investors unmask such manipulation. Consider the following examples.

(1) Unable to persuade customers to pay licensing fees for the use of its technology, SIT Company enters into 'advertising agreements' with some of them. Under the agreements, customers agree to carry out certain 'advertising' for SIT in exchange for technology licences. The advertising fees charged by the customers match the licensing fees SIT charges them so that SIT (and its customers) experience no net cash inflow or outflow as a result of the transactions. SIT books the licensing fees as current revenue but defers recognition of the advertising costs. As a result, it reports a profit from the exchange of services.

(2) AC, a carpet retail chain, states that its policy is to recognise revenue on a carpet sale only when the carpet has been delivered and fitted. The customer pays for the carpet before delivery occurs. As a result of pressure on store management to meet sales targets in a recent year, many stores brought forward the recognition of revenues on carpet sales made in the last two weeks of that year to the date of payment.

(3) B, a pharmaceutical company, normally books revenues when it ships goods to distributors. Recently, management became concerned that the company would not be able to meet stock

Exhibit 18.11 Unilever Group: summary income and balance sheet data, 1999–2001

In € million	2001	2000	1999
Consolidated profit and loss account (condensed)			
Group turnover	**51,514**	47,582	40,977
Group operating profit*	**5,174**	3,302	4,303
Share of operating profit of joint ventures	**84**	57	42
Other income from fixed investments	**12**	(4)	10
Interest expense, net	**(1,646)**	(632)	(14)
Profit on ordinary activities before taxation	**3,624**	2,723	4,341
Taxation on profit	**(1,547)**	(1,403)	(1,369)
Profit on ordinary activities after taxation	**2,077**	1,320	2,972
Minority interests	**(239)**	(215)	(201)
Net profit	**1,838**	1,105	2,771
Preference dividends	**(51)**	(44)	(20)
Dividends on ordinary capital	**(1,530)**	(1,414)	(1,245)
Result for the year retained	**257**	(353)	1,506
* After deducting 'Depreciation and amortisation'	2,845	1,954	1,147
Consolidated balance sheet at 31/12 (condensed)			
Fixed assets	**35,221**	37,463	9,606
Current assets other than cash	**15,876**	17,564	14,286
Cash	**1,862**	2,613	3,996
Borrowings, current	**(11,279)**	(16,675)	(2,936)
Trade and other creditors, current	**(11,933)**	(11,689)	(9,198)
Net current assets	**(5,474)**	(8,187)	6,148
Total assets less current liabilities	**29,747**	29,276	15,754
Borrowings, non-current**	**14,221**	13,066	1,853
Other long-term liabilities	**7,667**	7,423	5,561
Minority interests	**664**	618	579
Capital and reserves	**7,195**	8,169	7,761
Total capital employed	**29,747**	29,726	15,754
** Of which payable within five years (i.e. between years 2 and 5)	11,000	9,775	1,576

(*Source*: Unilever Group, *Annual Report and Accounts 2000 and 2001*.)

market expectations about annual sales and earnings growth. It persuaded distributors to increase purchases of its products at the end of its financial year by offering them 'bill and hold' terms. Under this policy, a distributor can delay paying for goods it buys. It orders goods from B and has them delivered to its warehouse. However, it pays for them only when they're shipped at a later date from the warehouse to the final customer (e.g. pharmacy, hospital, clinic). Meanwhile, B recognises revenue on delivery of the goods to the warehouse.

Required

Each of the above accounting policies creates a difference between profit and operating cash flow in the period. Identify the account or accounts where the difference appears. How might an investor use information from the cash flow statement to detect the manipulation of earnings in each case?

P18.4 Construction of a cash flow statement I

You are Emil. You have an eye for numbers. Geppetto, a puppet-maker, is troubled and asks for your help. 'We had a good year last year. After-tax profits were 13 million. How then can our cash have fallen by 2 million? Can you take a look at last year's accounts and tell me what's going on? I can't make head or tail of these accounts and people tell me you're quite a financial detective when it comes to balance sheets.'

He gives you the balance sheets of the company at 31 December x3 and x4. These are set out in Exhibit 18.12.

Exhibit 18.12

Geppetto Company
Balance sheets at 31 December x3 and x4
(amounts in millions, except per-share figures)

	x4	x3
Fixed assets		
Buildings and equipment:		
Cost	64	58
Less: Accumulated depreciation	−26	−25
Net book value	38	33
Investments	7	11
	45	44
Current assets		
Inventory	19	18
Accounts receivable	16	13
Cash	3	5
	38	36
Total assets	83	80
Shareholders' equity		
Share capital (par value 5)	22	20
Share premium	5	5
Retained profits	23	18
	50	43
Long-term liabilities		
Pension and other provisions	11	10
Bonds payable, net of discount	0	9
	11	19
Current liabilities		
Bank loan	8	2
Accounts payable and accrued liabilities	10	13
Corporate income taxes payable	4	3
	22	18
Shareholders' equity and liabilities	83	80

In addition, you uncover the following information about the company in x4. (All amounts except per-share figures are in millions.)

1 The company spends 21 on new buildings and equipment. It sells, for 9, fixed assets with a net book value of 11. Depreciation charged in the year is 5.
2 It sells investments with a carrying amount of 4 and reports a gain on sale of 1.5.
3 It pays a cash dividend of 1.5 a share during the year. At the end of the year, it declares and distributes a 10% share dividend to shareholders. There are no other issues of shares in the year.
4 Profit before tax is 20. Income tax expense is 7.
5 The bonds are retired at the start of the year and 9.5 is paid to bondholders.

Required

Prepare a cash flow statement for Geppetto Company, showing the flows of cash in x4 by activity. Draft a brief memo to Geppetto explaining the reason for the decline in cash in the year.

P18.5 **Construction of a cash flow statement II**

PaintPot is a manufacturer and distributor of decorative paints for use inside and outside the home. The company's x4 income statement and end-x3 and end-x4 balance sheets are set out in Exhibit 18.13. The notes to the accounts contain the following additional information. (All amounts save per-share amounts are in € millions.)

1 The company purchases equipment (tangible fixed assets) for 13.8 cash in x4.
2 PaintPot accounts for its stakes in associated companies by the equity method. It makes no new investments or disposals during x4.
3 All sales are on account. The company writes off bad debts of 8.9 in x4. Bad debt expense is included in 'Other operating costs' on the income statement.
4 The company issues one million new €5 par value shares at €12/share towards the end of x4 to finance the planned acquisition of a wallpaper manufacturer. Issuance costs of 0.4, all paid in the year, are charged against share premium.
5 Dividends are declared and paid in the same year.
6 PaintPot issued at par 10-year 10% bonds at the start of x1. The market rate of interest for debt of equivalent risk and maturity falls below 6% in x4 and the company decides to refinance the debt. It retires all the 10% bonds at the end of x4 and at the same time issues new 10 year 6% debt securities with a total face value of 35 at a price of 102 (per cent) yielding 5.73% to maturity.
7 Interest expense (income) is approximately equal to interest paid (received) in x4.

Required

Prepare a cash flow statement for PaintPot for x4, using balance sheet and income statement data. Present cash flows by activity. Use the indirect method to determine operating cash flow. Assume interest charges, investment income, interest income and taxes are classified as operating cash flows.

Check figure:
Net cash flow from operations   28.8

P18.6 **The cash flow statement: alternative format**

An investor asks you to explain some features of the cash flow statement of Thorntons, a UK confectionery producer and retailer, that puzzle her.

'Thorntons' cash flow statement has a strange format. It doesn't have the usual three-way split of operating, investing and financing cash flows. For example, take the statements for the years to end-June 2001 and 2002 (see [A] below: all the numbers are in £ millions). I can see an operating cash flow number but where are the investing and financing cash flow subtotals?

Exhibit 18.13 PaintPot Company: x4 income statement and end-x4 balance sheet

Consolidated income statement for x4
(in € million)

Sales revenue		474.3
Cost of sales		−275.3*
Other operating costs		−161.2
Operating profit		37.8
Exceptional items: Gain on disposal of tangible fixed assets	+4.8	
Loss on early retirement of bonds	−5.9	
		−1.1
Profit after exceptional items		36.7
Interest expense		−4.4
Interest income		+2.3
Profit before tax		34.6
Income tax expense		−11.3
Profit of consolidated companies after tax		23.3
Share of net profit of associated companies		+2.4
Minority interests		−2.9
Net profit for the year		22.8

* Includes depreciation of 10.8.

Consolidated balance sheets at 31 December
(in € million, save per-share amounts)

	x4	x3		x4	x3
Fixed assets			*Shareholders' equity*		
Tangible, at cost	104.6	105.5	Share capital (€5 par)	38.5	33.5
Less: Accumulated depreciation	−29.7	−32.3	Share premium	41.7	35.1
	74.9	73.2	Retained profits	66.7	64.0
Investments in associated				146.9	132.6
companies	10.5	9.6	Minority interests	11.8	9.7
	85.4	82.8		158.7	142.3
			Long-term liabilities		
Current assets			Bonds payable	35.7	30.0
Inventories	82.3	74.2	Restructuring provision	6.8	12.6
Trade receivables	102.1	91.2		42.5	42.6
Less: Allowance for bad debts	−7.7	−7.1	*Current liabilities*		
	94.4	84.1	Bank loans	31.0	22.5
Prepayments and accrued income	10.9	17.0	Trade payables	75.1	65.8
Cash at bank and in hand	63.5	43.4	Income tax payable	11.7	10.1
	251.1	218.71	Accrued expenses	17.5	18.2
				35.3	116.6
			Total shareholders'		
Total assets	336.5	301.5	equity and liabilities	336.5	301.5

[A]	2002	2001
Cash inflow from operating activities	21.2	21.1
Returns on investments and servicing of finance*	(3.5)	(4.1)
Taxation	0.5	0.9
Capital expenditure and financial investment	(2.8)	(1.6)
Equity dividends paid	(4.5)	(4.5)
Cash inflow before use of liquid resources and financing	10.9	11.8
Management of liquid resources	(2.3)	0.2
Financing – decrease in debt	(10.7)	(10.7)
(Decrease)/increase in cash in the period	(2.1)	1.3
* Interest received	0.3	0.2
Interest paid	(3.3)	(3.8)
Interest element of finance lease rental payments	(0.5)	(0.5)
Returns on investments and servicing of finance	(3.5)	(4.1)

'I'm also not sure about the "Cash inflow from operating activities" number. Thorntons seems to derive it from operating profit rather than after-tax profit. I'd like to compare the company's debt to OCF ratio with that of Swiss and Belgian chocolate makers that follow IAS. How do I adjust Thorntons' OCF number so that it's comparable? The company includes the following reconciliation in the notes to the 2001/02 accounts:

[B]	2002	2001
Operating profit	10.4	10.1
Loss on disposal of fixed assets	0.4	0.1
Depreciation and amortisation charges	13.5	13.1
Decrease in provisions	(0.5)	(0.7)
Operating cash flows before working capital movements	23.8	22.6
(Increase)/decrease in stocks	(0.8)	3.8
(Increase) in debtors	(1.7)	(1.4)
(Decrease) in creditors	(0.1)	(3.9)
Net cash inflow from operating activities	21.2	21.1

'One final point. Thorntons provides a reconciliation of net cash flow to the movement in net debt (see [C] below). I've not seen this in IAS-style cash flow statements before. On the face of it, this is a good idea. But the reconciliation makes me doubtful about the reliability of the numbers in the cash flow statement. For example, it shows net debt falling from £52.3 million at the start of 2000/01 to £37.2 million at the end of 2001/02, a decline of only £15.1 million.

[C]	2002	2001
(Decrease)/increase in cash in the period	(2.1)	1.3
Cash outflow from decrease in debt	10.7	10.7
Cash outflow/(inflow) from increase/(decrease) in liquid resources	2.3	(0.2)
Change in net debt resulting from cash flows	10.9	11.8
Inception of new finance leases	(3.7)	(4.1)
Translation difference	0.1	0.1
Movement in net debt in the period	7.3	7.8
Net debt at beginning of period	44.5	52.3
Net debt at end of period	37.2	44.5

'But according to the cash flow statement, net debt decreased by £22.7 million over the two years. Thorntons seems to have excluded the effect of new finance leases from the cash flow statement. Why have they done this? Surely the finance leases have a cash flow impact?'

Required

(a) Identify the cash flows in [A] that would be shown under 'Investing activities' and 'Financing Activities' in an IAS-style cash flow statement.

(b) Calculate the operating cash flow number that Thorntons would report in the bottom line of the 'Operating Activities' section of an IAS-style cash flow statement.

(c) Explain why Thorntons has excluded new finance leases from financing flows in the cash flow statement.

P18.7 Financing statement: conversion to cash basis

Spanish companies include a 'financing statement' in their published accounts in place of a cash flow statement. It shows the sources and uses of the company's *funds* in the period, where the term 'funds' indicates working capital (current assets less current liabilities) rather than cash. The statement can be converted to a cash basis. However, the resulting cash flow statement is approximate since key cash flow numbers (e.g. changes in working capital excluding the effects of acquisitions and disposals of businesses in the year) are not disclosed.

Compañía Logística de Hidrocarburos (CLH) is a company providing logistics services – mainly transport and storage of oil products – in mainland Spain and the Balearic Islands. Key operating data for the 1998–2001 period are given below:

In €m	2001	2000	1999	1998
Operating revenues	541	517	479	468
Net income	163	124	125	103

The company undertook a financial restructuring in 2001, replacing equity capital with debt. The aim, according to the company, was to increase returns on equity and thereby attract new shareholders.

CLH includes a financing statement in its 2001 accounts (*see* Exhibit 18.14). It describes it in the English-language version of the accounts as a 'statement of changes in financial position'.

Required

(a) Convert CLH's 2001 statement of changes in financial position to a cash basis. Analyse cash flows by operating, financing and investing activities. Use the 'Funds obtained from operations' figure as the starting point of the 'Operating activities' section. This figure is the sum of profit, depreciation and other long-term accruals.

(b) The company reported a major change in its financial balances in 2001 – from net cash of €153.3 million at the end of 2000 to net debt of €161 million a year later.

At 31 December	2001	2000
Short-term financial investments	1.4	152.3
Cash	22.4	2.7
– Long-term debt	(183.4)	(1.0)
– Short-term debt	(1.4)	(0.7)
Net cash/(debt)	(161.0)	153.3

Using the information in the cash flow statement you prepared in (a), explain the main reasons for the €314.3 million change in CLH's net financial position in 2001.

Check figure:
(a) Cash flow impact from change (€000)
in operating working capital +71,698

Exhibit 18.14   CLH: consolidated statement of changes in financial position, 2001

In €000	*2001*
Application of funds	
Tangible fixed asset additions	96,507
Dividends	506,745
Repayment, or transfer to short-term, of long-term debt	388
Provisions for contingencies and expenses	20,442
Total funds applied	**624,082**
Source of funds	
Funds obtained from operations	151,786
Fixed asset disposals	85,808
Tangible fixed assets	29,288
Long-term financial investments	56,520
Long-term debt	182,879
Reduction in working capital	203,609
Total funds obtained	**624,082**
Variation in working capital	
Inventories	(11,422)
Accounts receivable	74,588
Accounts payable	(135,331)
Short-term debt	(657)
Short-term financial investments	(150,906)
Cash	19,652
Accrual accounts	467
Total variation in working capital	**(203,609)**
Funds obtained from operations	
Income for the year	163,162
Add:	
Period depreciation and amortization	61,988
Provision for contingencies and expenses	19,726
Deferred corporate income tax asset	473
Less:	
Provisions transferred to income	453
Capital subsidies transferred to income	4,653
Gain on fixed asset disposals	62,227
Deferred corporate income tax liability	26,230
Total funds	**151,786**

(*Source*: Compañía Logística de Hidrocarburos (CLH), *Annual Accounts 2001.*)

Notes to Chapter 18

1 In the case of banks and other financial institutions, 'Operating activities' include the granting of loans and the acceptance of deposits. Similarly, stockbrokers classify the purchase and sale of securities they deal in as operating cash flows.

2 There are other dimensions to financial risk. For example, investors monitor price risk, that is the effect of changing prices (including changes in interest rates and exchange rates), on the company's business and its finances. We focus on credit risk because the cash flow statement is of most benefit in assessing this type of risk.

3 Sorter, G. and Benston, G. (1960), Appraising the defensive position of a firm: the interval measure, *The Accounting Review*, October: 633–640.

4 Empirical evidence supports this. For example, Dechow found that over various reporting periods (quarterly, annual, four-yearly) US companies' stock market returns were more closely associated with earnings than with cash flows. (Dechow, P. (1994), Accounting earnings and cash flows as measures of firm performance: the role of accounting accruals, *Journal of Accounting and Economics*, 18: 3–42.)

5 Barth, M., Cram, D. and Nelson, K. (2001), Accruals and the prediction of future cash flows, *The Accounting Review*, 76(1): 27–58.

6 Applying the EV/Ebitda multiple to a firm's current (or projected) Ebitda gives an estimate of the value of the *business* (i.e. the firm's net operating assets). To estimate the value of equity, subtract the firm's net debt at that date.

7 *See* Kotler, P. (2002), *Marketing Management*, 11th edition, Upper Saddle River, NJ: Prentice Hall, Chapter 11, for a fuller discussion of the concept of product lifecycles. *See also* Stickney, C. (1996), *Financial Reporting and Statement Analysis*, 3rd edition, Fort Worth, TX: Dryden Press, Chapter 2. Stickney applies the product lifecycle concept to corporate cash flows.

8 Dechow, P., Sloan, R. and Sweeney, A. (1996), Causes and consequences of earnings manipulation: an analysis of firms subject to enforcement actions by the SEC, *Contemporary Accounting Research*, 13(1): 1–36. Dechow *et al.* derive total accruals using balance sheet numbers (ΔCurrent assets – ΔCurrent liabilities – ΔCash + ΔShort-term debt – Depreciation and amortisation expense) since US firms were not required to publish cash flow statements before 1988. However, accruals are measured with error this way as the effects on working capital of businesses acquired or sold are not excluded from the changes in current assets and liabilities.

9 Where a firm has a bank overdraft (i.e. a bank loan that is repayable on demand), it may, under international rules, deduct it when computing the 'Cash and cash equivalents' figure.

10 If Figaro had *non-current* trade receivables and payables (i.e. where amounts are due more than one year after the balance sheet date), any increase or decrease over the year should be included – as an adjustment to profit – in calculating OCF.

11 International Accounting Standards Board, *IAS 7: Cash Flow Statements*.

12 Wolkenfeld, S. (1998), CFAR: a new tool for predicting credit quality, *Journal of Applied Corporate Finance*, 11(1): 121–124.

Financial statement analysis: basic framework

INTRODUCTION

In this chapter and the next, we explain and illustrate many of the techniques which investors use to analyse a company's financial statements. We draw on the accounting skills we've gained in the previous chapters to do so. It's possible to analyse financial statements with only a general knowledge of accounting. However, the deeper our understanding of corporate accounting and reporting practices, the sharper our analysis will be.

As we saw in Chapter 1, the users of financial statements – and their information needs – are many and varied. We focus in this and Chapter 20 on investors and their needs. Note that questions of concern to investors – How is the firm doing? What are its prospects? What are the potential risks from investing in it? – are also of interest to creditors, employees and customers. To help answer these questions, investors seek information about the firm's current and past profitability and risk from its published accounts. This is the core of financial statement analysis. (Some question one aim of such an analysis, namely to uncover mispricing of quoted securities, given the 'efficiency' of most capital markets. We examine this issue in Appendix 19.1.)

In this chapter we set out a simple framework for analysing a company's financial statements. This involves the following steps:

1 Understand the business environment it faces. Investors gather both firm-specific information (e.g. product mix, market focus, management skills) and general information about the industries and economies in which it operates.
2 Summarise the financial data in its accounts in a purposeful way. Investors plot trends in sales and earnings over time. They compare firms by common-sizing financial statements. They also use financial ratios to assess a firm's profitability and risk.
3 Interpret the ratios in the light of the knowledge gained about the firm and its environment.

We use the recent financial statements of a major European brewing company, Carlsberg, to illustrate the above steps.

A firm can make profits but fail to create wealth for its shareholders. Only if its profitability is greater than its cost of capital will shareholders be better off. In the final section, we show how investors estimate the shareholder wealth a firm has created – or destroyed – in a period.

Understanding the company and its environment

Investors do not analyse a company's financial statements in a vacuum. They need to have a good understanding of the industry the company operates in and the markets it serves. By analysing the economic conditions a company faces, investors can form expectations about its financial performance which they can then test against its published results.

The structure of an industry has a direct bearing on the profitability of companies in it. One well-known framework that relates profitability to industry structure is Porter's 'five forces of competition' model.[1] Exhibit 19.1 presents Porter's model in diagrammatic form.

Each of these five forces affects industry profitability. The more intense the competition within the industry, the more potent the threats from new entrants or substitute products, and the greater the bargaining power of suppliers or customers, the smaller the economic rents (returns in excess of the cost of capital) firms within the industry can earn.

Porter identifies the main constituents of each of the five forces. Consider rivalry within the industry. Competition is likely to be fierce where there are many firms in the industry all selling a similar product. In this case competition is price-based. But even in industries dominated by a few firms selling differentiated products, competition can erode profits if the firms are diverse (so they have difficulty agreeing to limit competition) and demand is stagnant or declining (so firms fight for market share). Note that if firms can differentiate their products, they will tend to compete through advertising and product innovation rather than on price.

Industry profitability is likely to be low if other firms can enter (and leave) the industry easily. So barriers to entry should raise industry profitability. Sometimes the barriers are inherent in the production or distribution process (e.g. production economies of scale). Sometimes they are created by government regulation or law (e.g. patents). Incumbent firms erect barriers to entry by differentiating their products and retaliating swiftly when new firms invade their markets.

There are substitutes for most goods and services. Whether buyers are willing to switch depends on how sensitive demand is to price changes. Where demand is price-sensitive (in technical terms, *price-elastic*), the threat posed by substitutes is greater and industry profitability

Exhibit 19.1 Industry structure and profitability: Porter's 'five forces of competition' model

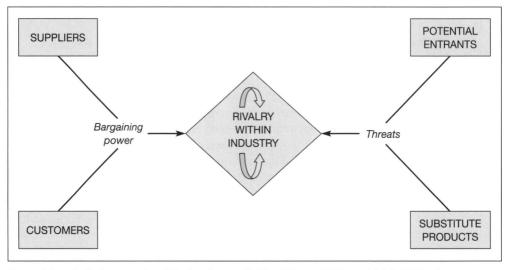

Source: Adapted with the permission of The Free Press, a Division of Simon & Schuster Adult Publishing Group, from *Competitive Strategy: Techniques for Analyzing Industries and Competitors* by Michael E. Porter. Copyright © 1980, 1998 by The Free Press.

will be lower. Firms may try to reduce this threat by distancing their products from substitutes. Again, the tactics they use include product innovation and advertising.

The bargaining power of customers and suppliers also affects industry profitability. Consider customers' bargaining power. A customer who is large (relative to a supplier) or has a large market share can put pressure on prices and drive down a supplier's profits. A customer is also in a strong bargaining position if there's little cost to switching suppliers or it can arrange the supply itself (e.g. through backward integration). As with substitutes, price is important. Where customers are sensitive to price changes – because of competitive conditions in their industry or because of the importance of the product in their own costs – their bargaining power is increased and suppliers' profitability suffers. Note that suppliers' bargaining power is the mirror image of that of customers.

Illustration: the brewing industry . . .

The company whose financial statements we'll analyse in this chapter is Carlsberg, a Danish-owned international beer producer. Before doing so, we examine briefly the brewing industry – its structure, products and markets – and consider the likely impact of Porter's five competitive forces on industry profitability.

Industry

The brewing industry consists of many small producers and a few very large ones. For example, in 2000 there were 1,650 breweries in the European Union employing 110,000 people and producing about 310 million hectolitres of beer. In Germany alone there were 1,141 plants each producing less than 100,000 hectolitres a year. At the other end of the scale, there were four groups with annual production of more than 50 million hectolitres. Carlsberg was one of them. The structure of the industry suggests there are two types of producer: the small brewer supplying a distinctive product to a local market, and the large company supplying standard beers to a national or international market. By concentrating production and setting up sophisticated distribution facilities, the big brewer can enjoy significant economies of scale. The estimated 2000 sales volume figures for the ten largest brewers are given in Exhibit 19.2.

Except for health regulations that apply to all food and drink producers, the production of beer is not regulated. However, the brewing industry does face restrictions on the sale of beer

Exhibit 19.2 **Top ten global brewers**

Rank	Company (country)	2000 sales volume (million hectolitres)	Leading brand(s)
1	Anheuser-Busch (USA)	158	Budweiser
2	SAB/Miller* (South Africa/USA)	109	Castle, Miller
3	Interbrew (Belgium)	87	Stella Artois, Labatt
4	Heineken (Netherlands)	72	Heineken, Amstel
5	Ambev/Quilmes* (Brazil)	68	Brahma
6	Scottish & Newcastle (UK)	55	Kronenbourg
7	Carlsberg (Denmark)	54	Carlsberg, Tuborg
8	Coors (USA)	39	Coors
9	Asahi (Japan)	35	Asahi
10	Kirin (Japan)	32	Kirin

* Pro forma, based on deals completed in 2001/02.

(*Source:* Canadean Beverage Market Research. Reproduced by permission of Canadean Ltd.)

since it is an alcoholic beverage. In most countries licensing laws limit the outlets that can stock it. Moreover, the sale of alcoholic beverages is either restricted to adults or, in the case of Muslim countries, banned outright.

Product

Beer is, in essence, a simple product – the result of fermentation using the malt of barley and other grains and flavoured with hops – which has been made in the same way for thousands of years. There are various types of beer (e.g. ale, lager, stout) but the material inputs are largely the same.

Why then is branding so widespread – and, in the case of the largest producers, so successful? Branding enables brewers to differentiate their products, allowing them to obtain higher prices and earn higher gross margins. The best-known brands provide reassurance to consumers: the taste and quality are the same over time and across countries. In addition, they have a signalling function. Through advertising a brand becomes associated with a particular lifestyle with which consumers identify.[2] Advertising also indicates the company's long-term commitment to the product.

Markets

As with most food and drink products, demand for beer is relatively stable. It varies little over the economic cycle. It is affected by the size and growth of the 18–35-year-old age group who are the largest consumers of beer in most countries. Demand is sensitive to changes in price and to weather conditions.

There are two types of market for beer. One is the market for standard beers which is dominated by the large national or international producers. The other is the market for specialist beers served by local producers ('craft' beers) and importers ('exotic' beers). Demand for standard beers is growing very slowly or even declining in developed economies but is expanding in many developing countries. By contrast, sales of specialist beers are increasing worldwide. Their share of the market has risen, especially in developed countries.

Europe illustrates these trends well. Beer sales have been stagnant in the poorer economies and have fallen in the richer ones. Overall, annual demand in the EU has declined in recent years. Annual per capita consumption in the 15 member states rose from 70 to 79 litres between 1970 and 1990. In the 1990s, demand dropped. Per capita consumption was around 75 litres in 2000, the same as in 1980. (The per capita figure is an average and conceals wide variations within Europe – from 28 litres in Italy to 128 litres in Ireland.) A decline in the 18–35 age group, campaigns against drinking and driving, and a shift in consumer tastes (e.g. to soft drinks) are all responsible. Exhibit 19.3 shows selected EU beer production and consumption statistics for the period 1970 to 2000.

Exhibit 19.3 **Brewing industry in the European Union: production and consumption, 1970–2000**

	1970	1980	1990	2000	Average real annual growth rate 70–80	80–90	90–100
Production (in hl. m)	247.7	296	321.6	309.2	1.8%	0.83%	−0.39%
Consumption (in hl. m)	228	266.8	286	284.4	1.58%	0.7%	−0.05%
Consumption (litres/head)	70.6	75.1	79.0	75.3			

(*Sources*: British Beer and Pub Association (2002), *Statistical Handbook*, reproduced by permission of Brewing Publications Ltd; UN (various) *Demographic Yearbook*, reproduced by permission of United Nations, the United Nations is the author of the original material.)

Take-home sales of beer have grown in Europe in recent years at the expense of sales in licensed premises. This has increased the bargaining power of large retail customers (e.g. supermarket chains). Some have started to market their own brands of beer.

Inputs

Production of standard beers is capital-intensive. This is where the economies of scale alluded to earlier arise. Key inputs besides plant are raw materials and packaging. In the case of large beer producers, their size relative to that of their suppliers and the competition among the latter mean that suppliers' bargaining power is low.

This short survey of the brewing industry suggests that, for standard beer producers, the opportunities for high profits are limited. They face strong competitive pressures from several directions: rivalry within the industry because of stagnant or declining demand, threats from substitutes (specialist beers, soft drinks) and, as take-home sales increase, the growing bargaining power of the large supermarket chains. The larger brewing firms have responded by acquiring competitors in order to obtain additional production and distribution economies and increase their own bargaining power. For example, Scottish & Newcastle purchased Danone's brewing interests (including the Kronenbourg brands) in 1999; Interbrew acquired two large brewing companies in the UK (Whitbread and Bass) in 2000 and one in Germany (Beck) in 2001; and South African Breweries (SAB) acquired US-based Miller Brewing in 2002.

● . . . and Carlsberg

We turn now to Carlsberg itself. Some companies have features which are unique or hard to replicate and this may give them a competitive advantage over rivals. Examples of such features are organisation, location, technology and reputation. Competition in the brewing industry may be fierce and profits low but Carlsberg has certain distinctive features which might enable it to earn above-average returns.

What are these distinctive features? The first is size. Carlsberg is a large company. It reported net sales of €4.6 billion in 2001. More significantly, it is one of the ten largest brewing companies in the world and has the leading share of the West European market.[3] Giant brewing companies like Carlsberg enjoy economies of scale not just in beer production but also in its marketing and distribution.

Carlsberg's second competitive strength is global reach. Over 90% of its sales are outside Denmark. In addition to exporting beer, the company has production sites – 90 of them – in 45 countries. In recent years it has invested heavily in Asia and eastern Europe, both growth markets. Its leading brands, Carlsberg and Tuborg, enjoy a high reputation internationally. They're produced under licence by 60 companies in over 40 countries. In nine European and six Asian countries (including China), awareness of the Carlsberg brand among consumers exceeded 80% of those polled.[4]

Third, the company has large soft drinks operations, especially in Scandinavia. It makes and sells Coca-Cola in Denmark and Finland and Pepsi in Sweden and Norway. Soft drinks are a substitute for beer. Carlsberg has hedged that competitive threat.

One other noteworthy feature of the company is its ownership structure. The Carlsberg Foundation is required by charter to own at least 51% of the shares of the holding company (Carlsberg A/S). This frees managers from the constraint of having to raise profits every period and allows them to take a longer-term view when evaluating potential investments. However, it also protects them from the threat of takeover, should the company underperform.

In sum, Carlsberg has certain characteristics which should give it a competitive advantage over other brewing companies. High reputation should permit premium pricing and size and global reach should yield scale economies. There is a question mark about the effect of its ownership structure. This may lead to greater organisational slack and, possibly, higher rewards to employees at the expense of shareholders.[5]

Trend and cross-section analyses of financial data

We move now from the general to the specific. We've collected the necessary background information and now have a better understanding of the target company and its industry. In this section, we look more closely at the company itself. We discuss certain techniques investors employ to analyse its accounts. We use the 2001 financial statements of Carlsberg – reproduced in Appendix 19.2 – to illustrate these techniques and to show how our newly acquired knowledge about the brewing industry helps us interpret better the numbers in them.[6]

Presented with a firm's accounts for a particular period, say year x7, our first concern as investors is to decide on a benchmark. Without a benchmark – a basis on which comparisons can be made – the numbers in the accounts have little meaning. There are various types of benchmark we can use. We can compare the firm's accounting numbers for x7 with those of prior periods (e.g. x2–x6). This is known as **trend analysis**. Alternatively, we can compare the firm's numbers for x7 with those of other firms – for example, in the same industry – for that year. We call this **cross-section analysis**. Of course, the two types of comparison can be combined and trends in accounting numbers monitored across firms.

Trend analysis

Trend analysis sheds light on how key numbers (e.g. sales, profit) have changed in the past. For example, investors are interested not only in the rate of growth of sales and profits but also in their variability. The simplest way of observing past trends is to present numbers graphically. In panel A of Exhibit 19.4, we plot Carlsberg's net sales and operating profits over the five years 1997–2001. (Carlsberg changed its financial year-end from 30 September to 31 December in 2000. Audited accounts for 1999/2000 were for 15 months. The exhibit shows the twelve-month (unaudited) figures that Carlsberg provides for comparison purposes.)

What do the numbers reveal? Carlsberg's sales and operating profits grew every year over the five years. There was a sharp increase in both in 1997/98 and again in 2001. Indexation tells the same story – but with more precision. From Panel B we see that sales grew faster than operating profits in 1997/98 but the reverse was true in 2002. It's evident that the operating margin ratio declined in both 1997/98 and 1998/99, recovered in 2000 and surpassed the 1996/97 level in 2001.

The answer to one question usually prompts others. For example, why did sales and operating profits grow so strongly in 1997/98 and 2001? The main reason is new ventures. Coca-Cola Nordic Beverages (CCNB), a new company majority-owned by Carlsberg, was formed in 1997 to bottle, sell and distribute Coca-Cola and other soft drinks in Denmark and Sweden. A year later it was extended to include Norway and Finland. The effect on the company's soft drinks sales is evident from Panel C: they rose from 15% to 27% of total output between 1996/97 and 1998/99. Carlsberg launched another venture in 2000, this time with Orkla, a Norwegian conglomerate. The two companies pooled their beverage interests in a new company, Carlsberg Breweries, in which Carlsberg has a 60% stake and Orkla the balance. Orkla had extensive beer and soft drinks operations in Scandinavia and Russia and, as controlling shareholder, Carlsberg was able to consolidate 100% of the results of these operations from the start of 2001 when they were transferred to the new company.[7]

For a deeper understanding of the trends in a company's results, we need to know the relative contributions of price, volume, product mix and exchange rate changes each year. Carlsberg

Exhibit 19.4 Carlsberg: revenues, operating profit and sales volume, 1997–2001

Panel A: Revenues and operating profit in nominal terms (DKr billion)

	Year to 30 September			Year to 31 December	
	1997	*1998*	*1999*	*2000**	*2001*
Revenues (net of excise duties)	14.9	22.1	24.2	25.7	34.5
Operating profit	1.26	1.55	1.67	2.09	3.40

Panel B: Revenues and operating profit in indexed form: 1997 = 100

	Year to 30 September			Year to 31 December	
	1997	*1998*	*1999*	*2000**	*2001*
Revenues (net of excise duties)	100	148	162	172	231
Operating profit	100	124	133	166	271

Panel C: Sales volume

	1997	1998	1999	2000*	2001
Beer and soft drinks (in hl million)	36.9	44.8	50.8	54.6	88.2
Indexed (1997 = 100)	100	121	138	148	239
Soft drinks as % of total sales	15	21	27	27	23

* Unaudited comparative figures. Carlsberg changed its financial year-end in 2000. Audited accounts for 2000 were for 15 months, 1 October 1999 to 31 December 2000.

(*Source*: Carlsberg Group, *Report and Accounts 2001*. Reproduced by permission of Carlsberg A/S.)

doesn't provide this information. For example, it discloses sales volumes for beer and soft drinks products – but not revenue and operating profit data by type of beverage. Thus it's not possible to compare revenue per litre – or operating profit per litre – for beer and soft drinks lines and assess the effect of changes in product mix on sales and profits.

Moreover, trends in a company's results can be distorted by changes in its activities. For example, in 2000 Carlsberg disposed of most of its non-beverage operations – in particular, a subsidiary making porcelain (Royal Scandinavia) – that had contributed around 10% of revenues in prior years. Total revenues per litre fell from DKr 5 in the 15 months to end-2000 to DKr 3.9 in 2001; excluding non-beverage operations, however, the fall was less dramatic – from DKr 4.36 to DKr 3.8. The expansion of its soft drinks operations in 1997/98 and 1998/99 raised its revenue per litre figure but the addition of Orkla's Russian beverage operations in 2001 with their low krone value reduced it.[8]

Cross-section analysis

As investors, we want to know how the target firm's financial performance and health compare with those of its competitors. This supplements data about trends in the firm's own profits and debt – and can be more important. For example, a firm reports a decline in profits; its main markets, we discover, are in economic recession. However, if the profit fall is smaller than that of its competitors, this suggests good relative performance on its part.

How can we compare accounting numbers when companies are of different size and/or their accounts are stated in different currencies? The answer is to arrange their accounts on a common basis. Each firm's balance sheet numbers are expressed as a percentage of its total assets and its income statement numbers as a percentage of its total revenues. This procedure is known as the **common-sizing** of financial statements.

We illustrate the information benefits from common-sizing. Exhibit 19.5 displays, in percentage terms, the 2001 balance sheets of Carlsberg and a major European rival, the Dutch brewing giant Heineken NV.

Common-sized balance sheets shed light on companies' operating activities and their financing decisions. For example, it's evident that both Carlsberg's and Heineken's operations are capital-intensive: tangible fixed assets (e.g. plant and equipment) represent around 50% of each company's total assets at end-2001. Neither firm carried much inventory at that date. This is consistent with the nature of their production activity: brewing requires inexpensive material inputs, has a short production cycle and, given the consumable nature of the final product, involves little storage. As for financing, the common-sized statements reveal the two companies pursued different strategies in 2001. Carlsberg relied more on debt capital than Heineken. Its net debt (long-term plus short-term debt less cash and securities) amounted to over one quarter of assets at end-2001; by contrast, Heineken had no net debt at that date. Not surprisingly, equity capital was more important to Heineken (43% of assets against Carlsberg's 31%). In parent company terms, the difference was even more marked (38% vs 20%): one-third of Carlsberg's equity capital was provided by minority shareholders in its subsidiaries (Coca-Cola in CCNB, Orkla in Carlsberg Breweries). Inspection of past balance sheets shows that Heineken has long pursued a low or zero debt policy whereas Carlsberg increased its leverage significantly in 1999/2000 following a change in the group's financing policies.

Not all differences in balance sheet structure are substantive, however. Consider the 'Receivables and prepayments' figures. Part of the large percentage difference in this item between Carlsberg (24% of assets) and Heineken (16%) can be traced to the two companies' different treatment of customer deposits on returnable packaging (e.g. casks, bottles). Heineken nets the deposits against receivables; Carlsberg records the deposits as a liability (under 'Provisions').[9]

As we've seen, common-sizing removes the effect of size differences. For an investor, this can be a mixed blessing: sometimes size counts. For example, Carlsberg's 2001 net sales (€4.6 billion at the end-2001 exchange rate of DKr7.44 : €1) were around 60% of Heineken's (€7.9 billion) but its tangible fixed assets (€2.7 billion) were 75% of Heineken's (€3.6 billion) at end-2001. Thus, although tangible fixed assets represent around 50% of total assets for both firms, it's clear that Heineken generates more sales per euro of them. Knowing the relative sizes of companies (as measured by sales) allows an investor to compare the efficiency with which they use assets.

Moreover, common-sizing cannot overcome differences in the way firms account for assets and liabilities. If material, these accounting differences can undermine conclusions drawn from

Exhibit 19.5 Carlsberg and Heineken: 2001 consolidated balance sheets common-sized

Consolidated balance sheets at 31 December 2001				
	Carlsberg		Heineken	
	DKr mn*	%	%	€ mn
Fixed assets				
Intangible	–	–	–	13
Tangible	20,326	49	50	3,614
Financial	4,767	12	8	531
	25,093	61	58	4,158
Current assets				
Inventories	2,865	7	10	692
Receivables and prepayments	9,820	24	16	1,192
Cash and securities	3,291	8	16	1,175
	15,976	39	42	3,059
Total assets	41,069	100	100	7,217
Group equity				
Shareholders' equity	8,059	20	38	2,758
Minority interests	4,454	11	5	381
	12,513	31	43	3,139
Long-term liabilities				
Long-term debt	12,042	29	11	797
Provisions and other long-term liabilities	3,702	9	15	1,046
	15,744	38	26	1,843
Current liabilities				
Bank loans and current portion of long-term debt	2,199	5	5	329
Payables and accruals	10,613	26	26	1,906
	12,812	31	31	2,235
Total equities	41,069	100	100	7,217

* Exchange rate at 31 December 2001: DKr 7.44 : €1.

(*Sources*: Carlsberg A/S, *Report and Accounts 2001*, reproduced by permission of Carlsberg A/S; Heineken NV, *Annual Report 2001*, reproduced by permission of Heineken A/S.)

common-sized figures. For example, Carlsberg values tangible fixed assets at (depreciated) historical cost whereas Heineken values them at replacement cost. Restating Heineken's tangible fixed assets to historical cost would reduce their reported amount – and raise the company's reported asset utilisation rate relative to that of Carlsberg.

We can 'common-size' other financial statements with equally productive results. For example, common-sized income statements bring to light differences in firms' cost structures. Assume two firms classify costs by nature. Common-sizing reveals the relative weights of material, labour and depreciation in each firm's cost structure. With this information, we can determine which firm uses labour and capital more productively. Unfortunately, we can't compare the cost structures of Carlsberg and Heineken directly because they classify costs differently: Carlsberg classifies them by function, Heineken by nature.

We can combine common-sizing and trend analysis. By performing the same common-sizing exercise over several periods, we can see how the composition of a firm's costs changes over time.

It also helps us understand why profit margins change too. Of course, the same insights can be gained by examining the trend in individual costs over time. We investigate the reasons for the change in Carlsberg's profit margin in a later section.

The investor's financial ratio toolkit

To many investors, financial statement analysis and financial ratios go hand in hand: the former implies calculation and interpretation of the latter. Financial ratios provide a simple and powerful way of summarising information in financial reports. By relating key numbers in the financial statements, e.g. profits to assets, debt to equity, investors assemble a 'toolkit' they can use to better gauge a company's financial performance and condition.

What's in the investor's ratio toolkit? In previous chapters we introduced the principal ratios on which investors rely when analysing accounts. They fall into one of two groups: those used to measure a company's profitability and those used to assess its financial risk. We look at each group of ratios in turn.

Profitability ratios

Three ratios that are widely used to measure a firm's profitability are:

- (rate of) return on assets (ROA);
- (rate of) return on equity (ROE);
- earnings per share (EPS).

We defined these ratios in earlier chapters. Exhibit 19.6 reminds us how each is calculated and what purpose it's intended to serve. We examine ROA and ROE more closely in this chapter and defer scrutiny of EPS to the next.

Return on assets

ROA shows how many cents of profit each euro of assets has generated in the financial year. It is an indicator of the success with which managers have employed the firm's assets in a period, irrespective of how those assets are financed.

Exhibit 19.6 Key profitability ratios: calculation and purpose

Ratio	How calculated	Purpose
Return on assets (RONOA)	$\dfrac{\text{Net operating profit after tax}}{\text{Average net operating assets}}$	Measures success with which managers have used firm's assets.
Return on equity (ROE)	$\dfrac{\text{Net profit attributable to ordinary shareholders}}{\text{Average ordinary shareholders' equity}}$	Measures success with which managers have used funds provided by firm's owners.
Earnings per share (EPS)	$\dfrac{\text{Net profit attributable to ordinary shareholders}}{\text{Weighted average ordinary shares outstanding}}$	Profit expressed in per-share terms. Permits comparisons with share price (P/E ratio) and dividend (payout ratio).

In Chapter 3, we calculated ROA by dividing operating profit by average assets. A more logical approach is to relate operating profit to *net operating assets* (i.e. operating assets less operating liabilities) rather than total assets. Operating assets include tangible and intangible fixed assets, inventories, trade receivables, prepayments and long-term investments in other companies while operating liabilities include trade payables, accrued expenses and provisions. This version of ROA is also known as **return on net operating assets (RONOA)**:

$$\text{RONOA} = \frac{\text{Net operating profit after tax (NOPAT)}}{\text{Average net operating assets (NOA)}} \qquad (19.1)$$

where:

NOPAT = Net profit + Net financial expense (NFE)

NFE = [(Interest expense − Interest income) + Losses (− Gains) from financial A/L] × (1 − *t*)

NOA = Operating assets (OA) − Operating liabilities (OL)

Defining return on assets in this way ensures that numerator and denominator are calculated on a consistent basis and the ratio truly measures the *operating* performance of the firm. We use this version of ROA throughout the rest of this chapter.

The numerator, NOPAT, is usually derived indirectly – by adding net financial expense to net profit. In this way, all special and exceptional items are captured in NOPAT: although non-recurring, they still relate to operations. Net financial expense (NFE) includes realised and unrealised holding losses (net of gains) on debt and marketable securities, as well as net interest charges. The tax rate (*t*) is the company's marginal corporate income tax rate. In evaluating a group's operating performance, the net profit figure in (19.1) should be consolidated net profit, i.e. *before* accounting for minority interests.

RONOA is equivalent to **return on capital employed** (**ROCE**), a ratio widely cited in the financial press. Closer inspection of the balance sheet shows that net operating assets and capital employed are identical.

OA + Financial assets (FA) = OL + Financial liabilities (FL) + Shareholders' equity   (19.2)

Rearranging (19.2) gives:

$$\text{OA} - \text{OL} = [\text{FL} - \text{FA}] + \text{Shareholders' equity}$$

or

$$\underbrace{\text{Net operating assets} \quad = \quad \text{Net debt} \quad + \quad \text{SE}}_{\text{Capital employed}}$$

Note that for ease of calculation we classify all cash and short-term investments as financial assets. In practice, part of a company's liquid assets is used in operations but management rarely disclose the amount in the financial statements. Long-term investments – and the income from them – are treated as operating items.

As we saw in Chapter 3, ROA is the product of two independent financial ratios, profit margin and assets turnover. RONOA can also be broken down in the same way:

$$\text{RONOA} = \quad \text{Profit margin (PM)} \quad \times \quad \text{Assets turnover (AT)}$$

$$\frac{\text{Net operating profit after tax}}{\text{Operating revenues}} \qquad \frac{\text{Operating revenues}}{\text{Average net operating assets}}$$

Profit margin and assets turnover can be broken down in turn. The profit margin is simply the residue of each sales euro after account is taken of the revenues absorbed by production, selling and other costs. This involves calculating cost ratios for the various types of cost incurred by

| Exhibit 19.7 | DuPont framework of profitability analysis: components of ROA |

RETURN ON ASSETS (ROA)

PROFIT MARGIN   ASSETS TURNOVER

which can be analysed by   *of which the major components*
examining individual cost-   *are:*
to-revenue ratios:

Cost of sales/Sales (revenue)	Receivables turnover $=$ $\dfrac{\text{Revenue from credit sales}}{\text{Average accounts receivable}}$
R&D costs/Sales	
Selling expense/Sales	Inventory turnover $=$ $\dfrac{\text{Cost of sales (or sales revenue)}}{\text{Average inventories}}$
Administrative expense/Sales	
Interest expense/Sales	(Tangible) fixed assets turnover $=$ $\dfrac{\text{Sales revenue}}{\text{Average tangible fixed assets}}$
Income tax expense/Sales	

the firm (e.g. COGS/sales, selling expense/sales, etc.). We can better understand changes in a firm's profit margin over time – and any differences among firms in the same industry – once we have calculated individual cost ratios each period.

As for assets turnover, this is affected by the rate of turnover of specific categories of asset, e.g. receivables, inventories, fixed assets. Exhibit 19.7 sets out the components of profit margin and assets turnover. This is known as the DuPont framework of profitability analysis, after the US chemical company of that name which first championed this approach.

Why does profitability, as measured by ROA, differ across firms? One reason is that firms differ in operational efficiency, that is, the efficiency with which they control costs and the efficiency with which they use their assets. The DuPont framework summarised in Exhibit 19.7 helps investors identify these efficiency differences.

Other reasons are industry-related rather than firm-specific. Industries differ with respect to: age; degree of competition among member firms; production process and input mix; and cyclicality of demand. These factors affect the level, composition and variability of ROA across firms. We consider each of them below.

1 *Age.* As we saw in Chapter 18, profit is likely to be negative during the introductory stage of a product's life and low (but increasing) during the growth stage (*see* Exhibit 18.2). As a result, ROA will be negative or low during this period. Firms whose products are mostly in the mature stage of the lifecycle tend to report higher ROA. Accounting rules contribute to this: the ROA denominator includes fixed assets whose carrying amount (under HC accounting) at the maturity stage is low owing to accumulated depreciation charges.

2 *Degree of competition.* Consider the effect of competitive forces on ROA. Where companies are many, their products are not differentiable and the costs of entering the industry are low, competition is likely to be fierce and ROA will be driven down to the company's cost of capital. Firms in industries where one or more of these conditions do not apply – e.g. the research-based pharmaceutical industry where new products enjoy patent protection and, as a result, entry into the industry is costly – are likely to report higher ROA.

3 *Production process and input mix.* The production process and the mix of capital and labour in it affect more the *composition* of ROA than its level. Note that a ROA of, say, 10% can be achieved with a PM of 5% and an AT of 2 or with a PM of 2% and an AT of 5. Consider firms in capital-intensive industries such as glass, steel or chemical manufacture. Given the heavy investment in equipment, such firms try to operate at or near capacity to spread fixed costs over more units and thereby lower unit costs. To increase output when the firm is operating at this level requires large capital expenditures since investment is 'lumpy'. Thus assets turnover is low and for technological reasons cannot easily be increased. However, the large initial investment in plant and equipment acts as a barrier to entry and normally enables firms to secure higher margins on their sales.

By contrast, in an industry such as food retailing a relatively small asset base can support a large amount of sales. Fixed assets (buildings, fittings) are not complex; inventory is kept low to avoid spoilage; receivables are small because most sales are for cash. The resulting high assets turnover does not result in high ROA because competitive conditions keep profit margins low.[10]

Nonetheless, there are circumstances where the input mix can affect the *level* of reported ROA. For example, certain service sector firms such as software providers, management consultants and advertising agencies often report high ROA because their main resource, the skills of their employees, does not appear as an asset on the balance sheet.

4 *Cyclicality of demand.* ROAs differ not only in level and composition but also in variability. The main source of ROA variability is the business cycle and its effect on demand for the firm's products. ROAs of companies in cyclical industries (e.g. construction, forestry products, heavy machinery) tend to fluctuate more than in industries such as food and drink where demand is relatively stable over the business cycle.

Note that operating leverage (the ratio of fixed to variable costs) can add to ROA variability. Capital-intensive firms like the glass, steel and chemical producers mentioned earlier have high operating leverage. For such firms, a unit change in output has a large impact on profit: costs alter little and so most of the change in revenue (from the output change) flows straight through to the 'bottom line'.

The earnings variability of 'cycle-sensitive' firms means that investors seek higher returns to compensate them for the higher risk. Thus the *expected* ROAs of such firms are higher.

The above points are summarised below.

	Return on assets (ROA)		
Factors affecting the . . . of a firm's ROA are:	*Level*	*Composition*	*Variability*
Age (of firm/industry)	✓		
Production process/input mix		✓	
Degree of competition	✓		
Cyclicality of demand			✓

Return on equity

ROE shows how many cents of profit each euro of shareholders' capital has yielded in the financial year. It is an indicator of the success with which managers have used owners' funds. The form of the ratio reflects this. The numerator is usually the net profit attributable to ordinary (common) shareholders: dividends to preference shareholders are deducted to arrive at this figure. Similarly, the denominator is usually the capital and reserves attributable to ordinary shareholders. Capital contributed by preference shareholders is excluded.

$$ROE = \frac{\text{Net profit attributable to ordinary (common) shareholders}}{\text{Average equity of ordinary (common) shareholders}}$$

In the case of a group, ROE can be calculated at group level or for parent company's shareholders only. In the latter case, the minority interest in subsidiaries' profits (or losses) must be excluded from the numerator and the minority interest in subsidiaries' net assets must be excluded from the denominator.

RONOA and ROE are linked. ROE can be viewed as the sum of two components: the firm's operating performance (RONOA) and the benefit (or cost) to shareholders from the firm financing its NOA with debt.[11]

ROE = Return on net operating assets + Gain (– Loss) from net financial leverage

The **gain from net financial leverage** can be broken down in turn. It's the product of two figures: (a) the difference – or **spread** – between a firm's operating returns and its net borrowing cost and (b) the leveraging of that spread through the use of debt. This latter ratio is known as the **net financial leverage effect** (**netflev**).

$$
\begin{aligned}
\text{Gain from net financial leverage} =\quad &\text{SPREAD} \qquad\qquad \times\quad \text{NETFLEV} \\[4pt]
= &\begin{bmatrix} \text{Return on} & \text{Net} \\ \text{net operating} - \text{borrowing} \\ \text{assets} & \text{cost (NBC)} \end{bmatrix} \times \begin{matrix} \text{Net financial} \\ \text{leverage} \\ \text{effect} \end{matrix} \\[6pt]
= &\left[\frac{\text{NOPAT}}{\text{Av. NOA}} - \frac{\text{NFE}}{\text{Av. net debt}} \right] \times \frac{\text{Av. net debt}}{\text{Av. SE}}
\end{aligned}
$$

where: Net debt = Financial liabilities – Financial assets
SE = Shareholders' equity

A company can raise the rate of return on its shareholders' funds by:

● improving its operating performance (via higher margins, faster assets turnover or both);
● reducing its net borrowing costs; and/or
● increasing its net financial leverage.

Note that higher operating returns benefits ROE both directly (through higher RONOA) and indirectly (through a larger spread).

Financial leverage increases risk as well as potential rewards to a firm's shareholders, since it magnifies any variability in its RONOA. When the firm is doing well (RONOA > NBC – or positive spread), owners benefit. Interest is a fixed cost: it does not usually vary with profit or revenues. As a result, owners do not have to share with creditors any increases in the firm's profits: they capture them all. However, when the firm is doing badly (negative spread), owners suffer. Debtholders are paid first – remember, their claims rank before those of the owners – and their return (interest) is fixed. In these circumstances, interest charges may absorb most of the firm's operating profits and owners are left with little.[12]

Exhibit 19.8 illustrates this. Assume a company finances its net operating assets (of 100) with a mixture of debt (40) and equity (60). The debt bears an annual interest rate of 10%. The exhibit shows returns to the firm's shareholders under three different RONOA assumptions: (a) below, (b) equal to, and (c) above the cost of debt. Taxes are ignored.

Notice the sensitivity of ROE to different levels of RONOA. When the firm's assets yield a return greater than the cost of debt (e.g. assumption (c)), owners benefit from financial leverage. The gain in case (c) (where RONOA is 15%) is 3.3%, the product of a positive spread of 5% and a (net) debt–equity ratio of 0.66. When, however, the firm's assets yield a return less than the

Exhibit 19.8 Effect of financial leverage on ROE under alternative RONOA assumptions

Facts

At start year 1, a company has net operating assets of 100, financed 60% with equity and 40% with debt bearing an annual interest rate of 10%. The table below shows year 1 ROE under the following RONOA assumptions: (a) 5%, (b) 10% and (c) 15%. Taxes are ignored.

Summary income statement for year 1

RONOA assumption	(a)	(b)	(c)
Operating profit	5	10	15
Interest expense [10% × 40]	−4	−4	−4
Net profit	1	6	11
RONOA [Operating profit/NOA (start-year)]	5%	10%	15%

Gain from net financial leverage:

	(a)	(b)	(c)
Spread [RONOA − NBC]	−5%	0	+5%
×	×	×	×
Netflev [Debt/SE]	0.66	0.66	0.66
	−3.3%	0	+3.3%
ROE*	**1.7%**	**10%**	**18.3%**

* Based on start-year shareholders' equity.

cost of debt (assumption (a)), financial leverage hurts shareholders. In our example, at a RONOA of only 5%, the company sustains a loss from financial leverage of 3.3%, cutting ROE to only 1.7%. Thus by substituting debt for equity in its capital structure, a firm increases the risks as well as the returns to its shareholders.

Empirical evidence indicates that ROA and ROE are highly correlated.[13] Most differences in interfirm ROEs are driven by the same factors that are responsible for differences in ROAs: age of firm/products, degree of competition, production process and input mix, cyclicality of demand. Moreover, the leverage effect of the (US) firms examined was remarkably stable in the period studied (1963–99).

● Financial risk ratios

In the business world, risk usually means the risk of financial loss. Creditors suffer financial loss when a firm is unable to meet its contractual obligations to them. Shareholders suffer financial loss when they are unable to recover their investment in the firm. This occurs when the market lowers its expectations about the firm's future earnings and the firm's market value falls as a consequence. Clearly, shareholders are likely to suffer financial loss before creditors do: a company may cut its forecast profit yet still be expected to pay its debts when they fall due.

Traditional analysis of financial risk focuses on the risks faced by creditors. For them, the risk of financial loss is less if the company under scrutiny has a history of profitable operations. Such a company has demonstrated that it can generate positive cash flows from operations (after debt servicing costs) on a continuing basis. Thus ROA or ROE can serve as a measure of risk as well as profitability.

There are other dimensions to risk. As we saw in earlier chapters, investors have devised specific ratios to assess liquidity and solvency risks. A company suffers liquidity problems when it is unable to pay its short-term debts when they are due. It is insolvent when its liabilities exceed

Exhibit 19.9   Key liquidity and solvency ratios: calculation and purpose

Ratio	How calculated	Purpose
Liquidity risk		
Current ratio (CR)	$$\frac{\text{Current assets}}{\text{Current liabilities}}$$	Shows extent to which short-term obligations are covered by cash and trading assets.
Quick ratio	$$\frac{\text{Cash, securities and A/R}}{\text{Current liabilities}}$$	As for CR but a more severe test of liquidity.
Defensive interval	$$\frac{\text{Cash, securities and A/R}}{\text{Projected operating outlays}}\ (\times\ 365)$$	Shows how long company can fund operations from existing cash and near-cash resources.
Solvency risk (financial leverage)		
Debt–equity ratio	$$\frac{\text{Net debt}}{\text{Shareholders' equity (of group)}}$$	Expresses interest-bearing debt (less cash) as a proportion of equity.
Debt-to-capitalisation ratio	$$\frac{\text{Net debt at MV}}{\text{Shareholders' equity at MV}}$$	As for debt–equity ratio, but debt and equity are measured at market rather than book values.
Times interest earned	$$\frac{\text{Profit before interest and tax expense}}{\text{Interest expense + Capitalised interest}}$$	Shows income cover for debt servicing costs.
Net debt-to-OCF ratio	$$\frac{\text{Net debt}}{\text{Operating cash flow}}$$	Shows how long it will take firm to pay off debt at current rate of cash flow generation.

its assets. Illiquidity does not imply insolvency: a firm may have sufficient assets to cover its debts but the assets cannot be converted quickly into cash. Exhibit 19.9 summarises the ratios most commonly used to measure these risks.

Liquidity ratios

How do we assess a firm's ability to pay its short-term debts? The usual approach is to establish what the firm's current liabilities are (those payable within a year) and to see whether it has the resources available to settle them.

One measure of 'available resources' is current assets: cash and other assets which are expected to be converted into cash within a year. The **current ratio** shows how many times a firm's current assets at a particular date cover its current liabilities then. A variant of this ratio, the **quick ratio** (or **acid test ratio**), adopts a tougher definition of available resources. Inventories are excluded from the numerator because they're usually the least liquid of current assets. Both ratios are widely used measures of a firm's liquidity.

They have weaknesses, however. First, both show a firm's liquidity on one date in the year only. Management can make both ratios look better by careful choice of the firm's financial year-end. In addition, either ratio can be raised by temporarily paying off loans or other current liabilities just before the year-end (but only if the ratio is already greater than one). Second, they equate 'liquid' with 'current'. Some *fixed* assets may be highly liquid. Remember that if management intends to hold shares or bonds of another company for longer than a year, the investment is classified as a fixed asset. If the securities held are quoted, management may be able to convert them into cash quickly.

As a result investors employ other ratios. For example, they check the firm's **defensive interval**. This relates a company's current liquid assets to its projected operating outlays in the next period. The ratio shows how long the firm can finance its operations from its cash and near-cash resources in the event it receives no cash from sales. It's adaptable – the numerator can be expressed net of current liabilities and actual operating outlays in the current period can be used in the denominator – and less easy for management to manipulate than the current ratio.

In addition, they use turnover ratios to estimate the firm's **operating cycle** in cash terms. *The operating cycle is the average period (in days) between payment for goods and supplies and receipt of cash from customers.* For a typical manufacturing company, it is estimated as follows:

	Ratio
Average credit period taken by customers	(365/Receivables turnover)
+ Average production and storage period	(365/Inventory turnover)
− Average credit period obtained from suppliers	(365/Payables turnover)
Average operating cycle (in days)	

We have already shown how the receivables and inventory turnovers are calculated (Exhibit 19.7 – and Chapters 10 and 9). The payables turnover is calculated as follows:

$$\text{Payables turnover} = \frac{\text{(Credit) purchases of goods and services}}{\text{Average accounts payable}}$$

Companies that present the income statement in a natural format usually disclose purchases of goods and services either on the face of the statement or in the notes. For those firms that classify expenses by function, investors must estimate purchases using cost of sales and inventory figures.

Operating cycles vary across industries, largely because of differences in the production period. What interests investors are intra-industry differences in the operating cycle and, in particular, any change in its length. A lengthening cycle usually indicates greater liquidity risk.

Solvency (or financial leverage) ratios

The ratios we describe as solvency ratios in Exhibit 19.9 carry other titles. Few firms are at risk of not being able to pay their debts. Nonetheless, other things being equal, that risk is greater, the greater is a firm's financial leverage (or gearing). Thus solvency ratios are often described as **financial leverage** (or **gearing**) **ratios**. As leverage is a broader term, we'll use it in place of solvency.

Investors measure a firm's financial leverage in various ways. The simplest approach is to relate net debt to shareholders' equity (the **debt–equity ratio** shown in Exhibit 19.9). Alternatively, net debt can be expressed as a proportion of financial capital (Net debt + Group equity). The numerator can be broadened to include all liabilities. A variant, the long-term debt to equity ratio, can be calculated to highlight the term structure of the firm's debt.

All the above debt ratios are based on book amounts. These may overstate a firm's true leverage. The market value of a firm's equity is often greater than its book value. The latter captures only the value of net assets 'in place' while market value includes the discounted value of expected above-normal future earnings (or 'growth opportunities') as well. Hence some analysts calculate a market value-based debt ratio. The **debt-to-(market) capitalisation ratio** relates the market value of a firm's debt to the market value of its equity. Nevertheless, leverage ratios based on book amounts are still popular, especially with creditors who argue that the collateral provided by growth opportunities is too uncertain.

Balance sheet leverage ratios have the same flaws as balance sheet liquidity ratios. They provide a snapshot of the firm's capital structure at one date only. They are manipulable: as we saw in earlier chapters, firms are adept at finding ways to keep debt off the balance sheet – or, at least, outside the liabilities' section of it. Above all, they tell us little about a company's ability to *service* its debt.

One solution is to calculate the burden of debt on profits. The **times interest earned ratio** (or **interest cover**) shows how many times a firm's profits before interest and tax cover its financial expenses in a period. Some financing costs may be 'off income statement', however. Analysts have devised a broader version of the TIE ratio, the **fixed charge coverage ratio**, to incorporate them. As discussed in Chapter 11, capitalised interest and the interest element in lease payments are considered part of a company's fixed (financial) charges which should be covered by profits from operations. The TIE and FCC ratios are reliable indicators of a firm's debt servicing ability so long as the profit figure in the numerator reflects recurring income.

If non-cash expenses (e.g. depreciation and increases in provisions) are large in relation to revenues, investors may substitute operating cash flow for profits in the TIE ratio. Another cash-based ratio is the **net debt-to-operating cash flow ratio**. The reasoning behind this ratio is the same as that for the defensive interval: the risk of financial loss to the creditor is less where a company has strong operating cash flows relative to its liabilities. Again, the ratio is adaptable. Some investors use projected OCF – or projected Ebitda – in the denominator; others estimate the firm's maintenance capital expenditures and deduct these from the OCF number to give a **net debt-to-free cash flow ratio**.

Financial risk and earnings variability

The problem with traditional risk ratios is that they're based on financial data of one date or period and they take no account of the nature of the company's business. The likelihood of a firm defaulting on its debt is a function not just of the level of that debt but also of the *variability of the firm's earnings over time*. This last point can be easily demonstrated. Consider two firms with similar profitability and capital structures. The probability of reporting losses – and thus the risk of being unable to service its debt – is lower for the firm with the more stable pattern of earnings.

What factors influence earnings variability? Two important ones are:

- the sensitivity of a firm's revenues to the economic cycle – in other words, the *variability of its revenues*; and
- the firm's cost structure and, in particular, its *operating leverage*.

Variability of revenues is the more important factor. High operating leverage will not result in high earnings variability without it. For example, gas distribution companies and electricity generating firms make major investments in plant and transmission equipment. Fixed costs such as depreciation are large relative to variable costs. Their operating leverage is high. Yet such firms usually avoid large variations in earnings because in most countries their business is regulated and, as a result, the variability of their revenues is low.

How is earnings variability measured? One approach is to calculate the deviation of a profitability ratio such as ROE from its mean over the business cycle. A statistic such as the **standard deviation** can be used. The larger the deviation, the more earnings have fluctuated in that period.

Note that firms whose earnings vary little do not necessarily have higher debt ratios. Their lower financial risk gives them higher debt *capacity*. Whether they exploit that capacity depends ultimately on the decision of their owners.

Bankruptcy prediction

Risk ratios also appear in bankruptcy prediction models. Researchers have found that certain financial ratios of failed companies differ markedly from those of healthy companies in the one to two years preceding bankruptcy. According to one widely used model, the variables that have the most discriminating power are:

1 profitability (ROA);
2 size (total assets excluding intangibles);
3 liquidity (current ratio);
4 cumulative profitability (retained profits/total assets);
5 capitalisation (market value of equity/market value of total capital, based on five years' average data);
6 earnings stability (standard deviation of ROA, based on ten years' data).

The ratios used are in parentheses. A model with these variables in it correctly classified over 90% of a sample of failed US firms at the date of the last published financial statements prior to bankruptcy.[14] It is reassuring that many of the risk factors we discussed earlier – profitability and history of profitability, liquidity, financial leverage, debt servicing ability, earnings stability – are captured in the model.

The profitability and risk ratios we've discussed above are the financial ratios most often found in the investors' toolbox. They're not the only ones, however. Investors devise other ratios – for example, by combining non-financial and financial data – in order to gain further insights into a firm's financial performance and condition. Examples are the revenue yield and capacity utilisation ratios used to evaluate firms in the air transport and hotel industries.

Profitability, risk and cash flow analysis illustrated

We now analyse Carlsberg's 2001 financial statements, drawing on the material in this and the previous chapter. Earlier we outlined the key economic characteristics of the brewing industry and Carlsberg's place in it. We summarise our findings below. By keeping in mind the business environment Carlsberg operates in, we'll make our analysis richer.

Carlsberg, we learned, is a major player in the European brewing industry. Important features of the market for beer in Europe are:

- *Stagnant or declining demand for standard beers.* Demography, health concerns and changes in consumer tastes are contributory factors.
- *Intense competition.* Given stagnant sales, standard beer producers battle for a higher market share. Substitutes (specialist beers, soft drinks) pose an additional threat.
- *Economies of scale.* Large producers enjoy production and distribution economies of scale. They extend them by acquiring or merging with brewing companies in new markets. Savings are channelled into brand promotion. Both inhibit the entry (or development) of additional large producers.
- *Growth in retailer bargaining power.* Take-home sales are increasing. Large supermarket chains have growing market share. Beverage producers compete for shelf access.

In light of the above – and what we know about Carlsberg as a company – what are our expectations about Carlsberg's profitability, leverage and cash flow profile?

- Competitive conditions in the brewing industry make it unlikely that the major players earn returns much above their cost of capital. Carlsberg's profits should benefit from its size and global reach. A capital-intensive production process means its asset turnover is likely to be low. Production economies should boost gross profit margins.
- Carlsberg's liquidity and debt ratios are likely to be strong, thanks to stable demand for beer and soft drinks and the group's healthy operating cash flows. The latter will be greater than profits because of large depreciation charges.
- Carlsberg should generate positive free cash flow owing to the maturity of its brands and the limited opportunities for internal growth.

Carlsberg's financial performance in 2001

To understand the present, we need to be aware of the past. Exhibit 19.10 shows the main profitability ratios of Carlsberg for 2001 and the preceding four years. (We show the calculation of Carlsberg's 2001 ratios, along with its consolidated 2001 financial statements, in Appendix 19.2.)

Return on assets

What do the profit ratios tell us about Carlsberg? The first impression is that the group performed well between 1997 and 2001. It was consistently profitable in this period. Its RONOA and ROE increased each year from 1999: in fact, its ROE in 2001 was more than double the 1999 level. (For 1999 and earlier years, Carlsberg's financial year ended on 30 September. The accounts for 2000 cover a 15-month period: for profitability ratio calculations, the income numbers have been apportioned.)

Closer inspection reveals that Carlsberg's performance was like the proverbial curate's egg – good in parts. The increase in RONOA and ROE between1999 and 2001 was, in fact, a recovery from depressed levels: the group suffered a sharp fall in profitability in 1999. RONOA had still not regained 1998 levels by 2001. Margins achieved new highs in 2001 but assets turnover remained sluggish. The increase in ROE was noteworthy but 60% of the improvement was due to higher gains from financial leverage. By increasing the proportion of debt in its capital structure, the group raised returns to shareholders but at the same time increased the riskiness of their investment.

Analysis of profit margin

What are the reasons for the improvement in the NOPAT margin between 1999 and 2001? Did the group raise prices, cut costs or shift sales to higher margin products? To what extent was the improvement due to special – and non-recurring – factors?

Exhibit 19.10 Carlsberg Group: key profitability ratios, 1997–2001

Financial period*	1996/97	1997/98	1998/99	1999/2000**	2001
Return on net operating assets	**10.5%**	**15.4%**	**9.1%**	**10.3%**	**13.9%**
Profit margin	6.3%	7.4%	5.2%	6.8%	9.0%
Assets turnover	1.67×	2.08×	1.76×	1.51×	1.55×
Gain on net financial leverage	**2.6%**	**1.1%**	**1.0%**	**5.5%**	**8.7%**
Return on equity	**13.1%**	**16.5%**	**10.1%**	**15.8%**	**22.6%**

* 2001: to 31 December; 1999/2000: 15 months to 31 December; 1998/99 and earlier years: to 30 September.
** Income statement numbers in ratios based on 12/15ths of reported numbers.

Carlsberg's accounts provide answers to most of these questions; industry and general economic data supply the rest. Increased prices contributed little to Carlsberg's bottom line in the 1997–2001 period: inflation in western Europe (responsible for 60% of Carlsberg's revenues in 2001) was low and, as we've seen, demand for beer in this market was stagnant or declining during this time. In fact, the change in the group's structure in 2001 contributed to a decline in revenue per litre.

	1996/97	1997/98	1998/99	1999/2000 (15 months)	2001
Beverage revenue/litre (DKr)	**3.5**	**4.2**	**4.1**	**4.4**	**3.8**
Beer sales (mn hl)	31.3	35.3	37	51	67.9
Soft drink sales (mn hl)	5.6	9.5	13.8	18.9	20.3
Beer sales (% of total)	85	79	73	73	77

Carlsberg benefited – in revenue/litre terms – from the expansion of soft drink sales in the late 1990s, following the setting-up of the Scandinavian joint venture with Coca-Cola that took effect in 1997. The merger of Carlsberg's and Orkla's beverage interests in 2001, however, resulted in a decline in revenue/litre. Orkla had extensive brewing operations in Eastern Europe and these sales had a relatively low krone value in 2001. (In addition, Carlsberg had to relinquish certain soft drinks operations in Scandinavia for anti-trust reasons which also contributed to the revenue/litre decline that year.)

Despite the adverse effects of the 2001 merger on per-unit revenues, Carlsberg's profit margins didn't suffer. Orkla's beverage operations had low krone costs. Exhibit 19.11 contains common-sized income statements for the three years to 2001.

Comparing Carlsberg's margins in 2001 with those in 1998/99 before the Orkla deal was even considered, we can see that Carlsberg spent less of each sales euro on production (down

Exhibit 19.11 Carlsberg Group: analysis of profit margin, 1999–2001

	Year to 30 Sept 1999	15 months to 31 Dec 2000	Year to 31 Dec 2001
Sales revenue	100%	100%	100%
Production costs	−52.6	−49.5	−50.5
Gross profit	47.4	50.5	49.5
Sales and distribution expense	−33.9	−35.9	−33.0
Administration expense	−7.2	−7.8	−8.0
Other operating income	+0.6	+1.6	+1.4
Operating profit	6.9	8.4	9.9
Special items*	+0.3	+1.2	–
Interest expense, net	−0.5	−0.7	−1.9
Other financial items**	+0.1	+0.1	+1.7
Profit before tax	6.8	9.0	9.7
Income tax expense	−2.0	−2.6	−2.1
Group net profit	4.8	6.4	7.6
$(1 - t)$ Interest expense, net	+0.4	+0.4	+1.4
Profit margin (Exhibit 19.10)	**5.2**	**6.8**	**9.0**

* Includes gain/loss from sale of businesses, restructuring charges, write-downs of tangible fixed assets.

** Includes gain/loss from sale of investments and write-downs of investments.

2.1 cents) and selling and distribution costs (down 0.9 cents) but more on administration (up 0.8 cents) in 2001 than in 1999. Other operating income contributed an additional 0.8 cents. But Carlsberg's bottom line in 2001 also benefited from one-off items – for example, gains on the sale of investments (in 'Other financial items') and a lower than normal effective tax rate (22% in 2001 against 29% in 2000 and 1999). In sum, not all of the improvement in NOPAT margin between 1999 and 2001 is sustainable. Carlsberg should be able to hold on to around three percentage points of the pre-tax gains as, according to management, they arise from production and distribution economies.

Assets turnover

Carlsberg's assets turnover in 2001 and 2000 was significantly lower than in 1999, offsetting the benefits from higher margins and depressing RONOA. Why was assets turnover sluggish in these two years? Exhibit 19.12 presents key activity ratios for the three years to 2001; these ratios are the major components of net operating assets turnover.

The ratios show that Carlsberg *improved* its utilisation of trade receivables, inventory and plant and equipment – three major operating assets – over the 1999–2001 period. In each case, it generated more revenues per euro of assets year-on-year and this, in turn, led to a shorter operating cycle. For example, from the inventory turnover figures we see that the average production and storage period fell from 61 days (365/6.02) in 1999 to 51 days in 2001. The increase in overall assets turnover in 2001 reflects the more intensive use of trade receivables, inventory and tangible fixed assets. The fall in the ratio in 2000 relative to 1999 was due to the impact of higher financial fixed assets and non-trade receivables (and *lower* operating liabilities).

Note that in some areas of asset management Carlsberg's *absolute* performance was still poor in 2001. For example, its customers took on average 64 days – i.e. over two months – to pay their bills that year.

Exhibit 19.12 Carlsberg Group: key activity ratios, 1999–2001

Financial period*	1998/99	1999/00	2001
Trade receivables turnover	5.43×	5.46×	5.67×
[Days' sales in receivables (365/trade RT)	67.2	66.9	64.4]
Inventory turnover**	6.02×	6.7×	7.18×
Tangible fixed assets turnover	1.81×	1.84×	1.87×
Net operating assets turnover (Exhibit 19.10)	**1.76×**	**1.51×**	**1.55×**

* 1998/99: year to 30 September; 1999/2000: 15 months to 31 December; 2001: year to 31 December. Figures for 1999/2000 are apportioned.
** Numerator is production costs. (For other turnover ratios, it is revenues net of excise duties.)

Return on equity

As we saw in Exhibit 19.10, Carlsberg raised returns on shareholders' funds even faster than returns on assets in the 1999–2001 period. Why was this? The main reason was management's decision to increase the group's financial leverage. Exhibit 19.13 charts the average net debt to equity ratio over the five years 1997–2001. The group's financial structure changed dramatically during this period – from a net *cash* balance of DKr 0.3 billion in September 1997 to net debt of almost DKr 11 billion at the end of 2001. Management decided in 1998 to finance future acquisitions from the company's own internal funds, where possible. If outside funding were needed, long-term debt would be used instead of equity.

Exhibit 19.13 Carlsberg Group: net financial leverage, 1997–2001

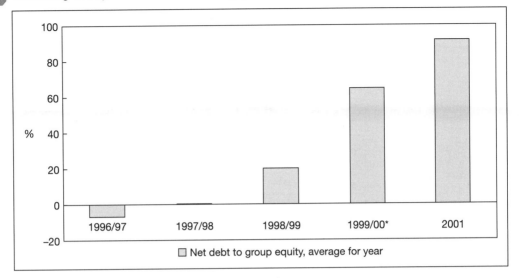

* 15 months to 31 December.

The increased financial leverage is only part of the story, however. To achieve *gains* from financial leverage, a company must generate positive 'spread' – the excess of RONOA over net borrowing costs – as well. In Carlsberg's case, 'spread' almost doubled in the 1999–2001 period.

	1998/99	1999/2000	2001
RONOA	**9.1%**	**10.3%**	**13.9%**
Gain from net financial leverage	**1%**	**5.5%**	**8.7%**
Spread [RONOA – NBC]*	*4.9%*	*8.5%*	*9.5%*
Netflev	*0.203*	*0.647*	*0.918*
ROE (group)	**10.1%**	**15.8%**	**22.6%**
* Net borrowing costs	4.2%	1.8%	4.4%

A postscript on ROE. What we have calculated above is the rate of return on the equity capital provided by Carlsberg's *group* shareholders. The return earned by its *parent company* shareholders was slightly greater than group ROE in 1999 and 2000 but much less in 2001.[15]

In DKr mn	1998/99	1999/2000	2001
Group net profit	1,156	2,227	2,615
Minority interests	8	–94	–1,109
Net profit, Carlsberg A/S share	1,164	2,133	1,507
ROE (parent company)	**11.6%**	**17.6%**	**17.6%**

This indicates that the ventures in which Carlsberg had a majority stake performed much better in 2001 than those that it owned outright. The reverse was true in 1999 and 2000. The significance to the group of the new subsidiary, Carlsberg Breweries, that combines Carlsberg's and Orkla's beverage interests and in which Carlsberg A/S has a 60% stake can be seen from the 2001 figure for 'minority interests' in the above table.

Exhibit 19.14 Carlsberg and main rivals: comparison of 2001 profitability

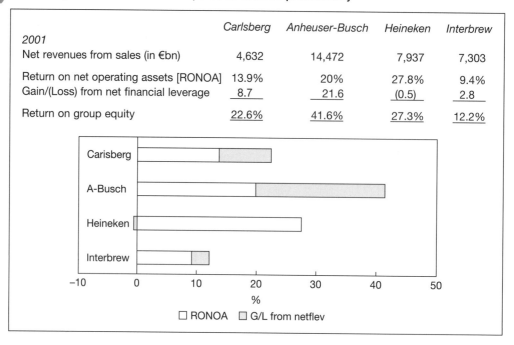

	Carlsberg	Anheuser-Busch	Heineken	Interbrew
2001				
Net revenues from sales (in €bn)	4,632	14,472	7,937	7,303
Return on net operating assets [RONOA]	13.9%	20%	27.8%	9.4%
Gain/(Loss) from net financial leverage	8.7	21.6	(0.5)	2.8
Return on group equity	22.6%	41.6%	27.3%	12.2%

Comparing Carlsberg's performance with its rivals'

Carlsberg earned high rates of return – on assets and equity – in 2001 compared with the returns it reported in earlier years. But how did its performance compare with that of its rivals? Exhibit 19.14 charts the 2001 ROE – and its main components, RONOA and gain/loss from net financial leverage – of Carlsberg and three of its main rivals, Anheuser-Busch, Heineken and Interbrew.

The exhibit reveals large differences in the four firms' operating performance and financial structure in 2001. Measured against Anheuser-Busch and Heineken, the leaders in the industry, Carlsberg's profitability in 2001 was disappointing. Its operating returns were only half those of Heineken and two-thirds those of Anheuser-Busch. This meant, in turn, that it had less 'spread' (RONOA – net borrowing cost) to lever up on its shareholders' behalf: Anheuser-Busch's spread was over 16% against Carlsberg's 9.5%.

Moreover, Carlsberg's and Heineken's reported profitability – in asset and equity terms – is overstated relative to Anheuser-Busch's. Both firms made sizeable acquisitions in the 1990s. Much of the purchase price of these acquisitions was assigned to goodwill which, under accounting policies then in force at the two firms, was written off against reserves. By contrast, Anheuser-Busch capitalised and amortised purchased goodwill during this time.

There is some consolation for Carlsberg's management. The company outperformed Interbrew, a much larger firm. It employed debt to its shareholders' benefit – which Heineken did not. And Anheuser-Busch with its domestic focus – the USA absorbed 95% of its beer output in 2001 – could reap production and distribution economies not available to a geographically dispersed group like Carlsberg.

Financial risk in 2001

Carlsberg was in good financial health in 2001. This is evident from its liquidity and financial leverage ratios that year. Exhibit 19.15 shows key financial risk ratios for the company and three of its main rivals in 2001.

Exhibit 19.15   Carlsberg and main rivals: financial risk in 2001

	Carlsberg	Anheuser-Busch	Heineken	Interbrew
Liquidity risk				
Current ratio	1.3	0.9	1.4	0.8
Quick ratio	1.0	0.5	1.1	0.6
Defensive interval (in days)	140	28	125	137
Financial leverage				
Debt–equity ratio	87.5%	97.3%	n/a*	50.5%
Times interest earned	6.0×	7.5×	16.5×	5.0×
Net debt / Operating cash flow	3.0	1.6	n/a	2.0

* n/a: not applicable (company has no net debt).

The risk of Carlsberg not being able to meet its short-term debts at the end of 2001 was small. For example, Carlsberg had one krone of 'quick' assets (cash, short-term investments, receivables) for every krone of current liabilities at the end of 2001. These assets were sufficient to finance 140 days of the group's operating outlays (including capital expenditures) that year. Heineken and Interbrew reported a similar 'defensive interval'. By contrast, Anheuser-Busch's cash and receivables were sufficient to finance barely a month of operating expenditures. Differences in operating environment are partly responsible for the difference in defensive interval. The three European brewers have extensive international operations that require them to carry larger cash balances than their US-focused rival.

Leverage ratios indicate low credit risk, too. Although Carlsberg's net debt at the end of 2001 was almost 90% of its group equity, its strong profits and cash flow meant it had no difficulty servicing these liabilities. For example, interest payments in 2001 were covered six times by earnings and, at the 2001 rate of (pre-tax, pre-interest) operating cash flow, the group could repay its debt in three years. Carlsberg's rivals revealed similar financial strength. As we saw earlier, Heineken had no net debt in 2001 (or in earlier years). More interestingly, Anheuser-Busch had greater balance sheet leverage but *higher* interest cover and *faster* debt-repayment ability that year.

Cash flow profile

Analysis of Carlsberg's cash flows sheds light on the company's past investing and financing decisions. Exhibit 19.16 presents summary cash flow data for the 1999–2001 period. (The figures for 2001 are taken from Carlsberg's 2001 accounts which are given in Appendix 19.2.)

Here is a synopsis of the cash flow 'story' for these years:

- Carlsberg's operations generated positive cash flows. After adjusting for special items in 1998/99 and the 15-month financial period in 1999/2000, operating cash flow grew year-on-year.
- The group continued to invest heavily in plant and equipment, despite little or no growth in demand for beer in its main west European markets. Capital expenditures exceeded depreciation every year.
- Increased capex was stimulated by the group's merger and acquisition activities. Carlsberg acquired majority stakes ('corporate acquisitions') and minority stakes ('financial investments') in brewing companies in Europe and Asia throughout this period. For example, in addition to the merger of its beverage interests with Orkla's at the start of 2001, Carlsberg made brewery purchases in Switzerland in 2000 and Poland and Turkey in 2001 and made or increased investments in breweries in South Korea (1999) and Malaysia (2001).

Exhibit 19.16 Carlsberg Group: analysis of cash flows, 1999–2001

In DKr million	1998/99	1999/2000 (15 months)	2001
Operating cash flow*	**730****	**2,305**	**2,215**
Capital expenditures, net	–2,024	–2,770	–3,551
Other investment income	+33	+38	+1,020
Dividends paid	–256	–256	–345
Free cash flow	**–1,517**	**–683**	**–661**
Other investing flows:			
Corporate acquisitions, net	–496	–4,309	–1,340
Financial investments, net	–399	+248	+192
Operating less investing cash flows	**–2,412**	**–4,744**	**–1,809**
Financed by:			
Disposal of securities	+1,427	+736	+821
Changes in financial liabilities and minority interests	–1,153	+3,797	+1,991
Net change in cash**	**–2,138**	**–211**	**+1,003**
* Depreciation	1,354	2,153	2,224

** After deducting special items of 1,091.
*** Excludes effect of exchange rate changes.

- Carlsberg was unable to finance capital expenditures let alone corporate acquisitions and financial investments out of operating cash flow. Free cash flow was negative every year. The group's net outflows after deducting all investing flows totalled almost DKr 9 billion in the 1999–2001 period.
- The group financed these net outflows by selling part of its portfolio of short-term investments (DKr 3 billion), raising capital through bank loans and via minority shareholdings in new subsidiaries (DKr 4.6 billion) and reducing its cash balance (DKr 1.3 billion). Carlsberg also assumed debt with its acquisitions. As a result, reported debt in the consolidated accounts grew by DKr 7 billion over the three years.[16]

Analysis of Carlsberg's 2001 financial statements: summary

How accurate were our predictions of Carlsberg's financial performance and health in 2001? Our expectations about the group's financial health were met but we overestimated its ability to generate superior returns. We also misjudged its cash flow profile. Carlsberg's cash flows in the 1999–2001 period were similar to those of a company in its growth phase – despite beer being a mature product in Carlsberg's main European markets.

1 *Profitability.* Carlsberg's performance in 2001 appears to be strong. RONOA and ROE both increased and, in the case of ROE, achieved its highest level in five years. However, by comparison with its main rivals, the group did not earn high operating returns. In particular, its operating margins were low. Moreover, its reported performance was overstated because of its policy of writing off goodwill against reserves.

2 *Liquidity and leverage.* As expected, liquidity was strong and, despite growing financial leverage, the group was able to service its debts with ease.

3 *Cash flows.* Surprisingly, free cash flow was negative – not just in 2001 but in the preceding two years, too. Note, however, that capex includes expenditures to expand as well as maintain its fixed asset stock and is affected by the group's merger and acquisition spree during this period. The net outflow was financed by disposals of short-term investments and by borrowing.

Residual income

We've seen that Carlsberg was profitable in accounting terms in the 1997–2001 period. The company generated positive RONOA and ROE each year during this time. But were the returns sufficient to make its shareholders richer? To answer this question we need to know the *cost* of the capital employed by Carlsberg. Only if the returns on the capital employed by Carlsberg were greater than its cost did the company increase shareholders' wealth. The excess of returns over cost of capital is known as 'economic profit' or **residual income**.

Calculating residual income (RI) is simple in principle. The usual approach is to deduct from after-tax operating profit a capital charge for the use of invested capital. Invested capital is defined as the book value of (net) debt and equity.

$$\text{Residual income} = \text{NOPAT} - (\text{CC} \times \text{BVCAP})$$

where NOPAT is net operating profit after tax, CC is the cost of capital, and BVCAP is the book value of debt and equity capital. 'Debt capital' includes short-term and long-term borrowing; it's usually stated net of cash and cash equivalents. Where RI is calculated for a group, 'equity capital' includes minority interests. BVCAP can be measured using start-of-period or average carrying amounts of debt and equity capital.

How do investors (and managers) estimate a company's cost of capital? A common approach is to combine the costs of its debt and equity capital on a weighted basis. Assuming a simple capital structure containing debt and ordinary share capital only, the **weighted average cost of capital (WACC)** is calculated as follows:

$$\text{WACC} = \left(\frac{\text{Debt}}{\text{Debt} + \text{Equity}} \times k_d (1 - t) \right) + \left(\frac{\text{Equity}}{\text{Debt} + \text{Equity}} \times k_e \right)$$

where k_d is the before-tax cost of debt, k_e is the after-tax cost of equity, and t is the tax rate associated with the tax shelter provided by interest. Since interest is tax-deductible but dividends are not, the cost of debt should be adjusted to an after-tax basis. Market values should be used in calculating 'Debt' and 'Equity'.

How are k_d and k_e computed? The cost of debt is the current interest rate on debt of equivalent risk and maturity. The cost of equity is harder to estimate. One widely used approach is to view k_e as the sum of a long-term risk-free interest rate and a market risk premium which is adjusted for the underlying volatility of the company's shares:[17]

$$k_e = \frac{\text{Long-term}}{\text{risk-free interest rate}} + \left(\frac{\text{Firm-specific}}{\text{volatility indicator}} \times \frac{\text{Market}}{\text{risk premium}} \right)$$

The interest rate on high-grade long-term government bonds is a proxy for the risk-free rate. The volatility indicator, known as 'beta', is stock market-linked. A company has a beta of 1 if the return (i.e. dividend and capital gains/losses) on its shares fluctuates in line with the return on the stock market. (The stock market is a proxy for all assets.) Such a firm is considered to be of average risk. A higher-risk (lower-risk) firm has a beta of more (less) than 1: the return on its shares fluctuates *more (less)* than the market return. The market risk premium is the additional return that investors demand for investing in risky securities (as represented by the overall stock market).

Obtaining an accurate estimate of beta is, in practice, a difficult task and is best undertaken by financial economists. Rather than trying to estimate Carlsberg's beta and thus the actual cost of its equity capital in 2001, we calculate below the company's *break-even WACC* in the year, that is, the cost of capital that results in zero RI. From this we can derive the break-even cost of equity capital. If Carlsberg's actual cost of equity is *less* than the break-even level, we can conclude that the company generated positive RI and created wealth for its shareholders in the period.

Carlsberg's breakeven WACC in 2001 – based on reported numbers – was 13.9%. Since 'invested capital' is equivalent to net operating assets, break-even WACC must be equal to RONOA:

$$\text{NOPAT}_t - [\text{WACC}_{B/E,t} \times \text{BVCAP}_t] = 0 \Rightarrow \text{WACC}_{B/E,t} = \text{RONOA}_t$$

As shown in Exhibit 19.10 (the calculation is set out in panel B of Appendix 19.2), Carlsberg's RONOA in 2001 was 13.9%.

To estimate the break-even cost of equity capital, we need to estimate the weights of debt and equity capital in Carlsberg's capital structure, using market values. At the end of 2001, the market value of the company's equity was DKr 20.9 billion. Assuming the market values of debt and minority interests approximate their book values, this implies that (net) debt represented around 30% of Carlsberg's end-2001 financial capital in market value terms.[18] The company's net borrowing cost in 2001 was 4.4% (*see* Appendix 19.2, panel B) and we assume that this approximates the company's after-tax cost of debt that year. Based on the above estimates of break-even WACC, debt (and equity) weights in the capital structure and the cost of debt, Carlsberg's break-even cost of equity was 18% in 2001:

$$13.9\% = [(0.3 \times 4.4\%) + (0.7 \times k_{e,B/E})] \Rightarrow k_{e,B/E} = 18\%$$

A break-even cost of equity capital of 18% is higher than Carlsberg's actual cost of equity in 2001 which, in view of the low-to-medium risk of investments in global beverage companies, was probably in the 10–15% range. At first glance, it appears Carlsberg added value for its shareholders that year.

A second – and closer – glance of the numbers reveals that Carlsberg's performance in 2001 was not so impressive. We mentioned earlier that Carlsberg wrote off against reserves any goodwill arising on acquisitions.[19] As a result, the reported balance sheet figure for shareholders' equity doesn't reflect the actual capital invested by shareholders. The amount of the understatement is large. According to management, Carlsberg wrote off DKr 7.5 billion of purchased goodwill up to the end of 2000 and a further DKr 1.6 billion in 2001. Adding back the cumulative goodwill write-off increases average invested capital to DKr 30.5 billion:

In DKr bn	*2001*
Reported average invested capital (or NOA), at book value	22.2
Cumulative goodwill write-off [7.5 + (1.6/2)]	8.3
Adjusted average invested capital	30.5

If 2001 NOPAT remains at DKr 3.08 billion (the reinstated goodwill asset is assumed to have an indefinite life and is not amortised), the break-even WACC falls from 13.9% to 10.1% (3.08/30.5) and break-even cost of equity from 18% to 12.5%. This figure is in the middle of the range of likely actual equity costs in 2001.

Adding back goodwill write-offs is only one of several adjustments that can be made to correct Carlsberg's capital figure so that it reflects more closely the resources invested in the business by shareholders and creditors. Other examples are the reversal of asset write-downs and the capitalisation of non-cancellable operating leases.[20] The net effect of including all such adjustments would be to lower further Carlsberg's break-even cost of equity – and increase the likelihood of it being *below* the company's actual cost of equity in 2001.

The company's failure to create wealth for its shareholders is evident more directly – in the share price. Set out below are end-year market prices of the company's B shares (the most widely held and traded class of its shares) between 1996 and 2001, along with the per-share dividend paid each year. Recall that the *market return* on an investment is the sum of the dividend yield and the percentage change in the share price during the period.

In DKr	1995/96	1996/97	1997/98	1998/99	1999/2000 (15 months)	2001
End-year market price of B shares	353	374	400	257	468	348
Dividend/share	3.4	3.6	4.0	4.0	5.4	5.0

Carlsberg's share price at the end of 2001 was approximately the same as at end-September 1996, $5\frac{1}{4}$ years earlier. The only return a shareholder investing in September 1996 enjoyed during the subsequent five years was dividend income – which, in yield terms, averaged around 1% a year.

Summary

In this chapter we show by example how investors analyse a company's financial statements. Three themes emerge from our investigation of Carlsberg's 2001 accounts.

1 There is no point in analysing financial statements in a vacuum. Before studying a company's accounts, we need to be familiar with the industries it operates in and the markets it serves. In particular, we should be aware of the likely effects – on its profitability, asset mix and capital structure – of technological and competitive forces on those industries and markets. Background knowledge such as this improves our understanding of the company and helps us interpret financial statements better.

2 Analysis involves making comparisons – with the company's competitors and with its past. A financial ratio is only high or low, strong or weak, relative to the benchmark chosen. Care must be taken to ensure the benchmark is appropriate. An important profitability benchmark is the firm's cost of capital. A firm creates wealth for its shareholders only if it earns a return on its assets greater than the cost of financing them.

3 As investors we should use all the data in financial statements. The profit margin, for example, reveals only part of the profitability story: the cost ratios, and their movement over time, tell us more. Similarly, insights we gain from the individual assets turnover ratios – receivables, inventory, fixed assets turnover – add to what we've learnt from the total assets turnover ratio. Moreover, we should test the internal consistency of financial statement numbers – making sure, for example, that the picture of the company portrayed in its income statement tallies with that in its cash flow statement.

A major reason investors analyse financial statements – for many, *the* reason – is to help them make investment decisions. They use them, in conjunction with other data, to make forecasts of corporate earnings and cash flows and, by extension, to value companies. But financial statements have limitations in this role. In the next chapter, we describe and illustrate these limitations and show how investors try to overcome them.

APPENDIX 19.1 Market efficiency and its implications

In recent years stock market professionals have questioned the benefit to investors of analysing published financial statements. They claim securities markets are efficient and thus the ordinary investor cannot profit from information which is publicly available. In this section, we ask:

● What is meant by 'market efficiency'? Are securities markets efficient?
● What are the implications for financial statement analysis if markets are efficient? if they're not?

Our discussion of market efficiency is brief. A fuller treatment can be found in finance texts.[21]

Market efficiency: theory and evidence

The definition of market efficiency is simple. A market is said to be efficient if prices in it reflect all available information. Securities markets bear the hallmarks of such a market, it's claimed. Rational investors value a security on the basis of the present value of its expected cash flows. If its market price is below (above) their valuation, they see an opportunity to make money and will buy (sell short) the security, bidding up the price (or driving it down) until the mispricing is removed and there are no further gains from trading. New information causes investors to revise their valuations and buy or sell accordingly. In an efficient market, investors act on new information as soon as it becomes available and the prices of securities adjust to it quickly and correctly.

What if investors are not rational? No problem, say supporters of the 'efficient market hypothesis' (EMH). If the investment decisions of irrational investors are *uncorrelated*, then their trades cancel each other out – in essence, their trading has a random pattern – and prices of securities continue to reflect fundamental values. If the investment decisions of irrational investors are *correlated* – that is, such investors exhibit herd-like behaviour – 'smart investors' such as arbitrageurs intervene in the market and restore prices to their fundamental values. Arbitrageurs earn their living from identifying mispriced securities and acting on that information.

To test the EMH, researchers needed more precise definitions of 'information' and 'gains from trading'. They proposed three information strengths. In its 'weak' form, security prices reflect fully the information contained in the past pattern of prices. This suggests that technical analysis, that is, plotting past price movements and looking for patterns in them, is of no help to investors since, in effect, prices move in a random way. In its 'semi-strong' form, security prices reflect fully all publicly available information. This includes published interim and annual reports, company announcements and general economic and financial data. In its 'strong' form, security prices reflect fully *all* available information, including information *not* publicly available but known to insiders only. Insiders are those with privileged access to corporate information: this group includes management and other employees and extends to those who through their work have access to information about the company which has not been made public (e.g. the firm's bankers). As for 'gains from trading', researchers measured them in risk-adjusted terms. They defined gains (and losses) as *abnormal returns*, that is, returns above (below) the normal returns an investor would demand given the risk assumed by investing in the security.

Many empirical studies in the 1960s and 1970s found evidence in support of the weak and semi-strong forms of the efficient market hypothesis. For example, early research showed that when the company announces its earnings for a past period, its share price already reflects the *expected* earnings for that period. In addition, the share price responds quickly to any *unexpected* component in the earnings figure. This suggests that investors constantly update their estimates of earnings *during the period* as new information – about the company or about events that may affect it – becomes available.

Efficient market hypothesis under attack

The EMH has been challenged in recent years. The attack has two prongs. Investors and researchers cite evidence from stock markets that is not consistent with the hypothesis. And some economists question the validity of the assumptions underlying it.

Many empirical studies were published in the 1980s that cast doubt on the EMH in its semi-strong (and even its weak) form. Some found that a security price reaction was still evident 60–90 days after the annual earnings announcement – evidence of an 'underreaction' to new information. By contrast, other studies found that the market overreacts to information. For example, 'growth' stocks – that is, firms that have achieved a very high rate of growth of earnings in the past and trade on a high price-to-book (P/B) or P/E ratio – underperform, while 'value' stocks (those with a low P/B or P/E ratio) outperform, in the future. This suggests that investors overreact: they bid up prices of growth stocks above, and drive down the prices of value stocks below, the level warranted by the discounted value of the company's expected future cash flows.

In addition to research studies, EMH sceptics point to stock market history. Why did the US stock market crash on 19 October 1987? What was the 'new information' that caused the 22.6% fall in the Dow Jones Industrial Average index that day? More recently, why did US and European stock markets become so overvalued during the dotcom bubble of the late 1990s? And why did the overvaluation persist so long, given the profitable opportunities available to arbitrageurs?

The theoretical foundations of the EMH have also been attacked. Some economists question whether investors are rational. They point to research findings in psychology which offer many examples of human behaviour that do not accord with the economist's notion of rationality. For example, human beings tend to make decisions heuristically, relying on patterns they observe in limited data sets from the past. (This helps explain investor overreaction to companies' past earnings history.) Moreover, market professionals doubt whether, in practice, arbitrageurs can counter the actions of irrational investors. Arbitrage requires a security to have a close substitute so that an arbitrageur can lay off the risk (i.e. buy a security similar to the one he or she has sold short). Close substitutes exist for derivative instruments (e.g. futures and options) but rarely for shares and bonds. Even where a close substitute for a share exists, arbitrage can be a risky activity. It may take a long time for the prices of the two securities to converge and, in the meantime, the arbitrageur must have the resources to maintain his or her position in them. Premature unwinding of that position may result in losses. As a result, securities may be mispriced – and the stock market over- or undervalued – for months if not years.

Not surprisingly, supporters of the EMH have been active in its defence. Empirical studies that indicate the market underreacts or overreacts to new information suffer from poor research design, they claim: researchers misspecify risk and so fail to measure risk-adjusted returns correctly. As for stock market 'anomalies', these can be explained by changes in discount rates. For example, a decline in the equity risk premium – that is, the extra return investors demand for investing in risky equities instead of risk-free government bonds – was responsible for high share values in the late 1990s, they argue. And they dispute the contention that arbitrage is, in practice, ineffective at removing mispricing of securities.

Implications for financial statement analysis

The controversy over the EMH continues. Meanwhile, investors are left wondering whether analysing financial reports is a worthwhile activity. For example, if markets are efficient, they will be unable to profit from financial statement analysis as the new information in a company's interim or annual accounts is impounded into its share price too quickly for them to act on it.

First, we should note there are circumstances when the efficiency – or inefficiency – of securities markets is of no direct concern to the financial statement user. For example, the securities of private companies and some state-owned companies are not publicly traded. Moreover, financial statement users are diverse and their reasons for analysing a company's financial statements are also varied. Banks use them to evaluate a loan request, unions to formulate a pay claim, governments to help shape tax policy.

Analysing quoted companies' accounts can still be fruitful even when securities markets are efficient. Investors check financial statements to confirm announcements by a firm of its past financial performance and condition. Interim and annual reports have 'reassurance' value: they help reduce investor uncertainty. In addition, investors consult them when assessing the riskiness of their investments.

But what if markets are not efficient, as EMH sceptics claim? Surely, analysing financial statements is a worthwhile activity in these circumstances? Yes – but the scope for investors to make money from it may be limited. For example, if a share is mispriced and arbitrage is unable to eliminate the mispricing, investors may have to wait until market sentiment towards the company changes before they can put their analysis of its accounts to profitable use. Experience in the 1990s suggests there can be periods when they have to wait a long time.

APPENDIX 19.2   Carlsberg Group: annual accounts and key ratios for 2001

Panel A   Carlsberg Group's financial statements for 2001*

PROFIT AND LOSS ACCOUNT 2001
(in DKr million)

Turnover	46,975
Production costs	17,393
Excise duties on beer and soft drinks, etc.	12,515
GROSS PROFIT	**17,067**
Sales and distribution expenses	11,386
Administration expenses	2,752
Other operating income, net	430
Profit before tax from participating interests in associated companies	41
OPERATING PROFIT	**3,400**
Special items, net	17
PROFIT BEFORE FINANCIALS	**3,417**
Income from other participating interests, etc.	688
Other interest income and similar income	1,210
Write-down of fixed asset investments, securities, etc.	78
Interest expenses and similar charges	1,878
PROFIT BEFORE TAX	**3,359**
Corporation tax	743
GROUP PROFIT	**2,616**
Minority interests	1,109
PROFIT FOR THE YEAR, Carlsberg A/S's share	**1,507**

* Reproduced by permission of Carlsberg A/S.

Panel A   Carlsberg Group's financial statements for 2001 continued

BALANCE SHEET AS AT 31 DECEMBER 2001

(in DKr million)

Assets	31/12/01	31/12/00
FIXED ASSETS		
Tangible fixed assets		
Land and buildings	7,683	6,805
Plant and machinery	7,983	5,984
Other fixtures and fittings, tools and equipment	3,061	3,230
Construction in progress	1,599	476
	20,326	**16,495**
Fixed assets investments		
Participating interests in associated companies	625	474
Loans to associated companies	63	195
Other investments and shareholdings	1,572	621
Other debtors	1,992	1,834
Deferred tax	480	1,076
Holding of own shares	35	0
	4,767	**4,200**
TOTAL FIXED ASSETS	**25,093**	**20,695**
CURRENT ASSETS		
Stocks and debtors		
Stocks	2,865	1,977
Trade debtors	6,580	5,564
Amounts owed by associated companies	209	969
Other debtors	2,542	2,380
Prepayments and accrued income	489	506
	12,685	**11,396**
Securities, cash and cash equivalents		
Shares	9	10
Bonds and other securities	117	1,212
Cash at bank and in hand	3,165	1,678
	3,291	**2,900**
TOTAL CURRENT ASSETS	**15,976**	**14,296**
TOTAL ASSETS	**41,069**	**34,991**

Panel A   Carlsberg Group's financial statements for 2001 continued

BALANCE SHEET AS AT 31 DECEMBER 2001

(in DKr million)

Equity and liabilities	31/12/01	31/12/00
EQUITY		
Share capital	1,278	1,278
Reserves	6,781	7,702
	8,059	**8,980**
Minority interests	4,454	1,651
TOTAL EQUITY	**12,513**	**10,631**
LIABILITIES		
Provisions		
Pensions and similar commitments	780	366
Liabilities for deposits on returnable packaging	1,239	1,142
Deferred tax	1,137	924
Other	546	699
	3,702	**3,131**
Long-term liabilities		
Bond loans	7,172	3,047
Credit institutions	4,804	2,887
Other	66	75
	12,042	**6,009**
Current liabilities		
Bond loans	598	1,170
Credit institutions	1,601	6,022
Trade creditors	3,414	2,651
Amounts owed to associated companies	348	150
Corporation tax	518	161
Excise duties and VAT	1,596	1,262
Other	3,312	2,278
Accruals and deferred income	1,105	1,181
Proposed dividend	320	345
	12,812	**15,220**
TOTAL LIABILITIES	**24,854**	**21,229**
TOTAL EQUITY AND LIABILITIES	**41,069**	**34,991**

● Panel A   Carlsberg Group's financial statements for 2001 continued

CASH FLOW STATEMENT 2001
(in DKr million)

Operating profit	3,400
Depreciation	2,224
Other adjustments	−407
Financial expense, net	−578
Corporation tax paid	−839
Cash flow from operations before changes in working capital	3,800
Change in debtors	−770
Change in stocks	−176
Change in creditors, excise duties, etc.	−639
CASH FLOW, OPERATIONS	**2,215**
Acquisition of tangible fixed assets, net	−3,551
Acquisition/disposal of companies, net	−1,996
Acquisition of fixed asset investments	−656
Disposal of fixed asset investments	848
Disposal of securities	821
Dividend received from associated companies	1,020
CASH FLOW, INVESTMENTS	**−3,514**
Dividend paid	−345
Receivables from sale of companies	656
Repayment of debt	−1,013
Minority interests	−513
Financial income and expenditure	3,517
CASH FLOW, FINANCING	**2,302**
CASH FLOW FROM OPERATIONS, INVESTMENTS AND FINANCING	**1,003**
Cash and cash equivalents, beginning of year	1,678
Currency translation adjustments of start-year cash and cash equivalents	−21
Acquired/sold cash at bank and in hand	505
Cash flow for the year	1,003
Cash and cash equivalents, end of year	**3,165**

Note: The statement of cash flow cannot be derived solely from the published annual accounts.

● Panel B   Derivation of certain financial ratios for 2001

Profitability ratios

Return on equity = Return on net operating assets + [(RONOA − Net bwg cost) × Net financial leverage]

$$\left[\frac{NOPAT}{Op.\ revenues} \times \frac{Op.\ revenues}{Av.\ net\ op.\ assets} \right] + \left[\left(\frac{NOPAT}{Av.\ NOA} - \frac{NFE}{Av.\ net\ debt} \right) \times \frac{Av.\ net\ debt}{Av.\ gp\ equity} \right]$$

NFE = Net financial expense = [Interest expense − Interest income] × (1 − t)
                                [1,878   −   1,210]   × (1 − 0.3)   **= 468**

t = Marginal tax rate   = 30% (Danish statutory tax rate in 2001)

NOPAT = Net operating profit after tax = Group net profit + Net financial expense
                                          2,616   +   468   **= 3,084**

NOA   = Operating assets − Operating liabilities = Net debt + Group equity

	End 2001	End 2000		
Long-term debt	12,042	6,009		
Short-term debt	2,199	7,192		
	14,241	13,201		
Less: Cash and securities	−3,291	−2,900		
Net debt	10,950	10,301	Av. net debt	**10,626**
Group equity	12,513	10,631	Av. gp equity	**11,572**
NOA	23,463	20,932	Av. NOA	**22,198**

Operating revenues   =   Turnover   −   Excise duties
                            46,975   12,515   **= 34,460**

In sum:
ROE = [Profit margin × Assets turnover] + [SPREAD   × NETFLEV]
                                              (RONOA − NBC)

$\dfrac{3,084}{34,460}$	$\dfrac{34,460}{22,198}$		$\dfrac{3,084}{22,198}$	$\dfrac{468}{10,626}$	$\dfrac{10,626}{11,572}$	
9%	×	1.55	[(13.9%	−	4.4%)	×	0.918]

                    13.9%   +   8.7%   **= 22.6%**
            Operating performance   *Gain from net financial leverage*

Activity ratios

Inventory turnover	$\dfrac{\text{Production costs}}{\text{Av. stocks}}$	$\dfrac{17,393}{2,421}$	**7.18×**
Receivables turnover	$\dfrac{\text{Turnover} - \text{Excise duties}}{\text{Av. trade debtors}}$	$\dfrac{34,460}{6,072}$	**5.67×**

Liquidity ratios

Defensive interval	$\dfrac{\text{Cash} + \text{Securities} + \text{Debtors, end-year}}{\text{Actual operating outlays in year}}$ ($\approx$ Op. costs (excl. depn) + Capex)	$\dfrac{12,622}{32,858}$ (× 365)	**140 days**

Problem assignments

P19.1 Alternative approach to financial statement analysis

Asked what she looked for when analysing a company's financial statements, a prominent fund manager, Florence Cash, gave a two-word reply: 'Cash flow'. Florence then elaborated: 'When evaluating a company, I don't spend time calculating profit margins or return on capital employed or any of the other traditional ratios favoured by financial analysts. The two questions that most concern me are: (1) Does the company generate positive free cash flow? and (2) Is free cash flow growing? I use these cash flow questions as a screening device. Only if the answer to both is yes, will I consider the company a candidate for investment and investigate it further.'

Required

Comment on Florence's approach to analysing financial statements. What are the advantages and disadvantages of this approach?

P19.2 Japanese production methods and profitability

Do Japanese production methods improve corporate profitability? This is a question that has long interested European and US managers. Recently, some researchers carried out a study of manufacturing companies in an EU member state to try to answer this question. They found that, for the sample of companies chosen, the profitability of high and low users of Japanese production methods was very similar, fluctuating between 6% and 8% in the period studied (1986–92). According to researchers, there was intense interest in Japanese production methods in Europe in the late 1980s; many of the EU firms adopting them did so in these years.

The researchers define profitability in the study as the ratio of operating profit to sales. Just-in-time (JIT) production, JIT delivery of supplies, cellular manufacture and quality circles are examples of Japanese production methods.

Required

Comment on the above findings. Is the operating profit to sales ratio the most appropriate measure of profitability in this case? Given the nature of Japanese production methods, what impact do you expect them to have on a firm's profitability?

P19.3 Effect of transactions on financial ratios

Pappacoda, a macaroni producer, has a current ratio of 1.5, a receivables turnover of 5, and an inventory turnover (cost of sales/average inventory) of 10.

Required

Consider the impact of each of the following events separately on Pappacoda's current ratio, receivables turnover and inventory turnover. Will the ratio increase, decrease or be unaffected?

(a) Purchase of flour and other materials on account. The company assumes a FIFO flow of costs.

(b) Payment of suppliers of materials which were purchased previously on account.

(c) Sale of macaroni on account. Sale price exceeds cost.

(d) Write-off of a bad debt. No provision has been made for doubtful accounts.

P19.4 Profitability: alternative ways of analysing ROE

FKI is a UK-based engineering group with interests in automated material handling, lifting products, and energy technology (e.g. electrical generators, transformers and switchgear). Sales rose 30% in the 2000/01 financial year but operating profits only managed a 12% increase so margins slipped. Summary income and balance sheet data from that year's consolidated accounts are set out below. All amounts are in £ millions.

Condensed profit and loss account for year to 31 March 2001

Turnover	1,740
Operating profit	202
Interest expense, net	−44
Profit on ordinary activities before tax	158
Tax on profit on ordinary activities	−55
Profit on ordinary activities after tax	103

Condensed balance sheet: average of end-March 2001 and 2000 figures

Tangible fixed assets		398	Capital and reserves	443
Goodwill and other fixed assets		522	Long-term borrowings	663
		920	Other long-term creditors and provisions	67
Stocks	249			730
Debtors	394		Short-term borrowings	18
Cash and short-term deposits	168		Trade and other short-term creditors	540
		811		558
Total assets		1,731	Total equities	1,731

Required

(a) Calculate FKI's return on equity for the year to 31 March 2001. Analyse ROE. What was the group's profit margin, assets turnover and return on net operating assets in 2000/01? How much did it gain or lose from financial leverage that year? (Assume 'Cash and short-term deposits' are all financial assets. The UK corporate tax rate was 30% in 2000/01.)

(b) Under an alternative approach, ROE is expressed as the *product* of return on assets and income and balance sheet leverage effects. The larger the interest expense in relation to net profit or the larger total liabilities in relation to total assets, the greater is the impact on ROE of these respective leverage effects.

$$
\text{Return on equity} = \underbrace{\frac{\text{NOPAT}}{\text{Average total assets}}}_{\text{Return on assets}} \times \underbrace{\frac{\text{Net profit}}{\text{NOPAT}}}_{\text{Income leverage}} \times \underbrace{\frac{\text{Average total assets}}{\text{Average shareholders' equity}}}_{\text{Balance sheet leverage}}
$$

What are the advantages, if any, of the method of analysing ROE outlined in the chapter (i.e. ROE = RONOA +/− gain/loss from financial leverage) over the above approach?

Check figure:
(a) Spread in 2000/01: 8%

P19.5 Profitability: comparing corporate performance

Kao Corporation is a Japanese toiletries and household products group. The range of its products is similar to that of US-based Procter & Gamble but the group is smaller (2001/02 sales of US$6.3 bn vs P&G's US$40 bn) and less international (domestic sales 75% vs 53% for P&G). Although Kao's profits have grown rapidly in the five years to 2002, its profitability in 2001/02 still lagged behind P&G's. P&G's group ROE in 2001/02 was 33.8%. By contrast, Kao's was only 12.9% that year. Kao's financial statements for 2001/02 are presented in condensed form in Exhibit 19.17.

Exhibit 19.17 Kao Corporation: condensed financial statements, 2002

Condensed income statement for year to 31 March 2002

	¥ million
Net sales	**839,026**
Cost of sales	–361,433
Gross profit	**477,593**
Selling, general and administrative expenses	–365,865
Operating income	**111,728**
Interest income, net of interest expense	31
Other non-operating expense, net	–3,818
Income before taxes and minority interests	**107,941**
Income tax expense	–45,778
Income before minority interests	**62,163**
Minority interests in earnings of consolidated subsidiaries	–1,888
Net income	**60,275**

Condensed balance sheets at end-March 2001 and 2002

	¥ million	
	2002	2001
Current assets		
Cash and short-term investments	**159,130**	173,250
Notes and accounts receivable, net of allowance for doubtful accounts	**102,244**	105,319
Inventories	**67,220**	69,903
Other current assets	**24,168**	17,739
Total current assets	**352,762**	366,211
Property, plant and equipment, at net book value	**295,563**	297,958
Intangible assets	**53,158**	57,370
Investments and other assets	**70,662**	62,221
Total assets	**772,145**	783,760
Current liabilities		
Short-term debt and current portion of long-term debt	**19,290**	26,272
Notes and accounts payable	**91,603**	98,627
Accrued expenses and other current liabilities	**103,759**	105,695
Total current liabilities	**214,652**	230,594
Long-term liabilities		
Long-term debt	**36,676**	43,142
Other long-term liabilities	**38,354**	26,314
	75,030	69,456
Minority interests	**22,732**	20,722
Shareholders' equity	**459,731**	462,988
Total liabilities and shareholders' equity	**772,145**	783,760

(*Source*: Kao Corporation, *Annual Report 2002*. Reproduced by permission of Kao Corporation.)

Summary income and balance sheet numbers taken from P&G's 2001/02 accounts are given below. (P&G discloses no information about minority interests. Group and parent company equity are assumed to be the same.)

	Procter & Gamble 30 June 2002 US$ bn
Financial year to:	
Net sales	40.24
Cost of sales	−20.99
Selling, general and administrative expenses	−12.57
Interest expense, net	−0.50
Other non-operating income, net	0.20
Income taxes	−2.03
Net earnings	4.35
Average net operating assets	23.27
Average shareholders' equity	12.86

Required

(a) Calculate Procter & Gamble's and Kao's return on net operating assets (RONOA) for each company's 2001/02 financial year. P&G's marginal tax rate is 35%, Kao's is 42% that year.

(b) Break down RONOA into its profit margin and assets turnover components. What are the reasons for P&G's higher profit margin?

(c) The president of Kao Corporation is puzzled. P&G's RONOA in 2001/02 is only around 3.7 percentage points greater than Kao's but its ROE that year is over 20 percentage points greater (33.8% vs 12.9%). Explain the reason for P&G's superior performance at the ROE level.

P19.6 Financial ratios: industry differences

Certain industries have distinctive economic traits and these can be seen in the financial statements of companies in the industry. Set out in Exhibit 19.18 are summary accounts of seven companies from seven different industries. In each case, numbers from the balance sheets and income statements of the three years to 2001 are averaged and then common-sized on net sales (i.e. expressed as a percentage of net sales).

Required

Match each company in the exhibit to one of the industries below. Give reasons for your choice.

1 Applications software development and production
2 Brandy distilling
3 Department store retailing
4 Drugs development and manufacture
5 Electricity generation and distribution
6 Supermarket retailing
7 Scheduled international air transport

The seven companies come from seven different countries. They do not all use the same accounting methods. Profitability ratios may be affected. However, industry differences in cost structure, activity ratios and financing should still be evident in the seven companies' accounts.

P19.7 Profitability: competitor analysis

The personal computer (PC) industry has experienced spectacular growth in the last 20 years. It started in the late 1970s when Apple, Atari and Commodore introduced the first personal computers. It took off in 1981 when IBM launched its first PC using an Intel microprocessor and operating software

Exhibit 19.18 Summary common-sized financial statements: average of 1999–2001 figures

	Company						
	(A)	(B)	(C)	(D)	(E)	(F)	(G)
Income statement							
Sales, net	100.0	100.0	100.0	100.0	100.0	100.0	100.0
Operating expenses							
(excluding D&A and R&D)	90.6	55.5	66.9	95.0	77.4	66.1	84.5
Depreciation and amortisation	8.0	5.0	3.6	2.9	2.9	18.8	3.6
Research and development	–	16.6	14.0	–	–	1.1	–
Interest expense (income), net	3.4	(0.8)	(0.7)	1.6	6.2	7.2	2.3
Income taxes	0.2	8.6	6.6	1.0	4.6	1.9	3.7
Other (income) expense, net	(1.9)	0.4	(0.1)	(1.9)	(0.6)	0.4	–
Total expenses	100.3	85.3	90.3	98.6	90.5	95.5	94.1
Group net profit (loss)	(0.3)	14.7	9.7	1.4	9.5	4.5	5.9
Balance sheet, end-year							
Tangible fixed assets:							
Cost (or value)	167.4	85.8	23.4	30.8	33.3	526.4	58.7
– Accumulated depreciation	–49.0	–28.9	–9.2	–10.8	–15.9	–297.3	–23.6
Net book value	118.4	56.9	14.2	20.0	17.4	229.1	35.1
Financial fixed assets	5.6	4.6	10.4	0.1	13.0	11.5	–
Other long-term assets*	0.9	0.2	3.9	16.8	89.5	14.1	9.8
Inventories	1.3	20.2	0.1	10.0	86.9	13.9	20.3
Trade receivables	9.5	16.7	33.4	2.4	21.5	6.6	14.6
Cash and securities	12.4	17.0	15.8	1.9	2.2	1.7	0.6
Other current assets	5.8	10.4	11.0	1.1	23.4	3.7	0.5
Total assets	153.9	126.0	88.8	52.3	253.9	280.6	80.9
Group equity	25.7	86.9	46.6	16.0	110.3	39.1	28.0
Debt (long-term and current)	81.8	8.9	3.6	21.9	87.2	183.9	31.0
Provisions and other long-							
term liabilities	15.7	7.6	4.3	3.3	11.3	34.4	6.7
Current liabilities	30.7	22.6	34.3	11.1	45.1	23.2	15.2
Total equities	153.9	126.0	88.8	52.3	253.9	280.6	80.9

* Including purchased goodwill and other intangibles.

Note: All income statement and balance sheet items are expressed as a percentage of net sales.

provided by Microsoft. Worldwide sales grew by over 15% a year throughout the 1990s. By 2000 annual PC sales had reached 130 million units and revenues exceeded US$150 billion that year. The main reasons for the growth in sales were: the accelerating power of PCs; falling unit prices, helped by falling prices for components (which represent 80–85% of a PC's cost); open standards based on Intel's microprocessor designs and Microsoft's operating software; and the impact of the Internet.

Rapid growth in sales has not translated into high profits for PC producers, however. Low barriers to entry have resulted in a fragmented industry – the largest firm holds no more than 15% of the worldwide market. Given the dominance of 'Wintel' technology, there's limited opportunity for product differentiation. Finally, PC producers are in a weak bargaining position relative to their customers (switching costs are low) and component suppliers.

Exhibit 19.19 Three PC producers: common-sized financial statements from 1999/2000

| | Company | | |
	A	B	C
Income statement			
Net sales	100	100	100
Cost of sales	−87.6	−79.6	−77.1
Gross profit	12.4	20.4	22.9
Selling, general and administrative expenses	−8.9	−10.3	−15.4
Research and development costs	−0.5	−1.5	−3.9
Operating income*	3.0	8.6	3.6
Financial income/(expense), net	+0.1	−	+0.3
Investment income/(loss)	−	+1.3	−1.9
Other non-operating income/(expense)	−	−	+0.2
Income before tax	3.1	9.9	2.2
Income tax expense	<0.1	−3.1	−0.8
Net income, group	3.1	6.8	1.4
Balance sheet			
Assets			
Cash and securities	10.8	16.7	7.3
Accounts receivable	6.6	9.6	18.7
Inventories**	8.7	1.4	5.1
Other current assets	1.7	2.3	4.8
Total current assets	27.8	30.0	35.9
Property and equipment, at cost	4.5	4.7	16.2
Less: Accumulated depreciation	−1.2	−1.6	−7.9
P&E, net	3.3	3.1	8.3
Long-term financial investments	0.8	9.0	9.3
Intangibles and other long-term assets	8.5	1.5	11.1
Total assets	40.4	43.6	64.6
Equities			
Accounts payable	9.4	13.7	10.7
Short-term debt	2.3	−	1.4
Other current liabilities	6.1	6.8	16.9
Total current liabilities	17.8	20.5	29.0
Long-term debt	0.3	1.8	0.7
Other long-term liabilities	−	2.2	1.6
Total liabilities	18.1	24.5	31.3
Minority interests	0.2	−	−
Shareholders' equity	22.1	19.1	33.3
Total equities	40.4	43.6	64.6
* After depreciation of	0.5	0.7	2.4
** Of which: Finished goods	5.9	1.0	3.1
Raw materials and work-in-progress	2.8	0.4	2.0

Note: All income statement and balance sheet amounts are expressed as a percentage of net sales.

Future prospects look bleak. The bursting of the dotcom bubble and the contraction of business investment in the EU, Japan and the USA saw a fall in unit sales and revenues in 2001 and 2002. Growth is not expected to resume until 2004. New competitors have established themselves in those markets that are still growing (e.g. China) and plan to invade the more mature western markets.

Three of the largest firms in the industry are Compaq (since 2002, part of the Hewlett Packard group), Dell and Legend. All three pursue a 'cost leadership' strategy – aiming to produce a similar product to their rivals but at lower cost – but each operationalises it in a different way. Some important characteristics of the three firms are summarised below:

1   *Compaq.* US company. World's largest PC producer, with total sales of US$42 billion in 2000. Founded in early 1980s. Focus on lowering production costs through just-in-time delivery of components and automated assembly lines with low labour content. Has diversified in recent years: half of 2000 sales consisted of servers and storage products and computer-related services, mainly to businesses.

2   *Dell.* US company. Founded in early 1980s. Total sales of US$32 billion in 2000. Pioneered direct sales of PCs to final customers. Assembly of PC is begun when customer places order (by phone or Internet).

3   *Legend.* Chinese company. Sales of US$3.5 billion in 2000. Founded in 1984 as distributor of foreign-made computer products. Began making own line of PCs in 1990. By 1997, largest producer in China. Pursues low price strategy – PC prices are 25% below those of equivalent foreign brands – made possible by reliance on China-sourced materials and components.

Exhibit 19.19 contains three common-sized balance sheets and income statements taken from recent accounts of the three companies.

Required

Given the brief information above about the operations and business strategies of Compaq, Dell and Legend, decide which set of accounts belongs to which company. What evidence from the exhibit did you use in making your decision?

P19.8 Residual income and measuring value creation

Michelin, the French tyre manufacturer, provides in its annual report to shareholders an assessment of its economic performance in the year. Management compare the group's actual return on capital employed with the target return to determine whether it has created or destroyed value in the period. The target return on capital is similar in concept to the weighted average cost of capital: Michelin's was estimated by management to be 10.7% in 2001.

Exhibit 19.20 contains summary income statement and balance sheet information for 2001 for the Michelin Group.

Required

(a) Calculate Michelin's residual income for 2001. According to your figures, did the group create or destroy value that year? Assume Michelin's marginal tax rate is 40% in 2001.

(b) In calculating actual and target returns on capital, Michelin include 'commitments under non-cancellable operating leases' as part of capital employed. Average operating lease commitments in present value terms were €602 million in 2001. Michelin also adjust the profit figure but do not disclose precisely how they do it. Indicate, in general terms, how Michelin's NOPAT (net operating profit after tax) should be adjusted for the effect of capitalising non-cancellable operating leases when calculating residual income. (There is insufficient information in the exhibit to compute the adjustment.)

Exhibit 19.20 Michelin Group: summary financial statements, 2001

Condensed income statement for 2001

	in € mn
Net sales	15,775
Operating income	1,011
Net interest expense	−321
Income tax expense	−329
Net income of fully consolidated companies	361
Share of losses of equity-method investments	−13
Amortisation of goodwill	−34
Net income before minority interests	314
Minority interests	−18
Net income	296

Condensed balance sheets at 31 December

in € bn	2001	2000		2001	2000
Fixed assets			*Shareholders' equity*		
Goodwill	319	283	Share capital and premium	1,879	1,879
Intangible assets	115	122	Retained earnings	2,117	1,964
Property, plant and equipment	6,410	5,943		3,996	3,843
Investments	493	532	Minority interests	330	311
	7,337	6,880	Group equity	4,326	4,154
Current assets			*Liabilities*		
Inventories	3,302	3,564	Debt	5,820	5,856
Trade receivables	3,390	3,340	Provisions for risks and charges	3,959	3,711
Other receivables and prepayments	2,414	2,427	Trade payables	1,451	1,590
Cash and cash equivalents	939	931	Other payables and accrued expenses	1,826	1,831
	10,045	10,262		13,056	12,988
			Total liabilities		
Total assets	17,382	17,142	*and shareholders' equity*	17,382	17,142

(*Source*: Michelin Group, *Financial Report 2001*.)

P19.9 Analysis of leverage

Deutsche Telekom (DT) is Germany's – and Europe's – largest telecoms group. Investors were concerned about DT's finances in 2002. Fierce competition in its home market resulted in a fall in the revenues and profits of its main division, fixed-line services, in 2001. Its other divisions – Systems, Mobile, and Online – all made losses that year and, in the case of Mobile and Online, are not expected to become free-cash-flow positive until the middle of the decade. Debt levels were already high owing to the funding of third-generation mobile licences which cost DT over €15 billion in 2000. They rose further with the acquisition of US wireless operators VoiceStream and Powertel. DT made an initial investment of €5.6 billion in VoiceStream's preferred stock in September 2000 (classified as a financial asset in DT's balance sheet). In May 2001 it completed the purchase of both companies by making a further cash payment of €4.9 billion and issuing new shares with a market value of €28.7 billion. The two companies were included in DT's consolidated accounts in 2001. They carried around €9.5 billion of debt on their books at the time of consolidation and were responsible for most of the increase in DT's intangibles (largely, mobile phone licences and goodwill) that year. Together they made a net loss of €3.1 billion in 2001.

Summary financial statements, taken from DT's 2001 consolidated accounts, are set out in Exhibit 19.21.

Exhibit 19.21 **Deutsche Telekom: extracts from 2001 consolidated accounts** (amounts in € billion)

	2001	2000
Consolidated income statement		
Net revenues	48.3	40.9
Results from ordinary business activities (before tax)*	(2.5)	6.5
Net income/(loss)	(3.5)	5.9
* After deducting: Depreciation and amortisation	15.2	13.0
Interest expense, net	4.1	3.1
Consolidated balance sheet (end-year)		
Intangible assets	80.0	35.8
Property, plant and equipment	58.7	54.1
Financial assets	8.0	16.7
Fixed assets	146.7	106.6
Inventories, receivables and other	14.3	13.3
Cash and short-term investments	3.6	4.3
Total assets	164.6	124.2
Group equity (including minority interests)	66.3	42.7
Provisions	18.5	11.4
Debt: Long-term	53.7	45.1
Current	13.3	15.2
Other liabilities	12.8	9.8
Total equities	164.6	124.2
Consolidated cash flow statement		
Net cash from operating activities**	11.9	10.0
Capital expenditures, net	−8.7	−6.9
Purchase of intangibles, net	−0.8	−16.0
Net purchase/disposal of financial assets and short-term investments	+8.8	−3.6
Acquisitions (less disposals) of companies	−4.7	−1.2
Net cash used for investing activities	−5.4	−27.7
Issuance/repayment (−) of debt	−2.9	16.5
Dividends	−1.9	−1.9
Proceeds from share offering	−	3.2
Net cash provided by/used for (−) financing activities	−4.8	17.8
Net increase in cash and cash equivalents	1.7	0.1
** After deducting interest paid (less interest received)	4.3	2.9

Segmental results for 2001

	Total revenues	Pre-tax results	Ebitda
T-Com (fixed-line services)	26.1	3.2	8.0
T-Systems	13.8	(0.3)	1.0
T-Mobile	14.6	(6.4)	3.1
T-Online	1.4	(0.2)	(0.1)

(*Source*: Deutsche Telekom, *Annual Report and Accounts 2001.* Reproduced by permission of Deutsche Telekom AG.)

Required

(a) Calculate the following ratios for 2000 and 2001:
  (i) end-year net debt–equity ratio;
  (ii) times interest earned ratio;
  (iii) end-year net debt-to-Ebitda ratio.

Based on your calculations of these ratios, was DT less or more able to service its debts in 2001 than in 2000? What other aspects of the group's operations or capital structure might give investors cause for concern about its financial health?

(b) An investor has doubts about the reliability of DT's published 2001 figures. He queries the group's reported debt and shareholders' equity numbers.
  (i) 'How can the group record a net repayment of debt on the cash flow statement when its balance sheet debt *increases* between the start and end of the year?'
  (ii) 'How can the group record an increase in group equity when it reports a loss in the year – and there's no evidence in the cash flow statement of a share issue in 2001?'

Answer the investor's questions. Explain why the group's debt and shareholders' equity increase in 2001 despite debt repayments and losses in the year.

Notes to Chapter 19

1 Porter, M.E. (1980), *Competitive Strategy*, New York: Free Press. Porter's model is discussed and illustrated in Grant, R.M. (2002), *Contemporary Strategy Analysis: Concepts, Techniques, Applications*, 4th edition, Oxford: Blackwell.

2 For a fuller discussion of the economic role of advertising and branding, *see* Kay, J. (1995), *Foundations of Corporate Success*, Oxford: Oxford University Press, chapter 16.

3 Euromonitor (2000), *World Drinks Marketing Directory 2000/01*, 2nd edition, Vol. 1, London: Euromonitor, chapter 1.

4 Research into brand awareness was carried out by Nielsen Research and is cited in Carlsberg's 2001 annual report.

5 A further distinctive feature – up to 2002 – was the protection Carlsberg enjoyed in its home market as a result of Danish bottling laws. Beverage containers had to be refillable. This raised importers' costs (since they couldn't distribute beer or soft drinks in cans) and represented a barrier to entry into the Danish market. The bottling laws, introduced in 1982 with the aim of encouraging recycling, were repealed in 2002, in response to legal action by the European Commission. The Commission claimed that the laws breached the EU's packaging directive and were a barrier to trade.

6 The analysis in this and subsequent sections is based on the original consolidated accounts for 2001 and earlier years. Following the new Danish Financial Statements Act of June 2001, Carlsberg adopted new accounting policies with respect to, among others, goodwill, restructuring charges, and the valuation of inventories and financial investments as from the first quarter of 2002. At the same time, it showed in summary form the effect of the new policies on the annual accounts of the previous four years.

7 To secure the agreement of Scandinavian competition authorities to the Orkla deal, Carlsberg was required to sell the Swedish and Norwegian operations of Coca-Cola Nordic Beverages, its joint venture with Coca-Cola.

8 We cannot compute the operating profit per litre – by type of beverage or even in total – since Carlsberg does not disclose the operating profits of its non-beverage activities.

9 This makes the difference in reported 'Provisions and other long-term liabilities' even bigger. Heineken carries larger provisions for pensions (and other staff costs) and deferred taxes.

10 For a fuller discussion of these points – and their implications for business strategy, *see* Selling, T. and Stickney, C. (1989), The effects of business environment and strategy on a firm's rate of return on assets, *Financial Analysts' Journal*, Jan/Feb: 43–52. Selling and Stickney define 'assets' as total assets when estimating ROA across industries.

11 A full exposition of this approach can be found in Nissim, D. and Penman, S. (2001), Ratio analysis and equity valuation: from research to practice, *Review of Accounting Studies*, 6: 109–154. Note that Nissim and Penman calculate ROE (RONOA) using start-of-year equity (net operating assets) instead of the average-for-the-year figure.

12 A company may report a loss from financial leverage if it carries net cash rather than net debt. In this case, netflev is negative.

13 For NYSE and AMEX-listed firms over the 1963–99 period, the Spearman correlation coefficient is 0.89: *see* Nissim and Penman, op. cit., table 2. US firms' median ROE was consistently greater than their median RONOA over the whole of this period, indicating a positive financial leverage effect.

14 Altman, E. (1993), *Corporate Financial Distress and Bankruptcy*, 2nd edition, New York: John Wiley. For a discussion of the problems associated with bankruptcy prediction models, *see* Foster, G. (1986), *Financial Statement Analysis*, 2nd edition, Englewood Cliffs, NJ: Prentice Hall, Chapter 15.

15 The ROE of the parent company's shareholders can also be derived by applying the following multiple to group ROE:

$$\text{ROE (parent company)} = \text{ROE (group)} \times \frac{\text{NI.PC/Group net income}}{\text{Av. SE.PC/Av. group equity}}$$

NI.PC is the net income attributable to the parent company's shareholders and SE.PC is the equity of the parent company's shareholders.

16 Carlsberg's 2001 financial statements in general – and its cash flow statement in particular – lack transparency. It is not possible to reconcile the cash flow statement data to the change in balance sheet numbers between end-2000 and end-2001. For example, there is no explanation in the accounts of the change in debt between the start and end of 2001. In addition, some entries in the cash flow statement are either puzzling or obscure. What is the source of the large dividend received from associated companies in 2001? What is included within 'Financial income and expenditure' under financing flows? Lack of transparency can be costly to a firm. Investors become suspicious and demand a higher return to compensate them for the additional perceived risk, thereby driving up the firm's cost of capital.

17 The following is a simplified description of an asset pricing model known as CAPM (capital asset pricing model). For a fuller discussion of the model and some of the problems associated with it, consult a finance textbook (e.g. Brealey, R. and Myers, S. (2001), *Principles of Corporate Finance*, 7th edition, New York: McGraw-Hill, Chapter 8).

18 Debt's 30% weighting is based on the following end-2001 figures: net debt of DKr 11 billion, minority interests of DKr 4.5 billion and equity of parent company shareholders of DKr 20.9 billion. Minority interests are assumed to be part of the equity weight for the purposes of the WACC calculation.

19 As a result of changes to its accounting policies implemented in 2002, Carlsberg now capitalises and amortises goodwill arising on acquisitions.

20 A US consulting firm, Stern Stewart, promotes just such a version of residual income. 'Economic value added' – or EVA as it's commonly known – includes a number of adjustments to both operating profit and invested capital that are designed to bring accounting numbers closer to a cash basis and, at the same time, undo the effects of conservatism in determining income. Stern Stewart claim EVA is superior to traditional profitability ratios as a measure of divisional and company-wide performance. For an independent appraisal of EVA, *see* O'Hanlon, J. and Peasnell, K. (1998), 'Wall Street's contribution to management accounting: the Stern Stewart EVA financial management system', *Management Accounting Research*, 9: 421–444.

21 *See*, for example, Brealey, R. and Myers, S. op. cit., chapter 13. For a critique of the efficient market hypothesis, *see* Shleifer, A. (2000), *Inefficient Markets*, Oxford: Oxford University Press.

20 Financial statement analysis: extensions

INTRODUCTION

Carlsberg's 2001 financial statements which we analysed in Chapter 19 present few problems for the investor. Carlsberg draws most of its revenues and profits from one activity, the production and distribution of beer and soft drinks. The company made no major changes to its operations or accounting policies in the year. Moreover, we restricted our analysis to Carlsberg's accounts so avoiding the problems that can arise when making intercompany comparisons.

This chapter has two goals. The aim in the first part is to look at some of the practical problems investors face when analysing more complicated financial statements. These practical problems arise because of:

- *Non-comparability of financial statements.* A firm's financial statements may not be comparable over time because it changes its operations or its accounting policies. In addition, an investor may have difficulty making cross-border comparisons because firms follow different accounting policies.
- *Overaggregation.* Consolidated financial statements may conceal important financial information about a diversified firm's business activities.
- *Lack of timeliness.* Investors want more timely information on the progress of the firm than is provided by annual accounts.

We examine each of these problem areas and show how, with the help of additional information which firms following international standards must now provide, investors can overcome them.

In section 2 of the chapter we confront a problem which occurs in even the toughest of regulatory environments: management may manipulate the numbers in their firm's financial statements. We discuss the reasons for and methods of 'creative accounting' and explain the steps investors take to unmask it.

Earnings per share is an important statistic used by investors when analysing financial statements. Certain firms are required to report it in their annual accounts. We show in the appendix how it's calculated.

Problem areas in financial statement analysis

Major changes in operating activities

The first problem area concerns the accounting effects of **major changes in a company's operations**. As we saw in Chapter 19, investors compare financial numbers and ratios of the current period with those of previous periods when analysing a company's financial statements. They use previous periods' numbers as a benchmark when evaluating the company's current financial performance and condition. Major changes to the company's operations – such as a large acquisition or the disposal of a segment of the business – make such comparisons difficult.

In addition, estimating a company's future earnings becomes harder. In making earnings forecasts, investors often take as a starting point the company's current recurring earnings. *Recurring earnings consist largely of the income from its continuing operations.* When a company sells or spins off a business segment, the operating results of these activities are no longer part of its income from continuing operations. They – and any gains or losses arising on the disposal itself – represent transitory profits (or losses). If they are not reported as such in the financial statements, investors will miscalculate the company's recurring earnings that period.

Illustration

Hero's 2002 results provide a good illustration of the problems that major business changes can cause. Hero is a Swiss consumer foods and baking aids group and the leading jam producer in Europe. In 2002 it acquired several businesses, including Schwartauer Werke, the German consumer foods group.

Hero's 2002 income statement shows the following sales and operating profit figures (amounts in SFr million):

	2002	*2001*	*% increase*
Net sales	1,386	1,179	17.5
Operating profit	144.9	89.6	61.7

Note the large increase in Hero's sales and profits in 2002. How much of the increase is attributable to the acquisitions that year? Hero discloses that sales from existing businesses (i.e. organic sales) rose only 2.7% in 2002 and acquisitions were responsible for the bulk of the sales growth that year. However, it doesn't provide similar figures for operating profits. As a result, it's more difficult for investors to construct a group profit forecast for 2003 and later years.[1]

● Disclosure requirements under IAS

Hero's limited disclosures are not atypical. The EU's 7th Directive states that where there has been a major change in the composition of a group, the consolidated accounts should provide information which makes the comparison of accounts over time 'meaningful' (Art. 28). Yet few EU companies show in detail the effect on sales and profits of significant acquisitions and disposals unless, as in Ireland and the UK, national accounting rules require it. One reason may be that the directive does not spell out precisely what information companies should disclose in these circumstances.

The IASB issued an accounting standard in 1998 that sets out disclosure requirements for firms *discontinuing* part of their operations. Where a firm sells or closes down a major component of its business, it should describe the activities to be discontinued and which lines of business they're in. In addition, it should show separately – on the face of the financial statements or in the notes – the following items which are attributable to the operations it's discontinuing:

- assets and liabilities in the current and previous year's balance sheets;
- revenues, expenses (including tax), profit and cash flows up to the date of disposal – and comparative figures for the previous year; and
- gain or loss on the disposal itself, showing the tax effect separately.[2]

The segregation of assets, liabilities, revenues and expenses occurs from the date the company is 'demonstrably committed' to the disposal. Evidence of this is either a binding sale agreement or a detailed formal plan of discontinuance from which the company cannot realistically withdraw. The standard lays down less stringent disclosure requirements for the period between the announcement of and firm commitment to discontinuance. The reason for the tightly drafted rules is to bring within the disclosure net firms that discontinue a line of business but sell its assets piecemeal. In addition, accounting regulators want investors to be aware of the impact of an impending disposal as early as possible.

Companies differ in how they present information about discontinued operations in their accounts. Some follow US/UK practice and highlight the revenues and trading results of such operations on the face of the income statement; other disclose the information in the notes. Exhibit 20.1 contains an illustration of the latter approach.

Xstrata is a Swiss-based natural resource group. Management carried out a major restructuring of the group in 2000 and 2001. They sold its Australian coal mining interests and aluminium reduction facility, its Argentinian oil and gas fields and a Chilean forestry trading company. They purchased a zinc mining, smelting and refining operation in Spain, acquired a magnesium scrap refining facility in the USA and increased the group's stake in an Australian vanadium project. The group discloses the gain or loss on disposal of operations on the face of the income statement (Exhibit 20.1, panel A) but shows the trading results of the discontinued operations in the notes to the accounts (panel B). It's evident from panel B that the discontinued operations contributed little to operating results in 2000 or 2001 (though the group made a large gain from disposal of its Argentinian oil and gas fields in 2000.) The group does not disclose separately the results of acquired businesses, but this information can be extracted from the note on segmental data, part of which is given in panel C. For example, the new zinc operation generated the same amount of revenues in 2001 as the long-established ferrochrome division but was less profitable (9% return on capital employed against ferrochrome's 26%).[3]

With the information on the group's discontinued operations and its segmental results, investors are better able to assess Xstrata's performance in 2001. And they have two years' comparable data about the group's continuing businesses to help them forecast its earnings for 2002 and later years.

Accounting changes

The second problem area we look at concerns **accounting changes**. You'll recall that one of the fundamental concepts in accounting is consistency. A company is supposed to apply the same accounting policies from one period to the next. This allows investors to compare its financial numbers over time. They have difficulty observing trends in, for example, cost ratios if a firm changes its accounting policies and does not restate prior years' accounts at the same time. Moreover, once a firm has closed its accounts for a period, it is not supposed to reopen them and alter the numbers.

Exhibit 20.1 Xstrata Group: income statement effects of 2000 and 2001 disposals

Panel A *Consolidated 2001 income statement (part)*

In US$ mn	2001	2000
Revenue	**613.6**	597.9
Cost of goods sold	**(474.5)**	(449.7)
Depreciation and amortisation	**(36.0)**	(21.7)
Operating earnings before effects of disposals and impairment	**103.1**	126.5
Gain/(loss) on disposal of operations	**(2.0)**	68.9
Loss from impairment of assets	**(45.5)**	–
Operating earnings	**55.6**	195.4

⋮

Panel B *Results of discontinued operations in 2000 and 2001*

	Forestry trading		Coal		Aluminium		Oil and gas	
In US$ mn	2001	2000	2001	2000	2001	2000	2001	2000
Revenue	**23.8**	54.8	–	35.4	–	18.1	–	–
Expenses	**(21.6)**	(52.7)	–	(39.0)	–	(17.0)	–	–
Operating earnings before effect of disposal	**2.2**	2.1	–	(3.6)	–	1.1	–	–
Gain/(loss) on disposal	**(1.8)**	–	**(0.2)**	–	–	0.1	–	68.8
Operating earnings/(loss)	**0.4**	2.1	**(0.2)**	(3.6)	–	1.2	–	68.8
Other	**(0.5)**	(0.4)	–	0.1	–	(0.2)	–	–
Income tax (charge)/credit	**(0.1)**	(0.2)	–	0.3	–	n.s.	–	–
Net earnings/(loss)	**(0.2)**	1.5	**(0.2)**	(3.2)	–	1.0	–	68.8

Panel C *Segmental information (part)*

2001 (US$ mn)	Metals and minerals				Energy		Forestry		
	Ferro-chrome	Vanadium	Zinc	Magnesium	Oil and gas	Coal	Plantation and trading	Other	Total
Revenue	257.7	63.5	266.6	n.s.	–	–	25.8	–	**613.6**
Op. earnings	66.2	(41.6)	47.5	(5.0)	–	–	(0.9)	(10.6)	**55.6**
Cap. employed	252.2	106.9	548.1	25.3	–	–	33.8	32.6	**998.8**

2000 (US$ mn)	Metals and minerals				Energy		Forestry		
	Ferro-chrome	Vanadium	Aluminium	Magnesium	Oil and gas	Coal	Plantation and trading	Other	Total
Revenue	419.3	68.5	18.1	–	–	35.4	56.6	–	597.9
Op. earnings	114.9	20.6	1.2	–	68.8	(3.6)	2.3	(8.8)	195.4
Cap. employed	363.5	206.2	–	3.7	–	39.9	50.5	20.4	684.2

(*Source*: Xstrata Group, *Annual Report 2001*. Reproduced by permission of Xstrata plc.)

However, in practice, firms do change their accounting policies. In addition, they sometimes restate the numbers in past years' accounts without changing their policies. In this section, we ask:

- Why do firms make accounting changes?
- How do they account for such changes?
- What is the impact of accounting practice in this area on financial statement analysis?

Reasons for accounting changes

A company may change the numbers in its past or current accounts for one of the following reasons:

- *Error.* It discovers a material error which requires it to adjust current and prior years' accounts.
- *New accounting rule.* It is forced to change accounting methods as a result of legislation or the introduction of a new accounting standard.
- *Management decision.* It changes its accounting policies voluntarily. Accounting policies embrace both accounting methods (for example, the straight-line or accelerated method of depreciation) and accounting estimates (the expected economic lives of various types of equipment, the proportion of receivables likely to prove uncollectible).

One reason for changing an accounting policy is that economic conditions have changed – for example, the rate of technological change has increased, shortening the economic lives of certain fixed assets – and management adjust accounting estimates or methods (or both) in response. Other reasons that management give are:

- to provide better matching of revenues and expenses;
- to bring the firm's accounting policies into line with those of other firms in the industry.

Presentation of accounting changes: three approaches

How might a firm report an accounting change? We focus on changes in accounting policy. Here are the three principal ways (others are variants of these):

1 **Restatement.** *The firm restates previous years' accounts. In the case of a new accounting policy, it applies the policy retroactively.* This ensures that current and prior years' accounts are prepared on a consistent basis, making it easier for an investor to analyse trends. However, it can be a costly exercise and, if done frequently, can undermine investor confidence in a company's published accounts.
2 **Cumulative catch-up.** *The firm adjusts the current year's accounts only. It shows the cumulative impact of the accounting change in one entry.* Current and prior years' accounts are no longer stated on a consistent basis – interperiod comparisons are undermined – but, in contrast to restatement, the effect of the accounting change is highlighted.
3 **Prospective adjustment.** *The firm adjusts the accounts of the current and future periods only. It makes no adjustment with respect to past periods.* Comparability of past and future accounts will suffer and the change is not highlighted. However, this may be the most appropriate approach where the reason for the change is the arrival of new information (i.e. information which could not have been known in the past).

Illustration

Assume Drosselmeyer Company, a toy-maker, starts business in year 1. From the outset, it spends 10 each year on developing new products (all amounts are in millions). Initially, it capitalises the costs of developing new toys and amortises them over five years. However, other firms in the industry expense development costs as they're incurred. Drosselmeyer decides to align its accounting policy with that of its rivals and, at the start of year 5, changes its method of accounting for development costs from capitalisation to immediate expensing.

Exhibit 20.2 shows the effect on Drosselmeyer's year 5 accounts of two of the three approaches: (a) cumulative catch-up and (b) restatement. (Prospective adjustment is reviewed later.) Comparative figures for year 4 are also given, since these would be shown in the year 5 financial statements. Under (a), they are unchanged from those shown in the year 4 financial statements. Under (b), they are restated.

Exhibit 20.2 Accounting change: cumulative catch-up and restatement approaches illustrated

Facts

Toymaker Drosselmeyer starts business in year 1. Up to start-year 5, it capitalises and amortises product development costs on a straight-line basis over five years. From year 5, it expenses them as they're incurred. Operating profit (before development costs) is 15, development costs 10 and dividends 5 each year. Start-year 1 net assets are 25. Taxes are ignored. Amounts are in millions.

Effect on year 5 accounts if change is accounted for by:

	(a) Cumulative catch-up		(b) Restatement	
	Year 4	Year 5	Year 4	Year 5
Income statement				
Operating profit	15	15	15	15
Development costs amortised	–8*	–	–	–
Development costs expensed	–	–10	–10	–10
Cumulative effect of change				
in accounting policy	–	–20**	–	–
Profit/Loss (–)	7	–15	5	5
Dividend	–5	–5	–5	–5
Retained profit/loss (–)	2	–20	0	0
Balance sheet				
Development costs, gross	40	–	–	–
– Accumulated amortisation	–20	–	–	–
Development costs, net	20	–	–	–
Other net assets	25	25	25	25
Total net assets	45	25	25	25
Share capital	25	25	25	25
Retained profit, 1/1	18	20	18	0
Prior period adjustment	–	–	–18***	–
Retained profit or loss (–) for year	2	–20	0	0
Retained profit, 31/12	20	0	0	0
Total shareholders' equity	45	25	25	25

Notes: Key numbers from years 1–4 accounts

	Year 1	Year 2	Year 3	Year 4
Development costs, gross	10	20	30	40
– Accumulated amortisation	–2	–6	–12	–20
Development costs, net	8	14	18	20**
Annual amortisation	2	4	6	8*
Profit for year	13	11	9	7
Retained profit (cumulative)	8	14	18***	20

Under the cumulative catch-up approach, a one-time adjustment is made to the accounts. If Drosselmeyer changes its accounting method at the start of year 5, it will make the following entries with respect to development costs that year:

Start-year 5
Dr. Cumulative effect of change in accounting policy (OE–)   20
Dr. Accumulated amortisation, development costs (CA–)   20
    Cr. Development costs (A–)   40
To record the cumulative effect of the change in accounting for development costs.

During year 5
Dr. Development expense (OE–)   10
    Cr. Cash (A–)   10
To record the immediate expensing of year 5 development costs.

Drosselmeyer's 'Development costs' asset has a gross cost of 40 at the start of year 5. This is the result of capitalising four years' expenditures at the rate of 10/year. The carrying amount of the asset is 20 then (*see* Exhibit 20.2 – under 'Notes' – for the calculation of this figure). As a result of the change in policy, the asset is written down to zero. Drosselmeyer shows the 'Cumulative effect . . .' as a separate item on its year 5 income statement, thereby highlighting the effect of the change. The year 5 income statement also bears the burden of a full year's charge for year 5 development costs. The company's cash flow is unaffected, however (assuming the change in policy has no tax impact).

Restatement affects not only the accounts in the year of change but also comparative figures given in that year's accounts. Thus in its year 5 financial statements, Drosselmeyer accounts for product development costs as if it had adopted the policy of immediate expensing *ab initio*. At the same time, it restates comparative year 4 figures and adjusts the start-year 4 balance in retained earnings. In this case, the **prior period adjustment** of 18 is the amount by which retained earnings would have been *lower* if Drosselmeyer had expensed development costs as they were incurred, starting in year 1.

If Drosselmeyer accounts for the change in accounting for development costs prospectively (not illustrated in Exhibit 20.2), it would record a prior period adjustment (of –20) to start-year 5 retained earnings and recognise development expense of 10 in its year 5 income statement. In contrast to the restatement method, it would not restate year 4's accounts. The result is that the figures for years 4 and 5 presented in year 5's accounts are not comparable. The year 4 figures assume development costs are capitalised and amortised while those for year 5 assume they're expensed immediately.

IAS requirements

Drosselmeyer is not free to choose the way it presents the change in accounting for product development costs. Firms that follow IAS must now account for changes in methods and estimates and for fundamental errors in the following way.[4]

Changes in estimates (e.g. asset lives, collectibility of debts, inventory obsolescence) *should be accounted for prospectively*. The change will affect the way a firm determines its current and future profits only. The firm does not alter its past financial statements.

Under international rules, there are two possible ways a firm can account for a *change in accounting method. One way is to apply the new method retrospectively and restate prior years' accounts.* This is the benchmark treatment. *The other – acceptable but not preferred – is the cumulative catch-up approach.* The 'Cumulative effect . . .' should be shown as an exceptional item (before pre-tax income) on the income statement. A firm may be forced to use this approach if it's not allowed, under national law, to restate prior years' numbers. Note that even in this case, it is encouraged to provide, on a pro forma basis, comparative information for prior years under the new method.[5]

What happens if the effect of the change on prior periods' accounts is not determinable? Suppose, for example, a firm is considering changing the method of valuing its inventory from FIFO to LIFO. For LIFO purposes, inventory consists of 'layers' of cost. The firm must determine when each layer arose and what was its cost. This could involve reconstructing inventory movements since the date the firm was founded, a costly if not impossible exercise. In this and similar cases, the IASC allows firms to apply the new method from the start of the year of change without retrospective adjustment.

Where a change in accounting method is voluntary, the firm must justify the change in its accounts. It must show that the new method 'will result in a more appropriate presentation of events or transactions' in its financial statements. If a company is forced to change its accounting policy as a result of a new international accounting standard, the standard itself will state how the change is to be handled.[6] Fundamental errors, when discovered, are accounted for in the same way as changes in accounting method – preferably by restatement but with cumulative catch-up as an allowed alternative.

Impact on financial statement analysis

Firms do not often change their accounting methods voluntarily. The law – or the accounting requirement that the new method must be preferable to the old – constrains them. Changing past accounting numbers because of fundamental error is also rare. However, with the introduction of new accounting rules – at national and international levels – *mandatory* changes in accounting method have become more common. The cumulative catch-up approach is widely favoured in these cases, on legal and cost grounds. However, unless the company discloses pro forma data showing past years' financials prepared according to the new method, investors will find it difficult to make interperiod comparisons or analyse trends.

Accounting for a change in *method* has one major benefit for investors. The change is highlighted in the firm's accounts. In contrast, investors may be unaware a firm has changed an accounting *estimate*. True, companies following international standards are required to show the effect on the accounts, if material, of *any* change in accounting policy – and that includes changes in estimates. But national rules are not always so strict. How can a reader of accounts discover if a company is changing accounting estimates surreptitiously – perhaps to boost profits or to smooth them? One way is to examine closely accounting items where such changes are likely. Examples are depreciable fixed assets, inventory and accounts receivable. Ratios in these areas – such as depreciation expense to gross fixed assets or bad debt expense to accounts receivable – should be monitored for unusual movements.

Intercompany differences in accounting policies

Accounting changes can undermine the trend in a firm's reported profits; **intercompany differences in accounting policies** can undermine cross-firm comparisons. We've already seen that, when given comparative figures restated or adjusted on a pro forma basis, an investor can overcome the first problem. What can he or she do about the second?

There are several possible remedies. One is to adjust accounts on a piecemeal basis in order to make them comparable. We call this **partial adjustment** since investors can rarely estimate the effects of all accounting differences between companies. Another – the **full adjustment** route – is to make use of supplementary, 'alternative GAAP' information a company may provide.

For example, many large international firms disclose in the notes to the accounts key financial numbers prepared according to alternative accounting rules (e.g. US GAAP). A third is to add **cash-based measures of performance and risk** to the armoury of accrual-based ones we discussed in Chapter 19. By definition, cash-based ratios are free of the accounting methods and estimates that underlie – and compromise – accrual-based ratios.

This problem is not trivial. Differences in accounting policy can affect virtually all items on corporate financial statements – revenues and expenses, liabilities as well as assets. They can have a major impact on firms' reported profitability – and on their risk ratios too. Accounting diversity is evident within countries but it's often most marked *between* countries.

Partial adjustment

Investors themselves can often adjust specific numbers in the financial statements from one accounting basis to another. There may be sufficient detail in the notes to the accounts to allow them to do this. For example, suppose Drosselmeyer, the toy-maker we met in the previous section, does not change its accounting policy but continues to capitalise and amortise product development costs. An investor can convert the company's accounts to the method used by its rivals – immediate expensing of development costs – by making the following adjustments:

1 Reduce Drosselmeyer's fixed assets and shareholders' equity by the end-year carrying amount of the asset, 'Development costs'.
2 Adjust Drosselmeyer's before-tax profit for the *difference* between development costs actually amortised and development costs incurred that year. (Under immediate expensing, development expense is equal to development costs incurred.) Profit is reduced if costs incurred exceed costs amortised.

Sometimes companies help. National law and accounting standards may require firms to provide alternative valuations of key assets and liabilities. For example, EU-based firms that value tangible fixed assets at other than historical cost must disclose either the HC of such assets or the valuation adjustment (4th Directive, Art. 33(4)). Quoted firms in the USA that value inventory on a LIFO basis must disclose its current cost at the balance sheet date (FIFO cost is considered a proxy for current cost).

By their nature, these item-specific disclosures, whether estimated by investors or provided by the company, are of limited value. They permit a partial adjustment of a firm's financial statements only. Where accounting policy differences are many, investors may be unable to fully reconstruct a firm's financials on the same basis as its competitors.

Full adjustment

The obvious solution to this problem is for firms to present financial statements on a standardised basis. Standardisation can be achieved, nominally at least, if all firms adopt a common set of accounting standards. This is the main purpose of IAS. However, international standards have not been universally adopted yet. In the meantime, many larger firms offer supplementary information on a standardised basis.

The supplementary information takes one of two forms. A firm may present an additional set of financial statements prepared according to international or US GAAP. This is the solution favoured by large Finnish and Norwegian companies.

Alternatively, it may show, in the notes to the accounts, key numbers such as net profit and shareholders' equity under international or US GAAP with a reconciliation to national GAAP. For example, non-US firms which arrange for their shares to be listed on a US stock exchange must provide certain key figures on a US GAAP basis if the primary statements filed with the SEC are prepared according to national GAAP. They must present, at a minimum, a reconciliation of (annual) net income between national and US GAAP and state what the end-year shareholders' equity would be under US GAAP.

Exhibit 20.3 illustrates this form of adjustment. It shows the reconciliation by Unilever, the Anglo-Dutch food and household products company, of its published 2001 profit and shareholders' equity figures to US GAAP. The information is taken from a note to the group's 2001 accounts.

Exhibit 20.3 Unilever Group: US GAAP disclosures in 2001 accounts (extracts)

Unilever's consolidated accounts are prepared in accordance with accounting principles which differ in some respects from those applicable in the United States. The following is a summary of the effect on the Group's net profit . . . and capital and reserves of the application of United States generally accepted accounting principles (US GAAP).

	€ million 2001
Net profit	**1,838**
US GAAP adjustments:	
Goodwill	**(124)**
Identifiable intangibles	**(118)**
Restructuring costs	**(18)**
Interest	**(55)**
Derivative financial instruments	**(119)**
Taxation effect of above adjustments	**108**
Net (decrease)	**(326)**
Net income under US GAAP before cumulative effect of change in accounting principle for derivative financial instruments	**1,512**
Cumulative effect of change in accounting principle for derivative financial instruments, net of tax benefit of €3 million	**(6)**
Net income under US GAAP	**1,506**

	€ million 2001	€ million 2000
Capital and reserves as reported in the consolidated balance sheet	**7,195**	8,169
US GAAP adjustments:		
Goodwill	**2,303**	2,926
Identifiable intangibles	**3,009**	3,067
Restructuring costs	**166**	185
Interest	**432**	487
Other comprehensive income effect of derivative financial instruments transition adjustment	**(101)**	–
Derivative financial instruments	**(128)**	–
Pensions and similar liabilities	**538**	437
Dividends	**1,059**	937
Taxation effect of above adjustments	**(920)**	(1,133)
Net increase	**6,358**	6,906
Capital and reserves under US GAAP	**13,553**	15,075

(*Source*: Unilever Group, *Annual Report and Accounts and Form 20-F 2001*.)

In a separate commentary (not given here), Unilever explains the reason for each of the itemised differences between the company's accounting principles and US GAAP. The most significant in 2001 concern goodwill and other intangible assets. Prior to 1998, Unilever wrote off against reserves goodwill and other intangibles that arose on the acquisition of stakes in subsidiaries and associated companies. Under US GAAP, goodwill and identifiable intangibles (principally trademarks) must be capitalised and amortised against profit. This is the policy that Unilever has followed since 1998.[7]

Amortisation of pre-1998 goodwill and other intangibles reduces Unilever's before-tax profit under US GAAP by €242 million. The balance sheet impact is much greater. Capitalisation of these intangibles increases end-2001 shareholders' equity by over €5,300 million. Note that this is the carrying amount (cost less accumulated amortisation) of the goodwill and other intangibles that Unilever wrote off before 1998.

The effect of all the differences between Unilever's own accounting principles and US GAAP is to reduce net profit by €326 million, an 18% reduction on the income statement figure of €1,838 million. End-year shareholders' equity, however, is much greater – and by a huge margin (€6,358 million – or 88%). As a result, profitability under US GAAP is much lower: 2001 US GAAP ROE is 10.5% against 23.9% using reported numbers. But balance sheet leverage is also reduced. The end-2001 debt–equity ratio is 163% under US GAAP against 295% under its own accounting policies. (Financial leverage is high because the group financed a major acquisition in 2000 largely with debt.)

The supplementary information provided by Unilever is helpful because it allows investors to compare a firm's profitability – and financial leverage – with that of other firms using US GAAP. Moreover, investors can use the information, in particular the type and size of income adjustments, to estimate the profitability, under US rules, of other firms that do *not* disclose such data.

The disclosures have also been used to judge the conservatism of accounting practices in various European countries relative to US GAAP. National accounting practices are considered more (less) conservative than those under US GAAP if they result in lower (higher) reported income. But characterising conservatism in this way can be misleading. National accounting rules may allow a firm to reduce its income when economic times are good, by building up provisions or writing down assets, and raise it when times are bad, by drawing down those provisions or revaluing the written-down assets. For example, by releasing provisions, Daimler Benz, the vehicle manufacturer, was able to report net profit of DM 615 million in 1993 under German rules. However, under US GAAP it reported a loss of DM 1,833 million that year. German accounting rules at that time encouraged balance sheet conservatism – understatement of assets, overstatement of liabilities – but because they permitted income smoothing, did not ensure income was stated conservatively.

A more satisfactory way of judging the (income) conservatism of a country's accounting practices is to look at the *timeliness* of earnings, in particular, how quickly bad news – such as a reduction in asset values – gets reflected in earnings. Researchers have found that there are national differences in earnings timeliness: companies in common-law countries tend to recognise bad news in earnings earlier than do those in code-law countries (*see* Box 20.1).

Cash-based accounting numbers

Investors do not always have access to standardised financial data. European firms rarely provide it unless they seek capital outside their domestic markets. What other steps can investors take to overcome intercompany differences in accounting policy?

One suggestion is to use cash flow in place of accrual-based numbers. As we showed in Chapter 18, operating cash flow – or a variant such as Ebitda – removes the effects of some or all accrual adjustments from profit. Accrual adjustments normally provide useful information

BOX
20.1

Accounting conservatism: international differences in earnings timeliness

'Anticipate losses but not gains.' This is the prudence principle we outlined in Chapter 7. It encapsulates what we mean by accounting conservatism. A company should recognise losses as soon as they arise but defer the recognition of gains until they are realised.

There are many examples of conservatism in accounting practice: impairment tests for fixed assets, the LOCOM rule in inventory valuation, the prohibition in many countries of tangible fixed asset revaluations. To better understand the accounting effects of conservatism, consider the case of Divergent Company. It has two depreciable assets, each costing €90,000 at the date of purchase (year 0) and subject to straight-line depreciation over its 10-year estimated life. At the start of year 2, new information leads Divergent to change its life estimates: to six years in the case of asset A and 12 years in the case of asset B. Under current international rules, Divergent must write down asset A – from €72,000 to €60,000 – immediately and recognise an impairment loss. It then increases the depreciation charge from €9,000 to €15,000 a year. By contrast, Divergent does *not* write up asset B. Instead, it amortises the depreciable amount (€72,000) over the asset's remaining life, thereby recognising a gain (in the form of a lower depreciation charge – €7,200 against the original €9,000 a year) only as the benefits of the asset are realised. The diagram below charts the carrying amounts of the two assets over their respective lives.

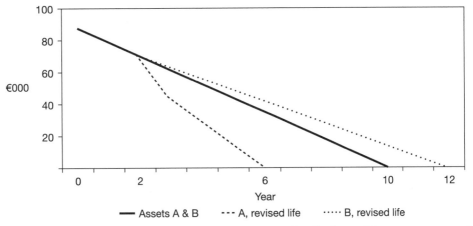

As our Divergent example shows, conservatism means that 'bad news' (e.g. an unexpected reduction in an asset's economic life) is reflected in earnings more quickly than good news (an unexpected increase in the asset's life). Moreover, because the good news gain is recognised only when realised, the earnings impact of good news lasts longer than that of bad news.

Empirical evidence confirms the differences in timeliness and persistence of good and bad news. Basu used stock market returns as a measure of news. He found that over the 1963–90 period, US companies' earnings were four to six times more sensitive to negative stock market returns (bad news) than to positive returns (good news). He also found a stronger association between current earnings and stock market returns than between current cash flow and stock market returns when news is bad. Our Divergent example suggests why. The company records a loss from the write-down of asset A against year 2 income but current cash flow is not affected as it's a non-cash charge.[8]

Are there international differences in accounting conservatism? Ball, Kothari and Robin argue it's more prevalent in common-law than in code-law countries. As we saw in earlier

Box 20.1 *continued*

chapters, ownership is more diffuse – and securities markets more important in corporate financing – in common-law countries. Ball *et al.* claim that accounting conservatism acts as an effective governance mechanism, allowing investors to monitor management of quoted companies more efficiently. If managers have to report corporate losses quickly, they'll move faster to stem them. Hence early in the development of corporate accounting, shareholders brought pressure on companies to adopt conservative practices such as the LOCOM rule. When regulatory bodies such as the SEC were established, they too favoured conservatism, imposing prohibitions on upward valuations of fixed assets and mandating equity accounting or full consolidation of subsidiaries. Companies in code-law countries faced, in the past, a different business and regulatory environment: stock markets were weak, many companies were family- or state-owned, governments set accounting rules. There was less call to use corporate accounts as a mechanism to police managers. Conservatism – in the income statement form outlined above – was rare.

Ball *et al.* tested their hypothesis on quoted companies from seven countries over the 1985–95 period. They found that the common-law countries examined (Australia, Canada, UK and USA) showed greater accounting conservatism than the code-law countries (France, Germany, Japan). Corporate earnings in the former were more closely associated with changes in stock market returns and more sensitive to negative than to positive stock returns. However, there was evidence of a change in French and German accounting practice over the 11 years. All countries (save Japan) exhibited greater accounting conservatism in 1991–95 than in 1985–90 but the change was most marked in the two European countries.[9] Developments since 1995 – especially, the growing influence of IAS on the corporate accounts of code-law countries – are likely to have further reduced the 'conservatism gap'.

to an investor and do not impede cross-company comparisons. However, where they are the result of different accounting methods, earnings are compromised as a performance measure. In these circumstances, 'cash flow smooths the playing field for companies with different accounting methods'.[10]

Cash flow data can also be used in cross-country comparisons of risk. We describe cash-based liquidity and leverage ratios in Chapter 18.

Making corporate accounts more comparable: a caveat

Trying to make corporate accounts more comparable – by using adjusted accrual-based data or focusing on cash flow numbers – may lead investors astray. First, comparability adjustments may reduce the usefulness of accounting numbers. For example, toy-maker Drosselmeyer may be justified in capitalising development costs. The future benefits from his outlays on product development may be more assured and easier to measure than is the case for his competitors. The difference in accounting captures the difference in the companies' economic circumstances.

Second, the accounting regime a company follows is not neutral. It influences people's behaviour. For example, German managers make investment decisions in the belief that the outcome of those decisions will be reported in the company's accounts according to German accounting rules. Faced with a different accounting regime, they may make different investment decisions. Investors should be mindful of this when making cross-country comparisons of corporate profitability and risk using adjusted data.[11]

Diversified operations

Investors face a further problem when they want to analyse the financial statements of *diversified* companies. Traditional consolidated accounts combine the revenues and expenses, assets and liabilities of all subsidiaries under the control of one company. Investors welcome such accounts because they can better understand the company as an economic entity – its size, profitability, liquidity and financial structure. The drawback is that the financial information is too aggregated. The accounts do not reveal how the components of the company have performed. As a result, investors lack vital information to help them assess the likely rewards and risks from their investment.

Thanks to legal, stock exchange and accounting rules, most diversified companies now supplement their consolidated accounts with summary financial information about their lines of business and their operations in various geographical areas. Such disclosures are known collectively as **segmental data**.

Benefits of segmental disclosures

Investors use segmental data to better understand a firm's past performance and to improve their forecasts of its future profits and cash flow. Investors usually forecast a firm's earnings in a two-stage process. They first forecast its sales and then apply an estimated profit margin ratio to that figure. When segmental data are available, they follow the same procedure but use the disaggregated numbers. Estimated consolidated profit is then the sum of forecast segmental profits (adjusted for any common costs or income). The following example, based on a firm with three business segments, illustrates the general procedure. All the numbers are assumed.

		Forecast sales		Estimated profit margin ratio		Forecast profit
Segment	A	100	×	15%	=	15
	B	250	×	8%	=	20
	C	150	×	12%	=	18
						53

Less: Expected common costs (net)
    (e.g. HQ costs, interest, income tax)   –5
    Forecast total net profit   48

Research indicates that profits forecasted in this way are more accurate than those based on consolidated figures alone.[12]

Segmental data can also shed light on the risk of a firm's operations. During the financial crisis in East Asia in 1997/98, investors consulted the segmental reports of international companies to discover the extent of their exposure to East Asian markets.

Illustration

The 2001 accounts of Benetton, the Italian clothing manufacturer and distributor, illustrate well the benefits of segmental disclosures to investors. According to the consolidated accounts, revenues grew by only 4% between 2000 and 2001 and contribution margin (defined by the company as gross profit less variable selling costs) did little better. The contribution margin ratio inched up to 37% in 2001.

Benetton Group	2001	2000	% change
Net revenues (in €m)	2,098	2,018	3.9
Contribution margin (in €m)	776	740	4.9
Contribution margin ratio	37%	36.7%	

However, the consolidated figures conceal a marked difference in the performance of the group's three main lines of business. Exhibit 20.4 gives a breakdown of Benetton's 2001 revenues and contribution margin by business sector and shows the change in sectoral revenues and contribution margin ratio between 2000 and 2001.

The segmental data in Exhibit 20.4 reveal the importance of 'casual wear' to the group results. It's by far the largest segment, responsible for 70% of total gross revenues. It's also the most profitable, with a contribution margin ratio of 40%. Moreover, 2001 was a good year for casual wear: revenues and contribution margin increased by 9.5% and 12%, respectively. Why, then,

Exhibit 20.4 Benetton Group: business segment data for 2001

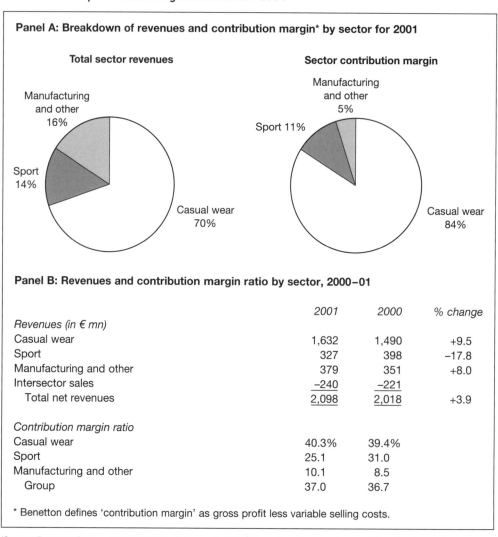

Panel A: Breakdown of revenues and contribution margin* by sector for 2001

Total sector revenues

- Manufacturing and other 16%
- Sport 14%
- Casual wear 70%

Sector contribution margin

- Manufacturing and other 5%
- Sport 11%
- Casual wear 84%

Panel B: Revenues and contribution margin ratio by sector, 2000–01

	2001	2000	% change
Revenues (in € mn)			
Casual wear	1,632	1,490	+9.5
Sport	327	398	−17.8
Manufacturing and other	379	351	+8.0
Intersector sales	−240	−221	
Total net revenues	2,098	2,018	+3.9
Contribution margin ratio			
Casual wear	40.3%	39.4%	
Sport	25.1	31.0	
Manufacturing and other	10.1	8.5	
Group	37.0	36.7	

* Benetton defines 'contribution margin' as gross profit less variable selling costs.

(*Source*: Benetton Group, *Annual Report and Accounts 2001*. Reproduced by permission of Benetton Group.)

was overall group performance so anaemic? The segmental figures provide the answer. The 'sport' sector – covering sportswear and equipment – suffered declines in both revenues and contribution margin in 2001 (due largely to a one-third contraction in sales of skates and skateboards, according to the company). This reverse largely offset the gains achieved in the other two sectors.

As well as explaining Benetton's past performance, the segmental data help investors improve their earnings forecasts and assessment of business risk. For example, casual wear is likely to remain the motor that powers the group's profits. Diversifying into sportswear and equipment gives Benetton the opportunity to build sales and profits outside the euro area (the Americas and Asia took 50% of 'sport' sales but only 15% of casual wear sales in 2001), but it brings added risk as the group's experience in the skate and skateboard product lines in 2001 illustrates.[13]

IAS disclosure requirements

Large companies, especially those whose securities are quoted and which have international operations, face a plethora of rules and guidelines on segmental reporting. In addition to observing national legal and stock exchange requirements, they must also take account of the guidelines of intergovernmental agencies such as the OECD and United Nations.[14] The reason for governmental interest in segmental reporting is self-evident. The operations of large companies can have a significant impact on a country's economic and social policies, especially in the areas of employment, competition and foreign trade. Companies themselves are reluctant to publish segmental data voluntarily since rival firms may find the information valuable and use it to their competitive advantage.

In drawing up segmental disclosure requirements, regulators must address the following issues:

- Which companies should be required to make segmental disclosures?
- How should a segment be defined?
- What information should be disclosed by segment?

The international standard on segmental reporting gives guidance on these issues. We summarise its main provisions below.[15]

Companies required to disclose segmental data

Only companies whose securities are publicly traded are required to publish segmental data. Moreover they only need provide it in their consolidated accounts.

Definition of segment

The international standard defines a segment in risk and return terms. The basis of segmentation can be either line of business (known as a 'business segment') or geographical area. The key point is that the business or geographical segment should be subject to risks and returns different from those faced by other segments of that type.

The novel feature of the standard is that it lays down different disclosure requirements for business and geographical segments. A company must first decide what is the 'dominant source and nature' of its risks and returns. If the dominant source is its lines of business, then the primary segmental report should focus on business segment activities. If it's the geographical areas in which it produces or sells its products, then the primary segmental report should focus on geographical segment activities. The less important segment is the subject of a secondary report. As we'll see, the primary report must contain more extensive segmental disclosures than the secondary report.

How does a company decide what is the 'dominant source and nature' of its risks and returns? The international standard is clear on this. The answer can be found in the way the company is organised. *A company's internal organisational and management structure and its system of internal financial reporting have evolved in response to external competitive pressures. They are therefore the logical basis for identifying its main risks and returns and for determining its primary and secondary segments.*

Defining segments by reference to a company's internal organisational structure has advantages for investors – and for the companies themselves. Investors get a better understanding of the way the firm operates. This should help them when they try to forecast its sales and earnings. Companies benefit because information-gathering costs are low: the segmental information can be taken directly from the internal reporting system. The main disadvantage for investors is that since firms' internal structures often differ, the segmental data may not be comparable across firms.

Segmental information to be disclosed

What information should a company provide by segment? First, the international standard introduces a materiality test. A company need only report information for larger segments. A 'reportable segment' is a business or geographical segment that earns a majority of its revenues from sales to external customers and whose sales or results (i.e. profits or losses) or assets are 10% or more of the respective totals for the group.[16] The 10% test limits the number of reportable segments and thus protects firms from costly and competitively damaging disclosures.

The standard lays down different disclosure requirements, depending on whether the reportable segment is a primary or secondary one. These requirements are summarised in Exhibit 20.5.

Exhibit 20.5 Disclosures by reportable segments: summary of main IAS requirements

Primary and secondary segmental reports	• Description of activities of each reported business segment and composition of each reported geographical segment. • Basis of pricing intersegment transfers.
Primary segmental report	For each segment: • Revenues,* external and intersegment • Profit or loss • Assets • Liabilities • Capital expenditures • Operating cash flow (or depreciation and other non-cash expenses) *plus:* Reconciliation of above items to the aggregated information in the main financial statements.
Secondary segmental report	For each segment: • Revenues, external only • Assets • Capital expenditures

* For geographical segments, revenues by location of *market* should be provided in addition, if they are significantly different from revenues by location of *production*.

As the exhibit shows, the disclosures a company must make in its primary segmental report are extensive and potentially very helpful to investors. For example, with segmental sales, profit and net asset data, investors can calculate each segment's return on net operating assets (RONOA) and break it down into its profit margin ratio and assets turnover components. Segment net operating assets are assumed to equal segment assets less segment liabilities. Usually these comprise operating assets and liabilities only, since management decide on the firm's capital structure (and thus the amount of net debt it carries) centrally. Note that estimates of segment RONOA may be affected by the amount of intersegmental sales and the basis on which they're priced – hence the importance of these two disclosures to investors.

Segmental capital expenditure figures allow investors to extend their analysis. They show how the company is allocating its investment outlays across business (and geographical) segments. An obvious question investors ask and the IASB's primary segmental disclosures help answer is: is the company channelling resources into its most profitable segments? Segmental capital expenditure figures are also needed to derive segmental free cash flow (operating cash flow less capex). This tells investors which segments are cash-generators and which cash-consumers. If a company doesn't disclose segmental OCF separately, it must break down depreciation and other non-cash expenses by segment so that investors can estimate it (i.e. OCF ≈ Profit + Non-cash charges).

Investors prize segmental disclosures and there is continual pressure on large, diversified companies to provide additional segmental data. As we'll see in the next section, those applying IAS now break down *interim* sales and profit figures by segment. Investors also want more detailed income statement data by segment. Some companies oblige. Benetton, for example, provides gross profit as well as contribution margin figures by business sector. (The company considers fixed selling expenses (e.g. advertising) and general and administrative expenses to be common costs and not assignable directly to lines of business.) There are calls on firms to release more general business data by segment. Ericsson's segmental report illustrates the kind of information investors are pressing for. The Swedish telecoms equipment producer publishes orders received from customers by segment – and by quarter. The major constraint on a firm supplying additional segmental data voluntarily is the fear that competitors will use the disclosures to its disadvantage.

Interim reporting

In analysing Carlsberg's financial results and condition in Chapter 19, we used the company's annual report as the main information source. From an investor's standpoint, a weakness of such reports is that the information in them quickly becomes dated. In Carlsberg's case, the group publishes in February annual accounts for the financial year ending in the previous December. An investor consulting Carlsberg's annual accounts in, say, January would learn of the financial impact of events that occurred 13–25 months earlier.

In order to satisfy investor demand for timely financial information, quoted companies publish **interim reports** during the year. An interim report usually comprises a management report, condensed consolidated financial statements and explanatory notes for the company and its subsidiaries for the quarter or half-year just ended.

Benefits of interim reports

Investors use interim financial data to revise their estimates of an investment's risk and return. Quarterly income statement numbers are particularly helpful. They give early warning of a change in business conditions and the impact on the firm. In addition, the sales and earnings of many firms – from ice-cream producers to gas utilities – display marked seasonal variations. By comparing the most recent quarter's sales and earnings with both the previous quarter's and those of the same quarter in the previous year, investors get early warning of a change in the company's fortunes. They can use the information to revise their forecasts of its future sales and earnings – and the sales and earnings of other firms in the same industry.

Illustration

Cisco Systems is a US-owned supplier of equipment for the Internet's infrastructure. No other company better exemplified the information technology boom years of the 1990s. Its sales and earnings grew by more than 30% a year throughout the decade. (Annual sales and earnings figures for the 1998–2002 period are set out in panel A of Exhibit 20.6.) For 43 consecutive quarters, it met or exceeded analysts' EPS forecasts. Its market capitalisation soared to over US$580 billion and made it, for a brief period, the most expensive company in the world.

The bursting of the dotcom bubble in 2000 dealt a punishing blow to Cisco's sales and profitability. Sales fell 30% between Q2 and Q3 2001. (The company's sales do not exhibit a seasonal pattern.) Despite a sophisticated information system that enabled the company to close its books in one day, management overestimated demand for the company's products and had to write off US$2.2 billion of excess inventory in April 2001. The write-off – and the

Exhibit 20.6 Cisco Systems: annual and quarterly earnings, 2000–02

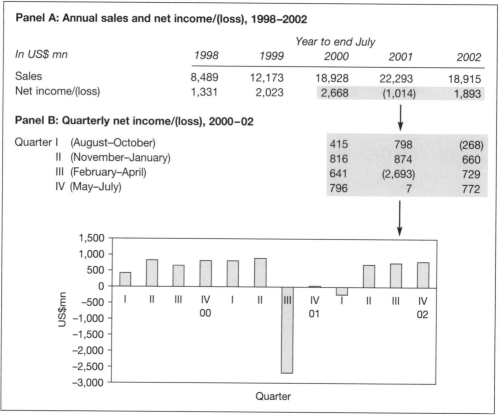

Panel A: Annual sales and net income/(loss), 1998–2002

In US$ mn	Year to end July				
	1998	1999	2000	2001	2002
Sales	8,489	12,173	18,928	22,293	18,915
Net income/(loss)	1,331	2,023	2,668	(1,014)	1,893

Panel B: Quarterly net income/(loss), 2000–02

Quarter		2000	2001	2002
I	(August–October)	415	798	(268)
II	(November–January)	816	874	660
III	(February–April)	641	(2,693)	729
IV	(May–July)	796	7	772

(*Data source*: Company; chart source; author.)

costs of laying off 18% of the company's workforce – were responsible for the US$2.7 billion loss reported in Q3 2001. (The company's financial year ends in July.) The company posted further large one-off charges in Q4 2001 and Q1 2002, resulting in low or negative earnings these quarters. Profit margins did not recover to 1999/2000 levels until Q2 2002. Panel B of Exhibit 20.6 charts the company's quarterly earnings over the three years from August 1999 to July 2002.

Cisco's quarterly reports provided investors with timely information about the change in its fortunes in 2001. Without them, investors would have had to wait until publication of annual data in August or September that year to learn of the sales collapse and its impact on profits. Note that Cisco's troubles in 2001 led to a sharp decline in its share price as investors revised their forecasts of future earnings. Its market capitalisation fell two-thirds between February and July 2001. With no sign of a resumption of sales growth, the share price continued to decline in the following financial year.[17]

Interim accounts: Integral and discrete approaches

There are two approaches to preparing interim financial statements, the integral and the discrete approaches. *Under the* **integral approach***, the year is considered the pivotal accounting period. The main accounts are the annual accounts and the accounts for each interim period are viewed as a sub-part of them.* Interim revenues and expenses are then apportioned annual amounts. For example, the bulk of maintenance work on North Sea oil production platforms is performed in the summer months when weather conditions are favourable. Assume Norse Oil Company's financial year runs to 31 December. It incurs maintenance costs of 60 million in the third quarter of the year. Under the integral approach, it estimates the costs and allocates them over the year, usually on a linear basis.

	Q1	Q2	Q3	Q4	Total
Maintenance expense	15	15	15	15	60
Maintenance expenditure			60		60

If actual outlays differ from expected, the expense charged in each of the remaining quarters of the year is adjusted.

Advocates of the integral approach claim the resulting earnings number is a better guide to company performance in the interim period. It is not distorted by decisions management make concerning the timing of discretionary costs and revenues *within* the year. In addition, for certain costs such as taxes, the accounting period *is* the year rather than a sub-part of it.

Under the **discrete approach***, an interim period is considered a distinct accounting period.* Moreover, it carries no less weight than the year in accounting terms. The company applies the same principles in its interim accounts as it uses in its annual accounts. Consider again Norse Oil's platform maintenance costs. If in the annual accounts the company expenses these costs as they are incurred, it accounts for them in a similar way in the interim accounts.

	Q1	Q2	Q3	Q4	Total
Maintenance expense	–	–	60	–	60

Allocating repair costs across quarters within the year – the integral approach – is avoided.

Advocates of the discrete approach argue that interim figures prepared on this basis are more transparent and reliable. Managers are not called upon to estimate total revenues and costs in the year before calculating interim figures. As a result, they have less opportunity to manipulate interim profits.

● Interim financial reporting in practice

Disclosure requirements

Interim reporting in the EU is heavily influenced by a 1982 directive on the subject.[18] Firms whose shares are listed on an EU stock exchange are required, by the directive, to issue a half-yearly report covering the first six months of each financial year. The report must be published within four months of the end of the half-year to which it refers. It must contain at a minimum the following information:

- net operating revenues;
- profit before and after tax;
- interim dividend, if paid or proposed;
- explanatory statement; and
- auditors' report, if the accounting information is audited.

Comparative figures should be shown for the corresponding six-month period in the preceding financial year. The explanatory statement should provide information to help investors assess the trend in the firm's sales and earnings and highlight any special factors that have influenced those figures in the half-year.

The USA and Canada impose more onerous requirements. For example, the US's SEC requires listed US companies to file quarterly reports – containing financial statements (with supporting notes) and management discussion of them – within 45 days of the end of each quarter. The filing deadline will be cut to 35 days by 2004.

North American practice is now finding an echo in other countries. Starting in 2003, listed companies in Malaysia and Singapore must publish quarterly reports. Japan's Financial Services Agency is considering introducing a similar requirement for listed Japanese companies from 2005. As part of its moves to improve corporate financial disclosure, the European Commission proposes that EU-listed companies file quarterly reports (with a 60-day filing deadline) starting in 2005. The Commission believes this will encourage international investment in European companies. Note that reporting more frequently than half-yearly is not a totally new idea in Europe. Some national stock exchanges already mandate quarterly or four-monthly reporting: in some cases (Norway, Spain), the ruling applies to all listed companies; in others, only a sub-group is affected (Germany's DAX-30 'blue chip' companies). Moreover, many large European multinationals disclose quarterly sales and earnings data on a voluntary basis.

Interim financial statements are usually unaudited, although the SEC requires those of US firms to be reviewed by external auditors.

Preparation of interim financial reports

The IASB issued an accounting standard on the preparation of interim financial reports in 1998. The standard is not mandatory. It's for the benefit of those companies which are required by stock exchange or other regulations to publish interim reports and which follow IAS in their annual accounts.[19]

The standard addresses two issues: what should an interim report contain and what accounting policies should a company follow when preparing it. As regards the first issue, the IASB views the interim report as a shortened version of the annual one. Thus the report should contain in condensed form a full set of statements (balance sheet, income statement, cash flow statement, statement of changes in shareholders' equity) and selected explanatory notes. It should shed light on year-to-date as well as the current period's figures. For example, the third quarter report would show income numbers for the first nine months of the year and the latest three months – and comparable figures in the previous financial year. Cash flow numbers would also be for the first nine months. In this way, the investor can see how the company's earnings and cash flows are developing over the year as well as learn about its trading performance in the most recent interim period.

The explanatory notes are intended to help investors interpret the interim figures. Thus the company should disclose in each interim report:

- segmental revenues and profit or loss (for business or geographical segments, whichever is the primary basis of segmental reporting);
- the effect of changes in the composition of the company (e.g. major acquisitions and disposals);
- important financing events (e.g. issue of shares, repayment of loans, dividend payments); and
- unusual items, such as restructuring charges and investment gains or losses.

The notes should also explain how the interim results are affected by seasonal or cyclical factors.

As for the second issue, the standard shows subtlety. At first sight, it appears to favour the discrete approach. 'An enterprise should apply the same accounting policies in interim financial statements as are applied in its annual financial statements. . . .' For example, if at the time of expenditure a cost fails an asset recognition test (for example, because of uncertainty of future benefits), the company should not defer the expense to a later interim period even if it believes that the uncertainty may be reduced by then. Nor should it accrue an expense unless it has a legal or constructive obligation to an outside party. Thus Norse Oil should not accrue in the first two quarters the costs of platform maintenance work scheduled for the third quarter.

However, the standard acknowledges the primacy of annual financial statements in the *measurement* of assets and liabilities. Companies should measure balance sheet items on a year-to-date basis. In this way, changes in estimates *during the year* are incorporated in the values of assets and liabilities.

Calculating interim income tax expense provides a good illustration of this approach. Tax authorities assess firms' profits to corporate income tax on an annual basis. Thus, under IAS, a company should accrue income tax expense in an interim period, using its estimated *annual* effective tax rate. This estimated tax rate should be updated each interim period to allow for progressivity in tax rates (e.g. in many countries low corporate income bears a lower tax rate) and events in the period which raise or lower the effective tax rate (e.g. new permanent differences, new tax credits).

For example, suppose Norse Oil estimates at the end of the second quarter that its annual effective tax rate will be 30%. Pre-tax profit in the first six months is 120 (million). By the end of third quarter, when year-to-date pre-tax profit rises to 150 (after deducting maintenance costs of 60), management revise the annual effective tax rate upwards to 32%. Norse Oil's third quarter interim report shows the following profit and tax expense numbers:

	Three months to 30 September	Nine months to 30 September
Profit before tax	30	150
Income tax expense	−12	−48
Net profit	18	102

The tax charge of 12 in the third quarter is the difference between the total tax expense for the first nine months (32% × 150 or 48) and that for the first six months (30% × 120 or 36).

● Future developments

Interim reports are likely to grow in importance in the future. Adoption of IAS by listed companies will result in more detailed reports – currently many firms do not provide interim cash flow or segmental data – and greater consistency in the preparation of interim financial statements.

Moreover, quarterly reporting will become more common, as a result of changes in stock exchange listing requirements and pressure from international, especially North American, investors.

There is unease in some quarters about requiring all listed firms to publish quarterly data, however. Having to produce interim reports quarterly rather than half-yearly imposes an additional regulatory burden on a company. And many wonder whether managers will become overly concerned about the short-term effect of their decisions – that is, the effect on the company's results next quarter – and reject profitable investments with longer-term payoffs. Nevertheless, the trend towards more frequent (and timely) reporting appears unstoppable. Already many retailing companies and airlines release *monthly* sales or revenue figures within days of the month-end.

SECTION 2 Accounting manipulation and its detection

From an investment standpoint, accrual accounting has much to commend it. Investors find profit and its revenue and expense components helpful for assessing a firm's financial performance and valuing it. Likewise, the balance sheet provides useful information about the firm's resources and obligations. But what gives accrual-based numbers their strength – the opportunity for a firm's managers to convey, through accounting methods and estimates, information about its future – can also be a source of weakness. The inherent flexibility of accrual accounting allows managers to manipulate reported numbers. They can take accounting as well as business decisions that result in the company appearing more (or less) profitable than otherwise.

Accounting manipulation takes many different forms. In some cases, it's simple 'window-dressing' – for example, delaying payment of suppliers at year-end to improve balance sheet liquidity ratios. More usually, earnings are involved – hence the other widely used phrase, 'earnings management'. Managers alter the timing of revenue or expense recognition to improve current or future years' profits. Although the activity is not necessarily illegal – the manipulation may not violate accounting rules and it can be hard to prove that managers' intent was to mislead investors – it is unethical. Moreover, it imposes costs on both investors and society at large. Resources are misallocated and, when the manipulation is exposed, firms' capital costs rise as investors seek higher returns to compensate them for the extra risk. The late 90s dotcom and telecoms bubbles and their aftermath illustrate this well.

Reasons for accounting manipulation

Why do managers manipulate accounting numbers? The reasons are many and varied. Four key ones concern taxes, capital-raising, debt contracts and management compensation.

1 *To reduce the tax and regulatory burden.* Taxes – and government-imposed regulations in general – are costs which firms seek to reduce. Subsidies and other reliefs (e.g. trade protection measures) are benefits which they seek to increase. In both cases, firms have an incentive to reduce reported profits (or increase reported losses).

2 *To raise capital more cheaply.* Firms that are perceived to have low operating and financial risk can raise debt and equity capital on favourable terms. Managers take actions to lower the perceived riskiness of the firm – either by reducing its reported leverage or by dampening the variability of its reported profits.

3 *To avoid violation of debt contracts.* To protect the interests of creditors, a debt contract usually imposes operating and financial restrictions on the debtor company. Financial restric-

tions are often expressed in terms of accounting numbers. Examples are minimum interest cover and maximum debt–equity ratios. If the debtor company fails to observe these limits, it may be forced to renegotiate the terms of the contract – probably to its disadvantage – or even to repay the debt before maturity. It has an incentive, therefore, to manage key accounting numbers (profit, interest expense, debt, equity) in order not to violate the debt contract.[20]

4 *To increase managers' wealth.* Managers' compensation may be linked directly to their firm's profitability. For example, they may receive bonuses linked to its reported profits. This does not mean that managers always have an incentive to bolster short-term profits. For example, the bonus plan may state that managers will receive no bonus if profits are below a stated minimum level. Should actual profits be below this, managers may be encouraged to lower them still further – by, in effect, charging future costs in the current period – in order to make it easier to earn a bonus in the future. A new management team may use similar 'big bath' tactics at the time of their appointment – to increase future profits during their tenure and so enhance their reputation and value as managers.

These are not the only reasons for manipulating accounting numbers. Managers resort to 'creative accounting' in other circumstances – for example, during takeover battles and in major wage negotiations with trades unions. In all these cases, managers are seeking to increase their own wealth and/or that of existing shareholders. If they succeed, they do so at the expense of governments, creditors, employees and prospective investors.

Methods of accounting manipulation

How a firm manipulates its accounting numbers depends on its goals. Exhibit 20.7 identifies three: to raise (or lower) short-term profits, to reduce earnings variability and to strengthen the balance sheet. The exhibit gives examples of the ways a firm can achieve these goals through creative accounting.

Many of the accounting devices listed – e.g. front-loading of revenues, deferring costs, smoothing profits through provisions, using off-balance-sheet financing techniques – have been described and illustrated in earlier chapters. Note that some have primary cash flow effects (even before taking account of any secondary tax impact). For example, bringing forward sales through limited-period incentives increases short-term profits and operating cash flow. Building up finished goods inventory can increase short-term profits (by capitalising in inventory more of the current period's production overhead) but may involve higher current outlays (e.g. additional storage costs).

The methods listed in Exhibit 20.7 assume a relatively stable corporate structure. However, additional opportunities for accounting manipulation arise when a company actively acquires and disposes of businesses. For example, an acquired business's operating assets such as inventories and plant and equipment may be written down and additional provisions booked in its accounts before consolidation takes place. By understating the net operating assets of an acquired business, the acquirer can flatter group results – via lower cost of sales, depreciation and other expenses – in the financial period following the acquisition.

Safeguards against accounting manipulation

Given the incentives to manipulate accounting numbers – and the number of ways to do it – why isn't the activity more widespread? An important reason is that managers' ability to manage accounting numbers is constrained, partly by institutional factors and partly by investor vigilance. (Of course, managers may reject it on ethical grounds.)

What are these institutional factors? One, obviously, is the set of accounting and reporting rules which a company must follow. These have become tougher in recent years. Consider, for example, the new international standards on provisions and intang-ible assets. The first limits when

Exhibit 20.7 Methods of accounting manipulation (in separate reporting environment)

Corporate goal	Method

*Raise short-term profits**	Bring forward revenues through:
	• accounting decisions
	   (e.g. lessor structures leases as sales-type leases)
	• 'real' decisions
	   (e.g. limited-period sales incentives to customers)
	
	Delay or cut expense through:
	• accounting decisions
	   (e.g. extend depreciable lives of fixed assets)
	• 'real' decisions
	   (e.g. build up finished goods inventories, cut expenditures on R&D, plant maintenance and employee training)

Reduce profit variability	• active use of provisions and allowances (e.g. for bad debts) • exceptional gains/losses (e.g. from asset disposals) to offset variable operating profits
Strengthen balance sheet	Bolster assets and equity through: • revaluation of fixed assets • disposal of fixed assets with large unrealised holding gains Keep debt off balance sheet through: • use of operating leases • financing via equity-accounted and unconsolidated affiliates • quasi-equity (e.g. preference share capital)

* Lowering short-term profits involves accounting or 'real' decisions which have the opposite effect (i.e. delaying revenues and bringing forward expenses).

a restructuring provision can be established and the second lays down strict recognition criteria. It is now harder for managers to smooth earnings through provisions and increase short-term profits by capitalising costs.

Another institutional factor is the external audit. An audit firm has an incentive to challenge those accounting practices of a client company it considers questionable. Its reputation may be damaged – and its partners' wealth reduced – if the courts later find the company and its advisers guilty of false accounting. (The partners of Arthur Andersen, one of the world's largest audit firms, forgot this lesson in the 1990s and, in the aftermath of the Enron accounting scandal, the firm disintegrated in 2001.) Should the audit firm fail to persuade the client's management to abandon such practices, it may qualify its audit opinion or resign the audit. Either action is a 'red flag' for investors.

Investigation of the annual accounts by independent auditors is an example of the way shareholders monitor – and ultimately control – management's actions. There are many other **corporate governance** mechanisms available to shareholders – from appointment of independent, non-executive directors to shareholder approval of top executive pay schemes. The more effective they are, the fewer are the opportunities for management to manipulate accounting numbers (*see* Box 20.2).

Corporate governance and financial reporting

In earlier chapters we characterised suppliers of capital as either 'insiders' or 'outsiders'. Insiders are managers and shareholders with a controlling interest in the firm. Outsiders are minority shareholders and creditors. When outsiders put capital into a business, they run the risk that the return on their investment will be less than they expected because insiders misuse it.

Capital gets misused in various ways. Insiders may steal it – directly or indirectly, by, say, selling corporate assets at below market price to another company they control. They may expropriate it by installing family members in managerial positions, awarding themselves excessive compensation or 'empire-building' (e.g. pursuing size rather than profitabilty goals). Outsiders try to protect themselves against such misuse of their capital. The mechanisms they use constitute the *governance* of a company.

Many factors contribute to effective corporate governance. The most important are the legal rights of shareholders and creditors and the system of enforcing them. We've seen examples of such rights in earlier chapters. For example, shareholders have the right to appoint directors, to sue them for misappropriating company funds and to vote in general meeting on major investment and financing decisions. Secured creditors can seize a debtor company's assets when it defaults on its debts.[21]

Accounting also plays a key role in good corporate governance. As we saw in Chapter 6, the law requires companies – all in the EU, only quoted ones in the USA – to publish financial statements periodically. The way the statements are prepared is also regulated, either by a government agency or by a private one supported by government. The accounting rules the agency lays down limit insiders' ability to manipulate financial information and thus make it easier for outsiders to monitor insiders' actions. Other corporate governance mechanisms reinforce accounting's role. Annual audits by external auditors – mandatory in all countries – and independent boards of directors serve to reduce the incidence of accounting manipulation.[22]

In the 1990s the prevailing wisdom was that countries with a common-law tradition – often referred to as 'Anglo-Saxon' countries – had more effective corporate governance than those in code-law countries. Investor rights were held to be stronger and better enforced in common-law countries. There was also less incidence of accounting manipulation, it was argued: accounting rules reflected conservatism in income measurement (*see* Box 20.1) and financial disclosures were more extensive.

The accounting scandals in the USA in the early 2000s led commentators to question the superiority of the Anglo-Saxon model. The US Congress and governments in other common-law countries also had doubts. They imposed new burdens on company executives and toughened audit regulation. For example, the US Sarbanes-Oxley corporate reform act of 2002 requires that the CEOs and chief financial officers of all US quoted companies certify their firms' financial statements. They face prison terms and heavy fines if they put their signatures to false reports. The act creates a new audit regulator, the Public Company Accounting Oversight Board. It will establish auditing standards and inspect at least triennially all audit firms, US and non-US, auditing companies listed on a US stock exchange.

However, empirical evidence indicates that many countries have a worse record of accounting manipulation than the USA. Leuz, Nanda and Wysocki studied the accounts of over 8,000 companies in 31 countries in the 1990–99 period. They found that earnings management was less evident in countries with large stock markets, diffuse corporate ownership, extensive investor rights and strong enforcement of them. Such countries are labelled 'outsider-oriented' by Leuz *et al.* They include – but are not limited to – richer common-law countries like the USA.[23]

Investor vigilance also deters managers from manipulating accounting numbers. Analysts and other financial experts scrutinise company accounts and draw attention to signs of 'low-quality' accounting practice.[24] The techniques they use are varied but usually include the following.

Monitoring of key operating numbers and ratios

Sales, operating margin, receivables turnover and inventory turnover are all studied carefully. Analysts are looking for signs of operating weakness (faltering cost control, slower receivables collection, inventory build-up) as well as accounting subterfuge (bringing forward sales, postponing costs).

Analysts also look at the relationship between operating and net profit. To what extent is the 'bottom line' inflated by non-operating income and non-recurring gains?

Cash flow check

Operating cash flow and profit are compared. As we saw in Chapter 18, a combination of rising profits and falling OCF acts as red flag (except, possibly, in the case of a rapidly growing firm investing heavily in working capital). It prompts analysts to investigate the company's accounting policies for signs of front-loading of income and deferral of costs.

The tax expense figure provides a further cash flow check. Analysts are wary of firms that boast a low current tax ratio (current tax expense/before-tax profit). Most countries' tax codes reveal a conservative bias: revenues are usually not taxed until cash is received; expenses are tax-deductible only when paid. Should a firm report a low current tax rate, this means its taxable profits are much less than its accounting profits. This may indicate skilful tax planning by the firm. However, it may also be evidence that the firm is using aggressive accounting methods (early recognition of revenue or late recognition of expenses) and that some of its accounting profits are illusory.

Examining the notes to the accounts

The notes to the accounts can be a mine of information. Analysts focus on the following:

- *The summary of accounting policies.* Analysts are on the look-out for unusual policies. When does the company recognise revenue? How does it account for inventory and depreciable fixed assets? Are the company's policies similar to those of other firms in the industry?
- *Financial investments.* There is scope here for concealing debt. For example, does the company have major equity-accounted investments in associates, incorporated joint ventures and unconsolidated subsidiaries? What is the financial leverage of these investee companies?
- *Commitments.* This note may also reveal evidence of debt concealment. For example, what are the minimum payments the company is committed to make under operating leases over the next five years? Are these commitments increasing relative to on-balance-sheet debt?

The above examples assume that analysts are searching for overstatement of profit and assets and understatement of liabilities. In countries where a uniform reporting tradition prevails, they may be concerned about possible understatement of net assets – through undervaluation of fixed assets and overprovisioning – which also makes profit an unreliable measure of corporate performance.

Accounting manipulation: an illustration

Accounting rules, external audits, independent directors and investor vigilance serve to limit accounting manipulation but they don't eliminate it. Sometimes warning signs are overlooked. MyTravel Group is a UK-based provider of all-inclusive holidays and other leisure travel services. It expanded abroad in the 1990s, and by 2001 owned travel companies in northern Europe and the USA. Revenues more than doubled between 1997 and 2001, exceeding £5 billion in the latter year. During 2002, the group suffered setbacks. It issued its first profits warning in March, citing the effects on the travel industry of the September 2001 terrorist attacks in New York. The second came at the end of September; a week later, the chief executive quit. October was an eventful month. The group issued a third profits warning after new auditors insisted that it change its accounting policies, the final dividend was scrapped and UK regulators began a review of the group's accounts. Meanwhile, the share price had plummeted – from 250p in January to 17p by the end of October. In late November, the group published preliminary results for the year to 30 September 2002. These showed a loss of £73 million and a restated profit (before tax) of only £62 million for the previous year, a quarter down on the original figure. Panel A of Exhibit 20.8 summarises the 2002 and restated 2001 figures.

MyTravel's travails in 2002 shouldn't have come as a total surprise to investors. The group's accounts for 2001 and its governance structure contained red flags. We summarise them below. (Key numbers are given in panel B of Exhibit 20.8.)

Exhibit 20.8 MyTravel Group: 2001 accounting 'red flags' and earnings restatement

---

Panel A: Summary 2002 and restated 2001 results

		Year to 30 September	
	2002	2001	
In £mn		Restated	As reported
Turnover	4,379.2	5,050.8	5,061.4
Operating profit/(loss) before exceptionals and goodwill	(20.4)	113.2	132.2
Finance income (charge)	8.5	(2.4)	(2.4)
Profit/(loss) before exceptionals and goodwill	(11.9)	110.8	129.8
Net exceptionals	(28.4)	(16.7)	(16.7)
Goodwill amortisation	(32.5)	(31.8)	(31.8)
Profit/(loss) on ordinary activities before tax	(72.8)	62.3	81.3

Panel B: Warning signs of declining earnings quality in 2001 accounts

		Year to 30 September			
In £mn, except ratios	2001	2000	1999	1998	1997
(1) Low and declining profit margins					
Group turnover	5,061	3,949	3,309	2,753	2,236
Profit margin ratios (in %)					
Profit before tax, exceptionals and goodwill	2.56	1.94	3.97	4.56	5.24
Exceptionals and goodwill amortisation	(0.96)	3.41	(0.17)	–	–
Profit before tax	1.6	5.35	3.8	4.56	5.24
(2) Deteriorating liquidity					
Operating profit before joint ventures and exceptionals	71.9	51.0	89.7	102.8	98.9
Accruals	(82.4)	82.9	9.5	(4.4)	57.0
Operating cash flow before tax	(10.5)	133.9	99.2	98.4	155.9
Net funds/(debt), end-year	(20.0)	158.9	104.2	266.0	313.9

(*Sources*: MyTravel Group plc, *Annual Report and Accounts 2001*, reproduced by permission of MyTravel Group plc; author's calculations.)

- *Low and declining profit margins.* The group's before-tax profit margin ratio, already low in 1997 (5.2%), declined year-on-year to 2000 and only recovered slightly in 2001. At 2.6%, the 2001 ratio was only half the 1997 figure. Moreover, these ratios are calculated before exceptional items and goodwill amortisation. Exceptional items had a significant impact on the group's bottom line in both 2000 and 2001. For example, without the £236 million gain on disposal of a joint venture in 2000, the company would have reported a loss that year.
- *Deteriorating liquidity.* Like profits, operating cash flows did not grow with revenues. Between 1998 and 2000 they hovered around £100 million, not enough to cover capital expenditures in these years. Ominously, OCF turned negative in 2001. Management attributed this to the closing down of the group's Belgian and French operations: the costs were provided for in 2000 and the cash disbursed in 2001. However, the operating profit figures indicate that the group's underlying cash flow generation was weak in both years.

   Weak cash flow led to greater reliance on debt financing. The group's financial year-end occurs in September – after the end of the summer holiday season in Europe and North America – when its cash position should be strong. However, the net cash balance halved between 1997 and 2000 and it reported net debt for the first time on its 2001 balance sheet.
- *Non-transparent accounting policies.* Firms like MyTravel that provide services have scope for front-loading income by taking an aggressive view of when services have been performed. Investors in such firms look for a clear statement of revenue recognition policies. The statement in MyTravel's 2001 accounts doesn't provide it:

   > Revenues and expenses relating to inclusive tours are taken to the Profit and Loss Account on holiday departure. Other revenues and associated expenses are taken to the Profit and Loss Account as earned. Certain expenses such as the cost of non-revenue earning flights, brochure and promotional costs are charged to the Profit and Loss Account over the season to which they relate.

   What are 'other revenues and associated expenses'? When is the earnings process completed for these items?

   The tax figures also raise doubts about the group's accounting policies. According to management, the tax rate (excluding exceptional items) was only 23% in 2001, well below the UK's statutory rate of 30% that year. The actual tax payments in 2000 and 2001 were only £8.9 million and £1.3 million, respectively; very low considering the company's pre-tax profits were £211.4 million and £81.3 million in those years.
- *Weak governance.* Although the positions of chairman and chief executive were split, the chairman of the company, David Crossland, was its founder and retained an executive role. Only three of the group's ten directors in 2001 were outsiders. Of the seven executive directors, one, the group finance director, was a former partner of Arthur Andersen, the group's auditors (before 2002), and worked on acquisition transactions for the group while at Andersen.

Poor business decisions were largely responsible for MyTravel's declining profits and cash flows. The group failed to integrate the businesses it purchased in the late 1990s – its newly acquired German business made heavy losses in 2000 and 2001 – and did not respond quickly enough to the slowdown in holiday travel following the September 2001 terrorist attacks in New York. However, the restatement of the 2001 results and part of the 2002 loss are attributable to accounting changes. For example, the new auditors, Deloitte & Touche, insisted that premium income on holiday insurance policies should be booked when the customer begins the holiday rather than when the policy is sold. The group was forced to abandon the aggressive accounting policies that the previous auditors had condoned.

It's easy to overlook warning signs. Successful companies present a special challenge. When a firm with a history of sales and profit growth encounters problems, there are always reassuring voices telling investors that the setback is temporary. Experience should put them on their guard.

In such companies, growth can become an imperative. If managers cannot find natural ways of increasing profits, they may turn to artificial ones.

Accounting quality

Some financial commentators refer to the 'quality' of a company's accounts. Investors assess quality in terms of the transparency of the numbers in the financial report, the robustness of the accounting policies underlying them and the predictability of earnings. Transparency flows from clear presentation and full disclosure, robustness from unbiased policies which avoid over- or understatement of profitability and leverage, earnings predictability from the absence of income smoothing devices. Clearly, accounting quality and manipulation are linked. Accounts that are judged to be of high quality are likely to contain little or no evidence of manipulation.

Unfortunately, accounting quality is often misconstrued as accounting conservatism. Consider the case of a mail-order company. Currently it expenses immediately all costs incurred in acquiring new customers. It wishes to change its policy and, in future, capitalise (and amortise) such costs. Management believes capitalisation better reflects the economics of its business since, based on past experience, the company retains customers on average for at least three years.

The problem is how to convince the investment community of the merits of the proposed policy. Analysts view capitalisation as a 'low-quality' practice, a device to defer costs in order to improve short-term profits. The share price may suffer if it's adopted. The company could try to reinforce its message but any additional steps it takes might prove costly. For example, disclosing more information about customers and retention rates could benefit competitors. It may be that the company must use means other than accounting policy – for example, signalling financial strength through substituting debt for equity – to communicate the economics of its business to investors.[25]

Summary

Investors face difficulties analysing a company's financial statements. The statements may not be comparable with those of past periods or competitors. They are aggregated and thus shed little light on the performance of diversified firms. Finally, the information annual accounts contain quickly becomes dated.

Accounting rule-makers (and stock exchanges) have tried to remedy these problems. A firm following international accounting standards must disclose:

- the sales and profits of any business it's discontinuing – and the gain or loss when the business is sold;
- the effect on its accounts from changing its accounting policies – if past periods' accounts aren't restated, then pro forma accounts based on the new policy should be provided;

and, if it's diversified:

- sales, assets and capital expenditures by business and geographical segment. Additional information – in particular, profit and operating cash flow – should be given for whichever of the two bases of segmentation, line of business or geographical area, is the main source of the firm's risks and returns.

Only publicly quoted firms are required to disclose segmental data. These are also the firms that are affected by stock exchange rules on 'alternative GAAP' disclosures and interim reports. Adjusting key accounting numbers to US or international GAAP helps investors compare companies in different countries. Interim accounts – styled, under international rules, on annual ones – provide more timely information.

Accrual accounting is inherently flexible. It allows managers to convey, through accruals, future-oriented information about the firm. However, accrual-based numbers are manipulable. Firms manipulate their accounts for one or more of the following reasons: to reduce tax and regulatory costs, to make capital-raising easier, to avoid violating debt and other contracts and/or to increase managers' wealth. To achieve these ends, they lower (or raise) short-term profit, reduce its variability and strengthen the balance sheet.

Accounting rules and other corporate governance mechanisms such as the external audit limit firms' accounting creativity but the most effective safeguard against manipulation is investor vigilance. The forensic techniques investors employ – monitoring operating ratios, checking profit against cash flow, analysing the notes to the accounts – require basic accounting skills.

Happily, these are skills you should now have. You've acquired them – at times painfully – while studying this book. May they serve you well.

APPENDIX 20.1 Earnings per share

Investors use EPS as a measure of corporate performance, in its own right and in combination with other market and accounting data (e.g. price–earnings ratio, dividend payout ratio). There are different ways of calculating EPS. This means that even when firms follow the same accounting policies, their EPS numbers may not be comparable.

To overcome this problem, international standards now lay down rules on how firms should calculate EPS.[26] The rules which we describe and illustrate in this appendix apply only to firms whose shares are – or will shortly be – publicly quoted: other firms are encouraged but not required to disclose EPS.

Basic EPS: calculation

EPS in its basic form is calculated as follows:

$$\text{Basic EPS} = \frac{\text{Net profit (or loss) in period attributable to ordinary shareholders}}{\text{Weighted average ordinary shares outstanding in period}}$$

EPS represents earnings per *ordinary* share. To calculate the numerator, the firm must deduct dividends declared to preference shareholders in the period. (If the preference shares are cumulative and the dividend is in arrears, then the dividend that should have been declared in the period is deducted.) In the case of a group, the ordinary shareholders are those of the parent company:

Group net profit (after extraordinary items)	xx
– Minority interests' share of profit	–xx
Net profit attributable to parent company's shareholders	xx
– Dividend to preference shareholders	–xx
Net profit attributable to parent company's ordinary shareholders	xx

Note that the net profit figure is *after* extraordinary items.

The calculation of the EPS denominator is more complicated. The ratio relates earnings for a period to the *average number of ordinary shares outstanding* in that time. The average should be weighted to take account of when during the period shares are issued or repurchased. (Own shares held by the company are considered issued but not outstanding and therefore should be excluded from the denominator.) For example, suppose a company with 1 million shares outstanding at 1 January year 6 issues for cash 200,000 shares on 1 October that year. The weighted average shares outstanding in year 6 will be:

Period	Fraction of year	Shares outstanding	Equivalent number of shares
1 Jan–30 Sept	9/12	1 million	750,000
1 Oct–31 Dec	3/12	1.2 million	300,000
			1,050,000

If a company declares a share dividend (bonus issue) or splits its shares, the denominator is adjusted from the start of the year. Figures for prior years are also restated in order to ensure comparability of EPS numbers over time. For example, suppose our company declares a 1 : 1 share split in June year 7. Shares outstanding increase from 1.2 to 2.4 million. There are no other changes to share capital in year 7. The weighted average shares reported in the company's year 7 accounts will be:

	Year 7	Year 6
Ordinary shares outstanding (in million)	2.4	2.1
		(2 × 1.05 million)

Reported EPS for year 6 (and prior years) in the year 7 accounts will be half the reported amount shown in the year 6 accounts.[27]

The denominator also includes the fully paid-up equivalent of partly paid shares. For example, if 200,000 partly paid shares are 75% paid-up, 150,000 are included in the weighted average share calculation.

Diluted EPS

Our EPS tale has another twist to it. A company disclosing basic EPS may have to disclose a second EPS figure, **diluted EPS**, if it has 'potential ordinary shares' in its capital structure. *Potential ordinary shares (POS) are ordinary shares that may be issued in the future as a result of*:

- *the conversion of bonds or preference shares;*
- *the exercise of warrants and employee share options; and*
- *the fulfilment of a contractual condition (e.g. achievement by acquired firm of profit targets agreed with acquirer).*

Diluted EPS is calculated as follows:

$$\text{Diluted EPS} = \frac{\text{Net profit/loss attributable to ordinary shareholders} \pm \text{Effect of POS on net profit/loss}}{\text{Weighted average ordinary shares and potential ordinary shares (POS) in period}}$$

A company must disclose diluted EPS as well as basic EPS if its POS are dilutive. For profitable companies, diluted EPS will always be less than basic EPS.

Why are investors interested in diluted EPS? Remember that investors use EPS for forecasting and valuation purposes. They want an EPS number that captures the effect of expected changes in a company's capital structure. In the 1960s, EPS was based on *actual* ordinary shares outstanding. Conglomerates and other acquisition-hungry companies in the USA found that reported EPS could be boosted by financing acquisitions with convertible securities and bonds issued with warrants. In this way, income increased thanks to the earnings of the acquired company and the low reported cost of the debt used to buy it while outstanding shares, the EPS denominator, remained unchanged. Higher EPS, managers believed, increased the company's share price and made future acquisitions cheaper. US accounting regulators brought in rules which forced companies to disclose the effect of potential ordinary shares on EPS. International regulators followed suit.

Diluted EPS is a hypothetical number. A company estimates earnings and outstanding shares as if all convertible securities in its capital structure have been converted and all options or warrants have been exercised. Conversion or exercise is assumed to take place from the start of the year – or the date of issue of the POS, if later. Should securities be converted or options/warrants exercised during the year, then the calculation of diluted EPS includes the effect of these POS only up to the date of conversion/exercise.[28]

In the case of convertible securities, the calculation of potential dilution is straightforward. The firm estimates the effect of conversion on both EPS numerator and denominator. This is known as the 'if converted' method. The EPS numerator increases – in the case of convertible bonds, by the interest saved (net of any tax effect) and, in the case of convertible preference shares, by the preference dividend avoided. The EPS denominator also increases – by the ordinary shares issuable under the conversion terms.

Estimating the potential dilutive effect of warrants and employee share options is more difficult. In contrast to convertible securities, the firm receives cash from the exercise of warrants or options which, in practice, is invested. What assumption should the firm make about the return on this investment? The international standard, following US practice, avoids this question. Under *IAS 33*, the firm assumes it purchases its own shares with the cash received from exercise. This is known as the 'treasury stock' method. If the warrants or options are 'in the money' (the market price is greater than the exercise price), they are dilutive: the number of shares issued on exercise exceeds the number of the company's own shares that can be bought back. Thus the EPS numerator is unchanged but the EPS denominator increases.

Exhibit 20.9 summarises the adjustments a firm makes to the EPS numerator and denominator when calculating diluted EPS.

As we stated earlier, a company must disclose diluted EPS if its POS are dilutive. *The international standard defines dilutive POS as securities that, after conversion or exercise, decrease the per-share profit from continuing, ordinary operations attributable to ordinary shareholders.* Note this benchmark profit figure. It excludes extraordinary items and the effect of discontinued operations. The impact on EPS of each issue or series of POS must be considered in turn, starting with the most dilutive. *If an issue or series of POS is anti-dilutive* (i.e. inclusion would result in an *increase* in per-share profit from continuing, ordinary operations), *it should be excluded from the diluted EPS calculation.* This procedure ensures the maximum dilution of basic EPS.

Example

We illustrate how basic and diluted EPS are calculated under IASB rules. Suizo-Hispania, designer and builder of luxury automobiles, reports net profits of €6 million in year 8. It has 12 million ordinary shares outstanding during the year. Its basic EPS is therefore €0.5. It has the following POS in its capital structure:

- *Employee share options.* There are 3 million shares under option in year 8 and their exercise price is €2.7. The average market value of the company's shares is €3.6 per share that year.
- *Convertible bonds.* At the start of year 7, the company issues, at par, €15 million of 3% ten-year convertible bonds. Holders can convert each €1,000 bond into 250 Suizo-Hispania ordinary shares starting in year 9. The tax rate is 30%.

Exhibit 20.9 Calculation of diluted EPS: adjustments to EPS numerator and denominator

Framework

$$\text{Diluted EPS} = \frac{\text{Net profit/loss attributable to ordinary shareholders} +/- \text{Effect of POS on net profit/loss}}{\text{Weighted average ordinary shares and } \textit{potential ordinary shares (POS)} \text{ in period}}$$

Source of dilutive POS	Adjustments to EPS numerator and denominator	
Convertible bonds	*Numerator*:	Add back interest saved (net of tax effect) as a result of conversion.
	Denominator:	Increase shares outstanding by shares to be issued on conversion.
Convertible preference shares	*Numerator*:	Add back preference dividend avoided as a result of conversion.
	Denominator:	Increase shares outstanding by shares to be issued on conversion.
Warrants and employee share options	*Numerator*:	No effect.
	Denominator:	Increase shares outstanding by *excess* of shares to be issued on exercise over the company's own shares purchasable with proceeds from exercise.

Exhibit 20.10 shows the calculation of Suizo-Hispania's basic and diluted EPS in year 8. In calculating diluted EPS, conversion of the bonds is assumed to take place at the start of year 8.

Suizo-Hispania's employee share options and convertible bonds both have a dilutive effect on EPS. We start the diluted EPS calculation with the share options because they are the more dilutive of the two POS. Since the market value of the shares exceeds the exercise price of the options, the shares issued on exercise of the options (3 million) are greater than the shares that can be bought back with the proceeds (€8.1 million/€3.6 = 2.25 million shares). In consequence, the EPS denominator increases by 750,000 while the EPS numerator is unchanged.

As for the convertible bonds, the company adds only €0.084 to its after-tax income for each share issued on conversion:

$$\frac{\text{Interest saved (net of tax)}}{\text{Shares issued on conversion}} = \frac{\text{€315,000}}{3,750,000} = \text{€0.084/share}$$

Since the company's EPS after accounting for the employee share options alone is €0.47 (€6,000,000/12.75 million shares), the marginal impact of the convertible bonds is dilutive. After adjusting for both POS, the company's year 8 diluted EPS is €0.38.

But what if Suizo-Hispania's net profit in year 8 is only €1 million? As stated earlier, the more dilutive of its two POS are the employee share options. Its EPS adjusted for the assumed exercise of these options is only €0.078 (€1 million/12.75 million shares). Since the interest saved on conversion of the bonds is greater than this on a per-share basis (€0.084/share), the effect of conversion is to *increase* EPS. Diluted EPS rises to €0.08 [(1.0 + 0.315)/16.5]. In this case, the convertible bonds are *anti-dilutive* and only the share options are included in the diluted EPS calculation.[29]

Exhibit 20.10 Diluted EPS calculation: effect of share options and convertible bonds

Facts

- Suizo-Hispania's net profit in year 8 is €6 million. The tax rate is 30%. There are 12 million average ordinary shares outstanding in the year.
- Three million share options have been granted to employees. The exercise price is €2.7. The average market price of SH shares in year 8 is €3.6.
- SH issued €15 million of 3% ten-year convertible bonds at par at the start of year 7. Holders can convert each €1,000 bond into 250 SH shares from year 9.

Year 8 EPS calculation

	Adjusted net profit to ordinary shareholders (Numerator)	Ordinary and potential ordinary shares (Denominator)	Earnings per share
Basic EPS	€6,000,000	12,000,000	€0.5
Employee share options	0	+750,000*	
	6,000,000	12,750,000	
*3% convertible bonds**	+315,000	+3,750,000	
Diluted EPS	€6,315,000	16,500,000	€0.38

Notes:

* Cash received on exercise: 3 million × €2.7 = €8.1 million. Shares purchasable: €8.1 million/ €3.6 = 2.25 million. Net increase in shares outstanding: 750,000.

** Interest saved, net of tax: €15 million × 3% × (1 − 0.3). Shares issued on conversion: 15,000 bonds × 250.

Presentation and disclosure of EPS

A company following international rules must report basic and diluted EPS on the face of its income statement for the current period and previous ones presented. It should also show how the numerator and denominator of the two EPS figures are arrived at. Loss-making firms (i.e. with negative EPS) must also disclose these EPS figures.

A company may disclose voluntarily per-share amounts of *components* of profit, such as extraordinary items and the profit or loss from discontinued operations. The IASB encourages firms to make these additional disclosures if management believe the information helps investors evaluate the performance of the company. The calculation should be consistent with the main EPS figures, that is the same weighted average number of ordinary shares should be used in the denominator.

EPS calculation and presentation: an unfinished story

The calculation and presentation of EPS are still evolving. There's still uncertainty about how the profit figure in the numerator should be calculated. Witness the IASB's open approach to the disclosure of per-share components of profit.

Investment analysts have their own views on this issue. Professional associations of analysts and credit rating agencies in various countries have constructed their own earnings formulas for use in performance appraisal and valuation of domestic companies. For example, the German Institute of Financial Analysts (DVFA) together with the German Association of Business Economics (SG) has devised an adjusted annual earnings number for German companies. The aims of the adjustments are to strip away tax-driven and transitory elements in reported profits and improve the comparability of German companies' results. Thus unscheduled depreciation (i.e. the difference between tax-based and normal depreciation) and gains and losses from major disposals of fixed assets are excluded from the adjusted earnings number. So, too, are changes in provisions that don't involve obligations to third parties. (This adjustment brings the earnings number closer to an IAS-based one.) Many German companies disclose DVFA/SG earnings (and EPS) figures in the annual report on a voluntary basis.

Note that the DVFA/SG earnings number cannot be computed without company assistance. By contrast, the 'core' earnings number that Standard & Poor's, the credit rating agency, calculates for leading US companies can be derived from published data.

Problem assignments

P20.1 Ebitda: investors' friend or foe?

Many companies now present an Ebitda (earnings before interest, tax, depreciation and amortisation) number in their annual and interim reports, usually among the 'financial highlights' or in the 'financial review' section of the report. Management claim they are merely responding to investor demand for a forward-looking earnings number. Disclosing the figure saves investors the trouble of calculating it themselves.

Financial regulators, however, warn investors to be wary of Ebitda and other so-called pro forma earnings numbers devised by management that are not supported by accounting standards or generally accepted accounting principles. Under SEC rules, companies listed on US stock exchanges must reconcile any 'pro forma' earnings number (such as Ebitda) to the US GAAP-based earnings number on the income statement.

Required

(a) Why do you think some investors are interested in Ebitda? What are the advantages of this earnings number over the earnings numbers – such as operating income, income before tax and net income – reported in the income statement?

(b) Why are financial regulators sceptical about Ebitda? What are the potential flaws of this earnings number as a performance measure?

P20.2 Restating accounts for new information

Under current accounting rules, companies – in countries where the practice is permitted – can restate past years' accounts in limited circumstances only. Restatement is required if material errors are discovered in past years' accounts. It may be required if a new accounting standard is introduced. It is permitted if the company changes an accounting method. Restatement is not permitted in other situations.

Many managers believe these rules are too restrictive. Consider, for example, the treatment of outlays on research. Even under the new international standard, it is difficult if not impossible for a firm to capitalise non-contractual research costs. At the time of the expenditure, future benefits are likely to be considered too uncertain to permit asset recognition. If later the research proves successful, the company cannot restate past years' accounts and recognise a research asset retrospectively since the circumstance – a revision of estimates of future benefits – does not qualify for restatement.

The economic consequences are potentially severe. Expenditures on intangibles are growing as a proportion of total investment as services increase their share of national output. In addition, there is evidence that technology is now changing at a faster rate – which implies rising corporate expenditures on research and development. These outlays are usually not capitalised and, as a result, balance sheets understate companies' economic resources. In some cases the understatement is extreme. For example, the book value of Microsoft's net assets was only 22% of their market value at the end of 2002.

Some financial experts have proposed that there should be continuous restatement of financial reports.[30] Under their proposal, companies would regularly revise past years' financial statements as new information becomes available and uncertainties about the future benefits of expenditures on intangibles are resolved. Note that this proposal is not as revolutionary as it sounds. Revising past periods' accounts to incorporate new information is a common practice in government accounting.

Required

Comment on the above proposal. Are there other advantages of continuous restatement of financial accounts in addition to those mentioned above? What are the potential disadvantages of this idea?

P20.3 Earnings impact of major changes in operations

Smith & Nephew plc, UK-based producer of medical devices, reorganised its operations in 2001. On 1 April that year it set up a joint venture (called BSN Medical) with Beiersdorf AG. S&N contributed its casting and bandaging and traditional woundcare businesses in return for a 50% equity stake in BSN Medical. (Beiersdorf contributed similar businesses to the joint venture for its 50% stake.) The results of these businesses prior to 1 April are shown in S&N's income statement as 'Operations contributed to the joint venture'. Exhibit 20.11 contains the group's profit and loss account for 2001.

S&N also acquired and disposed of other businesses in 2001. As part of its deal with Beiersdorf, it acquired the German company's advanced woundcare business. It sold its ear, nose and throat business during the year and made a £49 million gain on the disposal. The remaining businesses were grouped into four product areas – orthopaedics, endoscopy, advanced wound management and rehabilitation – and the company published segmental data for each of them in its 2001 accounts.

Exceptional items of 19.3 (£ million) shown under 'Ongoing operations' comprise:

- 2.9 of manufacturing rationalisation costs;
- 7.5 of rationalisation costs following the contribution of businesses to BSN Medical;
- 8.9 of integration costs in connection with the 2001 acquisition of the advanced woundcare business from Beiersdorf.

The exceptional items shown under 'Operations contributed to the joint venture' and 'Share of operating profit of joint venture' relate, in both cases, to manufacturing rationalisation costs. (The company also reported £4.3 million of such costs under exceptional items in the 2000 income statement.) Management estimate that the taxation charge on profits in 2001 *before* exceptional items and discontinued operations is £52.3 million.

Required

(a) You wish to calculate S&N's operating profitability (i.e. return on net operating assets) in 2001. Calculate the group's NOPAT (net operating profit after tax) that year. The UK statutory tax rate was 30% in 2001. (Note: RONOA cannot be calculated as no balance sheet information is given.)

(b) Calculate the 2001 turnover and operating profit figures you would use as the basis for forecasting S&N's group turnover and operating profits for 2002. Explain the basis of your calculation.

P20.4 Change in accounting policy

Volund, a metal fabricator, decides to build its own steel mill. The mini-mill costs 120, has a ten-year economic life and an expected scrap value of 10. (Amounts are in € million.) Volund depreciates the plant by an accelerated method (which it also uses for tax purposes). Depreciation in the first four years is: 20, 18, 16, 14.

During year 4, Volund decides to change the way it depreciates the mill in its published accounts. It switches to the straight-line (SL) method because it reckons the SL method better reflects the way the plant's services are consumed. It continues to depreciate the asset on an accelerated basis in its tax accounts. Volund's draft year 4 accounts *before the accounting change* are set out below in summary form:

Exhibit 20.11 Smith & Nephew: group profit and loss account, 2001

For the year ended 31 December	2001 £ mn
Turnover	
Ongoing operations	1,012.5
Operations contributed to the joint venture	35.3
Continuing operations	1,047.8
Discontinued operations	33.9
Group turnover	1,081.7
Share of joint venture	123.6
	1,205.3
Operating profit	
Ongoing operations:	
Before exceptional items	171.0
Exceptional items	(19.3)
	151.7
Operations contributed to the joint venture:	
Before exceptional items	3.6
Exceptional items	(1.8)
Continuing operations	153.5
Discontinued operations	0.5
	154.0
Share of operating profit of the joint venture:	
Before exceptional items	12.8
Exceptional items	(5.0)
	161.8
Discontinued operations – net profit on disposals	49.2
Profit on ordinary activities before interest	211.0
Interest payable	(17.4)
Profit on ordinary activities before taxation	193.6
Taxation	(64.0)
Attributable profit for the year	129.6
Ordinary dividends	(42.9)
Retained profit for the year	86.7

(*Source:* Smith & Nephew plc, *Annual Report and Accounts 2001*. Reproduced by permission of Smith & Nephew plc.)

	Year 4	Year 3
Statement of income and change in retained income		
Operating revenues	800	750
Income before tax	80	70
Tax expense (at 30%)	−24	−21
Net income	56	49
Retained income, start-year	124	93
Income available for distribution	180	142
Dividends paid	−20	−18
Retained income, end-year	160	124

	Year 4	Year 3
Balance sheet at year-end		
Steel mill, at net book value	52	66
Other assets	708	644
Total assets	760	710
Share capital and premium	200	200
Retained income	160	124
Liabilities (including provision for deferred taxes)	400	386
Total equities	760	710

Required

Adjust Volund's accounts to reflect the change in depreciation method for the steel mill. Assume Volund accounts for the change by the restatement method. Show the effect on pre-year 3 income as a 'prior period adjustment' to start-year 3 retained income.

Check figure:
Retained income, end-year 4   176.8

P20.5   Reconciling numbers to US GAAP: effect on profitability and leverage

Helping Hand is a business services firm that specialises in outsourcing services. Although based in a eurozone country – we'll call it Euroland, it has acquired businesses in other countries in recent years. Because of its growing international profile, it obtains permission to list its shares on the New York Stock Exchange. The company prepares its published accounts according to Euroland GAAP but provides a reconciliation of net income and shareholders' equity to US GAAP, as required by SEC regulations. The reconciliation given in its x9 accounts is set out in Exhibit 20.12.

Euroland GAAP differs from US GAAP in several important respects.

- Prior to x9, Euroland companies could write off purchased goodwill against reserves. Since the start of x9, they must capitalise and amortise it.
- Euroland rules for establishing provisions – for restructuring and other costs – are less strict than US ones so Euroland companies can set them up at an earlier date than US firms can.
- Euroland companies are permitted to revalue tangible fixed assets. Depreciation is calculated on the revalued amount of the assets. The revaluation surplus is credited to a non-distributable reserve and can be transferred to distributable reserves only when realised. US GAAP does not permit such asset revaluations.
- In estimating the cost of their defined benefit pension plans, Euroland and US companies use different actuarial methods.

Required

(a) Calculate Helping Hand's ROE for x9 under both Euroland and US GAAP. Clearly, goodwill is responsible for the large difference in reported profitability under the two accounting regimes. Why does Helping Hand *deduct* an amount for goodwill in arriving at US GAAP income but *add* a much larger amount under the same heading in arriving at US GAAP shareholders' equity?

(b) A condensed version of Helping Hand end-x9 balance sheet is set out below. It is prepared according to Euroland GAAP. Amounts are in € million.

Assets	
Fixed assets	6,404
Current assets other than cash	3,099
Cash and cash equivalents	497
Total assets	10,000

Exhibit 20.12 Helping Hand: reconciliation of x9 income and equity to US GAAP

(Amounts in € million)	x9	x8
Net income in accordance with Euroland GAAP	**526**	383
Adjustments to reported net income with respect to:		
Goodwill	**(103)**	(67)
Pension costs	**5**	(8)
Property revaluation	**3**	3
Provisions	**(29)**	(46)
Deferred tax effect of adjustments	**7**	12
Net income in accordance with US GAAP	**409**	277

(Amounts in € million)	**End-x9**	End-x8
Shareholders' equity in accordance with Euroland GAAP	**1,646**	1,207
Adjustments to reported shareholders' equity with respect to:		
Goodwill	**3,994**	3,412
Pension liabilities	**34**	39
Property revaluation	**(21)**	(24)
Long-term provisions	**20**	23
Shareholders' equity in accordance with US GAAP	**5,673**	4,657

Shareholders' equity and liabilities	
Shareholders' equity	1,646
Minority interests	235
Debt (including financial lease commitments)	4,178
Provisions and other long-term operating liabilities	761
Current operating liabilities	3,180
Total shareholders' equity and liabilities	10,000

(i) Using information in Exhibit 20.12, adjust the above balance sheet figures to (approximate) US GAAP.

(ii) Calculate Helping Hand's end-x9 net debt-to-group equity ratio under both Euroland and US GAAP.

(iii) On seeing your answers to (ii), an analyst remarks: 'No wonder the market has moved to cash flow measures of financial leverage. Balance sheet measures of leverage give absurd results.' What is the point the analyst is making? Under what circumstances do balance sheet measures of leverage give 'absurd results'?

P20.6 Analysis of segmental data

Swiss-based Nestlé is the world's largest food and beverage group with 2001 sales of SFr 85 billion. Its major brands include Nescafé, Perrier and Vittel in beverages and Maggi and Buitoni in prepared dishes. However, it uses the Nestlé name in milk products, ice cream and confectionery.

Nestlé follows IAS. Under 'Accounting policies', it defines its primary and secondary segment formats:

The primary segment format – by management responsibilities and geographic area – represents the Group's management structure. The principal activity of the Group is the food business, which is managed along three geographic zones. The other activities, mainly pharmaceutical products and water, are managed on a worldwide basis. The secondary segment format representing products is divided into five categories (segments).

(Nestlé, *Management Report 2001*)

Exhibit 20.13 shows the information Nestlé discloses under the secondary segment format.

Required

(a) Determine which product group in 2001:
   (i)   enjoyed the fastest sales growth;
   (ii) earned the highest margin on sales;
   (iii) was the most asset-intensive;
   (iv) earned the lowest return on assets.

Exhibit 20.13 Nestlé Group: segmental information by major product group for 2001 and 2000

In SFr millions	2001	2000	2001	2000
	Sales		Results	
Beverages	24,023	23,044	4,259	4,318
Milk products, nutrition and ice cream	22,953	21,974	2,572	2,620
Prepared dishes and cooking aids (and miscellaneous activities)	21,324	20,632	2,026	1,948
Chocolate and confectionery	11,244	10,974	1,234	1,166
Pharmaceutical products	5,154	4,798	1,255	1,212
	84,698	81,422	11,346	11,264
Unallocated items[a]			(2,128)	(2,078)
Trading profit			9,218	9,186

[a] Mainly corporate expenses, research and development costs, amortisation of goodwill and restructuring costs.

In SFr millions	2001	2000	2001	2000
	Assets		Capital expenditure	
Beverages	11,086	10,654	1,062	936
Milk products, nutrition and ice cream	11,127	11,215	573	530
Prepared dishes and cooking aids (and miscellaneous activities)	8,620	8,980	460	390
Chocolate and confectionery	6,347	6,685	249	250
Pharmaceutical products	2,859	2,589	99	113
	40,039	40,123	2,443	2,219
Administration, distribution, research and development			1,168	1,086
			3,611	3,305

(*Source*: Nestlé, *Management Report 2001*. Reproduced by permission of Nestlé S.A.)

(b) An analyst reviewing Nestlé's product group disclosures questioned their usefulness. 'A key expenditure is research and development which, according to the consolidated income statement, totalled SFr 1,162 million in 2001. Nestlé doesn't break down this figure by product group so the segmental profit and investment numbers are misleading.' Comment on this criticism. Do you agree?

(c) Nestlé publishes additional information under its primary segment format, in particular, liabilities and depreciation by segment. The capex and depreciation figures are shown below:

(In SFr millions)	Capital expenditure		Depreciation of property, plant and equipment	
	2001	2000	2001	2000
Food:				
Europe	954	946	806	890
Americas	747	766	695	767
Africa, Asia, Oceania	626	550	438	481
Other activities	1,169	949	558	519
	3,496	3,211	2,497	2,657
Corporate and R&D	115	94	84	80
	3,611	3,305	2,581	2,737

On comparing the capex and depreciation figures, an investor asks: 'The depreciation charge on Nestlé's food assets fell in every area between 2000 and 2001. Yet in Africa, Asia and Oceania and, to a lesser extent, in Europe, food capex rose between these two years. How can this be?'

Suggest possible reasons why the depreciation charge on a segment's fixed assets might decline in a period when expenditure on property, plant and equipment in that segment increases.

P20.7 Treatment of revenues and expenses in quarterly accounts

It's early April x5 and Demeter Company, a Mediterranean-based producer of horticultural equipment, is about to publish quarterly financial statements for the first time. The company has a December year-end and follows international accounting standards. Demeter's chief financial officer asks your advice on how the following items should be dealt with in the first quarter's report (to end-March x5). Set out below is the treatment she thinks is most appropriate for each revenue (expense) item.

Item	Proposed effect on Q1 net income	CFO's comments
Deferred maintenance charge	0	The cost incurred in Q1 was €50,000 but it really belongs in Q4 x4. The spending was deferred in order that the company could achieve its earnings target in x4. I think we should take the whole cost in Q4 x5 as an exceptional charge at year-end.
Dividend on financial investment	€20,000	No dividend was received in the quarter. The company expects to receive €80,000 over the year, the same as in x4. I reckon the income should be spread evenly over the year.
Cost of major advertising campaign	(€30,000)	The campaign was launched in early March and cost €90,000. The company expects to receive the benefits evenly over three months, March–May x5. I propose we split the cost and book one-third in Q1 and two-thirds in Q2.

Item	Proposed effect on Q1 net income	CFO's comments
Foreign currency transaction gain	0	The fall in the dollar in Q1 resulted in a €45,000 gain on the company's outstanding dollar debt. I don't think we should book any gain in Q1 because it's not realised and the dollar may recover later in x5.
Restructuring charge	(€17,500)	In Q1 the company announced plans to restructure one of its businesses. The plan is an outline only: there are no firm details. Expected total cost is around €70,000. No outlays were made in Q1. I propose we spread the expected cost evenly over the year.

Required

Advise Demeter's CFO. How should the company account for each of the above five items in its Q1 x5 income statement? Give reasons for the accounting treatment you propose.

P20.8 Calculation of earnings per share*

Spriggins Company is a small biotechnology company specialising in the development of new varieties of vegetable and field crop seeds. One of the company's most successful products is the high-growth, thick-stalk bean which founder Jack Spriggins developed.

Like most fast-growing companies, Spriggins is capital-hungry. It pays no dividends on its 15 million issued (ordinary) shares, ploughing back all profits into the business. It issued €10 million of ten-year convertible zero coupon bonds at the start of x2. The bonds raised €5.584 million giving a yield to maturity of 6%. Under the conversion terms, each €1,000 bond can be converted at any time into 80 ordinary shares.

The company launched a share option scheme for employees in x3, and 1,350,000 options were granted on 1 May. The options can be exercised from x5 at a price of €8.

Spriggins reports net profit of €9 million in x3. Interest expense on the bonds is €0.355 million that year and the tax rate is 30%. The average market price of the company's shares in x3 is €10.

Required

Calculate the company's basic and diluted earnings per share for x3.

Check figure:
Diluted EPS   €0.58

* Assignment draws on material in the appendix to this chapter.

Notes to Chapter 20

1 Investors can estimate organic profit growth in 2002, however. In a note to the 2002 accounts, Hero discloses the contribution of major acquisitions to group operating profits that year – and the contributions of the principal businesses disposed of in 2002 to 2001 as well as 2002 operating profits.

2 International Accounting Standards Board, *IAS 35: Discontinuing Operations.*

3 The sharp falls in the sales, earnings and capital employed of the ferrochrome division in 2001 are attributable to poor trading conditions: world demand for ferrochrome fell and Xstrata responded by cutting production capacity. As for the forestry segment, the end-2001 figures reflect the net assets of the group's eucalyptus plantation, the forestry trading business having been sold in 2001.

4 International Accounting Standards Board, *IAS 8: Net Profit or Loss for the Period, Fundamental Errors and Changes in Accounting Policies.*

5 The IASB announced in late 2002 that it planned to make restatement mandatory for all voluntary changes in accounting method. The cumulative catch-up approach would no longer be allowed. (Companies would not need to restate prior years' accounts if this involved undue cost.) Note that to implement the proposed IASB ruling some EU countries will have to amend existing accounting laws that require the opening balances of each financial year to *equal* the preceding year's closing balances. Such laws preclude restatement.

6 Companies switching to international from national accounting standards must restate prior years' accounts unless it's impracticable to do so or individual IAS require a different transitional treatment (Standing Interpretations Committee [of the IASC], *SIC-8: First-Time Application of IASs as the Primary Basis of Accounting*).

7 Other areas where differences in accounting have a significant impact on Unilever's 2001 accounts include interest, pensions and dividends. Unilever expenses all interest costs as incurred; US GAAP requires interest incurred during the construction of tangible fixed assets to be capitalised and depreciated over their useful lives. Pension and healthcare assets and liabilities are measured at fair value under US rules but at actuarial value under (then) UK rules, resulting in a higher net liability under the former. In the UK, dividends are provided for when proposed but in the USA they are not provided for until they become irrevocable.

8 Basu, S. (1997), The conservatism principle and the asymmetric timeliness of earnings, *Journal of Accounting and Economics*, 24: 3–37.

9 Ball, R., Kothari, S.P. and Robin, A. (2000), The effect of international institutional factors on properties of accounting earnings, *Journal of Accounting and Economics*, 29: 1–51.

10 Dreyfus, P. (1988), Go with the (cash) flow, *Institutional Investor*, August: 55–59.

11 This argument is developed in Choi, F. and Levich, R. (1990) *The Capital Market Effects of International Accounting Diversity*, New York: Dow Jones/Irwin.

12 Collins, D. (1976), Predicting earnings with sub-entity data: some further evidence, *Journal of Accounting Research*, Spring: 163–177.

13 Benetton's segmental disclosures, though helpful, are limited. The company provides no information on assets and liabilities by line of business so investors can't determine each sector's profitability. Moreover, it provides no information about how intersegment transfers are priced. This is important in the case of the manufacturing sector where over 60% of sales flow to the casual wear and sport sectors. Is casual wear's high contribution margin the result of low transfer prices being charged by manufacturing?

14 The main concerns of the OECD and UN are the disclosure of segmental data by geographical area. *See* Organisation for Economic Cooperation and Development (1976), *Guidelines for Multinational Enterprises*, Paris: OECD, and United Nations (1986), *The United Nations Code of Conduct on Transnational Corporations*, New York: UN.

15 International Accounting Standards Board, *IAS 14: Segment Reporting*. Segmental disclosures required under the EU's 4th Directive are modest. Large firms must break down annual sales, average staff numbers and staff costs by activity and geographical market where these activities and markets 'differ substantially from one another' (Art. 43(8) and (9)). The 7th Directive requires the same disclosures in the consolidated accounts. Neither directive states how a segment should be defined.

16 'Sales' here includes sales to other segments. As for profits, the firm divides its segments into profit- and loss-making ones and applies the 10% test to the profitable segments and loss-making ones separately.

17 Doubts about the quality of Cisco's earnings surfaced in 2001. The company's growth in the 1990s was fuelled by acquisitions. Analysts suspected that the company had boosted reported earnings during the decade by writing down the net assets of firms it acquired *before* consolidating their accounts. This reduced the costs it had to charge against income *after* the acquisition was effected. In addition, the write-offs Cisco booked in April 2001 helped to lift results in the following financial year since, in effect, the company brought forward 2002 costs to 2001. *See* Byrne, J.A. and Elgin, B. (2002), Cisco: behind the hype, *BusinessWeek*, 21 January, pp. 43–49.

18 European Commission (1982), *The Interim Reports Directive* (82/121/EEC), Brussels.

19 International Accounting Standards Board, *IAS 34: Interim Financial Reporting*.

20 The argument that debt and other contracts influence firms' accounting decisions is summarised and illustrated in Watts, R. and Zimmerman, J. (1986), *Positive Accounting Theory*, Englewood Cliffs, NJ:

Prentice Hall, Chapters 8–12. Most of the empirical work cited by Watts and Zimmerman is US-based. There have been few non-US studies to date. A recent interesting one found that Finnish firms manipulated profits under a dividend-and-tax strategy: they lowered them in 'fat' years to reduce taxes and raised them in 'lean' years to ensure dividends were covered by current earnings (Kasanen, E., Kinnunen, J. and Niskanen, J. (1996), 'Dividend-based earnings management: empirical evidence from Finland', *Journal of Accounting and Economics*, vol. 22, pp. 283–312).

21 For a fuller exposition of the argument that without legal safeguards outsiders' capital will be expropriated by insiders, *see* La Porta, R., Lopez-de-Silanes, F., Shleifer A. and Vishny, R. (2000), Investor protection and corporate governance, *Journal of Financial Economics*, 58: 3–27.

22 In a study of large, quoted US companies in the 1992–93 period, Klein found that decreases in the independence of boards of directors and audit committees were associated with increases in earnings management at these companies. *See* Klein, A. (2002), Audit committee, board of director characteristics, and earnings management, *Journal of Accounting and Economics*, 33: 375–400.

23 Leuz, C., Nanda, D. and Wysocki, P.D. (2003), Investor protection and earnings management: an international comparison, *Journal of Financial Economics*, forthcoming. Using cluster analysis, LNW found that countries fell into one of three groups: (1) 'outsider', (2) 'insider' with strong legal enforcement, and (3) 'insider' with weak legal enforcement. Common-law countries with well-developed capital markets dominate the 'outsider' group and code-law countries with a German or Scandinavian legal tradition the 'insider with strong legal enforcement' group. Earnings management increased across the three groups, being lowest among companies in group 1.

24 Each major stock market has its (unofficial) chronicler of creative accounting practices. For a US exposé, *see* Schilit, H. (2002), *Financial Shenanigans – How to Detect Accounting Gimmicks and Fraud in Financial Reports*, 2nd edition, New York: McGraw-Hill. For a UK exposé, *see* McBarnet, D. and Whelan, J. (1999), *Creative Accounting and the Cross-Eyed Javelin Thrower*, Chichester: John Wiley.

25 For a fuller development of this argument, *see* Healy, P. and Palepu, K. (1993), The effect of firms' financial disclosure strategies on stock prices, *Accounting Horizons*, March: 1–11.

26 International Accounting Standards Board, *IAS 33: Earnings per Share*.

27 If a company makes a 'rights issue' – in which new shares are offered first to existing shareholders at a discount to the current market price – the issue is treated for EPS purposes as part share dividend and part new share issue at the *full* market price. Comparative EPS figures for prior years are adjusted for the share dividend component of the issue.

28 If ordinary shares are contingently issuable (e.g. issuable on achievement by an acquired firm of profit targets agreed at the time of its acquisition), then for purposes of diluted EPS the denominator should include the contingently issuable shares even if the conditions have not been met in the period.

29 Our example is highly simplified. If earnings drop to €1 million, the share price is likely to fall, too. The dilutive effect of the employee share options will be reduced or, if the share price falls below the exercise price, eliminated.

30 Lev, B. and Zarowin, P. (1999), The boundaries of financial reporting and how to extend them, *Journal of Accounting Research*, Autumn: 353–385.

Glossary

Absorption costing. Dominant method of costing inventory in firms' published accounts. End-period work in progress and finished goods bear a share of the fixed production costs incurred during the period they were produced. (Such costs are 'absorbed' in inventory.)

Accelerated method. Depreciation method where proportionately more of an asset's cost is charged against revenues in the early years of its life. Examples are the *declining-balance* and *sum-of-years'-digits* methods.

Acceptance. *See Bill of exchange.*

Account. Document in which accounting transactions and events of a similar nature are recorded. The term can be applied to a specific category of asset, liability or shareholders' equity (e.g. ledger account) or a sub-part of it (e.g. individual customer account within receivables ledger account).

Account payable. Amount owed by firm to supplier under general credit arrangement. (Cf. *Note payable.*)

Account receivable. Amount owed to firm by customer under general credit arrangement. (Cf. *Note receivable.*)

Accounting policies. Accounting methods a company follows, and estimates its management make, when recognising and measuring its assets and liabilities. *See also Accounting principles.*

Accounting principles. Fundamental concepts underlying accrual accounting. Four main ones are: *going concern assumption*; consistency; prudence; *accruals concept.*

Accounting profit. Before-tax profit reported in published accounts. (Cf. *Taxable profit.*)

Accrual adjustment. Adjustment to update accounts for event which has economic impact on the firm in the period. The event may be the consumption of an asset, the settlement of a liability or the effect of the passage of time on either.

Accruals concept. Fundamental accounting principle. An event is recognised in accounts at time of its economic impact on firm. This may or may not coincide with receipt or payment of cash.

Accrue. To recognise revenue or expense (and related asset or liability) before cash is received or paid.

Accrued benefit valuation (ABV) method. Actuarial method of determining cost of pension (or other retirement) benefits. Benefits are based on services already rendered ('accrued') by employees.

Accumulated amortisation/depreciation. Cumulative amortisation/depreciation charges. Balance sheet account. Usually shown as contra account to related intangible/tangible fixed asset.

Accumulated benefit obligation. Measure of pension plan's liability (US). Actuarial present value of vested and non-vested benefits (computed under required *ABV method*), based on current salary levels.

Acid test ratio. *See Quick ratio.*

Acquisition accounting. Method of accounting for business combination. One firm is deemed to have bought another and records in consolidated balance sheet, at time of acquisition, the fair values of assets purchased and liabilities assumed. (Cf. *Merger accounting.*)

Actuarial gains/losses. Gains/losses that arise from (1) changes in actuarial assumptions underlying pension plan assets and liabilities and (2) experience adjustments (adjustments to plan assets and liabilities because experience – of labour turnover, inflation, etc. – differs from expectations).

Actuarial method. *See Interest method.*

Additional paid-in capital. *See Share premium.*

Affiliate/affiliated company. A company linked to another by shareholding (e.g. subsidiary, associate).

Allowance for bad debts. Valuation adjustment to accounts (or notes) receivable. Estimated amount of firm's trade debts outstanding at end of period which management consider are uncollectible. (Also known as *allowance for doubtful accounts* and *allowance for uncollectible accounts.*)

Amortisation. Allocation of cost over predetermined future period in a systematic way. The term is applied to:
– *intangible assets* – the predetermined future period is the asset's expected useful life;
– *discount/premium* (*on bonds*) – the predetermined future period is usually the period to maturity.
See also Depreciation.

Amortised cost. Method of valuing investment in debt securities. Debt securities are measured at historical cost adjusted for the amortisation of the issue (or purchase) discount/premium.

Annual accounts. For larger companies, these consist of balance sheet, income statement, cash flow statement, notes to the accounts, auditors' report.

Annual report. Accompanies annual accounts. Contains review by management of firm's activities during year.

Annuity method. Increasing-charge depreciation method. Cost of depreciable fixed asset is annuitised and interest element is then subtracted from asset's annual cost to give depreciation charge in period.

Asset. Resource expected to yield future benefits which is controlled by firm and acquired as a result of a past exchange.

Assets turnover. Sales revenue divided by (average) total assets. It measures the intensity with which a firm uses all its assets.

Associate/associated company. Investee company where investor firm exercises significant influence over its operating and financial policies, usually as a result of large minority shareholding (20–50%).

Audit. Examination of accounting records with aim of establishing that the firm's system of record-keeping is sound and financial statements prepared from them are reliable.

Auditors' report. Report by independent accountants appointed by shareholders which is included in annual accounts. It states whether the firm's accounts comply with legal requirements and convey faithful picture (in EU: 'give true and fair view') of its results and condition on dates indicated.

Available-for-sale investment. Investment in debt or equity securities that is neither *held-for-trading* nor *held-to-maturity investment*. Investment is carried at *fair value* and unrealised holding gains/losses are deferred in equity (unless investment is impaired).

Bad debt expense. Write-offs of bad debts in the period, net of past bad debts recovered. Where firm provides for estimated bad debts (via 'allowance for bad debts'), net write-offs are adjusted for change in required balance in allowance account.

Balance sheet. Statement of assets, and claims of owners and creditors on those assets, on a stated day.

Bearer share. Share whose owner is not stated on the share certificate. Ownership is transferred on delivery of the certificate. (Cf. *Registered share*.)

Betterment. Expenditure on tangible asset which is expected to increase its productive capacity. Expenditure is capitalised and depreciated.

Bill of exchange. Written agreement between seller/lender and purchaser/borrower setting out terms of payment. Lender draws up bill; borrower signs ('accepts') it.

Bill/billing. Invoice issued by supplier to customer under terms of contract. May be for work already done or in advance of work done.

Bond. Claim on assets of firm. Claim is usually of fixed duration and may offer periodic cash return (interest) to holder. It carries no ownership rights but ranks before claims of owners.

Bonus issue. *See Share dividend* (1).

Book reserve plan. *See Unfunded plan*.

Book value. *See Carrying amount*.

Book value per share. Share capital and reserves attributable to ordinary shareholders divided by ordinary shares outstanding at that date.

Capital. (1) Source of finance (e.g. debt capital) (2) Resources or assets, as in 'working capital' (net trading assets) and 'capital spending' (investment in fixed assets). (3) *Share capital*, as in 'Capital and reserves'.

Capital employed. The sum of *net debt* and *shareholders' equity* – or equivalently, operating assets less operating liabilities.

Capital lease. *See Finance lease*.

Capital reserve. *See Reserve*.

Capital stock. *See Share capital*.

Capital write-down. Reduction in nominal value and cancellation of part/all of share premium in order to eliminate accumulated losses.

Capitalisation issue. *See Share dividend* (1).

Carrying amount. Value at which asset or liability is stated ('carried') in the firm's books – hence also 'book value'.

Cash discount. Percentage reduction in invoiced amount available to credit customer who pays invoice within stated period.

Cash equivalents. Highly liquid investments such as short-term bank deposits and Treasury bills that mature within three months.

Cash flow. *See Operating cash flow*. The term is often used in annual reports and the financial press to mean profit/loss for the period plus depreciation and amortisation.

Cash flow hedge. Transaction in which a company uses hedging instrument (e.g. interest rate swap) to protect itself against changes in future cash flows of hedged item (e.g. variable-rate debt). If hedge is deemed effective, unrealised gains/losses on hedging instrument are deferred in equity until hedged cash flow affects income statement. (Cf. *Fair value hedge, Net investment hedge*.)

Cash flow statement. Statement explaining the change in firm's cash (and cash equivalents) balance in a period. Cash flows may be analysed by activity (operating, investing, financing).

Charge. (1) *See Debit* (b). (2) *See Expense.*

Chart of accounts. Listing of ledger accounts, including a coding system. May include guidance on accounting policies to be followed within the company.

Clean surplus accounting. All revenues and expenses, gains and losses, are recognised in the income statement and none is taken directly to reserves in the balance sheet.

Closing rate method. Method of converting accounts of foreign entity (expressed in local currency) into reporting currency. Assets/liabilities are translated at end-period exchange rate, revenues/expenses at rate prevailing at date of recognition (or end-period rate). Change in exchange rate gives rise to *translation adjustment*. (Cf. *Temporal method.*)

Common stock. *See Ordinary share.*

Completed-contract method. Method of recognising revenue from long-term contract. Revenue (and related expenses) are recognised at the date when the contract – to supply goods or services – is completed. (Cf. *Percentage-of-completion method.*)

Compound instrument. Security which has both debt and equity components.

Comprehensive deferred tax accounting. *See Full deferred tax accounting.*

Comprehensive income. Increase (or decrease) in shareholders' equity, excluding changes in contributed capital and profit distributions, in a period. Includes gains and losses taken directly to reserves in the balance sheet as well as net profit or loss reported in the income statement.

Consignment (inventory). Goods held by third party but still part of firm's inventory.

Consolidation accounting. Where one firm ('parent') controls another ('subsidiary'), the parent prepares additional set of accounts in which its and its subsidiary's accounts are combined. Intercompany balances and unrealised profits/losses on intercompany transactions are eliminated.

Consolidation difference. Difference between purchase price of net assets acquired and their carrying amount in subsidiary's books. It comprises fair value adjustments and *goodwill*. Sometimes used as synonym for goodwill alone. *See also Acquisition accounting.*

Constant purchasing power unit (CPPU). Alternative measurement unit to nominal currency. A firm's accounts are expressed in terms of the buying power of a currency as of a particular date.

Construction in progress. Building or plant which the company is constructing for its own use.

Consumables. *See Supplies.*

Contingent liability (asset). A liability (asset) where the obligation (resource) depends on the occurrence of a future event.

Contingent share issue. Issue of shares which is contingent on one or more future events (e.g. achievement of profit target). Often used by investor company as form of deferred payment to investee firm's former owners. Contingent shares are potentially *dilutive securities.*

Contra account. Account which is offset against (contra to) specific asset or liability. It is often used to write down carrying amount of asset or liability to a value below cost.

Contracts in progress (inventory). Unfinished goods (or services) which firm is contracted to produce. (Cf. *Work-in-progress inventory.*)

Contributory plan. Social security or company-sponsored welfare scheme to which employee as well as employer make cash contributions.

Convertible security. Bond or preference share with conversion option. Option gives holder the right to convert security into specified number of (ordinary) shares at predetermined conversion rate in future period.

Corporation tax. Income tax on companies.

Cost method. Method of accounting for investments. Investment is carried at cost, unless impaired. Income is only recognised when dividend or interest is received. (Cf. *Equity method, Fair value method* and *LOCOM method.*)

Cost of sales. The cost of the goods or services sold in the period. For retailer, 'cost' represents that of the merchandise only; for manufacturer, it includes production costs. In both cases, support costs such as marketing and administration are usually excluded.

Coupon rate. Annual interest paid on a bond (its coupon) divided by its face value. More generally, the stated rate of interest on fixed-rate debt.

Credit (Cr.). Shorthand for 'right-hand side of the account'. May be (a) adjective ('credit entry'), (b) verb ('to credit an account') or (c) noun.

Creditor. Individual or organisation to whom firm owes money, goods or services.

Cumulative catch-up method. Method of accounting for change in accounting policy. Cumulative effect of change in policy is shown as one-line entry on firm's income statement. (Cf. *Prospective method, Restatement method.*)

Current asset. (1) Cash or cash equivalent; or (2) financial asset held for trading purposes and expected to be converted into cash within twelve months; or (3) operating asset expected to be consumed or converted into cash within company's normal operating cycle.

Current cost. *See Replacement value*.

Current liability. Liability that falls due within 12 months or is expected to be settled within company's normal operating cycle.

Current rate method. *See Closing rate method*.

Current ratio. Current assets divided by current liabilities at balance sheet date. The ratio shows the extent to which firm's short-term obligations are covered by its cash and trading assets.

Current service cost. Cost of pension (or other retirement) benefits earned by employees for services rendered in current period.

Current tax expense (benefit). Portion of tax expense which is currently payable (refundable). *See Deferred tax accounting*.

Current value. *See Fair value*.

Days' sales in receivables. Number of days in period divided by receivables turnover in that period. The average credit period taken by customers.

Debit (Dr.). Shorthand for 'left-hand side of the account'. May be (a) adjective ('debit entry'), (b) verb ('to debit an account') or (c) noun.

Debt–equity ratio. *Net debt* divided by shareholders' equity. The ratio is an indicator of financial risk.

Debtor. Individual or organisation which owes money, goods or services to the firm.

Declining-balance method. Method of depreciation. Periodic charge is a predetermined, constant percentage applied to start-of-period carrying amount of fixed asset.

Deductible temporary difference. Excess of carrying amount of liability over its tax value. Excess of tax value of asset over its carrying amount.

Defensive interval. Liquidity measure. End-period cash and near-cash (e.g. *marketable securities, accounts receivable*) divided by next period's expected operating outlays and expressed in days. Shows how long company can continue operating in absence of operating receipts.

Defer. To recognise revenue or expense (and expiry of related liability or asset) after cash is received or paid.

Deferral method. Method of accounting for *tax credit*. Tax credit is deferred (via balance sheet account) and then amortised – and tax expense reduced – over life of related asset. (Cf. *Flow-through method*.)

Deferred tax accounting. Method of accounting for taxes on corporate income. Firm recognises tax impact, now (current tax expense/benefit) and in future (deferred tax expense/benefit), of current period's profit/loss.

Deferred tax asset. Amount of income taxes recoverable in the future as a result of *deductible temporary differences* and tax loss carryforwards. (Alternatively, tax effect of cumulative *timing differences* where expense is recognised earlier (and revenue later) in books than in tax return.)

Deferred tax liability. Amount of income taxes payable in the future as a result of *taxable temporary differences*. (Alternatively, tax effect of cumulative *timing differences* where expense is recognised later (and revenue earlier) in books than in tax return.)

Defined benefit (DB) plan. Pension (or other retirement benefits) plan in which benefits are specified but contributions are not. Plan may be funded or unfunded.

Defined contribution (DC) plan. Funded pension (or other retirement benefits) plan in which contributions are specified but benefits are not. Benefits are function of amount of contributions and fund's investment performance.

Depletion. Using up of exhaustible natural resource.

Depreciable amount. Cost less estimated residual value.

Depreciation. Allocation of cost (or depreciable amount) of tangible fixed asset over its expected useful life in a systematic way. *See also Amortisation*.

Derivative financial instrument. *See Financial instrument*.

Dilutive security. Security which is expected to result in increase in ordinary shares outstanding relative to earnings in the future, thereby reducing reported earnings per share. In-the-money employee share option is dilutive; convertible security is potentially dilutive. *See also Earnings per share*.

Direct costing. *See Variable costing*.

Direct financing lease. *Finance lease* in which lessor acquires asset and leases it to lessee. Lessor is usually a financial institution and lease is alternative to loan finance.

Discount (on bonds). Excess of maturity value of debt securities (or investment in them) over price at date of issuance (or purchase).

Discrete approach. Approach to preparation of interim accounts. Each interim period is considered a separate accounting period. Firm applies same accounting principles in both interim and annual accounts. (Cf. *Integral approach*.)

Dividend. Distribution to firm's shareholders – usually, from its profits and in cash.

Dividend cover. Earnings per share divided by cash dividend per share.

Dividend method. *See Cost method*.

Draft. *See Bill of exchange.*
Dual reporting. *See Separate reporting.*

Earnings. *See Result.*
Earnings per share (EPS). Net profit attributable to ordinary shareholders, divided by weighted average ordinary shares outstanding in the period. Firms may publish two types of EPS:
– *Basic EPS*. EPS calculation as above. No adjustment is made for *dilutive securities*.
– *Diluted EPS*. Hypothetical earnings per share. Profit and shares outstanding are adjusted for effect of *dilutive securities*.
Earnings yield. Earnings per share divided by end-period market price of ordinary share. Reciprocal of *price–earnings ratio*.
Ebit/Ebitda. Earnings before interest and tax (Ebit) and depreciation and amortisation (Ebitda). Earnings figures used in measuring corporate financial performance. Ebitda is popular where net profit is corrupted as a performance measure by effect of different tax systems and accounting rules across countries.
Economic value added. Operating profit less capital charge. Capital charge is product of weighted average cost of capital and invested capital (i.e. debt and equity capital). Operating profit and invested capital are adjusted to remove effects of conservative accounting rules. EVA is alternative performance indicator to *return on assets*.
Effective rate (of interest). *See Yield to maturity.*
Effective tax rate. Income tax expense divided by before-tax profit. A measure of the current and future tax burden on that profit.
Employee share option (ESO). Right to buy employer-firm's shares at predetermined price during specified future period. Right is earned after completion of service period (fixed ESO) or once performance goals are met (performance-based ESO).
Equity. Claim (of owner or creditor) on assets of firm (e.g. equities = assets). The term is often restricted to owners' claims only (e.g. equity capital, equity investments).
Equity accounting/equity method. Method of accounting for certain equity investments (in particular, *associates* in consolidated accounts). Investor firm records its share of ('equity in') investee's profit or loss in its income statement. The carrying amount of the investment in its books approximates its share of investee's net assets. (Cf. *Cost method, Fair value method, LOCOM method.*)
ESOP. Employee share ownership plan. Company sets up (and finances) trust that buys its shares. Trust allocates shares to employees but holds them until employees qualify for them (e.g. after service period, on retirement, etc.).
Exchange difference. General term for foreign currency exchange gain/loss. *See Transaction gain/loss, Translation gain/loss* and *Translation adjustment.*
Exercise price. Price at which holder of option or warrant can buy firm's shares.
Expenditure. Outlay of cash.
Expense. Cost associated with generation of revenue in a period. Cost can arise from consumption of asset or incurrence of liability.
Extraordinary. (1) General meaning: income, expense, gain or loss from event which is not part of firm's ordinary activities. (2) Technical meaning (according to international accounting standards): as in (1) but, in addition, the underlying event is unusual in nature and not expected to recur (e.g. flood in Sahara).

Face value. *See Nominal value.*
Factoring (of receivables). Transfer by firm of part/all of its receivables to outside party ('factor') for cash. Factor may have recourse to firm (i.e. be compensated by firm) if receivables are not collectible.
Fair value. General term indicating price of asset or liability today. Price may be determined by reference to market value, replacement value or present value (of expected future cash flows).
Fair value hedge. Transaction in which a company uses hedging instrument (e.g. commodity futures contract) to protect itself against changes in fair value of hedged item (e.g. stocks of commodity). Unrealised gains/losses on hedging instrument are recognised in income as they arise. (Cf. *Cash flow hedge, Net investment hedge.*)
Fair value method. Method of accounting for investments. Investment is carried at market value or at a current valuation. Unrealised gains and losses are recognised as they arise – in income statement or as separate item in shareholders' equity. (Cf. *Cost method, Equity method, LOCOM method.*)
FIFO. 'First in, first out'. Assumption about the flow of production or merchandise costs under historical cost accounting when prices change. The earliest costs are assigned to products sold; the most recent are assigned to ending inventory. (Cf. *LIFO, WAC.*)
Final salary plan. Pension plan in which benefits are linked to employee's pre-retirement salary. *See Defined benefit plan.*
Finance lease. Lease which is, in substance, the purchase of an asset with debt.
Financial fixed asset. Long-term investment (in debt or equity securities) or long-term loan/receivable.

Financial instrument. Any contract that gives rise to a financial asset for one party and a financial liability or equity instrument for another. Financial instruments are 'primary' (e.g. account receivable/payable; financial investment/share capital) or 'derivative' (e.g. financial option, interest rate swap) – in which part of financial risk attached to primary instrument is transferred.

Financing cash flow. Net amount of cash in/outflows on financing activities. These include issuance of debt and equity capital, their repurchase or retirement, dividends and, in some cases, interest paid. (Interest paid may be shown as operating outflow.)

Finished goods (inventory). Products completed but not yet sold.

Fixed asset. Asset used on a continuing basis to support firm's business.

Fixed charge coverage ratio. Profit before interest and tax expense divided by interest and other scheduled financial payments in a period. A more severe test of income leverage than *times interest earned*.

Flow-through method. Method of accounting for *tax credit*. Entire tax credit is deducted from income tax expense in period it is received. (Cf. *Deferral method*.)

Free cash flow. Operating cash flow less capital expenditures. Cash flow measure used in corporate valuations and risk assessment.

Full consolidation. *See Global consolidation*.

Full cost accounting. Method of accounting for exploration costs in oil and gas industry. All exploration costs – of dry as well as oil-producing wells – within hydrocarbon-producing area are capitalised. Costs are amortised, on production basis, over expected lives of oil-producing wells. (Cf. *Successful efforts accounting*.)

Full deferred tax accounting. Dominant approach to *deferred tax accounting*. Firm recognises tax effect of all *timing* or *temporary differences*.

Functional currency. Currency which dominates foreign entity's operations. If the local currency, entity is autonomous and *closing rate method* (of translation) is used. If the parent company's currency, entity is satellite of parent and *temporal method* is used.

Funded plan. Pension (or other retirement benefits) plan in which employer (and, if contributory, employees) make periodic contributions to entity separate from firm. Entity is responsible for investment of contributions and payment of pensions (or other retirement benefits).

Funds flow statement. Statement explaining the change in firm's working capital in a period.

Funds from operations. Profit/loss for the period adjusted for revenues and expenses that do not involve working capital.

Gain. Increase in net assets as a result of (1) transaction which is not part of firm's normal activities (gain on disposal of fixed asset); (2) transaction which is non-reciprocal in nature (windfall gain); or (3) upward (downward) adjustment to carrying amount of asset (liability) (holding gain).

Gearing. *See Leverage*.

General ledger. Collection of all ledger accounts.

Global consolidation. Combination of 100% of subsidiary's assets and liabilities, revenues and expenses, with those of the parent company, even when latter owns less than 100% of subsidiary's share capital. *See also Minority interest*.

Going concern assumption. Fundamental accounting principle. Assumption that firm will be able to continue trading, without threat to its existence, for the foreseeable future.

Goodwill. Excess of purchase price over fair value of the net assets of a business or company acquired. Shown as intangible asset if capitalised. Where fair value of net assets required exceeds purchase price, difference is known as 'negative goodwill'.

Gross margin ratio. Gross profit as percentage of sales revenue.

Gross profit. Excess of sales revenue over cost of sales.

Hedge accounting. Method of accounting for financial assets and liabilities. Asset or liability designated as hedging instrument is accounted for in same way as item being hedged ('hedged item').

Held-for-trading investment. Investment in debt or equity securities that investor company holds for speculative or trading reasons. Investment is carried at *fair value* and unrealised holding gains/losses are recognised in income as they arise. (Cf. *Available-for-sale investment, Held-to-maturity investment*.)

Held-to-maturity investment. Investment in debt securities that investor company intends to hold to maturity. Investment is carried at *amortised cost*. (Cf. *Available-for-sale investment, Held-for-trading investment*.)

Historical cost. Cost of purchasing or producing an asset. The cash received when a liability is incurred.

Holding gain/loss. Difference between *fair value* and carrying amount of asset (or liability).

Hybrid security. *See Compound instrument*.

Impairment. Fall in *recoverable amount* of fixed asset below its carrying amount.

Income. *See* (1) *Result* (e.g. net income for the year) and (2) *Revenue* (e.g. interest revenue).

Income statement. Statement showing firm's accomplishments (increases in net assets) and related efforts (decreases in net assets) from operating and incidental activities.

Increasing-charge method. Depreciation charge increases each period in a systematic way. *See Annuity method*.

Instalment method. Method of revenue recognition. Revenue (and related expenses) are recognised on a proportionate basis as the customer pays each instalment of the contract amount.

Instalment sale. Sale where title to good passes on delivery but payment is by scheduled instalment.

Intangible asset. Non-monetary fixed asset without physical substance and whose existence is, in most cases, evidenced by contract (e.g. purchased patent, trademark, licence). *See also Goodwill*.

Integral approach. Approach to preparation of interim accounts. Fundamental accounting period is the year; each interim period is a sub-part of it. Annual revenues and expenses are allocated to interim periods within year. (Cf. *Discrete approach*.)

Interest cover. *See Times interest earned*.

Interest method. Method of amortising debt *discount/ premium* arising at issuance (or purchase). Interest expense (income) is a constant percentage of start-of-period *carrying amount* of debt (investment in debt securities). Difference between interest expense (income) and interest paid (received) in period is amortised discount/premium.

Interim report. Financial report issued by publicly quoted company within its financial year – sometimes quarterly, most commonly in Europe half-yearly. Report contains condensed accounts – and management review of firm's activities – for interim period and year to date.

Interperiod tax allocation. *See Deferred tax accounting*.

Intrinsic value (of option). Excess of market price of share over exercise price of option on that share.

Inventory. For retailer/wholesaler, it comprises goods awaiting sale and supplies. For manufacturer, it comprises, in addition, raw materials and – this applies to some service providers too – products in the course of production. Advance payments to suppliers ('payments on account') are also included in this asset category.

Inventory profit/loss. *See Realised holding gain/loss*.

Inventory turnover. *Cost of sales* (or sales revenue) divided by average inventory in the period. It measures the speed with which a firm converts inputs into output – or, in the case of a retailer, merchandise purchases into sales.

Investing cash flow. Net amount of cash in/outflows on investing activities. These include the purchase and disposal of tangible, intangible and financial fixed assets, and dividends and interest received. (Dividends and interest received may be shown as operating inflows.)

Journal. Document in which all transactions are recorded initially – and in chronological order.

Ledger account. Summary record of all the accounting transactions and events affecting a particular category of asset, liability or shareholders' equity.

Legal reserve. Reserve to which firm transfers, by law, specified percentage of annual profits until minimum required level is reached.

Leverage. Ratio of fixed operating costs to total operating costs ('operating leverage') or of interest-bearing liabilities to shareholder's equity ('financial leverage'). Company uses capital-intensive production methods or debt-intensive financing to lever up returns (and risk) or owners.

Liability. Obligation of firm arising from past exchange. Settlement involves it transferring resources to outside party. Liabilities, in total, are the claims of creditors to a firm's assets.

Liability method. Method of measuring deferred tax asset/liability. Current tax rate is applied to *deductible/ taxable temporary differences* (or cumulative *timing differences*).

LIFO. 'Last in, first out'. Assumption about the flow of production or merchandise costs under historical cost accounting when prices change. The earliest costs are assigned to ending inventory; the most recent are assigned to products sold. (Cf. *FIFO, WAC*.)

Linear depreciation. *See Straight-line method*.

Liquidity. Cash and near-cash resources relative to short-term liabilities as of a particular date. Liquidity ratios (Cf. *current ratio, quick ratio*) measure firm's ability to pay short-term liabilities when they fall due.

LOCOM (method). 'Lower of cost or market'. Method of valuing inventories and financial investments. Asset is stated at the lower of its historical cost or its current market value. In the case of inventories, 'market' may be replacement cost. In the case of investments, 'market' may be determined on individual security or aggregate basis ('portfolio LOCOM'). (Cf. *Cost method, Equity method, Fair value method*.)

Loss. Decrease in net assets as a result of (1) transaction which is not part of firm's normal activities (loss on disposal of fixed asset); (2) transaction which is non-reciprocal in nature (loss from fire damage); (3) downward (upward) adjustment to carrying amount of asset (liability) (holding loss). *See also* (4) *Result* (e.g. loss for year).

Market value. Cash (or equivalent) expected to be received from selling an asset today in an orderly market. Cash required to settle a liability today.

Marketable securities. Debt and equity securities that can be traded in an active market. Usually classified as current asset.

Memorandum account. A summary record of transactions or events which have not (yet) been recognised in the firm's accounts.

Merchandise inventory. Goods held for resale.

Merger accounting. Method of accounting for business combination. The merging firms combine assets and liabilities at existing carrying amounts and revenues and expenses from start of year of merger. (Cf. *Acquisition accounting*.)

Minority interest. Share of subsidiary's net assets and of its profit or loss for the year which is attributable to shareholders other than those of parent company. Parent company shareholders have a majority interest; other shareholders have a minority interest.

Monetary asset. Asset where the cash to be received is contractually fixed.

Monetary liability. Liability where the cash to be paid is contractually fixed.

Money purchase (pension) plan. See *Defined contribution plan*.

Net assets. Total assets less total liabilities. Equivalent to shareholders' equity.

Net book value. Cost less accumulated amortisation/ depreciation of intangible/tangible fixed asset.

Net cash flow. The net change in cash and cash equivalents in the period (i.e. Operating cash flow +/– Investing cash flow +/– Financing cash flow).

Net debt. Interest-bearing liabilities less cash and *marketable securities*.

Net income. See *Net profit*.

Net investment hedge. Transaction in which a company uses hedging instrument (e.g. foreign currency loan) to protect itself against the effect of exchange rate changes on the carrying amount of a foreign investment. Unreaslised gains/losses on hedging instrument are deferred in equity until company disposes of investment (Cf. *Cash flow hedge, Fair value hedge*.)

Net profit. After-tax profit (for the period).

Net worth. See *Net assets*.

Nominal ledger. See *General ledger*.

Nominal value. Monetary amount assigned to bond or share when authorised. Amount is stated on bond or share certificate (hence 'face value').

Non-contributory plan. Social security or company-sponsored welfare scheme to which only employer makes cash contributions.

Note payable. Amount owed by firm to supplier under formal written agreement. (Cf. *Account payable*.)

Note receivable. Amount owed to firm by customer under formal written agreement. (Cf. *Account receivable* and also *Bill of exchange* and *Promissory note*.)

Off-balance-sheet debt. Debt which is not shown as a liability on the face of the balance sheet. It may be disclosed in the notes (e.g. financial commitments) or reported elsewhere on the balance sheet (e.g. as equity, asset sale, etc.).

On credit. Delayed payment terms granted by seller of goods or services to buyer. Also known as 'on (open) account'.

One-line consolidation. Effect of accounting for financial investment by *equity method*. Investor firm shows as one-line entry on balance sheet (income statement) its share of investee's net assets (profit or loss).

Operating cash flow. Net amount of cash in/outflows relating to main revenue-producing activities of firm. Corporate income tax payments (or refunds) are treated as operating flows or are shown separately.

Operating lease. Any lease other than a *finance lease*. Lease is treated as a rental transaction for accounting purposes.

Option price. See *Exercise price*.

Ordinary share. Ownership claim on firm's assets. Claim is a residual one, i.e. after claims of creditors have been met. Ordinary shareholder usually has right to share in management of company (by voting at shareholders' meetings) and in its earnings (via dividends).

Own shares. Shares bought back by firm and held 'in treasury' for later resale.

Own work capitalised. Costs incurred in period which relate to production of fixed asset for firm's own use. Costs are capitalised and, when asset is completed, are amortised over its useful life.

Owners' equity. See *Shareholders' equity*.

Par value. See *Nominal value*.

Partial deferred tax accounting. Minority approach to *deferred tax accounting*. Firm recognises tax effect of only those *timing/temporary differences* that are expected to crystallise (i.e. result in higher/lower tax bills) in foreseeable future.

Participating interest. Large (and influential) minority shareholding in another firm. Investor company has 'participating interest' in investee; investee firm is investor's *associate*.

Past service cost. Cost of pension benefits granted for past service by employees when plan is first adopted or when it is amended.

Payment on account. Advance payment for purchase of asset (usually, inventory or tangible asset).

Payout ratio. Cash dividend per share as percentage of earnings per share. Reciprocal of *dividend cover*.

Percentage-of-completion method. Method of recognising revenue from long-term contract. Revenue (and related expenses) are recognised during the term of the contract, based on the percentage of work completed during the period. (Cf. *Completed-contract method*.)

Period cost. Cost which is charged as expense in the period in which it is incurred.

Periodic system. System of inventory record-keeping in which amounts on hand and consumed in period – and their costs – are determined periodically (e.g. when inventories are counted). (Cf. *Perpetual system*.)

Permanent difference. Difference between accounting profit and taxable profit attributable to revenues/expenses not recognised in tax return (e.g. non-deductible expenses, tax-exempt income) or to items on tax return not recognised in books.

Perpetual system. System of inventory record-keeping in which inventory records are updated continuously to yield current information about amounts on hand and consumed in period – and about their costs. (Cf. *Periodic system*.)

Phantom shares. Notional shares awarded to employees – usually of unquoted firms – for meeting performance goals. Notional share yields dividends and capital growth according to predetermined formula.

Pooling-of-interests method. *See Merger accounting*.

Portfolio LOCOM. *See LOCOM*.

Potential ordinary share. *See Dilutive security*.

Preference share/preferred stock. Ownership claim on firm's assets which carries special rights (usually in form of priority over ordinary shareholders in profit distribution).

Premium (on bonds). Excess of price of debt securities (or investment in them) at date of issuance (or purchase) over maturity value.

Prepayment. Asset which is acquired as a result of advance payment for good or service.

Present value. Expected future cash flows attributable to asset or liability, discounted to present time.

Price–earnings ratio. End-period market price of ordinary share divided by earnings per share (of preceding 12 months). Stock market indicator of expected profit growth.

Price-to-book ratio. End-period market price of ordinary share divided by its end-period book value. Per-share book value is (ordinary) *shareholders' equity* divided by ordinary shares outstanding. Stock market indicator of expected profit growth.

Prior period adjustment. Adjustment to start-of-period retained profits (a) to correct earlier error, (b) to implement retroactive legislation, or (c) to otherwise restate prior years' accounts (e.g. for change in accounting policy).

Prior service cost. *See Past service cost*.

Product cost. Cost which is capitalised in inventory and not expensed (as cost of sales) until the related product is sold.

Pro forma. Term applied to hypothetical accounting numbers that are prepared under alternative accounting policies or that are based on alternative assumptions about company's operating activities.

Profit. *See* (1) *Gain*, as in 'profit on disposal of fixed asset', 'windfall profit' and 'inventory profit'; and (2) *Result* (e.g. profit for year).

Profit and loss account. UK terms for (1) *Income statement* and (2) *Retained profits*.

Profit margin (ratio). Profit (operating, before-tax profit, or net profit) as percentage of sales revenue.

Profit reserve. *See Reserve*.

Projected benefit obligation. Measure of pension plan's liability (US). Actuarial present value of vested and non-vested benefits (computed under required *ABV method*), based on expected future salary levels.

Projected benefit valuation (PBV) method. Actuarial method of determining cost of pension (or other retirement) benefits. Benefits employee will earn during expected service period with firm are estimated and the cost is then spread over that period.

Promissory note. Written agreement between seller/lender and purchaser/borrower setting out terms of payment. Borrower 'writes' note (makes promise to pay amount x on day y); lender is beneficiary.

Proportionate consolidation. Method of accounting for incorporated joint ventures. Investor company consolidates its proportionate share of venture's assets and liabilities, revenues and expenses.

Pro-rata consolidation. *See Proportionate consolidation*.

Prospective method. Method of accounting for change in accounting policy. Only accounts of current and future periods are adjusted for effect of change. (Cf. *Cumulative catch-up method, Restatement method*.)

Provision. (1) Estimated liability (e.g. provision for pension costs). (2) Valuation adjustment to asset (e.g. provision for bad debts). (3) Accrued expense (e.g. provision for repairs and maintenance).

Purchase method. *See Acquisition accounting*.

Quantity discount. Percentage reduction in listed price quoted by seller where number of items purchased by buyer in a period exceeds predetermined level.

Quick ratio. Current assets less inventories, divided by current liabilities. A more severe test of liquidity than the current ratio.

Raw materials (inventory). Materials used in production process and traceable directly to products.

Realisable value. Amount of cash (or equivalent) expected to be obtained by selling asset today in orderly market.

Realised holding gain/loss. Difference between current value and historical cost of asset (e.g. inventory, plant, investment) sold or consumed in the period. Gain (loss) shows the benefit (cost) of acquiring asset when the price was less (more) than the current price, a benefit which the firm captures ('realises') through sale or use. (Term may also be applied to liabilities.)

Receipt. Inflow of cash.

Receivables turnover. Revenue from credit sales divided by average accounts receivable. The ratio measures the speed with which the firm collects cash from its credit customers.

Recoverable amount. Higher of net selling price or value in use. Value in use is present value of estimated future cash flows generated by asset (including ultimate disposal). *See Impairment.*

Reducing-charge method. Method of depreciation. *See Declining-balance method.*

Registered share. Share whose owner (or nominee) is stated on share certificate. Ownership is only transferred when legal requirements regarding registration have been met. (Cf. *Bearer share.*)

Related party. Two parties are 'related' if one is able to control, or exercise significant influence over, the other. Individual (e.g. as shareholder) can be a related party of a company.

Replacement value. Cost today of purchasing or producing a similar asset. Cash obtained if the same obligation were incurred today.

Reporting currency. Parent company's currency (i.e. currency in which foreign entity's accounts are expressed after translation).

Reserve. Two general meanings: (1) contributed capital in excess of *share capital* (as in 'capital reserve' or *share premium*); (2) appropriated profits – as in 'profit reserves' or 'revenue reserves'. These include earned capital retained in business for legal reasons (e.g. legal reserve, statutory reserve) or economic ones (e.g. retained profits). Term also used in connection with: (3) surplus on revaluation of assets (e.g. revaluation reserve); and (4) deliberate understatement of firm's net assets by management (e.g. hidden reserve). Reserves in 'Capital and reserves' includes (1), (2) and (3) above. Legal rules determine which reserves are

'distributable' and 'non-distributable'. Term also used as synonym for 'provision' or 'allowance' (e.g. reserve for bad debts).

Residual value. Amount recoverable from disposal of tangible or intangible fixed asset at the end of its expected useful life.

Restatement method. Method of accounting for change in accounting policy. Prior years' accounts are restated as if new policy had been applied from the beginning. (Cf. *Cumulative catch-up method, Prospective method.*)

Restricted reserve. Reserve whose distribution is restricted under legal rules.

Restricted shares. Shares (or other equity instruments) granted directly to employee or purchasable at deep discount – but with vesting restriction. Vesting occurs only after service period has elapsed or performance goals have been met. Term also applies to shares where contract or law restricts sale for specified period.

Result. The firm's total revenues less expenses – plus gains less losses – for the period. Can also be used to describe a subset of revenues less expenses (e.g. operating result).

Retained earnings. *See Retained profits.*

Retained profits. Profits of current and prior periods which have been reinvested in the firm and not distributed.

Return on assets. After-tax operating profit as percentage of average assets. 'Assets' may be defined more narrowly as 'net operating assets'. The ratio measures the success with which managers have used firm's assets in a period.

Return on equity. Net profit attributable to ordinary shareholders as percentage of average ordinary shareholders' equity. The ratio measures the success with which managers have used funds provided by firm's owners in a period.

Revenue. Accomplishments of firm – from operating activities (e.g. sales revenue) or financial activities (e.g. interest revenue) – during a period.

Revenue reserve. *See Reserve.*

Reverse share split. Consolidation of shares. New shares carry higher nominal value than old ones but total nominal value of share capital is unchanged. (Cf. *Share split.*)

Rights issue. Issue of shares in which existing shareholders have right to subscribe first to the issue, in proportion to their holdings (and thereby preserve their proportionate stake in the firm).

Sales allowance. Adjustment to sales revenue for allowance against value of future purchases (e.g. vouchers) which the firm gives to customer who receives faulty goods or services.

Sales return. Adjustment to sales revenue for goods returned by customer.

Sales-type lease. *Finance lease* in which manufacturer/dealer leases asset to customer in place of direct sale. Lessor accounts for lease as asset sale with extended financing.

Salvage value. *See Residual value.*

Scrip dividend. *See Share dividend* (2).

Segment. Distinguishable component of firm's operations. Segmentation can be by product or geographical area (in which firm's products are produced or sold).

Separate reporting. Profit in published accounts is calculated according to accounting methods which are independent of those used to calculate profit in tax return.

Share. *See Ordinary share* and *Preference share.*

Share appreciation right. Right to shares or cash, based on increase in market value of share (or other equity instrument) over predetermined period.

Share capital. Nominal value of ordinary and preference shares which firm has issued. Strictly, the term is 'issued share capital' but prefix is often omitted. Other prefixes used in conjunction with 'shares' or 'share capital' are:
- *authorised* – shares which firm is permitted to issue according to its statutes;
- *subscribed* – shares applied for by investors;
- *called-up* – shares for which payment has been demanded by issuing firm;
- *outstanding* – issued shares held by outside investors. Those held by firm itself ('own shares') are excluded.

Share dividend. (1) Non-elective. Issue of free shares to shareholders, in proportion to their existing holdings, by means of capitalisation of reserves. (2) Elective (or optional). Profit distribution which shareholder elects to take in form of shares rather than cash.

Share premium. Market value of issued shares at time of issuance less their nominal value.

Share split. Subdivision of shares. New shares carry lower nominal value than old ones but total nominal value of share capital is unchanged.

Shareholders' equity. Claims of owners to firm's assets. Claims are residual, i.e. those of creditors take preference. Comprises share capital and reserves.

Solvency. Assets relative to liabilities as of a particular date. Solvency ratios (cf. *debt–equity ratio, times interest earned*) measure firm's ability to service its short- and long-term liabilities – or settle them when they fall due.

Specific identification. Method of determining costs of sales and inventory. Each item of inventory is tagged with its actual cost of purchase or production.

Spread. Difference between the return on a company's (operating) assets and the cost of debt used to finance them.

Stock. (1) Synonym for *Inventory*. (2) Debt securities ('loan stock'). (3) Synonym for *Share* ('common stock').

Stock dividend. *See Share dividend.*

Stockholders' equity. *See Shareholders' equity.*

Stockholding gain/loss. *Realised holding gain/loss* with respect to inventory.

Straight-line method. Method of depreciation of intangible/tangible fixed assets and of amortisation of bond discount/premium. Asset's depreciable amount is allocated evenly over its expected useful life; discount or premium is allocated evenly over period to maturity. Depreciation/amortisation charge is a constant amount each period.

Subsidiary. Investee company which the investor firm controls, usually as a result of majority (>50%) ownership of investee's voting shares.

Successful efforts accounting. Method of accounting for exploration costs of oil and gas companies. During exploration, all costs are capitalised. Results of exploration are then evaluated. Exploration costs of oil/gas producing wells ('successful efforts') are capitalised (and amortised over expected life) while those of dry wells are written off. (Cf. *Full cost accounting*.)

Sum-of-years'-digits (SoYD) method. Method of depreciation. Depreciation rate (applied to depreciable amount) is: the remaining number of years of asset's expected useful life divided by its SoYD. To calculate the SoYD, express the asset's life in digits and then sum them.

Supplies. Materials used in production and supporting activities (e.g. sales and administration) of the firm. In the case of production activities, materials are incidental to them and not traceable to products.

Synthetic debt. Debt whose risk characteristics have been changed – usually through swap arrangement.

Tangible fixed asset. Fixed asset which has physical substance. Examples are land, buildings, plant and equipment, fixtures and fittings, tools. Advance payments for such assets (payments on account) and buildings and plant under construction by firm are also included in this category.

Tax credit. Amount by which taxpayer can directly reduce tax liability in period as a result of, for example, investment in qualifying plant and equipment, R&D,

job creation. (It is a credit against government's tax receivable.)

Taxable profit. Taxable revenues less tax-deductible expenses.

Taxable temporary difference. Excess of carrying amount of asset over its tax base. Excess of tax base of liability over its carrying amount.

Taxes payable accounting. Method of accounting for taxes on corporate income. Firm recognises only tax impact now of current period's profit/loss. (Cf. *Deferred tax accounting*.)

Temporal method. Method of converting accounts of foreign entity (expressed in local currency) into reporting currency. Monetary assets/liabilities are translated at end-period exchange rate; non-monetary assets/liabilities at exchange rate appropriate to measurement basis used; revenues/expenses at rate prevailing when underlying event took place. Change in exchange rate gives rise to *translation gain/loss*. (Cf. *Closing rate method*.)

Temporary difference. Difference between tax base and carrying amount of asset or liability.

Third party (interest). *See Minority interest.*

Time value (of option). Fair value of option less its *intrinsic value*.

Times interest earned. Profit before interest and tax expense divided by interest payments in period. The ratio shows income cover for firm's debt servicing costs.

Timing difference. Revenue or expense recognised in books and tax return in different periods.

Trade creditors. *See Account payable.*

Trade debtors. *See Account receivable.*

Transaction gain/loss. Effect of change in exchange rate on unhedged foreign currency receivables and payables.

Translation adjustment. Effect, in reporting currency, of change in exchange rate on net assets of foreign entity (and movement in them) over a period. Taken to parent company's reserves and not recognised in income until foreign entity is sold.

Translation gain/loss. Effect, in reporting currency, of change in exchange rate on net monetary assets of foreign entity (and movement in them) over a period. Recognised in parent company's income immediately.

Treasury stock. *See Own shares.*

Treasury stock method. Method of calculating effect of options/warrants on diluted earnings per share. Firm assumes cash received on exercise of share options or warrants is used to buy back its own shares.

Trial balance. Listing of debit and credit balances in ledger accounts at end of financial period to check that balance totals agree.

Turnover. (1) Revenues from all operating activities (UK term). (2) Measure of intensity of asset use.

Unfunded plan. *Defined benefit plan* in which employer makes provision (or 'book reserve') for cost of pension (or other retirement) benefits but does not contribute cash to separate fund to meet future liabilities.

Uniform reporting. Profit in published accounts is calculated according to same accounting methods as those used in the calculation of profit in tax return.

Units-of-production method. Method of depreciation based on output or usage. Depreciation rate (applied to depreciable amount) is: output (or usage) of asset in the period divided by the total expected output (or usage) over its useful life.

Unrealised holding gain/loss. Difference between current value and historical cost of assets (e.g. inventory, plant, investment) held by firm at balance sheet date. Gain (loss) shows the benefit (cost) of acquiring asset when the price was less (more) than the current price.

Valuation allowance. Adjustment to reduce carrying amount of asset (e.g. inventory, investments, deferred tax) to amount that management consider is recoverable in future years.

Variable costing. Minority method of costing inventory in firm's published accounts. End-period work in progress and finished goods are measured at variable production cost. Fixed production costs are treated as period costs.

Vested. Attached to. Right to retirement benefits (pension) or shares (e.g. employee share options) is not conditional on continued service with the firm or job performance.

WAC. 'Weighted average cost'. Assumption about the flow of production or merchandise costs under historical cost accounting when prices change. Goods sold and in inventory are costed at weighted average cost per unit. Unit WAC is total cost of units available for use or sale divided by their number. (Cf. *FIFO, LIFO*.)

Warrant. Long-term call option. Right to buy specified number of shares at predetermined price in future period.

Work-in-progress (inventory). Products in course of manufacture or processing.

Working capital. Current assets less current liabilities.

Yield to maturity. Discount rate which equates present value of future payments under debt agreement to debt's current market value (current yield) or market value at date of issuance (historical yield).

Suggestions for further reading

You may wish to study in more depth topics we discuss in the book. The following are English-language references that could be useful to you. Check that the edition you use is the latest. Changes to accounting and reporting rules, at both the national and international levels, are frequent. The edition cited is the most recent one known to the author.

International accounting standards

- International Accounting Standards Board, *International Accounting Standards*, London: IASB. (This contains the text of all approved IAS and, since 2002, International Financial Reporting Standards (IFRS) as well as interpretations of IAS and IFRS. It's updated yearly. Information about proposed new and amended standards can be found on the IASB's website, www.iasb.org.uk).
- Epstein, B.J. and Mirza, A.A. (2003), *IAS 2003: Interpretation and Application of International Accounting Standards*, New York: John Wiley. (This explains and illustrates IAS and IFRS in considerable detail. Again, it's updated yearly.)

The major international accounting firms provide up-to-date information about the IASB's activities and IAS-related publications on their websites. Deloitte Touche Tohmatsu has a dedicated site for this purpose (www.iasplus.com).

Accounting and reporting practices in individual countries

There are a number of reference books in this area. Two with worldwide coverage are:

- Ordelheide, D. and KPMG (eds) (2001), *Transnational Accounting* (3 vols), 2nd edition, Basingstoke/New York: Palgrave. (Fourteen EU countries, Argentina, Australia, Canada, Japan and the USA are covered. There are separate chapters on individual company accounts and group accounts for each country.)
- Orsini, L.L., Gould, J.D., McAllister, J.P. and Parikh, R.N. (eds), *World Accounting* (3 vols), New York: Matthew Bender & Co. (Loose-leaf reference guide – with regular updates. Broader coverage than

Ordelheide. There are chapters on the larger emerging economies (Brazil, China, India and Mexico) and the four 'Asian tigers' (Hong Kong, Singapore, South Korea and Taiwan). Each country chapter contains a section on auditing as well as accounting practices.)

Some accounting guides have a regional focus. One that deals with national practices in Europe is:

- Alexander, D. and Archer, S. (eds) (2001), *European Accounting Guide*, 4th edition, New York: Aspen Law & Business. (The guide has separate chapters on almost all European countries. It is particularly strong on central and eastern Europe, with individual chapters on the Baltic States, Belarus, the Czech Republic, Hungary, Poland and the Russian Federation. Each chapter contains specimen financial statements taken from the published accounts of a company in that country.)

Some books combine country studies with comparative analysis of accounting practices. One widely cited example is:

- Nobes, C.W. and Parker, R.H. (eds) (2002), *Comparative International Accounting*, 7th edition, London: FT/Prentice Hall. (As with other accounting guides, there are separate chapters on accounting practices in particular countries, e.g. France, Germany, Japan, the USA. In addition, there are chapters on specific topics such as consolidation, liabilities, and foreign currency translation in which intercountry differences in these areas are examined.)

Because of the growing importance of international accounting standards, there is an increasing amount of published material that compares the accounting and reporting practices in a particular country with those laid down by IAS. An alternative approach – adopted by IFAD – is to focus on where national rules differ from IAS.

- International Forum on Accountancy Development (2002), *GAAP 2001: A Survey of National Accounting Rules in 53 Countries*, available at the IFAD website (www.ifad.net). (This contains an overview of differences between national written rules and IAS in 80 key areas of accounting and is effective as of end-2001.)

The above books and websites contain summaries of accounting and reporting requirements in individual countries. To gain a fuller understanding of these requirements, the original pronouncements of regulatory agencies in each country – and if necessary, independent commentaries on them – should be consulted.

Consider, for example, US accounting and reporting requirements. The Financial Accounting Standards Board (www.fasb.org) publishes a 'Current text' of its accounting standards (and technical bulletins) which is updated yearly. Companies that issue securities to the US public or are listed on a US stock exchange must observe the filing requirements of the Securities and Exchange Commission (www.sec.gov) which are contained in its 'Regulations S–X'.

Information about EU directives and regulations can be found on the European Commission's website (www.europa.eu.int). Navigating this website can be a daunting experience. The FEE's website (www.fee.be) provides easier access to EU accounting-related documents. The FEE (Fédération des Experts Comptables Européens) is a 'representative organisation for the accountancy profession in Europe' and serves some 41 professional bodies in 29 countries.

Business guides

As noted in the text, a country's accounting and reporting practices are shaped by many forces. Among them are its legal system, tax code and the ownership structure of its firms. Useful sources of information on a country's business environment are the business guides (*Doing Business In . . .*) published by certain international accounting and law firms. Their names and websites are listed below:

- BDO International (www.intax.co.uk)
- HLB International (www.hlbi.com)
- Lex Mundi (a worldwide organisation of independent law firms) (*see* www.hg.org)
- PricewaterhouseCoopers (www.pwcglobal.com)

Remember that an important audience for these guides are client firms that plan to set up or have already set up operations abroad.

Tax

The International Bureau of Fiscal Documentation produces loose-leaf taxation guides which contain more detailed information about national tax regimes than that available in the above 'business guides'. These guides cover the various regions of the world e.g. Europe, Asia-Pacific, Africa, and are regularly updated. Their 'Guides to European Taxation' series consists of six volumes. One of them is devoted to corporate tax:

- International Bureau of Fiscal Documentation, *Guides to European Taxation. Vol. II: The Taxation of Companies in Europe*, Amsterdam: IBFD.

Financial statement analysis

The following books are widely used in courses on financial statement analysis. Not surprisingly, the first three have a US slant.

- Palepu, K., Healy, P. and Bernard, V. (2000), *Business Analysis and Valuation*, 2nd edition, Cincinnati: Southwestern.
- Penman, S.H. (2001), *Financial Statement Analysis and Security Valuation*, New York: McGraw-Hill.
- Stickney, C.P. and Brown, P.R. (1999), *Financial Reporting and Statement Analysis*, 4th edition, Fort Worth, TX: Dryden Press.
- Walton, P. (2000), *Financial Statement Analysis: An International Perspective*, London: Thomson Learning Business Press.

Journals such as the *Financial Analysts' Journal* (published bimonthly by the Association for Investment Management and Research) and the *Journal of Applied Corporate Finance* (published quarterly by Stern Stewart Management Services) often contain articles which summarise recent academic research of interest to professional people working in the finance area.

Index

Note: The problem assignments are not indexed; nor is the glossary, which should be used in conjunction with this index. See also the list of abbreviations on pp. xiv–xvi.